Let's Go
ITALY

is the best book for anyone traveling on a budget. Here's why:

■ No other guidebook has as many budget listings.

Take Rome, for example. We list over 45 hotels and hostels for under $25 a night, and over 35 restaurants where you can dine for less than $10. We tell you how to get there the cheapest way, whether by bus, plane, or bike, and where to get an inexpensive and satisfying meal once you've arrived. We give hundreds of money-saving tips that anyone can use, plus invaluable advice on discounts and deals for students, children, families, and senior travelers.

■ Let's Go researchers have to make it on their own.

Our Harvard-Radcliffe researcher-writers travel on budgets as tight as your own—no expense accounts, no free hotel rooms.

■ Let's Go is completely revised each year.

We don't just update the prices, we go back to the place. If a charming café has become an overpriced tourist trap, we'll replace the listing with a new and better one.

■ No other guidebook includes all this:

Honest, engaging coverage of both the cities and the countryside; up-to-the-minute prices, directions, addresses, phone numbers, and opening hours; in-depth essays on local culture, history, and politics; comprehensive listings on transportation between and within regions and cities; straight advice on work and study, budget accommodations, sights, nightlife, and food; detailed city and regional maps; and much more.

■ Let's Go is for anyone who wants to see Italy on a budget.

Books by Let's Go, Inc.

EUROPE

Let's Go: Europe

Let's Go: Austria

Let's Go: Britain & Ireland

Let's Go: France

Let's Go: Germany & Switzerland

Let's Go: Greece & Turkey

Let's Go: Ireland

Let's Go: Italy

Let's Go: London

Let's Go: Paris

Let's Go: Rome

Let's Go: Spain & Portugal

NORTH & CENTRAL AMERICA

Let's Go: USA & Canada

Let's Go: Alaska & The Pacific Northwest

Let's Go: California & Hawaii

Let's Go: New York City

Let's Go: Washington, D.C.

Let's Go: Mexico

MIDDLE EAST & ASIA

Let's Go: Israel & Egypt

Let's Go: Thailand

Let's Go

The Budget Guide to

ITALY

1994

Mark C. Gordon
Editor

Anna H. More
Assistant Editor

Written by
Let's Go, Inc.
A subsidiary of
Harvard Student Agencies, Inc.

M
Macmillan Reference

HELPING LET'S GO

If you have suggestions or corrections, or just want to share your discoveries, drop us a line. We read every piece of correspondence, whether a 10-page letter, a velveteen Elvis postcard, or, as in one case, a collage. All suggestions are passed along to our researcher-writers. Please note that mail received after May 5, 1994 will probably be too late for the 1995 book, but will be retained for the following edition. Address mail to:

> **Let's Go: Italy**
> **Let's Go, Inc.**
> **1 Story Street**
> **Cambridge, MA 02138**
> **USA**

In addition to the invaluable travel advice our readers share with us, many are kind enough to offer their services as researchers or editors. Unfortunately, the charter of Let's Go, Inc. and Harvard Student Agencies, Inc. enables us to employ only currently enrolled Harvard students.

Published in Great Britain 1994 by Pan Macmillan Ltd., Cavaye Place, London SW10 9PG.

10 9 8 7 6 5 4 3 2 1

Maps by David Lindroth, copyright © 1994, 1993, 1992, 1991, 1990, 1989, 1986 by St. Martin's Press, Inc.

Published in the United States of America by St. Martin's Press, Inc.

ISBN: 0 333 61154 3

Let's Go: Italy is written by the Publishing Division of Let's Go, Inc., 1 Story Street, Cambridge, MA 02138.

Let's Go® is a registered trademark of Let's Go, Inc. Printed in the U.S.A. on recycled paper with biodegradable soy ink.

Acknowledgments

Researcher-Writers

Italy Team

Massimo Chiocca: Massimo's coverage of his home region benefited from his fluency in Neapolitese and his uncanny ability to cut through bureaucracy. Among other things, he taught us true Italian sign language.

Rebecca Hellerstein: At the last minute Rebecca seemed to appear out of nowhere and within days was in the Rome airport, staring at her shredded backpack as it rolled off the baggage carousel. Our undercover agent: look for her addition of soy-milk ice cream in Florence.

Finn Moore-Gerety: Finn celebrated his 19th birthday in a lonely desert town in Tunisia, writing his ever-flawless and voluminous copybatch. Somehow, he managed to find a Franco in every town and a vegetarian entree on every menu.

Frances Marguerite Maximé: As Fran flew through the north, she left a trail of broken hearts and accumulated a collection of jewelry to prove it. While she was dancing the night away in Torino, her mother graciously supplied the office with an Italian feast.

Catherine Springer: Surviving an initial week of bus strikes, bad weather, and the Justin Bernold Rome tour, Cathy quickly recovered and pursued her whirlwind itinerary, sacrificing herself to an accurate and first-hand description of Italian wine.

Rome Team

Justin Bernold: Where do we begin. Justin's favorite building in Rome is the Monument to Vittorio Emanuele. Need we say more? Never far from the North End, Justin's obsession with *gnocchi* was clear indication of his culinary insight into Italy.

Blythe Grossberg: Translator extraordinaire and true budget traveler, Blythe still managed to take on the Italian fashion challenge and now sports a Roman *coiffure*.

Bart St. Clair: Bart proved that the mustard trick really does work. He also provided us with some of the most accurate and amusing interpretaions of the Italian Baroque. He also never failed to give us the inside scoop on waiters from Stanford.

Everyone Else

The Jonathan Taylor room was never lacking in good humor, even when the air conditioning failed during the worst heat wave this century. You were all great to work with; Team Mexico (**Mike Ng** and Dr. **Sarthak Das**) provided the room with the best music, Team Thailand (**Alexis Averbuck, Andrew Kent,** and **Chuckra Chai**) gave us the best (and worst) marginalia, and Rome (**Justin Bernold**) kept us all awake with periodic shipments of Italian espresso beans.

By far the best Managing Editor that ever was or ever will be, **Jonathan Taylor** tirelessly worked to maintain the highest standards in our work and in our morale. There's as much of him in this book as there is of us. Thank you, Jonathan, for being superhuman.

We also would like to express our gratitude to the small, all-volunteer army of helpers who proofread, typed, solved computer mysteries, and made late-night runs to Store-24: Rachel, Brian, Deborah, Sue, Dd, Meredith, Andrea, Sidney, Ed, Dave Lurie. You were terrific, one and all.

There are a few others who deserve special mention: Angelo Schiffeo (for his inside information), Mike V. (for breaking in the floor), Lynne, Alex J., Ben W. (for looking so much like Shaun Cassidy), Amy D., Mimi (for loving Italy), and Oren ("C'mon, it'll be a great summer."). Also, a big thanks to our parents. —AM and MG

Contents

We can wire money to every major city in Europe almost as fast as you can say, "Zut alors! J'ai perdu mes valises".

How fast? We can send money in 10 minutes or less, to 13,500 locations in over 68 countries. That's faster than any other international money transfer service. And when you're *sans* luggage, every minute counts.

For more information call 39-6-67641 in Rome or visit your nearest American Express® Travel Service Office. In the U.S. call 1-800-MONEYGRAM.

INTERNATIONAL MONEY TRANSFERS.

Maps

▦ About Let's Go

Back in 1960, a few students at Harvard got together to produce a 20-page pamphlet offering a collection of tips on budget travel in Europe. For three years, Harvard Student Agencies, a student-run nonprofit corporation, had been doing a brisk business booking charter flights to Europe; this modest, mimeographed packet was offered to passengers as an extra. The following year, students traveling to Europe researched the first full-fledged edition of *Let's Go: Europe*, a pocket-sized book featuring advice on shoestring travel, irreverent write-ups of sights, and a decidedly youthful slant.

Throughout the 60s, the guides reflected the times: one section of the 1968 *Let's Go: Europe* talked about "Street Singing in Europe on No Dollars a Day." During the 70s, *Let's Go* gradually became a large-scale operation, adding regional European guides and expanding coverage into North Africa and Asia. The 80s saw the arrival of *Let's Go: USA & Canada* and *Let's Go: Mexico*, as well as regional North American guides; in the 90s we introduced five in-depth city guides to Paris, London, Rome, New York, and Washington, DC.

This year we're proud to announce three new guides: *Let's Go: Austria* (including Prague and Budapest), *Let's Go: Ireland*, and *Let's Go: Thailand* (including Honolulu, Tokyo, and Singapore), bringing our total number of titles up to twenty.

We've seen a lot in thirty-four years. *Let's Go: Europe* is now the world's #1 best selling international guide, translated into seven languages. And our guides are still researched, written, and produced entirely by students who know first-hand how to see the world on the cheap.

Every spring, we recruit nearly 100 researchers and an editorial team of 50 to write our books anew. Come summertime, after several months of training, researchers hit the road for seven weeks of exploration, from Bangkok to Budapest, Anchorage to Ankara. With pen and notebook in hand, a few changes of underwear stuffed in our backpacks, and a budget as tight as yours, we visit every *pensione*, *palapa*, pizzeria, café, club, campground, or castle we can find to make sure you'll get the most out of *your* trip.

We've put the best of our discoveries into the book you're now holding. A brand-new edition of each guide hits the shelves every year, only months after it was researched, so you know you're getting the most reliable, up-to-date, and comprehensive information available. And even as you read this, work on next year's editions is well underway.

At *Let's Go*, we think of budget travel not only as a means of cutting down on costs, but as a way of breaking down a few walls as well. Living cheap and simple on the road brings you closer to the real people and places you've been saving up to visit. This book will ease your anxieties and answer your questions about the basics—to help *you* get off the beaten track and explore. We encourage you to put *Let's Go* away now and then and strike out on your own. As any seasoned traveler will tell you, the best discoveries are often those you make yourself. If you find something worth sharing, drop us a line and let us know. We're at Let's Go, Inc., 1 Story Street, Cambridge, MA, 02138, USA.

Happy travels!

How To Use This Book

This book is designed to guide you through Italy, its Mediterranean islands, and Tunisia. It is intended to free your time and wallet from hassles and potential pitfalls of budget travel. Our researchers have been covering every corner of these regions for over twenty years, from the alpine meadows of Fruili-Venezia Giulia to the volcanic islands of Lípari to the remotest Saharan village in Tunisia. Every year, we discover the best bargains and update the listings contained here so that you, the budget traveler, can see the country from your own perspective.

In the first pages of this book, the **Essentials** section, we present the information which will help you prepare your trip, including advice on discount travel services, how to stay healthy and safe while abroad, and the documents you will need to cross over borders without difficulty. Furthermore, we give you access to the organizations specifically geared to student, senior, or budget travel both in your home country and in Italy. In the **Life and Times** section, we outline nearly 4000 years of the greatest civilization in the Western world. We also clue you in to the history of literature and the arts, from Machiavelli to Modigliani. We tell you what Queen Dido said! In the **Appendix** you will find a glossary of basic and not-so-basic phrases that should allow you to jump-start a conversation with anyone you meet.

The bulk of this book, of course, is dedicated to the cities and towns through which you will wander. Beginning with the Eternal City of Rome, it moves through Umbria, the green heart of Italy, to Florence, the gem of the Renaissance, around the sunny beaches of the Italian Riviera, across Italy's breadbasket, the Po valley, to the shimmering phantasm that is Venice. It is not our intention, however, to deepen the grooves etched into Italy by the tourist path. We therefore have been sure to include those areas not on everyone else's tourist map: the undiscovered mountain villages of Sardinia, the hidden walks of Rome, and miles of unspoiled Tunisian beaches.

Each town is divided into several sections. Following a brief introduction to the the area's culture and history, the **Orientation** describes its geography and layout and the **Practical Information** section lists essential schedules, offices, addresses, and phone numbers. **Accommodations, Food, Sights** and **Entertainment** will be true to their names. The listings we feel are the best bargains are given first and we will warn you against the biggest rip-offs around. In everything, we look for the unusual, since no one needs to be told how to find a slice of pizza in Napoli.

A NOTE TO OUR READERS

The information for this book is gathered by *Let's Go*'s researchers during the late spring and summer months. Each listing is derived from the assigned researcher's opinion based upon his or her visit at a particular time. The opinions are expressed in a candid and forthright manner. Other travelers might disagree. Those traveling at a different time may have different experiences since prices, dates, hours, and conditions are always subject to change. You are urged to check beforehand to avoid inconvenience and surprises. Travel always involves a certain degree of risk, especially in low-cost areas. When traveling, especially on a budget, you should always take particular care to ensure your safety.

LET'S USE CTS

USE CTS OFFICES TO TRAVEL IN THE RIGHT WAY

AREZZO.
Piazza Risorgimento, 116
Tel. (0575) 352716

BERGAMO.
Via del Pignolo, 16-A
Tel. (035) 244167

BOLOGNA.
Largo Respighi, 2
Tel. (051) 261802

BOLZANO.
Via Rovigo, 38
Tel. (0471) 934146

CAGLIARI.
Via Balbo, 4
Tel. (070) 488260

CATANIA.
Via P. Garofalo, 3
Tel. (095) 7150434

CATANZARO.
Via E. Scalfaro, 5
Tel. (0961) 724530

FERRARA.
Via A. Frizzi, 40
Tel. (0532) 205464

FIRENZE.
Via dei Ginori, 25-R
Tel. (055) 289721-289570

GENOVA.
Via S. Vincenzo, 117
Tel. (010) 564366

MILANO.
Via S. Antonio, 2
Tel. (02) 58304121

MILANO.
Corso di Porta Ticinese, 83
Tel. (02) 8372674-8378204

NAPOLI.
Via Mezzocannone, 25
Tel. (081) 5527975-5527960

PALERMO.
Via N.Garzilli, 28-G
Tel. (091) 332209-325752

PADOVA.
Via S. Sofia, 94-96
Tel. (049) 8751719

PERUGIA.
Via del Roscetto, 21
Tel. (075) 5727050-5731275

PISA.
Via S. Maria, 12
Tel. (050) 45431

RAVENNA.
Via G. Mazzini, 11
Tel.(0544) 39933-39342-32392

RIMINI.
Via Gambalunga, 56
Tel. (0541) 50580

ROME.
Via Genova, 16
Tel. (06) 46791

ROME.
Corso Vittorio Emanuele II, 297
Tel. (06) 6872672-3-4

SIENA.
Via C. Angiolieri, 49
Tel. (0577) 285008

TORINO.
Via Camerana, 3
Tel. (011) 534388- 535966

TRENTO.
Via Cavour, 21
Tel. (0461) 981549- 981533

TRIESTE.
Piazza Dalmazia, 3-B
Tel. (040) 361879

VENEZIA.
Dorso Duro Ca' Foscari, 3252
Tel. (041) 5205660-5205655

VERONA.
Largo Pescheria Vecchia, 9
Tel. (045) 8030951

VICENZA.
Contrà Porta Nova, 43
Tel. (0444) 545325-323864

VITERBO.
Via Garibaldi, 56
Tel. (0761) 344090

And in other 30 main Italian cities

SATA   ISTC

ESSENTIALS

PLANNING YOUR TRIP

The best way to start your vacation is beforehand. Creating a basic itinerary, but not setting it in stone, will allow you to call ahead for reservations without sacrificing spontaneity. Despite broad stereotypes, Italy is a large and diverse country. Above all, remember that small towns are just as Italian as the large cities, and usually considerably less congested. "Doing" Florence, Venice, and Rome may be a time-honored tradition, but it is also one of the most expensive of all possible Italian vacations. Visiting one of these cities, and then exploring the region around it, will give you a much better sense of Italy. It will also ensure that you don't spend all of your time amid other tourists.

Allow for leisure time in your itinerary—zipping through all of Italy in two weeks will sap both your sight-seeing energy and your social time. If you make an effort to be polite and friendly, so will most of the people you meet. And any attempt to speak Italian, however bungled, will be enthusiastically received.

A Note On Prices and Currency

This book's prices were researched in the summer of 1993, and the exchange rates above compiled in August 1993. Since rates fluctuate considerably, be sure to confirm them before you go by checking a newspaper. And be prepared for a noticeable increase in most prices; if prices seem consistently higher than *Let's Go's* by a certain amount, use that figure as a guideline as you travel.

■ Geography

In Italy, where there aren't hills, there are mountains: the Alpine ranges define Italy's northern border, the Apennines run its length and the Gargano and Sila Massifs, respectively, cross the spur and toe of the boot. This geography ensures that hill towns dominate the landscape everywhere. A case in point: the average Italian grandmother carrying home the groceries can beat the average American teenager up a hill, and the country has bred a unique form of human being, capable of simultaneously negotiating 3-inch heels, 13th-century stone cobblestone paving and a 60° incline. Though the largest Italian cities (*e.g.* Rome, Milan, Turin, Naples) now feature urban sprawl, the vast majority of the landscape remains a symbiotic mixture of well-tended countryside and well-enclosed cities. In some cities, notably Siena, farms and olive groves grow inside the old city walls.

The verticality of the landscape is broken by three substantial areas of plain: the largest is the valley of the Po River which stretches from Piedmont through a collection of low-lying Lombard cities and across the farmlands of Emilia-Romagna. A coastal plain also runs along the Tyrrhenian Sea from southern Tuscany through Lazio, and the *tavoliere* (chessboard) makes Apulia a rich farming region on the heel. The situation is not much different on the islands. Most of the smaller islands are mountains rising from the ocean. Sicily and Sardinia have mountainous interiors, though many of the major cities are tucked along the flatter coast.

Girding a peninsula roughly 1000km long and 150-250km across, the Italian coastline seems endless. Much of the coast will surprise only with its dullness, but the long wastelands serve to set off the astonishingly beautiful Amalfi coast (south of Naples), the crescent of Liguria (the Italian Riviera), and the Gargano Massif (the spur jutting into the Adriatic). Other attractive mainland seashores include Cala-

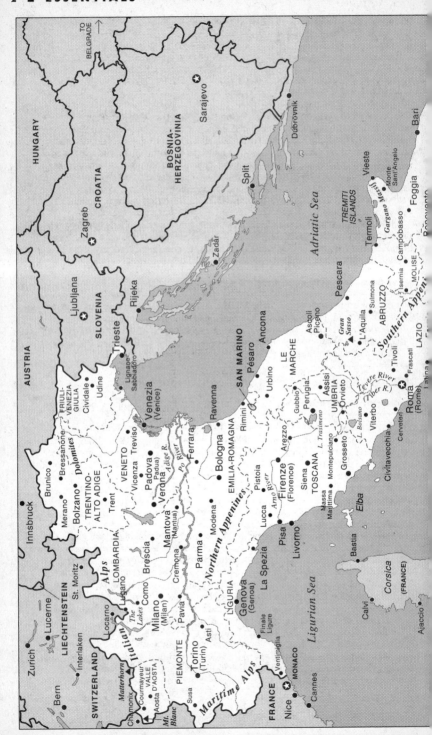

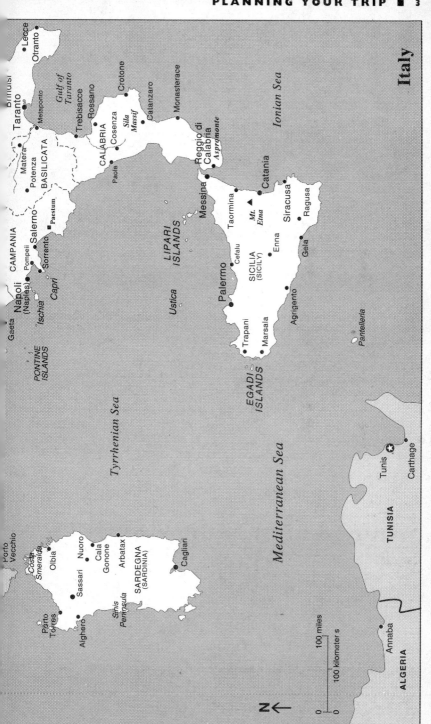

bria's Tyrrhenian coast, the wee southern coast of Lazio (near Gaeta), and the Monte Cónero cliffs (just south of Ancona). Sicily and Sardinia boast Greek ruins in romantic settings, as well as lots more sand. For the best swimming, venture to any of the smaller Italian islands—beyond the touristy Cápri and Amalfi and in the Aeolian Islands off Sicily, lies Italy's Mediterranean.

Italian wilderness has been whittled away over the millennia, but is selectively preserved in the great national parks: Abruzzo National Park in the Apennines and the alpine Gran Paradiso National park set between Valle D'Aosta and Piedmont.

■ When To Go

Without a doubt, the best time to see Italy is either in late-May-June or late-August-September when the summer crowds have not arrived or have just dispersed yet the weather is pleasant. Whenever you go, try to plan a rough itinerary based on the season: weather, festivals, and likely tourist congestion should all be considerations. A winter camping plan would face endless rain while a February visit that doesn't include a Carnevale celebration seems a loss.

Unfortunately for most people, summertime travel is the only option. The densest swarms of tourists choke Italy in July and August. At this time, the tourist-machine goes into overdrive: hotels are booked beyond belief, Michelangelo's *David* has hour-long lines, Elba is overrun with Germans, and the ocean view is always obstructed by seven levels of lounge chairs. Hotel rates go up almost without exception. There are, however, benefits: though many of the best restaurants are closed for holiday in August, some youth hostels and many campgrounds open *just* for the summer and museums and tourist offices maintain expanded hours. The best way to avoid the summer blues is by making reservations at least a few days in advance (unless you want to sleep on Cápri, Elba, the Amalfi coast where you should make reservations at least six months in advance).

Be aware that some areas have a *second* high season. The Dolomites and Alps are popular skiing destinations for Europe's wealthy: high season includes the two weeks after Christmas, mid-February to mid-March, and Easter. Easter week in Rome gets a little tight, as does Christmas in Venice. In general, though, visiting Italy between September and May means enjoying the benefits of the off-season. Traveling outside the summer months should give you a more accurate picture of Italian life. You'll be able to attend the fall wine harvests, the first olive pressings of early winter, or Holy Week processions in April.

Italy and August. A final word of warning: if you choose to travel in August, reservations are a matter of necessity; most Italians take their own vacations in August, and close up their businesses and restaurants. Some of the industrial cities of the north become complete ghost towns (scarcely one in a hundred Milan establishments remains open) and many other cities remain alive only as tourist-infested infernos.

■ Useful Addresses

Tourist Bureaus

Centro Turistico Studentesco e Giovanile (CTS), Via Genova, 16, 00184 **Roma** (tel. (06) 467 91; fax 467 92 05). With 90 offices throughout Italy, CTS provides travel, accommodation, and sight-seeing discounts, as well as currency exchange and information for students and young people. Sells the *Carta Verde* for discounts on train fares, the International Student Identity Card (ISIC), and the International Youth Cards (FIYTO and Euro Youth). Branch offices also in **London** and **Paris.**

Italian Cultural Institute, 686 Park Ave., **New York,** NY 10021 (tel. (212) 879-4242); 496 Huron St., **Toronto,** Ontario, M5R 2R3 (tel. (416) 921-3802). The Italian Government's cultural agency abroad. Information on Italian art, music, literature, and current events. They'll send the handy brochure *Italia,* containing everything from train and ferry schedules to where to yacht. Even if you don't bother writing anywhere else, consider calling them—they're friendly and helpful (though very busy in summer). Other offices in **Los Angeles** (tel. (301) 207-4737), **Montréal** (tel. (514) 849-3473), **Chicago** (tel. (312) 822-9545), **San Francisco** (tel. (415) 788-7412), **Washington, DC** (tel. (202) 387-5161), **Ottawa** (tel. (613) 236-0279), and **Vancouver** (tel. (604) 688-0809).

Italian Government Travel Office (ENIT), 630 Fifth Ave., #1565, Rockefeller Center, **New York,** NY 10111 (tel. (212) 245-4822; fax 586-9249). Write for their detailed (and indispensable) guide *Italia: General Information for Travelers to Italy* and for regional information. Branch offices: 500 N. Michigan Ave., **Chicago,** IL 60611 (tel. (312) 644-0990; fax 644-3019); 12400 Wilshire Blvd., #550, **Los Angeles,** CA 90025 (tel. (310) 820-0098; fax 820-6357); 1 Pl. Ville Marie, #1914, **Montréal,** Qué. H3B 3M9 (tel. (514) 866-7667; fax 392-1429); 1 Princes St., **London,** England WIR 8AY (tel. (01) 408 12 54; fax 493 66 95).

Italian Embassies and Consulates

U.S., Embassy of Italy, 1601 Fuller St. NW, **Washington DC** 20009 (tel. (202) 328-5500; fax 462-3605) and Italian Consulate General, 12400 Wilshire Blvd., #300, West **Los Angeles,** CA 90025 (tel. (310) 820-0622; fax 820-0727). Other consulates of Italy at 2590 Webster St., **San Francisco,** CA 94115 (tel. (415) 931-4924); 500 N. Michigan Ave., #1850, **Chicago,** IL 60611 (tel. (312) 467-1550); 630 Camp St., **New Orleans,** LA 70130 (tel. (504) 524-1557); 100 Boylston St., #900, **Boston,** MA 02116 (tel. (617) 542-0483); 535 Griswold St., #1840, **Detroit,** MI 48226 (tel. (313) 963-8560); 690 Park Ave., **New York,** NY 10021 (tel. (212) 737-9100); **student office,** 686 Park Ave., New York, NY 10021 (tel. (212) 879-4242); 100 Sixth St., #1026, **Philadelphia,** PA 19106 (tel. (215) 592-7329; fax 592-9808); 1300 Post Oak Blvd., #660, **Houston,** TX 77056 (tel. (713) 850-7520).

Canada, Embassy of Italy, 275 Slater St., **Ottawa,** Ont., K1P 5H9 (tel. (613) 232-2402); Consulate of Italy, 3489 Drummond St., **Montréal,** Qué. H3G 1X6 (tel. (514) 849-8351).

U.K., Embassy of Italy, 14 Three Kings Yard, **London,** W1 (tel. (071) 629 82 00); Consulate General of Italy, 38 Eaton Place, London, SW1X 8AN (tel. (071) 235 9371); Consulate General for Scotland and Northern Ireland, 32 Melville St., **Edinburgh,** EH3 7HA (tel. (031) 220 3695, for passport/visa inquiries 226 3631; fax 226 6260); Italian Consulate in Manchester, 111 Piccadilly, **Manchester,** M1 2HY (tel. (061) 236 90 24).

Australia, Embassy of Italy, 12 Grey St., Deakin, A.C.T. 2601, Canberra, G.P.O.B. 360 (tel. 273 33 33).

New Zealand, Embassy of Italy, P.O. Box 463, 34 Grant Rd., Wellington (tel. 473 53 39, fax. 472 72 55).

Budget Travel Services

Compagnia Italiana Turismo (CIT), 342 Madison Ave., #207, **New York,** NY 10173 (tel. (212) 697-2497); 6033 West Century Blvd., #980, **Los Angeles,** CA 90045 (tel. (310) 338-8615); 1450 City Councillors St., #750, **Montréal,** H3A 2E6 Qué. (tel. (800) 361-7799 or (514) 845-9137; fax 845-9137); 80 Tiverton Court, #401, **Toronto,** Ontario (tel. (416) 415-1060). New York office sells rail tickets wholesale; Montréal office specializes in tour packages.

Council on International Educational Exchange (CIEE), 205 E. 42nd St., New York, NY 10017 (tel. (212) 661-1414; for charter flights (800) 223-7402, in New York (212) 661-1450). CIEE offers information on budget travel as well as educational, volunteer, and work opportunities around the world. CIEE also offers discount airfares and issues ISICs (International Student Identity Cards) and International Youth Cards (for non-students under the age of 26). They publish various pamphlets and booklets on work and study abroad. (See Alternatives to Tourism.) Operates 56 Council Travel offices throughout the U.S., including: **Boston,** 729 Boylston St. #201, MA 02116 (tel. (617) 266-1926). **Chicago,** 1153 N. Dearborn St., IL 60610 (tel. (312) 951-0585). **Dallas,** 6923 Snider Plaza, B, TX 75205 (tel. (214) 363-9941). **Los Angeles,** 1093 Broxton Ave. #220, CA 90024 (tel. (310) 208-3551). **Portland,** 715 S.W. Morrison #600, OR 97205 (tel. (503) 228-1900). **San Francisco,** 919 Irving St. #102, CA 94122 (tel. (415) 566-6222). **Seattle,** 1314 N.E. 43rd St. #210, W**A 98105 (tel. (206) 632-2448).**

STA Travel: In U.S., 17 E. 45th St., New York, NY 10017 (tel. (800) 777-0112 or (212) 986-9470). Operates 10 offices in the U.S. and over 100 worldwide. Offers discount airfares for travelers under 26 and full-time students under 32; sells ISICs, HI memberships, and Eurail passes. **Boston,** 273 Newbury St., MA 02116 (tel. (617) 266-6014). **Los Angeles,** 7202 Melrose Ave., CA 90046 (tel. (213) 934-8722). **New York,** 48 E. 11th St., NY 10003 (tel. (212) 477-7166). **Philadelphia,** University City Travel, 3730 Walnut St., PA 19104 (tel. (215) 382-2928). **San Francisco,** 51 Grant Ave., CA 94108 (tel. (415)391-8407). In **Great Britain,** 86 Old Brompton Rd., London SW7 3LQ and 117 Euston Rd., London NW1 2SX England (tel. (071) 937 9921 for European travel; (071) 937 9971 for North American; (071) 937 9962 for long-haul travel; (071) 937 1733 for round the world travel). In **Australia,** 220 Faraday St., Melbourne, Victoria 3053 (tel. (03) 347 69 11). In **New Zealand,** 10 High St., Auckland (tel. (09) 309 9995).

Travel CUTS (Canadian Universities Travel Service), 187 College St., Toronto, Ont. M5T 1P7 (tel. (416) 979-2406). 35 offices throughout Canada. In **Britain,** 295-A Regent St., London W1R 7Y4 (tel. (071) 637 3161). Offers discounted flights with special student fares. Sells the ISIC, FIYTO, and HI hostel cards, and discount travel passes. The *Student Traveller* is available free at all offices and campuses across Canada.

Campus Travel, 52 Grosvenor Gardens, London SW1W 0AG (tel. (071) 730 8832, fax (071) 730 5739). Offers special student and youth fares on travel by plane, train, boat and bus, as well as flexible airline tickets. Also provides discount and ID cards for youths, special insurance for students and those under 35, and maps and guides.

London Student Travel, 52 Grosvenor Gardens, London WC1 (tel. (071) 730 3402).

USIT Ltd., Aston Quay, O'Connell Bridge, Dublin 2 (tel. (01) 679 8833, fax (01) 677 8843).

Hosteling Organizations

A one-year **Hosteling International (HI)** membership permits you to stay at youth hostels all over Italy and Tunisia at unbeatable prices. And, despite the name, you need not be youth: travelers over 25 pay only a slight surcharge for a bed. You can save yourself potential trouble by procuring a membership card before you leave home. Most budget travel organizations sell the membership. (For details on the Italian hostel network, see Traveling in Italy: Accommodations.)

Hosteling International Headquarters, 9 Guessens Rd., Welwyn Garden City, Herts, AL8 6QW, England (tel. (0707) 33 24 87).

American Youth Hostels (AYH), 733 15th St. NW, Suite 840, Washington, DC 20005 (tel. (202) 783-6161). Cards cost US$25 (renewals US$20, under 18 US$10, over 54 US$15); family cards US$35. Other countries' card prices are often lower.

Hosteling International-Canada, National Office, 1600 James Naismith Dr., Suite 608, Gloucester, Ont. K1B 5N4 (tel. (613) 748-5638).

Youth Hostels Association of England and Wales (YHA), 8 St. Stephen's Hill, St. Albans, Herts AL1 2DY (tel. (727) 855 215).

Australian Youth Hostels Association (AYHA), Level 3, 10 Mallett St., Camperdown, NSW 2050 (tel. (2) 565 16 99).

Youth Hostels Association of New Zealand (YHANZ), P.O. Box 436, 173 Gloucester St., Christchurch 1 (tel. (3) 379 9970, fax 365 4476).

An Óige, 39 Mountjoy Sq., Dublin 1 (tel. (01) 363 111, fax (01) 365 807). Membership for 1 yr. £7.50, under 18 £4, family £15.

Scottish Youth Hostel Association (SYHA), 7 Glebe Crescent, Sterling FK8 2JA (tel. (0786) 511 81).

Youth Hostel Association of Northern Ireland (YHANI), 56 Bradbury Pl., Belfast BT7 1RU (tel. (0232) 324 733).

HI has recently instituted an International Booking Network. To reserve space in high season, obtain a voucher from any national hostel association and send it to a participating hostel four to eight weeks in advance of your stay, along with US$2 in local currency.

Useful Publications

Forsyth Travel Library, P.O. Box 2975, Shawnee Mission, KS 66201 (tel. (800) 367-7984). Call or write for catalog of maps and guides, railpasses, timetables, and HI memberships.

Travelling Books, P.O. Box 77114, Seattle, WA 98177 (tel. (206) 367-5848). Mail order service specializing in books, maps, language aids, and other accessories. Call or write for a free catalog.

Wide World Books and Maps, 1911 N. 45th St., Seattle, WA 98103 (tel. (206) 634-3453). Open Mon.-Fri. 10am-7pm, Sat. 10am-6pm, Sun. noon-5pm. Books and hard-to-find maps.

Hippocrene Books, Inc., 171 Madison Ave., New York, NY 10016 (tel. (212) 685-4371; orders (718) 454-2360, fax (718) 454-1391). Publishes reference books, guides, maps, and foreign language dictionaries. Free catalog.

John Muir Publications, P.O. Box 613, Santa Fe, NM 87504 (tel. (505) 982-4078, fax (505) 988-1680). Publishes over 75 books on travel and environmental explorations, including the *Kidding Around* series of itinerary planners for the junior traveler. Several books by veteran traveler Rick Steves, including his *Europe through the Back Door* ($17.95), which shows you how to avoid tourist traps, and an Italian phrase book ($4.95).

Superintendent of Documents, U.S. Government Printing Office, Washington, DC 20402 (tel. (202) 783-3238, fax (202) 275-2529). Open Mon.-Fri. 8am-4pm. Publishes *Your Trip Abroad* ($1), *Safe Trip Abroad* ($1), *Health Information for International Travel* ($5), and "Background Notes" on all countries.

■ Documents and Formalities

When you travel, *always carry on your person two or more forms of identification, including at least one photo ID.* Never carry all identification, traveler's checks, and credit cards together. If you plan an extended stay, you might want to register your passport with the nearest embassy or consulate.

Passports

Citizens of the U.S., Canada, the U.K., Ireland, Australia, New Zealand, and S. Africa all need valid passports to enter both Italy and Tunisia and to re-enter their own country. Some countries will not allow entrance if the holder's passport will expire in less than six months, and returning to the U.S. with an expired passport may result in a fine.

As a precaution, carry a photocopy of your passport (separate from the original) and leave another one at home with a friend. Consulates recommend that you carry an expired passport or an official copy of your birth certificate in a separate part of your baggage and its wise to carry a few extra passport photos as well. If you lose your passport, notify the local police and your embassy or consulate immediately.

Your passport is a public document that belongs to your government and may not be withheld without your consent. Although you may be asked to surrender it to an Italian government official, if you don't get it back in a reasonable amount of time, you should inform the nearest mission of your country. In Italy and Tunisia, hotel proprietors are apt to ask you to leave your passport with them overnight as collateral. Even though this is an accepted custom, you are not required to leave it for any extended period of time (i.e. beyond the time it takes them to simply note the number). Offering to pay the full price up front is one way of avoiding this practice.

U.S. citizens obtain a passport ($65; under age 18, $40) by applying at any Passport Agency or a court or post office that accepts applications. All travelers to Italy, including infants, must have a passport in their name. You must submit: (1) proof of citizenship; (2) ID with your signature and either your photo or a personal description; (3) two identical, recent 2 in. by 2 in. photographs. You can renew your passport by mail (or in person) for $55. The passport office normally requires three to four weeks to process an application, but it is wise to apply several months in advance. Rush service is available for travelers who are willing to pay for express mail and can prove that they are departing within five working days.

Canadian citizens may apply in person at a regional office or at the **Passport Office,** Promenade du Portage, Place du Centre, Hull, Ottawa, mailing address Department of External Affairs, Ottawa, Ont. K1A 0G3, or, outside Canada, at the nearest Canadian embassy or consulate. An applicant must provide: (1) citizenship documentation; (2) two identical signed, certified, passport-size photographs less than one year old that indicate the photographer, the studio address, and the date the photos were taken; and (3) a CDN$35 fee. Citizens under 16 traveling with a parent may be included on the parent's passport. (Some countries require a child to carry his or her own passport whether or not traveling with a parent) If a passport is lost abroad, Canadians must be able to otherwise prove citizenship. For additional information, call (800) 567-6868; in Toronto, 973-3251; in Montréal, 283-2152.

British citizens: for a full passport, apply to the London Passport Office or by mail to a passport office located in Liverpool, Newport, Peterborough, Glasgow, and Belfast. Along with an application, submit: (1) a birth certificate and marriage certificate (if applicable); (2) two identical, recent, certified photos; (3) £18. Children under 16 may be included on a parent's passport. For a visitor's passport, valid for one year in western Europe only, apply at major post offices. You must bring ID, two photos, and the fee (around £9).

Irish citizens can apply for a passport by mail to one of the following two passport offices: Department of Foreign Affairs, Passport Office, Setanta Centre, Molesworth St., Dublin 2 (tel. (01) 671 16 33), or Passport Office, 1A South Mall, Cork (tel. (021) 27 25 25). First-time applicants should send their birth certificate and two photographs with the application. To renew, citizens should send the old passport (after photocopying it) and two photos. Passports cost IR£45. Citizens younger than 18 and older than 65 can request a 3-year passport that costs IR£10.

Australian citizens must apply in person at a local post office, a passport office, or an Australian mission overseas. A parent may file an application for a child who is under 18 and unmarried. You must submit: (1) proof of citizenship; (2) proof of your name; (3) two identical, recent, signed photographs (45mm by 35mm); (4) other ID. Fees are adjusted every three months; call the toll-free information service for current details (tel. 13 12 32).

Applicants for **New Zealand** passports must contact a Link Centre, travel agent, or Representative for an application to be mailed to the Passport Office, Documents of National Identity Division, Dept. of Internal Affairs, Box 10-526, Wellington (tel. (04) 474 81 00). You must submit: (1) proof of citizenship; (2) proof of identity; and (3) two certified photos. The fee is NZ$56.25 (if under age 16, NZ$25.30).

South African citizens can apply for a passport at any Home Affairs Office. Two photos, either a birth certificate or an identity book, and the 30R fee must accompany a completed application.

Visas

A **visa** is a stamp placed on your passport by a foreign government that permits you to visit that country. Tourists from the United States, Canada, Great Britain, Australia, New Zealand and South Africa do not need a visa to visit Italy for three months or less. If you wish to remain longer as a *bona fide* tourist with means of support, you may obtain a one-time, three-month extension from any local police station (*questura*). The Bureau of Consular Affairs warns that extensions are granted infrequently. If you intend to travel for more than three months, consider obtaining a long-term visa before departure. Travelers from countries other than those listed

DOCUMENTS AND FORMALITIES

above should be sure to check with an Italian Government Travel Office or Italian Embassy or consulate: Italy does require visas from citizens of many countries.

Entrance to Italy as a tourist does not include permission to study or work there. There are special requirements for student and work visas.

Italy requires foreigners to register at a local police station within three days of arrival in the country. Hotels are responsible for registering their guests, but if you aren't staying in a hotel, the responsibility is yours.

Customs

Unless you plan to import a BMW or a barnyard beast, you will probably pass right over the customs barrier and into the arms of relieved relations with minimal ado. Most countries restrict the importation of firearms, explosives, ammunition, fireworks, controlled drugs, most plants and animals, lottery tickets, and obscene literature and films. To avoid problems when you transport prescription drugs, ensure that the bottles are clearly marked, and carry a copy of the prescription. Officials may seize articles made from protected species, such as certain reptiles and big cats that roar.

Non-residents may import or export Italian or foreign bank notes and bearer securities up to 20 million lire before declaring them. Check with the tourist offices or the embassy for further details. Portable radios may require a small license fee upon entering Italy. Few other export restrictions apply, except on antiques and precious art.

United States citizens returning home may bring $400 worth of goods for personal use duty-free and must pay a tax on the next $1000. Retaining sales slips *could* save you hassle as you must declare all purchases. The goods cannot include more than 100 cigars, 200 cigarettes (1 carton), and one liter of wine or liquor. To be eligible for the allowance, you must have remained abroad for at least 48 hours and cannot have used this exemption within the preceding 30 days.

You can mail unsolicited gifts duty-free if they are worth less than $50, though you may not mail liquor, tobacco, or perfume. Mark the price and nature of the gift and the words "Unsolicited Gift" on the package. If you mail home personal goods of U.S. origin, you can avoid duty charges by marking the package "American goods returned." For more information, consult *Know Before You Go,* available from R. Woods, Consumer Information Center, Pueblo, CO 81009 (item 477Y). You can direct other questions to the U.S. Customs Service, P.O. Box 7407, Washington, DC 20004 (tel. (202) 927-6724).

Canadians abroad for at least a week may bring back up to CDN$300 worth of goods duty-free once every calendar year. Goods over the allowance will be taxed at 20%. You are permitted to ship articles home under this exemption as long as you declare them when you arrive. Citizens may import up to 200 cigarettes, 50 cigars, 400g loose tobacco, 1.14L of alcohol, and 355ml beer. For further information contact External Affairs, Communications Branch, Mackenzie Ave., Ottawa, Ontario, K1A 0l5 (tel. (613) 957 0275).

EC nationals who travel between EC countries no longer need to declare the goods they purchase abroad. Goods for personal use are not taxed further, provided that duty and tax are paid in the other country.

British citizens are allowed up to £36 of goods from outside the EC, including not more than 200 cigarettes, 100 cigarillos, 50 cigars, or 250kg of tobacco; and no more than 2L of wine plus 1L of alcohol over 22% volume. For more information contact H.M. Customs and Excise, Custom House, Heathrow Airport North, Hounslow, Middlesex, TW6 2LA (tel. (081) 750 1603, fax 081 750 1549). Notice #1 explains the allowances for people traveling to the U.K. both from within and without the European Community.

Irish citizens may return with the equivalent of IR£34 (IR£17 under 17) of goods purchased outside the EC, including: 200 cigarettes, 100 cigarillos, 50 cigars, or 250g tobacco; 1L liquor or 2L wine; 50g perfume; and 250ml toilet water. For more information, contact the Revenue Commissioners, Dublin Castle (tel. (01) 679 27 77; fax (01) 671 2021).

Australians may import AUS$400 (under 18 AUS$200) of goods duty-free, including 250 cigarettes, 250g tobacco, and 1L alcohol. For information, contact the nearest Australian consulate.

Each **New Zealand citizen** may bring home up to NZ$700 worth of goods duty-free if they are for personal use or are unsolicited gifts, including 200 cigarettes, 250g tobacco, 50 cigars, or a combination under 250g. They may also bring 4.5L of beer or wine and 1.125L of liquor. Consult the *New Zealand Customs Guide for Travelers,* available from customs offices, or contact New Zealand Customs, 50 Anzac Avenue, Box 29, Auckland (tel. 09 377 3520, fax 09 309 2978).

Each **South African citizen** may import duty-free: 400 cigarettes, 50 cigars, 250g tobacco, 2L wine, 1L of spirits, 250ml toilet water, and 50ml perfume. You can import other items up to a value of R500. Goods acquired abroad and sent home as unaccompanied baggage do not qualify for any allowances. You may not export or import South African Bank notes in excess of R500. For further information write to: The Commissioner for Customs and Excise, Private Bag X47, Pretoria, 0001.

Student and Youth Identification

The **International Student Identity Card (ISIC)** (US$15) is the most widely accepted form of student identification. Although in many cases establishments will also honor an ordinary student ID from your college or university, the ISIC is most universally recognized for discounts on sights, cultural events, accommodations, transport, and other services. It also provides insurance. In addition, cardholders have access to a toll-free Traveler's Assistance hotline whose multilingual staff can provide help in emergencies overseas. Many student travel offices issue ISICs (see Useful Addresses: Budget Travel Services). Applicants must be at least 12 years old and must be a student at a secondary or post-secondary school. The 1994 card is valid from Sept. 1993 through Dec. 1994. The new **International Teacher Identity Card (ITIC)** (US$16) offers similar discounts, in theory, but because of its novelty many establishments are reluctant to honor it. **Federation of International Youth Travel Organisations (FIYTO)** (US$10) issues its own discount card to travelers who are not students but are under 26. This one-year card offers many of the same benefits as the ISIC and is sold by many of the same organizations.

■ Money

For many tourists, especially students, the admirable pursuit of a bargain can become an obsession. This is not to say that traveling with a really light wallet doesn't have a certain legitimizing excitement. But careful budgeting can still allow you to experience the full Italian culture. If you plan ahead, you should be able to spend at least one night in a quiet pensione overlooking a garden. Save up for a *cappuccino* in Piazza Navona or at the Pantheon—such a break might cost you as much as L8000, but hey, it's the best *cappuccino* in the world. And be sure to pay the L10,000 entrance fees for the Vatican Museum and the Forum—they're worth it. Don't blow your budget, but don't let your budget blow Italy for you either.

Currency and Exchange

US$1 = 1587 lire(L)	L1000 = US$0.63
CDN$1 = L1203	L1000 = CDN$0.83
UK£1 = L2403	L1000 = UK£0.42
AUS$1 = L1075	L1000 = AUS$0.93
NZ$1 = L879	L1000 = NZ$1.38
SA R1 = L340	L1000 = SA R2.94

The Italian currency unit is the lira (plural: lire). The smallest denomination of Italian currency is the L10 coin, and the smallest note is the L1000 bill. Before leaving

Always travel with a friend.

Get the International
Student Identity Card,
recognized worldwide.

For information call toll-free **1-800-GET-AN-ID**.
or contact any Council Travel office. (See inside front cover.)

Council on International Educational Exchange
205 East 42nd Street, New York, NY 10017

home, most people buy about US$50 worth of lire to save time and hassle upon arrival. When exchanging money, look for *"cambio"* signs and shop around. Avoid exchanging at luxury hotels, train stations, and airports; the best rates are usually found at banks (although you still pay a commission of 1-2%). Changing currency is best done in the morning; banking hours are usually Monday-Friday, 8:35am until 1:35pm with an extra hour in the afternoon (often 3-4pm). Remember that unless a percentage rate is charged, you will lose a fixed chunk of money each time. To minimize such losses, exchange large sums at once, but never more than you can safely carry around. It also helps to plan ahead: if you are caught *sans lire* at night or on a Sunday, you may be forced into a particularly disadvantageous deal.

Traveler's Checks

Traveler's checks are the safest way to carry large sums of money. They are refundable if lost or stolen, and many issuing agencies offer additional services such as refund hotlines, message relaying, travel insurance, and emergency assistance. Although not all Italian establishments accept traveler's checks, your peace of mind will far outweigh the occasional inconvenience.

None of the major companies listed below supply traveler's checks in *lire,* so buy checks in your home currency. Aussies and New Zealanders may be better off by buying U.S. dollar or pound traveler's checks; the teller at the bank in the small town in Lazio may not even know where New Zealand is, let alone what its exchange rate is.

Refunds on lost or stolen checks can be time-consuming. To accelerate the process and avoid red tape, *keep check receipts and a record of which checks you've cashed in a separate place from the checks themselves*. Leave a photocopy of check serial numbers with someone at home as back-up in case you lose your copy. Never countersign checks until you're prepared to cash them. To protect yourself from clever thieves who take just one or two checks from the middle of the pile to escape detection, record the number of each check as you cash it.

American Express (tel. (800) 221-7282 in the U.S. and Canada; (0800) 52 13 13 in the U.K.; (02) 886 0689 in Australia, New Zealand, and the South Pacific with questions or to report lost or stolen checks. Elsewhere, call U.S. collect (801) 964-6665). AmEx travelers checks are the most widely recognized worldwide and easiest to replace if lost or stolen—just call the information number or the AmEx Travel office nearest you. AmEx offices cash their own checks commission-free (except where prohibited by law) and sell checks which can be signed by either of two people traveling together ("Cheque for Two"). Checks available in 7 currencies. Call and ask for AmEx's booklet *Traveler's Companion* which gives office addresses and stolen check hotlines for each European country.

Citicorp sells **Visa** traveler's checks. (Call (800) 645-6556 in the U.S. and Canada, (071) 982 4040 in London, from abroad call collect (813) 623-1709.) Commission is 1-2% on check purchases. Check holders automatically enrolled in Travel Assist Hotline (tel. (800) 523-1199) for 45 days after checks are bought. This service provides travelers with an English-speaking doctor, lawyer, and interpreter referrals as well as check refund assistance.

Mastercard (tel. (800) 223-9920 in the U.S. and Canada, from abroad call collect (609) 987-7300.) Commission varies from 1-2% for purchases depending on the bank. Issued in U.S. dollars only.

Thomas Cook distributes travelers checks with both the Mastercard and Thomas Cook names on them. In contrast to MC International, Thomas Cook handles the distribution of checks in U.S. dollars as well as in 10 other currencies. (Call (800) 223-7373 for refunds in U.S., (800) 223-4030 for orders. From elsewhere call collect (212) 974-5696.) Some Thomas Cook offices do not charge any fee for purchase of checks while others charge a 1-2% commission. You can buy Mastercard travelers cheques from Thomas Cook at any bank displaying a Mastercard sign.

Visa (tel. (800) 227-6811 in the U.S. and Canada; from abroad, call New York collect (212) 858-8500 or London (071) 937-8091.) Similar to the Thomas Cook/Mas-

MONEY

Don't forget to write.

Now that you've said, "Let's go," it's time to say
"Let's get American Express® Travelers Cheques." If they are lost or
stolen, you can get a fast and full refund virtually anywhere you
travel. So before you leave be sure and write.

tercard alliance, Visa and Barclay's Bank have formed a team by which Visa checks can be cashed for free at any Barclay's bank.

Credit Cards

Credit cards provide terrible temptations for the budget traveler, but they can prove invaluable in a financial emergency. Although many smaller establishments will not accept them—and those enticing, pricier establishments accept them all too willingly —used sparingly, they can get you through a cash crunch. The perks for a traveler are many. You can often reduce conversion fees by charging a purchase instead of changing travelers checks. With credit cards such as American Express, Visa, and Mastercard, associated banks will give you an instant cash advance in the local currency as large as your remaining credit line. Unfortunately, in most cases you will pay mortifying rates of interest for such an advance. In addition, holders of most major credit cards can now get instant cash around the clock at automated teller machines (ATMs) throughout Europe. In order to use this service, however, one must have a PIN number, available from your issuing bank. Also check with them about charges, interest rates, and ATM locations as well. Be forewarned that the shaky transatlantic connection still often prevents successful transactions.

If your income level is low, you may have difficulty acquiring a recognized credit card. American Express, as well as some of the larger national banks, have credit card offers geared especially towards students. Otherwise, you may have to find someone to co-sign your application. (If a member of your family already has a card, they can usually ask for another card in your name.) When using the credit card, beware of the hefty interest rate for failure to pay your balance each month.

Lost or stolen cards should be reported *immediately,* or you may be held responsible for forged charges. Write down the card-cancellation telephone numbers and keep them in a safe place separate from your cards. Always be sure that the carbon has been torn into pieces, and ask to watch as your card is being imprinted; an imprint onto a blank slip can be used later to charge merchandise in your name.

ATMs

Automatic Teller Machines are not quite as prevalent in Europe as in North America, but you will find that most banks in the larger cities are connected to a money network, usually PLUS or CIRRUS. Depending on the system that your bank at home uses, you may be able to access your account whenever you're in need of funds. ATM machines get the wholesale exchange rate which is generally 5% better than the retail rate most banks use (which is already better than the rate most places charge), but may charge hefty fees for each transaction abroad.

Sending Money

Sending money overseas is a complicated, expensive, and often extremely frustrating adventure. Do your best to avoid it by carrying a credit card or a separate stash of emergency traveler's checks.

The easiest way to get money from home is to bring an **American Express Card.** American Express allows green-card holders to draw cash from their checking accounts at any of its major offices and many of its representatives' offices (up to $1000 every 21 days, no service charge, no interest).

The next best approach is to wire money through the instant **international money transfer services** operated by **Western Union** (tel. (800) 225-5227) or **American Express** (tel. (800) 543-4080, in Canada (800) 933-3278). American Express serves more countries than Western Union, but Western Union tends to be a bit cheaper. The sender visits one of their offices or calls and charges it to a credit card; the receiver can pick up the cash at any overseas office abroad within minutes (fees are about US$22-50 to send US$250 and US$50-75 to send US$1000). To pick up the money, you'll need to show ID and/or answer a test question.

The least expensive but often cumbersome route is to **cable money** from bank to bank. Note that usually both sender and receiver must have accounts at the respective institutions. Transfer can take up to a few days; the fee is usually a flat US$20-30. Outside AmEx, avoid trying to cash checks in foreign currencies as they usually require weeks and a US$30 fee to clear.

Finally, if you are an American in a life-or-death situation, you can have money sent to you via the **State Department's Citizens Emergency Center,** Bureau of Consular Affairs, CA/PA, #5807, U.S. Department of State, Washington, DC 20520 (tel. (202) 647-5225; after hours and holidays, (202) 647-4000). For a fee of about US$25, the State Department will forward money within hours to the nearest consular office, which will then disburse it according to instructions. The agency prefers not to send sums greater than $500, and will enclose a message upon request. The quickest way to get money to the State Department is through Western Union.

Value-Added Tax

The **Value-Added Tax (VAT,** in Italian, *imposto sul valore aggiunta*, or **IVA**) is a form of sales tax levied in the European Economic Community. VAT is generally part of the price paid on goods and services. In Italy, the amount varies from item to item, averaging out at 19%. At certain large stores, visitors from outside the EEC can request a VAT refund if the pre-tax total in the shop exceeds L300,000. When you make your purchase, show the salesperson your passport, ask for an invoice and present both the certificate and goods to a customs officer upon leaving the country. Payment by credit card may speed up the processing of the refund check. For more information, contact **Italy Tax-Free Shopping**, Via Revere, 6, 21100 Varese (tel. (0332) 28 70 09, fax (0332) 28 53 36).

Bargaining

Bargaining is common in Italy, but use discretion: it is appropriate and warranted in dealings at markets, with street vendors, and over unmetered taxi fares (always settle your price *before* getting into the cab). But haggling over prices is out of place most everywhere else, especially in large stores. Hotel haggling is most often done in uncrowded, smaller *pensioni* or for *affitta camere* (*Let's Go* mentions when such activity is common). If you speak no Italian, memorize the numbers. Let the merchant make the first offer and counter with one-half to two-thirds of his or her bid. Never offer anything you are unwilling to pay—you are expected to buy if the merchant accepts your price.

■ Health

For **medical emergencies** in Italy, dial 113 or 112. **First Aid Service** (*Pronto Soccorso*) is available in airports, ports, and train stations. Every **pharmacy** (*farmacia*) in Italy lists the pharmacies open all night and on Sundays.

Common sense is the simplest prescription for good health while you travel: eat well, drink enough, get enough sleep, and don't overexert yourself. While it is rather difficult to lead a normal life when you are living out of a backpack, several tips will make preventative care easier.

Italy, especially the south, scorches in the summer. If you're going to be doing a lot of walking, take along some quick-energy foods. You will need plenty of protein (for sustained energy) and fluids (to prevent dehydration and constipation). Carry a water bottle. If you are prone to sunburn, be sure to bring a potent sunscreen with you from home (it can be expensive abroad), cover up with long sleeves and a hat, and drink plenty of fluids. Finally, remember to treat your most valuable resource well: lavish your feet with attention. Make sure your shoes are appropriate for extended walking, change your socks often, use talcum powder to keep dry, and have some moleskin on hand to pad hotspots before they become excruciating blisters. Don't be too anxious to embrace all the local customs—watch the caffeine intake; one person's five cups of espresso a day is another's poison. Italian tap water is safe to drink unless marked "*non potable*." Relying on bottled mineral water for a while minimizes chances of a bad reaction to the few unfamiliar microbes in Italian water. People with asthma or allergies should be aware that larger Italian cities often have visibly high levels of air pollution, particularly during the summer.

For minor health problems on the road, a compact **first-aid kit** should suffice. Some hardware stores carry ready-made kits, but it's just as easy to assemble your own. Items you might want to include are bandages, aspirin, antiseptic soap or anti-biotic cream, a thermometer in a sturdy case, a Swiss Army knife with tweezers, moleskin, a decongestant (to clear your ears if you fly with a cold), a motion sickness remedy, medicine for diarrhea and stomach problems, sunscreen, insect repellent, burn ointment, and an elastic bandage.

Travelers with chronic medical conditions should consult with their physicians before leaving. Always go prepared with any **medication** you may need while away as well as a copy of the prescription and/or a statement from your doctor, especially if you will be bringing insulin, syringes, or any narcotics into Italy.

Any traveler with a medical condition that cannot be easily recognized may want to obtain a **Medic Alert Identification Tag.** Their internationally recognized tag indicates the nature of the bearer's problem and the number of a 24-hr. hotline. Medical personnel can call this number to obtain information about the member's medical history. Lifetime membership begins at US$35. Contact Medic Alert Foundation, P.O. Box 1009, Turlock, CA 95381-1009 (tel. (800) 432-5378). The **American Diabetes Association**, 1660 Duke St., Alexandria, VA 22314 (tel. (800) 232-3472) provides copies of an article "Travel and Diabetes" and 18-language ID cards. Contact your local ADA office for information.

If you wear **glasses** or **contact lenses,** take an extra prescription with you and arrange for someone at home to send you a replacement in an emergency. If you wear contacts, you should take along a pair of glasses to rest tired eyes. Bring extra contact equipment, often exorbitant abroad. Remember that traveling does not always provide the most sanitary conditions for use of contact lenses.

Reliable **contraception** may be difficult to come by while traveling. Women on the pill should bring enough to allow for possible loss or extended stays. Although **condoms** are increasingly available, availability and quality varies in other countries. In Italy, condoms (*profilattichi*, or in common parlance, *preservativi*) are available over the counter at all pharmacies and in most supermarkets. A packet of six costs between L10,000 and L13,000.

The **International Association for Medical Assistance to Travelers (IAMAT)** provides brochures on health for travelers, an ID card, an immunization chart for 200 countries and territories, and a worldwide directory of English-speaking physicians. Membership is free (although donations are welcome) and doctors are on call 24 hrs. a day for IAMAT members. Contact chapters in the **U.S.,** 417 Center St., Lewiston, NY, 14092, (tel. (716) 754-4883); in **Canada,** 40 Regal Rd., Guelph, Ont., N1K 1B5, (tel. (519) 836-0102) and 1287 St. Clair Ave. West Toronto, Ont. M6E 1B8 (tel. (416) 652-0137); in **New Zealand**, P.O. Box 5049, 438 Pananui Rd., Christchurch 5 (tel. (03) 352-9053; fax (03) 352-4630).

While traveling, pay attention to signals of pain and discomfort that your body may send you. While you are on the road you are more susceptible to illness: some of the milder symptoms that you may safely ignore at home may be signs of more serious problems. The following paragraphs list some health problems commonly experienced by travelers, but should not be your only information source. Complete **health information** for travelers is available from a variety of published sources. Consult your local bookstore for books on staying healthy at home or on the road or write the **Superintendent of Documents,** U.S. Government Printing Office, Washington D.C. 20402 (tel. (202) 783-3238). You may also want to send for the **American Red Cross'** *First-Aid and Safety Handbook* ($14.95) by writing to your local office or to American Red Cross, 99 Brookline Ave., Boston MA 02215.

When traveling in the summer, protect yourself against the dangers of sun and heat, especially **heatstroke,** which can cause death within a few hours if not treated. It results from continuous heat stress, lack of fitness, or overactivity following heat exhaustion. In the early stages of heatstroke, sweating stops, body temperature rises, and headache develops, soon followed by confusion. To treat heatstroke, cool the victim off *immediately* with fruit juice or salted water, wet towels, and shade. Rush the victim to the hospital as soon as possible.

Extreme cold is no less dangerous—it brings risks of hypothermia and frostbite. **Hypothermia** is a result of exposure to cold and can occur *in the middle of the summer,* especially in rainy or windy conditions. Body temperature drops rapidly, resulting in the failure to produce body heat. Other symptoms are uncontrollable shivering, poor coordination, and exhaustion followed by slurred speech, sleepiness, hallucinations, and amnesia. *Do not* let victim fall asleep if he or she is in advanced stages—if he or she loses consciousness, it can result in death. To avoid hypothermia while traveling, always keep dry. Wear wool, *especially* in soggy weather. Dress in layers, and stay out of the wind, which carries heat away from the body. Remember that most loss of body heat is through your head, so always carry a wool hat with you. **Frostbite** occurs in freezing temperatures. The affected skin will turn white, then waxy. To counteract the problem, drink warm beverages and gently and slowly warm the frostbitten area in dry fabric or with steady body contact. *Never rub* frostbite.

Food poisoning can spoil any trip. Some of the cheapest and most convenient eating options are also most prone: street vendors, tap water, and carrying perishable food for hours in a hot backpack. One of the most common symptoms associated with eating and drinking in another country is **diarrhea.** Many people take with them over-the-counter remedies (such as Pepto-Bismol or immodium). Since dehydration is the most common side effect of diarrhea, those suffering should drink plenty of fruit juice and pure water. Rest, and let the heinous disease run its course.

Women traveling in unsanitary conditions are vulnerable to **bladder infections,** a very common and severely uncomfortable bacterial disease which causes its victim to suffer a burning sensation during urination. A strong antibiotic (available without a prescription in some countries) usually gets rid of the symptoms within a couple of days. Other recommendations are to drink enormous amounts of cranberry or another vitamin C-rich juice and plenty of water, and to urinate frequently. Untreated, bladder infections can become very serious as they lead to kidney infections or PID (pelvic inflammatory disease). Treat an infection the best you can while on the road; if it persists, take time out to see a doctor and definitely follow up with one when you get home.

If you plan to **romp in the forest,** try to learn of any regional hazards. Know that any three-leaved plant might be poison ivy, poison oak, or poison sumac—pernicious plants whose oily surface causes insufferable itchiness if touched. (As Marge Simpson tells Bart and Lisa before they leave for camp, "Leaves of three, let it be; leaves of four, eat some more.") Many areas have their own local snakes, spiders, insects, and creepy-crawlies.

Travelers in **high altitudes** should allow their body a couple of days to adjust to the lower atmospheric oxygen levels before engaging in any strenuous activity. Those new to high-altitude areas may feel drowsy, and one alcoholic beverage may have the same effect as three at a lower altitude.

AIDS

All travelers should be concerned about **Acquired Immune Deficiency Syndrome (AIDS),** transmitted through the exchange of body fluids with an infected individual (HIV-positive). Remember that there is no assurance that someone is not infected: HIV tests only show antibodies after approximately a six-month lapse. Do not have sex without using a condom or share intravenous needles with anyone. The Center for Disease Control's **AIDS Hotline** provides information on AIDS in the U.S. and can refer you to other organizations with information on Italy. (Tel. (800) 342-2437; TTD (800) 243-7889.) Call the **U.S. State Department** for country-specific restrictions for HIV-positive travelers. (Tel. (202) 647-1488; fax (202) 647-3000; modem-users may consult the electronic bulletin board at (202) 647-9225; or write Bureau of Consular Affairs, #5807, Dept. of State, Washington D.C. 20520.) The **World Health Organization** provides written material on AIDS internationally (tel. (202) 861-3200).

There are no restrictions on travelers with HIV or AIDS entering Italy, nor is there any obligation to report an infection on arrival in the country or if you find you have it once there. Italians are generally very sensible about medical treatment, and the medical professionals will not pry if you get tested; do double-check that your test is confidential, or even done anonymously if need be. AIDS education is becoming more prevalent throughout the country, and you will never have any problems finding condoms *(preservativi)* at any pharmacy. The **toll-free AIDS number** for Italy is 167 86 10 61. **Lege Italiano Lotte AIDS (LILA)** is a national AIDS activism organization (tel. (06) 89 99 76 or (06) 86 89 95 53 in Rome or (02) 498 46 78 in Milan).

AIDS tests can be performed at any **Analisi Cliniche** (a private lab which handles all sorts of tests, from allergies to pregnancy). Simply ask for the "AIDS test" or "HIV test"—there isn't an Italian word. (AIDS is pronounced AH-eeds in Italy.) Tests can be expensive (up to L150,000). Look in the Yellow Pages under *Analisi* for the private labs or refer to one of the following. The following are Analisi Cliniche located in Rome:

Unione Sanitaria Internazionale, Via V. Orsini, 18 (in Prati, north of the Vatican; tel. 321 50 53) or Via Machiavelli, 22 (Metro Linea A, P. Vittorio Emanuele stop). Open Mon.-Sat. 7am-7pm.

Analisi Cliniche Luisa, Via Padova, 96 (off Via Nazionale; tel. 44 29 14 06). Open Mon.-Fri. 7:30am-4:30pm, Sat. 8am-1pm.

Alessandrini, Viale Mazzini, 33 (tel. 321 79 99 or 323 05 04). Open Mon.-Fri. 7:30am-1:30pm and 4-7pm.

Cavour, Via Cavour, 238 (at Metro Linea B Cavour stop; tel. 474 39 48). Open Mon.-Fri. 7:30-11pm and 4-6pm, Sat. 7:30-11am.

Gynecology, STDs, and Abortion

Analisi Cliniche will perform tests for venereal disease *(malattia venerea)* as well as pregnancy tests, or you can buy home tests over the counter at pharmacies throughout the city. These labs also do pap smears and cryotherapy.

V.D. Clinic, San Gallicano, Via dei Fratte di Trastevere, 52A. (tel. 58 48 31). Small inexpensive clinic run (if you can believe it) by nuns. Crowded and chaotic. Open for tests Mon., Wed., Fri. 8:30-11:30am.

Abortion is legal in Italy, although not as a means of birth control. Local health units called *consultori* advise women on rights and procedures. In Milan, the office is **Consultorio Familiare ANCED,** Corso Buenos Aires, 75 (tel. (02) 670 15 79). There are also hospitals in most large cities that administer "morning after" contraceptives—as always, be sure they fully explain the side effects to you. The U.S. **National Abortion Federation's hotline** (tel. (800) 772-9100, Mon.-Fri. 9:30am-5:30pm) can direct you to organizations which provide information on abortion in other countries. The Vatican surrendered its right to interfere in Italian politics in the Lateran Treaty of 1929, and the anti-choice movement is fairly low-key. As it is a Catholic country, however, Italy isn't the easiest place to get an abortion.

International Medical Center, Via Amendola, 7 (1 block from Termini), 2nd floor (tel. 488 23 71; nights and Sundays 488 40 51). On call 24 hrs.; English spoken.

Referrals to English speaking doctors. Open Mon.-Sat. 8am-9pm; 24-hr. phone lines.

Ospedale San Camillo in Monteverde, Circonvallazione Gianicolense, 87 in Gianicolo (tel. 587 01). Abortion on demand is not available; women must have a gynecological exam, a discussion with the doctor, and possibly even undergo counseling. A D&C (simple abortion) runs about L600,000—the procedure is sometimes covered by insurance. Open Mon.-Sat. 8-11am.

■ Safety and Security

If you are ever in a potentially dangerous situation anywhere in Italy, call the **EMERGENCY ASSISTANCE NUMBER**—113 or 112. 113 is the Public Emergency Assistance number for the State Police, and usually has an English interpreter on hand; 112, the Immediate Action Service of the Carabinieri, should be your second choice. 115 is the nationwide telephone number for the fire department, and 116 will bring the ACI (Italian Automobile Club) if you need urgent assistance on the road.

Tourists are particularly vulnerable to crime for two reasons: they carry large amounts of cash and are not as savvy as locals. To avoid unwanted attention, blend in as much as possible. This is often harder than it sounds; even so, time spent learning local style will be well worth it. If you do feel nervous, walking purposefully into a cafe or shop and checking your map there is better than checking it on a street corner. Muggings are more often impromptu than planned; walking with nervous glances can be a tip that you have something valuable to protect. Carry all your valuables (including your passport, railpass, traveler's checks and airline ticket) either in a **money belt** or **neckpouch** stashed securely inside your clothing. These will protect you from skilled thieves who use razors to slash open backpacks and fanny packs. Making **photocopies** of important documents will allow you to recover them; carry one copy separate from the documents and leave another at home.

If you carry a purse, buy a sturdy leather one with a secure clasp, and carry it crosswise on the side away from the street with the clasp against you. (Even these precautions do not always suffice: moped riders who snatch purses and backpacks sometimes tote knives to cut the straps.) As far as packs are concerned, buy some small combination padlocks which slip through two zippers, securing a pack shut. Be particularly watchful of your belongings on buses, don't check baggage on trains, especially if you're switching lines, and don't trust *anyone* to "watch your bag for a second." Ask the manager of your hotel or hostel for advice on areas to avoid, and if you feel unsafe, look for places with either a curfew or a night attendant. Keep your valuables on you in low-budget hotels where someone else may have a passkey, and always in dormitory-style surroundings—otherwise a trip to the shower could cost you a passport or wallet.

When exploring a new **city,** extra vigilance may be wise, but don't go so far as to let fear inhibit your ability to experience another culture. When walking at night, day-time precautions should become mandates. In particular, stay near crowded and well-lit areas and do not attempt to cross through parks, parking lots, or any other large, deserted areas.

Among the more colorful aspects of Italian cities are the **con artists.** Tricks are many and adaptable. Be aware of certain classics: sob stories that require money, rolls of bills "found" on the street, mustard spilled (or saliva spit) onto your shoulder distracting you for enough time to snatch your bag. Hustlers often work in groups, and children, unfortunately, are among the most effective at the game. A firm "no," should communicate that you are no dupe. Contact the police if a hustler is particularly insistent or aggressive.

Trains are notoriously easy spots for thieving. Professionals wait for tourists to fall asleep and then carry off everything they can. When traveling in pairs, sleep in alternating shifts; when alone use good judgement in selecting a train compartment: never stay in an empty one. If you choose to sleep in an automobile, be aware that this is one of the most dangerous ways to get your rest; it is thus advisable to park in a well-lit area as close to a police station or 24-hr. service station as possible. Sleeping outside can be even more dangerous—camping is recommendable only in official, supervised campsites.

There is no sure-fire set of precautions that will protect you from all situations you might encounter when you travel. A good self-defense course will give you more concrete ways to react to different types of aggression but it might cost you more money than your trip. **Model Mugging** (east coast tel. (617) 232-2900; midwest tel. (312) 338-4545; west coast tel. (415) 592-7300) teaches a comprehensive course on self-defense (course prices vary from $400-500). Community colleges frequently offer self-defense courses at more affordable prices. **U.S. Department of State's** (tel. (202) 783-3238) pamphlet *A Safe Trip Abroad* ($1) summarizes safety information for travelers. It is available by calling the above number or by writing the Superintendent of Documents, U.S. Government Printing Office, Washington D.C. 20402. For the official Dept. of State travel advisory on Italy, including updates on crime and security, call their 24-hr. hotline at (202) 647-5225. Pamphlets are also available on traveling to specific areas. More complete information on safety while traveling may be found in *Travel Safety: Security and Safeguards at Home and Abroad,* from **Hippocrene Books, Inc.,** 171 Madison Ave., New York, NY 10016 (tel. (212) 685-4371; orders tel. (718) 454-2360; fax (718) 454-1391).

Drugs

Travelers should avoid drugs altogether. Italy enacted a "zero-tolerance" law in 1991; possession of any amount of narcotics or even "soft drugs" (i.e. marijuana) is now illegal. Sentences for violations are stiff: up to 15 years in jail and fines of up to L200,000,000. Travelers have been jailed for possessing as little as 3g of marijuana. Your home government is completely powerless to interfere with the judicial system of a foreign country and all foreigners are subject to Italian law. Even if you don't use drugs, beware of the person who asks you to carry a package or drive a car across the border. For more information, write for the pamphlet *Travel Warning on Drugs Abroad* from the **Bureau of Consular Affairs,** #5807, Department of State, Washington, DC 20520 (tel. (202) 647-1488).

■ Alternatives to Tourism

Study

Foreign study seems a fail-proof good time, but be aware that programs vary tremendously in expense, academic quality, living conditions, and exposure to local students and culture. Most American undergraduates enroll in programs sponsored by domestic universities, and many colleges staff offices give advice on study abroad. Take advantage of these counselors and put in some hours in their libraries. Ask for the names of recent participants, and impose on them.

Publications

CIEE's *Work, Study, and Travel Abroad: The Whole World Handbook* ($13.95, $1.50 postage), which describes over 1000 study programs and lists eligibility and application requirements for each. Contact the Information and Student Services Department, CIEE, 205 E. 42nd St., New York, NY 10017 (tel. (212) 661-1414).

Institute of International Education Books (IIE Books), 809 U.N. Plaza, New York NY 10017-3580 (tel. (212) 984-5412, fax (212) 984-5358), puts out several annual reference books. *Vacation Study Abroad* (US$36.95 + US$4 postage) and *Academic Year Abroad* (US$42.95 + US$4 postage) describe a myriad of study-abroad programs. Order from the above address (tel. (212) 883-8200). Also offers the free *Basic Facts on Foreign Study* and distributes several books published by

the U.K.Central Bureau for Educational Visits and Exchanges (all CB books are US$22.95 + US$4 postage each).

Organizations

Centro Turistico Studentesco e Giovanile (CTS), Via Genova, 16, 00184 Roma (tel. (06) 467 91; fax (06) 467 92 05) is connected with the Italian Ministries of Foreign Affairs and of Education, and provides information on study in Italy.

American Institute for Foreign Study, 102 Greenwich Ave., Greenwich, CT 06830 (tel. (800) 727-2437 or (203) 869-9090; high school students call Boston office at (617) 421-9575) offers courses in Italian, art history, and studio art in Florence in cooperation with Italian universities.

American Field Service (AFS) offers both summer- and year-long opportunities in Italy for high school students, ages 15-18. Write to AFS International/Intercultural Programs, 313 E. 43rd St., New York, NY 10017 (tel. (800) 237-4636 or (212) 949-4242).

Association of American College and University Programs in Italy, Corso Vittorio Emanuele II, 110, 00186 Roma (tel. (06) 68 80 47 52; fax 686 48 52).

Central Bureau for Educational Visits and Exchanges, Seymour Mews House, Seymour Mews, London W1H 9PE, England (tel. (071) 486 5101). Publishes *Study Holidays* (&7.75 in bookstores, postage extra) which gives basic information on over 600 language study programs in 25 European countries. Distributed in North America by IIE (see above).

Unipub Co., 4611-F Assembly Dr., Lanham, MD 20706-4391 (tel. (800) 274-4888). Distributes International Agency Publications including UNESCO's *Study Abroad* (US$24, postage US$2.50). International scholarships and courses.

World Learning, Inc., Summer Abroad, P.O. Box 676, Brattleboro, VT 05302 (tel. (802) 257-7751 ext. 3452, or 800-345-2929). Semester programs. Positions as tour group leaders are available world-wide. Applicants must be at least 24 and have established leadership abilities, language fluency, and in-depth overseas experience for the countries to which they apply. Group leaders have all their expenses paid and receive a US$200 honorarium. For the programs themselves, most U.S.

ALTERNATIVES TO TOURISM

colleges will transfer credit for semester work done abroad. Some financial aid is available.

Italian Universities

If your Italian is fluent, consider enrolling directly in an Italian university. Universities are overcrowded, but you will probably have a blast and develop a real feel for the culture. For an application, write to the nearest Italian consulate. In Rome, contact the Segretaria Stranieri, Città Universitaria, Piazzale delle Scienze, 2, Roma. Remember that visas are required of foreign students in Italy. Contact these organizations for more advice:

Amicizia, Via Mira, 4/10, 16129 Genova (GE) (tel. (010) 553 10 96; fax 553 11 52). International student organization for work and study in Italy.

Ufficio Centrale Studenti Esteri in Italia (UCSEI), Via Monti Parioli, 59, 00197 Roma (tel. (06) 320 44 91; fax 324 43 08). National organization for foreign students who have already started their course of study in Italy.

Another option is studying at an institute designed for foreigners but run by an Italian university. Write to the Italian Cultural Institute for a complete list of programs (see Useful Addresses: Tourist Offices). The following schools and organizations offer a variety of classes.

ABC Centro di Lingua e Cultura Italiana, Via de Rustici, 7, Palazzo Venerossi-Pesciolini, 50122 Firenze (tel. (055) 21 20 01; fax 21 21 12). Italian language school. Language, studio art, art history, and cooking courses for 1-24 weeks.

Centro Linguistico Italiano Dante Alighieri, Via B. Marliano, 4, 00162 Roma (tel. (06) 86 32 01 84; fax 860 42 03); Via dei Bardi, 12, 50125 Firenze (tel. (55) 234 29 84; fax 234 27 66). Language classes, cultural daytrips, extracurricular activities. Write 1-2 months in advance. Finds single rooms for L48,000 per day,

and doubles for L40,000 per person per day. Apartments (with kitchen, bathroom and 2 rooms) L1,500,000 per month, including utilities.

Instituto per l'Arte e il Restauro, Palazzo Spinelli, Borgo Santa Croce, 10, 50122 Firenze (tel. (055) 234 58 98; fax 24 07 09). Summer and year-long courses on Italian language, art, and art restoration.

Italia Idea, P. della Cancelleria, 85, 00186 Roma (tel. (06) 683 076 20, fax 689 29 97). Organizes courses on language, arts, and culture, including vacation courses at the seaside or in the mountains during summer months.

Koinè, Centro Koinè, Via de' Pandolfini, 27, 50122 Firenze (tel. (055) 21 38 81, fax 21 69 49). Offers group and 1-on-1 courses on Italian language and culture. Instruction centers in Florence and Lucca all year round, also Cortona, Bologna and Orbetello during spring and summer.

Università Italiana per Stranieri, Palazzo Gallenga, P. Fortebraccio, 4, 06100 Perugia (tel. (075) 574 61). Language classes, cultural instruction, daytrips, and extracurricular activities.

Volunteering

Volunteering is also a good way to immerse yourself in a foreign culture. Besides the personal satisfaction, you may even receive room and board for your work. *Volunteer! The Comprehensive Guide to Voluntary Service in the U.S. and Abroad,* (US$10.95, postage US$1.50) offering advice and listings, is available from **CIEE** (see Budget Travel Services above). Listings in Vacation Work's *International Directory of Voluntary Work* (£8.95; see ordering information under Work below) can be helpful.

Volunteers for Peace, 43 Tiffany Rd., Belmont, VT 05730 (tel. (802) 259-2759). Arranges placement in over 800 work camps in 37 countries, primarily in Europe. *International Workcamp Directory* (US$10 postpaid). Registration fee US$125.

Service Civil International/International Voluntary Service-USA, Rte. 2, Box 506, Crozet, VA 22932 (tel. (804) 823-1826). Arranges placement in workcamps

ALTERNATIVES TO TOURISM

in Europe, U.S., Russia, Turkey, Greenland, Asia and Africa. You must be 16 to work in European camps. Registration fees for the placement service in 1993 ranged from US$40-200 and will most likely go up for 1994.

Archaeological Digs

The **Archaeological Institute of America,** 675 Commonwealth Ave., Boston, MA 02215 (tel. (617) 353-9361) puts out the *Archaeological Fieldwork Opportunities Bulletin.* The 1994 edition (US$10.50 for non-members) is available from Kendall Hunt Publishers at (800) 338-5578. For information on anthropology, archaeological digs, and art history in Italy write to the **Centro Camuno di Studi Preistorici,** 25044 Capo di Ponte, Valcomonica (Brescia) (tel. (364) 420 91; fax 425 72). This research center offers volunteer work, grants, tutoring, research assistant positions, and training and apprenticeship in prehistoric and primitive art, research methods, and editing (publishes *BCSP,* the world journal of prehistoric and tribal art).

Work

The employment situation in Italy is grim for natives (especially in the South) and even worse for foreigners. Openings are coveted by herds of would-be expatriates, so competition is fierce. Foreigners are most successful at securing harvest work, restaurant or bar work, housework, or work in the tourism industry, where English-speakers are needed. The best tips on jobs for foreigners come from other travelers, so be alert and inquisitive.

Officially, you can hold a job in European countries only with a **work permit,** applied for by your prospective employer (or by you, with supporting papers from the employer). An employer must demonstrate that a potential employee has skills that locals lack. On the other hand, there is the cash-based, untaxable, **underground economy**—*economia sommersa* or *economia nera*—which makes up as much as one-third of Italy's economy. Many permitless agricultural workers go untroubled by local authorities, who recognize the need for seasonal labor. **Euro-**

pean Community citizens can work in any other EC country without working papers, and if your parents or grandparents were born in an EC country, you may be able to claim dual citizenship or at least the right to a work permit. Students can check with their university's foreign language departments, which may have official or unofficial access to job openings abroad.

Temporary and Seasonal

Long-term employment is difficult to secure unless you have skills in high-demand areas, such as medicine (including nursing) or computer programming. Other positions that tend to employ foreigners are:

Tour group leader: Summer positions are available with **Hosteling International (HI)** and **American Youth Hostels (AYH),** P.O. Box 37613, Washington, DC 20013-7613 (tel. (202) 783-6161). You must be at least 21, take a week-long leadership course and lead a group in the U.S. before leading one in Europe. See also **World Learning** above under Study.

Teaching English can be particularly lucrative. Local language schools are listed in the phone book. Professional English-teaching positions are harder to get. You may be able to secure a teaching position with an American school in Italy through one of these organizations: **U.S. Department of State,** Office of Overseas Schools, Room 245 SA-29, Department of State, Washington, DC 20522-2902 (tel. (703) 875-7800), which can send you a list of English-language schools abroad to contact directly; the **U.S. Department of Defense,** 2461 Eisenhower Ave., Alexandria, VA 22331 (tel. (202) 325-0885); and **International Schools Services,** P.O. Box 5910, Roszel Rd., Princeton, NJ 08540 (tel. (609) 452-0990). The ISS, which operates and assists English-speaking schools abroad, publishes a free pamphlet entitled *Your Passport to Teaching and Administrative Services Abroad.* The *ISS Directory* (US$29.95, $5.75 postage) can be obtained through Peterson's, Inc. (see Vacation Work below).

Publications

Start with CIEE's free *Work Abroad*, then graduate to the books put out by the following publishers:

Vacation Work, 9 Park End St., Oxford OX1 1HJ, England (tel. (0865) 24 19 78). Many of their books are available in bookstores, or from Peterson's Guides, 202 Carnegie Center, P.O. Box 2123, Princeton, NJ 08543 (tel. (800) 338-3282 or (609) 243-9111).

Inter Exchange Program, 161 6th Ave., New York, NY 10013 (tel. (212) 924-0446), provides pamphlets on work programs and *au pair* positions.

Addison-Wesley, 1 Jacob Way, Reading, MA 01867 (tel. (800) 447-2226), publishes *International Jobs: Where They Are, How To Get Them* (US$14.66, postage included).

World Trade Academy Press, 50 East 42nd St., #509, New York, NY 10017 (tel. (212) 697-4999) publishes the *Directory of American Firms Operating in Foreign Countries*, a list of jobs in private industry. Although the 3-volume set costs $195, World Trade also offers excerpts on specific countries (averaging US$10-15). You may also want to contact the Italian consulate for a listing of firms.

Remember that many of the organizations listed in books like these have very few jobs available and have very specific requirements.

Once in Italy, check the help-wanted columns in the English-language papers *Daily American* and the *International Daily News*. *Wanted in Rome* is available in English-language bookstores or from their office at Via dei Delfini, 17, 00185 Roma (tel. (06) 679 01 90). In Milan, you can place a free advertisement in the weekly *Secondamano* (also good for finding rides); in Rome, contact *Porta Portese*, Via di Porta Maggiore, 95 (tel. 73 37 48). The magazine *AAM Terra Nuova* (L8000 per issue), good for agricultural jobs, can be obtained by writing to: AAM Terra Nuova, Casella Postale 2, 50038 Scarperia (FI) (tel. and fax (055) 845 61 16). Radios will usually broadcast free advertisements, and prospective *au pairs* should consider placing advertisements in women's magazines.

■ Specific Concerns

Women Travelers

Italy and other Southern European and North African countries have long been viewed as particularly difficult areas for women traveling in groups or on their own. Yet although women travelers do face additional safety concerns, excessive caution can also impede the experience of safe aspects of a foreign culture. The best recipe for traveling safely is to inform yourself as much as possible about the conditions of the area to which you will travel. The following paragraphs are meant to be an introduction, rather than an exhaustive survey, of problems and possible means of avoiding them. Remember, when in doubt trust your instincts and err on the side of caution.

Italian culture, friendly in general, often overwhelms foreigners (especially, but not exclusively, women travelers and increasingly Italian women themselves). While the constant barrage of queries and catcalls can become annoying, most comments should not be taken as a preview of violence. Women, whether alone or in groups, can avoid most harassment by adopting the attitude of Roman women: walk like you know where you are going, avoid eye contact (sunglasses are helpful), meet all advances with silence, and, if still troubled, walk or stand near older women or couples until you feel safe. A walkman with headphones tells potential harassers that you're not listening (but be careful—purse-snatchers and pickpockets will take note of your musical oblivion as well; the sound need not be on). Wearing tight or suggestive clothing can attract unwanted attention, but so can attire that is more modest but obviously American (i.e. sweatshirts, college t-shirts, sneakers, hiking shorts, jean jackets).

If you feel at all uncomfortable, don't hesitate to seek out a police officer or a passerby. Memorize the **emergency numbers** in Italy (112 and 113) and always carry change for the phone and enough extra money for a bus or taxi. Self-defense courses suggest carrying a whistle or an airhorn on your keychain—a series of short blasts can call nearby passersby to your help. If you are physically harassed on the bus or in some other crowded space, don't talk to the person directly (this often encourages him). Body language, even a well-aimed knee or elbow, may make the point. Stepping hard on toes works admirably. Again, if you sense real trouble, ask the people around you for help. With luck, you may get the satisfaction of seeing your tormentor get an indignant, rapid-fire Italian tongue-lashing. When traveling on Italian trains, avoid empty compartments, especially at night. Look for compartments with nuns for maximum safety.

Budget **accommodations** occasionally mean more risk than savings. Avoid small dives and city outskirts; go for university dormitories or youth hostels instead. Centrally located accommodations are usually safest and easiest to return to after dark. Some religious organizations also offer rooms for women only. For a list of these institutions, contact the city's archdiocese or write to the provincial tourist office. Also helpful is the **Associazione Cattolica Internazionale al Servizio della Giovane,** which runs hostels for women throughout Italy. Their main offices are at Via Urbana, 158, 00184 Roma (tel. (06) 488 00 56), and Corso Garibaldi, 123, 20121 Milano (tel. 290 001 64; fax 290 042 52).

For additional information, see the following **publications.** *The Handbook for Women Travelers* (£7.99) by Maggie and Gemma Moss is published by Piatkus Books, 5 Windmill St., London W1P 1HF England (tel. (071) 631 0710). *Women Going Places* (US$14), a new women's guide geared towards lesbians, is appropriate for all women. Available from Inland Book Company, P.O. Box 120261, East Haven, CT 06512 (tel. (203) 467-4257).

Senior Travelers

Senior travelers are entitled to a number of travel-related discounts—always ask about these. The following organizations and publications provide information on discounts, tours, and health and travel tips. The **Bureau of Consular Affairs,** Superintendent of Documents, U.S. Government Printing Office, Washington, DC 20402 (tel. (202) 783-3238) provides information in *Travel Tips for Older Americans* ($1).

Elderhostel, 75 Federal St., 3rd floor, Boston, MA 02110. You must be 60 or over, and may bring a spouse who is over 50. Programs at colleges and universities in over 40 countries focus on varied subjects and generally last one week.

Gateway Books, P.O. Box 10244, San Rafael, CA 94912. Publishes Gene and Adele Malott's *Get Up and Go: A Guide for the Mature Traveler* (US$10.95, postage US$1.90). Offers recommendations and general hints for the budget-conscious senior. Call (800) 669-0773 for orders.

National Council of Senior Citizens, 1331 F St. NW, Washington, DC 20004 (tel. (202) 347-8800). For US$12 a year or US$150 for a lifetime, an individual or couple of any age can receive hotel and auto rental discounts, a senior citizen newspaper, use of a discount travel agency, and supplemental Medicare insurance (if you're over 65).

Pilot Books, 103 Cooper St., Babylon, NY 11702 (tel. (516) 422-2225). Publishes *The International Health Guide for Senior Citizens* (US$4.95, postage US$1) and *The Senior Citizens' Guide to Budget Travel in Europe* (US$5.95 postpaid).

Traveling with Children

Despite now having the lowest birthrate in Europe, Italians are well known for their love of children, and you will probably encounter more cooing than complications. Most hotels will put a cot in your room for a 30% price increase and even picky children tend to enjoy the simplest (and cheapest) of Italian foods: pizza, spaghetti and *gelato.* In addition, train systems in Italy sometimes offer discounts for groups or families. There are discount Eurailpasses for groups and children (children under 12 travel at half-price, children under four usually travel free), and an Italian kilometric ticket can be used by up to five at once. Even so, planning ahead and drawing up a detailed itinerary are especially useful for those traveling with small children. Remember that you may have to slow your pace considerably, and keep in mind that all the new sights and experiences are especially exhausting for kids—you may want to leave room for a mid-afternoon nap for everyone. For some families, it may be more convenient to travel by rental car, but train travel will often be cheaper, reduce the fidgets, and provide a novel, absorbing experience for children.

For more information see the following publications: **Wilderness Press,** 2440 Bancroft Way, Berkeley, CA 94704 (tel. (415) 443-7227) distributes *Backpacking with Babies and Small Children* (US$8.95) and *Sharing Nature with Children* (US$6.95), which present useful tips for the outward-bound family. **Lonely Planet Publications,** Embarcadero West, 112 Linden St., Oakland, CA 94607 (tel. (510) 893-8555 or (800) 275-8555) publishes *Travel With Children* (US$10.95, US$1.50 postage in the U.S.), a book chock-full of user-friendly tips and anecdotes; they also publish a free quarterly newsletter full of general travel advice and anecdotes, also available by writing P.O. Box 617, Hawthorn, Victoria, 3122, **Australia.**

Travelers with Disabilities

Italians are making an increased effort to meet the needs of people with disabilities. The **Italian Government Travel Office (ENIT)** provides listings of accessible hotels and associations for people with disabilities in various Italian cities and regions. When making arrangements with airlines or hotels, specify exactly what you need and allow time for preparation and confirmation of arrangements. In most **train stations**, a porter will assist you for L500 to L1000 per bag. Major train stations will provide aid as long as you make reservations by telephone 24hrs. in advance. Italy's rail system is modernized, so most trains are wheelchair accessible. For more information, call Italy's state **rail office** in New York (tel. (212) 697-2100) or **Rail Europe** in the U.S. (tel. (800) 345-1990; fax (914) 682-2821).

If you plan to bring a seeing-eye dog to Italy, contact your veterinarian and the nearest Italian consulate. You will need an import license, a current certificate of your dog's inoculations, and a letter from your veterinarian certifying your dog's health (see the section below on *Pets*).

American Foundation for the Blind, 15 W. 16th St., New York, NY 10011 (tel. (212) 620-2147). ID cards (US$10); write for an application, or call the Product Center at (800) 829- 0500. Also call this number to order AFB catalogs in Braille, print, or on cassette or disk.

Disability Press, Ltd., Applemarket House, 17 Union St., Kingston-upon-Thames, Surrey KT1 1RP, England (tel.(081) 549 6399). Publishes the *Disabled Traveler's International Phrasebook,* including French, German, Italian, Spanish, Portuguese, Swedish, and Dutch phrases (£1.75). Supplements in Norwegian, Hungarian and Serbo-Croatian (60p each).

Evergreen Travel Service, 4114 198th St. SW, #13, Lynnwood, WA 98036 (tel. (800) 435-2288 or (206) 776-1184). Arranges wheelchair-accessible tours and individual travel worldwide. Other services include tours for the blind and the deaf and tours for those not wanting a fast-paced itinerary.

The Guided Tour, Inc. Elkins Park House, Suite 114B, 7900 Old York Road, Elkins Park, PA 19117-2348. (tel. (215) 782-1370 or (800) 738-5843) Year-round travel programs for persons with developmental and physical challenges as well as those geared to the needs of persons requiring renal dialysis. Trips and vacations planned both domestically and internationally. Call or write for a free brochure.

Mobility International, USA (MIUSA), P.O. Box 3551, Eugene, OR 97403 (tel. (503) 343-1284 voice and TDD). International headquarters in Britain, 228 Borough High St., London SE1 1JX (tel. (071) 403 56 88). Contacts in 30 countries. Information on travel programs, international work camps, accommodations, access guides, and organized tours. Membership costs US$20 per year, newsletter

US$10. Sells updated and expanded *A World of Options: A Guide to International Educational Exchange, Community Service, and Travel for Persons with Disabilities* (US$14 for members, US$16 for non-members, postpaid).

Moss Rehabilitation Hospital Travel Information Service, 1200 W. Tabor Rd., Philadelphia, PA 19141 (tel. (215) 456-9603). Information on international travel accessibility: nominal fee charged for packet of information on tourist sights, accommodations, and transportation.

Society for the Advancement of Travel for the Handicapped, 347 Fifth Ave., Suite 610, New York, NY 10016 (tel. (212) 447-7284); fax (212) 725-8253). Publishes quarterly travel newsletter *SATH News* and information booklets (free for members, US$3 each for nonmembers). Advice on trip planning for people with disabilities. Annual membership is US$45, students and seniors US$25.

Twin Peaks Press, P.O. Box 129, Vancouver, WA 98666 (tel. (206) 694-2462, orders only (800) 637-2256). *Travel for the Disabled* lists tips and resources for disabled travelers (US$19.95). Also available are the *Directory for Travel Agencies of the Disabled* (US$19.95) and *Wheelchair Vagabond* (US$14.95). Postage US$2 for first book, US$1 for each additional.

Bisexual, Gay, and Lesbian Travelers

Gay and lesbian travelers may find Italians unwelcoming, particularly in the South. Holding hands or walking arm-in-arm with someone of the same sex, however, is common in Italy, especially for women, and sexual acts between members of the same sex are legal for those above the age of consent (16). People in large cities—Bologna, Milan, and Turin—tend to be more tolerant: just last year, Italians elected their first openly gay candidate to Parliament. Gay bars dot the nightclub scene in most cities (they also provide a refuge for women of all persuasions who want nightlife without incessant ogling), and a few gay beaches (*spiaggie gay*) dot the shores.

The Italian national gay organization, **ACRI-GAY,** is in Bologna, P. di Porta Saragozza, 2, P.O. Box 691, 40100 Bologna (tel. (051) 43 67 00; fax 42 36 36). *Babilonia*, a national gay magazine, is published monthly. Women's organizations and lesbian groups are often one and the same in Italy. The best source is the **ACRI-Donna** (at Via Mutilati, 3, in Verona; tel. (005) 801 28 54) which publishes the bimonthly newsletter *Bolettino Associazione Lesbiche Italiane*. The following sources should prove helpful in planning your trip; before ordering any publications, try the gay and lesbian sections of your local bookstores.

Are You Two Together?, (US$18) published by Random House and available at bookstores. A new gay and lesbian guide to spots in Europe. Written by a lesbian couple; covers Western European capitals and gay resorts.

Ferrari Publications, P.O. Box 37887, Phoenix, AZ 85069 (tel. (602) 863-2408). Publishes *Ferrari's Places of Interest* (US$14.95), *Ferrari's Places for Men* (US$13.95), *Ferrari's Places for Women* (US$12), and *Inn Places: USA and Worldwide Gay Accommodations* (US$14.95). Also available from Giovanni's Room (see below).

Gay's the Word Bookshop, 66 Marchmont St., London WC1N 1AB, England (tel. (071) 278 7654). Tube: Russel Sq. Open Mon.-Fri. 11am-7pm, Sat. 10am-6pm, Sun. and holidays 2-6pm. Mail order service available.

Giovanni's Room, 345 S. 12th St., Philadelphia, PA 19107 (tel. (215) 923-2960) (fax (215) 923-0813). International feminist, lesbian and gay bookstore with mail-order service.

Spartacus International Gay Guide, (US$29.95). Order from 100 East Biddle St., Baltimore, MD 21202 (tel. (410) 727-5677) or c/o Bruno Lützowstraße, P.O. Box 301345, D-1000 Berlin 30, Germany (tel. (30) 25 49 82 00); also available from Giovanni's Room (see above) and from Renaissance House, P.O. Box 292 Village Station, New York, NY 10014 (tel. (212) 674-0120). Extensive list of gay bars, restaurants, hotels, bookstores and hotlines throughout the world. Very specifically for men.

Women Going Places, (US$14) a new women's travel and resource guide emphasizing women-owned enterprises. Geared towards lesbians, but offers advice appropriate for all women. Available from Inland Book Company, P.O. Box 120261, East Haven, CT 06512 (tel. (203) 467-4257).

The Women's Traveler, (US$12), a travel guide for the lesbian community, provides listings of bars, restaurants, accommodations, bookstores, and services in over 50 cities worldwide. Available only in the U.S. or Canada from the Bob Damran Co., P.O. Box 11270, San Francisco, CA 94101 (tel. (415) 255-0404).

Pets

If you must bring an animal with you to Italy, know that there are a number of restrictions depending on the kind of beastie; contact the Italian Government Travel Office or a nearby Italian embassy. Bring a leash or muzzle if you have a dog; one or the other is required in public.

Specific Diets

Jewish travelers who keep kosher should consult local tourist boards for a list of kosher restaurants. Also useful is *The Jewish Travel Guide* (US$11.95, US$1.75 postage) from Jewish Chronicle Publications, 25 Furnival St., London EC4A 1JT, England, in North America, Sepher-Hermon Press, 1265 46th St., Brooklyn, NY 11219 (tel. (718) 972-9010).

Vegetarians should write the **Società Vegetariana Italiana,** Via dei Piatti, 3, 20123 Milano, for information on vegetarian restaurants, foods, and stores. *Let's Go* includes some vegetarian restaurants and you can always ask for a dish *senza carne* (without meat), though you may face incredulity. For more information, contact the **Vegetarian Society of the U.K.,** Parkdale, Dunham Rd., Altrincham, Cheshire WA14 4QG (tel. (061) 928 07 93). They publish the international *Vegetarian Travel Guide* (£3.99), listing vegetarian and health-conscious restaurants, guesthouses, societies, and health food stores throughout the world (half the book is devoted to the U.K.). The guide is also available for US$16 and US$2 postage from the **North American Vegetarian Society,** P.O. Box 72, Dolgeville, NY 13329 (tel. (518) 568-7970).

Minority Travelers

We have been hard-pressed to find any resources that advise members of visible minorities on specific travel concerns; if our readers have knowledge of any such institution, please write to us and let us know.

In certain regions, tourists of color or members of certain religious groups may feel unwelcomed by local residents. Furthermore, either historical or newly-developed discrimination against established minority residents may surface against travelers who are members of those minority groups. *Let's Go* asks that our researchers do not include known discriminatory establishments in our guides. If, in your travels, you encounter discriminatory treatment, you should firmly state your disapproval; make it clear to the owners that another hotel or restaurant will be receiving your patronage.

In terms of safety, we don't have any easy answers. Traveling in groups and taking a taxi whenever you are uncomfortable are always good ideas; your personal safety should always be your first priority. The best answer to xenophobic comments and other verbal harassment is no answer at all (they're just looking to get a rise out of you). Keep abreast of the particular cultural attitudes of the countries you're planning to visit. But above all, keep in mind that your own ethnicity or religion will not necessarily be problematic; you very well may find your vacation trouble-free and your hosts open-minded.

■ Packing

Pack light. Set out everything you think you'll need, eliminate half, and take more money. Once you're on the road you'll be thankful. If you find yourself packing "just in case," remember that almost all supplies are readily found in Italy (though not necessarily in Tunisia; and see Health for tips on medical and hygienic supplies you may want to bring from home).

Luggage

Backpack: Ideal if you're planning to hike over a lot of ground or camp; get one with several external compartments. Some convert into a more normal-looking suitcase. More cumbersome, an **external-frame** pack offers added support, distributes weight better, and allows for a sleeping bag to be strapped on. External-frame packs have been known to get caught and mangled in baggage conveyors; tie down loose parts to minimize risk. In any case, get a pack with a strong, padded hip belt to transfer weight from your shoulders to your hips. Quality packs cost anywhere from US$125 to US$300.

Light suitcase, carry-on/overnight bag, or large shoulder bag: Suitcases are best suited for people who plan to stay in cities and large towns and don't want to stand out as budget tourists. They're the worst for schlepping from city to city.

Daypack or courier bag: Bringing a smaller bag in addition to your pack or suitcase allows you to leave your big bag in the hotel while you carry a picnic to that beautiful spot by the river outside town. Make sure it's big enough to hold lunch, camera, water bottle, and *Let's Go*. Get one with secure zippers and closures.

Clothing and Footwear

No nation outdresses Italy. Although attempts to compete or blend in will prove difficult, do bring appropriate clothes for visits to art-encrusted cathedrals and churches, where shorts, skirts above the knees, and sleeveless or cut-off shirts are usually forbidden. In general bring few, but comfortable, clothes and keep accessories to a minimum. Climate should determine your wardrobe. Dark colors will not show the dirt they're bound to accumulate, but light colors will be cooler in hot weather. Natural fibers are also good choices—synthetics trap the heat. Laundry facilities are expensive in Italy and non-existent in Tunisia: bring non-wrinkling, quick-drying clothes that you can wash in a sink. Above all, shorts, university t-shirts, and running shoes brand you as a tourist and may be the cause of increased attention in Italy.

Women: During the summer, light cotton pants are the most appropriate travel-wear and are the only option for getting by cathedral dress codes. Your favorite pair of jeans may cause you problems on the road—they're hot, and hard to dry after a downpour. Shorts will definitely make you stand out and garner unwanted attention from men. Surprisingly enough, you might be just as comfortable and attract fewer stares in a knee-length miniskirt. Really.

Men: Again, cotton pants will be more comfortable than jeans and allow you to fit in (sort of). Shorts are more acceptable on men than on women and will give you a break from the heat, but remember that they will not pass in cathedrals.

Walking shoes: Not a place to cut corners. For **city** walking, lace-up leather shoes with firm grips provide better support and social acceptability than athletic shoes. If you plan to travel in the **rainy** fall or spring, waterproof your shoes. For alpine forays, a good pair of **hiking boots** is essential. Teva **sandals** are excellent for resting and airing out your feet after a long day—or buy a pair of Italian leather sandals once you get there. *Break in your shoes before you go.*

Don't forget: Raingear and a light sweater or jacket, even in summer. Gloves and thermal underwear are handy, perhaps even necessary, in winter.

Miscellaneous

The following is not an exhaustive list. For a **first-aid kit,** see Health.

Washing clothes: Laundry facilities in Italy are expensive and inconvenient. Washing clothes in your hotel sink is a better option. Bring a small bar of detergent soap, a rubber squash ball to stop up the sink, and a travel clothes line (available at camping stores).

Electric Current: Voltage is generally 220v in Italy, although some hotels offer 110v. Check before plugging in or you could fry your appliance into oblivion. U.S. and Australian gadgets need a prong adapter, available in Italy or from most travel stores. Converters and adapters are sold at many hardware stores. If you don't feel like going to the hardware store, order a converter or the free pamphlet *Foreign Electricity is No Deep Dark Secret* by mail from the Franzus Co., Murtha Industrial Park, P.O. Box 142, Beacon Falls, CT 06403 (tel. (203) 723-6664).

Film is expensive in Europe. Despite disclaimers, airport security X-rays can fog film. A lead-lined pouch, sold at camera stores, protects film. Pack it in your carry-on luggage, since higher-intensity X-rays are used on checked luggage. Although developing is inexpensive and fast in Italy, the use of non-standard chemicals sometimes does weird things.

Also valuable: alarm clock, plastic bags (for damp clothes, soap, food), sun hat, needle and thread, safety pins, sunglasses, Walkman, pocketknife, plastic water bottle, small flashlight, towel, moleskin (for blisters), and insect repellent.

Camping

Purchase **equipment** before you leave. As a rule, prices drop in fall when stores clear out their old merchandise. For **backpacks,** see Luggage, above.

Synthetic-filled sleeping bag: Cheaper, more durable, and faster drying than a down-filled one. Bags are rated according to the lowest temperature in which they can be used. A 3-season bag (US$110; down-filled US$135) keeps you warm even below freezing point. A less hard-core bag costs about US$40.

Pads: A cushion between your soft body and the hard ground. An **ensolite pad** (US$10-15) is warmer than the foam kind and keeps you warm and dry. A **Thermarest air mattress** (US$40) is a deluxe ensolite pad and air mattress that virtually inflates itself; like sleeping on air. Regular air mattresses start at US$50.

Tents: Last year's models are often drastically reduced. Get one with a rain fly and bug netting. For 2 people, a 2-person tent is a bit tight; consider a 4-person model.

Tarpaulin or **plastic groundcloth:** To put under the tent.

Campstoves: Don't rely on campfire cooking; some regions restrict fires. Simple stoves (US$40-125) burn butane or white gas. Also bring a mess kit and a battery-operated lantern.

Other: Waterproof matches, calamine lotion, and water-purification pills.

The following **organizations** provide advice and/or supplies.

Campmor, 810 Rte. 17 N, P.O. Box 997-LG92, Paramus, NJ 07653-0997 (tel. (800) 526-4784). Name-brand equipment at low prices.

National Campers and Hikers Association, Inc., 4804 Transit Rd., Bldg. 2, Depew, NY 14043-4906 (tel. (716) 668-6242). Sells the International Camping Carnet, required at some European campgrounds (US$30 includes membership in their association). Also has a short bibliography of camping travel guides and a list of camping stores in major European cities.

Recreational Equipment, Inc. (REI), Sumner, WA 98302 (tel. (800) 426-4840). Long-time outdoor equipment cooperative, favorite of outdoorsy northwestern types. Lifetime membership (not required) US$10. Sells *Europa Camping and Caravanning* (US$13), an encyclopedic listing of campsites in Europe.

GETTING THERE

■ From North America

Constantly fluctuating prices make estimating airfares impossible, but a few general rules do apply. Most airlines maintain a fare structure that peaks between mid-June and early September. Midweek (Mon.-Thurs.) flights run about US$30 cheaper each way than on weekends. If you plan on traveling elsewhere in Europe, consider beginning your trip outside of Italy; a flight to Brussels or Frankfurt could cost considerably less than one to Milan or Rome. The average price for a trip from New York to Rome in 1993 was around US$650.

Have a knowledgeable travel agent (or better yet, several) guide you through the options. Remember that travel agents might not want to do the legwork to find the cheapest fares (for which they receive the lowest commissions). Travel sections in newspapers often list bargain fares from the local airport. You might be able to out-fox airline reps with the phone-book-sized *Official Airline Guide* (at large libraries). This monthly guide lists every scheduled flight in the world (including prices). George Brown's *The Airline Passenger's Guerilla Handbook* (US$14.95; last published in 1990) is a more renegade resource.

Since inexpensive flights from Canada cost substantially more than the lowest fares from the U.S., Canadians may want to consider leaving from the States. Also check with Travel CUTS for information on special charters.

Commercial Carriers

If you decide to make your transatlantic crossing with a commercial airline, you'll be purchasing greater reliability, security, and flexibility—usually at a higher price. The commercial airlines' lowest regular offer is the **APEX (Advance Purchase Excursion Fare).** Specials advertised in newspapers may be cheaper, but have more restrictions and fewer available seats. APEX fares provide you with confirmed reservations and allow "open-jaw" tickets (landing in and returning from different cities). Reservations must usually be made at least 21 days in advance, with minimum and maximum stay limitations, and hefty cancellation and change fees. For summer travel, book early. **Alitalia** (tel. in the U.S. (800) 223-5730), Italy's national airline, is geared primarily to executives and well-heeled travelers, but they do offer APEX and off-season youth fares.

A few airlines offer other miscellaneous discounts. Look into flights to relatively less popular destinations or on smaller carriers. Call **Icelandair** or **Virgin Atlantic Airways** (tel. (800) 862-8621) for information on their last-minute offers.

Student Travel Agencies

Students and people under 26 with proper ID qualify for deliciously reduced air-fares. These are available from student travel agencies like **Council Travel, STA,** and **Travel CUTS** (see Budget Travel Services). In 1993, *peak* season round-trip rates from the east coast of North America to even the offbeat corners of Europe rarely topped US$700, and off-season fares were considerably lower. Change fees also tend to be low (around US$50). Most of their flights are on major scheduled airlines, though in peak season some seats may be on chartered aircraft.

Charter Flights and Ticket Consolidators

Ticket consolidators resell unsold tickets on commercial and charter airlines that might otherwise have gone begging. Look for their tiny ads in weekend papers and start calling. There is rarely a maximum age, tickets are heavily discounted, and may offer extra flexibility or bypass advance purchase requirements since you are not tangled in airline bureaucracy. Yet unlike tickets bought through an airline, you won't be able to use your tickets on another flight if you miss yours, and you will have to go back to the consolidator to get a refund. Pay with a credit card—you can't stop a cash payment if you never receive your tickets. Find out everything you can about the agency you're considering and get a copy of their refund policy *in writing*. Insist on a receipt that gives full details about the tickets, refunds and restrictions, and if they don't want to give you one or just generally seem clueless, use a different company.

It's best to buy from a major organization that has experience in placing individuals on charter flights. One of the most reputable is the CIEE-affiliated **Council Char-**

ter, 205 E. 42nd St., New York, NY 10017 (tel. (800) 800-8222). Their flights can also be booked through Council Travel offices.

Another organization is **Unitravel** (tel. (800) 325-2222). They offer discounted airfares on major scheduled airlines from the U.S. to cities in Europe and will hold all payments in escrow until completion of your trip. You should also try **Access International** (tel. 800 825-3633), **Interworld** (tel. (800) 331-4456; in Florida (305) 443-4929), **Rebel** (tel. (800) 227-3235), and **Travac** (800) 872-8800).

Consolidators sell a mixture of tickets. Some are on scheduled airlines and others on charter flights. The theory behind a charter is that a tour operator contracts with an airline (usually a fairly obscure one that specializes in charters) to use their planes to fly extra loads of passengers to peak-season destinations. Charter flights thus fly less frequently than major airlines and have correspondingly more restrictions. They are also almost always fully booked, schedules and itineraries may change at the last moment, and flights may be traumatically cancelled. Shoot for a scheduled air ticket if you can, and pay with a credit card. You might also consider travelers insurance against trip interruption.

Airhitch, 2790 Broadway #100, New York, NY 10025 (tel. (212) 864-2000) advertises a similar service: you choose a five-day date range in which to travel and a list of preferred destinations, and they try to place you in a vacant spot. Absolute flexibility—on both sides of the Atlantic—is necessary, but the savings might be worth it (flights cost US$169 each way when departing from the East Coast of the U.S., US$269 from the West Coast, and US$229 from most places in between). Airhitch usually gets you where you want to go, but they only guarantee that you'll end up in Europe. Check all flight times and departure sites directly with the airline carrier, and read *all* the fine print they send you and compare it to what people tell you. The Better Business Bureau of New York received complaints about Airhitch a few years ago. They still don't recommend them, but they don't discourage you from using them, either.

Last-minute **discount clubs** and **fare brokers** offer members savings on European travel, including charter flights and tour packages. Research your options carefully. **Last Minute Travel Club,** 1249 Boylston St., Boston, MA 02215 (tel. (800) 527-8646 or (617) 267-9800) is one of the few travel clubs which doesn't require a membership fee. Others include **Discount Travel International** (tel. (800) 324-9294), **Moment's Notice** (tel. (212) 486-0503; US$25 annual fee), **Traveler's Advantage** (tel. (800) 835-8747; US$49 annual fee), and **Worldwide Discount Travel Club** (tel. (305) 534-2082; US$50 annual fee). For US$25, **Travel Avenue** will search for the lowest international airfare available and then discount it 5-17% (tel. (800) 333-3335). The often labyrinthine contracts for all these organizations bear close study—you may prefer not to stop over in Luxembourg for eleven hours.

Courier Flights

Those who travel light should consider flying to Europe as a courier. The company hiring you will use your checked luggage space for freight and you're left with the carry-on allowance. Restrictions to watch for: most flights are round-trip only with fixed-length stays (usually short), you may not be able to travel with a companion (single tickets only), and most flights are from New York. Round-trip fares to Western Europe from the U.S. range from US$199-349 (during the off-season) to US$399-549 (during the summer). **Now Voyager,** 74 Varick St., #307, New York, NY 10013 (tel. (212) 431-1616), acts as an agent for many courier flights worldwide from New York, although some flights are available from Houston. They also offer special last-minute deals to such cities as London, Paris, Rome and Frankfurt which go for as little as US$299 round-trip. **Halbart Express,** 147-05 176th St., Jamaica, NY 11434 (tel. (718) 656-8279) and **Courier Travel Service,** 530 Central Avenue, Cedarhurst, NY 11516 (tel. (516) 374-2299), are other courier agents to try.

Check your bookstore or library for handbooks such as *The Insider's Guide to Air Courier Bargains* (US$14.95). The *Courier Air Travel Handbook* (US$10.70) can be ordered from **Thunderbird Press,** 5930-10 W. Greenway Rd., Suite 112, Glendale, AZ 85306, or by calling (800) 345-0096. **Travel Unlimited,** P.O. Box 1058, Allston, MA 02134-1058 (no phone), publishes a monthly newsletter that details all possible options for courier travel. A one-year subscription is US$25 (outside of the U.S., US$35).

■ From Europe

By Train

The great majority of budget travelers in Europe use the economical and efficient train system. **Eurailpasses** may be used to get to Italy from a number of European countries and are also valid for travel within Italy (but if you're only traveling in Italy, they're not worth it). If you're under 26, you may also purchase **BIJ** tickets, which cut regular second-class train fares on international runs by about 50%. BIJ tickets are sold by **Transalpino** and **Eurotrain.** Neither organization has a representative in the U.S., so Americans will have to purchase tickets in Europe. If you cannot find a Transalpino or Eurotrain office, try a large student or budget travel organization such as Council Travel, ISTC, or STA Travel. In Rome, you'll find **Transalpino** at P. Esquilino, 10Z (tel. 487 08 70; fax 488 30 94; open Mon.-Fri. 9am-6:30pm, Sat. 9am-1pm). There's also a booth in Termini, at track #22 (tel. 488 05 36; open Mon.-Sat. 8am-8:30pm; in summer also on Sun. 8:30am-5:30pm). When you buy a BIJ ticket, you must specify both your destination and route, and you have the option of stopping off anywhere along that particular route for up to two months. On an overnight ride, you might want also to purchase a *cuccetta,* the economy version of a full sleeping berth (about US$15—very worth it, as you will not be able to sleep a wink in a second-class seat).

Lenore Baken's *Camp Europe by Train* (US$16.95) covers all aspects of train travel. The *Eurail Guide* (US$15, postage US$3), published by **Eurail Guide Annual,** 27540 Pacific Coast Highway, Malibu, CA 90265, is widely touted as the best of European rail guides, listing train schedules, prices, services and cultural information. The ultimate reference is the *Thomas Cook European Timetable* (US$24.95, US$33.95 includes a map of Europe highlighting all train and ferry routes). In the U.S., order it from **Forsyth Travel Library,** P.O. Box 2975, Shawnee Mission, KS 66201 (tel. (800) 367-7984 or (913) 384-3440). Add US$4 for postage.

By Bus

Few people think of buses when planning travel to Italy, but they are available and cheap. **Magic Bus** runs direct service between many major cities in Europe. Their main office is located at 20 Filellinon, Syntagma, Athens, Greece (tel. (01) 32 37 471-4), but information is available from cooperating offices in many other cities. **London Student Travel** at 52 Grosvenor Gardens, London SW1W 0AG (tel. (01) 730 3402) operates express buses from London to destinations in Italy.

By Plane

Budget fares are available on high-volume flights between northern Europe and Italy, but usually only in the spring and summer. Carriers within Europe often offer student discounts. There are many good charter flights from London.

Air Travel Group Ltd., 227 Shepherds Bush Rd., **London** W6 7AS (tel. (081) 748 4999; fax 748 6381), acts as an umbrella organization for services including **Italy Sky Shuttle,** which programs flight assignments from seven U.K. hubs to 21 Italian cities. They also operate branch offices in Bologna, Milan, Naples, Rome, and Palermo. **London Student Travel,** 52 Grosvenor Gardens, London SW1W 0AG (tel. (01) 730 34 02), offers competitive fares all over the continent, and there's no age limit for many of their flights. Also check with **Magic Bus,** 20 Filellinon, Syntagma, Athens, Greece (tel. (01) 32 37 471-4), which operates inexpensive flights within Europe, despite its name.

ONCE THERE

■ Tourist Offices in Italy

The **Ente Nazionale Italiano di Turismo (ENIT)** is a national tourist office with bureaus in Rome (on Via Marghera, 2) and abroad. In provincial capitals, look for a branch of the **Ente Provinciale per il Turismo (EPT),** which provides information on the entire province. Many towns also have an **Azienda Autonoma di Soggiorno e Turismo (AST),** the city tourist board. The Azienda tends to be the most useful and approachable. The smallest towns sometimes sport a privately run **Pro Loco** office. Recently, a new brand of tourist office, the **Azienda di Promozione Turismo (APT)** has popped up. Watch out for these, because they are allowed to present you with a list of only those hotels that have paid to be listed and some of the hotels we recommend may not be on the list. Keep an eye out for the student-oriented **Centro Turistico Studentesco e Giovanile (CTS)** and the **Compagnia Italiana Turismo (CIT)** (see Useful Addresses, above for the central and foreign offices), the government-subsidized travel agency that specializes in outdoor activities such as camping and boating. Local offices are listed in the Practical Information section of each town.

■ Embassies and Consulates

Embassies in Rome have a tendency to close on holidays even the Romans don't know about. Call in advance to make sure your embassy is actually open before you wander over. All embassies answer the phone 24 hrs. in case of emergency, and have lists of English-speaking doctors and lawyers.

United States: Via Veneto, 121 (tel. 467 41). Passport and consular services open Mon.-Fri. 8:30am-noon and 2-4pm. Report stolen passports here; new passports can be issued in about an hour, for a US$65 fee (US$40 for minors).

Canada: Consulate, Via Zara, 30 (tel. 44 59 81 or 44 59 84 21; during non-business hours, 033 772 71 95; fax 44 59 89 05). Near the corner with Via Nomentana, on the fifth floor. Consular and passport services here open 10am-noon and 2-4pm. A passport issued here costs CDN$35. English and French spoken. Embassy, Via G.B. De Rossi, 27 (tel. 44 59 81).

U.K.: Via XX Settembre 80A (tel. 482 55 51; fax 487 33 24), near the Porta Pio and the corner with Via Palestro. Consular and passport services Mon.-Fri. 9:30am-12:30pm and 2-4pm; mid-July and Aug. open Mon.-Fri. 8am-1pm.

Australia: Via Alessandria, 215 (tel. 85 27 21; fax 85 27 23 00). Consular and passport services around the corner at Corso Trieste 25, open Mon.-Thurs. 9am-noon and 1:30-4pm, Fri. 9am-noon. They have lots of useful information for Australians (or any English-speakers) staying in Rome. Passport costs AUS$100.

New Zealand: Via Zara, 28 (tel. 440 29 28/29/30; fax 440 29 84). Consular and passport services Mon.-Fri. 8:30am-12:45pm and 1:45-5pm. Passport L104,000. If you need the passport after hours or during the weekend, a whopping L224,000 surcharge is added.

■ Emergencies

Few legal systems are as convoluted and ambiguous as Italy's. Interpretations of the law are as varied as the dialects of the land. Your consulate will provide an attorney and advice, but after that you are on your own; you will be subject to Italian law.

If you can't avoid the police system, at least know with whom you are dealing. The **Polizia Urbana,** or **Pubblica Sicurezza** (emergency tel. 113), are the non-military police who deal with local crime. Try to contact them first if you are robbed or attacked. The **Carabinieri** (emergency tel. 112) are actually a part of the Italian Army. They usually deal with the most serious crimes, such as terrorism (hence their intimidating, well-armed presence at airports). The **Vigili Urbani** manage less violent, less serious offenses, such as traffic violations. They also give directions to lost tourists. This book provides listings of police offices and medical emergency numbers in the Practical Information section of individual cities. Consult the Safety and Security section above for further notes on avoiding touristic misfortune.

■ Getting Around

Plane

Italy's train system is so efficient and airline prices so high that it makes little sense to fly Italy's three domestic airlines, **ATI, Alitalia,** or **Alisarda,** unless you need to go a long distance in speed-of-light time. Ask about discounts on domestic travel at one of their many offices.

Train

Ferrovie dello Stato (FS), the Italian State Railway, is one of the last European train systems to provide inexpensive service. The fare between Rome and Venice, one of the longer trips in Italy, is only US$32 one way, second-class. Moreover, passengers between the ages of 12 and 25 are eligible for reduced rates (see below).

Italian trains retain the romance and convenience that American railways have lost. Unfortunately, **they are not always safe.** While passengers sleep deeply, they may be molested, robbed or even attacked. Padlocking your pack to an immobile object (like the luggage rack) is a good idea; sleep wearing your money belt or neck pouch and, if you are traveling with a companion, try to sleep in shifts. Overnight travelers should know that compartments are sometimes gassed—be sure you open a window to thoroughly ventilate your compartment, and try to travel during the day whenever possible. (Women travelers should be cautious of empty compartments even during the day.)

Although the traveler touring only Italy will lose money on a **Eurailpass,** consider buying one if you will be traveling outside Italy as well. The **Eurail Flexipass** allows time to tour as well as traverse Italy. Passes available include those for five days of first-class travel 15 days (US$230), nine days of travel within 21 days (US$398), and 14 days of travel within one month (US$498), with half-price for children under 12. Travelers under 26 are eligible for a second-class **Youth Flexipass,** which allows a three-month window for 15 (US$340) or 30 days (US$540) of travel. Eurail also offers the **Saverpass,** a 15-day, discounted first-class pass for unlimited travel for two or more people traveling together (US$298 per person). From April 1 to September 30, three or more people must travel together. For more information or to purchase a pass, contact Council Travel, STA, Travel CUTS, or a travel agent.

The Italian State Railway offers its own passes, valid on all train routes within Italy. The **BTLC "Go Anywhere"** train pass is available in first- or second-class. Second-class passes cost US$136 for eight days, US$172 for 15 days, US$198 for 21 days, and US$240 for 30 days. Travelers must have the dates of validity stamped on the ticket at the first station of use. Unless you travel at a furious pace, however, there's no way to make this pass worth its price—train fares in Italy are simply too cheap.

The **Italian Kilometric Ticket** is good for 20 trips or 3000km (1875 mi.) of travel, whichever comes first, and can be used for two months by up to five people. Three thousand kilometers is a long way in Italy, so it's virtually impossible for one person to break even on the Kilometric Ticket. For a couple or a family traveling reasonably widely, however, it can pay off. Ticket holders may travel on Intercity, Eurocity, Rapido, and ETR450 (Italy's newest and fastest train providing express service to major cities), but must pay a supplemental fare. When used by more than one person, mileage per trip is calculated by multiplying the distance by the number of users. Children under 12 are charged half of the distance traveled, and those under four travel free. A first-class kilometric ticket is US$238, second-class, US$140, plus a US$10-per-person fee. When buying the ticket, be sure the sales agent stamps

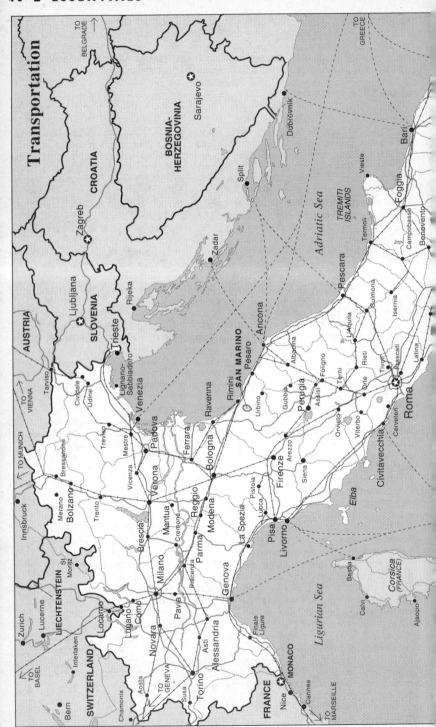

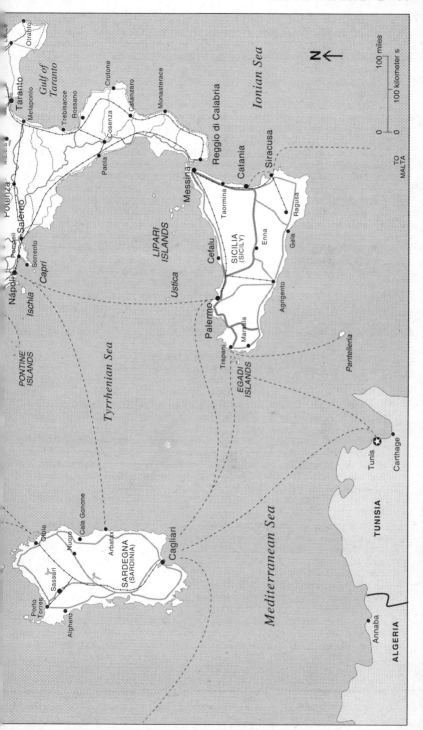

the date on it, or you may find yourself with a useless pass. Either pass may be bought from the Italian State Railway representative, 666 5th Ave., New York, NY 10113 (tel. (212) 697-2100), or in Italy (where purchase price is slightly lower) at major train stations and offices of the **Compagnia Italiana Turismo (CIT).** Be aware that while using this pass, you must go to the ticket booth and have your mileage stamped, otherwise you will pay hefty fines assessed for buying a ticket on the train.

The **cartaverde** is available to anyone under 26. The card costs L40,000, is valid for three years, and entitles you to a discount of 20% on any state train fare. They can be purchased only in Italy and if you're under 26, it should be your *first* purchase upon arrival. Families of four or more, or a group of up to five adults traveling together, qualify for discounts on Italian railways. Anyone over 60 with proof of age can get a 30% discount if they buy a **cartargento** ("silver card"), good for a year for L10,000. The discount is not available June 26-Aug. 14 and Dec. 18-28.

The Italian train system involves four kinds of regular trains. The *accelerato,* more commonly (and appropriately) referred to as a *locale,* usually stops at every station along a particular line, sometimes taking twice as long as a faster train. The *diretto* makes fewer stops than the *locale,* and the *espresso* stops only in major stations. The air-conditioned *rapido,* or *intercity (IC)* trains stop only in the largest cities. You will be charged more for a *rapido* ticket (waived for Eurail or BTLC holders), but it's often worth the money on long hauls (but check your train schedule; sometimes an *espresso* train is just as fast). Some *rapido* trains do not have second-class compartments, rocketing the cost of a ticket out of the budget traveler's range, and a few require reservations. On overnight trips, consider paying extra for a *cuccetta,* a fold-down bunk which typically comes six to a compartment (the cost will vary depending on the length of the journey—usually around $15). If you're not willing to spend the money on a *cuccetta,* consider taking an *espresso* train for overnight travel—they usually have compartments with fold-out seats. Finally, *freccie* trains run directly between cities that are normally connected only through other cities. There are 14 *freccie* that cover Italy, each running once per day.

Bus

Buses in Italy are neither faster nor cheaper than *diretto* trains. On the other hand, they are more punctual, comfortable, frequent, and they serve many points in the countryside that are inaccessible by train. Buses are also often crowded, so buy tickets in advance. Italy's bumpy terrain requires a strong stomach. As a reward for your possible sufferings, the scenery from many Italian buses often outshines the beauty of any final destination. Bus rides in the Southern Tuscan hills and the route from Bolzano to Cortina D'Ampezzo in the Dolomites are among the most incredible (and most nauseating).

Car

If you're pressed for time, or touring with friends or a large family, traveling by car may prove the most enjoyable and practical way to see Italy. Keep in mind, however, that much of Italy's infrastructure was constructed before the age of the automobile. Some towns will prove virtually unnavigable; consider parking on the outskirts and walking to town centers. (On the other hand, the Italian *Autostrade* are the worthy successors to the Roman roads, barreling through mountains and soaring over valleys.) Reckless drivers are not uncommon in Italy, and the convoluted street system often inflames tempers.

A car can cut severely into your budget. The *Autostrade* charge stunning tolls: the ride from Rome to Bologna will run you on the order of L40,000 in booth stops alone. Gas *(benzina)* computes to about L1500 a liter (about a quart) and renting a four-seater for one week will be at least US$200. **Auto Club of Italy (ACI)** has border offices and ENIT offices in Europe (only with foreign currency). The ACI is located at Via Marsala, 8 00185 **Roma** (tel. (06) 499 81). You may also wish to write for *Europe Free! The Car, Van, & RV Travel Guide,* 1842 Santa Margarita Dr., Fallbrook, CA 92028 (tel. (619) 723-6184).

You can rent a car from either a U.S.-based multinational with its own European offices, from a European-based company with local representatives, or from a tour operator, which will arrange a rental for you from a European company at its own rates. Not surprisingly, the multinationals offer greater flexibility, but the tour operators often strike good deals and may have lower rates. Always check if prices quoted include tax and collision insurance (some credit card companies will cover this automatically. This may be a substantial savings, but ask if a credit hold will be put on your account and if so, how much). Ask about student and other discounts and be flexible in your itinerary; it can be cheaper to pick up your car in some places than others. Ask your airline about special packages. Minimum age restrictions vary by country; rarely is it below 21. If you are a student or faculty member, inquire about special discounts or contact Council Travel or CTS. Reserving in the U.S. is usually much cheaper than renting once you've arrived. Many agencies require advance reservation made in the U.S.

The major firms renting in Italy are **Auto-Europe,** #10 Sharp's Wharf, P.O. Box 1097, Camden, ME 04843 (tel. (800) 223-5555); **Avis Rent-A-Car,** 900 Old Country Rd., Garden City, NY 11530 (tel. (800) 331-1084); **Budget Rent-a-Car,** 200 N. Michigan Ave., Chicago, IL 60601 (tel. (800) 472-3325), **Foremost Euro-car, Inc.,** 5430 Van Nuys Blvd., #306, Van Nuys, CA 91402 (tel. (800) 272-3299; (800) 253-3976 in Canada); **Hertz Rent-A-Car** (tel. (800) 654-3001); **Kemwel Group, Inc.,** 106 Calvert St., Harrison, NY 10528 (tel. (800) 678-0678); and **Maiellano Tours,** 441 Lexington Ave., New York, NY 10015 (tel. (212) 687-7725 or (800) 223-1616).

If you need a car for three weeks or more, **leasing** will be less expensive than renting. Most firms lease to drivers over 17 and rent to those over 20. Many companies also require a major credit card, and some offer discounts to foreigners.

If you're brave and know what you're doing, **buying** a used car or van in Europe and selling it just before you leave can provide the cheapest wheels on the Continent. Check with consulates for import-export laws concerning used vehicles, registration, and safety and emission standards. *Europe by Van and Motorhome* (US$13.95 postpaid, US$6 for overseas airmail) guides you through the entire process, from buy-back agreements to insurance and dealer listings. To order, write to 1842 Santa Margarita Dr., Fallbrook, CA 92028 (tel. (619) 723-6184). *How to Buy and Sell a Used Car in Europe* (U.S.$6 plus US$.75 postage) contains useful tips: write to Gil Friedman, P.O. Box 1063, Arcata, CA 95521. (tel. (707) 822-5001)

Caravanning, usually involving a **campervan or motorhome,** gives the advantages of car rental without the hassle of finding lodgings or cramming six friends into a Renault. You'll need those six friends to split the gasoline bills, however. Prices vary greatly, but for the outdoor-oriented group trip, caravanning can be a dream. Contact the car rental firms listed above for more information.

Do not leave valuables visible in your car. If you wish to leave an important or expensive article behind, try to find a parking garage (plentiful in major cities) where you can leave your car for around L4000 per day.

Foreign drivers in Italy need both an international driver's permit (or, if it's your own car, your license accompanied by a translation) and an international insurance certificate (or "green card"). Remember that all *Autostrada* direction signs are marked in green, all secondary roads in blue. Maps are essential, or you may find yourself confounded by Italy's labyrinth of small roads. It's good to have more than one map, as each emphasizes different roads. For any serious driving emergency, call the 24-hr. **nationwide auto service** at 116 (charges apply).

Mopeds and Scooters

Mopeds and scooters, an enduring feature of Italian life, provide an enjoyable way to tour the country, especially in coastal areas where the view demands frequent attention. They are, however, dangerous in the rain and on rough roads or gravel. Always wear a helmet and never ride wearing a backpack. If you've never been on a moped before, Italy is not the place to start. The Vespa-style motorbikes with small wheels and a center platform for your feet are particularly hazardous. Rentals are difficult to arrange in many places, but ask at bicycle and motorcycle shops. Rates are between L25,000 and L50,000 a day.

Bicycle

A bicycle's pace lets you feel truly a part of Italy. Anywhere outside the flat Po Valley, Italy's hills require a purpose-built touring or mountain bike with very low gears for any sustained expedition, along with an excellent set of lungs and legs. Since roads are generally in good condition, a touring bike with its more comfortable dropped bars and narrower, faster tires is probably preferable. For information about touring routes, consult national tourist offices or any of the numerous books available. *Europe By Bike*, by Karen and Terry Whitehill (US$14.95), offers specific area tours. *Cycling Europe: Budget Bike Touring in the Old World* is by N. Slavinski (US$12.95). Michelin road maps are clear and detailed guides. Be aware that touring involves pedaling both yourself and whatever you store in the panniers (bags which strap to your bike). Take some reasonably challenging day-long rides to prepare before you leave. Have your bike tuned up by a reputable shop. Wear visible clothing, drink plenty of water (even if you're not thirsty) and ride on the same side as the traffic. Learn the international signals for turns and use them. Although you may not be able to build a frame or spoke a wheel, learn how to fix a modern derailleur-equipped mount and change a tire before leaving, and practice on your own bike before you have to do it overseas. A few simple tools and a good bike manual will be invaluable.

Most airlines will count your bicycle as your second free piece of luggage. As an additional piece, it will cost about US$85 each way. Policies on charters and budget flights vary; check with the airline before buying your ticket. The safest way to send your bike is in a box, with the handlebars, pedals and front wheel detached. Within Europe, many ferries let you take your bike for free. You can always ship your bike on trains, though the cost varies from a small fixed fee to a substantial fraction of the ticket price. You may also be able to purchase an appropriate bike once you reach the home of Campagnolo and Bianchi.

If you want to transport your bicycle by train within Italy, label it and bring it to the *ufficio bagagli* at the railroad station; it should arrive within three days. If the train has a *bagagliaio* (baggage compartment), you and your bike can ride the rails together. The Touring Club Italiano publishes a helpful book (in Italian) called *Manuale Pratico di Cicloturismo*.

Long- and short-term rentals are readily available. The **French National Railroad (SNCF),** 610 5th Ave., New York, NY 10020 (tel. (800) 848-7245 or (212) 582-2110) rents bikes and has representatives in 11 countries, including Italy. With a ticket or railpass and identification, you can rent a bike for about US$3 a day with a US$20 deposit.

Getting all the necessary equipment together may be your biggest hassle. It is definitely worthwhile to buy proper equipment for touring; riding a bike with a frame pack strapped on it or your back is about as safe as pedaling blindfolded over ice. Bicycle accessories—panniers and other touring bags, lighting equipment, racks— are cheaper and of better quality in the U.S. Don't spend a penny before you scan the pages of *Bicycling* magazine and the Performance bicycling catalog for the lowest sale prices. **Bike Nashbar,** P.O. Box 3449, Youngstown, OH 44513-0449 (tel. (800) 627-4227) almost always offers the lowest prices, but when they don't, they cheerfully subtract 5¢ from the best price you can find. They regularly ship anywhere in the U.S. and Canada, and to overseas military addresses. Their own line of products is the best value. The first thing you should buy is a **bike helmet.** At about US$50, it's a lot cheaper and more pleasant than neurosurgery.

To increase the odds of finding your bike where you left it, buy a U-shaped lock made by **Citadel** or **Kryptonite**. They may seem expensive ($20-40) until you compare them to the price of buying a new bike in Italy.

By Thumb

> **Be sure to consider the risks involved before you hitch.** *Let's Go* does not recommend hitching as a means of travel in Italy or anywhere else.

Not everyone can be an airplane pilot, but almost every bozo can drive a car, and hitching means entrusting your life to a randomly selected person who happens to stop beside you on the road, risking theft, assault, sexual harrassment and unsafe driving. In spite of the risks, the gains are many: favorable hitching experiences allow you to meet local people and to get where you're going. The choice remains yours.

Women who decide to hitchhike in Italy should be forewarned: some men will consider you fair game for sexual harassment or worse. **If you're a woman traveling alone, don't hitch.** It's just too dangerous. Those who choose to hitch usually do so with a companion—a man and a woman are a safer combination, two men will have a harder time finding a ride, and three will go nowhere. Bulletin boards at hostels are often cited as a good place to start looking. Likewise, newspapers and university message boards sometimes carry ads seeking passengers to share driving and costs.

Italy has an excellent network of tollroads (*autostrade*) linking major cities. Hitching on the *autostrada* itself is illegal (as well as dangerous). Travelers more intent on seeing the countryside and meeting Italians than on making time often hitch the primary road system, which carries a large volume of short-range traffic.

Hitchhiking adepts usually refuse rides in the back seat of a two-door car, insure that the inside door handle operates before getting in, and they keep the door unlocked and their belongings close at hand—in case a quick escape becomes necessary, luggage locked in the trunk will probably stay that way. They also take care never to fall asleep in cars—some drivers may consider it tantamount to a wholesale sexual invitation. If a situation becomes uncomfortable for any reason, hitchers firmly ask to be let out, regardless of how unfavorable the spot seems for finding another ride. Hitching for women reportedly becomes more dangerous the further south or off the mainland one goes, and anywhere near a large city poses a particular risk.

The lighter hitchers travel, the easier rides are to find. They usually stack baggage carefully in a tight pile. A sign with the destination written in large letters is also reportedly useful. If long-distance traffic is scarce, some hitchers aim for the next large town on the road and scrawl out a new sign.

Europe: A Manual for Hitchhikers gives directions for hitching out of hundreds of cities, rates rest areas and entrance ramps and deciphers national highway and license plate systems. It's available from Vacation Work Publications (address in Work above).

■ Accommodations

Hostels

Hostels are great places to meet travelers from all over the world. If you are alone, there is no better place to find a temporary traveling companion. Italian youth hostels, *Ostelli Italiani*, are inexpensive and open to travelers of all ages; many are situated in historic buildings and areas of great natural beauty. They offer inexpensive meals and often provide services unavailable at hotels, including kitchen privileges, laundry facilities, and bike rental. On the other hand, you must adapt to curfews, daytime lockouts, and separate quarters for men and women (some hostels do have doubles). You should also be warned that many hostels close in late fall and winter. Hostels are not as abundant in Italy as in northern Europe, and their locations are often inconvenient. Security is also less certain than in a hotel room, so keep your valuables with you, or check them at the office.

Hostel accommodations usually consist of bunk beds, each with a mattress and blanket, in dormitory rooms. You may be required to use a **sleep sack,** a special sheet (you can purchase them from a number of travel and camping store, but most hostels which require them also provide them). The curfew is usually midnight in summer and 11pm in winter; some hostels turn off lights and hot water after this time. Rates vary by hostel, ranging from L10,000 to L17,000 per person including breakfast; dinners cost between L5000 and L13,000 (less for just a pasta course).

To stay in youth hostels affiliated with **Hosteling International (HI),** often you must be an HI member. For specifics on the Italian hostel organization, **Associazione Italiana Albreghi per la Gioventù (AIG)** and hosteling in Italy, see Useful Addresses: Hosteling Organizations.

Hotels

A provincial board inspects, classifies, and registers all hotels. No hotel can legally charge more than the maximum permitted by inspection, but some proprietors double their prices at the sound of a foreign voice—remember that an official rate card must adorn the inside of the door of each room, and that you should ask to look at the room (and the card) before committing to anything. Keep in mind that showers and breakfast often cost extra, and prices rise from year to year.

Given this system, you are unlikely to get ripped off by checking into the first place you find, or to find an unusual bargain by shopping around for hours. Differences between hotels of the same class are largely a matter of location and character, rather than price or facilities. In general, the most charming places are near the historic town center, while cheaper, nastier joints reside near the train and bus stations.

Hotels in Italy have recently been classified on a five-star system. Under this system, all accommodations should be called *hotels;* be aware, however, that a number of establishments retain their old classifications as *pensioni* (small one-to-three star hotels) or *locande* (the cheapest, usually one star, if any). *Albergo* is synonymous with hotel.

Prices fluctuate regionally; expect higher prices in the north and in Rome and Florence. The cheapest non-institutional singles generally start at about L18,000 and doubles at L26,000. Rates tend to be lower per person in a shared room. A room with a double bed is called a *matrimoniale* (though marriage is no longer a prerequisite). A double with separate beds is called a *camera doppia,* and a single is a *camera singola.* Showers, which are rarely in the room, usually cost L1000-2500 extra. Some places offer only full pension, meaning room and board (3 meals per day), or half-pension, meaning room, breakfast, and one other meal. Rooms with a private bath cost 30-50% more.

Italian law establishes a high and low season for areas popular with tourists. Remember that off-season months are different for alpine regions and seaside resort areas. When there is a difference in high and low season dates, *Let's Go* mentions it. Except in summer tourist spots such as Florence, Venice, the Riviera and Cápri, you usually needn't write for reservations. Without reservations, start looking for a room in the morning during high season, or call a day in advance. Pick up a list of hotels and their prices from the local tourist office (you can also call and have them quote rates over the phone). If you plan to arrive late, call and ask a hotel to hold a room for you. However, few hotels accept phone reservations more than a day in advance. Many small places don't have an English speaker, but this shouldn't dissuade a non-Italian speaker from calling. Instructions on making a room reservation in minimal Italian are included at the back of the book, and most *pensione* proprietors are used to receiving this type of call.

In many smaller towns (and some larger ones), householders rent rooms in their homes to passing travelers, sometimes with the blessing of the tourist authorities, sometimes without. Look for **affitta camere** signs posted around town or notes in store windows. Rates vary wildly; be prepared to bargain, but don't expect to pay much less than what a reasonable one-star *pensione* in town would cost.

Alberghi diurni (day hotels), found in town centers and near railroad stations, are good places to go when you need to clean up but don't have a room. Most are open 6am to midnight, and offer showers, barbershops, and luggage storage.

Student Accommodations

Student residences in Italy are inexpensive and are theoretically open to foreign students during vacations and whenever there is room. In reality, these accommodations are often nearly impossible to arrange. All university towns operate a *Casa dello Studente* to which you can apply. A useful source of information on student housing is the *Guide for Foreign Students,* from the **Italian Ministry of Education,** Viale Trastevere, Roma. The tourist office in university towns can also provide specific information.

The **Relazioni Universitarie** of the *Associazione Italiana per il Turismo e gli Scambi Universitari* operates a low-price-accommodations service for foreign students throughout the year in many of the major university towns. Discount student travel services also available. The main office is at Via Palestro, 11, 00185 Roma (tel. (06) 475 52 65).

The **Centro Turistico Studentesco e Giovanile (CTS)** can help you find and book accommodations in *pensioni* or dormitories. The London, Paris, and Athens offices can reserve a room for you in Italy for the first few nights. (See Useful Addresses: Budget Travel Services for complete information.)

Camping

Lakes, rivers, the ocean and the Alps are common backdrops for Italian campgrounds. Though there's often little space between sites, peaceful seclusion is usually only steps away. In August, arrive early—well before 11am—or you may find yourself without a spot. Rates average L6000 per person and another L6000 for the car. Many of the campgrounds are downright luxurious, boasting everything from swimming pools to campground bars, while others may be more primitive—you may want to shop around. The **Touring Club Italiano** (Corso Italiano, 10, 20122 Milano) publishes an annual directory of all camping sites in Italy, *Campeggi in Italia,* available in bookstores throughout Italy. A free map and list of sites is available from the Italian Government Travel Office or directly from **Federcampeggio,** Via V. Emanuele, 11, Casella Postale 23, 50041 Calenzano (Firenze) (fax (055) 882 59 18). An **International Camping Carnet** (membership card) is required by some European campgrounds but can usually be bought on the spot. The card entitles you to a discount at some campgrounds, and often may be substituted for your passport as a security deposit. In the U.S., it's available for US$30 through the **National Campers and Hikers Association, Inc.** (4804 Transit Rd., Bldg. #2, Depew, NY 14043, tel. (716) 668-6242). (Carnet price includes a membership fee.)

Wilderness Concerns

The first thing to preserve in the wilderness is you—health, safety, and food should be your primary concerns when you camp. See Health for information about basic medical concerns and first-aid. A comprehensive guide to outdoor survival is *How to Stay Alive in the Woods*, by Bradford Angier (Macmillan, US$8). Many rivers, streams, and lakes are contaminated with bacteria such as giardia, which causes gas, cramps, loss of appetite, and violent diarrhea. To protect yourself from the effects of this invisible trip-wrecker, always boil your water vigorously for at least five minutes before drinking it, our use an iodine solution made for purification. Filters do not remove all bacteria, but they can be useful for drawing water from streams that have

ACCOMMODATIONS

slowed to a trickle because of a drought. *Never go camping or hiking by yourself for any significant time or distance*. If you're going into an area that is not well-traveled or well-marked, let someone know where you're hiking and how long you intend to be out. If you fail to return on schedule or if you need to be reached for some reason, searchers will at least know where to look for you.

The second thing to protect while you are outdoors is the wilderness. The thousands of outdoor enthusiasts that pour into the parks every year threaten to trample the land to death. Because firewood is scarce in popular parks, campers are asked to make small fires using only dead branches or brush; using a campstove is the more cautious way to cook. Check ahead to see if the park prohibits campfires altogether. To avoid digging a rain trench for your tent, pitch it on high, dry ground. Don't cut vegetation, and don't clear campsites. If there are no toilet facilities, bury human waste at least four inches deep and 100 feet or more from any water supplies and campsites. *Biosafe* soap or detergents may be used in streams or lakes. Otherwise, don't use soaps in or near bodies of water. Always pack up your trash in a plastic bag and carry it with you until you reach the next trash can; burning and burying pollute the environment. In more civilized camping circumstances, it's important to respect fellow campers. Keep light and noise to a minimum, particularly if you arrive after dark.

Alternative Accommodations

Italian history comes alive when you stay in the guest house of a Roman Catholic **monastery.** Guests need not attend services but are expected to make their own beds and, often, to clean up after meals. Found in rural settings, monasteries are usually peaceful, and you shouldn't stay in one unless you want a quiet and contemplative experience. Carrying an introduction on letterhead from your own priest, pastor, or rabbi may facilitate matters, although many monasteries will accept only Catholic guests. For more information about specific regions and a list of convents, monasteries and other religious institutions offering accommodations, write to the archdiocese (*arcivescovado*) of the nearest large town. Many regional tourist boards also maintain a list of monasteries with guest houses.

For a quiet, non-religious atmosphere, stay in a **rural cottage** or **farmhouse.** Usually, you will be given a small room and asked to clean up after yourself, but you will have freedom to come and go as you please. For more information, write to the main office of **Agriturismo,** Corso V. Emanuele, 101, 00186 Roma (tel. (06) 651 23 42) or contact any of their offices in the region that you will be visiting.

If you plan to hike in the Alps or the Dolomites, you should contact the **Club Alpino Italiano,** Via Ugo Foscolo, 3, 20122 Milano, which owns about 600 huts (*rifugi alpini*) in the mountain districts and publishes a book with a map and information (including rating by difficulty). The **Touring Club Italiano,** Corso Italia, 10, Milano, (tel. (02) 852 61) publishes a number of books giving detailed hiking itineraries which include stopovers in the mountain refuges.

The **Associazione Cattolica Internazionale al Servizio della Giovane—Protezione della Giovane (PDG),** is a religious organization that helps women find inexpensive accommodations in its own hostels, convents, and *pensioni* throughout Italy. If you don't mind the occasional 10:30pm curfew, this service is extremely convenient. The PDG staffs offices in train stations of major cities and maintains centrally located bureaus in many towns. (See Specific Concerns: Women Travelers for more information.)

Sleeping in European train stations is a time-honored tradition, but while free and often tolerated by local authorities, it is neither fun, nor comfortable, nor safe (particularly dangerous for women and solo travelers).

■ Keeping In Touch

Mail

The postal system in Italy has justly drawn snickers from the rest of Western Europe, and now ranges from barely decent to deplorable. Aerograms and airmail letters from Italy take anywhere from one to three weeks to arrive in the U.S., while surface mail—much less expensive—takes a month or longer. Since postcards are low-priority mail, send important messages by airmail letter. Letters and small parcels rarely get lost if sent *raccomandata* (registered), *espresso* (express), or *via aerea* (air mail). Stamps (*francobolli*) are available at face value in *tabacchi* (tobacco shops), but you should mail your letters from a post office to be sure they are stamped correctly. Overseas letters are L1150; overseas postcards are L1050. Letters and postcards within Europe are L750 and L650 respectively.

Make sure anyone sending you mail from North America allows it at least two weeks to reach you. Mail from home can be sent to a hotel where you have reservations, or you can collect mail from most **American Express** offices if you have an American Express card or carry their traveler's checks. Have the sender write "Client Mail" on the envelope with the office's complete address.

Letters addressed to the post office with your name and the phrase **Fermo Posta** (General Delivery) will be held at the post office of any city or town. You must claim your mail in person with your passport as identification, and you may have to pay L250 per piece of mail. In major cities like Rome, the post office handling *Fermo Posta* usually is efficient and has long hours (though they close at noon on Saturdays and the last day of the month, and are also closed on Sunday). Since a city may have more than one post office, write the address of the receiving office if possible. It's also a good idea to have the sender capitalize and underline your last name to ensure proper sorting. Before writing a letter off as lost, check under your first name, too.

If you need to get something to or from Italy with celerity, both **Federal Express** and **DHL** operate in Italy, as do several Italian competitors. Shipments from North America to anywhere in Italy are guaranteed to arrive within 48 hours; shipments (up to 500g) from Italy are guaranteed anywhere in the world within two days. The cost from the U.S. to Italy for under 220g of documents is about US$25; shipping anything but documents usually involves filling out a commercial invoice. Contact the companies directly for more information. Federal Express: for delivery to Rome, call (2) 268 602 92 (the telephone code is (2) because the Milan office handles calls for Rome). In the **U.S.,** tel (800) 238-5355; in **Canada,** tel. (800) 463-3339. Other regional offices: **London,** tel. (081) 844 2344; **Sydney,** tel. (2) 317 66 66; **Auckland,** tel. (9) 256 83 00; **Dublin,** tel. (1) 847 34 73; **Johannesburg,** tel. (11) 921 7500. In Rome, **DHL** is located at Via Labicana, 78B (tel. (6) 790 83), southwest of Termini, about ¾km east of the Colosseum. (Open Mon.-Fri. 8:30am-6:30pm.) In the **U.S.** and **Canada** tel. (800) 225-5345; other regional offices in **London,** tel. (081) 890 9393; **Sydney,** tel. (2) 317 83 00; **Auckland,** tel. (9) 636 50 00; **Dublin,** tel. (1) 844 47 44; **Johannesburg,** tel. (11) 921 3600.

Telephones

Italian phone numbers range from two to eight digits in length. *Let's Go* makes every effort to get up-to-date phone numbers, but everyone is at the mercy of the Italian phone system, which this year is undergoing yet another in a seemingly endless series of major overhauls. Everywhere, phone numbers change with bothersome frequency; in Rome they change as quickly as traffic lights. If you call an old number, you may hear a recording of the new number in Italian, possibly even in English. For **directory assistance, dial 12.** Insert L200 if you are calling from a pay phone—the coins will be returned when you complete your call. Phone books often list two numbers: the first is the number at the time of printing, the second (marked by the word *prendera*) is what the number will be at some future, unspecified time. For an English-speaking operator, dial 170.

There are three types of telephones in Italy. Hold-outs from the dark ages of tele-communications take only tokens (*gettoni*) which are available (though increasingly rarely) for L200 from machines in train and bus stations, coffee shops, and tele-phone booths. *Gettoni* are also accepted as L200 coins, so there's no need to worry about buying too many. Instructions are posted on all phones; one *gettone* buys five minutes. You should usually deposit three or four, even if your call is local. If you underestimate, you may be cut off in the middle of your conversation. At the end of your call, press the return button for unused *gettoni*. To place long-distance calls, deposit six *gettoni* initially, and continue to feed the machine at every beep. For intercity calls, deposit eight or more. Thankfully, *gettoni* machines are being phased out. When using them, be sure to dial slowly as they sometimes misdial and discon-nect if you treat them roughly. Expect a couple of tries to get through successfully.

Scatti calls are made from a phone run by an operator (who may simply be the proprietor in a bar). Every town has at least one bar with a *telefono a scatti*, which can be used for international calls. A meter records the cost of your call, and you pay when you finish. Check with the operator before you lift the receiver, and remem-ber that he or she may tack on a substantial service fee.

The third type of phone is most common, and accepts either coins (L100, 200 or 500) or **phone cards.** Cards are an appealing, modern method. Cards can be bought for L5000 or L10,000 from machines, usually found near the phone. When you insert the card, a meter subtracts lire from it as you speak and displays the remaining value. Partially used cards can be removed and re-used. If you happen to run out in the middle of a call, you must insert another card, so buy more than one if you're planning a long conversation.

For the most part, it is not difficult to make **long-distance calls within Europe.** A person-to-person call is *con preavviso,* and a collect call is *contassa a carico del des-tinatario* or *chiamata collect.* For directory assistance for Europe and the Mediter-ranean, dial 176 (requires 5 tokens, or L1000).

Intercontinental calls can be made from phone card pay phones. In some small towns, however, international calls must be made from telephone company offices (SIP or ASST), generally found near the main post office and sometimes in major train stations, or from a *telefono a scatti.* To place a call at a telephone office, fill out a form at the counter. You will be assigned to a specific booth. Some offices ask for a L10,000 deposit. For intercontinental directory assistance, dial 17 90 (requires 5 tokens, or L1000). When direct-dialing is possible, you can dial two zeros and then the **country codes** (U.S. and Canada 1, Ireland 353, Great Britain 44, Australia 61, New Zealand 64, South Africa 27), followed by the area code and number. Calls to the U.S. cost L10,000 for three minutes and L3000 for each minute thereafter. Rates are highest on weekdays 8:30am-1pm, decrease after 6:30pm on weekdays and Sat-urdays from 1 to 10pm, and are at their lowest 11pm-8am, on holidays, and between 2:30pm on Saturday and 8am on Monday. Perhaps the simplest way to call long-dis-tance is to use the **AT&T** or **MCI Direct Service;** dialing a single number will con-nect you to an overseas, English-speaking operator who will then dial your collect call for you (you can also use a calling card). When calling the U.S. from most major cities in Italy, you can reach an AT&T operator by dialing 172 10 11 or an MCI oper-ator with 172 10 22. For MCI customer service call 167 87 90 73. To reach Canada easily, call **Canada Direct** at 172 10 01. Australia Direct and New Zealand Direct are similar, though not as extensive. For information call 0102 (Australia) or 018 (New Zealand). You may want to consider getting a calling card if you plan to make a lot of international calls; the cost is significantly lower. In order to receive a little card with the AT&T Direct numbers for most European countries, call AT&T at 1-800-874-4000. Beware once again that getting through often takes several tries.

Calls to Italy must be preceded by the country code **(39)** and the city code. When direct-dialing, the zero should be dropped from the beginning of each city code. Italians usually yell into the phone when calling long-distance, and you'll know the reason if you attempt an international call. The best connections are often abysmal; don't bother hanging up and 'rying again—it'll probably get worse.

Telegraphs and Fax Machines

The surest way to get an important message across the ocean is by wire service. **Telegrams** are sent from the post office and cost L1242 per word, including the address. **Faxes** may usually also be sent from the post office and increasingly from a number of private businesses in larger cities. If you're desperate, ask at the tourist office for the nearest fax service, sometimes you can use the fax at an upscale hotel for exorbitant fees. Fees are generally L10,000 a page. In the Rome post office, the staff may claim faxing to or from the U.S. is impossible, but insist.

Climate

Due to the cooling waters of the ocean and the protective Alps encircling the north, Italy's climate is for the most part temperate. The north grows fairly warm (and, in some places, very rainy) in the summer, while the south bakes in arid dry heat. Beware of Venice in August: the air is still, the canals stagnate, and the visitor swelters. In treeless Florence, it's a rare breath of air that musters up enough energy to provide relief. A breeze off the sea, however, cools the coast. Winter in the Alps is very cold, while Milan, Turin, and Venice turn chilly, damp, and foggy. Tuscany fares better, with temperatures in the 40s Fahrenheit, although rain is a sure bet. Southern temperatures usually remain in the 40s and 50s during the winter.

LIFE AND TIMES

■ History and Politics

Italian history is a complex fabric of events, personalities, and political parties with which no budget overview could aspire to keep pace. Duchies, kingdoms, republics, and Empires have washed over the Italian peninsula, a region united only under the Roman Empire and, recently by 19th-century nationalism.

The Ancient Peninsula

The discovery of a million-year-old village in Isernia in 1979 dated the earliest human settlement in Italy to the beginning of the Paleolithic era (1,000,000-70,000 BC). Starting around 2000 BC, Italic tribes inhabited scattered areas of the peninsula. Around 900 BC the first major unification occurred with the arrival of the **Etruscans** in central Italy who subjugated many of the Italic tribes. Scholars still debate their origin: a complex written language based on the Greek alphabet and recent archeological theories seem to support Herodotus' ancient opinion that they originated in Asia Minor. At Tarquínia, Veio, and Cervéteri, you can see the remains of their largest metropolises.

Beginning in the 8th century BC, the **Greeks,** who had already been trading and exploring around the boot for more than a millennium, began to settle in southern Italy. They first stopped along the Apulian coast and later founded metropolises in Calabria, Sicily, and Campania, which earned the title of *Magna Graecia* (Greater Greece). The Greek city-states were prone to internecine conflict but effectively survived until the 6th and 5th century BC. The Etruscan federation, which by that period ruled most of Northern Italy, eventually lost to the invading barbarian Gauls in the north and to the expanding Roman power in the south.

Rome

Myth has it that **Romulus and Remus,** twins, founded Rome in 753 BC. Wary of sharing power, Romulus slew Remus, initiating a tradition of ruthless, bloody politics. The new kingdom flourished during two centuries of Etruscan rule, until the son of **Tarquinius Superbus** raped the virtuous Roman maiden Lucretia. Lucretia committed public suicide, and the enraged Roman populace expelled the Tarquins in 509 BC.

The monarchy thus gave way to a **Roman republic** and the city quickly set about conquering its neighbors; by the 3rd century BC Rome controlled the entire peninsula except for the Greek cities. Although he won a series of battles against the Romans, Greece's Pyrrhus failed to press his advantage and was eventually defeated (hence the term "Pyrrhic victory").

Having conquered the Italian peninsula, the republic waged its most important battles, the three **Punic Wars** (260-146 BC), against Carthage for control of the Mediterranean. Rome, led by the evasive Fabius and the vindictive Scipio, and egged on by Cato the Censor, retaliated in the Third Punic War in 146 BC by razing Carthage. It was during the Punic Wars that Rome moved towards world power, consolidating its control over the Mediterranean and wiping out piracy in order to protect the supply routes for Rome, the capital city.

Under the umbrella of Roman military power, trade and shipping flourished. The spoils of war and taxes enriched Rome and its upper classes, creating an environment ripe for corruption. Social upheaval quickly followed: by 131 BC, slave, farmer, and plebeian demands for land redistribution led to popular riots against the corrupt patrician class, culminating in the **Social War** (91-87 BC), in which Latins and other Roman allies throughout the peninsula successfully fought for the extension of Roman citizenship. Sulla, the general who had led Rome's troops during the conflict, then led the Roman army into Rome (an unprecedented and taboo move), taking control of the city in a bloody military coup.

In the wake of this latest upheaval, **Spartacus,** an escaped gladiatorial slave, led a 70,000-man army of slaves and farmers in a two-year rampage down the peninsula. When the dust cleared, **Pompey the Great,** a close associate of Sulla, had taken effective control of the city, but soon found himself in conflict with his sometime co-ruler **Julius Caesar.** Caesar, the charismatic conqueror of Gaul, finally emerged victorious, but a small faction, fearful of Caesar's growing power, assassinated him on the Ides (15th) of March in 44 BC. His power eluded several would-be heirs before falling to his nephew, Octavian, who consolidated and concentrated power, assumed the title of **Augustus Caesar,** and inaugurated an imperial government in 27 BC.

Augustus' reign (27 BC-14 AD) is generally considered the **golden age of Rome:** the beginning of the *Pax Romana* (200 years of peace). Under Augustus and his successors, a professional army and imperial bureaucracy were created that were able to maintain the Empire and its borders under both good and bad emperors. Roman law and civic culture were extended out to the frontiers. These urban centers and their Romanized upper classes enabled the Emperor to rule over a vast empire with a small number of officials and troops. Rome reached its maximum geographical expansion under **Trajan** (98-117 AD). **Marcus Aurelius,** the stoic philosopher-emperor was forced to spend his reign fending off barbarian incursions. With his death in 180 AD, Rome entered into a period of decline.

The Moribund Empire and The Dark Ages

Weak leadership and the southward invasions of Germanic tribes combined to create a state of anarchy in the 3rd century AD. **Diocletian** secured control of the fragmented empire in 284 AD. He then established order, divided the empire into eastern and western halves and escalated the persecution of Christians in a period that became known as the "age of martyrs." The persecution began in 64 when the Emperor Nero needed a scapegoat for the immense destructive fire he was widely believed to have started. The Roman people were diverted by the sight of Christians dressed in the hides of animals and torn to shreds by savage canines, or set on fire as lamps so law-abiding citizens could do a little reading before bed. Despite this remarkably hazardous environment, by the end of Diocletian's violent reign approximately 30,000 Christians remained in Rome.

The fortunes of Christians took a turn for the better when **Constantine,** Diocletian's successor, claimed to have seen a huge cross in the wartime sky along with the letters, *"In hoc signo vincit"* (By this sign you shall conquer). Sure enough, victory followed the vision. Constantine, combining military strategy with spiritual conversion, declared Christianity the state religion in 315 AD. But soon provincial capitals decayed while armies of barbarian mercenaries patrolled the frontiers. In 410 **Alaric,** king of the Visigoths, deposed the last of Rome's western emperors and sacked the city. The ensuing scramble for power wasn't fully resolved until 476, when **Odoacer,** an Ostrogoth chieftain, was crowned King of Italy.

With the weakening and eventual disappearance of imperial authority in the Latin West, the Church and the papacy thus grew in power. Threatened by Lombards, the Pope was forced to call for Frankish assistance. Italian city-states dissipated their political energy and military strength in constant bickering, leaving themselves vulnerable to Hungarian attacks from the north and Saracen assaults on Sicily, Sardinia, and the western coast. Italy's relapse into near-chaos paved the way for increased papal authority. Although he was unable to repel the devastating Norman invasion of 1084, led by Robert Guiscard, **Pope Gregory VII** (1073-1085) did much to free Italy from outside rule, and from the 11th to 13th century, Rome grew as the administrative center of the Roman Catholic Church.

The Renaissance

Although the papacy eventually reasserted itself, the leaders who clasped the fallen scepter in the 14th through 16th centuries were secular politicos ruling the individual city-states. Left to their own devices, the leaders of these *communi* concentrated on extending their own economic and territorial power. Toward this end, they initiated a political fragmentation that would typify Italian history for centuries. Ironically, such instability planted the seeds of the greatest intellectual and artistic flowering of history—the **Renaissance.** Great ruling families like the Gonzaga in Mantua, the d'Este in Ferrara, and the Medici in Florence instituted important reforms in commerce and law, fertilizing the already rapid cultural and artistic flourishing of their respective cities. Princes, bankers, and merchants channeled their increasing wealth into patronage for the artists and scholars whose work defined the era. Unfortunately, power-hungry princes also cultivated the dark side of the Renaissance—constant warfare, usually among mercenaries. The weakened cities yielded easily to the Spanish invasions of the 16th century under Charles V and by 1556, both Naples and Milan had fallen to King Ferdinand of Aragon.

Disease and Disaster

Along with the humanist ideals, the creations of Michelangelo and Raphael, and the licentious exploits of *Carnivale*, Renaissance Italy encountered a humiliating arrest to its achievements: **syphilis**. The disease was probably imported to the continent in 1494 from either Africa or the West Indies, or from America by Christopher Columbus's crew. As French soldiers contracted syphilis from prostitutes in Naples they nicknamed it the "Neapolitan disease." The Italians, in turn, called it *morbo gallico* (disease of the Gauls). In Rome, the disease spread wildly, infecting seventeen members of the Pope's family and court, including Cesare Borgia.To add to the city's horrors, the Tiber produced a violent **flood** in 1495. Water gushed into the streets and surged through churches and homes. The ascetic Florentine friar **Girolamo Savonarola** soon proclaimed these calamities the wages of sin to and inaugurated a war on the excesses of Rome. He warned the city of famine, pestilence, and general catastrophe if it failed to clean up its act—he even envisioned a black cross rising from the hills of Rome emblazoned with the words, "The Cross of God's Anger." The pope tried to shut up the pesky friar, first by a decree forbidding him to speak, then by offering him a cardinal post. The friar refused the hat, claiming that one "red with blood" would be more appropriate. Excommunicated, Savonarola persevered until the Florentines themselves got sick of his continual haranguing and tortured, burned, and hanged him.

Jews In Renaissance Italy

Pope Sixtus IV (1464-71) was a strong and vocal defender of the Jews at the same time that he commissioned the Sistine Chapel as a great monument to Catholicism. Nevertheless, to the consternation of the Roman Jewry, he paid no attention to the first stirrings of the Inquisition. The expulsion of the Jews from Spain in 1492 sent many to Italy and to Rome to join the well-established Jewish community, where they set up shops and businesses.

Pope Leo X (1513-22), known more for his intense patronage of the arts than his religious devotion, involved a select number of Jews in his court. However, the Counter-Reformation ushered in a new period of intolerance toward the Jews. In 1556 all Roman Jews were herded into the Ghetto, a small, low-lying malarial district near the Tiber. The gates were locked at night, and during the day Jews were forced to wear yellow caps (for men) or veils (for women) if they ventured beyond the dreary zone. Jews were only allowed to work in outdoor markets or rag shops, though many pursued mystical practices, such as astrology and fortune-telling to make a living and it was not unheard of for patrician ladies of Rome to regularly have their palms read in the Ghetto. The walls of the Ghetto remained for two centuries.

The Borgia Family

One of Italy's leading Italian families, the **Borgias** have long been immortalized on stage, in song, and in print. All of 15th-century Europe trembled at the mere mention of this unscrupulous but charismatic family. While the very first Borgia Pope, Calixtus III, was harmless enough, his nephew and successor **Rodrigo Borgia** (1430-1503) was intent on founding a kingdom which would be ruled by his multitudinous progeny. You can still see Rodrigo's insatiable appetites in his face, captured in the unflattering frescoes done by Pinturicchio in the Vatican Museums.

While Rodrigo ruled in Rome, his son **Cesare** (1476-1507) went about the bloody business of carving out a new kingdom. Cesare swiped title after title from conquered nobles, ruthlessly pillaging cities as large as Urbino and Venetians and Florentines were certain they would be next. Notorious for his nonchalance while witnessing murders, he once invited four high-ranking officers to a banquet and continued munching on a drumstick while they were strangled in front of him.

Rodrigo's younger sister **Lucrezia Borgia** (1480-1519) certainly did her part to help out, marrying five times by the time she was 22, each time for a strategic purpose. In contrast to history's long-term view of her family, Lucrezia's personal story had a happy ending. Her marital bliss was crowned by a brood of children. Rodrigo and Cesare, on the hand, got their just deserts: the former may have been poisoned and the latter was struck down in battle.

After The Renaissance: Italian Irrelevance

Sixteenth century Spaniards brought a wonderful gift to Italy, in addition to their invading armies: the **Inquisition** became the primary method of suppressing Protestantism and the Jesuits, and rolling back the Counter-Reformation. Its victims included such noted intellectuals as Galileo Galilei and Giordano Bruno. The end of the 16th century brought the attenuation of Spanish control over the Italian states and a corresponding rise in the temporal power of the papacy. At the same time, the Duke of Savoy, Victor Amadeus II, extended his territorial control in Piedmont, leaving Italy a patchwork of political regimes.

The rise of **Napoleon** ushered in the new century. He united Italy for the first time since antiquity by bringing the southern provinces together with the Kingdom of Naples and the Roman Republic in 1798. Napoleon further stimulated Italian patriotism by arousing national resentment against the Austrian presence. After

Napoleon's fall in 1815, the **Congress of Vienna** carved up Italy anew, shuffling kingdoms and granting considerable control to Austria.

The Italian Nation

In subsequent decades, strong sentiment against foreign rule prompted a movement of nationalist resurgence called the **Risorgimento,** ultimately culminating in national unification in 1870. Success of the Risorgimento rests primarily with three Italian heroes: **Giuseppe Mazzini,** the movement's intellectual leader, **Giuseppe Garibaldi,** the military leader and commander of the "red-shirts," and **Camillo di Cavour,** the political and diplomatic mastermind. Although the much-revered Garibaldi and his army of 1000 defeated the Bourbons in the south, the credit for Italy's birth as a nation belongs to Cavour.

The new Kingdom of Italy, under **Vittorio Emanuele,** (whose statesmanship is commemorated by a *via* or piazza in seemingly every town) went on to annex Romagna, Parma, Mòdena, and Tuscany. France ultimately relinquished Rome on September 20, 1870, the pivotal date in modern Italian history. Once the elation of unification wore off, however, age-old provincial differences reasserted themselves. Northern regions wanted to shield their relative prosperity from the economic stagnation of the agrarian south, central city-states were wary of surrendering too much power to a central administration, and the Pope, whose Roman empire had been seized by the new kingdom, threatened Italian Catholics (98% of the population is Catholic, mind you) with excommunication for participating in politics. Disillusionment increased as Italy became involved in World War I, fighting to gain territory and vanquish Austria.

The chaotic aftermath of World War I paved the way for the rise of **fascism,** with its promise of order and stability. The Bolsheviks had recently gained control in Russia, and **Benito Mussolini** politically milked a "red scare" to destroy his strongest domestic opponents. Seeking to regain the glory of imperial Rome, "Il Duce" conquered Ethiopia in 1936. In 1940, Italy entered World War II and joined the Axis. Success came quickly, but was short-lived: when the Allies landed in Sicily three years later, Mussolini fell from his pinnacle of power. By the end of 1943, the government had changed direction, and declared war on Germany, which promptly invaded and occupied its former ally. Skirmishes between supporters of the deposed Fascist government and its democratic replacement further ravaged Italy.

The Constitution adopted in 1948 established a new Italian Republic with a president, a bicameral Parliament, and an independent judiciary. The president, elected for a seven-year term by an electoral college, is the head of state and appoints the prime minister. Chief executive authority rests with the prime minister and his Council of Ministers.

Within this framework, the **Christian Democratic Party** (DC), bolstered by American money and military aid (and, as has been recently and convincingly shown, Mafia collusion), bested the Socialists and surfaced as the consistent ruling party in the newly fashioned republic. But domination by a single party has not given the country stability: the republic has been mired in political turmoil, with more than 50 different governments since World War II. The Italian party system traditionally follows a pattern of "polarized centrism"—a multiparty system with most voters belonging either to the right-leaning Christian Democrats, or to one of the left-leaning parties: the **Socialist Unity Party** (PSU, though usually referred to by its old name, the PSI) or the **Democratic Party of the Left** (PDS, a much less radical version of the old Communist Party, the PCI). Since no single party can claim a majority of the voters, Italian governments are formed with volatile and tenuous coalitions forged between parties.

The instability of the postwar era, in which the Italian economy sped through industrialization at an unprecedented rate, gave way to violence and near-anarchy in the 1970s. The *autumno caldo* (hot autumn) of 1969, a season of strikes, demonstrations, and riots, came on the heels of the international mayhem of 1968 and foreshadowed the violence of the 70s: twenty percent inflation, spiraling unemployment rates, and the proliferation of terrorist groups left the Italian government at a loss to respond. Perhaps most shocking was the 1978 kidnapping and murder of ex-Prime Minister **Aldo Moro** by the *Brigate Rosse* (Red Brigades), a leftist terrorist group formed in Turin in 1970.

The extent of **mafia** power has waned somewhat in recent years, though in a desperate response to this situation it has actually stepped up attacks on individuals and famous sites in an attempt to intimidate political leaders and to frighten the general public as well as tourists. The loosely affiliated leaders of the nebulous organization still command great control over Italy's society, politics, and economy, especially in the *Mezzogiorno* and Sicily. As the leaders of the black market, the mafia has become the pillar, however crooked, of the Italian economy. Some of the *mafiosi's* success stems from the cultural acceptance of their activities, but today's mafia—with its heightened passion for drug-running and violence—inspires near-universal resentment among Italians. The Italian Parliament passed an unprecedented anti-mafia law in 1982, followed by the Palermo *maxi processi* (maxi-trials), the largest mafia trial in history. Sicily-based *La Rete* (the Network), a new political party with a strong anti-mafia platform, has become the most influential in Palermo—it won 15 Parliament seats in the April 1992 elections.

Divisions in Italy are not just between frightened citizens and organized criminals. Because the nation of Italy is still very young, city and regional bonds often prove stronger than nationalist sentiment. The most pronounced split exists between the north's highly industrialized European areas and the south's agrarian Mediterranean territories. Despite the many obstacles to modernization in the south, Italy has expanded with astonishing rapidity to become the world's fifth largest economy. Yet over the last 15 years, regional parochialism has been on the rise and northern patience with the wayward south is wearing thin: the right-wing **Lombard League** seeks to unite the fattest part of the north.

The chaos of Italian politics disillusions even its leaders. After three long years, Socialist **Bettino Craxi,** lamenting his inability to work with the Christian Democratic majority, resigned from the prime minister's chair in March 1987. After Craxi's fall, three Christian Democrats took office in quick succession. Then, following a rare period of relative stability, the musical chairs of Italian politics returned in April 1992: Christian Democrat **Giulio Andreotti,** who had been Prime Minister since July 1989, resigned, and President **Francesco Cossiga** also announced his retirement, citing Italy's "disastrous financial situation, the prominence of bad in our society, public disservice, and institutional paralysis." In the 1992 elections, the Christian Democrats gathered less than 30% of the vote for the first time since 1946, but managed to hold on to the presidency. On May 27, 1992, after disputes over voting procedures, a fist-fight between the neo-fascists and Christian Democrats (honest!), and 10 days and 15 rounds of voting that produced no majority, Oscar Luigi Scalfaro was finally elected Italy's new president, pledging his support for significant institutional reform of government, including a streamlining of the cabinet.

Since this time the slow and painful process of reforming electoral laws has resulted in *"tangentopoli,"* an unprecedented political crisis in which over 2600 politicians have been implicated in corruption scandals. Unlike past political schisms in the country, the current crisis has had immense reverberations in all aspects of Italian life. Reaction to continued uncovering and prosecution of mass corruption has included such pointed acts of violence as the May 1993 bombing of the Uffizi, Florence's premier art museum, and the "suicides" of ten indicted officials over the past two years, not to mention the unleashing of open Mafia retaliation against judges such as Falcone in Sicily. These are simply the most extreme manifestations of the numerous tremors running throughout the entire economic and political system, the complex structure of which English-language press has not fully captured.

■ Art and Architecture

Lump the whole thing! Say that the Creator made Italy from designs by Michael Angelo.

—Mark Twain

Any study of Italian art begins with the Roman Empire. The glory of Roman architecture is based on the **arch,** a deceptively simple innovation which yielded the famous Roman aqueducts, bridges, vaulted roofs, and triumphal arches. Rome's **Colosseum** (80 AD) typifies this marriage of Greek aesthetics and Roman technology; its **Pantheon** (117-125 AD), however, is proof that the arch was far more than a piece of architectural technology—it was a stroke of aesthetic genius.

The collapse of the Roman Empire and the rise of Christianity marked the beginning of a search for new aesthetic forms. The most pressing concern was the modification of the Roman temple to accommodate the Christian mass; for this purpose, the structure of Roman market-halls called "basilicas" were adopted. New trends in painting were slower to emerge; as early as the 5th century, however, Pope Gregory the Great was calling for art which would edify the illiterate masses and exalt the world beyond. The Christian art which emerged in the Middle Ages was thus crafted by men with an eye fixed firmly on heaven. These paintings combined a disregard for the physical world with a diminution of the individual in a larger, protective hierarchy of symbols and belief.

Although inspired by a different philosophy, Byzantine art was also religious and highly stylized. Byzantine architecture was notable both in the blueprint form of the Christian basilica and the domes and vaults atop these churches. Italian examples of Byzantine construction include the Church of San Vitale in Ravenna (547) and the Church of San Marco in Venice (1063-1073); the brilliant mosaics of the latter are also characteristically Byzantine.

Following these early years of the millennium, two great styles emerged to dominate art and architecture: Romanesque and Gothic, perhaps best understood in relation to one another. From 500-1200 AD **Romanesque** dominated Europe, with churches easily identified by small, rounded arches resting on massive stone piers. Great Italian Romanesque churches include the Cathedral of Pisa, San Ambrogio in Milan, the cathedral of Massa Marittima, and San Miniato in Florence.

The **Gothic** style of the 12th to 14th centuries resulted from the combination of the pointed arch and the flying buttress—together, they supported the heavy roof and allowed the Romanesque wall to be replaced by the glorious Gothic window. For some unknown reason, Italian Gothic never adopted the flying buttress and thus the incredible light-filled churches of France and Germany are absent in Italy. San Petronio in Bologna and the Cathedrals of Milan and Siena are lovely examples of this style. Great Gothic artists include **Simone Martini** and **Pietro Lorenzetti** (especially his Crucifixion in San Francesco, Siena).

As the 14th century neared, the economic and political conditions which nurtured the Renaissance were taking shape; the art was beginning to change as well, most notably with the work of **Giotto di Bondone** (1267-1337). In contrast to Byzantine and medieval art, Giotto used realistic proportions and backgrounds. His successor, **Masaccio** (1401-1428), is also worth noting for his work with light, shadow and color.

The **Renaissance** (14th-16th centuries), a period of renewed interest in humanity and its products, welcomed a flood of innovation and a rejection of dogmatic authority. Though a religious perspective no longer dominated the artist, religious art did not disappear altogether; it merely changed form. Renaissance art portrays human beings as individuals, often captured in action, and inserts them into specific, realistic backgrounds.

These new techniques revolutionized painting, sculpture, and architecture in Italy. One of the most prominent early Renaissance sculptors was **Lorenzo Ghiberti** (1378-1455). **Donatello** (1386-1466) revered the Roman style while producing

ART AND ARCHITECTURE

some of the most original work of his time. His close study of anatomy not only informed his sculpting, but made his statues the inspiration for anatomical accuracy and realism among later Renaissance painters.

The two most important architects of the early Renaissance are **Filippo Brunelleschi** (1377-1446) and **Leon Alberti** (1404-1472). Brunelleschi was an extraordinary engineer, often credited with the "discovery" of linear perspective in painting. His greatest accomplishment was raising the first great dome of the Renaissance over Santa Maria del Fiore in Florence. Alberti, whose style was less grandiose but more practical than Brunelleschi's, was the first to confront architecture in the context of town-planning. In the high Renaissance, their mantle would be taken up by **Donato Bramante** (1444-1514).

There is no doubt, however, that the peak of the Renaissance (1450-1520) was dominated by three men known as the Triumvirate of the High Renaissance: **Leonardo da Vinci** (1452-1519), **Michelangelo Buonarroti** (1475-1564), and **Raphael** (1483-1520).

The first of these three, da Vinci, was the original Renaissance Man—artist, scientist, architect, engineer, musician, weapons designer—and although he seldom finished what he started, his achievements were extraordinary. His monumental painting *The Last Supper* (Santa Maria delle Grazie in Milan) is a veritable handbook on Renaissance individualism in a religious theme. He also perfected the use of aerial perspective, defined standards of human proportional perfection, and stylized the use of *sfumato,* a technique that enables the artist to move smoothly from color to color and which revolutionized painting technique throughout Europe. That another genius of da Vinci's caliber existed at the same time—and in the same place—is stupefying. But Michelangelo painted and sculpted with as much skill as his contemporary—and perhaps with even greater results. The beautiful ceiling of the Sistine Chapel remains his great achievement in painting (after completing the project, he didn't paint again for 25 years). His architectural achievements are equally noteworthy—the master's designs for St. Peter's elevated Italian architecture to new heights. But sculpture is where Michelangelo's true genius lay. Classic examples are the formal, tranquil *Pietà* in St. Peter's, its half-finished, anguished counterpart in the Castello Sforzesco in Milan, the majestic, virile *David* in Florence's Academy, and the powerful *Moses* in Rome's San Pietra in Vincoli. Raphael is notable for his prolificacy and his technical perfection. Raphael invented the seated three-quarter-length portrait and the group portrait, and his frescoes in the Papal apartments in the Vatican are a must for lovers of Renaissance art.

When Rome was pillaged in 1527 by German and Spanish mercenaries, instability and conflict brought an end to the golden age of the Renaissance. The widespread disillusionment that followed was reflected in the emerging style of **mannerism.** Mannerists flouted Renaissance rules even as they revered them. This odd school was a short-lived link between the Renaissance and Baroque periods. A precursor to the Baroque period was the great architect **Andrea Palladio** (1508-1580), the originator of Palladian architecture (known for its classical, centralized proportions). Palladio's most important works were the Villa Capra at Vicenza and Il Redentore in Venice. The most lasting contribution to his art, however, may have been his *Four Books of Architecture,* which influenced many American and English architects.

The Baroque period that followed lasted into the 18th century. It signaled a concern for balance and wholeness, a new **realism.** At the beginning of this era, **Michelangelo de Caravaggio** (1573-1610) urged a return to naturalism—a commitment to portraying nature as is, whether ugly or beautiful. **Gian Lorenzo Bernini** (1598-1680), the most prolific artist of the high Baroque, designed the ornate colonnades of St. Peter's. **Tiepolo** (1696-1770) was the last of the great Italian decorative painters, and his sunny palate and strong frescoes marked the end of the tradition begun with Giotto.

Through French influence, the decorative **rococo** style and the sterner formalities of **neoclassicism** succeeded the Italian Baroque, to be succeeded themselves by the major trends of the 20th century. Two of Italy's greatest artists of this period were expatriates. **Amadeo Modigliani** (1884-1920) drew inspiration from the varied sources of mannerism, Renaissance art, and African primitivism, and did all his major work in France. **Giorgio de Chirico** (1888-1978) originated **metaphysical painting,** a precursor of surrealism, characterized by mysterious, somewhat threatening shapes occupying ambiguous space. Other modern Italian artists include **Sandro Chio** and **Enzo Cucci,** both neo-expressionists. **Francesco Clemente,** one of Italy's most talented new artists, paints to evoke dissatisfaction or disgust. Marcello Piacentini's monstrous fascist architecture looms at EUR in Rome, a built version of the vast, vaguely classical yet distorted urban spaces that de Chirico painted. To trace the current path of Italian art, you can visit modern art galleries in most major cities as well as at the Canova Museum at Passagno.

For further reading, you might want to try the bestseller (as of 1550) *Lives of the Artists,* a gossipy, informative glimpse into the artists of the Renaissance by Vasari, court artist for the later Medici. General books like H.W. Janson's *The History of Art* or E.H. Gombrich's *The Story of Art* contain everything you would ever need to know about art—Italian or otherwise.

■ Literature

Greek and Roman Mythology

Ovid's work is a principal source for our knowledge of Greco-Roman mythology. When the Romans plundered Greece, they even stole its divine pantheon. The anthropomorphic gods and goddesses lived as immortal beings with divine power, yet often descended to earth to intervene romantically, mischievously, or combatively in human affairs, sometimes disguised as animals or humans. Traditionally, 14 major deities preside: **Jupiter,** king of gods, his wife **Juno,** who watches over childbearing and marriage, **Neptune,** god of the sea, **Vulcan,** god of smiths and fire, **Venus,** goddess of love and beauty, **Mars,** god of war, **Minerva,** goddess of wisdom, **Phoebus,** god of light and music, **Diana,** goddess of the hunt, **Mercury,** the messenger god and patron of thieves and tricksters, **Pluto,** god of the underworld, **Ceres**, goddess of the harvest, **Bacchus**, god of wine, and **Vesta,** goddess of the hearth.

Literature Of The Empire

Early republican literature is not particularly inspiring; **Plautus's** farces, for instance, can best be seen as antique sitcoms. The poetry of Verona's **Catullus,** on the other hand, set a high standard for passion. **Livy** set down the authorized history of Rome during the first years of empire. **Julius Caesar** gave a first-hand account of the final shredding of the Republic; his *Commentaries* recount his experiences on the front lines of the Gallic wars. With Caesar's close contemporary **Cicero,** Latin prose is said to have reached its zenith: the dialogue *De Republica* asks, "is it better to be a statesman or a philosopher?" and resolves it magically with Scipio's dream.

The Rome of Augustus, despite a government prone to sudden banishment of the impolitic, produced the greatest Latin authors of antiquity. **Virgil,** revered as the only Roman poet worthy of comparison with Homer, wrote for the newly imperial city a creation myth worthy of its glory.

From the post-Augustan empire, **Petronius's** *Satyricon* is a bizarre, blunt look at the decadence of the age of Nero, while **Tacitus's** *Histories* summarize Roman war, diplomacy, scandal and rumor in the years following the death of Nero with unblinking even-handedness. His *Annals* look down from the upright Rome of Trajan's reign onto the scandalous activities of the Julio-Claudian emperors (Tiberius is a favorite target). Finally, **Marcus Aurelius's** *Meditations* bring us the musings of a philosopher-king on the edge of a precipice—it was all downhill after Marcus.

Italy had no *Beowulf* to brighten the Dark Ages, but the silence of a millennium was broken in brilliant fashion by a quite characteristic Italian cultural formation: a triumvirate. Any good Italian bookstore seems to devote a least a ceiling-to-floor case to annotated and critical editions of the works of **Dante Alighieri** (1265-1321), one of the first European poets to eschew Latin. He is consequently considered as much the father of the modern Italian language as of its literature. Dante peopled *The Divine Comedy,* his allegorical journey through the afterlife, with famous figures from his own lifetime; among the *Commedia's* chief virtues are Dante's acid opinions of Italian cities and their inhabitants.

If Dante is aptly described as a man with one foot in the Middle Ages and one in the Renaissance (quite a straddle), **Petrarch** (Francesco Petrarca, 1304-74) chose his side so emphatically as to be considered "the first modern man"; his subtle self-examination marks an individual, personal style unprecedented in medieval literature. The third member of the medieval literary triumvirate was a close friend of Petrarch's, but the style of **Giovanni Boccaccio** owes little to his melancholy chum. The *Decameron,* his collection of 100 stories told by ten young Florentines fleeing their plague-ridden city ranges in tone from bawdy to prim earnest, featuring pious maidens, licentious priests, carefree nobles, more licentious priests, pathetic paupers, scads of licentious widows, and the occasional licentious nun.

The Renaissance and Its Aftermath

15th- and 16th-century Italian authors were forced to create new genres to accommodate their expansive accomplishments. **Leon Battista Alberti** and **Palladio** (Andrea di Pietro) wrote treatises on architecture and art theory at either end of the Renaissance; **Baldassre Castiglione's** *The Courtier* instructed the inquiring Renaissance man on deportment, etiquette, and other fine points of behavior; **Vasari** took time off from ruinous redecorations of Florence's churches to produce a primer on art history and criticism *(The Lives of the Artists).* The most lasting work of the Renaissance, **Niccolò Machiavelli's** *Il Principe* (*The Prince*) was the first purely secular treatise ever written on politics. This sophisticated assessment of what it takes to gain and hold political power is candid, brutal, direct, Mansfieldian.

Both of the great Renaissance epic poets lived off the patronage of the same fabulously wealthy family—the Este clan of Ferrara. **Lodovico Ariosto's** *Orlando Furioso* is a study in irony; its gentle mocking of the literature of chivalry was the springboard off which *Don Quixote* leapt.

This being the Renaissance, people with perfectly good jobs in other areas felt compelled to add strings to their bows. Among Renaissance artists, **Benvenuto Cellini** wrote about that most interesting of all subjects, himself, in *The Autobiography;* **Michelangelo** wrote enough sonnets to fill a rather thick volume, while **Leonardo da Vinci** wrote about everything and anything *(The Notebook).* The scathing and brilliant **Pietro Aretino,** created new possibilities for literature when he began accepting payment from notable targets for *not* writing about them.

As Italy slid into international inconsequence, literary production again foundered. The Venetians frittered their time to the best effect; **Casanova's** *Life* makes good bedtime reading. Meanwhile, the prolific dramatist **Carlo Goldoni** transformed the traditional theater of the *commedia dell'arte* by replacing its stock figures with original, unpredictable characters in such works as *Il ventaglio.* The publication of **Alessandro Manzoni's** epic *I promessi sposi* (*The Betrothed*) marks the birth of the modern novel in Italy. A devout Catholic, Manzoni probed the suffering of humanity through the seemingly random course of history in this work and in his two tragedies, *Il conte di Carmagnola* and *Adelch.*

20th-Century Literature

Early in the 20th century, the playwright **Luigi Pirandello** (1867-1936) became the father of modern experimental theater with his explorations of the relativity of truth, exemplified by *Sei personaggi in cerca d'autore* (*Six Characters in Search of an Author*). Triestino **Italo Svevo's** three great works on the bourgeois mind are

Una vita (*A Life*), *La coscienza di Zeno* (*The Confessions of Zeno*), and *Senilità* (*Senility*).

Italy was also a center of Modernist innovation in poetry. The most flamboyant and controversial of the early poets is **Gabriele d'Annunzio,** whose cavalier heroics and sexual escapades earned him as much fame as his eccentric verse. In the mid- and late-20th century, **Salvatore Quasimodo, Eugenio Montale** and **Giuseppe Ungaretti** dominated the scene. Montale and Quasimodo founded the "hermetic movement" but both became more accessible and politically committed after the Second World War.

The 1930s heralded in the heyday of a generation of Italian writers who were much influenced by the experimental narratives and themes of social alienation in the works of U.S. writers. This school included **Cesare Pavese, Ignazio Silone, Vasco Pratolini,** and **Elio Vittorini.** The most prolific of these writers, **Alberto Moravia**, wrote the ground-breaking *Gli Indifferente* (The Time of Indifference) which launched an attack on the Fascist regime and was promptly censored.

As Italian literature approaches the end of the century, it is more difficult to determine what is a lasting masterpiece and to identify what schools are being developed. The works of the greatest of modern Italian authors, **Italo Calvino**, are unsurprisingly most widely available in English. Calvino's writing—full of intellectual play and magical-realism—is exemplified in *Invisible Cities,* a collection of cities described by Marco Polo to Kubla Kahn. The more traditionally narrative *If on a winter's night a traveler...* is a boisterous romp about authors, readers, and the insatiable urge to read, but perhaps most enjoyable for the traveler is *Italian Folktales*.

Most recently, **Umberto Eco's** wildly popular *The Name of the Rose,* a richly-textured mystery set in a 14th-century monastery, somehow managed to keep readers on edge while making the history of the revolutionary crisis in medieval Catholicism vaguely intelligible. *Foucault's Pendulum,* his latest, becomes rather precious in its complications, but wraps the story of the Knights Templar and half-a-millennium of conspiracy theories into a neat pocket-size package for transport.

■ Music

The Italians are musical tyrants, as anyone who's studied the piano, belonged to a school band, or belabored a violin can attest. Italians invented the systems for writing musical notation that persist today: **Guido D'Arezzo** came up with the musical scale, and a 16th-century Venetian printed the first musical scores with movable type. Cremona brought forth violins by Stradivarius; the piano is an Italian invention. Even so, for Italians, vocal music has always occupied a position of undisputed preeminence. Indigenous music languished until the 16th century, when Italians re-asserted themselves as choirmasters of the great cathedrals. In Venice, the Church of San Marco served as a showplace for the glory of the Republic. To befit a sanctuary of such splendor, church officials disregarded the more austere taste of Rome, calling for religious music with thunderous volume and dramatic instrumental accompaniment. **Palestrina** and his Roman colleagues, worried that the Council of Trent might banish polyphony in the liturgy, pre-empted such repression by eschewing Venetian flamboyance in favor of crystalline harmonies. At the same time, **madrigals,** free-flowing secular songs for three to six voices, grew in popularity.

Born in Florence, nurtured in Venice, and revered in Milan, **opera** is Italy's most cherished art form. Invented by the **Camerata,** an artsy clique of Florentine poets, noblemen, authors, and musicians, opera began as an attempt to recreate the dramas of ancient Greece by setting their lengthy poems to music. After several years of effort with only dubious success, one member, Jacobo Peri, composed *Dafne* in 1597, the world's first complete opera. Although *Dafne* has since been lost (not a tragedy, according to all contemporary accounts), a school of operatic composers soon emerged. As opera spread from Florence to Venice, Milan, and Rome, the styles and forms of the genre also grew more distinct. The first successful opera composer, **Monteverdi,** drew freely from history, blithely juxtaposing high drama, concocted love scenes, and bawdy humor. By charming his patroness the Duchess of Mantua, Monteverdi's jewel *Orfeo* (1607)—still performed today—assured the survival of the genre. Contemporaneous with the birth of opera was the emergence of the **oratorio,** which sets biblical text to dramatic choral and instrumental accompaniment. Introduced by the Roman priest, **Saint Filippo Neri,** who liked to preach against a background of dramatic music, the oratorio was soon incorporated into masses throughout Italy.

Instrumental music began to establish itself as a legitimate genre in 17th century Rome. **Vivaldi** wrote over 400 concertos while teaching at a home for orphaned girls in Venice. Under Vivaldi the concerto assumed its present form in which the virtuoso playing of the soloist is opposed to and accompanied by the concerted strength of the orchestra.

Eighteenth-century Italy exported its music; Italian composers coined the established musical jargon, their virtuosos dazzled audiences throughout Europe. At mid-century, operatic overtures began to be performed separately, resulting in the creation of a new genre of music; the **sinfonia** was modeled after the melody of operatic overtures and simply detached from their setting. Thus began the symphonic art form, which later received its highest expression in the hands of Italy's northern neighbors. At the same time, the composer **Domenico Scarlatti** wrote over 500 sonatas for the harpsichord. In opera, baroque ostentation yielded to classical standards of moderation, simplicity, and elegance.

To today's opera buffs, Italian opera means Verdi, Puccini, Bellini, Donizetti, and Rossini—all composers of the late 19th and early 20th centuries. With plots relying on wild coincidence and music fit for the angels, 19th-century Italian opera continues to dominate modern stages. **Verdi** became a national icon by mid-life, so much so that *Viva Verdi* was a battle cry of the Risorgimento. The music which he wrote as a young man includes both the tragic, triumphal *Aïda* and *La Traviata,* whose "foul and hideous horrors" shocked the London *Times.* Be aware as you listen that much of Verdi's work promoted Italian unity; his operas include frequent allusions to political assassinations, exhortations against tyranny, and jibes at French and Austrian monarchs. Another great composer of the era, **Rossini,** boasted that he could produce music faster than copyists could reproduce it, but he proved such a procrastinator that his agents resorted to locking him in a room until he completed his compositions. Finally, there is **Puccini,** composer of *Madama Butterfly,* noted for the beauty of his music and for the strength, assurance and compassion of his female characters.

Italian music continues to grow in the 20th century. **Ottorino Respighi,** composer of the popular *Pines of Rome* and *Fountains of Rome,* experimented with shimmering, rapidly shifting orchestral textures. **Gian Carlo Menotti,** now a U.S. resident, has written short, opera-like works such as *Amahl and the Night Visitors,* but is probably best known as the creator of the Two Worlds Art Festival in Spoleto (see the Spoleto—Umbria—listings below). **Luigi Dallapiccola** worked with serialism, achieving success with choral works such as *Canti di prigionia* (*Songs of Prison*) and *Canti di liberazione* (*Songs of Liberation*); both protest fascist rule in Italy.

Rock came to Italy in the 1960s, a reflection of musical trends set elsewhere, but endowed with a unique and indigenous character that blended folk and Mediterranean rhythms with pop beats. **Luigi Tenco** adapted the sound of be-bop to folk melodies while **Lucio Dalla** produced socially conscious rock. Both rock and politics continued to grow more radical as epitomized by the band **Area.**

No single trend has emerged to characterize Italian music over the last dozen years; a look at Italy's most popular performers reveals a surprising diversity of musical genres. **Luciano Pavarotti** remains universally adored. Although Italian discos rely primarily on English and American bands, when not dancing the night away, young Italians prefer the native singers and lyrics of *musica leggera,* (light Italian rock), as performed by **Claudio Bagliori, Bennato Edoardo,** and **Gianni Morandi.**

Opera season runs December to June. The productions at the Teatro alla Scala in Milan, the Teatro San Carlo in Naples, the Teatro dell'Opera in Rome, and La Fernice in Venice are especially spectacular, but Bari, Bergamo, Genoa, Mòdena, Trieste and Turin are also quite prestigious. Tickets are surprisingly cheap. Don't despair if you miss the season; throughout summer, you can enjoy open-air opera at the Baths of Caracalla in Rome, the Roman Arena in Verona, and at many major music festivals including the *Maggio Musicale Fiorentino* in Florence from May to June. The **European Association of Music Festivals,** 122, rue de Lausanne, 1202 Geneva, Switzerland (tel. (22) 732 28 03, fax (22) 738 40 12) publishes the booklet *Festivals 1993*; student rates and standing room are often available.

■ Film

For Rome's contributions to the arts in this century, don't go to the museum—go to the movies. Years before there was Hollywood, there were the **Cines** studios in Rome. Constructed in 1905-6, Cines created the Italian "super-spectacle," extravagant, larger-than-life re-creations of momentous historical events. The first "blockbuster" picture in film history was the 9-reel *Quo Vadis*, directed by Enrico Guzzani in 1912. The film featured real chariot races, real Christian-eating lions in the Colosseum, 5000 extras, mountainous three-dimensional sets, and a burning-of-Rome sequence that blazed the way for the scorching of Atlanta in *Gone With The Wind*.

Recognizing the popular power of cinema and its possibilities for propaganda, Mussolini created a national film school and the gargantuan **Cinecittà studios**, both of which are located in Rome. The presence of famous director **Luigi Chiarini** attracted many students, among them **Roberto Rosselini** and **Michelangelo Antonioni.** Mussolini's nationalized film industry (which lasted until 1943) produced no great films, yet sparked the subsequent explosion of **neo-realist cinema** (1943-50). The new style was characterized by the rejection of sets and professional actors in favor of location shooting and authentic drama. Neo-realists first gained attention in Italy with **Luchino Visconti's** 1942 *Ossessione,* a film based on James Cain's pulp-novel *The Postman Always Rings Twice.* Rossellini's 1946 tale of a Resistance leader trying to escape a Gestapo manhunt, *Roma, città aperta* (Open City), was filmed largely on the streets of Rome, just two months after the city's liberation, and won world-wide acclaim for the neo-realists. Perhaps the most famous and commercially successful neo-realist film, **Vittorio de Sica's** *The Bicycle Thief* (1948), is also set in Rome.

When neo-realism turned its wobbly camera from the Resistance to social critique, it lost its popular interest and, after 1950, gave way to individual expressions of Italian genius. Post-neo-realist directors **Federico Fellini** and **Michelangelo Antonioni** rejected logical narrative construction, turning away from the mechanics of plots and characters to a world of moments and witnesses. Fellini's *La Dolce Vita* (1960), regarded by many outside Italy as the representative Italian film, takes up Italy's ongoing fascination with its decadent aristocracy and questions the country's postwar love affair with American culture. This same theme was pursued a year later by Antonioni in *L'Avventura.* Antonioni's other films include *L'Eclisse* (1962), *Deserto Rosso* (1964), and his English-language film hit *Blow-Up* (1966).

Pier Paolo Pasolini, perhaps the most controversial of Italian directors, was also one of the greatest. Already regarded as Italy's premier poet when he started directing, Pasolini brought an intensely lyrical poetic vision to the screen. With *Hawks and Sparrows,* regarded by many as the director's masterpiece, Pasolini embarked upon an investigation of the philosophical and poetic possibilities of film.

By the late 60s it was clear to international critics that there were few young directors capable of carrying on the legacy of the previous two decades. Factional disputes regarding politics led to the disbanding of the National Association of Italian Filmmakers and the collapse of the Venice Film Festival in 1968. Despite this, the great tradition of Italian film has refused to choke and die. One of the most important and controversial Italian filmmakers of the seventies was **Lina Wertmuller;** her film *Swept Away* (1974) was an ironic approach to feminism which left many feminists furious. Those familiar with **Bernardo Bertolucci's** *Last Emperor* should see his *Spider Stratagem,* the story of a man's discovery of his father's ambivalent role in the Fascist period. Other major modern Italian films include de Sica's *Il giardino dei Finzi-Contini* (Garden of the Finzi-Contins) and **Francesco Rosi's** *Cristo si è fermato a Eboli* (Christ Stopped at Eboli), both based on the books of the same titles. The Oscar-winning *Cinema Paradiso,* directed by Giuseppe Tornatore, is the most recent invasion of America by Italian cinema.

■ Food and Wine: La Dolce Vita

A food glossary at the back of this book describes items commonly found on menus throughout Italy. Regional introductions and food sections of individual city listings describe local specialties.

Don't plan to lose weight in Italy. Any ground gained in health through mono-unsaturated olive oil and complex carbohydrate-rich pasta will certainly be buried under waves of *gelato,* cheesy pizza, indispensable coffee pit-stops, inescapable fried calamari, and the cholesterol heaven of the Italian dessert tray.

Italian cuisine, like virtually every other aspect of Italian life, differs by region. The north lays culinary claim to creamy sauces, exotic mushroom dishes, stuffed pasta, and flat, handmade egg noodles. Piedmont is best known for its delectable (but pricey) truffles, as is its southern neighbor Umbria; Lombardy specializes in cheeses and *biscotti* (sweet, shortcake-like biscuits); the coastal region of Liguria is noted for its seafood, pesto, and olive oil, while Germanic and Austrian influence on the Trentino-Südtirol/Alto Adige and Veneto regions have popularized dumplings, referred to as *gnocchi,* typically made of potatoes and flour. Central Italy serves richer, spicier dishes. Emilia-Romagna region is the world's pasta palace. Food here is loaded with meat, cream, cheese, and butter sauce. Tuscany draws justifiable acclaim for its pricey olive oil and bean dishes, while the Abruzzo is known for spicy, pepper-strewn food and a wealth of game meats. The food of the south is a bit coarser, but far less expensive than in the rest of Italy. Tomato sauces and tubular pasta originated in Campania, the birthplace of the most renowned "Italian" food; pizza as we know it hails from Naples. Greek influence can be detected in Calabrian cuisine, with its use of figs, honey, strong spices, and eggplant. Sicily produces luscious desserts, such as *cannoli,* sweet pastry stuffed with sweet cheeses and chocolate, and *cassata,* a rich ice cream. If you like fish, Italy will not disappoint. The lakes and endless coastline provide an astounding array of delicacies.

Most Italians begin the morning in a *bar* (a café) with a *cappuccino* and a brioche. **Lunch** is the main meal of the day in Italy. Almost everything closes down between 1 and 4pm, so you might as well take advantage of tradition. Though many Italians now take an American-style business lunch hour, most still find time to linger at midday over a few courses in a *trattoria.* Restaurants generally close from about 2pm until suppertime. If you don't want a big meal, grab lunch at an inexpensive *tavola calda* (literally, "hot table") or *rosticceria* (grill). Buy picnic materials at a *salumeria* or *alimentari,* both grocery stores. Fresh fruits and vegetables are best purchased at the open markets.

Italian **dinners** begin considerably later and last much longer than their American counterparts. The farther south you travel, the later dinner is served. A full supper begins with an *antipasto* (appetizer), which can be as simple as *bruschetta,* a type of garlic bread, or as fancy as *prosciutto* with melon. Next comes the *primo piatto* (the first course, usually pasta or soup), followed by the *secondo,* which consists of meat or fish. Ordering a *caffè* will get you strong Italian espresso; ask for *caffè macchiato* (literally "spotted coffee") if you would like some milk in it.

The *menù turistico* (referred to by *Let's Go* as *menù*) isn't always such a bargain. Since the government ensures fair dealing by controlling what is served, you will encounter no surprises. This may reassure non-Italians, but it also means the food is rather run-of-the-mill. When selecting a restaurant in Italy, keep in mind that family-run establishments charge less than those with hired help.

The billing at Italian restaurants can be a bit confusing. Most restaurants add a *pane e coperto* (cover charge) of about L1500 to the price of your meal, as well as a *servizio* (service charge) of 10-15%. In city restaurants, you may want to tip if the bill does not include service, but in family-run establishments without hired servers, tipping may be considered offensive. In a *bar*, look for a sign stating either *servizio compreso* (service included) or *servizio non compreso* (not included). In the case of the latter, drop some cash into the kitty on the bar. Café prices are lower—often half-price—if you don't sit down. The *Ricevuta Fiscale* (receipt) is an irritating device intended to hamper tax evasion. A restaurant must legally make up an R.F. and hand a copy to the client, who then must keep it until 60m from the restaurant (seriously!). If you are stopped (this happens rarely) and caught without it, both you and the restaurant may be fined.

Italy's rocky soil, warm climate, and hilly landscape have proven themselves ideal for growing grapes, and Italy produces more **wine** than any other country. Wine is the staple beverage (even served, slightly diluted, to children as young as 6). Italy's three greatest wine growing regions are Piedmont, Tuscany, and Veneto, but most every region has something to offer. Wines from the north tend to be heavy and full-bodied; most touted (and expensive) are Piedmont's *barolo* and *barbera,* but the equally famous and more affordable *Asti spumante* deserves a swig. Tuscany is regarded as Italy's wine-making capital; its rich *chianti,* similar to claret, is a universal favorite. Other good heavy red wines include *salerno* from Naples and *valpolicella* from the Venetian district. White wine connoisseurs should sample *soave* from Verona, *frascati* from Rome, *orvieto* from Umbria, *lacrima Christi* (Christ's Tear) from Naples, and *tocai* and *pinot grigio* from Friuli. Sparkling wines are also common in the north, and sipping them just before dinner at dusk imparts a sense of the *dolce farniente* (sweet apathy). The hotter climate of southern Italy and her islands produces stronger, fruitier wines than the north. Try the Sicilian *marsala,* which resembles a light sherry, or *cannonau,* from Sardinia.

You can usually order by the glass, carafe, or half-carafe, although bars rarely serve wine by the glass. *Vecchio* means "old," and *stravecchio* means "very old." *Secco* means "dry" and *abboccato* means "sweet." When in doubt, request the local wine—it will be cheaper (typically around L3500 a liter) and best suited to the cuisine of the region.

■ Sports and Recreation

In Italy, **il calcio** ("soccer" to the United States or "football" to the rest of the world) far surpasses all other sports in popularity. Some claim that Italy's victory in the 1982 World Cup did more for national unity than any political movement. Every city and town has its own team and major cities like Milan have more than one. Teams in the premier league pay huge sums to import the best players from around the world and pack their stadiums every Sunday. Italian football fans are called *tifosi,* that is, "typhoid-fevered." The Italian love of soccer divides as well as unites the Italian people, however. By kindling the deepest feelings of city loyalty, inter-urban rivalries—especially that between Naples and Rome—too often find expression in brawls.

Bicycling has long been popular in Italy. Besides manufacturing some of the best bikes in the world, Italians host the **Giro d'Italia,** a 25-day cross-country race in May. Professional basketball has also become a popular sport, importing players from the United States and other countries.

As the only country to encompass the entire 1400km arc of the Alps (along with the equally long stretch of the Apennines), Italy attracts thousands of **skiers** from December to April. **Summer skiing** is available on glaciers, as is hiking and mountain climbing throughout the north and in the Sila Massif in Calabria. **Swimming** has become rarer and riskier as Mediterranean pollution worsens. Try the beaches in the less-populated deep south, any of the Italian islands, or a lake. **Horseback riding** information is available from the Federazione Italiana Sport Equestri, v. Tiziano, 70 Roma.

■ Festivals and Holidays

Despite a dearth of national holidays, Italy suffers no shortage of town festivals. The most common excuse for a local festival is the celebration of a religious event. Virtually every town has a patron saint and has hosted a miracle or two, all of which are enthusiastically celebrated. An unmentionable number of festivals occur Easter weekend. Most bizarre is the May celebration of *Festi di San Domenico Abate* in Coculla, where people march through the city carrying a likeness of the saint draped with live snakes.

Less reptilian, though perhaps equally stomach-wrenching, is Italy's glut of jousting festivals, which tend to be held in late summer. Another medieval legacy, the Sienese *Palio,* features a bareback horse race in the town square, once in July and once in August. On the third Sunday in July, Venetians commemorate the end of the epidemic of 1575 with a gondola procession, and celebrate *Carnevale* in February with masks and some discreet street revelry. Carnevale action is much better in Ivrea, where anyone not wearing a red hat is likely to get dyed orange in the *Battle of Oranges.* Every June Florence stages a soccer match with its players in 16th-century costume to commemorate a match between the Florentines and the soldiers of Charles V, who were then laying siege to the city.

Italy also hosts plenty of equally delicious food and art festivals. Where food festivals and religious celebrations often end at nightfall, art festivals may span weeks or months. The month-long *Festival dei Due Mondi* (Festival of Two Worlds) in Spoleto, a delightful hodge-podge of classical art and cultural exhibits, follows this trend. For a list of festivals, write to the **Italian Government Travel Office,** 630 Fifth Ave., #1565, Rockefeller Center, New York, NY 10111 (tel. (212) 245-4822).

Take holidays, both legal and religious, into account when planning your itinerary. Banks, shops, and almost everything else shuts down, but merriment abounds. Italy officially closes on the following dates: January 1 (New Year's Day); January 6 (Epiphany); Easter Monday; April 25 (Liberation Day); May 1 (Labor Day); August 15 (Assumption of the Virgin); November 1 (All Saints' Day); December 8 (Immaculate Conception); December 25 (Christmas Day); and December 26 (Santo Stefano). Offices and shops in the following cities also shut down for feast days in honor of their respective patron saints: Venice (April 25, St. Mark); Florence, Genoa, Turin (June 24, St. John the Baptist); Rome (June 29, SS. Peter and Paul); Palermo (July 15, Santa Rosalia); Naples (Sept. 19, St. Gennaro); Bologna (Oct. 4, St. Petronio); Cagliari (Oct. 30, St. Saturnino); Trieste (Nov. 3, San Giusto); Bari (Dec. 6, St. Nicola); and Milan (Dec. 7, St. Ambrose). Be prepared for other surprises as you travel.

CENTRAL ITALY

Rome

Any attempt to capture Rome in its entirety fails—just as it is impossible to eat every goody in a sweets shop. There is always one more forgotten church, obscured cornice, or grinning gargoyle that eludes us. Rome is the study of failed human efforts to control a city, a civilization that grew from humble (lupine) origins into something divine. The foolish still attempt capture—Mussolini tried it only 60 years ago and was thwarted by the ancient ruins that kept sprouting up from beneath his efforts to create broad modern thoroughfares. And the millions of pilgrims who search Rome every year find themselves wearied by its twisting hot alleyways and multi-layered design. But no matter what you see or how long you stay, you will touch the city's spiritual core. Everything is sweet, everything tastes good—Rome is and always will be *bellissima*.

GETTING IN AND OUT OF ROME

By Plane

International flights touch down at **Leonardo da Vinci Airport** (tel. 659 51), referred to as **Fiumicino** for the coastal village in which it is located. This airport has a money exchange (a good place to get *lire* for the train, subway, or bus), a baggage check (24 hr.; L4,650 per day), and a post office. After you exit Customs, you'll find a tourist office (tel. 65 01 12 55) immediately to your left (open Mon.-Sat. 8:15am-7:15pm). The employees will provide you with maps of the city and try to find you a room. The **train** from Fiumicino into Rome leaves from the second floor of the international arrivals wing. Look for signs for the *Treno* (not the *Metropolitana*). This new line is the fastest and most convenient way into Rome, whisking you from the international and national terminals to the spanking new **Air Terminal Ostiense** inside the city. Buy your ticket (L6000) from one of the machines on the first floor; these make change and have English instructions. (Trains depart every 20-30min., 6:15am-12:45am, and the trip takes 25min. First and last trains from Ostiense to Fiumicino are at 5:40am and midnight.) Two new "bullet" trains now serve the airport, running from Florence's Santa Maria Novella Station and from Naples's Mergellina station. If you're headed to either of these cities, you can buy a 1-way ticket for L30,000 when you purchase an Alitalia plane ticket. Otherwise, the cost is L122,500 one-way.

At Air Terminal Ostiense there are phones, a money exchange, car rental booths and a branch of the student travel agency CTS (see above). If you arrive there on the train from Fiumicino, a series of elevated walkways takes you to either Linea B of the *Metropolitana* (you're at the Piramide stop; Linea B takes you to Termini for transfer to Linea A and the Vatican) or to any number of buses outside in Piazza dei Partigiani (#57 goes to Termini by way of Piazza Venezia; #95 follows the Via del Corso to Via Veneto and the Villa Borghese). Both bus and subway require that you buy a ticket before boarding. Buy subway tickets in the subway station, bus tickets in the bar at the train station. If you need a taxi, a cab from Ostiense is still much cheaper than one from Fiumicino, where the fare can run as high as L70,000. Use only yellow or white taxis. Refuse all offers of special prices or flat rates and insist that your taxi use the meter. Be *very careful* in this train station; pickpockets abound.

Most charter and domestic flights arrive at **Ciampino** (tel. 79 49 41). From here take the blue ACOTRAL bus to the Anagnina stop on Linea A of the *Metropolitana*

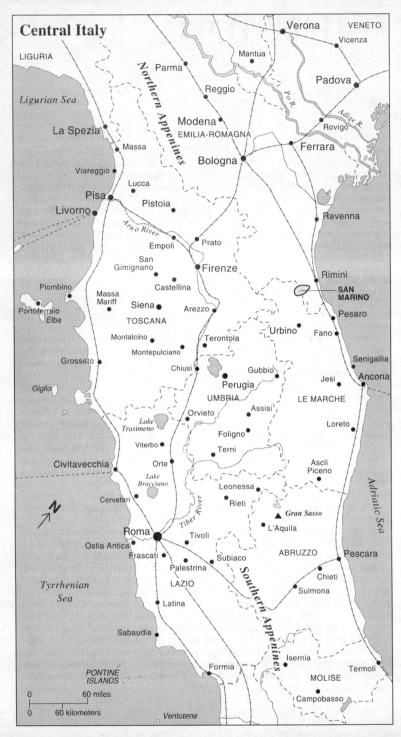

Central Italy

(L1000; departures every 30min. from 6am-9:30pm). Linea A takes you to Termini, the Spanish Steps, or the Vatican. Ciampino is inside the Rome city limits; do not allow a taxi driver to charge you the long-distance supplement.

By Train

Termini, named for the nearby baths (*thermae*) of the Emperor Diocletian, is the transportation hub of Rome, the focal point of most train and both subway lines. Termini is bursting with multilingual information booths, currency exchanges, baggage services, restaurants, bars, barbers, telephone offices, gift shops, and even an aquarium. The crowded railway information and Eurail offices are at the front, near Piazza dei Cinquecento. Train reservations must be made in person. The EPT tourist information booth is inside between tracks 2 and 3 (tel. 482 04 78 or 482 12 70; open daily 8:15am-7:15pm). The various stations on the fringe of town (**Tiburtina, Trastevere, Ostiense, San Lorenzo, Roma Nord, Prenestina, Stazione S. Pietro**) are connected by bus and/or subway to Termini. Watch out for pickpockets in and around the station. Never keep your wallet in your back pocket; if you carry a purse, wear it across your shoulder. Hold tightly to your luggage at all times. Luggage storage is available along tracks 1 and 22. (Open daily 5am-1am, L1500 per piece per day, bicycle storage 1 day only.) Improve the odds against theft by using the **waiting room** along track 1 when you can.

Sample trip lengths and prices given here are for *diretto* (direct) trains. To **Florence:** 2hr., L22,000; *rapido* supplement L9300. To **Venice:** 5hr., L40,200, *rapido* supplement L14,800. To **Naples:** 3hr., L15,400, *rapido* supplement L7300. To **Brìndisi:** 7-8hr., L43,500, *rapido* supplement L15,800.

By Car

Cars approach the city center by way of the **Grande Raccordo Anulare (GRA),** the beltway that encircles Rome. You can take any of several exits into the city. If you are coming from the north, enter on **Via Flaminia, Via Salaria,** or **Via Nomentana.** At all costs avoid **Via Cassia,** whose ancient two-chariot lanes can't cope with modern-day traffic. **Via Tiburtina** to the east is even worse. Follow the Grande Raccordo around to **Via del Mare** to the south, which connects Rome with **Lido di Ostia.** When leaving the city by car, don't attempt to follow the green **Autostrade per Firenze** signs; get on the Grande Raccordo instead and follow it around; it's longer but faster. From the south, **Via del Mare** and **Via Pontina** are the most direct connections from the coastal road from Naples. From the Adriatic coast, take **Via Appia Nuova** or **Via Tuscolana** off the southeastern quadrant of the Raccordo.

ORIENTATION

In his *Early History of Rome*, Livy concluded that "the layout of Rome is more like a squatter's settlement than a properly planned city." Two thousand years of city-planning later, Rome is still a splendid, unnavigable sea of one-way streets, dead-ends, clandestine *piazze*, incongruous monuments, and incurable traffic. Getting lost is as inevitable as death and taxes.

No longer defined by the Seven Hills, modern Rome sprawls over a large area between the hills of the **Castelli Romani** and the beach at **Ostia.** The central sights, however, lie within a much smaller compass. Rome was, until recently, a city built to be covered on foot. From Termini, the central locus and arrival point for most visitors to Rome, **Città Universitaria** and the student area of **San Lorenzo** are to the east, while most of the major tourist sights slope down between the hills to the west toward the Tiber. **Via Nazionale** is the central artery connecting Termini with the city center. At its base, Via Nazionale joins the immense **Piazza Venezia,** crowned by the conspicuous white marble pile of the **Victor Emanuele Monument.** From Piazza Venezia, Via dei Fori Imperiale leads southeast to the **Forum** and **Colosseum;** Corso Vittorio Emanuele heads west into the historic districts that fill the

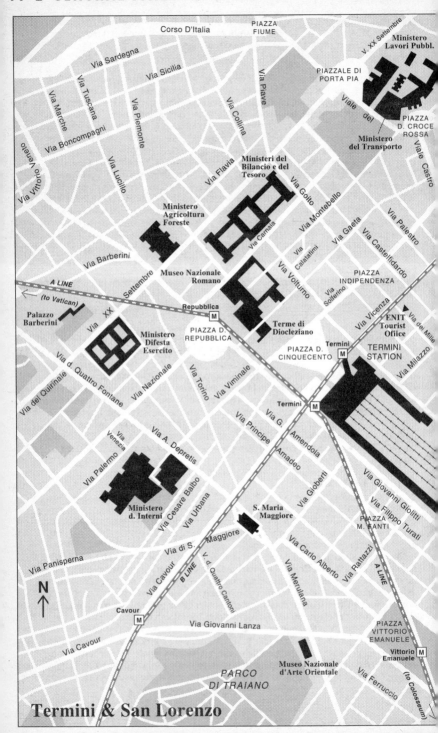

Termini & San Lorenzo

bend in the Tiber; the **Via del Corso,** the backbone of the city, stretches straight north to the **Piazza del Popolo** and the **Spanish Steps.**

The fourteen *rioni* (districts) of Rome, distinct in appearance and character, emerge from the snarl of traffic that fills these boulevards. To the north, the enormous **Villa Borghese** and **Pincio** parks border the Piazza del Popolo, the high-class shopping streets centering round the Spanish Steps, and the (now very faded) glamour of the **Via Veneto.** South of here, between Via Tritone and Via Nazionale, **Piazza Barberini** points the way to the stunningly restored **Trevi Fountain.** The **Forum** and **Colosseum** lead out of the city towards the ruins of the **Circus Maximus,** the **Appian Way** and the **Catacombs.** From Piazza Venezia to the west, the **Largo Argentina** marks the start of the Corso Vittorio Emanuele, which leads into the medieval and Renaissance tangle of alleys, towers, churches, and fountains around the **Pantheon** and **Piazza Navona** (north of the street) and **Campo dei Fiori** and **Piazza Farnese** (between Via Giulia and the river), before crossing the Tiber to the overwhelming prospect of **Castel Sant'Angelo** and the **Vatican City.** South of the Vatican (but more accessible from the other bank than from St. Peter's) is the medieval **Trastevere** quarter, home to countless *trattorie* and the best streets for wandering in the city. Back across the river, the historic **Tiber Island** and **Jewish Ghetto** lie in ruinous calm behind the Victor Emanuele Monument. Bounding the historic city at the south is the peaceful **Aventine Hill,** crowned with gardens and monasteries, and the delicious **Testaccio** district.

Touring Tips

Plan on getting lost, and make the most of it. Getting lost in the streets of Rome can be one of the most frustrating and enjoyable parts of your holiday. Rome's greatest treasures often lie hidden in the perplexing tangle of streets: the Pantheon emerges quite suddenly as you wind your way through narrow, cobbled streets and Bramante's Tempietto sits in the small courtyard of a lonely church.

Schedules and timetables are often unreliable, so it's best to call ahead whenever possible. Remember that the Roman lunch lasts from 1pm-4pm. Most shops and offices are open weekdays and Saturdays 9am-1pm and 4pm-8pm; in winter 3:30-7:30pm. Nearly everything closes down on Sunday and on Monday mornings, as well as on Saturday afternoons in summer, except for a few *caffè*, restaurants, and tourist services—the only people on the streets at these times carry guide books. Many museums are closed on Monday. Food shops close early on Thursday. But the seven major basilicas of Rome are open all day, every day. Smaller churches usually open with the first mass at 6 or 7am and close around 12:30pm. If no mass is planned, each church follows the divine caprices of its curate. Many churches reopen at 4pm for a few hours. Most museums and monuments close at 1:30 or 2pm. Plan your day strategically: important business (money changing, travel plans) first thing in the morning, museums and sights until afternoon, and then, if you haven't drifted into a post-prandial languor yourself, sights that don't observe siesta (the Forum, Colosseum, *piazze*, fountains, and the seven principal basilicas affiliated with the Vatican).

Secret Walks in Rome (tel. 39 72 87 28) is a new tour company that organizes 1½-hr. strolls through the oft-overlooked alleys of the city. English-speaking guides, many of them English and American expatriates, give tours focusing on Roman architecture, "talking statues," ancient Roman poetry, Italian politics, and even old wine shops (*enoteche*). Call the office to for the upcoming week's schedule.

Getting Around Rome

The most disconcerting thing about rush hour in Rome is that it lasts 24 hours a day. Droves of demon mopeds buzz through red lights and over sidewalks. A jaunt to the Colosseum at 3am to avoid the crowds will prove just how populated and active the city really is. On the up side, with so many Romans darting about, the public transportation system has developed to meet the demands. Bus and train service is surprisingly extensive, and the city is doing its best to lengthen Metro lines, despite delays caused by workmen uncovering ancient ruins with each shovelful. Be attentive while taking public transportation, however. Many well-dressed "undercover" pickpockets can razorblade a leather bag in seconds without your feeling a thing.

Buses and Trams

Rome's extensive bus system is a surprisingly efficient and comfortable means of getting through the city. Though the network of routes may seem daunting at first, the **ATAC** (*Aziende Tramvie Autobus Communali*) intra-city bus company (tel. 469 51) has ubiquitous booths and a friendly staff who can help you find your way. At the Termini ATAC booth (Piazza del Cinquecento, English spoken), you can buy a detailed map of bus routes (L1000). Each bus stop (*fermata*) is marked by yellow signs listing all routes that stop there, key streets on those routes, and routes with nighttime service (*servizio notturno*). Regular service route numbers are noted by red shields. Nighttime routes are indicated by black shields (on the newer signs) or at the bottom of the older, painted signs; they are often different from daytime routes of the same number, and far less frequent. The abbreviation *Pass.* on the signs lists the times the bus will pass that stop during the night. You must signal a nighttime bus to stop by standing right under its sign and waving an arm. Routes that do not have *servizio notturno* generally stop running at midnight.

Tickets for the bus cost L800. Stamp the ticket in the orange machine at the back of the bus as you board (you may only board a bus from the front or back doors, not from the middle); the ticket is then good for any number of transfers over the next ninety minutes. If you exceed 90 minutes during your last ride, stamp the other end of the ticket to prove that it was still valid when you boarded. Tickets are available at newsstands, *tabacchi*, and kiosks throughout the city. The **B.I.G.** daily ticket is valid for 24hrs. on the Metro and buses (L2800). A weekly bus pass (*biglietto settimanale*) is valid for eight nights and days but not for the Metro (L10,000, sold at Piazza dei Cinquecento). A monthly pass is also available (see under Subway). Trams use the same tickets as buses. You are on your honor to stamp your ticket; there is a strict L50,000 fine if you are caught without one, and playing dumb tourist won't help. Buy a number of tickets during the day, as they are difficult to come by at night. After midnight, ticket salesmen ride the *servizio notturno* buses and will sell you a ticket on board.

ACOTRAL bus service between Rome and the province of **Lazio** (tel. 591 55 51) has moved its departure points outside of the city proper to facilitate traffic; you need to take the subway to an outlying area and catch the bus from there. Take **Anagnina** (last stop on Linea A Metro) for Frascati and the Colli Albani; **Rebibbia** (last stop on Linea B Metro) for Tivoli and Subiaco; **Lepanto** (last stop on Linea A before Ottaviano) for Cerveteri, Tarquinia, Bracciano, Lago Vico, and Civitavecchia. For information, it may be easier to call CTS (tel. 467 91).

Subway

The two lines of the subway (*Metropolitana*) intersect in the basement of Termini and can be reached by the stairway inside the station. Entrances to all stations are marked on the street by a white "M" on a red square. **Linea A** runs from Ottaviano, near the Vatican, through P. di Spagna, P. Barberini, P. della Repubblica, and Termini, before heading to Anagnina and intervening stops in the southeastern suburbs of the city. **Linea B** runs from Rebibbia in the northeastern suburbs, through the university area around P. Bologna, to Termini, the Colosseum, Piramide (change here for the train to Fiumicino), and Magliana (change here for trains to Ostia and the beach) before terminating at Laurentina in EUR. The subway is fairly safe, but guard your valuables. The majority of Rome's sights are a trek from the nearest subway stop, but for covering large distances fast the subway beats the bus any day. (Linea A daily 5:30am-11:30pm; Linea B Sun.-Fri. 5:30am-9pm; Sat. and holidays 5:30am-11:30pm.) Tickets are L700 and can be bought in newsstands, *tabacchi*, or at coin-operated machines in the stations (there are bill-changers in the station but they are often broken). It is impossible to board the subway without a ticket. Trains to Ostia and the Lido beach are not part of the subway (buy an extra L700 ticket at the station of origin or at Magliana, where you change trains).

If you will be in Rome for more than a couple of weeks, consider purchasing the *abbonamente mensile*, which allows unlimited rides on one bus line (L18,000), one bus line and both subway lines (L22,000), or all bus lines and no subway lines (L22,000), and are good for a calendar month starting on the first of the month. Each pass is known as a *tessera* and is available wherever bus and subway tickets are sold.

Taxis

Taxis are a viable but expensive option. On call 24 hrs., they can be flagged down in the streets. Taxi stands are at Piazza Sonnino in Trastevere (at the end of Viale Trastevere before the bridge), at Piazza Venezia, Piazza della Repubblica, Via Nazionale, and at Piazza del Popolo. Ride only in yellow or white taxis, and make sure your taxi has a meter; then at least you'll know that you're being robbed legally. Official rates are L6400 for the first 3km or a waiting period of 9 min., then L1200 per km. Night surcharge L3000; Sunday surcharge L1000; each suitcase L500 (small parcels and lap dogs excepted). Radio taxis (tel. 35 70 or 66 45 or 49 94 or 881 77). Taxis from and to the airport cost around L70,000.

Car

If the aggression of other drivers, the weaving antics of moped maniacs, and the suicide squads of pedestrians don't totally unnerve you, keeping a car in the city does guarantee a high-adrenaline trip. It also assures a high-cost one. Parking is expensive and difficult to find, and if you don't keep your eyes peeled for the little signs, you may drive into a car-free zone and incur a fine. For more information contact **TCI (Touring Club Italiano)**, Via Marsala, 14, inside the shopping arcade. (Open Mon.-Fri. 9am-1pm and 4-7pm.) Also in the shopping arcade, **ACITOUR** (the travel agency run by ACI), Via Marsala, 14, (tel. 446 99 20; fax 445 27 02) can make reservations and help with travel plans. (Open Mon.-Fri. 9am-1pm and 2-6pm. Exchange open Mon.-Fri. 9am-1pm and 3-5pm.)

If you're still game to rent, Avis, Hertz, Maggiore, and Europcar all operate booths on the east side of Termini. By calling the central reservation numbers you can arrange to rent a car in Rome or in any part of Italy. All firms will let you drop your rental car off in any other Italian city where they have an office (with an extra charge of about L50,000 north of Rome and a monumental L300,000 to the south). English is spoken at all locations.

Maggiore, Main office, Via di Tor Cervara, 225 (tel. 22 93 51; fax 22 93 53 32), open Mon.-Fri. 8:30am-6:30pm; Termini (tel. 488 37 15), open Mon.-Sat. 7am-8pm; Air Terminal Ostiense (tel. 574 52 60); toll-free national number (1678) 670 67, open Mon.-Fri. 8:30am-6:30pm.

Avis, Termini (tel. 470 12 19), open Mon.-Fri. 7:30am-7:30pm, Sat. 8:13am-3:18pm; Main office, P. Esquilino 1C (tel. 470 12 16), open Mon.-Fri. 9am-1:30pm and 2:30-6pm; Fiumicino office (tel. 65 01 15 79 or 65 01 15 31), open 7:30am-11pm.

Hertz, Termini (tel. 474 64 05 or 474 03 89); Main office, Via Veneto, 156 (tel. 321 68 31), in the underground parking garage, accessible from the top of Via Veneto or from the P. di Spagna Metro stop (open Mon.-Fri. 7am-7pm, Sat. 7am-6pm, Sun. 8am-1pm); Fiumicino (tel. 65 01 14 48 or 65 01 15 53); toll-free national number (1678) 220 99.

Europcar, Reservations (tel. 52 08 12 00), open Mon.-Fri. 9am-6pm; Termini (tel. 488 28 54), open Mon.-Fri. 7am-8pm, Sat. 7am-1:40pm; Air Terminal Ostiense (tel. 574 57 85), open Mon.-Fri. 8am-8pm; Sat. 8am-1pm; Fiumicino (tel. 650 109 77 and 650 010 879), open 7am-11pm; toll-free national number (1678) 680 88, open Mon.-Fri. 9am-6pm.

Bicycles and Mopeds

Rome's many hills, cobblestone streets, dense traffic, and lunatic drivers make the city less than ideal for bikes and mopeds. In some areas, however, bikes can be a perfect way to explore the city; bike rides around Rome's parks are a welcome relief from a city of stone. A bike ride down the Appian Way may be the best way to see the many monuments, as well as the long stretches of countryside between them. Bicycles generally cost around L5000 an hour or about L15,000 per day, but the length of that "day" varies according to the shop's closing time. In summer, try the unmarked stands at P. di San Lorenzo at Via del Corso or Via di Pontifici at Via del Corso, both near P. di Spagna (open 10am-1am); at P. Sidney Sonnino, off Viale Trastevere; or at the Metro Spagna exit at Vicolo Bottino (open 9am-11pm). Rates average around L6000 per hr. Moped aficionados can rent mopeds and scooters for between L50,000 and L60,000 a day. You need to be at least 16 years old, but you don't need a driver's license. **Practice safe cycling and wear a helmet.**

I Bike Rome, Via Veneto, 156 (tel. 322 52 40), which rents from the Villa Borghese's underground parking garage. The subterranean entrance is near the intersection of Via di S. Paolo del Brasile and Via della Magnolie. Bikes L5000 an hour, L13,000 per day, or L38,000 per week. Tandems too. Open Mon.-Sat. 9am-8pm.
Scooters for Rent, Via della Purificazione, 84 (tel. 488 54 85), off P. Barberini. Bicycles L15,000 per day, L80,000 per week. Mopeds L50,000 per day. Vespas L60,000 per day. Open 9am-7pm. Visa, MasterCard, and AmEx accepted.

Safety

Rome is congested day and night with lost, bewildered, and distracted tourists, each loaded with cash and valuables in every pocket. The bright side is that Roman thieves, provided with so many thousands of easy targets, rarely resort to violence.

Never, ever count money in public, and watch to see that you are not followed after changing money. Roman thieves can empty your wallet even faster than your national government. Watch out for packs of children begging for change as they thrust flat pieces of cardboard or newspaper at your waist—underneath the flutter of paper they can probe pockets and unzip fanny pouches. These kids will do anything for a buck, including pulling down their pants and shrieking. The thieving hordes are especially thick around the Forum and the Colosseum, where people are blindly admiring the architecture, and on crowded buses like the #64 and the #492.

For a big city, Rome is relatively safe at night. Women and men will generally feel safe walking through the center of town during all but the darkest hours. Outside the *Centro Storico* (historical center), however, use caution. The area around Termini and to its south (especially near Piazza Vittorio Emanuele and the Colle Oppio, notorious drug areas) and Testaccio deserve special care; walk in groups at night. Bipedal mugging is particularly bad in the suburbs of Cinecittà and Centocelle. If for any reason you plan to sleep outside (an option we do *not* recommend) or simply don't want to carry everything with you, store your gear in Termini along track #1, or use a bus or train locker—although these are occasionally broken into. Women should also consult the section on Women Travelers in the Essentials section.

PRACTICAL INFORMATION

Tourist Offices:
EPT, in the Termini Station (tel. 487 12 70 or 482 40 78), between tracks #2 and 3. Lines can be horrendous. **Central Office,** Via Parigi, 5 (tel. 48 89 91 or 48 89 92 00, fax 481 93 16). Walk from the station diagonally to the left across P. dei Cinquecento (filled with buses) and go straight across P. della Repubblica. Via Parigi starts on the other side of the basilica, at the Grand Hotel. English spoken. **Fiumicino Office,** outside Customs (tel. 65 01 02 55). All 3 offices open Mon.-Sat. 8:15am-7:15pm. At any office, pick up a map and copies of *Romamor* and *Carnet di Roma e della Sua Provincia*. If you will be traveling in the region

around Rome, also ask for *Alberghi di Roma e Provincia*, which lists all hotels and *pensioni* registered with the EPT. All offices will help you find a room.

Enjoy Rome, Via Varese 39 (tel./fax 445 18 43), one block east of Termini station, perpendicular to Via Milazzo. A new tourist office with friendly, creative, English-speaking employees and a multitude of services and ideas. Hotel reservations for Rome and all of Italy (free). They also help with all kinds of alternative accommodations, including short- and long-term apartments (1-week's rent surcharge for long-term accommodations). Open Mon.-Fri. 8:30am-1pm and 3:30-6pm, Sat. 8:30am-1pm. They'll answer the phone Mon.-Sat. until 10pm.

ENIT, Via Marghera 2 (tel. 49 711); as you exit the tracks at Termini, head to your right—turn right onto Via Marsala, and take your first left onto Via Marghera; it's 2 blocks down on the left, across the street from the right-hand end of the shopping arcade. Some information on Rome, but mostly brochures and hotel listings for the rest of Lazio and the rest of Italy's provinces and major cities. Open Mon.-Fri. 9am-1pm, Mon., Wed., Fri. also 4-6pm.

Embassies: See the Essentials section for embassies and consulates in Rome.

Budget travel organizations:

Budget Travel Centro Turistico Studentesco (CTS), Via Genova, 16 (tel. 467 91), off Via Nazionale, about halfway between P. della Repubblica and P. Venezia. Branch offices at Termini (at track #22, tel. 467 92 54), at Via Appia Nuova, 434 (tel. 780 84 49), Corso Vittorio Emanuele II, 297 (tel. 687 26 72) and Air Terminal Ostiense (tel. 574 79 50) are open same hours as main office (see below). ISIC and YIEE cards L15,000 each. *Carta Verde* L40,000. Discount plane, train, boat and bus reservations and tickets, plus a free map, and currency exchange. Accommodations service, including out-of-town reservations (free). Bulletin boards with notices for rides, companionship, special services, etc. Lines can be aggravatingly slow; if information is all you need, it's better to phone (information tel. 467 91). Excellent English spoken at all locations. Main office open Mon.-Fri. 9am-1pm and 4-7pm, Sat. 9am-1pm.

Compagnia Italiana di Turismo (CIT), P. della Repubblica, 64 (tel. 479 43 49, fax 479 41). National travel agency that books discount train tickets and tours. In Termini (tel. 488 16 78, combined with *Sestante* travel agency), Via Veneto, 14c (481 43 82), Air Terminal Ostiense (tel. 574 57 42); general information tel. 479 41. All offices open Mon.-Fri. 9am-1pm and 2-5:30pm.

Italian Youth Hostels Association (Associazione Italiana Alberghi per la Gioventu), HI/IYHF, Via Cavour 44 (tel. 487 11 52, fax 488 04 92). Plenty of advice and a list of hostels throughout Italy. IYHA cards L30,000. Open Mon.-Thurs. 7:30am-5pm, Fri. 7:30am-3pm.

Post office: P. San Silvestro, 19 (tel. 67 71), between P. di Spagna and the Corso. Stamps at booths #31-33, *Fermo Posta* booth #65. Currency exchange (no checks) booths #25-28. Stamp machines and computer information in English in lobby. (Open Mon.-Fri. 8:25am-7:10pm, Sat. 8:20-11:50am. *Cambio* open Mon.-Fri. 8:20am-5:30pm, Sat. 8:20-11:50am.) Branch offices dot the city, and the **Vatican** runs a more efficient post office. The generic **postal code** for Rome is 00100; specific codes are elaborations on the 00101, 00102 theme. For *Fermo Posta* at S. Silvestro Post Office the code is 00186; at American Express, 00187.

Phones: SIP, in the Villa Borghese parking lot. Open 8am-9:30pm. Phone booths throughout the city. Booth in Termini across from aisle 6 (open Mon.-Sat. 8am-11pm, Sun. 9am-noon and 5-10pm) sells magnetic phone cards in L5000 or L10,000 units. These are also available at *tabacchi* and newsstands around the city.

American Express, P. di Spagna, 38 (tel. 676 41; lost or stolen cards toll-free 24hrs. 167 86 40 46; lost or stolen traveler's checks toll-free 24hrs. 167 87 20 00). Chaotic at times, but fairly efficient, and perfect English spoken. Mail held 30 days. Mail forwarded to another address by surface mail for a L7000 fee on arrival, or by airmail with prepaid postage. Postal code 00187. No need to change checks here; you'll find the same rates and shorter lines at any of the small *cambi* all over Rome. Good free maps of Rome. Open Mon.-Fri. 9am-5:30pm, Sat. 9am-12:30pm.

Currency Exchange: Large banks like **Banco d'Italia** or **Banco Nazionale del Lavoro** have offices all around the city. **Termini** has many *cambi*, usually with low rates and/or high commissions. The one by the train information booth is open 8am-8pm daily (with occasional unexplained lapses); if you arrive before or after those hours, there are **automatic tellers** that will change American dollars into *lire* at usurious rates. Machines besides the one in Termini are located at Via Marsala, 4; Via del Corso, 230 and 283; Via degli Uffici del Vicario, 78; P. San Silvestro; Via di Conciliazione (leading to St. Peter's); Via Veneto 7, 74 and 115 and elsewhere in the city center. Some **ATMs** accept Visa and MasterCard and give excellent exchange rates. Look for them around Via Veneto, the Vatican, P. Barberini, and the top of Via Giovanni Giolitti near Termini.

Lost Property: Oggetti Rinvenuti, Via Nicolo Bettoni, 1 (tel. 581 60 40), north of P. di Ponte Testaccio. Open Mon.-Sat. 10am-noon. **Termini,** at track #22 (tel. 473 06 02). Open 7am-11pm. **ATAC,** Via Volturno, 65 (tel. 469 51). Open Mon.-Fri. 9am-noon and 2-5pm. Also check at your **embassy** and with the police (listed below).

Late-night Pharmacies: Tel. 19 21 for recorded listings in Italian. *La Repubblica* and *Il Messaggero* newspapers publish a list of pharmacies open in Aug., and the closed pharmacies usually post a list. **Farmacia Internazionale Antonucci,** P. Barberini, 49 (tel. 482 54 56 or 487 11 95) above the P. Barberini Metro stop, near the Spanish Steps. **Farmacia Grieco,** Piazza della Repubblica, 67 (tel. 488 04 10 or 48 38 61), steps from Termini. **Farmacia Piram,** Via Nazionale, 228 (tel. 488 07 54). **Farmacia Risorgimento,** P. Risorgimento, 44 (tel. 372 46 22).

Hospitals: Vaccinazioni, Via Galilei, 3 (near S. Giovanni in Laterano). For shots and vaccines. Open Mon.-Sat. 9am-noon and 3:30-5:30pm. **Rome-American Hospital,** Via Emilio Longoni, 69 (tel. 22 55 71). Private emergency and laboratory services. English-speaking physician on call 24 hrs. **Policlinico Umberto I,** Viale di Policlinico, 255 (tel. 499 71) near Termini. Take Metro Linea B to the Policlinico stop. A free public facility. Open 24 hrs. **Dental Hospital: G. Eastman,** Viale Regina Elena, 287 (tel. 445 32 20). On call 24 hrs. Check in *Wanted in Rome* or *Metropolitan* for English-speaking dentists in private practices. **Red Cross:** Via Antonio Pacinotti, 18, (tel. 55 10) in Piazza della Radio.

Police: Ufficio Stranieri (Foreigner's Office), Via Genova, 2 (tel. 46 86 28 76). English spoken. Report thefts in person. Open 24 hrs. **Police Headquarters,** Via San Vitale, 15 (tel. 468 61). **Railway Police,** on track #1 in Termini (tel. 481 95 61 or 488 25 88).

Emergency Lines: First Aid (*Pronto Soccorso*) and **Police** tel. 113. **Carabinieri** tel. 112. **Fire** (*fuoco*) tel. 115. **Road Assistance** tel. 116. **Anti-violence hotline** (*Telefona Rosa assistenza contro la violenza*) tel. 683 26 90 or 683 28 20). Mon.-Fri. 10am-1pm and 4-7pm. Italian only. To report anti-gay violence, call the toll-free **Green Line,** tel. 1678 632 77.

Crisis Line: Samaritans, Via San Giovanni in Laterano, 250 (tel. 70 45 44 44). Native English speakers. Open for calls and visits 4-10pm.

Bookstores: Economy Book and Video Center, Via Torino, 136 (tel. 474 68 77), off Via Nazionale. Open Mon.-Fri. 9:30am-7:30pm, Sat. 9:30am-1:30pm; Oct.-May Mon. 3-7:30pm, Tues.-Sat. 9:30am-7:30pm. **Anglo-American Bookshop,** Via della Vite, 57 (tel. 679 52 52). Near P. di Spagna. Open Mon.-Fri. 9am-1pm and 4-8pm, Sat. 9am-1pm. **Open Door Bookshop,** Via della Lungaretta, 25 (tel. 271 69 00), off Viale Trastevere. Also has a fax (L4000 1st page, L2000 per additional page, plus phone charges). Open Mon. 4-8pm, Tues.-Sat. 10am-1pm and 4-8pm.

Women's bookstore: Al Tempo Ritrovato, Piazza Farnese, 103 (tel. 68 80 37 49), off Campo dei Fiori. Small section of English books about Italian and European feminism and politics, as well as American women's writing and lesbian literature. Open Tues.-Sun. 10am-7:30pm, Mon. 3-7:30pm, July-Aug. daily 10am-1:30pm and 4:30-8pm.

Feminist center: Via San Francesco di Sales, 1/2 (tel. 686 42 01). Seminars, cultural events, women's gatherings, and lesbian archives.

Community Bulletin Boards: Lion Bookshop, Via del Babuino, 181 (tel. 322 58 37). **Cinema Pasquino,** Vicolo del Piede in Trastevere (tel. 580 36 22). **All Saints Anglican Church,** Via del Babuino, 153 (tel. 679 43 57). Also check the area around the **University** for apartment listings, English-tutoring jobs, Italian tutors, and other services.

Laundromat: OndaBlu, Via Principe Amedeo, 70/b, off Via Cavour 2 blocks south of Termini. Wash L6,000 per 6.5kg load (40 min.). Dry L6,000 per load (20 min.).

Athletic Club: Roman Sport Center, Via del Galoppatoio, 33 (tel. 320 16 67) in Villa Borghese. One-day use of weight room, pool, sauna, turkish baths, aerobics classes, and squash courts costs L25,000 per person. Proper spandex-wear requested. Open Mon.-Sat. 9am-10pm.

ACCOMMODATIONS

In July and August, Rome bulges with tourists. A huge quantity of rooms meets this demand, but quality varies significantly and hotel prices in Rome are quite often astronomical. Although reservations help, they do not always guarantee that a room awaits you for the full length of your intended stay, or at the decided price, as large groups frequently take precedence over a reserved double in the minds of some proprietors. Make sure the hotel charges you no more than the price posted on the back of your room's door; it's the law.

The **tourist offices** in Rome will scrounge (reluctantly in peak season) to find you a room. The main office, at Via Parigi, 5 (tel. 48 89 91 or 48 89 92 00, fax 481 93 16), is the most helpful. The **Centro Turistico Studentesco e Giovanile (CTS),** Via Genova, 16 (tel. 467 91), and the **Enjoy Rome** agency (tel. 445 18 43) can also help you find a place. **Protezione delle Giovane,** Via Urbana, 158 (tel. 488 14 19) will assist women in finding convent accommodations and moderately priced rooms.

Termini is full of "officials" swarming around to find you a place. Many of them are the real thing, and have photo IDs issued by the tourist office. Still, some sneaky imposters issue themselves fake badges and cards, and direct you to dives charging 50% more than the going rate. Stay on the safe side. Ask them for maps and directions (since real officials will always have maps), but try to stay in places listed here.

If the queue at the tourist office extends to infinity, check your bags at the station and investigate nearby *pensioni*. It's usually not hard to find a place, several establishments often operate in a single building. During peak season, some hotels will try to charge more than the official prices, and will automatically tell the tourist office they are full. You may do better going to Enjoy Rome for help, or even calling and bargaining on your own. There are over 300 *pensioni* in Rome with prices comparable to those listed here. Be careful, but don't be afraid to set out on your own. **Always insist on seeing a room first,** though some proprietors are not always amenable. Check the mattresses, the bathroom, and the water pressure; most rooms come equipped with sinks. Check the security; test the locks (make sure your room key doesn't open the other rooms as well), ask about the curfew or when the front door locks, check how accessible the room-keys are to other guests or passers-by, and find out whether someone monitors the front desk at all times. Inquire about additional costs. Some hotels charge for hot showers, heat, or for bathrooms in the room. In the winter, check if the *pensione* has heat or you'll be sorry.

It is illegal and, well, stupid to "camp out" in the public places of Rome. Though violent crime is infrequent, dozing tourists invite trouble. If you must, sleep in groups with designated sentry watches in Termini (check your bags at the station's luggage storage room or risk serious material loss; Rome's best pickpockets hang out at Termini, waiting to prey on tired tourists). Check at the tourist office for a list of day-hotels. **Women, whether alone or in a group, should never sleep outdoors.** It is also a good idea to be careful even at designated campgrounds. See *Let's Go: Rome* for more information on accommodations and long-term stays.

North of Termini

Numerous clean, reasonably priced *pensioni* and hotels are within 10-15 minutes of Termini. When you exit the station, look for the big pink BNL (Banco Nazionale del Lavoro) building; that's north. Use the "Termini and San Lorenzo" map to orient yourself in this dense, *pensione*-rich area. Buses #3 and 4 take you directly to this *pensione* district. A fruit and vegetable **market** stands on Via Milazzo, between Via

Varese and Via Palestro (open Mon.-Sat. 6am-2pm). Another market is on Via Montebello, and several reasonable grocery and convenience stores dot the area.

Pensione Papa Germano, Via Calatafimi, 14A (tel. 48 69 19), off Via Volturno between Via Gaeta and Via Montebello. Mama, Papa, and the *bambini* Germano run this place with German discipline and Italian warmth. Deservedly popular with backpackers and students, reservations are a must during the summer months. Papa may try to match lone travelers with groups to fill a room. Singles L35,000. Doubles L50,000, with bath L60,000. Triples L75,000. Quads L22,000 per person. Reduction of 10% on all rooms Nov.-March. Visa and MC accepted.

Pensione Tizi, Via Collina, 48 (tel./fax 474 32 66 or 482 01 28). A 15-minute walk from the station. Take Via Goito from P. dell'Indipendenza, cross Via XX Settembre onto Via Piave, then take the first left onto Via Flavia, which leads to Via Collina. More safely located than many other accommodations around Termini, this family *pensione* has welcomed students for years to its comfortable rooms. Singles L40,000. Doubles L55,000, with shower L65,000. Triples L75,000.

Hotel Castelfidardo, Via Castelfidardo, 31 (tel. 474 28 94 or 494 13 78, fax 446 95 96). Completely new rooms, clean showers, and helpful management. Rooms lined with grey paint look like graph paper. Singles L40,000, with bath L50,000. Doubles L55,000, with bath L70,000. Visa, MC, and AmEx accepted.

Pensione Alessandro, Via Vicenza, 42 (tel. 446 19 58). Across the street from a *pizzeria rusticca,* near the corner with Via Palestro. Buzz #6 to get in. 30 beds in occasionally co-ed dorm rooms. The rooms aren't much to look at, but it's close to the station, the price is right, and the inimitable owner, Alessandro, is loved by locals and travelers alike. Check in 8am-midnight. No curfew, but ask for a key. L20,000 per person. Visa and MC should be accepted in 1994.

Hotel Home Michele, Via Palestro, 35 (tel. 444 12 04). Like Barbie's dreamhouse but Roman. Knickknacks everywhere, especially those of the pink fluffy sort. Small, so book early. Singles L30,000. Doubles L55,000. Triples L75,000.

Hotel Bolognese, Via Palestro, 15 (tel. 49 00 45). Stands out with still-lifes and terraces, a luxury in Termini. (The view stinks but the idea is liberating.) Suites available for families or groups. Singles L35,000, with bath L45,000. Doubles L55,000-65,000, with bath L70,000. Triples and suites L75,000, with bath L110,000.

Pensione Piave, Via Piave, 14 (tel. 474 34 47, fax 487 33 60). Off Via XX Settembre. Definitely a step up from the garden variety budget accommodation, and worth the extra *lire*. All rooms have private bath, telephone, and carpeted floors. The singles have double beds and one room even has a little fireplace. English spoken. Check-out at 10am but luggage can be left all day. Singles L35,000, with bath L50,000. Doubles L50,000, with bath L70,000. Triples L75,000, with bath L90,000. Quads L85,000, with bath L115,000.

Pensione Lachea, Via San Martino della Battaglia, 11 (tel. 495 72 56), off P. dell'Indipendenza. *Let's Go's* biggest fan, the warm-hearted owner will ensure every comfort. Newly renovated in 1993. Doubles L48,000-52,000. Triples L65,000-70,000. Bargaining is not out of the question if the place isn't full.

Pensione Reatina, Via San Martina della Battaglia, 11 (tel. 445 42 79, fax 44 41 27), downstairs from Pensione Lachea. Interior decorating ain't its forté (despite the Don Quixote bedspreads), but the cellar price for all 20 rooms includes breakfast (7:30-9:30am). Singles L35,000, with bath L39,000. Doubles L50,000, with bath L60,000. Triples L75,000. MC and Visa accepted.

Pensione Eureka, P. della Repubblica, 47 (tel. 482 58 06 or 488 03 34). Statues and murals in the entry make you feel right at Rome. English spoken. Not quite north of Termini; more west, off the far left corner of P. dei Cinquecento as you exit Termini. Curfew 1am. Singles L50,000. Doubles L80,000. Breakfast included.

Hotel Gexim, Via Palestro, 34 (tel./fax 444 13 11 or tel. 446 02 11). A 9-room *pensione* run by a young couple who prefer guests that stay more than one night. Light, airy rooms and no curfew. Singles L38,000. Doubles L55,000, with shower L70,000. Triples L75,000. Laundry sent out for L18,000 per load.

Pensione Monaco, Via Flavia, 84 (tel. 474 43 35 or 481 56 49), around the corner from Tizi. Dim, and no decor to speak of, but bathrooms and beds are spanking clean. Manager won't put up with much funny business—especially tipsy guests. Curfew midnight. One shower per day included, an extra one will cost you L2500. Singles L35,000. Doubles L50,000. Triples and quads L23,000 per person.

Pensione Restivo, Via Palestro, 55 (tel. 446 21 72). *La donna simpatica* who runs the place takes great pride in the blinding whiteness of her sheets. Laundry service. Singles L40,000. Doubles L60,000. Triples L75,000. Major credit cards.

Pensione Albergo Mary, Via Palestro, 55 (tel. 446 21 37) and **Pensione Albergo Mary 2,** Via Calatafimi, 38 (tel. 474 03 71, fax 482 83 13). Sister establishments. with moderate prices and clean rooms. Some employees speak a little English. 12:30am curfew at both. Singles L40,000, with bath L60,000. Doubles L60,000, with shower L80,000. Larger rooms available at Mary 2 for L30,000 per person. Prices soften in the low season. Visa, AmEx, and MC accepted.

Hotel Cervia, Via Palestro, 55 (tel. 49 10 57, fax 49 10 56). 21 rooms and 41 beds, so check here if you find the smaller *pensioni* full. A bit musty, but the helpful management speaks English. Curfew 1:30am. Singles L35,000-40,000. Doubles L50,000, with bath L75,000.

Pensione Katty, Via Palestro, 35 (tel. 444 12 16). No frills place at a no frills price. L2000 key deposit. Singles L30,000-45,000. Doubles L40,000-60,000, with bath L50,000-70,000. Triples and quads L20,000 per person.

Locanda Marini, Via Palestro, 35 (tel. 444 00 58), across the hall and in cahoots with Katty. Less-than-cheerful interior is warmed by the spritely proprietrix. Singles L25,000. Doubles L50,000-54,000.

Hotel Continentale, Via Palestro, 49 (tel. 495 03 82, fax 495 26 29). 2 yards from Termini. Recently renovated rooms have phones and some have balconies. Breakfast included. Some English spoken. Singles with shower L75,000. Doubles with shower and toilet L100,000. Quads with shower L180,000. Credit cards accepted.

Hotel Romae, Via Palestro, 49 (tel. 446 35 54 or 446 35 55, fax 445 20 24). With a bar, tile with pink accents, breakfast included, and a third bed free for children under 12, this hotel is perfect for a family of four. Recently renovated, it looks like a set from an outdated episode of Miami Vice. The prices we list represent a 20% discount for *Let's Go* adherents. All rooms come with antiseptic baths. Singles L70,000. Doubles L96,000. Triples L120,000.

Hotel Pensione Cathrine, Via Volturno, 27 (tel. 48 36 34). A stone's throw from Termini. The singles are worth it for beds that are, if not king-size, at least Siamese-twin-size. Two can fit comfortably in a single, even if they're not joined at the hip. The rates we list are specials for *Let's Go* readers. Singles L35,000-38,000, for two people L48,000. Doubles L50,000. Triples L69,000.

Hotel Ventura, Via Palestro, 88 (tel. 445 19 51). First-floor location is convenient, but noisy at night. Rooms are small but newly renovated, with TV's, telephones, and bathrooms. Singles L40,000. Doubles L60,000. Triples L75,000.

South of Termini

The area south of the station is generally busier, noisier, and seedier than the one to the north, but there are decent places and great bargains to be found with a little perseverance. Via Principe Amadeo runs parallel with the west side of the station two blocks over and can be reached by taking any of the side streets that intersect with Via Giolitti outside the west exit of the station. The closer you get to P. Vittorio Emanuele, the seedier the area becomes at night. Use extra caution if you're a woman traveling alone. In general, the farther one gets from the station, the better the neighborhood becomes. Via Giolitti, Via Filippo Turati, and Via Principe Amadeo can become intimidating at night (and as you travel farther down them from Via Cavour) so use appropriate caution and watch your pockets. Down Via Cavour, toward the Colosseum, the area takes on a more jovial character.

Pensione di Rienzo, Via Principe Amadeo, 79A (tel. 446 71 31). A tranquil retreat at a fabulous price. Lovely, large rooms, most with a balcony overlooking a peaceful cobblestone courtyard. Kindly manager speaks English. Singles L25,000, with bath L40,000. Doubles L50,000, with bath L80,000. Triples with bath L104,000.

Hotel San Paolo, Via Panisperna, 95 (tel. 474 52 13), at Via Caprareccia. Dirt-cheap but the swell proprietor, a cross between Grizzly Adams and Mickey Rourke in *Barfly*, makes up for the questionable decor. Singles L30,000. Doubles L45,000, with bath L50,000. Reservations accepted.

Pensione Sandy, Via Cavour, 136 (tel. 488 45 85), near the church of Santa Maria Maggiore. No sign; look for the Hotel Valle next door and prepare yourself for the arduous climb to the fourth floor. Tons of info for travellers. 25 hostel-style beds at L20,000 per person. L15,000 in winter (no heat but lots of blankets). Showers included. Lockers available for small valuables.

Hotel Orlanda, Via Principe Amadeo, 76 (tel. 488 06 37), at Via Gioberti. Sparse but clean. One has a wooden floor and is quite charming; the rest are the usual tile. Official curfew is midnight, but other arrangements can be made. Singles L35,000. Doubles L50,000, with bath L65,000. Triples L67,000. Quads L85,000.

Hotel Ferraro, Via Cavour, 266 (tel. 474 37 55), just past Via degli Annabaldi. A stone's throw from the Colosseum. A charming hotel with plants, statuettes, and cushy sofas. Singles L40,000, with bath L51,000. Doubles L51,000, with bath L65,500. Triples with bath L88,400. Quads with bath L111,000.

Hotel Scott House and **Hotel Eliana,** Via Gioberti, 30 (tel. 446 53 92 or 446 53 79, fax 446 49 86). Inexpensive and undergoing renovation in '93, some rooms have brown plastic walls, others have fresh paint. Breakfast room and roof patio coming in '94. Special prices for *Let's Go* readers. Singles with bath L30,000. Doubles with bath L50,000. Triples with bath L75,000. TV and phone in each room.

Pensione Pezzotti and **Hotel Cantilia,** Via Principe Amadeo, 79D (tel. 446 69 42 or 446 68 75, fax 446 69 04). Both owned by the same courteous management. New, pleasing, and pastel. **Pezzotti:** Singles with bath L40,000. Doubles with bath L55,000. Triples with bath L71,000. **Cantilia:** Singles L45,000, with bath L60,000. Doubles L60,000, with bath L80,000. Prices drop drastically in the off-season. Phones, balconies, and TVs. Major credit cards accepted.

Hotel Tony, Via Principe Amadeo, 79D (tel./fax 446 68 87). Tastefully done up in acqua wallpaper and murals of ruins. Charming and talkative (in English) manager. Singles L45,000. Doubles L60,000, with shower L70,000. Triples L90,000. 10% discount Nov.-March.

Around Piazza Navona and Campo dei Fiori

Il Centro Storico (The Historic Center) is the ideal, if increasingly expensive, base for living as the Romans do. By day, its winding cobblestone streets, hidden *piazze* and numerous *caffè* invite exploration; by night, the area swarms with boisterous Romans and tourists alike. Most major sights are within walking distance and the day market at nearby Campo dei Fiori yields bounties of cheap fruit and flowers. Unfortunately, hotel proprietors (mostly English-speaking) haven't failed to exploit their desirable location; you can expect to pay about 10-15% more to finance the charm and the deeper sense of Roman history absent from Termini accommodations. Reservations may be the only way to get a bed, especially in the summer. Most *pensioni*, unless otherwise indicated, do *not* accept credit cards.

Piazza Navona lies at the bend of the Tiber north of Corso Vittorio Emanuele II; Campo dei Fiori lies across the *corso* to the south. From Stazione Termini, take bus #64 (70 at night), and keep a keen eye on your belongings and friends. Bus #62 travels along Via XX Settembre to both areas, and is less popular with the pickpockets.

Albergo Della Lunetta, P. del Paradiso, 68 (tel. 686 10 80, fax 689 20 28), near the Church of Sant'Andrea della Valle. Take Via Chiavari off Corso Vittorio. Then take the first right off Via Chiavari. An economical eden in the heart of Old Rome, this is the best value in the Campo dei Fiori area. Homey blue-flowered wallpaper, tidy rooms with armoires, phones, and desks. Muse in the central garden or the TV lounge. Singles L35,000, with bath L65,000. Doubles L75,000, with bath L100,000. Triples L100,000, with bath L135,000. Reservations recommended.

Pensione Mimosa, Via Santa Chiara, 61 (tel. 68 80 17 53), off P. di Minerva behind the Pantheon. Will never be featured in the *Architectural Digest* hotels-of-the-world issue, but a fantastic location. A matronly woman presides over this kitschy abode, with puppy wall calendars and red checkered tablecloths in the breakfast room. Curfew 1am. Singles L45,000. Doubles L70,000. Triples L105,000. Quads L130,000. Breakfast (8-9am) L5000 per person.

Albergo Pomezia, Via dei Chiavari, 12 (tel. 686 13 71). The recently renovated section on the first floor is far nicer than the old one; all of the redone rooms have baths. Telephones, heat in the winter, matching furniture, and bathrooms (on the 2nd and 3rd floors) Joan Crawford would praise Christina for. Art-deco bar on the first floor (*caffè*, L1000). Curfew Sun.-Fri. 1:30am. Singles L50,000, with bath L85,000. Doubles L70,000, with bath L110,000. Triples L90,000, with bath L148,000. Prices drop in winter (Nov.-Feb., except for Christmas).

Hotel Piccolo, Via dei Chiavari, 32 (tel. 689 23 30 or 68 80 25 60), off Corso Vittorio Emanuele II, behind Sant'Andrea della Valle. Next to a bustling grocery but off the beaten path. Clean, quiet and comfortable, with warm wood trimmings in the bathrooms. Curfew 1:30am. Singles L58,000, with shower L70,000. Doubles L85,000, with shower L95,000, with bath L120,000. Triples with shower L95,000, with bath L120,000. Reservations recommended in summer. Visa, MC accepted.

Pensione Navona, Via dei Sediari, 8 (tel. 686 42 03, fax 680 38 02; call before faxing). Take Via de'Canestrari off P. Navona, cross over Corso del Rinascimento, and continue straight. A helpful Italo-Australian family runs a tight ship in this 16th-century Borromini building, which has served as a *pensione* for over 150 years. Call several weeks in advance and send a US$100 deposit to secure a room. Checkout 11am. Singles with bath and breakfast (8:30-9am) L65,000. Doubles L90,000, with bath and breakfast L95,000. Each extra person L43,000.

Pensione Primavera, P. San Pantaleo, 3 (tel. 68 80 31 09), off Corso V. Emanuele south of P. Navona. The entire *pensione* has been renovated, and the prices have risen with the quality. Black and white marble lobby with lime green accents, and rooms with a view of Palazzo Braschi. Doubles L80,000, with bath L90,000. Triples L120,000. Breakfast (8-10am) included. Prices drop 15% in winter.

Albergo Del Sole, Via del Biscione, 76 (tel. 654 08 73, fax 689 37 87). Off P. Campo dei Fiori. Top-notch furniture, plush lounging chairs, and dark wood armoires. Telephones too. Although many of the singles look like those near Termini station, the *pensione* is supposedly the oldest in Rome. Checkout at noon. Singles L70,000, with shower L75,000, with bath L85,000. Doubles L90,000, with bath L105,000-120,000. Triples with bath L160,000.

Albergo Abruzzi, P. della Rotonda, 69 (tel. 68 80 17 53). Here the humble can contemplate the great; this *albergo* is located smack dab in front of the Pantheon and its noisy admirers. While cleaner than the Pantheon, it could use some of the Pantheon's overhead lighting. Singles L48,000-62,000. Doubles L60,000-82,000. Reservations recommended in summer.

Near the Spanish Steps

This is the Italian equivalent of Paris's *Rive Gauche*; Beautiful People flock here to browse through boutiques and galleries. In an area where designer silk suits, leather loafers, mini-skirts, and face-lifts abound, inexpensive accommodations are scarce. Still, for fashion victims who find themselves lingering in front of Fendi after the buses stop running, the following safe havens are worth a try.

Residenza Brotsky, Via del Corso, 509 (tel. 361 23 39 and 323 66 41). A place of welcome for antique furniture and weary travelers. Climb up to the roof terrace for a view of St. Peter's. Color TV lounge. Singles with shower L55,000, with bath L60,000. Doubles L75,000-85,000, with bath L90,000. Triples with bath L90,000-105,000. Reservations recommended.

Pensione Parlamento, Via delle Convertite, 5 (tel. 679 20 82, for reservations 684 16 97 or 69 94 16 97), behind *La Rinascente* off Via del Corso on the street leading up to P. San Silvestro. High ceilings, a gorgeous terrace, and wonderful views. Management speaks English. Breakfast L12,000 (don't bother). Singles L61,000, with bath L85,000. Doubles L80,000, with shower L95,000, with shower and bath L105,000. Each additional person L25,000. Reservations recommended.

Pensione Panda, Via della Croce, 35 (tel. 678 01 79), between P. di Spagna and Via del Corso. Newly renovated with br'ght, fresh walls. Check first on the status of the noisy courtyard construction (should be done by '94). Singles L50,000-70,000. Doubles L85,000. Triples L110,000. AmEx and reservations accepted.

Pensione Fiorella, Via del Babuino, 196 (tel. 361 05 97), off P. di Spagna near P. del Popolo. Spruce set-up and a charming management that asks only that you respect their 1am curfew. If you can't, look elsewhere. If you can, they have *bath-tubs*. English spoken. Singles L40,000. Doubles L70,000. Breakfast included. No reservations, so arrive early in the morning.

Hotel Boccaccio, Via del Boccaccio, 25 (tel. 488 59 62), off Via del Tritone down from P. Barberini. A family establishment tucked back in peaceful Roman streets and stuffed with heirlooms. Singles L48,000. Doubles L60,000, with bath L80,000.

Pensione Jonella, Via delle Croce, 41 (tel. 679 79 66), between P. di Spagna and Via del Corso. A marble stairway becomes continually steeper and narrower on the ascent to these 5 effervescent rooms with high ceilings. Singles L45,000. Doubles and triples L35,000 per person.

Ottaviano

The *pensioni* on the other side of the Tiber aren't the cheapest in Rome, but they tend to be quiet, clean and friendly. Those in Ottaviano, near the Vatican, are attractive for their proximity to popular sights and a safer, residential area. Bus #64 from P. del Cinquecento and #81 from Via Cavour at Santa Maria Maggiore, as well as Metro Linea A, all run to Ottaviano. An indoor food **market** is nearby at the Piazza d'Unità, off Via Cola di Rienzo.

Residence Guiggioli, Via Germanico, 198 (tel. 324 21 13). At Via Paolo Emilia, 1st floor. Five of the best rooms in Rome. Beautiful antiques adorn pristine rooms. The wonderful proprietress will chat with you in Italian whether you understand her or not. Doubles L85,000; matrimonial suite with private bath L100,000.

Pensione Lady, same building as the Guiggioli, 4th floor (tel. 324 21 12). The same couple has been running this clean, peaceful *pensione* for 30 years. This explains the unintentionally campy '60s mod decor with portraits ranging from the good to the bad to the ugly. They prefer travelers who stay more than 1 night. Singles L55,000; *matrimoniale* and doubles L75,000. Closed 1-2 weeks in Nov.

Hotel Pensione Alimandi, Via Tunisi, 8 (tel. 39 72 39 48 or 39 72 39 41 or 39 72 63 00, fax 397 239 43). Take the steps off Viale Vaticano down to Via Sebastiano Veniero, and go straight—literally meters away from the Vatican Museum. A gorgeous place with a beautiful garden patio on the first floor and a terrace on the roof. Singles L54,000, with bath L70,000. Doubles L75,000, with bath L120,000. Triples with bath L120,000. L10,000 per extra bed. Children under 12 can share your room for free. Credit cards and reservations accepted.

Hotel Pensione Joli, Via Cola di Rienzo, 243, 6th floor (tel. 324 18 54 or 324 18 93; fax 324 18 93). At Via Tibullo. A sleek and snazzy hotel with blue pin-stripe walls and polished upholstered chairs. The joint sparkles. Singles L55,000, with bath 70,000. Doubles with bath L70,000. Triples with bath L128,000.

Hotel Florida, Via Cola di Rienzo, 243 (tel. 324 18 72; fax 324 18 57). On the 4th floor, below Hotel Joli. Trim, sparse modern rooms on their way toward charming. Telephones in each room. Friendly management. Singles L57,000, with bath L73,000. Doubles L77,000, with bath L99,000. Triples with bath L135,000.

Pensione Ottaviano, Via Ottaviano, 6 (tel. 370 05 33 or 39 73 72 53 or 39 73 81 38), off P. del Risorgimento north of P. San Pietro. Inches from St. Peter's, this is the only hostel-style *pensione* in the area—beds, and that's it. A fine but spare home to backpackers from various nations. English spoken. Dorm beds L20,000.

Trastevere

Hedonists and bohemians might prefer to stay in **Trastevere,** scene of much night-time revelry and home to many young expatriates. Buses #75 from P. Indipendenza, 60 from Via XX Settembre, and 170 from P. del Cinquecento all run from near Termini to Trastevere. A food **market** can be found at P. di San Cosimato.

Pensione Manara, Via Luciano Manara, 25 (tel. 581 47 13). Take a right off Viale di Trastevere onto Via delle Fratte di Trastevere to Via Luciano Manaro. Friendly management runs this homey establishment overlooking colorful P. San Cosimato in the heart of Trastevere. Truly a perfect location. English spoken. Doubles L58,000. Triples L75,000. Quads L95,000. Showers L3000 each, good and wet.

Pensione Esty, Viale Trastevere, 108 (tel. 588 12 01), about 1km down Viale di Trastevere from the Ponte Garibaldi. Spotless, professional rooms await in an Orwellian building somewhat removed from the rowdy heart of Trastevere. English spoken. Singles L40,000. Doubles 58,000. Triples L78,000. Quad L100,000. Often filled by Forestry Administration workers, so reserve in advance.

Student and Institutional Accommodations

If you are looking for a raucous time in Rome, institutions are not the place to go. While providing affordable accommodations, most of them are inconveniently located, difficult to arrange, and curfews at the HI hostel and various religious organizations keep you locked away from *la dolce vita*.

Ostello del Foro Italico (HI), Viale delle Olimpiadi, 61 (tel. 32 36 279 or 32 36 267, fax 32 42 613). Take Metro Linea A to Ottaviano (last stop) and then exit onto Via Barletta and take bus #32 (in the middle of the street) to "Cadorna." If you pass the Stadio del Nuoto, you've gone too far. The hostel is across the street, on the corner. Inconvenient location, but they sell bus and metro tickets (daily ticket L2800). 350 beds with lockers big enough for two packs. 3-day max. stay when full. Reception open noon-11pm. Lockout 9am-2pm. Lunch (1-2pm) or dinner (7-9pm) L12,000. Bar downstairs open 7:30am-11pm. Curfew midnight. L18,000 per person; L25,000 without HI/IYHF card (buy one at the desk for L30,000). Breakfast and showers included. Handicapped access.

Esercito della Salvezza (Salvation Army), Via degli Apuli, 41 (tel. 446 52 36, fax 445 63 06). Off Via dei Marsi, northeast of Termini. Take bus #492 or 415 from Termini to "Tibertina." 175 tiny but tidy rooms in a pretty quiet area. No lockout or curfew. Reserve 1 week in advance. Singles L28,000, with bath L40,000. Doubles L46,000, with bath L60,000.

The **Casa dello Studente** of the University of Rome, Via Cesare de Lollis, 20 (tel. 324 25 71) sporadically offers rooms to foreign students once its own students have left (up to 300 rooms, from mid-July to mid-September). Call in advance.

YWCA, Via Cesare Balbo, 4 (tel. 48 88 3917 or 48 80 460, fax 48 71 028), off Via Torino, south of Termini. Somewhat pricey, but entirely free from obnoxious Romeos. No men allowed unless they are married to their roommates. Colorful food and flower market outside (daily 6am-2pm). Curfew midnight. Singles L38,000. Doubles L64,000. Triples L78,000. Quads L104,000. Showers and breakfast (7:30-8:15am) included. No breakfast offered Sunday. Tell reception by 10am same day if you want lunch (1-2:15pm, L15,000).

Camping

You probably won't catch the malaria that killed Daisy Miller, but there are still plenty of mosquitoes menacing tourists in campgrounds near the city. Though there's often little space between sites, peaceful seclusion is usually steps away. In August, arrive early—well before 11am—or you may find yourself without a spot. Rates average L9000 per person and another L5000 for the car. If you're in Rome with a hopeless slash in your pack, substitute camping equipment can be found at **Cisalfa,** Largo Bríndisi, 5 (tel. 70 49 34 84), just outside the San Giovanni Metro stop (Linea A, direction Anagnina).

Seven Hills, Via Cassia, 1216 (tel. 371 08 26), 8km north of Rome. Take bus #910 from Termini to Piazza Mancini and transfer to #201; get off on Via Cassia and walk 1.5km down Via Italo Piccagli from Via Cassia. A camping commune in the hills that harkens back to the '60s. Blythe international campers play volleyball on the manicured grounds, laze poolside, and dance the night away in the disco

(9:30pm-1am). Reasonably priced bar, market, and pizzeria. They run a daily shuttle bus to the city center at 9:30am, returning at 1:30 and 5:30pm (L4000). L9200 per person, L4900 per tent, L4500 per car. Open March 15-Oct. 30.

Flaminio, Via Flaminia Nuova, 821 (tel. 333 26 04) is about 7km outside of Rome. Take bus #910 from Termini to Piazza Mancini, then transfer to bus #200. Get off on Via Flaminia Nuova when you see the "Philips" building on your right. Shady grass strewn with closely knit enclaves of tents, campers, and bungalows. Landscaping a little rough around the edges, but they're outfitted with 24-hr. pool, market, restaurant, bar, and a disco that rages long into the night. Coin-operated washing machines. L9000 per person, L4500 per tent, bungalows L37,000 (less per person with more people); open March-Oct.

FOOD

Meals in Rome are lengthy affairs, continuing for hours on end as each course is savored with deliberation. (Breakfast—a gulp of caffeine and a sticky bun—is the only exception.) Accordionists wail out Frank Sinatra (L100 tip expected), corks fly off the local *Castelli Romani* wines, and a crispy *bruschetta* (a piece of toasted bread garnished with oil, garlic, and herbs) begins the meal. Later, the *primo piatto* (first course) arrives, usually *risotto* (rice) or pasta, often prepared *alla carbonara* (with bacon and egg) or *all'amatriciana* (with bacon, white wine, tomato, and pepper). On Thursdays, many restaurants serve up homemade *gnocchi*, a doughy potato dumpling. Pasta and *risotto* in Rome, and even more so in the surrounding countryside, are prepared *al dente* (to the teeth), so expect to chew at great length.

An alternative to a traditional Italian meal is a moveable feast. Rome has innumerable picnic spots. Some of the best are the Villa Borghese, Villa Ada, the Janiculan Hill (Gianicolo), the Palatine Hill, the Botanical Gardens in Trastevere, and the Appian Way. *Alimentari* are your best bet for standard groceries. Food stores are open roughly Mon.-Wed. and Fri. 8am-1pm and 5:30-8pm, Thurs. and Sat. 8am-1pm. Outdoor **markets** can be found at P. Campo dei Fiori, P. Vittorio, and off Cola di Rienzo (indoors, near the Vatican). They generally operate Mon.-Sat. 6am-2pm, and sell a large variety of goods from food and housewares to clothing and antiques. Supermarket STANDA offers a huge selection of food, produce, toiletries, clothing, and anything else you can think of. There is one on Viale Trastevere, a few blocks down from Piazza Sidney Sonnino, and one on Via Cola di Rienzo, several blocks down from the Ottaviano Metro stop, and several blocks up from Piazza del Popolo.

Hop on a bus to reach the university district of **San Lorenzo** or the traditional area known as **Testaccio,** on the eastern banks of the Tiber. These are the last truly untouristed restaurant districts in Rome. The areas around **Piazza Navona** and **Campo dei Fiori** harbor romantic *trattorie*, and **Trastevere** has the liveliest *pizzerie*. The best places fill up quickly, so set out early to avoid the rush. Romans generally eat late—around 9pm. Most restaurants close for at least two weeks in August.

Piazza Navona

Authentic, inexpensive *trattorie* are easy to find in the Piazza Navona area, but steer clear of the main *piazze* where the restaurants milk tourists for their last *lira*. Venture into the alleys along Via Governo del Vecchio to eat Italian food with real-life Italians. Many of the best places for lunch are unmarked and don't have menus: look for doorways with bead curtains. There is no shortage of *alimentari*, *tavole calde*, and *pizzerie rustiche* lining Via di Ripetta and around the Pantheon. The best ice cream places in Rome surround the Pantheon and the main piazza.

Palladini, Via del Governo Vecchio, 29. Really a *salumiere* (deli) rather than a bona fide restaurant. No sign or place to sit, but bustling with a Roman lunch crowd eating seconds-old *panini*. Point to the fillings of your choice and eat outside. Favorites include *prosciutto e fiche* (smoked ham and figs) or *bresaola e rughetta* (smoked meat with arugula) sprinkled with parmesan cheese and lemon juice. A hearty sandwich costs L3500. Open Sept.-July Mon.-Sat. 8am-2pm and 5-8pm.

Il Giardinetto, Via del Governo Vecchio, 125 (tel. 686 86 93). Escape the hard, dusty cobblestones of the area, and dine beneath the leaf-lined ceiling of this Tunisian-run oasis. Try the *gnochetti* (L7000) or the *pennette alla gorgonzola* (L8000) and house wine (L8000 per liter). Portions generous enough to skip the *secondi* (L12,000-16,000). Open Tues.-Sun. 12:30-3pm and 7:30pm-midnight. Reservations and credit cards (Visa, MC, Diner's Club, and AmEx) accepted.

Pizzeria Baffetto, Via del Governo Vecchio, 114 (tel. 686 16 17), on the corner of Via Sora. A household name among Romans. Once a meeting place for 60s radicals; now you have to stand in line with Romans of all political persuasions to get your hands on the gigantic *pizza gigante*. Pizzas L5000-9000. *Vino* L6000. Cover L1000. Open Mon.-Sat. 6:30pm-1am.

Pizzeria Corallo, Via del Corallo 10/11, (tel. 68 30 77 03), off Via del Governo Vecchio. Unusual pizzas in a laid-back setting of green arches, crayon graffiti, and a metal palm tree. Try the *foccacia scamorza fiori di zucca e alici,* a pizza with scamorza cheese topped with zucchini flowers and anchovies (L12,000). Pizzas L6000-13,000. Cover L2000. Service 10%. Open Tues.-Sun. 7:30pm-1:30am.

Insalata Ricca 2, P. Pasquino, 73 (tel. 654 78 81), at the beginning of Governo Vecchio. This spin-off of the original (listed below in Campo dei Fiori) is just as good. Omelette cooked to order (L5500). Salads L4500-6000. *Gnocchi verdi al gorgonzola* L8500. *Secondi* L7000-10,500. Cover L2000. Open Tues.-Sun. 12:30-3pm and 7-11:30pm. Reservations recommended on Sat. Credit cards accepted.

Navona Notte, Via del Teatro Pace, 44-46 (tel. 656 92 78), one long block north off Via del Governo Vecchio. Touristy, but pretty cheap and generous portions. The *menù* (L15,000) features fresh mussels and a choice between pizza or spaghetti. Otherwise, pizzas and pastas are L7000, salads L3000, a liter of wine L8000, and *coperto* L1500. Open Thurs.-Tues. 7pm-3am.

Campo dei Fiori

While this is perhaps the most popular neighborhood among Romans to wine and dine, with its cobblestone streets, miniature *piazze*, and the grandness of Via Giulia, the area never feels too populated. Try Via Monserrato behind and to the west of the Campo, as well as the *piazze* to the front. *Caffè,* bars, pastry shops, and *alimentari* tempt and tantalize along Via dei Giubbonari.

L'Insalata Ricca, Largo di Chiavari, 85 (tel. 654 36 56), off Corso Vittorio Emanuele near P. Sant'Andrea della Valle. Funky modern art, innovative dishes, and an offbeat ambience are successfully combined here with neighborly service and savory, traditional *trattoria* food. Try the *gnocchi al sardi* (L6500) or request their title dish *insalata ricca,* a robust salad with everything on it (L6500, smaller portion L5500).Whole wheat pasta *integrale* L7000. Cover L2000. Open Thurs.-Tues. 12:30-3pm and 7-11pm. Open during *Ferragosto* except Aug. 14-16.

Hostaria Grappolo d'Oro, Piazza della Cancelleria, 80-81 (tel. 686 41 18), on Via Cancelleria off Corso Vittorio Emanuele II. Stellar—but inexpensive—gastronomic ecstasy. Words are too cheap for the *antipasti* (L8000) and *penne all'arrabiata* (L9000). The *spaghetti alle vongole* (clams) teases more flavor out of a clam than seems possible (L12,000). House white wine L6000. Cover L2500. Open Mon.-Sat. noon-4pm and 7pm-midnight.

Filetti di Baccalà, Largo dei Librari, 88 (tel. 686 40 18). Take Via dei Giubbonari off P. Campo dei Fiori; Largo dei Librari will be on your left. The ideal spot for informal *antipasti* and wine, this self-service favorite makes an unforgettable *filetto di baccalà* (deep fried cod filet, L4000). Wine L6000 per liter. Cover L1500. Open Sept.-July. Mon.-Sat. 5:30-10:30pm.

Ristorante La Pollarola, Piazza della Pollarola, 24-25 (tel. 68 80 16 54), take L. Chiavari two blocks south of C. Vittorio Emanuele II. A typical Roman *trattoria* with good eats, charming location, and tolerable prices. Outside dining in the summer. *Spaghetti alla carbonara* L8000. *Spaghetti con le vongole* (clams) L10,000. House wine L8000 per liter. Cover L3000. Open Sept.-July Mon.-Sat. 12:30-3pm and 7:30-11pm. Reservations and credit cards accepted.

Pizzeria Vergillo, Campo dei Fiori, 10 (tel. 68 80 27 46). One of the cheaper spots in a row of bustling cafes and *trattorie*. Delicious pizzas (L7000-12,000) and rich pasta dishes (the *fettucine al salmone* and *gnocchi alla gorgonzola* are both excellent, L12,000 each). Cover L2500. Open Thurs.-Tues. noon-3pm and 7pm-midnight. Major credit cards accepted.

Near the Spanish Steps

Caveat edax (let the diner beware): the high prices in this flashy district are no guarantee of quality. Although looking for inexpensive meals around Piazza di Spagna is like looking for a bargain at Armani—even the McDonald's features fountains and tile. There are, however, a few places that don't check for gold cards at the door. Opt for a hot *panino* with mozzarella and prosciutto, a fresh salad, or a piece of *pizza rustica* at one of the many bars in this area.

Centro Macrobiotico Italiano, Via della Vite, 14 (tel. 679 25 09), on the third floor, just off Via del Corso. Membership costs L30,000 per year (which reduces as the year progresses; in the summer months, membership is only about L13,000). They do allow tourists one meal with a L2000 surcharge and a passport. The dishes are all fresh and, unlike most Italian cooking, contain no butter. A full meal comes to about L15,000. *Cous-cous vegetale* L6800. Natural *gelato*, made with soy milk and honey, L6000. Open Mon.-Fri. 10am-7:30pm.

Er Buco, Via del Lavatore, 91 (tel. 678 11 54), steps from P. di Trevi. Possibly the oldest pizza oven in the city. The amicable owner, a young soccer-playing Stanford graduate who has traveled extensively in South America, is the sixth generation to take over the business. Pizzas L6000-10,000. *Bruschetta pomodoro* L2000. Cover L2000. Open Mon.-Sat. noon-4pm and 6:30-11:30pm.

La Cappricciosa, Largo dei Lombardi, 8 (tel. 687 84 80), right off Via del Corso and across from Via della Croce. The abstract New Age paintings inside are as soothing as Kitaro's best work. Helpful waiters bring you *primi* (L6000-8000), pizza (*alla Marinara*, L7000) and *dolci* (L5000). Cover L2000. Open Wed.-Mon. 12:30-3pm and 7pm-1am. Closed Aug. 24-31. Credit cards and reservations accepted.

Al Piccolo Arancio, Vicolo Scanderberg, 112 (tel. 678 61 39), near the Trevi Fountain in a quaint alley off of Via del Lavatore, which runs off P. di Trevi. The sign says "Osteria." Unusual and delicious pastas and appetizers. Tues. and Thurs., order the homemade *gnocchi al salmone* (L7000) or the *raviole di pesce* (L8000). Cover L2500. Arrive early. Open Sept.-July Tues.-Sun. 12:30-3pm and 7-11:30pm. Credit cards accepted.

Trattoria Da Settimio all'Arancio, Via dell'Arancio, 50 (tel. 687 61 19). Run by the same family that runs Al Piccolo Arancio. Excellent 3-course meals L23,000-26,000. Try the *ossobuco* (braised veal shank in sauce, L12,000). Delicious *antipasti*. Cover L2000. Open Mon.-Sat. 1-3:30pm and 7pm-midnight. Closed 1 week in Aug. Credit cards and reservations accepted.

Near the Colosseum and Forum

Despite its past glory, this area has yet to discover the noble concept of "the affordable restaurant." If you can't tear yourself from the Arch of Titus, try the following:

Taverna dei Quaranta, Via Claudia, 24 (tel. 700 05 50), 2 blocks up from the Piazza del Colosseo. This is the best food you can afford in the shade of the mighty amphitheater. At night, gaze by lantern at the ancient walls alongside the restaurant. *Pennette con melanzana* (eggplant) L7500. *Fritto misto vegetale* (fried mixed vegetables) L11,000. ½ liter wine L3,000. Cover L2500. Open noon-3pm and 8pm-1am. Open *all* of August. AmEx accepted.

Pizzeria Imperiale, Largo C. Ricci, 37 (tel. 678 68 71), at the start of Via Cavour opposite the Roman Forum entrance gate (on the right). Recover from ruins under shady umbrellas. Good pizzas; try the *peccato del frate* (red peppers, zucchini, spicy sausage, olives, and artichokes) for L9,500. Pasta L8000-12,000. Wine L10,000 per liter. Cover L1500. Open Mon.-Sat. noon-4pm and 7:30pm-midnight.

FOOD

Trastevere

Just across the river from the historical center and down the river from the Vatican, this is the site of the city's most elegant restaurants as well as the most raucous beer parlors, hopping pizza places, and a vocal bohemian population. By nightfall, the Piazza S. Maria di Trastevere is packed with hippies and boom boxes as well as the monied, somewhat ruffled diners in the piazza's costly restaurants.

Fieramosca, Piazza dei Mercanti (tel. 58154 69). A crowded, candle-lit pizzeria packed with Romans in the know. The self-serve antipasto spread is phenomenal (L10,000), and the pizzas are some of the best in Rome. Friendly waiters give out free menu posters to take home to Mom. Open Mon.-Sat. 7pm-midnight.

Taverna del Moro, Via del Moro, 43 (tel. 580 91 65), off Via Lungaretta in Trastevere. Beautiful *antipasto* spread (L7000). *Pizza con verdura* L12,000. Cheesecake L4000. Cover L2000. Open Tues.-Sun. 7-11pm. Credit cards accepted.

Mario's, Via del Moro, 53 (tel. 580 38 09). Take Via della Lungaretta off Viale Trastevere, and turn right after the church. Pasta is consistently phenomenal for a mere L4500-6500. *Menù turistico* L16,000. Wine L4400. Cover L1000. Open Sept. to mid-Aug. Mon.-Sat. noon-3pm and 7-11pm. Major credit cards accepted.

Pizzeria Ivo, Via di San Francesca a Ripa, 158 (tel. 581 70 82). Take Via delle Fratte di Trastevere off Viale Trastevere. Alas, the tourists have finally discovered this Trastevere legend, but the mouth-watering pizza's still well worth the long wait and chaotic atmosphere. Pizza L9500-13,000. Crisp, delicious wine, with the restaurant's own label, L9000. Cover L1500. Open Sept.-July Wed.-Mon. 6pm-1am.

Il Duca, Vicolo del Cinque, 56 (tel. 581 77 06). Off Via del Moro on the left as you head toward the river. A classic Roman *trattoria* on a lively nighttime street. Divine *bruschetta al carciofo* (L2500) and pastas (L8000-12,000). Wine L6000 per liter. Cover L2000. Open Tues.-Sun. 12:30-2pm and 7:30pm-midnight.

Il Tulipano Nero, Via Roma Libera, 15 (tel. 581 83 09), in P. San Cosimato. A friendly, rowdy pizzeria—dine outdoors in the summer. Iron palates can attempt the *rigatoni all'elettroshock* (very hot indeed, L8000). *Pizza tonno, mais, e rughetta* (with tuna, corn, and arugula, L7000) tastes far better than it sounds. Wine L9000 per liter. Cover L1500. Open Thurs.-Tues. 6:30pm-1am.

L'Ape sul Melo, Via del Moro, 17 (tel. 689 28 81). Great for lighter foreign appetites. Bistro atmosphere with a good beer and wine selection. Salads and snacks L6000-9000. 18 types of hot sandwiches (around L6500). Great desserts, including chocolate mousse (L4000). Open Thurs.-Tues. 7:30pm-2am.

The Vatican and the Borgo

The streets of the original Borgo (along the Leonine Wall north of Via di Conciliazione) fill with Romans heading to various restaurants, *birrerie,* and clubs, while the residential district around Via Cola di Rienzo is home to some of the best undiscovered bargains in town.

Armando, Via degli Ombrellari, 41 (tel. 686 16 02). North of Via di Conciliazione. Delicious lasagne is the house specialty at L8000; the *vino bianco* is a delight after a day of museum-trudging at L6000 *per litro*. Don't pass up the *antipasto*. Cover L2500. Open Thurs.-Tues. 12:30-3pm and 7:30-11pm.

L'Archetto, Via Germanico, 105 (tel. 312 55 92). A little off the beaten path. Piping hot pizzas (L6500), *filetti di baccalà* (fried fish, L5000) and *fiori di zucca* (fried zucchini flowers, L5000). Open Tues.-Sun. 7pm-midnight.

La Caravella, Via degli Scipioni, 32 (tel. 39 72 61 61). Near the entrance to the Vatican Museums. Cover L2000, pasta dishes L6000-9000. L15,000 gets a banquet with bread, soup or spaghetti, *secondi piatti* (meat dish), fries, salad, and dessert. Open Mon.-Sat. noon-4pm and 7-11pm. Credit cards accepted.

Hostaria dei Bastioni, Via Leone IV, 29 (tel. 39 72 30 34), off P. del Risorgimento near the Vatican Museums. A miraculous subterranean restaurant which rightly boasts of its seafood specialties. *Risotto alla pescatora* (rice with seafood sauce) L8000. Fresh fish dishes L12,000-15,000. Wine L6000 per liter. Noisy for outdoor lunch. Cover L2000. Service 10%. Open Mon.-Sat. noon-3pm and 7pm-1:30am.

Cucina Abruzzese, Via dei Gracchi, 27 (tel. 39 73 32 90). The somber decor hides some of the area's best home-cooking. A pretty arbor on the street shields you from the sun. Pasta L6000-8000. Cover L2500. Open Tues.-Sun. noon-midnight.

Testaccio

The oldest area of Rome, yet still unassailed by tourism, Testaccio remains a stronghold of Roman tradition. Dare to eat as the Romans do at restaurants that serve authentic local delicacies, such as *animelle alla griglia* (grilled calves' veins—tastiest when slightly chewy) and *fegata* (liver). The hippest nightclubs are (incongruously) located here as well, so you can boogie your oxtail-intake away.

Trattoria da Bucantino, Via Luca della Robbia, 84/86 (tel. 574 68 86). Take Via Vanvitelli off Via Marmorata, then take the first left. A Testaccio tavern with fabulous antipasta. Indigenous pasta delights like *bucatini all'amatriciana* (L8000). Wrestle with their *coda alla vaccinara* (L10,000). Wine L5000 per liter. Cover L2800. Open Aug. 27-July 21 Tues.-Sun. noon-3pm and 7:30-11pm.

Trattoria Turiddo, Via Galvani, 64 (tel. 575 04 47), in the Mattatoio district of Testaccio (take bus #27 from Termini or the Colosseum). Locals come here to taste the food they grew up on, like *rigatoni con pagliata* (with tomato and lamb intestine, L8000) and *animelle alla griglia* (grilled calf's veins, L11,000). Vegetarians strongly cautioned. Cover L2000. Open mid-Sept-mid-Aug. Mon.-Tues. and Thurs.-Sat. 1-2:30pm and 7-10:30pm, Sun. 1-2:30pm.

Trattoria Al Vecchio Mattatoio, P. Giustanini, 2 (tel. 574 13 82). A gutsy Roman eatery. Their *tonarello sugo coda* (thick spaghetti with tangy tomato oxtail sauce, L8000) seconded by *arrosto misto di frattaglie* (a mixed grill of liver, intestines, veins and back muscles, L12,000), washed down with some extra-strong wine (L5000 per liter), will put hair on anyone's back. Cover L2000. Service 12%. Open Sept.-July Wed.-Sun. 12:30-4pm and 7:30-11pm, Mon. 1-3pm.

San Lorenzo

A five-minute bus ride east of Termini on bus #71 or 492 (get off when the bus turns onto Via Tiburtina by the old city walls), San Lorenzo sits in the midst of the Città Universitaria. Many unpretentious *trattorie* and *pizzerie* offer grand cuisine for the university students here in an atmosphere that encourages conversation.

Il Pulcino Ballerino, Via degli Equi, 66/68 (tel. 49 03 01), off Via Tiburtina. A wonderful, artsy atmosphere with cuisine to match. Unusual *tagliolini del pulcino* (pasta in a lemon cream sauce, L9000) and *polpettine all'arancia* (meatballs in an orange sauce, L10,000). Try the *risotto alla fragola* (strawberry rice, L9000). Cover L1500. Open Tues.-Sun. 8pm-midnight. Closed first 2 weeks of Aug.

Pizzeria La Pappardella, Via degli Equi, 56 (tel. 446 93 49), off Via Tiburtina. A very inexpensive wood-oven pizzeria serving wafer-thin pizzas under a leafy canopy. Start off with a *bruschetta al pomodoro* (crisp bread with tomatoes and olive oil, L1500) for a basil *festa*. *Pizza Napoli* (mozzarella, tomato, anchovies) L6,000. *Crêpes* L7000. Open Tues.-Sun. 9:30am-2:30pm, 8-11:30pm.

Pizzeria L'Economica, Via Tiburtina, 46 (tel. 445 66 69), on the main road of the bus route. The name says it all. The large family who runs this place cooks up some of the most vicious pizza around (L4500-6000). Or try the *antipasto* dish for an incredible L5000. Wine L4000. Crowded, with lots of outdoor tables. Go early or late to avoid waiting. Open Sept.-July Mon.-Sat. 6:30-11pm.

Pizzeria Formula 1, Via degli Equi, 13 (tel. 49 06 10) in San Lorenzo, off Via Tiburtina. Romans know their pizza, so when it's as good and cheap as this, expect to wait. Pizza of all varieties L6000-8500. Try the zucchini flowers stuffed with mozzarella and anchovies. Open Mon.-Sat. 6:30pm-12:30am. It's anyone's guess really; the owner claims that the place is "sempre aperto!" (always open).

Il Capellaio Matto, Via dei Marsi, 25 (tel. 49 08 41). From Via Tiburtina take Via degli Equi and take the 4th right onto Via dei Marsi. Vegetarians rejoice! Numerous pasta and rice dishes for L7000-11,000. Crêpe dishes around L6500. Chicken dishes available for flesh-eaters. *Coperto* L2000. Open Wed.-Mon. 8pm-midnight.

Pizzeria il Maratoneta, Via dei Sardi, 20 (tel. 49 00 27), off Via Tiburtina. Four young marathoners bake pizza on the run (L5500-8500). Tomatoes and seafood cover half of their gorgeous *Pizza Mare e Monte,* while tomatoes, mozzarella, mushrooms, eggplant, onion, zucchini, and peppers bury the other half (L7000). No cover. Outdoor tables. Open Mon.-Sat. 5:30pm-12:30am.

La Tana Sarda, Via Tiburtina, 116 (tel. 49 35 50). Personable Sardinians rush from table to table, piling plates with delicacies. Romans rave about the *gnocchetti sardi* (twirled pasta with meat sauce, L7000) and the *ravioli sardi,* filled with flavored ricotta, L7000. For dessert, try the *dolcetti sardi* for L4000. Cover L2000. Open Sept.-July Mon.-Sat. noon-3pm and 7-11:30pm.

Near the Station

There is no reason to subject yourself to the gastronomic nightmare of the tourist-trapping restaurants that flank Termini; a 15-minute stroll from the station can take you to virtually any historic district this side of the Tiber—with quieter streets, tastier viands, and a more relaxing atmosphere. Still, when you've got corns on your feet and a desperate need in your belly, the following establishments provide excellent service for a largely local clientele.

Osteria con Cucina de Andreis Luciano, Via Giovanni Amendola, 73/75 (tel. 488 16 40). Take Via Cavour west from P. del Cinquecento; Via Giovanni Amendola is the first intersecting street. A green bead curtain screens the entrance to this haven for ravenous budget-travelers. Generous portions of pasta L3900-4500. Huge marinated half-chicken L6000. *Pollo e pepperoni* (chicken and peppers) is L6000. Half portions for half-price plus L400. Wine L2000 per liter. Cover L1000. Service 10%. Open Mon.-Fri. 9am-3pm and 7-9pm, Sat. 11:30am-5pm.

Il Ristorante Tudini, Via Filippo Turati, 5 (tel. 45 75 86), one block from Termini on corner with Via Gioberti. An appetizing reprieve from Termini fare, decorated with modish marble tables and greenery.*Veal scalloppine* L10,000. Cover L2000. Service 15%. Open Mon.-Sat. 12:30-11:30pm. A wide array of cards accepted.

La Cantinola da Livio, Via Calabria, 26 (tel. 482 05 19 or 474 39 62). Take Via Piave off Via XX Settembre, then take the 4th left onto Via Calabria. This cozy establishment specializes in *frutti di mare*—live lobsters wait tensely in tanks by the door. Stellar cuisine and impeccable service. Seafood fresh from Sardinia daily. *Spaghetti alla Cantinola* L9000. *Scampi* L16,000. *Antipasto di mare* L10,000. Open Mon.-Sat. 12:30-3pm and 7:30-11:30pm. Credit cards accepted.

Restaurant Monte Arci, Via Castelfidardo, 33 (tel. 474 48 90). Take Via Solferino past P. dell'Indipendenza off the east side of the station and then take the first left past the piazza. Boisterous waiters serve delectable *paglia e fieno al Monte Arci* (a pasta and spinach dish, L10,000) and *gnocchetti* (L7000). Cover L2500. Open Mon.-Sat. 12:30-2:30pm and 7-11:30pm. Visa and AmEx accepted.

Dolci (Desserts)

Giolitti, Via degli Uffici del Vicario, 40 (tel. 679 42 06). From the Pantheon, follow Via del Pantheon (at the northern end of the piazza) to its end and then take Via della Maddelena (in front of you) to *its* end; Via degli Uffici del Viccario is on the right. Simply orgasmic. Indulge yourself with their gargantuan 10-scoop "Olympico" sundae for L8000 and do penance on the thighmaster when you get home. The homemade *panna* is unbeatable. Open Tues.-Sun. 7am-2am.

Tre Scalini, Piazza Navona, 30 (tel. 687 91 48). Tre Scalini is famous for its perfect *tartufo,* a menacing hunk of chocolate ice cream rolled in chocolate shavings; but fame has brought tourists, and high prices with them. Get your *tartufo* at the bar for L4500; still a splurge, but *so* worth it. Open Thurs.-Tues. 8am-1:30am.

Palazzo del Freddo Giovanni Fassi, Via Principe Eugenio, 65/67 (tel. 446 47 40), off P. Emanuele west of Termini. This century-old *gelato* factory is worshiped by many. Some heretics argue that the *gelato* here beats Giolitti's hands down. Cones L2000-3000. Open Tues.-Fri. 1pm-midnight, Sat.-Sun. 10am-2am.

Gelateria Trevi di A. Cercere, Via del Lavatore 84/85 (tel. 679 20 60), near the Trevi Fountain. A small, family-run *gelateria* of yesteryear, whose infamous *zabaione* puts glitzy *gelaterie* down the street to shame. Small cones L2000. Open daily 10am-1am.

Caffè

Coffee is Rome's foremost fuel, and languorous pit stops are *de rigueur*. During the weekdays, most Romans rush in, down an *espresso*, and leave, but at night, the *caffè* come alive with thunderous cross-table conversations, bustling waiters, and shrill cashiers. In most *caffè* you pay one price to stand and drink at the bar and a higher price (as much as double) if you sit down at a table; there is usually a menu on the wall of the bar listing the prices *al bar* (standing up) and *a tavola* (at a table).

Caffè Sant'Eustachio, P. Sant'Eustachio, 82 (tel. 686 13 09), in the Piazza southwest of the Pantheon. Take Via Monterone off Corso Vittorio Emanuele II. Possibly the best *cappuccino* in Rome (L4000; L2000 at the bar). *Granita di caffè* with all the works L6000. Buy some of their *espresso* beans to take home (½kilo L15,000). Open Sept.-July Tues.-Sun. 8:30am-1am.

L'Antico Caffè Grèco, Via Condotti, 86 (tel. 678 25 54), off Piazza di Spagna. One of the oldest *caffè* in the world, this posh house has entertained the likes of European kings, movie stars, and John F. Kennedy since 1760. Waiters in tuxes serve the renowned *cappuccino* (L1700). Tea L2000. Open Mon.-Sat. 9am-8:30pm.

Caffè della Pace, Via della Pace, 3/7 (tel. 686 12 16), off P. Navona. Not just a L4000 cup of *cappuccino*, but an entire lifestyle. Chic and expensive, beneath vines and church façades. *Cappuccini:* daytime L1500 at bar, L4000 at table; nighttime L4000 at bar, L8000 at table. Open Tues.-Sun. 8:30am-3am.

Tazza D'Oro, Via degli Orfani, 84/86 (tel. 679 27 68), off the northeast corner of P. della Rotonda. No place to sit down, but a great brew at fantastic prices (*caffè* L1000). Superlative *granita di caffè* (L1200). Open Mon.-Sat. 7:30am-7:30pm.

SIGHTS

Rome wasn't built in a day, and it's not likely that you'll see anything of the city in 24 hours either. The city practically implodes with monuments—ancient temples, medieval fortresses, Baroque confections of marble and rushing water—crowding next to and even on top of each other on every serpentine street. No other city in the world can lay claim to so many masterpieces of architecture from so many different eras of history—not to mention the treasures of painting and sculpture hidden inside. Accept the fact that it's impossible to see everything the city has to offer. Relax and set out to see what you can, remembering that the city is a hot and dusty place in summer (and a crowded and chaotic one year-round), likely to sap the energy of even the most hardened sightseer. Pace yourself, make time for a stop in a bar or *caffè*, and carry a bottle of water (refillable at any of Rome's corner waterspouts; you'll see Romans bending to drink from the streams). See the color "Walks" map for suggested routes through the city. For more information see *Let's Go: Rome.*

Piazza del Popolo

The **Piazza del Popolo** was the first sight that greeted 19th-century travelers entering Rome from the north through the Porta del Popolo. The "people's square," as its name indicates, has always been a popular gathering place. Masked revelers once filled the square for the torchlit festivities of the Roman Carnival, and today the piazza remains a favorite arena for communal antics. The southern end of the square also marks the start of Rome's famous trident of streets: the central Via del Corso, which runs straight for over a mile to Piazza Venezia (you can see the gleaming white Vittorio Emanuele Monument at the end), the Via di Ripetta, built by Leo X for nonstop service to the Vatican, and the Via del Babuino, cleared in 1525 by Clement VII, which leads to the Spanish Steps. The great **Obelisk of Pharaoh Ramses II,** restored in 1984, commands the center of the piazza. The obelisk, some 3200 years old, was already an antique when Augustus brought it back as a souvenir from Egypt in the 1st century BC. Outside the Porta del Popolo (with a façade designed by Bernini) is an entrance to the **Villa Borghese Park.**

Nineteenth-century architect Guiseppe Valadier spruced up the once-scruffy piazza, adding the two travertine fountains on the western and eastern sides. To the west, a beefy Neptune splashes in his element with two of his hench-Tritons, while the opposite figures portray Rome flanked by the Anio and the Tiber. Behind its simple early Renaissance façade, the **Church of Santa Maria del Popolo,** tucked away on the north side of the piazza near the Porta del Popolo, contains some of the most important Renaissance and Baroque art in Rome. Immediately to the right as you enter, the **della Rovere Chapel** harbors an exquisite *Adoration* by Pinturicchio. Bramante designed the **apse** behind the altar. The **Cerasi Chapel,** immediately to the left of the main altar, houses two early Caravaggio paintings. The **Chigi Chapel,** second on the left, was designed by Raphael for the wealthy Sienese banker Agostino Chigi. (Open Mon.-Sat. 7am-noon and 4-7pm, Sun. and holidays 8am-1:30pm and 4:30-7:30pm. Mass daily 7, 8, 10am; holidays, on the hour 8am-1pm and 6:30pm).

From Piazza del Popolo, Via di Ripetta leads south toward the Tiber, ending in the Fascist-era **Piazza Augusto Imperatore.** The circular brick mound of the **Mausoleum of Augustus** once housed the funerary urns of the Imperial Roman family. Next door, the glass-encased **Ara Pacis** stands as a monument to the grandiosity of Augustan age propaganda. (Ara Pacis open Tues.-Wed. and Fri.-Sun. 9am-1:30pm; April-Sept. Tues. and Sat. also 4-7pm. Admission L3750).

The Spanish Steps and Piazza di Spagna

Designed by an Italian, paid for by the French, named for the Spaniards, occupied by the British, and currently under the sway of American ambassador-at-large Ronald McDonald, the **Spanish Steps** *(Scale di Spagna)* exude a truly international air as the center toward which most foreigners gravitate. When the steps were first built in 1725, Romans hoping to earn extra *scudi* as artist's models flocked to the steps dressed as the Madonna or Julius Caesar. Today, posers of a different sort abound: women beware—every eligible man in Rome (usually a self-awarded title) prowls here at night, along with drunken foreigners imitating their Italian counterparts.

The **Fontana della Barcaccia,** at the foot of the steps, was designed by Gian Lorenzo Bernini's less famous father Pietro. The fountain was built below ground level to compensate for the meagerness of the water pressure. The water from the spout is cool, refreshing, and, yes, potable. The rosy neo-classical façade of the **Church of Santa Trinità dei Monti** provides a worthy climax to the grand curves of the Spanish Steps, not to mention a sweeping view of the city. The interior is open 9:30am-12:30pm and 4-7pm, but the upper half is usually blocked by a gate. The whole church opens up only on Tuesdays and Thursdays 4-6pm.

In its day, the piazza has attracted many a creative spirit. Stendhal, Balzac, Wagner, and Liszt all stayed near here; at Caffè Greco, the well-known establishment on swanky Via Condotti, Goethe, Gogol, Berlioz, and Baudelaire used to linger over cups of *espresso*. Henry James and the Brownings lived at different times on Via Bocca di Leone, a small side street in the area, while Rubens and Poussin took flats on Via Babuino. A small plaque on the side of the pink house to the right of the Spanish Steps (P. di Spagna, 26) marks the home where Keats died in 1821. The second floor now houses the charming **Keats-Shelley Memorial Museum** (tel. 901 42 46; open Mon.-Fri. 9am-1pm and 3-6pm; admission L5000, discount for student groups). You can scrutinize a lock of Keats's hair, his deathbed correspondence, an urn containing Shelley's bones, and even some of Keats's curious drawings.

The streets between P. di Spagna and Via del Corso are the most elegant in Rome, their plate-glass windows gleaming with gaudy Italian fashions, and the reflections of preening window-shoppers. Boutiques litter **Via Condotti** and **Via Frattina; Via Borgogna** sparkles with jewelry stores; **Via della Croce** tempts with sumptuous foodstuffs; and **Via del Babuino** and **Via Margutta** supply expensive art fodder. This area was once the Bohemian center of Rome, and the site of numerous brothels; although gentrification has driven out most of the artists and ladies of the evening, a stroll along these back streets turns up the wares of the remaining dedicated few.

Along Viale Trinità dei Monti on the other side of Santa Trinità, the **Villa Medici** houses the **Accademia di Francia** (tel. 676 11). Founded in 1666 to give young French artists an opportunity to live in Rome (Berlioz and Debussy were among the scheme's beneficiaries), the organization now keeps the building in mint condition and arranges excellent exhibits, primarily of French art. (Academy temporarily closed to the public for restoration. Villa closed to the public except during exhibits. Opening and exhibition times vary.) The **Pincio,** a public park planted with formal gardens, extends up the hill beyond the villa (see Villa Borghese, below).

Trevi Fountain

Taking up most of the tiny piazza, the rocks and figures of Nicola Salvi's (1697-1751) famed and now sparkling clean **Fontana di Trevi** mount the back of **Palazzo Poli.** The aqueduct's name derives from the maiden who allegedly pointed out the spring to thirsty Roman soldiers. She is immortalized in one of the bas-reliefs above the fountain. The fountain is at its aesthetic best at night, when artificial lights make it glow in the darkness, while the reflected beams illuminate the faces of the teenagers thronging around the basin. In the most famous scene of Fellini's *La Dolce Vita*, Anita Ekberg takes a midnight dip in the fountain with Marcello Mastroanni and a kitten. Tradition claims that travelers who throw a coin into the fountain will return to Rome, but we urge you to refrain from the practice; the fountain is eroding (despite its recent renovation) from rust from the coins. Opposite the fountain is the Baroque **Church of Santi Vincenzo ed Anastasio,** rebuilt in 1630. The crypt preserves the hearts and lungs of popes from 1590-1903.

Piazza Barberini

Indifferent to the modern hum around the square, Bernini's Baroque **Triton Fountain,** with its muscle-bound figurehead, spouts its perfect stream of water high into the stirring air of Piazza Barberini. This cascade marks the fulcrum of Baroque Rome, as well as five major traffic-ways. Twisting north is the opulent stretch of **Via Veneto,** which has seen its *dolce vita* replaced by a flood of tourists forty years too late. The piazza showcases Bernini's **Fontana delle Api** (Bee Fountain); intended for the "use of the public and their animals," the fountain buzzes with the same motif that graces the aristocratic Barberini family's coat of arms. In stern rejection of Bernini's Baroque hedonism, the 1626 Counter-Reformation **Church of Santa Maria della Concezione,** further up Via Veneto, is a mausoleum housing the tomb of Cardinal Antonio Barberomo, who also founded the church; the tomb's inscription reads "Here lies dust, ashes, nothing." In the **Capuchin Crypt** downstairs, the artfully arranged bones of 4000 Capuchin friars keep him company, making this one of the most bizarre and elaborately macabre settings in Rome. (Open daily 9am-noon and 3-6pm. Donation requested.) The church makes an excellent haunted house on All Soul's Day (Nov. 2), when the chapels are illuminated.

In the other direction from the church, up Via delle Quattro Fontane, the sumptuous **Palazzo Barberini,** at Via delle Quattro Fontane, 13, houses the **Galleria Nazionale d'Arte Antica** (tel. 481 45 91), a collection of paintings dating from the 13th to 18th centuries. (Open Tues.-Sun. 9am-7pm. After 2pm, visitors are allowed only in the 1st floor galleries, and are admitted in small groups on the half hour. Admission to both galleries and apartments L6000.) Maderno, Borromini, and Bernini all had a hand in the architecture. Of the earlier works, note Filippo Lippi's *Annunciation and Donors*, Piero di Cosimo's *La Maddalena*, Holbein's *Portrait of Henry VIII*, and the superb canvases by Titian, Tintoretto, Caravaggio, El Greco, and Poussin. Most startling, however, is the entrance hall, whose ceiling glows with Pietro da Cortona's *Triumph of Divine Providence*, a glorification of the papacy of

SIGHTS

Urban VIII and his family, the Barberini. The family apartments on the second story merit a peek. (Open Mon.-Sat. 9am-2pm, Sun. 9am-1pm. Visits to the apartments are allowed every half-hour. Admission to both galleries and apartments L6000.)

Piazza del Quirinale and Via XX Settembre

Piazza del Quirinale, at the southern end of Via del Quirinale, occupies the summit of the tallest of Rome's seven hills. From the belvedere (reached by steps connecting the piazza with the Trevi Fountain below), the view takes in a sea of Roman domes, with St. Peter's—the mother of all domes—in the far distance. In the middle of the piazza, the heroic **statues of Castor and Pollux** (mythical warrior twins whom ancient Romans embraced as their special protectors) flank yet another of Rome's many obelisks. The President of the Republic officially resides in the **Palazzo del Quirinale,** a Baroque architectural collaboration by Bernini, Carlo Maderno, and Domenico Fontana.

Via del Quirinale leaves the piazza to the north, passing the modest façade of the **Church of Sant'Andrea al Quirinale** (tel. 48 90 31 87) on the right. Though the building lacks architectural complexity, Bernini's theatrical orchestration of the central altar is extraordinary. (Open Wed.-Mon. 8am-noon and 4-7pm.) Further along the street, the marvelous undulating façade of Borromini's **Church of San Carlo alle Quattro Fontane** (often called **San Carlino**) provides a sharp contrast to Bernini's neighboring work. San Carlino, small enough to fit inside one of the pillars of St. Peter's, is a triumph of rhythmical curves and concavities, its narrow interior governed by periodic pairs of pilasters. It also has the distinction of being Borromini's first and last work: though he designed the interior early on in his career, he finished the façade just before his suicide. (Open Mon.-Fri. 9am-12:30pm and 4-6pm, Sat. 9am-12:30pm. If the interior is closed, ring at the convent next door.)

Further down Via del Quirinale, a small square formed by the junction with **Via delle Quattro Fontane** showcases one of Pope Sixtus V's more gracious additions to the city. In an effort to ease traffic and to offer greater definition to the city's regions, the 16th-century pontiff straightened many of Rome's major streets and erected obelisks at important junctions. From the crossroads here, you can catch sight of the obelisks at Piazza del Quirinale, at the top of the Spanish Steps, and at Sta. Maria Maggiore, as well as (in the distance) Michelangelo's famous Porta Pia.

Via del Quirinale becomes Via XX Settembre at this point, which, after a few more blocks, opens into the Baroque **Piazza Bernardo,** site of Domenico Fontana's colossal **Moses Fountain.** The fountain, recently cleaned but already showing signs of new pollution, was built in 1587 at the point where the Acqua Felice aqueduct enters the city. The beefy statue of Moses was carved by Prospero Antichi who nearly died of disappointment after seeing the finished product. Across the way, the **Church of Santa Maria Della Vittoria** harbors Bernini's orgasmic *Ecstasy of St. Theresa of Avila* (1652) in the Cornaro Chapel, the last on the left. As the saint put it: "The pain was so great that I cried aloud but at the same time I experienced such infinite sweetness that I wished the pain would last forever... It was the sweet caressing of the soul by God." (Open daily 7am-noon and 4:30-6:30pm; dress code touted but sporadically enforced.) The **Church of Santa Susanna** to the left has a distinctive Counter-Reformation façade by Carlo Maderno. (Closed for restoration.)

Baths of Diocletian

Following Via delle Quattro Fontane south from P. Barberini to Via Nazionale, trek east or hop on any of the buses headed to P. della Repubblica, home to the **Fountain of Naiads** and the ruins of the **Baths of Diocletian.** Forty thousand Christian slaves took almost ten years—298-306 AD—to build what must have been the grandest community center of the age. In 1561, Pope Pius IV ordered Michelangelo, then 86, to convert the ruins into a church as a posthumous thanks to the 40,000 Christians. His original design imitated the architecture of the baths, but was much changed after both he and the pope died three years later. The eventual result is the **Church of Santa Maria degli Angeli.** Despite the departure from Michelangelo's plan and years of design screw-ups, the vast interior gives a sense of the magnitude and elegance of the ancient baths. The church was constructed in the ancient tepidarium (luke-warm baths). A door marked "Sacristy" leads to ruins of the frigidarium and an exhibit on the stages of the construction of the church (free). (Church open 7:30am-12:30pm and 4-6:30pm.)

Exiting the church to the right, on Via Giuseppe Romita, the Museo Nazionale Romano delle Terme (see below) has a separate exhibit on the baths. Statues on display include the 3rd-century BC *Hellenistic Prince*, and the 1st-century BC *Pugilist at Rest*. (Exhibit open daily 10am-1pm and 3-6pm; free.)

Around the corner on Viale Enrico de Nicola (across the street from the buses lined up in front of Termini Station), the **Museo Nazionale Romano delle Terme** (tel. 488 05 30) combines several important patrician collections with sculptures and antiquities found in Rome since 1870. The museum is located in the charterhouse built along with Santa Maria degli Angeli, and utilizes some of the rooms from the ancient baths. Don't miss the **Sala dei Capolavori** (Room of Masterpieces) and the so-called Ludovisi throne, a Greek statue dating from the 5th century BC. (Museum open Tues.-Sat. 9am-2pm, Sun. 9am-1pm. Admission L3000)

The Pantheon

The majestic **Pantheon** (tel. 36 98 31) has presided over its busy piazza for nearly 2000 years, its marble columns and pediment, bronze doors, and soaring domed interior (save superficial decorative changes) all unchanged from the day it was erected. While centuries of political chaos and urban neglect corroded most of ancient Rome's great monuments into ruins, the Pantheon has remained whole, a proud but bittersweet reminder of the eternal city's former glories. The temple has drawn visitors for centuries, in large part because it's one of the few Roman ruins that won't strain your imagination; the vast, serene interior not only preserves its perfect architectural proportions, but also retains the power to mystify, inspire, and even terrify as it must have done for the ancients.

The building as it stands today is the product of the Emperor Hadrian's fertile architectural imagination. Though it's unclear whether the emperor actually drew up the plans himself, it's certain that the 2nd-century AD philosopher-king, for whom architecture was a favorite hobby, had a hand in its design. (Hadrian also takes credit for the revolutionary design of the Temple of Venus and Rome in the Forum, for the sprawling fantasies of his Villa Adriana at Tivoli, and for his own mausoleum, now Castel Sant'Angelo.) The temple, dedicated to "all the gods," was conceived as a celebration of the abstract spatial harmonies and celestial order which the divine powers had bestowed on the universe. It's a study in (very carefully planned) contrasts and (very cleverly concealed) surprises. The classically proportioned façade, with its traditional triangular pediment, dedicatory inscription, and Corinthian columns, was designed to deceive the first time visitor into expecting an equally traditional interior.

Though the Senate voted to close all pagan temples during the 5th century AD, the Emperor Phocas (whose column stands in the Forum) gave the Pantheon to Pope Boniface IV for safekeeping in 609 AD Converted to the Church of Santa Maria ad Martyres (which title it retains to this day), the temple weathered the middle ages with few losses, though it sometimes did double duty as a fortress and even a fishmarket. Later artists and architects adored and imitated the building, which served as the inspiration for countless Renaissance and Neoclassical edifices, including Bramante's Tempietto, Palladio's Villa Rotonda and America's own Jefferson Memorial. Michelangelo, using the dome as a model for his designs in St. Peter's Basilica, is said to have designed his own dome one meter shorter in diameter than the Pantheon's, out of respect for his ancient model. The 17th century wasn't quite so deferential; when the vainglorious Pope Urban VIII Barberini melted down the bronze revetments from the roof of the portico down to make cannon for Castel Sant'Angelo and the *baldacchino* over the altar of St. Peter's, horrified Romans remonstrated, *Quod non fecerunt barbari, fecit Barberini* ("What the barbarians didn't do, Barberini did"). Adding insult to injury, Urban had Bernini add two clumsy turrets on either side of the pediment (visible in the famous Piranesi prints of the temple), which were almost immediately tagged the "ass-ears of Bernini." Saner minds removed the turrets in the last century. Later additions to the interior of the temple include several modest Renaissance frescoes, the tombs of Italy's first two kings, and the simple tomb of the Renaissance master Raphael Sanzio, whose eloquent epitaph reads, "Here lies one by whom, while he was alive, the great parent of all things feared to be conquered, now, as he is dead, she fears she herself will die." (Pantheon open Mon.-Sat. 9am-4pm, Sun. and holidays 9am-1pm; Oct.-June Mon.-Sat. 9am-2pm, Sun. and holidays 9am-1pm. Free.)

In the piazza before the temple, Giacomo della Porta's playful late Renaissance fountain (recently restored, and brilliantly so) supports an **Egyptian obelisk,** which was added in the 18th century, when obelisks, popular among ancient Romans, were once again à la mode. Around the left side of the Pantheon another obelisk marks the center of tiny **Piazza Minerva,** supported by Bernini's curious, winsome elephant statue. Behind, the unassuming façade (under restoration) of the **Church of Santa Maria Sopra Minerva** hides some of Renaissance Rome's artistic masterpieces. To the right of the entrance, six plaques mark the high-water level of floodings of the Tiber over the centuries. Inside the church, stained-glass windows cast a soft radiance on the Gothic interior and its celestial ceiling. The chapels in the right-hand aisle house a number of treasures, including (in the fifth chapel) a panel of the *Annunciation* by Antoniazzo Romano, and (in the sixth chapel) a statue of *St. Sebastian* recently attributed to Michelangelo. The south transept houses the famous **Carafa Chapel,** with a brilliant fresco cycle by Filippino Lippi, which was closed off for restoration in 1993. The altar of every Catholic church must house a holy relic or body part, and Santa Maria sopra Minerva got a great one—the body of St. Catherine of Siena, the famous 14th-century ascetic and church reformer, who died in a house nearby. (That's not her under the altar, just a wax copy.) To the left of the altar another medieval great, the painter Fra Angelico, lies under a fenced-off tomb slab. Between the two tombs, Michelangelo's great *Christ Bearing the Cross* stands guard. (Open 7am-noon and 4-7pm.)

From the northwest corner of Piazza del Pantheon, take Via Giustiniani to its intersection with Via della Scrofa and Via della Dogana Vecchia, halfway to the Corso del Rinascimento. Here stands the simple white façade of the **Church of San Luigi dei Francesi,** the French National Church in Rome and home to three of Caravaggio's most famous ecclesiastical paintings. (Church open 7:30am-12:30pm and 3:30-7pm.) Continuing past the intersection onto Via Salvatore, turn left at Corso del Rinascimento. On the left, the celestial **Church of Sant'Ivo** raises its famous corkscrew cupola over the Palazzo della Sapienza, the original home of the University of Rome, founded by Pope Sixtus IV in the 15th century. The entrance to the **cloister** on Corso del Rinascimento (#40) provides the best view of Borromini's intricate façade and cupola, designed in 1660 and recently restored. (Open Sept.-May daily 9am-noon.)

Via del Corso

Originally the Broad Street for the Roman Republic, Via del Corso became a prestigious address when the popes widened the street in the 15th century to accommodate the wild (often cruel) antics of Carnival. The storm of riderless horses and the hunchback races of the 18th century have been replaced by streams of crazed shoppers and the apocalyptic onslaught of buses and scooters. The nearby **Galleria Doria Pamphili** (in the *palazzo* of the same name at P. del Collegio Romano, 1A; tel. 679 43 65), houses the most important surviving collection of Roman patrician art. The gallery harbors treasures from the 15th through 18th centuries, including Caravaggio's *Flight into Egypt* and *Mary Magdalene,* Bellini's *Madonna,* Rubens's *Portrait of a Franciscan,* and Velázquez's *Portrait of Innocent X.* The private apartments contain some of the best paintings: Fra Filippo Lippi's *Annunciation* and Memling's *Deposition*. (Open Tues. and Fri.-Sun. 10am-1pm. Admission L6000. Guided tour of private apartments a worthwhile extra L3000.)

Piazza Navona

Despite popular belief, Emperor Domitian (81-96 AD) never used his 30,000-person stadium to shred naughty Christians. Instead, he used the site of modern day **Piazza Navona** as a racetrack. From its opening day in 86 AD, the stadium witnessed daily contests of strength and agility: wrestling matches, javelin and discus tosses, foot- and chariot-races, even mock naval battles. For these seafaring fracases, the stadium was flooded and floated with fleets of convicts. As the empire fell, real-life battles with marauding Goths replaced staged contests, and the stadium fell into disuse. Resourceful Romans used its crumbling outer walls as foundations for new houses, thus preserving the original outline of the stadium. Large crowds returned to the piazza with the Renaissance, and from 1477 to 1869, the space hosted the city's general market. Festivals and jousts were commonplace, as was the contest of the *cuccagna*, in which contestants shimmied up a greased pole to win fabulous prizes. Female travelers will have no problem getting lights for cigarettes or company for strolls, as prowling Romeos vie to test their English and their virility.

Bernini's exuberant **Fountain of the Four Rivers** (*Fontana dei Quattro Fiumi*), commands the center of the piazza. Each of the four male river gods represents one of the four continents of the globe (as they were thought of then): the Ganges for Asia, the Danube for Europe, the Nile for Africa (veiled since the source of the river was unknown), and the Rio de la Plata for the Americas. At the southern end of the piazza, the **Fontana del Moro** attracts pigeons and small children alike. Originally designed by Giacomo Della Porta in the 16th century, Bernini renovated it in 1653 and added *Il Moro*, the central figure perched on a mollusk (actually carved by Antonio Mari, one of Bernini's pupils). The tritons around the edge of the fountain were moved to the Giardino del Lago in the Villa Borghese in 1874 and replaced by copies. Adding balance to the whole scene is the **Fountain of Neptune,** flowing in the north end of the piazza. It too was designed by Della Porta in the 16th century, and spruced up by Bernini, but was without a central figure until 1878. Antonio Della Bitta then added the Neptune from which the fountain takes its name. The ruler of the sea frolics with nereids, sea horses, and a cockeyed octopus.

The piazza doesn't only have fountains; it was also the site of a genuine *miracolo*, marked by the **Church of Sant'Agnese in Agone.** According to Christian legend, Saint Agnes really meant it when she said no to the lascivious son of a low-ranking magistrate; consequently, she was stripped naked in Domitian's stadium. When her hair miraculously grew and covered her sinful nudity, the powers that were tried to burn her at the stake. When the flames didn't even singe her, efficient Diocletian decided to cut her head clean off. This time it worked. The church marks the spot where she was exposed, and houses her severed skull in its sacristy. (Open Mon.-Sat. 5-7pm, mass at 6pm; Sun. and holidays 10am-1pm, mass at noon.)

South of the church, **Palazzo Pamphili** was also built by the Rainaldis and the great Borromini. The façade of the **Church of San Giacomo degli Spagnoli** (a.k.a. **Madonna del Sacro Cuore**), on the southeast side of the piazza, hides a pristine Gothic interior, built in 1450 and restored in 1879.

From Piazza Navona, make your way west to the Vatican along narrow **Via del Governo Vecchio,** an ancient street now lined with off-beat art and antique galleries, vintage clothing stores and cheap *trattorie*. The narrow passage used to be a papal thoroughfare, lined with the townhouses of prosperous bankers and merchants. Though you probably won't be bumping into John Paul II anytime soon, you can still gawk at the medieval mansions overhanging the street, now filled with trendoid boutiques. Via del Governo Vecchio meanders into **Piazza dell Orologio,** where Borromini's Baroque clock-tower stands guard.

Campo dei Fiori

Across Corso Vittorio Emanuele II from Piazza Navona (down Via della Cancelleria), **Campo dei Fiori** is a flower-filled clearing in the middle of a dense medieval quarter. During papal rule, the area was the site of countless executions. In the middle of the Campo, a statue marking the death spot of one victim, Giordano Bruno (1548-1600), rises above the bustle, arms folded over his book. Scientifically and philosophically ahead of his age, Bruno sizzled at the stake in 1600 for taking Copernicus one step further: he argued that the universe had no center at all. Now the only carcasses that litter the piazza are those of the fish in the colorful **market** that springs up with fruit, fish, and flowers every day but Sunday from 7am to 2pm. The streets around the Campo are among the most picturesque in Rome and merit a few hours of exploration. The winding alleys may lure you to a cloistered fountain, a secluded piazza, or a hidden church, or spill you back onto noisy Corso Vittorio Emanuele II.

Several streets lead south from Campo dei Fiori into **Piazza Farnese.** The square is dominated by the huge **Palazzo Farnese,** considered the greatest of Rome's Renaissance *palazzi*. The Farnese, an obscure noble family from the backwoods of Lazio, parlayed Pope Alexander VI's affair with Giulia Farnese into a clutch of bishoprics for her son Alessandro, a fling at the papal throne, and eventually dukedoms in Parma and Piacenza. Alessandro Farnese refounded the Inquisition as Paul III, the first Counter-Reformation pope (1534-1549), and (more humanely) commissioned the best architects of his day—Antonio da Sangallo, Michelangelo, and Giacomo della Porta—to design his dream abode. (Unfortunately, the pope selected architects so advanced in their careers that they all died while in his employ.) Since 1635, the French Embassy has rented the *palazzo* for one *lira* per 99 years in exchange for the Grand Opera House in Paris, home of the Italian Embassy. (Palace definitely *not* open to the public.) In the 16th and early 17th centuries, the Farnese family hosted great spectacles in the square and had the two huge tubs (later converted into the present-day fountains) dug up from the Baths of Caracalla to serve as "royal boxes," from which members of the self-made patrician family could look on. Go around the back of the Palazzo Farnese for a glance at the gardens and Michelangelo's beautiful vine-covered bridge over Via Giulia.

Behind the elaborate Baroque façade of the **Palazzo Spada,** in Piazza della Quercia to the left (east) of the Palazzo Farnese, you'll find the jewel-like picture collection of the **Galleria Spada** (tel. 686 11 58). Seventeenth-century Cardinal Bernardino Spada bought up a grandiose assortment of paintings and sculpture, then commissioned an even more opulent set of great rooms to house them. The collection includes Titian's early *Portrait of a Musician* and Pietro Testa's *Allegory of the Massacre of the Innocents*. (Open in winter Tues.-Sat. 9am-2pm, Sun. and holidays 9am-1pm; in summer Tues.-Sat. 9am-7pm, Sun. and holidays 9am-1pm. L4000).

The Capitoline Hill (Campidoglio)

The physical center, the original capitol, and the most sacred part of the ancient Roman city, the **Capitoline Hill** still serves as the seat of the city's government and is crowned by a spectacular piazza of Michelangelo's design. In ancient times the hill was dominated by a gilded temple to Jupiter, chief god of the Roman pantheon, along with the state mint and the senatorial archives. The northern peak of the hill once held Juno's sacred flock of geese, which saved the city from ambush by the Gauls in 390 BC, by honking so loudly they woke the populace.

The north face of the hill, facing Piazza Venezia, has been completely swallowed by the gargantuan **Victor Emanuel Monument,** a colossal confection of gleaming white marble finished in 1911 to commemorate the short-lived House of Savoy, whose kings briefly ruled the newly unified Italy. At odds with its environs, it is often dubbed "the wedding cake" or Mussolini's typewriter." Around the right of the monument as you face it, a cluster of staircases rises to the top of the hill. The left-hand staircase has 124 steep medieval steps climbing to the unadorned façade of the 7th-century **Church of Santa Maria in Aracoeli.** The right-hand staircase, the curving Via delle Tre Pile (1692), climbs toward a small park. In the center rises Michelangelo's magnificent staircase **la cordonata,** a stepped ramp built in 1536 so that the Emperor Charles V, apparently penitent over his sack of the city a decade before, could ride his horse right up the hill to meet Pope Paul III during a triumphal visit. On your way up *la cordonata,* pause to note a **statue of Cola di Rienzo** (on your left), leader of a popular revolt in 1347 which attempted to reestablish a Roman Republic. The statue marks the spot where the disgruntled populace tore the demagogue limb from limb, where only a short while before they had elected him first consul amidst the ruins of ancient Republicanism.

At the top of the square, Michelangelo's spacious **Piazza di Campidoglio** is fronted on its long sides by the twin **Palazzo dei Conservatori** and **Palazzo Nuovo,** and between them at the back the turreted **Palazzo dei Senatori.** Paul III had the famous equestrian **statue of Marcus Aurelius** brought here from the Lateran Palace to serve as the focal point; but both man and steed proved too delicate to combat the assault of modern pollution and were removed for restoration ten years ago. The emperor now resides in climate-controlled comfort in the courtyard of the Palazzo dei Conservatori. Michelangelo also set up the imperious statues of the twin warriors Castor and Pollux, protector gods of the Roman populace, along with a set of marble trophies of arms and armor and, at the base of his ingenious split staircase, two reclining river gods converted into fountains. Note the exquisite geometry of the Florentine architect's pavement—the buildings face each other at just over a 90° angle in order to draw the visitor into the open space, and the ground slopes gently to the base of the non-statue; some have called this spot the navel of the world.

The **Musei Capitolini** are housed in the twin *palazzi* on either side of the piazza. One ticket covers entrance to both buildings. The museums' collection of ancient sculpture is among the largest in the world, but you may find the *pinacoteca*'s lackluster assortment of 16th-century Italian paintings a bit disappointing. (Museums open Tues.-Sun. 9am-1:30pm; in winter, also Tues. and Sat. 5-8pm, in summer, also Tues. 5-8pm, Sat. 8-11pm. Last entrance ½hr. before closing. Admission L10,000; L5000 with student ID; free on last Sun. of the month.) In the **Palazzo Nuovo** (on the left as you enter the piazza), note the morbid *Dying Gaul* with his chest pierced with wounds and his arm giving way to the heated swoon of death. The *Satyr Rising* on the windowed wall nearby is the "Marble Faun" that inspired Hawthorne's book of the same title. In the courtyard of the **Palazzo dei Conservatori,** fragments of a colossus of Constantine speak, like Ozymandias, of shattered glory. Among the statues in the halls above are the Etruscan *Capitoline Wolf* (Romulus and Remus included and suckling) and the wrenching and passionate *Spinario,* a sculpture of a young lad extracting a thorn from his foot. The **Pinacoteca** houses Bellini's *Portrait of a Young Man,* Titian's *Baptism of Christ,* Rubens' *Romulus and Remus Fed by the Wolf,* and Caravaggio's *Gypsy Fortune-Teller.*

To the right of the Palazzo dei Senatori, the Via del Campidoglio leads downward to a promontory with a panoramic view of the Forum and the Colosseum. Conversely, stairs lead up from the left of the Palazzo dei Senatori to the rear entrance of the **Church of Santa Maria in Aracoeli,** a 7th-century church filled with a jumble of monuments from every century since. Cross the pavement, studded with worn medieval tombs, to the stunning **Bufalini Chapel,** considered among the finest works of the incomparable Pinturicchio. (Open 7am-noon and 4-7pm.) Down the hill from the back stairs of the Aracoeli squats the gloom) **Mamertine Prison,** later consecrated as the **Church of Saint Pietro in Carcere** in commemoration of St. Peter's incarceration here. (Open daily 9am-noon and 2:30-6pm. Free.)

From the Campidoglio, two parks provide great spots for picnicking. Walk around Via delle Tre Pile to reach the first; climb up the stairs by the Museo Nuovo (passing through a *loggia*) to reach the wilder second, with views of the Palatine.

Near the Campidoglio, Via del Plebiscito leads left around the Palazzo Venezia to the Piazza del Gesù and **Il Gesù,** the mother Church of the Jesuit Order (on your left as Via del Plebiscito meets Corso Vittorio Emanuele II). The lighting here is almost theatrical; the nave remains relatively dark and by contrast, the large windows on the Eastern side of the church (in the drum of the dome) spotlight the altar with sunbeams. The Gesù became the prototype for endless churches built or rebuilt during the Counter-Reformation. Toward the front of the church, look to the left of the dome for the **Chapel of Sant'Ignazio di Loyola,** dedicated to the founder of the order, who lies buried under the altar. (Open 6am-12:30pm and 4-7:15pm.)

The Roman Forum and the Palatine Hill

The Forum was originally a marshy valley prone to flooding from the Tiber. Rome's earliest Iron Age inhabitants (1000-900 BC) eschewed its low, unhealthy swampiness in favor of the Palatine Hill, descending only to bury their dead. In the 8th and 7th centuries BC, Etruscans and Greeks using the Tiber Island as a crossing point for their trade brought prosperity to the area, and the forum was used as a weekly market. The early Romans came down from the Palatine, paved the area, drained it with a covered sewer (the **Cloaca Maxima**), and built their first religious shrines to the vital forces of fire and water. Commercial success went hand in hand with political power, and by the 6th century BC, the Romans had kicked out their Etruscan overlords and established a republic. The **Curia** (the meeting place of the Senate), the **Comitium Well** (or assembly place), and the **Rostra** (or speaker's platform) were built to serve the infant democracy, along with the earliest **temples** (to Saturn and to Castor and Pollux) dedicated in thanks for the civic revolution.

The conquest of Greece in the Punic War of the 2nd century BC brought new architectural forms home to the city, including the lofty basilica, which was first used as a center for business and judicial activities; the wealthiest Roman families (including Julius Caesar's) lined the town square in front of the Curia with basilicas, to the good of the public and of their own reputations. The Forum was never reserved for any single activity, and it was during these centuries that it was at its busiest, as senators debated the fates of far-flung nations over the din of haggling traders. The Vestal Virgins built their house over a street full of prostitutes, priests sacrificed in the temples, victorious generals led triumphal processions up to the Capitol, and pickpockets cased the tourists—as they still do today.

Start early in the day, take it slow, and be prepared to be exhausted. It's a big, complicated place, and it gets hot and dusty in the middle of the day. Take a bottle of water. From the entrance gate in Via dei Fori Imperiali (across from the end of Via Cavour), a ramp descends, past the Temple of Antoninus and Faustina on the left and the remains of the Basilica Aemilia on the right, to the basalt stones of the **Via Sacra,** the main thoroughfare of the Forum and the oldest street in Rome. The Via Sacra leads right to the slopes of the Capitol Hill. (Forum, Palatine, and Forum Antiquarium open Mon. and Wed.-Sat. 9am-6pm, Sun. and Tues. 9am-1pm; winter Mon. and Wed.-Sat. 9am-3pm, Sun. and Tues. 9am-1pm. Admission L10,000.)

The Civic Center

Turn right at the end of the entrance ramp; you will be on the Via Sacra facing the Capitoline Hill and the Arch of Septimus Severus. The Via Sacra cuts through the old market square and civic center of Republican Rome, bordered by the **Basilica Aemilia** (to your immediate right) and the intact brick **Curia** building (to your right as you walk down to the arch). The Basilica, built in 179 BC, housed the guild of the *argentarii*, or money-changers, who operated the first *cambi* in the city, providing Roman *denarii* for traders and tourists. The broad space in front of the Basilica is the **Forum** itself. The Curia, or Senate House, was one of the oldest buildings in the Forum, although the present structure dates from the time of Diocletian (303 AD); it was converted to a church in 630 AD and only restored in this century. Occasionally the interior is open; you can see an intricate (and very well-preserved) inlaid marble pavement and the steps where the Senators brought their own portable chairs to their meetings. The broad space in front of the Curia was the **Comitium Well,** or assembly place, where male citizens came to vote. The brick platform to the left of the Curia (as you face the Arch) was the **Rostra,** or speaker's platform, named for the beak-shaped prows of ships which were mounted here after a Roman naval victory at the Battle of Anzio in 338 BC. Senators and consuls orated to the Roman plebs from here, and any citizen could mount to voice his opinion. The hefty **Arch of Septimus Severus** at the end of Via Sacra is really an anomaly in this Republican square; dedicated in 203 AD to celebrate that emperor's victories in the Middle East, the arch reliefs depict the imperial family. Severus's son and successor Caracalla grabbed the throne by knocking off his brother Geta, and scraping his portrait off the arch. Halfway up the Capitol Hill, the grey tufa walls of the **Tabularium,** once the repository of Senate archives, now serve as the basement to the Renaissance **Palazzo dei Senatori** (closed off for renovation). Across the square to the left of the Temple of Saturn, the **Basilica Julia,** built on the site of an earlier basilica by Julius Caesar in 54 BC, followed the same plan as the Basilica Aemilia but was far more extensive. The Basilica was used by tribunals of judges for administering justice.

This part of the Forum, the original market square, was graced by a number of shrines and sacred precincts. Between the Curia and the Rostrum, a flat grey stone—the **Lapis Niger** (meaning *black* stone)—covers what may have been a *heroon,* or funerary monument, to Romulus, the legendary founder of the city. Closer to the Basilica Julia, the **Three Sacred Trees** of Rome—olive, fig, and grape-vine—have been replanted. On the other side, right across from the Basilica Julia, a circular tufa basin commemorates the **Lacus Curtius,** an ancient spring where, legend says, a gaping chasm opened in 362 BC, into which the Roman patrician Marcus Curtius threw himself in order to save the city. A relief records his sacrifice.

The three great temples of the lower Forum (to Saturn, to the Emperor Vespasian, and to Concord) have been closed off during excavations, although the columns of the **Temple of Saturn** are emerging from their shroud of scaffolding at the Capitoline end of the Basilica Julia. At the far end of the Basilica Julia, three white marble columns and a shred of architrave mark the massive podium of the **Temple of Castor and Pollux,** dedicated in 484 BC in celebration of the Roman rebellion against their Etruscan king, Tarquinius Superbus. Legend says that immediately after the battle the twin gods Castor and Pollux appeared in the Forum to water their horses at the adjacent **Basin of Juturna** (*Lacus Juturnae*), now marked by a reconstructed marble *aedicule* to the left of the gods' own temple. Across the street from the Temple of Castor and Pollux is the rectangular base of the **Temple of the Deified Julius,** which Augustus built in 29 BC to honor his murdered adoptive father, and to proclaim himself the son of a god. The circular pile of rocks inside probably marks the spot where Caesar's body was cremated in 44 BC (he was assassinated near Largo Argentina); pious Romans still leave flowers here on the Ides of March. The circular building behind the temple is the restored **Temple of Vesta,** on a foundation dating back to the time of the Etruscans. Built in imitation of an archaic round Latin hut, this is where the Vestal Virgins tended the sacred fire of the city.

The Upper Forum

The **House of the Vestal Virgins** occupied the sprawling complex of rooms and courtyards to the right and rear of the temple to Vesta, in the shade of the Palatine Hill. The six virgins who officiated over Vesta's rites, each ordained at the age of seven, lived in spacious and celibate seclusion here for thirty years above the din of the Forum. A tour through the storerooms and lower rooms of the house brings you back to the Via Sacra and the **Temple of Antoninus and Faustina** (to the immediate right as you face the entrance ramp), whose lofty columns and frieze were incorporated into the **Church of San Lorenzo in Miranda** before the 12th century (its façade dates from the Baroque). Antoninus, one of the "good emperors" of the 2nd century AD, had the temple built in honor of his wife Faustina, who died in 141; the Roman people returned the favor after his own death, and the temple now stands to commemorate the both of them. In the shadow of the temple (to the right as you face it), the archaic **Necropolis,** with Iron Age graves from the 8th century BC, was excavated earlier in this century, lending credence to the Romans' own legendary foundation date of 753 BC. The bodies were found in **tufa sarcophagi,** hollowed-out tree trunks. Here the Via Sacra runs over the **Cloaca Maxima,** the ancient sewer that still drains water from the otherwise marshy valley. The street then passes what is called the **Temple of Romulus,** a round building that still retains its ancient bronze doors from the 4th century AD. Not a temple at all, it probably served as the office of the urban praetor during the Empire (no admittance).

The Velia

The street now leads out of the Forum proper to the gigantic **Basilica of Maxentius** (also known as the Basilica of Constantine). The three gaping arches are actually only the side chapels of an enormous central hall whose coffered ceiling covered the entire gravel court, as well as another three chapels on the other side. Michelangelo studied its architecture before constructing St. Peter's Cathedral.

The Baroque façade of the **Church of S. Francesca Romana** (built over Hadrian's Temple to Venus and Rome) hides the entrance to the **Forum Antiquarium** (open the same hours as the Forum). Most of the rooms have been closed for years, but a few on the ground floor display funerary urns and skeletons from the necropolis. On the summit of the Velia, the shoulder running down from the Palatine, is the **Arch of Titus,** built by the emperor Domitian to celebrate his brother Titus's destruction of Jerusalem in 70 AD. The reliefs inside the arch depict the Roman sack of the great Jewish temple, including the pillage of a giant menorah. The Via Sacra leads to an exit on the other side of the hill, an easy way to get to the Colosseum.

The Palatine Hill

The flowering gardens and broad grassy expanses of the **Palatine Hill** are a refreshing change from the dusty Forum—an ideal place to picnic after a morning in the ruins. Though there are lots of ancient remnants to see here too, the cool breezes and sweeping views of Rome are the real reason to make the steep climb from below. The best way to begin is from the stairs (to the right after the street turns at the Arch of Titus) which ascend to the **Farnese Gardens.** Go through the gardens and past a *nymphaeum,* or enclosed fountain room, to a series of terraces with sweeping views of the Forum and the city. From the top, take a right through avenues of roses and orange trees until you reach another terrace, with a breathtaking view of the Forum, the Imperial Fora, and the Quirinal Hill. The gardens continue along the western side of the hill, where an octagonal box-hedge maze in the center follows the layout of a real maze excavated from the Palace of Tiberius underneath (this was excavated early in this century, but the practical Romans decided the gardens had really been nicer, and filled the dig back in). At the southwest corner (at the extreme top right of the gardens), another terrace looks out over the Capitoline Hill, the Republican temples of the Forum Boarium, and (across the river) the ridge of the Gianicolo. Stairs descend from the middle of the Farnese Gardens to the long, spooky **Cryptoporticus,** a tunnel which connected Tiberius's palace with the later buildings on this side of the hill. Used by slaves and imperial couriers, it may have been built by Nero for use as a secret passage. The short end of the tunnel brings you up to the vast ruins of the solemn **Domus Augustana,** the imperial palace built by Domitian (81-96 AD). The exterior walls, even in their ruined state, are so high that archaeologists are still unsure how they were roofed over.

Fori Imperiali

The **Fori Imperiali** sprawl across the street from the old Forum Romanum, a vast conglomeration of temples, basilicas, and public squares constructed by the emperors of the first and 2nd centuries AD, partly in response to increasing congestion in the old forum, partly for their own greater glory. In the 1930s, Mussolini, with imperial aspirations of his own, cleared the area of medieval constructions and built the Via dei Fori Imperiali to pass over the newly excavated remains. The *fora* were only partially excavated, and the broad, barren thoroughfare cuts across the old foundations at an awkward angle. All of the *fora* remained closed for renovation in 1993, with the exception of the Markets of Trajan (see below). The rest are all at least partially visible (except for the Forum of Vespasian) from street level.

The **Forum of Trajan,** the largest and most impressive of the lot, spreads across Via dei Fori Imperiali below two Baroque churches at the eastern end of Piazza Venezia. Eight years of restoration helped reveal the nearly perfectly preserved spiral of the **Trajan Column,** the greatest specimen of Roman relief-sculpture ever carved. The 200-meter-long continuous frieze wrapped around the column is one of the most dense and ambitious artistic endeavors of the ancient world. Down the street (but entrance on Via IV Novembre, 94, up the steps in Via Magnanapoli behind the Baroque churches) the **Markets of Trajan** provide a glimpse of daily life in the ancient city. The semicircular complex, built into the side of the Quirinal Hill, sheltered several levels of *tabernae,* or single-room stores, along cobbled streets. You can stroll along the basalt paving stones and climb to a spectacular view of Trajan's Forum and the Capitoline Hill. (Open Tues.-Sat. 9am-1:30pm, Sun. 9am-1pm; in summer Tues.-Sat. 9am-1:30pm and 4-7pm, Sun. 9am-1pm. Admission L3750.)

Across the Via dei Fori Imperiali, in the shade of the Vittorio Emanuele II Monument, the paltry remains of the **Forum of Caesar** lie beneath one of Rome's largest gypsy enclaves. A few reconstructed columns are all that remain of Caesar's **temple to Venus Genetrix** (Mother Venus, from whom he claimed descent), but the stone façades of the arcades he built to house Roman shops remain in better repair.

Colosseum

The **Colosseum,** accessible from the Metro stop of the same name (Linea B), stands as the enduring symbol of the Eternal City—a hollowed-out ghost of somber travertine marble that dwarfs every other ruin in the city. At its inauguration in 80 AD it could hold as many as 50,000 spectators; the first 100 days of operation saw some 5000 wild beasts perish in the bloody arena, and the slaughter didn't stop for three centuries. Gladiators fought each other here, and the elliptical interior could be flooded for mock sea battles. The outside of the arena, still well-preserved around three quarters of its circumference, provided the inspiration for countless Renaissance and Baroque architectural confections, the triple stories of Doric, Ionic, and Corinthian columns being considered the ideal orchestration of the classical orders. The raw interior comes as a bit of a disappointment; almost all the marble stands and seats were quarried by Renaissance popes for use in their own grandiose constructions, including the basilica of St. Peter's and the Palazzo Barberini. The floor (now gone) lay over a labyrinth of brick cells, corridors, ramps, and elevators used for transporting wild animals from their cages up to the level of the arena.

The ground level of the Colosseum is open Mon.-Tues. and Thurs.-Sat. 9am-7pm, Wed. 9am-1pm, Sun. 9am-1pm (until 6pm June-Aug.); *free.* An ascent to the upper floors provides better views of the whole city (and of the nearby Forum). Upper decks open Sun-Tues. and Thurs. 9am-6pm (in winter 9am-4pm), Wed. 9am-1pm, Fri.-Sat. 9am-7pm in summer. Admission L6000.

Between the Colosseum and the Palatine Hill lies the remarkably intact **Arch of Constantine.** After his conversion to Christianity by a vision of a flaming cross, Constantine built the arch to commemorate his victory over Maxentius at the Battle of the Milvian Bridge in 312. The triple arch, though well-proportioned, is constructed almost entirely from sculptural fragments pillaged from older Roman monuments.

Circus Maximus, Baths of Caracalla, and the Appian Way

Cradled in the valley between the Palatine and Aventine Hills (a few hundred feet down Via S. Gregorio from the west side of the Colosseum), the **Circus Maximus** today offers only a dusty shadow of its former glories. After its construction in about 600 BC, more than 300,000 Romans gathered here to watch the riotous, breakneck careenings of chariots round the quarter-mile track. The turning points of the track, now marked by a raised grassy hump, were perilously sharp by design, to ensure enough thrills and spills to keep the crowds happy.

At the eastern end of the Circus down Via dei Cerchi, **Piazza di Porta Capena** marks the beginning of the **Via Appia Antica,** built in 312 BC and rightly called the queen of roads ever since. The Via once traversed the whole peninsula, providing a straight and narrow path for legions heading to Brindisi and conquests in the East. Some of Italy's modern *autostrade* still follow the ancient path, but a sizeable portion leading out of the city remains in its antique state, with basalt paving stones, avenues of cypress trees, views of the Roman countryside, and crumbling necropoli of tombs both pagan and Christian.

It is difficult, if not impossible, to walk along the Via Appia Antica, as it is narrow, cobblestoned, and clogged with cars. You can walk as far as the end of Porta San Sebastiano; then grab **bus** #118 (which comes from the Colosseum) or the more frequent #218 (which comes from S. Giovanni in Laterano) for the last leg of the trip; get off at the Catacombs of S. Callisto to begin a tour on foot. Better yet, consider renting a bike from the city for an afternoon of pastoral exercise. Or take Linea B of the **metro** to Circo Massimo, and walk up Viale Aventino to Piazza di Porta Capena.

From the Piazza di Porta Capena, Via delle Terme di Caracalla passes the remains of the **Baths of Caracalla,** the largest of their kind in the city and the best preserved. Some 1600 heat-soaked Romans could sponge themselves off here at the same time. There is an entrance fee for the baths, but when the opera has taken up residence (and covered much of the site), entrance is sometimes free. (Open Tues.-Sat. 9am-3pm and Sun.-Mon. 9am-1pm; in summer Tues.-Sat. 9am-6pm. Admission L6000.)

Catacombs

Outside the city proper lie the **catacombs,** multi-story condos for the dead, stretching tunnel after tunnel for up to 25km and on as many as five levels. Of the 60 around Rome, five are open to the public; the most notable are those of **San Sebastiano, San Callisto,** and **Santa Domitilla,** next door to one another on Via Appia Antica south of the city. The Roman catacombs lie shrouded in mystery; no one can adequately explain how persecuted Christians found the time and the means to construct these elaborate structures. The best days to visit the catacombs are Friday through Monday, when the standard three are open. Take bus #118 from Via Claudia near the Colosseum (20min.; beware of infrequent service). The more frequent bus #218 also runs on Via Appia Antica; get off before it takes a sharp right turn up Via Ardeatina—you'll be at the entrance to **San Callisto,** Via Appia Antica, 110 (tel. 513 67 25 or 513 67 27), the largest catacomb in Rome (almost 22km of winding, subterranean paths). Its four serpentine levels once held eight popes, nine bishops, Santa Cecilia (the patron saint of music—her remains are now in the Church of Santa Cecilia in Trastevere), and thousands of early Christians interred in the first public Christian cemetery. Less appealing are the charred remains of babies who fell in vats of boiling oil. (Open Thurs.-Tues. 8:30am-noon and 2:30-5:30pm, until 5pm in winter. Admission L6000, under 10 free.) **Santa Domitilla,** Via delle Sette Chiese, 283 (tel. 511 03 42), beyond and behind San Callisto, enjoys acclaim for its paintings and for its collection of inscriptions from tombstones and sarcophagi. (Open Fri.-Wed. 8:30am-noon and 2:30-5:30pm, until 5pm in winter. Admission L6000.)

Perhaps the most impressive is **San Sebastiano,** Via Appia Antica, 136 (tel. 788 70 35; fax 784 37 45), which served as the temporary home for the bodies of Peter and Paul (or so ancient graffiti on its walls suggest). San Sebastiano is accessible from the entrance to San Callisto. Running for 7 miles among three levels, and accommodating 174,000 dead, the tunnels here are eerily decorated with animal mosaics, disintegrating skulls, and fantastic symbols of early Christian iconography. In the church above stands Bernini's statue to St. Peter. (Open Wed.-Mon. 8:30am-noon and 2:30-5:30pm, until 5pm in winter. Admission L6000, under 10 free.)

In all three catacombs, visitors follow a guided tour in the language of their choice; non-English tours are significantly less crowded (every 20min., free with admission). Santa Domitilla receives few visitors, so you're almost assured of a personalized tour. Because the catacombs have winding, uneven paths and the tours are conducted briskly, they are not recommended for people who are claustrophobic or have difficulty walking. The **Jewish catacombs** (Via Appia Antica, 119A) are at a fork in the road between Callisto and Sebastian but are not open to the public.

The Esquiline and Caelian Hills

The **Basilica of Santa Maria Maggiore** (four blocks down Via Cavour from Termini) occupies the summit of the Esquiline Hill. As one of the seven major basilicas of the city, it is officially a part of Vatican City. Both its front and rear façades are Rococo works (the front façade, not facing Via Cavour, is *in restauro*), but its interior, built in 352 AD, is the best-preserved example of a paleo-Christian basilica in the city. The coffered ceiling is believed to have been gilded with the first gold sent back from America by Columbus. To the right of the altar, a simple marble slab marks the **tomb of Gianlorenzo Bernini.** (Church open daily 7am-8pm; dress code enforced.)

From Piazza Santa Maria Maggiore, Via Santa Prassede leads, by an alley on the right of the piazza, to the **Church of Santa Prassede,** built in 822. The tiny **chapel of Saint Zeno** (lit by a coin-operated machine outside the door, L600) in the right aisle is the only chapel in Rome lined entirely in mosaic. The chapel also holds a portion of a column retrieved from Jerusalem in 1228 during the sixth Crusade. Possibly a site of historical scourgings, this is reputedly the column on which Christ was strapped and flagellated. (Open 7am-noon and 4-6:30pm.)

Down Via Carlo Alberto from Piazza Sta. Maria Maggiore lurks the shabby **Piazza Vittorio Emanuele,** home to Rome's biggest outdoor market, vending fresh fish and fruits, and non-edibles like clothes, shoes, and luggage. (At night, however, the wares are less Levi's and more lethal.) A few blocks to the west, steps on the left of Via Cavour (heading away from the station) lead you up and under the narrow archway of Via San Francesco di Paola to the piazza and **Church of San Pietro in Vincoli,** home to Michelangelo's unfinished *Tomb of Julius II*. The central figure, the imposing **statue of Moses,** is a masterpiece in itself. (Open 7am-12:30pm and 3:30-6pm.)

Though it is adjacent to the south side of the Esquiline Hill, perhaps the easiest way to begin an ascent of the **Caelian Hill** is from the valley of the Colosseum. Via di S. Giovanni in Laterano leads away from the Piazza del Colosseo (on the opposite side of the amphitheater from the entrance on Via dei Fori Imperiali) to the multiple **Churches of San Clemente** (about 1 block down on the left). True to Roman traditions of building, the complex incorporates centuries of architecture and handiwork. (Open Mon.-Sat. 9am-12:30pm and 3:30-6:30pm, Sun. and holidays 10am-12:30pm and 3:30-6:30pm.) Up the street, on the hill of Via dei Querceti (take your first right off S. Giovanni in Laterano after the Church of San Clemente, and head up Via SS. Quattro), the solemn **Church of Santi Quattro Coronati** lies fortified behind medieval battlements. The church itself is remarkable more for its strange shape and overly wide apse than for any decoration, but the little **chapel of Saint Silvester** off the entrance courtyard (to the right before the church entrance) contains an extraordinary fresco cycle of the life of the Emperor Constantine (ring the bell of the convent; the cloistered nuns will send you a key on a lazy susan; L1000).

Via dei Santi Quattro Coronati leads up the hill past the automechanics and left onto Via S. Stefano Rotondo. In the hectic piazza before you lies the grandiose **Church of San Giovanni in Laterano,** the cathedral of the diocese of Rome and, as such, the mother Church of the entire Catholic faith. The church is actually the oldest Christian basilica in the city, founded by Constantine in 314 AD. The traditional pilgrimage route from St. Peter's ends here, and the Pope still celebrates festival masses on occasion. The giant Gothic *baldacchino* over the altar houses two golden reliquaries with the heads of Saints Peter and Paul inside. Unfortunately, recent terrorists paid little attention (or perhaps too much) to the church's spiritual importance; a bomb heavily damaged the basilica in 1993, while a simultaneous blast devastated the Church of San Giorgio in Velabro (see below). Most of the damage was to the façade and some *frescoes* were left in danger of collapsing. When this guide went to press, San Giovanni was still closed to the public.

Across the busy Piazza di San Giovanni and to the right (marked by an **Egyptian obelisk** from the 5th century BC) the **Scala Santa** houses what are believed to be the marble steps used by Jesus outside Pontius Pilate's house in Jerusalem. Pilgrims earn an indulgence for ascending the covered steps on their knees; if you prefer to walk up to the chapel at the top, use the secular stairs on either side. (Scala Santa open 6:15am-12:15pm and 3:30-7:15pm, in winter 6:15am-12:15pm and 3-6:45pm.)

Piazza Mattei and the Jewish Ghetto

In **Piazza Mattei,** the graceful 16th-century **Fontana delle Tartarughe** (Tortoise Fountain) by Taddeo Landini marks the center of the **Ghetto,** the lowland quarter where Jews were confined from the 16th to the 19th century. While Dickens declared the area "a miserable place, densely populated, and reeking with bad odors," today's Jewish Ghetto is one of the most picturesque and eclectic (even chic) neighborhoods, with family businesses dating back centuries and restaurants serving up the tastiest food in Rome. Relatively speaking, Jews have fared better (and certainly longer) in Rome than almost any other place in Europe, but even here they have endured centuries of hostility, prejudice, and segregation.

There are no less than five Mattei *palazzi* in the area surrounding the Ghetto, traditionally controlled by that (ig)noble family. The **Tortoise Fountain** was actually designed by della Porta; Bernini added the turtles when he restored it in 1658. The local story of the fountain: Duke Mattei, a notorious and incorrigible gambler, lost everything in one night. His father-in-law-to-be was so disgusted by the Duke's flagrantly stupid behavior that he rescinded his approval of Mattei's marriage to his daughter. The Duke, in a bid to pull his name from the mud of scandal, had the fountain built in a single night to show that a Mattei could pull off anything, even when completely broke. He got the girl, though she ended up blocking up her window so she would never have to see the fountain that got her married to such a schlemiel.

Leaving the piazza on the east along Via dei Funari brings you past **Palazzo Mattei** (on the left), one of the many Mattei properties which stretch over several blocks. They made much of their money collecting tolls over the bridges to Trastevere, and later, from serving as sentinels for the Ghetto. The Mattei constructed their huge expanse of *palazzi*, often called the Island of Mattei, over a period of two centuries (1400-1600s). A papal housing decree in 1574 required all new buildings to be attached in some way, by courtyard or wall, to another; thus the Mattei *palazzi* are actually separated only by styles of architecture, and are not free-standing structures.

On the next block of Via dei Funari, the **Church of Santa Caterina dei Funari** (closed for renovation in 1993) towers austerely above the street of the same name, titled for the rope-makers who worked here. St. Ignatius founded the church to provide homes for poor and orphaned girls, who were then married off to local artisans. The bell-tower is a sorry addition to the church, and adding insult to injury, the recent restoration attempts have made the top look like a wedding-cake decoration, now called "the sacrilege of St. Catherine."

Down to the right is **Piazza di Campitelli,** a lovely and harmonious example of the Counter-Reformation Church's extreme efforts to beautify Rome above all other cities in order to demonstrate the superiority of the Vatican. To create the perfect space for the piazza, the **Church of Santa Maria in Campitelli** had to be moved and rebuilt. Carlo Rainaldi designed the church, which is arguably his best work ever. Like his Church of Sant'Andrea della Valle, this church exemplifies the theatrics of Baroque architecture to an even greater degree by creating a grand sense of space. (Open Mon.-Sat. for Mass at 7:30am and 7pm; Sun. and holidays 7:30am, 10am, 11am, noon, and 7pm.) From Via dei Funari, take Via Sant'Angelo in Peschiera off Piazza Lovatelli towards the river to Via Portico d'Ottavia. Several houses on this street, notably #13, #17, and #19 (part of the Portico d'Ottavia), date from medieval times. Note in particular the inscription on the building at Via Portico d'Ottavia, 1; after the patriotic invocation *Ave Roma*, it praises the owner for beautifying Rome. At the end of Via Portico d'Ottavia near the Tiber, facing the synagogue on the south, the façade of the **Church of San Gregorio a Ponte Quattro Capi** carries a Hebrew and Latin inscription (from Isaiah 65: 2, 3) admonishing Jews to convert to Catholicism. (Mass Mon.-Sat. 8am, Sun. 11am.)

Across the street from San Gregorio, the **Sinagoga Ashkenazita** (Synagogue of Rome; tel. 687 50 51) at Via Portico di Ottavia and Via Catalana, defiantly proclaims its divergent heritage in a city overrun with Catholic iconography and classical designs. There were originally five different *scuole*, or synagogues, in the Ghetto, reflecting the diversity of the Jewish settlers (of Spanish, Italian, and Sicilian heritage, to name a few), but they were destroyed in 1910. This synagogue reflects, in part, the unity of the Jewish people in Rome. Built between 1874 and 1904, the synagogue incorporates Persian and Babylonian architectural devices, purposefully avoiding any resemblance to a Christian church. The building is topped by a large metal dome, which, along with the Pantheon's, is visible from the top of the Gianicolo. The inside of the temple has a strictly Orthodox seating plan, with the women sitting above the men. Services, to which anyone is welcome, are given entirely in Hebrew. Since the 1982 attack on the synagogue, *carabinieri* and video devices keep terrorists at bay, and all visitors must be searched before entering.

The synagogue also houses the **Jewish Museum,** which displays ceremonial objects from the 17th-century Jewish community as well the original plan of the Ghetto. Several objects, like the green morocco leather prayer book from 1325 AD, attest to the tenaciousness of the Jewish Sephardic community over the centuries. The collection was hidden in a *mikvah* (a Jewish ritual bath) during the nine-month Nazi occupation of Rome. (No cameras. Synagogue open Mon.-Thurs. 9:30am-2pm, Fri. 9:30am-1:30pm, Sun. 10am-noon. Services Sun.-Fri. 7:45am, Sat. 8:30pm. Museum open July-Aug. Mon.-Thurs. 9:30am-6pm, Fri. 9:30am-2pm, Sun. 9:30am-noon; in winter Mon.-Fri. 9:30am-2pm, Sun. 9:30am-12:30pm. Hours fluctuate widely and the administrators advise checking for changes. Admission L5000.)

Also note the **Palazzo Cenci** on a slight rise (Monte Cenci) at the end of Via Catalana, named for the Spanish Jews who settled here. The *palazzo* was the scene of a September 9, 1598 scandal when Beatrice Cenci, aided by her brother and her step-mother, succeeded in having her father Francesco Cenci murdered. The whole clan was beheaded a year and two days later at the command of Pope Clement VIII, but the public sympathized with the group's plea of self-defense against the incestuous drug addict Francesco.

Nearby (back at the end of Via Portico d'Ottavia), a shattered pediment and a few ivy-covered columns are all that remain of the once magnificent **Portico d'Ottavia,** one of Augustus's grandest contributions to the architecture of the ancient city. The pediment crowned the side entrance to a long, rectangular enclosure whose 300 columns formed a sacred precinct around two important temples to Jupiter and Juno. Medieval Romans built around, inside, and on top of the marble portico, then filled the remaining open space with a fish market, which functioned until this century. The market lent its name to the **Church of Sant'Angelo in Pescheria** (still called the **Foro Piscario**), installed inside the portico in 755 AD. It was here that the Jews of the Ghetto were forced to attend mass every Sunday from 1584 until the 18th century—an act of aggressive evangelism which they quietly resisted by stuffing their ears with wax. The church is rarely open (under renovation in 1993). At #28 Via del Portico d'Ottavia, to the right of the old fish market, there is a plaque in memory of the 2091 Roman Jews who died in the Holocaust.

Theater of Marcellus

If you think the stocky **Theater of Marcellus** (Teatro di Marcello) next door looks like a Colosseum wanna-be, think again. The pattern of arches and pilasters on the theater's exterior, completed in 11 BC, actually served as a model for the great amphitheater across town. You can still make out the classic arrangement of architectural orders, which grows, in accordance with ancient principles, more complex from the ground up. Vitruvius and other ancient architects called this arrangement the most perfect possible for exterior decoration, inspiring Alberti, Bramante, Michelangelo, and countless other Renaissance architects to copy the pattern. Normally closed to the public, the park around the theater hosts classical concerts on summer nights (July 1-Sept. 30 every night at 9pm; call tel. 481 48 00 for more information).

Further down Via di Teatro di Marcello towards the Tiber, the remains of three more Roman temples jut out from the walls of the **Church of San Nicola in Carcere** (tel. 686 99 72). The three buildings were originally dedicated to the gods Juno, Janus, and Hope. The most complete temple lies to the right of the church, its Ionic columns littering the tiny lawn and supporting the church's wall. The left wall of the church preserves the Doric columns of another of the temples. The third temple lies buried beneath the sober little church. (Open Sept.-July Mon.-Sat. 4-7pm, Sun. mass at noon. Visits to the excavations Thurs. 10:30am-noon.)

One block further south along Via Luigi Pettroselli lies the **Piazza di Bocca della Verità,** the site of the ancient **Forum Boarium,** or cattle market. Now overgrown with weeds, the Forum could use some cattle today. The two ancient **temples** in the Forum Boarium capture one of the most important moments in the history of Roman architecture, the shift from native Italic to imported Greek styles which came hand in hand with Rome's conquest of Greece in the 2nd century BC. The rectangular **Temple of Fortunus** (on the right of the Forum from Via Pettroselli), which predates the conquest, follows archaic Italic models with its raised stone base, closed-off back and side walls, and severe front porch. The **circular temple** next door, also built in the 2nd century BC, shows how different the Greek take on religion was. Built at ground level, its symmetrical shape invites anyone to walk around and through its graceful colonnade. Once thought to be dedicated to Vesta (because of its similarity to the Temple of Vesta in the Forum), the real honoree of the round temple remains nameless to this day.

Across the piazza from the temples, Via del Velabro climbs a short way toward the Capitol Hill. Behind the hulking **Arch of Janus,** built in the 4th century as a covered market for cattle traders, the little **Church of San Giorgio in Velabro** was a marvelous medieval edifice, with a 9th-century porch and pillars, a simple basilican interior, and a *campanile* (bell tower) built of brick and stone arches. A terrorist car-bombing on July 27, 1993 reduced the church's famed portico to a single arch and part of a stone beam. To the left, the **Arch of the Argentarii** was erected by the money changers (*argentarii*) and cattle merchants who used the piazza as a market in the 3rd century AD, in honor of Emperor Septimius Severus and his family.

Closer to the river, past Piazza della Bocca della Verità, the exquisite **Church of Santa Maria in Cosmedin** (also called Church of S. Maria de Scuola Greca) harbors some of Rome's most beautiful medieval decoration. The front porch and bell tower, dating from the 12th century, welcome daily mobs of bus-borne tourists, all on their way to see the famous **Bocca della Verità,** in the portico. Originally a drain cover carved as a river god's face, the circular relief was credited with supernatural powers in the middle ages. It's said the hoary face will close shut on the hand of a liar, severing his other fingers. The caretaker-priest used to stick a scorpion in the back to bite the fingers of those little-white-liars. Clay replicas of the Bocca sell for L2000-65,000 (for big fat liars) in the shop of the church interior. (Portico open 9am-5pm. Church open 9am-noon and 3-5pm. Byzantine mass Sun. 10:30am.)

From the Bocca della Verità, the hazardous Lungotevere Aventino leads a short way to the Clivio di Rocca Savella, a lonely, cobbled ramp (on the right side of the street) that climbs between crumbling walls to the spacious gardens of the **Aventine Hill.** The ramp leads through an iron gate to a park on the same site, where orange trees frame a sweeping view of the Tiber and the southern part of the city, an ideal spot for picnicking. Across the park, another gate opens onto the courtyard of the **Church of Santa Sabina,** with a porch of ancient columns and a towering campanile. Via di Santa Sabina continues along the crest of the hill past the **Church of Sant'Alessio** to the **Piazza dei Cavalieri di Malta,** home of the ancient crusading order of the Knights of Malta. The keyhole in the gate offers a perfectly framed view of the dome of St. Peter's, which, to no one's comprehension, magnifies the sight. From Santa Sabina, Via di Valle Murcia descends past a public garden (where a rose show blooms in June and early July) to the **Circus Maximus,** where you can catch a stunning view of the ruined Palatine palaces and the churches of the Caelian Hill.

Testaccio

South of the Aventine Hill, the working-class district of **Testaccio** is known for its cheap and delicious *trattorie*, raucous nightclubs, and eclectic collection of monuments. The #27 bus runs from Termini down Via Cavour and across the river, entering Testaccio along Via Zabaglia. (Alternately, take Metro Linea B to the Piramide stop, where you will see the Pyramid of Caius Cestius, and then follow our directions backwards.) In ancient times the area served as the docklands of Rome, where grain, oil, wine, and marble were unloaded from river barges into giant warehouses. After the goods had been transferred to storage, Roman merchants tossed the leftover terracotta urns into a vacant lot. The pile grew and grew, and today the bulbous **Monte Testaccio** (from *testae*, or pot shards) rises 150 feet over the drab surrounding streets (to the right on Via Zabaglia). Though grown over with grass, the hill is punctured everywhere by fragments of orange clay amphorae. The park is no longer open to the public, and pilfering of pot shards is quite illegal.

Via Nicola Zabaglia turns left onto Via Caio Cestio, which runs along the length of the peaceful **Protestant Cemetery,** final resting place for many English visitors to the city, including Keats, Shelley, and Goethe's son Julius. Henry James buried his fictional heroine, Daisy Miller, here after she died of malaria. (Open Thurs.-Tues. 8-11:30am and 3:20-7:30pm; Oct.-Feb. 8-11:30am and 2:20-4:30pm. Ring the bell for admission at number 6. Free, but donation requested.) Outside the cemetery, past the well-preserved **Porta San Paolo,** the colossal **Pyramid of Caius Cestius** shares a burial plot with the Protestants. Like the collection of Egyptian statuary in the Vatican and most of the obelisks in the city, there's nothing Egyptian about this pyramid except its inspiration. When the Goths were marauding in the 3rd century, the emperor Aurelian had the pyramid built into his city walls as a bastion; nowadays it's the favored hangout of Rome's impeccably modish transvestite population.

Basilica San Paolo

From the pyramid, take Metro line B or grab bus #673, 23, or 170 down the boring Via Ostiense to the eery **Basilica San Paolo** (in the Ostiense neighborhood, Metro stop is "Basilica San Paolo"), the third of Rome's extraterritorial basilicas (with S. Giovanni and Sta. Maria Maggiore) and the largest church in the city after St. Peter's. St. Paul, who was martyred near the modern **EUR,** is believed to be buried under the altar (his body, that is; his head is in S. Giovanni), and the church was, until the construction of the new St. Peter's, the largest and most beautiful in Rome. Completely destroyed by fire in 1823, the present church is a modern reconstruction. (Open 7:30am-7pm.) The **cloister** is a peaceful remnant of the original construction, lined with twisted pairs of Cosmatesque columns and enveloping a rose garden. (Open 9am-1pm and 3-6pm.)

EUR

Rome is famous for monuments that hark back to ancient empires. South of the city stands a monument to a Roman empire that, fortunately, never was. The zone is called **EUR** (pronounced AY-oor), an Italian acronym for Universal Exposition of Rome, the 1942 World's Fair that Mussolini intended to be a showcase of fascist achievements. The outbreak of World War II led to the cancellation of the fair, and wartime demands on manpower and material ensured that EUR would never complete its mission of extending Rome to the sea, but the completed buildings house some of Rome's enormous museum overflow. Visit the area only to see the melba-toast museums or to see where the Cleavers would have lived if Wally were a strapping young fascist. EUR lies at the EUR-Palasport stop on Metro line B, or take bus #714 from Termini to Piazza G. Marconi. **Via Cristoforo Colombo,** EUR's main street, runs roughly north to south. From the metro stop, walk north up Via Cristoforo Colombo to **Piazza Guglielmo Marconi,** sprouting a 1959 modernist **obelisk** (the first of many bad takes on Classical Roman architecture).

Located to the right of the Piazza Marconi, the **Museo Preistorico ed Etnografico Luigi Pigorini,** at Viale Lincoln, 14 (tel. 592 30 57) houses an anthropological collection focusing on prehistoric Latium. (Open Mon.-Sat. 9am-2pm, Sun. 9am-1pm. Admission L6000.) The museum features objects from various parts of the Italian peninsula from the Stone, Bronze, and Iron Ages. In the same building, through the entrance at Viale Lincoln, 1 (walk to the end of the building and up the stairs to the right of the snack bar), the collection of the **Museo dell'Alto Medioevo** (tel. 592 58 06) dates from the Dark Ages. (Open Mon.-Sat. 9am-2pm, Sun. 9am-1pm; L2000.)

Continuing north, you will reach the **Viale della Civiltà del Lavoro.** To the east (right) stands the **Palace of Congress,** but the awkward **Palace of the Civilization of Labor,** at the west (left) end of the street, serves as EUR's definitive symbol, wrapping archlike windows around the "Square Colosseum" building, in an effort to evoke Roman ruins. Nearby **Piazzale delle Nazioni Unite** embodies the EUR that Mussolini had intended: imposing modern buildings decorated with spare columns attempt to meld the ancient empire with an empire to come.

Heading east from EUR, take Viale dell'Industria (on the right of Via C. Colombo) down to Via delle Tre Fontane. The **LUNEUR park,** an old-fashioned amusement center on Via delle Tre Fontane (tel. 592 59 33), features cheap thrills like the "Himalaya Railroad" for L3000. Farther down the road, at the intersection of Via delle Tre Fontane and Via Laurentina, stands the **Abbazia delle Tre Fontane** (Abbey of the Three Fountains), where St. Paul lost his head (literally). The legend says that Saint Paul's head bounced on the ground three times, creating a fountain with each bounce—hence the name. A millennia later, Saint Bernard, not yet in his dog days, stayed here during his 12th-century visit to Rome. The monks who live here today sell the monastery's own eucalyptus liquor (¼ liter for L6000) and special chocolate (L1000 per small bar). Store open Mon.-Sat. 11am-5pm, Sun. noon-5pm). South of EUR, across the lake (known simply as "the lake" or *il lago*) looms the **Palazzo Dello Sport** designed for the 1960 Olympic Games.

Trastevere

Trastevere has a proud, independent vitality, only becoming a part of Rome when Augustus insisted on incorporating it. The *Trasteverini* claim to be descendants of the purest Roman stock (*Romani di Roma*)—from Horatius, Scaevola, and others who defended the city from the Tarquinian invasion; some residents brag about never having crossed the river. Today, Trastevere's dark maze and medieval quarters, with webs of laundry strung across the buildings, and carefully grungy hippies lounging around the *piazze*, may give you a better sense of a traditional Roman community than any other part of the city. Take bus #170 from Termini to Viale Trastevere, an area packed with ice cream parlors, movie houses, and a McDonald's.

Right off the Ponte Garibaldi stands the statue of the famous dialect poet, Giacchino Belli, in the middle of his own piazza, which spills onto Viale di Trastevere, a busy thoroughfare. On the left, the **Torre degli Anguillara,** dating back to the 13th century, stands over a *palazzo* of the same name. Across the street, the **Church of San Crisogno** perpetuates yet another well-known Roman name, Cardinal Borghese's, etched into the façade. A block behind the church, the Via di Giulio Cesare Santini leads east into Via dei Genovesi (left of the McDonald's). The **Church** of **Santa Cecilia in Trastevere** lies two blocks ahead, on Via di S. Cecilia. Don't miss the **statue of Santa Cecilia** under the altar. (Open 10am-noon and 4-6pm.)

Via di S. Cecilia merges here with Via di S. Michele. The **Chiesa Grande** (tel. 581 67 32), at #22 Via di S. Michele, is the temporary home of the **Museo Borghese painting collection,** while the museum undergoes extensive renovations. The exciting collection of 16th-19th century works is crammed along the apse walls of a disused chapel. (Open Tues.-Sun. 9am-7pm, Sun.-Mon. 9am-1pm. Last entrance a half-hour before closing. L4000.)

Scurry back up Via di S. Michele to its left with Via della Madonna dell'Orto. Vignola designed a quirky façade for the **Church of Santa Maria dell'Orto** at the street's base. The six quadrangular obelisks atop the building do make a statement, though it may be at odds with the rest of the flowing Mannerist design. Via Anicia runs left from the church to Piazza San Francesco d'Assisi to find the **Church of San Francesco a Ripa,** one of the first Franciscan churches in Rome. Inside, you'll find Bernini's *Beata Lodovica Albertoni*, an ecstatic sculpture—I'll have what she's having. (Church open daily 7am-1pm and 4-7:30pm.) The largest flea market in Rome, the **Porta Portese,** takes place behind the church every Sunday morning.

From the piazza, take Via Tavolacci across Viale Trastevere to Via Morosini. Government ministries stoop to your left, while at your first right Via Roma Libera runs up into a piazza with a produce market (open daily 8am-2pm). Past the stalls in the upper right corner, Via di San Cosimato flows at last into Piazza di Santa Maria in Trastevere, the lungs of Trastevere. The grandiose **Church of Santa Maria in Trastevere** dominates the piazza. The church, built between 337 and 352 by Pope Julius II, was the first of Rome's hundreds of churches dedicated to the Virgin. The mosaics of the Virgin and the 10 saintly women lining the exterior are only a warm-up for the ones inside. (Open 7am-7pm; Mass at 9am, 10:30am, noon, and 6pm.)

From Piazza Santa Maria, Via della Scala leads past a church of the same name, with a warm melon-colored 16th-century façade, to the **Porta Settimania.** The gateway is part of the Aurelian Wall, which incorporated Trastevere in its grasp and fended off invasions in the 3rd century. Today you may pass freely though it, where Via Lungara leads north to the **Galleria Corsini,** on the first floor of the Rococo Palazzo Corsini. Sprawling across northern Trastevere from the Tiber to the foot of the Janiculan Hill, the gallery houses one half of the **Museo Nazionale dell'Arte Antica**—the worse half, unless you're a madonna fan. (The other half hangs in the Palazzo Barberini). The gallery's seven rooms (numbered clockwise) boast no fewer than 41 portrayals of the Virgin Mary, with 17 in one room alone, but despite the consistency of theme the collection's haphazard arrangement is uninspiring. If you do visit, concentrate on **Room 2,** with an eclectic assortment of 14th- to 17th-century masters. (Open Tues.-Sat. 9am-2pm, Sun. 9am-1pm. Admission L6000.)

Via Corsini skirts the side of the palace to meet Rome's breezy and umbrageous **Botanical Gardens.** This impressive and well-maintained assemblage of worldly flora stretches from valleys of ferns, through groves of bamboo, to a hilltop Japanese garden. (Entrance off of Via della Lungara. Grounds open Mon.-Sat. 9am-6pm, until 7pm in summer, Sun. and holidays 10am-2pm. Greenhouse open Mon.-Sat. 9am-1pm, Sun. and holidays 10am-2pm. Closed Aug. Admission L2000, children 6-11 L1000, under 6 free.)

Across the street from the Galleria Corsini the magnificent Renaissance **Villa Farnesina** houses several rooms frescoed by Raphael, Peruzzi, il Sodoma, and Giulio Romano. The villa was home to the Renaissance millionaire Agostino Chigi, who bankrolled the Vatican and hosted elaborate, dish-tossing parties. Check out the *Fables of Psyche*, which ring the ceiling, and Raphael's *Galatea*, in the left-hand room, which depicts the astrological position of the stars on the night of Chigi's birth. Il Sodoma's *Marriage of Alexander and Roxana* on the first floor and Peruzzi's *trompe l'oeil* perspective room next to it complete the highlights. (Open 9am-1pm; free.)

Adorned by busts of obscure 19th-century Italian heroes, **Janiculan Hill (Gianicolo),** Rome's lovers' lane, overlooks Trastevere from the northwest. To get to the summit take Via della Scala from Santa Maria in Trastevere to Via Garibaldi. Atop the hill sits the **Church of San Pietro in Montorio,** on the spot once believed to be the site of St. Peter's upside-down crucifixion. The church itself is nothing spectacular, but in the courtyard next door reposes Bramante's tiny, perfect **Tempietto** (1499-1502), a brilliant architectural marriage of Renaissance theory and ancient architecture. Its site is the precise spot where St. Peter was martyred. From the front of the Tempietto you have a vista of all of Rome. The roof of the Pantheon, Bramante's inspiration, rises straight ahead. (Tempietto open daily 8am-noon and 4-7pm.)

Back at the river, the elegant **Isola Tiberina,** lounging in the Tiber between Trastevere and the historical center, splits the river's unsavory yellow-green flow with banks swathed in marble and brick. According to Roman legend, the island shares its birthday with the Roman Republic: after the Etruscan tyrant Tarquin the Proud raped the virtuous Lucretia, her outraged husband killed him and threw his corpse in the river, where muck and silt collected around it...years later, Lucretia's family founded a new government, and the Tiber Island grew into dry land.

Villa Borghese

Take Metro Linea A to **Flaminia,** four stops past Termini heading toward Ottaviano. Rome's largest patch of public green, the park around the **Villa Borghese** occupies a large area north of Via Veneto. The cool, shady paths, overgrown gardens, scenic terraces and myriad fountains and statues are a refreshing break from the fumes and noise of daytime Rome.

Abutting the gardens of Villa Borghese to the Southwest is the **Pincio Hill,** first known as the "hill of gardens" (*Collis Hortulorum*) for the monumental gardens of the Roman Republic aristocracy built on it. The north and east boundaries of the Pincio are formed by the infamous **Muro Torto,** or crooked wall, known for its irregular lines and centuries-old dilapidation. Parts of the wall have seemed ready to collapse since Aurelian built it in the 3rd century. When the Goths failed to break through this precarious pile of rocks in the 6th century, the Romans decided Saint Peter was protecting it, and refused to strengthen or to fortify it.

The park contains three major museums: Museo Borghese, Museo di Villa Giulia, and the Galleria Nazionale D'Arte Moderna. Unfortunately, the **Museo Borghese** has been undergoing extensive repairs since 1984, and there's no end in sight. It's all but covered up by a screen of ugly scaffolding. The ground floor and its remarkable sculpture collection remain open, but the gallery's first-floor (and first-rate) painting collection (a cache of Titian, Caravaggio, Raphael, and Cranach) has been shipped off for the interim to the Chiesa Grande di San Michele a Ripa in Trastevere. (Open Tues.-Sat. 9am-7pm, Sun. and holidays 9am-1pm. Admission L4000.)

The **Galleria Nazionale d'Arte Moderna** is housed in the forbidding **Palazzo delle Belle Arti,** designed by Cesare Bazzani. The white marble façade incorporates four sets of double pillars, and several large pieces of sculpture sit in the foreground, including Guerrini's primitive *Personaggi* (1974) and Colla's stark *Grande Spirale* (1952). Inside, the museum's rooms are filled with the best Italian art of the 19th and 20th centuries. The most striking works, however, are by foreigners—Degas, Klimt, Monet, and Pollock. (Open Tues.-Sat. 9am-2pm. Sun. and holidays 9am-1pm. Admission L8000, students from the EEC under 19 free.)

A short walk towards the river along Viale delle Belle Arti takes you to the other temporal extreme: the **Museo Nazionale di Villa Giulia,** which houses the **Etruscan museum.** Villa Giulia itself was built under Pope Julius III who reigned 1550-55. The villa hosts **evening concerts** (usually classical or classical-jazz hybrid) from mid-June to late Aug.; tickets are L10,000-20,000. For concert information and schedules, call 678 07 42/3/4/5. (Tickets available at the museum Tues.-Sun. 9am-2pm, 9am-5pm on performance days, or at Via della Conciliazione, 4, Mon.-Tues. 9am-2pm and 4-7pm, Wed.-Fri. 9am-2pm.)

If all the museums are closed, don't lose hope; art is rampant even along the paths. In the **Giardino del Lago** (Garden of the Lake), find Jacopo della Porta's Tritons looking suspiciously like the ones in Piazza Navona. These are the real thing, moved here in 1984—the ones in Piazza Navona are copies. In the lake itself is a **Temple of Aesculapius.** Get a close-up from a rowboat. (Rentals 9:30am-1pm and 2-7pm; L4000 per person per 20min., with a 2-person minimum.)

ENTERTAINMENT

Check the various local listings for films, shows, concerts, and special events. On Thursdays, **La Repubblica** comes out with *Trova Roma*, a comprehensive list of concerts, plays, clubs, movies, and special events. Romans adore summer and hold myriad celebrations. At night, subdued Dionysian revelry claims the streets. Festivals erupt spontaneously in different *piazze*. In **Piazza della Repubblica,** there's often a Vegas-style crooner, while in **Piazza S. Maria in Trastevere,** you may run across the last vestiges of the flower children. The **Spanish Steps** host any number of sleazy, ersatz Romeos—you'd do well to skip these festivities. **Piazza Navona** bursts with fortune tellers and caricaturists (usually around L20,000), soused teenagers, and goggle-eyed tourists, while the **Pantheon** is a favored spot for bachelors to tipple a L15,000 *Campari* and to strut their stuff. **Via Giulia** makes a quiet and romantic evening *passeggiata*, or you can head over to the **Campo dei Fiori** for some low-key schmoozing. The **Gianicolo** serves as Lovers' Lane, lined wall to wall with quivering Fiats. You'll find the best mix of foreigners and Romans, outdoor strolling, and funky bars in **Trastevere.** Somewhat removed from the historical center, **Testaccio** is renowned for its hip club scene.

Pubs

There are numerous pubs in Rome, many with some sort of Irish theme. Most of the pubs cater to tourists and expatriates. If you want to meet Italians, you should probably avoid the pubs and head to a nightclub or jazz bar. The pubs and *birrerie* in Trastevere offer the best mix of foreigners and Romans.

Druid's Den, Via San Martino ai Monti, 28. Travelling south on Via Merulana from Via Santa Maria Maggiore, take your second right. An Irish hangout where Romans get to be tourists. Pints of Guinness L5000. Open 8pm-1am.

Jonathan's Angels, Via della Fossa, 16 (tel. 689 34 26). West of P. Navona. Take Vicolo Savelli Parione Pace off Via Governo Vecchio. Quite an experience. Jonathan is covered in tattoos and sports a huge gold-like medallion around his neck. Strange pictures of him adorn the walls too. Open Tues.-Sun 11pm-2am.

The Drunken Ship, Via dei Leutari, 34, off Corso Vittorio Emanuele II before P. Pasquino, which leads into the south end of P. Navona. Look for the twin Italian and American flags outside. Two expatriate American women run this facsimile of a fraternity bar. Slurp jello shots (L1000) under the flashing lights. For more refinement, sit outside and sip a Bud on tap (L3000) Open 8pm-2am every night.

Birreria Trilussa, Via Benedetta, 19/20 (tel. 71 54 21 80). Behind the fountain across the Ponte Sisto from Campo dei Fiori. A dark, woody pub that hums till all hours. Beer, wine and mixed drinks (L6000-8000), plus *bruschette* (L2500), pasta (L6000-8000) and an *antipasto* spread (L7000). Open 8pm-3am.

Music Clubs

Rome's music clubs attract a much hipper Italian crowd than the pubs; some even have dancing and are usually much cheaper than discos. Most are officially *associazione culturali*, which means they are private; some require a "membership" which means that you pay a one-time fee (often as little as L1000) for a card. Memberships are usually not exclusive, but on the weekends some of these clubs only allow members to enter (depending on how crowded the place is) and won't sell you a card. These charges sometimes include a drink. Call before setting out; opening hours tend to change seasonally and/or at the manager's whim.

Yes Brasil, Via San Francesco a Ripa, 103 (tel. 581 62 67), in Trastevere. Foot-stomping live Brazilian music in crowded quarters. A favorite hang-out of young Romans. Drinks L8000-10,000. No drink, no dance. Open Mon.-Sat. 3pm-2am. Music 10pm-midnight.

Caffè Latino, Via di Monte Testaccio, 96 (tel. 574 40 20), in the club district of Testaccio. This large fashionable place is built right into Monte Testaccio and the back wall is built out of pottery shards. One room for bands (mostly jazz) and one for videos and dancing. Drinks L5000-12,000. Open Oct.-June 9:30pm-2:30am. Membership fee L2000. **Caffè Caruso,** next door, has an almost identical set-up.

Big Mama, Via San Franscesco a Ripa, 18 (tel. 581 25 51). On the same street as Yes Brasil in Trastevere. Excellent jazz and blues for the diehard fan. Weekend cover (L20,000) makes it more of a commitment; weeknights are just as fun, although less crowded. Open 9pm-1:30am.

Clarabella, P. S. Cosimato, 39, in Trastevere. Live Brazilian Music. Obligatory first drink about L8000. Open Sept. to mid-July Tues.-Sun. 9:30pm-2:30am.

Discos and Dancing

Italians are really not great dancers, but they still pay over L20,000 to get into embarrassingly flashy discotheques circa 1984. Occasionally women get in free, but many of those places are gross pick-up scenes. Still, if your feet have to meet the beat, there are some exceptions. The really cool club scene changes as fast as Romans change outfits, so check *TrovaRoma*. Most places close up shop in the summer and move to the beach, so call before you head out.

La Makumba, Via degli Olimpionici, 19 (tel. 396 43 92), up Via Flaminia in the north of the city, across the Tiber from the Stadio Olimpico. One of the funkiest places. Hot Brazilian and African music, an old-fashioned mirrored ballroom with palm trees, a thatched roof, and Hawaiian drinks served in kitschy Kon-Tiki bowls. Prices vary. Open 11pm-3am.

Uonna Club, Via Cassia, 871, off Via del Foro Italico, north of the Stadio Olimpico. Rock-n-roll of various kinds, from reggae to garage-bands, underground Roman music, and New Wave. Prices and hours vary.

Radio Londra, Via di Monte Testaccio, 67. Small—nay, claustrophobic—club with loud house music for Romans until the wee hours. Mixed crowd of Romans, expatriates, gays, straights, and the occasional androgynatrix in black leather. In the summer, there's a lovely outdoor terrace with umbrellas. The best part—it's free. No drink purchase required. Crowded, so get here early. Open 11pm-6am.

Gay Clubs

Pick up a *Pianta Gay di Roma* at any bar or disco for a detailed map with complete listings of cruising spots, bars, and baths in Rome. Check the gay magazine *Babilonia*, *La Repubblica*'s *TrovaRoma*, or the *Rome Gay News* for more information.

L'Alibi, Via Monte di Testaccio, 44 (tel. 574 34 48), in the Testaccio district (Piramide metro stop). Especially during the warmer months, this is *the* gay club in Rome. Mostly men, but popular with women too. Sat. nights a steep L20,000 cover; Wed. and Fri. night no cover, first drink L10,000. Open 11pm-5am.

Hangar, Via in Selci, 69 (tel. 488 13 97). Centrally located (off Via Cavour where it bends near the Colosseum). Messalina, the wife of Nero, once lived in a house on this site. Small and often packed wall-to-wall. No cover, and the drinks are the cheapest in Rome. Open Wed.-Mon. 10:30pm-2am. Closed 3 weeks in Aug.

Joli Coeur, Via Sirte, 5 (tel. 839 35 23), off Viale Eritrea. Rome's primary lesbian bar is located a little out of the city center, east of Villa Ada. Sat. women only, Sun. mixed crowd. Open Sat.-Sun. 10:30pm-2am.

RadioLondra (see Discos) has a mixed crowd shaking to house music.

Music and Theater

Check with the tourist office for upcoming events—consult their free *Carnet di Roma,* keep your eyes peeled for posters, and scan the newspaper to keep up with the barrage of events. Concerts are held at the **Foro Italico** (tel. 36 86 56 25), **Stadio Flaminio** (tel. 323 65 39), and the Palazzo dello Sport (tel. 592 51 07).

Opera

In June, July and August the spectacular stage of the **Terme di Caracalla** (tel. 481 70 03) hosts lavish opera productions. Performances last from 9pm-1am, and special buses (L1200) ferry spectators home to various parts of the city. To get to the baths, take bus #90 from Piazza Venezia, or line B of the Metro to Circo Massimo, then bus #118 (or walk the 3 blocks). Tickets start at L30,000 and spiral up to L90,000, but since everyone moves down during the first act to empty seats in front, don't waste your cash on a high-end ticket. Semi-formal dress is appropriate; dress warmly even for summer nights. The season always begins with a production of Verdi's *Aida*, worth seeing for the lavish scenery alone. Buy tickets at the theater before the show, or at the opera's headquarters in P. Beniamino Gigli, 9, near Via Viminale (near Termini, or take the #70 bus from largo Argentina). From November to May, the opera moves back home to its aptly-named **Teatro dell'Opera** (in P. Beniamino Gigli, see above; tel. 48 16 01). Tickets may be bought weeks in advance.

Classical Music

The **Accademia Santa Cecilia** performs symphonies and chamber music in its auditorium at Via di Conciliazione, 4 (the street leading up to the Vatican). In summer, the company moves outdoors to the *nymphaeum* in the Villa Giulia. Special concerts are sometimes also held in P. di Campidoglio. Tickets cost L10,000 or L20,000. Call their information office at Via Vittoria, 6 (tel. 679 03 89). **L'Ippocampo** puts on an array of musical events in the ancient Auditorium of Maecenas (tel. 780 76 95). The **Amici di Castel Sant'Angelo** liven up Hadrian's mausoleum with classical music (tel. 854 61 92). **La Risonanza** performs masses in the Basilica di S. Eustachio Wednesdays at 9pm (tickets at the door). The **International Chamber Ensemble** plays classical music in late spring and early summer at the Chiostro del Bramante in the courtyard of Santa Maria della Pace on Via dei Coronari (tel. or fax 86 80 01 25).

In summer, **Concerti del Tempietto** performs symphonic and chamber pieces at night in the shadow of the Theater of Marcellus, at Via Teatro di Marcello, 44 (tel. 481 48 00).Concerts run from July 1 to Sept. 30 every night at 9pm. The **Villa Pamphili Park** (tel. 86 80 00 39) hosts a series of nighttime concerts in July. Though tickets are on sale, you can sit on an umbrella pine-covered hill above the seats and hear just fine. To get to the park, take bus #41 from the Vatican or #44, 75 or 710 from largo Argentina and Trastevere to the Janiculan Hill. The entrance to the park (where tickets are sold) is 200m down from the Porta San Pancrazio.

Rock 'n Roll

Tickets for rock concerts, held primarily at **Palazzo dello Sport,** start at L12,000. The acoustics suck and it's always jammed, but excellent groups perform. For tickets to and information on contemporary music events, visit the **ORBIS** agency at P. d'Esquilino (tel. 482 74 03), near Santa Maria Maggiore. (Open Mon.-Fri. 9:30am-1pm and 4-7:30pm, Sat. 10am-1pm.) The **Stadio Flaminio** (tel. 323 65 39) hosts big-name concerts, like U2 and Madonna (though no one came to her concert in '91 because there was a big Italian singer playing across town). *Rockerilla* is a popular music magazine that prints concert and ticket information; also check *Wanted in Rome*, *Metropolitana*, and in local record stores for information.

Theater and Ballet

The **Rome Opera Ballet** shares the stage and ticket office with **Teatro dell'Opera** (tel. 48 16 01 or 481 70 03). Call there for information. Tickets cost L30,000, L60,000, or L90,000. For **theater** listings check again with the tourist office or call the information number at **Teatro delle Arti,** Via Sicilia, 59 (tel. 474 35 64); **Teatro**

delle Muse, Via Forli, 43 (tel. 44 23 13 00); or **Teatro Ghione,** Via delle Fornaci, 37 (tel. 637 22 94), which has both music and theater performances.

Cinema

First-run cinemas in Rome tend to charge about L7000 and, though the movies are often American, they're generally dubbed into Italian. Try **Cinema Pasquino,** at Vicolo del Piede, 19/A (tel. 580 36 22) in Piazza Santa Maria in Trastevere, features undubbed American films. Take Via della Lungaretta to P. Santa Maria and turn right at the end of the piazza. Their program changes every few days. (Open nightly, closed July 27-Aug. 27. Admission L7000.) **Alcazar,** Piazza Merry Del Val, 14 (tel. 588 00 99), also in Trastevere, shows American films *in lingua originale* (admission L10,000). Monday nights from October to June, **Rouge et Noir,** Via Salaria, 31 (tel. 855 43 05), and **The Majestic,** Via SS. Apostoli, 20 (tel. 679 49 08), show new releases in English. Also check out the agenda section in the free English-language magazine **Metropolitan** at the newsstand next to Largo Torre Argentina, 11.

Sports

The best sources for sporting information (either to watch or to participate) are the tourist office and two magazines sold at newsstands, *Corriere dello Sport* and *Gazzetta dello Sport*. If you are in Rome between September and May, take in a **soccer** (*calcio*—pronounced cal-cho) game at the **Stadio Olimpico.** Of Rome's two teams, Roma and Lazio, Roma is the favorite, playing in the most competitive *serie A* league. If one of the two teams is playing *in casa* (at home), you'll witness a violent enthusiasm reminiscent of the Colosseum spectacles of yester-empire. The **Foro Italico** at the Stadio hosts the games (tel. 368 51). Each team sets its own price—in 1993, admission to Roma games was L22,000-25,000; admission to Lazio games was L27,000. Lazio tickets can be purchased at Lazio Point, Via Farina, 24 (tel. 482 66 88). Roma tickets can be bought at Enjoy Rome, Via Varese, 39 (tel. 445 18 43).

■■■ VATICAN CITY

Occupying 108½ independent urban acres entirely within Italy's capital, the state of Vatican City is the last toehold of a Catholic Church that once wheeled and dealed as a mighty European power. Under the Lateran Treaty of 1929, the pope remains supreme monarch of his tiny theocracy, exercising all legislative, judicial, and executive powers over the 300 souls who hold Vatican citizenship. According to this agreement, the pope remains neutral in national politics and Roman municipal administration, though the Vatican has generally relied on one or more political parties to fight for its causes at home (albeit with complications). The Vatican state maintains its own army in the form of the Swiss Guards, all descendants of the 16th-century mercenaries hired by Pope Julius II, who wear uniforms designed by Michelangelo. From the Baroque office complex known as the Curia, the priestly hierarchy governs the spiritual lives of hundreds of millions of Catholics around the world. On the western bank of the Tiber, Vatican City can be reached from Rome's center by Metro A to Ottaviano (walk south on Via Ottaviano toward the distant colonnade after leaving the station) or by buses #64 and 492 from Termini, bus #62 from P. Barberini, or #19 from San Lorenzo. The country also boasts a train station, St. Peter's. For official use only, trains service Viterbo and La Storta. See *Let's Go: Rome* for more information on the Vatican.

ORIENTATION AND PRACTICAL INFORMATION

Pilgrim Tourist Information Office, P. San Pietro (tel. 698 844 66 or 698 848 66), to the left of the piazza as you face the basilica. Free pamphlets. Money exchange with no commission. Open daily 8:30am-7pm.

ORIENTATION AND PRACTICAL INFORMATION

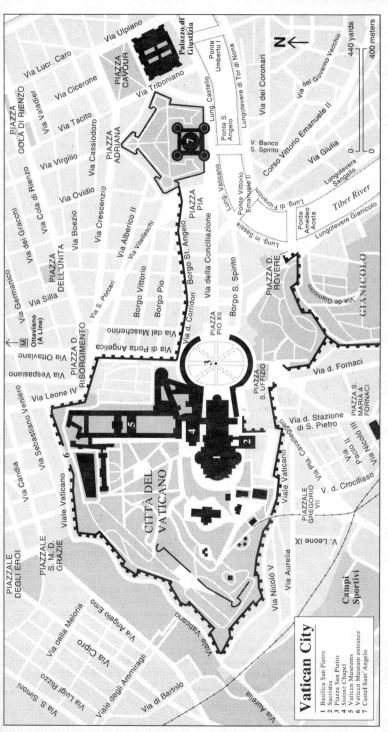

Vatican City

1 Basilica San Pietro
2 Sacristia
3 Piazza San Pietro
4 Sistine Chapel
5 Vatican Museums
6 Vatican Museum entrance
7 Castel Sant' Angelo

Tours and Sightseeing: Tours of the otherwise inaccessible **Vatican Gardens** (Mon.-Tues. and Thurs.-Sat. at 10am, 2hrs., L16,000; you can see them for free from the top of St. Peter's). Ask at the Tourist Office above, and book in advance.

The Vatican Post Office, P. San Pietro, is on the left as you face St. Peter's. A trailer office is set up in the piazza in summer. Service from Vatican City is more efficient than its Italian counterpart. (Open Mon.-Fri. 8:30am-7pm, Sat. 8:30am-6pm.) Branch office on 2nd floor of the Vatican Museum (open during museum hours). No *Fermo Posta* is available. Packages up to 1kg and 90cm, tied with string, can also be sent from the Vatican. Mail rates are the same as Italian rates.

To attend a **Papal Audience** apply in writing to the **Prefetture della Casa Pontificia,** 00120 Città del Vaticano, or go to the office by the bronze door of St. Peter's (to the right of the basilica; often indoors when it's hot or raining) the Monday or Tuesday before the audience you wish to attend (open 9am-1pm; tel. 69 82). Try to arrive early as there is limited seating. Tickets are free. The papal audiences are held Wednesday at 11am when the Pope is in Vatican City, 10am when he's at his summer estate south of Rome in Castel Gandolfo. The audiences are held in the Audience Hall behind the colonnade to the left of the basilica. During an audience, the Pope gives a message in several languages to about 2000-3000 people, greets the groups by name and country, and gives his blessing to all. Crowds of grouchy tourists may leave you feeling less than benevolent. In any case, wear subdued colors; women should wear dresses with sleeves; men should wear a tie and not wear informal clothing. **Multi-lingual confession** is also available inside St. Peter's. Languages spoken are printed outside the confessionals towards the main altar.

Public toilets are to the left of the Basilica, next door to the information office and in the right arm of Bernini's colonnade. A hospital, **Ospedale Santo Spirito,** awaits the sick at Via Borgo Spirito; capable nuns on call at Via S. Ufficio, to the left of the Basilica, fly to aid the wounded. (Open Wed. 8:30am-1pm, Sun. 9:30am-12:30pm.)

SIGHTS

Vastly more efficient and better maintained than any Italian institution (and also just plain vast), the pontiff's incomparable collection of architecture, painting, sculpture, decorative arts, tapestries, books, carriages, and cultural artifacts from around the globe merits enormous amounts of your time and energy. The official guidebook thoughtfully offers suggested itineraries for the flagging and the faint of heart, available at the Vatican Museum and tourist office (L12,000).

St. Peter's Basilica

Do not feed the clothing cops. **Appropriate dress** is always required in the Basilica. No shorts, miniskirts, or sleeveless shirts are allowed, but jeans and a t-shirt are fine for both men and women.

Begin outside, where Bernini's sweeping, elliptical Piazza San Pietro provides an impressive vestibule for the colossal church that dominates its western end. The colonnaded arms were meant to continue around the bottom end of the piazza; Mussolini's broad Via della Conciliazione, built in the 1930s to connect the Vatican with the rest of the city, opened up a view of St. Peter's that Bernini never intended (he had wanted the spacious marble piazza to greet pilgrims as a surprise after their wanderings through the medieval Borgo). The obelisk in the center, originally erected by the Emperor Augustus in Alexandria, is framed by two splashing fountains; round porphyry disks set in the pavement between each fountain and the obelisk mark the spots where, if you stand on them, the quadruple rows of Bernini's colonnades resolve into one perfectly aligned row.

As you ascend past the Swiss Guards to the porch of the basilica (you cannot enter in shorts or with bare shoulders), gaze into the courtyard they protect. Here, in the first century AD, thousands of Christians were slaughtered (and probably St. Peter among them). The **Porta Sancta** (holy door), the last door on the right, can only be opened by the pope, who knocks in its bricked-up center every 25 years with a silver hammer (next knocking will be in 2000). The basilica itself rests on the reputed site of its eponym's tomb, and a Christian structure of some kind has stood here since the Emperor Constantine made Christianity the state religion in the 4th century AD.

The overwhelming interior of the basilica measures 186 by 137 meters along the transepts. (Metal lines in the floor mark the puny-by-comparison lengths of other major world churches.) To the right, Michelangelo's sorrowful **Pietà** is protected by bullet-proof glass, since in 1978 an axe-wielding fiend attacked the famous sculpture, smashing the nose and breaking the hand off the madonna.

In the center of the crossing, Bernini's **Baldacchino** rises on spiralling solomonic columns over the plain marble altar, which only the Pope may use. The canopy, cast out of bronze pillaged from the porch of the Pantheon, was unveiled on June 28, 1633, by Pope Urban VIII Barberini. Vines and naked babies frolic their way up the twisting columns toward the cavernous vault of Michelangelo's cupola.

In the apse, more Bernini treasures gleam in marble and bronze. The convoluted **Cathedra Petri** is a Baroque reliquary which houses the original throne of St. Peter in a riot of bronze and gilt. On either side, the **tombs** of Popes Paul III and Urban VIII slumber in mixed-media (marble, bronze, and gilt, that is) splendor. To the left of the altar, Bernini's last work in St. Peter's, the gruesome **monument to Alexander VII,** is enlivened by the skeletal figure of Death raising an hourglass from an achingly fluid marble drapery and proclaiming *memento mori*—don't forget death.

Steps at the crossing, below Bernini's spear-wielding statue of St. Longinus, lead down to the **Vatican Grottoes,** the final resting place of innumerable popes and saints. The passages are lined with tombs both ancient and modern, and though the space is much modernized and well-lit, it's still creepy. The grottoes eject you back at the entrance. From here, you can cross round the left side of the porch to the entrance to the cupola. You can go up by stairs or elevator to the walkway around the interior of the dome, or go up some more fairly hellish stairs to the outdoor tippy-top ledge of the cupola. From here there's an excellent view of the roof of the basilica, the piazza, the Vatican Gardens, and the hazy Roman skyline. (St. Peter's open 8am-7pm. Dome closes 1hr. earlier and may be closed when the Pope is in the basilica, often Wed. morning. Admission on foot L5000, by elevator—though there's still a hefty climb—L6000. It's worth going up, even at L6000.) Mass is given several times per day in the church, with a particularly beautiful vespers service Sunday at 5pm.

On the left side of the piazza, through a gate protected by Swiss Guards, you can descend to the necropolis, one level below the grottoes. A double row of mausoleums dating from the first century AD lies here. Multi-lingual priests remind you that the center of the Catholic Church used to be a pagan burial ground, and tell the entrancing tale of the discovery of **St. Peter's tomb** here for L10,000. Only small, prearranged tours may enter. Apply to the *Ufficio Scavi* (excavation office) beneath the Arco della Campana to the left of the basilica (Mon.-Sat. 9am-noon and 2-5pm).

Vatican Museums

A ten-minute walk around the Vatican City walls (or the bus that drives from the piazza through the Vatican Gardens) brings you to the **Vatican Museums** (tel. 698 33 33). All the major galleries are open Mon.-Sat. 8:45am-1:45pm; during Easter and July-Sept. they are open Mon.-Fri. 8:45am-4pm, Sat. 8:45am-1:45pm. Last entrance 45 min. before closing. The museums are closed on major religious holidays. They are open the last Sunday of every month from 8:45am-1pm, when admission is **free**. Otherwise L12,000, L8000 with an ISIC card, children under 1m tall free.

The Vatican Museums constitute one of the world's great collections of art, a vast storehouse of ancient, Renaissance and modern statuary, painting, decorative arts, and sundry papal odds and ends. The galleries stretch over some four miles of the old papal palace and are stuffed with many more treasures than you could possibly see in one day. Though the entrance price is steep, consider making more than one visit. If you've only got a morning, invest some time planning your tour before you go—the galleries are so crowded and poorly labeled, and the distances between them so long, that simply wandering will leave you more frustrated and exhausted than enlightened. The best known and most noteworthy attractions in the collection are the **Pio-Clementine Museum** with its celebrated masterpieces of ancient sculpture, the brilliantly frescoed **Borgia Apartments** and **Raphael Stanze,** Michelangelo's incomparable **Sistine Chapel,** and the eclectic **Pinacoteca,** or picture gallery. From the collections lying off the beaten track, you can choose to see the specialized galleries of Egyptian, Etruscan, Greek or Roman art, each housing world-class collections of antiquities; the more esoteric **Pio-Christian Museum** (with early Christian sarcophagi), the exhibition rooms of the **Vatican Library,** or the intermittently-open **Ethnological Museum** (with artifacts from Third World cultures) and **Historical Museum** (with furnishings and carriages from papal households of the past). The remaining collections (of tapestries, maps, and modern religious art) are housed in long corridors leading to the Sistine Chapel.

In their most basic plan, the galleries function as a conduit for taking visitors from the entrance and the Belvedere Courtyard down to the papal apartments and the Sistine Chapel and back again. Two long, parallel corridors funnel the crowds through; at either end cluster the specialized galleries mentioned above. The museum management has laid out four color-coded tours and tries to make visitors follow one. Tour A hits only the barest essentials, making a swift trip to the Sistine Chapel and back, while tour D hits **absolutely everything**. Tour C will give clock-conscious art buffs to the magnificent Roman sculptures and Raphael rooms that A and B ignore. It's possible to pick and choose your way through, but remember that once you have passed a room or gallery, it's difficult to retrace your steps.

The entrance in Viale Vaticano leads to a strange bronze double-helix ramp that climbs to the ticket office, where there is also a money exchange, post office, cloakroom (large bags only), telephones, first aid station, and a booth selling a guidebook (L12,000) that's well worth the price. After the turnstiles a courtyard, with the intricately carved base of Antoninus Pius's column, confronts you with a choice of itineraries. Down the corridor and to the right is the entrance to the stellar **Pio-Clementino Museum,** the world's greatest collection of antique sculpture, featuring, amongst other gems, the sublime **Apollo Belvedere** and the tortured **Laocoön** group. The last room of the gallery contains the enormous red porphyry **sarcophagus of St. Helen**, mother of Constantine. Statues of Egyptian demigods hold up the ceiling and ogle a pair of sphinxes.

The next flight of the Simonetti Stairway climbs to the **Etruscan Museum** (open Wed., Sat., Sun. only), filled with artifacts from the necropoli of Tuscany and northern Lazio. Back on the landing of the Simonetti Staircase is the usually closed **Room of the Biga** (an ancient marble chariot outfitted with recent wheels and horses) and the entrance to the **Gallery of the Candelabra,** named for the ancient marble candleholders housed here, along with yet more examples of Roman statuary and decorative arts. Here begins the long trudge to the Sistine Chapel, through the **Gallery of the Tapestries,** the **Gallery of the Maps,** the **Apartment of Pius V** (here there is a shortcut stair to the Sistine Chapel), the **Sobieski Room,** and the **Room of the Immaculate Conception.** From the Room of the Immaculate Conception, a door leads into the first of the four **Raphael Rooms,** the sumptuous papal apartments built by Pope Julius II in the first decade of the 16th century. Raphael painted the astonishing **School of Athens** as a trial piece for Pope Julius, who was so impressed he fired his other painters, had their frescoes destroyed and handed the entire suite of rooms over to Raphael. The commission marked the beginning of Raphael's brilliant Roman career, and on his untimely death in 1520, his students completed the decoration according to his designs. The **Stanza della Segnatura** (which features the *School of Athens*) was painted entirely by Raphael and is considered his masterpiece. The four walls represent four branches of learning—theology, law, philosophy, and poetry. Depending on your itinerary, a staircase leads down to the Borgia Apartments and the horrid Museum of Modern Religious Art or, more directly, to the Sistine Chapel. The staircase descends into the **Room of the Sibyls.** Legend has it Cesare Borgia had his brother-in-law Alfonso D'Aragone murdered here, in order to free up his sister Lucrezia for marriage to the future Duke of Ferrara.

The Sistine Chapel

Stairs in the Vestibule of the Four Gates finally lead to the long-awaited **Sistine Chapel.** One of the few places in the museum outfitted with benches, this sacred chamber consistently overflows with weary, camera-laden tourists (though any form of photography is strictly forbidden in, and detrimental to, the chapel). If you do risk using your camera or video camera, a solemn guard in the chapel will shout "no video!" over the din of the crowd, and hundreds of tourists will glare at you.

The barrel vault of the ceiling, some 70 feet above the floor, gleams with the results of its recent, celebrated, and hotly debated restoration. Before craning your neck, first prepare yourself by taking in the frescoes on the side walls which predate Michelangelo's ceiling work. On the right wall, scenes from the life of Moses prefigure parallel scenes of the life of Christ on the left wall. The cycle, frescoed between 1481-83, was completed by a team of artists under the direction of Perugino that included Botticelli, Ghirlandaio, Roselli, the divine Pinturicchio, Signorelli, and della Gatta. Down the right wall are the *Journey of Moses* (Perugino; entirely covered for restoration in 1993), *Flight from Egypt* (Botticelli), *Crossing the Red Sea, Tablets of the Law, Punishment of Korah, Dathan, Abiram* (Botticelli), and the *Testament of Moses* (Signorelli); on the left wall, *Baptism of Christ* (Perugino; half-covered in 1993), *Temptation of Christ* (Botticelli), *Calling of the First Apostles* (Ghirlandaio), *Sermon on the Mount, Consignment of the Keys to Peter* (Perugino), and the *Last Supper.* Botticelli, Ghirlandaio, and Fra Damante painted the series of 26 early popes who stand in the niches between the high windows. On the right side of the far wall (the east entrance) is the *Disputation Over the Body of Moses,* by Matteo de Lecce, which replaces a lost work by Signorelli. On the left side of the wall is Arrigo Paludano's *Resurrection,* which fills the place once occupied by a Ghirlandaio piece.

Above stretches the undaunted genius, brave simplicity, and brilliant coloring of Michelangelo's unquestioned masterpiece—some have called these powerful frescoes the greatest works of Western art ever created. The fledgling painter chose to depict the history of mankind before the coming of Christ, thus linking the ceiling decoration with the stories of Moses and Christ on the side walls. He divided the vault into a monumental architectural scheme, each enclosing a separate scene from Genesis. These are, from west to east, *Separation of Light from Darkness, Creation of the Sun, Moon and Planets, Separation of Land and Sea and the Creation of Fishes and Birds, Creation of Adam, Creation of Eve, Temptation and Expulsion from Paradise, Sacrifice of Noah, Flood,* and the *Drunkenness of Noah.* These are framed by the famous *ignudi,* contorted naked male youths who cavort among the decorative vaulting. In the four spandrels are depictions of *David and Goliath, Judith and Holofernes,* the *Brazen Serpent,* and the *Punishment of Hanan.* These are surrounded by monumental figures of Old Testament prophets and classical sibyls, some pondering the events of Christian history to come, and some holding aloft books of revealed wisdom. The altar wall, covered by Michelangelo's apocalyptic vision of *The Last Judgement* (and the ensuing chaos of the last days of time) has been covered for restoration since 1981, but will theoretically be unveiled in 1994. (A paltry Polaroid dangles on the scaffolding in the meantime.)

Although the Sistine Chapel is a hard act to follow, the **Pinacoteca,** near the snack bar and the exit, holds the best art collection in Rome, including Filippo Lippi's *Coronation of the Virgin,* Perugino's *Madonna and Child,* Titian's *Madonna of San Nicoletta dei Frari,* and much, much more.

NEAR VATICAN CITY: CASTEL SANT'ANGELO

A short walk down Via d. Conciliazone from St. Peter's (and across from the angel-lined Ponte Sant'Angelo) stands the hulking mass of brick and stone known as **Castel Sant'Angelo.** Built by the Emperor Hadrian (117-138 AD) as a mausoleum for himself and his family, the edifice has served the popes of Rome in the centuries since as a convenient (and forbidding) fortress, prison, and palace. The complex, towering over a bend in the Tiber, consists of the original mausoleum, a suite of palatial Renaissance apartments built on top, and concentric rings of fortifications including the Ponte Sant'Angelo across the river and the Leonine Wall extending to the Vatican Palace. Hadrian, a dilettante architect as well as emperor, designed the mausoleum in imitation of his predecessor Augustus's more modest tomb across the river. He had the surviving round marble base crowned with an earthen tumulus and planted with cypress trees. But as the city fell to barbarian depredations, panicked Romans quickly converted the imposing structure to defensive purposes. When the city was wracked with plague in 590 AD, Pope Gregory the Great is said to have seen an angel sheathing his sword at the top of the citadel; the plague then abated, and the edifice has been dedicated to the angel, and called by his name, ever since. The fortress now contains a museum of arms and artillery, but the papal apartments and the incomparable views of Rome seen from them are the real reasons to pay a visit. (Open Tues.-Sun. 9am-2pm, last entrance at 1pm; Sun. 9am-1pm, last entrance at noon; Mon. 2-7pm, last entrance at 6pm; admission L8000.) Outside, the outer walls of the fort now enclose a large park (good for picnics), while the marble **Ponte Sant'Angelo,** lined with statues of angels designed by Bernini, leads back across the river, and is the starting point for the traditional pilgrimage route from St. Peter's to the Basilica of San Giovanni in Laterano on the other side of Rome.

LAZIO

The cradle of Roman civilization, Lazio (originally *Latium*, "the wide land") stretches from the low Tyrrhenian coastline through volcanic hills to the foothills of the Abruzzese Apennines. North and south of Rome, ancient cities maintain traces of the thriving cultures that were born there. Trains for Lazio locations leave from the Laziale section of Termini, and one private line serves Viterbo from the Roma Nord Station in P. Flaminio (outside P. del Popolo). **ACOTRAL buses** also serve the area.

■ Tivoli

In dramatic Tivoli, water is the inspiration and the attraction. Ancient Roman glitterati came to enjoy the delicious cool of the cascades. From Largo Garibaldi, the gardens of the **Villa d'Este** spill over watery terraces from the entrance in Piazza Trento. The property was shaped by Cardinal Ippolito d'Este (son of Lucrezia Borgia) to recreate the limpid sumptuousness of ancient Roman *nymphaea* and pleasure palaces. Immediately below the terrace is the **Fontane del Bicchierone,** a lumpy goblet of Bernini's design. To the left, a path leads down to the **Grotto of Diana**—a stuccoed nook favored as a shelter from the burning summer heat. Take another path (right) to the **Rometta,** or Little Rome, a series of fountains including one symbolizing the Tiber (the boat with the obelisk being the Tiber Island). The **Viale delle Cento Fontane** runs the width of the garden. At the other end from the Rometta, the **Fontana dell'Ovato** spurts one great sheet of water 15 feet into the air. Down the semi-circular steps from the center of the Viale delle Cento Fontane is the Fontana dei Draghi. Two great fishponds spread out from this point, stagnating amidst cypress and orange plantings. Nearby lurks the **Fontana della Civetta e degli Uccelli,** a water-work that is said to emit the chirps of birdsong. Across the ponds, the architectural behemoth, **Fontana dell'Organo Idraulico** once powered a complete water organ. Don't miss the **Fontana della Natura** with its colossal statue of Diana of Ephesus and her multiple, egg-shaped breasts, at the very bottom of the garden. (Open 9am to 1hr. before sunset. Admission L10,000 if water is at full power, L5000 otherwise.)

Across town in Via di Sibilla, you can pass through a pricey restaurant to two exemplary Republican temples, the **Temple of Vesta** and the **Temple of the Sibyl,** which command a high point overlooking the cascades of the Anio. Archaeologists have been scratching their heads for centuries over which gods were worshipped here, but it's pretty clear that the deities have long since taken their leave.

Back down Via di Sibilla and through Piazza Rivarola, take Ponte Garibaldi to the entrance of the **Villa Gregoriana,** which isn't a villa at all, but a natural park with paths descending through scattered ancient ruins to a series of lookouts over the cascades. From the opening of Gregory XVI's tunnel, the Aniene plunges 110 meters in the startling **Great Cascade.** (Open daily 9am-dusk. Admission L2500.)

In the valley below (take a bus, see above), the intriguing remains of the **Villa Adriana** (tel. (0774) 53 02 03) sprawl over another watery park. The largest and costliest villa ever built in the Roman Empire, it was apparently designed by the Emperor himself in the style of monuments he had seen before in his varied travels. The entrance gate leads you to the **Pecile,** built to recall the famous Painted Porch *(Poikile)* at Athens where Greek philosophers met to debate. At the northeast corner of the Pecile, Philosopher's Hall leads to the **Maritime Theater,** the emperor's private study and bedroom protected by its own moat (once outfitted with drawbridges). Underneath the broad **Court of the Libraries,** a shadowy **Cryptoporticus** kept the emperor's army of slaves hidden from view as they ran the enormous complex. The rest of the **Imperial Palace** sprawls nearby in well-labeled enclaves. South of the Pecile, beyond the main buildings, the **Canopus,** a murky expanse of water surrounded by plasters of the original architecture and sculpture found here, replicates a famous canal near Alexandria in Egypt (note the crocodile). The **Serapeum,** a Baroquish semicircular dining hall, anchors the far end of the canal. (Villa open daily 9am-dusk. Admission L8000.)

To get to Tivoli take the Metro Linea B to the last stop, Rebibbia (L700), then exit the station from the ACOTRAL terminal above. Tickets to Tivoli (L4600) are on sale here, and the **buses** leave from Capolinea 1 (30 min., 5am-midnight). After passing through smoggy factory areas and travertine quarries, the bus climbs to Tivoli, making a stop at Largo Garibaldi. Here a **tourist office** (tel. (0774) 212 49 or (0774) 33 45 22) gives out free maps and information on the sights, restaurants, and hotels in the city. (Open Mon.-Sat. 8am-6pm, in winter 8am-2pm.) To get to Hadrian's Villa, either take the ACOTRAL bus from Rebibbia and get off before Tivoli at Bivio Adriana, about 1.5km from the entrance to the park, or take the orange bus #4 from Tivoli itself, which leaves from Largo Garibaldi (tickets L800, available at the news kiosk; don't be confused by bus #4/, which does not go to the villa).

■ Subiaco

From Tivoli you can trace the Aniene back to its source in the stunning, untouched valley of **Subiaco,** a rocky town that dominates one of Lazio's emptier up-country quarters. As the road climbs inland, the sheer, forested crags of the Monti Simbruni rise above lush pastures and scattered vineyards. The town owes its origins to Nero, but its real fame is due to a more humble inhabitant—the young Benedetto di Norcia, a rich wastrel of the 6th century who after three years of seclusion founded a monastery, giving birth to the **Benedictine Order.**

ACOTRAL **buses** leave for Subiaco from the end of Metro Linea B (Rebibbia Station) every 50min. (6:20am-10:10pm, L4800; return buses 4:30am-7:30pm). About ½km before the bus terminus (in Piazza della Resistenza, the center of town), the bus passes the small stone **Ponte di San Francesco,** built in 1358, on the right. Debark here to cross the Anio to the stone **Chiesa di San Francesco,** filled with notable paintings, including frescoes in the third chapel on the left by il Sodoma, and an altarpiece of the Nativity by Pinturicchio. Back over the bridge, the road leads to the town and (on the right) the **tourist office** at Via Cadorna, 59 (tel. (0774) 822 013; open Mon. 8am-2pm, Tues.-Sat. 8am-2pm and 4-7pm, Sun. 9am-12:30pm). Get your map here.

From Piazza della Resistenza, the road leads straight out and up to a series of perilous hairpin turns—take the footpaths straight up the hill on the left once the road leaves town. Alternatively, blue ACOTRAL buses leave the piazza sporadically, heading toward Ienne, and pass near the entrances to the monasteries. (Tickets L1000, available at the *tabacchi* on Via Cavour just around the corner from Piazza Sant'Andrea.) After 2½km, the **Convento di Santa Scholastica** (tel. (0774) 855 25) rises on the right. The complex, a massive architectural hodgepodge, encompasses three different cloisters. In the first, a dull reconstruction of a Renaissance design, look for the words "Ave Maria" planted in artichokes. The second courtyard features an intricately carved Gothic arch and faded frescoes; the third and earliest court is the work of the 13th-century Cosmati family, whose twisted columns and bright mosaic work found their way into most of the churches in Rome. Off this court a Neoclassical church by Quarenghi (the Italian architect who designed much of Russian St. Petersburg) reposes. The library shelters the first two books printed in Italy. (Convent open daily 9am-12:30pm and 4-7pm; a monk leads guided tours every 30min. Free.)

The **Convento di San Benedetto** (tel. (0774) 850 39), another ½km up the hill, occupies one of the most spectacular hilltop sites in central Italy: from its honey-colored terraces the peaks and valleys of the Monti Simbruni recede as far as the eye can see. The sights inside the church complex, carved entirely out of its limestone cliff, aren't bad either. The monastery was founded on the site of the **Sacro Speco,** the rocky grotto where St. Benedict lived in penitential solitude for three years. Each generation of monks carved new chapels out of the rock and plastered them with precious frescoes. The *loggia* at the entrance to the upper church is decorated with the newest art in the place, a series of late 15th-century frescoes of the Madonna and Child and the Evangelists by the school of Perugino. Inside, the first section of the upper church boasts an elaborate cycle of 14th-century frescoes, done by a member of the Sienese school, depicting the Crucifixion and the Biblical events surrounding it. Stepping down from the altar, the lower church glows with the colorful paintings of Conxolus, a late 13th-century painter. The walls and vaults depict various scenes from the life of Saint Benedict, including his many miracles. To the right, the **Sacro Speco** is decorated only by a 17th-century marble statue of the monk.

Fourteenth-century Sienese frescoes of the *Triumph of Death* (including a gruesome skeleton on horseback) line the next staircase down. On the lowest level, the **Grotto dei Pastori** is revered as the place where Benedict taught catechism to local shepherds. Fragments remain of an 8th-century Byzantine fresco of the *Madonna and Child,* the oldest painting in this speluncular treasure-house. Outside you can see more spectacular views of the mountain valleys, as well as a rose bush with its own story to tell. Legend has it that St. Benedict resisted the temptations of Satan by throwing himself on a thorn bush. When St. Francis saw the thorns on his visit (some seven centuries later), he miraculously transformed them into roses, which took root and bloom to this day. (Convent open 9am-12:30pm and 3-6pm. Free.)

■ Ostia Antica

The romantic remains of ancient Ostia (tel. 565 00 22 for the ticket office at the park) offer a cooler, closer, and cheaper alternative to the more famous ruins at Pompeii and Herculaneum. The ruins are so sparsely visited you'll have no trouble finding a secluded spot for a picnic—and you'll need to bring one, since doing the site justice requires the better part of a day. Bring a water bottle as well.

The very first Roman colony, the settlement was developed as a commercial port and naval base during the 3rd and 2nd centuries BC. The ruins that remain all speak of the thriving activity the port once saw. Warehouses, shipping offices, hotels, bars, and shrines to the polyglot religious cults of slaves and sailors fill the site. Ostia's fortunes declined as Rome's did. The port fell into disuse during the onslaught of the Goths, and the silty Tiber eventually moved the coastline a mile or so to the west. Happily though, the mud effected a remarkable archaeological preservation. And the brick site was thus quarried and pillaged far less than the monumental marble precincts of Rome. Walking its main streets and narrow alleyways, you can easily imagine the din and flow of ancient city life.

The **Via Ostiensis,** paved with basalt blocks, leads through a **necropolis** of brick and marble tombs to the low remains of the **Porta Romana,** one of the city's three gates. The road is now the city's main street, the **Decumanus Maximus,** and leads into the center of the city. A few hundred yards inside, the **Baths of Neptune** rise on the right, paved with a mosaic scene appropriate for a harbor town: Neptune driving his chariot, surrounded by marine creatures. Off the Decumanus on the left of the Baths of Neptune, the **Via della Fontana,** a well-preserved street lined with stores and apartment houses, leads back to a **Fullonica,** or ancient dry cleaning shop.

The well-preserved but much-restored **Theater** rises next on the right. Beyond the theater, the expansive **Piazzale delle Corporazioni** (Forum of the Corporations) extends to the old river bank. Here importers and shipping agents from all over the Roman world maintained their offices. The sidewalk is lined with mosaic inscriptions proclaiming their businesses, the ancient precursors of modern welcome mats (look for fish and ships on the doorfronts of sailors). In the center of the piazza are the remains of a temple to Ceres, the goddess of grain, Ostia's lifeblood.

Several dozen meters from the Piazzale delle Corporazioni, on the theater side of the Decumanus, Via dei Molini leads to the **Casa di Diana,** the best-preserved Roman house at Ostia, and among the most complete in the world. Buildings like this, known as *insulae* (apartment blocks), once filled Rome and every city of the Roman empire. At the back of the ground floor, a dark, windowless room holds a **Mithraeum,** a shrine to the Persian sun god Mithras, whose cult was celebrated by worshippers sacrificing and feasting on sacred banquets on the two low couches.

Down the Via della Casa, which cuts in front of the house and leads to the left, is the **Thermopolium,** looking for all the world like a modern cappuccino bar, of which it was the ancestor. A few yards down the Via dei Molini, on the right side of the House of Diana, the **molini** (bakeries), which produced bread for the markets of Rome, jut into the street. Behind the House of Diana is the **Museum,** where a diverse collection of artifacts, both monumental and quotidian, are on display.

Back on the Decumanus, past the House of Diana, the street opens onto the **Forum of Ostia,** anchored, as at Rome, by the imposing **Temple to Jupiter, Juno,** and **Minerva** (called the **Capitolium**). Across the Forum a street leads to a **public latrine** (on the first left), and the vast **Terme del Foro** (Forum Baths). The Via del Tempio Rotondo runs parallel to the Decumanus and passes the 3rd-century AD **Round Temple,** a miniature Pantheon dedicated to the cult of all emperors.

At the fork in the Decumanus, the **Via della Foce** (which used to lead to the mouth of the Tiber) leads right to the sumptuous **House of Cupid and Psyche** (on the right), where the statue of the two lovers now in the museum was initially found. The house, amazingly intact, paneled in elaborate polychrome marble, was home to one of Ostia's wealthier merchants. Further down the street, a staircase descends to another eerie subterranean **Mithraeum,** from where an endless maze of sewers and cisterns spreads beneath the city.

Across the Via della Foce, the two-story **Casa di Serapide** has a central atrium with paintings and a relief of the god himself. The house opens into the **Baths of the Seven Wise Men,** named for a scatological fresco cycle found in one of the rooms. The circular mosaic hall was once heated by a system of hot air ducts and served as an exercise area for the bath. The next building, the **Casa dei Aurighi,** boasts two frescoes of charioteers and an arcaded courtyard. This building complex may have served as a hotel.

To reach Ostia Antica, take the Metro Linea B to the Magliana stop (L700), change to the Lido train and get off (20min.) at the Ostia Antica stop (you don't need to buy another ticket for this leg). The bar outside the train station has the only food or drink before the site. Cross the overpass and continue straight to the "T" intersection. Make a left and follow the signs to the entrance. The site is open daily 9am-6pm in summer, in winter 9am-4pm; admission L8000. The Bureau of Archaeological Digs (tel. 565 00 22) offers free guided tours at the excavations every Sunday morning from July to October. The tours are in Italian and follow a different route every time. Look for the schedule in the Sunday edition of *Il Messaggero*.

■ Viterbo

Heavy Allied bombing shattered Viterbo, and reconstruction has been slow. But the tinctured black city walls still stand, sheltering the vestiges medieval eminence. The city began as an Etruscan center but earned prominence as a papal refuge from Frederick Barbarossa's siege in the 12th century. The real architectural splurge commenced during the next century, as Viterbo became a Guelph stronghold in the aristocrats' civil war. It was here that the (literally) torturous process of papal elections first took shape. The *capitano* (city dictator) locked the cardinals in their palace until they chose a new pope. Threats to cut off food deliveries and to remove the roof from the conference room (so that the cold could creep in more easily) were added incentives for a quick decision. Today its streets brim with an eclectic mix of boys in uniform, the occasional punks, window shoppers, and senior citizens. And it still draws many to its sulphurous hot **Bulicane spring** (3km from the center), famous for its curative powers.

ORIENTATION AND PRACTICAL INFORMATION

At first glance, the inner city might intimidate you with its incongruous passages and what seem to be haphazardly scattered yellow signs misleading you down dead-end alleys. But don't worry—do follow the signs. The town walls form a trapezoid with the wide parallel side lining the eastern sector. **San Francesco** and **Santa Rosa** are in the northeast region (right inside the **Porta Fiorentina**), **San Sisto** and **San Pellegrino** (the historical center) in the southeast, and **San Lorenzo** west of center. **Piazza dei Caduti** is just north of **Piazza del Plebiscito** (which is practically dead center). The **bus station** is located just outside the northeast corner. Via Marconi and Via Cavour (which becomes Via Ascenzi south of P. del Plebiscito) converge at the tourist office.

When you arrive at the bus or train terminal, turn right on Viale Trieste, and walk along the city wall to the first opening, Porta Fiorentina (on the left), and descend along Via Matteotti to P. Verdi at the bottom of the hill. Via Marconi on the right takes you to P. dei Caduti and the EPT; the Azienda di Turismo is on the left, and Corso Italia, sloping up to the right, leads to the medieval San Pellegrino district.

Tourist Office: EPT, P. dei Caduti, 16 (tel. 30 47 95, fax 32 62 06). English spoken. Large map displayed outside. Open Mon.-Fri. 8:30am-2pm and 3:30-6pm, Sat. 8:30am-2pm. **Azienda di Turismo,** P. Verdi, 4 (tel. 22 66 66). No English, but a helpful wall map. Open Mon.-Sat. 8am-2pm. On weekends, the **EPT Tourist Office** at P. della Morte (tel. 34 52 29) in the southwest of town is open 3-7pm.
Post Office: Via Ascenzi (tel. 23 48 06), between P. del Plebiscito and the tourist office. Open Mon.-Fri. 8:10am-1pm, Sat. 8am-noon. Also P. della Rocca. Open Mon.-Fri. 2-7pm. **Postal code:** 01100.
Telephones: SIP, Via Calabresi, 7. Open Mon.-Fri. 8:10am-7:50pm, Sat. 9am-12:30pm. Also on Via Cavour, 31, just south of P. del Plebiscito. **Telephone code:** 0761.
Buses: Tickets can be purchased at the theater/snack bar at Viale Trento or at the ACOTRAL on Via Sauro (1 block east). All buses board passengers across from the theater. Buses to: Orvieto (1½hr., L3800); Civitavécchia (1¾hr., L4800); Tarquínia

(1hr., L4300); Caprarola (L1500); and Bolsena (L2800) as well as other cities in Etruria. To get to Viterbo from Rome take Metro Linea A to Flaminio. From the Flaminio station, follow the signs to the Roma Nord station outside. There, buy a combination train/bus ticket to Viterbo (L5300 1-way). The train goes first to Saxa Rubra (15min.; very isolated at night), and then you board an ACOTRAL bus to Viterbo (1½hr.). The last bus back to Rome leaves Viterbo at 7pm.

Emergencies: tel. 113. **Police: Questura,** Località Pietrare (tel. 34 06 91). **Hospital: Belcolle,** Strada Sammartinese (tel. 34 53 45), 2km from the center. **Red Cross:** tel. 30 40 33.

ACCOMMODATIONS AND CAMPING

Albergo Milano, Via della Cava, 54 (tel. 34 07 05). Located to the northeast by San Francesco and not far from the bus station. The kind grandmother will direct you to a clean room equipped with short-wave radio. Singles L27,000, with bath L35,000. Doubles L40,000, with bath L60,000. Renovating in 1993, so prices may rise.

Albergo Roma, Via della Cava, 26 (tel. 22 72 74 or 22 64 74). Comfy quarters at 2-star prices. Some rooms have mini-fridges and TVs. Singles L39,000, with bath L59,000. Doubles L59,000, with bath L85,000. Triples with bath L115,000. Quads with bath L140,000. Rates may drop if they're not busy. Visa, Am Ex, MasterCard accepted.

Camping: The nearest campgrounds are on the immaculate beach of **Lago di Bolsena,** 30km north. Most accessible by public transport are those in Bolsena itself (ACOTRAL bus, L3000): **Il Lago,** Viale Cadorna (tel. 79 91 91), L6000 per person, L6000 per tent, L4000 per car (open March-mid-Oct.). Prettier campgrounds near Bolsena off the Cassia in the towns of Capodimonte and Montefiascone. The tourist office has a list of campgrounds in the province of Viterbo.

FOOD

Local specialties include *lombriche* (earthworm-shaped) pasta and a chestnut soup, *zuppa di mosciarelle.* Try Viterbo's native *sambuca,* a sweet anise-flavored liqueur. Pope Martin IV experienced the sufferings of purgatory, according to Dante, for his weakness for a local dish, roasted eel from Bolsena. *Alimentari* can be found along Via dell'Orologio, or check out the huge **outdoor market** (Sat. 7am-2pm) in P. della Rocca. There is a **Supervivo supermarket** on Via Marconi, 40, before P. dei Caduti (open 8am-1pm and 4:30-8pm, closed Thurs. afternoon).

Porta Romana, Via della Bontà, 12 (tel. 30 71 18), in the southeast, near the Porta Romana gate. You tell her how much you're willing to pay, she tells you how much you're entitled to eat. Provincial specialties lauded by locals. Full meals about L18,000. Cover L2000. Open Mon.-Sat. 7-11:30pm.

Taverna del Padrino, Via della Cava, 22. Tasty pizzas and a lively atmosphere. Popular with conscripts. Pizzas average L7000. Cover L2000. Open noon-2:30pm and 7pm-3am.

SIGHTS

At the southern end of town is the medieval quarter's administrative center, **Piazza del Plebiscito.** The medallion-decked building with the tall clock tower is the **Palazzo del Popolo.** Large stone lions, the symbol of Viterbo, guard both. Between them lies the **Palazzo Comunale** in full Renaissance sprawl. (Open 8am-2pm. Free. Go upstairs to the office on your right and ask to see the Royal Room.) Outside, across from the large clock tower, the façade of the **Church of Sant'Angelo** incorporates a Roman sarcophagus that contains the body of the ineffably beautiful and virtuous Galiana. When she refused to marry an amorous Roman baron, he besieged the city, promising to spare it if she came to the wall. As soon as Galiana appeared, the baron shot her with an arrow, thereby ensuring her fidelity.

Curious *palazzi* line **Via San Lorenzo,** which wends its way from P. del Plebescito into Viterbo's medieval heart, P. San Lorenzo. A plaque on the seemingly peaceful thousand-year-old façade of the **Chiesa del Gesù** here recounts family murders that took place during a morning mass in 1271. In the Siena-influenced bell tower of the **cathedral** in Piazza San Lorenzo, pairs of slender, arched windows climb to a sharp peak. The **Palazzo dei Papi,** topped by a row of toothlike merlons, fills the far end of the piazza. From the *loggia,* enjoy a bird's-eye view of a complex of early Christian churches. This was the site of the papal conclave in which the roof was almost removed to freeze the clergy into a decision. (Open Mon.-Sat. 10am-12:30pm. Free.) The **Museum of Sacred Arts** inside the curia of the church contains medieval sculpture and painting (open 9:45am-1pm; free). At the end of Via San Lorenzo is the charming yet unfortunately named **Piazza delle Morte** (Square of Death), at the center of which is the 13th-century **Palazzetto of San Tomaso.** Just north of P. della Morte, Via Cardinale La Fontaine leads to Via San Pellegrino, which stumbles its way through the medieval quarter of **San Pellegrino.**

Back near the bus station at the northern end of town, the **Basilica of San Francesco** contains the tombs of two popes who died in Viterbo: Adrian V (1276, whom Dante put in hell with the misers) and Clement IV (1265-68). At the **Church of Santa Rosa** (near the basilica), the 700-year-old corpse of Viterbo's celebrated saint is preserved in a glass case. The people of Viterbo honor the saint every September 3 at 9pm, when one hundred burly bearers carry the *Macchina di Santa Rosa,* a towering 30m-high construction of iron, wood, and papier-mâché, through the illuminated streets. The bearers of the tributary lug it around town and then sprint uphill to the church. In 1814 the *macchina* fell on the *facchini* (bearers), and in 1967 it had to be abandoned in the street because it was too heavy. Several days of frenzied celebration surround this event.

Directly inside the Porta Fiorentina, the **National Archaeological Museum,** P. della Roca, 21 (tel. 32 59 29), contains exhibits on Viterbo's Etruscan heritage. (Open Tues.-Sat. 9am-2pm, Sun. 9am-1pm. Admission L4000.)

The **Festival Barocco** brings excellent classical music to Viterbo's churches in June. Ask at the tourist office about tickets (L12,000) and schedules.

Near Viterbo

Villa Lante (tel. (0761) 28 80 08), in the picturesque town of **Bagnaia,** is a particularly enjoyable example of the grandiose villas in vogue among 16th-century church bigwigs. Bus #6 leaves Viterbo from P. Mártiri d'Ungheria every half-hour for Bagnaia (15min., L1000; last bus back leaves Bagnaia at 8:30pm). From the piazza where the bus drops you, walk uphill and enter the villa's right-hand gate. To enter the gardens next to the villa ring at the gatehouse (on the left as you enter) and wait for a keeper to give you a tour of the verdant glories within. (Villa Lante open Tues.-Sun. 9am-7:30pm; March-April and Sept.-Oct. 9am-5:30pm; Nov.-Feb. 9am-4pm. Tours of the inner gardens every ½hr., L4000.) Farther along the same road lurks a pleasure garden of a different sort: the **Parco dei Mostri,** Park of the Monsters (tel. (0761) 92 40 29). Blue ACOTRAL buses depart from Viale Trento in Viterbo (6 per day, L1300) and drop you off in **Bomarzo,** 1km from the park. From where the bus leaves you, walk downhill and follow the signs for Palazzo Orsini (*not* Parco dei Mostri). Turn left down the stairs marked Via del Lavatio, and continue downhill to the park. A surreal wilderness of grotesque forms mocks the overly refined aristocratic sculpture gardens of the time. (Open 8:30am-7pm. Admission L10,000.)

ETRURIA

The Etruscans, an Italic tribe who may or may not have had roots in Asia Minor, dominated north-central Italy from the 9th to the 4th century BC. In the shadow of the new power to the south, most traces of the Etruscans' wholly original culture disappeared. What remains, excavated from their necropolises, is fascinating.

Unlike the stern, superstitious Romans, Etruscans enjoyed life to the fullest; their tomb paintings (at Tarquínia) celebrate life, love, eating and drinking, sport, and the rough countryside that they called home. Their *tumuli* (at Cervéteri) are carved out of the rock like houses in a friendly neighborhood. Vandalism has forced the government to close many tombs, and what artifacts have been excavated now reside in the Villa Giulia and Vatican Museums at Rome and in the national museums in Tarquínia and Cervéteri. Still, a visit to the ancient, rocky landscape of Etruria conjures up plenty of ghosts, and the deserted tombs have a quiet, shadowy appeal that's quite different from the pomp and grandeur that Rome has to offer.

■ Cervéteri

Outside Cervéteri (ancient *Caere*), the bulbous earthen tombs of the **necropolis** slumber in the tufa bedrock from which they were carved. Inside, the simple chambers are carved to resemble the wooden huts in which living Etruscans resided. As you enter a tomb, small rooms off the antechamber mark the resting place of slaves and lesser household members; the central room held the bodies of the rest of the family, and the small chambers off the back were reserved for the most prominent men and women. A triangular headboard on a couch marks a woman's grave, a circular one indicates a man's. Don't miss the **Tomb of the Shields and the Chairs,** the smaller **Tomb of the Alcove** (with a carved-out matrimonial bed), and the rowhouses where less well-to-do Etruscans rested in peace. Look for the colored stucco reliefs in the **Tomba dei Relievi.**

ACOTRAL **buses** run to Cervéteri from Rome at Via Lepanto (every ½hr., 1hr., L3800; take Metro Linea A to Lepanto, or bus #70 from Sta. Maria Maggiore or Largo Argentina). From the village, it's another 2km to the necropolis along a tree-lined country road; follow the signs downhill and then to the right. Whenever you see a fork in the road without a sign to guide you, choose the fork on the right. If you see lots of cows and a vineyard, you're lost. Bring a flashlight and a picnic lunch. Bring courage, too; few sounds chill the heart like the flapping of the giant grasshoppers which lurk in the abandoned tombs. (Site open Tues.-Sun. 9am-7pm; Oct.-April Tues.-Sat. 9am-4pm, Sun. 11am-4pm. Admission L8000; maps L1000.)

Also worthwhile is the **Museo Nazionale di Cervéteri,** P. Santa Maria Maggiore (tel. 995 00 03), located in **Ruspoli Castle,** displaying artifacts dug from the Caere necropolis in the last 10 years. (Open Tues.-Sun. 9am-2pm; in summer, open until 4pm. Free.) The last bus for Rome leaves at 9:30pm; if you're stuck, the **Albergo El Paso,** Via Settevene Palo, 293 (tel. 994 30 33; fax 995 03 03; ½km out the bottom left side of the main *piazza*) has doubles for L75,000. Shower included.

■ Tarquínia

When Rome was no more than a village of mud huts beside the Tiber, Tarquin kings held the fledgling metropolis under their sway. The tables turned, of course, and today little remains of the once-thriving Etruscan city. But the ravages of neither time nor Romans could wipe out the subterranean **necropolis** of tombs on the ridge opposite the city, and the vibrant frescoes remaining here are worth exploring.

Buses arrive in the Barriera San Giusto outside the medieval ramparts. The **tourist office** here (tel. 85 63 84; open Mon.-Sat. 8am-2pm and 5-7pm) provides a wealth of information and bus schedules. In adjoining P. Cavour stands the **Museo Nazionale** (tel. 85 60 36), one of the best collections of Etruscan art outside of Rome. Don't pass up the second-floor ramparts of the castle, where you can sun yourself and catch great views of the sea. (Open Tues.-Sun. 9am-2pm. Guided evening tours in summer Tues.-Fri.; inquire at the tourist office. Admission L8000.)

The same ticket admits you to the necropolis (tel. 85 63 08). Take the bus from Barriera San Giusto (any that go to the "Cimitero" stop) or walk (15min. from the museum). Head up Corso Vittorio Emanuele from P. Cavour and turn right down Via Porta. Then take Via Ripagretta to Via delle Croci, which leads to the tombs. You must wait for a group to form and for a guide to let you in. Because of their fragility, only four to six tombs may be seen on a given day (and even then only peered at from behind a metal railing in the doorway). All of the tombs are splendid works of art, decorated with scenes of Etruscan life, including banquets, sacrifices, and portraits, as well as animals and geometric designs (open Tues.-Sun. 9am-2pm).

Trip over Tarquínia by day. The site is a local stop on the Rome-Grosseto **train** line, and buses run from the station and beaches into town every 30 minutes until 9:10pm. (Trains leave from Roma Ostiense station starting at 7:20am; the last train back leaves Tarquínia at 10:48pm; 1hr; L7200 one-way, L12,200 round-trip). **Buses** also link the town with Viterbo (1hr., L3500), Civitavecchia (45min., L3200) and Rome (8 per day, 2hr., L6300). The bus from Rome leaves from Via Lepanto. For information on southern Etruria (Provincia di Viterbo), try the Azienda Autonoma di Turismo at P. Cavour, 1 (tel. (0766) 85 63 84), or at the EPT in Viterbo, P. dei Caduti, 16 (tel. 22 61 61). The cheapest hotel in Tarquínia is **Hotel San Marco**, P. Cavour, 18 (tel. 84 08 13; singles L53,000, doubles L78,000).

■ The Pontine Islands

A weekend playground for city-weary Romans, the Pontine Islands are Lazio's most splendid marine assets. After housing a series of exiles from ancient Rome, this stunning volcanic archipelago with its mountain spines and turquoise water was given to Bourbon King Charles III of Naples by his mother Elisabetta Farnese in 1734. The king soon started a program to colonize the islands, first sending farmers, hence the landscape of tiny vineyards growing on terraces. More families moved after the eruption of Mount Vesuvius in 1771. The Islands' subsequent population by wood-hungry Neapolitans led to the contemporary landscape of tiny vineyards, fragrant wild herbs, and flowers.

Ponza and **Ventotene** are the only two inhabited islands. Both offer several options for staying over as well as connections to various ports for day trips. Though crowded in July and August, the islands are geared mainly to Italians—a welcome change from the rampaging Germans on Elba and the international mayhem of Cápri.

The Islands can be reached by several ferry lines from Anzio, Terracina, Fiumicino and Formia, including **Med Mar** (Via Ofanto, 18, tel. 841 90 57; or P. Barberini, 5, tel. 482 85 79) and **CAREMAR** (in Naples, tel. (081) 551 38 82; in Ponza, tel. (0771) 46 16 00 or 227 10). From Rome the most inexpensive option is CAREMAR from Anzio (L17,100; train to Anzio L4300). The most convenient route is Via Fiumicino (to Ponza L40,000, Ventotene, L47,000). The Terracina-Ponza commute is L10,000 (once daily). If you're on an island spree, consider the journey from or to Cápri and Íschia. (Cápri-Ventotene on Med Mar is L25,000 but only runs June-Sept.)

> **Fiumicino-Ponza-Ventotene: Med Mar** departures daily 9am and 4:15pm, 2hr. 30min.; L47,000 to Ponza, L44,000 to Ventetone. Free shuttle bus runs from the airport to the port. Make reservations with a travel agent in Rome especially for weekend travel.
>
> **Formia-Ponza: CAREMAR** departures 9am and 4:30pm, L17,100 (2hr. 15min.). Returns 5:30am and 1:30pm.
>
> **Formia-Ventotene: CAREMAR** departures 9:10am and 1pm, (2hr. 15min.), L12,800. Return 5:30pm. If no one is at the information booth at the Ventotene port, inquire at the bar next door.
>
> **Ponza-Ventotene: Med Mar** departures 11am and 6pm, 30min., L18,000. Return 11am. **CAREMAR** departure 6:10pm, 35min., L15,500.

Ponza

> **Tourist Office: Pro Loco** (tel. 80 031). The office is in the large yellow building down at the port. Useful brochure with hotel listings available. Open Mon.-Sat. 9am-1pm and 4-8pm. Sept.-May open sporadically in the mornings.

Post Office: P. Pisacane, 32. Take the 1st right after the tourist office. The sign is on the left. Open Mon.-Fri. 8:30am-1:30pm, Sat. 8:30am-noon. **Postal code:** 04027. **Telephone code:** 0771.

Buses: main station Autolinee Ponzesi, Via Dante (tel. 804 47). Buses depart from here every 15min. to Le Forna (L1500). On the way back, flag down buses anywhere along Via Panoramica.

Emergencies: tel. 113. **Police:** Molo Musco (tel. 801 30). **First Aid and Medical Care: Poliambulatorio,** Via Panoramica (tel. 806 87). Open in the summer daily 4:30am-3am. Off season 4:30am-6:30pm.

Accommodations and Food   Unfortunately, Ponza isn't the fishing village it once was. Prices have skyrocketed over the past few years due to increasing tourism and free-lance camping was outlawed three years ago due to fire hazards. There are two helpful agencies to save you the trouble of searching for a site: **Agenzia Immobiliare "Arcipelago Pontino,"** Corso Piscane, 49 (tel. 806 78), and **Agenzia Afari "Magi,"** Via Branchina Nuova, 21 (tel. 80 98 41). They will help you find a room in **affitta camere** (private homes) for L40,000 in July and August, less during the off-season.

Pensione-Ristorante "Arcobaleno," Via Scotti D. Basso, 6 (tel. 80 315). As you ascend the stairs you may be cursing the writer who sent you here. When you reach the summit, however, you will understand why you were sent. Straight up the ramp, follow the street until it ends, then veer right until you pass the Bellavista Hotel. Turn left and follow the signs up, up, up. Wonderful people, the best views in Ponza and excellent food. Doubles L70,000. Off-season L30,000 and L50,000. Also: full meals are L25,000. These are special *Let's Go* prices. English spoken. Call ahead in summertime before you make the ascent.

Casa Vitiello, Via Madonna, 28 (tel. 80 117). In the historic part of town, this family-run *affitta camere* has simple rooms in a quiet location. Follow the signs to La Torre dei Borbini; it's across the street. Doubles, L80,000. Off-season L60,000.

The Pontine Islands are known for their lentil soup, fish, and lobster. Several comparable restaurants and bars surround the port and spark the island's nightlife. (Be careful if you're staying in Le Forna—Sept.-June the last bus is at 10pm; July-Aug. last bus at 3am.) Most restaurants also rent boats and organize island excursions by day.

Trattoria da Gina, Via Dante, 48/49 (tel. 80 064), at the port facing the sea. Follow the coastal street down on the left. A full menu from the day's catch, including water and wine, is only L25,000.

Ristorante Lello, Strada Panoramica, 10 (tel. 80 395), next door to the bus station. Specializes in regional dishes. Their *zuppa di lenticchie* (lentil soup, L5000) is especially tasty. *Primi* L7000, *secondi* L10,000.

Le Note Blu, Via Banchina T. di Fazio (tel. 80 507). Located directly on the waterfront, this "piano bar" with live music nightly is a good bet for jazz and drinks. (First drink L5000. Open 10:30pm-5am depending on the crowd.)

Sights   Ponza is full of grottos and hidden beaches. Explore either on foot (the best way to savor the breathtaking panoramic views) or by renting a boat (try the jutting pier to the right of the main launch—L80,000 and up for the entire day depending on boat size). For a guided boat tour, inquire at any of the portside restaurants that advertise (around L16,000 per person). Most trips visit the **Pilatus Caves,** an ancient Roman breeding ground for Muraena fish. The newest option (on the island) is to rent a **scooter** from the numerous rental places near the port (just look for an unusual number of scooters in one place). Prices don't differ much and are about L15,000 per hour and around L60,000 for the day.

The more isolated **beaches** can be reached by boat (usually around L10,000 round trip). For a more crowded area and cliff-diving action, try the *Piscine Naturali* (take the bus towards Le Forma).

Ventotene

If the crowds of Campania are driving you mad, tranquil Ventotene will provide a refuge for regrouping. Despite a barren landscape, this tiny island's unexploited charm will rejuvenate your weary traveling bones. Over the centuries, Ventotene has served in various capacities as a prison: ancient Roman women were succeeded in the 18th century by a co-ed clan of convicts (from Naples) sent to the island to reform themselves in arcadian bliss. After four scandalous years of license (1768-1772), they were tossed off the island and replaced by farmers.

The tiny **tourist office** is located right on the port and is managed by an affable English-speaking staff. **C.S.V.,** at P. Castello (Via Pozzo di S. Candida, 13), will help you find a room in a hotel, *affitta camere,* or private home for (singles L30,000 and doubles L60,000 during July and August). Prices drop from September through June. (Open June-Sept. daily, 9:30am-12:30pm and 4:30-7:30pm.) There are only a few hotels here and they are quite expensive. The only accessible one is **Albergo Isolabella,** Via Calarossano, 2 (tel. 85 027), near the beach at Cola Rossano and with a view of this small harbor. (Singles, L35,000. Doubles with bath, L80,000.) The **supermarket** at P. Castello will provide you with the basics. For fancier treats, head to **Il Forno,** Via Olivi, 35.

The **Archeological Museum** is also on P. Castello. (Open daily 10am-1pm and 7pm-midnight. Admission L3000. During the winter call the numbers posted outside to get the museum open.) Here you can also inquire about trips to Archaeological sites: **Villa Giulia** (2½hr. guided tour, L6000), **Cisterna Romana di Villa Stefania** (L5000). All tours are in Italian. **Coraggio,** on the Porto Romano rents rowboats (L10,000 per day), motorboats (L50,000 per day), and scuba diving equipment (L35,000 per day).

Two splendid **beaches** are Cala Rossano and Cala Nave, flanking either side of the port.

▨ Umbria

Christened the "Green Heart of Italy," Umbria has enjoyed renown since ancient times for its wooded hills, valleys, and rivers. This region inspired its sons, the Latin poets Plautus and Propertius, as well as Dante and Giosuè Carducci. Often shrouded in an ethereal silvery haze, the landscape also nurtured a mystic tradition that stretches from prehistory through to St. Benedict, who preached the doctrine of the marriage of work and worship, and to Umbria's most famous visionary, the nature-adoring ascetic St. Francis. Generations of visual artists also clambered about these hills, among them Giotto, Signorelli, Perugino and Pinturicchio.

Umbria's earliest inhabitants may have been the Umbrii, an ancient and reclusive tribe that withdrew to the east as first the Etruscans and then the aggressive Romans sought to expand their frontiers. Barbarian invasions in the 5th and 6th centuries provoked the inhabitants to retreat to the hill towns of the Etruscans, setting the stage for the rise of Medieval city-states. More than half a millennium of constant Guelph-Ghibelline warfare followed, finally allowing Pope Paul III to seize the weakened region for his own in the 1530s. Although the yoke of papal governance was lifted during the Risorgimento, its legacy of stagnation lingered well into this century. Umbria has now achieved a measure of prosperity by cultivating interest in its beautifully situated medieval cities and by promoting itself as a center of culture through such summer festivities as the pioneering Two Worlds Festival of Spoleto and the Umbrian Jazz Festival.

While trains link most major towns, buses provide the most convenient access, especially as they drop you off in the center of town rather than at the bottom of a steep hill. Thermal springs, clear streams, Etruscan ruins, and velvety ravines make the verdant countryside nearly as appealing as the numerous hilltowns.

■ Perugia

Perugians may be the politest people you'll meet in Italy, somewhat odd considering Perugia was long the country's most violent and disreputable town. From its roots as an Etruscan *polis* through Roman domination Perugia seems to have often been a troublemaker. Between attacks on its neighbors, though, it still found time for an annual festival called the *Battaglia de' Sassi* (Battle of Stones), during which two teams threw rocks at each other until a sufficient number of casualties or fatalities left a winner. Besides being celebrated as the town that once imprisoned St. Francis of Assisi (albeit during his dissolute, pre-preaching days), independent Perugia gets religious points as the birthplace of the Flagellants, the flesh-mortifying masses who wandered Europe whipping themselves in public, and as the deathbed of three popes (two died by poison). But the good times eventually ended, and Perugia found itself crushed underneath the Papal heel when it fell to Paul III in 1538.

Three centuries of mortification and economic misery as part of the Papal States apparently taught the Perugians some manners (though not subservience—they were rebelling against the Pope as late as 1859), for the present-day capital of Umbria claims a delightfully civilized atmosphere seasoned by the motley international crowd drawn to its universities and art academies. The *palazzi* that crowd Corso Vannucci, Perugia's main street, shelter the city's impressive collection of medieval and Renaissance art; interspersed are bars offering the city's contemporary masterpieces, the infamous chocolate *baci* (kisses).

ORIENTATION AND PRACTICAL INFORMATION

A few direct trains run from Florence and Rome to Perugia, but change at Foligno on the Rome-Ancona line, or catch one of the frequent trains from Teróntola on the Florence-Rome route for more service. Leaving from the train station, buses #26, 27, and 36 will leave you in P. Matteotti (L1000). Otherwise it's a treacherous 4km trek—uphill. From the bus station in P. dei Partigiani, follow the signs to the escalator (*scala mobile*) which takes you underneath the old city to Piazza Italia. Straight ahead, Corso Vannucci, the main shopping thoroughfare, leads to Piazza IV Novembre and the *duomo;* behind the *duomo* lies the university area. One block to the right of Corso Vannucci you'll find P. Matteotti, the municipal center. The new **Digi-plan** machines in the train station are extremely helpful, providing instant printout information (in Italian) on sights, museums, stores, restaurants, and more. Train information machines speak English.

Note: phone numbers in Perugia have recently been changed. If you have no luck with the one listed, try adding a 57 to the front (unless there is one already) and see if that works.

Tourist Office: P. IV Novembre (tel. 572 33 27), in the Palazzo dei Priori. Extremely friendly, patient, and knowledgeable staff gives accommodations and travel information. Artistic but misleading city map. Ask for the detailed walking guide, the *Umbria Informazione* brochure and the map of Umbria. Open Mon.-Sat. 8:30am-1:30pm and 4-7pm, Sun. 9am-1pm; in winter Mon.-Sat. 3:30-6:30pm.

Budget Travel: CTS, Via del Roscetto, 21 (tel. 576 16 95), off Via Pinturicchio towards the bottom of the street. Student center with travel and accommodations offices. Open Mon.-Fri. 9am-12:15pm and 4-7pm, Sat. 9am-noon. **CIT:** Corso Vannucci (tel. 260 61), by the fountain. Open Mon.-Fri. 9am-1pm and 3:30-7pm.

Currency Exchange: Best rates at the banks in town. At the train station, no commission for exchanges of less than L80,000, but worse rates.

Post Office: P. Matteotti. Open Mon.-Sat. 8:10am-7:30pm. **Postal code:** 06100.

Telephones: ASST, next to the post office in P. Matteotti. Open daily 7am-9:45pm. **SIP,** Corso Vannucci, 76. Open daily 8am-10pm. **Telephone code:** 075.

Trains: Fontivegge, P. Veneto. **F.S.** south to: Assisi (25min., L2700); Foligno (40min., L3600); Spoleto (1hr. 10min., L5400); Orvieto (1 3/4hr., L8800); Rome via Teróntola (3hr., L18,200). North to: Passignano sul Trasimeno (30min., L3300); Arezzo (1hr. 20min., L6500); Florence (2½hr., L14,200); Siena (L14,200). **Sant'Anna** station in P. Bellucci serves Città di Castello and Sansepolcro to the north and Todi to the south. **Information: F.S.,** P. Veneto (tel. 709 80). Open 8am-noon and 3-7pm. **Ferrovia Centrale Umbra,** Largo Cacciatori delle Alpi, 8 (tel. 239 47), near the bottom of the escalator on the 1st floor. The **ticket window** in the F.S. station is open 6am-9pm. **Luggage Storage:** L1500, open daily 6:30am-10:30pm.

Buses: P. dei Partigiani, down the *scala mobile* from P. Italia. City bus #28, 29, 36, or CD (L1000) from the train station. **ASP buses,** P. dei Partigiani (tel. 618 07) to most Umbrian towns, along with Urbino, Rome, and Florence. Information machines are English-competent.

Albergo Diurno: Viale Indipendenza, 7 (enter through the *scala mobile* under P. Italia). Open daily 8am-8pm. Toilet L400, shower L5000, bath L5500, towel L1500, soap L1000. Luggage storage L2500 per piece per day.

English Bookstore: Libreria Filosofi, Via dei Filosofi, 18/20 (tel. 573 04 73). Take bus CS from Via XIV Settembre. Out of the way, but a good selection ranging from last year's best-sellers to Faulkner and Eliot. Open Mon.-Fri. 9am-1pm and 4-8pm, Sat. 9am-1pm.

Higher Education: Università per gli Stranieri, Palazzo Gallenga, P. Fortebraccio, 4 (tel. 576 43 44 or 576 43 45). The university offers courses in Italian language and culture for foreigners. The student *caffè,* replete with pinball machines, is frequented by the young and the restless. A good place to meet other travelers. Check university bulletin board for cultural events and free concerts. Check with the registrar for rooms for rent (only for longer stays).

Laundromat: Lavanderia Moderna, Via Fabretti, 19, around the corner from the above university. L4000 per kg. Open Mon.-Fri. 8:30am-1pm and 4-8pm, Sat. 8:30am-1pm. Or try **Lavanderia GR,** C. Garibaldi, 34. L3000 per kg. Open Mon.-Fri. 8:30am-1pm and 3:30-7:30pm, Sat. 8:30am-1pm.

Swimming Pool: Piscina Comunale, Via Pompeo Pellini (tel. 576 51 60), near Santa Colombata. Open daily 1-7:30pm; off-season Mon.-Fri. 6:30am-8:30pm, Sat. 3-8pm. Admission L6000.

Emergencies: tel. 113. **Police: Questura,** P. dei Partigiani. **Medical Emergency:** tel. 572 41 11. **Hospital: Ospedali Riuniti-Policlinico,** Via Bonacci Brunamonti (tel. 57 81).

ACCOMMODATIONS AND CAMPING

Reservations are absolutely necessary during the Umbria Jazz Festival in July.

Centro Internazionale di Accoglienza per la Gioventù, Via Bontempi, 13 (tel. 572 33 27). From P. Matteotti walk up Via de' Fari, take a right on Corso Vannucci and go until you hit P. IV Novembre, then take the road leading off P. Dante away from the *duomo* past P. Piccinino (a parking lot) and take the right fork (Via Bontempi). This clean hostel offers many amenities: the 4-bed rooms have high ceilings, night tables, and firm bunks. The spacious kitchen is an excellent meeting spot. 3 week max. stay. Lockout 9:30am-4pm. Curfew midnight. L14,000; showers and use of kitchen included. Sheets L1000. Open mid-Jan. to late Dec.

Albergo Etruria, Via della Luna, 21 (tel. 572 37 30), down the passageway by Corso Vannucci, 55. This *pensione* sits at the precipitous end of an alleyway. The proprietor will show you through the 12th-century sitting room. Singles L32,000. Doubles L55,000. Showers L3500.

Albergo Anna, Via dei Priori, 48 (tel. 573 63 04), off Corso Vannucci. Walk up 4 flights to clean and cool 17th-century rooms, with daunting ceilings and peaceful views. Beds have beautiful linen. Singles L32,000. Doubles L44,000, with bath L50,000. Showers L6000. Breakfast L5000.

Pensione Paola, Via della Canapina, 5 (tel. 572 38 16). From the train station, take bus #26 or 27 and get off near Via della Canapina, across from a large municipal parking lot. Walk up the stairs; the *pensione* is on the right. A charming place with big, beautifully furnished rooms. Singles L33,000. Doubles L50,000. Breakfast included. Reservations recommended.

Camping: Paradis d'Ete, 5km away in Colle della Trinità (tel. 517 21 17). Take bus #36 from the station and ask the driver to leave you in Colle della Trinità. Hot showers and pool at no extra charge. L7000 per person, L6000 per tent, L3000 per car. Open year-round.

FOOD

Though renowned for chocolate, Perugia also serves up a variety of delectable breads and pastries; be sure to sample the *torta di formaggio* (cheese bread) and the *mele al cartoccio* (the Italian version of apple pie). Both are available at **Ceccarani,** P. Matteotti, 16, or at the **Co.Fa.Pa** bakery two doors down at #12 (both open Fri.-Wed. 7:30am-1pm and 5-7:45pm). For such local confections as *baci* (kisses), a combination of chocolate, nuts, and honey, follow your nose to **Bar Ferrari,** Corso Vannucci, 43 (open 7am-midnight). If you prefer your chocolate cold and creamy, head to the student-infested **Gelateria 2000,** Via Luigi Bonazzi, 3, off P. della Repubblica (open Mon.-Sat. 8am-midnight), whose product is excellence made edible (cones L1500-3000).

On Tuesday and Saturday mornings you can salivate over the **open-air market** in P. Europa; on other days, try the covered market in P. Matteotti for plenty of fruit, vegetables, and nuts (open Tues.-Sat. 8am-1pm). The entrance is below street level. On summer nights the market becomes an outdoor *caffè.* Buy essentials at the small markets in Piazza Matteotti (open during regular business hours, Mon.-Fri. 8am-1pm and 4-7pm, Sat. 8am-1pm). Complement your meal with the reasonably priced regional wines *Sagrantino Secco,* a dry, full-bodied red, or *Grechetto,* a light, dry white.

Trattoria Calzoni, Via Cesare Caporali, 12 (tel. 572 90 72), across from Albergo Eden. Home away from home for those who have always wanted (or miss) an Italian grandmother. The distinguished Signora Maria lovingly whips up the pasta of your choice before your very eyes (L9000 including beverage). A full meal will run you L16,000. Open Mon.-Sat. 12:30-2:30pm and 7:30-9:30pm.

Tavola Calda, P. Danti, 16 (tel. 572 19 76). Wide selection of meat and vegetables available cafeteria-style, outdoor seating. Pizza L1200 per slice, sandwiches from L3000, and a decent *rosticceria.* Baked ziti L3300. Rambunctious late-night crowd. Open Sun.-Fri. 9:30am-3:30pm and 7-11pm.

L'oca Nera, Via dei Priori, 78-82 (tel 21 889). Hidden in the caverns below the north-central quarter, this joint draws a crowd for its delicious food, funky atmosphere, and quick, pleasant service. Massive selection ranges from würtzel to *gnocchi* to hamburgers (avg. L5000 a dish).

SIGHTS

Piazza IV Novembre

The city's most important sights frame Piazza IV Novembre; all other monuments of distinction are within a 20-minute walk of this spot. In the center of town (the middle of the piazza) lies the **Fontana Maggiore,** designed by native son Fra' Bevignate and decorated by Nicolà and Giovanni Pisano. The bas-reliefs covering the majestic double basin depict scenes from religious and Roman history, the allegories of the months and sciences (lower basin), and the saints and other historical figures (upper basin).

The 13th-century **Palazzo dei Priori** presides over the piazza; its long rows of mullioned windows and toothlike crenulation embody archetypal Perugian bellicosity. This building, itself one of the finest extant examples of Gothic communal architecture, shelters the impressive **Galleria Nazionale dell'Umbria,** Corso Vanucci, 19 (tel. 203 16). The immense collection contains fine works by Tuscans Duccio, Fra' Angelico, Taddeo di Bartolo, Guido da Siena, and Piero della Francesca, but look particularly for its Umbrian art. Perugian Pinturicchio's gleeful use of color and disdain for Renaissance seriousness are not as evident in the works here as in Siena's *Picco-lomini Library* or San Gimignano's *Chapel of Santa Fina,* but viewing his efforts on the *Miracles of San Bernardino of Siena* is still the visual equivalent of eating a *bacio.* Perhaps too sweet for some tastes are the works of Pietro Vannucci, alias Perugino, the town's most celebrated artist. His newly-restored *Adoration of the Magi* is the gallery's premier piece. (Open Mon.-Sat. 9am-1:45pm and 3-7pm, Sun. 9am-1pm. Admission L8000.)

Next door in the **Collegio del Cambio** (Banker's Guild) (tel. 61 379), Perugino demonstrated what a talented artist could do with even a mundane commission. In his frescoes, he suffuses the entire piece with the characteristic gentle softness that he later passed on to his greatest pupil, Raphael. The latter is said to have collabo-rated on the *Prophets and Sibyls.* Notice also Perugino's self-portrait (*autoritratto*) on the left wall. In the small chapel adjacent to the chamber hang paintings of scenes from the life of John the Baptist by Giannicola di Paolo (1519), including an especially grisly decapitation scene with a grinning Salomé. Further toward the piazza, at #15, visit the **Collegio della Mercanzia.** This richly paneled room, begun in 1390, is the meeting-room for Perugia's merchant guild; to this day the guild's eighty-eight members meet here to debate tax law and local commerce. (Cambio and Mercanzia open Tues.-Sat. 9am-12:30pm and 2:30-5:30pm, Sun. 9am-12:30pm. Admission L2000, good for both.) You can visit the **Sala dei Notari,** containing interesting 13th-century frescoes, up the flight of steps across the fountain, for free.

At the end of the piazza rises Perugia's austere Gothic **duomo.** Though it was built in the 14th and 15th centuries, the façade was never finished. (Typically, the Perug-ini were going to use some marble they stole from Arezzo's cathedral-building sup-ply during a battle, but the Aretini made them give it back when they won the next round.) Fifteenth- to 18th-century embellishments of varying quality adorn the Gothic interior, but the town is most excited by the **Virgin Mary's wedding ring,** a relic they snagged from Chiusi in the Middle Ages. The ring is kept securely under lock and key—15 locks and keys, in fact.

Via dei Priori

Stroll along Via delle Volte della Pace (off Via Bontempi), which follows the city's old Etruscan walls; or follow Via dei Priori, which begins behind the palace, and Via San Francesco past the church of the same name, to the spartan **Oratory of San Bernadino,** near the end of Via dei Priori. Agostino de Duccio built it between 1457 and 1461 in the early Renaissance style, embellishing its façade with finely carved reliefs and sculpture. Inside a 3rd-century Roman sarcophagus forms the altar. Next door, only the pink-and-white façade of the 13th-century **San Francesco al Prato,** where San Bernadino used to stay, remains.

A medieval walk down Via Ulisse Rocchi, the city's oldest street, will take you through the northern city gate to the **Arco di Augusto,** a perfectly preserved Roman arch built on Etruscan pedestals and topped by a 16th-century portico.

Past the newly cleaned **Palazzo Gallenga,** at the end of a little byway off medieval Corso Garibaldi, lies the jewel-like **Church of Sant'Angelo.** The 5th-century church is the oldest in Perugia; the circular interior incorporates 16 columns appropriated from various ancient buildings. The small park in front of it makes for an alluring pic-nic spot. Behind the church, the gate **Porta Sant'Angelo** was built by the Perugian *condottiere* Braccio Fortebraccio ("arm strong-arm").

The East Side

At the opposite end of town from the Porta Sant'Angelo, near Via Cavour, towers the imposing **Church of San Domenico,** the largest in Umbria. The church's huge Gothic rose window (the largest in Italy) dramatically contrasts with the sobriety of its Renaissance interior. Don't miss the magnificently carved **Tomb of Pope Bene-dict XI,** finished in 1325, in the chapel to the right of the high altar; his bones lie in a box tied with a red ribbon on the wall. Next to the church, the **Museo Archeolog-**

ico Nazionale dell'Umbria occupies the old Dominican convent and showcases Etruscan and Roman artifacts. (Open Tues.-Sat. 9am-1:30pm and 2:30-6pm, Sun. 9am-1pm. Admission L4000.) Continue on Corso Cavour, past the Porta San Pietro, and you'll come to the **Church of San Pietro.** It maintains its original 10th-century basilica form: a double arcade of closely spaced columns leads to the choir. Inside, the walls (and visitors) are overwhelmed by paintings and frescoes depicting scenes of saints and soldiers; amidst the mass of paint, look for Perugino's *Pietà* along the north aisle. (Churches open 8am-noon and 3:30pm-sunset.)

At the far end of Corso Vannucci, the main street leading out from P. IV Novembre, lie the **Giardini Carducci.** These well-maintained public gardens are named after the 19th-century poet Giosuè Carducci, who wrote a stirring ode to Italy inspired by Perugia's historic zeal for independence. From the garden wall you can enjoy a broad vista of the Umbrian countryside: a castle or an ancient church crowns each hill. On the corner of the street below the gardens, a semi-circular lookout point shows you in which direction you're gazing and names the monuments in view. Go around the gardens and down Via Marzia to see the **Rocca Paolina,** the 16th-century fortress built by Sangallo, long a symbol of papal oppression; its interior juxtaposes Italian antiquity and dubious modern art. Pope Paul III had Sangallo demolish this section of the city in the 1500s in order to create this prison. In 1860, when Perugia was liberated from the rule of the Papal States and became part of the now-unified Italy, the Perugini spontaneously began hacking it to pieces. Today it serves as a pleasant and fanciful escalator-shelter surrounded by the remains of this medieval quarter. The **Porta Marzia,** the Etruscan gate in the city wall, opens onto Via Bagliona Sotterranea. This street within the fortress is lined with 15th-century houses that were buried when the gardens were built above. (Gate open Tues.-Sat. 8am-2pm, Sun. 9am-1pm.) The Rocca is also accessible by the escalator, which runs from 6am until 1am.

ENTERTAINMENT

Perugia's biggest annual event is the glorious **Umbria Jazz Festival,** which draws performers of international renown for 10 days in July. (Admission L15,000-35,000. Some events free.) For information, contact the tourist office.

July and August bring **Estate in Levare,** a series of musical, cinematic, and dance performances. In September a **Festival of Sacred Music** features concerts in various churches. Check Palazzo Gallenga for listings of English films and other events. The two most popular places for drinks are the two *caffè* called **La Terrazza,** one in P. Matteotti and one below P. Grimana by the University for Foreigners.

■ Lake Trasimeno

This placid and somewhat marshy lake, 30km west of Perugia, is the ideal spot to enjoy some arcadian tranquility while watching fishers mend their nets in the hamlets along the shore. Things have not always been so peaceful; in 217 BC, Hannibal's elephant-straddling army, fresh from the Alps, routed the Romans on the plain north of the lake. The names of the villages of Ossaia (place of bones) and Sanguineto (the bloody one) recall the carnage that left 16,000 Roman troops dead.

In the summer, landlocked Umbria becomes so stiflingly hot that splashing in the murky waters of Trasimeno can actually be pleasant. Getting to Castiglione del Lago (on the west shore) and Passignano sul Trasimeno (on the north) is simple. Each day, several buses depart Perugia's P. Partigiani for both lakeside towns (L8400 round-trip). **Passignano sul Trasimeno** is easily reached by bus or train (Perugia-Florence line). You may consider circling through both towns via train (L3300), ferry (L6500), and then bus back to Perugia. The **Pro Loco** (tourist office) is at Via Roma, 38 (tel. (075) 82 76 35) overlooking the peaceful city park (make a left if you're coming from the dock; go across the tracks and take a left if coming from the station). Here you'll find maps, hotel listings, and boat schedules. (Open Mon.-Wed. and Fri.-Sat. 9am-noon and 4-7pm, Thurs. and Sun. 9am-noon.) **Hotel Beaurivage,**

Via Pompili, 3 (tel. (075) 82 73 47) has spic'n'span doubles for L33,000, with bath L52,000. **Hotel Aviazione,** Via Roma, 54 (tel. (075) 82 71 62) has the same for L44,000, with bath L60,000. It also offers **bike rental** (1hr. L5000, ½day L10,000, full day L20,000). (Hotel open Dec.-Oct.) Boats leave from the dock for Isola Maggiore (28 per day, 20min., L4500, round-trip L8500). Food in both towns is expensive; plan a picnic on the lakeshore.

Follow in St. Francis's footsteps and spend a delightful day on **Isola Maggiore,** Lake Trasimeno's only inhabited island. A capriciously opened and staffed **tourist information booth** is by the dock. If no one's there, just take a good look at the large map of the island on the other side of the dock. As you leave the dock, take a right and follow the path to the tip of the island (being careful not to squish the green-brown salamanders who will accompany you) to the ruined **Guglielmi castle.** A bit further on is a tiny chapel enclosing the hard rock where St. Francis spent 40 days in 1211. From here, hike five minutes up to the **Chiesa di San Michele Arcangelo,** with a wonderful view of the island. (Open Sun. 10:30am-noon and 3-6pm.) **Castiglione del Lago,** a quiet town appropriately crowned by a castle, is accessible only by road or water. From the bus stop, a flight of steps ascends to the town center. The **tourist office** P. Mazzini, 10 (tel. (075) 96 52 484), will help you find a hotel (singles from L40,000, doubles from L52,000), a room in a private home, or a private flat (from L190,000 per week). You can also **change money** and get boat schedules here. (Open Mon. 8am-1:30pm, Tues.-Fri. 8am-1:30pm and 3-7:30pm, Sat. 8:30am-1pm and 3-7:30pm, Sun. 9am-1pm.) For food, try the shops lining Via Vittorio Emanuele, or hop into **Paprika,** Via Vittorio Emanuele, 107, whose local specialties include *spaghetti al sugo d'anguilla* (spaghetti with eel sauce from the lake). (Open Fri.-Wed. noon-2:30pm and 7:30-10pm.) Take Viale Garibaldi down to the dock, where eight boats daily make the ½-hr. trip to Isola Maggiore, the largest of the lake's three islands (L3300, round-trip L6400).

■ Assisi

Oh Lord, make me an instrument of your peace
—St. Francis of Assisi

Assisi's serenity originates in the legacy of St. Francis, a 12th-century monk who generated a revolution in the decadent Christian church of his time. He founded the Franciscan order, devoted to an unusual combination of asceticism, poverty, and chastity while promulgating what Francis taught as the abundance of the divine in this world. Present-day Assisi has become a center for Italian youths, who converge on it for conferences, festivals, and other religious activities. The young Franciscan nuns and monks who are the primary inhabitants of this city carry on his legacy with a kind of spiritual vigor as they fill the *piazze*, churches, and monasteries of the city; where Catholic youth sing songs accompanied by guitar-playing monks as they aim to become instruments of St. Francis' teachings.

ORIENTATION AND PRACTICAL INFORMATION

Towering above the city to the north, the **Rocca Maggiore** can help you re-orient yourself with a glance should you become lost among Assisi's winding streets. The center of town is **Piazza del Comune,** with Via Portica and Via Seminario connecting to the **Chiesa di San Francesco** toward the west end, and Corso Mazzini leading to the **Chiesa of Santa Chiara** in the opposite direction.

Tourist Office: P. del Comune, 12 (tel. 81 25 34), 1 doorway to left of the SIP. Information and accommodations service. Staff is not too enthusiastic and the map they provide misses many of the street names in Assisi. Ask about upcoming musical events. Open Mon.-Fri. 8am-2pm and 3-7pm, Sat. 9am-1pm and 4-7pm, Sun. 9am-1pm. Train and bus schedules posted outside. Beware: the tourist office on Corso Mazzini is actually a travel agency.

Post Office: P. del Comune. Open Mon.-Fri. 8am-7pm, Sat. 8am-1pm, Sun. 8am-12:30pm. **Postal Code:** 06081.

Telephones: SIP, P. del Comune, 11. The most beautifully frescoed phone building in the world. Open daily 8am-10pm; off-season 8am-7pm. **Telephone code:** 075.

Trains: Assisi lies on the Foligno-Teróntola **train line,** 30min. and L2400 from Perugia. At Teróntola change for Florence (L14,100); change at Foligno for Rome (L13,700) or Ancona (L11,300). Buses run from the station, below the town near the Basilica of Santa Maria degli Angeli, to the town (every ½hr., L1000).

Buses: ASP buses to Perugia (8 per day, L4200), Foligno (8 per day, L2000), and other surrounding hamlets, leaving from P. Matteotti. From P. Matteotti, walk down Via San Rufino past the *duomo* to P. del Comune.

Swimming Pool: Centro Turistico Sportivo, Via San Benedetto (tel. 81 29 91). Take the bus from P. del Comune. Open late July-Aug. daily 9:30am-7pm. Admission L6000.

Emergencies: tel. 113. **Police: Carabinieri,** P. Matteotti, 3 (tel. 81 22 39). **Hospital:** (tel. 81 391), on the outskirts. Take a city bus from P. del Comune. **First Aid:** tel. 81 28 24.

ACCOMMODATIONS

Reservations are crucial around Easter, and strongly recommended for the Festa Calendimaggio (early May) and in August. If you walk the few kilometers uphill to the hamlet of **Fontemaggio** along the road to Eremo delle Carceri, you will find a **youth hostel** and **campground** (tel. 81 36 36) offering single-sex, 10-bed rooms. The showers are hot, and there's a large market right next door. (Hostel L15,000 per night. Sheets included. Campground L6000 per person, L4500 per tent, L2000 per car. Open year-round.) The recently re-opened **Ostello della Pace (HI),** offers spanking new beds and breakfast for L16,000. (Lock-out 10am-5pm. Curfew 11pm.) If you prefer to be in town, ask the tourist office for a list of **religious institutions.** These are peaceful and cheap, but they shut down around 11pm.

Albergo La Rocca, Via di Porta Perlici, 27 (tel. 81 22 84). Follow the signs to the *duomo,* and then take the second cobblestoned street to the left of the *duomo* as you face it. A great choice away from the crowds. Commodious, attractive rooms. Singles L24,000. Doubles L41,000, with bath L56,000.

Alunni Camere Maria Bocchini, Via dell'Acquario, 3 (tel. 81 31 82), off P. Matteotti, very close to Albergo La Rocca. The house is up the stairs by the archway. Signora Alunni Bocchini welcomes with a motherly smile. Clean, cool rooms. Singles L30,000. Doubles L40,000.

Camere Maria Fortini, Via Villamena, 19 (tel. 81 27 15). Right on the main drag by P. Matteotti. Not marked as a *camere.* An assortment of colorful flowers on the front steps. Singles L30,000. Doubles L42,000, with bath L55,000.

Albergo Anfiteatro Romano, Via del Teatro Romano, 4 (tel. 81 30 25), off P. Matteotti. A large restaurant with modern rooms in a picturesque section of town. Romantic views. Singles L29,000. Doubles L38,000, with bath L60,000. Showers included.

St. Anthony's Guesthouse of the Franciscan Sisters of the Atonement, Via Alessi, 10 (tel. 81 25 42). The American sisters treat you like family. No room for asceticism here—the rooms are far too comfy. Gorgeous views of the town, a library full of English-language books, a garden, an orchard, and a relaxing terrace. 2-night minimum stay encouraged. Curfew 11pm. Singles L38,000. Doubles with bath L64,000. Breakfast included. Lunch L16,000. Open mid-March to mid-Nov.

FOOD

Assisi tempts you with a sinful array of nutbreads and pastries; *bricciata umbria,* a strudel-like pastry with a hint of cherries, is particularly divine. The **bakery** at P. del Comune, 32, offers the widest selection, but the **Pasticceria Santa Monica,** nearby at Via Portica, 4, boasts more palatable prices. (open 7am-1:15pm and 4-8pm). On

Saturday mornings there's a **market** on Via San Gabriele and Via Alessi. For well-made *panini* and picnic basics try **Micromarket Baldoni,** Via Fortabella, 61, near P. Unità and San Francesco. (Open Mon.-Sat. 8am-1pm and 3:30-8pm; closed Thurs. afternoon.)

Pizzeria Manzi Vincenzo, Via San Rufino, on the left immediately off P. del Comune. Endearing artist shows you his provocative sociopolitical paintings while feeding you the best pizza in Assisi. Slices L1500-3000. Open daily 8am-2pm and 4-7:30pm.

Ristorante La Fortezza, Vicolo della Fortezza, 2B (tel. 81 24 18), near P. del Comune. Reputedly the best restaurant in town. The award-winning meals include their homemade paté for an appetizer, then the *piccione alla fortezza* (pigeon). Full meals run L20,000-35,000, but *primi* start at L9000. Open daily noon-2:30pm and 7-9:30pm. AmEx, MC, Visa.

Trattoria Spadini, Piazza Chiara (tel. 81 30 05). Dine under low, white arches in a medieval Tuscan space now occupied by a single trattoria. Tourist menú (L18,500). Open Mon.-Sat. noon-3pm and 7-10pm.

Pallotta, Via San Rufino, 4 (tel. 81 23 07), near P. del Comune. A medieval atmosphere overseen by a graceful proprietor. Try their specialty *strangozzi alla pallotta* (pasta with mushrooms and olives, L8500). *Menù,* including wine and dessert, L20,000. Open Wed.-Mon. noon-2:30pm and 7-9:30pm.

SIGHTS

St. Francis, born in 1182, abandoned military ambitions at age 19 and rejected his father's wealth to embrace asceticism. His repudiation of the worldliness of the church, his love of nature, and his devoted humility earned him a huge following throughout Europe, posing an unprecedented challenge to the decadent papacy. He continued to preach chastity and poverty until his death in 1226, whereupon the order he founded was gradually co-opted by the Catholic hierarchy. The result was the paradoxical glorification of the modest saint in churches named for him and for his follower St. Clare, founder of the Poor Clares, the female order of the Franciscan movement.

The enormous and lavishly frescoed **Basilica di San Francesco** bears witness to this conflict of integrity and bureaucracy. When construction began in the mid-13th century, the Franciscan order protested: Francis had adhered to a stark asceticism, and the elaborate church seemed an impious monument to wealth. As a solution, Brother Elia, then vicar of the order, insisted that a double church be erected—the lower level built around the saint's crypt, the upper as a church for services. The subdued art in the lower church commemorates Francis's modest life, while the upper church pays tribute to his sainthood and consecration. This two-fold structure subsequently inspired a new Franciscan architecture.

The walls of the church are almost completely covered with Giotto's *Life of St. Francis* fresco cycle, dramatically lit from the windows above. Giotto's early genius is evident in his illustration of Francis's turbulent path to sainthood, which starts on the right wall near the altar and runs clockwise, beginning with a teen-aged Francis in courtly dress, surprised by a prophecy of his future greatness. The cycle closes with an image of the saint passing through the mystical agony of the "Dark Night," stripping himself of the clothes his father had bought him, signifying a break with his former life. The final stage of his approach to God occurs in the 19th frame, where St. Francis receives the stigmata. Sadly, Cimabue's frescoes in the transepts and apse have so deteriorated that they look like photographic negatives. Most frescoes and sculptures have "History Tell" machines; it costs L1000 to view the history of each work.

Pietro Lorenzetti adorned the left transept with an outstanding *Crucifixion, Last Supper,* and *Madonna and Saints.* Above the altar four sumptuous allegorical frescoes formerly attributed to Giotto are now thought to be the work of the so-called "Maestro delle Vele." Cimabue's magnificent *Madonna and Child, Angels,* and *St.*

Francis grace the right transept. Best of all are Simone Martini's frescoes in the first chapel off the left wall, based on the life of St. Martin. Descend through a door in the right side of the apse to a room that houses some of St. Francis's possessions: his tunic, his sandals, and sundry flesh-mortifying instruments. The precious piece which inspired the entire edifice, St. Francis's tomb, lies below the lower church (the steps to it are marked by a sign in the middle of the right aisle.) St. Francis's coffin was hidden in the 15th century for fear the war-mongering Perugians would desecrate it; it was only rediscovered in 1818. The stone coffin sits above the altar in the crypt, surrounded by the sarcophagi of four of his friends. (Mass in English in the upper church Sun. 8:30am. Tours in English of the whole structure Mon.-Sat. at 10am and 3pm; meet in front of the entrance to the lower church. Both churches open daily 6:30am-7pm, closed on Holy Days. Dress codes here are much more strictly enforced than in most Italian churches. No photography, no miniskirts, no shorts and no revealing shirts allowed—fashion police abound.)

Don't bypass the modern, well-lit **Museo Tesoro della Basilica,** with its graceful 13th-century French ivory *Madonna and Child,* 17th-century Murano glass work, and a fragment of the Holy Cross. (Open April-Oct. Tues.-Sun. 9:30am-noon and 2-6pm. Closed on holy days. Admission L3000.)

Via San Francesco leads away from the front of the Upper Church between Medieval buildings interspersed with 16th-century additions—note especially the **Sala del Pelegrino** (Pilgrim Oratory), frescoed inside and out. Via San Francesco boasts Italy's first public asylum, a 13th-century building at the corner of Via Fortebella. At the end of the street P. del Comune marks the old **Roman forum.** Here, bits of Roman Assisi alternate with buildings of the 13th-century commune. (Open daily 9:30am-1pm and 3-6:30pm. Admission L2500, students with university ID L1500. For non-students, a good deal is the *biglietto cumulativo* which allows entry into the forum, the Rocca Maggiore, and the Pinacoteca, L6500.) As you come upon P. del Comune, you see the **Temple of Minerva,** with its compressed front, next to the Romanesque **torre.** The **Palazzo del Comune,** on the downhill side, contains the **Pinacoteca,** housing Umbrian Renaissance art. (Open daily 9:30am-1pm and 3-7pm, in winter daily 10:30am-1pm and 3-6pm. Admission L2500, university students L1500. Cumulative ticket L6500.)

Via San Rufino climbs steeply up from P. del Comune between closely packed old houses, opening onto P. San Rufino to reveal the squat **duomo** with its massive bell tower. (The restored interior may be a disappointment after the decorative façade.) For an ascendant treat, continue uphill on the cobblestoned street to the left of the *duomo* as you face it, and take the steps that branch off to the left. At the top is the towering, dramatic **Rocca Maggiore,** an essential light to visit if you're just here for the day. The Keep has been recently restored, and views from up top are unparalleled. (Open daily 9am-8pm; in winter 10am-4pm. Closed in very windy or rainy weather. Admission L3000, university students L1500. Cumulative ticket L6500.)

The pink-and-white **Basilica of Santa Chiara** stands at the other end of Assisi, on the site of the ancient basilica where St. Francis attended school. (Open Mon.-Sat. 6:30am-noon and 2-7pm; in winter until 6.) The **Oratorio di San Francesco Piccolino,** in the upper part of vicolo di Sant'Antonio, is purported to be built around the stable where St. Francis was born, and the **Chiesa Nuova** nearby marks the site of his family's home.

ENTERTAINMENT

All of Assisi's religious festivals involve feasts and processions. An especially long dramatic performance comprises **Easter Week.** On Holy Thursday, a mystery play based on the Deposition from the Cross is acted out, and then on Good Friday and Easter Sunday, traditional processions trail through town. Assisi welcomes May with the **Festa di Calendimaggio** on May Day. A queen is chosen and dubbed Primavera (spring), and the various neighborhoods compete in a noisy musical tournament. Classical concerts and organ recitals occur once or twice per week from April to

October in the various churches. October 4 is the **Festival of St. Francis,** when a different region of Italy offers the oil for the Cathedral's votive lamp each year; that region's traditional dances and songs are performed in local costumes. During July and the beginning of August, the **Festa Pro Musica** features internationally known musicians and opera singers. For details, look for posters or ask at the tourist office.

Near Assisi

Several churches associated with St. Francis and St. Clare stand in the immediate vicinity of town. If you travel to Assisi by train, you'll see the huge **Basilica di Santa Maria degli Angeli.** The basilica itself shelters the **Porziuncola,** the first center of the Franciscan order (though actually owned by the Benedictines, to whom the Franciscans still pay the yearly rent—a basket of carp). In order to overcome temptation, St. Francis supposedly flung himself on thorny rosebushes in the garden just outside the basilica, thus staining the leaves forever red. The site grew popular when St. Francis instituted the annual **Festa del Perdono** (Aug. 2), during which an indulgence was (and is) awarded to all who come to the church. When he died in the adjacent infirmary, now **Capella del Transito,** the chapel began to attract throngs of pilgrims, and a whole ring of supporting chapels sprang up.

A pleasant hour-and-a-half hike through the forest above the town leads to the most memorable and inspiring sight near Assisi, the **Eremo delle Carceri** (Hermitage of Cells). Pass through the Porta San Francesco below the basilica and follow Via Marconi. At the crossroads take the left road, which passes by the Seminario Regionale Umbro. The site of St. Francis's retreats, this placid area better conveys the spirit of St. Francis than the opulent basilica. Inside the hermitage you can see the small cell where he slept, and back outside see the stone altar where he preached to the birds. (Hermitage open daily dawn to dusk.)

A 15-minute stroll down the steep road outside Porta Nuova takes you to the **Convent of St. Damian,** where St. Francis received his calling, and later wrote the *Canticle of the Creatures.* The chapel contains fine 14th-century frescoes as well as a riveting woodcarving of Christ. (Open daily 10am-noon and 3-6pm.)

■ Gubbio

Since 1960, this acutely picturesque town has been home to the National Board of Ancient Towns, an organization dedicated to preserving and restoring Umbria's historic hamlets. Today, cranes swing over the scaffolded ancient stone walls in a desperate attempt to hold on to what once was. A strategic checkpoint on the Roman transapennine road Via Flaminia, Gubbio, founded as "Iuvium" by the ancient Umbrian tribe, had long drawn pilgrims to the temple of a mountain god identified with Jupiter. From early on, the city also cultivated a bellicose attitude, taking on a succession of intimidating opponents including Romans, Lombards, Perugians, and even Napoleon. In 1387 the Montefeltro forced Gubbio into the Urbino orbit, encouraging artistic endeavors to match martial ones. Gubbio claims Italy's first novelist, Bosone Novello Raffaelli, as well as its own school of painting and ceramic tradition. The dual legacy of art and war survives in the profusion of china and crossbows in the store windows.

ORIENTATION AND PRACTICAL INFORMATION

Despite winding Medieval alleyways and bizarre conglomerations of buildings, Gubbio's layout is simple. **Piazza della Signoria,** the civic headquarters, set on a ledge of the hill on which the town is built, forms the center of the web. Buses will leave you off in P. Quaranta Mártiri. A short uphill walk on Via della Repubblica, the street bordering the *Loggia dei Tiratori* (Weaver's Gallery), will connect you with Corso Garibaldi, where you can find the tourist office.

Tourist Office: Piazza Oderisi, 6 (tel. 927 36 93), off Corso Garibaldi next door to the local Communist Party headquarters. Extremely helpful staff. English spoken.

Open Mon.-Fri. 8:15am-1:45pm and 3:30-6:30pm, Sat. 9am-1pm and 3:30-6:30pm, Sun. 9:30am-12:30pm; off-season, Mon.-Sat. afternoon hours are 3-6pm.

Post Office: Via Cairoli, 11 (tel. 927 39 25). Open Mon.-Sat. 8:10am-7:15pm. **Postal code:** 06024.

Telephones: Easy Gubbio, Via della Repubblica, 13. This brand-new office has phones, train information, and other tourist amenities. **Telephone code:** 075.

Trains: There are no trains to Gubbio itself; the nearest station is at Fossato di Vico, 19km away on the Rome-Ancona line (L5700 from Ancona, L13,700 from Rome). Buses connect Gubbio and the station (Mon.-Sat. 10 per day, 6 on Sun., L2000). For tickets, go to **Clipper Viaggi,** in P. San Giovanni, 15 (tel. 37 17 48), the piazza up the hill from P. Quaranta Mártiri. Open daily 9:30am-1pm and 3:30-7pm.

Buses: Via della Repubblica, 13-15 (tel. 927 15 44). Ticket office open daily 7:15am-1:45pm. To Perugia (12 per day, 1hr., L6200).

Emergencies: tel. 113. **Police: Carabinieri,** Via Matteotti (tel. 927 37 31). **Medical Emergency:** tel. 92 391. **Hospital:** P. Quaranta Mártiri, 14 (tel. 92 391).

ACCOMMODATIONS AND FOOD

Gubbio is an easy day trip from Perugia or on the way to the coast. The town can be seen in a few hours, and an overnight stay will drain your wallet unnecessarily. If compelled to stay, look for *affitta camere* if you encounter a dearth of hotel rooms.

Albergo Galletti, Via Piccardi, 3 (tel. 927 42 47), off P. Quaranta Mártiri. Small and photogenic on the edge of Medieval Gubbio. Hospitable proprietor. Singles L33,000. Doubles L50,000, with bath from L64,000. May be closed 2-3 weeks in June/July.

Pensione Grotta dell'Angelo, Via Gioia, 47 (tel. 927 34 38), off Via Cairoli. The angelic owners offer seraphic rooms. Singles with bath L45,000. Doubles with bath L70,000. Open Feb.-Dec.

Albergo dei Consoli, Via dei Consoli, 59 (tel. 927 33 35), 100m from P. della Signoria toward P. Bruno. Ask for rooms with a view. Singles with bath L48,000. Doubles with bath L70,000. Open Feb.-Dec.

Hotel Gattapone, Via Ansidei, 6 (tel. 927 24 89), off Via della Repubblica. Well-furnished rooms with carpets. Vacancies likely. Singles L48,000. Doubles L70,000. All rooms with baths. Open Feb.-Dec.

Guard against expensive meals in excruciatingly quaint settings. Go for the *salumeria* at P. Quaranta Mártiri, 36, across from the bus station, which makes great sandwiches for around L2500. (Open daily 7:15am-1:15pm and 3:15-8pm). Tuesday morning, there's a **market** under the *loggie* of P. Quaranta Mártiri. Local delicacies await you at **Prodotti Tipici e Tartufati Eugubbini,** Via Piccardi, 17. Here you can sample *salumi di cinghiale o cervo* (boar or deer sausage) and *pecorino* cheese or pick up some truffle oil (so your truffles don't get sunburned). (Open daily 8:30am-1pm and 3:30-8pm.)

Trattoria Fiorella, Corso Garibaldi, 86 (tel. 927 21 65). Centrally located. Excellent food in a family atmosphere. Complete meals including wine, *primi, secondi,* and fruit L18,000 and a more exotic *menù* for the same. Open Tues.-Sun. 12:15-2:30pm and 7:30-9:30pm.

Ristorante Il Bargello, Via dei Consoli, 37 (tel. 927 37 24), in a little piazza down the road from P. della Signoria. Vaulted 14th-century ceiling, wine bottles lining the walls, pleasant management. Outstanding pizza L4000-8000; Full meals from L25,000. Open Tues.-Sun. noon-3pm and 7-10pm. Major credit cards accepted.

San Francesco e il Lupo, at the corner of Via Cairoli and Corso Garibaldi (tel. 927 23 44), near the Azienda. A homey place with lupine servings at ascetic prices. *Menù* L20,000. Open mid-July through mid-June daily noon-2:30pm and 7-9:30pm.

SIGHTS

The first sight that greets you as you get off the bus is a pompous Fascist monument, erected in 1927. A grim and muscle-bound soldier stands guard, in a nightmarish martial vision. The ironically juxtaposed **Garden of the Forty Martyrs** (Giardini dei Quaranta Mártiri) honors those shot in reprisal for the assassinations of two occupying officials during World War II.

In **Piazza della Signoria** the stark, empty feeling of the square is offset by the panoramic view over its ledge. To the right stands the **Palazzo dei Consoli,** one of Italy's most graceful public buildings. The pre-Renaissance white stone palace (1332) achieves an unpretentious harmony with its rows of asymmetric windows and arcades, its slender campanile, and square Guelph crenulations. Enter to examine the **Museo Civico's** idiosyncratic mix of stone sculpture and old coins, featuring the puzzling *Tavole Eugubine.* Discovered in 1444 near the Roman theater outside the city walls, these seven bronze tablets (300-100 BC) are the main source of our knowledge of the Umbrian language. Their ritual text spells out the social and political organization of early Umbrian society, while providing the novice with good hints on how to take auguries from the livers of animals. Upstairs visit the stately rooms of the **Pinacoteca Comunale,** an eclectic collection of paintings, wooden crucifixes, and 14th-century furniture. (Open daily 9am-12:30pm and 3:30-6pm; Oct.-April daily 9am-1pm and 3-5pm. Admission L4000.) Across the piazza stands **Palazzo Pretorio.** Climb to the top of the town, where the 15th-century **Palazzo Ducale** and the 13th-century **duomo** face off. Federico da Montefeltro commissioned Luciano Laurana, designer of his larger palace in Urbino, to build a miniature version here. The *duomo,* an unassuming pink Gothic building, boasts fine stained-glass windows (late 12th century) and Pinturicchio's *Adoration of the Shepherds*.

Via dei Consoli will take you to the **Bargello** and its fountain. This 13th-century edifice is just one of the many Medieval buildings still in use; others nearby include the 13th-century **Palazzo del Capitano del Popolo,** on the street of the same name, and the 15th-century **Palazzo Beni** on Via Cavour. Follow the narrow streets downhill that run parallel to the Camignano stream. When you arrive in P. Quaranta Mártiri, the **Church of San Francesco** stands to the right. The church was constructed on the site of the house of the Spadalonga family, friends of St. Francis who gave him a tunic, eventually the prototype for today's Franciscan frock. The central apse holds the splendid *Vita della Madonna* (Life of the Madonna), a partially-destroyed 15th-century fresco series by Ottaviano Nelli, Gubbio's most famous painter. Across the piazza is the **weaver's loggia,** under whose shady arcades the 14th-century wool weavers stretched their cloth so that it would shrink evenly.

Besides wool, Gubbio's main industry in the Middle Ages was ceramics. Some particularly fine examples lie in the Palazzo dei Consoli Museum. Pottery and antiques can be found at the **Antica Fabbrica Artigiana,** Via San Giuliano, 3 (near the Bargello), a cavernous old palace.

During lunch, when all the museums close, take the seven-minute bird-cage chairlift (*funivia*) to the peak of **Monte Ingino** for a splendid view and prime picnicking (round-trip L6000. Open July-Aug. Mon.-Sat. 8:30am-7:30pm, Sun. 8:30am-8pm; Sept. Mon.-Sat. 9:30am-7pm, Sun. 9am-7:30pm; Oct.-Feb. Thurs.-Tues. 10am-1:15pm and 2:30-5pm; June Mon.-Sat. 9:30am-1:15pm and 2:30-7pm, Sun. 9am-7:30pm.) While you're there, visit the **basilica and monastery of Sant'Ubaldo,** Gubbio's patron saint. The basilica houses the three *ceri,* the large wooden candles carried in the Corsa dei Ceri procession each May. On your way back to the center of town, stop at the **Church of Santa Maria Nuova,** near the funicular station, contains the lyrical *Madonna del Belvedere* by Ottaviano Nelli. Ask the custodian at Via Dante, 66, to let you in.

ENTERTAINMENT

Corsa dei Ceri (May 15), a 900-year-old tradition and one of Italy's most noted processions, witnesses the three *ceri,* hourglass-shaped wooden towers brought to P.

della Signoria from the basilica of Sant'Ubaldo. They are surmounted by wax statues of Sant'Ubaldo (in whose honor the festival is held), San Giorgio, and Sant'Antonio Abate. After 12 hours of flag-twirling and elaborate traditional preparations, squads of husky runners (*ceraioli*) clad in Renaissance-style tights heft the heavy objects onto their shoulders and race up Monte Ingino at a dead run. Making occasional pit stops for alcoholic encouragement, they eventually reach the basilica of Sant'U-baldo, and plop down the *ceri* for safe-keeping until the following May.

During the **Palio della Balestra,** held on the last Sunday in May, archers from Gubbio and nearby Sansepolcro gather in P. della Signoria for the latest installment of a fierce crossbow contest dating back to 1461. If Gubbio wins, an animated parade ensues. (Gubbio's major industry these days is the production of toy crossbows for *balestra*—tourists.)

■ Spoleto

Like its peers in Umbria and southern Tuscany, Spoleto offers a picturesque hilltop setting and almost unbearably charming medieval streets. The town's biggest draw, however, is its summer arts festival, the *Festival dei Due Mondi* (of the Two Worlds). The composer Gian Carlo Menotti selected Spoleto in 1958 to be the test site for his claim that art need not be merely the *dolce* after *pranzo* (sweet after dinner), but could become a community's bread and butter. His optimism has not been betrayed: Spoleto's transformation into an internationally renowned center for the arts has brought prosperity to the town. Prices run as high as the cutting-edge aesthetic sensibility that has spawned expressionist pizza parlors and abstract Mondrianesque one-star hotels. Art of all sorts explodes around the town in late June and usually lingers through the summer. If you wish to rub shoulders with the pretentious and artistically inclined, remember to reserve six months ahead.

ORIENTATION AND PRACTICAL INFORMATION

Spoleto is typically Umbrian in that its narrow, cobblestoned streets make it difficult to navigate. **Piazza del Mercato** is the social center of the city, with many shop-lined streets radiating off it. Via Brignone connects P. Mercato with **Piazza della Libertà,** home of the tourist office and city bus stop. The adjacent **Piazza del Municipio** and **Piazza del Duomo** which contain most of the city sights, are close to P. Mercato as well.

Tourist Office: P. della Libertà, 7 (tel. 22 03 11). A warm and savvy office with an excellent if unwieldy map. English spoken. Open daily 9am-1pm and 4:30-7:30pm; off-season 9am-1pm and 3:30-6:30pm.

Post Office: P. della Libertà, 12 (tel. 46 727). Open Mon.-Sat. 8am-12:30pm and 3-7:30pm. **Postal code:** 06049.

Telephones: During the festival, a **SIP** office appears on Via Brignone between p. Mercato and P. Libertà (open daily 10am-midnight). At other times, forage for phones in bars and hotels. **Telephone code:** 0743.

Trains: (tel. 48 516) in P. Polvani. From: Rome Via Orte (2hr., L10,500); Ancona (2½hr., L12,100); Perugia (10 per day, 1hr., L4400). From the station, take any orange bus to **Piazza della Libertà** and the tourist office (L1000); otherwise it's a ½hr. uphill trek. Ask for a free city map at the newsstand in the station.

Buses: from P. della Libertà and P. Garibaldi, except service to Urbino and Rimini, which leave Mon.-Sat. mornings in the summer from Via Flaminia (near the API gas station). 2 per day to Perugia and Assisi. Check at the tourist office for current schedules.

Emergencies: tel. 113. **Police: Carabinieri,** Via dei Filosofi, 57 (tel. 49 044). English-speaker available. **Hospital:** Via Loreto, 3 (tel. 21 01), outside Porta Loreto.

ACCOMMODATIONS AND CAMPING

Finding accommodations is difficult during the summer music festival. If you're organized enough to make reservations, do so as early as possible. Otherwise, the youth hostel in **Foligno** is an easy commute, as trains run all night long. Performances take place during the day, so getting back before curfew shouldn't infringe on your festival experience.

HI youth hostel, P. San Giacomo, 11 (tel. (0742) 52 882), in Foligno, 26km away. Curfew 11pm. L14,000 per person. Hot showers and breakfast included. Open March-Aug.

Camere Marcella Venanzi, Vicolo II°, 1 (tel. 44 050), off Corso Mazzini, 42. A private home with high ceilings, a delightful proprietor, and an optimal location. Singles L25,000. Doubles L40,000.

Albergo Anfiteatro, Via Anfiteatro, 14 (tel. 49 853). Whitewashed rooms with modern furnishings. Singles L37,000, with bath L55,000. Doubles L50,000, with bath L75,000.

Hotel Panciolle, Via del Duomo, 3-4 (tel. 45 598). Newly graduated from *camere* to hotel. Friendly management and modern facilities. Doubles with bath L80,000.

Fracassa, Via Focaroli, 15. Head toward the Roman Theatre, off Via del Gesuiti. 7 tidy rooms managed by a charming proprietor. Singles L27,000. Double L35,000.

Camping Monteluco (tel. 22 03 58), behind the church of San Pietro, a 15-min. walk from P. della Libertà. Take Viale Matteotti out to the tennis courts, then to the left across the highway. On the far side of the highway, take Via San Pietro to the church, to the left, and up the hill. A short distance past the church a dirt path branches to the right and leads directly to the campground. Pleasant and shaded. L6000 per person, L4500 per tent, L2000 per car. Open April-Sept.

Camping Il Girasole (tel. 51 335), next to a vast sunflower field (hence the name) near the small town of Petragnano. Hourly buses connect it with the train station. Quiet, with plenty of shade and hot showers. L7000 per person, L7000 per tent, L2000 per car. Price goes down for longer stays. Open Easter-Sept.

FOOD

An open-air market enlivens **Piazza del Mercato** Monday through Saturday from 8:30am to 1pm. At other times, try the **Lo Sfizioso** market at P. Mercato, 26 (open Fri.-Wed. 7:30am-1:30pm and 4:30-7:30pm).

Ristorante Pentagramma, Via Tommaso Martini, 4, off P. della Libertà, (tel. 37 233). The finest traditional restaurant cooks up only Umbrian specialties. *Zuppa di ceci* (chickpea soup, L9000). (Open Tues.-Sun. noon-2:30pm and 7-10pm.)

Trattoria Del Panciolle, Via del Duomo 3-4 (tel. 45 598). Simple country fare; full meals L18,000-25,000. Specialties include *caciotta,* a delectable local cheese (L5000). Some outside tables on a shady porch overlooking the tree-laden piazza. Open Thurs.-Tues. noon-2:30pm and 7:30-10pm.

Borgo In, Corso Garibaldi, 94 (tel. 22 21 91). Vivacious staff serves excellent calzones for L2200 apiece. *Primi* and pasta from L5000. Pizza from L2000. Open daily 7:30am-10:30pm.

Gelateria, Via Mazzini, across from Vicolo II° between P. della Libertà and San Filippo Church. The finest *gelato* in Umbria.

SIGHTS

Tucked on a ledge midway between the great papal fortress above and the Roman Anfiteatro below rests Spoleto's monumental Romanesque **duomo.** It was built in the 12th century and then augmented by a portico (1491) and 17th-century interior redecoration. An utter amalgam of styles and materials, its soaring bell tower was cobbled together from fragments of Roman structures and is held up by incongruous flying buttresses. Eight rose windows animate the façade, the largest of which bears the four symbols of the evangelists. Inside, brilliantly colored scenes from the life of the Virgin by Fra' Filippo Lippi fill the domed apse. Lippi died here while working on these frescoes. Lorenzo the Magnificent asked the Spoletini to send his body back, but with tourism waning from lack of noble corpses, Spoleto insisted on keeping it. Lorenzo could only commission Lippi's tomb, which lies in the right transept and was decorated by the artist's son, Filippino. (*Duomo* open 8am-1pm and 3-7pm, in winter 7:30am-noon and 3-5pm.)

Santa Eufemia, across the piazza to the side of the *duomo,* lacks both the stature and the frescoes of the latter; poor Eufemia never amounted to much in the eyes of the Vatican. The beautiful Romanesque church named for her, however, was built with Umbria's first *matronea* or "women's balconies." (Open 8am-8pm.)

Spoleto's many classical ruins testify to its prominence in Roman times. The first-century **theater** stands just outside the Roman walls, visible from P. della Libertà. Walk through the theater to the *loggia* next to it and then to the **Museo Archeologico,** with ceramic and statuary finds from the area. (Open Mon.-Sat. 9am-1:30pm and 3-7pm, Sun. 9am-1pm. Free.) The **Arco Romano** at the top of Via Bronzino marked the entrance to the town, and farther along, the **Arco di Druso** marked the entrance to the forum (now P. del Mercato). On nearby Via de Visiale you can enter a restored **Roman house.** (Open April-Sept. Mon. and Wed.-Sat. 9:30am-1pm and 3-7:30pm, Sun. 10am-1pm and 3-6pm, Tues. 3-7:30pm. Admission L2000; L5000 ticket includes admission to the Pinacoteca and Modern Art Museum as well.) Most of the Roman buildings have been recycled and their stones used to build churches, including **San Salvatore** (1km from the town center), one of the earliest surviving Christian churches in Italy, which retains some of its 4th-century architecture. (Open 7am-7pm; Oct.-May 7am-dusk.)

The **papal fortress,** or **Rocca,** sits on the hillside above Spoleto. The fortress, until recently a prison, was used during the war to confine Slavic and Italian political prisoners; in 1943 the prisoners staged a dramatic escape to join the partisans in the Umbrian hills. Follow the walk that curves around the fortress for panoramic views of Spoleto and the countryside. Farther on, you will reach one of the region's most stunning architectural achievements, the **Ponte delle Torri.** The 80m-high bridge and aqueduct, built in the 14th century on Roman foundations, spans the channel of the river Tessino. On the far bank rise the craggy Medieval towers for which the bridge was named.

On the far side of the bridge, take the left fork past elegant villas and ancient churches to **Monteluco,** Spoleto's "mountain of the sacred grove." An invigorating 1½hour climb through an ilex forest leaves you at the tiny Franciscan **Sanctuary of Monteluco,** once the refuge of St. Francis and San Bernadino of Siena. (Open May-Sept. 8am-1pm and 4-8pm. Buses leave P. della Libertà for Monteluco approximately every 1½hrs. when it's open. Ask at the newsstand for schedules and tickets; the bus costs L2000.) A five-minute stroll down the right fork brings you to the Romanesque **Church of San Pietro,** on whose tan façade a menagerie of bas-relief beasties appears, cavorting among cosmological diagrams and scenes from popular fables. Note the wolf wearing a monk's cowl and holding a book to the right of the door. Beyond the bestiary, you'll spot the remains of mosaics laid in the 5th century.

The **Museum of Modern Art** hosts exhibits of art displayed during the summer arts festival. From Corso Mazzini, turn left on Via Sant'Agata, then right on Via delle Terme. The museum lies ahead on your right. (Open Mon. and Wed.-Sat. 9am-1pm and 3-7:30pm, Sun. 10am-1pm and 3-6pm, Tues. 3-7:30pm. Admission with L5000 cumulative ticket.) **Pinacoteca** (art gallery) is located in the Palazzo del Municipio on the piazza of the same name. (Admission with L5000 cumulative ticket.)

ENTERTAINMENT

The **Festival dei Due Mondi,** held from mid-June and mid-July, has become one of Italy's most important cultural events. The festival features numerous concerts, operas, and ballets with performances by well-known Italian and international artists. Film screenings, modern art shows, and local craft displays abound. (Tickets L15,000-200,000; a few events are free. Purchase well in advance from travel agents in most large cities or by mail.) The opera season, which includes a number of modern and experimental works, runs from late August to September.

■ Near Spoleto: Trevi

Trevi, perched on a hilltop of olive trees about ½hr. north of Spoleto by train, is a delightful place to spend an afternoon. The town is a spectacular sight as one approaches, splaying in almost complete verticality along a hillside. In **Piazza del Comune,** the city center, you'll find the **Palazzo del Comune,** home to the **Pinacoteca Comunale.** The museum contains a replica, by Pinturicchio, of his *Madonna e Bambino,* now in London's National Gallery, as well as archaeological finds from the area. Halfway along the road to Trevi's center from the train station (2km) is the **Chiesa della Madonna della Lacrime.** The church is on the site of a house on whose wall a Mother and Child with St. Francis had been painted in 1483. Two years later blood-colored tears were seen on the image, inspiring the construction of first a chapel, then a temple, then finally a church on the site. Perugino's frescoed *Adoration of the Magi, Saints Peter and Paul,* and *Annunciation,* from 1521, decorate the interior. The **Illumination Procession,** a candle-lit parade through town in honor of St. Emiliano, is held on January 27 in Trevi, while during the first three weeks in August the town celebrates "Trevi in Piazza," with musical and theatrical performances in P. del Comune.

Trevi is easily reached by train from Foligno (L1100) or Spoleto (L1400). From the station, it's 4km uphill to town. Ten city buses run per day to town (L600), the last at 7:50pm; nine buses per day run to the station, the last at 7:30pm. There is no place at the train station to buy bus tickets, so run into the *tabaccheria* 50m uphill from the stop. The bus leaves you at P. Garibaldi; from there, take Via Roma to P. del Comune (also known as P. Mazzini). **Pro Trevi,** the information office, is at the far end of the piazza at #16; Trevi's **telephone code** is 0742.

Albergo Cochetto, (tel. 78 229) is off P. Comune/Mazzini down Via Dogali, and has well-furnished, if slightly overpriced, rooms. Singles run L34,000, with bath L52,000; doubles are L48,000, with bath L74,000. **La Cerquetta,** is found at Via Flaminia, km 144 (tel. 78 366). Singles are L28,000, with bath L38,000. Doubles run L42,000, with bath L56,000. **La Casarecchia,** P. Garibaldi, 19 (tel. 98 03 43), by rights a *pizzeria,* also rents out rooms (about L38,000 per person). (*Pizzeria* open Tues.-Fri. 9am-1:30pm and 3pm-midnight, Sat. 9am-midnight, Sun. 5pm-midnight.)

■ Todi

According to legend, an eagle led the founders of Todi to this destination when it absconded with a tablecloth to a rocky crag. Reclaiming it, the intrepid ancestors celebrated the recovery of their picnic set by establishing Todi in this aerial setting. History seems to have bypassed the steep, narrow streets of this isolated town; as a result it retains traces of its Etruscan, Roman, and Medieval past.

ORIENTATION AND PRACTICAL INFORMATION

In the Todi of today, there's barely room for cars, let alone eagles with tablecloths. All areas in the city which don't house an important sight (and some which do) seem to have transmogrified into parking lots. **Piazza del Popolo,** the center of town, houses the *duomo* and sundry *palazzi;* P. Jacopone and Umberto lie around the corner. Corso Cavour, Via Roma, Via Matteotti, and Viale Cortesi, form one street leading steeply downtown and out the ancient city walls to the hotels.

Tourist Office: P. del Popolo, 38 (tel. 88 31 58 or 894 25 26), under the stairs of the Palazzo del Capitano. Buy the map for L3000, since the photocopy they'll hand you is illegible. Open Mon.-Sat. 9am-1pm and 4-7pm, Sun. 9:30am-12:30pm and occasionally 4-6:30pm; in winter closed Sun. afternoon. They also have **telephones. Telephone code:** 075.

Post Office: P. Garibaldi (tel. 894 22 02). Open Mon.-Fri. 8:10am-6:25pm, Sat. 8am-noon. **Postal code:** 06059.

Trains: The private **Ferrovia Centrale Umbria** (Central Umbrian Railway) provides infrequent service to Todi from Perugia, via Spoleto and Terni. City bus B runs to the station 15min. before every train; it'll carry you the 4km up to the town center (L1000).

Buses: ASP runs 7 buses per day to P. Jacopone from Perugia (80min., L4600). The last bus for Perugia departs at 5pm from the Church of Santa Maria della Consolazione, a 1km pleasant downhill walk from the town's center.

Emergencies: tel. 113. **Police: Carabinieri,** Via Angelo Cortese (tel. 894 23 23). **Hospital: Ospedale degli Infermi,** Via Matteotti (tel. 88 34 47).

ACCOMMODATIONS AND FOOD

Hotels in Todi are expensive, scarce, and inconveniently located. The **Hotel Zodiaco,** Via del Crocefisso, 23 (tel. 894 26 25), outside Porta Romana, has singles for L32,000 and doubles for L45,000, with bath L70,000. Further down the hill, **Hotel Tuder,** Via Maestà dei Lombardi, 13, off Via Cortesi (tel. 894 21 84), proffers luxurious doubles with bath for L92,000. Both of these hotels lie along a busy highway; be careful walking here at night.

Pick up basics at the *alimentari* at Via Cavour, 150. (Open Mon.-Sat. 7:45am-1:30pm and 5:30-8:30pm, closed Wed. afternoon.) Fresh fruit and veggies are at the **Frutta e Verdura market** on the corner of P. Jacopone (open Mon.-Wed. and Fri.-Sat. 7am-1:30pm and 4-8pm, Thurs. 7am-1:30pm).

AgriTodi, Via San Lorenzo, 1 (tel. 894 23 96). Facing the *duomo* in P. del Popolo, take the small street to the right under the portico. Not only do they have the most interesting menu, but they also have the lowest prices in town. *Bruschette* L3000-8000, *primi* L7000-8000, *secondi* L7000-10,000. Lots of local wines for sale. Open Dec.-Oct. Wed.-Mon. 10:30am-2:30pm and 4:30-10pm.

Ristorante Cavour, Via Cavour, 21-23 (tel. 894 24 91). Excellent, filling meals L22,000. Pizza around L5000. Specialty is *tortellini al tartufo nero* (with black truffles, L10,000). Try to get a seat in the cool medieval dungeon. Open Feb.-Dec. Thurs.-Tues. noon-3pm and 7:30-9:30pm for meals, until 2am for pizza. Am Ex.

Bar 'Icopertio, Via G. Matteotti, 120 (tel. 894 39 57). For those who wish to avoid the exorbitant expense of full-fledged restaurant dining. It's a trip downhill from P. Jacopone for delicious pizza, lasagna, *bruschette,* fried vegetables, etc. L10,000 for a healthy portion of 2 items.

SIGHTS

Piazza del Popolo is a stately ensemble of glowering palaces and a somber *duomo;* the square's air of authority is only slightly diminished by the cars which whiz around its edge. This piazza has been Todi's focal point since Roman times and remains its high point in altitude and architectural achievement. The **Palazzo del Capitano** (1290) stretches its cavernous portico across the east end of the piazza with peaked Gothic windows on the second floor, lending relief to the imposing façade. (Open 10am-12:30pm, 4-8pm.) The **Pinacoteca Civica** occupies the fourth floor; keep climbing for the fascinating frescoes in the **Sala del Capitano del Popolo** at the top of the exterior marble staircase. Huge wooden arches soar across the immense hall. The adjoining **Palazzo del Popolo** with its distinctive crenulated profile was begun in 1213. Across the piazza from the *duomo,* the tower and façade of the **Palazzo dei Priori** (1297-1337) retain visages of medieval gloom despite the rows of Renaissance windows carved out in the early 16th century.

Directly across the piazza the rosy-faced **duomo** rests solidly atop a flight of broad stone steps. The central rose window and arched doorway command attention with their intricate decoration. Inside, Romanesque columns with Corinthian capitals support a plain wall punctuated by slender windows. The delicate Gothic side arcade, added in the 1300s, shelters an unusual altarpiece: the Madonna's head emerges in high relief from the flat surface of a painting. A strangely halcyon scene

ORVIETO

of the Last Judgment (16th century) occupies the church's back wall. (*Duomo* open daily 8:30am-12:30pm and 2:30-6pm.)

Neighboring **Piazza Garibaldi** opens to a superb vista. On the right side of the *piazza* stands the Renaissance **Palazzo Atti** with a sadly deteriorated façade but beautiful rusticated stone corners. From the piazza, follow the signs leading off Corso Cavour to the remaining walls of the **Foro Romano** and the nearby 12th-century **Chiesa di S. Ilario.** From here, it's a brief jaunt to the **Fonti Scarnabecco,** whose 13th-century porticoes still house one solitary working tap. Return to P. del Popolo and take Via Mazzini to the majestically angular **Church of San Fortunato.** Built by the Franciscans between the 13th and 15th centuries, the church boasts Romanesque portals and a Gothic interior. The story of the sacrifice of Isaac decorates the space between the first and second columns to the right of the door. Note Masolino's fresco of the Madonna and angels.

To the right of San Fortunato, a path bends uphill toward **La Rocca,** a ruined 14th-century castle. Next to the castle, follow a sinuous path, appropriately named **Viale della Serpentina,** to a breathtaking belvedere constructed on the remains of an old Roman wall. Further down stands the isolated Renaissance **Church of Santa Maria della Consolazione.**

The **Mostra Nazionale dell'Artigianato** (National Exhibit of Crafts) takes place in August and September. For some years there has also been a national exhibit of antique and modern woodwork in April, since Todi, after all, is home to some of the finest woodcarvers in Italy. The city's most colorful festival is the **Mongolfieristico,** a three-day hot-air balloon show which occurs in mid-July. For information, contact the tourist office.

■ Orvieto

Set atop a volcanic plateau, the town of Orvieto lies hidden from the rolling farmlands of southern Umbria. The dark closeness of its streets recall its origin as one of the cities of the Etruscan *Dodecapolis*, but it is the medieval legacy that colors the city more strongly today. A papal refuge from the Middle Ages through the Renaissance, Orvieto reached its historical peak in the 13th century. While Thomas Aquinas lectured in the local academies, Crusades real and imagined were planned within the city walls. A well-preserved medieval center provides the backdrop for the stunning 13th-century *duomo*, which has rewarded Orvieto's piety with touristic fame and wealth. Oenology has held special import for the region since it saved the city from a Barbarian sack in the early centuries. Local lore tells us that marauders stealing off with precious chalices from the ancient temples were amazed when their booty transmogrified into "liquid gold"—actually the local wine. Nonplussed, the barbarians partook of the miracle until they were quite drunk and the locals drove them down the city cliffs. Sample the product that saved the city, the excellent white *Orvieto classico* wine.

ORIENTATION AND PRACTICAL INFORMATION

Orvieto lies midway on the Rome-Florence line. From the train station, cross the street to take the funicular up the volcano. When you reach the top you can walk up **Corso Cavour** to the city center (10 min.) or take a **shuttle** to Piazza del Duomo. (Funicular departs every 15 minutes, L1000, with shuttle L1300.) Corso Cavour is the town's backbone, site of most of the city's restaurants, hotels, and shops. Via Duomo branches off C. Cavour and ends at P. del Duomo.

Tourist Office: P. del Duomo, 24 (tel. 417 72). Friendly staff seems frazzled but patient. Get the incredibly complete pamphlet on hotels and restaurants, sights, and practical information. Complete information on trains and buses; city **bus tickets** for sale. Open Mon.-Fri. 8am-2pm and 4-7pm, Sat. 10am-1pm and 4-8pm, Sun. 9am-8pm. Also has **telephones. Telephone code:** 0763.

Post Office: Via Cesare Nebbia which begins after the Teatro Mancinelli, next to Corso Cavour, 114 (tel. 412 43). **Stamps** are available at tobacco shops and mail drops dot the town. Open Mon.-Sat. 8:15am-6:40pm. **Postal code:** 05018.

Trains: To Florence (L13,800); Rome (L10,500); and Perugia (L8800). **Luggage Storage:** L1500.

Buses: ACOTRAL, P. Cahen. 7 per day to Viterbo (L4500). **ACT,** P. Cahen, 10 (tel. 419 21). To: Perugia (L10,700) and Todi (L7700). Buy tickets at the *tabacchi* up Corso Cavour or on the bus.

Emergencies: tel. 113. **Police:** P. della Repubblica (tel. 400 88). **Hospital:** P. del Duomo (tel. 30 91).

ACCOMMODATIONS

Da Fiora, Via Magalotti, 22 (tel. 411 19), just off P. della Repubblica through small P. dell'Erba (take minibus B to Erba). The best deal in town. Not technically a hotel; the proprietress rents private rooms. Modest but spotless. Prices go down in winter. Singles L20,000. Doubles with bath L40,000. If it's full, she'll make up beds on the couch or floor for L10,000 per person.

Hotel Posta, Via Signorelli, 18 (tel. 419 09), near the Torre del Moro, between Corso Cavour and P. Scalza. Great location. Leafy garden and pleasant lobby. Curfew 11:30pm. Singles L35,000, with bath L50,000. Doubles L50,000, with bath L70,000. Closed sporadically for vacation Dec.-Feb. Call first.

Hotel Duomo, Via Maurizio, 7 (tel. 41 887), off Via Duomo. *Really* great location. Tall windows spill light across marble floors and dark wood furniture. Singles L33,000, with bath L50,000. Doubles L45,000, with bath L74,000.

Camping Orvieto (tel. (0744) 95 02 40), on Lake Corbara 14km from the center of town. Call from the station and they'll pick you up. Swimming pool and hot showers included. L7500 per person, L6500 per tent, L2500 per car. Open Easter-Sept.

FOOD

Most of the fixings will fix you for broke. At least the wine is cheap. An excellent *alimentari* sits below P. della Repubblica at Via Filippeschi, 39 (open Mon.-Tues. and Thurs.-Sat. 7:30am-1:30pm and 5-8pm, Wed. 7:30am-1:30pm).

Cooperativa al San Francesco (tel. 433 02), on Cerreti off Via Lorenzo Maitani off the front side of P. del Duomo. Follow the large signs, your nose, or the crowd. Extremely popular with locals. A huge restaurant, self-service cafeteria, and *pizzeria* all rolled into one. Cheap and wholesome. Dine at outdoor tables on a peaceful piazza or indulge in the cavernous interior. Pizza (at night only) and wine L11,000. Full meals L14,000. Open daily noon-3pm and 7-11pm. All brands of credit cards accepted.

Da Fiora, Via Magalotti (tel. 411 19). Just below her rent-a-room residence, Signora Fiora has established a bustling restaurant enterprise with the best deals in town. Pasta, meat, and beer or wine (L12,000) will fill you as you take in a spaghetti Western on TV or enjoy the company of what appears to be the local Boys' Club.

SIGHTS AND ENTERTAINMENT

The shuttle bus drops you off in P. del Duomo. The first glance at the 1290 **duomo** (Orvieto's fervor and pride) promises to be overwhelming: its fanciful façade, intricately designed by Lorenzo Maitani, dazzles and enraptures the admirer with intertwining spires, mosaics, and sculptures. The bottom level features exquisitely carved bas-reliefs of the Creation and Old Testament prophecies, and a final panel of Maitani's realistic *Last Judgment*; the bronze and marble sculptures (1325-1964) emphasize the Christian pantheon, set in niches surrounding the rose window by Andrea Orcagna. The fabulous mosaics provide a day-long performance of light and shadow. Thirty-three architects, 90 mosaic artisans, 152 sculptors, and 68 painters worked for over six centuries to bring the *duomo* this far, and the work continues; the bronze doors were only installed in 1970. The cathedral's 700th anniversary two years ago provoked a flurry of restoration that has left its masterpieces better than ever, among them the **Capella della Madonna di San Brizio** (sometimes called the **Capella Nuova**) off the right transept (and, sadly, undergoing lengthy restoration). Inside are Luca Signorelli's dramatic **Apocalypse frescoes,** considered to be his *chef d'oeuvre.* Begun by Fra Angelico in 1447, they were supposed to be completed by Perugino, but the city grew tired of waiting and enlisted Signorelli to finish the project. His mastery of human anatomy, dramatic compositions, and vigorous draftsmanship paved the way for the genius of Michelangelo. On the left wall hangs the *Preaching of the Antichrist.* The prominent Renaissance dandy in a shimmering crimson costume to the left of the Antichrist is the painting's patron; behind the bald man to the patron's left is the red-hatted poet Dante. The woman with the outstretched hand on the other side is Signorelli's mistress, seen as a prostitute engaged in the basest act imaginable to a good Catholic of the day—taking money from a Jew. Behind her stand Columbus, Petrarch, Cesare Borgia, and Dante (again). Far off in the corner, Signorelli and Fra Angelico, in black, observe the proceedings. On the opposite wall, muscular humans and skeletons pull themselves out of the earth in the uncanny *Resurrection of the Dead.* Beside it is the *Inferno*, with Signorelli (a blue devil) and his mistress embracing beneath the fiery display. In the **Cappella del Corporale** off the left transept, Lippo Memmi's *Madonna dei Raccomandati* hangs with abashed pride. This chapel also holds the gold-encrusted **Reliquary of the Corporale** (chalice-cloth), the *raison d'être* of the whole structure. The cloth inside the box caught the blood of Christ which dripped from a consecrated host in Bolsena in 1263, thereby substantiating the doctrine of transubstantiation, which the papacy was still having some trouble putting over. (The *duomo* is open all year 7am-1pm, but the afternoon hours vary each month—2:30-5:30pm is a safe bet. Free.)

The austere 13th-century **Palazzo dei Papi** (Palace of the Popes) sits to the right of the *duomo.* Here, in 1527, Pope Clement VII rejected King Henry VIII's petition to annul his marriage with Catherine of Aragón, condemning both Catherine and English Catholicism to a dim prospect. Now the *palazzo* houses the **Museo Archaeologico Nazionale,** where you can examine Etruscan artifacts from the area, and even walk into a full-size tomb. (Open Mon.-Sat. 9am-1:30pm and 3-7pm, Sun. 9am-1pm. Free.) Across from the *duomo*, the **Museo Claudio Faina,** in the "Museo Civico" building, harbors more Etruscan finds. (Closed indefinitely for restoration.)

A 10-minute walk down Via del Duomo and then Via Constituente puts you in P. Capitano del Popolo. Here, the 13th-century **Palazzo del Capitano del Popolo** sports the standard motif of Romanesque Orvieto architecture: a checkerboard band surrounding its windows. Return to Corso Cavour and continue through P. della Repubblica into Orvieto's **medieval quarter.** The soils of the verdant slope below P. San Giovanni are enriched by the graves of thousands who perished in the Black Death of 1348. Drop by the small church **San Lorenzo de Arari,** with dozens of luminous frescoes and an Etruscan altar beneath its Christian successor.

On the eastern edge of town, down Via Sangallo off P. Cahen, you can descend the **Pozzo di San Patrizio** (St. Patrick's Well). Having fled just-sacked Rome, Pope Clement VII wanted to ensure that the town did not run out of water during a siege, and in 1527 commissioned Antonio da Sangallo the Younger to design the well. (Open daily 9:30am-7pm; in winter daily 10am-6pm. Admission L6000, L10,000 includes the Museo Greco.) After cooling off in the clammy well shaft, enter the **Fortezza,** where a fragrant sculpture garden and lofty trees crown battlements overlooking the Umbrian landscape. (Open 7am-8pm, Oct.-March 9am-7pm.)

For the most complete tour of Etruscan Orvieto, consider the **Underground City Excursions** departing from the tourist office. Speleological guides lead groups on a labyrinthine path past tunnels, quarries, cellars, wells and cisterns that were dug from the tufa 3000 years ago. (Tour lasts 1½hrs., L10,000.)

On Pentecost (42 days after Easter), Orvieto celebrates the **Festa della Palombella.** Small wooden structures filled with fireworks and connected by a metal wire are set up in front of the *duomo* and the Church of San Francesco. At the stroke of noon, the San Francesco fireworks are set off, and a white metal dove shoots across the wire to ignite the explosives. **Concerts** are held in the *duomo* on August evenings. In June, the **Procession of Corpus Domini** celebrates the Miracle of Bolsena.

Near Orvieto: Civita

Civita, not just another quaint town teeming with tourists, is slightly off the beaten path but well worth the hike. Literally a one-horse town, Civita is crammed onto the pinnacle of a small mountain, accessible via foot-bridge from Bagnoregio (take a bus from Orvieto, 30min., L3000 round-trip; last bus returns at 5:20pm) or by a path through the valley between the two mountain towns. Civita's residents (all 20 of them) will invite you into their backyards or basements where you can see their private collections of Etruscan and Roman relics for a small fee. Take a picnic lunch or dine in the lone café.

TUSCANY (TOSCANA)

The archetypal Italy springs from Tuscany. Its landscapes, familiar from Renaissance paintings, mix sere ochres with groves of holly and olive trees, lines of cypresses and parasol pines. Grapevines and sunflowers follow the contours of the hills that roll from the rocky, forested Apuan Alps to the sea and the hills of the south. Its towns, often walled, preen upon the heights, quintessential hill towns. Its Renaissance culture—an unprecedented explosion of art, architecture, and humanist scholarship—became the culture of Italy, while Tuscan, the language of Dante, Petrarch, and Machiavelli, is today's textbook Italian.

Despite its appearance of eternal eminence, everything of importance in this region occurred within one outstanding half-millennium. A backwater in both Etruscan and Roman times, the region was far from the center of succeeding barbarian kingdoms. Toward the end of the 10th century, increasingly powerful local aristocrats wrested control of towns, creating the free *comuni,* independent city-states. Many of the fortifications that surround Tuscan towns today first sprang up during this period of upheaval. In the 1100s, the free *comuni* of Tuscany began to engage in their two most characteristic activities: inter-city warfare and artistic production, with the Renaissance emerging out of the glorious mayhem. The bubble burst in the early 16th century, when the rich, leisured Tuscans, who had long since left their warfare to hired hands *(condottiere)*, fell to the invading armies of the French and the Habsburgs. The entire region was then placed under the rule of the Medici, a family of bankers that ruled republican Florence for a century and presided over Tuscany's descent from the apex of the High Renaissance into a cultural and political non-entity. Protected by their centuries of irrelevance, the cities and towns of Tuscany remain almost unchanged.

The region has only one drawback: it's too popular. Though Tuscans are generally very gracious, your English may induce sighs from natives, especially in Florence. Efforts to speak Italian, however mangled, will be much appreciated.

An extensive and convenient transportation system makes it easy to tour Tuscany's countryside. The state railroad serves all major towns and many smaller ones, though the many hill towns are better reached by bus. Hitching is not uncommon in the area, although *Let's Go* never recommends hitchhiking. Given the ease of transportation and the overcrowding of sightseers, plan your itinerary wisely. Florence, Siena, and Pisa are unmissable; consequently, no tourist misses them. Once you've seen them, consider devoting a little time to three of the most hospitable and beautiful of Tuscan cities: Montepulciano, Cortona, and northern Lucca. The only area to avoid is the unattractive coast. To list all of the Tuscan hilltowns worth visiting would take a book twice this size, so we've only included the larger and more historically and culturally significant places; if you plan an extended stay in the region, exploring on your own will lead you to innumerable towns crowning hills and clustering in valleys. If you ask in almost any restaurant, they'll tell you who lets rooms.

Youth hostels abound in Tuscany, but hotels are on the expensive side. Reservations are advisable all summer, especially in Florence, Siena, and Pisa. Camping is possible at the many lakes, mountains, and coastal resorts.

As familiar as Tuscany seems visually, its cuisine may surprise you: neither southern pasta and tomatoes nor northern *risotto* and *polenta* are staples of the Tuscan table. White beans *(fagioli)* are a regional obsession, so join locals and enjoy them in everything; tasteless Tuscan bread, however, is best eaten when hidden in such local concoctions as *crostini* (roasted bread topped with liver pate or cheese). Other local specialties include *ribollita* (bean and cabbage stew) and *fiori di zucca fritti* (fried zucchini flowers). Meat dishes include *coniglio* (rabbit), *trippa* (tripe), *lepre* (wild hare), *cinghiale* (wild boar), *salsicce* (grilled sausages), and the famous and costly beef steak *bistecca alla fiorentina.* Tuscany's gastronomic triumph, however, is its wine. The region's most popular is *chianti,* from the area around Florence and Siena. Tuscany's premier red wine, however, is the expensive *brunello di Montalcino.* A unique Tuscan wine is *vin santo,* a sweet, sauternes-like wine made from grapes hung in lofts to dry for several months before being crushed; drink it as Tuscans do—with a plateful of *cantuccini di Prato* (crispy almond cookies) for dipping.

■■■ FLORENCE (FIRENZE)

Fiorentius, the city that flowers, was the Roman name granted this city, presaging according to many Florentines, its protagonist role in the flowering of artistic genius during the Renaissance. Medieval Florence saw many monastic orders establish churches here to serve as community centers for the rapidly growing population. Fueled by an innovative banking system, the city evolved from a booming, 13th-century wool and silk trading town into the archetype of political experimentation and artistic rebirth. Periodic civil wars disrupted Florentine civic life until the ascendancy of the Medici clan and their establishment of peace in the 15th century under Lorenzo the Magnificent. From this period Renaissance culture, locating its epicenter in Florence, began its most splendid years of production. At its apex in the mid-15th century, Florence was the unchallenged European capital of painting, sculpture, architecture, medicine, astronomy, physics, commerce, and political thought.

Since the Renaissance, Florentines have sculpted the city's character with a sensibility of denouement: to maintain their self-identity as cultural protagonists they devote their energies to preserve the city's Renaissance heritage and quietly discourage other cultural art forms from encroaching here. Florentines are by and large resigned to the constant inundation of tourists but the 20th-century deluge of commercialism should not divert the visitor's appreciation from the city's incomparable heritage.

ORIENTATION

Florence is easily accessible by train from Milan, Bologna, Venice, and Rome. From the Stazione Santa Maria Novella, it is a short walk on Via de' Panzani to the center of Florence. This area, the heart of the city, is bordered by the *duomo* in the north, the Arno River in the south, and the Bargello and Palazzo Strozzi in the east and west.

Major arteries radiate from the *duomo* and its two *piazze:* **Piazza San Giovanni** encircling the baptistry and **Piazza del Duomo** around the cathedral. The city's main street, **Via dei Calzaiuoli,** runs from between the baptistry and the *duomo* to **Piazza Signoria** in the direction of the river Arno. Parallel to Via dei Calzaiuoli on the west, **Via Roma** leads from Piazza S. Giovanni through **Piazza della Repubblica** (the city's largest open space) to the **Ponte Vecchio,** which spans the Arno to the district called the **Oltrarno.** Parallel to Via dei Calzaiuoli on the east, Via del Pronsolo runs to the **Badia** and the **Bargello**. Heading north (away from the river) om P. S. Giovanni, Borgo San Lorenzo runs to **Piazza San Lorenzo** and parallel ia dei Servi to **Piazza SS. Annunziata.**

For guidance through Florence's tangled center, pick up a free map (ask for the ne with the street index) either inside the station from the booth marked *Infor-uazioni Turistiche Alberghiere* or just outside at the red and white tourist booth. A nore detailed map is the *Litografia Artistica Cartografica* (L3000 at newsstands).

Artistic and historical sights are scattered throughout Florence, but the city's com-actness ensures that few sights lie out of the pedestrian's range. Orange ATAF city uses will ferry foot-weary sightseers most everywhere. Florence's streets are num-ered in red and black sequences. Red numbers are for commercial establishments, vhile black numbers (occasionally blue) denote residential addresses (including nost sights and hotels). Black addresses will appear here as a numeral only, while ed addresses are indicated by a number followed by an "r." The two sequences lmost never coincide (28 black might abut 86r); if you get to an address and it's not vhat you're looking for, then you've probably got the wrong color.

As in the rest of Italy, most establishments close for two to four hours in the after-oon. On major holidays, including the festival of Florence's patron saint San Gio-anni (June 24), everything but the occasional *bar* will close.

For entertainment information, consult the monthly *Firenze Spettacolo* (L2500), old at newsstands. Hotels, hostels, and most restaurants and tourist information ureaus distribute free copies of *One, Three, Five...Days in Florence,* a slim publica-ion chock-full of museum hours, musical events, and friendly suggestions.

▶RACTICAL INFORMATION

Tourist Offices: Consorzio I.T.A. (tel. 28 28 93) in the train station by track #16, next to the pharmacy. Give them a price range and they will find you a room, though perhaps not the best value and probably near the station. No booking by phone. You pay the first night's rent plus a L3000-5000 commission. Open daily 8:30am-9pm. **Azienda Promozionale di Turismo (APT) offices** at Chiasso Bar-oncelli, 19r (tel. 230 21 24), and at Via Cavour, 1r (tel. 27 60 382) and at Via Man-zoni, 16 (tel. 247 81 41). Open Mon.-Sat. 8am-7pm. Other offices at Piazzetta Guelfa, 3 (tel. 28 40 15) and Via Martelli, 6 (tel. 21 38 93.) Open Mon.-Sat. 9am-3pm. **Consortium Italian Tourist Association,** Viale Gramsci, 9a (tel. 247 82 31). **Informazione Turistica,** at the red and white booth outside the train station (exit by track #16). Officially open daily 8am-9pm; in practice their hours can be sporadic. **Associazione Cattolica Internazionale al Servizio della Giovane** (tel. 29 46 35), by track #1 in the train station. Free accommodations service.

Budget Travel: S.T.S.-Student Travel Service, Via Zanetti, 18r (tel. 28 41 83). Sells student discounted train, plane, and bus tickets. Open Mon.-Fri. 9:30am-12:30pm and 3:30-6:30pm, Sat. 9:30am-12:30pm.

Consulates: U.S., Lungarno Vespucci, 38 (tel. 239 82 76), at Via Palestro near the station. Open Mon.-Fri. 8:30am-noon and 2-4pm. **U.K.,** lungarno Corsini, 2 (tel. 28 41 33). Open Mon.-Fri. 9:30am-12:30pm and 2:30-4:30pm. Call the U.K. Embassy in Rome for after-hours emergencies (tel. (06) 475 55 51). Canadians, Australians, and New Zealanders only have representatives in Rome and Milan.

Currency Exchange: Local banks have the best exchange rates. Open Mon.-Fri. 8:20am-1:20pm and 2:45-3:45pm. A number of banks are open Sat. morning until ll:20am. **Cassa di Risparmio di Firenze** now has automatic tellers that will exchange money at Via de' Bardi, 73r; Via de' Tornabuoni, 23r; Via degli Speziali, 16r; and Via dei Servi, 40r. Open 24hrs.

American Express: Via Dante Alighieri, 20-22r (tel. 50 981). From the *duomo,* walk down Via Calzaiuoli; turn left onto Via dei Tavolini. Am Ex is on the little piazza at its end. Cashes personal checks for cardholders. They also hold mail (free for card and checkholders, L3000 per inquiry—whether you have mail or not—for everyone else). L3000 to leave messages. L10,000 to forward mail. Does not accept wired money. Open Mon.-Fri. 9am-5:30pm, Sat. 9am-12:30pm. Also has a **branch office,** Via Guicciardini, 49r (tel. 27 87 51), across the Ponte Vec-

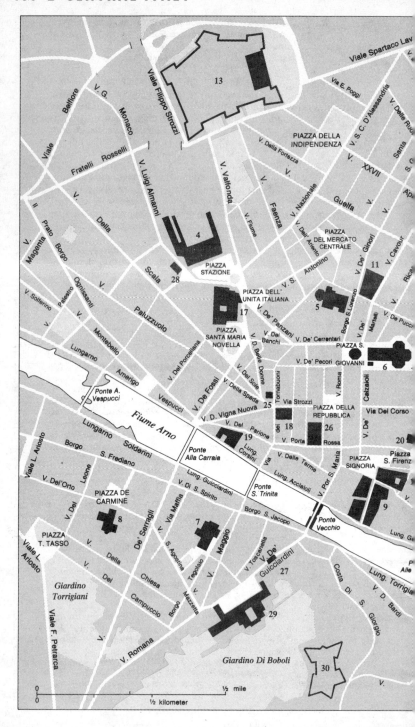

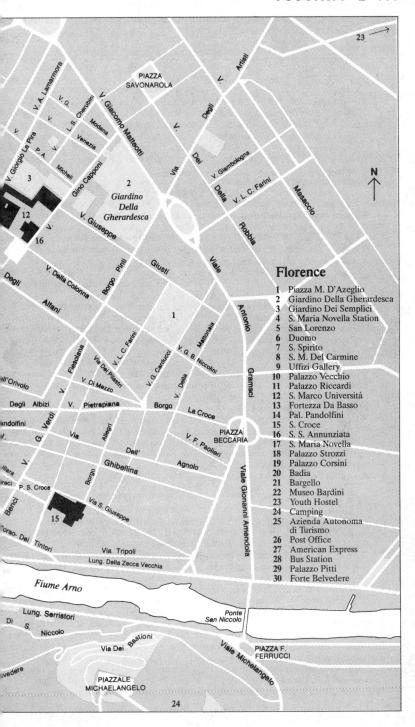

PIAZZA
SAVONAROLA

Giardino
Della
Gherardesca

Florence

1   Piazza M. D'Azeglio
2   Giardino Della Gherardesca
3   Giardino Dei Semplici
4   S. Maria Novella Station
5   San Lorenzo
6   Duomo
7   S. Spirito
8   S. M. Del Carmine
9   Uffizi Gallery
10 Palazzo Vecchio
11 Palazzo Riccardi
12 S. Marco Università
13 Fortezza Da Basso
14 Pal. Pandolfini
15 S. Croce
16 S. S. Annunziata
17 S. Maria Novella
18 Palazzo Strozzi
19 Palazzo Corsini
20 Badia
21 Bargello
22 Museo Bardini
23 Youth Hostel
24 Camping
25 Azienda Autonoma
    di Turismo
26 Post Office
27 American Express
28 Bus Station
29 Palazzo Pitti
30 Forte Belvedere

PIAZZA
BECCARIA

Fiume Arno

Ponte
San Niccolo

Lung. Serristori

Di   S. Niccolo

Via Dei   Bastioni

PIAZZA F.
FERRUCCI

PIAZZALE
MICHAELANGELO

Viale Michelangelo

FLORENCE

chio from the old city down Via de Guicciardini on the left. If you pass the Palazzo Pitti, you've also passed the office. Financial services and rail reservations only. Open Mon.-Fri. 9am-5:30pm.

Post Office: (tel. 21 61 22), on Via Pellicceria off P. della Repubblica. Stamps at windows #21 and 22; Fermo Posta at windows #23 and 24. To send packages, go to the back of the building to Via dei Sassetti, 4. Open Mon.-Fri. 8:15am-7pm, Sat. 8:15am-noon. **Telegram** office in front open 24hrs. **Postal Code:** 50100.

Telephones: ASST, Via Pellicceria, (tel. 21 41 45) at the post office. Make international collect calls here. Open 24hrs. Phones also at Via Cavour, 21r. Open daily 9am-9pm; winter 9am-8pm. **SIP,** in the train station near track #5 with phone books available. Lines usually shorter than at ASST. 1 booth available for international calls. Open daily 7:30am-9:30pm. Buy the phone cards here rather than the ones at the newsstand at the train station which often do not work. **Telephone code:** 055.

Fax/Photocopy: Firenze Riproduce, Via Pietrapiana, 70r (tel. and fax 248 09 22). Send and receive for around L3000 a page plus phone costs. Open Mon.-Fri. 9am-1pm and 3-7:30pm, Sat. 9am-1pm but fax receives calls 24hrs. a day.

Flights: Amerigo Vespucci Airport, Florence. Via del Termine, 1 **Peretola** (tel. 37 34 98 or 31 80 00, fax 31 87 16). SITA runs regular buses to the airport from Via S. Caterina da Siena, 157 (tel. 48 36 51). **Galileo Galilei Airport,** tel. (050) 500 707, in Pisa. Take the airport express (1hr., L6300) from the Florence train station (every hr., 5:55am-8pm). In Florence, call for flight information (tel. 27 88) or ask at the "air terminal" (tel. 21 60 73) at platform #5 in the Florence train station, where you can also check in, register baggage, and get an embarkation card for L2500 (open daily 7am-8pm).

Trains: Santa Maria Novella Station, near the center of town. Information office (tel. 27 87 85) open daily 9am-5pm. You can also use the bright-yellow (English-speaking) computers outside the office to plan your trip. Do not buy phone cards here (see Telephones, above). Every hr. to: Bologna (1hr., L7200, *rapido* supplement L2700); Venice (3½hr., L18,700, *rapido* supplement L6400); Milan (3½hr., L22,000, *rapido* supplement L9300); and Rome (2½hr., L22,000). Almost all trains arrive here except a few trains to and from Rome, which use the **Campo di Marte** station on the east side of town. Bus #19 connects the 2 stations about every 20min. around the clock (25min.).

Metropolitan Transport: City buses (ATAF), P. del Duomo, 57r (tel. 58 05 28). Tickets (L1100 for 70min., L1600 for 2hr., 8 60-min. rides L8000 (8 per day), 24-hr. ticket L5000) must be bought *before boarding* and are available at the train station or at *tabacchi*. L34,100 fine for ticketless passengers. Bus routes are posted at stops; for a comprehensive map go to the ATAF booth in the railway station. Metropolitan bus #7 serves Fiesole.

Buses: SITA, Via Santa Caterina da Siena, 15r (tel. 48 36 51 Mon.-Fri., 21 14 87 Sat. and Sun.). Frequent buses to Siena (2hr., L8300), Volterra (6 per day, L9000), San Gimignano (13 per day, L7100), Greve (1 per hr., L3000), and Poggibonsi (many, L5300). **CAT,** P. Stazione, 15 (tel. 28 34 00), to Arezzo (7 per day, 9:30am-6:30pm, 2hr, L6000). **CAP,** Via Nazionale, 4 (tel. 21 46 37), to Prato (L2400). **LAZZI,** P.Via Stazione 4-6r, (tel. 21 51 54), to Pisa (L8700), Prato (L2400), Lucca (L7100), and Pistoia (L4000). **LAZZI Eurolines** to Rome, Naples.

Bike and Moped Rental: Promotourist, Via B. Bandinelli, 43 (tel. 70 18 63). **Program,** Borgo Ognissanti, 135r (tel. 28 29 16). **Ciao and Basta,** Via Alamanni, under the Central Station (tel. 21 33 07). **MotoRent,** Via S. Zanobi, 9r (tel. 49 01 13). Bikes start at L7000 per 3hr., L15,000 per day. Mountain bikes run about L30,000 per day. Mopeds begin at L5000 per hr., L30,000 per day, L180,000 per wk. No license necessary, but bring ID indicating you are at least 16.

Hitchhiking: Hitchers take the A-1 north to Bologna and Milan or the A-11 northwest to the Riviera and Genoa, or take bus #29, 30, or 35 from the station to the feeder near Peretola. For the A-1 south to Rome and the extension to Siena, they take bus #31 or 32 from the station to exit #23, Firenze Sud. As always, **hitchhiking is extremely risky;** *Let's Go* **does not recommend hitching.** The **International Lift Center,** Corso Tintori, 39 (tel. 28 06 21), matches passengers with drivers for a fee. Open Mon.-Sat. 9am-7:30pm, Sun. noon-3pm.

Lost Property: For objects left on a train, go to the **Ufficio Oggetti Rivenuti** in the train station (tel. 235 21 90). Otherwise, the **Ufficio Oggetti Smarrito,** Via Circondaria, 19 (tel. 36 79 43). If your car gets towed, call **Parco Auto Requisite,** Via dell'Artovata, 6 (tel. 35 52 31). They're right next to each other. Take bus #23 (A, B, or C) from the station. Open Mon.-Wed. and Fri.-Sat. 9am-noon.

English Bookstore: After Dark, Via del Moro, 86r (tel. 29 42 03), near P. Santa Maria Novella Book-swap (see Shopping). Sells *Let's Go* for L3000 less than anywhere else (L30,000). Open Mon.-Sat. 10am-1:30pm and 3-7pm, Sun. 3-7pm; in Aug. 10am-1pm. **Paperback Exchange,** Via Fiesolana, 31r (tel. 247 81 54). Open Mon.-Sat. 9am-1pm and 3:30-7:30pm; mid-Nov. to mid-March closed Monday. **BM Bookstore,** Borgo Ognissanti, 4r (tel. 29 45 75). Open Mon.-Sat. 9am-1pm and 3:30-7:30pm, Sun. 9am-1pm; Nov.-Feb. closed Sun.

Library: Biblioteca Marucelliana, Via Cavour, 43, a communal library 2min. from the *duomo.* Open Mon.-Fri. 8am-1pm and 4-7pm, Sat. 8am-1pm. **Biblioteca Storia dell'Arte,** Via della Pergora, 37, a beautiful library concentrating on the history of art. Open Mon.-Fri. 8am-2pm. The largest in Florence, **Biblioteca Nazionale,** P. D. Cavalleggeri, requires you to go through a time-consuming bureaucratic process but the reading rooms are beautiful and one can request books from the extensive collection. Open Mon.-Fri. 9am-7pm and Sat. 9am-1pm.

Bulletin Boards: Listings of people seeking Anglophone roommates, English teachers, baby-sitters and notices of Anglophone religious, musical, and theatrical activities: **CarLie's American Bakery,** Via Brache, 12r (tel. 12 51 37), near Via dei Neri. Open Sept.-July 15 Mon.-Sat. 8am-noon and 4-7pm. **The American Church,** Via Rucellai, 16 (tel. 29 44 17), near the train station off Via della Scala. Open Mon., Wed., Fri. 9am-12:30pm and Sun. 9-11am. The **British Institute,** Via Tornabuoni, 2, between P. Santa Novella and P. della Repubblica. **The Paperback Exchange,** (see Bookstores above). **La Raccolta,** Via Leopardi 10 (tel. 247 90 68). A center for alternative activities with listings for roommates, apartments, activities (i.e. demonstrations) and classes.

Ticket Agency: Box office at Via della Pergola, 10r (tel. 24 23 61, fax 234 02 57). Advance booking for shows, concerts, and theater. Open Mon.-Sat. 10am-8pm.

Laundromat: Wash and Dry Lavarapido, Via dei Servi, 105, two blocks from the *duomo.* Self-service L3000 per kg. **Elensec,** Via dei Neri, 46r (tel. 28 37 47), near P. San Remigio. L3000 per kg. Open Mon.-Fri. 8:30am-1pm and 3:30-7:30pm. **Lavaria Express,** P. S. Pier Maggiore. L3000 per kg. Open Mon.-Fri. 8:30am-1pm.

Public Toilets: upstairs in the Mercato Centrale, in the Palazzo Vecchio, in the Palazzo Pitti, and in the train stations.

Public Baths: Bagno S. Agostino, Via S. Agostino, 8 (tel. 28 44 82), off P. Santo Spirito. Bath L3000. Soap and towel L1500. Open Tues. and Thurs. 3:30-6:45pm, Sat. 8:30am-noon and 3:30-6:45pm. Another option is to ask at a *pensione* near the station, where an understanding proprietor may let you shower for about L5000.

Gym: Gymnasium, Via Palazzuolo, 49r (tel. 29 33 08). Latest in workout equipment, daily step aerobics, body building, and stretching classes. L15,000 to enter for one day. L120,000 for ten admissions. Sauna available by appointment to soothe those sore limbs, L12,000 per sitting. **Tai Chi, Yoga** and similar classes offered at **La Raccolta,** Via Leopardi 10 (tel. 247 90 68). See its descriptions under the food section.

Swimming Pools: Bellariva, Lungarno Colombo, 6 (tel. 67 75 21). Bus #14 from the station or a 15-min. walk upstream along the Arno. Open June-Sept. daily 10am-6pm. Free. **Costoli,** Viale Paoli (tel. 67 57 44), in a huge sports complex at Campo di Marte. Take bus #17 from P. Unità toward the *duomo.* Arrive early. Open daily 10am-6pm. Admission June-Sept. L6000, children L2000, over 60 free.

Late-Night Pharmacies: Farmacia Comunale (tel. 28 94 35), at the train station by track #16. **Molteni,** Via Calzaiuoli, 7r (tel. 28 94 90). **Taverna,** P. S. Giovanni, 20r (tel. 28 40 13). All open 24hrs.

Medical Assistance: Misericordia, P. del Duomo, 20 (tel. 21 22 22 or 21 95 55). They will send an ambulance. **Tourist Medical Service,** Via Lorenzo il Magnifico, 59 (tel. 47 54 11). A group of general practitioners and specialists with someone on call 24 hrs. Around L80,000 for a home visit. Sometimes they give out advice over the phone. **Medical First Aid:** tel. 47 48 91. **Drug Addiction Service:** tel. 48 30 10. A list of French- and English-speaking doctors is available from the U.S. consulate.

Emergency: tel. 113. **Police: Questura** (headquarters), Via Zara, 2 (tel. 49 771). On weekends or after hours go around the corner to Via Duca D'Aosta. English-speaking personnel usually available. **Ufficio Stranieri** (for visa, work-permit, or passport problems), at the same address and phone number. **Fire:** tel. 115.

ACCOMMODATIONS

Florence abounds with one-star *pensione* and private homes with *affitta camere,* so no matter when you arrive, the search for accommodations shouldn't leave you in a bind. If you arrive late in the afternoon, check with the accommodations service at the train station; they'll know who still has room and at what prices. Many reputable hotel proprietors including those listed in this book may approach you when you disembark at the train station. Check their review in a hotel listing: this is a convenient way to be assured of a room. For L3000 or so, they will also reserve a hotel room for you. The best places go early, so reservations (*prenotazioni*) are wise, especially if you plan to visit at Easter or in summer. The vast majority of *pensioni* prefer to take reservations in the form of a letter with at least one night's deposit in the form of a postal money order, either in dollars or lire. From June to August, and around Easter, there's almost no chance you will find any space in the best lodgings without prior reservations (with a deposit). Calling a day or so in advance may make things easier, but remember that without a deposit most hotels will only hold reservations until noon. Also realize that it is good form and important for their business to show up if you have called ahead, or to cancel if you can't make it. This simple courtesy avoids untold aggravation not only for proprietors but also for hapless travelers who otherwise may be turned away. Be sure to check out by the time listed on the door and to tell the proprietor as early as possible when you plan to leave so they can accept reservations from other guests. It is considered polite to leave L1000 per day on the pillow for the person who cleans your room. While this practice is not always followed, use your own discretion. If you have any complaints talk first to the proprietor, and then to the **Ufficio Controllo Alberghi,** Via Cavour, 37 (tel. 27 601).

Sleeping in Florence's train stations, streets, or parks is a poor idea and police discourage it.

The city's best budget lodgings can be found at **Pensionale Pio X** and **Istituto Gould** in the Oltrarno, but clean and inexpensive lodgings are dispersed throughout the city. **Long-term housing** can be secured rather easily in Florence. If you plan on staying a month or more, check the classified ads in *Le Pulce,* a bi-weekly paper (L3500) that has apartment, sublet, and roommate listings. Prices range from L350,000-800,000 a month. If you only want to stay a month, try and strike a bargain with someone who's looking for a roommate; they might be willing to take someone short term while seeking a permanent roommie. Also check the **bulletin boards** (see Practical Information).

Hostels

Istituto Gould, Via dei Serragli, 49 (tel. 21 25 76), across the river in the Oltrarno. Leave the station by track #16, turn right and walk to P. della Stazione. Go straight ahead down Via degli Avelli, with the church Santa Maria Novella on your immediate right. Cross P. Sta. Maria Novella and continue straight down Via dei Fossi, over the Ponte alla Carraia, and down Via dei Serragli (15min.). Or take bus #36 or 37 from the station to the 1st stop across the river (more trouble than walking). One of the best lodgings in Florence: accommodating staff is happy to answer questions and the sunny rooms are spotless. Altruistic spirits will find satisfaction in staying here—all the profits go to support a local orphanage. There are only two drawbacks: it's impossible to check in or out on Sundays (the office is closed) and the rooms overlooking the street are often noisy. Open Mon.-Fri. 9am-1pm and 3-7pm, Sat. 9am-1pm. Singles L35,000, with bath L38,000. Doubles L50,000, with bath L54,000. Triples with bath L69,000. Quads with bath L84,000. (Lone travelers can take a bed in a quad for L18,000.) Sheets and towels included. Rooms are scarce during the academic year. Reserve 3-4 months in advance with deposit in spring. Arrive by 8am to get in line for a room.

Pensionato Pio X, Via dei Serragli, 106 (tel. 22 50 44). Follow the directions to the Istituto Gould (above) then walk a few more blocks down the street. Quiet, no daytime lock-out, gregarious management, only 4 or 5 beds per room. Clean rooms and bathrooms. 2-day min. stay, 5-day max. stay. Check-out 10am. Curfew midnight. L18,000 per person; showers included, but L3000 more for a room with bath. No reservations. Usually full in summertime, but turnover is high. On weekends arrive before 9am.

Ostello della Gioventù Europa Villa Camerata (HI), Via le Augusto Righi, 2-4 (tel. 60 14 51), northeast of town. Leave the station by track #5, then take bus #17B (20-30min.). You can also take this bus from P. del Duomo. In a gorgeous villa with *loggia* and gardens. Tidy and popular, though far away. Reception open Mon.-Fri. 9am-1pm and 3-7pm. Check-out 9am. Curfew midnight. L18,000 per person. L14,000 to stay in beds in tents outside without breakfast, L5000 per night extra for those without hostel card. Sheets and breakfast included. Dinner L12,000. Open 2-11:30pm; off-season 3-10:30pm. Reserve by letter only.

Suore Oblate dello Spirito Santo, Via Nazionale, 8 (tel. 239 82 02), near the station. Numbers on Via Nazionale are tricky; ask along the street for help. The nuns take in women, married couples, and families. 30 beds in huge rooms with modern bathrooms and a good security. Curfew 11pm. Doubles with bath L70,000. Triples and quads L25,000 per person. Breakfast included. Phone reservations accepted, but it's better still to write in advance. Open July-Oct. 15.

Ostello Santa Monaca, Via S. Monaca, 6 (tel. 26 83 38), off Via dei Serragli near Istituto Gould in the Oltrarno. This hostel tends to crowd many beds into high-ceilinged rooms, but the best price for this central location. Curfew 1am. No breakfast. Shower included. Sign-up sheet posted 9:30am-1pm, with as many spaces as there are beds open. No reservations. Open 8-9:30am and 4-11:30pm.

Piazza Santa Maria Novella and Environs

Standing in front of the station, you will see the back of the Basilica of Santa Maria Novella. Beyond the church and in the immediate vicinity you'll find excellent budget accommodations galore. Ask for rooms overlooking the piazza. In this area you'll be close to the *duomo* and *centro,* and it's a short walk from the station.

Pensione La Mia Casa, P. Santa Maria Novella, 23 (tel. 21 30 61). A 14th-century *palazzo* with clean rooms with textured, flowery wallpaper and quiet views. Every night, the proprietor screens—in English, and for free—a documentary on Florence (8pm) and a relatively recent American film (9pm). Curfew midnight. Singles L28,000. Doubles L43,000, with bath L54,000. Triples L58,000, with bath L73,000. Quads L73,000, with bath L92,000. Breakfast L6000.

Locanda La Romagnola and **Soggiorno Gigliola,** Via della Scala, 40 (tel. 21 15 97 and 28 79 81). Leave the station by track #5, walk across the street, and turn right onto Via della Scala after a block. Friendly, simple, and likely to have rooms. Curfew midnight. Singles L33,000, with bath L45,000. Doubles L51,000, with bath L68,000. Triples L65,000, with bath L81,000. Showers L3000.

Albergo Montreal, Via della Scala, 43 (tel. 238 23 31). Clean, friendly, professional. Beautiful, quiet, outdoor terrace where one can sit and read, write or reflect. Curfew 1:30am. Singles L38,000. Doubles with bath L63,000 (with shower only L59,000). Triples with bath L80,000. Quads with bath L100,000.

Hotel Visconti, P. Ottaviani, 1 (tel. 21 38 77). Friendly proprietor. Fussily decorated singles L35,000. Doubles L52,000, with bath L67,000. Triples L98,000, with bath L113,000. Quads L126,000, with bath L145,000. Breakfast included.

Hotel Elite, Via della Scala, 12 (tel. 21 53 95). Proprietor is deservedly proud of his well-maintained, 8-room hotel. English spoken. Single with shower L45,000; with bath L55,000. Doubles with bath L75,000. Triples L100,000. Breakfast L10,000. Send 1 night's deposit to reserve a room, or call ahead and show up by noon.

Near the Station

As you leave the station, a left onto Via Nazionale will plunge you into a neighborhood swarming with travelers. If you can't avoid this quarter, at least walk away from its heart. Here along **Via Nazionale, Via Faenza, Via Fiume, Via Guelfa,** and nearby streets, cheap establishments abound—often several to a building.

Via Faenza, 56 houses no fewer than 6 separate *pensioni*. From the station follow the directions to Via Nazionale, on which Via Faenza is the 2nd intersection. **Pensione Azzi,** (tel. 21 38 06) styles itself as the "locanda degli artisti"—the artists' inn. Even the art-inept will enjoy the friendly management, large, immaculate rooms, and elegant dining room and terrace. They also boast a small but growing library, ranging from Stephen King to art history (with, as of now, not much in between). Curfew 1am. Singles L40,000-50,000. Doubles L55,000-80,000. Triples L90,000. Breakfast L3000. Solo travelers can get beds in dorms with 7-8 beds for L25,000 per person. **Albergo Anna,** (tel. 239 83 22). Lovely rooms—some ceilings with frescoes, others with fans. Singles L45,000. Doubles L70,000. Triples L95,000. Breakfast L8000. **Albergo Merlini,** (tel. 21 28 48). Light and airy. Hip and breezy. Breakfast served on the terrace, which looks out over a garden to the *duomo* beyond. Curfew 1am. Singles L38,000. Doubles L60,000, with bath L75,000. Triples L69,000. **Albergo Armonia,** (tel. 21 11 46). Clean and adequate. Doubles L75,000. Triples L105,000. Quads L132,000. Quints L150,000. Breakfast and shower included; prices significantly lower in winter. **Albergo Marini,** (tel. 28 48 24). Simple white rooms with comfy beds. Curfew 1am. Doubles with bath L70,000. Triples with bath L81,000. Quads with bath L100,000. Breakfast L10,000. **Locanda Paola,** (tel. 21 36 82). Relaxed, but the furniture doesn't all match. Doubles with private shower (but no toilet) L70,000. Triples L75,000, with shower L90,000. Discounts for longer stays.

Hotel Nazionale, Via Nazionale, 22 (tel. 238 22 03), near P. Indipendenza. Sunny rooms and friendly French management. Breakfast included and served in your room. Curfew midnight. Singles L46,000, with bath L56,000. Doubles L72,000, with bath L80,000. Triples L94,500, with bath L108,000. MC, Visa accepted.

Pensione Daniel, Via Nazionale, 22 (tel. 21 12 93), near P. Indipendenza. Small but the walls are painted over in pinks, yellows, and blues reminiscent of a Fra Angelico fresco. Strict midnight curfew. L24,000 per person in dorms. Doubles with bath L50,000. Breakfast L5000.

Locanda Nella e Pina, Via Faenza, 69 (tel. 21 22 31 and 28 42 56). Kindly proprietress will take care of you. One double has view of a spectacular garden. Curfew midnight. Singles L35,400. Doubles L52,000. Triples L70,000. Quads L90,000. **Locanda Giovanna,** (tel. 238 13 53), is located in the same building. 7 small, well-kept rooms, some with garden view. Singles L35,000. Doubles L40,000-63,000. Triples L80,000. **Hotel Soggiorno d'Erico,** same address, 4th floor (tel. and fax 21 55 31). Small rooms have nice views of the hills around Florence, free kitchen use, and laundry done for L1000 per kg. Singles L36,000. Doubles L44,000. Triples L74,000. Am Ex, Visa.

Ausonia e Rimini, Via Nazionale, 24 (tel. 49 65 47). Leaving the station from track #16, take a right, and then a left onto Via Nazionale. Welcoming owners. The spotless rooms are nicely decorated and well-lit. Curfew 1am. Singles L42,000, with bath L55,000. Doubles L68,000, with bath L86,000. Triples L90,000, with bath L111,000. Quads L120,000, with bath L132,000. Breakfast included. Nov. 10-Jan. prices should be about 10% lower. Am Ex, Visa.

Near Piazza San Marco and the University Quarter

This area is considerably calmer and less tourist-ridden than its proximity to the center might suggest.

La Colomba, Via Cavour, 21 (tel. 28 91 39). Sunny, white modernity. Windows peer out across a picturesque Florentine roofscape. Italo-Australian proprietor Rosanna is helpful and friendly, and sociable tots Angelo and his little brother Stefano enjoy companions from other lands. Husband often goes to the train station to recruit guests. Negotiable curfew 1:30am. Singles L55,000. Doubles L90,000, with bath L100,000. A *real* continental breakfast is included. **Hotel Sofia,** just upstairs (tel. 28 39 30), offers pleasant, plain rooms at good prices. Curfew 1am. Singles L36,000. Doubles L55,000. Triples and quads L23,000 per person.

Hotel Tina, Via San Gallo, 31 (tel. 48 35 19 or 48 35 93). Small *pensione* with high ceilings and artsy posters. Fantastic owners offer excellent advice on everything from local discos to hidden architectural gems in Florence. Breakfast included. Singles, L40,000. Doubles L60,000, with bath L70,000. Triples with bath L90,000.

Albergo Sampaoli, Via San Gallo, 14 (tel. 28 48 34). A peaceful hotel with a proprietress proud of her history with American tourism since the 1950s. Antique furniture and spic-n-span bathrooms make the *pensione* an enduring gem. Refrigerators on each floor keep your drinks chilled. Doubles L56,000, with bath L70,000. Triples with bath L90,000. Quads L88,000. The proprietor does not accept written reservations; call the night before you're arriving.

Hotel Globus, Via Sant'Antonio, 24 (tel. 21 10 62, fax 239 62 25). The sun shoots through these breezy rooms. Outgoing, professional management. Singles L38,000. Doubles L55,000, with bath, L80,000. Triples L70,000, with bath L95,000. Show your *Let's Go* to get these prices. Breakfast L7000.

Pensione Casci, Via Cavour, 13 (tel. 21 16 86, fax 239 64 61). Only 3min. from the *duomo*. A tranquil, restored *palazzo* with ceilings and floors as they were in the 14th century. Rossini lived here for several years in the 1950s. Enthusiastic multilingual proprietors. Singles with bath L68,000. Doubles with bath L100,000. Triples with bath L130,000. July and Aug. Rent a bed in a dorm-style room for L35,000. Prices fall in low season. All-you-can-eat continental breakfast included.

Hotel San Marco, Via Cavour, 50 (tel. 28 42 35) offers 3 floors of airy, modern rooms. Curfew 1:30am. Singles L40,000, with bath L55,000. Doubles L80,000, with bath L90,000. Triples with bath L125,000. Am Ex, MC, Visa.

Old City (Near the Duomo)

The daily flood of tourists somehow misses many of the establishments in this ancient quarter.

Locanda Orchidea, Borgo degli Albizi, 11 (tel. 248 03 46). Dante's wife was born in this 12th-century *palazzo,* which features a still-intact tower. English-speaking proprietor presides over 7 exquisite rooms (some overlook a charming garden). Singles L32,000. Doubles L48,000, with shower L55,000. Triples L66,000, with shower L72,000. Quad L88,000, with shower L92,000. Quint L100,000. Reservations strongly recommended in summer.

Soggiorno Brunori, Via del Proconsolo, 5 (tel. 28 96 48), off P. del Duomo. Sufficiently hygienic rooms in a beautiful and conveniently located building. Friendly manager speaks English and goes out of his way to make your stay pleasant. Curfew 12:30am. Doubles L54,000, with bath L68,000. Triples with bath L90,000. Quads L96,000, with bath L120,000. Breakfast L8000 served in your room.

Soggiorno Bavaria, Borgo degli Albizi, 26 (tel. 234 03 13). From P. della Repubblica walk straight up Via del Corso, which becomes Borgo Albizi; Bavaria is on the left, inside the courtyard and up the stairs to the right. A renovated *palazzo.* Majestic rooms with decorated ceilings. The room looking over the city and the *duomo* is the closest to a room with a view you will find in Florence. One of the best deals in Florence for its quality, price and location. Singles L47,000. Doubles L63,000, with bath L70,000. Triples, quads L30,000-40,000 per person depending on the season. Breakfast included. Reserve by July for Aug. stays.

Hotel Aldini, Via Calzaiuoli, 13 (tel. 21 47 52 or 21 24 48; fax 21 64 10). If you're contemplating going all-out for a hotel, this is the place to do it. Antique freestanding fireplaces in all the newly renovated and spotless bedrooms. A/C, color TV. Singles with bath L85,000. Doubles with bath L140,000. Triples with bath L191,000. Breakfast included (we should hope so). MC, Visa.

Albergo Costantini, Via Calzaiuoli, 13 (tel. 21 51 28). Big, airy, clean rooms. Curfew 2am. Singles L45,000, with bath L60,000. Doubles L60,000, with bath L90,000. Triples with bath L120,000. Pay in advance. Breakfast L10,000. Call 3 days ahead to get a room.

Albergo Firenze, P. Donati, 4 (tel. 21 42 03 and 26 83 01), off Via del Corso. Tidy, friendly, and central. Singles L43,000, with bath L52,000. Doubles L66,000, with bath L77,000. Triples L95,000, with bath L105,000. Breakfast included.

Hotel Maxim, Via dei Medici, 4 (tel. 21 74 74, fax 28 37 29). Another entrance at Via dei Calzaiuoli, 11. Cheerful proprietor lets clean, sunny rooms near the *duomo.* Doubles L64,000, with bath L84,000. Triples L97,000, with bath L120,000. Breakfast included. Laundry L16,000 a load (5kg). Am Ex, MC, Visa.

Soggiorno Panerai, Via dei Servi, 36 (tel. 26 41 03), near the *duomo.* A tidy, quiet 5-room *pensione* run by a helpful American. Doubles L50,000. Triples L66,000. Quad L88,000. All rooms without bath, but 2 rooms share a big shower. Breakfast included. To reserve more than 2 days in advance, send 1 night's deposit.

Universo Hotel, P. Santa Maria Novella, 20 (tel. 28 19 51). Adequately cleaned rooms, some with views of the church and piazza. Singles L60,000, with bath L86,000. Doubles L90,000, with bath L110,000. 20% discount with *Let's Go* in July and Aug. Am Ex, MC, Visa accepted.

Pensione Zurigo, Via Oriuolo, 17 (tel. 234 06 44). Neat, clean, and simple. Large bathrooms with tubs. Curfew 1:30am. Singles L40,000. Doubles L70,000, with bath L85,000. Triples L75,000, with bath L95,000. Breakfast included. MC, Visa.

Pensione Esperanza, Via dell'Inferno, 3 (tel. 21 37 73). From Via Parione between P. Goldoni and Via Tornabuoni, go through the arch called Volta della Vecchia, turn left on Via Purgatorio, then immediately turn right. 9 rooms with old furniture, some with balconies. Peaceful. Proprietor Ilva is accommodating and attentive. Curfew 1am. Singles L30,000. Doubles L45,000. Showers L2000.

In the Oltrarno

Only a 10-minute walk away from the *duomo,* but literally "outside the Arno," *pensioni* in here offer a welcome respite from the bustle of Florence's hub. Rooms are generally quiet and airy and some overlook the Arno, tranquil *piazze,* or well-kept gardens.

Pensione Sorelle Bandini, P. Santo Spirito, 9 (tel. 21 53 08). Old-world elegance and happy staff on the top floor of a large *palazzo.* Beautiful sun-drenched *loggia.* Terrace with view of the hills of Florence looks over the piazza. English spoken. Doubles L90,000, with bath L95,000. Triples L118,000, with bath L133,000. Show your *Let's Go* to get these prices. Breakfast included. Reservations accepted.

Hotel La Scaletta, Via Guicciardini, 13 (tel. 28 30 28), across the Ponte Vecchio towards the Pitti Palace. Spectacular views of the Boboli gardens and the city from rooftop terraces. Rooms furnished with an English touch. Singles with bath L69,000. Doubles L90,000, with bath L115,000. Breakfast included. MC, Visa.

Camping

Italiani e Stranieri, Via le Michelangelo, 80 (tel. 681 19 77), near P. Michelangelo. Take red or black bus #13 from the station (15min., last bus 11:55pm). Extremely crowded, but offers a spectacular panorama of Florence. Fantastic facilities, including a well-stocked food store and bar. They may post a *completo* sign or tell you the same by phone, but if you show up without a vehicle they will often let you in. L6000 per person, L7000 per tent, L4000 per car, L2500 per motorcycle. Open mid-March to Nov. 6am-midnight.

Villa Camerata, Viale A. Righi, 2/4 (tel. 61 14 51), outside the HI youth hostel on the #17B bus route. Catch the bus at the train station or at P. del Duomo. L6000 per person, L7500 per small tent. Open April-Oct. 7:30am-1pm and 3-9pm; if it's closed, stake your site and come back later to register and pay.

Camping Panoramico, Via Peramonda, 1 (tel. 59 90 69), outside the city near Fiesole. Take bus #7 from the station to Fiesole (last buses 11:25pm and 12:30am, L1100). L8500 per person, L15,000 per tent, auto included.

Villa Favard, Via Rocca Tedalda. Take bus #14. Free campsite. A fenced-in area with a security guard, though you should keep an eye on your valuables just the same. No hot water, but running cold water and toilets. Open in summer only.

FOOD

Florence's hearty Tuscan cuisine is rooted in the peasant fare of the surrounding countryside and reflects the city's self-conscious preservation of its unsophisticated side. Yet, Tuscan food, typified by only the freshest ingredients and simple preparations, contends among the world's best cuisines. White beans and olive oil form the two main staples of Florentine food, and most regional dishes will come loaded with one or the other, if not both. Specialties include such *antipasti* as *bruschette* (grilled Tuscan bread doused with olive oil and garlic, and sometimes topped with tomatoes and basil). For *primi* Florentines have perfected the Tuscan classics *minestra di fagioli* (a delicious white bean and garlic soup) and *ribollista* (a hearty bean, bread, and black cabbage concoction). Florence's classic *secondo* is *bistecca alla Fiorentina,* thick sirloin steak (with a characteristic squeeze of lemon), each inch more succulent and expensive than the last. You will gain murmurs of admiration if you order it as Florentines do: *al sangue* (very rare—literally "bloody"). Other typical *secondi* include *trippa alla fiorentina* (tripe cooked in a tomato and cheese sauce), and grilled pork sausages. The best local cheese is *pecorino,* made from sheep's milk. Wine is another Florentine staple, and the local *chianti* is superb. Genuine *chianti classico,* the highest quality, commands a premium; it is also called *gallo nero* after the black rooster on its neck label. A liter of house wine typically costs L6000-7000 in Florence's *trattorie,* while stores sell bottles of delicious wine, even *chianti classico,* for as little as L4000. Florentine refinement shines through in the local dessert, *cantuccini di prato,* (almond cookies made with tons of egg yolks) dipped in *vin Santo* (a rich dessert wine made from raisins).

For lunch, visit one of the many *rosticcerie gastronomie,* or browse over pushcarts throughout the city. Buy your own fresh produce, tripe and meats at the **Mercato Centrale,** between Via Nazionale and the back of San Lorenzo. (Open Mon.-Sat. 8am-1pm; Oct.-May Mon.-Sat. 6:30am-1pm and 4-8:30pm.) For staples, head to **Supermercato STANDA,** Via Pietrapiana, 1r (open Tues.-Sat. 8:30am-8pm, Mon. 3-8pm), or to any of the small markets throughout the city.

Vegetarians and health-conscious travelers will find several health-food markets operating throughout the city. The best are two stores named after the famous American book, **Sugar Blues.** The first is a 5-min. walk from the *duomo* at Via XXVII Aprile, 46r (tel. 48 36 66). (Open Mon.-Fri. 9am-1pm and 5-7pm, Sat. 9am-1pm.) The second is in the Oltrarno, right next to the Institute Gould at Via dei Serragli, 57r (tel. 26 83 78). (Open Mon.-Fri. 8:30am-1:30pm and 4:30-8pm.) Both stock vitamins, algae, homemade take-out vegetable torts, organic vegetables and more, all with an Italian touch. Also try **La Raccolta,** at Via Leopardi, 10 (tel. 247 90 68), downstairs: a center for health food and a meeting place for an alternative community in Florence. (Open Tues.-Fri. 10am-2pm and 4-7:30pm.)

Santa Maria Novella and environs

Amon, Via Palazzuolo, 26-28r. Some of the best Middle Eastern food to be found on any continent. Try the refreshing *moussaka,* a pita filled with baked eggplant, hot sauces, and heated. Falafel L3000, shish kebab L4000. Beer L1800. Stand-up or take-out only. Open Mon.-Sat. noon-3pm and 7-11pm.

Trattoria da Giorgio, Via Palazzuolo, 100r. Filling, down-home-style meals including *primo, secondo,* salad and wine for L14,000. Menu changes daily. There's usually a wait to get in. Open Mon.-Sat. noon-3pm and 6:30-10pm.

Trattoria Contadino, Via Palazzuolo, 69r. Just down the street from da Giorgio, and the same deal. Meals *alla buona* for L14,000.

Il Giardino, Via della Scala, 67 (tel. 21 31 41). Enjoy a hearty portion of hand-made *tagliatelle* (L6000) under the vines of the garden inside. The roast veal is enough

FLORENCE

to encourage anyone on to a 2nd course (L9000). Cover L2000. Service 10%. Open Wed.-Mon. noon-3pm and 7-10pm. Credit cards accepted.

La Scogliera, Via Palazzuolo, 80r (tel. 21 02 57). Good pizzas in an authentic Italian environment, heightened by the Italian cadences of the proprietor's English and the Italian folk music playing in the background. Tourist *menú* L14,000. Dine in the small terrace outside and do some star-gazing. Open Mon.-Fri. noon-3pm and 7-11pm. Am Ex and Visa accepted.

The Station and University Quarter

Trattoria Antichi Cancelli, Via Faenza, 73r (tel. 21 89 27). Home-style and hearty. Try a great bowl of vegetable soup (L5500). Open Tues.-Sun. noon-3pm and 7-10:30pm. Am Ex, MC, Visa accepted.

Trattoria da Zà-Zà, P. Mercato Centrale, 26r (tel. 21 54 11). Soups are a specialty in this hip-hopping *trattoria;* try the *tris* (mix of 3) bean, tomato, and vegetable for L7000, or the other-worldly *tagliatelle al pesto* made fresh every morning, L7000. Cover L1800. Open Mon.-Sat. noon-2:30pm and 7-10pm. Reservations suggested. Am Ex, Visa.

Trattoria Mario, Via Rosina, 2r. Share huge wooden tables with the crowds of locals that flock here for lunch. Menu changes daily. *Primi* L3000-5000, *secondi* L4500-9000. Open for lunch noon-3:30pm.

Rosticceria di Barone, Via Guelfa, 40r (tel. 21 70 39). Newly opened Persian specialty rosticceria with a marvelous vegetable dish *melanzano affumicaté* (smoked eggplant in sauce) that is combined with *visoverde* (green rice) imported from the Middle East. Served only on Wednesdays. Full meal, including beverage, L8000. Open Mon.-Fri. noon-10pm, Sat. noon-9pm.

Ristorante Bella Cina, Via Guelfa, 24 and Via dei Gineri. Just opened. This new Chinese restaurant serves up fresh, delicious food for very low prices. Air-conditioned. Try the *melanzani in salsa piccante* (L4000). Open daily noon-3pm and 7-11pm. Am Ex.

Caffé Carocal—Mexican Restaurant, Via de Ginori, 10r. Bar atmosphere in which to munch on decent nachos, burritos (L14,000), or tostadas (L14,000). Happy hour 6-7pm. Open Thurs.-Tues. 6pm-1am.

Old City (The Center)

Trattoria da Benvenuto, Via dei Neri, 47r. Filling portions of *gnocchi* (L4500). Only L7000 for grilled *braciola* (veal chop). Open Mon.-Tues. and Thurs.-Sat. noon-3pm and 7:15-10pm.

Acqua al Due, Via Vegna Vecchia, 40r, behind the Bargello. Florentine specialties in a cozy, air-conditioned and popular with young Italians. The *assaggio,* a dish of 5 types of pasta, demands a taste (L9800); getting a table, however, usually demands a reservation. Open Tues.-Sun. 7pm-2am. MC, Visa.

Aquerello, Via Ghibblelina, 156r, (tel. 234 05 54), Pseudo-Memphis decor and superb, offbeat food. Duck when your *spaghetti flambé all' Aquerello* (L8000) arrives—it's on fire. Or have your duck *à l'orange* (*anitra all'arancia,* L15,000). Cover L3000. Open Fri.-Wed. 11am-3pm and 7pm-1am. Am Ex, MC, Visa.

La Maremmana, Via dei Macci, 77r (tel. 24 12 26). A rare combination: simple, generous, and affordable. *Menù* starting at L18,000. Tablecloths, cut flowers, pasta, *secondi,* side dishes, a fruit dessert and wine included. Justifiably busy. Open Sept.-July Mon.-Sat. 12:30-3pm and 7:30-10:30pm. MC, Visa.

Trattoria l'che c'è c'è, Via de Mangalotti 11r, (tel. 21 65 89). The owner/chef cares about his food, as you'll taste. *Topini (gnocchi) al gorgonzola,* L7500. Try a Tuscan *secondo* like *salsicce e faglioli* (sausage and beans), L10,000. Cover L2000. Open Tues.-Sun. 11:30am-2pm and 7:30-10:30pm. Reserve in advance.

The Oltrarno

Oltrarno Trattoria Casalinga, Via Michelozzi, 9r, near P. Santo Spirito. Delicious Tuscan specialties in relaxed, if crowded, atmosphere. Ravioli made with spinach and ricotta, L6000. *Secondi* about L7500. Menu changes daily. Cover L1500. Open Mon.-Sat. noon-3pm and 7-9:30pm.

Il Borgo Antico, P. Santa Spirito, 61 (tel. 21 04 37). A hip-hopping restaurant with an impressive array of slightly offbeat (but tasty) dishes. Enormous and flamboyant salads like no others found in Italy (L10,000). Try the *ravioli alla crema di SalVia* , in a sweet-cream rosé sauce (L8000). Pizzas L8000-12,000. Cover L3000. Reservations recommended for outdoor seating. Open Mon.-Sat. 12:30-2:30pm and 7:30-11pm. (Pizzeria open until 12:30am.)

Ristorante Il Fiacchere, Via Ardigliore, 22 (tel. 29 47 44), off Via Serragli. A rare find in Florence, hidden away with simple, well-crafted decor and attention to detail in the food that makes it particularly fine. Try their popeye-inspired *Risotto Braccio di Ferro* with spinach in a cream sauce (L7000) or *Tagliatelle Maremma* with *porcini* mushrooms (L7000). Open daily 7:30-11pm.

Baked Goods

CarLie's Bakery, Via Brache, 12r (tel. 21 51 37). Behind Via de'Benci, near the river. From P. Signoria, walk between the Palazzo Vecchio and the Uffizi. Head along Via dei Neri and turn left onto Via Brache. Even non-Americans will wax nostalgic over the fudge brownies and gooey chocolate chip cookies. The proprietors dole out sympathy and advice to weary American travelers along with their confections. Open Tues.-Sun. 10am-1:30pm and 3:30-8pm. Open Sept. 1- July 15.

Pasticceria Naturale Troponais, Via Santiallo, 92r (tel. 48 30 17). Health food devotees can find delicious Italian bread here.

Gelaterie

No dinner in this gelato capital of Italy would be complete without a luscious lick from one of the many *gelaterie.* Set off on your own odyssey, but before plopping down L2500 for a cone, assess the quality of any establishment by checking out the banana. If it's bright yellow, it's been made from a mix—keep on walking. You know you've found a true Florentine *gelateria* when the banana is slightly off-grey, indicating only real live bananas are inside. Vegans can find soy-milk gelato at **De Herbore,** Via del Proconsolo, 6 (tel. 234 09 96) in scrumptious banana, cacao, vanilla, and multiple fruit flavors.

Gelateria Dei Neri, Via dei Neri, 20-22r. A prodigal upstart with sinfully scrumptious gelato. A truly mythical "Mitica" (chocolate ice cream with just about everything mixed in). Cones L2500-5000. Open daily 10:30am-midnight.

Il Granduca, Via dei Calzaiuoli, 57r. Delicious *gelato* with fresh fruit and sweets.

Vivoli, Via della Stinche, 7, behind the Bargello. The most renowned of Florentine *gelaterie,* with a huge selection. No cones, only cups (from L2500). Open Sept.-July Tues.-Sun. 8am-midnight.

Perchè No?, Via Tavolini, 19r, off Via Calzaiuoli. Though the decor doesn't show it, this is the oldest *gelateria* in Florence—it opened in 1939. Open Wed.-Mon. 8am-12:30am.

SIGHTS

> *Florence! One of the only places in Europe where I understood that underneath my revolt, a consent was lying dormant.*
> —Albert Camus

It takes quite a city to reduce an existentialist to acquiescence. The same secret spell that Florence has cast over intellectuals from Goethe to Camus can overwhelm the first-time visitor. Beware the well-documented "Stendhal Syndrome," the dizziness and palpitations of the heart that result from aesthetic overload (named for the famed French author who first described an ailment which overcame him in the church of Santa Croce.

In past years visitors have had to battle the crowds to see the most popular museums—the Uffizi, the Accademia, the Bargello. This is no longer true, but the explanation for this phenomenon is unfortunate for the budget traveler: All Florentine museums (in fact, most Italian museums) recently doubled their admission price, making art-viewing an extremely costly endeavor—L4000-10,000 at most major venues. Florence merits budget-bending for its museums, but choose what you want to see carefully, and plan to spend a healthy chunk of your day at each museum. Before writing off the Uffizi or the Bargello (L10,000), remember that they house the best collections of Renaissance painting and sculpture in the world, and perhaps reconsider. Fill in those gaps left by budget strictures by exploring Florence's churches, most of which double as treasuries of great works of art.

Piazza del Duomo

Florentines often refer to their cathedral as "Santa Maria del Fiore"; asking a local about *"il duomo"* may leave both of you confused. In 1296 the city fathers commissioned Arnolfo di Cambio to erect a cathedral and carry out the project "with the most high and sumptuous magnificence so that it is impossible to make it either better or more beautiful with the industry and power of man." Filippo Brunelleschi won the inevitable competition to direct the construction of the Europe's largest dome since the Roman Pantheon. To accomplish the task, Brunelleschi came up with the revolutionary idea of building a double-shelled dome with interlocking bricks that would support itself during construction. He also supervised every step of the building process, personally designing the system of pulleys and constructing kitchens between the two walls of the cupola so that the masons would not have to descend for lunch. Alberti described the dome as "large enough to shelter all of Tuscany within its shadow...and of a construction that perhaps not even the ancients knew or understood"—the ultimate compliment in a period awed by the genius of Greece and Rome. Michelangelo paid tribute to its harmonious proportions in a ditty he composed upon receiving the commission for the dome of St. Peter's: *"Io farò la sorella,/Già più gran ma non più bella"* ("I'm going to make its sister/Bigger but not more beautiful"). The cupola was finished in 1436, but the half-completed Gothic-Renaissance façade was taken down by an overly ambitious 16th-century Medici rebuilding campaign and not replaced until 1871, when Emilio de Fabris, a Florentine architect influenced by the Gothic style, received the commission.

Inside, the nave's sheer immensity overwhelms the art. In the form of a Latin cross, the church claims the world's third longest nave, behind St. Peter's in Rome and St. Paul's in London. The fresco illustrating the *Divine Comedy* in the left aisle, by a student of Fra Angelico, pays tribute to Dante, who was forced to flee to Florence after backing the losing side (white) in the struggle between the black and white Guelphs. The *orologio*, a 24-hour clock designed by Paolo Uccello, is perhaps the interior's most interesting piece. The clock, which hangs on the cathedral's back wall, above the entrance, runs backwards.

Climb up the 463 steps around the inside of the dome (the tallest structure ever built in Medieval Italy at 110m) to the **lantern** (tel. 230 28 85) and on the way survey the city from the external gallery. (*Duomo* open daily 10am-5pm. Masses are held 7-10am and 5-7pm. Lantern open Mon.-Sat. 10am-4:45pm. Admission L5000.) You can also visit the **crypt** to see the tomb of Brunelleschi, some 13th century tombs, and bits of mosaic. (Crypt of open Mon.-Sat. 10am-5pm. Admission L3000.)

Most of the *duomo's* art has been placed in the **Museo dell'Opera di S. Maria del Fiore** (tel. 230 28 85), behind the *duomo* at P. del Duomo, 9. Up the first flight of stairs is a late *Pietà* by Michelangelo. Frustrated by his own work, he intentionally damaged the figure by taking a hammer to it and severing Christ's left arm. Soon thereafter a pupil touched up the work, leaving parts of Mary Magdalene's head with visible "scars" and removing a leg. There are other masterpieces here as well: Donatello and Luca della Robbia's wonderful *cantorie* (choir balconies with bas reliefs of cavorting children and *putti*); Donatello's *St. Mary Magdalene* (1555); and a silver altar by Michelozzo, Pollaiuolo, and Verrocchio. The art that once covered the campanile's exterior includes Donatello's prophets and Andrea Pisano's

Progress of Man cycle of small reliefs. The museum now houses four of the frames from the baptistry's *Gates of Paradise* (see below), and after restoration will house the entire collection. (Open Mon.-Sat. 9am-7:30pm; in winter, Mon.-Sat. 9am-6pm. Admission L5000.)

Though it was built sometime between the 7th and 9th century, by Dante's time Florentines thought their **baptistry** had originally been a Roman temple, a proper medieval complement to this little masterpiece of green and white marble. The interior contains 13th- to 15th-century Byzantine-style mosaics, whose stylized, cartoon-like execution seem to foreshadow modernist art. The lowest circle is thought to be the work of Cimabue. Along the wall rests the elegant, perfect early Renaissance *Tomb of the Anti-Pope John XXIII,* by Donatello and Michelozzo, arranged so that the sculpted figure lies directly in line of Christ's blessing.

The commission to execute the famous bronze doors of the baptistry was among the most coveted in Florence. In 1330, Andrea Pisano (1270-1349) was imported from Pisa, and Venetian foundry-workers were brought in to cast the first set of doors, which now guard the south side (toward the river). In 1401, the cloth guild announced a new competition to determine who would forge the remaining doors. The original field of eight contestants narrowed to two youngsters, Brunelleschi (then 23) and Ghiberti (20). Each was given a year to complete a panel, and Ghiberti, whose entry more elegantly molded its subject to the quatrefoil Gothic frame, was awarded the commission. (The competition pieces, panels depicting the sacrifice of Abraham, now hang in the Bargello.)

Ghiberti's doors, on the north side away from the river, start with Pisano's framework, but add detail, movement, and classical draperies. His work was so admired that the last set of doors was commissioned from him as soon as he finished the first, in 1425. The **"Gates of Paradise,"** as Michelangelo reportedly called them, are nothing like the two earlier portals, abandoning the quatrefoil framing and the 28-panel design for 10 large, entirely gilded squares, each of which incorporates mathematical perspectives to recess the scenes into startlingly deep space. Originally intended to stand as the third set of doors on the north side, they so impressed the Florentines that they were switched with the second doors and placed in their current honored position facing the cathedral. The doors were finished in 1452, after 24 years of labor, and three years before Ghiberti's death. The panels have been under restoration since a 1966 flood and will eventually reside in the Museo del Duomo, while replicas hang in the baptistry. The baptistry's doors open only on June 24, the feast of Florence's patron saint St. John the Baptist. (Open Mon.-Sat. 1:30-6pm, Sun. 9am-1pm.)

Next to the *duomo* rises the 82m **campanile,** the "lily of Florence blossoming in stone." Giotto, then the official city architect, drew up the design and laid the foundation, but died soon after construction began. Andrea Pisano added two stories and Francesco Talenti completed the tower in 1359, but only after doubling the thickness of the walls to support the weight. The original exterior decoration now resides in the **Museo del Duomo.** (The 414 steps are open daily 8:30am-6:50pm; Nov.-March 9am-5:30pm. Admission L5000.)

Palazzo Vecchio and Piazza della Signoria

From P. del Duomo, **Via dei Calzaiuoli,** one of the city's oldest streets, leads to P. Signoria. Laid out as part of the original Roman *castrum* (camp), today Via dei Calzaiuoli bustles with crowds, chic stores, ice cream shops, and vendors peddling their wares in the sidewalks. At the far end, the area around the **Palazzo Vecchio** (tel. 276 84 65) forms the civic center of Florence.

The fortress-like *palazzo* was built between 1298 and 1314 according to the plans of the ubiquitous Arnolfo di Cambio, who intended it to replace the Bargello as the seat of the commune's government; its interior apartments served as living quarters for the seven members of the *signoria* (council) during their rotating, one-month terms in office. By the time of Cosimo di Medici's autocratic rule, however, the building's role as a symbol of communal government was simply an irony.

The courtyard, rebuilt by Michelozzo in 1444 and ruined by Vasari in 1565 to please a Medici bride, contains a copy of Verrocchio's charming 15th-century *putto* fountain and several stone lions (the heraldic symbol of the city). Michelangelo and Leonardo da Vinci were commissioned to paint opposite walls of the **Salone dei Cinquecento,** the meeting room of the Grand Council of the Republic. Although they did not get around to executing the frescoes, their preliminary cartoons, the *Battle of Cascina* and the *Battle of Anghiari,* were studied by all young Florentine artists and copied for mass production by engravers. The tiny, windowless **Studio of Francesco I,** built by Vasari, is a treasure house of mannerist art, with paintings by Bronzino, Allori and Vasari, and bronze statuettes by Giambologna and Ammannati. The best of the art waits in the **Mezzanino.** Look for Bronzino's portrait of the poet Laura Battiferi and Giambologna's *Hercules and the Hydra.* (Open Mon.-Fri. 9am-7pm, Sun. 8am-1pm. Admission L8000.)

A vast space by medieval standards, **Piazza della Signoria** was created in the 13th Century by the destruction of the house-towers belonging to the Uberti clan. For a long time, no one of means wanted to own or build on the site. In 1497, Savonarola convinced Florentines to light off the **Bonfire of the Vanities** in the square, a grand roast that consumed some of Florence's best art. A year later, disillusioned Florence sent Savonarola up in smoke on the exact same spot.

Symbolic sculptures cluster around the front of the *palazzo:* Donatello's *Judith and Holofernes,* Michelangelo's *David* (only a copy is on display; the original stood here over a century ago), Giambologna's *Equestrian Monument to Cosimo I* and Bandinelli's *Hercules.* The awkward Neptune statue to the left of the Palazzo Vecchio occasioned the following quip by Michelangelo: "Oh Ammannato, Ammannato, what lovely marble you have ruined!"

Built as a space for civic speakers, the graceful 14th-century **Loggia dei Lanzi** gradually became a misogynist sculpture gallery under the Medici dukes. Here you can see Benvenuto Cellini's *Perseus Slaying Medusa,* which Cellini signed on Perseus' sash; Giambologna's *Rape of the Sabines* whose spiral quality invites viewing from any angle; and the dynamic and violent *Rape of Polyxena* by Pio Fedi.

The Uffizi

In May of 1993, a bomb was detonated in the Uffizi, killing five people in nearby buildings and destroying priceless works of art. The bombing came as a terrible shock to Florentines and Italians alike, who cherish the Uffizi as a symbol of their precious Renaissance heritage. The symbolic implications of the bombing are immense: with each work of art destroyed, Florentines feel that a small part of themselves has been destroyed as well. No group has taken responsibility for the acts of violence, and the authorities have apprehended no one, but the common consensus blames the current transition from an older political regime to a newer one as much as any specific group.

The political disruptions caused by these bombings are matched by the cultural disruptions: half the rooms in the Uffizi remain closed to the public and will not open for several years as reconstruction of the bombed out rooms carefully goes ahead. A list of the several works destroyed and the almost 40 works seriously damaged can be obtained from the tourist office. Rooms 25-35 and 41-45 remain closed to the public but three important works, Michelangelo's *Doni Tondo,* Caravaggio's *Bacchus,* and Titian's *Flora* have been moved to a room near the entrance so the public will continue to have access to them as reconstruction continues. Do not skip the Uffizi because of the closed rooms: it continues to display an unparalleled collection of Renaissance works. Consider your visit an act of solidarity with Florentines against senseless acts of destruction.

The Rooms

The **Uffizi** (offices, tel. 21 83 41) form a double row behind the *loggia*. Vasari designed the Uffizi in 1554, when Duke Cosimo demanded housing for his consolidated administration of the Duchy of Tuscany. The street makes a strong political statement, framing the tower of Palazzo Vecchio at one end and the Medici Forte Belvedere across the Arno at the other. Giambologna's bust of Cosimo oversees the entire complex at the Arno end. Vasari included a secret corridor in the structure, between Palazzo Vecchio and the Medici's Palazzo Pitti; it runs through the Uffizi and over Ponte Vecchio and houses more art, including a special collection of artists' self-portraits. The city can thank the Medici for the most stunning collection of Renaissance art in the world: the very last Medici, Anna Maria Ludovica (1667-1743) bequeathed the entire clan's hoard of art to the people of Tuscany, provided that it never be moved from Florence.

Before heading up to the main gallery on the second floor, ascend the stairs to the first floor to see the exhibits of the Cabinet of Drawings and Prints. The few drawings displayed here only hint at the much larger collection they keep squirreled away for scholars. Upstairs, the long main corridor wrapping around the building is holds an impressive collection of Hellenistic and Roman marbles, inspirations for many Renaissance works.

The collection is arranged chronologically, and provides a complete education on Florentine painting of the Renaissance, with detours into a select collection from the German and Venetian Renaissances. Despite the hefty admission, it would be inadvisable to try to see everything in the Uffizi in a day.

Room 2 starts you off in the late 13th and early 14th century with three great *Maestà*, huge panels of the enthroned Madonna by Cimabue, Florence's first remembered genius, Sienese Duccio di Buoninsegna, whose riot of color clearly marks him as a foreigner, and Giotto, whose vastly informed use of perspective and naturalistic flesh foreshadows the onset of the Renaissance (still 100 years away). **Room 3** moves to Siena to fill out the 14th century with the delightful Gothic works of Simone Martini and the Lorenzetti brothers, because, as Room 4 shows, the Florentines weren't very busy then. Rooms 5 and 6 contain some nice Italian bits of International Courtly Gothic, but in no way prepares for the explosion of the early Renaissance in **Room 7.**

Perhaps the most charming room in the museum, Room 7 houses two minor Fra Angelicos, and an over-painted Masolino Madonna and Child (whose central figures are by Masaccio) in addition to its three masterpieces. The softly colored, innovative *Sacra Conversazione* by Domenico Veneziano is one of the master's few known works, and one of the first paintings to incorporate the Madonna and Saints into a unified space. Piero della Francesca's double portrait of Duke Frederico and his wife Battista Sforza, recently restored, glows in translucent color and intricate detail. Rounding off the room, Paolo Uccello's famed *Rout of San Romano* is an absurd and disturbing perspective play where rabbits hop behind huge, toy-like fighting warhorses (this is only the central panel of a triptych—the Louvre and London's National Gallery each have a side). **Room 8** contains Filippo Lippis, each brown; the Pollaiuolo brothers share space with a (probably) forged Filippino Lippi in **Room 9.**

Rooms 10-14 are a vast Botticelli shrine: *Primavera, Birth of Venus, Madonna della Melagrana,* and *Pallas and the Centaur,* glow with luminous color after their recent restoration; the recently installed glass and difficult lighting go largely unappreciated. **Room 15** moves into High Renaissance gear with Leonardo's remarkable *Annunciation* and perhaps more remarkable (though unfinished) *Adoration of the Magi,* both of which receive comic counterpoint in Piero di Cosimo's *Perseus Liberating Andromeda.* **Room 18,** an octagonal Tribuna designed by Buontalenti to hold the Medici treasures, is more impressive for its collection of portraits, many by Bronzino. **Room 19** features Piero della Francesca's students Perugino (the *Portrait of a Young Man* is thought to be of his student Raphael) and Signorelli. **Rooms 20** and **22** make an incongruous detour into German territory, and **Room 21** sandwiches the major Venetians between them. Ponder Bellini's famous *Sacred Allegory,* an inexplicably moving work, before examining Mantegna's little *Triptych* in **Room 24.**

Note: these rooms will be **closed** for the next 2-3 years for reconstruction. As you cross to the gallery's other side, glance out the windows of the south corridor over Florence—the Medici commissioned an impressive view. The second half of the Uffizi rounds out the Florentines in **Rooms 25-27** with Michelangelo's only oil painting, the proto-mannerist *Doni Tondo,* a string of Raphaels unaccountably accompanied by Andrea del Sarto's *Madonna of the Harpies,* and Pontormo's odd *Supper at Emmaus.* Florence cares less for the museum after this, and you'll find rooms sporadically closed. If they're open, the best bits are Titian's influential *Venus of Urbino* and Parmigianino's completely preposterous *Madonna of the Long Neck,* an apparent cross-breed between God and a giraffe, both found in Room 30; a clutch of Caravaggios, including his *Sacrifice of Isaac* and *Bacchus* in Room 43; and Room 44's two Rembrandt self-portraits, one young, one old. (Open Tues.-Sat. 9am-7pm, Sun. 9am-1pm. Admission L10,000.)

The Ponte Vecchio

From the Uffizi, head down to the Arno and turn right. The nearby **Ponte Vecchio** has spanned the Arno at its narrowest point since Roman times. Until 1218 this was Florence's *only* bridge over the Arno. The Medici, in an effort to "improve" the area, kicked out the butchers and tanners, whose shops lined the bridge in the 1500s, and installed the goldsmiths and diamond-carvers whose descendants remain today. The commander leading the German army's retreat across the river in 1944 could not bear to blow up the bridge, and instead destroyed the medieval towers and nearby buildings on either side to make the bridge impassable. Today, the peddlers and artisans who line the bridge by day make way for nocturnal street musicians.

Around the Bargello

The heart of Medieval Florence lies between the *duomo* and the Signoria around the 13th-century **Bargello,** in Piazza San Firenze. The Bargello fortress was once the residence of the chief magistrate and later the police headquarters. Now it houses the **Museo Nazionale** (tel. 21 08 01), a treasury of Florentine sculpture. Upstairs on the first floor in the Salone del Consiglio Generale, Donatello's remarkably effeminate bronze *David,* the first free-standing nude since antiquity, exemplifies the early period of Renaissance sculpture. Compare it with the marble *David,* also by Donatello, along the wall to the left. Completed about thirty years earlier (1408), this statue appears more a Roman patrician than a shy young boy. Along the wall to the right hang two beautiful bronze panels of the *Sacrifice of Isaac,* submitted by Ghiberti and Brunelleschi for the baptistry door competition (see Piazza del Duomo). Towards the other end of the room resides a series of della Robbia terra-cotta Madonnas. In the *Loggia* (also upstairs on the first floor), one finds a menagerie of bronze animals created by Giambologna for a Medici garden grotto. Downstairs on the ground floor Michelangelo's early works dominate the first room, including a debauched *Bacchus,* a handsome bust of *Brutus,* an early unfinished *Apollo* or *David,* and a tondo of the *Madonna and Child.* Devote your attention to Cellini's work on the other side of the room, especially the models for Perseus and the *Bust of Cosimo I.* Giambologna's *Oceanus* reigns in the Gothic *cortile* outside, while his *Mercury* twirls off his pedestal back in the Michelangelo room. (Open Tues.-Sat. 9am-2pm, Sun. 9am-1pm. Admission L6000.)

The **Badia,** across Via del Proconsolo from the Bargello, was the church of medieval Florence's richest monastery. Filippino Lippi's *Apparition of the Virgin to St. Bernard,* one of the most famous paintings of the late 15th century, greets you on the left as you enter. (Open 9am-noon and 4-6pm.) Around the corner in Via S. Margherita you can visit the **Casa di Dante** (tel. 28 33 43), the reconstructed house of the great poet. (Open Mon.-Tues. and Thurs.-Sat. 9:30am-12:30pm and 3:30-6:30pm, Sun. 9:30am-12:30pm. Free. Closed during August for vacation). The small museum outlines Dante's life, but you'll get a better idea of a characteristic 14th-century dwelling at **Palazzo Salviati,** a few blocks away on Via della Vigna Vecchia at Via dell'Isola delle Stinche.

Equidistant from the *duomo* and the Signoria is the intriguing **Orsanmichele,** Via dei Calzaiuoli (tel. 28 47 15). Built in 1337, it is the only surviving example of the Florentine Gothic architectural style. Originally built as a granary and *loggia,* and only later partially converted into a church, Orsanmichele today mixes secular and spiritual concerns in the statues along its façade: they represent the patron saints of the major craft guilds. These niched figures make up another gallery of Florentine art: look for Ghiberti's *St. John the Baptist* and *St. Stephen,* Donatello's *St. Peter* and *St. Mark,* and Giambologna's *St. Luke.* Inside, Bernardo Daddi's miraculous *Virgin* is encased in a Gothic tabernacle designed by Andrea Orcagna. Temporary exhibits are shown in the *saloni* on the top floor; it's worth the climb just for the view of the cityscape. (Open daily 8am-noon and 3-6:30pm. Free.)

Markets, Palazzi, and Santa Maria Novella

After hours of contemplating great Florentine art, visit the area which financed it all. In the early 1420s, 72 banks operated in Florence, most in the area around the **Mercato Nuovo** and **Via Tornabuoni.** Trade generated profits that were then reinvested in land and the manufacture of wool and silk. The Mercato Nuovo arcades, constructed in 1547, housed the gold and silk trades. Pietro Tacca's ferocious statue *Il Porcellino* (The Little Pig), actually a wild boar, was added some 50 years later. Its snout remains brightly polished—rubbing it supposedly brings good luck. The starkly neoclassical **Piazza della Repubblica** replaced the Mercato Vecchio, the old market, in 1890. Today, the inscription *"Antico centro della città, da secolare squalore, a vita nuova restituito"* ("The ancient center of the city, squalid for centuries, restored to new life"), seems ironic, emblematic of a more determinedly progressive age. The statue in the center, on the corner near the UPIM store, is a facsimile of Donatello's statue of *Abundance,* which once presided over the square. Here you'll find several of the city's most popular *caffè.*

As Florence's 15th-century economy expanded, its bankers and merchants showed off their new wealth by erecting palaces grander than any seen before. The great Quattrocento boom commenced with the construction of the **Palazzo Davanzati,** Via Porta Rossa, 13. Today the *palazzo* has been reincarnated as the **Museo della Casa Fiorentina Antica** (tel. 21 65 18), and illustrates the lives of affluent 15th-century merchants. The building houses furniture, tapestries, utensils, and paintings typical of a wealthy family during the Renaissance. See a video on the history of the building at 10am, 11am, and noon on the fourth floor (about 40min., either in Italian or English, depending on the crowd). (Open Tues.-Sat. 9am-2pm, Sun. 9am-1pm. Admission L4000.)

The relative modesty of the Palazzo Davanzati soon gave way to more elegant and extravagant *palazzi.* The **Palazzo Strozzi** (tel. 21 59 90), on Via Tornabuoni at Via Strozzi, begun in 1489, may be the most august of its kind. With its regal proportions and carefully rusticated façade, it is the best example of the Florentine *palazzo* type, which has spawned endless permutations the world over. (Open Mon., Wed., and Fri. 4-7pm. Free.) Alberti's architectural triumph of half a millennium ago, the **Palazzo Rucellai,** Via della Vigna Nuova, 16, is renowned for its delicate classical façade. Its newly renovated interior now houses the **Alinari Museum of Photographic History** (tel. 21 33 70), with temporary exhibits from the vast Alinari photo archives. (Open Thurs.-Tues. 10am-7:30pm. Admission L5000, students, children, and senior citizens, L3000.)

Many owners of the earlier *palazzi* also commissioned family chapels in the **Church of Santa Trinità** (tel. 21 69 12), on Via Tornabuoni, so as to spend eternity in the best company. The fourth chapel on the right houses remains of a fresco cycle of the life of the Virgin and, on the altar, a magnificent *Annunciation* by Lorenzo Monaco. Scenes from Ghirlandaio's life of St. Francis illuminate the Sassetti chapel in the right arm of the transept. The famous altarpiece of the *Adoration of the Shepherds*, also by Ghirlandaio, rests in the Uffizi; the one you see here is a copy. (Open Mon.-Sat. 7am-noon and 4-7pm.)

The wealthiest merchants built their chapels in the **Church of Santa Maria Novella** (tel. 21 01 13), near the train station. Built from 1246 to 1360, the church boasts a green and white Romanesque-Gothic lower façade. Giovanni Rucellai commissioned Alberti to design the top half and then had a chapel built inside. Frescoes covered the interior until the Medici commissioned Vasari to paint others in their honor; they ordered most of the other walls whitewashed so their rivals would not be remembered. Fortunately, Vasari respected Masaccio's powerful (but misnamed) *Trinity,* the first painting to use geometric perspective. About halfway down the left side of the nave, Masaccio's fresco creates a tabernacle in the wall; its perspectival sense creates both projection and recession into space to include the worshipper in a brooding and prophetic vision of the mercy seat. The **Cappella di Filippo Strozzi,** just to the right of the high altar, contains frescoes by Filippo Lippi, including portrayals of a rather green Adam, a wooly Abraham, and an excruciatingly accurate *Torture of St. John the Evangelist.* The tomb of Filippo Strozzi by Benedetto da Mareno lies behind the altar. After making a bet with Donatello over who could create a better crucifix, Brunelleschi made the realistic wooden crucifix that can be found in the **Gondi Chapel,** to the left of the high altar. The **Sanctuary** is covered by a fantastic series of Ghirlandaio frescoes. Unfortunately, the sacristy, off the left aisle, is missing Giotto's masterful wooden crucifix. Under restoration, it should be returned to the church in 1994. (Open Mon.-Sat. 7-11:30am and 3:30-6pm, Sun. 3:30-6pm.) Next door, visit the cloister to see Paolo Uccello's frescoes, including *The Flood* and *The Sacrifice of Noah.* Even more fascinating, the adjoining so-called **Spanish Chapel,** the **museo** of the church (tel. 28 21 87), harbors the important 14th-century frescoes of Andrea di Bonaiuto. (Open Mon.-Thurs. and Sat. 9am-2pm, Sun. 8am-1pm. Admission L4000.)

Around San Lorenzo

The Medici staked out an entire portion of the city north of the *duomo* in which to build their own church, the spacious **Basilica of San Lorenzo** (tel. 234 27 31), and the Palazzo Medici. San Lorenzo was begun in 1419 following Brunelleschi's plans. The Medici loaned the city the necessary funds to build the church and in return were given control over its design. Their coat of arms, with its six red balls, is carved all over the nave; their tombs fill the two sacristies and the Cappella dei Principi behind the altar. (Cosimo's is cunningly placed in front of the high altar, thus making the entire church his personal mausoleum.) Michelangelo designed the church's exterior, but the profligate Medici ran out of money to build it, so it stands bare. (The rough brick is at least consistent with the rusticated Palazzo Medici—officially called P. Medici Riccardi—diagonally across the piazza.) Inside the basilica, two massive bronze pulpits by Donatello command the nave. (Open daily 7am-12:15pm and 3:30-5:30pm.) Next door, the **Biblioteca Mediceo-Laurenziana** (tel. 21 07 60) illustrates Michelangelo's architectural virtuosity with its recasting of the vocabulary of classical architecture in a Mannerist mode. Inside is one of the largest and most valuable collections of codices and manuscripts in the world. Changing exhibitions on themes such as Dante or Virgil can be seen in the library from April to June and September to October. At other times of year, atmospheric conditions would damage the collection. (Open Mon.-Sat. 9am-1pm. Free.)

To reach the **Cappelle Medicee** (tel. 21 32 06), go outside and walk around the church through the market to the back entrance on P. Madonna degli Aldobrandini. Intended as a grand mausoleum, Matteo Nigetti's **Cappella dei Principi** (Princes' Chapel) emulates the baptistry. Except for the operatic gilded portraits of the Medici dukes, the decor is oppressive, a rare moment of the Baroque in Florence. Michelangelo's **New Sacristy** (1524) comes as a welcome contrast, its starkly simple architectural design reflecting the master's study of Brunelleschi. Michelangelo sculpted two impressive tombs for Lorenzo and Guiliano de' Medici, representing the four stages of the day. On Guiliano's tomb recline the figures of night (the sleeping woman), and day (the alert man). In contrast, Lorenzo's tomb supports dawn (the woman who refuses to wake up), and dusk (the man tired from a hard day's work). The sculptural treatment of the female figure is especially intriguing; her unnatural look may derive from Michelangelo's refusal to work from female models. (Open Tues.-Sat. 9am-2pm, Sun. 9am-1pm. Admission a steep L9000.)

According to art historians, Brunelleschi proposed a sumptuous design for the **Palazzo Medici** (tel. 276 01), but had it rejected. With its arched window frames and Michelangelo's "kneeling" windows on the southwest corner, Michelozzo's *palazzo* set the trend in palace styles. The private chapel inside features Benozzo Gozzoli's ornate 15th-century tapestry-like murals of the three Magi as well as portraits of the Medici and their family. It's closed indefinitely for restoration. (First floor exhibition hall open Mon.-Tues. and Thurs.-Sat. 9am-1pm and 3-7pm, Sun. 9am-noon. Admission free.)

Around Piazza Santissima Annunziata

The complex of religious buildings encircling P. Santissima Annunziata emanates serenity. The *loggia* of the **Spedale degli Innocenti** (tel. 24 36 70; on the right), designed by Brunelleschi and built in the 1420s, was copied on the other side by Antonio da Sangallo a century later. The visual unity so pleased contemporary tastes that the *loggia* was continued across the façade of the church in 1601. The statue of Ferdinando de' Medici stands over the piazza in a position intentionally reminiscent of that of Marcus Aurelius in Rome's Campidoglio. The **Galleria dello Spedale degli Innocenti** contains Botticelli's *Madonna e Angelo* and Ghirlandaio's *Epiphany*. (Open Mon.-Tues. and Thurs.-Sat. 9am-1pm and Sun. 8am-noon. Admission L3000.)

The miraculous works of Fra Angelico exalt the **museum** of the **Church of San Marco** (tel. 21 07 41), one of the most peaceful and deeply spiritual spots in Florence. A large room to the right contains some of the painter's major works, including the altarpiece used in the church. Mount the stairs to see Angelico's most famous *Annunciation,* a rainbow celebration that greets you at the top. In the dormitory each cell contains its own Fra Angelico fresco, painted in flatter colors and sparse forms so as to facilitate the monks' meditation on the scene. Michelozzo's library is one of the most successful examples of Brunelleschian serenity, and on the whole, you might feel like following in the footsteps of Cosimo I, the patron of the convent, who retired here. His cell, unsurprisingly, is the largest. Look for Savonarola's cell as well, and imagine that fiery personality contemplating his tender fresco. (Open Tues.-Sat. 9am-2pm, Sun. 9am-1pm. Admission L6000. The exterior is currently under renovation.)

The **Accademia** (tel. 21 43 75) lies between the two churches at Via Ricasoli, 60. Most of the museum is off-limits, but the collection itself remains on display. Michelangelo's triumphant *David* stands in self-assured perfection under the rotunda designed just for him. He was brought here from P. della Signoria in 1873 after a stone hurled during a riot broke his left wrist in two places. Note the opaque finish—during a cleaning the original polish was inadvertently removed. Leading up to *David* are Michelangelo's *Prisoners,* a series of five sculptures. The master left these statues intentionally "unfinished;" envisioning a prisoner inside the stone, he sculpted each block only enough to "liberate" it. (Open Tues.-Sat. 9am-2pm, Sun. 9am-1pm. Admission L10,000.)

From P. SS. Annunziata, take bus #6 (get off at Via Andrea del Sarto) to Sarto's **Cenacolo di San Salvi,** Via di San Salvi, 16 (tel. 67 75 70). This abbey refectory houses the Sarto's stupendous *Last Supper* (1519) alongside other 16th-century Florentine paintings. (Open Tues.-Sat. 9am-2pm, Sun. 9am-1pm. Admission L2000.) The **Cenacolo di Sant'Apollonia,** in the **Museo di Andrea del Castagno,** Via 27 Aprile, 1 (tel. 28 70 74), is no less impressive. This mid-15th-century fresco of the

Last Supper takes up an entire wall, and is del Castagno's masterpiece. (Open Tues.-Sat. 9am-2pm, Sun. 9am-1pm. Free.)

Around Santa Croce

The Franciscans built the **Church of Santa Croce** (tel. 24 46 19) as far away as possible from San Marco and their Dominican rivals. Despite the ascetic ideals of the Franciscans, it is quite possibly the most splendid church in the city. The church was begun in 1294 on a design by di Cambio, but the façade and Gothic bell tower were not added until the 19th century. Originally the nave was covered by Andrea Orcagna's master fresco cycle. Never heard of Orcagna? Maybe it's through the good offices of Vasari, who not only destroyed the entire cycle, but left Orcagna out of his famous *Lives of the Artists*. On the right of the altar, the tempera murals of the **Peruzzi Chapel** vie with the frescoes of the **Bardi Chapel;** Giotto and his school decorated both. Among the famous Florentines buried here are Michelangelo, who rests at the beginning of the right aisle in a tomb designed by Vasari, and humanist Leonardo Bruni, shown holding his precious *History of Florence* on a tomb designed by Bernardo Rossellino—a wonderful little Brunelleschian piece of architecture. Between the two sits Donatello's gilded limestone *Annunciation*. The Florentines, who banished the living Dante, decided that his corpse would not make much trouble and eventually got a tomb all ready; Dante died in Ravenna, however, and the literary necrophiliacs there have never sent him back, leaving the tomb empty. A bit closer to the altar lies Machiavelli, on whose sarcophagus no extravagance was lavished. In the right aisle is the tomb of the Pisan Galileo. The organ here is the largest in Italy. (Open Mon.-Sat. 8am-12:30pm and 3-6pm, Sun. 3-5:30pm.)

The barn-like Gothic of Santa Croce contrasts with the brittle delicacy of Brunelleschi's small **Pazzi Chapel,** at the end of the cloister next to the church. This is an excellent example of the innovations of early Renaissance architecture as well as the perfect place to recover your energy, surrounded by cool *pietra serena* pilasters, Luca della Robbia tondos of the apostles, and rondels of the evangelists by Donatello. The second cloister, also by Brunelleschi, offers even more calm. Doze against a column in perfect tranquility. The **Museo dell'Opera di Santa Croce** (tel. 24 46 19; through the *loggia* in front of the Pazzi Chapel) is still recovering from the disastrous 1966 flood that left many works, including the great Cimabue *Crucifixion,* in a tragic state. The one-time refectory contains Taddeo Gaddi's imaginative fresco of *The Tree of the Cross,* and beneath it, the *Last Supper.* (Open Thurs.-Tues. 10am-12:30pm and 2:30-6:30pm; Oct.-Feb. 10am-12:30pm and 3-5pm. Admission L3000.)

From the museum, follow Via dell'Oriuolo two blocks past P. Saluemini and turn right on Via Buonarroti to reach the **Casa Buonarroti,** Via Ghibellina, 70 (tel. 24 17 52), which houses Michelangelo memorabilia and two of his important early works, *The Madonna of the Steps* and *The Battle of the Centaurs.* Both are in the first rooms to the left of the landing on the second floor. He completed these panels when he was about 16 years old; they show his transition from bas-relief to full sculpture. (Open Wed.-Mon. 9:30am-1:30pm. Admission L5000, students L3000.)

A few streets north of Via Ghibellina stands the **Synagogue of Florence,** also known as the **Museo del Tempio Israelitico,** Via Farini, 4, at Via Pilastri (tel. 24 52 52 or 24 52 53). Said to be the most beautiful synagogue in Europe, and built between 1872 and 1874 by the architects Micheli and Treves, the Sephardic temple is decorated in a modified Moorish style, enhanced with elaborate geometrical designs. (Open Mon.-Thurs. 11am-1pm and 2-5pm, Fri. 11am-1pm, Sun. 10am-1pm. Admission L3000, students L2000. Frequent informative tours.)

In the Oltrarno

Historically disdained by downtown Florentines, the far side of the Arno remains a lively, unpretentious quarter. Even in high season, when most Florentines avoid public places, P. Santo Spirito bustles.

Start your tour a few blocks west of P. Santa Spirito at the **Church of Santa Maria del Carmine.** Inside, the **Brancacci Chapel** houses a group of revolutionary 15th-century frescoes that were declared masterpieces in their time. In 1424 Felice Brancacci commissioned Masolino and his partner Masaccio to decorate his chapel with scenes from the life of St. Peter. While Masolino probably designed the series, which applies perspective techniques not fully grasped by previous artists, it was Masaccio who executed these revolutionary frescoes before his death in 1428, imbuing his figures with a solidity and sober dignity that built upon the innovations of Giotto. Fifty years later a respectful Filippino Lippi completed the revered cycle. Note especially the *Expulsion from Paradise* and *The Tribute Money,* which are credited to Masaccio alone. (Open Mon. and Wed.-Sat. 10am-5pm, Sun. 1-5pm. Admission L5000.)

As Brunelleschi designed it, the **Church of Santo Spirito** (tel. 21 00 30) would have been one of the most exciting pieces of sacred architecture ever. He envisioned a four-aisled nave encircled by hollow chapels, which the exterior would reveal as a series of convex bumps. Brunelleschi died when the project was only partially completed, and the plans were altered to make the building more conventional. Nonetheless, it remains a masterpiece of Renaissance harmony, similar to but far less busy than San Lorenzo. (Open daily 8am-noon and 3:30-6:30pm, in winter 4-6pm.)

Luca Pitti, a *nouveau-riche* banker of the 15th century, built his *palazzo* east of Santo Spirito, against the Bóboli hill. The Medici acquired the *palazzo* and the hill in 1550 and enlarged everything possible. The courtyard was redesigned by Ammannati; the columns captured in the rough blocks reflect the 16th-century preoccupation with the theme of nature versus art. The **Pitti Palace** (tel. 21 34 40) now houses no less than five museums. The **Museo degli Argenti** (tel. 21 25 57), on the ground floor, exhibits the Medici loot. Browse among cases of precious gems, ivories, and silver, then peruse Lorenzo the Magnificent's famous collection of vases. (Open Tues.-Sat. 9am-2pm, Sun. 9am-1pm. L6000 admission gets you into the costume and porcelain museums as well.) The **Museum of Costumes** (tel. 21 25 57) and the **Porcelain Museum** (tel. 21 25 57) host more Medici debris. (Museum of Costumes open Tues.-Sat. 9am-2pm, Sun. 9am-1pm; admission L6000. Combined ticket with Museo degli Argenti. The Porcelain Museum temporarily closed.) The **Royal Apartments,** (tel. 28 70 96) on the main floor, preserve their furnishings from the residence of the Royal House of Savoy, together with a few treasures from the Medici period. (Open Sat. 10:30-11:30am. Admission by appointment only.) The **Galleria Palatina** (tel. 21 03 23) was one of only a handful of public galleries when it opened in 1833. Today its collection includes a number of Raphaels (most, unfortunately, behind glass), and works by Titian, Andrea del Sarto, Rosso, Caravaggio, and Rubens. Note the neoclassical Music Room and the Putti Room, dominated by Flemish works. (Open Tues.-Sat. 9am-2pm, Sun. 9am-1pm. Admission L8000.) The fifth and final museum, the **Galleria d'Arte Moderna** (tel. 28 70 96), houses one of the big surprises of Italian art: the early 19th-century proto-impressionist works of the Macchiaioli school (from Livorno, of all places). The collection includes neoclassical and Romantic works as well. Look for Giovanni Dupré's sculptural group *Cain and Abel.* (Open Tues.-Sat. 9am-2pm and Sun. 9am-1pm. Admission L4000.)

The elaborately landscaped **Bóboli Gardens** (tel. 21 34 40), behind the palace, stretch to the hilltop **Forte Belvedere** (tel. 234 24 25), once the Medici fortress and treasury. Ascend Via di Costa San Giorgio (off P. Santa Felicità, to the left after crossing Ponte Vecchio) to reach the villa, an unusual construction with a central *loggia* designed by Ammannati. Buontalenti built this star-shaped bastion for Grand Duke Ferdinand I; now the fortress hosts summer exhibitions and sun-tanning exhibitionism. (Gardens open Tues.-Sun. 9am-7:30pm; April-May and Sept. 9am-6:30pm; March and Oct. 9am-5:30pm; Nov.-Feb. 9am-4:30pm. Admission L5000. Fort open 9am-10pm; in winter 9am-5pm. Free.)

The splendid view of Florence to be had from the fort is matched only by the pic-ture-perfect panorama from **Piazzale Michelangelo.** Go at sunset for the most spec-tacular vista of the city, from Ponte Vecchio to Santa Croce and beyond.

Above the *piazzale* is **San Miniato al Monte,** one of Florence's oldest churches, and one of the best examples of the early Romanesque. (Take bus #13 from the sta-tion or climb the stairs from P. Michelangelo.) The inlaid marble façade with its 13th-century mosaics is only a prelude to the incredible pavement inside, which is patterned with lions, doves, and astrological signs. Inside the Cardinal of Portugal's chapel you'll find a collection of superlative della Robbia terra-cottas (ask the sacris-tan to let you in). (Church open Mon.-Sat. 8am-noon and 2-7pm., Sun. 2:30-5:30pm; in winter Mon.-Sat. 8am-noon and 2-6pm., Sun. 2:30-5:30pm.)

ENTERTAINMENT

For reliable information on what's hot and what's not, consult *Firenze Spettacolo* (L2500). The **passeggiata** promenades along Via dei Calzaiuoli; afterwards Floren-tines frequent the ritzy *caffè* in P. della Repubblica. Street performers draw crowds to the steps of the *duomo,* the arcades of the Mercato Nuovo, and P. Michelangelo.

Florence vies with England for the honor of having invented modern soccer, and every June the various *quartieri* of the city turn out in costume to play their own medieval version of the sport, known as **Calcio Storico.** Two teams of 27 players face off over a wooden ball in one of the city's *piazze.* The line between athletic contest and riot is often blurred in these games. Check newspapers or the tourist office for the dates and locations of either historic or modern *calcio.* Tickets (start-ing at about L15,000) are sold at the Chiosco degli Sportivi on Via dei Anselmi (tel. 29 23 63).

To rub shoulders with the most chic of the jet-set Florentines, head over to **La Dolce Vita,** in P. del Carmine, *the* hot-spot of the moment (July 1993) and conve-nient to the budget lodgings in the Oltrarno. Just two blocks away, P. Santo Spirito hops with a good selection of bars and restaurants. A raucous crowd of Beautiful People frequent **Lo Sfizzio,** on Lungarno Cellini, 1, where they carouse over enor-mous drinks on the outdoor terrace (open until 1am). For a quieter evening of wine tasting, **Fuori Porta,** Monte alle Croce, 10r, offers an impressive selection of *vino* by the glass, from L4000. (Open Mon.-Sat. 10am-midnight.) **The Red Garter,** Via dei Benci, 33r, is definitely the place you want to be if you're a woman scoping out Italian men: pick up a date while listening to classic American rock. (Though there must be nicer ways to meet locals.) For an authentic Irish pub serving (you guessed it!) cider, Guinness, and other draught beers (L6000 a pint), try **The Fiddler's Elbow,** P. Santa Maria Novella, 74. It's crowded and convivial but plagued by for-eigners. (Open daily noon-12:15am.) **Angie's Pub,** Via dei Neri, 35r, (tel. 29 82 45), is an Italian place (despite the name) catering mostly to students, and therefore usu-ally uncrowded in the summer months. A selection of imported beer & cider on tap from L4000 a glass. Angie's also serves hamburgers on its own special rolls (L5000-6000; open Tues.-Sat. 12:30-3pm and 7pm-1am). For live jazz, **Jazz Club,** Via Nuova dei Caccini, 3, at borgo Pinti, lives up to its billing. (Disregard the "members only" sign on the door. Open Sept. 21-July 14.) For entertainment Italian-style, why not—bowl! **Pin's Club Bowling,** Via Faenza, 71 (tel. 238 13 80), has 11 regulation lanes. (L5000 per person per game, Sat.-Sun. L6000. Shoes L1000.) There's also pool, ping-pong, and video games. Call ahead to reserve a lane, especially if you want to bowl in the evening. (Open daily 3pm-midnight.)

Dancing

Note that many of the discos listed below cater almost exclusively to tourists, with a sprinkling of Italians who have designs on foreigners. Near Santa Maria Novella, **Space Electronic,** Via Palazzuolo, 37 (tel. 29 30 82), reflects a young international crowd with its multitudes of mirrors. Beer L7000, mixed drinks L8000. Free *karaoke.* Open Sun.-Fri. 10pm-2am, Sat. 10pm-3am. Sept.-Feb. closed Mon. Cover with 1 drink L20,000, with a copy of *Let's Go* L15,000. Or try **Yab Yum,** Via dei Sassetti, 5r (tel. 28 20 18), off P. della Repubblica. Cover with first drink L15,000. Open nightly 11pm-4:30am. In summer, Yab Yum's business moves to **Capitale** in the Parco delle Cascinè, in front of the Hotel Michelangelo (tel. 35 67 23). Take bus #17C from the *duomo* or station. Open daily. The trendy spot for Italian students is **Rockafè,** Borgo degli Albizi, 66 (tel. 24 46 62). American infiltration not yet complete. Cover L15,000. Open Sept.-June Tues.-Sun. 10pm-4am. In a tiny alleyway across P. della Signoria from the Palazzo Vecchio is **Tabasco Gay Club,** P. S. Cecilia, 3r (tel. 21 30 00), Florence's most popular gay disco. Minimum age 18. No cover, but minimum 1 drink. Open Tues.-Sun. 10pm-3am.

Festivals

The most important of Florence's traditional festivals, that of St. John the Baptist on June 24, centers around a tremendous fireworks display which rips over the city from P. Michelangelo. Easily visible from the Arno, they start at about 10pm. The summer swings with music festivals, starting in May with the **Maggio Musicale,** which draws many of the world's eminent classical musicians. The **Estate Fiesolana** (June-Aug.) fills the Roman theater in nearby Fiesole with concerts, opera, theater, ballet, and movies. For information on tickets, contact the Biglietteria Centrale in the Teatro Comunale, Corso Italia, 16 (tel. 21 62 53 or 277 92 36), or Universalturismo, Via degli Speziali, 7r (tel. 21 72 41), off P. della Repubblica. In September, Florence hosts the **Festivale dell'Unità,** with organized music and concerts at Campi Bisenzia (take bus #30).

The **Florence Film Festival,** generally held in December, is justly famous. For more information contact the film festival office at Via Martiri del Popolo (tel. 24 07 20). The **Festa dei Porcini,** an annual festival celebrating and presenting a variety of mushrooms for three days in August.

SHOPPING

The Florentine flair for design comes through as clearly in the window displays of its shops as in the wares themselves. **Via Tornabuoni's** swanky boutiques and the goldsmiths on the **Ponte Vecchio** proudly serve a sophisticated clientele. Florence makes its contribution to *alta moda* with the bi-annual Pitti Uomo show, Europe's most important exhibition of menswear (held mid-Jan. and July), and its companion Pitti fashion shows. If you're looking for high-quality used and antique clothing, try **La Belle Epoque,** Volta di S. Piero, 8r (tel. 21 61 69), off P. S. Pier Maggiore, or **Lord Brummel Store,** Via del Purgatorio, 26r (tel. 28 75 40), off Via Tornabuoni. These city boutiques make for great window shopping, but save your shopping money for the better prices you'll find elsewhere.

The city's artisan traditions continue to thrive at the open markets. **San Lorenzo,** the largest, cheapest, and most tourist-oriented, sprawls for several blocks around P. San Lorenzo, trafficking in anything made from leather, wool, cloth, or gold. (Open Mon.-Sat.) High prices are rare, but so are quality and honesty. For almost anything from potholders to parakeets visit **Parco delle Cascinè,** a park that begins west of the city center at P. Vittorio Veneto, and stretches along the Arno River. (At night the park transforms into a "strip" where dozens of transvestites solicit customers from an endless stream of cars, driven mostly by curious onlookers).

For clothing and shoes, the market held Tuesday mornings in **Parco delle Cascinè** (take bus #9, 17C, 26, or 27 from the station) is a better bet. For a flea market specializing in old furniture, postcards, and bric-a-brac, visit **Piazza Ciompi,** off Via Pietrapiana (walk out Borgo degli Albizi). Virtually undiscovered, it's one of the city's best. (Open Tues.-Sat.) Florentines are not hagglers: bargaining usually won't get you very far, but try it if you feel the asking price is truly outrageous.

Books and art reproductions are some of the best souvenirs you can carry away from Florence. Famed **Alinari,** Via della Vigna Nuova, 46-48r (tel. 21 89 75), stocks the world's largest selection of art reproductions and high-quality photographs,

L5000-8000 apiece. (Open Mon.-Sat. 9am-1pm and 4-8pm.) Rizzoli's *Maestri del Colore* series of color reproductions is a bargain. **Feltrinelli,** Via Cerretoni, 34 (tel. 29 63 20), has an unbeatable selection of art books. (Open Mon.-Fri. 9am-7:30pm, Sat. 9am-1pm.) **After Dark,** Via del Moro, 86r (tel. 29 42 03), is an English language bookstore with a book swap, magazines, and a bulletin board. The atmosphere in the afternoon is that of a literary social club, as a hip English-speaking crowd gathers to browse and converse. (Open Mon.-Sat. 10am-1:30pm and 3-7:15pm, Sun. 3-7pm.)

Cartolerie (stationery stores) and many gift shops carry samples of the famous **carta fiorentina,** paper covered in an intricate floral design. Florentine **leatherwork** is generally of high quality and is frequently affordable. Leather shops fill the city, but P. Santa Croce and Via Porta Santa Maria are particularly good places to look. A number of smaller shops, such as **Bagman,** Via dell'Alberto, 19, off Via della Scala, let you peek in at the artists. Check for such opportunities in other stores too, especially in jewelry stores: many of them sell only goods made on the premises.

One of the best leather deals in the city hides in one of its most beautiful churches. The **Santa Croce Leather School** (tel. 24 45 33/34 and 247 99 13), in the back of the church to the right, offers some of the best quality artisan products in the city, but has prices to match. (Open 9am-12:30pm and 3-6:30pm and 7:30-10:30pm.)

■■■ NEAR FLORENCE:
THE ARNO VALLEY

■ Fiesole

Atop the olive-covered hills just 8km to the northeast of Florence, Fiesole has long been a welcome escape from the sweltering summer heat of the Arno valley below. Built originally as a Roman outpost, the tiny village actually became a refuge for Etrucan fleeing the Romans. Since then it has had a quiet existence as a satellite of Florence, as well as a source of inspiration and a resting place for numerous well-known figures—among them Alexander Dumas, Anatole France, Marcel Proust, Gertrude Stein, Frank Lloyd Wright, and Paul Klee. Da Vinci even used the town as a testing ground for his flying machine. Fiesole's location affords incomparable views of both Florence and rolling countryside to the north, so beloved by Renaissance masters. A perfect place for a picnic or a day-long *passegiata*.

Orientation and Practical Information Bus and car afford the only access to Fiesole. ATAF city bus #7 from Florence leaves the Florence train station, from P. del Duomo, and from P. San Marco every 15-20min. during the day, less frequently at night (about 20min., L1100, standard ATAF ticket available at the machines). The last bus back to Florence leaves Fiesole at 11pm. The bus from Florence drops you off in **Piazza Mino da Fiesole,** at the center of town; the **tourist office** (tel. 59 87 20) is at #37, offering loads of advice and pamphlets. (Open Mon.-Sat. 8:30am-2pm.) The principal thoroughfare is **Via Gramsci,** also known as *La Principale.* At #5 you'll find the **Post Office.** (Open Mon.-Fri. 8:15am-5:30pm, Sat. 8:15am-noon.) The **Postal Code** is 50014; the **Telephone Code** is 055. In cases of **Emergency,** tel. 113. **Tourist Medical Service** (tel. 47 54 11) is a group of English-speaking general practitioners with someone always on call.

Accommodations, Camping, and Food Fiesole's natural beauty and tranquility unfortunately caters primarily to wealthier tourists. Budget travelers aren't out of luck, though—you can enjoy a full day in Fiesole and still have time to return to Florence for the night. If you're dying to stay, try **Villa Sorriso,** Via Gramsci, 21 (tel. 59 027), a plain and simple place with frank, friendly management. (Singles L60,000. Doubles L88,000-98,000—some with bath, some with shower only.) **Camping Panoramico,** Via Peramonda, 1 (tel. 59 90 69), is 3km out of town with a back-breaking hill at the end of the journey. Take bus #70 from Fiesole, which runs about 12 times per day, the last one at about 7pm (L1100) and encounter beautiful facilities, including a store and a bar. (L8500 per person, L13,900 per tent, auto included.) Overpriced, tourist-trap restaurants abound in Fiesole. Opt for one of the several markets and fruit stands on **Via Gramsci,** and make a picnic, or stop and shop at the **COOP supermarket,** Via Gramsci, 20. Indulge in a feast of bread, S. Daniele prosciutto, ripe tomatoes, basil, ricotta, olives, and artichokes. (Open Sun.-Tues. and Thurs.-Fri. 8am-1pm and 5-8pm, Wed. 8am-1pm.)

Sights and Entertainment Directly across P. Mino da Fiesole from the tourist office you'll see the 11th-century **Cattedrale di San Romolo.** Upstairs to the right of the Salutati Chapel lies the tomb of the bishop of the same name and his altar, both works of Mino da Fiesole (1430-1484). The marble of the tomb, with its delicate carvings, resembles a translucent jewel. (Open daily 7:30am-noon and 4-7pm.)

The **Bandini Museum,** behind the *duomo,* houses a select collection of Renaissance works, including an *Annunciation* by Taddeo Gaddi, Cosimo Rosselli's *Crowning of the Virgin,* and paintings by Jacapo di Firenze. (Open Wed.-Mon. 9:30am-1pm and 3-7pm. A ticket to the Bandini Museum, Teatro Romano, and Antiquarium Constanini costs L6000. A separate ticket to the Bandini Museum costs L3000, students L2000.)

Hiding just around the corner from the Museo Bandini, on Via Portigiani, 1, are the **Teatro Romano** and **Museo Civico Archeological Zone.** The theater hosts performances year-round, more frequently during the July and August **Estate Fiesolana,** a series of music, dance, and theater performances. Call the theater for details (tel. 594 77). The archaeological museum, modeled after an Ionic temple, houses an attractively presented collection of artifacts from excavations in and around Fiesole. (Open 9am-7pm; Oct.-March Wed.-Mon. 10am-6pm. Admission L6000, including the Constanini and Bandini museums. L5000 for the theater or archeological museums alone, students L2500.)

If you take Via San Francesco up the steep hill from the main *piazza,* you'll be rewarded with an unsurpassed view of Florence and the valley that the Arno has chiseled into the surrounding hills. Further along the street you'll arrive at the **Church of Sant'Alessandro.** Don't let its white-washed, modern façade dissuade you from entering. Within is the nave of a 4th-century basilica graced by antique Eubean (Greek) columns made of rare *marmo cipollina* (onion marble), topped by delicate Ionic capitals. (The church keeps erratic hours and is usually closed. Ask at the tourist office or just hike up; the views outside are spectacular anyway.)

■ Prato

The grace of Northern Italy begins 30min. from Florence. The machine shops and textile mills outside this hamlet have earned it the nickname "the Manchester of Tuscany." A self-governing republic in the 12th century, Prato flourished in textile production and the arts, and maintained schools of mathematics and theology. The Ghibelline-Guelph feud split the city, and Prato became part of the Florentine Republic. The present city is not one of the highlights of the region, but it does make a pleasant day trip from Florence (30min. by bus or train).

ORIENTATION AND PRACTICAL INFORMATION

There are two stations in Prato; get off at Stazione di Porta al Serraglio (from Florence ½hr., L2400), which is in fact more centrally located than Stazione Centrale. From the station, walk straight down Via Magnolfi to the **Piazza del Duomo.** CAP buses also run frequently from Florence, ending up in piazza Filippo Lippi, just behind the P. Duomo (3 per hour, L2400). From the *duomo,* head down Via Mazzoni and take a left on Via Cairoli to find the **tourist office** at #48. The city is surrounded by ancient walls.

Tourist Office: Via Cairoli, 48 (tel. 24 112). Thorough, detailed brochures and a list of *affita camere* and *agriturismo* homes in and around Prato. Open Mon.-Sat. 9am-1pm and 4-7pm.

Post Office: Via Archivescovo Martini, 8 (tel. 49 001). Open Mon.-Fri. 8:15am-7pm, Sat. 8:15am-noon. **Postal Code:** 50047.

Telephones: SIP, P. del Duomo, 33. **Telephone Code:** 0574.

All-Night Pharmacy: P. Mercatale, 146/A (tel. 30 327); P. Ospedale, 5.

Emergencies: tel. 113. **Police: Polizia Municipale,** tel. 423 91. **Hospital: Guardia Medica,** Via de' Mazzamati, (tel. 38 438). **Ospedale di Prato,** (tel. 49 42 54), **Misericordia,** Via del Seminario, 26 (tel. 21 666). They will send an ambulance.

ACCOMMODATIONS AND FOOD

Albergo Il Giglio, P. San Marco, 14 (tel. 370 49), 3 blocks from train station. Same management as the Roma, but more upscale. Shower included. Curfew 1am. Singles L46,000, with bath L58,000. Doubles L69,000, with bath L84,000.

Pick up fruit and vegetables at the **market** in P. Filippo Lippi, behind the *duomo* (Mon.-Sat. 8am-1pm.) One of the *bar* should do the trick for lunch: the best is **Pizzeria/Bar La Paglietta,** Via Magnolfi, 30, 100m from P. del Duomo. Renato, who has been written up in local papers for his friendly countenance and hearty fare, serves delicious slices of his "grand passion" for L2000. (Open Mon.-Sat. 7am-8pm.)

SIGHTS

In P. del Duomo, the **Cathedral of San Stefano's** Romanesque and Gothic façade, with alternating bands of white stone and green marble, endows the structure with rare elegance. The *duomo's* most unusual feature is the pagoda-like **Pergamo del Sacro Cingolo** (Pulpit of the Sacred Belt), a reproduction of which projects from the cathedral's façade at its right corner. The original resides in the Museo dell'Opera del Duomo next door. The pulpit represents a brilliant collaborative effort: Donatello sculpted the fine bas-relief *putti,* the sprightly and sensuous cherubs that dance around the smooth marble exterior, while Michelozzo contributed the delicately classical canopy and the supporting entablature. The pulpit was commissioned to honor the local legend of the *sacro cingolo.* When the apostle Thomas asked to see Mary's tomb as proof of her Assumption, he found it filled with flowers. Looking to heaven, he saw the Virgin herself, who gave him her belt as confirmation, and doubting Thomas doubted no more. This gift is celebrated five days a year (Easter, May 1, Aug. 15, Sept. 8, and Dec. 25), when church dignitaries ascend to the pulpit and display the *sacro cingolo* to enthusiastic crowds. Other works from the cathedral that are now housed in the museum include the recently revived *Death of St. Jerome* by Prato native Filippo Lippi.

The *duomo* holds a number of artistic treasures. To the left of the entrance is the **Chapel of the Sacro Cingolo,** which Agnolo Gaddi decorated with frescoes depicting the life of the Virgin. Giovanni Pisano sculpted the *Madonna and Child* on the chapel's altar. Halfway up the nave on the left is another pulpit, the work of Antonio Rossellino and Mino da Fiesole, who carved it with scenes from the lives of St. Stephen and St. John the Baptist (the patron saints of Prato and Florence, respectively). In the apse a masterful fresco series by the libertine monk Filippo Lippi depicts the chaste lives of St. Stephen and St. John. The vivid action and attention to courtly detail suggest an artistic temperament ill-suited to monastic life. And in fact, Lippi's model for Salome, a brown-eyed nun, gave birth to their illegitimate son, Filippino, who became a distinguished painter himself. The Pope pardoned the sinning couple and (belatedly) released them from their vows. The **Museo dell'Opera del Duomo** (tel. 293 39), contains Filippo Lippi's *Death of S. Girolamo,* and Filippino's *St. Lucy.* (Open Mon. and Wed.-Sat. 9:30am-12:30pm and 3-6:30pm, Sun. 9:30am-12:30pm. Admission L5000; under 18 and over 60 free.)

The ticket to the museum permits entrance to two other museums in Prato, the **Galleria Comunale** (tel. 45 23 02) and the **Museo di Pittura Murale.** For the Galleria, turn left from the steps of the *duomo* onto Via Manzoni and proceed to P. Comune, which is dominated by the **Palazzo Pretorio,** the seat of executive authority under the ancient republican government of Prato. Inside the Galleria offers a small but distinguished collection of painting and sculpture. On the second floor, a gallery of 13th- and 14th-century altarpieces displays works by father and son Lippi, including Filippo's warm and humorous *Nativity with St. Vincent.* **The Museo di Pittura Murale,** P. San Domenico, 18, down Via Guasti from P. del Comune, has only recently opened to the public. Bernardo Daddi's important work, *The Story of the Holy Girdle,* can be found in this museum, along with other handily restored frescoes from the Prato area. (Both museums open Mon. and Wed.-Sat. 9:30am-12:30pm and 3-6:30pm, Sun. 9:30am-12:30pm.)

Walk back to P. del Comune, go straight two blocks, and turn right to arrive at the **Church of Santa Maria delle Carceri** (1484-1492), by Giuliano da Sangallo. Andrea della Robbia authored the refined frieze. (Open daily 6:30am-noon and 4:30-7pm.)

◼ Pistoia

Pistoia came into its own in 1177, when it joined a handful of other Italian city-states in declaring itself a free commune. Despite this bold debut, Pistoia's neighbors soon surpassed it in military, political, and economic sophistication. Coveting Pistoia's dagger-producing smithies, Florence vied with Pisa and Lucca for possession of the city. Not until the fall of the Medici did Pistoia regain its independence. Pistoia's claim to fame (or infamy) is the tool of war it perfected in the 16th century—the pistol. Today, the city is home to one of the world's leading train manufacturers. Beyond the factories, fields of bright flowers undulate with the hills: this city of steel is also one of Europe's leading greenhouses. Pistoia makes a good day trip from Florence (35min.), but if you're on a tight schedule, head to the less steel-edged towns of Tuscany first.

Orientation and Practical Information From the train station, the center is easily reached by walking straight up Via XX Settembre and straight on to Via Vanucci, Via Cino, and Via Buozzi, at the end of which you turn right for the *duomo* (15min). You can also take bus #10, 12, 26, 27, or 28 to the *duomo* from the station (buy tickets at the COPIT office outside the station, L800). Or take the Lazzi bus (tel. 25 132; L4800); last bus returns to Florence at 9pm. The **Tourist Office** is in Palazzo dei Vescovi, P. del Duomo (tel. 21 622). Open Mon.-Sat. 9:30am-12:30pm and 3:30-6:30pm, Sun. 9:30am-12:30pm and 3:30-6pm; off-season Mon.-Sat. 9:30am-12:30pm and 3:30-6pm. The **Post Office** is at Via Roma, 5 (tel. 22 756), off P. del Duomo. Open Mon.-Fri. 8:30am-7:30pm, Sat. 8:30am-1pm. **Postal Code:** 51100. **Telephones** are in Piazza Garibaldi. Open 24 hrs. **Telephone Code:** 0573. There's a **Late Night Pharmacy,** in Piazza del Duomo. If they're not open, they'll have the address of the nearest one that is. For **Emergencies** dial 113. **Police: Carabinieri,** tel. 21 212. For medical assistance call **Misericordia,** 20 321.

Accommodations and Food A reasonable room at a reasonable price is a rare find in Pistoia. It makes more sense to see Pistoia on a daytrip from Florence. If you do spend the night, try **Albergo Firenze,** Via Curtatone e Montanara, 42 (tel. 231 41), near Via Buozzi at Via degli Orafi. Singles L42,000, with bath L52,000; doubles L75,000, with bath L85,000. Breakfast L8000. Visa, MC.

Cruise side streets for grocery and inexpensive specialty shops. Market junkies will want to browse at the slightly touristy **open-air market** held in P. della Sala every Wednesday and Saturday (7:30am-2pm). A daily fruit and vegetable **market** is also held on weekdays in P. della Sala, near the *duomo* (8am-2pm). For a sit-down meal try **Pizzeria Tonino,** Corso Gramsci, 159b (tel. 33 330), behind the Palazzo

LUCCA

Marchetti. Try the wonderfully tasty and filling *gnocchi* (L7000), or a Tuscan favorite like the grilled *salsicce* (sausage, L7000). Open Tues.-Sun. noon-2:30pm and 7:30pm-midnight. Visa, AmEx.

Sights and Entertainment Geographically and culturally, Pistoia converges on the **Piazza del Duomo,** with the **Cattedrale di San Zeno** on the right. Originally erected in the 5th century, the church has since been rebuilt three times. Inside the *duomo* you'll find an impressive store of early Renaissance art; look for the della Robbia lunette over the central door and several sculptures by Verrocchio. Most remarkable is the *Dossale di San Jacopo,* an enormous silver altarpiece that rests in a plain chapel on the right wall. (Cathedral open Mon.-Sat. 7am-noon and 4-7pm, Sun. 7am-1pm and 4-7pm except during services.) The octagonal 14th-century **baptistry** across from the *duomo* presents a modest exterior enlivened by Nino and Tommaso Pisano's *Virgin and Child* in the tympanum. (Open Tues.-Sun. 9:15am-12:30pm and 46:30pm.)

To the left of the *duomo* stands the **Palazzo Comunale.** Built in the 13th and 14th centuries, the *palazzo* has a curious detail on its façade: left of the central balcony an arm reaches out of the wall, brandishing a club above the black marble head below—a tribute to the 1115 Pistoian victory over the Moorish king Musetto.

The **Centro Marino Marini** houses the Pistoian artist's drawings, etchings, and sculptures. On the first landing is Marini's *Erode* (Herod), a portrayal of the king holding a dead child at his side. At the top of the stairs, ask the guard to let you into the Assembly Room to the left; in the far corner, you'll find Agenore Fabbri's *Ancora una Pietà,* in which the tortured bodies of Christ and his mother evince a visceral agony. (Open Tues.-Sat. 9am-1pm and 3-7pm, Sun. 9am-12:30pm. Free.) Upstairs the **Museo Civico** hosts a collection of happier paintings from the 13th through 19th centuries. (Open Tues.-Sat. 9am-1pm and 3-7pm, Sun. 9am-12:30pm. Admission L3000, under 18 and over 70 free; Sat. afternoon free.)

Exit P. del Duomo by Via del Duca and continue up Via dei Rossi; the typical Pisan Romanesque façade of the **Church of Sant'Andrea** will appear on the left. Here Giovanni Pisano carved a pulpit that almost shows up his efforts in Pisa. The sculptor saved the most impressive scene, the *Massacre of the Innocents,* for the panel most clearly visible from the nave. (Open daily 8am-1pm and 4-7pm.)

At the southern end of the city, on Via Cavour at Via Crispi, don't miss the 12th-century **Church of San Giovanni Fuorcivitas.** The single-naved interior is a vast, box-like space. The church contains Luca della Robbia's vibrant *Visitation,* and a font by Giovanni Pisano. (Open daily 8am-1pm and 4-7pm.)

The thousand or so remaining flower children of western Europe converge annually on Pistoia for the **Pistoia Blues** concert series held during the last weekend of June. For information and tickets (L40,000 for the weekend, L26,000 for one evening), inquire at the tourist office or the *Comune di Pistoia* (tel. 37 11). The summer festival culminates with the **Giostra dell'Orso** (Joust of the Bear), held in P. del Duomo on July 25, the feast of St. James (patron saint of the city). The *Giostra* began in the 14th century as a bloody contest between 12 mounted knights and a dressed-up bear.

■ Lucca

Overshadowed by its neighbors Pisa and Florence, Lucca conserves within its tree-topped ramparts a hospitable old-world quiescence, contentedly undiscovered. Once a Roman colony, Lucca was regarded as the capital of Tuscany by the Goths and Lombards after the fall of the Roman empire. Silk trading from the 12th through 14th centuries earned Lucca prestige and prosperity that found a lasting expression in fine religious and secular buildings.

ORIENTATION AND PRACTICAL INFORMATION

Trains provide the most convenient form of transportation to Lucca, from either Florence (Florence-Viareggio line, 90min., L5700) or Pisa (30min., L2400). The station lies just outside the city walls; from the station, walk left on Viale Cavour and enter the first city gate on the right. Inside the walls, head left on Via Carrara; Via Vittorio on your right will lead you to **Piazza Napoleone** (also known as P. Grande), the hub of the city. **Lazzi** buses also run to Pisa and to Florence, stopping in many other towns in the immediate area (to Pisa L2600, Florence L7400, Prato L6000, Pistoia L4800). To get to the tourist office, head to the far end of P. Napoleone (one big parking lot), turn left on Via Vittorio Emanuele II, and follow it until it hits the city wall. The white building to your right is the tourist office.

Centro Accoglienza Turistica, P. Verdi. (tel. 53 592). An office immured within a former city gate, from which the enthusiastic staff gives out brochures and rents bikes (L2000 per hr., L10,000 per day; rental open 10am-7pm). Also **exchanges currency**—though at these rates it's gateway robbery. Office open daily 9am-7:15pm; Nov.-March 9am-1:30pm; exchange open Mon.-Sat. 9am-1pm and 3-7pm.
Currency Exchange: Credito Italiano, P. S. Michele, 47 (tel. 47 546). Open Mon.-Fri. 8:20am-1:20pm and 2:45-4:15pm.
Post Office: Via Vallisneri (tel. 45 690), off P. del Duomo. Open Mon.-Fri. 8:15am-7pm, Sat. 8:15am-noon. **Postal code:** 55100.
Telephones: Via Cenami, 15-19 (tel. 55 366), off P. San Giusto. Open Mon.-Sat. 8:45am-12:30pm and 3:30-7pm. **Bar Casali,** P. San Michele. Open 8am-10pm. **Telephone code:** 0583.
Pharmacy: Farmacia, P. San Michele, 42. Open Mon.-Sat. 9am-1pm and 4-8:30pm.
Emergencies: tel. 113. **Police: Carabinieri,** tel. 112. **Hospital:** Campo di Marte (tel. 97 01). **Medical Assistance: Misericordia,** tel. 49 23 33.

ACCOMMODATIONS AND FOOD

The **CIV-EX travel agency,** at Via Veneto, 28 (tel. 56 741), provides an accommodations service and a list of families in Lucca who rent rooms in private houses.

Ostello della Gioventú Il Serchio, Via Brennero, 673 (tel. 34 18 11). Take bus #1 or 11 from P. Giglio (last bus 8pm), or walk out Porta S. Maria. Turn right onto Via Batoni and then left onto Viale M. Civitali and follow the signs for the *ostello* (20min.). Charmless and cheek-by-jowl. Check-out 9am; office open 4:30-11:30pm. Curfew 11:30pm. L14,000 for bunk bed, shower, and breakfast. There is also a bar which serves food (plate of spaghetti L5000). Hostel card required, but they may slip you in if you don't have one.
Albergo Diana, Via del Molinetto, 11 (tel. 49 22 02), off P. San Martino. Attractive rooms, grandfatherly manager. Singles L40,000. Doubles L65,000, with bath L80,000.
Albergo Melecchi, Via Romana, 37 (tel. 95 02 34). Attractive rooms, but a bit out of the way. Go out the city walls at porta Elisa, and walk straight out Viale Cadorna. At its end, 2 or 3 blocks on, turn left onto Via Tiglio, and make your first right onto Via Romana. Singles L27,000. Doubles L52,000.

Eating out is no problem in Lucca, where an abundance of cheap *trattorie* serve delicious Tuscan food and just as many well-stocked *pizzicherie* (delicatessens) offer great sandwiches, fresh fruit, and veggies. The **central market** occupies the large building at the west side of P. del Carmine. (Open Mon.-Sat. 7am-1pm and 4-7:30pm.) An **open-air market** overruns P. Anfiteatro every Wednesday and Saturday (8am-1pm). The **Supermercato STANDA** stands at Via Emanuele, 50, off P. Napoleone.

Ristorante Da Guido, Via Battisti, 28 (tel. 47 219), at Via degli Angeli. The local sports culture inhabits this small rooms filled with the sounds of the latest soccer match or cycling race on the television as locals enjoy the cheap and filling meals.

Gentile proprietor who welcome tourists adds the perfect touch. *Penne all'arrabbiata* (made with lots of hot pepper) only L3500. Most *secondi* L6000, including roasted veal or rabbit. Open Mon.-Sat. noon-2:30pm and 8-10pm.

Pizzeria Rusticanella 2, Via San Paolino, 30, between P. Verdi and P. San Michele. Float indoors on the aroma of their mouth-watering pizzas and order one under the ceiling light straight out of Dickens. Slices from L1000. If you're not up for pizza, try the *tortelle casalinghe* (L5000) or *salsicce* (sausage, L5000). Open Mon.-Sat. 11am-3pm and 6-10:30pm.

SIGHTS AND ENTERTAINMENT

Piazza Napoleone, in the heart of Lucca, is the town's busy administrative center. The 16th-century **Palazzo Ducale** houses government offices. Head down Via del Duomo to the noble **Piazza San Martino,** where the ornate, asymmetrical **duomo San Martino** leans against its bell tower on one side and the post office on the other. The architects designed the façade around the pre-existing bell tower, which had been constructed two centuries earlier. The 12th- and 13th-century reliefs include Nicola Pisano's *Deposition* and *Nativity* above the right door, and reliefs depicting St. Martin's life and the *Labors of the Months* between the doors. Matteo Civitali, Lucca's famous sculptor, designed the floor, contributed the statue of St. Martin to the right of the door, and executed two beautiful sculptures of angels for the altar. His prize piece is the **Tempietto** half-way up the left aisle, which houses the *Volto Santo,* a wooden crucifix said to be the true image of Christ. Sculpted by Nicodemus right after Calvary, the statue passed into the hands of Bishop Gualfredo. Somewhat ignorant of navigational technique, the bishop set off in a boat without a crew or sails, but, miraculously, the boat landed safely at Luni. To settle the ownership dispute that arose between Lucca and Luni, the statue was placed on an oxcart and the oxen were left to choose the rightful site; they turned immediately toward Lucca. (The *Volto* is taken for a ride through the town every September 13 in commemoration.) In an alcove in the left transept is the delicately sculpted *Tomb of Ilaria del Caretto,* by Jacopo della Quercia. The sacristy contains the beautiful and well-preserved *Madonna and Saints* by Ghirlandaio, and Tintoretto's *Last Supper* waits in the third chapel on the right. (Open daily 7am-noon and 3:30-6:30pm; Oct.-Feb. 7am-noon and 3-5:30pm.)

From the cathedral, return to P. Napoleone past the 12th-century Church of San Giovanni, turn right on Via Beccheria, and continue to central **Piazza San Michele,** the old Roman forum, which is ringed by impressive brick *palazzi* typical of Medieval Lucca. The annual **Palio della Balestra,** a crossbow competition dating back to 1443, takes place here. The participants appear in traditional costume on July 12 and September 14 for the competition, which was revived as a tourist draw in the early 1970s. The **Church of San Michele in Foro,** again with multi-patterned columns, epitomizes Pisan-Lucchese architecture. (Open 8:30am-12:30pm and 3:30-7:30pm.)

From the piazza, stroll along nearby **Via Fillungo,** Lucca's best-preserved Medieval street. Off P. Scalpellini rises the **Church of San Frediano,** an imposing Romanesque structure graced by a huge polychrome mosaic—*The Ascension* by Berlinghieri—on its façade. Within, the second chapel to the right holds the decaying (officially incorruptible) **mummy of Santa Zita,** the beloved Virgin of Lucca. One chapel over to the left are the frescoes of the *Legend of the Volto Santo* by Amico Aspertini—drop a L100 coin into the box to illuminate the intricate designs of the sparkling tiles. (Open 8:30am-12:30pm and 4-7:30pm.)

From the church, cut across P. Anfiteatro (former site of a Roman amphitheater) to Via A. Mordini. A right on Via Guinigi will bring you to the **Palazzo Guinigi,** a splendidly preserved complex of Medieval palaces alternating red brick and white marble columns. Climb the 230 steps to reach the lofty tower of **Torre Guinigi,** crowned by flowers and small oak trees. From here you can survey as far as the Apuan Alps. (Open Mon.-Sat. 9am-7pm. Off-season 10am-4pm. Admission L3000.)

Conclude your tour of Lucca with a walk or bike ride around the perfectly intact city walls. The shaded, breezy 4km path, which is closed to auto traffic, meets grassy parks and cool fountains along the *baluardi* (battlements), from which you can appreciate both the layout of the city and the beautiful surrounding countryside high above the moat.

Lucca's calendar groans with dance and classical music events. The musical delights of the **Estate Musicale Lucchese** linger from July to September. The **Teatro Comunale del Giglio's** opera season is September. During the summer, you can take in an Italian-language **film** under the stars in Piazza Guidiccioni. (June-Aug. nightly at 9pm, L7000; students, children, and those over 60, L4000.) The **Settembre Lucchese** is a lively jumble of artistic, athletic, and folklore presentations. Pick up a calendar of events from the tourist office.

■■■ PISA

Shameless contemporary exploitation obscures the splendor of Pisa's republican history and cultural clout. Medieval Pisa rivaled Genoa, Amalfi, and Venice on the seas, extending its Mediterranean empire as far as Corsica, Sardinia, and the Balearics. From the 11th through 13th centuries, the revenues from these colonies, the profits from ferrying the First Crusade, the spoils from the sack of rival Amalfi, and money from honest trade with the Near East carried the maritime republic to the height of its power. Pisa's renowned ensemble of cathedral, baptistry, and leaning tower exemplify the innovative architecture of the Pisan Romanesque period, whose instantly recognizable stripes and blind arcades are featured on cathedrals from Sardegna to Apulia. Post-war tourism has once again revived Pisa, after five centuries of slumbering in Florence's shadow.

ORIENTATION AND PRACTICAL INFORMATION

Pisa lies on the Tyrrhenian coast of Italy at the mouth of the Arno, directly west of Florence. **APT** runs both intra- and intercity buses, connecting Pisa with other towns along the coast, including Tirrenia and Livorno. **Lazzi** buses embark on longer routes, serving destinations such as Florence, though hourly **trains** are more convenient.

The town centers not around its beautiful *duomo,* as do most Italian cities, but rather around the Arno. Most of Pisa's important sights lie to the north of the Arno; the train station unaccountably rests far to the south. To get to the **Campo dei Miracoli** ("Field of Miracles"; home to the *duomo* and leaning tower) from the station take bus #1 (buy tickets to the left outside the station, L900) or walk on Via Crispi out of P. Sant'Antonio (next to P. Emanuele), and cross the river. Via Roma leads to P. del Duomo (1.5km).

Tourist Office: P. della Stazione, 11 (tel. 42 291). Friendly staff hands out detailed maps. No accommodations service, but will call around to see who has space. Open Mon.-Sat. 9:30am-1pm and 3:30-7pm. A **branch** office at P. del Duomo (tel. 56 04 64), behind the leaning thing. Open Mon. and Fri. 9:30am-3pm and 3:30-6:30pm, Tues.-Thurs. 9:30am-3pm and Sat. 9:30am-noon and 3-6pm.

Budget Travel: CTS, Via Santa Maria, 45/B (tel. 45 431). Daytrips, international tickets, and boats to nearby islands. Be prepared to wait at least 30min. English spoken. Open Mon.-Fri. 9:30am-12:30pm and 4-7pm, Sat. 9:30am-12:30pm.

Currency Exchange: Your best bet is a bank near the center of town, but the train station offers reasonable rates and is open 24hrs. *Don't* change money anywhere near P. del Duomo.

Post Office: P. Emanuele, 8 (tel. 24 297), near the station. Go to the windows on your left. Open Mon.-Fri. 8:15am-7pm, Sat. 8:15am-noon. **Postal code:** 56100.

Telephones: at the train station. Open 24 hrs. **Telephone code:** 050.

Airport: Galileo Galilei (information: tel. 28 088). Charter, domestic, and international flights. Trains make the 4-min. trip (L900) from the train station, coincident with departures.

Trains: P. della Stazione (tel. 42 291 or 41 385), in the southern end of town. Ticket office open 8:30am-8:30pm. Trains run between Pisa and Florence every hr. (1hr., L6700), stopping in Lucca on the way (20min., L2600). The main coastal line links Pisa to Livorno (L1800), Genoa (L13,400), and Rome (L26,300).

Buses: Lazzi, P. Emanuele, 11 (tel. 46 288). Frequent service to Lucca, Pistoia, Prato, and Florence. **APT,** P. Sant'Antonio (tel. 23 384), near the station. Frequent service to Livorno and Volterra.

Late Night Pharmacy: Farmacia, P. del Duomo. Open all night.

Emergencies: tel. 113. **Police:** tel. 50 15 13. **Hospital:** on Via Bonanno, (tel. 59 21 11), near P. del Duomo. **Medical Assistance:** P. San Fredino, 6 (tel. 50 11 00).

ACCOMMODATIONS AND FOOD

Pisa has plenty of cheap *pensioni* and *locande*, but demand is always high and the new hostel is a bit of a hike. Call ahead and make reservations, or pick up the hotel map at the station, take the bus to the *duomo* and start looking.

Centro Turistico Madonna dell'Acqua, Via Pietrasantina, 15 (tel. 89 06 22). Take bus #3 from the station and ask the driver to let you off at the *ostello*. A spanking-new hostel beneath an old sanctuary. Check-out 9am. Office open 6-11pm. L17,000 per person includes shower and sheets. Singles for L30,000. L20,000 per person for beds in double or triple rooms. Sells cold drinks and bottled water.

Casa della Giovane, Via F. Corridoni, 29 (tel. 43 061), a 10-min. walk from the station. Turn right as you leave. An ACISJF hostel for women only. The staff is extremely accommodating. Reception open 7am-10pm. Curfew 10pm. L22,000 per person in clean and bright doubles, triples, and quads. Breakfast included.

Albergo Gronchi, P. Archivescovado, 1 (tel. 56 18 23), adjacent to P. del Duomo. Pretty gardens in back put you just beyond the range of the Tower, should it topple. Curfew midnight. Roomy, cool singles L28,000. Doubles L44,000.

Hotel Galileo, Via Santa Maria, 12 (tel. 40 621). Spacious rooms sporting tiled floors and frescoed ceilings more than compensate for the dark and depressing entranceway. Singles L32,000. Doubles L44,000. Triples L57,000. Quads and quints also available.

Locanda Serena, Via D. Cavalca, 45 (tel. 24 491), near P. Dante. Dingy, but spacious and cheap and in the heart of the traditional quarter. Curfew midnight. Singles L30,000. Doubles L42,000. Breakfast L4000.

Albergo Helvetia, Via Don G. Boschi, 31 (tel. 55 30 84), off P. Archivescovado, 2min. from the *duomo*. Tidy, spartan rooms. Owners speak English. Curfew midnight. Singles L32,000. Doubles L48,000, with bath L56,000. Breakfast L4000.

Camping: The 3 campgrounds near Pisa can be dreadfully hot and crowded in summer. For information call 56 17 94. **Campeggio Torre Pendente,** Viale delle Cascine, 86 (tel. 56 06 65), 1km away, is the closest. Follow the signs from P. Manin. At least L7800 per person and L5000 per tent. Open March 15-Sept. 30. **Camping Internazionale** (tel. 36 553), on Via Litoranea in Marina di Pisa, is 14km away, on a private beach with a bar and restaurant. Take an ACIT bus to San Marina di Pisa. Open April-Oct. 15. **Camping Mare e Sole** (tel. 32 757), on Viale del Tirreno, in nearby Calambrone. Bungalows on the beach. L7000 per person, L8000 per tent. Open April-Sept.

For a more authentic ambience than that manufactured by the touristy *trattorie* near the *duomo,* head toward the river. You'll find an **open-air market** in P. Vettovaglie (take Via Vigina off Lungarno Pacinotti), at the heart of the residential quarter preferred by Pisans. Bakeries and *salumerie* also abound. Buy staples at the **COOP supermarket** at P. Don Minzoni and Via S. Agostino (open daily 8am-8pm). The local specialty is *torta di ceci* (or *cecina*) a delicious pizza made with chickpeas, available at most *bar-pizzerie* for L2000 per slice.

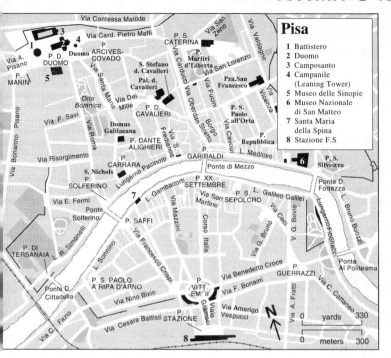

Pisa

1 Battistero
2 Duomo
3 Camposanto
4 Campanile
  (Leaning Tower)
5 Museo delle Sinopie
6 Museo Nazionale
  di San Matteo
7 Santa Maria
  della Spina
8 Stazione F.S

Trattoria da Matteo, Via l'Aroncio, 46. Off Via S. Maria, near the Hotel Galileo. Friendly proprietor whips up a wide range of culinary treats. The *gnocchi al pomodoro* (L6000) are an excellent start. For a *secondo* try the *scaloppina in umido con i funghi* (veal with mushrooms, L7000). *Pizze* L6000-9000. Open Sun.-Fri. noon-3pm and 7-10:30pm.**Pizzeria Nando,** Corso Italia, 103, between P. Vittorio Emanuele and the river. Piping hot pizzas fly to the customers straight from the mouth of the oven blazing behind the counter (L5500-7000). Fantastic *panini* created from bread that's baked to order (L3000-5000). Open Mon.-Sat. 10am-2:30pm and 4-10pm.

SIGHTS

Piazza del Duomo, also known as the **Campo dei Miracoli** (Field of Miracles), contains the **cathedral, baptistry, camposanto, and Leaning Tower,** which rise from a rare blanket of green grass enclosed by the ancient city wall. The city offers an all-inclusive ticket to the baptistry, Camposanto, the Sinopic, and the Museo del Duomo for L12,000 (individual admission for each is L5000).

The black-and-white façade of the **duomo** is the archetype of the Pisan Romanesque period. Begun in 1063 by Buscheto, the cathedral was the first structure of the Campo. Enter the five-aisled nave through Bonanno Pisano's bronze doors (1180). Though most of the interior was destroyed by fire in 1595, paintings by Ghirlandaio along the right wall, Cimabue's mosaic *Christ Pantocrator* in the apse, and the remains of the Cosmati pavement on the floor remain in good condition. Giovanni Pisano's last and greatest **pulpit,** no doubt designed to outshine his father's in the baptistry, is the *duomo's* highlight. Relief panels depict classical and biblical subjects, the *Nativity,* the *Last Judgment* and *Massacre of the Innocents* being among the most striking. (Open daily 7:45am-12:45pm and 3-6:45pm; in winter 7:45am-12:45pm and 3-4:45pm. Closed for mass 10-10:45am.)

The **baptistry,** an enormous barrel of a building that mixes the Tuscan Romanesque and Gothic styles—the lower half in typical Tuscan stripes, but for the upper half Nicola Pisano and son Giovanni created a stunning Gothic ensemble of gables, pinnacles, and statuary set in lacy tracery. Nicola Pisano's **pulpit** (1260), to the left of the baptismal font recapture the sobriety and dignity of classical antiquity, and is considered one of the harbingers of Renaissance art in Italy. Astoundingly, the dome's acoustics are such that an unamplified choir singing in the baptistry can be heard from 20km away. (Open daily 8am-7:40pm. In winter daily 9am-4:40pm. Admission L5000, or buy the inclusive ticket—see above.)

The **Camposanto,** a long, white-cloistered cemetery filled with earth brought back from Mt. Calvary by the Crusaders holds, among other things, Roman sarcophagi whose reliefs inspired Nicola Pisano's pulpit. Fragments of frescoes shattered by Allied bombs during World War II line the galleries. Enter the Cappella Ammannati to view the haunting frescoes of an unidentified 14th-century artist known for these works as the Master of the Triumph of Death. (Open daily 8am-7:40pm; off-season 9am-4:40pm.)

Cross the square from the Camposanto to the **Museo delle Sinopie,** which displays *sinopie* (preliminary fresco sketches by Traini, Veneziano, Gaddi and others) discovered during restoration after World War II. (Open daily 9am-12:40pm and 3-6:40pm; off-season 9am-12:40pm and 3-4:40pm. Admission L5000, or buy the inclusive ticket—see above.)

Leaning Tower

The last and greatest miracle in the Campo dei Miracoli is the **Leaning Tower.** Intended as the *duomo's* campanile, it was begun by Bonanno Pisano in 1173 and had reached the height of 10m when the soil beneath it unexpectedly subsided, leaning six inches. The belfry contains seven bells, each corresponding to a note on the diatonic scale. The tilt has intensified as post-World War II tourists ascended in ever-increasing numbers, and the tower continues to slip 1-2mm every year. The Tower has been **closed** indefinitely, to the dismay of thousands of visitors. More drastic measures are being taken to halt its slow collapse—for instance steel cables wrapped around the bottom story, the walls of which were thought to be in danger of fracturing. The possible construction of an aqueduct to Pisa might solve the problem, allowing the closure of all wells in the surrounding area. (Groundwater depletion by thirsty Pisans and shower-mad American tourists is thought to cause the Tower's settling.)

The new **Museo dell'Opera del Duomo,** located behind the Leaning Tower, displays artwork from the three buildings of P. del Duomo, including the ivory *Madonna and Crucifix* and *Madonna and Child* by Giovanni Pisano. (Open daily 8am-7:30pm; off-season 9am-12:30pm and 3-4:30pm.)

Beyond the Campo dei Miracoli, museums, Romanesque churches, and *piazze* dot the city. The **Museo Nazionale di San Matteo,** on the Arno not far from P. Mazzini, includes panels by Masaccio, Fra Angelico, and Pietro Lorenzetti, and sculpture by the Pisano clan. (Open Tues.-Sat. 9am-7:30pm, Sun. 9am-1:30pm. L6000.)

Piazza dei Cavalieri, designed by Vasari during Medici rule, once the Roman forum, was the civic center during the Middle Ages. Today it is the seat of the **Scuola Normale Superiore,** one of Italy's premier universities, thanks to the Medici transferring Florence's university here in the 16th century. The administrative offices of the Scuola occupy the beautiful **Palazzo dei Cavalieri,** its façade decorated with busts of the Grand Dukes of Tuscany and with graffiti.

Vasari also designed the 16th-century **Chiesa di San Stefano,** next door to the *palazzo.* (Open daily 8am-12:30pm and 4-7pm.) The patchy structure of the **Palazzo dell'Orologio,** across the piazza, incorporates the remnants of two towers.

Of Pisa's numerous churches, two merit special attention. Don't miss the **Chiesa di Santa Maria della Spina,** a spectacle of Gothic art, which faces Lungarno Gambacorti against the river. From the Campo, walk down Via Santa Maria and over the bridge. Originally an oratory, the church was enlarged in 1323 and renamed Chiesa della Spina (Church of the Thorn) because it claims to house one of the thorns from Christ's crown. (Open daily 8am-noon and 3:30-7pm.) Another worthy sidetrack from the P. del Duomo is the **Church of San Nicola,** between Via S. Maria and P. Carrara, dedicated to Pisa's patron saint. See him in the famous altarpiece of the fourth chapel on the right, breaking and deflecting the arrows a wrathful God aims at Pisa. The bell tower of the church inclines slightly, not unlike its more famous cousins. (Open daily 8am-noon and 4-6:30pm.)

ENTERTAINMENT

Occasional **concerts** are given in the *duomo,* where the acoustics are astounding. A former church on **Via San Zeno** holds performances of experimental music, and on the last Sunday in June, the annual tug-of-war, the **Gioco del Ponto,** revives Pisa's medieval color and pageantry.

■ Livorno

Overwhelmed by the monstrous liners awaiting departure for Sardegna, Corsica, Greece, and Spain, Livorno is something of a rough-and-ready port town. It has long maintained a strong cosmopolitan tradition: already an important trading center by the early 16th century, the city passed legislation providing asylum for any person suffering religious, racial, or political persecution in 1577. The population of Jews, Greeks, and other persecuted peoples subsequently swelled. Liberal thinking has marked Livornese history even into the 20th century; the P.C.I. (Partito Comunisto Italiano) was established here in 1921. Very heavy Allied bombing during World War II splintered its old city. The largely rebuilt town remains on most tourist itineraries only as a spot to hop a ship to some other destination; but at least spend your pre-departure hours exploring the few remaining monuments or enjoying the excellent local seafood.

ORIENTATION AND PRACTICAL INFORMATION

A major station on the coastal train line, Livorno is easily accessible by train from Pisa (15min., L1800), Florence (1hr., L8700), Rome (3hr., L23,700), and Piombino (1hr. 30min., L5400). Take bus #1, 2, or 8 from the train station (buy tickets outside at machines or inside at the *tabacchi* for L1000) to reach **Piazza Grande,** the center of town. Or cross the park in front of the station and walk straight down Viale Carducci, which becomes Via dei Larderel, to Piazza Repubblica. Cross the piazza and take Via delle Galere to Piazza Grande.

> **Tourist Office:** P. Cavour, 6 (tel. 89 81 11), up Via Cairoli from P. Grande. Friendly and helpful. Open Mon.-Sat. 8:30am-2pm, Tues. and Thurs. 3-6pm also. Branch office at Calata Carrara, near the Corsica departure site (tel. 21 03 31). Open June 15-Sept. 30 Mon.-Sat. 9am-noon, and some afternoons.
> **Post Office:** Via Cairoli, 12-16 (tel. 89 76 02). Open Mon.-Fri. 8:15am-7pm, Sat. 8:15am-1pm. **Postal code:** 57100.
> **Telephones: ASST,** P. Grande, 14. Open Mon.-Sat. 7:30am-11:30pm. **Telephone code:** 0586.
> **Ferries:** It is a good idea to reserve tickets about 2 weeks in advance in July and August, especially if you are traveling with a bicycle, motorcycle, or car. Be sure to check where and when your boat leaves; schedules change unpredictably with little advance notice. To add to the hassle, many of the companies listed apply hellishly complicated fare schedules for their runs to Sardinia, with up to 8 different prices for a one-way ticket. Call ahead to make sure you can afford your planned excursion or check at the tourist office which has complete information on all ferries and can decipher their fare schedules. **Corsica Marittima,** at the Stazione Marittima (tel. 89 78 51, 89 89 52, or 88 04 56). Sails to **Bastia, Corsica,** and **Livorno-Bastia:** mid-April-mid-Sept. Sat. at 3pm or 6pm. July-Aug. also Thurs. at 3pm (3hr., L38,000; April-June and 2nd week of Sept., L33,000). From P.

Granda, walk down Via Logorano, across P. Municipio to Via Porticciolo, which becomes Via Venezia, which in turn leads to the port and the Stazione Marittima. **Moby Lines:** ferries and hydrofoils to **Corsica** and ferries only to **Sardinia.** Hydrofoils to Bastia, Corsica: mid-June-mid-Sept. Mon.-Fri. at 9:30am (2hr., L49,000). Ferries to Bastia: Early June-late Sept. 1-3 per day, always a sailing at 8:30am (4hr., L34,000-45,000). Ferries to **Olbia, Sardinia:** mid-June-early Sept. 1-2 boats per day (at 10:30am or 10:30pm or both). Spottier schedule at other times. (9hr., L75,000—high season and weekends, to L37,000—off-season, morning and midweek departures.) **Corsica and Sardinia Ferries,** Calata Carrara (tel. 88 13 80 or 88 63 28), at the Stazione Marittima. Ferries to, well, **Corsica** and **Sardinia.** To Bastia, Corsica: June-mid-Sept. 1-3 boats per day (always a sailing at 8:30am). Mid-Sept.-June 2-6 boats per week. (4hr., L40,000, L34,000 off-season and midweek). To Olbia, Sardinia: ferries run mid-April-early Oct. Two sailings per day mid-June-early Sept. (at 9:30am and 9:30pm, 9-10hr., L36,000-75,000). **Emergencies:** tel. 113. **Hospital: Pronto Soccorso,** tel. 40 33 51 or 42 13 98.

ACCOMMODATIONS AND FOOD

Finding a room is easy even in summer, since most people stay here only one night before catching a boat. Avoid the train station and port areas and head into the center of town.

Hotel Goldoni, Via Mayer, 42 (tel. 89 87 05). Take Via Rossi 1 block out of P. Cavour. Clean, modern if slightly cramped rooms. Central, with compact garden. Favorite of local workers. Amiable staff. Doubles L60,000, with bath L70,000.

Hotel Corsica, Corso Mazzini, 148 (tel. 88 22 80). Lovely garden in back features a well-placed copy of Verrocchio's *puttino* fountain. Very quiet. *Caffè* inside. Singles L40,000, with bath L50,000. Doubles L57,000, with bath L70,000.

Livorno owes its culinary specialties, like its livelihood, to the sea. An **open-air market** sprawls along Via Buontalenti (Mon.-Sat. mornings 8am-1pm). Fill your brown bag at the **STANDA supermarket** off P. Grande at Via Grande, 174. (Open daily 8:30am-1pm and 4-8pm.)

La Cantonata, Corso Mazzini, 222 (tel. 88 14 42). Smiling owner dishes out huge plates of *spaghetti ai frutti di mare* (seafood spaghetti, L7000), the freshest fish, and brimming glasses of *chianti*. Other-worldly *riso nero* (rice turned black from squid ink) only L7000. *Secondi* L8000. Cover L2000. Service 10%. Open Tues.-Sun. noon-2:30pm and 7-11pm.

Trattoria Il Sottomarino, Via dei Terrazzini, 48 (tel. 23 771), off P. della Repubblica at the end of Via Pina d'Oro. Not cheap, but people come from all over Tuscany just to taste their *cacciucco,* a fiery and delicious seafood stew. Open Aug.-June Fri.-Wed. 12:30-2:30pm and 7:30-10pm.

SIGHTS AND ENTERTAINMENT

Located in the heart of the quarter known as **Piccola Venezia** for the many canals coursing through the neighborhood, the **Fortezza Nuova** is protected by a complete moat. Completed in the early 1600s by the Medici family, the fortress now houses a well-maintained public garden and park. Compare this fortress to the massive, sprawling **Fortezza Vecchia** (from the new fortress, walk to P. Municipio, and then down Via S. Giovanni). Built by the powerful Marquises of Tuscany in the 9th century, the portly tower in the middle was the first fortification on the site. When Pisans conquered Livorno, they built a fort around the tower. In the 16th century the Medici surrounded the ensemble with robust brick walls to consolidate their hold on Livorno, by then the chief Tuscan port.

Livorno has inspired two important contributions to painting. Foremost is the group of 19th-century painters "I Macchiaioli" (literally, "the blotters"), led by Giovanni Fattori . In the **Museo Civico Giovanni Fattori** (tel. 80 80 01) in Villa Fabbricotti at Via della Libertà, 20, you can see their proto-impressionist work. (Open

Tues.-Wed., Fri., and Sun. 10am-1pm, Thurs. and Sat. 10am-1pm and 4:30-7:30pm; admission L4000.) Livorno's second gift to art history was 20th-century painter Amadeo Modigliani.

Livorno's chief festival, the **Palio Marinaro,** takes place just off this stretch of coast. In mid-July, rowers from the various neighborhoods of the city race traditional craft toward the old port, to the roars of spectators crammed onto the banks.

■ Elba

"Lucky Napoleon!" Dylan Thomas exclaimed in a letter written from Elba to his friends. Once you've witnessed the island's deep turquoise waters, dramatically poised mountains, and velvety beaches, you'll share the sentiment. A surviving fragment of the giant peninsula that once joined Corsica to the Tuscan shore, Elba first drew Etruscan settlers, who mined its hills for iron. Jason and his Argonauts made a stop, but the jeering Greeks named it Aethalia (Soot Island). Roman patricians saw the island's beauty through the smoke and built their summer villas here. The present proprietors rent it out to vacationing Germans. Fortunately, the best parts of the island lie off the beaten track, and if you come in the off-season you will have virtually the whole place to yourself.

In July and August, vacationing Italians flock to Elba, so without a reservation made at least several months ahead, it is impossible to find lodging on the island. During June and September the weather is perfect and the beds plentiful. Camping may be the best way to go on Elba, but beware—camping space come as dear as a hotel on the island and often needs reserving. There are also about 100 **affita camere** on the island and about 30-40 **agriturismo** locations, depending on the month.

GETTING THERE

The only real way to reach Elba is by ferry from Piombino Marittima (also called Piombino Porto) to **Portoferraio,** Elba's largest city. Trains on the Genoa-Rome line stop at Campiglia Marittima, from which a tiny commuter train leaves for the ferries in Piombino Marittima (wait for the *porto* stop). From Florence change at Pisa to arrive at Campiglia Marittima. Both **Toremar** (1hr., L8000, hydrofoil 30min., L16,000) and **Navarma** (1hr., L8000 Mon.-Fri., L10,000 Sat.-Sun.) run frequent boats to Elba, a total of about 18 per day during the summer months. Talk directly to Toremar (tel. (0565) 91 80 80) or Navarma (tel. 22 12 12) at Piazzale Premuda, 13, in Piombino.

TRANSPORTATION

On Elba, **ATL** buses constitute the only form of public transportation between the major cities of Portoferraio, Marina di Campo, Marciana Marina, and Porto Azzurro (all L2700 from Portoferraio). Popular **boat excursions** cover various parts of the coast; contact **Etruria** in Portoferraio (tel. 90 42 73) for details. Renting a **moped** allows you to see the more isolated parts of the island; park it anywhere while you hunt out unexplored beaches.

ORIENTATION

Each of the different zones of the island attracts a distinct variety of loyal visitor, from families in **Marina di Campo** and **Marciana Marina**, to party-hard beach fanatics in **Capo Civeri**, to the private-yacht set in Porto Azzurro. The coast is mostly sandy from Procchio, around Portoferraio, down the east coast and around to Marina di Campo. Elba's western shore, with its stone-slab waterfront, remains relatively unfrequented. Wherever you decide to go, bypass Portoferraio, a chaotic port-city with the most overcrowded beach on the island. Head over to the **tourist office** as soon as you land to pick up the essential *"notizie Utili per il Turista,"* which gives information for the entire island on beaches, hotels, restaurants, entertainment of any kind, and a decent map of Elba.

■ Portoferraio

PRACTICAL INFORMATION

Tourist Office: Azienda Promozionale di Turismo, Calata Italia, 26 (tel. 91 46 71), on the 1st floor, across from the Toremar boat landing. Polyglots and information galore: accommodations, a map, bus schedule, and brochure. They have information on **agriturismo** and **affita camere** rooms in home in the cities and countryside of Elba. Open Mon.-Sat. 8am-1pm and 4-7pm. There's also a **tourist information booth** at the bus station on Viale Elba, 20, which cheerfully provides brochures, reserves rooms, holds luggage (L1500) and sells bus tickets. Open June 15-Sept. 15 Mon.-Sat. 8am-8pm. **Associazione Albergatori,** Calata Italia, 21 (tel. 91 47 54). Free room-finding. Open Mon.-Fri. 8:30am-1pm and 3-7pm; off-season 8:30am-1pm and 3-6pm.

Post Office: P. Hutre, off P. della Repubblica. Open Mon.-Fri. 8:15am-7pm, Sat. 8:15am-1pm. **Postal code:** 57037.

Telephones: SIP, Calata Italia, across Viale Elba from Hotel Massimo. Open daily 8am-10pm. In Marina di Campo, try **Pietre Bigiotteria,** Via Roma, 41. Open Mon.-Sat. 8am-10pm, Sun. 10am-noon. **Telephone code:** 0565.

Buses: ATL, Viale Elba, 20 (tel. 91 43 92). Open June-Sept. Mon.-Sat. 8am-8pm, Oct.-May 8am-1pm and 5-7pm. A list of places to buy tickets on Sun. is posted on the door. There are also public toilets here. **Luggage storage** L1500 per piece. Open daily 8am-8pm.

Ferries: Toremar, Calata Italia, 22 (tel. 91 80 80). Hydrofoil tickets available at the **Toremar Aliscati booth** on the waterfront in front of the main Toremar office. **Navarma,** Viale Elba, 4 (tel. 91 81 01).

Bike/Moped Rental: Rent Ghiaie, Via Cairoli, 26 (tel. 91 46 66), in front of the Ghiaie beach. Easily the best place to rent mopeds and bikes on the island. Rent a well-maintained bike (L16,000 for 9am-7:30pm, L20,000 for 24hrs.) or moped (daily L32,000, L36,000 for 24hrs., less in Sept.-July). You can also rent from or drop off at any of their other branches around the island (at Marciana Marina, Porto Azzurro, Lacona, or Marina Di Campo; flat L10,000 fee for returning rentals to a different branch, regardless of how many or what kind). They also give lessons; auto driver's license required. MC and Visa accepted at the Portoferraio office only. Open 9am-1pm and 3:30-7:30pm.

Emergencies: tel. 113. **Police:** (tel. 92 006), on Via Garibaldi. **Hospital: Ospedale Civile Elbano** (tel. 91 74 21), off Via Carducci. **Ambulance:** P. Repubblica, 37 (tel. 91 40 09).

If you decide that Portoferraio's charm outweighs its drawbacks, your best bet for clean, economical accommodations in this town is the **Bagni Elba,** Via dei Gasperi (tel. 91 51 78), across from the Villa Ombrosa Hotel right on the beach. Light and breezy doubles with private baths and balconies over the beach (L75,000). Reservations necessary from the middle of June through August. Infested with overpriced tourist restaurants, Portoferraio is not the place to indulge the appetite. Sustain yourself at the *rosticeria* **Pane Calda,** Via Carducci, 25, where you can find vibrantly colored rice salads for L7400, and filling *secondi* like *cotoletta alla Milanese* for L8700. Across from the port, basic picnic fare can be found at the **Margherita Supermarket,** #6 Calata Italia. (Open 7:30am-1:30pm and 4:30-8:30pm.)

If caught in Portoferraio with some time to spare, consider stopping by the **Archaeology Museum,** Fortezza dell Lingrella (tel. 91 73 98) which guides you through the history of Elba from prehistoric times to the present. (Open Mon.-Sat. 9:30am-12:30pm and 6-9pm, Sun. 6-9pm. Admission L4000, children L2000.)

■ Marina di Campo

Marina di Campo's fine sandy beaches, winding their way for miles along the coast, attract masses of vacationing families with strollers and countless boxes of diapers. The numerous campgrounds around Marina di Campo are popular with young people. You can either bake in the sun or rent sporting equipment like **windsurfers** (starting at L15,000 per hour) at "Tropical Bagni" during the day—no office or phone, just go to the beach and you'll see them. **Hotel Lido** Via Mascagni, 29 (tel. 97 60 40), in the center of town. Only a minute from the beach, with clean and comfortable rooms. (Singles L42,000, with bath L56,000. Doubles with bath L63,000.) You must reserve by Easter for July and August. Campgrounds abound in Marina di Campo. Try **La Foce** (tel. 97 64 56), a three-star place, or **Del Mare** (tel. 97 62 37), a two-star campground, both located in La Foce, which borders the left-hand side of Marina di Campo's waterfront. The **Canabis Resturant,** Via Roma, 41-43 (97 75 55), bakes the best food around, including killer crêpes stuffed with cheese and prosciutto for around L6000 (open daily 7am-2am). No brownies, though. Via Roma, along the waterfront, is also chock full of *alimentari,* where you can provision yourself for next to nothing. In summer, the party moves to **Marina 2000** at night for dancing and carousing.

■ Porto Azzurro

If you intend on staying in Porto Azzurro, brace yourself for massive financial outlay. Playspot of the too-thin and too-rich, Porto Azzurro naturally shelters some of the finest beaches on the island, but the beauty comes dear. **La Lanterna,** *affitta camera,* located above La Lanterna restaurant, is the lodging that comes closest to a bargain, charging only L44,000 for a double, with bath L58,000. In summer they might require you to take half-pension for a total of L65,000. **The Grill,** Via Marconi, 26, near the Blumarine Hotel, offers copious portions of *penne* with a choice of tomatoes or clams for L7500. (Open daily 8:30am-2:30pm and 6pm-1am.)

■ Marciana Marina

The strip of pebble beach that borders Marciana Marina's waterfront is just one of the countless beaches that hide in isolated coves along this part of the island. **Casa Lupi,** Via Amedeo, (tel. 99 143), is your best bet here. It's a bit of a hike (5-10min. uphill from the beach), but it sports clean rooms and a terrace that looks out over a vineyard to the sea below. (Singles L32,000, with bath L38,000. Doubles L46,000, with bath L56,000. In summer they require half- or full pension, L60,000 for half, with bath L65,000. Full pension L70,000, with bath L75,000.)

Marciana Marina is also the perfect base to explore the less developed western half of Elba. You can reach the numerous beaches along the western coast that are inaccessible on foot via boat; rentals available in Capo Sant'Andrea for about L100,000 per day. Bring a few friends with you and the mission to secure your own beach doesn't really cost that much. From Marciana Marina, partiers head to the **Claxon** in nearby **Procchio** to hear live music at night.

From Marciana Marina, a possible side excursion is a visit to **Monte Capanne.** From the top of this 1019m mountain one can see the entire island, and even as far as Corsica on a clear day. The strenuous uphill trek takes two hours, but a cable car will carry you up for L7500, round-trip L12,000 (open 10am-12:15pm and 2:30-6pm). To get to Monte Capanne take the bus from Marciana Marina to Marciana, and get off at the Monte Capanne stop (15min.).

From Mariana one can also walk to the **Romitorio di San Cerbone** and the **Santuario della Madonna del Monte,** two sanctuaries described by one Italian writer as "dense with mysticism," surrounded by pines. If interested in guided hikes to explore Elba's natural beauty contact **Il Genio del Bosco, Centro Trekking Isola d'Elba** in Antiche Saline, near Portoferraio (tel. (0565) 93 03 35).

■ San Gimignano

From the road approaching San Gimignano the hilltop village appears almost to be a collection of skyscrapers in some great, distant city. Only upon arrival does one see that the looming towers are actually individual houses in the tiny but perfectly preserved medieval town. The 14 towers, survivors of an original 72, recall a tumultuous period when warring families fought pitched battles within the city walls, using their towers for grain storage during sieges. They also proved to be convenient for dumping boiling oil on passing enemies. Many 13th-century Italian cities emulated San Gimignano's skyline; Florence's towers are said to have numbered in the hundreds. With the rise of the commoners in the 14th century, however, most towers were demolished. The ones that remain here are relics of San Gimignano's medieval descent into obscurity.

Tried for centuries by bloody feuds and petty wars, the prosperous pilgrimage-town of San Gimignano finally met its abrupt end with the onset of the Black Death of 1348. The Ardinghelli family made a bid to revive local fortunes by ceding control of the town to a reluctant Florence in 1353, but only succeeded in stripping themselves and the rival Salvucci of power. For the next six centuries, San Gimignano stagnated in poverty, until its punctuated horizon proved a sure lure to postwar tourists, whose custom also resuscitated production of the golden *vernaccia* wine. An overnight stay promises blissful tranquility—but joining the hordes of daytrippers will more suitably evoke the city's chaotic medieval past.

ORIENTATION AND PRACTICAL INFORMATION

TRA-IN buses run to Florence and Siena every 1-2 hours, and less frequently to Volterra. Change buses at Poggibonsi, also the nearest train station (20min., L2100). Buses arrive at Porta San Giovanni just outside the town. To get to the center, enter through the *Porta* and continue on straight up the small rise to **Piazza Dante** where the tourist office will be on your left. Follow the crowd up the hill to **Piazza della Cisterna** and **Piazza del Duomo,** which are linked.

Tourist Office: Associazione Pro Loco (APL), P. del Duomo, 1 (tel. 94 00 08). Reams of pamphlets. No accommodations service, but a complete list of hotels and rooms in private homes. Also **changes currency** and sells bus tickets. English spoken. Open daily 9:30am-1pm and 3-7pm. **Ufficio Informazioni Turistiche (UIT),** Via S. Giovanni, 125 (tel. 94 08 09) will reserve hotel rooms. Open Mon.-Sat. 9:30am-1pm and 3-7:30pm.

Post Office: Behind the *duomo.* Open Mon.-Fri. 8:15am-12:30pm and 2:45-6:30pm. **Postal code:** 53037.

Telephones: at the APL office. Also at **SIP,** Via San Matteo, 13. Open daily 8am-midnight. **Telephone code:** 0577.

Buses: TRA-IN buses leave from P. Martiri outside Porta San Giovanni. Schedules and tickets available in the UIT office, or the gift shop outside Porta San Giovanni. Change at Poggibonsi for Florence (75min., L8000), Siena (50min., L6300), Volterra (40min., L5700). Buses run direct to Volterra and Siena mid-June-mid-Sept.

Pharmacy: Via San Matteo, 13 (tel. 94 20 29). All-night availability to fill urgent prescriptions. Open Mon.-Sat. 9am-1pm and 4-7pm.

Emergencies: tel. 112. **Police: Carabinieri,** tel. 94 03 13. **Hospital:** Via Folgore da San Gimignano (tel. 94 03 12). **Ambulance: Misericordia,** tel. 94 02 63.

ACCOMMODATIONS

San Gimignano caters almost exclusively to tourists from the north, making most accommodations well beyond budget price range. Fortunately, a fantastic hostel and peaceful convent save the day if you arrive early. **Affitta camere** provide another alternative to overpriced hotels, with singles for about L40,000 and doubles about L60,000. Get a list from either the tourist office or **La Rocca,** an accommodations service at Via dei Fossi, 3/A (tel. 94 03 87), outside the walls near Parco della Rocca. The manager will be more than happy to provide names and addresses of private rooms to let, or to reserve them for L5000. (Open daily 9am-1pm and 3-9pm.)

Ostello della Gioventù, Via delle Fonti, 1 (tel. 94 19 91, fax 94 19 82), at Via Folgore di S. Gimignano. A splendid place run by congenial young people. The panoramic views, bar, and recently renovated bathrooms make this one of the most welcoming hostels in Italy. English spoken, bus tickets sold, and regional info distributed. No membership required. Reception open 7:30-9:30am and 5-11:30pm. Curfew 11:30pm. L20,000 per person. Showers, breakfast, and sheets included. Open mid-February-mid-December.

Convento di Sant'Agostino (tel. 94 03 83), in P. Sant'Agostino. Marvelous rooms (some with views) set around an otherworldy courtyard. Singles L28,000. Doubles L40,000. Triples L55,000. Write 1 mo. in advance for summer reservations. In a pinch, the manager or the monk in the gift shop will try to squeeze you in.

Ostello del Chianti (HI), Via Roma, 137 (tel. (055) 807 70 09), in **Tavernelle Val di Pesa.** It's not really anywhere near San Gimignano, but it's a nice place anyway. Take the SITA bus to Tavernelle, changing at Poggibonsi (1hr., L3400). Connections are poor, so check the schedule before you go. A superb 54-bed hostel in a beautiful setting. Membership required. Reception open 6:30-10:30pm, but you may get a key. L14,000 per person. Showers and breakfast included.

Albergo/Ristorante Il Pino, Via S. Matteo, 102 (tel. 94 04 15). Rustic simplicity. In the quiet quarter by the convent. Doubles L40,000. Showers included.

Camping: Il Boschetto, at Santa Lucia (tel. 94 03 52), 2½km downhill from Porta San Giovanni. Buses run from town to the site (L1000), but it's not a bad hike. Bar, market, and pizzeria. Office open 8am-1pm, 3-8pm, and 9-11pm. L5500 per person, L4500 per small tent, L2100 per car, L1600 per cycle. Hot showers included. Open March 27-Oct.15.

FOOD

Boar and other wild-game are San Gimignano's specialities, but the town caters to less daring palates with mainstream Tuscan fare at fairly high prices. Whether you're looking to save, or simply to savor, try the **open-air market** in P. del Duomo (Thurs. morning). The famous **Vernaccia di San Gimignano,** one of Italy's finest white wines, can be purchased at the deconsecrated church of **San Francesco** on Via San Giovanni. A **small market** with cheap, filling sandwiches and take-out pasta, salads and drinks is at 19 Via S. Matteo. (Open Mon.-Sat. 8am-1:30pm and 4-8pm.)

Pizzeria Perucà, 4 Via XX Settembre. A new 3-table pizzeria with young and enthusiastic proprietors. Take-out pieces, L1500, sit-down L4500-8500. Try the *calzone alla casa,* (filled with proscuitto, mozarella, funghi, and other assorted vegetables). Open daily noon-3pm and 4-9:30pm.

Rosticceria/Pizzeria Chiribiri, (tel. 94 19 48), the 1st left off Via San Giovanni as you enter town. Pizza sold by the slice, and plentiful pasta from L4500. Heavenly fare at down-to-earth prices. Open Thurs.-Tues. 11am-10pm.

L'Antica Trattoria, Via Cannici, 4 (tel. 94 05 81), just down the hill after you exit through Porta S. Matteo. Try some of the wild game specialties like *pappardelle alla lepre* (pasta with wild hare, L9500) or the *bocconcini di cinghiale* (boar stew L12,500). Open Tues.-Sun. noon-3pm and 7-10:30pm. MC, Visa.

Osteria Le Catene, Via Mainardi. Fast tomorrow, feast tonight in this renovated interior with medieval arches complemented by modern art posters. *Primi* from L8000, *secondi* from L15,000. Cover L3000. Service 10%. Call in advance. Open Thurs.-Tues. 12:30-2pm and 7:30-9:30pm. AmEx, Visa, and MC.

SIGHTS AND ENTERTAINMENT

Famous by the 14th century as *Città delle belle torri* (City of Beautiful Towers), San Gimignano always had enough tourist appeal that no artist could turn down a commission. They came in droves, and the resulting collection of *trecento* and *quattrocento* works luminously (and sometimes ludicrously) complements San Gimignano's asymmetric cityscape. The city rightfully treats itself as a unified work of art—one ticket (L10,000, students L7500; available at any museum or tourist sight) allows entry to almost all of San Gimignano's sights. Opening hours are also coordinated: sights are open April-Sept. daily 9:30am-12:30pm and 3:30-6:30pm; Oct.-March Tues.-Sun., same hours.

Via San Giovanni, the principal street, runs from the city gate to **Piazza della Cisterna.** The triangular *piazza,* surrounded by towers and *palazzi,* ajoins **Piazza del Duomo** where the impressive tower of the **Palazzo del Podestà** is located. To its left is the **Palazzo del Popolo** (open Tues.-Sun. 9am-7:30pm) riddled with tunnels and intricate *loggie.* To the right of the *palazzo* rises its **Torre Grossa,** the highest tower in town and the only one you can ascend; it's well worth the climb. On the left stand the twin towers of the Ardinghelli, truncated thanks to a zoning ordinance that prohibited the building of structures higher than the Torre Grossa.

Within the Palazzo del Popolo, the frescoed Medieval courtyard leads to the **Sala di Dante.** The poet spoke here in 1299 as the ambassador from Florence, hoping to convince the city to join the Guelph league. On the walls, Lippo Memmi's sparkling *Maestà* blesses the accompanying *trecento* scenes of hunting and tournament pageantry. In the **Museo Civico** Taddeo di Bartolo's altarpiece, *The Story of San Gimignano,* teaches proper respect for the bishop of Mòdena, for whom the city is named. San Gimignano calmed oceans, exorcised demons, saved the city from the Goths, and even fought the devil himself with his trusty cross—which he is pictured bringing with him as he sneaks off in the middle of Mass to relieve himself. The museum maintains an excellent collection of other Sienese and Florentine works, most notably Filippino Lippi's long-fingered *Annunciation,* crafted in two circular panels, and Pinturicchio's serene *Madonna in Glory.* The best part of the museum is the room of wedding frescoes off the stairs, a unique series of *trecento* scenes that take a couple from initial courtship to a shared bath and wedding bed.

Piazza Luigi Pecori, a courtyard behind the *palazzo,* houses the equally dull **Etruscan Museum** and **Museo d'Arte Sacra** in the same building. The latter contains some interesting medieval wood statues among the usual religious robes, but unless you're trying to get the most out of your admission stub, don't bother.

The misnamed **Piazza del Duomo** shelters not a cathedral (the town doesn't have one), but the **Collegiata,** whose bare façade hides a Romanesque interior covered with exceptional Renaissance frescoes. Start with the **Chapel of Santa Fina** off the right aisle (open same hours as Museo Civico). A marvel of Renaissance harmony designed by Giuliano and Benedetto Maiano and adorned by Ghirlandaio's splendid frescoes, the chapel is devoted to the most saccharine saint in Italy. In the main church, Bartolo di Fredi contributed Old Testament scenes along the north aisle while Barna De da Siena provided the appropriate, if less enthusiastic, New Testament counterparts along the south aisle. Taddeo di Bartolo's **Last Judgement** frescoes over the entrance are unfortunately a bit faded, but concentrated staring leads the nature of the torments endured by the damned to become clear. At the other end of town, Benozzo Gozzoli created the poignant and sensitive fresco cycle recounting the life of St. Augustine in the **Church of Sant'Agostino.** (Open 8am-noon and 3-6pm; off-season 2-5pm.)

Dinner finishes early in the hills, and the *passeggiata* along Via San Giovanni and Via San Matteo (passing by the towers of the Salvucci clan) provides the principal entertainment. During the summer pass the evening under the stars at the **Rocca** fortress where you can take in movies at San Gimignano's outdoor summer music theater (L6000; weekly showings during July and Aug.; check with the tourist office for information).

■ Volterra

When you finally find Volterra, you'll think that you've reached the edge of the world. Perched atop a huge bluff, the town broods over the surrounding checkerboard of green and yellow fields. Drawn by the cliffs' impregnability, the Etruscans established Velathri, which by the 4th century BC had become one of the most powerful cities of the Dodecapolis, surrounded by three great circuits of still-extant walls. Medieval Volterra shrank to one-third the size of its ancestor, leaving a still-palpable sense of decline and desolation. Today, the medieval mystique gives way to mercantilism: the town increasingly depends on weekend tourists to nourish its alabaster production and trade.

ORIENTATION AND PRACTICAL INFORMATION

Although nearer to San Gimignano and Siena, Volterra is linked administratively to Pisa, from which **TRA-IN** bus service is most frequent (change at Pontederra, L6800). **SITA** buses run from Florence (4 per day, 2½hr., L9000), Siena (5 per day, 2hr., L6300), and San Gimignano (4 per day, 1hr., L5100). There is a small train station 9km west of town at Saline di Volterra, with trains from Pisa (L6500) and the coastal line. **APT** buses synchronized with the trains run between Saline and Volterra (7 per day, L1900). All buses arrive and depart from **Piazza della Libertà,** where you can buy tickets from the vending machine or in the bars down the street. From P. della Libertà, take the only street leading out of the piazza, and turn left onto central **Piazza dei Priori.** From October to May bus service is less direct and you will have to change buses at intermediate stops. Ask before you go.

> **Tourist Office:** Via Turazza, 2 (tel. 86 150), just before P. dei Priori. Provides bus and train information and sells tickets. Distributes a list of only those hotels that have registered with the agency. Few pamphlets or brochures about the city or environs. Has **telephones.** Open Mon.-Sat. 9am-12:30pm and 3:30-6:30pm; Sun. (in summer only) 9am-noon and 4-6pm. **Telephone Code:** 0588.
>
> **Post Office:** P. dei Priori, 14 (tel. 86 969). Open Mon.-Fri. 8am-7pm, Sat. 8am-noon. **Postal Code:** 56048.
>
> **Public Baths: Albergo Diurno,** Via delle Prigioni, 3, off P. dei Priori. Toilets L300. Open Fri.-Wed. 8am-7pm.
>
> **Emergencies:** tel. 113. **Medical Assistance: Misericordia, Pronto Soccorso,** P. San Giovanni (tel. 86 164).

ACCOMMODATIONS AND FOOD

The spacious youth hostel, convent, campgrounds and inexpensive hotel contribute to the abundance of cheap beds in Volterra. Signs for **affitta camere** frequently appear in shop windows, facilitating a search for rooms in private homes.

> **Youth Hostel** (tel. 85 577), Via del Poggetto, across from *fortezza* near Porta A Selci. A squeaky clean hostel with a lush garden out back. Small rooms with terrific views over the city wall to the valley below. Reception open 8-10am and 7-11pm. Curfew 11:30pm. L15,000; no membership required. Breakfast L3000.
>
> **Conventa Sant'Andrea** (tel. 86 023), P. S. Andrea, next door to the church, about a 5-minute walk exiting the city from Porta A Marcoli. Quiet, private rooms off frescoed hallways. L22,000 per person, L28,000 per person in rooms with bath.
>
> **Camping: "Le Balze,"** farther down the road at Via Mandringa, 15 (tel. 87 880). This attractive campground has bungalows, a restaurant, and a refreshing pool, plus tennis, volleyball, bocce, fishing, horseback riding, and a view over Le Balze. L6500 per person, L6000 per tent, L2000 per car, L1000 per cycle. 4-person bungalow L50,000. 6-person bungalow L60,000. Hostel attached to the campground, L15,000 with breakfast. Open early March-late Oct. Reservations accepted.

An excellent selection of Volterra's game dishes and local cheeses is available at **alimentari** on Via Guarnacci and Via Gramsci. Sample *salsiccia di cinghiale* (wild boar sausage) and *pecorino* (goat) cheese. Any of the local *pasticcerie* will sell you *Ossi di Morto,* a rock-hard local confection made of egg whites, sugar, hazelnuts, and a hint of lemon. Do your bulk shopping at the **COOP supermarket,** on Via delle Casine outside the city walls. (Open Mon.-Tues. and Thurs.-Sat. 7:30am-12:30pm and 4:30-7:30pm, Wed. 7:30am-12:30pm.)

> **Il Pozzo degli Etruschi,** Via dei Prigioni, 30. Ample portions of hearty Tuscan fare served in a private garden. Try the *penne ai porcini* (pasta with mushrooms,

L5000). For *secondo* pig out on a serving of *cinghiale con olive* (wild boar with olives, L9000). Cover L2000. Service 10%. Open Mon.-Sat. 7:30am-12:30pm and 4:30-7:30pm; closed Wed. afternoons. AmEx, MC, Visa.

L'Ombra della Sera, Via Gramsci, 70 (tel. 86 663), off P. XX Settembre. Wild boars' heads on the wall create a rustic atmosphere in which you can feast on a copious portion of *tortellini* made with prosciutto and cream, L6500. *Secondi* average L10,000, for entrees such as *coniglio alla contadina* (rabbit with tomatoes and vegetables). Open Tues.-Sun. noon-3pm and 7-10pm. AmEx, Visa.

Pizzeria/Birreria Ombra della Sera, Via Guarnacci, 16. Great pizza, great prices. Pizzas L5000-7000. Open Tues.-Sun. noon-3pm and 7pm-midnight.

SIGHTS AND ENTERTAINMENT

Volterra's **Fortezza Medicea,** an elegant remnant from the period of Florentine domination used since its 1472 completion as a jail, is the first structure you'll see as you ascend to the town. Volterra revolves around **Piazza dei Priori,** a Medieval center surrounded by sober, dignified *palazzi.* The **Palazzo dei Priori,** the oldest governmental palace in Tuscany (1208-1254), presides over the square. (Open Mon.-Sat. 9am-1pm.) Across the piazza sits the **Palazzo Pretorio,** a series of 13th-century buildings and towers.

Located behind the Palazzo dei Priori, the **duomo** documents haphazard construction. Initiated in Pisan-Romanesque in the 1200s, desultory work continued for three centuries without reaching completion. Immediately on the left, the oratory houses a series of moving wooden statues depicting the life of Jesus from nativity to crucifixion. The chapel off the transept holds frescoes by Rosselli, including the brilliantly colored *Mission per Damasco.* Over the main altar stands the huge 12th-century polychrome wood sculpture group *Deposition from the Cross* above which is an intricate alabaster tabernacle by Mino da Fiesole. (*Duomo* open daily 7:30am-12:30pm and 2-7pm.)

Across the piazza down Via dell'Arco is the massive, 3rd-century BC **Etruscan arch,** one of the city's oldest gates. The black lumps of stone on the outside were once sculpted human heads that symbolized beheaded enemy prisoners. On the other side of the P. dei Priori on Via dei Sarti the **Pinacoteca Comunale** occupies the **Palazzo Minucci-Solaini** (tel. 87 580), an elegant building with a gracefully arcaded courtyard. Inside, Taddeo di Bartolo's graceful *Madonna and Saints* altarpiece will surprise anyone who has seen his gruesome *Last Judgement* in San Gimignano. A Luca Signorelli *Annunciation* and a gleaming Ghirlandaio altarpiece enhance the collection. But the art professors and students making the pilgrimage to Volterra have come for the treasure in the last room on the first floor. In his frenetic *Deposition* (1520), Rosso Fiorentino exploded High Renaissance conventions of order and restraint with a cacophony of colors swirling towards a shockingly green body of Christ. Rosso was never revisited by such dramatic vision, outside the currents of both Renaissance and Mannerist art; after the sack of Rome in 1527, he spent his time covering the walls of Francis I's gallery in Fontainebleau with pre-Baroque fluff. (Open daily 9:30am-1pm and 3-6:30pm; mid-Sept. to mid-June 10am-2pm. Admission L5000, students L2000.)

Volterra's other major attraction is the **Museo Etrusco Guarnacci,** at Via Minzoni, 15 (tel. 86 347). It displays over 600 finely carved Etruscan funerary urns from the 7th and 8th centuries, and an enormous collection of dramatic bas-reliefs depicting voyages to the underworld. On the first floor you can find the museum's most famous piece, the oddly elongated bronze figure dubbed *L'Ombra della Sera* (Shadow of the Evening), the present-day symbol of Volterra. (Same hours as the *pinacoteca.* Admission L8000, students L6000. Ticket also good for the *pinacoteca.*)

Take a left on Via Lunga le Mura del Mandorlo (before Porta Marcoli) for a spectacular view of the surprisingly intact **Teatro Romano.** Continue past the *teatro* to the **Church of San Francesco** on the edge of town. The **Capella della Croce,** off the right aisle, encloses frescoes by Cenno Cenni that relate the story of the True Cross. (Open daily 7:30am-12:30pm and 2-7pm.)

Volterra's most spectacular natural sight lies a 20-minute walk outside of town at **Le Balze.** Where cliffs formed by erosion tower hundreds of feet over the valley floor. These gullies have been growing over the millenia, swallowing churches in the Middle Ages and uncovering an Etruscan necropolis in the 18th century. Precariously perched at the edge of the Balze you can see a 14th-century monastery of the Camoldotesi order, now under restoration and hoping not to be engulfed.

∎∎∎ SIENA

Today, Siena lies in the shadow of its ancient rival Florence, but during the 13th century its flourishing wool trade, crafty bankers, and sophisticated quasi-republican civil administration marked it as one of the principal cities of Europe—easily Florence's equal. In 1230, the belligerent Florentines catapulted excrement and dead donkeys over Siena's walls in an effort to trigger an irreparable plague. The rude ploy failed, and in 1260 Siena routed the Florentines at the Battle of Montaperti. The century of grandiose construction that followed this brief ascendancy endowed the city with its flamboyant Gothic cathedral, the harmonious Piazza del Campo, and a multitude of *palazzi*. In 1348, half of Siena's citizens succumbed to the first of three plagues, and the weakened city bid adieu to its glory days, falling prey to the ambitions of the papacy, the Visconti, and the vengeful Florentines. In 1554, the Medici teamed up with the infinitely ambitious Habsburg despot Charles V to smash Siena into a ghost town. The Florentines then took pains to ensure that Siena would henceforth never amount to anything more than a provincial backwater. It is to this enforced stagnation that Siena owes the unmatched integrity of its Medieval Gothic townscape, carefully preserved today thanks to judicious city planning.

Sienese are determined to maintain their identity as more than just a Florentine satellite. They boast their own painting tradition, led by Duccio, Simone Martini, and the Lorenzetti brothers, who built upon decorative elements of Gothic art with exuberant clashes of color and narrative flair, ignoring the sober Renaissance restraint their rivals were producing to the north. They eschew Florentine hard-headedness in other spheres as well, harkening to a mystic tradition that produced the 15th-century Saint Catherine, an ecstatic illiterate who brought the papacy back from Avignon, and Saint Bernadine, who roamed the peninsula reviving the teachings of St. Francis. But there's nothing mystical about the pageantry and bravado of the most characteristic of Sienese rituals, the wild *Palio* and the *contrade* (Medieval neighborhood) competition that swirls around it. The *Palio* is the keystone of Siena's principal industry, tourism; the city's avocation is represented by the resurrected 15th-century Monte dei Paschi di Siena, now a major national bank.

ORIENTATION AND PRACTICAL INFORMATION

Siena once lay on the main road between Rome and Paris—modernity finds it on a secondary train line off the Rome-Florence route. Change at Chiusi from Rome and the south, at Empoli from Florence and the north. Frequent buses link Siena to Florence and the rest of Tuscany, making this an ideal base for exploring the smaller Tuscan hill towns (alternately, many of the smaller hill towns make a more pleasant, rustic base for visiting Siena). Buses stop outside the city's historic center at P. San Domenico. Across the street from the train station, you can take any bus (buy tickets from the vending machines by the station entrance or at the *biglietteria* window for bus tickets, L1000) to P. Matteotti. Follow the signs to **Piazza del Campo** (also called *Il Campo*). Walking to the center can be a pleasant way to orient yourself in the city, but be prepared to spend at least a 45-min., and procure a decent map before you leave the station.

Tourist Office: Azienda di Promozione Turismo, Via di Città, 43 (tel. 42 209). Turn right on the street just before the Campo. Rather harried, but can help students (only) find rooms to rent for longer stays in Siena. Open Mon.-Fri. 9am-1pm

SIENA

and 4-7pm. The **branch office,** P. Il Campo, 56, has a list of *affitta camere* available to non-students for shorter periods (from a few days to a few weeks) for about L25,000 per person. The agency in the Campo also has a travel agency, which **changes money** for outrageous rates and sells bus, train, and boat tickets. (Tourist office open in theory Mon.-Sat. 8:30am-7:30pm; travel agency open Mon.-Fri. 9am-1pm and 3:30-7pm, Sat. 9am-1pm.) There are also **tourist information booths** in the train station and bus stations that will help with hotels and general orientation. Open Mon.-Sat. 9am-1pm and 4-7pm.)

Budget Travel: CTS, Via Cecco Angiolieri, 49 (tel. 28 50 08), off P. Tolomei. Student travel services. Open Mon.-Fri. 9:30am-12:30pm and 4-7pm.

Post Office: P. Matteotti, 36. Fermo Posta, window #12, stamps, #11. Open Mon.-Sat. 8:15am-7pm; last day of each month, 8:15am-noon. **Postal code:** 53100.

Telephones: SIP, Via dei Termini, 40. Open Thurs.-Tues. 7:30am-1:15pm and 2-7:30pm, Wed. 7:30am-1:15pm. Also Via Donzelle, 8; open 7am-midnight. Via Cecco Angiolieri; open 7am-10pm. Via Pantaneto, 44; open 7am-11pm. Viale Vittorio Emanuele, 21; open 7am-midnight. All the local SIP offices are notorious for arbitrary changes in office hours; if the SIP office of your choice is closed, try pay phone booths in P. Matteotti. Also, SIP offices post a list of other places to go if they're closed. **Telephone code:** 0577.

Trains: P. Rosselli. Hourly departures to Florence (via Empoli, L7200) and Rome (via Chiusi, L18,700). Open daily 7:30am-6pm.

Buses: TRA-IN/SITA, P. San Domenico, 1 (tel. 22 12 21). Service to all of Tuscany, including Florence (express bus, L8300), San Gimignano (L5600), Volterra (L6300), Montepulciano (L6500), Pienza (L5000), Arezzo (L6600), and Montalcino (L4200). Open daily 5:50am-8:15pm.

Car Rental: Hertz and **Intercar,** Via S. Marco, 96 (tel. 41 148). Fiat Panda for L154,700 per day or L666,000 per week. Must be 21 years old and have a driver's license. Vespas an outlandish L77,000 per day. Must be 18 and have a driver's license. Open daily 8:30am-1pm and 3-7:30pm.

Bike Rental: Poggibonsi Ciclo Sport, Via Trento, 82 (tel. 92 85 07), in Poggibonsi.

English Bookstore: Feltrinelli, Via Banchi di Sopra, 66. A wide selection. Open Mon.-Sat. 9:30am-8pm. **Libreria Senese,** Via di Città, 62-66 (tel. 28 08 45). Penguin classics and bestsellers. Open Mon.-Sat. 9am-8pm.

Laundromat: L'Olandesina Self-Service, Via Malta, 38 (tel. 28 81 91), just inside Porta Camollia—on your right as you enter the city. Leave your load and 3hrs. later it's done. Wash and dry L14,000, students, L13,000. Open Mon.-Fri.

Emergencies: tel. 113. **Police: Questura,** Via del Castoro, near the *duomo.* **Hospital:** P. del Duomo, 1 (tel. 29 01 11). **Ambulance: Misericordia,** Via del Porrione, 49 (tel. 28 08 28).

ACCOMMODATIONS AND CAMPING

Finding a room in Siena is usually simple enough, but call a few days in advance during July and August, and book months ahead for either *Palio*. For stays of a week or more, rooms in private homes provide an attractive alternative, with singles L30,000-60,000. The tourist office has a list and will phone for you (see above).

Ostello della Gioventù "Guidoriccio" (HI), Via Fiorentina, 89 (tel. 52 212, fax 56 172), in Località Lo Stellino, a 20-min. bus ride from the *centro.* Take bus #4 or 15 across from the station or from P. Matteotti. If coming from Florence by bus, get off at the stop after you see the large black-and-white sign announcing entry into Siena. Considering the availability of inexpensive rooms in the *centro* and the extra expense and inconvenience of bus tickets to the hostel, you might plan on searching for a spot inside the city's walls before making the journey. 120 beds. Curfew 11pm. L18,000 per person. Breakfast included. Dinner L12,000.

La Casa del Pellegrino, Via Camporegio, 31 (tel. 44 177), behind San Domenico. A hotel run by nuns—enjoy stunning views of the *duomo* from the spotless and secure rooms. Free discourse on the state of sin and salvation. Opens at 7:30am.

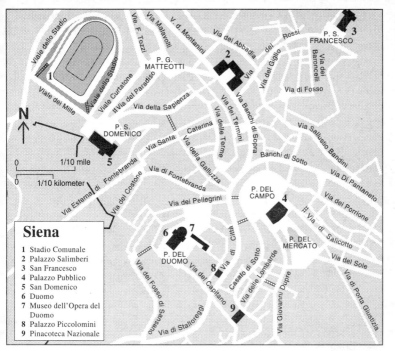

Siena

1 Stadio Comunale
2 Palazzo Salimberi
3 San Francesco
4 Palazzo Pubblico
5 San Domenico
6 Duomo
7 Museo dell'Opera del Duomo
8 Palazzo Piccolomini
9 Pinacoteca Nazionale

Curfew 11pm. Singles L32,000, with bath L40,000. Doubles with bath L58,000. Triples with bath L79,000. Quads with bath L95,000. Reservations preferred.

Locanda Garibaldi, Via Giovanni Dupré, 18 (tel. 28 42 04), behind the Palazzo Pubblico, close to P. del Campo. A homey establishment with 8 cozy doubles for L55,000. Curfew midnight. Fills early.

Albergo La Perla, Via delle Terme, 25 (tel. 47 144), on P. dell'Indipendenza off Via Banchi di Sopra. Gregarious management and a central location. Lots of decent rooms. Curfew 1am. Singles with bath L38,000. Doubles L68,000.

Piccolo Hotel Etruria, Via Donzelle, 1-3 (tel. 28 80 88), off Banchi di Sotto, near Il Campo. Newly renovated rooms and propinquity to the Campo makes this a popular hotel. Curfew 12:30am. Singles L45,000, with bath L55,000. Doubles L54,000, with bath L80,000. Triples L80,000, with bath L108,000. Breakfast L4000. Major credit cards.

Albergo Tre Donzelle, Via Donzelle, 5 (tel. 28 03 58). Just 1 door up from the Etruria. Airy rooms around a light-flooded stairwell. Curfew 1am. Singles L30,000. Doubles L50,000, with bath L63,000. Triples L67,500, with bath L108,000.

Albergo Cannon d'Oro, Via Montanini, 28 (tel, 44 321), near P. Matteotti. Well-decorated, well-maintained rooms with garden and hillside views. 3 singles with bath L55,000. Doubles L60,000, with bath L85,000. Triples L90,000, with bath L105,000. Breakfast L8000. April and Sept. are the busiest months. MC, Visa.

Camping: Colleverde, Strada di Scacciapensieri, 47 (tel. 28 00 44). Take bus #8 from P. Gramsci. L9000 including car and tent or camper. Swimming pool L3000. Open mid-March to mid-Nov.

FOOD

Siena specializes in rich pastries, the most famous being *Panforte,* a dense concoction of honey, almonds, and citron. Sample it at the **Bar/Pasticceria Nannini,** the oldest *pasticceria* in Siena, with branches at Via Banchi di Sopra, 22-24, and elsewhere in town. **Enoteca Italiana,** in the Fortezza Medicea, near the entrance off Via

Cesare Maccari, purveys the finest of the regional wines in Italy, from Brunello to Barolo, Asti Spumante to Vernaccia, at the lowest prices around. Sample before buying, only L2000 per glass. (Open daily 3pm-midnight.) Siena's **open-air market** fills La Lizza each Wednesday (8am-1pm). Shoestringers can pick up supplies at the **Consortio Agrario supermarket,** Via Pianigiani, 5, off P. Salimberi (open Mon.-Fri. 7:45am-1pm and 5-8pm, Sat. 7:45am-1pm) or at **COOP,** close to the train station (take bus #1; open Mon.-Tues. and Thurs.-Fri. 8:30am-1pm and 4-8pm, Wed. and Sat. 8:30am-1pm).

Rosticceria Monti, Via Calzoleria 12. Where locals come to buy prepared food. Pick up a crispy and aromatic roast chicken (L3500) or a heaping serving of *gnocchi* cooked to order (L4500). Great Tuscan bean specialties, including bean soup (L3000) and bean salad (L2500). Open Sat.-Thurs. noon-3pm and 6:30-11pm.

Osteria Le Logge, Via Porrione, 33 (tel. 48 013), off P. del Campo. A famous and cozy resturant only a short walk from Torre del Mangia. *Primi* offerings include their specialty, *malfatti osteria* (spinach and ricotta in egg pasta, coated with meat sauce and baked, L8000). Amongst their *secondi* (about L14,000), try the *tagliata alla rucola,* (thinly sliced beef cooked with garlic, olive oil, pepperoncini, and rugola). Cover L2000. Service 10%. Open Mon.-Sat. 12:30-3pm and 7:30-10:30pm. Reservations are a good idea in this popular place. MC, Visa.

Grotta del Gallo Nero, Via Porrione, 65-67 (tel. 22 04 46), just down the street from Osteria Le Logge, behind P. del Campo. One of the most popular places in town. Italian rock hits blare as a young staff serves excellent Tuscan specialties at unbeatable prices. Hearty dish of homemade *pici* (fat spaghetti) with porcini and sausage for L8000, or the juicy *vitello arrosto* (roast veal) for L10,000. Open Tues.-Sun. noon-3pm and 7pm-1:30am, Mon. noon-3pm. **Bibo,** Via Banchi di Sotto, 61-63. When the *mensa's* closed, come here for generous sandwiches (L3500) and beer (L4000). Homemade *gelato*. Open Tues.-Sun. 7:30pm-1am.

SIGHTS

The Campo

Where other Italian towns center on their *duomo,* Siena radiates from the **Piazza del Campo,** the shell-shaped, salmon-colored brick square designed expressly for civic events. The paving stones of the piazza are allegedly divided into nine sections representing the city's Medieval "Government of Nine," though numerate observers count 11. The *campo* has always been the center stage. Dante described the real-life drama of Provenzan Salvani, the heroic Sienese *condottiere* who panhandled around Il Campo in order to ransom a friend. A little later, Sienese mystics like San Bernadino found the piazza a natural auditorium. *Il Palio* reduces the Campo to splendid mayhem twice each summer as horses race around its outer edge.

At the highest point in Il Campo's central axis, you'll find the **Fonte Gaia,** a pool surrounded by reproductions of native son Jacopo della Quercia's famous carvings (1408-1419). Closing the bottom of the shell is the **Palazzo Pubblico,** a graceful Gothic palace. A gluttonous watchman who doubled as a bellringer gave his nickname to the **Torre del Mangia,** the clock tower that rises like a scepter to the left. Siena's Council of Nine commissioned a tower whose republican might would overshadow any skyscraper the nobility or clergy could erect in town; a pair of Perugian architects gave them the second tallest structure raised in Medieval Italy (102m; Cremona has the tallest). In front of the *palazzo* is the **Cappella di Piazza,** built in 1348 in gratitude for the end of the Black Death which claimed half the population. It took exhausted Siena 100 years to complete the Cappella; you can trace the transition from Gothic to Renaissance architecture as pointed arches give way to gracefully rounded ones halfway up the walls.

The Museo Civico

The Palazzo Pubblico holds the masterpieces of Sienese art in the **Museo Civico.** The two rooms that provide the best introduction to both Sienese art and the spirit of the city are the **Sala del Mappamondo** and the **Sala della Pace.** In the first, named for a lost series of astronomical frescoes, lies Simone Martini's *Maestà* (Enthoned Virgin) and *Guidoriccio da Fogliano.* These two frescoes, facing each other across the vast room, illustrate the contradictions of Sienese Medieval government. On the one hand, Siena looked to the Virgin, the town's patron saint, for justification and legitimacy; on the other hand, it hired mercenary soldiers (*condottiere*) like Guidoriccio to defend the city. In the next room, the Sala della Pace (also called Sala dei Nove), Sienese civic pride shines through in Pietro and Ambrogio Lorenzetti's frescoes of the *Allegories of Good and Bad Government and their Effects on Town and Country.* On the right side, in the elaborate, chiliastic *Allegory of Good Government,* people dance in the streets, artisans toil happily, and contented farmers labor on vast stretches of fertile land that unfold to the horizon. The fortunate citizenry's destiny is overseen by Justice, who is counselled by Wisdom and Compassion. On the left side, that of bad government, a gloomy, desolate landscape is populated only by thieves, sinners, devils, and sundry lost souls, their fate sealed by ruling Pride, Wrath, and Avarice. The frescoes in the room, once the deliberating chamber of the Council of Nine, might well have shamed the Sienese government into civic decency, but the rule of the Nine came to an end shortly after the frescoes were completed. In a case of life not imitating art—the Allegory of Good Government is remarkably well-preserved, while the Allegory of Bad Government is chipping its way into oblivion. Upstairs, on the Loggia dei Nove, you'll find the original della Quercia sculptures from the Fonte Gaia, now sadly debilitated. Step into the next room to witness Matteo di Giovanni's particularly ghastly rendition of the *Slaughter of the Innocents.* Head back downstairs to the entrance, cross the courtyard, and climb the tower's 300-odd narrow steps to bask in the spectacular view of the *duomo* and the entire city. (*Palazzo* and museum open Mon.-Sat. 9:30am-6:45pm, Sun. 9:30am-1:45pm; Nov.-March daily 9am-1:45pm. Admission L6000, students L3000. Torre del Mangia open daily 10am-7pm, mid-April to mid-June and mid-Sept. to mid-Oct. 10am-6pm, mid-March to mid-April and mid-Oct. to mid-Nov. 10am-5pm, mid-Nov. to mid-March 10am-1:30pm. Admission L4000.)

The Duomo

The striped **duomo,** perched atop one of Siena's three hills, took so long to build that it spanned two architectural epochs, incorporating Romanesque arches and Gothic pinnacles. Civic pride demanded both enormous scale and prominent position, but the limited size of the hill gave architects trouble. Because of these limitations, the apse would have hung in mid-air over the edge of the hill, had the Sienese not built the **baptistry** below it to support the structure. The obscurely placed baptistry is thus missed by many travelers, and those who do visit are further challenged by the miserly lighting. However, those who concentrate are rewarded by the Gothic and Renaissance styles of the **baptismal font** (1417-30). In the bronze panels that decorate the lower part of the font, compare Ghiberti's *Baptism of Christ* to the adjacent *Herod's Feast* of his contemporary Donatello. Ghiberti's Gothic panel is a supremely crafted and finished celebration of tactile pleasures, while Donatello's Renaissance work is a more reserved, intellectual study of perspective and movement. Other panels are by della Quercia (*Birth of John the Baptist*) and the six bronze angels are by Donatello. (Open mid-March to Sept. 7:30am-7:30pm, Oct. to early Nov. 7:30am-6:30pm, Nov. to mid-March 7:30am-1:30pm and 2:30-5pm.)

Ascending a flight of steps will lead you to the **Piazza del Duomo** and the front façade, but on the way you'll pass a free-standing, striped wall. This is the sole remnant of Siena's early 14th-century plan to rebuild their cathedral in response to Florence's commencement of their great domed *duomo*: Siena's was to be the largest in the world but building was halted forever by the bubonic plague. As you see Siena's present building, you'll hardly regret that they were halted in their ambitions; it would be hard to imagine a more wonderful Christian church than Siena's completely finished, unbelievably decorated edifice. Giovanni Pisano carved the lower part of the façade; the statues of prophets, sybils, and philosophers you see are copies of his ground-breaking works, whose interacting postures and oddly proportioned figures were the first to be sculpted with the idea of the awed upward-staring viewer in mind. (The originals are in the Museo dell'Opera Metropolitana, where you can see the rough-cut, deeply grooved chiselling that created the effect.)

If you're overwhelmed upon entering, perhaps it would be best to look down at the floor, whose inlaid **pavement** is mostly covered (in a rotating cycle) to help preserve the marble masterpieces, the two-century effort of a string of Siena's best artists. The ideal time to visit is August 15 through September 15, when the best works, by the Marchese d'Adamo, are exposed. Halfway up the left aisle you'll find the **Piccolomini altar,** a complete architectural structure designed by Andrea Bregno in 1503. At the bottom on either side are statues of St. Peter and St. Paul, two oft-forgotten works by Michelangelo executed during the same years as his *David.* The **pulpit** nearby is one of Andrea Pisano's best, with allegorical and biblical reliefs wrapping around the barrel (though you may feel an inappropriate urge to laugh at the children-suckling she-wolves that support the mismatched columns of the base).

Farther down this aisle is the lavish **Libreria Piccolomini,** commissioned by Pope Pius III to house the elaborately illustrated books of his uncle Pius II, whose collection still lines the walls. The library also contains the Roman statue **The Three Graces,** and some 15th-century illuminated lyrical scores. (*Duomo* open mid-March to Sept. 7:30am-7:30pm, Oct. to early Nov. 7:30am-6:30pm, Nov. to mid-March 7:30am-1:30pm and 2:30-5pm. Strict sartorial standards apply: no tank-tops or shorts above the knee. Library open mid-March to Sept. 9am-7:30pm, Oct. to early Nov. 9am-6:30pm, Nov. to mid-March 10am-1pm and 2:30-5pm. Admission L2000.)

The **Museo dell'Opera Metropolitana** (cathedral museum), under the arches of P. Jacopo della Quercia, which adjoins P. del Duomo, houses all the extra art that formerly graced the cathedral. The first floor contains some of the foremost Gothic statuary in Italy, all by Giovanni Pisano. Upstairs is the *Maestà,* by Duccio di Buoninsegna, originally the screen of the cathedral's altar. (Open mid-March to Sept. 9am-7:30pm, Oct. to early Nov. 9am-6:30pm, Nov. to Dec. 9am-1:30pm, Jan. to mid-March 9am-1pm. Admission L5000.)

Around the City

Siena's **Pinacoteca Nazionale,** down the street from the cathedral museum at Via San Pietro, 29, features works by every major artist of the Sienese school: the seven magnificent followers of Onccio, Simone Martini, the Lorenzetti brothers, Bartolo di Fredi, Sano di Pietro, Il Sodoma, and many others. (Open Tues.-Sat. 8:30am-7pm, Mon. 8:30am-2pm, Sun. 8:30am-1pm; in winter Mon.-Sat. 8:30am-2pm. L8000.)

The **Sanctuary of St. Catherine,** on Via del Tiratoio, pays homage to the most renowned daughter of Siena, a simple girl who influenced popes, founded a religious order, and was proclaimed patron saint of Italy by Pope Pius XII in 1939. The structure offers a pleasant sojourn among roses and geraniums. (Open daily 9am-12:30pm and 3:30-6pm.)

As in other Italian towns, the Franciscans and the Dominicans have set up rival basilicas at opposite ends of Siena. The **Church of San Domenico** contains Andrea Vanni's portrait of St. Catherine and dramatic frescoes by Il Sodoma (1477-1549). The *cappella* also contains the requisite macabre relic, this one depicting Catherine's head. (Church open daily 8:30am-1pm and 4-7pm.) The **Church of San Francesco** houses two mournful frescoes by Pietro and Ambrogio Lorenzetti. The huge, stark space offers a sharp contrast to the *duomo.* (Open daily 9am-1pm and 4-7pm.) The adjacent **Oratory of San Bernardino** (ring the bell at #22 for the doorkeeper) houses several more Il Sodomas.

Via Banchi di Sopra, via Banchi di Sotto, and **Via di Città** trisect Siena, intersecting above Il Campo. Via di Città begins with the **Loggia della Mercanzia** and continues past the towers of various medieval families to the **Palazzo Chigi-Saracini,** a magnificent Gothic structure that now houses the Accademia Musicale Chigiana.

ENTERTAINMENT

The Accademia Chigiana sponsors an excellent music festival, the **Settimana Musicale Senese,** Siena's Musical Week (late July). Siena also hosts a **jazz festival** in July, which features internationally known bopsters. Check the posters or the tourist office for details.

The **Palio di Siena** takes place on July 2 and August 16. As the race approaches, Siena's emotional temperature rises steadily. Ten of the 17 *contrade* (chosen by lot—there's limited space in Il Campo) make elaborate traditional preparations. Young partisans sporting the colors of their *contrada* chant in packs on the street. Five trial races take place over the three days leading up to the race, and a final trial is run the same morning. Just before the race, each horse is brought into the church of its respective *contrada* to be blessed. A procession of heralds and flagbearers prefaces anarchy with regal pomp—the last piece in the procession is the *palio* itself, a banner depicting the Madonna and Child, drawn in a cart by white oxen. Officials pad the buildings of the piazza with mattresses, for many a rider has lost control and careened off the track. The horses tear three times around Il Campo, unsaddled jockeys clinging to their backs. Riders alternate whip strokes between their mounts and their competitors. Packed in the center of Il Campo and hanging from the balconies of the surrounding *palazzi,* the throng roars with excitement. Second place brings dishonor, shame, and occasional suicides.

To stay in Siena during the *Palio,* book rooms at least four months in advance—especially for budget accommodations. Write the APT in March or April for a list of individuals and companies that let rooms, or to reserve a seat in the stands. You can stand in the "infield" of the piazza for free. Access to the piazza closes early, so stake out a spot early in the day. The two-hour parade takes place immediately before the 7pm race, which lasts about 70 seconds. The night before the race everyone revels until 3am or so, strutting and chanting their way around the city, pausing only to eat and drink. After the race, nine of the 10 competing *contrade* languish in bleary-eyed agony. For the full scoop on *Il Palio* ask at the tourist office and pick up their excellent program. To witness a less touristed phase of *Il Palio,* attend *La Tratta* (the choosing of the horses), which takes place on June 29 and August 13 at 10am.

SOUTHERN TUSCANY

■ Monte Oliveto Maggiore

Perched on a knoll halfway between Montepulciano and Siena, the **Monastery of Monte Oliveto Maggiore** typifies the wealthy Benedictine abbey. Founded by such tired Sienese merchants as Bernardo Tolomei and Ambrogio Piccolomini, both of whom retired here in 1313, the monastery is home to the Olivetan Order, approved by the pope six years after the gold-encrusted monks arrived. Money breeds money, and by the 1400s, Monte Oliveto had so much that a rebuilding program turned the monastery into a Renaissance prodigy. Thanks to its isolation, the place functions today much as it did during the Middle Ages, and remains relatively untouristed. The monks still make their own wine, honey, olive oil, and a strange herb liqueur called *Flora di Monte Oliveto,* all sold at the small shop within the abbey.

The real treasures of Monte Oliveto Maggiore lie in the **Chiostro Grande.** On the wall of this large cloister, to the right as you exit from the church, you'll find a cycle of frescoes depicting the life of St. Benedict. Commissioned to execute the entire cycle, Luca Signorelli died before he completed the job, painting only nine of the 36 panels in 1947-8. Il Sodoma took over the commission, extending the cycle both back into the life of S. Benedict and forward in time from where Signorelli left off. Sodoma's frescoes can thus be found on the first, second, and fourth walls of the cycle, and Signorelli's on the third. Don't miss Il Sodoma's *Come Florenzo Manda*

Male Femmine al Monastero ("How Florenzo Sends Feminine Evil to the Monastery"), in which bewildered monks look to St. Benedict for guidance when confronted with a bevy of voluptuous, scantily-clad women.

The **Chiesa Abbazia** off the Chiostro Grande, thoroughly renovated in the 18th century, contains treasures from disparate eras. Note the wood-inlaid, 16th-century stalls by master Fra Giovanni da Verona lining the nave and the modern stained-glass work. (Abbey open daily 9:15am-12:30pm and 3-7pm; off-season 9:15am-12:30pm and 3-5:30pm. Ring if the door is closed.)

Rooms are available for visiting students: reserve by mail. (Write to the Abbazia di Monte Oliveto Maggiore, 53020 Siena.) Free **camping** in the area surrounding the abbey is a possibility. At the entrance to the abbey grounds, in the old tower and gate house, **Ristorante La Torre** serves sandwiches (L3000-4000), pizza (L4500-7000), and full meals (around L20,000). The monks also operate a *bar-pasticceria*, which sells basic necessities as well as drinks.

Many people find that the easiest way to reach Monte Oliveto from Siena is to take the train to Asciano (almost hourly, L2800) and then hitch a ride up 11km of country road to Monte Oliveto. The best chances for hitching are on Sunday, when traffic to the monastery is more plentiful. **Always use extreme caution when hitchhiking** (See section on safety). A bus also runs from Siena to **Chiusure,** a walkable 2km from Monte Oliveto (Mon.-Sat. leaves 2pm, returns 7am, round-trip L6500).

■ Massa Marittima

The locals simply call their home "Massa," for indeed even though it's surnamed "Marittima" this burg is anything but close to the waves. An ancient Etruscan mining town, this may not be the place to come for fun in the sun, but it does have one of Tuscany's most spectacular Romanesque *duomos,* and the authenticity of an untouristed Tuscan hill town.

Orientation and Practical Information TRA-IN buses link Massa Marittima to Siena, leaving from Via Ximenes and arriving at P. San Domenico in Siena (twice daily at 8:30am and 5:30pm, 1hr. 30min., L7400). FMF buses run between Piombino and Massa Marittima, making Massa a convenient stopover ere you see Elba (4 per day, 1hr., L4800). The surest way to reach Massa is by way of Follonica (every ½hr., L2700), a local stop on the main Tyrrhenian line from Pisa (L8800). Buy bus tickets at the travel agency at P. Garibaldi, 18 (open 8am-8pm) or at the *paninoteca* next door when business hours are over. The **tourist office** (tel. 90 22 89) is next to the cathedral the Medieval **Palazzo del Podestà**, along with the **Museo Archeologico** and the **Pinacoteca Comunale.** The tourist office in the lobby is generous with information and pamphlets. The **telephone code** is 0566.

Accommodations and Food The only hotel in the town's center is the **Hotel Cris,** Via Roma, 9-10 (tel. 90 38 30), on the corner of Via Cappellini. (Singles L22,000. Doubles L37,000.) Downstairs a family-run restaurant offers reasonably priced home-style fare. They prepare a delectable dish of homemade *tortelli ai funghi porcini* for only L6000. (The restaurant may be closed in August.) For a more memorable meal, head to **Trattoria da Alberto,** Via Parenti, 35, which serves hearty Tuscan food under grapevines in an outdoor garden. It would be a shame not to try their homemade *tagliatelle* topped with *cinghiale* (wild boar) in a spicy tomato sauce (L6000). Wash it down with a carafe of their respectable house wine.

Sights and Entertainment The 13th-century **duomo,** with a marvelous Pisan-Romanesque façade, dominates **Piazza Garibaldi,** in the center of town. The stairs leading to the church are a work of art in themselves—at the corner, they converge like a fan into a flat wall. Individually carved heads reign atop the pilasters of the façade's blind arches. To the right of the door lies the enormous baptismal font, sculpted in 1267 from a single block of marble. To the left hangs a series of 11th-century bas-reliefs depicting Jesus and his apostles staring out at you. Behind the high altar in the choir see the *Arca di San Cerbone,* the tomb of the city's patron saint (1324). The chapel to the left of the high altar houses a *Madonna delle Grazie* by Duccio. (Open daily 9am-noon ar.d 3-8pm.)

The *museo,* on the first floor of the **Palazzo del Podestà,** contains prehistoric, Etruscan, and Roman artifacts. Upstairs, the *pinacoteca* displays Sienese paintings, including Ambrogio Lorenzetti's flashy and innovative *Maestà* that infuses a typically iconic subject with narrative focus through the addition of a vast supporting cast of saints worshipping the enthroned Madonna and the trio of allegorical figures on the steps below her. (Open Tues.-Sun. 10am-12:30pm and 3:30-7pm; Nov.-March Tues.-Sun. 9am-1pm and 3-5pm. Admission to both museums L3500; under 18, students and seniors L2500.)

From P. Garibaldi, ascend the Via Moncini. As you pass through the fortress wall at the top of the street, you will see a soaring arch bridging the wall and the campanile, which dominates P. Matteotti. Right on Corso Diaz and left on Via Populonia brings you to the **Antico Frantoio,** a house containing an 18th-century olive press, where you can examine the process by which the oil is extracted from the olive. (Open Tues.-Fri. 10am-noon, Sat.-Sun. 10am-noon and 4-7pm. Admission L2000; students, under 18 and seniors L1000.)

Visit Massa on the Sunday following May 20 or the second Sunday of August to catch the **Balestro del Girifalco.** This lively procession in medieval costume culminates in a crossbow match between the *terzieri* (three sections) of the town. Operas and concerts are held every week in P. Garibaldi: check the tourist office.

■ San Galgano

Only slightly removed from a winding country pass between Siena and Massa Marittima, the ruined 13th-century Cistercian abbey of San Galgano was once one of the richest and most powerful in Tuscany. Its monks served as treasurers and judges for the communes of Siena and Volterra, helped construct the *duomo* in Siena, and became bishops and even saints. Their vast fortune permitted the monks to construct an abbey of noble proportions, but by the mid-16th century, due to their corruption, most of the church had crumbled to dust.

Its very dilapidation makes San Galgano an unforgettable sight. Nature has been kind to the massive old building, the foremost specimen of Cistercian Gothic architecture in Italy; it has removed the roof completely without harming the majestic columns within. Gothic windows and rosettes frame Tuscan landscapes, and nestfuls of birds chirp from odd corners.

San Galgano, the abbey's patron saint, is renowned for having renounced war for a life of religion and peace with the miraculous gesture of thrusting his sword into a stone. The rock and weapon are enshrined only a short walk away in the **Chapel of Monte Siepi,** a beautiful Romanesque church on a hill overlooking the abbey. The rotund church supports a starkly impressive black-and-white striped cupola and contains, in addition to the miraculous stone, frescoes by Ambrogio Lorenzetti, in its chapel. The chapel also contains the hands of a villain who upon trying to burn the hut of San Galgano, was torn to shreds by wolves who had befriended the saint. The hands are preserved as a symbol of friendship between the townsfolk and the beasts of the woods. (Open daily 8am-1pm and 4-6pm.)

To reach San Galgano, take the TRA-IN bus that runs between Siena and Massa Marittima, and get off at the San Galgano stop. Four buses run per day between the two cities, so wait for the next one and continue on.

■ Montalcino

Montalcino has changed little since medieval times, when it was a Sienese stronghold. With few historic monuments to attend to, Montalcino has concentrated on making the heavenly *brunello di Montalcino,* a smooth full-bodied wine that is widely acknowledged as Italy's finest red.

Nearly impregnable behind its walls, in 1555 Montalcino sheltered a band of republicans escaping from the Florentine siege of Siena. There, they and the citizens staged the republic's last stand, holding out against the Medici for another four years. The city walls still stand, along with the remains of the town's original 19 fortified towers. Montalcino's **Rocca,** or fortress, watches over the southeast corner of town. Two courtyards beckon inside the fortress, one sunny and cheered by tiger lilies, the other sylvan and shaded by foliage. You can explore the Rocca's 14th-century walls, chambers, and turrets, which afford a stunning view of the exquisite landscape. (Open Tues.-Sun. 9am-1pm and 2-8pm. Free.) On the way down, stop at the small *enoteca* in the *fortezza's* cavernous main room; try the tasty sandwiches (L3500) as you sample the local wines (L4500 per glass). Montalcino's most inspiring sight lies 9km away down a serpentine country road. Built in the 12th century on the remains of a 9th-century church allegedly founded by Charlemagne, the **Abbazia di Sant'Antimo** (tel. (0577) 83 56 69, ask for Padre Andrea) rates as one of Tuscany's most beautiful Romanesque churches, with its rounded apse and alabaster capitals. (Open Tues.-Sun. 10:30am-12:30pm and 3-6pm. Buses run Mon.-Sat. 4 per day, Sun. 2 per day; L1000.)

The most compelling reason to visit Montalcino is its world-class wine. *Brunello,* a dry wine with a pronounced aromatic persistence, is produced from the Sangiovese Grasso variety of grape. The wine pressed from this vine can be given one of three classifications. The first, *vino rosso di Montalcino,* indicates that the wine has been aged only one year in wooden barrels before being bottled, yielding a younger, brighter wine. *Brunello,* the second classification, means that the wine has been aged for four years, and that the wine has aged at least six months in the bottle before sale. Due to its lack of sediment and other special qualities, *Brunello* has an exceptional capacity to age, and should improve for up to thirty years. The final classification, the *Riserva,* denotes a wine that has aged five full years in the bottle, producing a truly exceptional wine. *Rosso* should run around L6000-8000 and the *Brunello* costs roughly L20,000, while the *Riserva* begins at L30,000 a bottle. The best deals on *Brunello* are found at the **COOP Supermarket** off P. del Popolo. To gain a real appreciation for the local vineyards, head 5km down the road to the **Fattoria dei Barbi** in Sant'Antimo (tel. (0577) 84 82 77). You can also visit the **Azienda Agricola Greppo,** which produced the first *Brunello* in 1888, and can be found 3km away from Montalcino on the road to Sant'Antimo. Call before heading out in order to arrange a tour of the cellars (tel. (0572) 84 80 87). Contact the tourist office for information about guided tours of the local vineyards. To sample some of the exotic honey products made in Montalcino hop over to **Apicoltura Ciacci** on Via Ricasoli, 26, up the street from the Chiesa di S. Agostino, where you'll discover every honey product imaginable, including honey soap, honey-biscuits, honey-Grappa, honey-milk, and honey candies. (Open 10am-12:30pm and 4-7pm.)

Not only do local products tickle the vinophile's throat, but the superb *trattoria* **Il Moro,** Via Mazzini, 46, is itself reason enough to visit Montalcino. Sample the local catch of *cinghiale* (wild boar) with *pappardelle* (a homemade pasta) for L5000 or the mixed grill for L10,000. (Open Tues.-Sun. noon-2:30pm and 7:30-10:30pm.) There's a **market** for picnics on Saturdays (7:30am-1pm) on Viale della Libertà. Rooms are scarce and expensive in Montalcino, so try to find a bed in a private home. The **Tourist Office,** Costa del Municipio, 8 (tel. and fax (0577) 84 93 21), can help you find lodging. (Open Tues.-Sun. 9:30am-1pm and 3:30-7pm.) You might also try **Affitacamere Casali,** Via Sagna, 3, (tel. (0577) 84 80 83), which lets adequate doubles with bath (L50,000; use of kitchen L15,000).

Ten **TRA-IN** buses make the one-hour trip daily from Siena to Montalcino (L4200). If coming from Pienza or Montepulciano, change buses at Torrenieri. Visit in June, when the old town comes alive for a *Teatro* festival. Contact the tourist office for tickets (about L10,000).

■ Montepulciano

This small medieval town, stretched along the crest of a hill, occupies the finest location in Italy for the melding of beautiful countryside and fine wine. Though the smooth, garnet-colored *vino nobile* has gained the town fame, the landscape and museums alone make the town an excellent choice for a daytrip from Siena.

At the **tourist office,** Via Ricci, 9 (tel. (0578) 75 74 42), off P. Grande, pick up the helpful booklet *Montepulciano—Perla del Cinquecento,* in English and French. It contains loads of useful information, including a list of *affitta camere.* Check before you trek, however, as such information is subject to change. (Open Tues.-Sat. 10am-1pm and 4-7pm, Sun. 10:30am-1pm and 3:30-7pm.)

TRA-IN buses run to Montepulciano from Siena, Florence, Pienza, and Chiusi. Montepulciano is an easy daytrip from Siena (Mon.-Sat. 6 per day, 2hr., L6600, change at Buonconvento). Hourly trains to Chiusi make Montepulciano a convenient stopover on the Florence-Rome line; take the bus from there (45min., L2700).

ACCOMMODATIONS AND FOOD

The mild trauma of hotel prices in Montepulciano makes the town more attractive as a daytrip from Siena.

Affitta Camere Bella Vista, (tel. 75 73 48) rents small but adequate rooms. The logical choice at L35,000 for a single, L45,000 for a double with bath (L55,000 for double with a bath and balcony). Call for reservations.

Albergo La Terazza, (tel. (0578) 75 74 40; fax 75 76 61). Spacious rooms, with access to a terrace where *aperitifs* are served among the flowers. Doubles with bath L78,000-88,000. Triples with bath L75,000. Mini-apartments also available. Breakfast L3500. Reserve ahead—this place is popular.

Ristorante Cittino, Vicolo della via Nuova, 2 (tel. 75 73 35), off Via di Voltaia nel Corso. Clean and homey. Singles L30,000. Doubles L50,000. The restaurant serves superb homecooked food. Full meals around L25,000. Open July to mid-June. Restaurant and hotel closed Wed., but you can check in Wed. night if you call ahead.

Montepulciano offers a smorgasbord of excellent, affordable restaurants. Ristorante Cittino is one of the best deals (see above). There are **minimarkets** all along the *Corso* and a larger **supermarket** in P. Savonarola at the bottom of the *corso,* as well as an **open-air market** in P. Sant'Agnese (Thurs. 8am-1pm).

Trattoria Diva e Maceo, Via Gracciano nel Corso, 92 (tel. 71 69 51). Where locals go to socialize over a plate of cannelloni stuffed with ricotta and spinach (L8000) or a divine *ossobuco* (L11,000). Open Wed.-Mon. noon-3pm and 7-10pm.

Rosticceria di "Voltaia," Via di Voltaia nel Corso, 86. Tasty homecooked dishes to eat in or take out. Full meals around L20,000, take-out cheaper. Open Mon.-Sat. noon-3pm and 7-11pm.

SIGHTS AND ENTERTAINMENT

Montepulciano boasts an impressive assemblage of 16th- and 17th-century Renaissance and Baroque *palazzi.* The town's main drag, the **Corso,** divides nominally into four parts: Via di Gracciano nel Corso, Via di Voltaia nel Corso, Via dell'Opio nel Corso, and Via del Poliziano nel Corso. It winds langorously up the hill, passing near the summit where the Piazza Grande and the *duomo* are located. Impressive *palazzi* line the lowest quarter of the Corso, Via di Gracciano. On your right at #91 is **Palazzo Avignonesi** (1507-1575), attributed to Vignola. The elegant windows of the second floor are in sharp contrast to the bold protruding windows of the ground floor, marking different stages of construction. The lions' heads on either side of the door belong to the same pride as the lion on top of the **Marzocco Column,** in front of the *palazzo.* The lion, the heraldic symbol of Florence, replaced the she-wolf of Siena in this spot when Florence took the city in 1511. The original lion now rests in the **Museo Civico.** Farther up on the other side of the street at #70 rises the asymmetrical façade of **Palazzo Cocconi,** attributed to Antonio da Sangallo the Elder (1455-1534). Cross the street to #73, the **Palazzo Bucelli,** whose base is inset with Roman and Etruscan reliefs, urn slabs, and inscriptions collected by the 18th-century proprietor, Pietro Bucelli.

The **Church of Sant'Agostino** dominates P. Michelozzo, farther up the street. The lower part of the façade demonstrates Michelozzo's masterful classicism, while the second level "quotes" the Gothic style. Just in front of the church of Madonna di Fatima looms the **Torre di Pucinella,** constructed in 1524 of wood and metal plating. Punctually on the hour, the Pucinella gongs the bell, keeping time for the surrounding neighborhood. Back on the Corso, which becomes Via di Voltaia nel Corso at #21, stop at the U-shaped **Palazzo Cervini.** This *palazzo's* external courtyard is typical of country villas but rare in urban residences. Here it serves a double purpose as a symbol of the family's grandeur and as a magnanimous civic gesture in making the clan's private space public.

To reach **Piazza Grande** and the **duomo** at the top of the hill you can either meander around and up Il Corso, or scale the steep alleys to the right. The unfinished *duomo,* the Palazzo Tarugi, the Palazzo Cantucci, and the 14th-century Palazzo Comunale ring the piazza. The unpretentious *duomo,* with its simple stone and brick exterior and unfinished façade, clothes an even sparser interior. It houses a poignant *Assumption of the Virgin* by Taddeo di Bartolo in a triptych above the altar. (Open 9am-1pm and 3:30-7:30pm.) The austere **Palazzo Comunale** took nearly a century to build, and was finally completed in the mid-1400s by Michelozzo. On a clear day you can take in a view that ranges from Siena's towers in the north to the snow-capped Gran Sasso massif in the south from the palazzo's tower. (Open Mon.-Sat. 8am-1pm. Free.) The remaining two *palazzi* were both designed by Antonio Sangallo the Elder. The elegant white façade of **Palazzo de' Nobili-Tarugi** faces the *duomo;* two arches on the bottom left allow one to enter a deep vaulted *loggia* that cuts through the entire corner of the building.

The Palazzo Neri-Orselli, Via Ricci, 10, houses the **Museo Civico,** one of Montepulciano's foremost attractions. The museum contains a collection of enameled terracotta by della Robbia, Etruscan cinerary urns, and over 200 paintings. (Open Wed.-Sun. 9:20am-1pm and 3-6pm. Admission L3000.)

The **Church of San Biagio,** outside the town walls, is Sangallo's masterpiece. Walk the steep ½km down the hill to appreciate the balance of its centralized plan and its graceful details.

Around August 15, the **Bruscello** (a series of amateur theatrical productions) takes place on the steps of the *duomo.* To buy tickets (around L10,000), contact the tourist office. Visit Montepulciano the last Sunday in August to see the raucous **Bravio** (Barrel Race), held to commemorate the eight neighborhood militias who fended off the Florentines and Sienese. Pairs of youths, dressed in costumes bearing their team markings, roll barrels up the steep incline of the Corso, exchanging insults and blows as they battle their way to the Piazza Grande.

■ Pienza

Known as "the Pearl of the Renaissance," Pienza was planned and built virtually overnight by Bernado Rossellino to satisfy the utopian vision of Aeneas Silvius Piccolomini. After becoming Pope Pius II in 1458, he fulfilled a humanist dream by transforming his native hamlet into a tiny paradise subsequently dubbed "Pienza" in his honor. The plan called for a group of monumental structures to be erected around a piazza: a cathedral, a papal *palazzo,* a town hall, and a public well. Completed between 1459 and 1462, the mini-city exemplifies the Tuscan Renaissance. In fact, Piazza Pio II is classical almost to a fault; there isn't the slightest element of disorder in the textbook façade of the **cathedral.** The luminous interior is purely Gothic, the work of Renaissance masters Vecchietta and Giovanni di Paulo. Ask the custodian in the sacristy on the right aisle to let you visit the underground crypt, which contains a baptismal font by Rossellino and fragments of Romanesque sculpture from the church which formerly stood here. (Open daily 7am-1pm and 3-7:30pm.)

Palazzo Piccolomini, to the right of the piazza as you face the church, is widely considered to be a copy of the Palazzo Rucellai in Florence, though there is still some debate in art historical circles. Within rest various collections of weapons and medals drawn from the Pope's personal possessions. (Open Tues.-Sun. 10am-12:30pm and 4-7pm; off-season Tues.-Sun. 10am-12:30pm and 3-6pm. Admission L3500.) Behind the *palazzo,* a three-story *loggia* overlooks an amazing garden hanging along the edge of a cliff. Inside the **Palazzo Civico,** facing the cathedral, you can exhaust the stores of the resourceful **tourist office** (tel. (0578) 74 85 02; open June-July Mon.-Sat. 10:30am-12:30pm and 3:30-5:30pm, Sun. 10am-12:30pm and 3-5:30pm; Aug.-May daily 10:30am-12:30pm and 3:30-6:30pm). To the left as you face the cathedral is the **cathedral museum.** (Open March-Oct. Wed.-Mon. 10am-1pm and 4-6pm; Nov.-Feb. Wed.-Mon. 10am-1pm and 3-5pm. Admission L2000.)

Aeneas Silvius was baptised at the church **La Pieve di S. Vito,** a 25-minute walk from the center of town along Via Fonti (which begins on the back right-hand corner of the park). With a round bell tower and low thick walls, this Romanesque church was begun in the 8th century, but not completed until the 12th century.

Come to town on the first Sunday of September for the **Fiera del Cacio,** when Pienza celebrates the local *pecorino* (sheep cheese) by recreating the medieval marketplace. The **Sabato Serenata** is held the day before the sheep cheese fest, and features a philanderer sporting traditional threads, who serenades a matron perched in a window of the Palazzo Piccolomini with old Tuscan folk songs.

Inexpensive lodgings are uncommon in Pienza, but if the tranquility and charm convince you to stay for the night, head over to the **Ristorante il Prato,** P. Dante Alighieri (tel. 74 86 01), which has tiny but clean rooms. (Singles L30,000; doubles with bath L60,000.) More expensive, but with tremendous panoramic views of the countryside from its balconies, is **Il Corsignano,** Via della Madonnina (tel. (0578) 74 31 38). (Singles with bath L60,000; doubles with bath L90,000.) **Trattoria La Buca delle Fate,** Corso Il Rossellino, 38/A (tel. (0578) 74 84 48) graces Pienza with exceptional local cuisine, including delicious homemade *pici* (hollow spaghetti, L7000) and a fragrant *coniglio in umido* (rabbit in a light brown sauce, L10,000). (Open Tues.-Sun. noon-3pm and 7-11pm.)

TRA-IN buses run between Pienza and Siena (Mon.-Sat. 7 per day, 1½hr., L5000). Pienza is best seen, however, as a daytrip from Montepulciano (9 per day, L1800).

◄ Arezzo

Quoth a 19th-century British traveler of Arezzo, "Its subtle air has been asserted to be peculiarly favorable to genius." Indeed, little Arezzo has had its share of visionaries: the poet Petrarch, the humanist Leonardo Bruni, the artist and historian Giorgio Vasari, and Guido d'Arezzo, inventor of the musical scale. Masaccio, Paolo Uccello, Piero della Francesca, and Michelangelo were born in the surrounding countryside. Yet most moved on to more beautiful and cosmopolitan settings. Petrarch left for the papal court in Avignon, Bruni became the intellectual leader and chancellor of Florence, Guido headed for Ferrara, and though Vasari built and frescoed his house in Arezzo, he spent most of his time in Florence with the Medici. The partial exception to this exodus was local son Piero della Francesca, who stayed here long enough to paint one of the most moving fresco cycles in Italy. But while the cycle undergoes restoration, only an eclectic gathering of good Medieval and Renaissance pieces keeps Arezzo on the art pilgrim's tour. The less devoted might better follow the example of the early Aretini—and flee.

ORIENTATION AND PRACTICAL INFORMATION

Arezzo lies on the Florence-Rome train line, an hour from Florence (L6500) and two hours from Rome (L17,100). Buses connect it with nearby hilltowns, including Cortona (LFI, 1½hr., L3700) and Sansepolcro (CAT, 1hr., L4500). Four buses run daily to Siena (1½hr., L7000), returning to Arezzo in the afternoon.

Arezzo's train station and modern quarter lie at the bottom of a hill which ascends through the historic center and peaks at the *duomo*. Follow **Via Guida Monaco,** which begins directly across from the station in Piazza della Repubblica, up into the medieval and Renaissance old town, and continue with Via Cesalpino up to the top. You can leave your bags in **luggage storage,** to your left before you enter the station from the tracks (L1500; open daily 8am-7pm).

Tourist Office: To the right as you leave the station in P. della Repubblica, 22 (tel. 37 76 78). A little overwhelmed by the tourist onslaught, but more than happy to give out free maps and other information. Open June-Oct. Mon.-Sat. 9am-1pm and 4-7pm, Sun. 9am-1pm. Nov.-May open Mon.-Sat. 9am-1pm and 3-6pm, and Sundays when there is an antique fair, 9am-1pm.

Post Office: Via Monaco, 34, to the left of P. Monaco when facing uphill. Open Mon.-Fri. 8:15am-7pm, Sat. 8am-12:30pm. **Postal code:** 52100.

Telephones: SIP, P. Monaco, 2, in the shopping arcade. Open 24 hrs. Also at Via Margaritone, off Via Niccolò Aretino near the Archeological Museum. Open Mon.-Sat. 8:30am-12:30pm and 3:30-6:30pm. **Telephone code:** 0575.

Buses: (tel. 38 26 44), on Viale Piero della Francesca in front of the train station. Open Mon.-Sat. 6:15am-8:35pm, Sun. 9:10-11:15am and 3:20-7:15pm.

Emergencies: tel. 113. **Police:** off Via Fra' Guittone, near the train station. **Guardia Medica** (tel. 30 04 44). **Hospital:** (tel. 35 67 57; at night and Sun. 35 18 00), on Via Fonte Veneziana.

ACCOMMODATIONS AND FOOD

The hotels of Arezzo fill to capacity during the Fiera Antiquaria (Antique Fair) on the first weekend of every month. Reservations are also necessary in the last four days of August during the **Concorso Polifonico Guido d'Arezzo,** a vocal competition. Otherwise, you should have little trouble finding a room—but maybe you should take that as a sign.

Ostello Villa Severi, Via Redi, 13 (tel. 29 047). Take bus #4 (L800) from the right-hand-side of Via Guido Monaco (100yd. up Via G. Monaco from the train station), and get off at the stop after the Ospedale Civile (about 7 minutes). A restored villa in the countryside overlooking hills and vineyards. 68 beds, 6 beds per room. Open 8am-4:30pm and 6:30pm-midnight. L18,000 per person, breakfast included. Dinner L15,000, but if you reserve ahead you can get half-pension (bed, breakfast, and 1 meal) for L34,000, or full pension (room and 3 meals) for L42,000.

Hotel 129, Via Adigrat, 1 (tel. 90 13 33), near the station. This modest hotel offers basic rooms with schoolchairs, desks, and institutional but very clean floors. Singles L27,000-30,000. Doubles L45,000-50,000.

Hotel Astoria, Via Monaco, 54 (tel. 24 361). Miniscule rooms. A good option in a pinch. Singles L38,000, with bath L49,000. Doubles L60,000, with bath L80,000. Breakfast L8000. AmEx, MC, Visa.

Skip a restaurant lunch and check out alternative food options, such as the **supermarket Santa Prisca** at Via Monaco, 84 (open Sun.-Fri. 8am-1pm and 4:30-8pm, Sat. 8am-1pm). Try the **open-air market** held Tuesday, Thursday, and Saturday in P. Sant'Agostino. For excellent cheese, especially *pecorino,* a sharp sheep's cheese and local specialty, the best bet is **La Mozzarella,** Via Spinello, 25 (open 8am-1pm and 4:30-7:30pm, Wed. 8am-1pm). Eat in the park behind the *duomo,* the one place in Arezzo that affords a peaceful and impressive view onto the Tuscan countryside.

La Scaletta, P. del Popolo, 11 (tel. 35 37 34), to the right when facing the post office. The earthy proprietor/cook takes pride in his tasty and copious cuisine. Try the *scallopa al limone e vinobianco* (L10,000). Pizzas L5000-8000. Open Fri.-Wed. noon-3pm and 7pm-midnight.

Otello, P. Risorgimento, 16 (tel. 22 648), 1 block away from Albergo Milano and in front of the tourist office. Fashionable young customers, tasteful modern decor, and fantastic food. Try the *crostoni* (L10,000-12,000). Open Mon.-Sat. 5pm-1am, Sept.-June Tues.-Sun. 5pm-1am. AmEx accepted.

SIGHTS AND ENTERTAINMENT

The **Church of San Francesco** at P. S. Francesco forms the spiritual and physical center of Arezzo. This 14th-century structure guards Piero della Francesca's famous fresco cycle *Legend of the Cross,* the story of the wood used for Christ's cross from seed to crucifix. The city planned to have finished the restoration for 1992, the 500th anniversary of Piero's birth, but the best laid plans often go delayed in Italy. Now that the 500th has passed, the urgency seems to have evaporated. It's now anybody's guess as to when the restoration (now covering the right half) will be completed. (Open daily in summer 8am-noon and 1:30-7pm; off-season 8:30am-7pm.)

Contrast this Franciscan art with the decoration of the rival Dominican order on the other side of town. The **Church of San Domenico** contains a superb Cimabue crucifix (1265), Spinello Aretino's *Annunciation* in the chapel to the right of the altar, and the Marcillat rose window over the door. (Open 7am-noon and 3:30-7pm.) Beyond the church on Via XX Settembre, 55, is **Vasari's house.** Filled with heroic frescoes, the house merits a trip just for an idea of what Hallmark might have accomplished during the Renaissance. (Open Mon.-Sat. 9am-7pm, Sun. 9am-1pm. Free.)

The massive **duomo,** on Via Ricasoli, encloses Piero della Francesca's *Mary Magdalene* just to the right of Bishop Guido Tarlati's tomb. Light filters into the cathedral through a series of 20-ft. stained glass windows by Marcillat onto the altar, a wildly complex assemblage of 14th-century local carvings. (Open 7am-noon and 3-7pm; off-season 7am-noon and 3-6:30pm.) Between the *duomo* and the fortress, a leafy park gives magnificent views out onto the countryside beyond its edge.

If you backtrack down Corso Italia, on the left you'll see the Pisan-Romanesque **Church of Santa Maria della Pieve,** Arezzo's most important architectural monument and something of a city emblem. Its tower is nicknamed "the tower of a hundred holes" for the Romanesque windows that pierce the structure on all sides. A brilliantly restored polyptych, *Il Politico* by Pietro Lorenzetti, sits on the elevated presbytery, depicting the Annuciation and the Madonna and Child. (Open daily 8am-noon and 3:30-7pm; in off-season 8am-12:30pm and 3-6pm.)

Behind the Pieve is **Piazza Grande,** surrounded by a chronological succession of Arezzo's best architecture. Next to the arches of the Pieve's rear elevation, the **Palazzo della Fraternità dei Laici** mixes Renaissance and Gothic styles. A reconstruction of the Petrone, a column where criminals were exhibited and proclamations read, rises at the piazza's high point.

The **Giostra del Saracino,** is a medieval joust performed the last Sunday of August and the first Sunday in September. "Knights" representing the four quarters of the town charge with lowered lances at a wooden effigy of a Saracen. Feasting and processions accompany the event, and the winning region carries off a golden lance.

■ Sansepolcro

Lost in a valley among Tuscany's densely forested hills, medieval Sansepolcro is the birthplace of Piero della Francesca and hosts some of his finest works. The town is most easily accessible by the hourly CAT line bus from Arezzo (1hr., L3300), the last bus returning to Arezzo at 7:30pm. This bus ride is not for the weak of stomach, though the incredible views of the countryside are worth the punishment. The bus drops you off on Via Vittorio Veneto. To get to the museum, take a left from the bus station, then turn left again at the next street, Via Niccolo, and walk three minutes until you come to the street light; the museum will be on your right.

The **Museo Civico,** Via Aggiunti, 65, houses some of Piero della Francesca's most famous works. The *Resurrection,* his masterpiece, features a triumphant and determined Jesus wearing a red and white banner as he prepares to stride over the side of his tomb. Also by Piero is the *Madonna della Misericordia,* a polyptych with a huge goddess of a Madonna hiding a confraternity under her cloak. The museum also contains a *Crucifixion* by Luca Signorelli, Piero's best student. Don't miss Antonio and Remigio Cantagallina's *Ultima Cena,* with Judas in the foreground holding his money bag and looking nonplussed as a devil on the floor spits blood on him. (Open daily 9-11:15am and 2:30-7:15pm. Admission L5000.)

The **Palio della Balestra** takes place the second Sunday in September. Stay overnight and join in the revelry generated by this competition between archers of Gubbio and Sansepolcro. To reach Sansepolcro's **tourist office,** on Via della Fonte (tel. (0575) 73 02 31 or 74 05 36) from the museum, turn right on Via Niccolo and then take the first left on P. Garibaldi; the tourist office is one block ahead on the left. (Open daily 10am-1pm and 4-7pm.) They're more than happy to provide maps and sell guidebooks to the region. Should night fall or hunger strike, try the comfortable **Albergo Fiorentino,** Via Luca Pacioli, 60 (tel. (0575) 74 03 50; fax 74 03 70), two blocks from the Museo Civico (singles L26,000, with bath and TV L40,000; doubles L42,000, with bath and TV L65,000; triples with bath and TV L81,000; quads with bath and TV L95,000; showers L4000; breakfast L6000) and the **Ristorante Da Ventura,** Via Aggiunti, 30 (tel. 76 560), which serves outstanding homemade pasta dishes, including the house specialties: ravioli with spinach and ricotta filling or *tagliatelle* with porcini mushrooms. Whole roasts are carved right at the table. (*Primi* L7000, *secondi* L10,000; open Sun.-Fri. noon-2:30pm and 7-10pm.)

Another important stop on any Piero della Francesca odyssey is the tiny chapel halfway between Arezzo and Sansepolcro, outside the town of **Monterchi.** 24 km outside of Arezzo on highway 73, there is a fork in the road; take the right fork (highway 221) to the chapel. Within, marvel at the unusual *Madonna del Parto,* Piero's rendition of the Madonna immaculately pregnant with Bambino. (Open daily 10am-12:30pm and 3-7pm.) The Arezzo-Sansepolcro bus stops nearby in Le Ville (where you can follow the signs to the chapel, about a 20-min. walk).

■ Cortona

The ancient town of Cortona preens on a mountaintop with all the hubris of a town that knows it's closer to heaven than earth. Older than Troy, Cortona enjoyed independence on several occasions in its history but earned its reputation under foreign domination. After the usual Guelph-Ghibelline internal strife and some squabbles with neighbors Perugia and Arezzo, the ruling family spent the last years of the 14th century bumping each other off, leaving the city to be plucked by the king of Naples, who promptly sold it to Florence in 1409. Under Florentine rule, Cortona exported Luca Signorelli to its owner and in return received Fra Angelico, who sojourned here for a decade and painted an *Annunciation* that rivals the one in Florence's San Marco. The town's high-altitude perch has allowed little room for expansion; consequently, old Cortona has changed little in the last 600 years. The inexorable medieval ambience has lured many modern *literati,* Henry James and Germaine Greer among them.

ORIENTATION AND PRACTICAL INFORMATION

The easiest way to reach Cortona is by train, either from Rome (90min., L13,800), from Florence (1hr., L8800), or from Arezzo (30min., L2400). As Cortona is not directly on the line, you must get off at either charmless Terontola-Cortona or barren Camucia-Cortona, both of which are connected to Cortona by the LFI buses that run about every hour to Piazza Garibaldi in Cortona (L2000 and L1600 respectively).

Buses leave you at **Piazza Garibaldi** just outside the main gate in the city's wall. Enter through this gate and follow **Via Nazionale,** passing the **Tourist Office** almost immediately on your left, to the town's center at **Piazza della Repubblica.** From there, cross the piazza diagonally to the left to reach the other main square, **Piazza Signorelli.**

Tourist Office: Via Nazionale, 72 (tel. 63 03 52). Friendly and helpful, with lots of maps and brochures. Open Mon.-Sat. 8am-1pm and 3-6pm.
Post Office: off P. della Repubblica. Open Mon.-Fri. 8:30am-7pm, Sat. 8:30am-noon. **Postal code:** 52044.
Telephones: SIP, Via Guelfa, off P. della Repubblica. Open daily 8am-midnight. **Telephone code:** 0575.
Swimming Pool: tel. 60 13 74, 7km away at Sodo. Take the bus for Arezzo and ask the driver to let you off at the *piscina*. Water slides! Open daily 8am-midnight. Admission L6000.
Emergency: tel. 113. **Police:** Via Dardano, 9 (tel. 60 30 06). **Medical Assistance: Servizio Guardia Medica Turistica,** Via Roma, 3 (tel. 60 18 17). For emergencies. Open 8am-8pm. **Ambulace: Misericordia,** tel. 60 30 83. **Hospital:** Via Maffei (tel. 62 941).

ACCOMMODATIONS AND FOOD

Cheap hotels are scarce in Cortona, but institutional arrangements take up the slack. The hostel is one of Italy's best, a converted 13th-century house with exceptionally friendly management, and the nuns down the hill will do right by you.

Ostello San Marco (HI), Via Maffei, 57 (tel. 60 13 92). From the bus stop, walk up steep Via S. Margarita and follow the signs to the hostel, about 5min. A perfectly clean and cozy place with a cavernous dining room. 1 double (open to couples). Laundry facilities available. Open 7-10am and 4pm-midnight. L14,000 per person. Breakfast and sheets included. Showers included, but hot water shuts off late at night. Dinner L12,000. Open mid-March through mid-Oct. and year-round for groups.
Istituto Santa Margherita, Viale Cesare Battisti, 15 (tel. 63 03 36). Walk down Via Severini from P. Garibaldi; the *istituto* is at the corner of Via Battisti, on the left. Echoing marble hallways take you to spacious rooms, all with bath. Curfew midnight. Singles L24,000. Doubles (no unmarried couples) L38,000. Triples L48,000. Dormitory-style rooms for L18,000 per person. Breakfast L5000.
Albergo Italia, Via Ghibellina, 5 (tel. 63 05 64), off P. Repubblica. High ceilings, firm beds in recently renovated rooms. Pleasant, vigorous management. Singles with bath around L50,000-55,000. Doubles with bath around L60,000-70,000.

With several *trattorie* featuring immense pasta dishes and an abundance of grocery, fruit, and *rosticcerie* (prepared food) stores, even a pauper won't starve in Cortona. The best local wine is the smooth *bianco vergine di Valdichiana*. True penny-pinchers can pick up a bottle (L3000) at the **Supermercato A&O,** in Piazza della Repubblica. (Open daily 8am-1:30pm and 4:30-10pm.) On Saturday the same piazza metamorphoses into a great **open-air market.**

Trattoria La Grotta (tel. 63 02 71), P. Baldelli, 3, off P. della Repubblica. Delectable fare in a homey atmosphere. Sample the homemade *gnocchi alla ricotta e spinaci* (ricotta and spinach balls in tomato and meat sauce, L8000). Continue sampling with one of their grilled specialties, perhaps the *fegato di Vitello* (calf's liver, L9000). Open daily Aug.-Sept. noon-3pm and 7-11pm; Oct.-July Wed.-Mon. noon-3pm and 7-11pm.
Trattoria Dardano, Via Dardano, 24, (tel. 60 19 44) caters mostly to locals in one long, breezy room. *Primi,* including a hearty *lasagne al forno,* L5000-6000. *Secondi* L6000 and up (their specialty is roasted meats, L6000-7000). Open daily noon-3pm and 7pm-midnight.
Trattoria Etrusca, Spaghetteria e Birreria, Via Dardano, 35. Specializes in *primi,* serving up marvelously unique pasta creations. Try the house specialty, *tagliatelli colle zucchine* (pasta with zucchini, L7000). Full meals for under L12,000. Kitchen open daily 12:30-2:30pm and 7:30pm-1am; Oct.-May closed Thurs. *Bar* and *birreria* open 9am-2am. MC, Visa.

SIGHTS

The most stunning sights in Cortona are the incredible vistas of the surrounding valleys and hills afforded by Cortona's elevation. From the ancient citadel of the **Fortezza** on the summit of Cortona's rugged hill (Mont. S. Egidio), you can see the entire town spread out below, and gaze out over Tuscany. On the walk up to the fortezza, one passes several small meadows with beautiful views and no people—perfect for a picnic. On the other side of town, at P. Garibaldi, lean out over the iron fence to peer down the jagged cliff to the floor of the valley below, where you can see Hannibal's beloved Lake Trasimeno and Umbria beyond.

In P. della Repubblica stands the 13th-century **Palazzo del Comune,** with a clock tower and monumental staircase. **Palazzo Casali,** to the right and behind the Palazzo del Comune, dominates P. Signorelli. Only the courtyard walls with their coats-of-arms and the outside right wall remain from the original 13th-century structure—the façade and interlocking staircase were added in the 17th century. Inside the courtyard, steps lead to the **Museo dell'Accademia Etrusca,** which cherishes many treasures and artifacts from the Etruscan period, as well as an overflow of carvings, coins, paintings and furniture from the first through the 18th century. In the first gallery is a circular bronze chandelier from the 5th century BC, mounted in a glass case suspended from the ceiling. With 16 voluminous oil reservoirs, it weighs 58kg when empty. A rare example of intricate Etruscan metalwork, the *lampadario* was discovered by a local farmer plowing his field. The same room contains a two-faced *Janus,* depicted as a full figure rather than the usual bust. In the third gallery you'll find 12th- and 13th-century Tuscan art, including works by Taddeo Gaddi, Cenni di Francesco, and Bici di Lorenzo. The museum wraps up with the 20th-century work of local boy Gino Severini, including lithographs, collages, and an intriguing *Maternità.* (Open Tues.-Fri. 9am-1pm and 4-7pm; Oct.-March Tues.-Sun. 9am-1pm and 3-5pm. Admission L8000.)

To the right and downhill from the Palazzo Casali is **Piazza del Duomo.** On the façade of the *duomo* note the brick entry of the original Church of S. Maria, poking out like a sore thumb from the stone fronting. During renovations, enter the church from the side door, near the Palazzo Vescovile. Inside, you'll find an impressive Baroque canopied high altar, completed in 1664 by Francesco Mattioli. The two-floored **Museo Diocesano** across from the *duomo* houses a stunning *Annunciation* by Fra Angelico in the upstairs gallery on the right. Across the corridor on the left, Christ's pain-wrenched face confronts you in Pietro Lorenzetti's fresco of *The Way to Calvary.* Vasari's staircase leads to a frescoed oratory on the lower level containing a painted cross by Lorenzetti. (Open April-Sept. Tues.-Sun. 9am-1pm and 3-6:30pm; Oct.-March 9am-1pm and 3-5pm. Admission L5000.) Perhaps the best example of Luca Signorelli's work is *The Deposition,* which resides in the 16th-century **Church of San Niccolò,** up the hill beyond the youth hostel. Ring the bell if the church isn't open, and, after the kind woman shows you the painting, ask her to activate the nifty mechanism that turns the panel around so you can see Signorelli's *Madonna and Saints* on the other side. (Church generally open 9am-12:30pm and sporadically in the afternoon.)

When afternoon sedates Cortona, head up to the **Fortezza Medicea** for a splendid view and a refreshing breeze. Take Via San Cristoforo, which winds up the hill between tall cypresses from the small church of the same name. You will pass the remains of Etruscan and medieval city walls, the site of an ancient temple dedicated to Mars, god of war, and a stone explaining how Santa Margherita administered her first miraculous cure. At the top enter the tree-filled fortress, built on the remains of an Etruscan fortification. (Open mid-July to Aug. Tues.-Sun. 10am-1pm and 4-7pm.)

The Renaissance **Church of Santa Maria delle Grazie al Calcinaio,** designed by Francesco di Giorgio Martini, eagerly awaits visitors about 2km down the road near Camucia. The soft gray *pietra serena* stone is beautifully carved in the interior, and the white walls create a cool tonality. Paintings of the Signorelli school hover near the altar and a Marcillat stained-glass window energizes the opposite wall. (Open daily 8:30am-noon and 3:30-7pm.) Ask at the tourist office for information about the **Meloni del Sodo,** recently discovered Etruscan tombs near Sodo.

ENTERTAINMENT

Of the numerous gastronomic festivals throughout the year, the most important is August 14-15's **Sagra della Bistecca,** when the whole town pours in to feast upon the superb local steak. Various musical and theatrical events take place thoughout the year, clustering in the summer months. The Azienda's informative "Cortona '93" will give you the lowdown. Relax in the **public gardens** or join in the evening *passeggiata* along the park's *parterre.* Italian movies are screened here in summer.

NORTHERN ITALY

▨ Liguria

The crescent-shaped coastal strip of Liguria (the Italian Riviera) stretches 350km along the Mediterranean between France and Tuscany. Genoa, in the center, divides the coast into the *Riviera di Levante* (rising sun) to the east, and the *Riviera di Ponente* (setting sun) to the west. Ligurians are known for their cultural isolation; claiming Nordic, not Latin, ancestry, they have their own vocabulary and an accent incomprehensible to other Italians, let alone foreigners. Its distinctive character, however, has not prevented Liguria from playing a leading role in the unification of the Italian peninsula. Giuseppe Mazzini, known as the father of the *Risorgimento*, and its most popular hero, Giuseppe Garibaldi, were both Ligurians.

Protected by the maritime Alps from the more severe weather to the north, Liguria cultivates its crops and a lively tourist trade all year long, and is one of Italy's most prosperous regions. In summer the landscape comes ablaze with deep reds and purples, while lemon and almond blossoms scent the air; in winter, the olive trees that shade the robust flower beds produce what may be Italy's best oil (a title contested by Tuscany).

The character of the Italian Riviera differs from that of its French neighbor. Here you'll find neither the arrogance nor the cultural sterility of Cannes or St. Tropez. The palm-lined boulevards and clear turquoise water are the same, but above these rise *città vecchie* or *alte* (old or upper cities)—distinctly Italian mazes of narrow cobblestoned streets and tiny *piazze*. Unless you're coming from France, you might do best by starting at the eastern edge of Liguria and working your way only as far as Genoa. Although slightly more expensive, the eastern (Levante) coast is the most inviting of the two: it is less congested than Ponente, and the dramatic juxtaposition of Alps and ocean creates a landscape where pine forests hover thousands of feet above the water and tiny beaches are wedged between sharply chiselled escarpments. If you plan to stay closer to the French border in Ponente, consider Finale Ligure, a resort town with medieval ambience and infinite stretches of sandy beach. The area of the Ponente from Imperia to the French border is known as the Riviera dei Fiori (Riviera of Flowers). Adjacent to gaudy Sanremo and other hyped-up vacation spots, it's the least interesting portion of the coast, unless you really have a thing for palm trees.

All the coastal towns are linked by frequent trains on either the Genoa-La Spézia or Genoa-Ventimiglia line and even more frequent intercity buses that pass through all major towns. Boats connect the resort towns, and local buses run to the hill towns inland.

■■■ GENOA (GÉNOVA)

Its name comes from the latin word, *janua*, meaning gate, which is appropriate: for packed between the lofty peaks and the now semi-polluted waters of the Liguraian Sea, Genoa's entanglement of delightfully narrow shop-filled streets co-exist with a wild trading port. A strategic location brought it security and trade; by the late 13th century, having defeated Pisa, the reach of the Genoan empire extended as far as North Africa, Syria, and the Crimea. Crusades and colonial profits allowed its leading families to endow the city with parks, palaces, and a generous store of art. Venice overwhelmed Genoa in 1380, and the city languished under foreign domination

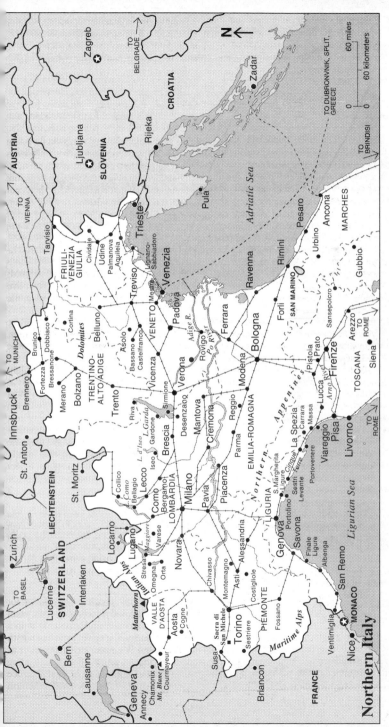

Northern Italy

until it was swept up in the fires of the Risorgimento. Renowned *Genovesi* include Christopher Columbus, the Risorgimento ideologue Giuseppe Mazzini, and virtuoso violinist Niccolò Paganini. These days it is the Genovese industrialists, with a sense of fashion and an understanding of international business to rival the Milanese, who define the city.

Genova occupies three dimensions, north-south, east-west, and, most importantly, up-down. The most useful form of public transportation in this city of rapidly ascending streets are the prolific public elevators and cog-rail *funiculare* trollies. Heavily rebuilt after World War II bombing, the city's commercial center does not necessarily merit a visit. Instead, stick to the *creuze,* the narrow footpaths, and the charming *vicoli* that wind their way upwards among houses, overhanging gardens, and numerous cats; these trails offer spectacular views and a peaceful respite from the chaos of the modern city.

ORIENTATION AND PRACTICAL INFORMATION

Unlike most Italian cities, Genoa's center does not lie at the *duomo,* or even in the oldest quarter of the *centro storico,* but around the decidedly more modern 19th-century P. de Ferrari. Most visitors arrive at one of Genoa's two train stations, **Genova Principe** or **Genova Brignole.** Buses #33 and 37 connect the two stations (25min., L1000). From Brignole take bus #40 and from Principe take #41 to the center of town at P. de Ferrari. The city stretches along the coast; the main streets leading west to Stazione Principe from P. de Ferrari are **Via XXV Aprile, Via Garibaldi** and then **Via Balbi. Via XX Settembre** runs east in the direction of Stazione Brignole. The tourist offices give out free maps, but their street indexes are woefully inadequate, and most of the smaller streets' names aren't marked. This map will probably serve only to get you completely lost, especially if you attempt to venture into the *centro storico.* Procure a decent map at the *edicola* (newsstand) to be found right in the train station; just five-minute walk from any point to another— Genoa's tangled streets can stump even a native.

Genoa's double sequence of **street numbers** (red for commercial establishments, black for residential or office buildings) is confusing, especially since dirty red numerals often appear black. Don't be fooled if you come to the supposed address of a place and it is not there; chances are that you have simply come to the number of the wrong color.

The *centro storico* preserves many of Genoa's most important monuments; unfortunately, it is also the city's most dangerous quarter, riddled with drugs and prostitution at night. The problem is complicated by the labyrinthine streets; you'll need a sixth sense of navigation, even with a map, and it's an extremely bad place to get lost. Don't wander the area after dark or on shop-closed Sundays, and be cautious in deserted Genoan August. But do visit: the sights are well worth seeing.

Tourist Office: EPT, Via Roma, 11 (tel. 54 15 41, fax 58 14 08), up 2 flights off P. Corvetto. From Stazione Brignole, go right on Via de Amicis to P. Brignole, then continue up Via Serra to P. Corvetto. From Stazione Principe, take bus #33 or 37 and get off at P. Corvetto, or go on foot by way of Via Balbi, through P. Annunziata, along Via Bensa, Via Cairoli (which becomes Via Garibaldi) through P. Nunziata, and continue straight through P. Fontana Marose, which leads you to P. Corvetto. Friendly but slightly disorganized with its little store of useful information on hotels and museums. Some English spoken. Open Mon.-Fri. 8am-1:30pm and 2-5pm, Sat. 8am-1:30pm. There are train station **branches** at both the Principe (tel. 26 26 33) and Brignole (tel. 56 20 56) stations. Open daily 8am-8pm. Also, try Città di Genoa-Servicio Informaziona Videotel across from Palazzo Municiple (tel. 20 98 27 19). Good for a better free map and student travel info. Make sure to pick up the indispensable "Genovagiovane" guide for students. Open Mon.-Fri. 9am-noon and 1-5pm.

Budget Travel: CTS, Via San Vincenzo, 117r (tel. 56 43 66 or 53 27 48), off P. Verdi near Stazione Brignole. Student fares to all destinations. **Associazione**

Albergatori per la Gioventù, Via Cairoli, 2 (tel. 29 82 84), near P. Nunziata. HI cards. Both open Mon.-Fri. 9am-12:15pm and 3-7:30pm.

Consulates: U.S., P. Portello, 6 (tel. 28 27 41). Business matters and emergencies only. For passports and visas contact the consulate in Milan (tel. (02) 290 018 41). Open Mon.-Fri. 9am-noon. **U.K.,** Via XII Ottobre, 2 (tel. 56 48 33). Open Mon.-Fri. 9am-noon and 4-7pm.

Currency Exchange: Banks abound: Sat.-Sun. head to the train station, which gives slightly lower rates, but only takes L500 (and sometimes no) commission. Open daily 7am-10pm.

American Express: Viatur, P. Fontane Marose, 3 (tel. 56 12 41), inside a travel agency. L3000 for mail inquiry without AmEx card or AmEx traveler's cheques. Does not actually handle money, but will authorize **check cashing** for cardmembers (they give you an authorization, which you take to a bank to get your *lire*). Open Mon.-Fri. 9am-1pm and 3pm-7pm.

Post Office: Central office, Via Boccardo, off Via Dante at P. de Ferrari. **Another office** at Via D'Annuzio, 32 (tel. 160 for central information at either office), for **Fermo Posta** or express mail service. From P. de Ferrari, follow Via Dante 2 blocks to P. Dante; take Via D'Annunzio, on your right. The post office will be on the left-hand side, on the pedestrian level above the roadway. Both open Mon.-Sat. 8:15am-7:40pm. Convenient offices (without Fermo Posta) in the Stazione Principe and across the street from the Stazione Brignole. All open Mon.-Fri. 8:15am-8pm, Sat. 8:15am-1pm. **Postal Code:** 16100.

Telephones: ASST, in the post office, has the shortest lines. Open daily 8am-8pm. Other ASST phones at Via XX Settembre, 139 (open Mon.-Sat. 8am-11:50pm, Sun. 8am-9pm) and Stazione Brignole (open 8:15am-9:15pm). **Telephone Code:** 010.

Flights: C. Colombo Internazionale (tel. 24 11), in Sestiere Ponente. European destinations. Buses depart for the airport from the last platform in the *piazza* 1hr. before scheduled flights (L4000).

Trains: Stazione Principe (tel. 26 24 55), in P. Acquaverde. **Stazione Brignole** (tel. 58 63 50), in P. Verdi. For train information, call 28 40 81, 7am-11pm. Trains run from both stations to points along the Ligurian Riviera and to major Italian cities. To Turin (10 per day, 2hr., L12,100) and Rome (15 per day, 5-6hr., L33,600).

Buses: AMT, Via D'Annunzio, 8r (tel. 599 71). One-way fares L1000. All-day tourist passes L3000 (foreign passport necessary). Tickets good for 1½hrs. and can be used for *funiculare* and elevator rides.

Ferries: Stazione Marittima, tel. 26 14 66. Major destinations are Porto Torres (Sardinia), and Palermo, but each could be reached more cheaply and conveniently from elsewhere. Listed fares are 1-way deck class. **Grandi Traghetti** (tel. 58 93 31 or 26 71 28). To Sicily (19hrs., July 23-Aug. 10, L310,000). **Tirrenia** (tel. 25 80 41). To Sardinia (L41,800-53,500). **Corsica Ferries:** (tel. 59 33 01). To Corsica (6hr., L44,000).

Boat Excursions: Cooperativa Battellieri del Porto di Genoa, tel. 26 57 12. Guided boat tours of Genoa's port from the Stazione Marittima (daily at 10am and 2pm, 40min., L4000). Trips to the Cinque Terre (L17,000, round-trip L27,000) and Portofino (L10,000, round-trip L17,000).

Hitchhiking: Hitchers take bus #17, 18, 19, or 20 from Stazione Brignole to the Genoa West entrance, where highways lead to points north and south. It is illegal to hitchhike on the highway itself. Remember that hitchhiking is very risky; **women especially should excercise extreme caution, and should never hitch alone. Furthermore,** Let's Go **does not recommend hitchhiking for anyone.**

English Bookstore: Bozzi, Via Cairoli, 2r (tel. 29 87 42). Open Mon.-Fri. 8:30am-12:30pm and 1:30-7pm, Sat. 8:30am-12:30pm and 1:30-8:30pm. Closed 1 wk. in Aug.

Public Baths: Diurno, Sottopassaggio de Ferrari, 67r (tel. 56 49 80), in the underpass in front of the bombed-out theater in P. de Ferrari. Showers L6600, bath L8300. Towels included. Shampoo L100, soap L600. Open Mon.-Sat. 8am-8pm, Sun. 8am-noon.

Swimming Pool: Piscina Communale, Via G. B. d'Albertis. Admission L2500. Open Mon., Wed., and Fri.-Sat. 8:30am-noon and 4-7:30pm. Also at Stadio del Nuoto (Albaro) (tel. 36 84 09).

Pharmacies: tel. 192 for the name of an all-night pharmacy. **Pescetto,** Via Balbi, 185r (tel. 26 26 97), is usually open all night.

Laundry: Lavanderia Contini, P. Paolo da Novi, 37 (tel. 56 24 83). Near Stazione Brignole. L9000 per load for washing, L11,000 for drying. (Figure out a way to air-dry your clothes!) Open Mon.-Fri. 8:30am-12:30pm and 3:30-7:30pm.

Emergencies: tel. 113. **Police:** Via Diaz (tel. 536 61). Ask for the *ufficio stranieri* (office for foreigners). **Hospital: Ospedale San Martino,** Viale Benedetto XV, 10 (tel. 353 51). **Ambulance:** tel. 570 59 51 or 651 12 36.

ACCOMMODATIONS AND CAMPING

Genoa must have more one-star hotels per capita than any other city in Italy, so finding cheap shelter isn't a problem. Finding someplace you'd also want to stay is. Almost without exception, budget lodgings in the *centro storico* (historical center) and near the port prefer to rent rooms by the hour, and no one should stay here at night. Go for the hostel, or stick to the area around Stazione Brignole; the establishments are substantially nicer and more secure. Rooms get scarce only in October, when Genoa hosts nautical conventions.

Ostello Per La Gioventù (HI), Via Costanzi, 120 (tel. 24 22 457 or 58 64 07). From Stazione Principe, take bus #35 for 5 stops, then transfer to bus #40 (which you can take direct from Brignole). Ride #40 to the end of the line, just uphill from the hostel. Recently built pink and gray building with panoramic views of the city and incredible facilities: free luggage lockers outside each room, reading lights by each bed, elevators, bar and self-serve restaurant (L12,000 per meal). TV and reading rooms, laundry (L12,000 for 8kg) and maps and brochures. Excellent wheelchair access. Parking and payphones available, too. Bus every 10min. to the *centro.* Max. 3-day stay. Office closed 9am-3pm. Checkout 9am. Hot showers from 6pm-11pm. Curfew 11:30pm. HI card required. L18,000 per night, sheets and breakfast included.

Casa della Giovane, P. Santa Sabina, 4 (tel. 20 66 32 or 28 18 02), near P. Annunziata. Women only. An excellent deal, it's clean and safe (old moms guard the front desk like hawks). Rooms most plentiful on weekends and in the summer as students who go to the nearby university take off. Strict curfew 10:45pm. Singles L18,000. Doubles L36,000. Triples L45,000. Quads L52,000. Breakfast included. Meals in restaurant only L10,000.

Pensione Mirella, Via Gropallo, 4/12 (tel. 83 93 772). From Stazione Brignole, go right on Via de Amicis to P. Brignole and go right again. In a beautifully maintained and secure building. Large, clean, and elegantly furnished rooms and pleasant proprietor. Singles L35,000. Doubles L50,000. Make reservations. **Albergo Carola** (tel. 89 13 40), 2 flights up. An excellent alternative. Singles L35,000. Doubles L60,000.

Pensione Barone, Via XX Settembre, 2/23 (tel. 58 75 78), off Via Fiume. Small establishment on the 3rd floor. Baroque designs on the ceilings make up for dark rooms and peeling wallpaper. Midnight curfew. Singles with shower L35,000, with shower and private toilet L45,000. Doubles with shower L55,000, with shower and private toilet L65,000. MC, Visa. If they are full, ask about their other hotel, The Garden, Via Calatafimi, 7 (tel. 839 93 31) near P. Corvetto. Singles L40,000. Doubles L60,000.

Camping: The area around Genoa teems with campgrounds, but many are booked solid during July and Aug. Options in the city are scarce and often unsavory; try for something on the beach. **Villa Doria,** Via Vespucci, 25 (tel. 58 64 07), in Pegli. Take the train or bus #1, 2, or 3 from P. Caricamento to Pegli, then walk or transfer to bus #93 up Via Vespucci. The closest campground west of the city. English spoken. L5000 per person, L12,000 per tent.

FOOD

Partaking of the culinary offerings of Genoa may inflict grave damage on your waistline, but your wallet and tastebuds will thank you. *Trattorie* and their local specialties are ubiquitous. *Pesto,* the Genovese pride and joy, is an incomparable pasta sauce made from ground basil, pine nuts, garlic, and *parmigiano,* and served with olive oil. Although *pesto* is enjoyed throughout the world, you can only taste the real product in Genoa, for the basil has a special smooth quality to it, without the slight taste of mint; eat it in the traditional manner, over *trenette* cooked with potatoes. Other Genovese specialties include *pansotti,* ravioli stuffed with spinach and ricotta, served with a creamy walnut sauce; also try the *farinata,* a fried bread made from chick-pea flour, and the *polpettone,* a baked composite of mashed potatoes and beans sprinkled with bread crumbs. Accompany any meal with loads of olive oil-soaked *focaccia,* a delicious flat bread topped with herbs, olives, onions, or cheese, and a specialty of nearby Recco. The *centro storico* hosts the best *trattorie* at the best prices, so eat a big lunch and skip dinner, because you don't want to navigate this area at night. Near Brignole, Borgo Incrociati teems with small family-run restaurants; wander around to check out daily specials—your best bet for dinner.

Osteria da Colombo e Bruno, Borgo Incrociati, 44r. A traditional *trattoria* frequented at lunch by local workers. The *menù* (L11,000), including *primo, secondo,* vegetable, fruit, bread, water, and wine, can't be beat. Open Sept.-July Mon.-Sat. 12:30-2:30pm and 7:30-10pm.

Sa Pesta, Via Giustiniani, 16r (tel. 20 86 36), south of P. Matteotti. Sa Pesta knows *pesto;* everyone from doctors to dockworkers converge here for lunch to wolf down incomparably prepared Genovese specialties like *farinata* (fried chick peas) and *minestrone alla genovese* (with pesto). *Primi* L5000-7000; *secondi* L6000-8000. Fixed-price menu offered. *Focaccia* and *pizzato* for take out. Open Sept.-July Mon.-Sat. noon-2:30pm.

Trattoria da Maria, Vico Testadoro, 14r (tel. 58 10 80), off Via XXV Aprile. Maria's serves the absolute best of quintessential Genovese cuisine. The menu changes daily—everything's extremely fresh. Wonderful staff helps translate the menu, *prezzo fisso* L12,000 (includes *primi, secondi,* and water or wine). Open Sun.-Thurs. noon-2pm and 4:30pm-7pm.

Bakari, Vicolo della Fieno, 16r, to the Northwest of P. San Matteo in the *centro storico.* A chlorophyll-colored restaurant with stone columns supporting a low arched ceiling. Packs 'em in at lunch. Choose from 6 different fixed-price *menùs,* including 3 different vegetarian dinners. Prices range from L13,900 for a beggar's banquet to L23,000 for a regal feast. All meals include at least *primo, secondo,* vegetable, dessert, water, wine, and bread. Open Mon.-Tues., and Thurs. noon-2:30pm and 7-9:15pm, Wed. and Fri. noon-2:30pm. (Dinners cost 10% more than lunch.)

Kilt 2 Self Service, Vicolo Doria, in the shade of P. San Matteo in the *centro storico.* A cafeteria set-up that dishes out otherworldly gourmet meals for a fixed price of L14,000. Menus change daily, but keep an eye out for the *mussels marinara*—they would send even Julia Child into ecstasy. Open Mon.-Sat. 12:45-2:30pm.

Brera Express, on Via Brera, (tel. 54 32 80). Just off Via XX Settembre, near Stazione Brignole. *Pizzeria* and full-service, but the best deal is the cafeteria-style *prezzo fisso* menu—L14,500 for a full meal including beverage. Open Mon.-Fri. 11:30am-2pm and 7pm-midnight. (Self-service closes at 10pm.)

Focacceria Daniel, Via San Vicenzo, 185r (tel. 56 67 70), off Via XX Settembre. Bakes up a wide variety of tasty *focacce* (L1600 per *etto*). Open daily 7am-7:30pm.

Antico Forno, Via di Porta Soprana, 15, on the corner of Via Notare. The smell will draw you in for a piece of fresh bread, sweetbread, focaccia or pizza all between L1000-3000. Open Mon.-Sat. 9am-9pm.

Moody, Via XII Ottobre, 8. Self-Service. Great fixed price menu for L13,500. The restaurant is as busy and bustling as the street surrounding it. Open 'til 1:30am Sat. and Sun.

Il Fornaio, Via San Luca, 95, off Via Lomelina. The place to come for the tastiest Italian biscotti. Open daily 8am-8pm.

Gelateria Biza, Via San Vincenzo, 65. Thirty different kinds of scrumptuous gelato are sure to please anyone's palate. Open daily 11am-7:30pm.

SIGHTS

From Principe to the Centro Storico

Because of its longstanding commercial strength Genoa has managed to collect some of the finest 16th- and 17th-century works of Flemish and Italian art. It is also a city well-endowed with the *palazzi* and *ville* of its famous merchant families. From the open and airy Stazione Principe, graced by a small square with a statue of Christopher Columbus, one can see the distant view of the port.

This is an excellent place to begin an exploration of the city; nearby, just before the *palazzo*-lined **Via Balbi** on Via S. Giovanni, lies one of Genoa's oldest monuments, the Romanesque church **San Giovanni di Pre'.** The stone vaulted roof and the feeble light that filters into the church add to its Romanesque weight and cavernous solidity. Next door, **La Commenda,** built in the late 12th century, quartered the Knight Commanders of St. John.

Via Balbi, the heart of Genoa's university quarter, preserves some of the most lavish *palazzi* in Genoa. At #10, the fine courtyard of the 18th-century **Palazzo Reale** (Royal Palace) once opened onto a beautiful seaside garden; now it looks out on a major road and city sprawl. Upstairs, the **Galleria d'Arte** (tel. 247 06 40) provides a glimpse into the lifestyles of 18th-century Genovese nobility, with paintings by Tintoretto, van Dyck, and Bassano. Across the street is the **Palazzo Balbi.** (Open daily 9am-1pm. Admission L4000. Under 18 free.) The street runs into P. Nunziate, formerly called "Gaustato" (broken) for the large number of ruins in the square. Today it typifies the Genovese square: small, irregular, and distinguished by formal *palazzi.* The severe neoclassical façade (1843) of the **Church of SS. Annunziata** (1591-1620) conceals an incongruously rococo interior which resembles King Midas's personal residence. The gold-washed interior was almost entirely reconstructed after suffering heavy damage during World War II bombing raids. Although the chapels that line the aisles do not preserve any great masterpieces, they form an impressive gallery of 17th-century art. (Open daily 6:30am-11:30pm and 4-7pm.)

Bookstores line Via Cairoli on its way to **Via Garibaldi,** the most impressive street in Genoa, bedecked with elegant *palazzi.* A glance inside their courtyards reveals impressive frescoes, fountains, or leafy gardens complete with goldfish pools.

The **Palazzo Bianco** (1548, rebuilt 1712) at Via Garibaldi, 11 (tel. 29 18 03), now houses one of the city's most important collections of Ligurian art as well as its best Dutch and Flemish paintings. **Palazzo Rosso,** Via Garibaldi, 18, built in the 17th century, houses magnificent furnishings and a lavishly frescoed interior. Today it plays host to the **Galleria di Palazzo Rosso** (tel. 28 26 41). Several full-length van Dyck portraits grace the second floor, as does Bernardo Strozzi's masterpiece, *La Cuoca.* (Both *palazzi* are open Tues.-Sat. 9am-7pm. Note that they occasionally alternate weeks open due to lack of staff. Admission L4000. Under 18 free.) Next door to the Palazzo Bianco at Via Garibaldi, 9, **Palazzo Doria Tursi (Palazzion Municipale),** now the city hall, showcases Niccolò Paganini's violin, the *Guarneri del Gesù.* The sounds of this instrument broke the hearts of many, drove others to suicide, and persuaded the rest that they were hearing angels singing. The violin is still used on rare occasions to perform Paganini's works, but with less extreme consequences. (Open Mon.-Fri. 8:30am-noon and 1-4:30pm. Free.)

The *galleria* faces the vigorous Renaissance façade of the **Palazzo Municipale** (1564-70) and its beautiful roof gardens. The courtyard of the **Palazzo Podestà** (1565), Via Garibaldi, 7, contains an unusual grotto fountain and an intriguing stucco decoration of a merman. **Palazzo Parodi** (1578), Via Garibaldi, 3, boasts an elegant doorway with noseless telemons, a tribute to the owner's ancestor, Megollo Lecari, who took revenge on his enemies by chopping off their noses and ears. Via Garibaldi spills into P. Fontane Marose, from which you take Via Interiano to P. del Portello, the base for a public elevator (runs 6:50am-10:30pm; L400) that whisks you up to **P. Castelletto.** The *piazza* maintains an extraordinary vista over the entire city and port. From P. Portello you must take the *funicolare* (L1000) for the **Chiesa di Sant'Anna.** A harmonious Renaissance work, Sant'Anna is also notable for its location, poking out precariously from the steep hillside among leafy gardens. One of Genoa's most beautiful and peaceful *creuze* (footpaths) descends from the church among trees, *palazzi,* and omnipresent felines.

From P. Fontane Marose, Salita di Santa Caterina takes you to Piazza Corvetto. The **Villetta Di Negro** spreads out along the hill to your left, inviting you to relax amid waterfalls, grottos, and terraced gardens. Its summit houses a real treasure, the **Museo d'Arte Orientale E. Chiossone** (the museum of Oriental art, tel. 54 22 85). The first floor houses impressive sculptures; check out the dimunitive dog-dragon. (Open Tues.-Sat. 9am-7pm, Sun. 9am-12:30pm. Admission L4000. Under 18 free.) From P. Corvetto, Via Roma leads to **Piazza de Ferrari,** the city's bustling center, home to a monstrous fountain resembling, naturally, a raised hubcap.

Off P. de Ferrari lie P. Matteotti and the **Palazzo Ducale,** once the home of the city's rulers. Inside, visit the two beautiful courtyards, one punctuated by an elegant 17th-century fountain. On the opposite corner to this imposing palace stands the ornate **Church of the Gesù** (also known as SS. Ambrogio e Andrea; 1549-1606). This Baroque edifice features *trompe l'oeil* effects, double cupolas, and two important Rubens canvases, *The Circumcision* and *St. Ignatius Healing a Woman Possessed of the Devil.*

The Centro Storico

The unkempt and often dangerous historical center is a mass of duplicitous streets bordered by the port, Via Garibaldi, and P. de Ferrari. Due to its crime, prostitution and drugs, the historic center is an advisable spot for tourists only during weekdays when stores are open; at night the quarter's underground elements crawl out and not even the police venture in. But the *centro storico* is also home to Genoa's most memorable monuments: the *duomo* S. Lorenzo, the church of San Luca, and the medieval Torre Embraici. Keep an eye out for the numerous sculpted and painted tabernacles, or "Madonette," that adorn the corners of buildings (about 3m up the walls).

Off P. Matteotti resides the **Duomo San Lorenzo.** Already in existence in the 9th century, the church was enlarged and reconstructed in the 12th through 16th centuries, resulting in the characteristically striped Gothic façade and uncharacteristically lopsided appearance—only one of the two planned bell towers was completed. The carved central portal decorated with lions, sirens, and vines opens to a severe and simple interior of black and white, like a chessboard. The chapel of St. John the Baptist along the left wall is decorated with statues of Adam and Eve by Matteo Civitali. A vintage American bomb adorns the right wall of the church, miraculously unexploded after having crashed through the roof during World War II. (Open Mon., Wed., and Fri.-Sat. 10am-noon and 2-5pm, Sun. 10am-noon.) Behind the *duomo* Via Arrivescovato leads to Genoa's most characteristic and charming square, **Piazza San Matteo.** It contains the houses and family chapel of the Doria family, members of the medieval oligarchy that ruled Genoa. The animal reliefs above the first floor are the trademarks of the masons who built the houses. Chiseled into the façade of the **Church of San Matteo** (1125) are descriptions of the Dorias' great deeds, and to the left, a small door protects a lovely 14th-century cloister. Nearby, down Vicolo delle Vigne, resides one of Genoa's oldest churches, **Chiesa Santa Maria delle Vigne.** Dating from the 10th century, it still maintains its Romanesque arc-spired bell tower (open 8am-noon and 3:30-7pm).

GENOA

From here head down Via Greci to **Via San Luca,** the main artery of the old quarter, where you'll find many of Genoa's most important monuments. The **Church of San Siro** was Genoa's first cathedral (rebuilt 1588-1613). A dome crowns the little **Church of San Luca,** a 12th-century treasure in the shape of a Greek cross. (Both open Mon.-Fri. 4-6pm. Free.) **Palazzo Spinola,** in P. di Pellicceria, 1 (follow the yellow signs), exemplifies Genoa's mercantile wealth from the 16th through 18th centuries. In the *palazzo's* rooms, which retain most of their original decoration and furnishings, works of art donated by the Spinola family mingle with later additions, constituting the **Galleria Nazionale di Palazzo Spinola** (tel. 29 46 61). Don't miss the portraits of the four evangelists by van Dyck in the Sala da Pranzo. (Open Tues.-Sat. 10am-7pm, Sun. 9am-1pm. Admission L4000. Under 18 free.)

Medieval arcades (Portici di Sottoripa) border one side of P. Caricamento, by the port on the other side of P. Banchi. Across the piazza, the **Palazzo San Giorgio,** a part-Gothic, part-Renaissance structure, once housed the famous Genovese bank of St. George. Intense World War II bombing left much of the area in need of reconstruction, but some interesting churches remain scattered among the old tenements and medieval ruins. The **Church of Santa Maria di Castello,** a labyrinth of chapels, courtyards, cloisters, and gardens, once served as a crusaders' church and hostel. In the chapel to the left of the high altar check out the *Crocifisso Miracoloso*—Jesus' beard supposedly grows longer every time crisis hits the city. Nearby, the medieval **Torre Embriaci** looms over Santa Maria di Castello, with Guelph battlements jutting out from the rough stone surface. Head down Vico della Pace to P. San Cosimo to visit the **Chiesa di Santi Cosma e Damiano,** built in the 1100s and typical of Genovese Romanesque architecture with its austere façade and beautifully preserved octagonal campanile.

Finally, the newest addition to the old city, the **Museo dell'Architettura e Scultura Ligure** occupies the former monastery of Sant'Agostino at P. di Sarzano (tel. 20 16 61). This museum attempts to explicate Genoa's history through its surviving art. Giovanni Pisano carved the museum's most outstanding piece, the funerary monument of Margherita of Brabant, in 1312. Fragments of this monument have been scattered to various corners of the continent, but the museum hopes to eventually reassemble it. (Open Tues.-Sat. 9am-7pm, Sun. 9am-noon. Admission L4000.) From P. di Sarzano Via Ravecca leads back to the medieval **Porta Soprana,** which flaunts its enormous twin towers and noble arched entryway, the emblem of this district. Walk past the reputed boyhood home of Christopher Columbus (his father was the gatekeeper of Soprana) and the ruins of the 12th-century cloister of the **Church of Sant'Andrea.**

To pay tribute to Italy's greatest patriot and political thinker (save, of course, Niccolò Machiavelli), take bus #34 from Stazione Principe to the **Cimitero di Staglieno.** Here, in one of Europe's only modern necropolises, lies the **Tomb of Giuseppe Mazzini** (1805-1872), which honors the Genovese native known as the father of the Risorgimento. Other national figures such as Lorenzo Pareto (1800-1865), the famous Italian scientist and scholar, have also chosen to spend eternity here. (Cemetery open daily 8am-5pm.)

ENTERTAINMENT

In July **Genoa Jazz** presents jazz concerts at Villa Imperiale, drawing musicians from Europe and the United States. Seats start at about L15,000, but you can buy a ticket for the entire series for about L60,000. For information check with the tourist office, or call Kamarillo, Via San Vincanzo, 109r (tel. 58 74 55). For listings of other music, theater, and dance performances, pick up one of the numerous pamphlets at any tourist office.

Nightlife booms at **Charlie Christian,** Via S. Donato, 20r, a smoky bar with live jazz and blues, hiply named after the father of jazz guitar (open Mon.-Sat. 8pm-1am). Hoofers head to **Cristina's,** in Piazza Tommase (tel. 36 86 52), where they can vogue to the latest vibes. (Open Tues.-Sat. 10pm-2am.) In summer the action moves to **Nervi,** only minutes away by train or bus, where people bar-hop or stroll along the *lungomare,* lapping *gelato.*

RIVIERA DI LEVANTE

■ Camogli

Camogli takes its name from the wives who ran the town while their husbands manned its once-huge fishing fleet ("Camogli" is a contraction of "Casa Mogli"—"Wives' House"). Lest this generate any unenlightened visions of long-gone tranquility, bear in mind Dickens's evaluation of Camogli: "the saltiest, roughest, most piratical little place." The husbands are back now, and this "piratical little place" has mellowed into a small, peaceful resort of 6,000. Those seeking a budget version of the more glamorous Portofino, might find Camogli to be just the place.

Orientation and Practical Information The town climbs uphill from the sea into pine and olive groves and a promontory separates the pebble beach from the fishing harbor below. Like many Riviera towns, Camogli came into money long after its six-story, blank-walled houses had been built. The *nouveau riche* Camogliesi hired painters to decorate their homes with *trompe l'œil* balconies, pilasters, moldings, and rustication, and other fripperies. After a long absence, the style has re-emerged and the solid, green-shuttered homes once again sport more playful façades.

Camogli can be reached by *locale* train on the Genoa-La Spézia line (from Genoa 20 trains per day, 40min., L2400; from La Spézia 10 trains per day, 1hr. 30min., L5000; from Sestri Levante 35 per day, 30min., L2400) or from Santa Margherita by bus (35min., L1700) or train (10min., L1500). **Tigullio** buses depart across from the station to nearby towns. Buy tickets at Bar Aldo, next to the station. (To: Santa Margherita, 18 per day, L1500; Portofino Vetta—*not* Portofino Mare, the port—3 per day, L1400.) Buses also stop at P. Schiaffino, across from the tourist office (on Via XX Settembre). You can buy tickets close by at the *tabaccheria* at Via Repubblica, 25. Ferries are more expensive, but offer incredible views of the peninsula's cliffs. From Camogli, **Golfo Paradiso,** Via Scala, 2 (tel. 77 20 91) ferries take you around the rugged headland to **San Fruttuoso** (May-Sept. 15 7-12 per day, L6000, round-trip L10,000). They also run a nighttime trip to Portofino (leaving at 9:30pm and returning at about 11:45pm; round-trip L16,000). Buy tickets on the boat. Or you may just want to forget all about the boats and make the three-hour hike to San Fruttuoso; pick up the Camogli tourist office's useful trail map if you do, or just follow the double blue dots of the well-marked path.

The **tourist office** at Via XX Settembre, 33 (tel. 77 10 66), to your right as you leave the station, helps you find a room and cheerfully answers even the silliest questions, all in broken English. They also have **telephones.** (Open Mon.-Sat. 9am-12:30pm and 4-7pm, Sun. 9am-12:30pm; Sept.-June Mon.-Sat. 9am-12:30pm and 3:30-6:30pm.) Camogli's **telephone code** is 0185. Exchange your money at the **Banco di Chiavarie della Riveria Ligure,** Via XX Settembre, 9 (tel. 77 25 76). The **post office** accepts mail at Via Cuneo, 1 (tel. 77 01 14), to the left of the station. (Open Mon.-Fri. 8:10am-6pm, Sat. 8:10-4pm.) The **postal code** is 16032. You'll find a **pharmacy** (tel. 77 10 81) at Via Repubblica, 4 (open Mon.-Sat. 8:30am-12:30pm and 3:30-7:30pm). For more serious medical concerns there is a **hospital** at Corso Mazzini, 96 (tel. 74 102). The **Red Cross** is located at Via XX Settembre, 58 (tel. 77 00 85) and the **police** at Via Cuneo, 30F (tel. 77 00 00).

Accommodations and Food Your best bet is unquestionably **Albergo La Camogliese,** Via Garibaldi, 55 (tel. 77 14 02). Walk down the long stairway near the

SAN FRUTTUOSO

train station to #55, near the seafront. The clean, commodious rooms are a joy, and the proprietors have indisputably found their calling. They refer to *Let's Go* readers as "Let's Go amici" and offer them special discounts. (Singles with bath L45,000. Doubles L55,000, with bath L60,000-80,000, depending on size and view. Breakfast L4000. Show them your book and make reservations.) The pleasant **Pensione Augusta,** Via Schiaffino, 100 (tel. 77 05 92), at the other end of town, has clean and simple rooms enlivened by the ceaseless rumbling of nearby trains. (Singles L50,000; doubles L67,000-75,000. All rooms with bath.) If these are full, walk left from the station past the post office to **Albergo Selene,** Via Cuneo, 16 (tel. 77 01 49). (Singles L46,000. Doubles L76,000.) If you still can't find anything, talk to the owner of La Camogliese and he will probably be able to find you a reasonable room in town. For a do-it-yourself meal, the scores of foodstuff shops on Via Repubblica should suffice. **Revello,** Via Garibaldi, 183 (tel. 77 07 77), at the end of Via Garibaldi, offers a huge array of snacks to choose from. Locals make a morning stop there for the Riviera's best *focaccia,* but their secret treat is the *camogliese al rhum,* a choc-olate-covered cream puff with a rum-spiked filling (both are L2600 per *etto*). These sinfully delicious treats have been pleasing visitors ever since they were first created here in 1970. (Open daily 7:30am-1pm and 3:30-7:30pm.) An open-air **market** in the main piazza is open Wednesdays 7am-1:30pm for food, clothes, and bargain fish-hooks. If it's nighttime, and you're desperate to groove, there's only one disco option: **La Loggia** at Via Aurelia, 31 (tel. 77 32 86).

Sights and Festivals Camogli is famous nationally and internationally for its enormous fish-fry, the **Sagra del Pesce.** On the second Sunday in May, tourists descend on Camogli to partake of the free fish, fried up in a giant, four-meter-across pan, which holds 2000 sardines at once, and adorns a wall at the entrance to the town when not in use. Though best-known for its pebble beach and holiday atmo-sphere, Camogli has its share of sights to see on a cloudy day: you can start with the **church** off P. Colombo in the old town. From the church, stone steps lead left to the **Acquario Tirrenico** (aquarium; open daily 10am-noon and 3-7pm; admission L4000). The **maritime museum, "Gio Bono Ferrari,"** across from the station, is dedicated to sailors who traveled from Cape Horn to Rangoon. (Open Mon., Thurs., Fri. 9am-noon; Wed., Sat., Sun. 9-11:45am and 3-5:45pm.)

■ San Fruttuoso

The tiny fishing hamlet of San Fruttuoso, set in a natural amphitheater of pines, olive trees, and green oaks by the sea, is much too expensive for a prolonged stay or even a meal, but it's still worth a daytrip. The town is accessible by foot (1½hr. from Portofino Mare or Portofino Vetta) or by boat. Both **Golfo Paradiso** (tel. (0185) 77 20 91; 12 boats per day from Camogli, L6000, round-trip L10,000) and **Servizio Marittimo del Tigullio** (tel. (0185) 28 46 70; 15 boats per day from Portofino, L6000, round-trip L10,000) provide service.

For a great view, walk to the left of the bay to the medieval **lookout tower** (admis-sion L2000), constructed by the Doria family. Fifteen meters offshore and 18m underwater stands a bronze statue with upraised arms, the *Christ of the Depths,* erected in memory of casualties at sea. The statue now serves as protector of scuba divers, and, in late August, the townlet sponsors a **festival** commemorating those lost at sea. Be sure to visit the Benedictine **Abbazia di San Fruttuoso di Capo di Monte** (tel. (0185) 77 27 03), for which the town was named. Here the non-amphib-ious can see an exact replica of the *Christ of the Depths* and activate a musical nativ-ity scene. (Open May-Oct. Tues.-Sun. 10am-1pm and 2-6pm; Nov.-Jan. Sat.-Sun. 10am-1pm and 2-4pm; March-April Tues.-Sun. 10am-1pm and 2-4pm. Admission L5000.)

■ Portofino

Gorgeous Portofino was discovered long ago by the well-to-do. Today the yachts of the wealthy fill the harbor and boutiques line the streets, but the curve of the shore and the tiny bay may be enjoyed by paupers and princes alike. A nature reserve surrounds Portofino; trek through it to San Fruttuoso (90min.) or Santa Margherita (2½hr.). If you choose to hang around town, you can escape to the cool interior of the **Chiesa di San Giorgio** by following the signs uphill from the piazza at the bay. A few more minutes up the road to the **castle** will set you in a fairy-tale garden with a view of the clear bay. Look for the footpath marked "Al faro" to reach the lighthouse (20min.—don't step on the salamanders!) and a breathtaking coastline vista. The *gelateria* here is open April-Sept. daily 9:30am-8pm.

There's no train to Portofino, but Tigullio **buses** run along the coastline to and from Santa Margherita. (Every 30min., L1400; make sure you take the bus to Portofino Mare, not Portofino Vetta, and buy tickets on board.) Maps and English brochures are available at the **tourist office,** Via Roma, 35 (tel. 26 90 24), on the way to the waterfront from the bus stop. Some English spoken. A large signboard of the arrivals and departures from Sta. Margherita is posted outside. (Open Mon.-Tues. and Thurs.-Sat. 8:30am-7pm, Wed. 9am-12:30pm, and Sun. 9:30am-noon; off-season, Mon.-Sat. 9am-6pm, Sun. 9am-1pm.) Currency may be exchanged at the **bank** on Via Roma, 14 (tel. 26 91 64). The **post office** is at Via Roma, 32 (tel. 26 90 40). Portofino's **telephone code** is 0185; use the **telephones** at the tourist office. For emergencies the **police** are at Via del Fondaco, 8 (tel. 26 90 88) and there's a **pharmacy** at P. Martiridella Lebertà, 6 (tel. 26 91 01). To sustain yourself on the hike to San Fruttuoso, head to **Alimentari Repetto,** under the arches to the left of the bay, for warm *focaccia* and cool drinks (open daily 7am-10:30pm).

■ Santa Margherita Ligure

Santa Margherita Liguria evokes the elegance of an era now past. For decades it was the vacation spot known for its whispers of restless glamour complete with a tourist industry accustomed to striving for the best. It now possesses a muted, serene quality expressed in the soft hues of blue, orange, octane and pink of its *trompe l'oeil* façades and by the graceful old ladies who continue to summer here, taking their evening *passeggiette* through town in softly flowing dresses. Abandon other overtouristed destinations and come here to escape, indulge in the fantasy of its former elegance and explore the rest of the Italian Riviera from this affordable base.

ORIENTATION AND PRACTICAL INFORMATION

Major inter-city trains along the Pisa-Genova line stop at Rapallo, the next town over. From there, catch the frequent local trains for the 3 min. ride to Santa Margherita or take an orange city bus outside the station labeled Santa Margherita (every 15min., 10 min., L1800). Tickets at the *tabacchi* in the station. Santa Margherita spreads in an arc around its small port. Facing away from the port, from the Piazza Martiri Libertà, Via Gramsci winds around the port to your right, below the train station, while Via Solmano, the street of shops and boutiques is straight ahead and to its right. Via XXV Aprile leads to the tourist office, continuing on to become Corso Matteotti.

Tourist Office: Via XXV Aprile, 2b (tel. 28 74 85). Turn right from the train station onto Via Roma, then right on Via XXV Aprile. Information, town map, and accommodations service. English spoken. Open daily 8:45am-12:30pm and 3:30-7pm.

Post Office: Via Roma, 36 (tel. 28 88 40), to the right of the station. Open Mon.-Fri. 8:10am-6:30pm, Sat. 8:10am-noon. **Postal Code:** 16038. **Telephone Code:** 0185.

Trains: (tel. 28 66 30), in P. Federico Raoul Nobili at the summit of Via Roma. To: Genoa (3 per hr. 4:30am-midnight, L2600); La Spézia (2 per hr. 6am-2am, L5600).

Luggage Storage: L1500 per piece. Ticket window and luggage storage open Mon.-Sat. 5:45am-7:50pm, Sun. 6:15am-8:35pm.

Buses: Tigullio buses depart from P. Martiri della Libertà at the small green kiosk on the waterfront. *Biglietteria* open daily 7am-8pm. Service to Camogli (15km, L2000) and Portofino (5km, L1700). Tickets can easily be bought on board for Portofino.

Ferries: Tigullio, Via Palestro, 8/1/B (tel. 28 46 70). Boats leave from the docks at P. Martiri della Libertà. To: Portofino (L4000, round-trip L7000); San Fruttuoso (L9000, round-trip L15,000); and Cinque Terre, Monterosso, or Riomaggiore (July-Sept. 15 only, L18,000, round-trip L25,000).

Bike Rental: Motonoleggio, Via Pagana, 5b (tel. 28 34 08). From the waterfront, follow Via Gramsci up the hill past the Hotel Helios. Bikes L10,000 for 3 hours, L20,000 per day. Tandems and motorbikes for slightly higher prices. Open June-Sept. daily 9am-12:30pm and 2:30-7:30pm. Oct.-May open sporadically, but you can call ahead and try to reserve.

Emergency: tel. 113. **Police:** (tel. 28 71 21), on Via Vignolo. **Hospital: Ospedale Civile di Rapallo,** P. Molfino, 10 (tel. 502 31), in Rapallo near the train station. For late-night and weekend medical attention, **Guardia Medica:** tel. 60 333 or 27 33 82.

ACCOMMODATIONS

Stay away from the water. Your room won't have a view and you'll have to trek a bit, but the reward will be peace, quiet, and an extra L10,000 in your pocket.

Corallo, Via XXV Aprile, 14 (tel. 28 67 74), about a block from the tourist office. Let yourself in the green gate and go through the garden. The kindly gent who runs the place has been in the business for years. His tidy, simple rooms have been recently repainted, and he's now turning his attention to the garden in front. Curfew 2:30am (get keys in the Bar Vanni out front to get in after midnight). Singles L28,000. Doubles L48,000. Call ahead or try to show up before noon.

Angelo's Hotel Terminus, Piazzale Nobili, 4 (tel. 28 61 21), to the left as you exit the station. The proprietor, Angelo, a former London restaurateur, dedicates his days and much of his rights to recreate the grace of the Italian Riviera's famed hotel culture. Clean, well-furnished rooms with new bathrooms and insulated windows that block the noise of the station some with fantastic views of the water and the hills of Santa Margherita. Singles L50,000, with bath L70,000. Doubles L75,000, with bath L90,000. Triples L100,000.

Hotel Nuova Riviera, Via Belvedere, 10 (tel. 28 74 03). A beautiful old villa set in a garden perfect for vacationing children. Spacious, elegant rooms. Singles L40,000-50,000. Doubles L60,000-80,000. Breakfast included. ½-pension sometimes required in summer at L75,000 per person. Reservations recommended.

Albergo Annabella, Via Costasecca, 10 (tel. 28 65 31), off P. Mazzini, not far from the beach. Capacious, clean, and contemporary rooms. Singles L35,000. Doubles L53,000. Triples L70,000. Showers L2000. Breakfast L6000. High season ½-pension required: L65,000 per person.

Hotel Conte Verde, Via Zara, 1 (tel. 28 71 39). An 18th-century villa expanded into the present hotel set in a very pleasant garden. Clean, modern rooms whose furnishings vary according to price. Singles L50,000-65,000. Doubles L90,000-120,000. Bicycles lent out free to guests.

Albergo La Piazzetta, Via Gramsci, 1 (tel, 28 69 19, fax 28 80 26). Clean rooms, with pretty ceilings, tiled floors and modern furnishings. Singles L45,000, with bath L50,000. Doubles L65,000, with bath L75,000. Breakfast included. MC, Visa.

FOOD

Supermarkets, bakeries, fruit vendors, and butcher shops line Corso Matteotti. On Fridays from 8am to 1pm, the shops oust the cars and spill onto the *corso*. The **COOP Supermarket** 9c Corso Matteotti, stocks all the basics including soy products for vegetarians. (Open Mon.-Sat. 8am-1pm and 4-8pm.)

FINALE LIGURE

Trattoria Baicin, Via Algeria, 9 (tel. 28 67 63), off P. Martiri della Libertà near the water. Papà Tommaso is the master chef, Mamma Beatrice rolls the pasta and boils the sauces, and brothers Piero and Rossano and cousin Andrea work the tables, making for a friendly and traditional Ligurian meal courtesy of the Famiglia Giovanuzzi. Try Mamma's homemade *Trofie alla Genovese gnocchi* mixed with potato, string beans, and pesto (L6500). A full meal sets you back L18,000 (cover included, 10% service not). Cover L2000. Open Tues.-Sun. noon-3pm and 6:45-midnight. AmEx traveler's checks, Visa.

Ristorante A Begudda, Via Tripoli, 5/A (tel. 28 09 86), off Via Roma. Savor the homemade pasta worked into local delicacies by Fortuna, the chef, as her husband presides over the rustic dining room decked out with colorful oddities and local art. Try the *Liguria Pansotti in Salsa di Noci* (L7000). Visa.

Trattoria Da Pezzi, Via Cavour, 21 (tel. 28 53 03), offers the most interesting daily specials in town: *ravioli di verdura e ricotta in salsa noci* (vegetable ravioli in sweet walnut-cream sauce) on Thurs. and Sun. (L5000). Cover L1200. Open Sun.-Fri. 11:30am-2:15pm and 6-9:30pm. Also a snack bar and take-out service at the entrance—open Sun.-Fri. 10am-2:15pm and 5-9:20pm. Am Ex accepted.

Rosticceria Revelant, Via Gramsci, 15 (tel. 28 65 00), east of P. Martiri della Libertà. Scrumptious take-out meals. Try the lasagna (L1350 per *etto*). Open Thurs.-Tues. 8am-1pm and 4:30-8:30pm, Sun. 7:30am-1pm.

SIGHTS AND ENTERTAINMENT

One of Santa Margherita's attractions remains its tranquility and proximity to Camogli and Portofino. From 8am to 12:30pm, you can ogle the day's catch at the local **fish market** on Lungomare Marconi, or come between 4 and 6pm to watch the fleet bring in its haul. (Market closed Wed. afternoon.) More exalted sights include the rococo **basilica** on P. Caprera, dripping with gold and crystal, which houses some good Flemish and Italian works. To reach the **Church of the Cappuccini,** a favorite feline hangout, walk along the waterfront past P. Martiri della Libertà and mount the stone ramp behind the stone castle. For human companionship, chalk up a pool cue at the **Old-Inn Bar,** P. Mazzini, 40 (open daily 7am-1am).

RIVIERA DI PONENTE

■ Finale Ligure

Eschewing the glamor and arrogance of other Riviera towns, Finale Ligure attracts a young crowd with its soft sand, luxurious flora, and relaxed, medieval character spiced up by a thriving boardwalk beach scene. If you yearn for bumpercars, tie-dye t-shirt shops, and gelaterias, your prayers have been answered.

ORIENTATION AND PRACTICAL INFORMATION

The city divides into three sections: **Finalpia** to the east, **Finalmarina** in the center, and **Finalborgo,** the old city, to the west. Most of the places listed below, including the **train station,** are located in Finalmarina.

Tourist Office: IAT, Via San Pietro, 14, (tel. 69 25 81 or 69 25 82), on the main street overlooking the sea (as opposed to the *lungomare,* which is really more of a promenade than a street). Luisa has been here for over 30 years and knows her stuff. She will gladly offer motherly advice for all of your problems, as well as a great map. Open Mon.-Sat. 8am-1pm and 4-7pm; off-season Mon.-Sat. 8am-1pm and 3-6pm, Sun. 8:30am-12:30pm. The **Associazione Alberghi** (tel. 69 42 52), across from the station in a camper-like office, helps you find rooms in the summer. Open June-Sept. 15 Mon.-Fri. 9am-8pm, Sun. 9am-8:30pm.

Currency Exchange: Try the **Casa di Risparmio,** Via Garibaldi, 4. Open Mon.-Fri. 9am-1:30pm and 3-4pm, Sat. 8:20-11:50am. The **Banco San Paolo** changes money with a L5000 commission.

Post Office: Via Concezione, 29 (tel. 69 28 38). Open Mon.-Fri. 8:10am-6pm, Sat. 8:10-noon. **Postal code:** 17024.

Telephones: SIP, Via Roma, 33. Pay phones, directories, and vending machines selling tokens and phone cards. Open June 1-Sept. 30 8am-11pm; Oct. 1-May 31 8am-8pm. If it's late, try the phones at **Bar Casanova,** Via Brunenghi, 75 (tel. 69 56 15), behind the train station. Open Mon.-Sat. 6:30am-1:30am. Also a phone in the station. **Telephone code:** 019.

Trains: P. Vittorio Veneto (tel. 69 27 77). Frequent service to: Genoa (L6000), Ventimiglia (L7000), and Santa Margherita Ligure (L8200).

Buses: SAR, Via Aurelia, 28 (outside and to the left of the train station). Ticket office open Mon.-Sat. 7am-1pm. On Sunday, buy tickets at Bar Sport, across the *piazza,* or at one of the other listed agents. To: Borgo Verezzi (L1100), Savona (L2800), Albenga (L2200), and other towns. All buses leave from in front of the station. Orange **city buses** to Finalborgo, L1000.

Bike Rental: Oddone, Via Colombo, 20 (tel. 69 42 15), on the street behind the tourist office. Bikes: 9am-12:30pm, L8000; 3-8pm, L10,000; 9am-8pm L15,000. Tandems: 9am-12:30pm, L20,000; 3-8pm, L22,000; 9am-8pm, L25,000. Mountain bikes: L10,000 for 1hr., L30,000 half-day, L50,000 full day. You must leave your passport and a deposit. Open daily 8am-12:30pm and 3-8pm. MC, Visa.

Pharmacy: Communale Via Ghiglieri, 2 (tel. 69 26 70) off Via Pertica. Open Mon.-Fri. 8:30am-12:30pm and 4-8pm. A posted sign shows which pharmacies are open when this one isn't.

Emergencies: dial 113. **Police:** Via Brunanghi, 68 (tel. 69 26 66). **Guardia Medica:** 8pm-8am and Sat. 2pm-Mon. 8am, tel. 64 77 77. If you need to get to the **hospital** (tel. 69 07 95), call one of the following *Auto Lettiga* service numbers—cheaper and more reliable than a taxi: (tel. 69 23 33 in Marina, 69 13 25 in Borgo, 69 83 32 in Varigotti, 64 66 66 for the hospital's own service). **First Aid: P. A. Croce Bianca,** Via Torino, 16 (tel. 69 23 32).

ACCOMMODATIONS

A visit to the Associazone Alberghi prior to seeking shelter could save you time and legwork. In July and August the youth hostel is always your best bet. Rooms in private homes can be arranged through the tourist office.

Youth Hostel: Castello Uvillermin (HI) (tel. 69 05 15), on Via Generale Caviglia in a turreted castle overlooking the sea. From the station, take a left onto Via Torino. At the tiny P. Milano, turn left and go up the stairs. Cross the street and continue uphill (via staircase); when you get to the top, turn right onto Via Caviglia. A small sign and, yes, another set of steps marks the way up to the castle, on your left. The view makes the climb worthwhile. Crowded in summer, with the (somewhat rustic) facilities strained almost to their breaking point, but still cheap and convivial. Cristina fixes great meals (L12,000). No phone reservations, and no groups in July-Aug. Reception open 7-9:30am and 5-10:30pm. Curfew 11pm; July-Aug. 11:30pm. Check-in 5pm, but you can leave your bags 7-9:30am. Doors locked until 7am. L14,000 per person for HI cardholders, (without card add L5000 or buy one for L30,000), sheets and breakfast included. Open March 15-Oct. 15.

Albergo San Marco, Via della Concezione, 22 (tel. 69 25 33), the street facing the beach, down from the station. Friendly proprietors keep spotless rooms, all with bath. Doubles L60,000. Triples L70,000. Breakfast included. June-Sept. full pension required: L55,000 per person in June, L62,000 in July, L70,000 Aug. 1-15, L65,000 Aug. 16-31, L57,000 Sept. 1-15, L52,000 Sept. 16-30. Remember to lock your door, even in a safe area such as this. Closed Oct.-Nov.

Albergo Cirio, Via Pertica, 15 (tel. 69 23 10), in the center of town. Super-friendly family atmosphere. Singles L25,000, with bath L30,000. Doubles L55,000, with bath L60,000. Triples L60,000, with bath L70,000. Breakfast included. Full pension L55,000 per person. In July-Aug. half-pension is required at L45,000 per person. AmEx, MC, Visa.

Camping: Del Mulino (tel. 60 16 69), on Via Piemonte. To get here from the station, take the bus for Calvisio from the stop outside at Via Torino and get off at the Boncardo Hotel. From here, take Via Porro, go left under an arch onto Via Castelli; follow it uphill and look for the signs for the campsite. Believe it or not, this is the closest campground to the beach. Bar and restaurant on the premises, but no proper laundry. L7000 per person, L6000 per tent; off-season L6000 and L4500. Open April-Sept.

FOOD

Trattorie and *pizzerie* line the streets closest to the beach. Pay less for comparable fare farther inland along Via Rossi and Via Roma.

Spaghetteria Il Posto, Via Porro, 21. An elegant and creative pasta house with an unusual menu. Try the *penne zar* (pasta with salmon and caviar, L8500) or the *penne pirata* (with shrimp and salmon, L8500). Cover L1500. Open Tues.-Sun. 7:30-10:30pm. Closed for approx. 1 month after Easter.

Salumeria Della Chiesa, Via Pertica, 13 (tel. 69 25 16), near the train station, is the perfect place to pack a picnic lunch for the beach. *Insalata di mare* (seafood salad) L3500 per *etto*. Lasagna L1500 per *etto*. Open daily 7:30am-1pm and 4-8pm; Oct.-May Mon.-Wed. and Fri.-Sat. 7:30am-1pm and 4-7pm, Thurs. 7:30am-1pm. The same management runs a restaurant around the corner on Via Gandolino, with *primi* from L6000. Open Mon.-Sat. noon-2pm.

Paninoteca Pilade, Via Garibaldi, 67 (tel. 69 22 20), off P. Vittorio Emanuele. Some of the best *panini* on the Riviera (L3000-5000). Pizza by the slice (L1800). Beer L2500-4000, wine L1300. MTV, old Coke posters, and cheap food—you get the picture. Open daily 10am-1am; off-season 10am-2:30pm and 4-8pm.

Bei Gisela, Via Colombo, 2 (tel. 69 52 75). *Jawohl!* Too expensive for a full meal, but if you're hankering for kitsch, a bit of Deutschland, or just good beer on tap, here's the place. Löwenbräu memorabilia everywhere. *Primi* from L6000, beer on tap L2200. Cover L1500. Open daily 10:30am-2:30pm and 6:30-10:30pm for dinner, 3:30pm-midnight. Sept.-June closed Wed.

SIGHTS AND ENTERTAINMENT

Enclosed within its still-intact ancient walls, **Finalborgo,** a 1km walk up Via Brunenghi from the station, is a Renaissance city in miniature. The Baroque **Basilica di San Biago,** inside the city walls through the *Porta Reale* entrance off Via Brunenghi, boasts an elegant 13th-century octagonal clock tower, while the giant 12th-century **Castel San Giovanni** still stands guard nearby (closed to the public). The **Chiostro di S. Caterina,** a five-minute walk across town from the *Porta Reale,* is a 14th-century edifice housing the **Museo Civico.** (Open Tues.-Sat. 10am-noon and 3-6pm, Sun. 9am-noon; Oct.-May Tues.-Sat. 9am-noon and 2:30-4:30pm. Admission L5000.)

At the waterfront in **Finalmarina,** you can climb the steps at the intersection of Via Colombo and Via Torino to the lofty 14th-century **Castelfranco.** World War II ravaged much of this structure, but it has recently been restored, and the view is tremendous. Ask at the tourist office for hours and admission charge, if any.

The towns surrounding Finale Ligure invite discovery. Take an SAR bus (L1100) to tiny **Borgo Verezzi.** Get off at the first stop in the town of Borgio. From here, five buses leave daily for Verezzi. From mid-July through August, performances animate **Teatro di Verezzi,** the town's outdoor theater in the main *piazza.* The performing company is one of Italy's most renowned, featuring many noted Italian thespians. (Admission about L25,000. Call the Borgo Verezzi tourist office at (019) 61 51 54 or 61 51 16 for details.)

Nighttime fun in Finale throbs and bobs at the **Sporting Club** (tel. 69 13 22), a combination swimming pool/disco. The club runs a free shuttle, which leaves every hour 10am-midnight from the Hotel Boncardo, Corso Europa, 4, to the club in nearby San Bernardino. (Open June-Sept. 15 for swimming only, daily 11am-7pm, L8000 per person; for swimming and dancing, daily 9:30pm-3am, Sun.-Fri. L15,000 per person, Sat. L25,000 per person. Cover includes one drink.) Or try the pricier, meat-market type discos: **Scotch Club,** on Via S. Pietro (tel. 69 24 81; cover L20,000); **Caligola,** (tel. 60 12 84), on Via Torino (open Wed. and Fri.-Sun.;cover L20,000); **Il Covo,** (tel. 60 12 84), Capo San Donato (open Thurs.-Sun.; cover L15,000; Sat. L20,000; drinks L10,000).

Also worthy of a visit in Finale is the **Archeological Museum,** P. Santa Caterina (tel. 69 99 20). (Open Tues.-Sat. 10am-noon and 3-6pm, Sun. and holidays 9am-noon; in winter Tues.-Sat. 9am-noon and 2:30-4:30pm, Sun. and holidays 9am-noon. Admission L5000.)

■ Sanremo

The first and still the largest resort on the Italian Riviera, Sanremo was once the glamorous retreat of high-rollers from around the world. The high prices persist, though tawdry casinos, shabby cabanas, and hyperactive tourism are all that remain of its one-time eminence. Like Sestri Levante on the Riviera di Levante, Sanremo is an expensive, avoidable annoyance—unless you're looking for a gambling opportunity. The terminally optimistic can relive Sanremo's glory days at the Edwardian **Casino,** Corso Inglesi, 18 (tel. 53 40 01). The entrance fee is only L15,000, though you must be 18 to enter and men must wear coat and tie. Blackjack begins at 8:30pm, but early gamblers can play roulette starting at 2:30pm. The "American Room" of one-armed bandits has neither dress code nor entrance fee, and lures early risers with its 11am opening. All the "fun" stops at 2:30am. San Remo's **tourist office** is located at Corso So. Cavallotti, 59 (tel. 50 57 62). San Remo's **postal code** is 18038; the **telephone code** is 184. The **museum "hotline"** is (tel. 54 19 42).

■ Dolcedo

An unforgettable excursion into the Ligurian hinterland can be launched from Imperia (a drab, modern town along the Riviera). A 7km-trip through sunny groves that produce Liguria's best olive oil leads to the medieval village of **Dolcedo.** Bridges cross the river Prino, ancient oil mills grind, and the 15th-century chapel of Santa Brigida is also nearby. The bridge on which the Knights of Malta carved "mcclxxxxii die 3 juli hoc opus perfectum fuit" ("on 3 July 1292 this work was finished") leads to the old market square, an area that seems utterly unchanged since the Middle Ages. Make a right on Via de Amicis to the **Church of San Tommaso,** a parochial church with 17th-century arcades. Its striking pink and green exterior, seems to have partially inspired the peculiar half-pink-and-green and half-blue-and-gold interior. At the moderately priced **Ristorante Da Tunu** (tel. 28 00 13), a full meal costs less than L15,000, wine L5000 per three-quarters of a liter. *Cinghiale* (wild boar) is an autumn specialty. (Cover L1500. Open Tues.-Sun. noon-2:30pm and 7-9:30pm.) Riviera Trasporti buses (towards Prela) leave P. Dante in Imperia for Dolcedo 11-15 times per day. Buy tickets at any *tabaccheria* in town (L1800).

The medieval hillside village of **Cervo,** is a picturesque retreat from the larger beach towns of the Riviera. Its white houses, red roofs, stone archways and tiny *piazze* are well worth the simple excursion: take the *locale* along the Ventimiglia-Genoa line. Cervo hosts an international chamber music festival in July and August, held in front of the Baroque **Church of San Giovanni Battista.**

■ Bordighera

Bordighera is known as the "City of Palms." Legend has it that Sant'Ampelio brought the seeds from Egypt and planted them in the town's fertile soil. The town's green thumb persists: it proudly supplies the Vatican with the palm leaves for Holy Week. One of the most popular resorts on the Riviera di Ponente, Bordighera has hosted an upscale crowd in its dramatically situated gardens and fortified old town for decades.

Orientation and Practical Information The bus from Ventimiglia (15min., L1300) drops you off along the main street, **Via Vittorio Emanuele II,** which runs west from the city's train station. Most of the offices and shops line Via Vittorio Emanuele, while the residential area sits uphill and farther inland. For a wealth of useful information visit the **Tourist Office** at Via Roberto, 1 (tel. 26 23 22; fax 26 44 55), just past the small park. From the train station, go left on Via Vittorio Emanuele, then take the first right on Via Roberto. Marvelous Marisa doles out maps, hotel listings and information in English. She doesn't book rooms, but will give you some good suggestions. Open Mon.-Sat. 9am-12:30pm and 3:30-6pm, Sun. 9am-noon; Oct.-May Mon.-Sat. 9am-12:30pm and 2:30-5:30pm. A **currency exchange** is conveniently located at Via Vittorio Emanuele, 165 (tel. 26 36 54). The **post office** (tel. 26 23 74) is located just to the left of the station in P. Eroi della Libertà. Open Mon.-Fri. 8:10am-6:30pm, Sat. 8:10am-noon. (**Postal code:** 18012.) Across from the tourist office are **telephones** at the **SIP** office Via Roberto, 18. Pay phones only. Open daily 8am-8pm. (**Telephone code:** 0184.) **Trains** on the Ventimiglia-Genoa line arrive at the **Stazione F.S.** in P. Eroi della Libertà (tel. 26 22 09). A **pharmacy** (tel. 26 12 46) at Vittorio Emmanuele, 145 stocks the basics. **Hospital/Medical Services** can be obtained at Via Aurelia, 66 (29 10 25), and for an **ambulance** dial 26 45 33. In case of **emergency call** 113.

Accommodations and Food In summer, most hotels want clients to stay several days and require that they accept full or half-pension. Though a bit of a hike to get there, the nuns at **Villa Loreto,** Via Giulio Cesare, 37 (tel. 29 43 32) provide the lowest prices and best company around in their palatial, tranquil residence graced by palm and lemon trees. Take Via Vittorio Emanuele left from station for 200m then go right on orange-tree-lined Via Rossi and left on Via Aldo Moro, which leads into Via Cesare. Women and married couples only. Curfew 10:30pm; Sept.-June 9pm. They only give rooms with full pension (L53,000-55,000 per person, depending on the size of the room and whether it's with bath). Closed Oct.-Nov. About 100m down from the station, off Via Vittorio Emanuele you'll find **Villa Miki,** Via Lagazzi, 14 (tel. 26 18 44). Small rooms, but a serene setting, firm beds, and balconies overlooking the town and valleys. L28,000 per person. Showers and breakfast included. Full or half-pension required during summer and Easter, L45,000-55,000 per person. A warm reception and private showers await you at the friendly **Albergo Nagos,** P. Eroi della Libertà, 7 (tel. 26 04 57). New furniture and nice views make up for small room sizes. Singles L28,000. Doubles L40,000. Full pension (L55,000) required July-Aug., half-pension (L45,000) required May-June and Sept.

The *trattorie* in the old city serve the cheapest sit-down meals. For picnics, try the **mercato coperto,** P. Garibaldi (open Tues.-Sat. 7am-1pm) or the **Supermercato STANDA,** Via Libertà, 32 (open Mon.-Sat. 8:30am-12:30pm and 3:30-7:30pm). **Trattoria degli Amici,** Via Lunga, 2 in the *città alta,* serves *lasagne con funghi porcini* (with fresh mushrooms) for L8500. Cover runs a hefty L4000. (Open Jan.-Oct. Tues.-Sun. noon-2pm and 7-11pm.)

Sights and Entertainment If you're up for a long but worthwhile walk, head east along Via Romana. Fork off onto Via Rossi, where cannons still stand sentinel above an awesome expanse of deep blue sea. Take the steps down to the **Church of Sant'Ampeglio,** built around the grotto where Ampeglio the hermit holed up. (Open Sun. at 10am or knock on the door. Also open May 14, for the festival of Sant'Ampeglio.) The **Giardino Esotico Pallanca** ("exotic garden," tel. 26 63 44) at Via Madonna della Ruota, 1, contains over 3000 species of cacti and other rare South American flora. For inspiration of a more melodic nature ask at the tourist office about the Museum of Italian Song. **Lungomare Argentina** named after Evita

Peron who herself inaugurated it, follows along Bordighera's biggest attraction, the **beach**.

In late July and August, Bordighera holds the **Salone Internazionale Umorismo** (tel. 26 17 27), an international humor festival with performances and exhibits in the Palazzo del Parco (the same building as the tourist office).

■ Ventimiglia

A former Roman municipality, Ventimiglia has long lost all vestiges of the splendor of its ancient and medieval past. The relics of a Roman theater remain to the east of town, and the 11th-century old city's winding streets across the river to the west may be of interest. For most visitors, however, Ventimiglia serves primarily as a point of departure for the French Côte d'Azur; it is within easy reach of all the famous Riviera oases, yet more affordable than similar towns in France.

ORIENTATION AND PRACTICAL INFORMATION

As the "western door of Italy," on the French-Italian border, Ventimiglia is an important gateway in and out of the country. Frequent buses link it to the rest of the Riviera dei Fiori and parts of France while trains run to the Italian and French Riviera. From the train station, cross the street and walk down Via della Stazione. The second cross road is **Via Cavour,** and the third is **Via Roma.** Most of what you'll need can be found on these two streets.

Tourist Office: Via Cavour, 61 (tel. 35 11 83). City maps and lots of brochures. Open Mon.-Sat. 9am-1pm and 3-7pm, Sun. 9am-noon and 3-6pm.

Currency Exchange: Via Stazione 3/A (tel. 35 12 15), outside the station. No commission. Open Mon.-Sat. 8am-12:30pm and 2:30-7pm. Also in the train station. Open 24 hrs.

Post Office: Via della Repubblica, 8 (tel. 35 13 12), toward the water. Open Mon.-Fri. 8:10am-5:30pm, Sat. 8:10am-noon. Closes at noon on the last working day of each month. **Postal Code:** 18039.

Telephones: At the restaurant in the train station (tel. 35 19 35). Open 24 hrs. **Telephone Code:** 0184.

Buses: Riviera Trasporti, Via Cavour, 61 (tel. 35 12 51), next to the tourist office. Open Mon.-Sat. 7:30am-noon and 4-7pm, Oct.-March Mon.-Sat. 8:30am-noon and 4-7pm. On Sundays, get tickets at **Pasticceria Viale,** Via Cavour, 626 (open daily 8am-noon and 3-8pm). To: Sanremo (L2200), Bordighera (L1500), Imperia-Porto Maurizio (L5000, change in Sanremo), as well as other local towns.

Trains: Piazzale Stazione (Nice: 10-25 per day, 40min., L6900; Genoa: 15 per day, 2hr. 30min., L12,100; Cannes: 25 per day, L18,800; Marseille: 9 per day, L35,100).

Bike Rental: Eurocicli, Via Cavour, 85/A (tel. 35 18 79). L3000 per hour, L10,000 per day. Open Mon.-Sat. 8:30am-7:30pm, Sun. 9am-7:30pm; mid-Oct.-May Mon.-Sat. 8:30am-7:30pm.

Emergencies: tel. 113.

Police: P. della Libertà, 1 (tel. 35 75 75 or 35 75 76).

Hospital: Ospedale Santo Spirito, on Via Basso (tel. 35 67 35).

ACCOMMODATIONS AND FOOD

Ventimiglia is one of the Riviera's most inexpensive places to stay, but it fills up in July and August, so reserve a room in advance. Consider crossing the border and staying in the **youth hostel** (tel. (033) 93 35 93 14) in the nearby French town of **Menton** (15 min. by train, L1600).

Cavour, Via Cavour, 3 (tel. 35 13 66). Make a right on Via Cavour as you come from the station. Respectable rooms and polite management. Singles L30,000, with bath L40,000. Doubles L40,000; with bath L55,000.

XX Settembre, Via Roma, 16 (tel. 35 12 22). Friendly and clean. Singles L17,000. Doubles L30,000. Full pension L52,0000. Its restaurant serves a well-prepared

L17,000 meal. Restaurant open Fri.-Wed. noon-3pm and 7:30-9:30pm. May be closed for vacation in June—call ahead.

Hotel Vittoria, Via Hanbury, 5 (tel. 35 12 31). Make a left on the 1st cross street after exiting the station. Sparkling rooms and sweet owners. Curfew 12:30am. Singles L35,000, doubles L60,000. Breakfast included. Doubles without breakfast L54,000. AmEx, MC, Visa.

Camping Roma, Via Peglia, 5 (tel. 33 580 or 35 76 13), 400m from the waterfront. Across the river from the station side of town, or at the "right" side of the old town as you approach it. L12,000 per person, L12,000 per tent; Sept.-July L7000 per person, L7000 per tent.

You will pay dearly for quality, sit-down meals. The two restaurants in the *pensioni* above serve good meals. The covered **open-air market,** which sprawls every morning along Via della Repubblica, Via Libertà, Via Sant'Ambrosio, and Via Roma is the best place to grab fresh produce. Many of the *pizzerie* lining the beach prepare personal-size take-out pizzas for about L3000.

Self-Service Hotel Suisse, P. Battisti, 34 (tel. 35 11 28). An excellent option, located outside the train station. Daily pasta specials start at L5000, entrees with side veggies at L7000; cover runs L1000. Open daily noon-2:30pm and 7pm-midnight.

Supermercato STANDA, at the corner of Via Roma and Via Ruffini, is well-stocked with staples. Open Mon.-Sat. 8:30am-7:30pm.

SIGHTS AND ENTERTAINMENT

Most visitors to Ventimiglia never venture beyond the the beach, but for those willing to sacrifice a day of tanning there are a number of worthwhile sights to see. The Gothic **Cathedral** with its intricate portal and adjoining 11th-century baptistry, are easy to find in the old town. Take Via Banchieri after the bridge, and from there take Via Falerina. **San Michele,** a Romanesque church of the same vintage, is on the other side of town. Follow the signs off Via Garibaldi to P. Colleta (open Sun. 10:30am-noon). The well-preserved **Roman theater** anchors the **archeological zone** (tel. 381 31) off Corso Genova to the east of the town. Turn left on Via Cavour, and continue about 1km to find it between gas stations and railroad tracks. (The zone is now "closed," but you can view it perfectly well from Corso Genova.)

A trip to the **Balzi Rossi** (Red Cliffs, tel. 381 13), 9km from Ventimiglia toward France, offers you a glimpse of an even earlier civilization. The blue Riveria Trasporti bus from the corner of Via Cavour and Via Ruffini in Ventimiglia (9-12 per day, 20min., L1500) takes you to a series of caves where you can view the remains of Cro-Magnon troglodytes. The most spectacular artifacts are housed in Balzi Rossi's **Prehistoric Museum** near the seaside. (Open Tues.-Sun. 9am-noon and 2:30-6:30pm. Admission L4000, under 18 free.) The world-famous botanical **Hanbury Gardens** (tel. 229 507) stretch from the summit of Cape Mortola down to the sea and contain some of the world's most exotic flora, taken from three continents. Take the blue Riveria Trasporti bus (L1500) from Via Cavour and Via Martiri della Libertà to La Mortola. (Open daily 9am-6pm; off-season Thurs.-Tues. 10am-4pm. Admission L8500.)

■ Near Ventimiglia

Of the many valleys fanning inland from Ventimiglia, **Val di Nervia** is the most accessible. On foot, continue past the Roman theater to the Val di Nervia road on your left. You can also take the blue Riveria Trasporti bus from the train station in Ventimiglia (Campo Rosso is the nearest; 15min., L1500).

Riviera Trasporti also runs buses to the surrounding castle-topped hills. **Dolceacqua,** 9km from Ventimiglia, is crowned by a medieval castle and an old city whose narrow, twisting stone streets are still bustling with activity (L1800 by bus from the Ventimiglia train station). Turn right at the bottom of the new city and walk across the arched Roman bridge to the orange, pink, and green rococo **cathedral** at the bottom of the old city, then continue up the narrow streets to the wonderful **Castello dei Doria.** (Open Sept.-June daily 9am-noon and 3-7pm, July-Aug. Wed.-Mon. 10am-noon and 3-5:30pm. Admission L2000.) Visitors and locals alike come from miles around for the biggest and tastiest pizza in the region at **Pizzeria La Rampa,** Via Barberis, 11 (tel. 20 61 98), on the left side of the main *piazza* in the new town (overlooking the bridge and old city). (Open daily 7pm-midnight.) On August 15, the village celebrates **Ferragosto** with swirling regional dances, traditional costumes, and mouth-watering local pastries.

▨ Piedmont (Piemonte)

Fertile Piedmont is not only the source of the mighty Po River; it also has long been a source of fine food and wine. From the 11th century this abundance served the French House of Savoy, whose fortunes became increasingly intertwined with those of Italy. In the early 19th century, after Napoleonic occupation, Piedmont became the crucible for the unification movement. It was the Savoy king Vittorio Emanuele II and his minister Camillo Cavour who ushered in the *Risorgimento,* enlisting France's help to drive the Austrians out of Italy in 1859. From 1861-1865 Turin was the capital of the newly formed Kingdom of Italy. But first Florence and then Rome usurped this title. The suddenly idle Piedmontese aristocracy quickly turned its hand to industry; now only Lombardy exceeds the region in wealth and productivity. Piedmont also continues to be an area of occasionally violent political activity: both the Red Brigades and latter-day monarchists have based their operations here.

The area falls into three zones. The **Alpine,** with the two stellar peaks of Monviso and Gran Paradiso, contains a string of ski resorts and a huge national park that spills across the regional border into Valle D'Aosta. The **Pianura,** the beginning of the fecund Po valley, encompasses industrial Turin, the wineries of the Asti region, and Italy's only rice paddies. The **hills** north and south of the Po contain many of the region's isolated castles.

■■■ TURIN (TORINO)

Turin's peaceful, Baroque elegance is the direct result of years of urban planning, as well as the later influence of the giant Fiat auto company, which has become synonymous with the city. Just beyond the train station, cars circle neatly around the putting-green grass of P. Carlo Felice, where only the occasional jogger disturbs well-rooted cosmopolitans perusing their morning *La Stampa.* Piazza Castello, the city center, pulses with university students and Armani-clad businessmen. The Turin you're likely to encounter is cultured and courteous, but it can't be mere coincidence that the train station sends you out facing north. Most Fiat employees live and work in the south end in the giant modern slum of Mirafiori, the birthplace of the Red Brigades. These radical crimson troopers of the 1970s drew on the same legacy of revolutionary ideology that established Turin as the fountainhead of Italian political unification in the 18th and 19th centuries. The fact that Turin is capital of Italian extremism, however, is something you may not suspect, and probably won't experience, as you admire the elegant, arcaded avenues and *piazze* of the city center.

ORIENTATION AND PRACTICAL INFORMATION

Turin lies on a broad plain on the north bank of the Po River, flanked by the Alps on three sides. **Stazione Porta Nuova,** in the heart of the city, is the best place to dis-

Turin

1 Santa Cristina
2 San Carlo
3 Egyptian Museum
4 Palazzo Carignano
5 Palazzo Madama
6 Palazzo Reale
7 Duomo
8 San Giovanni
9 Mole Antonelliana
10 Castello Valentino
11 Galleria d'Arte Moderna
12 Stazione Porta Nuova

embark. The city itself is an Italian rarity in that its streets meet at right angles, making it easy to get around either by bus or on foot. The three main streets are **Corso Vittorio Emanuele II,** running past the station to the river; the elegant **Via Roma,** housing the principal sights and running north through P. San Carlo and P. Castello; and **Via Garibaldi,** stretching from **Piazza Castello** to **Piazza Statuto** and the **Stazione Porta Susa.**

Tourist Office: APT, Via Roma, 226 (tel. 53 59 01; fax 53 00 70), under the left arcade on the small, divided piazza just before P. San Carlo. English spoken. Extensive literature on Turin and its province. Your best bet is the pocket-sized guide called "Torino Giovani: A Young Visitors's Tourist Guide" available free in English or Italian. Open Mon.-Sat. 9am-7:30pm. Smaller office at the **Porta Nuova** train station (tel. 53 13 27; open Mon.-Sat. 9am-7pm). Both offices will help you find a room. **Informa Giovani** ("Youth Information"), Via Assarotti, 2 (tel. 57 65 49 76 or 57 65 49 77), off Via Garibaldi between P. Castello and Porta Susa. From feminist groups to fortune tellers, they'll give you the word. Youth hostel membership (L25,000 plus photo), as well as information on renting bikes, getting a job, or finding an apartment in Turin. Open Mon. and Wed.-Sat. 10:30am-6:30pm.

Budget Travel: Centro Turistico Studentesco, Via Camerana, 3 (tel. 53 43 88), 2 streets over to the left of the station as you exit, and 1 block off Corso Vittorio Emanuele II. Travel information, discount train (BIJ) and air tickets for students under 26. ISIC cards. English spoken. Open 9:30am-12:30pm and 3-6:30pm, Sat. 9:30am-12:30pm.

Currency Exchange: The exchange in the Porta Nuova Station is the easiest and offers a decent rate. The banks along Via Roma and Via Alfieri also offer good rates, as does an automatic exchange machine by the tourist office near P. San Carlo.

Post Office: Via Alfieri, 10 (tel. 53 58 91 or 562 81 00), off P. San Carlo. Telex, fax and telegram service. Open Mon.-Fri. 8:15am-5:20pm, Sat. 8:15am-1pm. **Fermo Posta** open Mon.-Sat. 9am-noon and 3-7pm, Sun. 9am-noon. **Postal code:** 10100.

Telephones: ASST, Via Arsenale, 13, off Via S. Teresa, around the corner from the post office. Open Mon.-Sat. 8am-7:45pm. Coin- and card-operated phones available 24 hrs. at the **SIP,** Via Roma, 18, where you can purchase phone cards from a machine. **ASST** office in Porta Nuova, open daily 8am-7:45pm. **Telephone Code:** 011.

Flights: Caselle Airport, (tel. 577 84 31 or 577 84 32). European destinations. Take a bus from the ATIV agency on Corso Siccardi, 6, at Via Cernaia (every 45min. 5:15am-11:15pm, L5000; ticket office open Mon.-Fri. 9am-1pm and 2-7pm, Sat. 9am-1pm, but you can also purchase tickets on the bus). From Caselle to Turin, buses leave approximately every 30min. 6:30am-11:30pm, 35min., L5000. Stops at P. XVIII Dicembre (near Porta Susa) and the station at Corso Inghilterra, 3. From there, take city bus #9 or #15 (L1000) to Porta Nuova.

Trains: Porta Nuova, (tel. 561 33 33). To: Milan (every 30min., 1hr. 45min., L12,100); Venice (11 per day with change at Milan, 4 per day direct, 4hr. 30min., L30,300); Genoa (every hr., 2hr., L12,100); Rome (9 per day, 9-11hr., L96,800); Paris (3 per day, change at Lyon, 7hr. 30min.-10hr., L97,000). **Luggage Storage:** in Porta Nuova, L1500. Open 24 hrs.

Buses: Autostazione Terminal Bus, Corso Inghilterra, 3 (tel. 44 25 33). Timetable available from tourist office. Take bus #9 or #15 from Porta Nuova to the station. Buses serve ski resorts, the Riviera, and the western valleys of Susa and Pinerolo. To: Courmayeur (21 per day, 3hr., L13,200); Aosta (every hr., 2hr., L10,300); Milan (15 per day, 2hr., L17,500); Chamonix (3 per day, 3hr. 30min., L28,500).

Metropolitan Transit: City buses cost L1200. Tickets must be bought at *tabacchi* before boarding. The system is easy to navigate and a helpful map is available at most terminal offices. Buses run until 12:30am.

Taxis: tel. 57 37/57 30/ 57 44, or 57 48. L4000 plus L1000 per km. L3000 surcharge at night and L1500 Sun. and holidays.

Bike Rental: Parco Valentino on Viale Matteoti in Parco Valentino, a 15-min. walk down Corso Vittorio Emanuele as you exit Porta Nuova to the right. Open Tues.-Sun. 9:30am-12:30pm and 3-7pm. L2000 per hour, L7000 per day. You must leave an ID and a L5000 deposit.

Lost Property: Ufficio Oggetti Smarriti, Via Chatillon, 19 (tel. 85 54 37), open 8:30am-12:30pm. Also at Porta Nuova (tel. 55 69 33 15), open 8am-noon and 3-7pm.

English Bookstore: The British Bookstore, Libreria Internazionale Luxembourg, Via Accademia delle Scienze, 3 (tel. 561 38 96), across from Palazzo Carignano. A wide and worldly selection. Open Tues.-Sat. 9am-12:30pm and 3-7:30pm.

Laundromat: Lavanderia Vizzini, Via S. Secondo, 30 (tel. 54 58 82). Wash and dry: 4 kg, L15,000, 6 kg, L20,000. Open Mon.-Fri. 8am-12:30pm and 3-7:30pm, Sat. 8:30am-12:30pm.

Public Baths: Albergo Diurno (tel. 54 49 72), just outside Porta Nuova, on the left side as you leave the tracks. Clean and elegant. Showers L7500. Towels included. Toilets L1500. Open Mon.-Sat. 7am-7pm, Sun. 7am-noon.

Swimming Pool: Piscina Comunale Stadio Civile, Corso G. Ferraris, 294 (tel. 319 93 09). Take bus #41 from Corso Vittorio Emanuele near the station. Open June-Sept. Tues.-Sun. noon-7pm, L5000, Sun. L7000. Changing room L3000.

Late-Night Pharmacy, Corso Vittorio Emanuele II, 66 (tel. 53 82 71). Open 24 hrs.—well, almost; they're closed for lunch 12:30-3pm. Ring to summon the pharmacist after dark.

Emergencies: Tel. 113. **Police:** Corso Vinzaglia, 110 (tel. 558 81). **Medical Assistance:** Tel. 57 47. **Hospital: Mauriziano Umberto,** Largo Turati, 62 (tel. 50 801). **Red Cross:** tel. 51 77 51.

ACCOMMODATIONS AND CAMPING

Hotels abound but prices can be steep, even for the most bare-bones of rooms. Accommodations are actually easier to find in summer than during the rest of the year, and more easily uncovered on weekends than during the week.

Ostello Torino (HI), Via Alby, 1 (tel. 660 29 39; fax 66 04 45), a small street off Via Gatti. Take bus #52 from Stazione Porta Nuova. Get off at the 3rd stop after crossing the Po River, and follow the road uphill immediately to your right through Piazzale Luserna. Via Alba branches off Viale Thovez at the top of the *piazzale;* the hostel is at the corner of Via Gatti. Located in a hilly residential neighborhood dotted with art nouveau mansions. Contemporary, clean, and comfortable. Desk open 7-9am and 6-11:30pm, Oct.-March 7-9am and 6-10:30pm. Curfew 11:30pm, in winter 10:30pm. L16,000 per person. Breakfast and sheets included. Lockers are available for a L15,000 deposit. Dinner or packed lunch L12,000. Laundry (wash and dry) L7000 a load. Non-members pay an extra L5000 per night. To purchase HI membership stay 6 nights at this price at any hostel or pay the equivalent extra (L30,000) to validate the card immediately.

Pensione San Carlo, P. San Carlo, 197 (tel. 56 27 46), on the 4th floor. In the midst of the action, yet set back from the noisy piazza. Red carpet rolled out for guests in ski-lodge style rooms. Singles L45,000, with bath L55,000. Doubles L55,000, with bath L75,000. Triples L75,000.

Pensione Alfieri, Via Pomba, 7 (tel. 839 59 11), under the right archway where the piazza dead-ends. Caring owners, but a rather somber ambiance, and sometimes a dearth of rooms. Often occupied by long-term residents, many of whom are students. Singles L25,000. Doubles L40,000. Reserve ahead.

Hotel Bellavista, Via Galliari, 15 (tel. 669 81 39; fax 66 87 89), on a street slightly behind and to the right of Porta Nuova as you exit. Large, airy rooms and a sunny hallway. TVs and phones in the rooms. Singles L45,000. Doubles L75,000, with bath L90,000. Triple with bath L130,000.

Hotel Magenta, Corso Emanuele, 67 (tel. 54 26 49), left of the train station. Very chic. If it's not full you can probably talk the manager's price down. All rooms have TV and firm beds. Singles L54,000, with bath L87,000. Doubles L64,000, with bath L104,000.

Camping: Campeggio Villa Rey, Strada Superiore Val S. Martino, 27 (tel. 819 01 17). L4000 per person, L3500 per tent. Open March 1-Oct. 30.

FOOD

Piedmontese cuisine is a sophisticated blend of northern Italian peasant staples and elegant French garnishes. Butter replaces olive oil in cooking; cheese, mushrooms, and white truffles are used instead of tomatoes, peppers, and spices. *Agnolotti* (ravioli stuffed with lamb and cabbage) are the local pasta specialty, but *polenta*, a cornmeal mush often topped with fontina cheese, is the more common starch. Many *secondi* involve flesh or fowl simmered in wine sauces, not surprising in a region where excellent wine is so abundant. Three outstanding red wines (Barolo, Barbaresco, and Barbera) available in Turin's supermarkets or restaurants are worth the extra price. The cheapest sustenance is found on Via Mazzina, where fruit, cheese, and bread shops abound. There's also a supermarket, **Metà,** at #42. (Open Mon.-Sat. 8:30am-12:30pm and 4-7:30pm; closed Wed. afternoon.)

Turin serves delectable local pastries, including the remarkably rich *bocca di leone,* a doughnut filled with whipped cream, fruit, or chocolate (about L2500). You can sample it at **Cossolo il Pasticciere,** Via Gramsci, 1, and Via Garibaldi, 9. Their *sospiri* (chocolate rum pastries, L1100) are as light as air and almost as cheap. (Open Mon.-Sat. 7:30am-8:30pm.)

Several trendy *gelaterie* ice the near side of P. Castello coming from the station. Try the spiffy **Bar Blù** (tel. 53 14 24, open Tues.-Sun. 7am-2am) or **Ra Palino** (tel. 89 82 82, open Tues.-Sun. 11:30am-1am), where you can sample the exotic flower flavors *rosa* and *viola.* The **open-air market** at P. della Repubblica runs Mon.-Fri. 8am-1pm. On Saturday (8am-6pm), an assortment of non-edibles are also sold here— everything from baskets to underwear. There is also the **Market Rossini,** Via Rossini, 1 (tel. 839 77 13), at the corner of Via Lagrange. Open Mon.-Tues. and Thurs.-Sat. 8:30am-1pm and 4-7:30pm, Sun. and Wed. 8:30am-1pm. To mingle with the fashion nobility, try **Caffè Torino,** Via Roma, 204, on P. San Carlo (tel. 54 51 18), a Turin institution. If you're in an extravagant mood, sit down and savor the solicitous service provided by tuxedo-clad waiters. (Cappuccino L5500 if you sit, L1500 if you stand. Open Wed.-Mon. 7:30am-1am.)

Ristorante Taverna Fiorentina, Via Palazzo di Città, 6 (tel. 54 24 12), off P. Castello. A small, family-run restaurant. Try the *capretto Sardo al forno* (baked lamb, Sardinian-style, L7000). Plate of the day L6000-9000. Cover L2500. Open Aug.-June Sun.-Fri. noon-3pm and 7-10pm.

Ristorante da Michele, (tel. 88 88 36) on P. Vittorio Veneto. Old "Coke" posters and mirrors with a homey atmosphere. Popular—get there early. Brick-oven pizza from L6500 and *primi* L8000-18,000. Open Wed.-Mon. noon-2:30pm and 7:30-11:30pm.

Trattoria Amelia, Via dei Mercanti, 6 (tel. 562 84 78), off Via Garibaldi. A homey *trattoria* in the center of town. Family-style cooking. *Primi* L5000. *Secondi* L7000-8000. Tourist menu L15,000. Open Sun.-Fri. noon-2:30pm and 6:30-9:30pm.

Trattoria Messico, Via Bernadino Galliari, 8 (tel. 650 87 98), 2 streets south of Via Vittorio Emanuele, near Porta Nuova. No sombreros here, just tourists afraid to stray too far from the station and a smattering of locals. Terrific pasta and *fettuccini al messico* (L6000). Wine L6000 per liter. Cover L2000. Open Mon.-Sat. noon-2pm and 7-10pm.

Trattoria Toscana, Via Vanchiglia, 2 (tel. 812 29 14), off P. V. Veneto near the university. This hit with locals rewards those who undertake the walk. Don't miss the *bistecca di cinghiale* (boar steak, L6500), which clashes with the rose-covered tables. Open Sept.-July Sun.-Fri. noon-4:30pm and 7-9:30pm.

Café Gran Corso, C. Vittorio Emanuele, 63 (tel. 562 93 49). Less than a 5-minute walk to the left of the Stazione Porto Nouva. The Regoni family is sure to please with fresh *panini* (L3000) made to order, to eat there, or to go. Open 6:30am-8pm. Closed Sundays.

Seven-Up, Via Andrea Doria, 4. Crêpes or silky *risotto* (both L6000) in a crisp-and-clean, no-caffeine atmosphere. Pizza (L4500-8500). Open Tues.-Sun. noon-2:30pm and 6:30-11pm.

Brek, P. Carlo Felice, 22. In the center of the action off Via Roma. Chic and delicious self-serve fare.

Il Punto Verde (Vegetarian), Via Belfiore, 15F (tel. 650 45 14). Good place for lunch. Open Tues.-Fri.

Ex Finestra Sul Cielo (Vegetarian), Via Massena, 1 (tel. 562 22 03). Reserved for members of ARCI, a youth club (membership available at the restaurant). Open Mon.-Sat.

Erewhon (Vegetarian), Via Calandra, 16 (tel. 88 24 50). Macrobiotic and vegetarian. Reserved for members of ENDAS, another youth club (membership available at restaurant). Open Mon.-Sat.

SIGHTS

It's hard to say which the Turinese revere more: their successful auto industry or the (now somewhat tarnished) Holy Shroud. Whatever the preference of locals, the city has wealth to offer those who are neither religious pilgrims nor auto buffs. Turin's museums, architectural sights, and serene gardens are on par with some of the great capitals of Europe, and its managable size and relative safety make it an excellent city to explore for visitors of all interests and budgets.

From Piazza Carlo Felice at the Porta Nuova station, **Via Roma**, flanked by generous arcades and lined with stores, heads straight into the heart of the city. Just ahead, **Piazza San Carlo** displays all the formality and grandeur the 17th-century Baroque was capable of bestowing. In the center of this perfect rectangle, the statue of Duke Filiberto Emanuele stands proudly above the crowds—and cars—on his horse. The piazza is embellished by elegant Baroque buildings and the twin churches of **Santa Cristina** and **San Carlo,** both the work of Filippo Juvarra, architect to King Vittorio Amadeo II.

Beyond P. San Carlo, Via Roma ends in **Piazza Castello,** the historic center of the city, dominated by the imposing **Madama Palace** (tel. 436 14 55), so-called because the widow of Vittorio Amadeo I, "Madama Reale," Marie Christine of France, lived here. (Natives often refer to it as the Palazzo Reale, however, which is a bit confusing as there is another royal palace in Turin.) The colossal two-story pilasters and columns are set against Juvarra's richly decorated façade, which hides a jumble of fragments—including a Roman gate and a 13th-century castle—all incorporated in the building. The **Museo Civico di Arte Antica** (tel. 57 65 39 18) inside contains a fine collection of medieval and Renaissance objects. (Both palace and museum were closed for restoration in 1993.) The **Armeria Reale** (Royal Armory) of the House of Savoy (tel. 54 38 89) is located just across P. Castello at #191, and contains the best collection of medieval and Renaissance tools of war in the world. Upstairs to the library you'll find Leonardo da Vinci's self-portrait (*autoritratto*) in red ink. (Open Tues. and Thurs. 2:30-7:30pm and Wed. and Fri.-Sat. 9am-2pm. Admission L6000.)

Though the city owes its glory to political rather than ecclesiastical leadership, unadulterated splendor blesses the the interior of the **Church of San Lorenzo** in P. Castello. Constructed between 1668 and 1680, it is Guarini's most original creation—follow the moldings as they weave in and out of side chapels, or count the myriad columns of every color, shape, size, and texture imaginable. The dome is the highlight, a multi-layered kaleidoscope of wishbones and starfish with ribs in a dynamic, swirling composition. (Open 7:30am-noon and 4-7:30pm.) Cross the courtyard to see the **Palazzo Reale** (tel. 436 14 55), a plain apricot building that the Princes of Savoy called home from 1645 to 1865. Its red-and-gold interior houses an outstanding collection of Chinese porcelain vases. The small but sumptuous garden was designed by Louis le Nôtre (1697), who is more famous for his work on the *jardins* of Versailles. (Palace open Tues.-Sun. 9am-5pm. Admission L6000. Gardens open daily 9am-6pm. Free.)

The **Cathedral of San Giovanni,** behind the Palazzo Reale where Via XX Settembre crosses P. San Giovanni, is also a must-see, although it houses a has-been. Guarini's remarkable creation, the **Cappella della Santa Sindone** (Chapel of the Holy Shroud, 1668-1694), rests here. His unrestrained, whirling black marble dome (under renovation in 1993, but still open to tourists) caps the somber rotunda that houses a silver vessel containing one of the strangest relics of Christianity, the **Holy Shroud of Turin.** This is the piece of linen in which it was thought that Christ was wrapped for burial after his crucifixion. Although scientists have finally refuted the claim that this was Christ's shroud, they haven't been able to account for it. The piece apparently dates from the 12th century, but no one has been able to explain the unique front and back impressions of a crucified body. Before leaving the cathedral, don't miss Luigi Gagna's oil reproduction of Leonardo's *Last Supper* above the front door, considered the world's best copy of the Renaissance masterpiece. (Tel. 436 61 01. Chapel open Tues.-Sat. 9am-noon and 3-5:30pm. *Duomo* open daily 7am-noon and 3-5:30pm.)

The **Palazzo dell'Accademia delle Scienze,** at #6 of the Via of the same name, houses two of Turin's best museums. Crammed into two floors of this Guarini masterpiece, the **Egyptian Museum** (tel. 561 77 76) houses one of the finest collections of Egyptian artifacts in the world outside Cairo. Here you will find several copies of the Egyptian *Book of the Dead* and an intact sarcophagus of Vizier Ghemenef-Har-Bak, which stands out among the large sculptures and architectural fragments on the ground floor. Upstairs is the fascinating and well-furnished tomb of 14th-century BC architect Kha and his wife, one of the few tombs spared by thieves. (Museum open Tues.-Sun. 9am-2pm. Admission L10,000.) The third and fourth floors house the **Galleria Sabauda** (tel. 54 74 40). This gallery, with masterpieces from the House of Savoy, is renowned for its paintings by Flemish and Dutch artists: van Eyck's *St. Francis Receiving the Stigmata,* Memling's *Passion,* van Dyck's *Children of Charles I of England,* and Rembrandt's *Old Man Sleeping.* The Sabauda is also home to several Mannerist and Baroque paintings, including a noteworthy Poussin, several Strozzis, and Volture's *Decapitation of John the Baptist.* Major works from Palazzo Madama reside here while it undergoes restoration. (Open Tues.-Sun. 9am-2pm. Admission L6000.)

P. San Giovanni at Corso Regina Margherita, 105 (tel. 521 22 51), houses several beautiful Greek and Roman busts, a collection of Greek and Cypriot ceramics, and pieces from the treasury of Marengo. There are also several pre- and proto-historic artifacts from the Piedmont and Valle d'Aosta regions. (Open Tues.-Sat 9am-1pm and 3-7pm, the 1st and 3rd Sundays of the month 9am-1pm. Admission L6000.) The **Galleria d'Arte Moderna,** Via Magenta, 31 (tel. 562 99 11), off Largo Emanuele, contains representative works of late 19th- and 20th-century masters, including Chagall, Picasso, Courbet, and Renoir.

The **National Cinematographic Museum,** P. San Giovanni, 2 (tel. 436 11 48), occupies the Palazzo Chiablese. The museum contains an excellent collection of pre-cinematic and cinema stills, and maintains a library (tel. 521 47 84). Turin was the birthplace of Italian cinema; the seminal silent film *Cabiria* was filmed along the banks of the Po. (Library open Tues.-Sat. 10am-noon and 3-6pm. The museum's exhibits may have moved for restoration—check with the APT for current museum location, hours and admission costs.)

The Palazzo Carignano contains the **Museo Nazionale del Risorgimento Italiano** at Via Accademia delle Scienze, 5 (tel. 562 11 47), but enter from P. Carlo Alberto on the other side. One of the great Baroque palaces of Europe, its façade is a masterpiece of white marble relief and elegant statuary. In the 19th century, this palace housed the first Italian parliament and the cradle of Prince Vittorio Emanuele II. The museum today contains historic documents and other paraphernalia of national interest. On Sundays from 10:30am to noon there is a free guided tour of the exhibits. (Open Tues.-Sat. 9am-6:30pm, Sun. 9am-12:30pm. Admission L5000.)

Also of interest: **The Stupinigi Palace,** (tel. 358 12 20) at Pallazina de Caccia. The residence of former King Vittorio Amadeo II and his court (admission L8,000 includes a guided tour in Italian).

For the culture-weary, a siesta in the shady **park** at P. Cavour is ideal, as is an amble along the banks of the Po through gorgeous gardens to the **Valentino Castle** (tel. 669 93 72). A "medieval" castle built in 1884 for a world exposition, it looks like something from *Alice in Wonderland*. The guide takes you through room after room of objects and oddities—a sink in the shape of a castle, a throne that converts to a potty. Unfortunately, both the dungeons and towers are inaccessible. (Open Tues.-Sat. 9am-6pm, Sun. 10:30am-6pm. Admission L6000, free Fri.)

No Italian city would be complete without its expression of civic virility; in modern Turin, you can skip prowess-testing stairs and take a glass elevator to the top. The **Mole Antonelliana,** Via Montebello, 20 (tel. 839 83 14), a few blocks east of P. Castello, began, in a flurry of political intrigue, as a synagogue, but ended up as a Victorian eccentricity. The view inside the dome as you ascend to the top is dizzying. (Open Tues.-Sun. 9am-7pm. Admission L4000.)

ENTERTAINMENT

The newspaper **La Stampa** publishes an excellent section on current events, all types of music, cinema, and theater, as well as annual festivals. Turin comes alive with the sound of music, theater, and dancing shoes from the beginning of June through July 6 when the city invites international companies to the **Sere d'Estate** festival. For information and programs, contact the **Assessorato per la Cultura,** P. San Carlo, 161. (Tel. 57 65 37 40. Open Mon. 3-7pm, Tues.-Sat. 9am-1pm and 3-7pm; in winter Mon. 2-6:30pm, Tues.-Sat. 9am-6:30pm. Admission to events will run you between L15,000 and L30,000.) **Settembre Musica** is a month-long extravaganza of classical concerts performed all over the city. Contact the Assessorato or the tourist office for a program.

Cinemas are prevalent in Turin, offering the latest in both big-budget blockbusters as well as more obscure art films. During the academic year, a number of foreign films are shown in their original languages. For a list of the titles, times and locations, contact the Informa Giovani. Find a listing of summer films in *Arena Metropolismi.*

During his time as a student in Turin, Erasmus said that magic pervaded the city, and Turin has since extended its reputation as a center of the occult. Get your palm read at the porta Pila, or flirt with the world of black garb and magenta walls at **Inferno,** Via Carlo Alberto, 55 (tel. 83 25 02) and Via Po, 14 (tel. 839 74 42). Local punks come to chat more than to shop. (Both open Mon. 3:30-7:30pm, Tues.-Sat. 9:30am-12:30pm and 3:30-7:30pm.) If you seek more traditional attire, but can't afford the chic shops lining Via Roma, try the **department store** at Via Lagrange and Via Teofilo Rossi.

■ Near Turin

When Turin was besieged by the French on September 6, 1706, King Vittorio Amadeo II made a pact with the Virgin Mary to build a magnificent cathedral in her honor if the city could resist. Turin was unconquered, and the result was the magnificent **Basilica of Superga** (tel. 89 00 83), erected on the summit of a 672m hill. The Basilica's neoclassical deep-porched form and high drum support a magnificent dome. From the spacious terrace, you can survey the city, the Po Valley, and the Alps. Half the fun is getting there. Take tram #15 from Via XX Settembre to Stazione Sassi and then board a small cable railway for a 20-minute ride through fragrant countryside. (Open daily 8am-noon and 2:30-6:30pm. Free.) The funicular departs on the hour (June to Sept., L2000). The tourist office also has information about boat trips on the Po, which normally run mid-June to mid-September (L3000-10,000).

Turin is about two hours from many excellent **hiking areas** and **ski slopes** in the Alps. An hour up the nearest mountain, alpine refuges begin appearing, on the way to **Sestriere** (2035m). Only an hour and a quarter from Turin, it boasts a comprehensive resort with four cableways, 20 ski lifts, excellent runs, and a skating rink. Bus service connects the area with Oulx (on the Turin-Paris train line) and Turin. The **Venini,** a *rifugio alpino* (alpine hut) on the town's outskirts, supplements the town's conventional lodgings. For more information contact Sestriere's **tourist office,** Piazzale Agnelli, 11 (tel. (0122) 75 54 44). **Alagna Valsesia** (1200m), 156km from Turin and 138km from Milan, boasts the second-largest lift in the area. Farther north looms **Macugna** (1327m), 183km from Turin and 141km from Milan, with its own enormous ski lift (1540m). The ski season runs November through May; ask in Turin about snow conditions before boarding a bus. All areas are linked with Turin by bus and train. For more information and a list of accommodations, write to the tourist office in Turin and request a booklet on *settimane bianche* ("white weeks," cheaper weekly skiing deals), as well as an *Annuario Alberghi* and their booklet *Orizzonte Piemonte: Dove la Neve è "Più Neve."*

■ Susa

Though far the capitol, Susa never lets the visitor forget its Roman origins. Surrounded by mountains and divided by a river, this tiny hamlet of 7,000 was once the seat of the Gaul Cottius, a prefect of the Empire. Brimming with Roman artifacts and graced with a beautiful cathedral, Susa is the perfect escape from Turin's occasionally oppressive elegance, and a pleasant stopover on the way to the ski resorts further up the Susa Valley.

Orientation and Practical Information To get to Susa from Turin, take the train to Bussoleno (10 per day) and change there for Susa (Turin-Susa 53 km, 1hr., L4300). From the station, walk up Corso Stati Uniti 50m to your right. The white stand at the corner of the small park is Susa's **Pro Loco,** a friendly tourist office with maps and brochures. (Open daily 9am-5pm, in winter Tues.-Sat. 8:30am-noon.) The **SAPAV bus** line (tel. 62 20 15) serves Susa, with departures to Turin, Oulx (L10,000), and Sestriere, the most fashionable of the Piedmont ski resorts. Buses leave from outside the train station, Corso Stati Uniti, 33. **First aid** (*pronto soccorso,* tel. 316 31) is across the street from the train station, up toward the tourist office. Susa's **postal code** is 10059; its **telephone code** is 0122.

Accommodations and Food If you plan to stay, try **Hotel Stazione,** C. Stati Uniti, 2 (tel. 62 22 26), across from the station. Marco and Loris will fill you in on Susa's history, and will give you spotless rooms as well. (Singles L29,000, with bath L35,000. Doubles with bath L55,000.) Tuesday mornings a **market** offering everything from clothes to fresh cheese winds the length of Via Palazzo di Città and Via Martiri della Libertà. Tasty, fresh *focaccia* (L1200) is available at Via Mazzini, 2 (next to the bridge, open Mon.-Sat. 9am-1pm and 4-7:30pm); (tourist *menu* L18,000).

Sights A typically Italian historical jumble, Susa's cultural wealth centers on its collection of antique Roman remnants and operational medieval constructions. Medieval Susa centers on the **Cathedral of San Giusto,** a 1029 structure that houses the 14th-century *Triptych of Rocciamelone,* a Flemish portrayal of the Virgin and saints in brass, and a fine 10th-century baptismal font, carved in serpentine. Beside the cathedral, the **Porta Romana** (5th century) hints with many-windowed splendor at the Roman remains around the town. From the front of the cathedral, in P. Savoia, follow the yellow signs uphill to the **Arco d'Agosto** the **Castle of Maria Adelaide,** and the Roman **aqueduct.** If the two-minute uphill walk tires you out, quench your thirst with a drink of natural spring water from the "mouth" of the gatekeeper statue. Cottius, then a mere chieftain, built the arch as a tribute to the Emperor Augustus in 9 BC; Augustus returned the favor by elevating Cottius to a prefecture in the Roman Empire. If archeological treasures aren't enough, you can savor the spectacular mountain vistas from the grounds of the castle. Around the own, the complete Roman tour takes in the **Amphitheater** and the **Baths** (follow the ubiquitous yellow signs), while the medievalist can continue on to the Romanesque church of **Santa Maria Maggiore,** with its handsome campanile. The Gothic 13th-century **Convento di San Francesco,** founded by one of the Savoys, includes a lovely little cloister. When the Savoys came to town, they holed up in the collection of 12th- and 13th-century houses along **Borgo dei Nobili,** reached by heading down Via S. Francesco from the convent.

■ Sacra di San Michele

Perched on a bluff 1000m above the town of Avigliana, the massive stone **Sacra di San Michele** (tel. 93 91 30) looms precariously over the approaching traveler. Umberto Eco based the monastery in *The Name of the Rose* this edifice, and even in summer it's not hard to imagine monks falling to snowy deaths from the windows, or turning up in a vat of pig's blood stowed in some dank corner.

Orientation and Practical Information Although it's easier going by car, the 12km hike from nearby Avigliana (easily reached by train—15 per day, L2400—from Turin) will make you feel like a real pilgrim. From P. del Popolo in Avigliana follow the main road, Corso Laghi, around Lago Grande. Every time the road splits, take the right fork until you hit Via Sacra di San Michele on its steep and winding tour up the mountainside (allow two to three hours for the entire walk). Passing motorists are few once you hit Via Sacra di San Michele, but workers on the Sacra's restoration project occasionally pass by on their way to the summit. **Buses** to the top leave only on Sundays in July and August at 8am from P. Carlo Felice in Turin. (Martoglio bus line, tel. 937 60 28, round-trip L10,000.) There are **public toilets** outside the entrance, but bring your own paper. For more information, Avigliana's helpful **Informazione Turistica** (tel. (011) 93 86 50), will supply you with maps. (Open Mon.-Sat. 9am-12:30pm and 3-6pm.)

Sights The **Sacra,** (St. Ambrogio; tel. (011) 93 91 30) a monastery founded in 1000 AD, perches atop Mt. Pirchiriano, making the place notable both for its interior and for the views its location affords. Upon entering the structure, the impressive "Stairway of the Dead," an immense set of steps helping to buttress the building leads outside to the beautifully carved wooden doors depicting the arms of St. Michael with the Serpent of Eden. As you enter the vast Romanesque-Gothic interior, the fresco to your left depicts the *Burial of Jesus, the Death of the Virgin,* and the *Assumption,* by Secondo del Bosco (1505). Down the small steps in the middle of the nave is the shrine of St. Michael. As your eyes get accustomed to the dark, you'll see three tiny chapels. The largest one, to your left, with a back wall of solid rock, was built in 966 AD by St. John Vincent and supposedly consecrated by angels. In the crypt you'll find the tombs of medieval scions of the Savoy family. (Sacra open Mon.-Sat. 9am-12:30pm and 3-5pm, Sun. 9am-noon and 3-5pm, Oct.-March Mon.-Sat. 9am-12:30pm and 3-5pm, Sun. 9am-noon and 2:30-5pm.)

ASTI AND THE MONFERRATO AREAS

Vineyards predominate around Asti, providing it with both an economic base and widespread renown: the sparkling Asti Cinzano and Asti Spumante, among others, begin their effervescing here. Many of these wineries remain under family control, and a warm reception awaits visitors who take time to explore less-trafficked areas. The area is also an important center of paleontology; remains of mastodons, rhinoceri, and other gargantuan fauna have been unearthed at **Cinaglio, Valleadona,** and **Villafranca d'Asti.** So important are these discoveries that a paleological epoch has been named after the area, the Astian period.

ASTI

■ Asti

The modern city of Asti takes its name from the ancient Lugurian village "Ast" ("high hill"). In 89 BC, the settlement became one of the most important Roman outposts in ancient Liguria, "Hasta Pompeia," and by the 13th century, Asti had emerged as one of the richest and most powerful provinces in Italy. For the next 500 years, control of the region bounced between native princes and the House of Savoy. Although the resulting wars destroyed the city several times, 120 13th-century towers survive. Asti has prospered since that time–you'll see a lot of Armani suits here–and is now famous for its poet Vittorio Alfieri and his cousin Count Beneddeto, an architect who designed much of this quiet city.

ORIENTATION AND PRACTICAL INFORMATION

Asti is easily accessible by train from Turin (every 30min., 40min., L4300) and Alessandria (every 30min., 20min., L3200). A direct train leaves daily for Milan (2hr., L10,500). The **train station** in P. Stazione (tel. 503 11) is a few short blocks south of the heart of the town, **Piazza Vittorio Alfieri.**

> **Tourist Office:** P. Alfieri, 34 (tel. 50 357). Assists in finding accommodations (no reservations made) and provides information on daytrips to wineries and castles. Pick up the *Guide to Asti and its Province* and the indispensable map of town. English spoken. Open Mon.-Fri. 9am-12:30pm and 3-6:30pm, Sat. 9am-12:30pm.
> **Currency Exchange: Instituto Bancario di San Paolo di Torino,** Via Battisti, 3 (tel. 39 41) at P. Alfieri and Corso Dante. Change located on the second floor. Open Mon.-Fri. 8:25am-1:25pm and 2:40-4:10pm.
> **Post Office:** Corso Dante, 55 (tel. 59 28 51 or 32 917) off P. Alfieri. Open daily 8:15am-7pm. **Postal Code:** 14100.
> **Telephones: SIP,** P. Alfieri, 10 (tel. 550 11). Open Mon.-Fri. 8:30am-12:30pm and 3-7pm, Sun. 9am-4pm. Automatic phones next door, open daily 7am-10pm. **Telephone Code:** 0141.
> **Buses:** P. Marconi (tel. 536 72), across the piazza from the train station. To: Costigliole (7 per day, 30min., L2500) and Isola d'Asti (every hour, 10min., L1600), as well as Acqui (2 per day, 1hr., L 4400), and Canelli (9 per day, 45min., L3100). Buy tickets on the bus.
> **Emergencies:** tel. 113. **Police:** Corso XXV Aprile, 5 (tel. 41 81 11). **Hospital: Ospedale Civile,** Via Botallo, 4 (tel. 39 21). **Red Cross:** tel. 21 78 83.

ACCOMMODATIONS AND FOOD

Across from the train station, **Hotel Cavour,** P. Marconi, 18 (tel. 53 02 22), offers modern, clean singles for L38,000, with bath L50,000. Doubles are L55,000, with bath L70,000 (open Sept.-July). Though you'll be a good hike from the action, you might want to take bus #2 to the corner of Corso Torino and Corso XXV Aprile (L800) to **Antico Paradiso,** Corso Torino, 329 (tel. 21 43 85). Religious motifs adorn its white-washed walls (singles for L34,000 and doubles for L50,000; closed Mon.). In the center of it all, **Hotel Reale,** P. Alfieri, 6 (tel. 50 240), holds true to its "royal" title, renting singles for L80,000 and doubles for L150,000. You can camp at **Campeggio Umberto Cagni,** Via Valmanera, 152 (tel. 27 12 38). From P. Alfieri, turn onto Via Aro, which becomes Corso Volta, then take a left on Via Valmanera. (L4000 per person, L5000 per tent, electricity L1800. Open April-Sept.)

At the **Campo del Palio,** across the street from the station, vendors hawk every kind of fruit and vegetable imaginable (open Mon. and Wed. 8:30am-1pm). Mornings also rouse a market into action at P. Catera, off Via Carducci in the heart of town. The **Super Gulliver Market,** Via Cavour, 81, could feed an army of Lilliputians. (Open Mon.-Sat. 8:30am-7:30pm.) The **Mercato Coperto Alimentari,** at P. della Libertà (between P. Alfieri and Campo del Palio) is a great place to see where you would probably shop if you had a place to cook. Raw meats, cheeses, vegetables, and pastas abound—each merchant has a separate kiosk. (Open Mon.-Fri. 8am-1pm and 3:30-7:30pm; closed Thurs. afternoons). **Leon d'Oro,** Via Cavour, 98 (tel.

59 20 30) is a great spot for a fresh, filling meal in a relaxed, but elegant atmosphere—pink tablecloths, dark cherry wood and mirrored walls, and pink marble bar. (Pizza L6000-8000, *antipasti* L6000-10,000, *primi* L6000-7000. Some veggie entrees as well as veggie pizza. Open daily 10am-midnight.) **Ristorante Dorta Torino,** Viale Partigiani, 144 (tel. 21 68 83). Take a right at Corso Alfieri where the Torre Rosa lies. Paste just L4500—try the *penne picante* if you like hot stuff; salad just L2000, a large beer a mere L2500. (Open Sat.-Thurs. noon-2:30pm and 7-10pm.) **Trattoria del Mercato,** Corso Einaudi, 50 (tel. 59 21 42) at Campo del Palio, serves a typical risotto and tortellini for about L5000. Groups get a discount. (Open 8am-3pm and 6-8pm. Closed Dec., March, and Sept.) **Gran Caffè Italia,** Via Cavour, 129 (tel. 59 42 22) is on the corner of the rotary opposite the train station. Fresh *panini* (L2500) and a *menú* (L10,000) served. (Open Oct.-Aug. Mon.-Sat. noon-2:30pm; bar open 6:30am-8:30pm.) **Pizzeria da Gianni,** Corso Alfieri, 83, toward the hospital, throws pizza for L4000-7500, *primi* for L3000-4000, and *secondi* for L6000-7000. The house specialty is *lumache alla parigiana* (Parisian snails, L7000). Cover is L2000. (Open Wed.-Mon. 6pm-1am.) For *gelato* try **Cercena's,** Via Cavour, 115. (Open 9am-9pm.)

SIGHTS

From **Piazza Vittorio Alfieri,** the heart of the town, a short walk west on Via Garibaldi to P. San Secondo will take you to the 18th-century **Palazzo di Città** (City Hall), and the medieval **Collegiata di San Secondo**. The Romanesque-Gothic church was built on the very spot where San Secondo, Asti's patron saint, was decapitated. (Open daily 7am-noon and 3:30-7pm.) At the end of Corso Alfieri stands Asti's oldest tower, the **Torre Rossa** (Red Tower), a 16-sided cylinder where the saint was imprisoned prior to his execution. The tower, with foundations dating back to the time of Augustus, adjoins the elliptical 18th-century **Church of Santa Caterina.** If you walk to the left of the piazza as you exit the church, you'll be able to see the dome of the **Santuario della Madonna del Portone** (Sanctuary of the Madonna of the Gate). This splendid Byzantine church can be reached by going south from P. Santa Caterina to Via S. Anna.

North of Corso Alfieri, several medieval streets lead to P. Cattedrale, dominated by the eclectic **Cathedral of Asti,** whose size and grandeur make it one of the most noteworthy Gothic cathedrals in Piedmont. The cathedral was begun in 1309; in the 16th and 17th centuries local artists, including native son Gandolfino d'Asti, covered every inch of the walls with frescoes. Decaying 11th-century mosaics blanket the floor of the altar. If you wander about for a few minutes, the caretaker might come out and give you an exhaustive private tour (open daily 7:30am-noon and 3-7pm). Up Via delle Valle from Corso Alfieri, off P. Medici, is the 13th-century **Torre de Troya**, the highest tower in Piedmont. Asti also has its own wine cellar, near P. Alfieri, which can be visited on Wednesdays (ask at the tourist office). The **Giardini Pubblici,** between P. Alfieri and Campo del Palio, provide refreshing flora for picnicking human fauna. On the far end of the Corso is the 15th-century **Church of S. Pietro** with a 12th-century octagonal baptistry. (Open Tues.-Sat. 9am-noon and 3-6pm, Sun. 10am-noon.) Exhibits of local artists are often shown in the baptistry and the complex stays open later. The church served in WWII as an army hospital; Romans, friars, and war dead all share the space beneath the courtyard.

SEASONAL EVENTS

The series **Asti Teatro,** held during the first three weeks of July, offers theatrical productions from the medieval to the modern. The venue varies, so call for information; reservations are suggested. (Teatro Alfieri, Via Teatro Alfieri, 16; tel. 39 91. Open daily 2:30-7:30pm. Admission around L18,000, discounts for children and students.) The theater takes to the streets with the **Palio di Asti,** held annually on the third Sunday of September. The Palio recalls the town's liberation in 1200 with man and mare alike draped in medieval garb. A procession commences at 2pm from the cathedral, passes through the town, and ends at Piazza Alfieri, where the horses are relieved of their costumes for the festival's finale, the oldest horserace in Italy. Astian vintners have made a tradition of courting prospective buyers with annual Bacchanalias, each dedicated to a different fruit of the vine. In spring you can celebrate the exposition **Vino Nuovo del Lunedì Marzo,** during the last week of March in the Salone delle Manifestazione, P. Alfieri. In June and July the Asti Teatro Festival incorporates jazz, drama, dance, music at the Collegio and Michelerio Palaces. Donkey races and amaretto-throwing are popular, though unusual, festivities which take place a the end of June in Mombaruzzo. In September, agricultural Asti revels in the **Douja d'Or,** a week-long festival celebrating the splendor of the grape.

■ The Monferrato and Le Langhe

Asti is surrounded by numerous vineyards and castles worth visiting. **Costigliole,** a brief bus ride away, is home to a medieval castle complete with drawbridge. Costigliole's **tourist office** can be reached at (0141) 96 60 31. Also a short distance from Asti and accessible by bus are **Isola d'Asti,** with its two medieval churches (the bus passes Isola d'Asti on its way to Costigliole), and **Canelli,** surrounded by the muscat vineyards which produce the fruity *Asti spumante.* (Ask at Asti's tourist office for the *Carta dei Vini a D.O.C. Della Provincia di Asti,* a map of vineyards in the region offering wine tastings). Phone the Distelleria Bocchino, Via G. B. Giulani, 88 (tel. 81 01) to make an appointment at the wine factory. Closed weekends. The same holds true for the **Distelleria Beccaris,** Via Alba, 5 (tel. 96 81 27) in Costigliale. On weekdays, for wine-tasting and a gastronomical tour call the **Cantina Sociale,** Via L. Bosca, 30 (tel. 82 33 47 or 83 18 28) to set up an appointment in Canelli, or while in Costigliole try the **Associazione Produttori Viticoli,** Traz. Bionzo, 54 (tel. 96 83 59 or 96 84 58).

■ Aquitermi

If it were located on the coast Aquitermi could easily be mistaken for Miami. Though surrounded by green countryside dotted with evidence of past greatness, such as the Roman aqueduct, the first thing one notices is the number of people "taking the cure." Every year people arrive in droves to receive natural treatment for their afflictions: with thermal springs heating up to a steamy and sulphuric 75°, *fangi* (mud baths), and treatment centers for everything from rheumatism to poor circulation, it's like the mythical "cocoon" people have been searching for—Ponce de Leon's "fountain of youth." Don't despair, however, if you're healthy and in good shape, for there are still parks, museums, and sights to be seen.

Orientation and Practical Information Aquitermi is located about 34km from Alessandria, in the province of the same name. From Milan, take any train en route to Alessandria, and from Genoa, go by way of Ovada (about 40min., trains run every hour; about L4,000) to the station at P. V. Veneto in Aquitermi (tel. 20 45). To reach the **tourist office (APT),** Corso Bagni, 8, tel. (0144) 32 21 42) from the station, take a left on Via Alessandria, another onto Via Monteverde, which leads to Corso Bagni. Very helpful English-speaking staff gives out a free map and great info about where to rent bikes, ride horses, eat, or stay. Open Mon.-Fri. 8am-12:30pm and 3:30pm-6:30pm, Sat. 8am-12:30pm. **Currency exchange** is at **Cassa di Risparmio di Torino,** Corso Dante, 26 (tel. 570 01). Via Trucco holds the **post office** (tel. 29 84 or 29 86; **postal code:** 15011), while **telephones** are found at **S.I.P.,** P. Matteotti, 31 (tel. 187). **Emergencies:** Via Sorprano, 122 (tel. 28 00).

Accommodations and Food The best places to stay are located across the Bormida river. From the information office, take Corso Bagni across the river to Viale Einaudi, the first left (notice the huge pool on the right). **Albergo Piemonte,** Via Einaudi, 19, is run by a talkative young proprietor and her husband who wish to bring more youth to the town. (Singles L30,000, with bath L35,000; doubles L60,000, with bath L70,000). **Hotel Belvedere,** Via Einaudi (tel. 32 27 48), a former private villa with back and front patios and is now enclosed by white picket fence and geraniums. (Singles L32,000; doubles L48,000, with bath L59,000). **Albergo Giaccobe,** Via Einaudi, 15 (tel. 32 25 37), has gloriously furnished rooms—flower print bedspreads abound—some with balconies. Singles L35,000, with bath L50,000. Doubles L50,000, with bath L70,000.

When you get hungry, head to **Vecchio Borgo,** P. della Bollente, 3 (tel. 32 26 15). Pizzas from L5000, primi and antipasti from L8000-10,000. Cover L2000. **Bue Rosso,** Via Cavour, 62 (tel. 32 27 29), will serve up a home-cooked meal at a reasonable price.

Sights If you like archeology, head to the **Museo Civico Archaeologico Castello dei Paleogi** (tel. 575 55; open Wed.-Sat. 4-7pm, Sun. 3-6pm). Constructed in the 11th century, it focuses on the Roman history of the region. The Paleontological Castle was partially destroyed in 1646, but was restored in 1815 and again more recently, where tombs, sarcophagi, and mosaics abound. The Romanesque **Duomo of San Guido** is adorned with multiple ceiling frescoes and painted purple columns. It houses the famous *Trittico* of Ruebens (Madonna and Child) in the sacristy—ask to see it. As you cross the river, the Acquedotto Romano is a beautiful backdrop to the sunset. Don't miss actually feeling the steamy, bubbling sulphuric water from P. Bollente. At 75°, it's about the only thing here that's hot besides the scenery.

VALLE D'AOSTA

The gorgeous Valdostan expanse inspires torrents of superlatives. With the collapse of mining and agriculture, Valle d'Aosta's economy looks now to Tourism (with a capital T). Skiers and hikers visiting the area often swear they've found paradise—that is, until they inspect Aosta's sky-high price-tags.

Train service in the region runs only as far as Pre-St-Didier, but fearless bus drivers bank 180-degree turns with gut-wrenching efficiency, making most of the valley accessible. The most spectacular entrance to the area is indisputably the international cable car connection from Chamonix (about L65,000). Be aware that Courmayeur, the connection on the Italian end, has combined forces with Cervinia to try to bring the Olympic games to Valle d'Aosta, and if unchecked inflation were the criterion, the ambitious twosome would stand a good chance. Unless you've got lots of money to burn, head to the lesser-known valleys and enjoy the high peaks at lower prices.

Hiking

The Valle d'Aosta is a paradise for hikers. Each valley's tourist office provides information on routes (usually very well-marked) and the comprehensive network of huts and refuges, which allows the intrepid to stay high for days at a time. Trails often bring you above 10,000 feet, so dress and pack carefully. You'll need a sweater, a windbreaker, a pair of gloves, heavy wool socks with polypropylene liners, a compass, and a first-aid kit. Because even the easiest trails have tricky stretches, you'll need a pair of good hiking boots. Don't forget that the strength of the sun intensifies with altitude—wear plenty of sunscreen even on cloudy or chilly days.

The best time of the year to hike is in July, August, and the first week of September, when all the snow has melted. In April and May, thawing snow often causes avalanches. Obtain a reliable map—*Kompass* maps (available at kiosks and hiking stores in the area) are the most accurate. Also beware of poisonous snakes, which have flourished as the birds that normally gobble them fall victim to illegal hunting. These most often hang out on the rocky tracts at low altitudes.

The tourist offices in Aosta and in each smaller valley give out a list of camp-grounds, bag-lunch (al sacco) vendors, and mountain huts and bivouacs (ask for the elenco rifugi bivacchi). Most regional offices also carry the booklet Alte Vie (High Roads) with maps, photographs, and helpful advice pertaining to the two serpentine mountain trails that link many of the region's most dramatic peaks. Long stretches require virtually no expertise and offer panoramic views and a taste of Alpine adventure. Both trails are subdivided into shorter hikes and assessed with regard to difficulty and availability of food and accommodations.

Similarly, **rifugi alpini** (mountain huts) are not the exclusive abodes of veteran mountaineers. Some are only a cable car ride or a half-hour walk from main roads, and many offer half-pension (L28,000-33,000). Public refuges, or bivacchi, though generally empty shells, are free, while those run by caretakers cost L13,000-18,000 per night. For more detailed information on all things mountainous, contact **Inter-guide,** at Via Monte Emilius, 13 (tel. 44 448; fax 44 448), in Aosta, or the **Club Alpino Italiano,** P. Chanour, 8 (tel. 40 194; fax 36 32 44) open Mon., Wed.-Thurs. 5-7pm, Tues. and Fri. 8-10pm, above Aosta's tourist office. They offer insurance and membership deals with discounts on refuges.

Skiing

Skiing in Valle D'Aosta is sublime, but it's not the bargain it used to be. **Settimane bianche,** "white-week" packages for skiers, are one source of discount rates and may keep you from devoting the bulk of your après-ski hours to the contemplation of financial woes. In the off-season, one-star full pension runs about L340,000, half-pension L300,000, and bed and breakfast L225,000, while weekly lift passes average L170,000. In high season, prices jump by as much as 20%. Winter reservations should be made in writing directly through the hotels. For more specific information, write to the **Ufficio Informazioni Turistiche,** P. Chamonix, 8, 11100 Aosta, and request their pamphlet **White Weeks: Winter Season, Aosta Valley.**

Courmayeur and **Cervinia** are the best known ski resorts in the 11 otherwise tranquil valleys, basking in the glory of Mont Blanc and the Matterhorn. **Val d'Ayas** and **Val di Gressoney** offer equally challenging terrain for lower rates. If cross-country is more to your taste, head to **Cogne,** or to **Brusson** half-way down Val d'Ayas.

In Cervinia and Courmayeur, tank tops sometimes replace parkas for **summer skiing** (play it safe and bring both), and in June and late September it's possible to find a room without reservations. Arrange summer package deals, similar to those available in winter, through the tourist office in either Cervinia or Courmayeur (they're still quite expensive).

Other Sports

Kayaking, rafting, and swimming in the rivers of Valle d'Aosta provide cheaper adrenaline fixes than skiing. The most navigable rivers are: the **Dora Baltea,** which runs through the valley; the **Dora di Veny,** which branches south from Courmay-eur; the **Dora di Ferre,** which wanders north from Courmayeur; the **Dora di Rhêmes,** which flows through the Val di Rhêmes; and the **Grand Eyvia,** which courses through the Val di Cogne. Seven kayaking lessons and a week of camping on the Dora Baltea cost about L260,000 through the **Scuola di Canoa di Courmay-eur,** c/o Emanuele Pernasconi, Casella Postale, 11013 Courmayeur. A day-long raft-ing expedition costs L75,000. (Courses offered June 29-Sept. 6.) **Rafting Adventure,** in Villeneuve, also offers group trips (tel. (0165) 950 44). The Aosta tourist office distributes a list of **mountain bike** rentals throughout the valleys.

■ Aosta

Aosta is the hub of a region whose economy is increasingly dependent upon tourism. And while Aosta itself sits in the flatlands, its prices have more in common with the nearby peaks of Monte Emilius (3559m) and Becca di Nona (3142m). On the plus side, Aosta has benefitted aesthetically from its 2000-year history as a substantial city in a region of diminutive hamlets. Remains of bridges, triumphal arches, and theaters recall Aosta's importance as a Roman center and a medley of towers and churches provide architectural diversity from the Middle Ages. Day trips to the *real* alpine valleys from Aosta are tricky to schedule if you want to return before night falls, so plan ahead.

ORIENTATION AND PRACTICAL INFORMATION

Aosta sits roughly in the center of the region bearing its name, and is most easily reached by train from Turin (11 per day, *diretto* 2 hr., *locale* 4 hr., L10,500). Alp-bound visitors arriving from the east should change trains at Chirasso. Trains stop at Piazza Manzetti, which lies at the opposite end of the Avenue du Conseil des Commis from Piazza Chanoux, Aosta's central piazza. Buses stop just around the corner from Piazza Chanoux in Piazza Narbonne.

Tourist Office: P. Chanoux, 8 (tel. 23 66 27; fax 34 657), straight ahead and down Avenue du Conseil des Commis from the train station. Ask for the booklets *Aosta: Architecture, Art, Archeology* and *Aosta Valley* and pick up copies of the regional listings of hotels, campgrounds, and *rifugi.* The compact yearly *Orari* contains comprehensive schedules of Val d'Aosta's transportation services, including cable cars. Open daily 9am-1pm and 3-8pm, Sun. 9am-1pm.

Currency Exchange: Banco Valdostano A. Berard and C., P. Chanoux, 51 (tel. 31 845). Efficient and friendly. Visa for cash advances accepted. Open Mon.-Fri. 8:20am-1:20pm and 2:40-4pm.

Post Office: P. Narbonne (tel. 44 138). Open Mon.-Fri. 8:15am-7:30pm, Sat. 8:15am-1pm. **Postal Code:** 11100.

Telephones: SIP, Viale Pace, 9 (tel. 43 997), off Via Chanoux. Open Mon.-Fri. 8:15am-12:15pm and 2:30-6:30pm, Sat. 8:45am-12:15pm and 3-6:30pm, Sun. 8am-3pm. **Telephone Code:** 0165.

Trains: P. Manzetti (tel. 20 36 57). Frequent service to Chivasso and the intermediate stations at Chatillon, Verrès, and Pont-St-Martin which offer access, respectively, to the valleys of Valtournenche, Ayas, and Gressoney. To: Chivasso (15 per day, 1hr. 30min., L7200) with stops at Chatillon (L2400), Verrès (L3200); Pont-St-Martin (L4300). Also to Turin (11 per day, 2-4hr., L10,500) and to Milan (9 per day with a transfer at Chivasso, 3-4hr. 30min., L15,400). **Luggage Storage:** L1500. Open 9am-12:30pm and 2:30-6:30pm. **Photocopy machine:** L200 per copy.

Buses: P. Narbonne (tel. 26 20 27), off P. Chanoux on Via Ribitel Arcidiacono. To: Cogne (9 per day, 50min., L3200); Courmayeur (12 per day, 1hr., L3600); Great St. Bernard Pass (2 per day, 45min., L7400); Fenis (5 per day, 30min., L1600); Valtournenche (7 per day, 2 hr. 15min., L5800).

Alpine Information: Club Alpino Italiano, P. Chanoux, 8 (tel. 40 194), upstairs from the tourist office. Open Mon., Wed., and Thurs. 5-7pm, Tues. and Fri. 8-10pm. During the rest of the week, try contacting the **Società Guide,** Via Monte Emilius, 13 (tel. 44 448).

Snow Conditions: tel. 32 444.

Emergencies: tel. 113. **Police:** Corso Battaglione Aosta (tel. 36 15 45). **Hospital: Ospedale Regionale,** Viale Ginevra, 3 (tel. 30 41). **Ambulance:** tel. 30 42 11. **Alpine Emergency: Società Guide,** tel. 44 448 or 23 82 22.

ACCOMMODATIONS

"High season" in Aosta Valley is generally considered to be from late December to mid-January, all of February and March, and the second and third weeks of April. In high season, most hotels will not accept reservations for fewer than three nights. Tradition decrees that all advance reservations be done by mail with a 30% deposit.

La Belle Epoque, Via d'Avise, 18 (tel. 26 22 76), centrally located off Via Aubert. Good-sized clean rooms, balconies, and palatial hall bathroom. Restaurant downstairs crowded with locals (*menù* L16,000). Singles L28,000. Doubles L50,000. The best deal in the Aosta Valley.

Mancuso, Via Voison, 32 (tel. and fax 34 526). From the station, hang a left on Via Carducci as you exit, and another left under the tracks. Peaceful, family atmosphere, with a restaurant downstairs (*menù* about L15,000). All rooms with bath, some with terraces. Singles L35,000-40,000, doubles L55,000-58,000. Off-season L30,000-34,000 and L45,000-50,000 respectively.

Monte Emilius, Via Carrel, 9 (tel. 35 692), a skip and a jump to the right from the train station. Friendly management, and dulcet serenading nightly by passing traffic. Singles L22,000. Doubles L40,000.

Camping: Camping Ville d'Aoste (tel. 32 878 or 25 07 79), in Les Fourches, 1km from Aosta. The cheapest. L4500 per person, L4700 per tent. Open June-Sept. **Camping Milleluci** (tel. 442 74 or 423 74; fax 23 52 84), in Roppoz, also 1km from Aosta. L6400 per person, L6800 per tent. Open year-round.

FOOD

The strategy of any frugal gourmet in Aosta should be to supplement a hearty one-dish meal with a sampling of local cheeses. Prospective picnickers feast their eyes and imaginations on the food shops lining Via de Tillier and Via Pretoriane. Here, the siren song of pastries might entice you to hurl yourself upon the local bakeries. The most divine divas are *tegole,* wafer-thin cookies containing an assortment of ground nuts, though the generous *krapfen* at **La Corbeille à Pain,** Via P. Pretoriane, 22, are worth a try (L1000), as are the L900 *brioches d'Aosta* at the *panettoria* at Via de Tillier, 24. The **STANDA supermarket** on Via Torino sells more generic merchandise. (Open Mon.-Sat. 8:30am-12:30pm and 3:30-7:30pm.) (Open 8:30am-noon and 2:30-6pm. Closed Sat. afternoon and Mon. morning.) The chic **Cafe Roma,** Via E. Aubert, 28 (tel. 26 24 22) serves cappucino to those who want to see and be seen while **Gelateria Linus,** to the left of Cafe Roma, spoons out the best *gelato* around (about L2000).

Trattoria Praetoria, Via S. Anselmo, 9 (tel. 44 356), just past the Port Pretoriane. An intimate dining room where Valdostan chatter flows as freely as the wine. *Primi* L6000-8000, *secondi* L9000-12,000. Cover L3000. Open Fri.-Wed. 12:15-2:30pm and 7-9:30pm.

Grotta Azzurra, Via Croce di Città, 97 (tel. 26 24 74), uphill from where Via de Tillier becomes Via Aubery. Fake wood paneling and delicious fare. Locals come for the fish specialties. Try the *gnocchi alla gorgonzola* (L8000). Pizza L6000-12,000; *primi* L4000-10,000. Cover L2000. Service 15%. Open Aug.-June Thurs.-Tues. noon-2:30pm and 6-11pm.

SIGHTS

Ruins dating from the time of Augustus (the town's original name was "Augusta Praetoria") have given Aosta its nickname the "Rome of the Alps." The virtually intact **Arco d'Augusta** marks the entrance to the ancient town. The **Porte Pretoriane,** toward P. Chanoux down Via Sant'Anselmo, stands at the eastern limits of the old city walls. Within the Roman bounds, active excavation continues to unearth a growing number of historical monuments. The sprawling remains of the **Roman Theater** are the most spectacular. (Open daily 9:30am-noon and 2:30-6:30pm. Off-season 9:30am-noon and 2-4:30pm.) The forum's present incarnation is a tiny, sub-ground-level park, the **Criptoportico Forense.** (Open daily 10am-noon and 2:30-6pm. Off-season 10am-noon and 2:30-4:30pm.) Jump ahead 400 years to the 5th century AD and round off the archaeological tour with a visit to the digging sites at the **Church of San Lorenzo.**

Begin your medieval itinerary at the **Church of St. Ursus,** better known as **Sant'Orso,** whose Romanesque campanile dwarfs Aosta's horizon at a height of 46m. The Sant'Orso complex combines an 11th-century structure with a Gothic façade. St. Ursus, who pioneered the orthodox community after fleeing the heretical practices of delinquent Bishop Placcano, lies interred in the barren crypt, the story of his life narrated in the 40 sculpted columns that gird the adjacent cloister.

ENTERTAINMENT

Those with a penchant for royalty should come to Aosta to witness an annual coronation ritual with a decidedly Valdaostan twist. Every October brings the **Bataille de Reines** (Battle of the Queens), a bovine head-butting bash in which approximately 200 well-trained Bessies engage in elimination rounds of brain-battering. On a more sedate note, the **Foire de St-Ours,** the region's most prestigious crafts fair, is held during the last days of January.

■ Near Aosta

Turreted fortresses adorn the valley. You can get a preview by flipping through the photo-strewn pages of *Castelli della Valle d'Aosta* at a local bookstore or the free booklets at the tourist office. **Fénis** (tel. (0165) 76 42 63) comes with turrets of all shapes and sizes. The interior of the castle is equally noteworthy for its 14th-century Gothic paintings (easily reached by bus from Aosta—5 per day, ½-hr., round-trip L2900). Farther down the valley, 1km from Verrès (15 trains per day, 35min., L3200), rests the artistic treasure trove of the **Issogne** fortress (tel. 92 93 73). (Both open Wed.-Mon. 9am-7pm, Dec.-Feb. 9am-12:30pm and 2-5:30pm.)

Valle del Gran San Bernardo

This sparsely populated valley links Aosta to Switzerland via the Great St. Bernard Pass. Napoleon trekked through here with 40,000 soldiers in 1800, but the pass is better known for the **Hospice of St. Bernard,** founded in 1505, home base for the patron saint of dogs' best friends. The legendary life-saver, Barry, was stuffed for posterity and may still be seen if you drive through the pass—a bit worse for the wear. The hospice (just across the Swiss border—bring a passport) offers amazing views of international peaks just a brisk walk uphill past the dog museum to the summit of a crag. **Mont Velan** (tel. 78 207) in Saint-Oyen charges L18,000 per person, and **Des Alpes** (tel. 78 09 16) in Saint-Rhêmy, steps up a notch in price and altitude with singles for L20,000 and doubles for L39,500. **Camping Pineta** (tel. 78 113) in Saint-Oyen offers riverside plots for L6000 per person and per tent (open year-round). The smaller branch of the valley leading to Ollomont and Oyace is even more serene and offers longer hikes. **Mont Gelé** (tel. 73 220) in Ollomont charges L24,000 per single, L40,000 per double (L2000 less for each in off-season). For more information, contact the tourist office in Aosta or call the **ski-lift office** at St. Remy (tel. 78 09 13 or 78 00 46) or St. Oyen (tel. 78 218 or 78 258). The valley is in the Aosta telephone area and uses the **telephone code** 0165.

The first of the spectacular bus rides departs from Aosta at 8am, the last return bus at 4:15pm (4 per day, 1 hr. 15min., L6000, round-trip L9200). L14,100 will take you from Aosta to Martigny in Switzerland (4 per day, 3-4hr.).

Valtournenche

The **Matterhorn** ("Cervino" in Italian) is a wonder to behold. **Cervinia-Breuil** is not. The nondescript buildings differ only in purpose: some serve expensive food, others offer expensive accommodations, and those remaining rent expensive sports equipment. Many fresh air fiends, however, consider these man-made deterrents a small price to pay for the opportunity to climb up or glide down one of the world's most famous glaciers. A cable car provides year-round service to **Plateau Rosa** (round-trip L30,000) where summer skiers frequently tackle the slopes in swimming gear. Don't forget your passport since a number of the trails spill over into Switzerland. Hikers can forgo the lift tickets and attempt the three-hour ascent to **Colle Superiore delle Cime Bianche** (2982m), with tremendous views of Val d'Ayas to the east. Ninety minutes on the same trail leads to the emerald waters of **Lake Goillet.**

The **tourist office** (tel. 94 91 36 or 94 90 86) on the main street inundates visitors with information on "white weeks packages" as well as *settimane estive,* their summer equivalent. (Open 8:45am-noon and 2:45-6:30pm). **Du Soleil** (tel. 94 95 20), across from the tourist office, lacks many of the luxuries of its glitzier, ritzier competitors, but has the best rates going (half-pension L230,000). Six-day lift passes are L205,000 for the unrestricted, international variety. If you plan to stick it out for a week during the summer months, look into the *Carta Estate,* a guest pass providing discounts on multitudes of post-ski activities.

Hotel Lac Bleu (tel. (0166) 94 91 03; fax 94 93 07), 2km downhill from Cervinia, offers singles at L35,000 and doubles at L70,000 (off-season L28,000 and L60,000). Also quite reasonable is **Leonardo Carrel** (tel. 94 90 77) in the locality of Avouil. (Singles L31,000, doubles L51,000 year-round.) Camp year-round at **Glair Lago di Maen** (tel. (0166) 92 077), 39km from Aosta (L5300-6300 per person). **Guide del Cervino** (tel. 94 83 69) can be reached by 3½ hours of hiking or by the cable car to Plateau Rosà. **Theodule** (tel. 94 94 00), a half-hour walk or 10 minute schüss from Plateau Rosà, has the odd distinction of tendering summer yoga classes. Both *rifugi* cost in the ballpark of L12,000 nightly, half-pension available at L38,000. For outdoor escapades complete with a fearless leader, contact the **Società Guide** (tel. 94 81 69), which organizes group outings.

Restaurant prices are as steep as the Matterhorn itself, so consider stocking up at the **Despar supermarket** by the bus stop. You can also save some dough by buying bread across the street and then heading for the nearest *Fontina* sign to purchase fillings. Try **Pizzeria Copa Pan** (tel. 94 91 40), a few doors past the tourist office, which is one of the only restaurants to serve dishes in the four-digit price range (open Fri.-Wed.). Downhill in Valtournenche, an **outdoor market** is held on Friday mornings in summer.

Six buses per day run to Cervinia-Breuil from Châtillon on the Aosta-Turin train line. Two direct buses also arrive daily from P. Castello in Milan. The **telephone code** is 0166.

Val d'Ayas

Sports enthusiasts who value economy over name-dropping should consider stopping here and bypassing the more ostentatious pleasure grounds to the west.

In Brusson, **Beau Site** (tel. 30 01 44) has the best deal on "white weeks": L250,000 for full board except at Easter and Christmas when prices leap up to L280,000. **Cai Casale** (tel. 30 76 68), a refuge in St. Jacques, 3km north of Champoluc, charges L15,000 per person, L38,000 with full pension. **Aquila** (tel. 30 01 26), in Brusson, is a stone's throw from 45km of cross-country trails, and asks L20,000 per person. In Crest, 4km from from Champoluc and accessible by cable car, **Cre Fornè** (tel. 30 71 97) lets singles for L22,000 (high season L24,000) and doubles for an unbeatable L30,000 (high season L32,000). **Camping Deans** (tel. 30 02 97), also operates in Brusson (L5000 per person, L4000 per tent. Open year-round).

Mountain bikes and skis can be rented at **Sport 4** (tel. 30 65 30) on the way into Champoluc, or at myriad other spots as well. Contact the **Società Guide** (tel. 30 71 94) for hiking advice, or read through the list of itineraries on the map in Champoluc's central piazza. The *telecabina* will take you up to the mountain community of Crest, a convenient base for further excursions (lift operates daily 8am-12:50pm and 2-5:50pm, round-trip L8000). Before setting off, you might want to fuel up with a *crostata salata Valdostana* (L2000 per *etto*) or one of the meatier pastries at the *gastronomia/salumeria* between the Champoluc bus stop and the cable car.

Eight **buses** run daily to Champoluc from the train station at Verrès (1hr., L3200, round-trip L5500). Thirteen **trains** run to Verrès from Aosta (40min., L3200, round-trip L5400), while a comparable number cover the 90min. of track from Turin. If you can spare some time from outdoor pursuits, visit the **parish church** in Antagnod which the most ornate Baroque high altar in all of Val d'Aosta.

The central **tourist office** in Brusson (tel. 30 02 40; fax 30 06 91) and smaller branches in Champoluc (tel. 30 71 13) and Antagnod (tel. 30 63 35) provide trail maps and hotel information. The **telephone code** for the Ayas Valley is 0125.

Val di Cogne

When Cogne's mines ran dry in the 1970s, the townspeople resorted to more genteel pursuits—delicately prying cross-country skiers apart from their money. The quiet village has consequently become a harmonious blend of authentic and self-conscious rusticity for the entertainment of visitors, women in traditional garb make lace and craftsmen sculpt wood in the open air. In winter, Cogne functions as the head of a 50km entanglement of cross-country trails, although a cable car also transports Alpine addicts to the top of the modest downhill facilities (round-trip L10,000, L140,000 for a 7-day pass). In summer, however, the pastoral community is better known as the gateway to the **Gran Paradiso National Park** (tel. 74 812).

Given the resemblance of the whole of Val d'Aosta to a mammoth nature reserve, one might wonder what sets this park apart from its surrounding areas. The answer: ice and fauna. In addition to offering a seemingly endless network of hiking trails and a population of 5000 ibex, the park hosts the highest glacier (4061m) to exist entirely within Italian borders.

For accommodations in Cogne, try the **Hotel Stambecco** (tel. 74 068; L34,000 per person. All rooms with bath). **Du Soleil** (tel. 740 33), on the main strip into town, has singles for L28,000 and doubles for L43,000, as well as the most economical *settimana bianca*—L240,000 for a week of bed and breakfast. Campers can choose between **Camping Gran Paradiso** (tel. 74 105, open June-Sept.), which charges L4800 per person and L4700 per tent, or the more popular **Lo Stambecco** (tel. 741 52, open June-Sept. 20) in the *località* of Valnontey (L5300 per person, L5000 per tent). For pizza (under L10,000), try **Pizzeria Edelweiss,** Viale Cavagnet (tel. 74 92 44).

Valnontey is a wee hamlet in the midst of the national park, notable for its convenient *alimentari,* its cluster of two-star hotels, and the **Giardino Alpino Paradisia.** The inspiration for constructing a botanical garden amidst a barren scrubland at an altitude of 1700m struck during the Cogne Mountain Festival in 1955, no doubt aided by several bottles of wine. Practical complications notwithstanding, the thriving gardens boast a wide array of rare alpine vegetation, including a comprehensive display of lichen. (Open June 13-Sept. 13, 9am-12:30pm and 2:30-6pm. Admission L3000.) The **Mining Museum** in Cogne (tel. 74 92 64) is open daily 10am-8pm. (Off-season Tues.-Sun. 10am-12:30pm and 2:30-6pm. Admission L4000.) For those who find cross-country a little too staid, there's always the bungee option through two companies: **Jumping Club** (58m; tel. (022) 36 72 23, fax 67 18 68, info line (040) 67 18 68), P.O. Box CH 1211, Geneve, 2 Depot or **Rafting Adventure** in Aosta (tel. (0165) 95 082).

Cogne's **tourist office,** P. Chanoux, 34 (tel. 74 040, fax 74 91 25), distributes maps of the park and hiking and transport info. The **post office** (tel. 74 061) is on P. Chanoux. There's a **bank** (tel. 74 020) on Via Dr. Grappein and a **pharmacy** (tel. 74 001) on Via Gran Paradis. Also on Via Dr. Grappein are the **police** (tel. 74 026). For other **emergencies** call the following: **ambulance** (tel. 74 024), **first aid** (tel. 74 907), **alpine aid** (tel. 74 244, 74 92 86, 74 204,or 74 026). For information on services call: **hotel info** (tel. 74 835; fax 74 050), **ski school** (tel. 74 200), **taxi** (tel. 74 000/062/ 065). Cogne is an easy **bus** ride from Aosta (8 per day, 50min., L2100). The **telephone code** is 0165.

Courmayeur

Italy's oldest Alpine resort has become the jet set's newest playground. **Monte Bianco** (Mont Blanc) is the main attraction: its jagged ridges and unmelting snowfields lure tourists with unsurpassed opportunities for hiking and skiing. Prices are astronomical and rooms are booked solid summer and winter (reserve 6 months ahead), but in June the city shuts down while the shopkeepers take their own vacations.

The **AGIP** station at Strada Regionale, 76 (tel. 84 24 27), 1km north on Via Roma, charges the lowest rates in the city, singles going for L27,000, and doubles for L45,000 (L5000 more for each during high season). **Venezia** (tel. 84 24 61), up the hill to the left from P. Monte Bianco, has spiffy, elegant singles for L32,000 and doubles for L48,000. Pitch tent at **Cai-Uget,** Mt. Bianco (tel. (0165) 89 215). (Open Aug.-Sept. L5,000 per person.)

Picnicking is the best option in this town of Michelin-starred eateries. At **Pastificio Gabriella,** Passaggio del Angelo, 94, toward the *strada regionale* end of Via Roma, you'll find excellent cold cuts and pâté garnished with Alpine violets. (Closed for 2 weeks in July.) **Il Fornaio,** at Via Monte Bianco, 17, serves up scrumptious breads and pastries. Try the *Veneziane* (L1000). Wednesday is **market day** (8:30am-2pm) at nearby Dolonne (1km from Courmayeur).

Even "white-week specials" are exorbitant—bed-and-breakfast deals under L230,000 are a dream. Ski passes average L190,000, falling to L160,000 during the summer months. Pick up the seasonal brochure *Courmayeur: Mont Blanc* for a complete list of athletics facilities and rental shops. For even pricier thrills, take the *Funivia del Monte Bianco* to the border summit (L23,000, round-trip L32,000); from here, a descent into French Chamonix costs 153F (about L39,000).

For hiking excursions in Italy, catch the bus that departs hourly from Viale M. Bianco to **Combal Lake.** A beautiful six-hour hike awaits you on the road up the valley past *Rifugio Elisabetta* to where the path (marked by a "2" in a triangle) branches off to the left and clambers up to the Chavannes Pass (2603m). The trail then runs along Mont Perce, beneath the crest, until it reaches Mont Fortin (2758m), where it descends once again to Lake Combal. The view from Mont Fortin is breathtaking. The bus finally deposits you back at Courmayeur. A map is crucial on these jaunts; arm yourself with tips at the **Ufficio delle Guide** (tel. 84 20 64) in P. Abbe-Heurl, facing the stone-steepled church. (Open 9am-12:30pm and 3:30-7pm).

19th-century English gentlemen brushed off the **Giro del Monte Bianco** as a two- or three-day tour for "less adventurous travelers." Today, more level-headed guides suggest that travelers take a week or more to complete the trip. The trail leads around Monte Bianco, past Chamonix and Courmayeur, and then into Switzerland. Refuges and hotel dormitories are spaced five or six hours apart all along the route. You need not invest your whole vacation: one leg of the larger trail makes an ideal daytrip, and two sections can amply fill a weekend. This is serious mountaineering for which you should be thoroughly equipped and trained before you head out.

Buses access Courmayeur from all directions: Aosta (11 per day, 1 hr., L3600); Turin (6 per day, L11,000); and Chamonix (8 per day, L9000). Pick up a schedule at the **tourist office** (tel. 84 20 60), on P. Monte Bianco at the base of the town by the main road. The same omnipotent office complex houses the **bus station** (tel. 84 93 17), **currency exchange** (open 7:30am-8pm), and **post office** (tel. 84 20 42, **postal code:** 11013, open Mon.-Fri. 8:15am-6:30pm and Sat. 8:15am-1:40pm).

▓ The Lake Country

Some of Stendhal's most florid prose came while trying to describe the Italian lakes, and most visitors find that even a simple postcard home suffers the same fate. After you've visited, you too can bore your friends with the sort of breathless, enchanted effusions 19th-century Romantics produced by the dozen.

There are distinct differences in the personalities of each of the lakes. Garda draws a younger crowd with sailboard-speckled waters by day and an assortment of nightclubs after sunset. Como hosts the sophisticates from nearby Milan, while Lago Maggiore doggedly retains a supine elegance with its elderly luxury hotels lining the shore. The cleaner waters of Garda and Orta are preferable for swimmers, but any lake will do if you prefer to contemplate placid ripples from *terra firma.*

Restaurant prices have soared to rival the mountains; plan on a picnic or two (small *alimentari* abound). Local cheeses include *robiola* (a cream cheese), *caprino* (goat cheese), the soft, tangy *taleggio,* and the piquant *fontale.* All cost about L1200 per *etto,* enough for several sandwiches. A specialty of the Como region is *agone,* sun-cured fish from the lake. *Brianza* is the trademark name of most local wines.

LAKE COMO (LAGO DI COMO)

An air of poetic sublimity lingers over Lake Como's northern reaches. The shores combine the atmospheres of the Mediterranean and of the mountains—lavish villas tucked into a craggy backdrop, warmed by the heat of the Riviera sun and cooled by lakeside breezes. The lake itself is actually a forked amalgam of three long lakes joined in the Centro Lago area of Bellaggio, Tremezzo, Menaggio, and Varenna. The dense green slopes are peppered with villages—take the boat for Colico and get off at the first stop that strikes your fancy. Regular boat service connects towns in all three areas of the lake, as do convenient buses.

■ Como

Situated on the southwestern tip at the receiving end of the Milan rail line, Como is the lake's token industrial center. The city is famous for silk manufacturing, and the preponderance of hyper-efficient lunch-time pit-stops removes the city from the languorous atmosphere permeating most lake towns.

ORIENTATION AND PRACTICAL INFORMATION

Como is a half-hour from Milan by train (every hr., L2700). As you leave the station (tel. 26 14 94), the town is straight ahead and the lake is to your left. There is another train station on the other side of town, **Ferrovia Nord Milano** (tel. 26 63 13), on Via Manzoni off Lungo Lario Trieste, which serves only Milan (every 30min. morning and evening, every hr. 2-5pm, L4600).

Tourist Office: P. Cavour, 16 (tel. 27 40 64), in the largest lakeside piazza near the ferry dock. From the train station, walk down to Via Gallio which becomes Via Garibaldi and leads to the inland side of P. Cavour by way of P. Volta. Open Mon.-Sat. 9am-12:30pm and 2:30-6pm.

Currency Exchange: Banca Nazionale del Lavoro, P. Cavour, 34 (tel. 31 31), across from the tourist office. Dependable rates and cash advances on Visa. Open Mon.-Tues. and Thurs.-Fri. 8:20am-1:20pm and 2:30-4pm, Wed. 8:20am-5:50pm. Sat. and 4-6pm, try the tourist office or the train station.

Post Office: Via T. Gallio, 4 (tel. 26 93 36). Stamps at #11. Open Mon.-Fri. 8:15am-7:30pm, Sat. 8:15am-noon. There is another office in the center of town at Via V. Emanuele, 99. Open Mon.-Fri. 8:15am-1:30pm, Sat. 8:15am-11:40am. **Postal Code:** 22100.

Telephones: SIP office recently closed and no information exists regarding a future office. In the meantime the many telephones in the train station and in P. Cavour must suffice. **Telephone Code:** 031.

Buses: SPT, Matteotti (tel. 30 47 44), at the bend in Lungo Lario Trieste. To: Menaggio (L3000); Bellaggio (L3500); Gravedona (L4700); Bergamo (L7300). **Information** open Mon.-Fri. 8am-noon and 3-6pm, Sat. 8am-noon.

Public Transportation: Tickets available at *tabacchi.* L1000 for an inter-city, one-use ticket.

Ferries: tel. 27 33 24 or 26 02 34. Daily to all lake towns. Fares L1300-11,200. Departures from the piers along Lungo Lario Trieste, in front of P. Cavour. Pick up the booklet *Orari e Tariffe* for a comprehensive listing of prices and departures.

Swimming Pool: Lido Villa Olma (tel. 57 09 68). Sadly, Como's dirtied waters no longer permit ablutions. The grassy plot here is more lawn than beach, but the pool does the job—it's wet. L7000, L5000 if you buy tickets at the youth hostel. Open daily 10am-7pm.

Bike Rental: the youth hostel rents them to guests for L6000 per day.

Emergencies: tel. 113. **Police:** Viale Roosevelt, 7 (tel. 27 23 66). **Hospital: Ospedale Valduce,** Via Dante, 11 (tel. 32 41).

ACCOMMODATIONS

Less expensive campsites and hostels line the shores of the lake (ask for a list at the tourist office), but if you must stay in town...

Ostello Villa Olmo (HI), Via Bellinzona, 6 (tel. and fax 57 38 00), on the inland side of Villa Olmo. From the station it's a 20-min. walk down Via Borgovico (which becomes Bellinzona) to your left or take bus #1, #6, #11, or #14 (L1000). Multilingual staff, bar facilities, and discounts on assorted tickets. Slightly crowded rooms with lockers. Laundry L5000. Ironing L1000. Play it safe and call ahead in summer. Curfew 11pm. L13,000 per person with breakfast. Full meals L12,000. Bag lunches L10,000. Open March-Nov. daily 7:30-10am and 4-11pm. Off-season, groups by reservation only. MC, Visa.

Protezione della Giovane, Via Borgovico, 182 (tel. 57 43 90), on the way to the youth hostel. Take bus #1, #2, or #6. Run by nuns; women only. Clean singles and doubles, some more modern than others. New bathrooms shine. A spacious building with a central courtyard and garden. Free laundry and kitchen use. Curfew 10pm. L15,000 per person. Lunch or dinner L15,000

Albergo S. Antonio, Via Coloniola, 10 (tel. 30 42 77), behind the bus station. Neat rooms with showers, and a good restaurant downstairs (*menù* L18,000). Singles L40,000. Doubles L57,000.

FOOD

Many of Como's residents eat lunch *alla Milanese,* downing a quick, satisfying meal in an inexpensive self-service joint. The food is wholesome, the atmosphere energetic, and cover charges rare. Unfortunately, finding an affordable *dinner* can be a challenge. Picnickers will appreciate the long hours of the **G.S. supermarket** on the corner of Via Recchi and Viale Fratelli Rosselli, across from the park. (Open Mon. 2-8pm, Tues.-Sat. 8:30am-8pm.) Lakeside benches are great for free *al fresco* dining, although solo women should go prepared with "vai via" (go away) in their vocabulary. Mountainous loaves of *matalok* can be purchased at the **Franzi bakery** at the corner of Via Vitani and Via Francensco Muratto.

Ristorante Carducci, Via Carducci, 4 (tel. 27 63 88), in the old part of town near the Basilica di San Fedele. An inexpensive ACLI-run *mensa* in a functional room. Full meals L9500. Open Mon.-Fri. 11:30am-2:15pm, Sat. 11:30am-1:30pm. Closed 2 weeks in Aug.

Gerald's, Via Bianchi Giovani, 6 (tel. 30 48 72), off P. Cavour. Inhale decent food elbow-to-elbow with complete strangers. This green-tiled feeding machine will suck you in and spit you out in less than 30min., but you'll eat well if you don't get lost in the sea of consumers. *Primi* L4500, *secondi* L6000, with *contorno* L8,000. Bar open Mon.-Sat. 7am-8pm, meals lunchtime only.

Taverna Messicana, P. Mazzini, 5/6 (tel. 26 24 63). Inexpensive *primi* and *secondi* (from L6000 and L8000 respectively) and a million variations on the pizza theme ranging from L5000 to 12,000 (for a salmon and vodka adventure). Cover L2000. Open Tues.-Sun. 11am-2pm and 7pm-midnight.

SIGHTS AND ENTERTAINMENT

Como's **duomo** harmoniously combines Gothic and Renaissance elements. The vigorous sculptures that animate the exterior of the church are the work of the Rodari brothers. Note especially Como residents Pliny the Elder and Pliny the Younger on either side of the door. Against the *duomo* is the sturdy **Broletto,** the former communal palace, with thick pillars, colonnaded windows, and colorful marble balconies. The **Church of San Fedele,** two blocks from the *duomo,* bears an unsurprising resemblance to Ravenna's Byzantine churches, since the oldest parts of the church (notably the altar and the blind arcade) were built by the Lombards during the same period.

A 20th-century version of the communal palace is Giuseppe Terragni's **Casa del Fascio.** Built in 1939 to house the local fascist government, it is the antithesis of the traditional "fascist architecture" of heavy masonry and Roman imagery, becoming instead an icon for the entirely different language of modernist architecture.

After visiting Como's monuments, take the *funicolare* up to **Brunate** for excellent hiking and eye-exploding views. The cars leave from the far end of Lungo Lario Trieste every half-hour (L3500; round-trip L6100, L4000 if purchased through the youth hostel; children L2100, round-trip L3700). Be aware that the last car comes down from Brunate at 10:30pm. The other option is spending the night in one of the three rough-and-ready *baite* (guesthouses) along the trail, which provide room and board in either private or dormitory-style rooms (about L27,000). Check with the tourist office in the off-season to make sure they're open.

■ Centro Lago

The endless villas and towns of the Centro Lago can be explored at your leisure while staying at one of the two excellent youth hostels in **Menaggio** (on the west shore) and **Domaso** (on the north side). In Menaggio, **Ostello la Prinula (HI),** Via IV Novembre, 38 (tel. (0344) 32 356), is one of the jollier and better-kept hostels around. It offers great cuisine (dinner L12,000), family suites, a washing machine, and cooking equipment. (Lockout 10am-5pm. Curfew 11pm. L12,000 per person. Open mid-March to mid-Nov.) The **hostel (HI)** in Domaso is at Via Case Sparse, 12 (tel. (0344) 960 94). It lies 16km from Como by bus, but the boat is more convenient. (L12,000 per person. Open March-Oct.) You can also crash at one of the secluded **campsites** that dot the northwest lakeside. The Como tourist office has complete camping information.

Once your baggage is properly ensconced, hop on a ferry and hop off whenever a villa, castle, or village beckons you. Among the innumerable possibilities, we humbly suggest whistle stops at **Varenna,** on the western shore, for its perfect cluster of houses below the castle Vezio, and **Isola Comacina,** also on the western shore, for its breathtaking "Oratory of San Giovanni". The magnificent Villa Balbianello (on the extreme tip of the headland that cradles Comacina) can only be seen during the boat ride because, unfortunately, it's closed to the public.

LAKE MAGGIORE (LAGO MAGGIORE)

Lacking only the hustle of its easterly cousins, Lake Maggiore cradles the same temperate mountain waters and picture-perfect shores. A glaze of opulence coats the waters here, and a stroll past any of the grandiose shore-side hotels reveals that Maggiore is a preferred watering hole of the elite. Modest *pensioni* tucked away in the shadows of their multi-storied superiors, however, enable travelers to partake of the lake's sedate pleasures for a surprisingly reasonable sum.

■ Stresa

Stresa retains much of the charm that brought visitors here in droves during the 19th and early 20th centuries. Splendid views of the lake and the mountains around it lie at each turn of the cobbled streets. Only an hour from Milan on the Milan-Domodossola train line (every hr., L5300), the town is a convenient base for further expeditions in the region. The **tourist office** (tel. 30 150 or 30 416) is at Via Principe Tomaso, 72. From the station, turn right on Via Carducci and follow the signs. (Open Mon.-Sat. 8:30am-12:30pm and 3-6:15pm, Sun. 9am-noon; Oct.-April Mon.-Fri. 8:30am-12:30pm and 3-6:15pm, Sat. 8:30am-12:30pm.) The **post office** is at Via Roma, 5, near P. Congressa. (Open Mon.-Fri. 8:15am-6:30pm, Sat. 8:15-11:40am.) **Postal code:** 28049.) Stresa's **telephone code** is 0323. For **emergency medical assistance** (*Guardia Medica*), phone 31 844. The funky sign at Via De Martini, 20, reading **"Hopital,"** is, in fact, the place to go with a medical complaint (tel. 30 428).

Accommodations and Food Albergo Luina, Via Garibaldi, 21 (tel. 30 285), offers quiet comfort in the thick of the cobbled center. The kind, English-speaking proprietors reserve the right to request a minimum three-day stay during high season. (Singles L40,000. Doubles with bath L75,000.) **Orsola Meublé,** Via Duchessa di Genova, 45 (tel. 31 087), offers a resting place just downhill from the station. Some rooms have terraces. (Singles L30,000, with bath L40,000. Doubles L40,000, with bath L55,000.) Go uphill and pass under the tracks to find the beautiful breezy rooms of **Hotel Mon Toc,** Via Duchessa di Genova, 67-69 (tel. 302 82; fax 93 38 60). (Singles L45,000. Doubles L70,000. Occasionally mandatory full pension L65,000 per person.)

Taverna del Pappagallo, Via Principessa Margherita, 40 (tel. 30 411), serves up appetizing and affordable meals in this area bereft of a supermarket. *Primi* begin at L5000, *secondi* at L10,000. Pizza hovers around L8000. (Cover L2000. Open Thurs.-Mon. 11:30am-2:30pm and 6:30-10:30pm.) Follow the diagonal continuation of Via de Amicis past Via P. Tomaso, and you'll stumble upon a number of appetizing dining possibilities. **Salumeria Bianchetti Augusto,** Via Mazzini, 1 (tel. 30 402) is great for a slice (L1500) to munch on as you walk along the *"lago."*

Entertainment From the last week in August to the third week in September, some of the finest orchestras and soloists in the world gather in Stresa for the internationally acclaimed **Settimane Musicali di Stresa.** (Student prices of L15,000 available for certain concerts.) Write or call the ticket office for information (Palazzo dei Congressi, Via R. Bonghi, 4, 28049 Stresa; tel. 31 095). You can also ask about the **Estate Chitarristica sul Lago Maggiore,** an international extravaganza of classical guitar held in August in nearby Verbania; many of the concerts are free.

Near Stresa: Islands

The beauty of the **Borromean Isles, Isola Madre, Isola Bella,** and **Isola dei Pescatori,** has been amply touted over the past 300 years. Daily excursion tickets allow you to hop back and forth among the islands at liberty. L11,000 will buy a ticket to Pallanza and the intermediate islands (ticket office tel. 44 555). The L13,400 variety allows you to extend your itinerary even further to **Villa Tàranto** with its impressive botanical gardens. (Open daily April-Oct. 8:30am-7:30pm. Admission L8000, ages 6-14, L5000). Enclosed gardens are a recurring theme in any tour of this end of the lake, and if you save your money by eschewing the flora, you will often find yourself with only a small plot of land to pace upon while waiting for the next ferry to rescue you. **Isola dei Pescatori** is the only garden-free island, and vendors have capitalized on the unrestricted space by erecting souvenir stands on all sides. You have the run of the island, but mid-day tourist congestion makes it difficult even to walk.

Isola Madre (tel. and fax 31 261 for information) is the longest and quietest of the three islands. Lancelotto Borromeo was the first of the noble family to begin work on the palaces and gardens, renting the island in 1502. Count Renato bought it in

1609 and continued the project, resulting in an elegant 16th-century villa. The palace contains a great number of portraits of the family and, no expense having been spared for the Borromeo *bambini,* a famous collection of dolls. The botanical garden has a stupendous array of exotic trees, plants, and flowers. (Open March 27-Oct. 24 daily 9am-noon and 1:30-5:30pm. Admission L9000, ages 6-15, L4000.)

The sprawling opulence of the Palazzo e Giardini Borromeo has made **Isola Bella** (tel. (0323) 30 556, fax (02) 72 02 00 38) the most famous of the islands. The palace, built in 1670 by Count Borromeo, is a monument to the Baroque. The ten terraces of the gardens, liberally punctuated with statues, rise up in true wedding-cake fashion to the Borromeo family emblem, the unicorn. By the way, the Borromeo family motto is "Humilitas." (Same hours and prices as Madre.)

Pallanza, on the far side of Isola Madre, offers little of artistic interest, but lakeside dining is cheaper here and you might consider having a meal before cruising "home." Stresa's navigation offices are located in P. Marconi, and tickets are sold from 8am-8pm. For additional information, contact the central office at Arona, Viale Barracco, 1 (tel. (0322) 46 651).

■ Lake D'Orta (Lago D'Orta)

Lake d'Orta remains the Lake Country's unspoiled refuge, surrounded by hills and forests and graced by several small towns. Nietzsche retreated here in 1883-1885 to script his final work, *Thus Spoke Zarathustra.* Lake d'Orta lies on the Novara-Domodossola **train** line (10 per day from Novara, 1hr. 30min., L7200). Get off at Orta Miasino, 3km above Orta, and then either walk down or catch one of the four buses that travel to Orta. Like any true retreat, the lake is cursed—and thus blessed—by a dearth of public transportation. Connections from nearby Lago Maggiore are difficult and indirect, but on weekdays in summer **buses** leave twice a day from Baveno and Stresa (contact the tourist offices). Beware of the train station's peculiar hours if you're counting on an evening departure. (Open 6:20-11:30am and 1:30-3:30pm).

Practical Information Orta's **tourist office** is at Via Olina, 9/11 (tel. 90 354, fax 90 56 78). (Open Tues.-Sat. 9am-noon and 3-5:30pm, Sun. 10am-noon and 3-5pm.) If you arrive on a Monday or are bound for a different town, check the office at Via Panoramica across the street and down from the Eastern-influenced Villa Crespi (tel. 90 56 14). (Open Mon. and Wed.-Fri. 10am-1pm and 4-7pm, Sat.-Sun. 10am-1pm and 4-8pm). The **post office** is at P. Ragazzoni. (Open Mon.-Fri. 8:30am-noon and 2-6pm, Sat. 8:30-11am.) The **postal code** is 28016. The **telephone code** is 0322.

Accommodations and Food Restaurant prices (and the solicitous treatment accorded tourists) are a relief after those of the more commercialized lakes, but affordable accommodations await only a happy few. **Ristorante Olina** (tel. 90 56 56), across from the tourist office, offers beautiful doubles with private baths (L75,000, use of kitchen L5000). Family suites with kitchens are also available, some with glimpses of the lake. The **Taverna Antico Angello,** Via Olina, 18 (tel. 90 259), provides central one-star economy hung with wisteria. (Singles L28,000. Doubles L38,000.) **Conca d'Oro** (tel. 90 252), to the left on the descent into town, offers a greater number of lesser rooms. (Singles L35,000. Doubles L54,000.) A good-sized **open-air market** sells out on Wednesday mornings in P. Motta. Remember that Lago d'Orta is known as the home of *tapulon* (donkey meat, minced and well-spiced, cooked in red wine). For this and other warm comestibles, consider hopping on a boat to **Ristorante San Giulio,** with an 18th-century dining room and lakeside terrace, on the tiny island of the same name. *(Primi* run L5000-7000 and *secondi* are L10,000. The cover is L2000.)

Sights Set high in the cool, verdant hills above town is the **Sacro Monte,** a monastic complex devoted to St. Francis of Assisi. The sanctuary was founded in 1591, and its 20 chapels boast some 376 life-sized statues and 900 frescoes whose combined forces tell the life story of Italy's patron saint. **Isola di San Giulio,** across from Orta, has an interesting Romanesque **basilica** from the 12th century, built on 4th-century foundations. (Open Mon.-Sat. 9:30am-11pm and 2-7pm, Sun. 9:30-10:45am and 2-7pm.) A circular route around the island snakes through the narrow streets past ivy-covered walls and tiled roofs. Bring L3000 to buy a bag of *pane di San Giulio* from the nuns in the adjacent convent. Small motor boats weave back and forth constantly during the summer (round-trip L3000; tickets sold on board). Winter service is restricted to just a couple of runs per day.

▨ Lombardy (Lombardia)

Over the centuries Roman generals, German emperors, and French kings have vied for control of Lombardy's bounty. The agricultural riches of the region have since been augmented by industrial and financial resources, making it the cornerstone of the Italian economy. In fact Lombardy has in many ways more in common with its northern neighbors than with the rest of the peninsula, and Lombardians make periodic calls for an end to the subsidization of the Roman bureaucracy and the historically backward South. Yet since World War II Lombardy's "new Italy" has attracted legions of ambitious southerners, and the province has recently become a magnet for immigrants from North Africa and the Middle East. Tension between long-time denizens and immigrants persists, but thanks in part to this diversity, residents of Lombardy are today among the least provincial Italians.

Although cosmopolitan Milan, with its international reputation for high style and finance, may loom largest in foreigners' perceptions of the region, Lombardy is in fact far more than a metropolis and its countryside. Bergamo, Brescia, and Mantua, with their hints of Venetian influence, are culturally foreign to their western neighbor. The beginnings of the Alps are not far from the southern plain, combining an Italian climate with strains of Swiss and Austrian culture.

■■■ MILAN (MILANO)

In a country often inclined to rest on its cultural laurels, Milan is a fresh exception—a frenetically industrious city where the achievements of modernity seem most to outstrip historical legacy. Even the *duomo,* the city's sophisticated emblem, anticipates its 20th-century skyscraping counterparts.

The Romans made Milan the capital of the western half of the empire between 286 and 402 AD. Milan's influence continued to grow. In the 15th century Lodovico Sforza's patronage attracted Leonardo da Vinci and Donato Bramante to his court, ushering in the Renaissance in Milan. The modern era arrived with the French troops in 1797. The city later became headquarters of the Italian unification movement in the mid-19th century. After suffering bombing during World War II, Milan was speedily rebuilt. Milan is relentless in its pursuit not of erstwhile glory but of the modern—a preoccupation that makes it an international center of *haute couture.*

Despite its size, Milan in fact fosters a rather suburban feel with large apartment buildings and little bars lining wide, tree-shaded streets. It is also a relatively safe city, and surprisingly enough, during the early hours of the morning as well as the entire month of August, the city really "shuts down." As in any city, normal precautions should be taken to avoid being a victim of crime (see section on Safety).

ORIENTATION

Milan is linked by train to all major cities in Italy and Western Europe. The layout of the city resembles a giant target, encircled by a series of concentric ancient city walls. In the outer rings lie suburbs built during the 1950s and 60s to house southern immigrants. The **duomo** and **Galleria Vittorio Emanuele II** comprise the bull's-eye, roughly at the center of the downtown circle. Within this inner circle are four central squares: **Largo Cairoli,** near Castello Sforzesco, **Piazza Cordusio,** connected to Largo Cairoli by Via Dante, **Piazza Duomo,** at the end of Via Mercanti, and **Piazza San Babila,** the business and fashion district along Corso Vittorio Emanuele. Northeast and northwest lie two large parks, the **Giardini Pubblici** and the **Parco Sempione.** Farther northeast is the **Stazione Centrale,** Mussolini's colossal train station built in 1931. The area around the train station is a mishmash of skyscrapers dominated by the sleek **Pirelli Tower** (1959), still one of the tallest buildings in Europe. From the station a scenic ride on bus #60 takes you to the downtown hub, as does the more efficient commute on subway line #3. The station is also connected to the downtown area by **Corso Buenos Aires,** where prices for clothing are actually reasonable.

The **subway** (Metropolitana Milanese, abbreviated "MM") is the most useful branch of Milan's extensive public transportation network. **Line #1** (red line) connects the *pensioni* district east of Stazione Centrale to the center of town and extends as far as the youth hostel (Molino Dorino fork). **Line #2** (green line) links Milan's three train stations and crosses MM1 at Cadorno and Loreto. The new **Line #3** (yellow line) runs from just north of the Stazione Centrale to the southern sprawl of the city, intersecting with line #2 at Stazione Centrale and #1 at the *duomo.* The subway operates from approximately 6am to midnight. Among the many useful train and bus routes, **trams #29** and **30** travel the city's outer ring road, while **buses** #96 and 97 service the inner road. **Tram #1,** which runs during the wee hours, also departs from Centrale and runs to Piazza Scala. Tickets for buses, trams, and subways must be purchased in advance at newsstands or from ticket machines—bring small change. A ticket (L1100) is good for one subway ride or 75 minutes of surface transportation. All-day passes (L3500) are available from the **ATM** office at the Duomo and Centrale stops and are good from the first time you use them rather than from the time you buy them. Those planning a longer stay should consider the weekly pass (L8400, photo required), valid for any form of public transportation. It is a good idea to have extra tickets on hand in the evening, as *tabacchi* close around 8pm and vending machines are unreliable. (L20,000 fine for riding without a ticket.)

PRACTICAL INFORMATION

Tourist Office: APT, Via Marconi, 1 (tel. 80 96 62/63/64; fax 72 02 24 32), in the "Palazzo di Turismo" in P. del Duomo, to the right as you face the *duomo.* Comprehensive local and regional information, and an especially useful map and museum guide (in Italian). Will not reserve rooms but will phone to check for vacancies. Some English spoken. Open Mon.-Sat. 8am-8pm, Sun. 9am-12:30pm and 1:30-5pm. Branch office at **Stazione Centrale,** (tel. 669 05 32 or 669 04 32; open Mon.-Sat. 8am-7pm) and **Linate Airport** (tel. 74 40 65; open Mon.-Fri. 9am-4:30pm). For hotel information and reservations, call the hotel owners' association, **Hotel Reservation Milano** (tel. 76 00 60 95), which may request a deposit during busy periods. The **Associazionne Turistrea Giovanile,** Via del Amicis, 4 (tel. 89 40 50 75), near the Porta Ticinese, has some discounts and helpful information for young travelers. Open Mon.-Fri. 9:30am-1pm and 2-6:30pm, Sat. 9:30am-1pm.

Budget Travel: CIT, Galleria Vittorio Emanuele (tel. 86 66 61). The most central travel agency. Also **changes money.** Open Mon.-Fri. 9am-5:50pm. Another office at the **Stazione Centrale** (same hours). **Centro Turistico Studentesco,** Via S. Antonio, 2 (tel. 583 041 21). Open Mon.-Fri. 9:30am-6pm, Sat. 9:30am-noon; Sept.-May Mon.-Fri. 9:30am-1pm and 2:30-6pm, Sat. 9:30am-noon. **Transalpino Tickets:** Next to the train information office in the upper atrium of Stazione Cen-

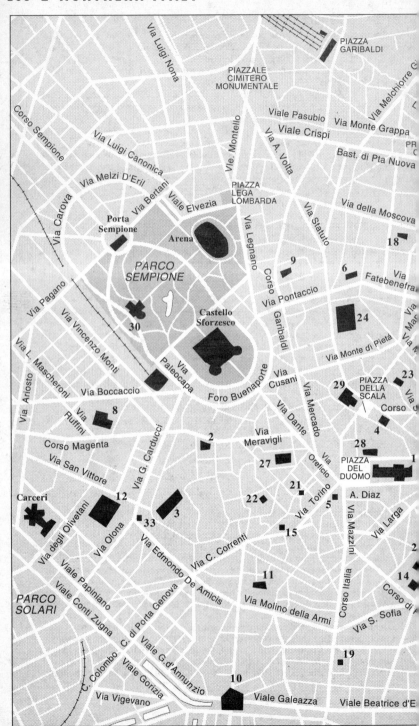

Milan

1 Duomo
2 Monastero Maggiore
3 Basilica di Sant'Ambrogio
4 Chiesa di S. Fedele-Palazzo Marino
5 Chiesa di S. Satiro
6 Chiesa di S. Marco
7 Chiesa di S.M.di Passione
8 Chiesa della Grazie
9 Chiesa di Simpliciano
10 Cheisa di S. Eustorgio
11 Chiesa di S. Lorenzo Maggiore
12 Chiesa di s. Vittore-Museo Nazionale della Scienze e della Tecnica
13 Chiesa di S. Maria della Pace
14 Chiesa di S. Nazaro
15 Maggiore con la Cappella Trivulzio
16 Basilica di S. Giorgio al Palazzo
17 Chiesa di S. Carlo

18 Chiesa di S. Bábila
19 Chiesa di Sant'Angelo
20 Chiesa di S. Maria alla Fontana
21 ex Palazzo Reale-Arcivescovada
22 Palazzo dell'Ambrosia
23 Palazzo Borromeo
24 Palazzo Poldi Pezzoli
25 Palazzo Moriggia-Palazzo di Brera
26 Palazzo del Senato ex Ospedale Maggiore
27 Palazzo della Ragione
28 Galleria Vittorio Emanuele II
29 Teatro alla Scala-Museo Teatrale
30 Palazzo dell'Arte
31 Civico Planetario
32 Palazzo Sormani
33 Pusterla di Sant'Ambrogio

trale (tel. 670 51 21). Open Mon.-Sat. 8am-8pm, Sun. 8:30am-12:30pm and 2:30-6:30pm. When closed, go to **Italturismo,** to the right from the station, under the grand drive-thru. Open daily 6:45am-8pm; Sept.-July Mon.-Sat. 6:45am-8pm.

Consulates: U.S., Via P. Amedeo, 2/10 (tel. 29 00 18 41). Open Mon.-Fri. 9am-1pm. **Canada,** Via Vittor Pisani, 19 (tel. 669 74 51; emergencies tel. 66 98 06 00). Open Mon.-Fri. 9am-12:30pm and 1:30-5:15pm. **U.K.,** Via S. Paolo, 7 (tel. 869 34 42). Open Mon.-Fri. 9:15am-12:15pm and 2:30-4:30pm. **Australia,** Via Borgogna, 2 (tel. 76 01 33 30). Open daily 9:15am-noon and 2-4:30pm. **New Zealand** citizens should contact their embassy in Rome.

Currency Exchange: All **Banca d'America e d'Italia** and **Banca Nazionale del Lavora** branches give cash advances on Visa cards. (The former are usually open Mon.-Fri. 8:30am-1:30pm and 2:45-4:15pm, the latter Mon.-Fri. 8:20am-1:20pm and 2:30-4pm.) The **Banca Nazionale delle Comunicazioni** at Stazione Centrale has pretty standard rates if you need to change money right away. (Open Mon.-Sat. 8am-6:30pm, Sun. 9am-1pm. L3000 fee.)

American Express: Via Brera, 3 (tel. 85 571), on the corner of Via dell'Orso. Walk through the Galleria, across P. Scala, and up Via Verdi. Holds mail free for American Express members, otherwise L800 per inquiry. Will accept wired money for a fee of US$30 per US$1000. Open Mon.-Fri. 9am-5pm.

Post Office: Via Cordusio, 4 (tel. 869 20 69), near P. del Duomo in the direction of the castle. Stamps at #1 and 2. Fermo Posta c/o the CAI-POST office to the left. Open Mon.-Fri. 8:30am-5:30pm, Sat. 8:30am-1pm. **Postal Code:** 20100.

Telephones: SIP, in Galleria Vittorio Emanuele. Open 7am-midnight. **ASST,** in Stazione Centrale. Open 7am-midnight. **Linate Airport: ASST,** open 7am-11:45pm. **Malpensa Airport,** open 7am-8pm. **Telephone Code:** 02.

Flights: Malpensa Airport, 45km from town. Intercontinental flights. Buses leave every half hour in the mornings, hourly in the afternoon from P. Luigi di Savoia, on the east side of Stazione Centrale (L12,000). **Linate Airport,** 7km from town. Domestic/European flights and intercontinental flights with European transfers. Much easier logistically. The bus to Linate leaves Stazione Centrale every 20min. 5:50am-9pm (L4000). It's cheaper (L1200) to take bus #73 from P. San Babila (MM1). **General Flight Information** for both airports, tel. 74 85 22 00.

Trains: Stazione Centrale, P. Duca d'Aosta (tel. 67 500), on MM2. The primary station. To: Genoa and Turin (both every hr., 1hr. 30min. and 2hr., L12,100); Venice (20 direct per day, 3hr., L18,700); Florence (every hr., 3hr., L33,500 with supplement); Rome (every hr., 5hr., L59,300 with supplement). Information office open daily 7am-11pm. Eurail passes and *Cartaverde* available outside the building. **Luggage Storage:** L1500. Open 4am-2am. **Lost and Found:** (tel. 67 71 26 77) next to *binario* 21. Open daily 7:20am-8:45pm. **Stazione Nord** (tel. 851 16 08) connects Milan with Como, Erba, and Varese, **Porta Genova** (tel. 59 10 01 43) has lines to the west (Vigevano, Alessandria, Asti), **Porta Garibaldi** (tel. 655 20 78) links Milan to Lecco and Valtellina to the northwest.

Buses: ATM (tel. 87 54 95), in the P. del Duomo MM station. Municipal buses require pre-purchased tickets (L1200). Day passes for non-residents L3800. Open Mon.-Sat. 8am-8pm. Also at **Stazione Centrale** (same hours). **Intercity** buses are less convenient and more expensive than the trains, but **SAL, SIA, Autostradale,** and many others depart from P. Castello and the surrounding area (MM: Cairoli) for Turin, the lake country, Bergamo, Certosa di Pavia, and points as far away as Rimini and Trieste.

Taxis: In P. Scala, P. del Duomo, P. S. Babila, and Largo Cairoli. Or contact them by radio (tel. 67 67 or 83 88). The official Milan taxis are yellow and uniformly expensive, starting at L4000, with a nighttime surcharge of L4000.

Car Rental: Hertz (tel. 20 483, Galleria delle Carrozze office 670 30 62). Outside the station, to the left as you exit. The **Guida Italia** package offers a Fiat for 7 days for under L500,000, with reservations a week ahead. Open Sept.-July Mon.-Fri. 7:40am-8pm, Sat. 7:40am-2:10pm. Also check with **Europcar** (tel. 167 86 80 88) and **Avis** (tel. 669 02 80) at the same place: same rates, similar hours.

English Bookstore: The American Bookshop, Via Camperio, 16 (tel. 87 09 44), at Largo Cairoli. The best selection in Milan. Open Tues.-Fri. 10am-7pm, Sat. 10am-1pm and 3-7pm, Mon. 3-7pm. Closed 2 wks. in Aug. **Hoepli Librería Inter-**

nazionale, Via Hoepli, 5 (tel. 86 54 46), near P. Scala. Open Mon.-Sat. 9am-7pm. **Rizzoli's,** Galleria Vittorio Emanuele (tel. 86 46 10 71) has only a small English collection, but is well stocked with *Let's Go*.

Library: United States Information Service, Via Bigli, 11A (tel. 79 50 51), near P. S. Babila. Library with U.S. publications for perusal. Open Mon.-Tues. and Thurs. 9:30am-1pm and 2:30-6pm, Wed. 9:30am-1pm. **British Council Library,** Via Manzoni, 38 (tel. 78 20 16), near USIS. Open Tues.-Wed. 10am-7:30pm, Thurs.-Fri. 10am-6pm, Sat. 10am-12:30pm.

Day Hotel: Albergo Diurno (tel. 669 12 32), beneath P. Duca d'Aosta, reached by stairs underground as you leave the center of the Stazione Centrale. Toilets L500, with soap and towel L2000, with shower L5000, with bath L8000. Open Thurs.-Tues. 7am-8pm. **Luggage storage** (same hrs.), L1500 per 24 hrs.

Laundromat: Lavanderia Automatica, Corso Porta Vittoria, 51 (tel. 55 19 23 15), beyond largo Augusto behind the *duomo*. The most central, but consult the yellow pages for the *lavanderia* nearest you. **Acqua e Zapone,** Via Allesandario Tadino, at the corner of where Via Tunisia meets Corso Buenos Aires. Self-service laundry close to hotels, near the Porta Venezia stop on the Metro. Wash and dry L6000 each for 7kg. Open daily 8am-10pm.

Swimming Pool: Cozzi, Viale Tunisia, 35 (tel. 659 97 03), off Corso Buenos Aires. Out of a dozen, the closest to Stazione Centrale. Open Tues.-Sat. 12:30-6:30pm; admission L4500. In summer, move outdoors to **Giulia Romano,** Viale Ponzia, 35 (tel. 29 22 24). **Lido di Milano,** P. Lotto, 15 (tel. 39 26 61 00), near the youth hostel. Open daily 11am-7pm. Admission L4500. Indoor pool open Sept. 10-June 10am-5:30pm.

AIDS Hotline: Centralino Informazioni AIDS, (tel. 62 08 70 70). Open Mon.-Fri. noon-8pm, Sat. 9am-noon. Also **Centri AIDS,** P. XXIV Maggio, Ex Casello (tel. 89 40 24 06), Via Fantoli, 7 (tel. 506 13 91), and Via Masaniello, 23 (tel. 45 314 25).

Women's Center Hotline: Centro Azione Milano Donne, Viale Tibaldi, 41 (tel. 58 10 40 67). Advises women on legal rights.

Handicapped/Disabled Services: Settore Servici Sociale, Largo Treves, 1 (tel. 62 08 69 10).

Late-Night Pharmacy: Though nocturnal duty rotates among Milan's pharmacies (call 192 to find out who is on the night shift), the one in Stazione Centrale never closes (tel. 669 07 35 or 669 09 35). During the day, try the **Italo-English Chemist's Shop** on Corso Europa, 18 (tel. 76 00 18 28 or 78 16 02) and also on P. Duomo, 21 (tel. 86 46 48 32).

Hospital: Ospedale Maggiore Policlinico, Via Francesco Sforza, 35 (tel. 55 031), 5min. from the *duomo* on the inner ring road.

Emergencies: tel. 113. **Police:** tel. 77 271. **"SOS for Tourists":** tel. 545 65 51 for legal complaints. **Medical Emergency:** tel. 38 83. **Ambulance:** tel. 77 33.

ACCOMMODATIONS

There are over 50 "on-paper" bargains in Milan, but if you want a clean room in a safe and reasonably convenient location, only a few choices are worth your while. Every season is high season in Milan (except August), and a single room in an upright establishment for under L35,000 is a real find. Even resort areas like the Riviera and the Alps offer better bargains than Milan. For the best deals, it is advisable to make the trip from the station to the city's center or its southern periphery. In all cases, make reservations well ahead of time.

Ostello Pietro Rotta (HI), Viale Salmoiraghi, 2 (tel. 39 26 70 95). From any train station, take MM2 to Cadorna and change to MM1 going out to Molino Dorino. Get off at QT8—a district in the leafy outskirts. Take a right when you exit the metro and follow the orange hostel sign straight for about 10 minutes—the hostel is on the right. Modern hostel with 380 beds (6 per room), a sunny garden, and a helpful staff. Run on a mechanized regimen. English spoken. HI card strictly required, but non-members can purchase it at the hostel (L5000 per night for 6 nights). Open 7-9am and 5-11:30pm. Unbending enforcement of daytime lockout.

MILAN

Depending on the management's whim, lights suddenly die between 11:20pm and midnight. Curfew 11:30pm. L20,000 per person. Breakfast, sheets, and lockers included. Use of washer and dryer L6000 each for a 3kg load. Individuals may not make reservations. Open Jan. 13-Dec. 20.

Near Stazione Centrale

Due Giardini, Via Settala, 46 (tel. 29 52 10 93 or 29 51 23 09; MM2: Caiazzo). Go left from the station on Via Scarlatti. Via Settala is the 4th road on the right. "Feel-the-springs" beds but clean and neat. The main attraction is the expansive garden outside. Open all night. Singles L50,000. Doubles L70,000. Triples L90,000. No reservations taken—come early in the morning.

Hotel San Marco, Via Piccinni, 25 (tel. 204 95 36 or 29 51 63 16 or 29 51 64 14; MM1-2: Loreto). From station head left to P. Caiazzo and turn onto Via Pergolesi which becomes Piccinni. Comfortable rooms with TV and telephone compensate for the unending street noise below. Friendly management speaks some English. Singles L45,000, with bath and breakfast L62,000. Doubles L64,000, with bath and breakfast L88,000.

Near Piazza Loreto

Albergo "Villa Mira," Via Sacchini, 19 (tel. 29 52 56 18; MM1-2: Loreto), off Via Porpora 2 blocks from P. Loreto. A family-run establishment with rooms out of a Mr. Clean commercial, plus a bar downstairs. Singles L39,000. Doubles with bath L55,000.

Hotel Winston, Via Catalani, 21 (tel. 266 47 80; MM1-2: Loreto), off Via Porpora. A quiet retreat of modern rooms, some overlooking a tranquil garden. Singles L35,000. Doubles L50,000.

Hotel Ca' Grande, Via Porpora, 87 (tel. 26 14 52 95 or 26 14 40 01; MM1-2: Loreto), about 7 blocks in from P. Loreto in a building protected by a spiked fence. Clean rooms with hospital-style beds. Street below can be noisy. English spoken. Singles L40,000, with bath L60,000. Doubles L60,000, with bath L80,000.

Around Corso Buenos Aires

All of these hotels are near the Porta Venezia stop on MM1.

Viale Tunisia, 6. This building houses two budget hotels, each equidistant from the station and the city center. Some English is spoken at the **Hotel Kennedy** (tel. 29 40 09 34), 6th floor. Very tidy rooms, with dreamscape decor imported from the 60s. Singles L45,000. Doubles L60,000, with bath L85,000. Triples with shower L105,000. Reservations are recommended. Closes at midnight, checkout by 11am. The **Hotel S. Tomaso** (tel. 29 51 47 47) is on the 3rd floor. Orderly rooms with hardwood floors, some overlooking a courtyard. Communication in English is not a problem. Singles L40,000, with bath L45,000. Doubles L70,000. Prices may be a bit higher in Sept. and Oct., a bit lower in Dec. and Jan.

Hotel Aurora, Corso Buenos Aires, 18 (tel. 204 92 85 or 204 79 60). Street noise is muted by the interior courtyard, and behind a grungy façade lies a spotless labyrinth of modern rooms. English spoken. Singles L50,000, with bath L65,000. Doubles with bath L80,000.

West and South of the City Center

Hotel Jolanda, Corso Magenta, 78 (tel. and fax 46 33 17; MM1: Conciliazione), in a quiet neighborhood popular with university students. Tasteful, wood-floored rooms that are essentially unattainable without a reservation 2 wks. in advance. Singles L40,000. Doubles L60,000-70,000, with bath L90,000. Open Sept.-July.

Pensione Cantore, Corso Genova, 25 (tel. 835 75 65; MM2: Genova), a 15-min. walk southwest of the *duomo,* farther down Via Corso Correnti. A bit out of the way, but grand and immaculate rooms. Friendly atmosphere. Closes at 2am. Doubles L60,000. Reserve ahead.

Camping

Il Bareggino (tel. 901 44 17; MM1: Molino-Dorino line), on Via Corbettina in Bareggino. Hard to reach without a car, though you can take an *extraurbane* bus from P. Lotto. L5300 per adult, L2900 per child, L5200 per tent.   ·

Autodromo (tel. (039) 38 77 71), ir. the park of the Villa Reale in Monza. Train or bus from Stazione Centrale to Monza, then a city bus to the campground. A step down. L3200 per person and per tent, L2000 per child under 6. Open April-Sept.

FOOD

Like its fine *couture,* Milanese cuisine is classic, understated, and overpriced. Specialties include *risotto giallo* (rice with saffron), *cotoletta alla milanese* (a breaded veal cutlet with lemon), and *cazzouela* (a mixture of pork and cabbage). *Pasticcerie* and *gelaterie* crowd every block. Try the Milanese sweet bread *panettone,* made with raisins and lemons. The newspaper *Il Giornale Nuovo* lists all the restaurants and shops open in the city. The largest **markets** are around Via Fauché or Viale Papiniano on Saturday and sometimes Tuesday, and along Via Santa Croce on Thursday. On Saturday, the **Fiera di Sinigallia** occurs on Via Calatafimi—a 400-year-old extravaganza of the commercial and the bizarre.

Splurge on the local pastry at **Sant'Ambroeus** (tel. 76 00 05 40), a Milanese culinary shrine, under the arcades at Corso Matteotti, 7. (Open Tues.-Sat. 8am-8pm, Mon. 3:30-8pm.) For supermarkets, try **Pam,** off Corso Buenos Aires at Via Piccinni, 2 (tel. 20 27 15), or the air-conditioned store at Via Piane, 38B. (Both open Tues.-Sat. 8:30am-7:30pm, Mon. 2-7:30pm.) There is also a useful **S & B Market** farther down at Via Casati, 3 (open Tues.-Sat. 8:30am-1pm and 3:30-7:30pm, Mon. 8:30am-1pm). For a balanced meal at reasonable rates, sit down with the Milanese office workers at one of the countless self-service restaurants that now cater to professionals under time constraints. The **Brek** restaurant on Via Lepetit by Stazione Centrale and the strategically positioned **Ciao** in P. del Duomo are particularly convenient. (At both, *primi* average L4500, *secondi* L7500.)

South of Stazione Centrale and near Corso Buenos Aires

Pizzeria da Sasa, Via Pergolesi, 21 (tel. 669 26 74), about 5min. from the train station. Family-run with kids to prove it. Pizza and calzones L6500-9500. *Primi* L9000-L12,000. Cover L2000. AmEx, Visa.

Pizzeria Columerina, Via Felice Casati, 5 (tel. 29 51 84 27; MM-1: Porta Venezia). Red tablecloths and mosaic-style stone floors. Pizza L5000-65000. Daily specials L8000-18,000. Drinks L1000-6000. Cover L2000.

Pizzeria del Nonno, Via Andrea Costa, 1 (tel. 26 14 52 62; MM1-2: Loreto), off P. Loreto. Surprisingly genteel decor for a hungry, rowdy crowd. Enormous pizzas (L7000-10,000) keep their mouths full. Special of the day runs L6000-12,000. Cover L1500. Open Tues.-Sat. noon-2:30pm and 7pm-12:30am, Sun. 6pm-12:30am.

Tarantella, Via le Abruzzi, 35 (tel. 29 40 02 18), just north of Via Plinio. Lively and leafy neighborhood place with sidewalk dining. Great *antipasti.* Immense specialty salads L10,000. Pizza L8000-20,000 (try the *gorgonzola). Primi* begin at L8000, *secondi* range from L14,000 to seafood fantasies in the L20,000 range. Open Sept.-July Sun.-Fri. noon-3pm and 7-11:30pm.

Isola del Panino, Corso Buenos Aires and F. Casati. Art-deco atmosphere serves up 47 different kinds of super-fresh *panini* for just L3500-5000. (It's not uncommon to have two.) Open Tues.-Sat. 7:30am-midnight.

La Piccola Napoli, Viale Monza, 13 (tel 26 14 33 97; MM1-2: Loreto). A haunt for local night owls. Pizza L7000-10,000 (L1000 less at lunch). Open mid-Aug. to mid-July Tues.-Sun. 6pm-3am.

Near Piazza del Duomo

Flash, Via Bergamini, 1 (tel. 58 30 44 89; MM1: Duomo), at P. San Stefano. Mobbed—and with good reason. The chef spins delectable Neapolitan pizza L7000-11,000. Wine L5000 per ½ liter. Many types of delicious *panini* (including vegetarian) at the bar L3500-4000. Cover L2000. Open Tues.-Sun. noon-3pm and 7pm-1am.

Peck, Via G. Cantù, off Via Dante near the *duomo*. Milan's premier *rosticceria*. Pizza and pastries by the kilo—L3000 will buy a large slice of either. You cannot leave without trying the chocolate mousse (about L3000). Open Tues.-Sat. 8am-1pm and 3:30-7pm.

Between Largo Cairoli and Piazza Cordusio

Le Briciole, Via Camperio, 17 (tel. 87 71 85 or 80 41 14), 1 street over from Via Dante. Lively and popular with young people. Pizza L6500-9000. Spectacular *antipasto* buffet L10,000, *secondi* L7500-14,000. Cover L3000. Open Tues.-Fri. and Sun. 12:15-2:30pm and 7:15pm-midnight.

Near Via Torino and Corso di Porta Ticinese

This once-affordable neighborhood is muddling through the early stages of gentrification. The chic vs. cheap battle is on, so check it out before chic wins out.

Be Bop Caffè/Ristorante, Viale Col di Lana, 4 (tel. 837 69 72; MM2: Sant'Agostino or Genova), off the far side of P. XXIV Maggio. Understated decor with a jazz soundtrack, except after hours when the young staff pumps up the volume. Salads are generously proportioned here (L14,000-18,000). All-inclusive lunch *menù* L14,000. Open Sept. to mid-Aug. Mon.-Sat. noon-2:30pm and 7:30pm-1am.

La Crêperie, Via Corso Correnti, 24 (tel. 837 57 08), the continuation of Via Torino. Fruit crêpes L3000, liqueur dessert crêpes L4000, and the "real food" variety L6000. L9000 lunch special combo. Sip a lemon-and-celery juice to the nonstop music. Open Mon. and Wed.-Fri. noon-midnight, Sat. noon-1:30am, Sun. 4pm-midnight.

Mergellina, Via Molino delle Armi, 48 (tel. 89 40 13 33), in a banana-colored building by the actual Porta Ticinese. 10-min. walk from the *duomo*. Terrific pizza L6000-10,000. Cover L2000. Open Sept.-July Thurs.-Mon. 11am-3pm and 7pm-1:30am, Wed. 7pm-1am.

Portnoy, Via de Amicis, 1 (tel. 837 86 56), at Corso di Porta Ticinese. Ultra-hip: where black will always be in. Young, socially conscious management displays new paintings and poetry. Writers give readings of their work followed by discussion. *Panini* L2000-4500. Open Mon.-Sat. 7am-2am. Poetry readings 7:30-8:30pm; no showings in Aug. Some classical music nights also (no extra charge).

Between Via Pontaccio and Piazza XXV Aprile

Pizzeria Grand'Italia, Via Palermo, 5 (tel. 87 77 59). Go for pizza at L5800-7000, or sample a multitude of other dishes. Open Wed.-Sun. 12:15-3pm and 7pm-2am.

Spaghetteria Enoteca, Via Solferino, 3 (tel. 86 47 20 20; MM2: Moscova) in the basement. A monument to the tangled and inextricably wonderful world of spaghetti. Everything is prepared *all'instante* (on the spot). *Assagini* (small portions) of 5 types of spaghetti L8500. Cover L2500. Open Sept.-July Tues.-Sun. from 7:30pm. Lively *birreria* next door.

Gelaterie

After World War II the Viel family (first the brother, then the cousins), began selling tutti-frutti *gelato* from a little cart outside the *duomo*. The enterprise quickly took off and today the name Viel is synonymous with exotic, fresh fruit *gelati* (L1700-4000) and *frullati* (whipped fruit drinks, L2500) all over Milan. For the freshest and fanciest, take your taste buds to the jolly **Viel Frutti Esotici Gelati** on the left as you face the Castello from Largo Cairoli (MM1: Cairoli). At **Viel,** Via Marconi, 3E, next to the tourist office, you can buy a cone packed with four scoops and take it to the outside tables, one of the cheapest places to sit near the *duomo* (L1500-5000 for a large cup).

Jack Frost Gelateria, Via Felice Casati, 25 (tel. 669 11 34; MM1: Porta Venezia), off Corso Buenos Aires at Via Lazzar tto. Creamy *gelato* and fairy-tale decor. Try their *bacio* (a chocolate and hazelnut "kiss"). Open Thurs.-Tues. 10:30am-1am.

Gelateria Milanodoc, P. Cantore, 4 (tel. 89 40 98 30), near the Navigli. A household word in Milan. Under a thatched roof enclosed by hedges. Open Tues.-Sun. 8am-1am.

SIGHTS

Around the Duomo

The **Piazza del Duomo** marks both the geographical and conceptual focus of Milan. The **duomo,** a radically vertical Gothic creation with vaguely classical proportions, presides over the piazza. Gian Galeazzo Visconti founded the cathedral in 1386, hoping to flatter the Virgin into granting him a male heir. Construction proceeded sporadically over the next four centuries and was finally completed at Napoleon's command in 1809. In the meantime, 2245 statues, 135 spires, 96 gargoyles, and kilometers of tracery accumulated. The unusual triangular façade juxtaposes Italian Gothic and Baroque elements under a filigree crown. Inside, the 52 columns rise to canopied niches that shelter statues reaching almost the full height of the ceiling—48 meters. The church, a five-aisled cruciform, seats 40,000 worshipers. Narrow side aisles extend to the grand stained glass windows, said to be the largest in the world. The imposing 16th-century marble tomb of Giacomo de Medici in the right transept was inspired by Michelangelo. From outside the north transept, you can climb to the top of the cathedral, where you will find yourself surrounded by florid outbursts of turrets and spires (admission L4000, with elevator L6000). This rooftop magical kingdom is crowned by a gold-plated Madonna. (Open daily 7am-7pm; Oct.-May 9am-4:30pm. No shorts, miniskirts, or sleeveless shirts or dresses.)

The **Museo del Duomo,** P. del Duomo, 14 (tel. 86 03 58), is across the piazza in the Palazzo Reale. The newly renovated museum hosts a collection of treasures from the cathedral. (Open Tues.-Sun. 9:30am-12:30pm and 3-6pm. Admission L7000.) It also houses the **Museo d'Arte Contemporanea.** Upstairs is a fine permanent collection of Italian Futurist art, though Picasso figures in, too. (Open Tues.-Sun. 9:30am-5:30pm. Free. Wheelchair accessible.)

On the north side of the piazza is the monumental entrance to the **Galleria Vittorio Emanuele II.** The four-story arcade of *caffè,* shops, and offices is covered by a glass barrel vault and a beautiful glass cupola (48m). The gallery extends from the *duomo* to the **Teatro alla Scala** (also known as **La Scala),** the world's premier opera house, a simple neoclassical building completed in 1778. La Scala rests on the site of the Church of Santa Maria alla Scala, from which it took its name. To see the lavish, multi-tiered hall, enter through the **Museo Teatrale alla Scala** (tel. 805 34 18). Here a succession of petite rooms are lined floor to ceiling with opera memorabilia, including plaster casts of the hands of famous conductors, and Verdi's mythologized top hat. (Open Mon.-Sat. 9am-noon and 2-6pm, Sun. 9:30am-12:30pm and 2:30-6pm; Oct.-April Mon.-Sat. 9am-noon and 2-6pm. Admission L5000.)

Passing the 16th-century Palazzi Marino, which is opposite La Scala and is now the mayor's office, and the side of the church of San Fedele (1569), you arrive at the curious **Casa degli Omenoni** (1565), embellished with eight giant figures of the worldly Atlas. The street ends at **Piazza Belgioioso,** a pleasant square of old Milan dominated by the 18th-century Belgioioso *palazzo* and the picturesque house of 19th-century novelist Alessandro Manzoni. The **Museo Manzoniano,** at Via Morone, 1 (tel. 87 10 19), is devoted to his life and works. Among the portraits of his friends is an autographed likeness of Goethe. (Open Tues.-Fri. 9am-noon and 2-4pm. Free.) Farther along down Via Morone brings you to **Via Manzoni.** A fitting beginning for this street, medieval **Porta Nuova** is a Roman tomb sculpture and a Gothic niche cradling statues of saints. The **Museo Poldi-Pezzoli,** Via Manzoni, 12 (tel. 79 48 89), an outstanding private collection of art bequeathed to the city in 1879, housed in the former home of the founder. The museum's masterpieces are hung in the

MILAN

Golden Room, which overlooks a verdant garden (visible through a Palladian window). The paintings include a Byzantine *Virgin and Child* by Andrea Mantegna, Bellini's *Ecce Homo, St. Nicholas* by Piero della Francesca, the magical *Gray Lagoon* by Guardi; and the museum's signature piece, Antonio Pollaiolo's *Portrait of a Young Woman.* (Open Tues. and Fri. 9am-12:30pm and 2:30-6pm, Sat. 9:30am-12:30pm and 2:30-5:30pm, Sun. 9:30am-12:30pm. Admission L5000.)

Near Castello Sforzesco

After the cathedral, the enormous 15th-century **Castello Sforzesco** (tel. 62 36 39 47, MM1: Cairoli), restored after heavy bomb damage in 1943, is Milan's best-known monument. The first interior court is so vast that architectural details seem to disappear; while the more enclosed, lesser courtyards are noted for their Renaissance arcades. On the ground floor is a sculpture collection renowned for Michelangelo's unfinished *Pietà Rondanini,* his last work. The picture gallery features paintings by Mantegna, Bellini and other Renaissance masters, as well as *Madonna with Angels* by Fra Filippo Lippi. (Open Tues.-Sun. 9:30am-5:30pm. Free.)

Via Verdi, alongside La Scala, leads to **Via Brera,** another charming street lined with small, brightly colored palaces and art galleries just a few steps from the *duomo* (MM1: Cordusio; for doorstep service, catch bus #61 from MM1: Moscova). The **Pinacoteca di Brera** (Brera Art Gallery), Via Brera, 28 (tel. 86 26 34), presents an impressive collection of paintings in a 17th-century *palazzo.* Paintings include Bellini's *Pietà* (1460); Andrea Mantegna's brilliantly foreshortened *Dead Christ* (1480); Raphael's *Marriage of the Virgin* (1504); Caravaggio's *Supper at Emmaus* (1606); and Piero della Francesca's 15th-century *Madonna and Child with Saints and Duke Federico di Montefeltro.* The vibrant, animated frescoes by Bramante from the *Casa dei Panigarola* provide comic relief from the dramatic intensity of these works. A limited but well-chosen collection of works by modern masters including Modigliani and Carlo Carrà serves as an even more striking contrast. (Open Tues.-Sat. 9am-2pm, Sun. 9am-1pm. Admission L8000.)

The **Church of Santa Maria delle Grazie,** on P. di Sta. Maria delle Grazie and Corso Magenta off Via Carducci (MM1: Cairoli, or take bus #21 and 24), is renowned for the splendid tribune Bramante added in 1492. Inside, the Gothic nave with its tunnel-like vaults is juxtaposed with the airiness of the Bramante addition. To the left, a door leads to an elegant square cloister, the artist's other contribution to the church. (Open Mon.-Sat. 6:50am-noon and 3-7:30pm, Sun. 3-7:30pm.) Next to the church entrance in what was the monastery's refectory is the **Cenacolo Vinciano** (tel. 498 75 88), containing **Leonardo's Last Supper.** In late afternoon, the natural light that streams through the windows elegantly complements the lighting in the fresco. The fresco captures the apostles reaction to Jesus' prophecy that "One of you will betray me." Scaffolding for an eternal restoration project covers only the bottom of the fresco, leaving the rest in full view. (Open Tues.-Sun. 8:15am-1:45pm. Admission L6000. Wheelchair accessible.)

To further your study of Leonardo, explore the **Museo Nazionale della Scienza e della Tecnica "Leonardo da Vinci,"** Via San Vittore, 21 (tel. 48 01 00 40, MM1: San Ambrogio or bus #50 or 54), off Via Carducci. A large section is devoted to applied physics and a huge room is filled with wooden models of Leonardo's most ingenious and visionary inventions. Open Tues.-Sun. 9am-5pm. Admission L6000.)

The **Church of Sant'Ambrogio** (MM1: San Ambrogio), which served as a prototype for Lombard-Romanesque churches throughout Italy, is the most influential medieval building in Milan. Ninth-century reliefs in brilliant silver and gold decorate the high altar. The crypt contains the gruesome skeletal remains of Sant'Ambrogio and two early Christian martyrs. The tiny 4th-century **Chapel of San Vittore,** with exquisite 5th-century mosaics adorning its cupola, is through the seventh chapel on the right. As you leave the church on the left, you will pass under the peculiar **Portico della Canonica** (1492) by Bramante, the end columns of which have notches resembling those of tree trunks.

Continue your spiritual pilgrimage to the land of the dead. The vast grounds of the **Cimitero Monumentale**, several blocks east of Stazione Porta Garibaldi, are a labyrinthine network of three-story mausoleums in architectural styles ranging from Egyptian pyramids to art deco jukeboxes.

From Corso di Porta Romana to the Navigli

The distances between sights are greater here—consider public transportation.

At the **Church of San Nazaro Maggiore**, on Corso di Porta Romana (accessible from the *duomo* by tram #13), a medieval Lombard-Romanesque structure conceals the remnants of a 4th-century basilica. The Renaissance funerary chapel of the Trivulzio in front is the work of Bramante's pupil Bramantino (1512-1547). The tomb bears the famous epigraph: *Qui numquam quivit quiescit: Tasc* (he who never knew quiet now reposes: Silence). (Open daily 8:30am-noon and 3-6:30pm.)

The **Church of San Lorenzo Maggiore**, on Corso Ticinese (MM2: Porta Genova, then bus #59), the oldest church in Milan, testifies to the greatness of the city during the paleochristian era. The building began as an early Christian church in the mid-4th century, and although it was rebuilt later (12th-century *campanile* and 16th-century dome), it retains its original octagonal plan. On the four cardinal sides are large, semicircular screened spaces behind which runs an ambulatory, in the manner of San Vitale at Ravenna. To the right of the church sits the 14th-century chapel of Sant'Aquilino. Inside is a 4th-century mosaic of a young, beardless Christ among his apostles. A staircase behind the altar leads to the remains of an early Roman amphitheater. (Church open Mon.-Sat. 8am-noon and 3-6pm, Sun. 10:30-11:15am and 3-5:30pm.) Near the front of the church is the 12th-century **Porta Ticinese.**

Farther down Corso Ticinese (bus #15) stands the **Church of Sant'Eustorgio**, founded in the 4th century to house the reputed bones of the Magi, spirited off to Cologne in 1164. The present building (erected in 1278) has a typical Lombard-Gothic interior of low vaults and brick ribs supported by heavy columns. The real gem of this church, and one of the great masterpieces of early Renaissance art, is the **Portinari Chapel** (1468), attributed to the Florentine Michelozzo (L500 to open the gates in the back of the apse). A *Dance of Angels* is carved around the base of the multicolored dome, and frescoes depict the life and death of Peter the Martyr. In the center of the chapel is the magnificent Gothic tomb of St. Eustorgius (1339), sculpted by Giovanni di Balduccio of Pisa. (Church open daily 8am-noon and 3-7pm.)

Through the neoclassical Arco di Porta Ticinese (1801-1814) or outside the Porta Genova station (MM2), you will find the **navigli district**, the Amsterdam of Italy: canals, small footbridges, open-air markets, picturesque alleys, and trolleys. This is the part of the medieval canal system (whose original locks were designed by da Vinci) that linked northern cities and lakes.

South and East of the Duomo

One of the largest constructions of the early Renaissance is the 1456 **Ospedale Maggiore** on Via Festa del Perdono near P. Santo Stefano. The "General Hospital"—now the University of Milan—contains nine courtyards. Inside is a magnificent 17th-century court and a gracious smaller one credited to Bramante. In 1479, Bramante designed the mystical **Church of San Satiro** on Via Torino, a few blocks (or a few minutes ride on bus #15) from the *duomo*. Despite its modest proportions, the interior creates the illusion of wide spaces. Compare the imaginary and the real by standing at the back of the church and then behind the high altar.

Following Via Spadari off Via Torino and then making a right onto Via Cantù will deposit you at the lilliputian but lovely **Pinacoteca Ambrosiana**, P. Pio XI, 2 (tel. 80 01 46). The 14 rooms of the Ambrosiana house exquisite works from the 15th through 17th centuries, including Botticelli's *Madonna of the Canopy,* Leonardo's *Portrait of a Musician,* Raphael's cartoon for the *School of Athens,* Caravaggio's *Basket of Fruit,* the first example of still-life painting in Italy, and the two paintings of *Earth* and *Air* by Breughel. (Open Sun.-Fri. 9:30am-5pm.)

East of the *duomo,* **Corso Vittorio Emanuele,** between P. del Duomo and P. San Babila, is the major shopping street of the city. The street was entirely rebuilt after the war. Off P. San Babila, **Via Monte Napoleon,** the most elegant street in Milan, is lined with early 19th-century *palazzi* and late 20th-century Armanis and Cardins. The part of **Corso Venezia** bordering the Giardini Pubblici is a broad boulevard lined with sumptuous palaces. Don't miss a stroll through the English-style **Giardini Pubblici** on a sunny afternoon. (Open roughly 7am-10pm.) A small zoo lies within the grounds (open 9:30am-5pm).

The **Galleria d'Arte Moderna,** Via Palestro, 16 (tel. 70 23 78), is next to the Giardini Pubblici in the neoclassical Villa Comunale (MM2: Porta Venezia). Napoleon lived here with Josephine when Milan was capital of the Napoleonic Kingdom of Italy (1805-1814). Important modern Lombard art is displayed here, as well as works by Picasso, Matisse, Renoir, Gauguin, and Cézanne. (Open Wed.-Mon. 9:30am-12:15pm and 2:30-5:30pm. Free.) Another worthwhile museum is the **Museo di Milano** (tel. 70 62 45) on Via Sant'Andrea, 6, which shows Italian art and shares an 18th-century mansion with the petite **Museo di Storia Contemporanea** (Museum of Contemporary History; tel. 76 00 62 45; MM2: San Babila). (Both open daily 9:30am-5:30pm. Free.) Also check out the **Museo Civico di Storia Naturale** (Museum of Natural History) on Corso Venezia, 55, in the Giardino Pubblico (tel. 62 08 54 05). This quarters extensive geology and paleontology collections, including a room of complete dinosaur skeletons. (Open daily 9:30am-5:30 pm. Free.)

ENTERTAINMENT

Music and Theater

Emblematic of the pastiche of populism and posh that characterizes the arts scene in Milan is the **Musica in Metro** program, a series of summer concerts performed by local music students dressed in their black-tie best in subway stations. These kids probably hope to perform someday at **La Scala,** which traditionally opens its season on December 7. Though good tickets are usually sold out long in advance, gallery seats (notorious for inducing altitude sickness) go for as little as L30,000. (Box office tel. 72 00 37 44 or 80 960, open Tues.-Sun. 10am-1pm and 3:30-5:30pm. On performance days tickets go on sale 5:30-9:30pm. Unsold gallery seats and standing room are available 1hr. before curtain.) The **Conservatorio,** Via del Conservatorio, 12 (tel. 76 00 17 55 or 76 00 18 54), near P. Tricolore, offers more classical music, while the **Teatro Lirico,** Via Rastrelli, 6 (tel. 80 00 46), south of the *duomo,* is Milan's leading stage, offering everything from ballet to avant-garde plays. (Ticket office open Mon.-Sat. 10:30am-6:30pm; admission from L20,000). Summer brings special programs of music and culture: **Milano d'Estate** (Milan in Summer) in July, and **Vacanze a Milano** (Vacation in Milan) in August.

The **Piccolo Teatro,** Via Rovello, 2 (tel. 87 76 63), near Via Dante, began in the post-war years as a socialist theater and is now owned by the city. (Performances Tues.-Sun. nights.) **Ciak,** Via Sangallo, 33 (tel. 71 34 01), near P. Argonne east of the *duomo,* is a favorite haunt of young *milanesi* for theater, films, and occasionally cabaret. Take train #5 from Stazione Centrale to Viale Argonne.

The **Teatro di Porta Romana,** Corso di Porta Romana, 124 (tel. 518 11 26 or 518 11 44; bus #13 from Via Marconi off P. del Duomo), is building a reputation for experimental productions and first-run, mainstream plays (admission about L20,000). In what has become an annual project, the **Teatro dell' Elfo,** Via Ciro Menotti, 11 (tel. 71 67 91), sponsors the **Festival dei Festival,** showcasing the best of the many local theater festivals staged throughout Italy. (Performances throughout July. Admission about L25,000.) For a different brand of street theater, the **Carnivale** in Milan is increasingly popular. As the crowds in Venice sport fewer costumes and more cameras each year, many come here instead for the friendlier atmosphere. Tickets for all performances are sold at the corresponding venue but can also be purchased through **La Biglietteria,** Corso Garibaldi, 81 (tel. 659 01 88 or 659 89 56).

Movies

Milan's cinematic scene thrives. Check any Milanese paper (especially the Thursday edition) for showings and general information. Between late June and late August, the **Cinema nel Parco** festival offers outdoor showings of recent films (L3000). Old movies can be seen at the **Cineteca Italiana/Museo del Cinema,** Via Manin, 2/B (tel. 79 92 24, open Mon.-Fri. 3-6:30pm, admission L3000).

Clubs

The **Navigli** and **Porta Ticinese** areas, once home to prostitutes and black-marketeers, are now alive with clubs, *birrerie* (beer halls), and *paninoteche* (sandwich bars). Another safe, attractive, and chic district lies by **Via Brera;** here you'll find art galleries, small clubs, and restaurants.

Rock and all that's Hot: After Bologna, Milan supports the best rock scene in Italy. **Rolling Stone,** Corso XXII Marzo, 32 (tel. 738 10 00), east of the *duomo.* Easy on hip and heavy on chic. Cover L20,000 (1 beer included). Open Thurs.-Sun. until 3am. **Plastic** (officially **Il Killer Plastico**), is close to Viale Umbria, 120. Verging on disco, it swings between a punk/new wave and a fashionable New York crowd. Cover L15,000, Sat. L18,000. Open Tues.-Sun. until 3am. **Bella Epoque,** P. XXIV Maggio, 8 (MM2: Porta Genova, then bus #59). Come here for a quick Beatles fix. Open Fri.-Sun. until 3am. **New Magazine,** Strada Via Piceno, 3 (tel. 73 09 41). Close to Rolling Stone and Plastico. Crunchy atmosphere accentuated by peanut shells on the floor softens the bright orange and yellow neon paintings. Busier in winter. Cover Fri. L12,000, Sat. L15,000. Closed Mon.

Jazz and Folk: Capolinea, Via Ludovico il Moro, 119. Walk out Corso Italia toward the Navigli and Porta Ticinese, south of the *duomo.* A student crowd. Open Tues.-Sun. until 1:30am. **Le Scimmie,** Via Ascanio Sforza, 49, beyond the Capolinea. Milan's premier jazz spot. Open daily 8pm-2am. **Biblo's,** Via Madonnina, 17, in the Brera area, welcomes folk performers. Open daily. Admission L10,000-15,000.

Discos: Gimmi's (formerly called USA), Via B. Cellini, 2 (tel. 540 09 58), near Corso Porta Vittoria. One of Milan's top discos, a beautiful people club and suitably expensive. Cover L30,000 (includes first drink). Open Wed.-Sun. 10:30pm-3:30am. **American Disaster,** Via Boscovich, 48, near Stazione Centrale. Disasterously tacky (don your glow-in-the-dark shirts), but less expensive. Open Thurs.-Sat. **No Ties,** Foro Buonaparte, 68. A chic, both gay and straight place with a long line at the door. Cover L10,000-12,000, Wed. 2-for-1 admission. Open Wed.-Sun. 10pm-3am. **Nuova Idea,** Via de Castillia, 30 (MM2: Gioia). A huge and notably gay hangout, famous throughout Italy. Cover L8000-10,000. Open Tues. and Thurs.-Sun. 9:30pm-1 or 2am. **Contatto,** Corso Sempione, 76 (MM1: Cairoli, then bus #57), behind the Castello Sforzesco. A gay club.

Neither Fish nor Fowl: Zimba ("lion" in Swahili), Via Besenzanico, 3 (tel. 40 091 90). Has shocked xenophobes by becoming one of the city's biggest hangouts. Conga, rhythm and blues, and Carribean music. Open Thurs.-Sat. 10:30pm-3am. **Magia Music Meeting,** Via Salutati, 2 (MM2: San Agostino). New bands looking for a break start out here. Go for dinner while you listen (about L8000). Open daily until 3am.

SHOPPING

Milan's most elegant boutiques are found between the *duomo* and P. S. Babila, especially on the excessively chic **Via Monte Napoleone.** If you can tolerate the stigma of being an entire *season* behind the trends, famous designer brands may be purchased from **blochisti** (wholesale clothing outlets). Try **Monitor** on Viale Monte Nero (MM2: Porta Genova, then bus #9), or **Il Salvagente,** on Via Bronzetti off Corso XXII Marzo (bus #60). More affordable, yet still well-designed, is the clothing sold along **Corso Buenos Aires,** and both **Via Torino,** near the *duomo,* and **Via Sarpi,** near Porta Garibaldi, are decked out in inexpensive department stores and boutiques catering to a younger crowd. Shop around the area of Corso di Porta

Ticinese for *chic ma non snob* (hip) attire (MM2: Porta Genova, then bus #59). **Eliogabalo,** P. Sant' Eustorgio, 2 (tel. 837 82 93), named after a Roman Emperor renowned for his preoccupation with matters sartorial, offers the latest in *haute couture*. Reasonable prices for everything from clothes to groceries can be found at the **STANDA** department store at Via Torino, 37 (tel. 86 67 06), five blocks from the *duomo*. Photo booth (L3000), photocopy machine (L200), and shoe repair on the third floor. (Open Tues.-Sun. 9am-7:30pm and Mon 2-7:30 pm.) True Milanese bargain hunters attack the giant street markets on Saturday and Tuesday to buy their threads. These are on **Via Fauché** (MM2: Garibaldi), **Viale Papinian** (MM2: Sant'A-gostino) and the 400-year-old **Fiera di Sinigallia** on Via Calatafimi (Sat. only). For used clothing try the Navigli district or Corso Garibaldi. Shop at the end of July for the pre-Ferragosto sale wars (20-50% off). (Clothing stores are generally open Mon. 10am-noon, Tues.-Sat. 10am-noon and 2-7:30pm.)

■ Pavia

The Pavia of today has returned to a state of prosperity with the help of agricultural and industrial development. Romanesque churches dating from Pavia's tranquil years as a Milanese satellite are scattered throughout the historic sector, and the 14th-century university continues to flourish. The once-prominent city's status as an offbeat tourist locale is evinced by the confidence with which non-Italians persevere in mispronouncing its name (hint: emphasize the second syllable).

Once an important Roman outpost, Pavia weathered Attila the Hun in 452 before entering the limelight as the Lombard capital during the 7th and 8th centuries. Spanish, Austrian, and French forces governed Pavia in rapid succession from the 16th century until 1859, when Italy's movement for national independence—a particular concern for Pavia—liberated the city.

ORIENTATION AND PRACTICAL INFORMATION

Pavia is a mere 35km south of Milan, on the train line to Genoa (30min.). The city sits on the banks of the Ticino river not far from its intersection with the Po. The train station overlooks **Piazzale Stazionale** in the modern, west end of the town, which is linked to the historic center by **Corso Cavour.**

Tourist Office: Via F. Filzi, 2 (tel. 22 156; fax 32 221), in a characterless section of town. Take a left on Via Trieste from station and then right on Filzi. Good city map. Ask for the booklet *Pavia and its Province*. Open Mon.-Sat. 9am-12:30pm and 2:30-6pm.

Post Office: P. della Posta, 2 (tel. 21 251), off Via Mentana, 1 block over from Corso Mazzini. Stamps and Fermo Posta at #5. Open Mon.-Sat. 8am-7pm. **Postal code:** 27100.

Telephones: SIP, Via Galliano, 8 (tel. 30 45 11), around the corner from the post office. Open Mon.-Sat. 9am-12:30pm and 2:30-7:30pm, Sun. 9am-2pm. **Telephone code:** 0382.

Trains: at the head of Viale V. Emanuele II at the western end of town (tel. 230 00). To: Genoa (every ½hr., L8800); Milan (every hr., L3200); Cremona (4 per day, L5700); Mantua (1 per day, L10,500). **Luggage Storage:** L1500. Open 7am-9pm.

Buses: SGEA (tel. 302 020), departing from the new space-age station on Via Trieste (left from the train station). To Milan (every hr., 6am-10pm, 50min., L4100) via the *certosa* (charterhouse, 10min., L1800).

Taxi: tel. 314 71.

Swimming Pool: Via Mascherpa, 10 (tel. 52 53 62). Via Folperti (tel. 46 95 52).

Pharmacy: tel. 29 748.

Emergencies: tel. 113. **Police:** P. Italia, 5 (tel. 112). **Hospital: Ospedale S. Matteo,** P. Golgi, 2 (tel. 38 81). **Medical Assistance:** tel. 39 01, nights and holidays tel. 52 76 00.

ACCOMMODATIONS

A dearth of reasonably priced places to stay makes Pavia most appealing as a daytrip.
Inquire at the tourist office about the current condition of the youth hostel at Vagh-
era.

Hotel Splendid, Via XX Settembre, 11 (tel. 24 703), off Corso Cavour near P. del
Duomo. Indeed ironic, but the Splendid is the last of Pavia's one-stars that has not
been converted to student housing. Clean sheets and floors, white-washed walls
and slightly mildewy shower. Singles L30,000. Doubles L54,000.

Camping: Ticino, Via Mascherpa, 10 (tel. 52 53 62). Walk down Viale Vittorio
Emanuele II from the station. At the statue of Athena, the wise thing to do is turn
right and cross the bridge. Swimming pool. L6200 per person, L4000 per tent.

FOOD

Coniglio (rabbit) and *rana* (frog) are the local specialties, but if you don't eat things
that hop, stick to the local pastries on display in shop windows along Corsos Cavour
and Mazzini. **Esselunga** is an intimidatingly oversized supermarket at the far end of
the mall complex between Via Trieste and Viale Batisti (open Tues.-Sat. 8am-8pm,
Mon. 1-8pm).

Trattoria da Andrea, Via Teodolina, 23 (tel. 24 210), off P. del Duomo. A homey
room saturated with tantalizing smells. The brothers in charge perfected their art
long ago. *Menù* L16,000. Pasta around L6000. Wine L8000-16,000 per bottle.
Open Sat.-Thurs. noon-3pm and 6:30-11pm.

Ristorante Pizzeria Marechiaro, P. Vittoria, 9 (tel. 23 739). Delicious pizza with
exquisite crust, prepared before your eyes, for L5000-9000. Crowded, cozy atmosphere. Summertime diners overflow onto the piazza. Cover L2000. Open Tues.-
Sun. 11am-3pm and 7pm-3am.

Gelateria de Cesare, Corso Garibaldi, 15c (tel. 25 074), parallel to Corso Mazzini
on the river side. The pride and glory of Pavia's *gelato* connoisseurs, this modest
cubbyhole has none of the glitz of its competitors, but scoops out mighty fine
gelato. Open Sept.-July Tues.-Sun. 9am-midnight.

SIGHTS AND ENTERTAINMENT

For centuries the **Church of San Michele** (tel. 26 063) was the favored venue for
coronations of Northern Italian kings, including Charlemagne in 774 and Frederick
Barbarossa in 1155. The original 7th-century church was entirely rebuilt in the
Romanesque style at the end of the 11th century. Decorating the chancel are a 1491
fresco of the *Coronation of the Virgin* and bas-reliefs from the 14th century. The
8th-century silver crucifix of Theodote graces the chapel to the right of the presbytery. To get to San Michele, go down Corso Garibaldi and turn right after Via della
Rochetta. (Open Tues.-Sat. 9-11:30am and 2:30-6:30pm, Sun. 9am-noon.)

From San Michele it's a short walk to what's left of Pavia's layered brick **duomo.**
The **Torre Civica,** adjoining the *duomo,* collapsed in the spring of 1989, killing several people and taking with it a good portion of the *duomo's* left-hand chapel, as
well as some nearby houses and shops. Disputes over what ought to be done with
the rubble have led to a lackadaisical restoration, and the piazza is still garnished
with barricades and scaffolding. The shaky brick exterior of the *duomo,* recently
reinforced by concrete columns, conceals an impressive interior. Begun in 1488 and
influenced by the designs of Bramante, Macaluso, and Leonardo, the *duomo* was
one of the most ambitious undertakings of the Renaissance in Lombardy—naturally,
much of it was not actually completed until 1895-1933. The huge interior space in
the form of a Greek cross is typical of a Renaissance central-plan church.

The prestigious **University of Pavia,** founded in 1361 (tel. (382) 38 71), sprawls
along strada Nuova. It claims such famous alumni as Petrarch, Columbus, and the
Venetian playwright Goldoni. The university's most electrifying exponent, however, was the physicist Alessandro Volta (his experiments are on display at the uni-

versity). And the patron of the university, Galeazzo II of Visconti, earned notoriety for his research into human torture. The three towers rising from the university's property on P. Leonardo da Vinci are vestiges of the more than 100 medieval towers that once pierced the city's skyline, and as of summer 1993 were scaffolded on account of the city's understandable concern with structural failure.

Strada Nuova ends at the **Castello Visconteo** (tel. 33 853), a colossal medieval castle (1360) set in a park that once extended to the Certosa di Pavia, the Visconti's private hunting ground 8km away. The castle's vast courtyard is bordered on three sides by richly colored windows and elegant terracotta decoration. The fourth wall was destroyed in 1527 during the Franco-Spanish Wars. Pavia's **Civic Museum** (tel. 33 853), located here, houses a picture gallery and an extensive Lombard-Romanesque sculpture collection. (Open June-Nov. Tues.-Sat. 9am-1:30pm, Sun. 9am-1pm. Off-season Tues.-Sat. 9am-1:30pm. Admission L5000.)

From the front grounds of the castle, you can see the low rounded forms of the **Church of San Pietro in Ciel d'Oro** (tel. 30 30 36). Another exquisite example of the Lombard-Romanesque style, it was consecrated in 1132. Inside on the high altar is a marble reliquary containing the remains of St. Augustine in an ornate Gothic ark. (Open daily 7am-noon and 3-7:30pm.)

Near Pavia

Eight kilometers north of Pavia stands the **Certosa di Pavia** (Charterhouse of Pavia; tel. 92 56 13. Ask to speak with polyglot Padre Tebreab). Both buses and trains can deposit you nearby. **Buses** leave Pavia from P. Piave opposite the station (L1500) and Milan from P. Castello (L3000). From the bus stop, the *certosa* awaits you at the end of a long road lined by trees. From the **train** station, go to the left around the outside wall of the monastic complex and turn inside to the right at the first opening. This Carthusian monastery and mausoleum was built for the Visconti who ruled the area from the 12th to 15th centuries, and summarizes four centuries of Italian art, from early Gothic to Baroque. The exuberant façade (late 1400s-1560) revels in sculpture and inlaid marble, representing the apex of the Lombard Renaissance. The Old Sacristy houses a Florentine triptych carved in ivory, with 99 sculptures and 66 bas-reliefs depicting the lives of Mary and Jesus.

The monks lead delightful tours of the complex whenever a large enough group has gathered (usually every 45min.), leaving from inside the church. (Open Tues.-Sun. 9-11:30am and 2:30-6pm, March-April. and Sept.-Oct. Tues.-Sun. 9-11:30am and 2:30-5pm, Nov.-Feb. Tues.-Sun. 9-11:30am and 2:30-4:30pm. Free.)

■ Cremona

Agriculturally prosperous Cremona is home to some of the most remarkable architecture in Lombardy. For the past 500 years, however, it has been Cremona's musical contributions that have made the world take note. In 1530, Andrea Amati created the violin and established the Cremonese violin-making dynasty. Having learned the fundamentals as apprentices in the Amati workshop, Antonio Stradivari (1644-1737) and Giuseppe Guarneri (1687-1745) lifted the art of violin-making to unprecedented heights. Students from all over the world still come to learn the legendary craft at the International School for Violin-Making, ever hopeful of stumbling upon the formula of Stradivari's secret varnish. Though Cremona's earth-toned buildings create a somewhat sober atmosphere, its continuing interest in all things musical and an ever-active concert season at the Ponchielli Theater lend the city a more than compensatory dose of color and life.

ORIENTATION AND PRACTICAL INFORMATION

En route from the train station to the cluster of *piazze* at the city's historical core **Via Palestro** first becomes **Via Campi** and then **Via Verdi**. A left at Piazza Cavour or Piazza Pace leads to the **Piazza del Comune.** If the 15-min. walk doesn't appeal to you, jump on bus #1 (L1200). Most Cremonese desert the city in July and August.

Tourist Office: P. del Duomo, 5 (tel. 23 233). The staff is obliging, but English not necessarily spoken. Open Mon.-Sat. 9:30am-12:30pm and 2:30-9pm.
Post Office: Via Verdi, 1 (tel. 22 619). Open Mon.-Fri. 8am-7pm, Sat. 8am-1pm. **Postal Code:** 26100.
Telephones: SIP, P. Cavour, 1 (tel. 23 911). Open Mon.-Sat. 9am-12:30pm and 2:30-7:30pm, Sun. 9am-1pm. **Telephone Code:** 0372.
Trains: Via Dante, 68 (tel. 22 237). Ask for P. Stazione. To: Milan (9 per day, 1hr. 30min., L72,500); Pavia (4 per day, 1hr. 15min., L6200); Mantua (15 per day, 1hr., L5300); and Brescia (12 per day, 45min., L4700).
Buses: Autostazione di Via Dante (tel. 29 212), to left of the train station. To Milan (7 per day, 2hr., L5500); Bergamo (5 per day, L7300); and Brescia (almost every hr., L5000). Tickets at **La Pasticceria Mezzadri,** Via Dante, 105 (tel. 25 708), or at the station, open 7:20am-1pm and 2:15-6:30pm.
Emergencies: tel. 113. **Police: Sicurezza Pubblica,** Via Tribunali, 6 (tel. 48 81). **Medical Assistance:** tel. 37 74. **Hospital: Ospedale** (tel. 40 51), past P. IV Novembre to the east.

ACCOMMODATIONS AND FOOD

While lodging runs cheap in Cremona, it can be difficult to find a room, especially during the week. If you want to stay, reserve far ahead in summer.

Albergo Touring, Via Palestro, 3 (tel. 21 390). From the station, walk across Via Dante and straight down Via Palestro. Singles L30,000. Doubles L37,000
Albergo Brescia, Via Brescia, 7 (tel. 43 46 15). An unpleasant 20-min. walk to the left down Via Dante and a left at P. Libertà, or take bus #1, 3, 4, or 6 from the station. Nice management and functional rooms that are booked solid during the week. Singles L40,000. Doubles L50,000. Open Aug. 10-July 10.
Albergo Bologna, P. Risorgimento, 8 (tel. 24 258). Very small singles only. L25,000. Open Aug.-first week of July.
Camping: Parco al Po (tel. 27 137), on Via Lungo Po Europa southwest of town. From P. Cavour, walk 20min. down Corso Vittorio Emanuele. L4900 per person, L4200 per tent. Electricity L1500. Open May-Sept.

First whipped up in the 16th century, Cremona's bizarre *mostarda di Cremona,* consists of a hodgepodge of fruits—cherries, figs, apricots, melons—preserved in a sweet mustard syrup and served on boiled meats. Bars of *torrone* (nougat with an egg, honey, and nut base) are less adventurous but equally steeped in Cremonese confectionary lore. *Mostarda* can be found in most local *trattorie,* while *torrone* can be purchased in the sweet shops on Via Solferino. **Spelari,** at Via Solferino, 25, has been keeping dentists in business since 1836 (*torrone*) L11,000. (Open Tues.-Sat. 8:30am-12:30pm and 3:30-7:30pm, Mon. 8:30am-12:30pm.) On Wednesday and Saturday from 8am-1pm, an **open-air market** in P. Marconi, past P. Cavour on Corso Verdi. Two **supermarkets** compete on P. Risorgimento (open 8am-12:45pm and 4-7:45pm).

Italmense Agnello Ristorante, Via Vianello Torriani, 7 (tel. 22 119), off Via Boccaccio north of the *duomo.* Popular with students and office workers. Pasta L3000. *Secondi* L5500. Open Mon.-Fri. noon-2pm. Closed 2 weeks in Aug.
Pizzeria allo Stagnino, Corso Garibaldi, 85 (tel. 39 153), at Via Oberdan. Bronzed soccer players come here after games. In their absence, relative calm prevails. Pizzas L6-10,000. *Coperto* L2000. Open Wed.-Mon. 10am-2:30pm and 6pm-2am.
La Bersagliera, P. Risorgimento (tel. 21 397). Cremonese *cognoscenti* lavish praise on this family-owned establishment. Pizzas L10,000. Wine L7000 per carafe. Cover L2000. Open Fri.-Wed. noon-2:30pm and 6:30-10pm.

SIGHTS AND ENTERTAINMENT

Violins and their production are the primary attraction in Cremona. Closest to the train station, the small **Museo Stradivariano,** at Via Palestro, 17 (tel. 29 349), provides a fascinating introduction to the art of Stradivari and his contemporaries. (Open Tues.-Sat. Admission L5000, includes the Museo Civico around the corner and the Violin Room.) On the second floor of the **Palazzo del Comune** in P. del Comune, decorated with 16th-century Renaissance terra-cottas, the **Saletta dei Violini (Violin Room)** showcases five masterpieces attributed to Andrea Amati, his grandson Nicolò Amati, Stradivari, and Guarneri. (Open June to mid-Aug. Mon.-Sat. 7am-noon and 3-7pm, Sun. 9am-6pm; mid-Sept. to May Mon.-Fri. 9am-noon and 3-6:45pm, Sat.-Sun. 9am-noon. Hours sometimes change according to the whims of the guard. Admission L5000—includes Museo Civico, too.)

Directly facing the *palazzo* is the 12th-century pink marble **duomo,** a fine example of the Lombard-Romanesque style. The interior houses a cycle of 16th-century frescoes. (Open Mon.-Sat. 7am-noon and 3-7pm, Sun. 7am-1pm and 3:30-7pm.) To the left of the cathedral stands the late 13th-century **Torrazzo,** at 108m the tallest campanile in Italy. (Scale the heights mid-March to Oct. Mon.-Sat. 10:30am-noon and 3-6pm, Sun. 10:30am-12:30pm and 3-7pm. Admission L5000.) The dome of the solid 1167 **baptistry** rises in a perfect, unadorned octagonal pattern to a small oculus. (Open daily 9am-12:30pm and 3-7pm. Closed for restoration in 1993.) The **Loggia dei Militi,** across from the baptistry, completes the square. Erected in 1292 in Gothic style, it functioned as a meeting place for the captains of the citizens' militia. The Gothic **Church of Sant'Agostino** (1345), near Via Plasio, contains Bonifacio Bembo frescoes and a *Madonna with Saints* by Perugino (1494).

Cremona is also endowed with fine Renaissance buildings, including the **Palazzo Fodri** (1499) at Corso Matteotti, 17. The columns in the courtyard bear French royal insignias in homage to Louis XII of France, who occupied the duchy of Milan in 1499. The **Palazzo Affaitati** (1561), Via Ugolani Dati, 4, flaunts an impressive grand staircase of marble that leads to the **Museo Civico** (tel. 29 349), with Caravaggio's San Francesco contemplating a *memento mori* (skull), as well as 15th-century codices which recall Renaissance politics. (Hours and prices same as at Museo Stradivariano. Entrance included with admission to Museum.)Take Via Ghisleri from P. della Libertà or bus #2 from P. Cavour to the remarkable 15th-century **Church of San Sigismondo** on Via Marmolada. When the Milanese duchess Bianca Maria Visconti wed Francesco Sforza, her family presented this church as her dowry.

Cremona is alive with the sound of music all year long. **Cremona Jazz** in March and April eases the way into the summer season with a series of concerts throughout the city (tickets begin at L12,000). **Cremona Rock** gets serious at the stadium at the end of June, and they'll be dancing in the streets with **Salotto in Piazza,** evenings in June and July when P. del Comune becomes an outdoor piano bar. On a more sedate note, **Luglio in Musica** is a series of free concerts of sacred works . The September **Festival di Cremona** kicks off the Teatro Ponchielli fall season with a classical series heavy on the strings (tickets L20,000-25,000), and it all reaches a crescendo with the **opera season,** from mid-October through early December (tickets begin at L18,000). For ticket information on the Festival contact the Teatro Ponchielli ticket booth at Corso Vittorio Emanuele, 52 (tel. 40 72 73; open daily 4-7pm).

■ Mantua (Mantova)

Despite a bit of fame as the home town of Virgil, Mantua's early years as a Roman colony passed by in relative obscurity. After enduring periods of domination, Mantua achieved sudden glory in 1328 with the unexpected ascension of the Gonzaga family, which sprouted from peasant roots to become one of the most formidable Renaissance dynasties. In the years that followed, the Gonzagas zealously sought to obliterate any taint of provincialism by importing known artists and cultivating whatever promising talent existed locally. Alberti designed their churches of San Sebastiano and Sant'Andrea, Monteverdi spun madrigals for their pleasure, and Mantegna painstakingly applied his paints to their palace walls. Today's industrial eyesores sprawl along the outskirts of the modern city, but the historic center preserves much of the unhurried rustic flavor its rulers sought so fiercely to repudiate.

ORIENTATION AND PRACTICAL INFORMATION

A few kilometers north of the Po, Mantua is girded on three sides by the torpid waters of the Minro lagoons, producing a stubby, peninsular projection in which the better part of the historic center is concentrated. The unrestricted land at the far end has given way to modern expansion. The train station lies a 10-min. walk along Via Solferino e S. Martino and Via Fratelli Bandiera if you embark from Mantua's three central *piazze:* P. Mantegna, P. Concordia, and P. Marconi.

Tourist Office: P. Mantegna, 6 (tel. 35 06 81, fax 36 32 92), adjacent to the church of Sant'Andrea. From the train station take a left on Via Solferino through P. S. Francesco to Via Fratelli Bandiera and turn right on Via Verdi. Ask for *Mantova e la Festa Padana,* a calendar of events in the province, and ask about **agriturismo** lodgings, around L20,000 a night. Open Mon.-Sat. 9am-noon and 3-6pm.

Currency Exchange: Banks are a dime a dozen. **Banca Nazionale del Lavoro,** P. Cavallotti, 3, where Corso Vittorio Emanuele II becomes Corso Umberto, has dependable rates and cash advances on Visa. Open Mon.-Wed. and Fri. 8:20am-1:20pm and 3-4:30pm, Thurs. 8:20am-5:50pm.

Post Office: P. Martiri Belfiore, 15 (tel. 32 64 03 or 32 71 43), up Via Roma from the tourist office. Open Mon.-Fri. 8am-7pm, Sat. 8:20am-1:20pm. **Postal code:** 46100.

Telephones: SIP, Via Corridoni, 13 (tel. 32 77 11 or 187 33 21). Open Mon.-Fri. 8:30am-noon and 2-4:30pm. **Telephone code:** 0376.

Trains: P. Don Leoni (tel. 32 16 46), at the end of Via Solferino e S. Martino, southwest of town. To: Cremona (every hr., 45min., L8600); Verona (every hr., 40min., L5400); and Milan (6 per day, 2hr. 30min., L20,600). **Luggage Storage** L1500, open 6:10am-9:15pm.

Buses: APAM P. Mondadori (tel. 32 72 37), across and to the right as you leave the train station. Cross Corso Vittorio Emanuele II to Via Caduti. Buses to Brescia (15 per day, 4hr., L6000). Tickets sold Mon.-Sat. 7am-1:15pm and 3-7:15pm.

Bike Rental: Ferrari Umberto, Via Conciliazione, 6 (tel. 92 30 92), off Corso Vittorio Emanuele II near the bus station. L2500 per hr., L12,000 per day. Open Tues.-Sat. 8:30-11:15am and 3-7pm, Mon. 3-7pm.

Emergencies: tel. 113. **Police:** P. Sordello, 46 (tel. 32 63 41). **Hospital: Ospedale Civile,** Viale Albertoni, 1-3 (tel. 32 92 61 or 36 82 51).

ACCOMMODATIONS AND FOOD

Ostello Sparafucile (HI) (tel. 37 24 65), in the nearby hamlet of Lunetta di San Giorgio. From the train station, exit to your right and walk left down Corso Vittorio Emanuele to P. Cavallotti (5min.), then take bus #2 or 9 (L1200) from in front of the UPIM and get off near the gas station (hostel is on the left). Or, walk through P. Sordello along Via S. Giorgio Via Legnano to the stone tower at the far end (1km). Lovingly restored 16th-century tollbooth. Lockout 9am-4pm. Curfew 11pm. HI card required. L14,000 per person. Open April-Oct. 15.

Locanda La Rinascita, Via Concezione, 4 (tel. 32 06 07), near P. Virgiliana. From the train station, walk left on Viale Pitentino (15min.), then right on Via Zappetto, which intersects with Via Concezione. Breezy, reasonably clean rooms and. Gossip can be passed easily from balcony to balcony. Singles L25,000. Doubles L40,000. Reserve 4 or 5 days in advance.

Albergo Roma Vecchia, Via Corridoni, 20 (tel. 32 21 00), down from P. Belfiore. Another entrance around the corner at Via Buozzi, 1. Large, clean rooms with good mattresses. Doubles L42,000, with bath L55,000. Towels L2000. Open Aug. 23-Dec. 19 and Jan. 4-July 31.

Camping: Sparafucile tel. 37 24 65, next to the youth hostel. In a comfortable setting. L4000 per person, L3500 per tent. Cold showers included. Hot showers L1000. Light L2500. Breakfast served in the adjoining hostel at 7:30am.

Self-Service Virgiliana, P. Virgiliana, 57 (tel. 32 23 77). From P. Sordello, take Via Fratelli Cairoli to P. Virgiliana. On the left corner of the piazza. A clean *mensa* with excellent values. Full meals under L11,000. Open Mon.-Fri. noon-2pm.

MANTUA

Ai Ranari, Via Trieste, 11 (tel. 32 84 31), the continuation of Via Pomponazzo, near Porto Catena. A slightly more chic place specializing in regional dishes. *Primi* L7000-8000, *secondi* L9000-14,000. Don't leave without trying the Mantuan delight of *tortelli di zucca* (L7500). Wine L8000 per carafe. *Coperto* L1500. Open Thurs.-Tues. noon-3:30pm and 7-11pm.

SIGHTS AND ENTERTAINMENT

Cobblestoned **Piazza Sordello** forms the center of a vast complex built by the Gonzaga. The **Palazzo Ducale** (tel. 32 02 83) dominates the piazza, a monument to Gonzagan "modesty." The 500 rooms and 15 courtyards, constructed over a period of 300 years (14th-17th centuries), now house an impressive collection of antique and Renaissance art. The **Magna Domus** and the **Captain's Palace,** two 14th-century Gothic structures, constitute the main part of the palace. Near the entrance is the Hall of Dukes where you'll find Antonio Pisanelli's frescoes (1439-44), discovered in 1969 under thick layers of plaster. The Gonzaga's Summer Room looks out onto a hanging garden (1579) bordered on three sides by a splendid portico. From the Paradise Chambers you enter the Dwarves' Apartments, tiny low rooms built as much to amuse the court as to house its substantial dwarf contingent. (Open Mon.-Sat. 9am-1pm and 2:30-6pm, Sun. 9am-1pm. Admission L10,000 lets you into everything in the Palazzo.)

Formerly a fortress, the **Castello di San Giorgio** (1390-1406) is the most formidable structure in the palace complex. It was converted into a wing of the palace. Andrea Mantegna's famed frescoes of the Gonzaga family (1474) in the **Camera degli Sposi** (Marriage Chamber) spin about the walls. (Open Tues.-Sat. 9am-pm and 2:30-5pm, Sun.-Mon. 9am-1pm. Admission L10,000.)

Despite its 18th-century façade, the **duomo** was conceived centuries earlier as revealed by the Romanesque campanile and the Gothic elements on its side. Its interior hails from the late Renaissance, but the baptistry below the campanile was frescoed in the 13th century. (Open daily 8:30am-12:30pm and 3:30-7:30pm.)

Piazza delle Erbe, just south of P. Sordello, opens onto the **Rotonda di San Lorenzo.** The circular, 11th-century Romanesque rotunda (rebuilt early this century) is also known as the Matildica for the powerful noblewoman who, expiring heirless, left the rotunda to the pope. Opposite the rotunda rises Mantua's most important Renaissance creation, Leon Battista Alberti's **Church of Sant'Andrea** (1471-1594). The façade combines the classical triumphal arch motif—barrel-vaulted portal and flanking pilasters—with an antique pedimented temple front. The gargantuan interior was the first monumental space constructed in classical style since imperial Rome. The plan—a vaulted church with a single aisle, flanking side chapels, and a domed crossing—served as a prototype for ecclesiastical architecture for the next 200 years.

The **Palazzo d'Arco** (tel. 32 22 42), off Viale Ritentino, is blessed with an extraordinary zodiac chamber by Fontanello. From P. Mantegna, follow Via Verdi to the *palazzo.* (Open Tues.-Wed. and Fri. 9am-noon, Thurs. and Sat.-Sun. 9am-noon and 3-5pm; Nov.-Feb. Sat.-Sun. 9am-noon and 2:30-4pm. Admission L4000.)

Contrast to the luxurious palaces and academies can be found at the spartan home of **Andrea Mantegna** on Via Acerbi, 47 (tel. 36 05 06). Built in 1476, it frequently hosts traveling exhibits. (Open 9am-12:30pm and 3-6pm. Free.) Opposite the house stands Alberti's **Church of San Sebastiano** (1460), whose Greek cross layout initiated the Renaissance propensity for centrally-planned churches.

A trek through P. Veneto and down Largo Parri leads to the opulent **Palazzo del Te** (tel. 32 32 66 or 36 58 86). Built by Giulio Romano in 1534 as a suburban retreat for Francesco II Gonzaga, it is widely regarded as the finest building of the Mannerist period. The rooms inside demonstrate the late Renaissance fascination with the Roman villa type, along with a willingness bend the rules of proportion and use of materials. Idyllic murals of Psyche, remarkable for their vividness and eroticism, fresco Francesco's banquet hall. Another wing of the palace features regular shows of modern Italian artists alongside a collection of Egyptian art. (Open Tues.-Sun. 10am-6pm. Admission L10,000, under 18, L4000.)

The **Teatro Sociale di Mantova,** P. Cavallotti (tel. 32 38 60), off Corso Vittorio Emanuele, stages operas in October and plays November through May. (Cheap seats around L20,000.) Some of the best productions in the country stop here, albeit only for a couple of nights. The **Spazio Aperto** series brings dance, music, and cinema events to various *piazze* and *palazzi* around town. Mantua also hosts a chamber music series in April and May. Most fun is the **Concorso di Madonnari** on August 15; the *madonnari,* street artists whose chalky madonnas wash away with the first rains, hold a competition in nearby Grazie di Curtatone.

Near Mantua

Make the trip to **Sabbioneta,** 33km southwest of Mantua, founded by Vespasiano Gonzaga (1532-91) as the home for his feudal court. Its importance as an artistic center in the late Renaissance earned it the title "Little Athens of the Gonzagas." Inside the well-preserved 16th-century city walls lie the **Ducal Palace,** the **Olympic Theater,** and the **Palazzo del Giardino,** all fascinating Renaissance structures. Only the guided walk enables you to visit the otherwise inaccessible interiors. The 45-min. tour in Italian (L8000) leaves roughly every 20min. from the **tourist office,** Via Gonzaga, 31 (tel. (0375) 52 039; open Tues.-Sat. 9am-noon and 2:30-5pm). In summer Sabbioneta stages a **Festival di Musica e Danza,** and from mid-March to mid-April antique aficionados come for the exhaustive **Mercato del Antiquariato.**

Sabbioneta's **Tourist Office** is located at Via Vespasiano Gonzaga, 31 (tel. (0375) 52 039). (Open daily 9am-noon and 2:30-6pm.)

■■■ BERGAMO

Bergamo, like the *Commedia dell'Arte* it fostered, is endowed with a multitude of personalities. A bustling commercial and industrial center, an artistic hot-spot, and a focal point of both history and legend, the city is divided physically and spiritually into two parts. The hilltop *città alta* recalls its medieval origins with narrow, cobblestone streets shaded by solemn ecclesiastic façades. The rapid-paced *città bassa* below is a temporal world apart, providing an intriguing juxtaposition of a Venetian fortress and a modern metropolis.

ORIENTATION AND PRACTICAL INFORMATION

Poised at the juncture of the Brembana and Seriana valleys, Bergamo is an easy train ride from Milan, Brescia, and Cremona. The train station, bus station, and budget hotels are all in the *città bassa.* To get to the more interesting *città alta*, take bus #1 or 3 (L1100) to the funicular, which ascends from Viale Vittorio Emanuele II to the Mercato delle Scarpe (every 15min., L1100), or walk up the old footpath to the city, starting from behind the funicular station on Viale Vittorio Emanuele II (10-20 min).

Tourist Office: APT (città bassa), Viale Papa Giovanni XXIII, 106 (tel. 24 22 26), straight ahead through P. Marconi from the train station, on the left. Open Mon.-Fri. 9am-12:30pm and 3-6pm. Weekends head to *città alta:* **APT,** Vicolo Aquila Nera, 2 (tel. 23 27 30), off P. Vecchia. Open daily 9am-12:30pm and 3-6:30pm.

Currency Exchange: Banca Nazionale del Lavoro, Via Petrarca, 12 (tel. 39 81 11), off Viale Vittorio Emanuele II near P. della Libertà. Good rates and Visa deals. Open Mon.-Tues. and Thurs.-Fri. 8:20am-1:20pm and 3-4:30pm, Wed. 8:20am-5:50pm. After-hrs. money exchange at **Hotel Excelsior San Marco,** P. della Repubblica, 6 (tel. 23 21 32), off Viale Vittorio Emanuele II. Cash only.

Post Office: Via Masone, 2A (tel. 21 22 70), at Via Locatelli. Take Via Lelasco from Viale Vittorio Emanuele II. Stamps and Fermo Posta at #7. Open Mon.-Fri. 8:15am-8pm, Sat. 8:30am-1pm. **Postal Code:** 24122.

Telephones: SIP, Largo Porta Nuova, 1 (tel. 21 92 95), where Viale Papa Giovanni XXIII becomes Viale Vittorio Emanuele II. Open Mon.-Sat. 9am-12:30pm and 2:30-

7pm., Sun. 9am-1pm. After hours, go to **Hotel Cappelle d'Oro,** Via Papa Giovanni XXIII, 12 (tel. 21 83 65). In *città alta,* try **Caffè Tasso,** P. Vecchia, 3 (tel. 23 79 66). **Telephone Code:** 035.

Trains: P. Marconi (tel. 24 76 24). To: Milan (every hr., 1hr., L3900); Brescia (15 per day, 1hr., L3900); Cremona (6 per day, 1hr. 30min., L4500). Information open daily 7am-8:30pm. **Luggage Storage:** L1500. Open 6am-10pm.

Buses: across from the train station (tel. 24 81 50). To: Milan (every 30min. 5:40am-10:30pm, L6500); Cremona (every 30min. 5:05am-7:30pm, L7500); Como (9 per day 6:55am-6:20pm, L7300); Brescia (8 per day 6:50am-6:45pm, L6100).

Emergencies: tel. 113. **Police:** Via Monte Bianco, 1 (tel. 27 61 11). **Medical Emergency:** tel. 25 02 46. **Hospital: Ospedale Riuniti,** Largo Barozzi, 1 (tel. 26 91 11).

ACCOMMODATIONS

The higher the altitude, the higher the price. Ask the tourist office about **Agriturismo** (for lodging in rural houses) as well as other alternatives.

Ostello Città di Bergamo (HI), Via G. Ferraris, 1 (tel. and fax 34 23 49). Take bus #14 from Porta Nuova to località Monterosso. The uphill hike is rewarded with an unparalleled view of an unattractive apartment complex. On the positive side, a well-stocked supermarket serves the community at the base of the hill. Open 7-9am and 6pm-midnight, but you can lounge around downstairs during the day. L12,000 per person, breakfast included. Meals L11,000. (Still closed for renovation in 1993.)

Albergo S. Antonino, Via Paleocapa, 1 (tel. 21 02 84), a left off Viale Papa Giovanni XXIII past the tourist office. The disheartening exterior disguises clean, dependable rooms and a hospital-like feel. ACLI *mensa* downstairs. Curfew midnight. Singles L25,000, with bath L32,000. Doubles L42,000, with bath L48,000.

Locanda Caironi, Via Torretta, 6 (tel. 24 30 83), off Via Borgo Palazzo. About a 20-min. walk, or take bus #5, 7, or 8 out on Via Angelo Maj. A family-run affair in a quiet, residential neighborhood. The *trattoria* downstairs is considered one of Bergamo's best-kept culinary secrets. Singles L20,000. Doubles L35,000.

FOOD

Casonsei, a meat-filled ravioli dish, is a Bergamasco culinary delight, as are the *branzi* and *taleggio* cheeses. *Valcalepio* red and white wines have distinguished local viniculture. Streets in *città alta* are lined with *pasticcerias* selling yellow *polentina* confections topped with chocolate blobs intended to resemble birds. Be forewarned about this sweet (and pricey) take-off on Bergamo's most ancient culinary tradition: many natives have never even tasted these for-tourists-only treats. For necessities, shop at **Roll Market,** on the right-hand side of Viale Vittorio Emanuele II just before the hill to *città alta* (open Tues.-Sat. 8:30am-1pm and 3:30-8pm, Mon. 8:30am-1pm).

Città Bassa

Mensa ACLI, Via Paleocapa, 1, in the basement of the Albergo S. Antonino. 2 dishes, *contorno,* and bread for L10,700. Wine L11,000. Open Mon.-Fri. 11am-2:15pm and 7-8:15pm.

Trattoria Casa Mia, Via S. Bernardino, 20 (tel. 22 06 76), off Via Zambonate. Follow Via Tiraboschi from Porta Nuova. An inviting, unpretentious place serving complete meals (including wine, water, coffee, bread, and service) for under L14,000. Open Sept.-July Mon.-Sat. 8am-3pm and 5:30-10:30pm.

Ristorante Self-Service Dany, Via Taramelli, 23/B (tel. 22 07 55). From the station walk down Viale Papa Giovanni XXIII, turn right on Via San Francesco d'Assisi, then left. *Primi* from L2000, *secondi* from L3500. Open Mon.-Fri.

Città Alta

Though you may withstand the temptations of the first bakery you pass on Via Colleoni or Via Gombito, be prepared to undergo the same trial at 20m intervals. The makings of a moderately balanced meal, however, lurk among the sweets.

Forno Tresoldi, Via Colleoni, 13 (tel. 24 39 60). Costs a little more than three coins, but the spinach pizza is otherworldly (about L2500 per slice). Open Tues.-Sun. 8:30am-1:30pm and 3-8pm.

Trattoria Barnabò, Via Colleoni, 31 (tel. 23 76 92), past P. Vecchia. One of the finest restaurants in Bergamo, with *menù* under L15,000. They sculpt a vast menagerie of *polenta* breads—enhanced with cheese, mushrooms, and sausage. Open Sept.-June Fri.-Wed. noon-2:30pm and 7pm-midnight.

Trattoria 3 Torri, P. Mercato del Fieno, 7/A (tel. 24 43 66), a left off Via Gombito when heading away from P. Vecchia. This enticing little corner establishment entertains with elegance, and is always full (there are only about 6 tables). Try the *real* polenta (L13,000). *Menù* around L30,000, but *primi* begin at L8000. Cover L2000. Open Thurs.-Tues. noon-2:30pm and 7-10pm. Reservations strongly recommended.

SIGHTS

Città Bassa

Begin a tour of the city at **P. Matteoti,** the heart of Bergamo Bassa and a favorite meeting place for the evening *passeggiata*. In the **Church of San Bartolomeo,** at the far right of the piazza, rests a superb altarpiece of the *Madonna and Child* by Lorenzo Lotto. Via Tasso on the right of San Bartolomeo leads to the **Church of Santo Spirito.** Note the strange infernal-looking sculpture on the façade. Its fine Renaissance interior (1521) houses paintings by Lotto, Previtali, and Bergognone. **Via Pignolo** connects the lower city with the upper and winds past a succession of handsome palaces (16th to 18th centuries). Along the way is the tiny **Church of San Bernardino,** whose polychromatic interior is the humble backdrop to a splendid altarpiece by Lotto. A right on Via San Tommaso brings you to the astounding **Galleria dell'Accademia Carrara** (tel. 39 94 26), one of the most important art galleries in Italy. Housed in a glorious neoclassical palace, the 15 rooms of the second floor represent virtually all the Italian notables, joined by the canvases of Brueghel, Van Dyck, and El Greco. (Open Wed.-Mon. 9:30am-12:30pm and 2:30-5:30pm. Admission L3000, students free.)

Città Alta

From the Carrara gallery, a terraced walkway (Via Nora) ascends from the lower city to **Porta Sant'Agostino,** a 16th-century gate built by the Venetians as part of their fortifications for the city. Via Porta Dipinta leads to the heart of Bergamo Alta, first passing the Romanesque **Church of San Michele** (12th-13th centuries), decorated inside with colorful frescoes (tel. 24 76 51 to make an appointment) and then the neoclassical **Church of Sant'Andrea,** which contains an altarpiece by Moretto. The street continues as narrow and steep Via Gombito, lacing by a massive 12th-century tower of the same name. The *città alta* can also be reached along the white marble **Porta San Giacomo,** which overlooks the *città bassa's* main thoroughfare.

Via Gambito ends in **Piazza Vecchia,** a majestic ensemble of medieval and Renaissance buildings flanked by restaurants and *caffè*. On the right is the white marble **Biblioteca Civica** (1594), the repository of Bergamo's rich collection of manuscripts, modeled after Venice's Sansovino Library. Across the piazza is the massive **Palazzo della Ragione** (1199), with its robust arcade. To the right, and connected to the *palazzo* by a 16th-century covered stairway, stands the 12th-century **Torre Civica** (Civic Tower). Its 15th-century clock sounds the curfew at 10pm.

A passage between the two buildings leads to **Piazza del Duomo.** Ahead is the multicolor marble façade of the masterful **Colleoni Chapel** (1476). It was designed by G. A. Amadeo (also responsible for the Charterhouse of Pavia) as a tomb and chapel for Bartolomeo Colleoni, a celebrated Venetian mercenary. (Open daily 9am-noon and 2-6pm.) To the right of the chapel is the octagonal **baptistry** graced by a red marble gallery. It is actually a reconstruction of a 14th-century baptistry that at one time stood in the **Basilica of Santa Maria Maggiore.** This basilica, which adjoins the Colleoni Chapel to the left, was constructed in the second half of the 12th century. The understated Romanesque exterior contrasts sharply with the flourishing Baroque interior. Other points of interest include the Victorian tomb of the composer Gaetano Donizetti (1797-1848). (Open Mon.-Sat. 8:30am-noon and 3-7pm, Sun. 9am-10:30pm and 3-7pm.)

For a romantic conclusion to the tour, return to P. Mercato delle Scarpe and proceed left on Via alla Rocca. Sitting on a site occupied by fortifications since Roman times, the present Rocca is home to the **Risorgimento Museum** (tel. 24 71 16). The surrounding grounds have been dubbed the **Park of Remembrance** in honor of those soldiers who died for the Italian cause (museum currently under restoration).

If you find yourself in Bergamo during concert season, you might be drawn into more sedentary pursuits. The **drama season,** featuring Italy's most prestigious companies, occupies center stage at the Donizetti Theater from November to April at which point the spotlight shifts to the two-month-long, universally acclaimed **International Piano Festival,** co-hosted by Brescia. In September, Bergamo unabashedly celebrates its premier native-born composer with a festival of Donizetti's lesser-known works. For further information, contact the tourist office or the theater itself at P. Cavour, 14 (tel. 24 96 31). The indispensable summer-fun pamphlet, *Vivi la Tua Città,* available at the tourist office, is chock-full of music, dance, theater, and film with times and places (but no prices).

■ Brescia

Situated between Milan and Verona, Como and Garda, Brescia has long been overlooked by tourists bound for bigger things. The comparatively slow pace of tourism may be a by-product of the city's multifaceted character, which defies succinct promotional slogans. Roman ruins and fascist *piazze* co-exist within the thoroughly urbanized center, and, lest a single style of cathedral be thought undiplomatic, Brescia has not one *duomo* but two. Relative prosperity has been the one constant over the years. Today the city owes its place in the prosperous Lombardian economy to weapons production, giving Brescia the frenetic pace of a modern industrial center.

ORIENTATION AND PRACTICAL INFORMATION

Brescia is approximately midway between Milan (1hr.) and Verona (45min.) on the direct train line to Venice, and is the main point of departure for buses to the western shores of Lake Garda. Most of the city's architectural gems are concentrated in the piazza-packed *centro storico,* linked to P. della Repubblica by Corso Martiri della Libertà and Via Porcellaga. Continuing through the center and out the other end, you will come to two aptly named streets, **Via del Castello** and **Via del Musei.** The first leads uphill to the castle—the latter slopes down to museum row and the Roman archaeological site.

> **Tourist Office:** Corso Zanardelli, 34 (tel. 434 18), the arcaded continuation of Corso Palestro which branches to the right off Corso della Libertà/Via Porcellaga en route to the center. Set off slightly from the street. Helpful map. Open Mon.-Fri. 9am-noon and 3-6:30pm, Sat. 9am-12:30pm.
>
> **Post Office:** P. Vittoria, 1. Stamps and Fermo Posta at #6. Open Mon.-Fri. 8:15am-5:30pm, Sat. 8:15am-1pm. **Postal Code:** 25100.
>
> **Telephones: SIP,** Via Moretto, 46 (tel. 375 12 74). Open Mon.-Sat. 9am-12:30pm and 2:30-6pm, Sun. 9am-1pm. **Telephone Code:** 030.
>
> **Trains:** at the opposite end of Viale Stazione from P. della Repubblica. To: Milan (every 45min., 1hr., L6500); Verona (every hr., 45min., L5000); Venice (every hr.,

2hr. 15min., L13,800); Bergamo (15 per day, 1hr., L3900); Padova (every hr., 1hr. 45min., L10,500); Vicenza (every hr., 1hr. 15min., L8800); Cremona (8 per day, 50min., L4300). Information open 8am-noon and 3-6pm. **Luggage Storage:** L1500. Open 24 hrs.

Buses: by the train station (tel. 377 42 37). East-bound buses are to your right and under the bridge from the train station. To: Verona (6:45am-7:50pm, 2hr., L9200); Mantua (6am-7:15pm, 1hr., L7700); Cremona (6:30am-7:50pm, 1hr., L6700). West-bound buses leave from the **SIA** station, just to the left of the train station. Ticket office open Mon.-Sat. 6am-8pm, Sun. 7-11am and 3-6pm. Daily to Milan (5:50am-9:20pm, 1hr. 45min., L11,000).

Emergencies: tel. 113. **Police:** (tel. 425 61), on via Boticelli. **Medical Assistance:** tel. 399 55 45. **Hospital: Ospedale Civile,** tel. 399 51.

ACCOMMODATIONS AND FOOD

Accommodations are reasonably priced in Brescia, but often fill with businesspeople during the week. Call a week ahead for reservations. You'll be fortunate to find any sort of bargain in the historic center.

Servizio della Giovane (ACISJF), Via Fratelli Bronzetti, 17 (tel. 375 53 87). From the station, take Viale Stazione to P. della Repubblica, and pick up Via dei Mille on the far side. Via Filli Bronzetti is on the right after a couple of blocks. Women only. Run by friendly nuns. Spotless bathrooms off triples that are so newly furnished they look like promotional photos. Kitchen facilities another perk. Curfew 10pm. L10,000 per person.

Albergo Rigamonti, Via Mansione, 8 (tel. 40 332). Modern, tidy, and respectable. TV room, bar, and car park. Singles L30,000, with bath L45,000. Doubles L50,000, with bath L60,000.

Albergo San Marco, Via Spalto S. Marco, 15 (tel. 45 541). From the station take Via Foppa, turn right on Via XX Settembre, make the next left, and turn right onto Via Emanuele, which becomes Via Spalto S. Marco. Rooms are clean, the clientele young and fun. Singles L26,000. Doubles L45,000. Closed in Aug.

Open-air vendors do their thing in P. Mercato and P. Rovetta (Tues.-Fri. 8am-noon and roughly 3-6pm). The **Oviesse** clothing store off P. Rovetta at Corso Mameli, 23, conceals a grocery store in its basement (open Tues.-Sat. 9am-12:25pm and 3-7:20pm, Mon. 3-7:20pm). Whatever and wherever you choose to eat, or even if you're not eating at all, be sure to submerge yourself in one of the local wines. *Tocai di San Martino della Battaglia,* a dry white wine, *groppello,* a medium red, and *botticino,* a dry red of medium age, are all favorites in Brescia and beyond.

Ristorante Rosticceria Mameli, Corso Mameli, 53 (tel. 375 95 02), near P. Loggia. An enticing array of prepared foods sold downstairs for take-out, and upstairs in the restaurant. Salads L1500-5000 per *etto. Primi* around L7000, *secondi* L11,000. Open Tues.-Sun. 8am-midnight.

Trattoria Al Frate, Via Musei, 25 (tel. 375 14 69), by the base of the ascent to the castle. Plentiful food and the ever-present imbibers who rise only for a refill are living testimonials to the fine wines. *Primi* L8500, *secondi* L11,000-17,500. Cover L3500. Wine begins at L9600 per liter. Open Tues.-Sun. 10:30am-3pm and 5pm-2am.

SIGHTS AND ENTERTAINMENT

Down from **Piazza della Vittoria,** the first sight encountered in the center of town, is the **Piazza della Loggia,** built when when Venice ruled the city. On one side of this square stands the **Torre dell'Orologio,** modeled after the clock tower in Venice's Piazza San Marco, with an astronomic clock and two stone fellers that strike the hours. Across from the tower, the Renaissance **loggia,** the work of a gaggle of architects including Sansovino and Palladio, boasts intriguing carvings. An elaborate door underneath the portico leads to a monumental staircase and a room adorned with paintings from the 16th century.

The **Piazza del Duomo,** across Via X Giornate, is dominated by its heavily manneristic **duomo nuovo** (1604-1825). Next door is the old *duomo,* or **Rotonda,** a refreshingly simple Romanesque building with endearing patchwork and uneven windows scattered over its two-story circular plan. (Open April-Sept. Wed.-Mon. 9am-noon and 3-7pm. Contribution desired, but not required.) The **Broletto Palace,** next to the *duomo nuovo,* is a typical Lombard medieval town hall crowned by an 11th-century tower.

Down Via dei Musei from the center is Emperor Vespasian's vast **Tempio Capitolino,** part of the yield of ongoing archaeological efforts to unearth monuments from Brescia's classical roots as the Roman colony of Brixia. Upstairs is a small museum with mosaics, a medieval road map, and excellent bronzes. (Museum and temple open Tues.-Sun. 10am-12:45pm and 2-6pm. Admission L3000.)

A few paces farther down Via dei Musei you'll find the 16th-century **Church of Santa Guilia,** now the home of a **museum of Christian art.** Its greatest treasure is the 8th-century cross of Desiderius, encased in silver and encrusted with hundreds of jewels and cameos; note especially the inset 3rd-century portraits. Also look for the biblical carvings on a 4th-century ivory chest. (Open daily 10am-8:30pm. Admission L5000. Closed for restoration in 1993.)

From the Tempio Capitolino walk through P. Foro to Via Gallo, which becomes Via Crispi and leads to Brescia's principal attraction, the **Pinacoteca Tosio-Martinengo.** The solemn 22-room *palazzo* displays a good collection of works by Brescian masters (notably Moretto), but better still is Raphael's effeminate *Cristo benedicente.* There are also first-rate works by Veneziano, Tintoretto, Clouet, Vicenzo Foppa, and Lorenzo Lotto. (Open Tues.-Sun. 9am-12:30pm and 2-5pm. Admission L4000.)

Fender-benders should check out the **Museo della Chitarra** (Guitar Museum), Via Trieste, 34. (Open Mon.-Tues. and Thurs.-Fri. 2:30-7:30pm. Free.) If you have more time, visit the **castello** hovering on the high ground behind Via dei Musei. This array of architectural styles houses a sad little zoo, an observatory, the Risorgimento Museum, and the Luigi Marzoli Museum of Arms. Down Via Piamarta is an intact Roman gate.

The bulk of Brescia's high-brow cultural events take place in the splendor of the Teatro Grande. December to April marks the annual **Stagione di Prosa,** a long-running series of dramatic performances. From April to June, the focus shifts to the **Festive Pianistico Internazionale,** co-hosted by nearby Bergamo. **Estate Aperta** includes an impressive series of concerts, theatrical performances, and films, held June through September in churches, courtyards, and *piazze.* Pick up a schedule at the tourist office, or call the coordinating forces at the **Centro Teatrale Bresciano** (tel. 375 63 54).

VENETO

The Veneto stretches from the Austrian Alps down across the foothills of the Dolomites and the Venetian Alps to the fertile plain of the Po and its delta. The territory encompasses not only an extremely wide range of terrains, but a multitude of culturally independent towns and cities nominally lumped together by Venetian rule. By the time this took place (14th century), however, the Germanic and Milanese influence in the region was so profound that 400 years later when Venetian Empire was dissolved by the Napoleonic invasions, the independent cultures already established were scarcely ruffled. A good indicator of unity can always be found in the transcendent medium of cuisine. Rice and *polenta* provide the starch base, the latter a cornmeal concoction used with most local seafood dishes. Wine is strictly regional, featuring the dry white *soave,* the dry, sparkling *prosecco,* the light red *bardolino,* and the full-bodied *valpolicella.*

■■■ VENICE (VENEZIA)

She is the Shakespeare of cities—unchallenged, incomparable, and beyond envy.

—John Addington Symonds

As unreal as it appears, Venice convinces even the most skeptical visitor that its fantastic heritage has not been lost. Buildings rise out of the water and as the tide comes in and laps at the threshold of their doors, you may wonder if they have risen high enough. Land in the lagoon was at a premium, so only narrow pedestrian passages, most of which are old canals now filled with earth, connect the *campi* (squares). During the day, boats ferry everything from food supplies to building debris to camera-happy tourists. An evening stroll through the illuminated streets returns the city to its past: Venice has more historic buildings and inspiring vistas per square inch than any other city in Italy. Enjoy the architecture in the cool of the night, with colored lights reflected in the sloshing waters and gondolas lazily passing by. Despite its crowds and inflated prices, Venice beckons anyone interested in the roots of Italian culture to make at least one visit its sublime combination of water, stone and light.

First driven by Attila's hordes, then by conquering Lombards, Roman refugees joined fishermen on the low barrier islands of the swampy lagoon. An unsuccessful attack by Charlemagne in 810 led to the settlement of the inner islands that underlie the modern city. In 828, when two Venetian merchants stole St. Mark's remains from Alexandria, they established the city's eminence under a new patron saint. By the 11th century, ties to Constantinople and marine prowess had established Venice as the dominant entrepôt for trade with the Middle East. In 1204, Venice sent the penniless armies of the Fourth Crusade to raid Constantinople and the spoils of this campaign filled Venetian squares and treasuries with new prosperity. After consolidating its oligarchic government in the 14th century, the Venetian Republic defeated its rival Genoa in 1380 and expanded onto the Italian mainland. Over the next three centuries, jealous European powers to the west and the unstoppable Ottoman Turks to the east whittled away *La Serenissima's* empire, while the discovery of ocean routes to the Far East robbed it of its monopoly on Asian trade. By the time Napoleon conquered it in 1797, idle Venice was little more than a decadent playground. French and Austrian rule capped off the glory days as the development of industry at Mestre drew away the archipelago's working population.

ORIENTATION

Venice is composed of 117 bodies of land distributed throughout the Venetian lagoon, and is protected from the the Adriatic by the Lido, an island which lies 2km

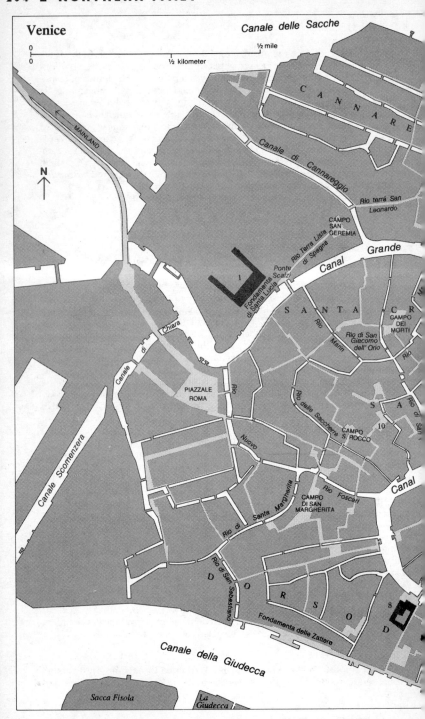

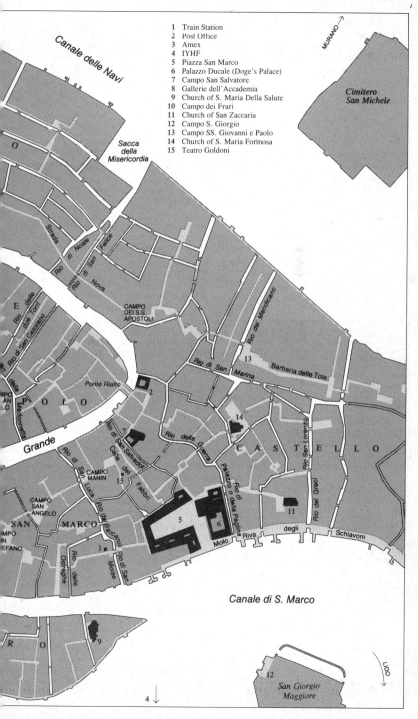

1 Train Station
2 Post Office
3 Amex
4 IYHF
5 Piazza San Marco
6 Palazzo Ducale (Doge's Palace)
7 Campo San Salvatore
8 Gallerie dell'Accademia
9 Church of S. Maria Della Salute
10 Campo dei Frari
11 Church of San Zaccaria
12 Campo S. Giorgio
13 Campo SS. Giovanni e Paolo
14 Church of S. Maria Formosa
15 Teatro Goldoni

further out to sea. A 4km causeway links the urban center to the mainland. The **Santa Lucia train station** lies on the northwestern edge of the city, while the garages, car rentals, and bus terminals are across the Grand Canal in nearby **Piazzale Roma**—the last stop for all land-bound transportation. If you're in a rush to get to **Piazza San Marco** (and the central tourist office) from the station or Piazzale Roma, take *vaporetto* #2. For a splendid introduction to the *palazzi* along the Grand Canal, take #1 or #34. The 40-min. walk to San Marco starts left from the station onto Lista di Spagna, and following the signs (and the crowds).

Yellow signs placed around Venice guide you to the **Rialto** (the bridge connecting San Marco and San Polo), the **Accademia** (Dorsoduro), San Marco (at the border of San Marco and Castello), Piazzale Roma (Santa Croce), and the *ferrovia* (Cannaregio). They can help you navigate the labyrinth of Venice from one end to the other, yet in doing so they can actually take you on the longer route, making you their prisoner. Moreover, these signs are the leading cause of the "pedestrian freeway" phenomenon. Liberate yourself with a real map (do not rely on the freebies at the tourist office, nor on the oversimlified maps given out at the AmEx office). The *Edizioni Storti* map-guide of Venice (L5000) shows all the major streets, and is color coded, in addition to having an invaluable street index. You will certainly get lost in Venice, but with a map in hand you might not feel helpless and overwhelmed.

For deviating from the main pathways you will be rewarded with cheaper prices, local hangouts, quiet *campi*, beautiful vistas, and friendly Venetians. It is true that many of the sights cluster around the grand canal, but it is easy enought to choose a route, find the site and then return back to the tranquil waterways.

Orientation begins with a fundamental comprehension of the **sestieri,** the sections of the city. Within each section, there are no individual street numbers, but merely one long and haphazard sequence of numbers (roughly 6000 per *sestiere*). Every building, however, is also located on some type of a "street"—*fondamente, calli, campi, salizzade, canali, rii, ponti,* and *rii terrà,* (foundations, narrow streets, squares, paved roads, channels, small channels, bridges, and old channels that are now streets, respectively). To add to the confusion, it is often unclear which *sestiere* you are in at any given moment as the boundaries are not clearly indicated. *Let's Go* supplies the *sestiere,* the number, then the street name when possible, and supplements this by mentioning the nearest landmark—beyond that, try asking the locals.

The **Grand Canal,** the central artery of Venice, can be crossed on foot only at the **ponti** (bridges) **Scalzi, Rialto,** and **Accademia.** *Traghetti* (gondola-like ferry boats) may seem too picturesque for practical use, but in fact they are used fairly frequently for canal crossings where there is no bridge. North of the Canal, from the station to about the Rio dei Santi Apostoli lies the *sestiere* **Cannaregio.** Continuing clockwise around the Canal, **Castello** is just south of the Rio di S. Giovanni Crisotomo, and **San Marco** extends from the Mercerie and P. San Marco to the Ponte Accademia. The easternmost extension of Venice is the **Santa Elena** *sestiere.* Cross the Rialto bridge from P. San Bartolomeo, and you will find yourself in the **San Polo** district. West of San Polo and encompassing Piazzale Roma is the *sestiere* of **Santa Croce.** Now trace an imaginary line from Cà Rezzonico on the Grand Canal to the church of Santa Maria Maggiore on the *rio* of the same name: the land south of this and hooking around to the Punta della Dogano is **Dorsoduro.** And don't make the mistake of trying to rinse off your sticky *gelato*-laden hands in the Canal—those stone stairs leading into the water have been gathering moss since Michelangelo was a boy.

High tides (usually November-April) cause *acque alte,* the periodic floodings that swamp parts of the city, notably San Marco, under as much as three feet of water. If you don't like wet feet, check ahead with the tourist office and consult the signs posted at all ACTV landing stages. *Acque alte* usually last two to three hours, and planks or platforms are laid out across most major thoroughfares.

If you plan to drive to Venice, take the "Ponte della Libertà" causeway which ends in Piazzale Roma. Parking facilities can be found in P. Roma in the garages *comu-*

nale and San Marco, with additional parking on the adjacent island of Tronchetto (follow the road signs). Parking on the Tronchetto "car park island" with 5000 parking spaces could cost you as much as L35,000 per day, while parking in the garages at the P. Roma runs up to L42,000 for a 24-hr. period. In another strange Italian pricing decision, the garages provide a list of cars and makes. The mini-econo cars are charged one price to park, the midsize another, and the Rolls and Jaguars, yet another higher price. Motorists should consider leaving their cars in the parking lot at the Mestre train station on the mainland (about L8000 per day) and taking a train into Venice (L1200 each way; all trains into and out of Venice stop at Mestre).

Vaporetti

The alternative to walking is taking the **vaporetti** (motorboat buses), which skim the Venetian waterways. Most principal boats run 24 hrs. but frequencies are reduced after 11pm. A 24-hr. *biglietto turistico,* available at any ticket office, allows you unlimited travel on all boats except #2 (L12,000). You can also purchase a three-day ticket for L17,000. Neither is really worthwhile unless you're on a kamikaze tour. If you plan to stay more than four days on Giudecca, or plan to visit some of the outlying islands, a **Cartavenezia** might be useful. With this, the *diretto* is only L1200 and the *accelerato* L1000. It's valid for one month. (Bring L10,000 and a passport photo to the information office at Fondamenta Nuova.) The ACTV office offers a special three-day ticket for holders of the **Rolling Venice Pass** (see tourist offices under Practical Information) for L16,000.

Not all stations sell tickets all the time—buy extras, but make sure to get the type that can be machine-validated (upon boarding) at any station. Tickets may be bought both at the booths in front of the *vaporetti* stops and at various self-serve dispensers (located at the ACTV office at P. Roma and at the Rialto stop). Tickets may also be bought from the conductor after boarding (L500 surcharge). Be sure to count your change carefully when buying tickets at the station booths. Tourists dashing for a departing *vaporetto* sometimes find themselves short a few *lire* once the boat is on its way. The fine for riding the *vaporetti* without a ticket is L15,000, but enforcement can be lax.

PRACTICAL INFORMATION

Tourist Offices: APT (tel. and fax 71 90 78), at the train station. Usually mobbed. The longer of the 2 lines is just for accommodations. They provide *Un Ospite di Venezia* (A Guest in Venice), a bilingual biweekly (monthly in the winter) booklet packed with information and entertainment listings. Open Mon.-Fri. 9am-noon and 3-6pm, Sat. 8am-2pm. **Main office: San Marco,** Ascensione, 71/F (tel. 522 63 56), opposite the basilica. English spoken. Shorter lines. Open Mon.-Sat. 8:30am-7pm. **A 3rd office: Lido** at Gran Viale 6/A (tel. 526 57 21). Open Mon.-Sat. 9am-2pm. **Hotel Information: AVA,** P. Roma, 540/D (tel. 522 86 40) makes reservations in 1- and 2-star hotels with a deposit. Officially open daily 9am-10pm, Oct.-April 9am-9pm, but in practice at the management's whim. Also an office inside the train station (tel. 71 50 16), in the same cubbyhole as the tourist office. **Youth Discount Card: Rolling Venice,** at the train station (tel. 72 01 61 or 72 05 19). Next to the APT office. Open June 15-Sept. 30 daily, 8am-8pm. Main office at San Marco (tel. 270 76 50 or 270 76 45), near the tourist office. For ages 14-29. Offers great tourist services as well as a discount card for admission to museums, shops, restaurants, and events throughout Venice, also an invaluable guide filled with inside information culled from locals and students. Worth it whether you're in Venice for 1 day or 1 month. Bring L5000 and a passport photo (L3000 at the booth in the station).

Budget Travel: CTS, Dorsoduro, 3252 (tel. 520 56 60, fax 523 69 46) on Fondamenta Tagliapietra. Off the Dorsoduro-to-San Marco route, near Campo S. Margherita. Take Calle Piove to Calle Larga Foscari and turn right after crossing the bridge, on the bank of Rio Foscari. Open Mon.-Fri. 9am-12:30pm and 3:30-7pm. **Transalpino** (tel. and fax 71 66 00) for international train tickets, to the right as you exit the station. Open Mon.-Sat. 8am-8pm.

Consulates: U.K., Dorsoduro, 1051 (tel. 522 72 07). Open Mon.-Sat. 9am-noon and 2-4pm. The closest U.S., Canadian, and Australian consulates are in Milan; New Zealand and South African citizens should contact their embassy in Rome.

Currency Exchange: The best rates are found in Padua. In Venice, **Banca Ambrosiano Veneto** on Calle Larga XXII Marzo, San Marco 2378, between San Marco and the Accademia. Open Mon.-Fri. 8:20am-1:20pm and 2:35-4:05pm. L4500 commission. If you insist upon changing money at the station, save time and get slightly better rates by walking 400m to **Banco San Marco,** next to the bridge spanning the canal (Open Mon.-Fri. 8:30am-1:30pm and 2:45-4:15pm).

American Express: San Marco, Sal S. Moise, 1471 (tel. 520 08 44), off P. San Marco. Take Calle Seconda dell'Ascensione from the end of the piazza opposite the basilica and follow it for a couple of blocks (look for the AmEx directional mosaic underfoot). L1500 inquiry charge on mail for those without card or traveler's checks. Mediocre exchange rates. Office open Mon.-Fri. 9am-5:30pm, Sat. 9am-12:30pm. Exchange service open in summer Mon.-Sat. 8am-8pm.

Post Office: San Marco, 5554 (tel. 528 62 12), on Salizzada Fontego dei Tedeschi near the eastern end of the Rialto bridge off Campo San Bartolomeo. Fermo Posta at desk #4; stamps at #12. Open Mon.-Sat. 8:15am-6:45pm. **Branch office** through the arcades at the end of P. San Marco. Open Mon.-Fri. 8:15am-1:30pm, Sat. 8:15am-12:10pm. Stamps sold in the *tabacchi* at the station. Also close to the train station in an alley off Lista di Spagna, Calle del Spizier. **Postal Code:** 30124.

Telephones: ASST, train station. Open Mon.-Fri. 8am-7:45pm, Sat. 8am-1:45pm. Also **Iritel** at San Marco, Fontego dei Tedeschi, 5550, next to the main post office. Open Mon.-Sat. 8am-7:45pm. **SIP,** in P. Roma and along Viale Santa Maria Elisabetta on the Lido. Open daily 8am-9:30pm. **Telephone Code:** 041.

Flights: Aeroporto Marco Polo (tel. 541 54 91). ACTV (tel. 528 78 86) local bus #5 runs to the airport every 1½hr. (30min., L1000), or take the ATVO coach (tel. 520 55 30) with luggage space for L5000.

Trains: Stazione di Santa Lucia (tel. 71 55 55, lost and found 71 61 22). Information office in station across from tourist office. Open daily 7:10am-9:30pm. To: Padua (every 15min., 30min., L5400 round-trip); Bologna (14 per day, 1hr. 30min., L12,800); Milan (18 per day, 2hr. 30min.-3hr., L17,000); Florence (6 per day, 2hr. 30min.-3hr., L18,700); Rome (4 per day, 5hr. 15min., L40,200). **Luggage Storage:** L1500 per day. Open 24 hrs.

Buses: ACTV, the local line for buses and boats (tel. 528 78 86) in P. Roma. Open Mon.-Sat. 8am-2:30pm. Closed the last 2 wks. in Aug. **ATP** is the long distance carrier. Roughly every 30min. To: the villas on the Riviera del Brenta (Malcontenta L1000, Mira L2300, Strà L3100), Padua (L3800), Mestre (L1000), Treviso (L2600). Ticket office open daily 7:30am-11pm. Information office open Mon.-Sat. 8am-6:30pm. Fine for riding without a ticket: L30,000.

Car Rental: Europcar, P. Roma, 496/H (tel. 523 86 16). The best rates in Venice, which ain't saying much. Open Mon.-Fri. 8am-1pm and 2-7pm, Sat.-Sun. 8:30am-noon. **Avis,** Piazzale Roma, 496/G (tel. 522 58 25). Open Mon.-Sat. 8am-8pm, Sun. 8am-1pm; Nov.-March Mon.-Sat. 8am-noon and 3-7pm.

English Bookstore: Il Libraio a San Baranabà, Dorsoduro, 2835/A (tel. 522 87 37), Fondamenta Gherardini, off Campo San Baranabà. Classics, American fiction set in Venice, and *Let's Go* guides. Open Mon.-Tues. and Thurs.-Sat. 10:30am-1pm and 4-8pm. All the same is at **Libreria Serenissima,** Marzaria S. Zulian, 739. On San Marco, between the Rialto and San Marco, on one of the major routes.

Laundromat: Lavaget, Cannaregio, 1269 (tel. 71 59 76), on Fondamenta Pescaria off Rio Terà San Leonardo beside the Ponte Guglie. Self-service. L12,000, soap included. Open Mon.-Fri. 8:15am-12:30pm and 3-7pm.

Public Baths: Albergo Diurno (Day Hotel), San Marco, 1266, in the *ramo secondo* (2°), off the west end of P. San Marco. Showers L4000. Toilets L500. Luggage storage L2000-3000. Showers open daily 8am-4pm. Also in the station—next to *binario* 1. Showers L4000. Soap and towel each L500. Open daily 7am-8pm. **Toilets** are scattered throughout town. *Gabinetti* (also *toilette*) can be found on either side of the Rialto, on the waterfront near P. San Marco, and under the Dorsoduro side of the Accademia bridge (L500), to name but a few locations. Also at

P. Roma near Treponte and in Castello, Calle Morosina, 4052/A. Toilet (L500), shower (L3000), with towels (L4000). Open daily 8am-7pm.

Late-Night Pharmacy: check the *Ospite di Venezia* or call 192.

Hotel Crises: Questura, on Fondamenta San Lorenzo in the Castello (tel. 270 36 11). The people to contact if you have a serious complaint about your hotel.

Emergencies: tel. 113. **Police: Carabinieri,** P. Roma (tel. 523 53 33 or 112 in an emergency). **Medical Assistance:** tel. 520 32 22. **Hospital: Ospedale Civili,** Campo SS. Giovanni e Paolo (tel. 529 45 17). **Boat ambulances:** tel. 523 00 00.

ACCOMMODATIONS

Plan on spending slightly more on rooms here than elsewhere in Italy. In summer, reservations, preferably made as much as a month in advance, will preserve your sanity. To avoid the crowds and expense of summertime stays in Venice, visit the city while based in one of the towns nearby (Padua and Treviso, each 30min. away, are good places to secure a room). Many *locande* will hold a room until 10 or 11am. The **APT** at the train station and the **AVA** hotel service near the bus station will book rooms, but if you go there directly they are more willing to bargain.

The singles listed below vanish in summer. If the situation becomes desperate, you can always resort to one of the campgrounds at Mestre (ask at the tourist office) or Padua's youth hostel (closes at 11pm, last train at 9:15pm). The police frown on impromptu crashing in parks or on beaches.

Dormitory-type accommodations are always available in Venice without reservations, even during August and September. Such accommodations often have irregular operating seasons, so check with the tourist offices to see which are open. In *pensioni,* look out for L10,000 breakfasts and other forms of bill-padding, and always agree on what you'll pay before you hit the sack or surrender your passport.

Institutional Accommodations

Ostello Venezia (HI), Fondamenta di Zitelle, 86 (tel. 523 82 11, fax 523 56 89), on Giudecca. Take *vaporetto* #5 (*sinistra*) from the station (25min., L2500), #5 (*destra*) or #8 from San Zaccaria near San Marco (5min., L2500). Get off at Zitelle and walk right. A recently-renovated warehouse on the canal. English spoken. In summer arrive in the morning to secure a place—the tourist office at the train station will let you know if they're already full. Open daily 7:30-9am and 2-11:30pm. Curfew 11:30pm. L20,000 per person, membership required. HI cards L5000 over 6 nights. Breakfast included. Full meals L12,000. No phone reservations.

Ostello Santa Fosca, Cannaregio, 2372 (tel. 71 57 75), on Fondamenta Canal, just across the bridge and then to your left from Campo San Fosca. From the train station (15min.), take the Lista di Spagna and continue on this wide street across 3 bridges. Run by students. Dormitory-style rooms. A few singles and doubles available. Courtyard and kitchen facilities. Check-in 10am-noon and 6-11:30pm. Check out 9am. Lockout 9am-6pm. Dorm L18,000 per person. Single/Double L22,000 per person. Rolling Venice: L1000 discount. Open July-Sept.

Foresteria Valdese, Castello, 5170 (tel. 528 67 97). Take the *vaporetto* to San Zaccharia, then walk to Campo Santa Maria Formosa (5min.). From the campo, take Calle Lunga S. M. Formosa, just over the 1st bridge. The 18th-century guesthouse of Venice's biggest Protestant church. Check-in 9am-1pm and 6-8pm. Lockout 9:45am-1pm. Dorms with bunk beds L25,000 per person, L21,000 each additional night. Breakfast included. Reserve 1 mo. ahead for their 2 beautiful doubles (L56,000). 2 apartments with bath and kitchen, L90,000-110,000 for 2; L15,000 for each additional bed up to maximum 5 in the apartment. Phone reservations suggested.

Domus Civica, ACISJF, San Polo, 3082 (tel. 72 11 03/52 40 46), across the street from a bar in both directions, on the corner of Calle Chiovere, Calle Campazzo, and S. Rocco, between the Frari Church and Piazzale Roma. Along the road, follow the yellow arrows between Piazzale Roma and the Rialto. Both men and women welcome. Student housing in the winter. Run by a church-affiliated organization. Everything the heart could desire: ping-pong tables, a TV room, a piano.

Check-out 7:30-10am. Curfew 11:30pm. Singles L28,000. Doubles L50,000. Open mid-June to mid-Oct. Rolling Venice: 20% discount.

Instituto S. Maria del Soccorso, Dorsoduro, 2591 (tel. 52 20 96). Near Campo di S. Margerita in Dorsoduro. Form the train station. Take Vaporetto #5 and get off at S. Basilio, then follow Fondamento S. Basegio, in front of you. Across Campo S. Basilio, until it turns right onto Fonda del Soccorso. A beautiful lodging with a gorgeous interior garden. Nun-run. Tidy, comfortable rooms. Friendly hosts. No lockout. 60 beds. Open 7:30am-11pm. Curfew 11pm. L28,000 for the first night, L25,000 for subsequent nights. Singles and doubles with breakfast L34,000 per person, in groups of 10 or more or with Rolling Venice. Reservations necessary. Open June 25-Sept. 20.

Suore Cannosiano, Fondamenta del Ponte Piccolo, 428 (tel. 522 21 57), also on Giudecca. Take boat #5 to Sant'Eufemia, and walk to your left and over the Ponte Piccolo bridge as you descend. Women only. Run by solicitous nuns. You can arrive at any time of day to leave your bags. Check-out 6-8:30am. Lockout 8:30am-4pm. Curfew 10:30pm. Dorm-style rooms L16,000 per person.

Hotels Cannaregio (From the Station to the Rialto)

The area around the station on and near Lista di Spagna offers the best and most convenient selection in the city.

Hotel Calderon, Cannaregio, 283 (tel. 71 55 62), in P. San Geremia at the end of Lista di Spagna. A short walk from the station. Fine rooms, with matching furniture, some overlooking the square or the park behind. Friendly, family-run hotel. No English spoken. All rooms without private bath. No curfew; you are given your own set of keys. Singles L35,000. Doubles L50,000. Triples L75,000. Quads L80,000. Breakfast L4000. Reserve ahead Aug.-Oct. Am Ex, Eurocard, MC, Visa.

Locanda Antica Casa Carettoni, Cannaregio, 130 (tel. 71 62 31), along Rio Terà Lista di Spagna, to the left of the station. Rooms steeped in antiquity described by the proud proprietor as "truly Venetian." But for the experience and the price you might have to settle for a cold shower. Curfew: midnight. Singles L28,000. Doubles L48,000. Triples L69,000. Open March-July and Sept.-Jan.

Hotel Minerva and Nettuno, Cannaregio, 230 (tel. 71 59 68, fax 524 21 39), on your left on Lista di Spagna from the station. Spacious, remodeled rooms and convenient locale make this a prime choice. Singles L47,000, with bath L61,000. Doubles L68,000, with bath L89,000. Breakfast included. MC, Visa.

Albergo Adua, Cannaregio, 233/A (tel. 71 61 84), on Lista di Spagna. Courtly rooms with flowery wallpaper, most with wall-to-wall carpeting. Small, family-run, and quiet for the neighborhood. Singles L42,000. Doubles L58,000, with bath L90,000. Extra beds: 35% more per bed. Breakfast L7500. MC, Visa.

Dorsoduro and Santa Croce

Cà Foscari, Dorsoduro, 3887/B (tel. and fax 522 58 17), on Calle della Frescada, at the foot of Calle Crosera where it hits Calle Marconi. Take *vaporetto* #1 or #34 to San Tomà. Look for the camouflaged sign. Family-run, with pride. Tastefully decorated rooms. Singles L40,000. Doubles L70,000. Breakfast included. Call in advance—rooms held until noon. Open Feb.-Nov.

Locanda Montin, Dorsoduro, 1147 (tel. 522 71 51). From Campo San Barnabà, go south through the passageway Casin dei Nobili, across the bridge, right on the Fondamenta Lombardo, and around the corner onto Fondamenta di Borgo. Modern paintings and restored antiques abound. Singles L40,000. Doubles L65,000. Breakfast included. Reserve with 1 night's deposit. Closed 20 days in Jan. and 10 days in Aug. AmEx, DC, MC, Visa.

Hotel Messner, Rio Terra Spizier, 217 (tel. 522 72 66), near the Chiesa della Salute, and closest to the #1 stop of that name. Discounts can be arranged for large groups. Singles L55,000. Doubles L74,600. The annex is L18,000 cheaper for all rooms. Breakfast included. AmEx, Diners, MC, Visa.

San Marco (From the Basilica west to the Grand Canal)

Locanda Casa Petrarca, San Marco, 4386 (tel. 520 04 30). From Campo San Luca, go south on Calle dei Fuseri, take the 2nd left and then turn right onto Calle Schiavone. English spoken. Singles L40,000. Doubles L70,000-75,000, with bath L90,000-99,000. Extra beds: 35% more per bed. Breakfast L6000.

Locanda San Salvador, San Marco, 5264 (tel. 528 91 47), on Calle del Galliazzo, off Campo San Bartolomeo. Good views and a spacious terrace. Right in the middle of the action. Singles L40,000, with bath L50,000. Doubles L65,000-70,000, with bath L85,000-95,000.

Locande San Samuele, San Marco, 3358 (tel. 522 80 45). Follow Calle deghe Botteghe from Campo San Stefano and take a left on Salizzata San Samuele. Rooms and bathrooms are small and somber. Singles L39,000. Doubles L51,000, with bath L80,000. Breakfast L7000.

Alloggi Alla Scala, San Marco, 4306 (tel. 521 06 29). From Campo Manin take Calle de la Vida o dela Locande then a left on Corte Contarini del Bovolo. Located in a quiet and historic courtyard. An elegant staircase is surrounded by a garden next door. Colorful rooms *alla carnevale.* Doubles L70,000-80,000. Triples L90,000-110,000. Doubles L65,000, with bath L75,000. Breakfast L7000. Reserve with 1 night's deposit. Closed in Aug. Reserve with 1 night's deposit.

Alloggi Massetto, San Marco, 1520/A (tel. 523 05 05), on Ramo Primo Corte Contarina at the Boca de Piazza west of San Marco. Good prices and locale. Only 5 rooms. Proprietress has a penchant for small birds and lets them fly free in the house. Singles with bath L30,000. Doubles with bath L40,000. Triples L50,000, with bath L55,000.

Castello (From San Marco to the Island of Sant'Elena)

Pensione Casa Verardo, Castello, 4765 (tel. 528 61 27). Take Rimpetto la Sacrestia out of Campo SS. Filippo e Giacomo (just east of San Marco) across the bridge. Without a doubt *the* find in this part of town—run by a hospitable, outgoing family. Large rooms with eclectic furnishings. No surface is spared in decoration! Singles L42,000-44,000. Doubles L60,000, with bath 85,000. Triples L120,000-130,000. Quad L130,000-140,000. Breakfast L7000. Reserve with 1 night's deposit. They have another establishment, **Hotel da Bepi,** Santa Croce, 160 (tel. 522 67 35), on the Fondamento Minotto, near P. Roma. Singles L45,000. Doubles L70,000, with bath L90,000. Breakfast included. MC, Visa.

Hotel Caneva, Castello, 5515 (tel. 522 81 18), 2 min. from the Rialto. Take Calle Stagneri from P. S. Bartolomeo, cross the bridge, and turn right after Campo della Fava. Off a quiet, alternative route to S. Marco. Many rooms overlook a canal and about half are carpeted. Doubles L66,000, with shower L74,000, with bath L97,000. Triples L87,000. Quads L100,000. Nov.-March prices drop by L10,000.

Locanda Silva, Castello, 4423 (tel. 522 76 43). Take Calle dell'Anzolo (it starts next to San Marco), then make the 2nd right, continue across the bridge, and go left when you hit Fondamenta del Rimedio. On a canal. Large and fastidiously kept. Singles L45,000. Doubles L65,000, with shower, L80,000, with bath L95,000. Triples L90,000, with bath L125,000. Quads L115,000, with bath L145,000. Includes breakfast. Open Feb.-Nov.

Locanda Corona, Castello, 4464 (tel. 522 91 74; *vaporetto:* San Zaccharia). Head north on Sacrestia, from Campo SS. Filippo e Giacomo, take the 1st right, and then the 1st left onto Calle Corona. Fine rooms, limited hot water supply. Drop by the Fucina degli Angeli (Angel's Forge) next door for a look at glass-blowing. Singles L34,000. Doubles L48,000. Showers L3000. Breakfast L8500.

Locanda Sant'Anna, Castello, 269 (tel. 528 64 66). Take Via Garibaldi, which becomes Fondamenta Santa Anna, turn left on Ponte Santa Anna, then right at Corte del Bianco (*vaporetto:* #1 or 4 to Giardini). Worth the hike. Friendly family proprietors and a refreshing absence of tourists. Starched sheets and sparkling rooms. TV downstairs. Curfew midnight. Singles L47,000. Doubles L68,000, with bath L96,000. Triple L99,000, with bath L125,000. Quads L122,000, with bath L150,000. Breakfast included. Reserve ahead with 1 night's deposit.

The Outskirts of La Serenissima

Situated between the airport and the islands, **La Fenice** is a country estate/farm-house turned hotel. It offers modern rooms, all with bath. Country cooking and an outdoor garden and patio. Both rooms and campgrounds are available. (Singles L45,000. Doubles L65,000. Triples L75,000. Quads L90,000. Breakfast L6000.) Camping: L5000 per person, L2000 per car, L3000 per tent. Open April-Oct.

Camping

The **Litorale del Cavallino,** on the Adriatic side of the Lido, east of Venice, is one endless row of campgrounds on the beach. From San Marco, *vaporetto* #14 winds its way to Punta Sabbioni (40min., L3300). **Camping Miramare,** Lungomare Dante Alighieri, 29 (tel. 96 61 50, fax 530 11 50), about 700m along the beach to your right as you descend from the Punta Sabbioni *vaporetto* stop, charges L10,800 per person and L5000 per tent depending on the time of year. Bungalows L46,500 for 4 people. Open April-Nov. **Cà Pasquall,** Via Poerio, 33 (tel. 96 61 10), charges a mere L4500 per person and L12,000 per tent space. (Open May-Sept.)

Another option is **Campeggio Fusina,** Via Moranzani, in the locality of Malcontenta (tel. 547 00 55), which costs L8000 per person, L6000 per tent, and L18,000 per tent and car. (English spoken. Call ahead.) From P. Roma, take bus #4 (L1100) to Mestre and change to bus #13 (across the street from Supermarket Pam). Ride to the last stop (1hr., last bus at 9pm). The boat trip is more picturesque and convenient but also more expensive. Take *vaporetto* #5 (L2500) left to Zattere and then take #16 (L3500) for 20 min. to Fusina.

FOOD

It is becoming difficult to actually sit down to a good meal in Venice at terrestrial prices. To avoid paying a fortune, visit any *bar* or *osteria* in town and make a meal from the vast display of meat- and cheese-filled pastries, tidbits of seafood, rice, and meat, and *tramezzini,* triangular slices of soft white bread with every imaginable filling. (Venetians have long cultivated the tradition of just such a between-meal repast, known as the *cicchetto,* always washed down by *un'ombra,* a glass of local wine). Good deals on tourist *menùs* converge along the broad **Via Garibaldi,** a lovely 15-min. walk along the waterfront from P. San Marco.

If you're going to spend big bucks on dinner, try one of the local seafood dishes. *Seppie in nero* is a tasty, soft squid coated with its own ink and usually served with *polenta,* a bland cornmeal mush. A plate of *pesce fritta mista* (mixed fried seafood, at least L9000) usually includes *calamari* (squid), *polpo* (small octopus), shrimp, and the catch of the day. *Fegato alla veneziana* is a simple but celebrated dish of liver and onions.

Kosher food is served in Europe's oldest Jewish quarter, in Cannaregio at the end of a series of Hebrew and Jewish signs. Call ahead to reserve a space at the **Casa Israelitica di Reposo,** 2874 (tel. 71 80 02), located across the Campo del Ghetto Nuovo from the Museo Ebraico. (Open June-Sept. Sun.-Fri. 10am-7pm, Oct.-May, 10am-4pm.)

The Veneto and Friuli regions produce an abundance of excellent and inexpensive **wines.** A good local white wine is the sparkling, dry *prosecco della Marca,* or the *collio,* another dry white. In reds, try a, merlot or *marzemino. Osteria* or *Baccari,* simple and usually authentic wine and snack bars, can be found in alleys and streets throughout the city. Venetians drop by in the late afternoon, before dinner.

There are a few **street markets** in town. Of course, the most famous and the historic center of trade and merchandise for the old Venetian Republic is the area surrounding the **Rialto** (San Polo side). Fruit stands line the Ruga degli Orefici, and on the right are the *Erberia* (vegetables) and *Pescheria* (fish) markets. Another morning market also appears in Cannaregio on Rio Terra S. Leonardo, just past Ponte Guglie. It disappears in the mid-afternoon.

Locals shop on the side streets near **Campo Beccarie** in San Polo near the Rialto. Less entertaining but more convenient are the *alimentari*. In Cannaregio, **STANDA,** on Strada Nova, 3660, near Campo S. Felice, has groceries in the back (Open daily 8:30am-7:20pm). In Castello near San Marco, there's **Su. Ve.,** 5816, on Calle del Mondo Novo, off Campo Santa Maria Formosa. (Open Thurs.-Sat. 8:45am-7pm, Wed. 8:45am-1pm.) In Dorsoduro, go to **Mega I** at Campo Santa Margherita, 3019/B, an unmarked entrance between a phone booth and a *caffè*. (Open Sun.-Fri. 9am-1pm and 4:30-7:30pm, Sat. until 7:45pm, and Wed. 9am-1pm.) In Giudecca, **Vivo Supermarket,** on Fondamenta de Zittele, 203A, to the left of the church *redatore*, is your nearest grocery outlet. (Closed Sun. and Wed. afternoon.)

Cannaregio

Cafe da Poggi, Campo della Maddalena, 2103 (tel. 71 59 71). On the main route from the station to San Marco. A popular student hangout with coffee, drinks, sandwiches and loud music. Open daily, early to late.

L'Arca di Noe, Cannaregio, 5401 (tel. 523 81 53). On Calle Larga Giacinto Gallina. Vegetarian restaurant. Organic dishes and brown rice. Indian food every Wed. Primi piatti, L8000-10,000. *Menù* L28,000. Reservations. Open Fri.-Wed. 9am-3pm and 5-11pm. Eurocard, MC, Visa.

Osteria al 40 Ladroni, Fondamenta della Sensa, 3253 (tel. 71 57 36). Next to Ponte de la Malvasia. On the canal's edge back in the quiet residential quarter. Indoor and outdoor seating. Casual, with great prices and paper tablecloths. *Primi* L5000. Open Mon.-Sat. 8am-11pm. Lunch 1-4pm and dinner 8-11pm.

Ristorante al Ponte, Cannaregio, 2352 (tel. 72 07 44), quite literally *on* Ponte del'Anconeta, the 2nd bridge after you turn left from the station, just past P. San Geremia. The reasonable *menù* (L12,500) includes everything but beverage and spotlights regional specialties such as *seppie nere alla Veneziana* (black cuttlefish in a sauce of oil, white wine, and tomatoes). Cover L3000. Service 12%. Open Wed.-Mon. 11:30am-2:30pm and 6:30-9:30pm.

Ai Promessi Sposi, Cannaregio, 4367 (tel. 522 86 09). From the Strada Nova, take a left on Calle del Duca just before Campo S. Apostoli, then a right on Calle del'Oca. Mellow music and magnificent meals. Try their specialty, *spaghetti bigoli in salsa* (thick spaghetti with anchovies and onions, L7000). *Menù* L16,000. Cover L1500. Open Thurs.-Tues. noon-2:30pm and 7-10pm.

Trattoria Casa Mia, Cannaregio, 4430 (tel. 528 55 90), on same alley as Promessi Sposi. One look at the family-filled interior and you may choose to make it *la casa tua*. *Bigoli in salsa* is L5500 per person for a min. of 2, and fish entrees begin at L10,000. Cover L1500. Service 12%. Open Wed.-Mon. noon-3pm and 6-10pm.

San Polo and Santa Croce

Pizzeria alle Oche, Santa Croce, 1552 a/b (tel. 524 11 61). Near Campo San Giacomo. Rumor has it amongst the Venetian student population that it's the best pizzeria in town. Open for lunch and dinner.

Trattoria/Pizzeria All'Anfora, Santa Croce, 1223 (tel. 524 53 25), on Lista Vechia dei Bari. A "lowbrow" eatery populated by local folks. Vine-covered patio dining out back. *Primi* L5-10,000. Pizza L5-10,000. Open Tues.-Sun. for lunch and dinner. Am Ex, MC, Visa.

Trattoria alle Burchielle, Santa Croce, 393 (tel. 523 13 42), on the Fondamenta Burchielle, off the corner of P. Roma over the bridge at Campazzo Tre Ponti, the 3-bridge intersection. A trattoria since 1503 along the banks of a small canal. Pasta L6000. Cover L1500. Service 10%. Open Tues.-Sun. noon-3pm and 7-10:30pm

Osteria do Spade, San Polo, 860 (tel. 521 05 74), in Sottoportego delle Do Spade near the Rialto. Tucked away under an archway before the Do Spade bridge south of the fish market. Serves sumptuous little sandwiches (L1200-1800). Try the house wine (L800 per glass) or any of the hundreds of Friuli and Veneto whites and reds. Especially good is *inferno* from the Val Telina (L2200 per glass). Open Sept.-July Mon.-Sat. 9am-1pm and 5-8:30pm. Closed Sun. and Thurs. afternoon.

Osteria do Mori, San Polo, 429 (tel. 522 54 01), down the street from the above. Venetians have frequented this snack-and-wine bar since 1571. Standing room only. Wine L1200-7000 per glass. *Tramezzini* L1400. Open late Aug.-July Mon.-Tues. and Thurs.-Sat. 8:30am-1:30pm and 5-8:30pm, Wed. 8:30am-1:30pm.

Alla Rivetta, San Polo, 1479 (tel. 522 42 46), on canal's edge in Campiello dei Meloni on the way to Rialto. Expect better prices than service. Fried fish L8000. Cover L1500, service 10%. Open Tues.-Sun. 7am-noon and 2-9:30pm.

Aliani Gastronomia, San Polo, 655 (tel. 522 49 13), on Ruga Vecchia San Giovanni, after a left off Ruga Orefici, the street that leads to the Rialto bridge on the San Polo side. The best and most central take-out deli. Cheeses and cold cuts, lavish lasagna (L1550 per *etto*), roasted half chicken (L9800), and lots of vegetables. (Open mid-Aug. to July Mon.-Sat. 8am-1pm and 5-8pm.)

Mensa Universitaria di Cà Foscari, S. Polo, 2480 (tel. 71 80 69), on Calle del Magazen. Full meals including drink and dessert L6000 with student ID. Open Mon.-Sat. 11:45am-2:30pm and 6:30-8:30pm, Sun. noon-2pm.

Dorsoduro

El Chef, Dorsoduro, 2765 (tel. 522 28 15), on Calle Lombardo, under the archway from Campo S. Barnabà. If a dish of fish is not your wish, go elsewhere. Local wines L8500 per liter. Open mid-March-Dec. Tues.-Sun. noon-3pm and 6:30-10pm.

Crepizza, Dorsoduro, 3760 (tel. 522 62 80), on Calle San Pantalon off Calle Crosera across from da Silvio. Look for the hanging sign. Crêpes (about L8000, sweet crêpes from L6000) and pizza (L6000-10,000) served with zeal. Cover L1500. Service 10%. Open Wed.-Mon. noon-2:30pm and 7-10:30pm. Eurocard, MC, Visa.

San Marco

Rosticceria San Bartolomeo, San Marco, 5424/A (tel. 522 35 69), in Calle de la Bissa off Campo San Bartolomeo near the Rialto Bridge, under a sign for Rosticceria Gislon. Top-notch self-service. Venetian specialties such as *seppie con polenta* (cuttlefish with cornmeal pudding, L14,000). 15% discount with *cartagiovane*. Open Feb.-Dec. Tues.-Sun. 10am-2:25pm and 4:50-9pm.

Vino, Vino, San Marco, 2007/A (tel. 523 70 27), on Calle del Sartor da Veste, off Calle Larga XXII Marzo, which runs from the Ponte Moisè due west of P. San Marco. Praised in the *New York Times,* and, like the paper, it's black and white, and red all over. A river of wines (L2500-8000 per glass) and a sea of tourists. Cover L1000. Rolling Venice discount. Open for drinks Wed.-Mon. 10am-11:30pm; for eats, noon-4pm and 7-11:30pm.

Da Zorzi, San Marco, on Calle dei Fuseri, 4359 (tel. 522 39 14). Near Campo San Luca. Vegetarian restaurant and *caffè*.

Leon Bianco, San Marco, 4153 (tel. 522 11 80), on Salizzata San Luca which runs between Campo San Luca and campo Manin, northwest of P. San Marco. Snarf tasty food while standing at marble counters, shoulder to business-suited shoulder. Main courses L5500. *Risotto* L4000. *Tramezzini* L1500. Tasty fried snacks L1000-1300. Open Mon.-Sat. 8am-8pm.

Alfredo, Alfredo, near San Marco, in Campo S. Filippo e Giacomo (tel. 523 97 27). For a restaurant and cafe atmosphere and near the Rialto, across from the main Post Office. For fast food and pizza, Salizada del Fontego, 5549 (tel. 528 52 49), near Ponte l'Olio. Venice's answer to McDonalds. Open daily 11am-midnight and in S. Filliop e Giacomo, open daily 11am-2am. AmEx checks, AmEx, MC, Visa.

Castello

Osteria Al Mascaron, Castello, 5225 (tel. 522 59 95), on Calle Longa Santa Maria Formosa, which runs off Campo Santa Maria Formosa, northeast of P. San Marco. The ultimate in informal *osteria* eating—dark, comfortable and crowded. Filled with chattering Venetians taking a wine break or enjoying delicious specialties like *spaghetti alle vongolenere* (with black clams, L12,000). Cover L2000. Open mid-Jan. to mid-Dec. Mon.-Sat. 11am-3pm and 6-11pm.

Trattoria Alla Rivetta, Castello, 9625 (tel. 528 73 02). Off Campo SS. Filippo e Giacomo which lies just east of P. San Marco—the restaurant's squeezed into a space right before the Ponte San Provolo. One of the only genuine and reasonable places in the area. Try the *pesce fritta mista* (large portion L14,000). Cover L2000. Service 12%. Open Tues.-Sun. 10am-10pm. Closed Aug.

Antiche Botteselle, Via Garibaldi, 1621 (tel. 523 72 92), on a broad street that penetrates Castello near the Arsenale stop. A 15-min. walk from S. Marco. *Menù* L13,000 if you mention *Let's Go,* otherwise L12,000 plus cover and service. 36 types of pizza (L4800-8000). *Primi* L5000-14,000. *Secondi* L6000-19,000. Wine L8000 per bottle. Open Thurs.-Tues. 8:30am-3pm and 6-10pm (bar til midnight).

Cip Ciap, at Ponte del Mondo Novo, 5799/A (tel. 523 66 21), off Fondamenta Santa Maria Formosa, southwest of the campo, deserves highest praise for its pizza (L5000-10,000, slices L1200); the *disco volante* (literally "flying saucer," stuffed with mushrooms, eggplant, ham, and salami, L9000) is out of this world. (Open Dec.-Oct. daily 9am-8pm.)

Gelaterie and Pasticcerie

Gelateria Santo Stefano, San Marco, 2962/A (tel. 522 55 76), in the northwest corner of Campo Morosini San Stefano, is said to have the best *nocciola* (hazelnut) and *panna* (whipped cream) in the world. Cones L2000-4000. Open April-Sept. Tues.-Sun. 7:30am-midnight. Off season 7:30am-9pm. Closed Dec.-Jan.

Gelati Nico, Fondamenta Zattere, 922 (tel. 522 52 93), in Dorsoduro near the *vaporetto* stop of the same name, is the pride of Venice. The prices are similar to San Stefano's, but the portions are huge. *Gianduiotto,* a slice of dense chocolate hazelnut ice cream dunked in whipped cream, is their specialty (L3200). Open in summer Fri-Wed. 7am-11pm. Mid-Jan. to mid-Dec. 7am-9pm.

Il Doge, Campo Santa Margherita, Dorsoduro, 3058/A (tel. 523 46 07) is seldom without a line of salivating customers. Tasty *granite* (flavored ices, L2000), and *frappé* (fruit shakes, L3000), along with *gelato* comprise the holy frozen trinity. Open for worship Feb.-Oct. daily 10:30am-midnight.

Causin, P. Santa Margherita, 2996 (tel. 523 60 91), accross the Campo. A *caffè-gela-teria* that has pleased customers since 1928. The best and cheapest place in Venice. Two-scoop cone L1500. Five-scoop bowl L3000. Open daily 8am-8pm.

Pasticceria Pitteri, Cannaregio, 3844, on Strada Nova, the central street (open Mon.-Sat. 8am-8:30pm.) Buy the dense and nutty *pane dei dogi* (L2700-3100 per *etto*) and repent at your leisure.

A. Rosa Salva, San Marco, 5020 (tel. 522 79 34), on Marzaria San Salvador, 5021, near the Rialto bridge. Locals claim that it is Venice's premier bakery and the famous *budino di semolino* (a rich pudding cake, L1000 each) affirms this. Open Mon.-Sat. 8am-8pm. Closed last week in July and first week in Aug.

SIGHTS

> In Venetian churches a strict dress code applies. No shorts, sleeveless shirts or miniskirts allowed.

If you plan to visit several Venetian museums consider buying the city's **Biglietto Cumulativo** (Special Museum Ticket, L18,000). This ticket gets you into the Palazzo Ducale, the Museo Correr, the Museo del Risorgimento, the Cà Rezzonico Museo del Settecento, the Galleria d'Arte Moderna di Cà Pesaro, the Museo Vetrario di Murano, the Palazzo Mocenigo, the Museo Guidi, and the Casa di Goldoni. It is available at any of the above museums and is valid through the end of the calendar year. Also keep your eyes open for special art exhibits tucked away in churches and schools.

The Grand Canal

The Grand Canal bisects the main islands which constitute the city of Venice. Most important activity in the city happens on or near these shores. The façades of the opulent *palazzi* that crowd its banks testify to a history of immense wealth. From the *vaporetto* #1 or #34 you will enjoy a tour of some of the greatest works of Renaissance architecure. The palaces share the same structure despite the external decorative features, which reflect the styles of various historical periods. From early on, cramped island life didn't permit the luxury of a central courtyard. Instead, Venetian *palazzi* were constructed with central halls running front to back, providing the necessary air circulation and light. The ground floor (*androne*) served as an entrance hall (from the canal), while the living quarters occupied the *piano nobile* (second floor). The overall effect, unlike that of the dense, massive urban palaces of the Florentine Renaissance, is one delicate, inviting openness.

The oldest surviving palaces, some from the 13th century, were influenced by Byzantine and early Christian tastes. Look for rounded arches in low relief, like those on the **Cà da Mosto,** the *palazzo* on the S. Marco side of Grand Canal shortly past the Rialto bridge towards the train station. Further on toward the station on the same side of the canal is the **Cà d'Oro** whose name derives from the gold leaf that once adorned the tracery of its renowned façade. Built in 1440, the Cà d'Oro represents the pinnacle of the Venetian Gothic (see Cannaregio below).

On the other side of the canal, one can see what is now the **Gallery of Modern Art.** The majestic Baroque edifice is known as the **Palazzo Pesaro** because of the grotesques grimacing out from its façade. Closer to the station stands the **Fondaco dei Turchi,** a Turkish warehouse until 1838. Today, the **Natural History Museum** stands in lieu of the Ottoman merchants.

Many of Venice's Renaissance edifices are the works of three major Venetian architects: Mauro Coducci, Jacopo Sansovino, and Michele Sanmicheli. Coducci's early **Palazzo Corner-Spinelli** (directly to the right of the S. Angelo stop in between the Rialto and the Accademia Bridges, 1510) and **Cà Vendramin Calergi** (directly to the right of the S. Marcuola stop, near the station), both on the east bank, were the first *palazzi* to depart from the traditional Venetian style, infusing classical and Byzantine elements. Coducci's leadership inspired Sansovino's stately **Palazzo Corner della Cà Granda** (located on the San Marco side of the canal, directly left of S. Maria del Giglio stop, past the Accademia, 1550), and Sanmicheli's **Palazzo Grimani di San Luca** (the second palazzo to the left of the S. Angelo stop, just past the Rialto), also on the east bank.

San Marco and Castello Piazza San Marco and Environs

Piazza San Marco is the city's nucleus. Water and land traffic merge at the Molo and Riva degli Schiavoni, from where Venice radiates in unsurpassed magnificence. The numerous domes and spires of the church of San Marco, along with the pink, Rococo decorations of the Doge's Palace, contrast with the Classical façade of Sansovino's. Above the piazza soars the solid brick **campanile.** The campanile (96m high) originally served as a watchtower and lighthouse for the city. The most recent tower was rebuilt as an exact replica of the 16th-century campanile, after it collapsed during the earthquake of 1902. (Tel. 522 40 64; open daily 9:30am-9:30pm, winters until 7:30pm. Admission L4000.) A fine photo spot, though cheaper admission, shorter lines, and better views are available at the **Campanile di San Giorgio** across from P. San Marco on the small island of San Giorgio (see Outlying Sights, below).

Construction of the **Basilica of San Marco** (tel. 522 52 05) began in the 9th century, when two Venetian merchants stole St. Mark's remains from Alexandria, packing them in pork to hoodwink Arab officials. The caper is commemorated in a mosaic to the left of the three entrance arches. The basilica's cruciform plan and five bulbed domes, a direct architectural reference to the Church of the Holy Apostles in Constantinople, suggest a prestige which was intended to rival both Byzantium and St. Peter's. Rebuilt after a fire in the 10th century, it was continually enlarged and embellished over the next half-millennium. The result is a unique synthesis of Byzantine, Western European, and Islamic influences. (Open daily 9:45am-7:30pm. Basilica is free, L2000 to see the Golden Screen and go into the upper galleries.)

The church sparkles with mosaics of all ages—perhaps the best are those on the atrium's ceiling. Underfoot, 12th-century confections of marble, glass and porphyry confuse the eyes with endless geometric intricacies. The basilica's main treasure is the **Pala d'Oro** (tel. 522 56 97), a Veneto-Byzantine gold bas-relief encrusted with precious gems. In the area behind the screen are Sansovino's bronze reliefs and his sacristy door. The ticket to this area will also get you into the small **treasury**, a hoard of gold and relics left over from the spoils of the Fourth Crusade. (Open Mon.-Sat. 9:45am-6:30pm, Sun. 1:30-5:30pm. Admission L2000.) Through a door in the atrium is the **Galleria della Basilica** (tel. 522 52 05)—worth it for a better view of the mosaics on the walls and floors. The recently restored *Horses of St. Mark* (originals) are on display here. (Open daily 10am-6:30pm. Admission L2000.) Guided tours of the basilica are given April-June and Sept.-Oct. Mon.-Sat. at 11am. Call the **Curia Patriarcale** for further information (tel. 520 03 33. English spoken).

As you come out of San Marco you'll find Coducci's ornate **Torre dell'Orologio** (1499), a florid arrangement of sculpture and sundials on your right. Two oxidizing bronze Moors strike the hours. The arch below marks the beginning of the **Mercerie,** Venice's main commercial street leading to the Rialto.

Between San Marco and the lagoon stands the **Palazzo Ducale** (Doge's Palace; tel. 522 49 51). The *palazzo,* built in the 14th century after the original was destroyed by a fire, is a magnificent example of Venetian Gothic. The exterior design is a combination of arcades and light-colored stone cladding which lends a light and delicate appearance to a potentially massive and monolythic structure. This clever design was also employed when the extension to the palace was added one century later. The sculpted Virtues of Temperance, Fortitude, Prudence, and Charity that adorn the **Porta della Carta** are attributed to the 15th century duo of Giovanni and Bartolomeo Bon. At the side of San Marco stand the *Quattro Mori,* statues of four Roman emperors that crusaders "borrowed" from Constantinople in 1204. Rizzo's **Scala dei Giganti,** sweeping up to the second floor in the left end of the courtyard, is crowned with Sansovino's *Mars and Neptune.* Up his famous **Golden Staircase** preside the Senate Chamber and the Room of the Council of Ten (the much-feared secret police of the Republic), both shrouded in paintings. The route then returns to the second floor, where after passing some enormous globes, you can wander through the echoing **Grand Council Chamber.** The room contains the huge, resplendent *Paradiso* by Tintoretto as well as Veronese's *Apotheosis of Venus.* This room contains the portraits of all the doges of Venice except Marin Falier. An empty frame commemorates this over-ambitious doge, who was executed for treason after his unsuccessful coup attempt in 1355. Throughout the building are slits in the walls where secret denunciations were inserted to be investigated by the Ten. (Open daily 9am-7pm. Admission L8000.) For a **Secret Itineraries Tour** through the palace and then over the bridge of sighs through the prison, call 249 51. You must call ahead for reservations, since there is no tour info at the doge's palace. (Tours Thurs.-Tues. 10am and noon, 1hr.)

From the Council Chamber, a series of secret passages leads across the **Ponte dei Sospiri** (Bridge of Sighs) from the back of the palace to the prisons. Casanova was among those condemned by the Ten to walk across into the hands of sadistic Inquisitors. The name alludes to the bitter groans of prisoners pondering the slim prospects of ever regaining their freedom.

Facing the Palazzo Ducale across P. San Marco are Sansovino's greatest hits, the elegant **Libreria** (1536) and the **Zecca** (mint, 1547). The main reading room of the **Biblioteca Marciana** (tel. 520 87 88), on the second floor, is adorned with frescoes by Veronese and Tintoretto. (Entrance at #12. Open Mon.-Fri. 9am-1pm. Prior permission required.) Venetian artists received their quota of classical cultivation from the sculptures in the **Museo Archeologico,** P. San Marco, 52 (tel. 522 59 78), next door. (Open Mon.-Sat. 9am-2pm, Sun. 9am-1pm. Admission L4000.)

Under the portico at the opposite end of the piazza from the church is the entrance to the **Museo Civico Correr** (tel. 522 56 25). It houses a couple of Bellinis and Carpaccio's *Courtesans,* not to mention such sundry curiosities of daily Venetian life as the foot-high platform shoes once worn by sequestered noblewomen. (Open Wed.-Mon. 10am-5pm. Admission L5000, students L2500.)

VENICE

Two famous *caffè* face off in the piazza. Eighteenth-century supporters of the Austrians ruling the city patronized **Caffè Quadri,** P. San Marco, 120-123, on the side of the piazza farther from the water. (Tel. 523 92 99. Open daily 10am-midnight. Oct.-April Tues.-Sun., 10am-midnight.) Patriotic Venetians frequented **Caffè Florian,** across the piazza at San Marco, 56/59. (Tel. 528 53 38; open daily 9am-midnight; Oct.-April Thurs.-Tues. 9am-midnight.) There is no more seductive way to spend a Venetian evening than to sit in the piazza, listening to the competing orchestras while sipping a cappuccino. Both *caffè* have a L3500 cover charge during "concerts," so if you sit down with a caffè (L4500), you might as well take off your coat and make yourself at home. **Harry's Bar,** favored hangout of "Ernesto" Hemingway and real men ever since, lies on Calle Vallaresso, in front of the San Marco *vaporetto* stop. (Drinks L7500. Service 20%. Open Tues.-Sun. 10:30am-11pm.)

The Mercerie

Starting under the arch of the Torre dell'Orologio in San Marco, the shop-filled and tourist-clogged Mercerie leads up to the **Church of San Giuliano,** commissioned by the Venetian doctor Tommaso Ragone as a monument to himself. His portrait by Sansovino glowers over the door, framed by inscriptions and allegories. The Mercerie then passes by **Campo San Salvatore.** The church consists of three square crosses stuck together. The church was originally designed and built in the early 16th century, yet the façade was not completed until 1633; it contains Giovanni Bellini's *Supper in Emmaus* and Titian's *Annunciation* (1566). (Open daily 9:30am-noon and 4:30-7pm. Free.)

Around San Marco

North of P. San Marco stands the **Church of Santa Maria Formosa.** At the bottom of the campanile leers a hideous, carved head, which, to Ruskin, "embodied the type of evil spirit to which Venice was abandoned, the pestilence that came and breathed upon her beauty." Coducci's Greek-cross plan, a rebuilding of an ancient church, houses Palma il Vecchio's painting of St. Barbara, here the exemplar of female beauty in Renaissance Venice. Across the bridge, a twisted alleyway leads to the haunting **Palazzo Querini-Stampalia** (tel. 522 52 35), whose intriguing aristocratic rooms house paintings dating from the 14th through 18th centuries. (Open Tues.-Sun. 10am-12:30pm and 3:30-6pm. Off-season closed in the afternoon. Admission L8000.)

North of Campo Santa Maria Formosa, Calle Lunga and Calle Cicogna lead to Campo **SS. Giovanni e Paolo** and to the church of the same name (*San Zanipolo* in the Venetian dialect). This grandiose Gothic structure, built by the Dominican order over the course of two centuries (mid-13th to mid-15th), resembles a brick barn, and the monuments to various doges along the sides are no improvement. However, there is a wonderful polyptych by Giovanni Bellini hanging over the second altar of the right-hand nave. From the left transept you enter the **Cappella del Rosario** (Rosary Chapel) which, although damaged by a fire in 1867, still preserves four marvelous paintings by Veronese. If you cross the Ponte Rosso and go straight, you'll come to the Lombardos' masterpiece, the **Church of Santa Maria dei Miracoli.**

To the east of San Marco, off the Riva degli Schiavoni, stands the beautiful 15th-century **Church of San Zaccaria** (tel. 522 12 57). Coducci designed this striking façade, an enlarged version of his San Michele. Inside, the second altar on the left houses Bellini's masterpiece *The Madonna and Saints.* (Open daily 10am-noon and 4-6pm.) Around the corner, on the waterfront, is Massari's **Church of the Pietà** (built in 1475, façade of 1906), containing celebrated Tiepolo frescoes. Vivaldi was concertmaster here at the beginning of the 18th century, and concerts featuring his music are held in the church throughout the summer. (Open summers daily 9:30am-12:30pm and 3-6pm, Off-season only for masses and concerts.)

For a real treat, make your way through the *calli* to the **Scuola di San Giorgio degli Schiavoni,** Ponte dei Greci, 3259 (tel. 522 88 28). Here, between 1502 and

1511, Carpaccio decorated the ground floor with some of his finest paintings, depicting episodes from the lives of St. George, St. Jerome, and St. Trifone. (Open Tues.-Sat. 10am-12:30pm and 3:30-6pm, Sun. and Mon., 10am-12:30pm.) The nearby **Museo dei Dipinti Sacri Bizantini** (tel. 522 65 81), at Ponte dei Greci, 3412, displays religious paintings from the Byzantine and post-Byzantine periods. (Open Mon.-Sat. 9am-1pm and 2-5pm. Admission L4000.) For the tale of *La Serenissima's* maritime supremacy, visit the **Museo Storico Navale** (tel. 520 02 76) on the waterfront of the Castello district where Via Giuseppe Garibaldi hits Riva dei Sette Mártiri. (Open Mon.-Sat. 9am-1pm. Admission L2000.)

Playing up the water theme, Venice has its own **Aquarium,** Calle Albanesi, 4259 (tel. 520 77 70), just off Campo SS. Filippo e Giacomo, which features examples of the local sealife of the lagoon. (Open daily 9am-8pm. Admission L3500.) A bit farther down the waterfront lie the **Giardini,** which every two years plays host to the biennial International Exhibition of Modern Art, known as the **Biennale.**

Cannaregio From the Rialto to the Ghetto

Heading north from the Rialto bridge on Salizzada San Giovanni, you reach the last of Coducci's churches, **San Giovanni Crisostomo,** a refined Greek cross. The interior contains works by Giovanni Bellini and an altarpiece by Sebastiano del Piombo. Marco Polo supposedly lived under the arch in corte Seconda del Milione.

From the Crisostomo church, head left toward the *rio* of the same name. Cross two bridges and two small squares to find the **Church of SS. Apostoli,** with an unassuming Tiepolo painting of Santa Lucia's first communion. Nearby is the **Cà d'Oro** (whose inaccessible front door taunts you from the Grand Canal), where the **Galleria Giorgio Franchetti** (tel. 523 87 90) opened in 1984. This formerly private collection displays works of minor Flemish painters and a few major pieces, including Titian's *Venus,* Mantegna's *St. Sebastian* and Durer's *Deposition.* (Open Mon.-Sat. 9am-1:30pm, Sun. 9am-12:30pm. Admission L4000.) North of here the **Church of the Gesuiti** (tel. 523 06 25) boasts a florid green-and-white marble interior (rebuilt by Giorgio Massari in 1724), Titian's *Martyrdom of St. Lawrence*, and Tiepolo's alterpiece and ceiling fresco. In the northern corner of Cannaregio the **Church of Madonna dell'Orto** patiently awaits the venturesome. Take scenic *vaporetto* #5 (*destra*) to the Madonna dell'Orto stop (L2500). Tintorettos, notably his *Sacrifice of the Golden Calf, Last Judgement* and *Presentation of the Virgin*, reside within. (Open daily 9:30am-noon and 3:30-5:30pm.)

Between the church and the train station lies the **Jewish Ghetto,** the first in Europe. The term *ghetto* itself originated in Venice, as the quarter was named after the knife-grinders who previously worked here. Established by ducal decree in 1516, the Ghetto Nuovo remained the enforced enclave of the Jews in Venice until Napoleon's victory over the Venetian Republic in 1797. Upon entering the ghetto through the underpass off Fondamenta di Cannaregio, you can still witness the grooves in the marble where the nightly gate formerly stood, barring movement outside the ghetto at night. The area contains the tallest tenement buildings in Venice and five synagogues, of which three are open to the public. The **Sinagoga Grande Tedesca** is less opulent but more intriguing than the **Sinagoghe Spagnole** and **Levantina.** Tedesca is also the oldest, dating back to 1528. Drop by the **Museo Ebraica** (tel. 71 53 59) in the Campo del Nuovo Ghetto for a diminutive but fascinating exhibit documenting five centuries of Jewish presence in Venice. Inquire here about guided tours of the Old Ghetto, every 30min. starting at 10:30am. (Museum open June-Sept. Sun.-Fri. 10am-7pm; Oct.-May Sun.-Fri. 10am-4pm. Admission L4000, students L2000.)

San Polo and Santa Croce

The **Ponte Rialto,** spanning the Grand Canal, is the entrance to this commercial district. In the center of the **Erberia,** the grocery section of the open market, is the **Church of San Giacomo di Rialto,** the oldest in Venice. A stubby column with a staircase to the top stands in front of it, supported by a bent stone figure. The col

VENICE

umn served as a podium from which state proclamations were issued. The statue, called *il Gobbo* (the hunchback), has served as a bulletin board for public responses since Roman times.

From the **Rialto** bridge, drift with the crowd down the Ruga degli Orefici, then turn left and follow Ruga Vecchia San Giovanni to the **Church of San Polo** (*San Apponal* in the local dialect); the young Giandomenico Tiepolo completed the dramatic 14 stations of the Cross in the chancel. Nearby, in the great Gothic Franciscan **Basilica dei Frari** (1340-1443; tel. 522 26 37), Donatello's wooden *St. John the Baptist* keeps company with a later Florentine statue of the saint by Sansovino and three purely Venetian paintings: Giovanni Bellini's triptych of the *Madonna and Saints* over the sacristy, Titian's famous *Assumption of the Virgin*, and his *Madonna of Case Pesaro*. (Open Mon.-Sat. 8:30am-noon and 3-6pm, Sun. 3-5:30pm. Admission L1000, Sun. and holidays free.)

The *scuole* of Venice were a combination of guilds and religious fraternities. Members paid annual dues for the support of their needy fellow members and for the decoration of the *scuola's* premises. Among the richest and most illustrious was the **Scuola Grande di San Rocco** (tel. 523 48 64), across the *campo* at the end of the Frari. Tintoretto, who set out to combine, in his words, "the color of Titian with the drawing of Michelangelo," covered the inside with 56 paintings. To see the paintings in chronological order, start on the second floor in the Sala dell'Albergo and follow the cycle downstairs. (Open daily 9am-5:30pm. Off-season, Mon.-Fri. 10am-1pm, Sat. and Sun. 10am-4pm. Admission L6000, with Rolling Venice: L5000.)

Dorsoduro

The Ponte dell'Accademia crosses the Grand Canal at the **Gallerie dell'Accademia** (tel. 522 22 47). This temple of Venetian-school art should top your list of things to see. Among the galleries, Room II stands out for Giovanni Bellini's *Pala di San Giobbe*, a sublime marriage of perspectival sense and Venetian sensibility. Room IV encloses more Bellinis (Giovanni and father Jacopo both) as well as an early Piero della Francesca, but Room V surpasses this, with a pair of certifiable Giorgione canvases, *La Tempesta* and *La Vecchia*. Rooms VI-IX build up High Renaissance anticipation, which receives its payoff in Room X. Displayed here, Veronese's huge rendition of the Last Supper enraged the leaders of the Inquisition with its indulgent improvisation—a Protestant German and a monkey figure among the guests—and Veronese was forced to change the name to *Supper in the House of Levi* to avoid having to make changes at his own expense. This room also contains several brilliant Tintorettos and Titian's last work, a brooding *Pietà*. Rounding off the collection are a number of works by Tiepolo, Canaletto, and Longhi, whose refined cityscapes are considered the height of early urban art. The wonderful cycle of *The Legend of St. Ursula* by Carpaccio (1490-95) in Room XXI boasts a scene of Ursula, 11,000 virgins in tow, trooping off to Cologne to meet martyrdom at the hands of the Huns. (Open Mon.-Sat. 9am-7pm. Off-season Mon.-Sat. 9am-1pm. Admission L8000.)

The **Cà Rezzonico** (*vaporetto* stop of the same name) is on the fondamenta Rezzonico, across a bridge from Campo San Baranabà. Designed by Longhena, it's one of the great 18th-century Venetian palaces. Inside, recall notorious intrigues and love affairs in the **Museo del Settecento Veneziano** (Museum of the 18th Century; tel. 522 45 43). The small bedrooms and boudoirs on the second floor house delightful works by Tiepolo, Guardi, and Longhi. (Open Sat.-Thurs. 10am-5pm. Admission L5000. Seniors and children under 12, L3000.)

The **Collezione Peggy Guggenheim,** Dorsoduro, 701 (tel. 520 62 88), housed in the late Ms. Guggenheim's Palazzo Venier dei Leoni, near the tip of Dorsoduro, is an small and eclectic collection of modern art. It has rapidly become one of Venice's most popular museums, and deservedly so. Aesthetic and tasteful presentation complements the diversity of the collection itself. The collection includes works by Brancusi, Marino Marini, Kandinsky, Rothko, Max Ernst, and Jackson Pollock. The grounds also feature a sculpture garden. (Open Wed.-Mon. 11am-6pm. Admission

L7000. Students with ISIC, or Rolling Venice card, and seniors, L4000.) Just down the street from the Guggenheim Collection is a **Cenedesa Glass Blowing Factory** in Campo San Gregorio, 174. Witness the technique here without traveling to outer islands. (Open Mon. and Wed.-Sat. 10am-1pm and 2-5pm. Free.)

The **Church of Santa Maria della Salute** (tel. 522 55 58), standing at the tip of Dorsoduro, is the most theatrical piece of architecture in Venice. It was designed by Longhena as the site of the dramatic *Festa della Salute* (Nov. 21), which celebrates the deal struck by the church and the festival with God, a deal that purportedly saved Venice from the plague of 1630. In the sacristy are several Titians and a Tintoretto. (Open daily 9am-noon and 3-6:30pm. Admission to sacristy L500.)

A bit north of Fondamenta Zattere, toward the western end of town, lies the 16th-century **Church of San Sebastiano.** It was here that Paolo Veronese took refuge in 1555 when he fled Verona, apparently after killing a man. By 1565 he had filled the church with some of his finest paintings and frescoes. On the ceiling, you'll marvel at his breathtaking *Stories of Queen Esther.* To get a closer look at the panels, climb to the nuns' choir. Here you'll also see the artist's moving fresco *St. Sebastian in Front of Diocletian.* Ask the custodian to turn on the lights (tip L500). Approach the church by sea from the San Basilio stop on *vaporetto* #5 or 8 (L2500).

Outlying Sights

Many of Venice's most beautiful churches are a short boat ride away from San Marco. Two of Palladio's most famous churches are visible from the *piazza.* The **Church of San Giorgio Maggiore,** across the lagoon (take boat #5 or 8, L2500), graces the island of the same name. The church houses Tintoretto's famous *Last Supper.* Ascend the **campanile** (tel. 528 99 00) for a superb view of the main islands. (Open daily 9am-1pm and 2-6pm. Admission L2000.)

A bit farther out on the next island, Giudecca, is Palladio's famous **Church of Il Redentore** (the Redeemer). During the pestilence of 1576, the Venetian Senate swore that they would build a devotional church and make a yearly pilgrimage there if the plague would leave the city. Palladio accommodated the pilgrims by enlarging the church's tribune and still managed to preserve the coherence of the building's layout. Take *vaporetto* #5 or 8 (L2500).

The tiny **Church of San Michele in Isola,** on its own island on the far side of the lagoon, is a Venetian masterpiece and the final resting place of the sometimes madman (not to mention fascist sympathizer), poet Ezra Pound. Begun by Coducci in 1469, the pristine marble façade with its delicate scallops was Venice's first Renaissance structure. The small hexagonal chapel to the left is a later addition. Take *vaporetto* #5 to the *cimitero* (cemetery) stop (L2500).

The Islands of the Lagoon

Accessible by *vaporetto* #1 and 2, the **Lido** was the setting for Thomas Mann's *Death in Venice* and Visconti's boring film version, both of which give an unforgettable impression of the sensuality and mystery for which Venice is famous. Lovers of the *belle époque* will enjoy a visit to the fabled Grand Hôtel des Bains. From the *vaporetto* stop, follow the crowd that troops daily down Gran Viale Santa Maria Elisabetta or take bus A (L800).

Boat #12 departs from Fondamenta Nuove, near Campo dei Gesuiti, for the islands of Murano, Burano, and Torcello. (Murano is also serviced by the #5.) **Murano** has been famous for its glass since 1292, when Venice's artisans decided to transfer their operations there. Today, serious glass-making and tourist enterprises coexist, affording opportunities to witness the glass-blowing process. The **Museo Vetrario** (tel. 73 95 86) on Fondamenta Giustinian, along the main canal, has a splendid glass collection dating from Roman times onward. (Open daily 10am-5pm. In off-season Thurs.-Tues. 10am-3pm. Admission L5000, students, seniors and children L3000.) Also located on Murano is the exceptional **Basilica SS. Maria e Donato,** built in the 7th century but owing its exterior a 12th century renovation. **Burano,** P. Galuppi, a half-hour out of Venice by boat #12 (L3500), caters to tourists. It is famous for its lace, which is hawked all over Venice. The small **Scuola di Merletti di Burano** (tel. 73 00 34) documents the craft. (Open Tues.-Sat. 9am-6pm, Sun. 10am-4pm. Admission L3000.)

Today **Torcello,** the remaining island, is the most rural of the group. Of the first-time visitor to Venice, John Ruskin wrote, "let him not...look upon the pageantry of her palaces...but let him ascend the highest tier of the stern ledges that sweep round the altar of Torcello." The **Cathedral** (tel. 73 00 84), founded in the 7th century and rebuilt in the 11th, has Byzantine mosaics inside so incredible that a 19th-century restorer took a few back to Wales with him. (Cathedral open daily 10am-12:30pm and 2-5pm. Admission L1500. Adjacent **museum** (tel. 73 07 61), Palazzo del Consiglio, open Tues.-Sun. 10am-12:30pm and 2-5:30pm. Admission L3000.)

Never too far from water, prosperous Venetians built their farming villas along the Brenta River which connects Venice and Padua. To call on the villas, take the ACTV buses from P. Roma. **Villa Malcontenta** (also Called "Villa Foscari"), built by Palladio on a temple-like plan, is one of the most revered in the western world. (Tel. (041) 547 00 12. Open May-Oct. Tues., Sat., and the first Sun. of the month 9am-noon. Admission L10,000.) **Mira** (also "Palazzo Foscari"), one of the most attractive villas on the Brenta, is now open for tours. (Tel. 42 35 52. Open Tues.-Sun. 9am-6pm. Admission including guided tour L7000, seniors L5000.) **Strà** (also "Villa Pisani"; tel. (049) 50 20 74) is renowned for its grand design by Figimelica and Preti and its interior decoration by Urbani and Giambattista Tiepolo. (Open Tues.-Sun. 9am-6pm. Admission L6000.) To get to Villa Malcontenta, take bus #16 from P. Roma (L700). To reach the other two villas, hop on the bus (not the direct line) that leaves about every half-hour for Padua (L2400) from P. Roma.

ENTERTAINMENT

The weekly booklet *Un Ospite di Venezia* (free at tourist offices) lists current festivals, concerts, and gallery shows. Also ask for *Venice, 1993 Events.* There are concerts once or twice a week in the larger churches such as San Marco and the Frari. The **Teatro La Fenice** (tel. 521 01 61) has an excellent summer program, featuring mostly music, with many guest artists (admission L10,000-30,000, with the Rolling Venice card half-price). The **Festival Vivaldi** takes place in early September. In summer, Vivaldi's music is also featured in a concert series in the church of **Santa Maria della Pietà,** where he was choirmaster.

For a historical introduction to the city, check out Steven Wolf's three-talk series *Venice in English: The Art and History of Venice,* an entertaining way to gain perspective on what's around. (Mon.-Sat. 7pm at the Hotel San Cassiano at S. Croce, 2232. Tel. 524 17 68.) From the Rialto Bridge, follow the signs to the Contemporary Art Museum Cà Pesaro until you find directions for the Hotel San Cassiano. Free aperitifs are served during the break. (Admission L10,000, students L7000. The third talk is free, but one should be sufficiently enlightening.)

Mark Twain Called the **gondola** "an inky, rusty canoe," but only the gentry can really afford to ride one. The authorized rate starts at L70,000 for 50 minutes, which inflates to L90,000 after sundown, but mercenary gondoliers will frequently quote prices in the six-digit range. Rides are most romantic if procured about 50 minutes before sunset, and barely affordable if shared with 5 people. Venice was built to be traveled by gondola and you will never truly get a feel for the city and its architecture until you slide quietly down the canals, passed by the front doors of the houses and institutions and travel on the original pathways. There is, however, a sneaky way to get a cheap ride just for the experience. There are several points along the Grand Canal where many Venetians need to cross, though there is no bridge. To solve the problem, *gondole* operate a short, cross-canal service. Each trip lasts only a minute or so, but this stand-up style of transportation averages a mere L700.

For theatrical entertainment **Commedia in Campo,** a classical Venetian-type of theater operates outdoors in various campos throughout the city, alternating places on different nights. Tickets are L20,000, but you may be able to catch a glimpse through the curtains.

The famed **Venice Biennale** (tel. 521 87 11 for public relations), centered in the Giardini di Castello, takes place every odd-numbered year, with a gala exhibit of international modern art. (Admission to all exhibits L10,000, less to see individual bits and pieces.) The **Mostra Internazionale del Cinema** (Venice International Film Festival, tel. 520 03 11) is held annually from late August to early September. Tickets (about L10,000-30,000) are sold at the Cinema Palace on the Lido (where the main films are screened) and at other locations—some late-night outdoor showings are free. Contact the tourist office with questions about cinema.

After an absence of several centuries, Venice's famous **Carnevale** was successfully (in a monetary if not entirely festive sense) revived as an annual celebration in 1979. During the ten days preceding Ash Wednesday, masked Venetians and camera-happy tourists jam the streets. Write to the tourist office in December for dates and details, and be sure to make lodging arrangements months in advance. Venice's next most colorful festival is the **Festa del Redentore,** originally to celebrate the end of the plague (third Sun. in July). The Church of Il Redentore is connected with Zattere by a boat-bridge for the day, and a magnificent round of fireworks shoots off between 11pm and midnight on the Saturday night before. On the first Sunday in September, Venice stages its classic **regata storica,** a gondola race down the Grand Canal, preceded by a procession of decorated gondolas. The religious festival **Festa della Salute** takes place on November 21 at Santa Maria della Salute, with another pontoon bridge constructed, this time over the Grand Canal. Again the occasion for celebration is the end of the plague.

If **shopping** is your bag, a few caveats are in order. Do not make purchases in P. San Marco or around the Rialto bridge. Not only do shops outside these areas boast products of better quality and selection, they charge about half the price. Venetian glass is best bought toward the Accademia bridge from San Marco, and between the Rialto and the station in Cannaregio, though for fun you may want to look in the showroom at the glass-blowers' factory behind the Basilica of San Marco. The map accompanying the Rolling Venice lists many shops offering reductions to pass-holders. For the most concentrated and varied selections of Venetian glass and lace, trips to the nearby islands of Murano and Burano, respectively, are in order. *Vaporetto* #5 (L2500) serves Murano while #12 (L3500) serves both Murano and Burano. Both boats leave from the Fondamenta Nuove stop.

Nightlife

Although many places shut down surprisingly early, circa midnight, there are quite a few good places to go before or after the bewitching hour. The principal after-midnight strip is Fondamenta della Misericordia in Cannaregio, just past the "Ghetto." From Lista di Spagna, cross the first main bridge, turn left on Fondamenta di Cannaregio, and look for the underpass to your right and signs pointing to the main square of the Ghetto Nuovo. Go to the square then take another bridge over the large canal in front ice you cross and take a right down the Fondamenta. Continue a few blocks, walking parallel with the canal and you should be in the center of the action. But Venice's selection of nightclubs is paltry, not to mention a meat-market. Respectable Venetians go to Mestre and the mainland when they want to party and most people seem to prefer mingling and dancing in the city's streets. Try **El Souk** (tel. 520 03 71), a swanky place in Calle Contarini Corfù, 1056/A, near the Accademia. It's a kasbah run like a private club. (Open 5pm-4am. Cover L15,000 includes first drink.) Beyond this, the Lido is your best choice—there you can hit **Nuova Acropoli** (tel. 526 04 66), at Lungomare Guglielmo Marconi (go right after you hit the beach). (Open in the off-season only, Fri. and Sat., L12,000-20,000.)

Paradiso Perduto, Fondamenta della Misericordia, 2540. Bar, jazz club and restaurant. Well-known amongst locals and natives, this place is young and hip. Dark setting with cafe-type paintings. Adorning the walls and long wooden tables lit by candle-light. Outdoor seating by the canal also a possibility. Sundays, live Jazz and Salsa. Typical Venetian fish dishes. Open 7:30am-late (depending on the night and the crowd.) Closed Wed., Jan. 6-20, and August 1-5.

Iguana, Fondamenta della Misericordia, 2515 (tel. 71 67 22) Cannaregio. Yes, there is Mexican food in Italy. Iguana is a Mexican bar and restaurant and a favorite hangout for Venetian students. Open Wed.-Mon. 8am-3pm and 5pm-1am. Lunch discount with Rolling Venice card.

Kinky Pub, Fondamenta della Misericordia, 2578 (tel. 72 19 87) Cannaregio. English pub theme. English lettering everywhere. Features beer, darts and board games. Open Thurs.-Tues. 9am-1pm and 3pm-2am.

Codroma, Dorsoduro, 2540 (tel. 520 41 61). A popular student spot. Drinks, board games. Cold snacks. Open Fri.-Wed. 10am-1am. Closed 15 days in Aug.

Devil's Forest, San Marco, 5185 (tel 520 06 23). On Calle Stagneri off Campo S. Bartolomeo and near the Rialto bridge. Upscale English pub atmosphere with stout, ale and lager on tap, afternoon teas, cold snacks and diverse crowds. Open Tues.-Sun. 8am-midnight.

Haig's Bar, San Marco, 5266 in Campo S. Maria del Giglio, not too far from the P. San Marco. Exit on the far end of the piazza across from the basilica. Travel straight on Sal. S. Moise past the AmEx office, cross 2 bridges and look for the bar at the side of a restaurant by the same name. A small, elegant indoor bar with patio seating outside in the Campo. Frequented by locals and visitors : gondoliers, business-types, and their friends gather here. Open Thurs.-Tues. 9am-2am.

■■■ PADUA (PÁDOVA)

In 602, Padua fell victim to marauding Lombards, and the once-prosperous Roman municipal center was reduced to a pile of rubble. Five and a half centuries later, the city had recuperated sufficiently to declare its independence from Byzantine and Lombard rule. The new republic quickly made up for lost time as, despite a series of tyrannical rulers and military defeats, Padua became one of the intellectual hubs of Europe. The "Bo" was founded in 1222, and is second in seniority only to Bologna among Italy's universities. Luminaries such as Dante, Petrarch, Galileo, and Copernicus all contributed to the collective genius, while the visual arts flourished, abetted by the visits of Florentines Giotto and Donatello and by the local talent of Mantegna. Reconstruction following World War II has given rise to a number of eyesores that threaten to engulf the once picturesque town, but the flourishing university and wealth of mid-millennium masterpieces safeguard Padua's reputation as a city of culture. Additionally, the city's beautiful youth hostel, within close reach of Venice, draws many budget travelers to Padua.

ORIENTATION AND PRACTICAL INFORMATION

Intercity buses and its location on the Venice-Milan and Venice-Bologna train lines make Padua a convenient destination on almost any northern Italian itinerary. The train station is at the northern edge of town, just outside the 16th-century walls. A 10-min. walk down the Corso del Popolo—which becomes **Corso Garibaldi**—will take you into the modern, commercially-minded heart of town. Another 15min. will bring you to **Il Santo,** the cathedral of Padua's patron saint, Anthony. **ACAP** city buses #3, 8, and 18 (L1000) will take you directly downtown. For L3000, you can purchase a 24-hr. tourist ticket valid for all urban lines.

Tourist Office: in the train station (tel. 875 20 77). Accommodations information and bus schedules for villas outside Padua. No accommodations service. Pick up a map and a copy of the sometimes-available entertainment brochure, *Padova Today,* for free, or *Padova Welcome* (the office's own comprehensive city guide; at L1000 it's worth the investment). Open Mon.-Sat. 8am-6pm, Sun. 8am-noon. A 2nd office in the Museo Civico (tel. 875 11 53) is open Tues.-Sun. 9am-7pm.

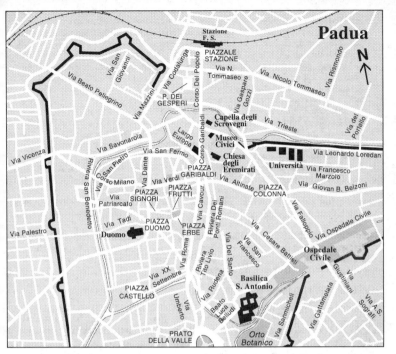

Budget Travel: CTS, Via Santa Sofia, 94/96 (tel. 875 17 19), at Via Gabelli. Student IDs and travel information. BIJ and other train tickets. English spoken. Open Mon.-Fri. 9:30am-12:30pm and 3:30-7pm.

Currency Exchange: Banco Atnoniana, Via VIII Febbraio, 5 (tel. 83 91 11). The best rates and no commission. Central branch located behind Caffè Pedrocchi, in the center of town. There are 8 other branches in town, including one at Piazzale Statione, 7 (tel. 875 10 50). Open Mon.-Fri. 8:20am-1:20pm and 2:35-3:35pm, Sat. 8:20-11:50am.

American Express: Tiare Viaggi, Via Risorgimento, 20 (tel. 66 61 33), near P. Insurrezione. No exchange service. Open Mon.-Fri. 9am-1pm and 3-7pm, Sat. 3-7pm.

Post Office: Corso Garibaldi, 25 (tel. 820 85 17). Fax service and Fermo Posta. Open Mon.-Fri. 8:15am-7:30pm, Sat. 8:15am-12:30pm. **Train Station Office:** Open Mon.-Fri. 8:15am-1pm. **Postal code:** 35100.

Telephones: Iritel, Corso Garibaldi, 3 (tel. 65 17 60). Open daily 8am-11:30pm. **SIP,** Riviera dei Ponte Romani, 40 (tel. 66 60 88), in the passageway by Caffè Pedrocchi. Open daily 9am-noon and 3:30-6:45pm. **Telephone code:** 049.

Trains: P. Stazione (tel. 875 18 00), in the northern part of town at the head of Corso del Popolo, the continuation of Corso Garibaldi. To: Venice (every 15min., 30min., L3200, round-trip L4800); Verona (every hr., 1hr. 30min., L6500); Milan (every hr., 2hr. 30min., L17,100); Bologna (every 30min., 1hr. 30min., L8800). Open daily 7:20am-7pm. **Luggage Storage:** L1500. Open daily 6:30am-2pm and 3:30-10pm.

Buses: ATP, Via Trieste, 42 (tel. 820 68 33; fax 820 68 14), near P. Boschetti, 5min. from the train station. To: Bassano del Grappa (every 30min., 1hr. 15min., L5000); Vicenza (every 30min., 30min., L4200); Venice (every 30min., 45min., L4200); Strà (every hr., L1700). Buses operate roughly between the hours of 6am-9pm. Office open Mon.-Thurs. 8:30am-1pm and 2-5:30pm, Fri. 8:30am-1pm.

Bike Rental: in P. del Municipio at the Comune di Padova. Downtown, near Caffè Pedrocchi. Free bike rental for touring inside the city walls (although with a little persuasion, you can also take them on local trips to nearby villages). ID required as collateral.

Car Rental: There are several agencies just outside and in front of the train station. **Avis,** P. Stazione, 1 (tel. 66 41 98). **Europcar,** P. Stazione, 6 (tel. 36 094). **Hertz,** P. Stazione, 5 (tel. 65 78 77).

English Bookstore: Draghi Libreria Internazionale, Via Cavour, 17-19 (tel. 876 03 05). An alcove full of classics (including the *Let's Go* series). Open Tues.-Sat. 9am-12:30pm and 3:30-7:30pm, Mon. 3:30-7:30pm. **Supermercato del Libro,** Corso Garibaldi, 14 (tel. 65 29 76; fax 875 47 56). More English classics. Open Mon.-Sat. 8:30am-12:30pm and 3:30-7:30pm.

Laundromat: Fast Clean, Via Ogni Santi, 6 (tel. 77 57 59), near the *portello* and the *segretaria* of the university. Take bus #7, 9, or 15. Self-service. 1-4kg L7000; 4-7kg L9000. Soap L550 (use that useless L50 piece!). Dryer L1500. Open Mon.-Fri. 9:30am-11:30pm and 3:30-6:30pm, Sat. 9:30am-12:30pm.

Swimming Pool: Municipal, in Abano Terme. A 20-min. bus ride from Padua. Catch the local bus **MT** or **AT** (there's a stop in Prato della Valle) on Via Mazzini. Another **pool** can be found on Via Giarre (tel. 81 14 49).

Emergencies: tel. 113 or 112. **Police:** Via Santa Chiara (tel. 83 31 11). **Ufficio Stranieri** (Foreigners' Office), Riviera Ruzzante, 13 (tel. 66 16 00). English interpreters available Mon.-Fri. 10am-12:30pm. **Hospital: Ospedale Civile,** Via Giustiniani, 2 (tel. 821 11 11), off Via San Francesco.

ACCOMMODATIONS

Cheap lodgings abound in Padua, but tend to fill quickly. If you can't get into the places listed below, try any of the hotels near **Piazza del Santo,** or call the **APT** (local tourist board; tel. 875 20 77) or the **provincial tourist board** (tel. 820 15 54) for private rooms in a local home. For summer housing options at the university call or write to **Centro Universitario,** Via Zabarella, 82 (tel. 65 42 99) or **Cattolici Popolari,** c/o Palayyo del Bó (tel. 828 31 11, ext. 399). In summer, start your search as early as 7am.

Ostello Città di Padova (HI), Via Aleardi, 30 (tel. 875 22 19; fax 65 42 10), off Via Camposampiero. Take bus #3, 8, or 12 from the station. Get off Prato della Valle, a 10-min. walk to the hostel. Take Via A. Memmo towards Torresino Church. Quiet location with large, immaculate, crowded rooms. Accommodating staff. English spoken. There's a cheap and friendly hostel bar in back—the best place to meet local travelers. Flexible 5-day max. stay. Open daily 8-9:30am and 6-11pm. Register and drop off your stuff anytime Mon.-Fri. (closed for lunch 1-4pm). Curfew 11pm. L16,000 per person, hot showers and breakfast included. Dinner available in the bar (Mon.-Fri. 8-9:30pm). *Primi* L3800, *secondi* L5000-7000. Complete meals L10,000 includes ½ liter of wine. If out-of-the-way castles suit your imagination, consider staying at the hostel in **Montagnana** (see description under Near Padua).

Casa della Famiglia (ACISJF), Via Nino Bixio, 4 (tel. 875 15 54), off P. Stazione. Go right as you leave the station—it's a small street to the left. Women under 29 only. Their reception office in the station is open daily until 5pm. The good sisters reserve the right to turn away "undesirables." Curfew 10:30pm. Modern and tidy doubles, triples, and quads about L20,000 per person. Study and a kitchen open for use at night. Open July-Aug.

Pensione Bellevue, Via L. Belludi, 11 (tel. 875 55 47), off Prato della Valle. Gorgeous rooms overlooking ivy-covered courtyard. Restaurant downstairs has a tourist *menú* for L18,500. Singles L35,000, with bath L40,000. Doubles L40,000, with bath L64,000.

Albergo Pavia, Via del Papafava, 11 (tel. 875 57 44), right down the street from the Pace. Rooms in front of the garden have wooden floors; rooms in back have been recently renovated. Rooftop clotheslines where the management will let you have a corner for your laundry. Doubles L34,000, with bath L43,000.

Camping: Montegrotto Terme, Strada Romana Apponanse, 104 (tel. 79 34 00). A 15km bus ride from Padua. Take the ACAP bus "M." Stop at the Hotel Cristallo, then walk 1km on foot. Tennis, disco, stores and restaurants in the vicinity. L9,000 per person, L14,000 per tent. Open March-Nov. 10.

FOOD

Markets are held on both sides of the Palazzo della Ragione. During the academic year, student *mense* pop up all over town, so ask around. Supermarkets and alimentari can be found at the following locations. Downtown, across from Caffè Pedrocchi: **PAM,** on Via Cavour in P. della Garzeria (open Mon.-Sat. 8:30am-7:30pm, closed Wed. afternoons and Sun.), **Supermarket Despar,** on Via S. Sophia, 44 (open Mon.-Sat. 8:30am-1pm and 4-7:30pm, closed Wed afternoon). You can sample a glass from the nearby Colli Euganei winery district, or try the sparkling *lambruschi* of Emilia Romagna. Two of the most distinctive whites are produced by **Trattoria da Nane della Giulia,** Via Santa Sofia, 1, off Via San Francesco (open Mon.-Sat. 11:30am-2:30pm and 6pm-midnight, closed Mon. morning and Sun.), and **Spaccio Vini Carpanese,** Via del Santo, 44 (tel. 30 581; open Mon.-Sat. 9-11:30am and 4-6pm). Delicious wines run L2000-4000 per glass.

Mensa Universitarià, Via San Francesco, 122 (tel. 66 09 03). The most pleasant and convenient *mensa*. Come for the bulletin boards, helpful if you're looking for a used car, motorcycle or a summer sublet. Full-meal price of L9000. Open 11:45am-2:30pm and 6:45-9pm. Check here for information on the other *mensas'* schedules. Their opening times tend to be erratic.

Brek (tel. 875 37 88), in the piazza off Via VIII Febbraio, across from the Caffè Pedrocchi. (Just look for the outdoor book market in front.) Self-service restaurant. New, upscale appearance, and prices to rival the university *mensa's.* Pick up a full meal including wine for L11,000. These restaurants appear to be the newest phenomena in Northern Italy. Look out for them in other towns, as well. (Open Sat.-Thurs. 11:30am-3pm and 6:30-10:30pm.)

Al Pero, Via Santa Lucia, 72 (tel. 365 61), near Via Dante. Bustling neighborhood eatery with fantastic food. To visit Veneto without tasting *polenta* is a sin. Fulfill your vows by ordering the *salamini arrosti con polenta* (with small roasted sausages, L4500). *Primi* L3500, *secondi* L4500-5000. Wine L4000 per liter. Cover L1500. (Open Mon.-Sat. noon-2:30pm and 7-9:30pm.)

Pizzeria al Santo (tel. 66 14 73), P. del Santo in front of the Basilica. Outdoor seating. Prime view of the church and excellent people-watching post. Pizza L6500-9000. Wine L3500 per ½ liter. (Open Wed.-Mon. until late.)

Alexander Bar, Via San Francesco, 38 (tel. 65 28 84), off Via del Santo, which runs roughly parallel to Via Roma 2 blocks east. One hundred beers and about 60 types of *panini* (L3000-5000). Open late (Mon.-Sat. 8:30am-2am), so you can take your time deciding.

Lunanuova, Via G. Barbarigo, 12 (tel. 875 89 07) in the *zona duomo.* Vegetarian restaurant complete with comfortable, quiet setting, mellow jazz and political bulletin boards as well as an array of books and pamphlets on veggie vacations in Italy. A good resource center for those inclined. The restaurant features brown bread—a rarity in Italy. Also, lunch and dinner selections from L5500-7000. For beverages, choose between beer, wine and succhi di frutta or herbal tea remedies. Coperto L2000. (Open Mon.-Sat. 12:30-2:30pm and 7:30-midnight. No lunch served Mon.)

Lucifer Young, Via Altinate, 75 (tel. 875 22 51). Enter Dante's Inferno! A bar in 3-D the decorator took his or her lessons from the lowest circle in the Divine Comedy. Near the University. Mostly drinks (there's a wicked house brew). Some food. (Open Mon., Tues., Thurs., and Fri. at 7pm, Sat. at 5pm and Sun. at 4pm.)

SIGHTS

Despite four centuries of Venetian dominance, Padua proudly preserves its distinct civic identity, taking pride in the legend of its founding by the Trojan Antenor, in paying tribute to its local saint, the Franciscan Sant'Antonio (patron saint of lost and found and target of an unbelievable number of pilgrims), and in its illustrious university. The frugal may buy a ticket good at most of the museums of Padua **(Cappella degli Scrovegni, Museo Civico, Orto Botanico, Palazzo della Ragione, Battistero del Duomo),** and the **Oratorio di San Giorgio).** It costs L15,000 (L10,000 for students and groups), is available at any of the above sights, and is valid for one year.

The **Cappella degli Scrovegni** alone merits a pilgrimage to Padua. The chapel contains the master fresco cycle of the celebrated Florentine Giotto. Executed over the course of three years between 1303 and 1305, these thirty-six perfectly preserved panels illustrating the Redemption story are one of the most influential works of art from this period. Giotto's ability to realistically portray the third dimension was unprecedented in Medieval art, and his achievements influenced Italian painting for centuries to follow. (Open April-Sept. daily 9am-7pm; Oct.-March Tues.-Sun. 9am-6pm. Admission L10,000. Students L7000. School groups L4000 per person. Admission to chapel on Mon. L4000. Tickets must be bought at the Museo Civico and are good for both the chapel and museum.) The adjoining **Museo Civico** houses an art gallery with Giorgione's *Leda and the Swan* and a Giotto crucifix.

Next door, the **Church of the Eremitani** boasts an imposing exterior and a beautifully carved wooden ceiling that was successfully reconstructed after a devastating bombing in 1944. Unfortunately, the cycle of frescoes by Andrea Mantegna that once rivaled the Giotto next door in innovative beauty were almost entirely lost. (Open Mon.-Sat. 8:15am-noon and Sun. 9am-noon and 3:30-6:30pm; Oct.-March Mon.-Sat. 8:15am-noon and Sun. 9am-noon and 3:30-5:30pm. Free.)

A complex of buildings on P. del Santo pays homage to Il Santo, as Padua's patron is familiarly called. The 14th-century **Basilica di Sant'Antonio** (tel. 66 39 44), where the saint is entombed, is a Medieval architectural oddity, a fantastically absurd conglomeration of eight domes, a pair of octagonal campaniles, and some supporting minarets. The mecca of progressing pilgrims looking for everything from lost love to lost limbs keeps the church perpetually crowded. The brilliance of the frescoed arches of the interior provide an odd backdrop to Donatello's bronze sculptures on the high altar. These seven statues, watched over by the artist's *Crucifixion,* must be grouped together in the mind (their present arrangement dates to the mid-19th century) in order for one to appreciate the subtle interplay of their expressive postures. The **Cappella di San Felice** on the right displays the 14th-century works of Altichiero da Zevior, one of Giotto's preeminent students. Saint Anthony's tongue and voice box are contained in an appropriately head-shaped reliquary in the apse of the church. (Basilica open daily 6:30am-7:45pm.)

The adjoining **Oratorio di San Giorgio** houses examples of Giotto-school frescoes, as does the **Scuola del Santo,** including three by the young Titian. (Both open daily, 9am-12:30pm and 2:30-7pm, Oct.-Jan. 9am-12:30pm, Feb.-March 9am-12:30pm and 2:30-4:30pm. L2000 for both, group rate L1000 per person.)

In the center of P. del Santo sits Donatello's pioneering bronze equestrian statue of **Gattamelata,** a mercenary general remembered for his agility and ferocity in all fields (his name means "calico cat"). In true Renaissance spirit, Donatello modeled the statue after the Roman equestrian statue of Marcus Aurelius at the Campidoglio in Rome.

A verdant refuge lies a block away in the **Orto Botanico** (tel. 65 66 14), the oldest in Europe (est. 1545), where Goethe and other prurient vegophiliacs studied the sex lives of plants. (Open Mon.-Sat. 9am-1pm and 3-6pm, Sun. 9am-1pm; Nov.-March Mon.-Sat. 9am-1pm. Admission L5000, students L3000.)

The **Palazzo della Ragione,** build in 1218, with the external loggias and keel-shaped roof added in 1306 by Fra Giovanni degli Eremitani marks the city center. Surrounding it are three *piazze*—P. Erbe, P. Frutti, and P. Signori host daily morning markets inside the Palazzo. Traveling art exhibitions are also displayed. (Open Tues.-Sun., 9am-7pm; off-season 9am-1pm and 3-6pm. Admission L5000; special exhibits L10,000, students L7000.)

The **Duomo** in P. Duomo (tel. 66 28 14) was erected between the 16th and 18th centuries. Michelangelo was said to have participated in the design. The Battistero next door was built in the 12th century, although retouched in the 13th. Inside you will find yet another significant cycle of religious frescoes. Recently restored, painted by Giusto de Menabuoi from 1376-78. Giotto sparked a movement dedicated to fresco painting. Developments in this medium can be traced through the many notable works about town. (Open Tues.-Sun. 9:30am-12:30pm and 3-6pm. Admission L3000. Students L1500.)

The **university** campus is scattered throughout the city but its headquarters is found in Palazzo Bò (tel. 828 31 11). (In Venetian dialect *bò* means steer or castrated bull and derives from the sign of the inn that formerly occupied the *palazzo's* site.) The **teatro anatomico** (1594) unfortunately has been closed for several years for restoration. It was the first of its kind in Europe and hosted the likes of Vesalius and the Englishman William Harvey, who discovered the circulation of blood. Almost all Venetian noblemen received their mandatory instruction in law and public policy in the Great Hall, and the "chair of Galileo" is preserved in the **Sala dei Quaranta,** where the physicist used to lecture.

Caffè Pedrocchi (tel. 755 20 20), across the street, was the headquarters for 19th-century liberals who supported Giuseppe Mazzini. When it was first built, the *caffè's* famous neoclassical façade had no doors and was open around the clock—every university student was entitled to a free newspaper and a glass of water. The battle between students and Austrian police here in February 1848 was a turning point in the Risorgimento. Capture the spirit for the price of a cappuccino (L2600; open Tues.-Sun. 7:30am-1am).

ENTERTAINMENT

Padua's nightlife is elusive. The best way to get the inside scoop on the goings on of the collegiate crowd is to keep your eyes peeled for posters around the university and to scan the *mensa* bulletin. The evening *passeggiata* happens in P. Garibaldi and up Via Cavour. The walkway is lined with *caffè,* Pedrocchi among them. The *caffè* in nearby P. delle Frutta also come to life at night, and prices here are a bit easier to stomach. Check the posters around Palazzo Bò or pick up a copy of the newspaper *Il Mattino* for concert and film listings. In July the city organizes the **Cinema Città Estate,** a film series presented in the Arena Romana. Call the tourist office (tel. 875 20 77) or the Assessorato di Turismo (tel. 820 15 30) for further information. On February 8, Padua celebrates the **Festa della Matricola,** in which students and professors take the day off from classes, wear ancient academic costumes, and play practical jokes on each other.

On the third Sunday of each month there is an **antique market** in the Prato della Valle.

■ Near Padua

The **Colli Euganei** (Eugan Hills), southwest of Padua, offer a feast for the senses. Padua's tourist office has pamphlets suggesting various itineraries. The volcanic hills are rich not only in soil, the consequent richness of their wines, and hot mineral springs, but in extraordinary accommodation options as well. Contact the **Agriturist** office at Via Mártiri della Libertà, 9 (tel. 66 16 55), in Padua for information on staying in a real, working farm. Most of the participating farms offer a bed in a double or triple for about L25,000, including breakfast and showers. If you've always dreamed of life in a castle, realize your aspirations with a night at the **Youth Hostel (HI)** in **Montagnana.** The town is just outside of the *colli,* an hour by bus from either Vicenza or Padua (round-trip L10,000). The hostel (tel. (0429) 81 07 62) offers 70-beds within the Rocca degli Alberi. For L12,000, enjoy a soft bed and hot showers under the auspices of a warm-hearted management. The Montagnana **tourist office** is in P. Maggiore (tel. (0429) 813 20). Take the bus to Pojana and walk the two or three kilometers.

■ Treviso

Treviso means "three faces" and, while the name may be without historical significance, it seems particularly well-suited to this provincial capital. The tourism industry promotes the first two faces, *città d'acque* (city of water) and *città dipinta*
(painted city). On the water side, rivulets from the Sile loop through town, disap-
pearing only to resurface where least expected, and as for the paint, the frescoed
façades of the buildings that line the city streets still display hints of their former
glory. The third face of Treviso needs no glossy brochures to catch the visitor's eye:
Treviso is rolling in dough. Benetton was born here, and though there are only four
official outlets in town, Benetton's lucre-laden wings hover over the whole province. For those of you who wish to buy your B's from the source, a warning: buy
big. For Treviso is also the birthplace of that most dastardly of desserts: *Tiramisù* .
Since Treviso's affluence keeps bargains at bay, the town is best seen as a daytrip
from Venice.

ORIENTATION AND PRACTICAL INFORMATION

Treviso lies a half-hour inland from Venice. The historic center is contained within
the old city walls which are bordered alternately on the inside and outside—sometimes both—by flowing water. Via Roma is the entrance to town, and a curving
street that changes names at each bend on its way to P. dei Signori, the center of
Treviso. Pedestrian-dominated Via Calmaggiore leads to the *duomo*.

> **Tourist Office:** Via Toniolo, 41 (tel 54 76 32, fax 54 13 97). Via Roma becomes
> Corso del Popolo as you cross the Fiume Sile; take this to P. della Borsa, easily
> identified by the face-off of rival banks. Via Toniolo is to the right. Don't miss *Tre-
> viso Città Dipinta,* including a walking itinerary of the best-preserved exterior
> fresco-work. There's also info galore on the Ville Venete (see Central Veneto
> below). Open Mon.-Fri. 8:30am-12:30pm and 3-6pm, Sat. 8:30am-noon.
>
> **Post Office:** P. Vittoria, 1 (59 72 07). Stamps and Fermo Posta at #1. Open daily
> 8:15am-7:30pm. **Postal Code:** 31050.
>
> **Telephones: SIP,** Via XX Settembre, 1. Between P. della Borsa and P. dei Signori.
> Open Mon.-Sat. 9am-12:30pm and 4-7:30 pm. **Telephone Code:** 0422.
>
> **Trains:** P. Duca d'Aosta (tel. 54 13 52), at the southern end of town. Treviso lies on
> the Venice-Udine line. To: Venice (every 30min., 30min., L2400); Udine (every
> 30min., 1hr. 30min., L8800); Milan (every hr., 3hr. 30min., L20,400). **Luggage
> Storage:** L1500. Open daily 6am-8:30pm.
>
> **Buses:** Lungo Sile Mattei, 21 (tel. 41 22 22), to the left just before Corso del Popolo
> crosses the river. Comprehensive service throughout the Veneto and to the villas.
> To: Padua (every 30min., L4500); Vicenza (every 1 hr., L2800); Bassano (9 per
> day, L1200); Ásolo (every 1 hr., L3800).
>
> **Emergencies:** tel. 113. **Hospital: Unit Sanitaria Locale,** tel.3221. Take bus #1.

ACCOMMODATIONS AND FOOD

Unfortunately for the budget traveler Treviso's wealthy climate has spawned a number of hotels (singles, L50,000) but few cheaper budget accommodations. Around
the outskirts of town you can find a couple of one-star hotels for less, Al Giardini and
Al Mercato. Consult the tourist office for more info.

Treviso is famous for its cherries, *radicchio* (red chicory), and *tiramisù,* a heavenly local creation of espresso-and-liquor-soaked cake topped with sweet cream
cheese. Cherries peak in June, *radicchio* in December. If *primi* and *secondi* seem to
be merely an inconvenient delay, begin with dessert at **Nascimben,** Via XX Settembre, 3 (tel. 15 12 91, open Tues.-Sun. 7am-2am). The unnamed liquor store (look for
the *Birra Vini* sign) at Via Mura di S. Teonista at the end of Borgo Cavour is living
proof of *radicchio's* celebrated status in the community. Admire the artistically
labeled bottles of *grappa al radicchio rosso* (L15,000). More conventional table
wines begin at L3000 a bottle. For your basics, shop at **Pam Supermarket,** P.
Borso, 18 (tel. 539 13) in the corner of the piazza behind Banco Nationale del

Lavoro. Closed Sun. and Wed. afternoon, open Mon.-Sat. 8:30-1 and 3-7:30.) Pizzeria, bar, and **Ristorante da Max** (tel. 54 59 74) on Via Paris Bordone, 11, is downtown and dirt cheap. The booth and tile atmosphere is a welcome anomaly to upscale Treviso. Good pizza for L5000-9000. (½L wine L3000.) (Open 10:30am-3pm and 6pm-midnight. Closed Fri. late July-early Aug.) **All'Oca Bianca,** Vicolo della Torre, 7 (tel. 54 18 50), on a side street off central Via Calmaggiore, is a casual *trattoria* in the thick of things. Delight in inexpensive drinks and pastries. Main courses average L10,000. (Open Thurs.-Tues. 8am-4pm and 6pm-midnight. Closed Tues. evening.)

SIGHTS

The **Palazzo dei Trecento** (tel. 54 17 16), which abuts P. dei Signori loudly asserts Treviso's successful reemergence from a 1944 air raid (on Good Friday), which demolished half the town. Ascend the stairs on the outer wall and look for the clearly marked signs underfoot which mark the pre-bomb extension of the walls. Post-war reconstruction and new building blend with the original townscape, and spiraling prosperity allows the city to devote its resources to endless restoration. (Open Mon-Sat. 8:30am-12:30pm. Free.)

Back in P. dei Signori, one can join in Via Calmaggiore's endless *passeggiata* and walk beneath the arcades to the seven-domed, patchwork-style **duomo.** The **Cappella Malchiostro** was inserted in 1519 and contains frescoes by Pordenone and Titian's *Annunciation.* It's a strange combination considering the two artists were sworn enemies. (Open weekdays 7:30am-noon and 3:30-7pm; Sun. 7:30am-1pm and 3:30-8pm.) From P. del Duomo, Via Risorgimento leads to the large Dominican church of **San Nicolò** on Via San Nicola. The mammoth, 14th-century brick structure sports a triple apse, along with some frescoed saints by Tomaso da Modena. (Open in summer Mon.-Fri. 8am-noon and 3:30-7pm; in winter Mon.-Fri. 9am-noon and 3-5:30pm. Free.)

The **Museo Civico** at Borgo Cavour, 22 (tel. 513 37) houses Titian's *Sperone Speroni* and Lorenzo Lotto's *Portrait of a Dominican,* conveniently hung in the same room. The ground floor protects Treviso's archaeological finds, most impressive among which are the 5th-century BC bronze discs from Montebelluna. (Museum open Tues.-Sat. 9am-noon and 2-5pm, Sun. 9am-noon. Admission L1000.)

■ Bassano del Grappa

At the foot of Monte Grappa, Bassano del Grappa is a hideaway for refined Italian and Austrian tourists. Mushrooms, wrought iron, pottery, *grappa* brandy, and the emblematic covered bridge have all earned the city fame. Locals, though, claim that Bassano's greatest asset is its proximity to the mountains, so you may want to split your time between Bassano and the surrounding countryside.

ORIENTATION AND PRACTICAL INFORMATION

The majority of historical and interesting areas lie between the train station and the River Brenta. From the station take Via Chilisotto (to the right) to find the downtown area. The center is split between Piazza Garibaldi and Piazza Liberta, only one-half block apart.

Tourist Office: Largo Corona d'Italia, 35 (tel.52 43 51). From the station, walk down Via Chilesotti, across the larger Viale delle Fosse, and through the gap in the stone wall to the new office complex. The tourist office is the older, detached building to the right. The monthly, trilingual *Bassano Mese*, featuring hotel listings, restaurants, practical information and a town map, is invaluable. Bicyclists and motorists looking to tackle the region will benefit from *Bici e Vai,* an itinerary-packed brochure of the nearby towns. Open Mon.-Fri. 9am-12:30pm and 3-6:45pm.

Post Office: (tel. 22 111), on Via XI Febbraio, near the *duomo.* Open Mon.-Fri. 8:15am-7:45pm, Sat. 8:15am-6:40pm. **Postal Code:** 36061.

Telephones: Caffè Danieli, P. Garibaldi (tel. 29 322). Open daily 8am-1am. Closed Tues. afternoon and Wed. **Telephone Code:** 0424.

Trains: at the end of Via Chilesotti (tel. 52 50 34), a couple blocks from the historic center. Ticket counter open 5:10am-9 pm daily. To: Padua (10 per day, 1hr., L3900); Venice (15 per day, 1hr., L8600); Trent (5 per day, 2hr., L7200); Vicenza Via Cittadella (8 per day, 2hr., L5400). **Luggage Storage:** L1500. Open daily 6:30am- 8:40pm.

Buses: in P. Trento (tel. 25 025). As you come up Via Chilesotti, turn left on Viale delle Fosse. A few different bus companies service the various surrounding towns: **Autoline Rossi** (tel. 32 150), **F.T.V.** (tel. 30 850). To: Vicenza (every 30min., L4500), Asiago (5 per day, L5300), Maróstica (every hr., L1800), Thiene (every hr., L3600). **La Marca Line** (tel. in Treviso (0422) 41 22 22). To: Treviso (L5200), Masèr (L3100)and Asolo.

Bike Rentals: Signora Ernesto at the **Cooperativo Feracina,** Via delle Fosse,12 (tel. 20 244), near a big park, inside the parking garage behind the ancient wall. L3000 for 3 hrs., L5000 per day.

Club Alpino Italiano (tel. 52 93 40; fax 52 93 41), on Via Colomba, 1/B. For hiking and mountain information. Open Tues. and Fri. 9-10:30pm and Wed. 5-7pm.

Emergencies: tel. 113. **Police:** Via Cá Rezzonico (tel. 21 22 22, or 112 for emergencies). **Hospital: Ospedale Civile,** Viale delle Fosse, 43 (tel. 21 72 52), **Night and emergency medical care** (tel. 21 72 60), rotating nighttime pharmacy consult "Bassano Mese" for most current phone number.

ACCOMMODATIONS AND FOOD

Low-budget hotels seem to be in danger of extinction in Bassano. Reserve ahead or consider accommodations elsewhere—yet another town to visit as a daytrip.

Instituto Cremona, Via Chini,6 (tel. 52 20 32), past the main post office on Via Emiliani. This school-turned-hostel offers bargain-basement rates. L12500 per night, L16,000 for bed and breakfast. 11pm curfew and no daytime lockout. Open late-June-early-Sept. Mon.-Fri. only. Check in 9am-noon and 6-8pm.

Locanda Hotel Bassanello, Via Trozzetti, 2 (tel. 353 47), on the other side of the tracks. Family-run, inexpensive rooms. Singles L28,000. Doubles L40,000, with bath L60,000. Breakfast L5000.

The town's most spirited claim to fame is *grappa,* a potent liquor distilled from the seeds and skins of grapes. For authenticity, buy a bottle from the **Nardini** distillery by the Ponte degli Alpini. Bassano is also famous for its white asparagus. Depending on the season, this and other produce can be purchased at the **open-air market** on Thurs. and Sat. 8am-1pm in P. Garibaldi. For sumptuous cooked food on the run, try the gourmet, deli-style fare at **Venzo** on Via da Ponte or **Guido Merlo** around the corner at Via Roma, 15.

Ottone Birraria, Via Matteotti, 50 (tel. 22 206). From Hungarian goulash (L12,500) to hot sandwiches (L6000-8000). Pasta L8000. Open Wed.-Mon., 9:30am-3:30pm and 6:30pm-1:30am. Closed Mon. evening. Eurocard, MC, Visa.

Al Saraceno, Via Museo, 60 (tel. 52 25 13). A local hangout with seafood specialties and an impressive pizza repertoire. *Primi* L5000-7000, *secondi* L5000-12,000. Pizza L4500-7000. Cover L2000. Open Tues.-Sun. 10am-2:30pm and 5:30pm-1am.

SIGHTS AND ENTERTAINMENT

Bassano's charm is epitomized in the small **Ponte degli Alpini,** a covered wooden bridge dating from 1209 and redesigned by Palladio (1568-70) to resemble a fleet of ships anchored in midstream. The bridge is named for the Alpine soldiers died fighting the Austrians and Germans during WW I. The **Museo Civico** in P. Garibaldi (tel. 52 22 35), houses masterpieces by Jacopo da Bassano (1517-1592), including *Flight into Egypt* and *St. Valentine Baptizing St. Lucilla.* (Open Tues.-Sat. 9am-12:30pm and 3:30-6:30pm, Sun. 3:30-6:30pm. Admission L2000, students L1000.)

Next door stands the Romanesque-Gothic church of **San Francesco,** completed in the early 14th century. The spacious interior unfortunately has few traces left of the original frescoes, but the *Madonna and Child* by Lorenzo Martinelli beneath the arches of the entrance has recently been restored.

■ Vicenza

This quiet provincial city boasts one of the highest average incomes in Italy, thanks to a recent boom in high-tech manufacturing and services that now augments the traditional industries of textiles and gold-working. Vicenza is best known, though, as the city of architect Palladio (Andrea di Pietro, 1508-1580), whose Renaissance interpretations of the classical Roman canon mingle with Venetian Gothic on the city's streets.

ORIENTATION AND PRACTICAL INFORMATION

Vicenza lies in the heart of Veneto. The train station is in the southern part of town. **AIM** city buses #1 and #7 run to the center of town and P. Matteotti (L1000). Next to the train station is the intercity **FTV** bus station. To walk into town, orient yourself with a glance at the helpful map outside the station and set out on Viale Roma. Take a right on Corso Palladio (the central street), and turn right. P. Matteotti is at the other end, 10min. away.

Tourist Office: P. Matteotti, 12 (tel. 32 08 54), next to the Teatro Olimpico. For the disabled, there's a city map of wheelchair-accessible facilities. Open Mon.-Sat. 9am-12:30pm and 2:30-5:30pm, Sun. 9am-12:30pm; mid-Oct.-mid-March Mon.-Sat.2-5:30pm.

Budget Travel: AVIT, Viale Roma, 17 (tel. 54 56 77), before you reach the supermarket PAM. BIJ/Transalpino tickets. Avis and Hertz rental cars. Open Mon.-Fri. 9am-1pm and 3-7pm, Sat. 9:30am-12:30pm.

Car Rental: Avis, Viale Milano, 88 (tel. 32 16 22, fax 32 62 61). Car rental with credit card, 23 and older. For the best rates reserve at home at Tour Europe Rate. Around L100,000 per day, L150-200,000 per weekend and L650,000 per week, all with unlimited mileage. Open 8am-12:30pm and 3-7pm, Sat. 8am-12:30pm.

Post Office: Contrà Garibaldi (tel. 32 24 88), near the *duomo.* Stamps at window #11. Fermo Posta at #6. Open Mon.-Fri. 8am-7:30pm, Sat. 8am-1pm. **Postal Code:** 36100.

Telephones: SIP, P. Giuseppe Giustu, 8 (tel. 99 01 11), off Corso SS. Felice e Fortunato. Open daily 9am-1pm and 4-7pm. After 7pm, go to **Ristorante La Taverna,** P. dei Signori, 47 (tel. 54 73 26). Open until 1am. **Telephone Code:** 0444.

Trains: P. Stazione (tel. 32 50 45), at the end of Viale Roma. To: Venice (every 30min., 1hr., L5000); Padua (every 30min., 30min., L3200); Milan (every 30min., 2-3hr., L13,800); Verona (every 30min., 30min., L4300). **Luggage Storage:** L1500, open daily 7am-9pm.

Buses: FTV, Viale Milano, 7 (tel. 54 43 33), to the left as you exit the train station. To Bassano (every hr., L4500), Asiago (every hr., L6100), Padua (every 30min., L4500; Thiene (every 30min., L4500), Schio (every 30min., L3600), Montagnana (3 per day, L5300). All buses run approximately 6am-9:30pm. Office hours 7am-8pm.

Swimming Pool: Piscina Comunale, Via Giurato, 103 (tel. 51 37 83), northwest of town, near the U.S. army base. Open Mon.-Fri. 10am-7pm, Sat.-Sun. 9am-7pm. Admission L4800. Also at Via Ferrarin (tel. 92 47 31). Open Mon.-Fri. 10am-6:30pm, Sat.-Sun. 9am-6:30pm. Admission L5000, under 18, L4000.

Emergencies: tel. 113. **Police:** Via Muggia, 2 (tel. 50 77 00). **Medical Emergency/ambulance**: (tel. 99 34 11 or 51 00 00). **Hospital: Ospedale Civile,** Viale Rodolfi, 8 (tel. 99 36 66). **Night and weekend medico:** tel. 99 34 70.

ACCOMMODATIONS AND FOOD

Vicenza's bourgeois inclinations render it an unpromising home for inexpensive *pensioni*. To compound the problem, many establishments close for vacation in early August, and most are packed in September during the annual architecture course. Consider the youth hostel in Verona.

Hotel Vicenza, Stradella dei Nodari, 5/7 (tel. 32 15 12), off P. Signori in the alley across from Ristorante Garibaldi. Meticulously scrubbed and centrally located. Management may store your luggage after check-out. The babble of voices in the square, however, continues to the wee hours of the morning and is hardly a lullaby. Singles L40,000, with bath L55,000. Doubles L60,000, with bath L76-80,000.

Albergo Due Mori, Contrà Do Rode, 26 (tel. 32 18 86, fax 32 61 27), around the corner from Hotel Vicenza. Bright, sparkling, newly furnished rooms. Singles with bath L52,000. Doubles L68,000.

Hotel Italia, Via Risorgimento, 3 (tel. 32 10 43 or 56 58 51), take a right on the busy street that runs in front of the station. Simple, fresh and well-kept rooms. Amiable owners also have a restaurant downstairs. Singles L40,000 with bath, TV, telephone and microbar L70,000. Doubles L50,000, with bath, bar, etc. L85,000.

Camping: Campeggio Vicenza, Strada Pelosa, 241 (tel. 58 23 11), out past the main U.S. army base. Take bus #1 from the train station (20min.). L6800 per person. L8000 per tent, with car L16,000.

Produce is marketed outdoors every day in P. dell'Erbe behind the basilica, and on Tuesday and Thursday mornings you can hunt for edibles among the bizarre clothes that are sold in the central piazza. Thursday's market is the biggie, winding throughout the town. Cheese, chicken, and fish tend to proliferate in P. del Duomo. For more staid shopping, turn to **Supermercato PAM,** Viale Roma, 1 (open Mon.-Tues. and Thurs.-Sat. 8:30am-1pm and 3-7:30pm, Wed. 8:30am-1pm).

Righetti, P. del Duomo, 3 (tel. 54 31 35), with a better marked entrance at Contrà Fontana, 6. Self-service with reasonable fare and great ambience, including outdoor seating in P. Duomo. *Primi* L3000, *secondi* L5000, and a L500 cover that includes unlimited bread. Open Sept.-late-July Mon.-Fri. noon-2:30pm and 7-10pm, bar open 9am-midnight.

Al Bersagliere, Contra Orefice, 11 (tel. 32 35 07), off P. Erbe. A hole-in-the-wall with great prices and a relaxed, if inelegant, atmosphere. *Primi* L5000-6000 *Secondi* L7000-11,000. Cover L1500. Open Mon.-Sat. 8am-2am.

SIGHTS

Piazza dei Signori is the town center. It was the town's forum when Vicenza was Roman and the town's showpiece when it was Venetian. Palladio began and ended his architectural career in this square. His treatment of the **basilica** (tel. 32 36 81) first made the young architect famous. In 1546, Palladio's patron, the wealthy Giovan Giorgio Trissino, agreed to fund his proposal to shore up the collapsing Palazzo della Ragione, a project that had frustrated some of the foremost architects of the day. Ingenious variation of pilaster widths in the twin *loggie* masks with Renaissance harmony the irregular Gothic structure beneath. Palladio continued to work on the basilica until his death. Look at the **Torre di Piazza** next door to get an idea of the basilica's former appearance. (Basilica open Tues.-Sat. 9:30am-noon and 2:30-5pm, Sun. 9:30am-noon.)

Across the piazza, the **Loggia del Capitano** illustrates a later Palladian style. Palladio left the façade unfinished at his death, having completed only the three bays and the four sets of gigantic columns. The two symbolic columns of Venice complete the piazza.

Behind the Loggia del Capitano, the **Palazzo del Comune** faces **Corso Palladio,** Vicenza's main street. Vicenzo Scamozzi's precise design for the *palazzo* demonstrates a much sharper interpretation of classical architecture than that embodied in the buildings of Palladio, his mentor. Corso Palladio, lined with Renaissance *palazzi*, runs the length of Vicenza, from Porta Castello in the east to the Teatro Olimpico on the banks of the Bacchiglione River. In P. Castello, a medieval gate is all that remains from the castle that once guarded the town's entrance. In front of the gate, on the left, the two bays of the **Palazzo Porto-Breganze** are an imposing fragment of the structure begun by Scamozzi according to Palladio's designs. Scamozzi did manage to finish the **Palazzo Bonin,** also designed by Palladio (at #13 on the right-hand corner of corso Palladio).

Contrà Vescovado leads out of the piazza next to Palazzo Porto-Breganze to the **duomo,** a large Gothic structure in brick with a graceful apse and a Palladian cupola. The **Casa Pigafetta** on nearby Via Pigafetta shows that Palladio wasn't the only architect to influence Vicenza; this unique early Renaissance house successfully fuses Gothic, Spanish, and classical styles.

Farther south, on the banks of the Retrone near Ponte San Michele, stands the **Palazzo Civena,** an early Palladian home.

The area north of Corso Palladio is crammed with Renaissance *palazzi,* each striving to outdo its neighbors in conspicuous expenditure. For more Palladio, try the **Palazzo Valmarana-Braga,** Corso Fogazzaro, 16, the sculpted figures on the corners distinguish it from its neighbors. Vasari considered Palladio's unfinished **Palazzo da Porto-Festa** on Contrà Porti the most magnificent of all, but others prefer the other two on the street, either the grandiose **Palazzo Porto-Barbaran** or the **Palazzo Thiene,** a felicitous blending of Palladio's and Lorenzo da Bologna's architectural genius. The **Palazzo Schio** is a refreshingly non-Palladian masterpiece.

At the far end of Corso Palladio, on what was once a lawn sloping to the river, Palladio built the villa-like **Palazzo Chiericati** which now houses the well-stocked **Museo Civico** (tel. 32 13 48). The collection in the *pinacoteca* on the first floor includes some of Bassano's best endeavors, works by Bartolomeo Montagna (notably *Madonna Enthroned),* a Memling *Crucifixion,* Tintoretto's *Miracle of St. Augustine,* and a rare and refined *Madonna* by Cima da Conegliano. (Open Tues.-Sat. 9:30am-noon and 2:30-5pm, Sun. 10am-noon. Admission L4000, Sun. L3000. Admission good for the Teatro Olimpico.)

The nearby **Teatro Olimpico** (tel. 32 37 81) embodies the same classicism cultivated by the 16th-century *palazzo*-building patrons. The *Accademia Olimpica,* as the noble literati called themselves, met in the pseudo-Roman theater for performances of their own plays. The city still hosts productions here every year June through September, with both local and imported talent. (Open Mon.-Sat. 9:30am-12:20pm and 3-5:30pm, Sun 9:30am-12:20pm; Oct. 16-March 15 Mon.-Sat. 9:30am-12:20pm and 2-4:30pm, Sun. 9:30-12:20pm. Admission L4000, Students. L3000.)

ENTERTAINMENT

Manifestazioni 1992, available at the tourist office, will guide those in search of high culture. Besides the performances in the **Teatro Olimpico** (tel. 32 37 81; admission L15,000-40,000, students L12,000-20,000), there is the summer concert series **Concerti in Villa.** Check with the tourist office for the foreign film series.

Near Vicenza

Though most of the Palladian villas scattered through the Veneto are a bit of a strain to get to (see Ville Venete below), there are a few great villas close to town. Goethe considered the **Villa La Rotonda** (also called Villa Capra; tel. 32 17 93; walk from town or take bus #8 or #13 from near the station) one of the most magnificent architectural achievements ever. Everyone seems to have agreed—this villa was a model for Palladian buildings in France, England, and the U.S., most notably Jefferson's Monticello. (Interior open March 15-Oct. 15 Wed. only. Exterior open Tues.-Thurs. 10am-noon and 3-6pm. Admission L5000, to the exterior L2000.) Palladio's unfinished **Villa Thiene** (tel. 55 68 99 or 55 90 09) is stately and a bit forlorn, remaining aloof despite the encroaching suburbs of Quinto Vicentino. (Open Mon.-Sat. 8:30am-12:30pm. Free.)

■ Central Veneto

The arc of land stretching from Treviso through Bassano del Grappa to Vicenza makes up the heartland of the Veneto. This region happily bore the brunt of the celebratory Venetian decoration of the *terra firma,* leaving a choice collection of indefensible castles, strikingly charming towns, and Renaissance villas. Two small train lines run through the region, one linking Treviso to Vicenza by way of Castelfranco Veneto and Cittadella, and the other traveling north from Padua through Castelfranco to Bassano del Grappa. Most of the other sights in the region can be reached easily by bus, but the unwieldy schedules (see Treviso, Bassano, and Vicenza Practical Information) might prompt you to hop on a bike or moped, or gather a group to rent a car.

Ville Venete

Venetian expansion to the mainland which began in the early 15th century provided infinite opportunity for Palladio's talents. As Venice's wealth accumulated and its maritime supremacy faded, its nobles began to turn their attention to the acquisition of real estate on the mainland. The Venetian Senate stipulated that they build villas rather than castles to preclude any possibility of becoming independent warlords. The architectural consequences were stunning: Veneto is now home to hundreds of the most splendid villas in Europe.

Although villas abound in the Veneto, they are difficult to reach, have unpredictable schedules, and often allow tours of their exteriors only. Phone ahead or contact the **APT** in Vicenza on Via Gazzolle,1 (tel. 39 91 11). The affable staff has mountains of well-written booklets on the villas. The tourist offices in Vicenza and Treviso provide good literature on Palladio's works, but they have written information only on the villas in their immediate provinces. Check in local bookstores for more complete guides to the *Ville,* in English and Italian.

The bus from Vicenza to Bassano stops at Thiene. Here, make the change to head for the tiny village of **Lugo** to see two famous Palladian villas at close range (5 per day, 2 on Sun., L3200). The simple **Villa Godi-Valmarana** (a.k.a. "Malinveri," tel. (0445) 86 05 61) was the architect's first. (Grounds open March-Nov. Tues., Sat.-Sun., and holidays 2-6pm. Admission L4000. Interior, by prior appt. only). A few yards up the street is the more elegant and expansive **Villa Piovene** (tel. (0445) 86 14 81). The villa may be viewed only from the outside; for a close look, pay L3000 to enter the wonderful park around it. (Open daily 2:30-7pm.) Seven kilometers to the east of Ásolo (near Vicenza) lies the most famous of the villas, the **Villa Barbaro-Volpi,** at **Masèr,** built in 1560 by Palladio. Wander to the base of the hill to see the exquisite circular temple that Palladio built for the owners. (Interior open Tues., Sat.-Sun., and holidays 3-6pm; Oct.-May Tue., Sat.-Sun., and holidays 2-5pm. Admission L6000. Call (0423) 56 50 02 for more information.) Masèr is an easy bus trip from Bassano (6 per day, L2900). Conclude your immersion in Palladian architecture with a train ride from Castelfranco to Fanzolo (on the Padua-Belluno line) to see **Villa Emo** (tel. (0423) 48 70 40). Considered along with Masèr to be one of the most characteristic Palladian villas, the interior frescoes balance fluently with the architecture and are the masterworkings G.B. Zelotti. (Open Feb.1 to mid-Dec. Sat. 3-6pm, Sun. and holidays 3-7pm. Admission L5000, groups L4000.)

■■■ VERONA

The city of rose-colored marble is no less romantic today than it was for Shakespeare. In fact, the city's artistic strength is in part inspired from its two-thousand-year stint as a major metropolis. Even during its formative years as a Roman colony,

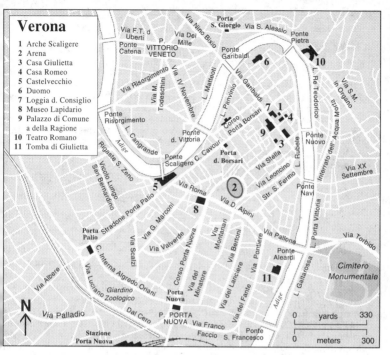

Verona

1 Arche Scaligere
2 Arena
3 Casa Giulietta
4 Casa Romeo
5 Castelvecchio
6 Duomo
7 Loggia d. Consiglio
8 Museo Lapidario
9 Palazzo di Comune
  a della Ragione
10 Teatro Romano
11 Tomba di Giulietta

Verona was an important crossroads, and the remarkably well-preserved remains are tangible evidence of the colony's preeminence. In the 13th and 14th centuries, Verona experienced another cultural heyday under the rule of the della Scala clan. A synthesis of statuesque remains and opulent *palazzi* marks Verona, whose gracious interweaving of past and present manifests itself best in the celebrated summer opera season held within the Arena, an amphitheater of epic proportions erected in 100 AD.

ORIENTATION AND PRACTICAL INFORMATION

The heart of the Verona lies between **Piazza Brà** and the **Arena.** From the center **Corso Porta Nuova** is the artery that leads south to the bus and train transportation. Most of the scenic portions of town are contained within the lazy loop of the **Adige River.** Piazza Brà is a 20-min. walk up Corso Porto Nuova from the train station, or a ride aboard **AMT** bus #2. Bus tickets (L1200) are available at the booth across from the station, as are day passes (L3000).

Tourist Office: Via Dietro Anfiteatro, 6 (tel. 59 28 28), which translates to "behind the amphitheater." Multilingual staff, accommodations consultations. Open Mon.-Sat. 8am-8pm, Sun. 8:30am-1:30pm. **Branch:** P. Erbe, 38 (tel. 800 66 97), on the end intersected by Corso Borsari. Open Mon.-Sat. 8am-8pm. **Youth Info Caravan:** at the Porta Nuova train station. Open Mon.-Sat. 9am-7pm, Sun. 9am-1pm. **Youth Info Center:** Corso Porto Borsari, 17 (tel. 801 07 95 or 59 07 56). Open Tues.-Wed., Fri.-Sat. 10am-1pm, Mon. 3-5pm. **Hotel Booking Office:** Via Patuzzi, 5 (tel. 800 98 44; fax 800 93 72). Open Mon.-Fri. 9am-12:30pm and 2-6pm.
Budget Travel: CIT, P. Brà, 2 (tel. 59 17 88). Open Mon.-Fri. 9am-1pm and 3-7pm, Sat. 9am-1pm. **Centro Turistico Giovanile,** Via Seminario, 10 (tel. 800 45 92), across the river and off Via Carducci, on the 3rd floor. Open Mon.-Fri. 3-7pm.

VERONA

CTS, Largo Pescheria Vecchia, 9/A (tel. 803 09 51), near the Scaligeri tombs. Open Mon.-Fri. 9:30am-12:30pm and 4-7pm.

Currency Exchange: Cassa di Risparmio, P. Brà, centrally located on the corner of Via Roma. Open Mon.-Fri. 8:20am-1:20pm and 2:35-4:05pm.

American Express: Fabretto Viaggi, Corso Porta Nuova, 11 (tel. 800 90 40), 2 blocks down on the left from P. Brà. Won't sell traveler's checks, but changes them for no commission after 4pm. Open Mon.-Fri. 8:30am-12:30pm and 3-7pm.

Post Office: P. Poste (tel. 800 39 98), also known as P. Francesco Viviani, adjacent to P. Indipendenza near Ponte Nuovo. Stamps and Fermo Posta at #13, 14, and 16. Open Mon.-Sat. 8:15am-7:30pm. **Postal Code:** 37100.

Telephones: SIP, Via Leoncino, 53, as you leave P. Brà. Open Mon.-Sat. 9am-12:30pm and 3-7:30pm. 24-hr. phone bank and *schiede* dispenser 3 doors down. **Telephone code:** 045.

Trains: P. XXV Aprile (tel. 59 06 88), linked with P. Brà by Corso Porta Nuova. To: Venice (every hr., 2hr., L8800); Milan (every hr., 1hr. 30min., L17,800); Bologna (every hr., 2hr., L8800); Trent (every hr., 1hr., L7200); and Rome (6 per day, 6hr., L48,700). **Currency exchange:** open 7am-9pm, wretched rates. **Luggage Storage:** L1500. Open 24hrs.

Buses: APT, P. XXV Aprile (tel. 800 41 29). To: Riva del Garda (every hr. 7:45am-6:45pm, L7400); Sirmione (every hr., L3500); Brescia (every hr., L3900); Montagnana (3 per day, L7800). Ticket window open daily 6am-8:30pm.

Taxis: tel. 53 26 66.

Car Rental: Hertz (tel. 800 08 32), at the train station. "Affordable Europe Rates," L661,000 per week. Open Mon.-Fri. 8am-noon and 2:30-7pm, Sat. 8am-noon.

Bike Rental: Paolo Bellomi, Via degli Alpini (tel. 800 70 40), off P. Brà. L4000 per hr., L15,000 per day. Open daily 9:30am-10pm; off-season 10am-7pm.

Swimming Pool: Centro Nuoto Piscina Coperta, Via Col. Galliano (tel. 56 78 25 or 56 76 22). Take bus #7 from P. Erbe or Castelvecchio to the beginning of Corso Milano and ask for directions. Olympic-sized. Olympic-caliber people-watching to boot, despite unflattering mandatory headwear. Open in summer daily 10am-8pm. Admission L5000, ½-day L4000, over 60 or under 14 L3500.

English Bookstore: The Bookshop, Via Interatto dell'Acqua Morta, 3 (tel. 800 76 14), across Ponte Navi and to the left. Also a community bulletin board with occasional bargains of an unpredictable nature. Open Mon. 3:30-7:30pm, Tues.-Fri. 9:15am-12:30pm and 3:30-7:30pm, Sat. 9:15am-12:30pm.

Pharmacy: tel. 192.

Emergencies: tel. 113. **Police: Questura,** tel. 59 67 77. **Ufficio Stranieri:** Lungoadige Porta Vittoria (tel. 809 05 05). Interpreter available, Mon.-Fri. 8:30am-12:30pm. **Hospital: Ospedale Civile Maggiore,** Borgo Trento, P. Stefani (tel. 807 11 11).

ACCOMMODATIONS

Make reservations during the opera months of July and August.

Ostello Verona (HI), Salita Fontana del Ferro, 15 (tel. 59 03 60), on the southern slope below Castel San Pietro. From the train station or downtown, take day bus #72 (from the "f" platform of the train station) or night bus #91 across the river (on Ponte Nuovo). The bus is small and not always backpack-friendly. Get off in P. Isolo. Walk ahead to Via Ponte Pignolo at the end of the piazza, turn right (you'll see the hostel sign), go to the end, then turn left, take the first right, and finally the first left. One of the most beautiful and well-run in Europe, the hostel is also the only one adorned with 15th-century frescoes. The master chef gladly caters to vegetarians if notified in advance, and fabulous Fabio (fab Fab) has become legendary. You can also **camp** in the villa's garden. Rooms open at 6pm, but arrive earlier to register and drop off your stuff. Curfew 11pm, with special provisions for opera-goers. Hostel L14,000 per person, including hot showers, breakfast, and sheets that give starch new meaning. Camping L7000 per person, all-inclusive (L5000 without tent). Restaurant-caliber dinners L11,000. 5-night maximum stay. 220 beds.

Casa della Giovane (ACISJF), Via Pigna, 7 (tel. 59 68 80), off Via Garibaldi, accessible by bus #71. Get off at P. Duomo or Via Garibaldi. Women only. Spotless rooms in an optimal location. Flexible lockout 9am-6pm. Curfew 10:30pm, unless you have opera tickets. L15,000 per person in 8-bed rooms. Singles L20,000. Bed in a double L19,000, in a triple L17,000.

Locanda Catullo, Vicolo Catullo, 1 (tel. 800 27 86), set off the street between 1/D and 3/A, off Via Mazzini. Some newly redone doubles have French doors and terraces. Singles L37,000. Doubles L50,000, with bath L70,000.

Locanda Volta Cittadella, Via Volta Cittadella, 8 (tel. 800 00 77), near P. Cittadella. Spartan but clean rooms. Singles L27,000. Doubles L36,000.

Campeggio Castel S. Pietro, Via Castel S. Pietro, 2 (tel. 59 20 37), over the hill from the hostel, just down and around the bend from the castle. Take bus #3 to Via Marsala. Hot showers, a bar, and other conveniences. L5500 per person, L4000-7000 per tent depending on size, L3000 per car. No trailers allowed. Open mid-June to mid-Sept.

Campeggio Romeo e Giulietta, Via Bresciana, 54 (tel. 851 02 43), inconveniently located on the road to Peschiera de Garda. APT bus to Peschiera from train station (L2000). Alert bus driver that you're going to the campground (last bus from Verona 8pm). Hot showers, plenty of space, store, and pool, but no romantic balconies. Check in 8am-11pm. L5200 per person, L6800 per tent. Open year-round.

FOOD

Verona is famous for its wines: *soave* (dry white), *valpolicella,* and *bardolino* (both red). The vendors in Piazza Isolo offer better prices than those in Piazza delle Erbe. For a large sampling, try **Oreste dal Zovo,** Via S. Marco in Foro, 7/5 (tel. 803 43 69), off Corso Porta Borsari. The congenial owner has shelves of every wine imaginable. Serve yourself *grappa* from a mini-barrel (L2500) and crunch on microscopic snacks (L100) or small *panini* (L1000). For other essentials go to **Supermarket PAM** (tel. 803 28 22), Via Dei Mutilati, 3, near P. Brà off Corso Porta Nuova. (Open Mon.-Tues. and Thurs.-Sat. 8:30am-7:30pm, Wed. 8:30am-noon.)

In The Center

Trattoria Fontanina, Piazzetta Chiavica, 5 (tel. 803 11 33), down the street from the tombs of the Scaligeri. Streetside terrace. *Primi* L7000, *secondi* L8000-12,000. Cover L1500. Service 12%. Open Wed.-Sun. noon-2pm and 7-9:30pm, Mon. noon-2pm.

La Bottego di Nonno Francesco, Via Leoni, 4 (tel. 59 67 37), near Ponte Navi. Gastronomic goodies to go. Open Mon.-Tues. and Thurs.-Sat. 8:15am-1:45pm and 4:30-7:45pm, Wed. 8:15am-1:45pm.

Élite Gastronomica, Corso Porta Nuova, 2 (tel. 803 00 74), closer to the Arena. Make a picnic of their tempting seafood salads in the shade of P. Brà's park. Open Mon.-Tues. and Thurs.-Sat. 9am-1pm and 4-7:30pm, Wed. 9am-1pm.

Across the River

Unless the gravitational tug of the Arena proves overwhelming, cross the water to this university quarter when in search of satiation.

Nuovo Grottina, Via Interrato dell'Acqua Morta, 38 (tel. 803 01 52), off Via Carducci by Ponte Nuovo. A favorite with students during the school year, and priced to stay that way. Pizza L4500-8500. *Menù* L14,000. Wine L3000 per ½ liter. Cover L1000. Open Fri.-Wed. 9:30am-2:30pm and 6pm-1am.

Trattoria Al Cacciatore, Via Seminario, 4 (tel. 59 42 91), the 4th left off Via Carducci, which begins at Ponte Nuovo. A genuine neighborhood joint with delicious food. *Primi* L3500, *secondi* L7500. Cover L1500. Open Mon.-Fri. 8:30am-2:30pm and 6:30-10pm, Sat. noon-2:30pm.

Trattoria dal Ropeton, Via San Giovanni in Valle, 46 (tel. 30 040), below the youth hostel. Very authentic, very popular, and very hard to get the best courtyard tables. Consider reservations. *Primi* L6000, *secondi* L11,000. Cover indoors L1500, courtyard L2500. Open Wed.-Mon. 12:30-3pm and 7:30-11pm.

Il Grillo Parlante, Vicolo Seghe San Tomaso, 10 (tel. 59 11 56), tucked in a tiny corner alley behind the old bus station in P. Isolo. Bright red doors and a tropical motif mark Verona's vegetarian hotspot. *Primi* L6000, *secondi* L6500-7000. Cover L2500. Open Fri.-Sun. and Tues.-Wed. noon-2pm and 7:30-10pm, Thurs. noon-2pm.

SIGHTS

The majestic pink **Arena** (tel. 800 32 04) in P. Brà dates back to 100 AD, and among Roman amphitheaters it is surpassed in size only by the one at Capua and the Colosseum in Rome. The Arena's superb condition testifies to Verona's municipal pride (Open Tues.-Sun. 8am-6:30pm, in opera season 8am-1pm. Admission L6000, students L1500.)

From P. Brà, Via Mazzini takes you into **Piazza delle Erbe,** the former Roman Forum. The center of the piazza holds the Madonna Verona fountain, installed by Cansignorio della Scala in 1368. At the far end rises the 1523 column of St. Mark, symbol of four centuries of Venetian domination. The **Gardello Tower,** built in 1370, stands between the imposing Baroque **Palazzo Maffei** and two buildings with frescoed façades and spacious terraces that Verona's first families, the Scaliger (della Scala) and the Mazzanti, once called home. In the center of the piazza, almost hidden by fruit vendors' awnings, stands the Berlina—during medieval times, convicts were tied to the marble structure to be pelted with rotten fruit.

The **Arco della Costa,** called the "Arch of the Rib" for the whale rib hung from it, separates P. delle Erbe from **Piazza dei Signori.** The delicate **Loggia del Consiglio** (1493), built in the Venetian Renaissance style, stands adjacent to the *prefettura.* The grey **Palazzo della Ragione** stands on the corner. This densely knit brick and marble ensemble was the seat of the della Scala dynasty for centuries. The Scala was a violent and dogged family, as their names suggest: Cangrande (Big Dog), succeeded by Mastino II (The Mastiff), and then Cansignorio (Head Dog). Yet, like many of their brutish peers, the della Scala were also sensitive patrons of the arts. Dante passed many months here as the guest of Cangrande, and eventually dedicated his *Paradiso* to the powerful warlord.

Through the arch at the far end of P. dei Signori lie the peculiar outdoor **Tombs of the Scaligeri,** further testimony to the Scala family temperament. The **Casa di Romeo,** long the home of the Montecchi family (model for the Montagues), has slowly deteriorated into a disappointing coffee bar (around the corner from P. dei Signori at Via Arche Scaligori, 2). At Casa Capuletti, Via Cappello, 23, more commonly known as **Casa Giulietta** (tel. 803 43 03), you will find a tall, ivy-covered wall next to a balcony where you can wait your turn in line to spot your Romeo among the trinket stands. It doesn't help that the feuding dal Capellos (Capulets) never lived here. (Open Tues.-Sun. 8am-6:30pm. Admission L5000, students L1000.)

At the other end of Via Arche Scaligeri, Corso Sant'Anastasia leads to the Gothic **Basilica of Sant'Anastasia** whose interior bulges with art treasures. Don't miss Pisanello's *St. George Freeing the Princess* (in the Giusti Chapel in the left transept), considered one of his best paintings, and the frescoes by Altichiero and Turone. Walk down Via Duomo from the basilica to the **duomo,** decorated with medieval sculpture by local stone carvers. The first chapel to the left features Titian's ethereal *Assumption of the Virgin.* The **Biblioteca Capitolare** (tel. 59 65 16), the oldest library in Europe, maintains a priceless medieval manuscript collection, which shameless sinners can see by donning a specious scholarly visage to trick the priest (Cathedral open daily 7am-noon and 3-7pm. Library open Mon., Wed., and Sat. 9:30am-12:30pm, Tues. and Fri. 9:30am-12:30pm and 4-6pm. Free.)

Over the Roman Ponte Pietra (across the Adige) the recently uncovered **Teatro Romano** (tel. 800 03 60) now provides a venue for Shakespearean plays. The theater was built during the Augustan and Flavian years at the foot of what is today called St. Peter's Hill. It affords a wonderful view of Verona, especially in the evening. (Complex open Tues.-Sun. 8am-6:30pm, off-season and performance days Tues.-Sun. 8am-1:30pm. Admission L5000.)

At the bottom of the hill, the Interatto dell'Acqua Morta leads to the 15th-century **Church of Santa Maria in Organo.** Although Sammicheli made a significant contribution to the façade, the most delicate inlay work was completed by Giovanni da Verona. Behind the church the **Giardino Giusti** (tel. 803 40 29), a delightful 18th-century garden, beckons. (Open daily 8am-8pm. Admission L5000, students L2000.)

The della Scala fortress, the **Castelvecchio** (tel. 59 47 34), was carefully reconstructed after devastation during World War II. The many-leveled interior is decked out with walkways, parapets, an extensive collection of sculptures and paintings including Pisanello's *Madonna and Child,* Luca di Leyda's *Crucifixion,* which balances passion and compositional rhythm, and works by Andrea Mantegna, Francesco Morone, Tintoretto, and Tiepolo. (Open Tues.-Sun. 8am-6:30pm. Admission L5000.)

The church of **San Zeno Maggiore,** upstream from the Castelvecchio is one of the finest examples of Italian Romanesque architecture. Built and expanded upon from the 10th to 12th centuries, the massive brick church of Verona's patron saint surpasses its more central counterparts in artistic wealth. The 17th-century sculpted bronze doors sparked a craze throughout Italy. The interior structure is notable for its wooden "ship's keel" ceiling and the spacious crypt area. The two-story apse contains a Renaissance altarpiece by Mantegna. (Open daily 8am-noon and 3-7pm.)

ENTERTAINMENT

Verona has parlayed the romance of its pervasive rosy marble and vast Roman arena into the city's premier cultural event, an opera and ballet extravaganza that takes place in July and August. Ticket prices start at L25,000 for unreserved gallery seats. For more information, call 59 01 09 or 59 07 26, or go directly to arch #8 or #9 to make a reservation or a purchase. If you opt for general admission seating, be prepared to encounter crowds of operaholics who camp out up to two hours before the gates open to ensure for themselves marginally better views.

The Teatro Romano stages Shakespeare productions (in Italian) every summer. (Tickets start at L19,000. Reserve ahead at arch #18. Open in season Mon.-Sat. 10:30am-1pm and 4-7pm. For information call 807 71 11, for reservations 59 00 89). *Verona for You* (available at the tourist office) lists current exhibits and events.

▧ Friuli-Venezia Giulia

Overshadowed by the touristed cities of Veneto and the mountains of Trentino-Alto Adige, Friuli-Venezia Giulia has traditionally received less than its fair share of recognition. Trieste has been a long-standing exception to this rule, and today increasing numbers of beach-goers flock to the least expensive resorts on the Adriatic.

Friuli-Venezia Giulia was once a number of distinct provinces, as its name suggests. Finally the local clergy unified and maintained autonomy from the church and other states from the 6th to 15th centuries. The entire region was then appropriated by the Venetian Republic, only to be reabsorbed, Venetians and all, into Austria-Hungary. The present region is the product of a postwar union between Udine, Pordenone, Gorizia, and Trieste. The historical differences between these provinces, and the area's vulnerability to Eastern forces given its marginal geographic location in the north of Italy, combine to give Friuli-Venezia Giulia a hybrid character and culture. The mix of political intrigue and coffee-culture elegance brought by the Austro-Hungarian Empire attracted intellectuals of varied provenance to turn-of-the-century Friuli: James Joyce lived in Trieste for 12 years, during which he wrote the bulk of *Ulysses;* Ernest Hemingway's *A Farewell to Arms* draws part of its plot from the region's role in World War I; Freud and Rilke both worked and wrote here. The mixture of Slovenian, Friulian, and Italian peoples has produced an indigenous literary tradition of its own, which includes Italo Svevo and the poet Umberto Saba.

The Tagliamento and Natisone River Valleys shelter fertile farmlands, and local dialect and hearty culinary traditions are the legacy of the society's peasant origins. The Carnian Alps to the north and the Julian Alps to the east present copious opportunities for hiking, rock-climbing, and skiing, and provide an alternative climate to the beaches of the southern coast.

■■■ TRIESTE

The unofficial capital of Friuli-Venezia Giulia lies at the end of a narrow strip of land sandwiched between Slovenia and the Adriatic. Given its strategically placed harbor and proximity to Austrian and former Yugoslavian borders, Trieste has been a bone of contention over the centuries. Even as an independent city from the 9th to 15th centuries, and Venice's main rival in the Adriatic until La Serenissima overtook it, Trieste was always coveted by the Austrians. Austria finally got its crack at a real Adriatic port in the post-Napoleonic real estate market, and proceeded to rip the medieval heart from Trieste, replacing it with neo-classical bombast. The equally heavy-handed style of government the Habsburgs brought succeeded in turning the mostly Italian population into fervent *irredentisti* clamoring for the return of the vaguely Italian province to Italy. They emerged victorious in 1918 when Italian troops occupied the Friuli, but unification only brought more trouble: Mussolini's thicket of fascist statuary provided appropriate counterpoint to the Austro-Hungarian architecture, while his policies of cultural chauvinism offended anyone not already alienated by the Habsburg rulers. The achievement of its citizens' dream also succeeded in wiping out Trieste's reason for existing: Italy already had a choice collection of Adriatic ports.

Today, evidence of Trieste's multinational history lingers in the numerous buildings and monuments of Habsburg origin and the Slavic nuances in the local cuisine. The city's Italian identity, on the other hand, is vehemently asserted by the persistence of fascist and anti-Slav parties, and more tangibly in the formidable **Piazza Unità d'Italia.** The cumulative product of these conflicting forces is a cosmopolitan transportation hub—a logical departure point for travelers to Eastern Europe.

ORIENTATION AND PRACTICAL INFORMATION

Trieste is a direct train ride from Venice or Udine, and several trains and buses cross over daily to neighboring Slovenia and Croatia. Less frequent ferry service runs the length of the Istrian Peninsula. The grey, industrialized quays catering to ferries and fishermen taper off into Trieste's equivalent of a beach—a stretch of tiered concrete, populated with bronzed bodies, which runs 7km from the edge of town out to the castle at Miramare. Moving inland one encounters **Piazza Oberdan,** which opens onto the ever-busy **Via Carducci.** Shopping sprees are common on the fashion-oriented streets that intersect with this central artery near P. Goldoni. The artistically inclined can head to the pride and glory of Trieste, **Piazza Unità d'Italia,** which looks out to the harbor. Public transportation runs throughout the city, and most buses stop in the immediate vicinity of the train station. Everything in Trieste except public services closes on Monday.

Tourist Office: in the train station (tel. 42 01 82), around the corner to the left after exiting from the main entrance. Copious information on Trieste including a list of *manifestazioni* (cultural events) occasionally encompassing international programs as well. For cheap accommodations also ask about staying at private homes. English spoken. Open Mon.-Fri. 9am-3pm and 3-8pm. Another branch is located in the **Castello di San Giusto** (tel. 30 92 98).

Budget Travel: CTS, P. Dalmazia, 3 (tel. 36 18 79). Agency for air and train tckets plus a variety of other vacation information. Less helpful is **Aurora Viaggia,** Via Milano, 20 (tel. 60 261), 1 block from Via Carducci. Information on transportation and lodging in the former Yugoslavian territory. Open Mon.-Fri. 9am-12:30pm and 4-7pm, Sat. 9am-noon.

Consulates: the **U.S.** no longer has a consulate here, but it does have an honorary representative at Via Roma, 15 (tel. 66 01 77). Ask for Sig Bearz. Otherwise try the consulate in Milan. **U.K.,** Vicolo delle Ville, 16 (tel. 30 28 84), available Tues. and Fri. 9am-12:30pm. The closest **Canadian** and **Australian** consulates are in Milan. **New Zealand** citizens should contact their embassy in Rome. To check on the current state of visa requirements for travel east, contact the **Consulate General of Yugoslavia,** Strada del Friuli, 54 (tel. 41 01 25). Open Mon.-Fri. 9am-noon.

Currency Exchange: Banca d'America e d'Italia, Via Roma, 7 (tel. 63 19 25). Cash advances on Visa cards. Open Mon.-Fri. 8:20am-1:20pm and 2:35-3:50pm. Also try **Assomar Cambio** in the bus staion in P. della Libertà (tel. 42 53 07). Open daily 7:30am-8pm. No commission, except for traveler's checks.

Post Office: P. Vittorio Veneto, 1 (tel. 36 67 42), along Via Roma, the 2nd right off Via Ghega coming from the train station. Fermo Posta at counter #21, stamps at #30. Fax downstairs. Open Mon.-Sat. 8am-7:30pm. **Postal Code:** 34100.

Telephones: SIP, Viale XX Settembre, 5. Open Mon.-Fri. 8:30am-noon and 2-7:30pm, Sun. 8:30am-3:30pm. Another office at P. Oberdan. Open Mon.-Fri. 8:30am-noon and 2-3:50pm. **ASST,** Via Pascoli, 9, off P. Garibaldi. Open 24 hrs. **Telephone Code:** 040.

Trains: P. della Libertà (tel. 41 82 07), down Via Cavour from the quays. Train info open daily 8:30am-12:30pm and 3:30-6:30pm. To: Udine (15 per day, 1hr. 30min., L5700); Venice (16 per day, 2hr., L12,100); Milan (1 per day, 5hr. 30min.-7hr. 30min., L30,300); Ljubljana (6 per day, 3hr. 30min., L14,500); Budapest (1 or more per day, L60,000). **Luggage Storage:** L1500. Open daily 5am-midnight.

Buses: Corso Cavour (tel. 336 03 00), in the fringe of P. della Libertà near the train station. To: Udine (8 per day, L6000); Rijeka/Fiume (2 per day, L11,400). **Luggage storage** L1500. Open daily 6:20am-8pm. There are also several smaller lines that run throughout the region. Check at the station.

Public Transportation: ACT, Via d'Alviano, 15 (tel. 77 951). Open Mon.-Fri. 9am-1pm.

Rental Cars: Hertz, in bus station, P. della Libertà. Open Mon.-Fri. 8:30am-12:30pm and 3-7pm. Closed Sat. afternoon and Sun. Another **Hertz** office at the airport (tel. 77 70 25), as well as **Avis** (tel. 77 70 85). **Europcar** (tel. 77 89 20), **Eurodollar** (tel. 77 98 66), and **Budget** (tel. 77 91 66).

Ferries: Agemar Viaggi, P. Duca degli Abruzzi, 1/A (tel. 36 37 37; fax 77 723), by the waterfront next to the canal. Will arrange trips with **Adriatica di Navigazione.** To: Grado (15min., L8500); Lignano (1hr. 15min., L10,000); Parenzo (2hrs. 10min., L23,000); Rovigno (3hrs. 10min., L26,000); Piran (1hr. 30min., L13,000); Umag (2hr. 30min., L18,000); Pula (4hr. 30min., L32,500).Prices do not include harbor tax. Office open Mon.-Fri. 8:30am-1pm and 3-7:30pm.

Taxis: tel. 545 33 or 30 77 30.

English Bookstore: Libreria Cappeli, Corso Italia, 12B. English books and travel guides. Open Tues.-Sat. 8:30am-12:30pm and 3:30-7:30pm. Closed Sun. and Mon.

Laundromat: Via Ginnastica, 36 (tel. 36 74 14). Coin-operated. Open Tues.-Fri. 8am-1pm and 4-7pm, Sat. 8am-1pm. Closed Sun. and Mon.

Public Baths: in P. Ponterosso. Open during the morning market. L200.

Swimming Pool: Piscina Communale "Bruno Bianchi," Riva Gulli, 3 (tel. 30 60 24), along the waterfront. Indoor. Open Oct.-July, Mon.-Sat. noon-3pm, Sun. 9am-1pm. L3500. Lockers L1100.

Late Night Pharmacies: tel. 192. Insert 3 telephone tokens.

Emergencies: tel. 113. **Police:** Via del Teatro Romano (tel. 37 901), off Corso Italia. **Hospital: Ospedale Maggiore,** P. dell'Ospedale (tel. 77 61), up Via Tarabocchia from Via Carducci. **Ambulance:** tel. 118.

ACCOMMODATIONS

Watch out for weekdays, when companies often fill up the smaller *pensioni* with workers. Consult the tourist office, which leaves a helpful list of Trieste's hotels and *pensioni* taped to the door for those who arrive after hours.

Ostello Tegeste (HI), Viale Miramare, 331 (tel. 22 41 02). From station take bus #36 (L1000). You'll find the bus stop #36 on Viale Miramare, the street to the left of the station. The hostel is located on the seaside, just down from the castle Miramare, about 6km from the city center. Get off of the bus just before it stars heading up the hill. Also look out for signs to the castle. There is a popular garden bar at the hostel and the view over the sea back towards town is terrific. Live bands play here periodically, othertimes loud recorded American music fills the air. Average of 4 bunks per room. Hot showers included, but hot water only available 5hr. per day until 9am. After 6pm personal lockers with locks provided free of charge. HI members only. Registration noon-11:30pm. Checkout 9:30am. Lockout 9:30am-noon. Curfew 11:30pm. L17,000 includes showers and breakfast. Also serves lunch and dinner (*menù* L13,000—although you can eat 1 or 2 parts for less). Call or write ahead to reserve a bed during suntanning season.

Julia, Via XXX Ottobre, 5 (tel. 37 00 45). Big, well-lit rooms with shower, sink and toilet. Singles L29,000. Doubles L46,000.

Centrale, Via Ponchielli, 1 (tel. 63 94 82). Located centrally, as the name suggests, right off the canal. Large, yet standard 1-star hotel rooms. Clean, no frills. Singles L30,000, with shower L34,000, with bath L45,000. Doubles L50,000, with shower L54,000, with bath L65,000.

Centro, Via Rome, 13 (tel. 63 44 08). Small, adequate rooms with high ceilings. Downtown. Singles L30,000. Doubles L55,000. **Marepineta** (Campground, tel. 29 92 64), along the coast, SS #14, provides beachside luxury. L4500-9000 per person, L8250-18,000 per tent and L4000-5000 per car (or any sort of camper). Hot water, electricity, and a bar included. Open May-Sept. Alongside the campground is a charming 2km trail billed as the **Rilke Sentiere** after the poet Rilke, who lived in **Duino,** the village at the other end of the trail. Duino presides over the haunting ruins of the **Duino castle.** (Open by reservation only; tel. 20 81 20.) Camping Marepineta is located in Sistiana; buses leave from the terminal every hr. (L2400).

Camping Obelisco, Strada Nuova Opicina, SS # 58 (tel. 21 16 55), is 7km from Trieste in Opicina, a suburb on the rocky *carso*—a sparsely beautiful place to camp for those not umbilically attached to the beach. Fewer facilities than Marepineta, and correspondingly lower prices. L3500-5000 per person, L7000-10,000 per tent, light L1500. Trains leave frequently from the station (L2600), or take the tram from P. Oberdan (L1600).

FOOD

Many dishes in Trieste's restaurants have Eastern European overtones (usually Hungarian) and are often loaded with paprika. The city is renowned for its fish; try *sardoni in savor* (large sardines marinated in oil and garlic). Monday is a non-day in Trieste: many shops and restaurants close. To fend for yourself, visit one of the several **alimentari** on Via Carducci or try the **Bosco Supermarket** in P. Goldoni (open Tues. and Thurs.-Sat. 8am-1pm and 4:30-7:30pm, Mon. and Wed. 8am-1pm). If you're near the waterfront, go to **Supermercato Despar** across from the public pool (open Mon.-Fri. 8:30am-1:30pm and Tues., Thurs., and Fri. 4:30-7:30pm, Sat. 8:30am-7:30pm). While in town, sample a bottle of **Terrano del Carso,** a dry red wine with a low alcohol content that has been valued for its therapeutic properties since the days of ancient Rome. To purchase grapes in their unadulterated form, stroll through the open-air **market** in P. Ponterosso, by the canal. (Open Tues.-Sat. 8am-5:30pm.)

Paninoteca Da Livio, Via della Ginnastica, 3/B (tel. 63 64 46), inland off Via Carducci. Small, smoky shop boasts monster *panini* (L2500-7000), dozens of brands of beer, and crowded with customers. Open Mon.-Sat. 9am-3pm and 5-10pm. Closed last week of July and first of August. **Pizzeria Barattolo,** P. Sant'Antonio, 2 (tel. 64 14 80), along the canal. Amazing pizza (L6000-12,000). Also bar and *tavola calda* offerings. Open Tues.-Sun. 8am-1am. AmEx, Diner, MC, Visa accepted.

Brek, Via San Francesco, 10 (tel. 73 26 51) or on Viale Cami Elisi (tel. 77 46 23). Self-service restaurant. Economical, efficient and tasty. Everything is *alla carta* so pick and choose between fresh fruit, wine, pasta and more. Via Francesco open Sat.-Thurs. 11:30am-3pm and 6:30-10:30pm. Viale Cami Elisi open Tues.-Sun. same hours.

SIGHTS

In honor of the Habsburg empress, 19th-century Viennese urban planners carved out a large chunk of Trieste to create Borgo Teresiano, a district of straight avenues bordering the waterfront and the canal. Facing the canal from the south is the district's one beautiful church, the Serbian Orthodox **San Spiridione.** Unfortunately, the church is surrounded by a steel barricade, so you'll have to admire it from afar. The **Municipio** at the head of **Piazza dell'Unità d'Italia,** a monument to the limits of ambition, sags under the weight of its heavy ornamentation and oversized tower. In the corner of the piazza stands an allegorical fountain with statues representing four continents. The surreal effect is completed by the stone warehouses rotting slowly along the waterfront.

The 15th-century Venetian **Castle of San Giusto** presides over **Capitoline Hill,** the city's historic center. You can take bus #24 (L1000) from the station to the last stop at the fortress, and ascend the hill via the daunting **Scala dei Giganti** (Steps of the Giants—all 265 of them) rising from P. Goldoni. It offers a great view of the sea and downtown Trieste, and is a prime sunset-watching spot, if the bora winds don't blow you away. Within the walls is a huge outdoor theater where film festivals are held in July and August (pick up a copy of *Trieste '94, Eventi Luglio-Agosto* at the tourist office). Directly below are the remains of the old Roman city center, and across the street is the restored **Cathedral of San Giusto.** Its irregular plan is due to its origin as two churches built simultaneously from the 5th through 11th centuries, one dedicated to San Giusto, the other to Santa Maria Assunta. Inside are two splendid mosaics in the chapels directly to the left and right of the altar. Walk around the ramparts of the castle (open daily 8am-7pm), or peek into the museum, which has temporary exhibits in addition to its permanent collection of weaponry (tel. 30 77 44; open Tues.-Sun. 9am-12:45pm; admission L2000).

Down the other side of the hill, past the *duomo,* lies the eclectic **Museo di Storia de Arte** and **Orto Lapidario** (Museum of History and Art and Rock Garden; tel. 37 05 00 or 30 86 86) at Via Cattedrale, 15, in P. Cattedrale. The museum provides archaeological documentation of the history of Trieste during and preceding its Roman years, and boasts a growing collection of Egyptian art and artifacts from southern Italy. (Open Tues.-Sun. 9am-1pm. Admission L3000, students with ID L1500.) Descending the hill towards the ruins of the *teatro romano* you end up only a few short blocks from P. Unità d'Italia.

The **Teatro Romano** on Via del Teatro Romano off Corso Italia was built under the auspices of Trajan (1st c. AD). Gladiatorial contests were originally held here, later Greek tragedies were shown.

An excellent collection of drawings and a less impressive selection of paintings by Tiepolo, Veneziano, and others has been moved from the Capitoline Hill to an elegant 18th-century villa at Largo Papa Giovanni XXIII, 1, which is now the **Museo Sartorio** (tel. 30 14 79). The museum is easily reached by walking along the quays, a short distance from the center. (Open Tues.-Sun. 9am-1pm. Admission L3000.)

Back in the thick of things, stop at the **Museo del Risorgimento,** Via XXIV Maggio, 4 (tel. 36 16 75), in a *palazzo* by Umberto Nordio off P. Oberdan. The museum contains the cell of Guglielmo Oberdan, the 19th-century Irredentist who met his death at the hands of the Austrians in 1882 and posthumously gave his name to the piazza. (Open Tues.-Sun. 9am-1pm. Admission charged.)

ENTERTAINMENT

The regular opera season of the **Teatro Verdi** runs November to May, but a six-week operetta season is held in June and July. Purchase tickets or phone for reservations at P. Verdi, 1 (tel. 36 78 16; open Tues.-Sun. 9am-noon and 4-7pm; seats from L10,000). Inquire at the tourist office about other performances in the **castle** or **Teatro Romano.**

Caffé Tommaseo, in P. Tommaseo along the canal (closed on Mon.), and **Caffé San Marco,** on Via Battisti, preserve the city's turn-of-the-century coffee culture (the latter frequently offers live musical performances). (Open 7am-midnight. Closed Wed.) Coffee in Trieste is an art form, thanks to the influence of the Viennese. It comes to you on a silver platter, with a glass of water and frequently a few sweet pastries (typically L3000-5000). Locals gather indoors at the Tergesteo, a sunlit, covered arcade. More caffes and table seating ia a grand old structure from 1842. Located next to the stock exchange building in P. della Borsa. The liveliest *passeggiata* takes place along Viale XX Settembre, a cool and largely traffic-free tree and *caffé*-lined avenue—a good place to relax in the shade.

■ Near Trieste

West of Trieste you can sunbathe along the rocky coast and visit the **Castello Miramare** (tel. 22 41 43), the Disneyesque castle of Archduke Maximilian of Austria, who ordered its construction in the middle of the 19th century. Maximilian didn't live to see the completion of the grounds—he went to serve as Napoleon III's "Emperor of Mexico" and ended up being shot. Miramare acquired a bad reputation after Maximilian's widow Carlotta went mad. It was rumored that anyone spending the night here would come to a bad end, a belief helped along by the decision of Archduke Ferdinand to spend the night here on the way to his assassination at Sarajevo. Poised on a high promontory over the gulf, Miramare with its white turrets is easily visible from the Capitoline Hill in Trieste or from the train on the journey through the *carso*. Miramare's extensive parks are open to the public at no cost and range from marble fountains to secluded, bark-strewn paths. To reach Miramare, take bus #36 (30min., L1000). (Castle museum open daily 8am-7pm. Admission L6000, L7500 with tour in Italian. English tours available for L20,000.) Fortunately, each room has a description and history provided in English. In July and August, a series of **sound and light shows** transforms Miramare into a high-tech playground. (Shows Tues, Thurs., and Sat. at 9:30pm and 10:45pm. The show is in English. Admission L7000. Call the Tourist Office for more info.)

Near the castle, a **marine park** (tel. 22 41 47) sponsored by the World Wildlife Fund conducts several programs throughout the year, including guided introductions to the coast's marine life. The park itself is the area marked by buoys off shore surrounding Castle Miramare. It is forbidden to swim here without a guide. Guided water tours—both snorkeling and scuba are offered. (Open Wed. and Fri. Admission L25,000, children L15,000. In Italian. Call the office to make reservations, which are required. Office open Mon.-Fri. 9am-7pm, Sat. 9am-5pm. You can also rent snorkel, fins and mask—together L25,000 or separately.)

About 15km from Trieste in Opicina, you'll find the **Grotta Gigante** (tel. 32 73 12), the world's largest accessible cave. Staircases wind in and around the 90m-high interior, which the brochure claims could hold the whole of St. Peter's. (Open Tues.-Sat. 9am-noon and 2-7pm, Nov.-Feb. 10am-noon and 2:30-4:30pm. L8000. Transportation from P. Oberdan and admission. You can also take bus#45; 5 per day, L1300.)

■ Aquileia and Palmanova

Aquileia

Aquileia was founded in 181 BC on the banks of the now-defunct Natisone-Torre River. Between 200 and 452 AD it flourished as the Roman capital of the region, serving as the gateway to the Eastern Empire and as the principal trading port of the Adriatic. The Patriarchate of Aquileia was established here in 313, but as the Huns and Lombards descended to sack the city in the 5th and 6th centuries, the Patriarch fled to Grado and then moved on to Cividale del Friuli. Aquileia finally regained control in 1019, celebrating by rebuilding its great basilica, and from here the Patriarchate successfully defied the popes until it faded into obscurity. Meanwhile, the port silted up and malaria set in. The disgruntled Patriarch moved on to Udine and dwindled into an archbishop, leaving behind a perfect open-air museum of Roman and early Christian art, the most important archeological remains in northern Italy.

Aquileia can be reached by bus from Udine (16 per day, 1hr., L3800), and local buses travel to Cervignano, a train station on the Trieste-Venice line (every 30min., L1200). The **tourist office** (tel. (0431) 91 94 91; open April-Oct. Fri.-Wed. 9am-1pm and 4-6pm) is a block from the bus stop in P. Capitolo.

Across the piazza from the tourist office stands Aquileia's **basilica.** The basilica is a tribute to the town's artistic heritage, offering a sampling of artwork from across the centuries. The floor, a remnant of the original church, is a 4th-century mosaic of unequalled magnitude, animating over 700 square meters with geometric designs and realistic bestial depictions. The 9th-century crypt beneath the altar contains several 12th-century frescoes illustrating the trials of Aquileia's early Christians and scenes from the life of Christ. In the *Cripta degli Scavi,* directly to the left upon entering, excavation has uncovered three distinct layers of flooring, providing vivid evidence of the building's varied history. (Basilica open daily 7:30am-7:30pm; in winter 8am-12:30pm and 3-6pm. Crypt open Mon.-Sat. 9am-3pm., Sun. 9am-1pm.)

Omnipresent yellow signs and clearly delineated tourist maps make it easy to find the various ruins, but the cypress-lined alley behind the basilica runs parallel to the once-glorious **Roman harbor** and is a pleasant alternative to Via Augusta as a path to the **forum.** Continue from there to the **Museo Paleocristiano** (tel. 91 11 30), where displays explain the transition from classical paganism to Christianity, and moss covers the ubiquitous mosaics. (Open Tues.-Sat. 9am-6:30pm, Sun. 9am-1pm and 2-6:30pm, Mon. 9am-2pm; in winter Mon.-Sat. 9am-2pm, Sun. 9am-1pm. Free.)

Camping Aquileia, Via Gemina, 10 (tel. (0431) 91 042; in winter 91 037), up the street from the forum, is a shady spot with a swimming pool. (L4500 for adults, L5500 July-Aug.; under 12 L2800-3500. Tent sites L7200-L8500, wooden bungalows or trailers for two L26,000-50,000. Open May 15-Sept. 15.) The **Albergo Aquila Nera** (tel. (0431) 910 45), down Via Roma in the P. Garibaldi, offers more central accommodations. (Singles with bath L35,000. Doubles with bath L60,000. Additional bed L10,000. Breakfast L7000. Complete dinner for about L18,000—be sure to ask the proprietor for a glass of local white wine. Open April-Dec.) The **Desparo Supermarket** on the Udine end of Via Augusta is a penny-pincher's salvation (open Tues.-Sat. 8am-1pm and 4pm-midnight, Sun. 8am-1pm), and the **Trattoria Augusta** upstairs serves a decent *menù* for L15,500 (open Tues.-Sun. 9am-3pm and 5pm-midnight).

Palmanova

Palmanova, a town girded by a nine-sided Venetian fortress, lies between Udine and Aquileia on the bus route to Grado (16 per day, 20min., L2200). With a hexagonal central piazza and six main streets radiating out to the ramparts, Palmanova is an exceptionally well-preserved example of Renaissance military planning. The **tourist office,** Borso Udine, 4/C (tel. (0432) 92 91 06) is on the ground floor of the **Museo Civico,** which displays manuscripts and artifacts documenting Palmanova's military history. (Both open Tues.-Sun. 10am-noon.)

■ Udine

If you venture here you should congratulate yourself on your unorthodox itinerary: Udine is an unexpectedly captivating town. In addition to Italian, natives speak some German, some Serbo-Croatian, and the old *Friulàn* dialect, an obscure relative of equally obscure Swiss Romansch. The linguistic intermingling of Central European, Balkan and Italian influences typifies the exotic composite of Udinese life. Given its turbulent history—conquered by Venice in 1420, appropriated by Austria in the late 18th century, and heavily bombed during WWII—Udine is fortunate to have escaped with its landmarks intact.

As a more significant legacy of WWII, Udine had the only concentration camp in Italy, which occupied a converted rice factory. Naturally, this fact cannot be found in any of the tourist brochures. It has now been memorialized as a park on Viale della Vittoria, on your right as you head out of the city center.

The present town is notable primarily for its graceful Gothic and Renaissance architecture, and for works of the rococo pioneer Giambattista Tiepolo. Udine today is small, tidy, and upscale. Shoppers and businesspeople stream through the streets. The local attractions are limited although it could serve as a comfortable base for those who want to explore Friuli Venezia Giulia.

ORIENTATION AND PRACTICAL INFORMATION

Udine's train and bus stations are both on Viale Europa Unita in the southern part of town. All bus lines pass by the train station, but only buses #1, 3, and 8 run from Viale Europa Unita to the center of town, by the **P. della Libertà** and **Castle Hill.** You can also make the 15-minute walk: from the station, go right to Piazzale D'Annunzio, then take a left turn under the arches to Via Aquileia. Continue up Via Veneto to P. Libertà.

Tourist Office: P. 1° Maggio, 7 (tel. 29 59 72). From P. della Libertà, turn right on Via Manin and left on P. 1° Maggio, then look for the pink-arched façade, or take bus #2, 7, or 10 to P. 1° Maggio. Wonderful maps, copious information. Be sure to pick up the booklet *Udine: Eight Itineraries* for an exhaustive overview. English spoken. Open Mon.-Fri. 9am-1pm and 3-6pm.

Currency Exchange: Credito Italiano, Via Manin, 2 (tel. 50 32 33), near P. della Libertà. Open Mon.-Fri. 8:20am-1:20pm and 2:35-4:05pm, Sat. 8:20am-11:50pm.

Post Office: Via Veneto, 42 (tel. 50 19 93). Fermo Posta and stamps through the left door at desk #9. Fax at window #3. Open Mon.-Sat. 8:15am-7:30pm. Also a smaller branch at Via Roma, 25, straight ahead from the train station. Open Mon.-Sat. 8:10am-1pm. **Postal Code:** 33100.

Telephones: SIP, Via Savorgnana, 13 (tel. 27 81), off P. Duomo. Open Mon.-Fri. 9am-12:30pm and 4-7:30pm. **Telephone Code:** 0432.

Trains: on Viale Europa Unita (tel. 50 36 56). **Information** office open 7am-9pm. Trains to: Venice (22 per day, 2hr., L10,500); Trieste (19 per day, 1hr. 30min., L6500); Milan (4 per day, 5hr., L23,500); Vienna (6 per day, 7hr., L70,000). **Luggage storage,** L1500. Open daily 7:30am-10:30pm.

Buses: on Viale Europa Unita (tel. 20 39 41), 1 block to the right of the train station as you exit. The station itself is defunct, but head through, then turn left when you see the bus parking garage and find the office for **Autolinea Ferrari** (tel. 50 40 12). Service to Trieste (9 per day, 1hr., L6000); Lignano (17 per day, 1hr., L6000); Venice (1 per day, 2hrs., L9900); Grado (16 per day, 1hr., L4000); Cividale (24 per day, 30min., L2300); Palmanova (23 per day, 20min., L2300); Aquileia (18 per day, 40min., L3800). Bus line offices housed in the "Pullman Bar" next door (tel. 50 24 63).

Mountain Information: the bulletin board of the **Club Alpino Italiano,** inside city hall on Via B. Odorico. Information on upcoming trips and skiing. For information on hikes within the Friuli-Venezia Giulia, contact **Gruppo Attività ed Informazione Ambientali,** Via Monterotondo, 22 (tel. 60 18 92). **Società**

Alpina Friulana, Via Odorico, 3. Open Mon.-Sat. 5-7:30pm, Thurs. and Fri. 9-11pm. Alpine information and excursions.
Swimming Pool: Piscina Comunale, Via Ampezzo, 4 (tel. 26 967 or 26 929), near P. Diacono. Indoor pool open Sept.-May; outdoor June-Aug. Open Mon.-Sat. 2-7pm, Sun. 10am-1pm. L6000.
Late Night Pharmacy: tel. 192.
Emergencies: tel. 113. **Police:** Via Prefettura, 16 (tel. 50 28 41). **Medical Emergency:** tel. 118. **Hospital: Ospedale Civile** (tel. 55 21), in P. Santa Maria della Misericordia. Take bus #1 north to the last stop.

ACCOMMODATIONS

Luckily the large map outside the train station is clearly marked with the locations of Udine's hotels, some of which are real bargains. Now for the bad news: local workers probably snagged the best spots long ago. Many single rooms tend to be booked by the month. During June and July students taking exams also vie for these vacancies.

Suite Inn, Via di Toppo, 25 (tel. 50 16 83). Take bus #1 from the station, get off at Via Gemona or Piazzale Osoppo, and walk up Via di Toppo. Sweet proprietor is eager to please. Cozy sitting room with TV and piano. Tidy rooms, spotless bathrooms, and phones. Singles L30,000. Doubles L50,000. Breakfast L5000.
Locanda Da Arturo, Via Pracchiuso, 75 (tel. 29 970). Take bus #4 from the station, get off at P. Oberdan, and walk down Via Pracchiuso on the far side of the piazza. Restaurant downstairs has a *menù* for L16,000. Quiet, with only a few rooms. Call ahead for reservations. Singles L18,000. Doubles L36,000. Closed either July or Aug.
Locanda Piccolo Friuli, Via Magrini, 9 (tel. 50 78 17). From P. Garibaldi take Via Brenari to Via Poscolle and continue on Vicolo Gorgo. A bit more expensive, but worth it: a beautiful old building with antique fixtures. Creaky wood floor, big sitting room, and frescoes create the quaint atmosphere. Singles with bath L45,000-50,000. Doubles with bath L65,000-70,000. Triples with bath L80,000-85,000. Breakfast L8000.
Al Vecchio Tram, Via Brenari, 32 (tel. 50 25 16). Just off P. Garibaldi. Elegant staircase and large, adequate rooms. Restaurant downstairs. Singles L29,000-30,000. Doubles L46,000-50,000.

FOOD

A pastiche of earthy Italian, Austrian, and Slovene, Udinese cuisine tends more toward the hearty than the *haute*. A typical regional specialty is *brovada e museto,* a stew made of marinated turnips and boiled sausage. Shop for produce weekday mornings in the **open-air market** at P. Matteotti near P. della Libertà, or head for Via Redipuglia or P. 1° Maggio on Saturdays between 8am and 1pm. Buy staples at the **Desparo Supermarket,** at Viale Volontari della Libertà, 6, off P. Osoppo. (Open Mon. and Wed. 8:30am-1pm, Tues., Thurs., and Fri. 8:30am-1pm and 4-7pm, Sat. 8:30am-7pm.) Also try **Lavoratore Supermercati,** Via Stringher, 10, down the street from the duomo. (Open Mon. and Wed. 9am-1:30pm, Tues. and Thurs.-Sat., 9am-1:30pm and 4-7:30pm.) Other **Lavatore** include one on the mall on Via Canciani, off Via Poscolie Interno, 3. (Open Tues.-Fri. 9am-12:30pm and 4-8pm, Sat. 9am-12:30pm and 3:30-8pm.) Cheap pizzerias and trattorias cluster around Via Pracchiuso, including Pizzamania, Via Pracchiuso, 63. (Slices and takeout only.)

Zenit, Via Prefettura, 15. A cross between a '50s diner and a pre-school cafeteria in decor, but reasonable as a self-service place. Popular with local businesspeople. *Primi* L4500-6500. *Secondi* L6000-8000. Cover L500. Open Mon.-Sat. 11:45am-2:30pm and 6:30-9:30pm.
Ristorante/Pizzeria Ai Portici, Via Veneto (tel. 50 89 75), under the arcade before P. della Libertà. Pizza for L7000-8000 is a reasonable price, given the chic

ambience. *Primi* L8000. *Secondi* L14,000-25,000. Cover L1500. Open Wed.-Mon. 9am-midnight or 1am.

Mangiamitutto, Via Vittorio Veneto, 27 (tel. 29 93 41) and Via Antonio Caccia, 18 (tel. 450 57), by P. Le Osoppo. A casual, cheap, and tasty sandwich shop. Their symbol is two pairs of the "Rolling Stones" tongue and lips. Sandwiches L4000-6000. Beer on tap L2500 and L5000. Open Tues.-Sat. 7am-midnight.

SIGHTS AND ENTERTAINMENT

The heart of Udine is **Piazza della Libertà,** an elegantly elevated square. Along its higher side runs the Renaissance **Arcade of San Giovanni.** The two symbolic columns of Venice in the piazza commemorate the conquest of Udine by the Venetian Republic; while across the piazza stands the delicate, candy-striped **Loggia del Lionello,** another architectural reminder of the conquerors' presence in Udine. Originally built in 1448, the beloved *loggia* was severely damaged by a fire in 1876, but reconstructed shortly thereafter by popular demand.

The rugged **Arco Bollani** (1556, designed by Palladio) (tel. 50 18 24), in the corner near the clock tower, allows you through the walls enclosing the **Chiesa di Santa Maria** and the **castello** of the Venetian governors. The *castello* is home to the **Museo Civico,** which exhibits a myriad of notable frescoes including a frieze and several *putti* by Giambattista Tiepolo. (Open Tues.-Sat. 9:30am-12:30pm and 3-6pm, Sun.-Mon. 9:30am-12:30pm. Admission L3200, students L1600.)

In P. del Duomo, 50m from the more hectic P. della Libertà, stands the Roman-Gothic **duomo,** with several Tiepolos on display in the Baroque interior (the first, second, and fourth altars on the right side). There is a small **museum** (tel. 50 68 30) in the squat brick *campanile,* which is comprised of two chapels with 14th-century frescoes by Vitale da Bologna. (Museum closed for renovation in 1993.) Udine has been called the city of Tiepolo, and some of this Baroque painter's finest works adorn the **Oratorio della Purità** (tel. 50 68 30), across from the *duomo.* The *Assumption* frescoed on the ceiling (1759) and the *Immaculate Conception* of the altarpiece represent Tiepolo's world of light, air, and awe. (Ask the cathedral sacristan to let you in. Tip expected.)

A sizeable sampling of earlier Tiepolo frescoes is housed in the **Palazzo Arcivescovile** (tel. 50 43 14), P. Patriarcato, 1, at the head of Via Ungheria. Here, from 1726 through 1730, Tiepolo executed an extensive series of Old Testament scenes. (Open Mon.-Fri. 9am-noon. Free. Closed for restoration in 1993.) Several blocks south from P. della Libertà along Via Stringher, off P. XX Settembre, stands the **Chiesa di San Francesco.** This architectural gem of the early Renaissance is considered Udine's most beautiful church. Unfortunately, it opens only for exhibitions.

There are also a number of interesting museums, including an excellent **Gallery of Modern Art** at P. P. Diacono, 21 (tel. 29 58 91), on the ring road that circles the old city. The museum transports you to the idiosyncratic world of De Kooning, Lichtenstein, Chagall, Picasso, and every major 20th-century Italian artist. (Open Tues.-Sat. 9:30am-12:30pm and 3-6pm, Sun. 9:30am-12:30pm. Admission L3200, students L1600.) The **Friulian Museum of Popular Arts and Traditions,** Via Viola, 3 (tel. 50 78 61), northeast of the P. XXVI Luglio, exhibits a collection of regional costumes and folk art. (Open Tues.-Sat. 9:30am-12:30pm and 3-6pm, Sun. 9:30am-12:30pm. Admission L3200, students L1600. Closed for restoration in 1993.)

■ Cividale del Friuli

At the far edge of Italy and unknown to most travelers, sleepy Cividale saw its glory days come and go during the darkest of the Dark Ages. In the 6th century AD, land-hungry Lombards seized what was then *Forum Iulii* and made the vanquished Roman trading center the capital of the first Lombard duchy. By the 8th century, Patriarch of Aquileia had moved in to grab a piece of the action, setting off a building frenzy. Since then things have been generally quiet, despite devastating earthquakes that have twice crumbled the city's monuments. Cividale thus remains the only place in Italy to see magnificent medieval art from the least known century of Italian history.

This tiny town can easily be seen in an afternoon. No need for a map, simply wander through the ancient portal and follow the yellow metal or natural wood signs past the restaurants, shops and cafes to the historical points of interest.

Orientation and Practical Information Cividale is easily reached by train from Udine, which lies at the end of a *locale* line that connects the two cities (every hr., 20min., round-trip L3600). The **train** and **Rosina bus stations** (tel. 63 10 46; open Mon.-Fri. 8:30am-12:30pm, Sat. 8:30am-1pm) open onto Viale Libertà and are a brief walk from the **center** and **tourist office** at Largo Boiano, 4 (tel. 73 13 98). (Bus to Udine L2300.) From the train station head directly onto Via Marconi, turning left through the **Porta Arsenale Veneto** when the street ends. Bear right in the P. Dante, then left onto Largo Boiano. The staff is extremely helpful. (Open Mon.-Fri. 9am-1pm and 3-6pm, Sat. 9am-1pm.) The **post office,** at Largo Boiano, 37 (tel. 73 11 57), is just down the street from the tourist office and has an exchange service that accepts traveler's checks. (Open Mon.-Fri. 8:30am-5:30pm and Sat. 8:30am-1pm.) The **postal code** is 33043. In case of **emergency,** call 113, or seek out the **police** on P. A. Diaz (tel. 73 14 29). The **hospital (Ospedale Civile)** is in P. dell'Ospedale (tel. 70 81).

Accommodations and Food Accommodations are certainly not Cividale's forte. The two-star **Al Pomo d'Oro,** P. S. Giovanni (tel. 73 14 89), has singles with bath for L48,000, doubles with bath for L75,000, and breakfast for L5000. (A lovely old building in the medieval quarter with a restaurant downstairs. AmEx, Eurocard, MC, and Visa.) The specialties of the area are *gubana* (a fig- and prune-filled pastry laced with *grappa*) and *Picolit,* a pricey dessert wine rarely sold outside of the Natisone Valleys. Most bars stock pre-packaged *gubana,* but for fresh mouth-watering rings, look for the "Gubana Cividalese" sign on your right as you near the **Ponte del Diavolo,** located at Corso D'Aquileia, 16. P. Diacono hosts Cividale's **open-air market** every Saturday from 8am to 1pm. The management of **Antica Trattoria Dominissini,** Stretta Stellini, 18 (tel. 73 37 63), serves up *cucina friulana* in the shadow of **Chiesa S. Francesco.** Ask to sit outside in the vine-roofed area with a view of the church's tower. (*Primi* L5000, *secondi* L5000-10,000. Open Sun.-Fri. 8:30am-3pm and 4-11pm.) The **Taverna Roma,** Piazza A. Picco, 15 (tel. 73 01 25), is said to be a popular spot with the young crowd. (Open Tues.-Sun.)

Sights and Entertainment Built and expanded upon over a period of centuries, Cividale's *duomo* (directly on your left as you leave the tourist office) is an odd melange of architectural styles, but most of the credit is given to Pietro Lombardo, who completed the bulk of the construction in 1528. Walk to the far end of the *duomo* to view the 12th-century silver **altarpiece of Pellegrino II,** with its 25 saints and pair of archangels. Move on to the Renaissance **sarcophagus of Patriarch Nicolò Donato,** located to the left of the entrance. Annexed to the *duomo* is the **Museo Christiano.** This free display includes the **Baptistery of Callisto,** a wonderfully sculpted piece of architecture commissioned by the first Aquileian patriarch to move to Cividale. More significantly, the museum houses the **Altar of Ratchis,** a delicately carved work from 749, one of the few surviving masterpieces of the Middle Ages. (Open Mon.-Sat. 9:30am-noon and 3-7pm, Sun. 3-6:45pm. Museum also open Sun. 9am-noon. Both free.)

The greatest Italian work of the 8th century can be found downhill and upstream at the **Tempietto Longobardo,** built on the remains of Roman homes (follow the signs). Although the "little temple" suffered greatly from the earthquakes of 1222 and 1976, exhaustive efforts have restored a famous sextet of 8th-century stucco figures to their original form. The beautiful 14th-century wooden stalls partially compensate for the loss of the original frescoes. Another bonus is the spectacular view of river and mountains, obtained from the entrance overlooking the rocky riverbed. The green, lush countryside rolls on into the distance, and on a high vista sits the picturesque **Castelmonte Stara Gora.** (The Tempietto is open daily 10am-1pm and 3:30-6:30pm. Admission L2000, students L1000.) For a similarly stunning vista, try the **Ponte del Diavolo,** an impressive stone bridge of indeterminate age. For a better look at the bridge itself, descend the stair to the water on the far side. Local legend has it that the devil himself threw down the great stone in the center of the river on which the bridge was built.

On the sixth of January, the **Sword Mass** follows a procession to the *duomo.* This event commemorates the investiture of the Patriarch Marquando of Randek, and the sword used today is the gift presented to him by the townspeople in 1336.

■ Trentino-Alto Adige

"Grüss Gott!" Travelers to Italy's northern reaches often hear this and fear they have stumbled into Austria. And they have in all but name; the influence of Austrian culture exceeds that of Italian in much of the region. Trentino in the south is predominantly Italian-speaking, while Südtirol (South Tirol) in the north is largely German-speaking and encompasses most of the mountain region known as the Dolomites. Long an integral part of the Holy Roman Empire, the provinces were conquered by Napoleon only to pass into the hands of the Austro-Hungarian Empire. At the end of World War I, however, Trentino and the Südtirol fell under Italian rule. Germany curtailed Mussolini's brutal efforts to Italianize the Südtirol during the 1920s, but not before he had supplied every German name in the region with an Italian equivalent.

The intermingling of Austrian and Italian traditions permeates everything from art to cuisine. North of Bolzano, you may get better service by trying to speak German; in Trent, Italian is the ticket.

■ Dolomites (Dolomiti, Dolomiten)

Stunning limestone spires shoot skyward from billowing fields and pine forests. These amazing peaks—fantastic for hiking, skiing, and rock-climbing—start west of Trent and extend north and east to the Austrian frontier.

Finding accommodations in the Dolomites is easy. There are the hundreds of alpine huts and the rooms in private homes advertised by the *zimmer/camere* signs. Pick up the complete *Südtirol Hotel Guide,* free at the provincial office in Bolzano and in local tourist offices. These offices also provide listings of campgrounds in the region, but travelers camp almost anywhere—with discretion.

The **SAD** (Società Automobilistica Dolomiti) deploys an armada of **buses** that covers virtually every paved road in the area with surprising frequency.

Hiking

Even the least intrepid can become avid Dolomitists. The terrain varies from wide, gentle trails to vertical cliffs. **Alpine huts** (*rifugi*) abound, making forays into the mountains easier and safer. All huts are clearly marked on the *Kompass Wanderkarte,* the best map of the region, available at most newsstands and bookstores. Huts generally operate from late June through early October, but at higher altitudes the hut season is likely to be shorter. The provincial tourist offices in Trent and Bolzano supply information in English on their respective provinces. The Alpine desk of the office in Bolzano is run by Dr. Hannsjörg Hager, a noted Alpinist who speaks English and can help you pick a suitable route, making sure the huts are open before you get into the mountains. Hut prices increase with altitude, but average about L12,000 per dormitory cot and L18,000 per bed. All offer a *menù* for roughly

L10,000; bring your own food if possible. Pick up information about winter walking paths from the tourist office. For further information about Trentino huts, contact the SAT at Via Manci, 57 (tel. 98 18 71 or 98 64 62), in Trent (open Mon.-Fri. 8am-noon and 3-7pm).

Skiing

The Dolomites offer amazingly popular downhill skiing enhanced by sunny skies and perfectly powdery snow. The **regional tourist office** in **Bolzano** (tel. (0471) 99 38 09) is a good source of information. For more specific information concerning prices, deals and snow conditions contact **Club Alpino** (See Essentials: Camping). Major ski centers near Bolzano, include **Alta Venosta** (around Lake Resia) and **Colle Isarco**; near Trent, **Folgaria, Brentonico, Madonna di Campiglio,** and **Monte Bondone** (especially close to the city); near Bressanone, **Val d'Isarco,** the **Zona dello Sciliar,** and **Val Gardena;** and near Corvara, **Alta Badia.**

One of the cheapest and most convenient ways to enjoy a skiing holiday in the Dolomites is to get a **settimana bianca** (white week) package deal from any CTS or CIT office. Prices start around L500,000 and include a week's room and board and ski passes. If you want to travel the region by bus or car, or if you're planning to stay in the region of interlocking trails around the Gruppo Sella, consider purchasing the **Superski Dolomiti** pass, good on all 430 cablecars and lifts in the Dolomite area (around L40,000 per day, L200,000 per week).

■ Trent (Trento, Trient)

Trent's strategic importance, located inside of the Alpine threshold, yet connected back to the Veneto by a long, deep valley, made the city an important gateway. The Romans created two imperial roads throughTrent. During the centuries to follow, fortress-like castles proliferated in the region. In the 16th century the Council of Trent pondered the problems of Lutheran contagion for 18 years. Cultural and physical ownership of the city itself was contested in the 19th century, but was settled once and for all at the conclusion of World War I, when Trent became an Italian city. In contrast to the disputes which have surrounded the city, its pleasant, frescoed *piazze* and numerous parks make Trent a relaxing stop.

ORIENTATION AND PRACTICAL INFORMATION

Behind Trent's train station flows the Adige River; in front are the public gardens. A right turn on Via Pozzo will take you past a helpful signboard map at the corner of the garden to Via Orfane which becomes Via Cavour and leads to P. del Duomo. An earlier left on Via Roma leads in the direction of the Castello del Buonconsiglio. Virtually everything of importance is concentrated within the small historic center.

Tourist Office: Azienda Autonoma (City Tourist Office), Via Alfieri, 4 (tel. 98 38 80, fax 94 71 88), diagonally across P. Dante and the public gardens to the right from the train station. Open Mon.-Sat. 9am-noon and 3-6pm, Sun. 10am-noon; Sept.-June Mon.-Fri. 9am-noon and 3-6pm, Sat. 9am-noon. **Azienda per la Promozione Turistica del Trentino** (Regional Tourist Office), Corso III Novembre, 132 (tel. 98 00 00, fax 23 15 97), a 15-min. walk away on the continuation of Via Santa Croce.

Budget Travel: CTS, Via Cavour, 21 (tel. and fax 98 15 33), near P. del Duomo. Student IDs, plane and train tickets, Transalpino tickets, and occasional organized outings. English spoken. Open Mon.-Fri. 10am-1pm and 4-8pm.

Post Office: Via Calepina, 16 (tel. 98 72 70), at P. Vittoria. Open Mon.-Fri. 8:10am-7:30pm, Sat. 8:10am-1pm. Another office to the left from the train station on Via Dogana. Same hours. **Postal Code:** 38100.

Telephones: SIP office, P. della Portella, 2/B, the 1st right from Via Pozzo. Open Mon.-Sat. 8:30am-noon and 3:30-7pm, Sun. 8am-1pm. Phones also on Via Belenzani, 30. Open daily 8:30am-9pm. **Telephone Code:** 0461.

Trains: Tel. 23 45 45. To: Verona (every hr., 1hr., L7200); Bolzano (every hr., 45min., L4300); Bologna (11 per day, 3hr., L15,400); Venice (7 per day, 3hr., L12,100). **Luggage Storage:** L1500. Open 24 hrs.

Buses: Atesina, Via G. Marconi, 3 (tel. 82 10 00), next to train station. To Riva del Garda (every hr., 1hr., L5000). Extensive local service. Ask at the information booth in the station for schedules.

Cableways: Funivia Trento-Sardagna, Via Lung'adige Monte Grappa (tel. 23 21 54). Up and over the tracks; past the bus terminal take a right on busy Cavalcavia San Lorenzo, and you'll find the Funivia on the other side. This lift gets you up onto Mt. Bondone, specifically to Sardagna (daily 7am-6:30pm, L2500).

Bike "Rental": Next to the tourist office on Via Alfieri, 2, and also at the parking garage "Autosilo," Via Petrarca. A free bike for 3hr. Be warned: the free bike business is slow; look around for the caretaker. Other depot at the hostel. ID and a L10,000 deposit required Open March-Nov. Mon.-Fri. 8am-8pm, Sat. 8am-1pm.

Hiking Equipment: Rigoni Sport, P. Battisti, 30/31 (tel. 98 12 39). Open Tues.-Sun. 9:10am-noon and 3-7pm, Mon. 3-7pm. **Mountain Shop,** Via Buonarotti, 4 (tel. 82 42 58), near the campground. Inexpensive.

English Bookstore: Libreria Disertori, Via M. Diaz, 11 (tel. 98 14 55), near P. Battisti. Open Tues.-Sat. 9am-noon and 3:30-7pm, Mon. 3:30-7pm. MC, Visa.

Swimming Pool: Nuova Lido Piscina Coperta, Via Fogazzaro, 4 (tel. 91 10 06), off Viale Verona. Outdoor and indoor. Open July-Sept. daily 9am-8pm; Oct.-June Tues.-Sun. with slightly shorter hours. Admission L4700, children L2100.

Emergencies: Police, tel. 112. **Medical,** tel. 118. **Civic,** tel. 113. **Police: Questura,** P. Mostra (tel. 98 61 13). **Hospital: Ospedale Santa Chiara,** Largo Medaglie d'Oro (tel. 90 31 11), past the swimming pool and up Via Orsi. **Alpine Emergency: CAI-SAT hotline,** tel. 23 31 66. The **fire station,** tel. 115, can also reach alpine help.

ACCOMMODATIONS

Trent has plenty of rooms for rent except in August, when private rooms are impossible to find without reservations. Check with the tourist office about Agriturismo.

Ostello Giovane Europa (HI), Via Manzoni, 17 (tel. 23 45 67), a continuation of Via Torre Verde. Hotel turned hostel. 1- to 6-person rooms. Bar and TV. Check-in from 7:15am. Lockout 9am-5:30pm. Curfew midnight. L15,000 per person; breakfast included. Lunch and dinner for groups only (L12,000). Temporarily closed.

Casa della Giovane, Via Prepositura, 58 (tel. 23 43 15). Take a right off Via Pozzo from the station at the 1st real intersection, and turn left at P. da Vinci. Set back from the street behind a housing complex that conveniently soundproofs. Catholic-run organization (ACISJF). Spotless rooms with the latest in modern plumbing. Women only. Filled with students Sept.-early June. Check-out by 9:30am. Curfew midnight. Singles L28,000, with bath L25,000. Doubles with bath L25,000 per person. Prices go down for extended stays.

Hotel Venezia, P. Duomo, 45 (tel. 23 41 14), a *dipendenza* of the hotel of the same name around the corner. Both have clean, standard rooms, some with a view of the *duomo*. Quality and prices are the same. Singles L32,000, with bath L47,000. Doubles L52,000, with bath L73,000. Breakfast L6000.

Al Cavallino Bianco, Via Cavour, 29 (tel. 23 15 42), down the street from the *duomo*. Spacious rooms, but the main draw is the uninhibited paint job in the living room—enjoy the great outdoors from the comfort of your hotel! Singles L31,000, with bath L47,000. Doubles L52,000, with bath L73,000. Triples with bath L93,000. Closed in Dec. and 1 week in June. MC, Visa.

Camping: Camping Trento (tel. 82 35 62), on Lungadige Braille, a 20-min. walk upstream along the river. Take bus #2. After the Centrale Elettrica, walk 500m up to the pharmacy. Reception closes at 11pm. L5500 per person, L7500 per site. Open March-Oct. 15. Closed for repairs in 1993.

FOOD

The **market** in P. Lodron behind the *duomo* does its thing every morning from 8am to noon and occasional afternoons. **Open-air markets** spring up on Thursday in Via Maffei, Prati, Esterle, Torrione, and Borsieri, as well as P. d'Arogno. Budget buys await at **Supermarket Orvea**, Via Belenzani, 49 (tel. 96 03 33; open Mon.-Fri 8:30am-12:30pm and 3:30-7:30pm, Sat. 8:30am-12:30pm) and at **Supermarket Poli,** near the station at the corner of Via Roma and Via delle Orfane (open Mon.-Fri. 8:30am-noon and 3:10-7:10pm, Sat. 8:30am-noon).

Birreria Pedavena, Via S. Croce, 15 (tel. 98 62 55). Leave P. del Duomo on Via S. Vigilio and go with the flow. A good introduction to the north-south hybrid cuisine. *Pasta e fagiole* L4500, *wurstel* dishes L5500-7000. Cover L1500. Open Aug.-June Wed.-Mon. 8:30am-midnight.

Ristorante/Pizzeria Chistè, Via delle Orne, 4 (tel. 98 18 46). Serves huge portions that are popular with the locals. *Primi* about L5500. Pasta about L11,000. Cover L1000. Open Aug. 20-July 19 Tues.-Sun. noon-2pm and 6:30-11pm.

Pizzeria Duomo, P. Duomo, 22 (tel. 98 42 86). Pizza any way you want it. Loosen your belt and tackle the *luna,* a double-calzone specialty (L12,000). Open Sun.-Fri. noon-2pm and 6-10:30pm.

La Cantinota, Via S. Marco, 24 (tel. 98 03 61), at the other end of Via Manci from Via Roma. Everything, including the red carpet, is rolled out for you here. Enjoy the irreproachable cuisine, and humor the management by dropping by the piano bar after dessert. *Risotto* for at least 2 people L9000; *wurstel alla griglia* L9000. Cover L2000. Open Aug.-June Fri.-Wed. noon-3pm and 7-11pm. Piano bar open 7:30pm-2:30am.

SIGHTS AND ENTERTAINMENT

The pointed dome of Trent's Gothic-Romanesque **duomo,** also known as the **Cathedral of Saint Vigilio,** rises in modest emulation of the looming Alps. The famed Council's decrees were delivered in front of the huge cross in the Chapel of the Holy Crucifix. (Open daily 6:30am-noon and 2:30-8pm.) The remains of a 6th-century paleochristian basilica were recently uncovered beneath the *duomo.* Admission to this underground church is included in the admission to the **Museo Diocesano,** P. Duomo, 18 (tel. 23 44 19). (Open mid-Feb. to mid-Nov. Mon.-Sat. 9:30am-12:30pm and 2:30-6pm. Admission L2000, students L1000.)

Take a right at the end of **Via Belenzani** onto Via Roma to get to the **Castello del Buonconsiglio,** Trent's other main sight. Once the home of the bishop-prince who governed Trent, the castle was incorporated into the city walls. The castle also houses the **Museo Provinciale d'Arte.** (Castle and museum tel. 23 37 70. Open Tues.-Sun. 10am-7pm. Admission L4000 for ages 18-60, others free.)

If you arrive in the summer, try to catch a play or performance at one of the private castles (admission free-L10,000). Check with the tourist office for information.

Mountains Near Trent

Monte Bondone rises majestically over Trent and begs for pleasant daytrips and overnight excursions. Check with the tourist office (tel. and fax 94 71 88) in **Van-eze,** halfway up the mountain, about accommodations, ski lifts and maps. **Ski School Monte Bondone** (tel. 47 211) gives lessons and rents equipment. Pick up a map at the tourist office in Trent, and then catch the cable car from ponte di San Lorenzo, between the train tracks and the river, to **Sardagna,** a great picnic spot (cable car runs daily 7am-6:30pm, L2500; in Trent tel. 91 03 32 or 38 10 00). From there, a 10-12km hike takes you to the **Mezavia Campground** (tel. 94 81 78; L5000 per person, L7000 per tent; open June to mid-Sept.).

■ Bolzano (Bozen)

Bolzano attempts to ease linguistic feuds with mandatory instruction in both Italian and German for its youth, but the disproportionately large number of fair, rosy-cheeked bilinguists reveals the city's true Austrian bent. Underlying tensions however, do not appear to have not interfered with Bolzano's prosperity. The historic center is a combination of spacious *plätze/piazze* and arcaded alleys, presenting a congenial face to the mountain-bound traveler.

ORIENTATION AND PRACTICAL INFORMATION

Bolzano's historic center rests in the hollow of the converging Isarco and Talvera rivers, and is linked by bridge to the more modern, industrial sectors to the west. Bolzano's street signs somewhat comically manifest its bilingualism, redundantly repeating themselves bilingually in both languages repetitiously (we generally include only the Italian name). A brief walk up Via Stazione from the train station, or via Alto Adige if you've arrived by bus, leads to P. Walther.

Tourist Office: For Bolzano only, P. Walther, 8 (tel. 97 56 56 or 97 06 60). Lists of every accommodations option, including **Agriturismo.** *Walks and Hikes* suggests nearby hikes of varying lengths and difficulty. *Manifestazioni* includes several pages of tourist-oriented phone numbers. English spoken. Open Mon.-Fri. 8:30am-6pm, Sat. 9am-12:30pm. **Provincial Tourist Office for South Tyrol,** P. Parrocchia, 11 (tel. 99 38 08), just down from P. Walther, across from the *duomo*. A must for those setting out for the mountains.

Budget Travel: CTS, Via Rovigo, 38 (tel. 93 41 46), across the river, off Via Milano just past P. Matteotti. Open Mon.-Fri. 9am-12:30pm and 3:30-7pm, Sat. 9am-noon. **CIT,** P. Walther, 11 (tel. 97 85 16). Transalpino tickets and skiing packages. Open Mon.-Fri. 8:30am-12:30pm and 3-6:30pm.

Currency Exchange: Banca Nazionale del Lavoro, at the end of Via Stazione. Best rates, Visa services. Open Mon.-Fri. 8:20am-1:20pm and 3-4:30pm.

Post Office: Via della Posta, 1 (tel. 97 94 52), by the *duomo*. Open Mon.-Fri. 8:15am-5:15pm, Sat. 8:15am-12:45pm. **Postal Code:** 39100.

Telephones: SIP, P. Parrocchia, 17, to the left of the post office. Office open Mon.-Sat. 8:30am-12:15pm and 3:30-7:45pm, Sun. 8am-1pm. Booths open daily 7:30am-8pm. **ASST,** via Roma, 36/M, across the river near P. Adriano. Open Mon.-Sat. 8am-8pm. **Telephone Code:** 0471.

Trains: P. Stazione (tel. 97 42 92). To: Trent (14 per day, 45min., L4300); Verona (27 per day, 1hr. 15min., L10,500); Merano (every 45min., 45min., L3200); Milan (2 per day, 4hr., L20,400). **Information** open Mon.-Sat. 7am-8pm, Sun. 9am-1pm and 2:30-5:30pm. **Luggage Storage:** L1500. Open 24 hrs.

Buses: SAD buses, Via Perathoner, 4 (tel. 97 12 59, fax 97 00 42), between the train station and P. Walther. To: Alpe di Siusi (13 per day, 1hr. 30min., L5900); Collalbo (5 per day, 50min., L2600); Cortina d'Ampezzo (4 per day, 3hr. 30min., L14,500); Merano (13 per day, 1hr., L4000); Brunico (about 6 per week, about 6 per weekend, 1hr. 45min., L8400). Less frequent service on weekends. **Local buses: ACT,** Via Conchpelli, 60 (tel. 97 12 59). Bus service extends throughout the city. All lines stop in P. Walther.

Cableways: 3 cableways, lying at the edges of Bolzano, will quickly take you 1000m or more up and over the city, to the nearest trailhead. To Colle (Kohlern): take the world's oldest cableway, the Funivia del Colle (or as the locals call it, the Kohlerer Seilbahn; tel. 97 85 45), Via Campiglio (Kampillerstraße). Every hr. on the hr. To Renon (Ritten) take the Funivia del Renon (tel. 97 84 79) departing from Via Renon (only 5 min. walk from train station). Round-trip L7200. To Salto high plateaus take Funivia S. Genesio (Jeneseiner Seilbahn; tel. 97 84 36) on Via Sarentino, the farthest from the station. Cross the river, Talvera. Tickets around L3000, round-trip L5000. Bike and pet transport possible.

Car Rental: Avis, P. Verdi, 18 (tel. 97 14 67). **Hertz,** Via Alto Adige, 30 (tel. 97 71 55).

Bike "Rental": Via Stazione, near P. Walther. Borrow a bike for 4hr. by leaving a L10,000 deposit and ID information. Intercity cruisers, not mountainworthy.

Hiking Information: Club Alpino Italiano (CAI), P. Erbe/Obstplatz, 46 (tel. 97 81 72), and **Alpenverein Südtirol (AVS),** Via dei Bottai/Bindergasse, 25 (tel. 97 87 29). These are, respectively, the Italian and Austrian Südtirol Alpinist clubs. Weekend daytrips about L15,000 (CAI trips Sun. only). *Kompass Wanderkarte* for the area, billboard with offers of used ski equipment. CAI open Mon.-Fri. 11am-noon and 5-7pm. AVS open Mon.-Fri. 3:30-7:30pm.

Camping Equipment: Sportler, Via dei Portici/Laubengasse, 37/A (tel. 97 40 33). Expensive, extensive selection. Open Mon.-Fri. 9am-12:15pm and 2:30-7pm, Sat. 9am-12:15pm. You may get a better deal down the street at **Sport Reinstaller,** Via Portici, 23. Open daily 8:30am-noon and 3-7pm.

Swimming Pool: Lido di Bolzano, Viale Trieste. Outdoor pool. Open June to mid-Sept. daily 10am-6pm. **Piscina Coperta,** Viale Trieste (tel. 91 10 00), across the river. Indoor pool. Open Oct.-June Tues.-Fri. 12:30-2:30pm and 7-9pm, Sat. 4-6pm and 6:30-8:30pm, Sun. 3-6pm and 6:30-8:30pm.

Laundromat: Lavanderia Automatica Westinghouse, P. Matteotti, 3 (tel. 91 44 46), across the river off Via Torino. Washing your own clothes can be yours for the price of a good dinner (L15,000). Open Mon.-Fri. 8am-noon and 2:30-7pm.

Emergency: tel. 113. **Police:** tel. 94 76 11. **Medical Emergency:** tel. 90 83 30. **Hospital: Ospedale Regionale San Maurizio,** Via Lorenz Böhler (tel. 90 81 11). **Medical Assistance: White Cross,** tel. 27 44 44.

ACCOMMODATIONS

Bolzano has innumerable budget deals in the spring and fall; in summer and winter, however, you'll be hard pressed to find anything affordable. Given the magnificent surroundings, it is almost a pity to stay in the city. Try the mountain options or ask about the **Agriturismo** program at the tourist office.

Magdalena Weinstube, Sta. Maddalena di Sotto, 22 (tel. 97 43 80). Worth the hike toward St. Magdalena. Beautiful farmhouse with a stupendous view of the city. All rooms with bath. L28,000 per person, but you must stay more than 1 night. Singles available only if you stay 1 week or more. Breakfast included.

Pensione Reiseggerhof, Sta. Maddalena di Sotto, 24 (tel. 97 86 94), uphill from Weinstube. More great views, along floral trim on the furniture in the sunny doubles. All rooms with bath. Doubles L25,000 per person. Breakfast included.

Schwarze Katz, Sta. Maddalena di Sotto, 2 (tel. 97 54 17). Not feeling too excited about the steep uphill hike with pack? Then look to your left. You have arrived at hotel "Black Cat," a family-run, friendly place with rooms and a garden restaurant. L22,000 per person, with bath L30,000.

Croce Bianca, P. del Grano (Kornplatz, 3) (tel. 97 75 52). Spacious, old style rooms. Singles L30,000. Doubles L50,000, with bath L68,000.

Camping: Moosbauer, Via San Maurizio, 83 (tel. 91 84 92). Take bus #10A from the station (last at 8:30pm). Get off at the hospital stop, then walk down San Maurizio 1km. L7500 per person, L6000 per site.

FOOD

Rindsgulasch is a delicious beef stew, *Speck* is tasty smoked bacon, and *Knödel* (dumplings) come in dozens of rib-sticking varieties. Fall spotlights the local vineyards with the week-long Südtiroler Törgelen tasting spree. Festive P. dell Erbe (Obstplatz) has an all-day produce **market** every day but Sunday, and two **Despar supermarkets** thrive at Via della Rena, 40, and Via dei Bottai, 29 (both open Mon.-Fri. 8:30am-12:30pm and 3:45-7:15pm, Sat. 8am-12:30pm). For baked goods, revel among the delectable selections at **Panificio/Backerei Lemayr,** Via Goethe, 17 (open Mon.-Fri. 7am-12:30pm and 3:30-7:15pm, Sat. 7:30am-12:30pm). If you arrive in July, there are plenty of eating options on Via dei Bottai.

Restaurant Weisses Rössl, Via dei Bottai/Bindergasse, 6 (tel. 97 32 67), the continuation of Via Laurin and Via dei Grappoli, at the end of Via dei Portici. A cheap place with Austrian atmosphere. Nearly 100 regional and Italian dishes listed plus a daily *menù* (L7500-12,000). Open Aug.-June Mon.-Fri. 7am-1am, Sat. 7am-3pm.

Spaghetti Express, Via Goethe, 20 (tel. 97 53 35). A noisy, fun place with a young crowd. Try any of the umpteen kinds of pasta (L8000-10,500); the dish with crab-meat, risotto, cream, and brandy is great. Cover L1500. Open Mon.-Sat. noon-2pm and 7-10pm. Also at Via Orazio, 57 (tel. 42 611).

SIGHTS AND ENTERTAINMENT

Piazza Walther is altogether clean and attractive—even the McDonald's on the corner is tasteful. It is dominated by the 14th-century Gothic **duomo,** and delicate, lace-like tower designed. (Open Mon.-Fri. 9:30am-6pm, Sat. 9:30am-noon.) The 14th-century **Church of the Francescani** rests in a peaceful garden off the piazza. (Open daily 6am-noon and 2:30-6pm.) The firetowers of the 13th-century **Castel Mareccio** (tel. 97 66 15), on *passeggiata* Lungo Talvera, are later additions. (Open Mon.-Sat. 10am-noon and 3-6pm.)

Across the Talvera River, the quarter around P. Gries has two imposing churches, the Baroque **Church of the Benedictine Abbey of Muri** on the piazza (open 9-11:30am and 3-6pm; ring side bell.), and the **Gries Parish Church** (tel. 28 54 87), off the piazza. (Open Feb.-Oct. Mon.-Fri. 10:30am-noon and 2:30-4pm. Call ahead.)

The bike-borrowing option is the best way to visit the castles that cluster in the nearby valleys. **Castello Mareccio,** closest to the center, has a core structure which dates back to the 13th century. A 15-minute ride up Via Weggerstein to Via S. Antonio will take you past **Castello Roncolo** (tel. 98 02 00), the most impressive of the lot. Guided tours of the frescoed rooms are available for groups, preferably by reservation. (Open April-Nov. Tues.-Sat. 10am-5pm. Admission L1000.)

■■■ LAKE GARDA
(LAGO DI GARDA)

Garda is the grandest and most popular of the Italian lakes, thanks to its breezy summer and mild winter. Overlooked in favor of its western neighbors in the last century, it now boasts a more contemporary air. Of the lake's major towns, three in particular warrant a visit: Riva for its seclusion, reasonable prices, and splendid swimming, Gardone Riviera for the morbidly fascinating villa of Gabriele D'Annunzio, and Sirmione for its extensive Roman ruins and beautifully situated medieval castle. If you're coming from Verona, consider a daytrip to the tiny but stunning bay at **Punta San Vigilio** (just past Garda) for swimming, sunning, and picnicking.

Desenzano lies on the Milan-Venice train line, two hours from Venice, 25 minutes from Verona and Brescia, and one hour from Milan. Once there, it's easy to get to the lake towns by buses, hydrofoils, and ferries. Check the schedules carefully and plan ahead, as buses and ferries stop running early in the evening. For shorter trips, take the ferry—it's cheaper than the hydrofoil and you can sit on deck. It makes the Riva-Desenzano trip in only two hours (L23,200), while the regular ferries leave infrequently (only about 4 per day) and take four hours (L10,400). **Campgrounds** surround the lake but are concentrated between Desenzano and Salò. Unofficial camping is discouraged. Many private residences rent rooms (mostly doubles) in Lake Garda's larger towns. Get a list of these from the tourist office.

■ Sirmione

Alas, shrewd developers realized the potential of what Catullus once lauded as the "jewel of peninsulae and islands." The Space Boat Disco has landed just off shore, and the expansive Garda Village is forthcoming. In the off-season, however, the crowds thin out, and the surviving cypress and olive groves that cluster at the peninsula's farthest point provide an attractive haven from the man-made wonders in the center of town.

Practical Information Buses run to Sirmione every half-hour from Brescia and Verona (1hr., L3900 and L4400 respectively), and from Desenzano, the closest train station (L2000). The ride down the peninsula's central artery concludes in Sirmione on Viale Marconi, next to the **tourist office** in the disk-shaped building at #2 (tel. 91 61 14), where you can arm yourself with maps and accommodations information. (Open Mon.-Fri. 9am-12:30pm and 3-7pm, Sat. 9am-12:30pm.) Next to the tourist office you may find the new **hotel booking office** (open daily 12:30-3:30pm and 6:30-10:30pm). **Bikes** can be rented at **Green Walk,** Via Verona, 47 (tel. 990 40 34) or on Via XXV Aprile (L3000 per hr., L17,000 per day). The **postal code** for Sirmione is 25019. The **telephone code** for both Sirmione and Desenzano is 030. In **emergencies,** dial 113. For **medical emergencies,** call toll-free 167 82 10 49.

Accommodations and Food Sirmione is best visited on a daytrip. If you arrive in July or August without a reservation, plan on sleeping in the lake. **Albergo Flora,** at San Salvator, 7 (tel. 91 60 27) has large rooms for reasonable prices. (Singles L33,000. Doubles L50,000, with bath L64,000). **Sirmioncino** (tel. 91 90 45), in Colombare behind the Hotel Benaco, usually has camping space (L8000 per person, L1700 for tent and per site). Lugana boasts two campsites in **Il Tiglio** (tel. 990 40 09) and **Lugana Marina** (tel 91 91 73).

Food prices drop marginally outside the castle's immediate vicinity. If the inescapable waterfront views have you craving seafood, the **Osteria del Pescatore** does the trick at Via Piana, 20. Try the *trota dorato alla saliva,* a trout dish fried in butter and sage, whose merits overshadow any misinterpretations of its name (L10,000). Sirmione's **market,** Piazzale Montebaldo, happens on Fridays from 7:30am to 1pm.

Sights and Entertainment Dominating the central piazza is the conspicuous **Rocca Scaligora,** built in the 13th century. You can roam around the interior and climb the lofty towers for the equally lofty sum of L6000 (open Tues.-Sun. 9am-6:30pm, in winter 9am-1pm). At the far end of the peninsula, the **Grotto di Catullo** offers the ruins of a Roman villa and bath complex. (Open Tues.-Sun. 9am-6pm. Admission L6000.) Between the ramparts and the ruins lie a clean and quiet public beach and the **Church of San Pietro in Mavino.** The hilltop house of worship was originally constructed in the 9th century, with handsome interior frescoes from the 13th-century.

■ Gardone Riviera

Formerly the playground of the rich and famous, Gardone Riviera is now home to Lake Garda's most famous sight, D'Annunzio's villa **Il Vittoriale.** In summer the town experiences a crush of German tourists in search of the perfect tan and memories of days gone by. Still, the crowds can be avoided in the hills behind Gardone, which are threaded with walking paths, and aging lemon groves scent the air.

Practical Information The **tourist office** is at Corso Repubblica, 35 (tel. 20 347), in the center of Gardone Sotto. When you get off the boat, turn left onto the corso. Pamphlets are few, but the amiable staff fills in the gaps. Ask for the map of nearby walks. Information on rooms, but no reservations. Open Mon.-Sat. 9am-12:30pm and 3:30-6:30pm, Sun. 9am-12:30pm; in winter Mon.-Sat. 9am-12:30pm and 3-6pm. The **Post Office,** at Via Roma, 8 (tel. 20 862) is open Mon.-Fri. 8:10am-1:30pm, Sat. 8:30-11:40am. **(Postal code: 25083. Telephone code: 0365.) Buses** (tel. 21 061) run to and from Brescia (every 30min., L3400), Desenzano (6 per day, 2hr. 30min., L2500), Milan (3 per day, 3hr., L11,400), and Riva (6 per day, 1hr.

15min., L3700). In the case of an **emergency** call 113 or 112 (for **police** call 201 79). For **medical assistance,** call 413 nights and holidays.

Accommodations and Food Gardone is better seen as a day trip. Rooms are expensive and breakfast is often required. If you must stay, the views from **Pensione Hohl,** Via del Colli, 4 (tel. 20 160), might ameliorate the financial pain (singles L30,000, doubles L44,000). **Pizzeria/Ristorante Sans Souci,** Vicolo al Lago off Corso Repubblica on the lake side, serves food in the cool calm of a cellar and veranda. *Primi* L5000-10,000. (Open Tues.-Sun. 11am-3pm and 6pm-3am.)

Sights and Entertainment Above Gardone sprawls the sunset playground of Gabriele D'Annunzio (1863-1938), the poet, novelist, and latter-day Casanova. Parked in the garden is the prow of the battleship *Puglia*, the emblem of D'Annunzio's popularity. After World War I, he raised an army of poetry lovers and steamed across the Adriatic to retake Fiume from infant Yugoslavia.

Even Mussolini found D'Annunzio's ultra-nationalist squawking embarrassing, and in 1925 presented the poet with a lovely rural villa in an attempt to keep him quiet. D'Annunzio regularly went into debt to stuff his house with the most expensive and useless bric-a-brac available. The fascist rummage-sale effect is most pronounced in his bathroom, which is strewn with 2000 bizarre objects and fixtures. The *Sala del Mappamondo* contains a huge globe on which to dream dreams of global conquest, while the *Sala del Lebbroso* houses the cradle/coffin in which D'Annunzio would lie to contemplate death and the surrounding leopard skins.

The Vittoriale is up the hill from Gardone, best reached along Via Roma and Via dei Colli. Visit the house early—before the crowds arrive. Taped tours of the house play in German, English, French, and Italian. (Open Tues.-Sun. 9am-12:30pm and 2-6:30pm, until 5:30pm in winter. Admission L5000 to grounds, L15,000 for both grounds and house.) Visit the **botanical gardens** laid around a stately villa halfway up the hill to Il Vittoriale to recover from the perversity. (Open March-Oct. daily 8:30am-7pm. Admission L4000.)

The **Fondazione "al Vittoriale"** (tel. 20 130 for info, 21 551 for ticket info) puts on a summer program of plays, concerts, and dance in the outdoor **Teatro del Vittoriale** (mid-July to early Aug., cheapest seats L15,000).

■ Riva del Garda

Presiding over Lake Garda's northernmost point, Riva's dramatic juncture of mountain and water announces the lake's extension into the Trentino region. This is the riveting landscape that once lured Thomas Mann and Friedrich Nietzsche. Riva wavers between its Austrian heritage, a legacy of Habsburg rule up to 1918, and its more recent affiliation with Italy. The question is partly settled by the Teutonic firmness with which weekending families take over the town. Join the flotilla of windsurfers at play in Riva's steady breezes, or explore the drier options afforded by a network of nearby hiking trails.

Practical Information Riva is easily reached by **bus** from Trent (8 per day, 1hr., L4700), and buses run frequently to and from the closest train station at Roverto (20min., L2900). The Roverto Sud exit of the Brennero Autobahn is only 15km away. The **tourist office,** Giardini di Porta Orientale (tel. 55 44 44), to the left of the castle as you face the water. The electric board out front will help you locate hotel vacancies, and hiking maps are posted in back. Ask for a schedule of events on Riva and other nearby lake towns. (Open Mon.-Sat. 9am-noon and 2:30-6:30pm, Sun. 9am-noon.) **Bike rental** is at Via Fiume, 19, off P. Gazzoletti. L10,000 per day, mountain bikes run L15,000. The **hospital** is inland from the center on Largo Inviolata (tel. 55 40 04). Riva's **telephone code** is 0464 and its **postal code** is 38066.

Accommodations and Camping Riva is one of Lake Garda's few affordable destinations. An off-season visit is far more reasonable, or make reservations for July and August many months ahead of time. The **Ostello Benacus (HI),** P. Cavour, 9 (tel. 55 49 11; fax 55 65 54), next to the church in the center of town, was renovated in 1988, with new doubles and triples for women. (Hot showers. Reception open 8-10am and 6pm-midnight, but the happy proprietor never stays away for long and the daytime lock-out is not enforced. HI members only. L13,000 per person, breakfast at the adjacent *mensa* L3000. In summer advance reservations (with 30% deposit) are recommended. Open March-Oct.) The **Garni Carla,** Via Negrelli, 2 (tel. 55 21 40) has sparkling rooms, cool balconies, and a small garden with some peculiar tropical shrubbery. From the Church of the Inviolata walk up Viale dei Tigli, turn left on Via Rosmini, then right onto Via Negrelli. (Singles with bath L30,000. Doubles with bath L60,000. Additional L2000 charge if you are staying for only 1 night.) The **Locanda La Montanara,** Via Montanara, 20 (tel. 55 48 57) is very central. (Singles L22,000. Doubles with bath L44,000. Breakfast L5000. ½- and full-pension provided in cozy downstairs *trattoria.* Reserve at least a month ahead for summer. Open April-Oct.) The **camping** option is **Bavaria,** Viale Rovereto, 100 (tel. 55 25 24), on the road toward Torbole. Right on the water, with a *pizzeria* on the premises. L13,500 per person, tent included. Open April-Oct.)

Food A large **open-air market** comes to Riva every other Wednesday on Vias Dante, Prati, and Pilati, while the **supermarket** inland from the tourist office is open on a regular basis. **Alimar SRL,** P. Cavour, 6 (tel. 55 49 11), is next to the hostel and provides the usual *mensa* combo of cheerless appearances and heavenly prices. (*Primi* L4500, *secondi* L6000. All-inclusive meals L10,000. Open Mon.-Fri. 11am-3pm and 6:30-8pm, Sat. 11am-3pm.) A less institutional choice is the **Birrera Spaten,** Via Maffel, 7 (tel. 51 36 70). Good food, garish plaids. (Pizza begins at L5500, *primi* at L5000, *secondi* L4000-9000. Open daily 10:30am-3pm and 5:30pm-midnight, off-season Tues.-Sun.)

Sights Riva's most prominent structure is the 12th-century **Rocca** (castle), surrounded by water and graced by a small shady park. Also worth a visit is the Austrian-influenced **Church of the Inviolata** (1611), up Viale Roma, an unusual example of Baroque architecture. For an excursion from Riva visit **Cascata Varone** (3km from Riva), a 100m waterfall surrounded by a breathtaking natural gorge. Buses to Varone from Riva are few and oddly timed, but you can hike or rent a bike. **Musica Riva** in July is an internationally known festival of performances by well-known young musicians. (Ask at the tourist office for a program. Admission varies from free to L15,000.)

BOLOGNA

Emilia Romagna

Go to Florence, Venice, and Rome to sightsee. Come to Emilia Romagna to eat. Italy's wealthiest wheat and dairy producing region covers the fertile plains of the Po river valley and fosters the finest culinary traditions on the Italian Peninsula. Plan to go over budget while in Emilia Romagna, as you gorge on Parmesan cheese and prosciutto, Bolognese fresh pasta and *mortadella*, Ferrarese *salama* and *grana* cheese. Complement these with the respectable selection of regional wines, including reds like the sparkling *lambrusco* from Parma and Sangiovese from Romagna.

Though the Romans settled this region originally, most of the ruins one sees are actually remnants of medieval structures. Developed as autonomous *comuni* during this chaotic time, the towns later fell under the rule of great Renaissance families whose names still adorn every *palazzo* and piazza in the region. In the 19th century the Italian Socialist movement was born here and the area remains a stronghold of the left; Bologna is the buckle of Italy's "Red Belt," which extends from Emilia-Romagna through Tuscany and Umbria.

Emilia Romagna looks different than the rest of Italy. Muted yellows and browns predominate, and the farm buildings are low, square, and flat-roofed. The uninterrupted plains seem to stretch forever, and the illusion of distance is magnified by the cold gray fog of winter—replaced in summer by a silver haze and stifling heat that make distant towns shimmer. A naturalistic spirit imbues the local architecture—cathedrals' arches seem to have grown into their places, and cloisters' carved columns resemble ivy-clad trees.

■■■ BOLOGNA

With one forkful of Bologna's *tortellini*, it becomes clear that this city appreciates the better things in life. Indulgence of the mind began 900 years ago when the city founded the first university in Europe. The **Università di Bologna** has since graduated the likes of Dante, Petrarch, Copernicus, and Tasso, and has made Bologna the urban epitome of culture and prestige. The wisdom and eloquence of its scholarly halls spills over into the streets, where endless porticoed walks, *nobili signori* and *signore,* and a general opulence belie wealthy Bologna's contradictory position as the outpost of the Italian Communist Party.

ORIENTATION AND PRACTICAL INFORMATION

At the heart of northern Italy, Bologna is the hub for rail lines to all major Italian cities, as well as to both the Tyrrhenian and Adriatic coasts. Buses #25 and #30 shuttle between the train station and the town's historical center at P. Maggiore (tickets L1300 at most *tabacchi* and newspaper stands). On the northern edge of P. Maggiore is Piazza del Nettuno. From here, **Via Ugo Bassi** runs to points west, **Via dell'Indipendenza** runs north, back toward the train station, and **Via Rizzoli** runs west to **Piazza Porta Ravegnana,** site of the two towers. After dark, women should take the bus instead of walking to the town center, or stick to Via dell'Indipendenza.

> **Tourist Office: Main office** in Palazzo Comunale, P. Maggiore, 6 (tel. 23 96 60), in the building on the right side of the piazza as you face the basilica. Modern, genial, and efficient. Computer terminal "Tutto Bologna" has reams of information in English (branch terminals sprinkled throughout the city). Open Mon.-Sat. 9am-12:30 and 2:30-6:30pm, Sun. 9am-12:30pm. In the **train station** (tel. 24 65 41), near the main exit to the street. Stop here to book a room free. Pick up a copy of *Bologna Dove* for the latest information and a respectable free map. Open Mon.-Sat. 9am-7pm. Another well-stocked **branch office** at the airport, near the international arrivals (tel. 38 17 22). Open Mon.-Sat. 10:30am-2:30pm.

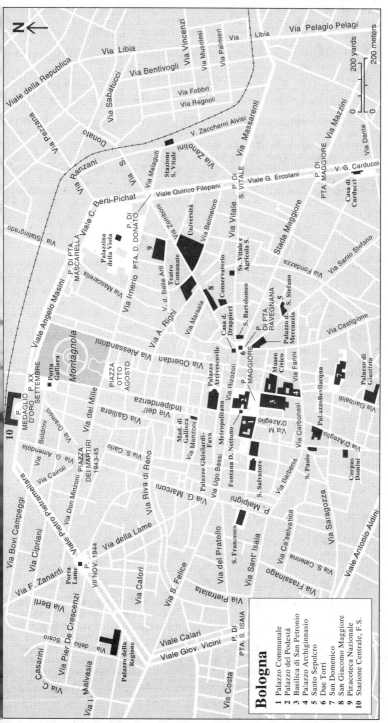

Bologna

1 Palazzo Communale
2 Palazzo del Podestá
3 Basilica di San Petronio
4 Palazzo Archiginnasio
5 Santo Sepolcro
6 Due Torri
7 San Domenico
8 San Giacomo Maggiore
9 Pinacoteca Nazionale
10 Stazione Centrale, F.S.

Budget Travel: Centro Turistico Studentesco (CTS), Via delle Belle Arti, 20 (tel. 26 48 62). Open Mon.-Fri. 9:30am-12:30pm and 3:30-6:30pm, Sat. 9:30am-noon. Closed the last week of July and the 1st week of Aug. **University Viaggi,** Via Zamboni, 16/E (tel. 22 85 84 or 23 62 55). Open Mon.-Fri. 9am-12:30pm and 3-6pm; closed 2 weeks in Aug. Both issue BIJ tickets and HI cards. Big discounts on sea and air travel. Arrive in the early morning to avoid lines.

Currency Exchange: banking hours Mon.-Fri. 8:20am-1:20pm and 2:30-3:30pm or 2:45-3:45pm, or change at the *cambio* at the train station (no commission, decent rates). Open 7:15am-1:15pm and 2:15-7:30pm. After 9pm, go to ticket booth #6.

Post Office: P. Minghetti (tel. 22 35 98), southeast of P. Maggiore, off Via Farini. Fermo Posta at #20 in the Casellario Abbonati wing. Open Mon.-Fri. 8:15am-6:40pm, Sat. 8:15am-12:20pm. **Postal Code:** 40100.

Telephones: ASST, P. VIII Agosto, 24, off Via dell'Indipendenza. Open 7am-10pm **SIP,** Via Fossalta, 4/E, off P. Nettuno. Open daily 8am-9:30pm. Also at the train station. **Telephone Code:** 051.

Flights: Aeroporto G. Marconi (tel. 31 15 78 or 31 22 59), at Borgo Panigale northwest of town center. Take blue (suburban) bus #91 from the station. European flights. Many charters available.

Trains: Information, tel. 24 64 90. Open 8am-8pm. The harried staff rarely answers the phone. Instead try the tourist office in P. Maggiore, and pick up free copies of any national train schedule. Trains to: Florence (every 30min., 1hr.-1hr. 30min., L6300); Venice (every hr., 2hr.-2hr. 30min., L10,800); Milan (every hr., 2hr. 30min.-3hr., L13,700); Rome (every hr., 3hr.-3hr. 30min., L27,100).

Buses: ATC buses for nearby cities depart from the terminal on the far side of P. XX Settembre (tel. 24 83 74). Walk left from the train station. Bologna's efficient urban buses, also run by ATC (tel. 35 01 11), get crowded in early afternoon and evening. Inner-city tickets cost L1200 and are valid for 1hr. after they are punched. Fine for evaders L50,000.

Taxis: (tel. 37 27 27, 37 37 50, or 37 47 18). Fare L7000 for the first 2 km, L1400 for each additional km.

English Bookstore: Feltrinelli, Via dei Giudei, 6/C (tel. 26 54 76), off P. Porta Ravegnana. Browse with the university students. Large selection of English books and travel guides, including *Let's Go.* Open Mon.-Sat. 9am-7:30pm.

Laundromat: Self-Service Acqua Lavasecco, Via Todaro, 4 (tel. 24 07 40). Open daily 8am-11pm.

Public Baths: Diurno, in town center at Via Montegrappa, 2 (tel. 22 84 09), off Via dell'Indipendenza. Showers (*semplice*) L9000. Shampoo and 2 towels included. Bathrooms L500. Open Mon.-Fri. 8:30am-12:30pm and 3:30-7pm, Sat. 8:30am-12:30pm. Another day hotel at P. Re Enzo, 1/B, bordering P. Maggiore to the north. Showers, shampoo, and towels L10,000. Bathrooms L1000. Same hours.

Late-Night Pharmacy: at the train station (tel. 24 66 03) and at P. Maggiore, 6 (tel. 23 85 09) in the town center. Open Mon.-Sat. 7:30am-11pm, Sun. 8am-10pm.

Emergencies: tel. 113. **Police:** P. Galileo, 7 (tel. 23 33 33). **Ufficio Stranieri:** tel. 33 74 73 or 33 74 75. **Medical Emergency:** tel. 33 33 33. **Hospital: Ospedale Policlinico Sant'Orsola-Malpighi,** tel. 636 21 11 or 636 31 11.

ACCOMMODATIONS

Prices are high and rooms scarce due to the glut of students and business travelers. The situation improves very slightly in January, July, and August. But don't despair: Bologna has an affordable youth hostel.

Ostello Di San Sisto (HI), Via Viadagota, 5 and14 (tel. and fax 50 18 10, English spoken, and 51 92 02), in the Località di San Sisto 6km northeast of the center of town, off Via San Donato. Ask at the tourist office for the map giving specific directions. Take bus #93 running away from P. dei Martiri from Via Irnerio/dei Mille, which peels off Via dell'Indipendenza 3 blocks from the train station. (Mon.-Sat. every 30min., last bus at 8:15pm). Get off at the 2nd stop after the rotary and follow the signs. On Sun. you must take bus #20B, which heads from town center toward the station on Via dell'Indipendenza and turn onto Via Irnerio. Get off at the 1st stop after the bus leaves Via San Donato, and walk the 2km to the hostel. A villa set among green pastures. New, clean and well designed. Open 7-9am and 5-11:30pm. Lockout between 9am-5pm, impossible even to drop your bag off during these hours. L17,000 per person, nonmembers L22,000. Breakfast included. Dinner 8pm, L12,000.

Protezione della Giovane, Via Santo Stefano, 45 (tel. 22 55 73), off P. Porta Ravegnana. Women only. Clean, but often filled with students in the winter. Curfew 10:30pm. L15,000 per person. Breakfast (7:30-9am) and shower included.

Albergo Panorama, Via Livraghi, 1 (tel. 22 18 02 or 22 72 05). Off Via Ugo Bassi, near the intersection with Via N. Sauro. True to its name, this cozy hotel has large rooms with panoramic views of the hills behind Bologna. Very clean with a super-friendly management. Singles L40,000. Doubles L65,000.

Albergo Apollo, Via Drapperie, 5 (tel. 22 39 55). Near P. Maggiore, off Via Rizzoli. Clean white rooms with plenty of space. Couldn't be closer to the center of town. Singles L36,000. Doubles L60,000, with bath L76,000.

Pensione Marconi, Via Marconi, 22 (tel. 26 28 32). Bear right from the station onto Via Amendola, which becomes Marconi. Spotless. Desk monitored all night. Singles L38,000, with shower L48,000. Doubles L62,000, with bath L75,000.

Albergo Minerva, Via de' Monari, 3 (tel. 23 96 52), off Via dell'Indipendenza between Via dei Mille and Via Ugo Bassi, about a 10-min. walk from the station. Optimal location and decent rooms. Singles L45,000. Doubles L59,000.

Albergo Il Guercino, Via L. Serra, 7 (tel. and fax 36 98 93). Turn left out of the station and go left over the tracks on Via Matteotti. Turn left on Via Tiarini and then immediately right on Via Serra. The best of the high-priced "budget" hotels in Bologna, but an inconvenient location. The young, friendly English-speaking owner lets quiet and comfortable rooms with phones. Midnight curfew. Singles L38,000, with bath L65,000. Doubles L60,000, with bath L85,000.

Albergo Arcoveggio, Via Spada, 27 (tel. 35 54 36). Behind the train station, take Via Matteoti. New hotel with clean rooms and friendly management. Singles L35,000. Doubles L60,000, with bath L72,000.

FOOD

Bologna's cuisine centers around fresh hand-made egg pasta in all shapes and sizes. The best of the stuffed pastas are *tortellini,* bursting with ground meat, and *tortelloni,* made with ricotta cheese and spinach. Don't miss Bologna's namesake dish, *spaghetti alla Bolognese,* pasta with a hefty meat and tomato sauce. Bologna is also renowned for salamis and hams of all kinds, including (surprise!) "bologna," known locally as *mortadella.*

Restaurants cluster on side streets only minutes away from the town center; the areas around Via Augusto Righi and Via Piella, as well as the neighborhood of Via Saragozza, are especially good for cheap, traditional *trattorie.* **Mercato Ugo Bassi,** Via Ugo Bassi, 27, a vast **indoor market,** sells produce, cheeses, and meats. (Open Mon.-Wed. 7:15am-1pm and 5-7pm, Fri. 7am-1pm and 4:30-7:30pm, Thurs. and Sat. 7:15am-1pm.) Or shop Bologna's crowded **outdoor market** in Via Pescherie Vecchie, off P. Maggiore (same hours). You'll find the large, American-style **Supermarket Coop** off Via dei Mille at P. Martiri (Open Tues.-Sat. 8:30am-7:30pm and Mon. 2:30-7:30pm). Near the university is **Superconad supermarket**, Via della Bella Arti, 31/C. (Open Mon.-Sat. 8:30am-1:30pm and 4-7:30pm. Closed Thurs. afternoon.)

Mensa Universitaria, P. Puntoni, 1, where Via Zamboni meets Via delle Belle Arti. Show the guard a student ID to buy a meal ticket (L1000-7800) which entitles you to pasta, *secondo, contorno, vino,* and *frutta.* Students are usually eager to meet foreigners; strike up a conversation while waiting. Inside a bulletin board lists jobs and apartments. Open Sept.-July Mon.-Sat. 11:45am-2:30pm and 6:45-9pm.

Trattoria Da Maro, Via Broccaindosso, 71/D (tel. 22 73 04), off Strada Maggiore. Students and locals gather here to lunch on satisfying plates of *tagliatelle* or *tortellini* (L5000) and any of the standard *secondi* (L7000). Cover L2000. Open Sept.-July Mon.-Fri. noon-3pm. Closed Aug.

BOLOGNA

Antica Trattoria Roberto Spiga, Via Broccaindosso, 21/A (tel. 26 00 67). A modest, miraculous Bolognese relic: one room, a couple of servers, and a surfeit of good food. Complete meals L18,500 with wine or water. Sublime *gnocchi* L5000. Wine L1000 per glass. Open Mon.-Sat. noon-2pm and 7-10pm. Closed Aug.

Trattoria Della Santa, Via Urbana, 7/F. Heart-felt pasta, but portions are petite. *Tortelloni* with ricotta, spinach and herbs, L7000. Tasty grilled meat *secondi* (starting at L8000). Open Sept.-July Mon.-Sat. 12:30-2:30pm and 7:45-10:30pm.

Oggi Si Vola, Via Urbana, 7/E (tel. 58 53 08). Entirely macrobiotic, a rarity in Italy. Cheerful and homey interior with an open kitchen. Miso soup and such macrofaves as grilled vegetables, L8000. Open Mon.-Sat. noon-2:30pm and 8-10:30pm.

Trattoria Da Danio, Via S. Felice, 50 (tel. 55 52 02). A 10-min. hike up Via San Felice off Via Ugo Bassi rewards you with a large and appetizing menu at this humble, authentic *trattoria*. Try the *lasagne verdi* or the *tagliatelle verdi pancetta e pomodoro* (L7000 each). Daily pasta specials L7000. Cover L2500. Open Sept.-July Mon.-Sat. noon-2:30pm and 7:30-10pm. Closed for 2 weeks in Aug.

Lazzarini, Via Clavature, 1 (tel. 23 63 29), off P. Maggiore. Touristy but affordable snack bar with an exquisite self-service restaurant upstairs. The menu changes daily, but look for the *tortellini alla panna* (L5800). Other pasta dishes L6000. Entrees L7000-9000. Restaurant open Mon.-Fri. 11:30am-3pm. Snack bar open Mon.-Sat. 7am-8pm. Visa, MC, AmEx.

Ristorante Clorofilla, Strada Maggiore, 64 (tel. 23 53 43), near P. Porta Ravegnana. Although the name sounds like a throat medicine, the food here is innovative, healthy, and almost exclusively vegetarian. Bulletin board is the communication center for local environmental and social action groups. Try one of their imaginative salads (L5500-8000), or tea (L3000). Desserts L3500-5000. Open Mon.-Sat. 11am-3pm and 7pm-midnight, in the winter tea served 4-7pm. A small **health-food market** a few doors down sells whole-wheat bread, organically grown fruit, and delicious cookies. Open Mon.-Fri. 8am-1pm and 4-7pm, Sat. 8am-1pm. Both are closed in Aug.

Pizzeria La Mamma "Self Service," Via Zamboni, 16. A popular hangout frequented by boisterous university and military students (any student ID will get you a 10% discount). Table service also available. Delicious pizza (L5500-10,000). Open daily noon-2:30pm, 7-10pm. Karaoke on Sun. 8pm-2:30am.

SIGHTS

Bologna's most remarkable sight is the endless series of porticoes lining buildings throughout the city. Begun during the 14th century, porticoes offered a solution to the housing crisis of a growing city; buildings expanded into the street while leaving room for mounted riders to pass underneath. The building frenzy lasted several centuries, resulting in a diverse mix of architectural styles, from Gothic to Renaissance to Baroque.

The tranquil expanse of **Piazza Maggiore,** the heart and center of the city, reflects both Bologna's historical wealth, exhibited in its collection of tidy monuments, and its modern-day prosperity, evidenced by the city's commitment to maintaining the piazza in well-swept repair. The **Basilica di San Petronio,** designed by Antonio da Vincenzo (1390), was built to overawe. The Bolognese originally planned (like many cocky Italian towns) to make their basilica larger than St. Peter's in Rome, but the jealous Church ordered that the funds be used instead to build the nearby Palazzo Archiginnasio. The marble façade of the *duomo,* displaying the town's heraldic red and white, extends to the magnificent central portal. Jacopo della Quercia (1367-1438) carved the eroded marble *Virgin and Child* and the expressive Old and New Testament reliefs. The cavernous Gothic interior has played host to such historic events as meetings of the Council of Trent (when not meeting in Trent) and the 1530 ceremony in which Pope Clement VII gave Italy to the German king Charles V. According to legend, the pomp and pageantry of the exercises here drove a disgusted Martin Luther to reform Germany. The zodiacal sundial is the largest in Italy—it measures hours, days, and months when the sun shines through the ceiling opening onto the floor. (Open daily 7:30am-7pm.)

Behind San Petronio, through one of Bologna's busiest porticoes, visit the **Palazzo Archiginnasio,** formerly a university building, covered with memorials to and crests of notable scholars. It now houses the town library; there's an old anatomical theater upstairs, but you have to ask the *portiere* to open it. Shattered during the bombing of 1944, the theater was subsequently reconstructed from thousands of rubbly bits. (Open Mon.-Sat. 9am-12:30pm. Free.)

Piazza del Nettuno adjoins P. Maggiore. The famous 16th-century bronze *Neptune and Attendants* statue and fountain, the work of Giambologna, grace the square. Affectionately called "The Giant" by town citizens, Neptune reigns over the seas and a collection of extremely erotic sirens and water-babies. To the right, a clock tower, a beautiful terra-cotta *Madonna* by Nicolò dell'Arca, and a Menganti bronze statue of Pope Gregory XIV, punctuate the large brick block of the **Palazzo Comunale.** (Open Tues.-Sat. 9am-2pm, Sun. 9am-12:30pm. Free.) The Romanesque **Palazzo del Podestà,** across the piazza (facing San Petronio) was remodeled by Fioravanti's son Aristotle, who later designed Moscow's Kremlin.

Via Rizzoli leads from P. Nettuno to **Piazza Porta Ravegnana,** where seven streets converge in Bologna's medieval quarter. The two towers here are the emblem of the city. Of the 200 towers built in the 12th and 13th centuries by aristocratic Bolognese families only a dozen or so remain. Legend has it that the two principal families of Bologna, the Asinelli and the Garisendi, competed to build the tallest and best-looking tower. The Garisendi plunged into the construction of their tower without suitably reinforcing the foundation. It sank on one side and the upper portion fell off; all that remains is the leaning section. The Asinelli were more cautious and built their tower to a sleek 97m (number four on the big list of tallest Italian towers—after Cremona, Siena, and Venice, in case you're keeping score). Reality tells a simpler, if less dramatic, story: land movement botched an attempt to build an observation tower for the civic defense system (the lower, tilting tower), so the city started again and found greater success nearby. Climb the **Torre degli Asinelli** for an amazing view of the city; the arches of Lorraine ogli Estara are particularly breathtaking. (Open daily 9am-6pm. In winter, 9am-7pm. Admission L3000.)

Going down Via Zamboni to P. Verdi, one enters the **Zona Universitaria,** Europe's oldest university campus. Keep your eyes peeled, though, or you might miss it. Only the signs over the doors let you know that these are the ancient halls of the learned—the buildings at first don't appear to be affiliated to a university. The political posters plastered everywhere reflect the idealistic bent of Bologna's college crowd. If you're in town in June, look for the traditionally vulgar posters lampooning the lives of graduating students.

Back at the two towers, the Strada Maggiore leads east past the **Basilica of San Bartolomeo.** Stop here and see the exquisite *Madonna* by Guido Reni in the left transept before proceeding to the **Church of Santa Maria dei Servi,** a remarkably intact Gothic church. Inside columns alternate with octagonal pillars to support a unique combination of ogival arches and ribbed vaulting. In a left-hand chapel behind the altar hangs Cimabue's great *Maestà.* Giovanni Antonio Montorsoli, a pupil of Michelangelo, executed the exquisite Renaissance altar.

Via Santo Stefano leads from the two towers past the pointed arches of the portico of the **Palazzo di Mercanzia,** opening onto the triangular **Piazza Santo Stefano.** The **basilica's** four interlocking Romanesque churches are all that remain of the original seven. The most spectacular church, the round **Chiesa del San Sepolcro,** is the center of the group. San Petronio, patron saint of Bologna, lies here, buried under the pulpit. In the courtyard in the rear is the **Basin of Pilate**—the governor supposedly absolved himself of responsibility for Christ's death in this bath-size tub. Flanking San Sepolcro is the oldest church in the group, the **Church of SS. Vitale e Agricola.** Its arched interior incorporates bits of Roman temples, capitals, and columns. A labyrinth of little chapels opens off the side of "Pilate's courtyard," and in the back you'll come upon the dark **Church of the Trinity.** You can skip the small religious museum on the top story with a good conscience. (Open daily 9am-noon and 3:30-7pm. Admission L2000.)

From P. Maggiore, follow Via dell'Archiginnasio to Via Farini and then Via Garibaldi to the **Church of San Domenico.** San Domenico, founder of the Dominican order, is buried here. Nicolò dell'Arca earned his nickname for the work he did on the saint's tomb, or "ark." His statues rival the Michelangelos in the tomb and the softly modeled 13th-century reliefs by Nicola Pisano. To tell whose work is whose, consult the informative schema hanging near the entrance to the chapel. Look for Filippino Lippi's *Visit of St. Catherine* at the end of the right aisle.

The **Church of San Giacomo Maggiore,** in P. Rossini is a successful melange of the Romanesque and Gothic styles. The edifice was designed in the late 13th century, when the Dominican and Franciscan brotherhoods, who favored the Gothic design, began to influence the aristocratic clergy, adherents of the Romanesque style. The adjoining Romanesque **Oratorio di Santa Cecilia** (ask the sacristan to let you in through the back of the church) presents a cycle of Renaissance frescoes by Amico Aspertini. Behind, in the ambulatory, is the **Bentivoglio Chapel,** commissioned by these 15th century tyrants of Bologna. Lorenzo Costa painted the frescoes; one depicts the Bentivoglio clan. On the altar is a Francesco Francia altarpiece.

The **Museo Civico Archeologico,** Via Archiginnasio, 2 (tel. 23 38 49), has innumerable Roman inscriptions and Bronze and Stone Age tools on display along with various artistic antiquities. (Open Tues.-Fri. 9am-2pm, Sat.-Sun. 9am-1pm and 3:30-7pm. Admission L5000, students L2500.)

The **Pinacoteca Nazionale,** Via delle Belle Arti, 56 (tel. 22 32 32), ranks among Italy's best galleries. Follow the progress of Bolognese artists from primitivism to mannerism and beyond. Bolognese artists may have missed the boat on the Renaissance but the Pinacoteca doesn't. The first section contains a Giotto altarpiece, and the Renaissance wing contains Raphael's *Ecstasy of Santa Cecilia,* Perugino's *Madonna in Glory,* Guido Reni's *Madonna,* and Parmigianino's *Madonna di Santa Margherita.* One room holds great works by the three Carracci, Bolognese natives who helped spark the Baroque revolution. (Open Tues.-Sat. 9am-2pm, Sun. 9am-1pm. Admission L6000.)

The **Museo Civico Medioevale e del Rinascimento** (tel. 22 89 12), in the 15th century Palazzo Ghisilardi Fava at Via Manzoni, 4, contains, in addition to a number of exquisite curios, a superb collection of the sculpted tombs of medieval Bolognese professors, which typically show the professor reading to students. The diligent students are shown dozing, daydreaming, and gossiping. The "Stone of Peace," depicts the Virgin and Child flanked by kneeling students who came to terms with the *comune* in 1321 after protesting the execution of a fellow student. (Open Mon. and Wed.-Sat. 9am-2pm., Sun. 9am-1pm. Admission L5000, students L2500.)

The *piazzola,* a large and diverse **open-air market,** takes place on P. VIII Agosto (Sept.-July Fri.-Sat. 8am-2pm). Literature buffs may want to drop by the **museum and house of Giosuè Carducci,** P. Carducci, 5, to see the poet's works and sundry possessions. (Open Mon.-Sat. 9am-noon and 3-5pm, Sun. 9am-1pm).

ENTERTAINMENT

Bologna Spettacolo News available at the tourist office (free) or any newsstand (L800) has all the information you need about upcoming concerts and music festivals, whether it be 17th-century chamber music or a 20th-century love-in. The city sponsors daily **open-air discos,** in July and August in Parco Cavaioni, on the outskirts of the city. (Action begins about 10pm. Free. The main disco is called "Frigo".) To get to the park, take bus #52 from P. Minghetti into the hills 5km out. Once there make friends fast, as bus service may end by 10pm. Bologna's newest nighttime summer entertainment is the city-sponsored **Bologna Sogna** (Bologna Dreams series, which features concerts at *palazzi* and museums around town through July and August. Ask the tourist office for a schedule of events.

During the academic year, current **English-language movies** are screened every Monday at **L'Adriano,** Via S. Felice, 52 (tel. 55 51 27; admission L6000).

Bologna's tremendous university population makes for lively nighttime diversion during the academic year. Try *osterie* and bars in the university district, particularly along Via delle Belle Arti and on P. Verdi. Also check out **Cantina Bentivoglio** at Via Mascarella, 4/B, for jazz, and the **Old West Pub** at Via Saragossa, 55, for folk music.

■ Ferrara

Ferrara earned its laurels as the home turf of the Este dynasty from 1208 to 1598. Between murdering sundry relatives, these sensitive aesthetes proved themselves some of the most enlightened (and also bloodthirsty) patrons of their age. Their court and university attracted Petrarch, Ariosto, Tasso, Mantegna, and Titian, among others. Ercole I's early 16th-century city plan broke new ground with its spacious, harmonious design, and here the modern theatre, with curtains, stage, and seated audience, was invented. But the balding dukes eventually went heirless, and Ferrara succumbed to two and half centuries of cruel neglect. Today, an air of retrospective melancholia permeates the deserted *palazzi* and hangs heavy above the medieval town center.

ORIENTATION AND PRACTICAL INFORMATION

Ferrara lies on the train line between Bologna and Venice. When you walk out of the train station, turn left and then right on Viale Cavour, which leads to the Castello Estense at the center of town (1km). Buses #1, 2, and 9 also travel this route (L1000).

Tourist Office: P. Municipio, 19 (tel. 20 93 70). Well-stocked. Exceptionally knowledgeable folk eager to discuss everything from local politics to your dining preferences. Open Mon.-Sat. 9am-1pm and 2:30-7pm, Sun. 9am-1pm.

Post Office: Viale Cavour, 27 (tel. 34 504), 1 block toward the train station from the *castello.* Open Mon.-Fri. 8am-7:30pm, Sat. 8am-1pm. Fermo Posta at window #7. **Postal Code:** 44100.

Telephones: SIP, Largo Castello, 30 (tel. 49 791), off Viale Cavour at the *castello.* Open 8am-8pm. From midnight to 8am, try **Hotel Ripagrande,** Via Ripagrande, 21 (tel. 76 52 50). **Telephone Code:** 0532.

Trains: Information, tel. 77 03 40; open Mon.-Sat. 8:30am-noon and 3-7pm. To Bologna (33 per day, 40min., L3900, round-trip L5000); Venice (24 per day, 1hr. 30min., L8800); Ravenna (14 per day, 1hr., L5700); Padova (L5700).

Buses: ACFT, tel. 47 268 and **GGFP,** tel. 20 52 35. Main terminal on Via Rampari San Paolo. Open 9:30am-11:30pm. Most buses can also be taken from the train station (buy tickets at **Bar Fiorella,** across from the train station), or from P. Municipio (buy tickets from the information booth at P. Municipio, 10). To Ferrara's beaches (12 per day, 1hr., L7900). Buses to Mòdena depart from the train station (11 per day, 1hr. 30min.-2hr., L7900).

Swimming Pool: Via Porta Catena, 103 (tel. 75 03 67). Take bus #3 and get off at the corner of Viale XXV Aprile. Go up Via Azzo Novello and turn right on Via Porta Catena. Open June 11-Aug. Admission L10,000, children L5000.

Emergencies: tel. 113. **Police:** Corso Ercole I d'Este, 26 (tel. 20 75 55), off Largo Castello. **Ufficio Stranieri:** assistance in English, tel. 26 9 44. **Hospital: Ospedale Sant'Anna,** Corso Giovecca, 203 (tel. 29 51 11).

ACCOMMODATIONS AND CAMPING

Ferrara's decent budget accommodations are likely to be full. Reserve at least a day or two in advance if possible.

Albergo San Paolo, Via Baluardi, 9 (tel. 76 20 40). Walk down Corso Porta Reno from the *duomo,* turn left on Via Carlo Mayr, take the 1st right, and then the 1st left. Entrance on Via Baluardi, 9. Ferrara's best option. New rooms in a quiet, central location. Singles L35,000, with bath L55,000. Doubles L55,000, with bath L75,000. Reservations advised.

Albergo Nazionale, Corso Porta Reno, 32 (tel. 20 96 04), on a busy street that runs between the castle and the *duomo.* Clean rooms fill quickly. Friendly manager knows everything about America. Singles L35,000, with bath L45,000. Doubles with bath L75,000.

Albergo Tre Stelle, Via Vegri, 15 (tel.10 97 48). Basic, bathless, clean rooms. Impossible to squeeze in—call ahead for reservations. On a romantic, cobblestoned street. Singles L20,000. Doubles L30,000.

Camping: Estense, Via Gramicia, 5 (tel. 75 23 96). Take bus #11. L5000 per person, L4000 per child. Open Easter-Oct.

FOOD

Ferrara produces an enticing array of local specialties. Don't miss the chance to gorge on *capelletti,* delicious triangular meat *ravioli* served in a broth, or *capellacci,* stuffed with squash and parmesan cheese and served in a light sauce of butter and sage. The gastronomic symbol of the city is its robust *salama da sugo,* an aged, ball-shaped sausage of meats soaked with wine, served hot in its own juices. The traditional Ferrarese dessert consists of a chunk of luscious *pampepato,* a chocolate-covered almond and fruit cake. **Negozio Moccia,** Via degli Spadari, 19 (tel. 353 75), sells the renowned *pampepato Estense* brand in ½kg (L7950) and 1kg (L13,500) sizes. (Open Mon.-Sat. 9am-1pm and 4:30-9pm.) For picnic goodies, stop by the **Mercato Comunale,** Via Mercato, off Via Garibaldi next to the *duomo,* or **Supermarket Conad,** Corso Garibaldi, 51/53 (open Mon.-Wed. and Fri.-Sat. 8:30am-7:30pm, Thurs. 8:30am-1pm). All shops in Ferrara close on Thursday afternoon.

Trattoria da Giacomino, Via Garibaldi, 135 (tel. 20 56 44). The best place in town. The *tortelloni di ricotta* are tasty pumpkin-filled pasta (L5500). Cover L2000. Open Sept.-July Sun.-Fri. noon-2pm and 7:15-9:30pm. Closed Sat.

Trattoria Da Noemi, Via Ragno, 31/A (tel. 76 17 15), off Corso Porta Reno. The smells of Ferrarese cooking have wafted out of this *trattoria* for over 30 years. The *salamina* (L8000) is as succulent as ever, and a plate of their home-made *gnocchi* (L7000) makes a divine dinner. A veranda stretches out back. Cover L2500. Open Wed.-Mon. noon-2:30pm and 6:30-10pm.

Osteria Al Brindisi, Via G. degli Adelandi, 11 (tel. 370 15). The oldest *osteria* in Italy. Recently blessed by a full-fledged cardinal, so you can dig in without fear Copernicus and Cellini did. No joke. Try delicious sandwiches (L4500) paired with one of their 600 varieties of wine. Open Mon.-Sat. 10am-11pm.

Al Postiglione, Vicolo Chiuso del Teatro, 4 (tel. 20 49 73). Pasta dishes L2500-3500. Delicious sandwiches like the *paradiso,* with prosciutto, artichokes, mushrooms, tomato, and cheese (L4500). Wine L1000 per glass. House specialty is *lasagne* (L5000). Open Mon.-Sat. 8am-3pm and 5-10pm.

SIGHTS

Towered, turreted, and moated, the awesome **Castello Estense** (tel. 29 92 79) stands precisely in the center of town, constructed as a refuge from attack by their subjects. Corso della Giovecca lies along the former route of the moat's feeder canal partitioning the medieval section of town from that which was planned by the d'Este's architect, Biagio Rossetti. The Salone dei Giochi and the surrounding rooms retain rich frescoes on their ceilings, the best of which are in the Loggetta degli Aranci. The Lombardesque **Cappella di Renata di Francia** (Chapel of Renée of France) seems a bit out of place here—as Renée herself, a Protestant married to a Catholic, must have felt. Parisina, the wife of Duke Niccolo d'Este III, was killed with her lover, the Duke's natural son, Ugolino in the damp prison underneath. This domestic spat beneath the castle's surface of unruffled elegance inspired Browning to pen "My Last Duchess." (Open Tues.-Sat. 9:30-12:30pm and 1:30-6:30pm; Sun. 10am-6pm. Admission L6000. Entrance inside the courtyard.)

Walk down Corso Mártiri della Libertà to P. Cattedrale and the *duomo*. Alongside the church under the double arcade, little shops and vendors operate much as they did in the Middle Ages. Reshaped by every noble with designs on Ferrara, the cathedral and the castle remain the effective center of town. The tall slender arches and terra-cotta that ornament the apse were designed by Rossetti, the town planner; Alberti (1404-1484) executed the pink campanile covered with Estense seals and crests. Notice the *faux* rose windows in the left and right portions of the façade. (Church open Mon.-Sat. 6:30am-noon and 4-7:30pm, Sun. 7:15am-1pm and 4-7:45pm.) The best pieces now reside in the **Museo della Cattedrale** upstairs: Cosmè Tura's 15th-century *San Giorgio* and *Annunciation* from the Ferrarese school, and Jacopo della Quercia's *Madonna della Melagrana.* (Museum open Mon.-Sat. 10am-noon and 3-5pm. Free.)

On the fringes of the city center stand the d'Este *palazzi*. Only the carved door of the **Palazzo Schifanoia,** Via Scandiana, 23 (tel. 641 78), hints at the wealth of frescoes inside. The magnificent frescoes in the Saloni dei Mesi offer one of the most accurate and vivid depictions of 15th-century courtly life. (Open daily 9am-7pm. Admission L5000, 2nd Sun. and Mon. of the month free.) The **Palazzo Ludovico Il Moro,** Via XX Settembre, 124, features a courtyard designed by Rossetti. Inside, the **Museo Archeologico Nazionale** houses extensive finds from the Greco-Roman city of Spina and an outstanding collection of Athenian vases.

The **Casa Romei,** Via Savonarola, 30 (tel. 403 41), was the 15th-century dwelling of a Ferrarese merchant, filled with some of the most beautifully decorated rooms of the period. The museum displays statues and frescoes salvaged from destroyed churches in Ferrara. (Open Tues.-Sun. 10am-5pm. Admission L4000.)

The **Palazzo dei Diamanti,** at Corso Ercole I d'Este and Corso Rossetti (the continuation of Corso Porta Po), on the other side of town, outshines all other ducal residences. Inside, the **Pinacoteca Nazionale** (tel. 20 58 44) contains the best work of the Ferrarese school. Most impressive are the *Passing of the Virgin* (1508) by Carpaccio and the incredibly overworked *Massacre of the Innocents* by Garofalo. (Open Tues.-Sat. 9am-2pm, Sun. 9am-1pm. Admission L6000.) On the ground floor, the **Galleria Civica d'Arte Moderna** often mounts special exhibits by well-known contemporary Italian and European artists. (Open daily 9am-1pm and 3-5:30pm. Admission varies from exhibit to exhibit.) Down Corso Porta Mare at #9 you'll find the **Palazzo Massari** museum complex. The most interesting **Museo Documentario della Metafisica** (tel. 20 69 14) documents the inception of metaphysical art in a collection of works by Giorgio de Chirico, Carlo Carrà, Tino Puenté, and Giorgio Morandi, Italy's greatest 20th-century painters. Other museums in Palazzo Massari include the **Museo Boldini,** filled with paintings by the 19th-century Italian painter Giovanni Boldini; the **Museo Ferrarese dell'Ottocento,** which houses a hodgepodge of 19th-century Italian paintings; and the tiny **Galleria della Fotografia** and **Galleria Civica,** both of which display local work. (All museums in the complex open daily 9:30am-1pm and 3:30-7pm. Admission L8000, on first Sun. and Mon. of the month free.) Fans of Italian literature will want to make a pilgrimage to the **tomb of Ariosto** in the **Palazzo Paradiso,** Via Scienze, 17 (tel. 20 73 92). (Open Mon.-Fri. 9am-7:30pm, Sat. 9am-1pm.)

At #170 on the Giovecca visit the recently restored **Palazzina di Marfisa d'Este,** (tel. 20 74 50) a splendid palace in miniature. (Open Mon.-Sun. 9am-12:30pm and 3-6pm. Admission L3000.) Walk by the **Palazzo dei Bentivoglio,** at Via Garibaldi, 90, a fantastic showpiece of the mannerist liberties that evolved into the Baroque style. The pervasive sense of history in Ferrara is nowhere stronger than in the **Cimitero Israelitico** (Jewish cemetery) at the end of Via delle Vigne off Corso Porta Mare. Here the Finzi and Contini are buried as well as most of Ferrara's 19th and 20th-century Jewish community. Ring the bell and the custodian will let you in. Look for the monument to Ferrara Jews murdered at Auschwitz.

MÒDENA

ENTERTAINMENT

In July and August, Ferrara hosts **Ferrara Estate,** a music and theater festival that brings diverse performances to the city's *piazze* (contact the tourist office for specific information). During the rest of the year, avant-garde theater shakes up the **Sala Polivalente,** Corso Porta Mare, 7, behind Palazzo Massari. For more information, contact the Museo della Metafisica (tel. 20 69 14). At the end of June, the city sponsors the **Aterforum,** a series of classical music concerts in Ferrara's churches and palaces (check with tourist office). Tickets (L8000-10,000) at the **Teatro Comunale,** Corso Giovecca, 10/12 (tel. 20 26 75), or at the performance site. Each year on the last Sunday of May, Ferrara re-creates the ancient **Palio di San Giorgio.** This event, dating from the 13th century, is a lively procession of delegates from the city's eight *contrade* (districts) followed by a series of four races in P. Ariostea: the boy race, the girl race, the donkey race, and finally, the great horse race. The flag-waving ceremony of the eight *contrade* takes place two weeks earlier in P. del Municipio. During the summer, local bands play next to the *duomo* for free (tel. 76 20 02). Try **Casanova,** Via Frizzi, 14 (tel. 20 91 90), a stylish but not terribly cheap *enoteca* and bar where many students and young folks hang. (Closed Tues.)

■ Mòdena

It is fitting that Mòdena is the hometown of Luciano Pavarotti—operatic tenor virtuoso and avid eater—as well as of Ferrari and Maserati factories. Like all three, Mòdena purrs with prosperity. Conquered by the Romans in the 3rd century BC, the city owed its early prominence to its location: the region's principal road, the Via Emilia, ran through the heart of this town. The city is best visited as an excursion from Bologna or Parma or as a stopover between the two.

ORIENTATION AND PRACTICAL INFORMATION

Mòdena lies roughly midway between Parma and Bologna. From the train station, take bus #7 or 11 (L1100) to **Piazza Grande** and the center of town. The alternative is a walk that takes you left on Via Crispi, right down Corso Emanuele, right around the Palazzo Ducale, and finally to **Via Emilia** (Mòdena's main street) and the **Piazza** by way of Via Battisti.

Tourist Office: Via Scudari, 30 (tel. 22 24 82; fax 21 45 91). From P. Grande, walk right on Via Emilia. Open Mon.-Fri. 9am-12:30pm and 3:30-4:30pm, Sat. 9am-12:30pm. **Informa Giovani,** Via Scuderi, 12 (tel. 20 65 83). Just a few doors down from the tourist office. Geared specifically to young people. The office also keeps bulletin boards with job and housing notices. Drop by even to just chat. Open Mon.-Tues. and Thurs.-Sat. 10:30am-12:30pm and 4-7pm.

Budget Travel: Hersa Viaggi (CTS), Via Emilia Est, 429 (tel. 37 28 63). Information and numerous student discounts. Open Mon.-Fri. 8am-12:30pm and 3-7pm, Sat. 8am-12:30pm; closed Aug. 9-24. Also try **Agenzia Viaggiatori Iter,** Via S. Carlo, 5 (tel. 22 23 70 or 24 11 46), off Via Emilia 1 block from P. Grande. Similar discount services. Open Mon.-Fri. 8:30am-12:30pm and 3-7pm.

Currency Exchange: Credito Italiano, Via Emilia, 108.

Post Office: Via Emilia, 86 (tel. 24 20 30). Open Mon.-Sat. 8:15am-7:40pm. **Postal code:** 41100.

Telephones: SIP, Via Università, 23, off Corso Canal Grande. Open daily 8am-8pm. **Telephone code:** 059.

Trains: P. Dante Alghieri (tel. 21 82 26 or 22 31 01). To: Bologna (every 30min., 20min., L3200); Parma (every 30min., 30min., L4300); and Milan (16 per day, 1hr. 45min., L13,800). **Luggage:** L1500. **Bike Rental:** L1000 per hr. for first 2 and L500 thereafter. Both open 6-10am, 11am-4pm, and 5-8pm.

Buses: ATCM, Via Fabriani (tel. 30 88 01), off Viale Monte Kosica, which leads from the train station. Bus #7 to Ferrara (every hr., L5400), bus #7 to Maranello (several daily, L3500).

Pharmacy: Via Emilia, 167. Open 8am-noon and 1:30-7:30pm.

AIDS hotline: 24 43 44.
Emergencies: tel. 113. **Police:** Viale Rimembranze, 14 (tel. 22 51 72). **Hospital: Nuovo Policlinico,** tel. 36 10 24. Take bus #7 east and get off at Via del Pozzo.

ACCOMMODATIONS, CAMPING, AND FOOD

Locanda Sole, Via Malatesta, 45 (tel. 21 42 45), off Via Emilia at P. Muratori, west of P. Grande. Only 100m from town center. Cool and airy, basic rooms catering to students. Singles L27,000. Doubles L45,000. Showers included.

Albergo del Pozzo, Via del Pozzo, 72/A (tel. 36 03 50), slightly east of town center. Take bus #7 east and get off at Via del Pozzo. Adequate but often full; call 2-3 days before arrival. Singles L27,000. Doubles L45,000, with bath L58,000.

Albergo Astoria, Via Sant'Eufemia, 43 (tel. 22 55 87), parallel to and south of Via Emilia, off P. Grande. 50 budget rooms—kept clean by incredibly friendly management. Singles L25,000. Doubles L40,000. Showers L3000.

Camping: International Camping Mòdena, Via Cave Ramo, 111 (tel. 33 22 52), in Località Bruciata. Take bus #19 to within ½km of the site. L9600 per person and per tent. Open March 15-Oct.

Luxuriating in the low plains area around the Po river basin, the city and its environs till some of the most fertile soil in the Italian peninsula. Mòdena, like nearby gastronomic centers Bologna and Parma, produces unsurpassed *prosciutto crudo,* and the bright, sparkling *lambrusco* red wine. Mòdena's own claim to gastronomic fame derives from the curiously tame but fragrant and full-bodied balsamic vinegar, which Modenese sprinkle liberally over salads, vegetables, and even fruit. Balsamic vinegar can be aged for decades, and the finest vinegars can do damage upwards of L50,000 for a lilliputian bottle. Top off a meal with the local *vignola* cherries, considered to be among the tastiest in Italy.

Stock your picnic basket at the **STANDA supermarket,** Via Emilia, 119, across from the post office (open Mon.-Wed. and Fri.-Sat. 8:30am-12:30pm and 3:30-7:30pm, Thurs. 8:30am-12:30pm). To watch local Modenese society in action, drop into **Bar Molinari,** Via Emilia next to STANDA, immediately before lunch and dinner or in the evening. Small pastries L1200, large ones (all you'll need for lunch) L3200. Try the delicate *torta Elizia.* (Open daily 7am-12:30am.)

Trattoria Da Omer, Via Torre, 33 (tel. 21 80 50), off Via Emilia across from P. Torre. Look for the hand-painted sign among the jewelry and fur stores. Chef Omer is the saving grace of Mòdena with his reasonably priced, meticulously prepared delicacies. *Tortellini fiocco di neve,* filled with fresh cheeses and seasoned with butter and sage, is pasta at its prime for L9000. Zesty vegetable buffet L4000. *Coperto* L3000. Open Mon.-Sat. 12:30-2:30pm and 7:30-10:30pm.

Ghirlandina Mensa, Via Leodoino Vescovo, 9 (tel. 23 72 55). From the *duomo* take Largo Sant'Eufemia and turn left onto Via Leodoino Vescovo: the mensa hides on your left. One of Mòdena's best cafeterias: tasty food and consistent quality. Menu changes daily. *Primi* L2500-3000. *Pasta al salmone* L3000. Secondi L4000-5000. Open Sept.-July Sun.-Fri. noon-2pm and 7-9pm.

Cioè, Viale Monte Kosica, 140 (tel. 21 03 96), behind the bus station in a rougher part of town. Traditional Italian fare. Pasta L5000. *Secondi* L7000-10,000. Open Aug. 20-Aug. 10 Mon.-Fri. noon-2:30pm. Closed for two weeks in Aug.

Italy, Italy, Via dell'Università, off Corso Canal Grande. A modern, informal Italian fast-food restaurant actually patronized by Italians. Extremely congenial staff. Marble and glass interior with decent pasta offerings (L4000). All-you-can-eat salad bar L5000 (small plate L2800). Open Tues.-Fri. 10am-11pm, Sat.-Sun. noon-10pm.

SIGHTS

One of the best-preserved Romanesque cathedrals in Italy, Mòdena's **duomo,** in P. Grande, dates from the early 12th century. Its patron, the Marchioness Matilda of Canossa, held a fiefdom that backed the Holy Roman Emperor, especially the merchant *comune* of Mòdena. Thus the stylistic innovations on the religious buildings sponsored by the Marchioness often bore political significance.

The sculptor Wiligelmo and his school decorated most of the *duomo* with stylized carvings that draw on local, Roman, Biblical, and even Celtic themes. Carvings around the doors depict scenes from the Old Testament and San Gimignano, Mòdena's patron saint, traveling to Asia. (*Duomo* open daily 7am-noon and 3:30-7pm.)

Looming high over the *duomo* is the 95m **Ghirlandina Tower,** Mòdena's symbol. Built in the late 13th century, it incorporates Gothic as well as Romanesque elements. A memorial to those who died fighting the Nazis and Fascists during World War II has been added to the base. The tower opens only a few days a year—the porter at the *municipio* (town hall) in P. Grande can tell you when.

The **Palazzo dei Musei,** in Largo Sant'Agostino at the western side of Via Emilia, contains both the **Biblioteca Estense** (Este Library, tel. 22 21 45 or 23 50 04) and a picture gallery. The library's permanent display of masterpieces includes a 1501 Portuguese map of the world and a 1481 copy of Dante's *Divine Comedy*. Don't miss the **Bible of Borso d'Este,** a 1200-page tome partially illustrated by Taddeo Crivelli, a 15th-century Emilian painter. (Open Tues. and Wed. 9am-2pm and Thurs, Fri. and Sat. 9am-7pm, Sun. 9am-1pm. Free.)

The **Galleria Estense** (tel. 22 21 45 or 23 50 04), on the floor above the library, is a well-stocked and meticulously organized collection. The long gallery on the right after you enter begins with earthy Emilian primitives and peaks in Cosmè Tura's *St. Anthony of Padua*. Beyond, an excellent Flemish section features Joos van Cleve's *Virgin and Child with St. Anne*. The Mannerist and Baroque galleries which follow contain some Venetian works by Tintoretto and El Greco, as well as Velàzquez's famous portrait of Francesco I d'Este. (Open Tues.-Wed. and Fri. 9am-2pm, Thurs. and Sat. 9am-7pm, Sun. 9am-1pm. Admission L4000.) On the second floor of the **Palazzo dei Musei** discover the newly restored **Archaeological Museum,** which focuses on topics such as the art of Florentine paper-making, early electromagnetic experiments, and paleolithic stone tools. (Open Tues.-Sat. 9am-1pm. Tues. and Thurs. 3-6pm. Sun. 9am-1pm. Admission L3000.)

Mòdena's real claim to international fame is the **Ferrari** automobile. The factory is located southwest of Mòdena in **Maranello.** (Bus #7 from the bus terminal, every hr., 30min., L3700.) Though you're not allowed to sniff around the inner-workings of this top-secret complex, you can, however, view a truly astounding display of antique and modern Ferrari cars and Formula One racers, as well as trophies at the nearby **Galleria Ferrari,** the company museum, Via Dino Ferrari, 43 (tel. (0536) 94 32 04). To reach the museum from the Ferrari factory stop, continue along the road in the same direction as the bus for about 200 yards, and then screech a right at the sign that says Galleria Ferrari; the museum is located in an oversized glass-and-steel amalgamation on the left, about 100 yards down the street. Over twenty Ferraris are on display; fantasize over the stately antiques of yesteryear or the flashy turbos of the 90s. (Open Tues.-Sun. 9:30am-12:30pm and 3-6pm. Admission L7000.)

ENTERTAINMENT

The city sponsors a summer music, ballet, and theater series called **Sipario In Piazza** during July and August. You might even happen on a performance by native son Luciano Pavarotti. Contact the Ufficio Sipario in Palazzo Comunale, Piazza Grande (tel. 20 64 60), for information and tickets (L10,000-20,000). Winter brings **opera** to Mòdena's **Teatro Comunale,** Corso Canal Grande, 85 (tel. 22 51 83). On the fourth weekend of every month, the city puts on the **Fiera d'Antiquariato** at the Ex Ippodromo park, northwest of the town center (take bus #7), a boisterous celebration of food, wine, and local customs. To experience Modenese life in the fast lane, check out the list of **discos** at the tourist office or at Informa Giovani. (Unfortunately the discos are all outside the city limits and fairly hard to reach without a car.)

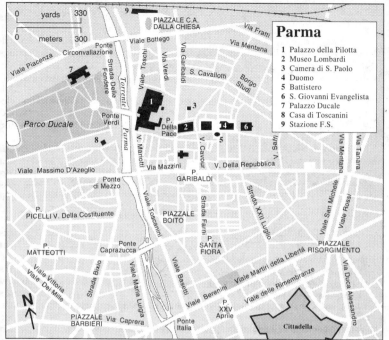

■■■ PARMA

Parma's place in the international limelight derives not from its splendid history or culture but from the dedication with which "i Parmigiani" (people from Parma) craft their incomparable delicacies. Parmesan specialties include a sweet and buttery-smooth *prosciutto crudo,* the sharp and crumbly *parmigiano* (Parmesan) cheese, and a bright sparkling red wine called *lambrusco.*

The city's market-town prosperity has long financed robust cultural activity: here 16th-century Mannerist painting came to full bloom under Il Parmigianino, while Giuseppe Verdi became so enamored of the local countryside that he remained in Parma to compose his greatest music. Stendhal, then an unknown French functionary, made the city the setting of his 1839 novel *The Charterhouse of Parma.* Twentieth-century Parma has given the world maestro Arturo Toscanini. Today Parma cultivates an air of mannered elegance and prosperity recalling the refinement of 19th-century rule. The town is blanketed in tranquility, overtrafficked by neither cars nor tourists.

ORIENTATION AND PRACTICAL INFORMATION

Parma lies about 200km northwest of Bologna, conveniently served by the Bologna-Milan train line. The historical center lies on the eastern side of the **Torrente Parma,** during the heat of the summer a dry river bed that bisects the city. Walk left from the station to **Via Garibaldi,** then right 1km to the town center. Turn left on Via della Repubblica to reach **Piazza Garibaldi.** The main streets branch off this piazza, with **Via Mazzini** running west, **Strada Cavour** heading north toward the *duomo,* **Via della Repubblica** extending east, and **Strada Farini** branching south in the direction of the **Cittadella,** Parma's park and the site of its youth hostel.

Tourist Office: P. del Duomo, 5 (tel. 23 47 35). From the station, walk left and turn right down Via Garibaldi, then make a left onto Strada Pisacane. Information on all nearby towns, but not necessarily in English. Price list of Parmesan accommodations. Open Mon.-Fri. 9am-12:30pm and 3:30-6:30pm, Sat. 9am-12:30pm, Oct.-April Mon.-Fri. 9am-12:30pm and 3-6pm, Sat. 9am-12:30pm.

Currency Exchange: Credito Romagnolo, Via Mazzini, 68. Open Mon.-Fri. 8:20am-1:20pm and 3-4:30pm, Sat. 8:20-11:50am. Try the **train station** as a last resort. Open 5:25am-11pm.

Post Office: on the street that runs between Strada Garibaldi and Strada Cavour, near the *duomo*. Open Mon.-Fri. 8:15am-6:40pm, Sat. 8:15am-12:20pm. Also a **branch** across the street from the station, at Via Verdi, 250. Open 8:30am-6:40pm, in Aug. 8:30am-2pm. **Postal code:** 43100.

Telephones: SIP, (tel. 23 84 81), in P. Garibaldi in the front of the city hall. Self-service phones. Beware: loud and chaotic at night. Open daily 7:30am-11pm. **Telephone code:** 0521.

Trains: P. Carlo Alberto della Chiesa (tel. 77 11 18, rarely answered). To: Milan (20 per day, 1 hr. 20min., L10,500); Bologna (34 per day, 1hr., L6500); Florence (7 per day, L13,800). **Luggage Storage:** L1500.

Buses: (tel. 23 38 13), on Viale P. Toschi before the Ponte Verdi. More convenient than trains to provincial towns. To: Colorno (6 per day, L2200); Fontanellato (nearly every hr., L3200); Torrechiara (nearly every hr., L3200); Busseto (6 per day, L5250); Bardi (5 per day, L6200); Montechiarugolo (several daily, L2200).

Pharmacy: Strada Farini, 42A.

Fine Art and History Info Line: tel. 23 58 25.

Emergencies: tel. 113. **Police: Questura,** Borgo della Posta (tel. 23 88 88). **Hospital: Ospedale Maggiore,** Via Gramsci, 14 (tel. 967 20), over the river past the *Palazzo Ducale.* **Ambulance:** tel. 25 90 84. **First Aid:** tel. 28 58 30.

ACCOMMODATIONS AND CAMPING

Ostello Cittadella (HI), Via Passo Buole (tel. 58 15 46). Take bus #9 (make sure you ask the driver if he's going towards the *ostello*) from in front of the station (last bus 8pm; L700). Get off after about 15min. when you see a small white sign that says *ostello*. Walk down Via Pasao Buole until you reach a large white portico surrounded by ancient walls. Walk inside to the hostel on your left. From P. Garibaldi, take bus #2 or 6. The hostel occupies a 17th-century fortress. Spacious, 6-bed rooms, fresh bathrooms (ask downstairs for toilet paper), and luxurious hot showers. 3-day stay limit. Reception open all day. Lockout 9:30am-5pm. Curfew 11pm. HI members only, but sometimes accepts student ID. L12,000 per person.

Casa della Giovane, Via del Conservatorio, 11 (tel. 28 32 29 or 28 59 23). Women only. Beautiful rooms, sturdy furniture, and polished wood floors. When rooms are tight, younger women receive preference. Curfew 10pm but women over 18 can stay out until 11:30pm on Thurs. ½-pension L25,000 per person for women under 25, L17,000 for room only. Women over 25 (exceptional cases only) L32,000 for ½-pension, L20,000 for room only. Breakfast included.

Albergo Croce di Malta, Borgo Palmia, 8 (tel. 23 56 43). Peaceful rooms kept sparkling. Restaurant downstairs. Singles L40,000. Double L55,000.

Locanda Lazzaro, Borgo XX Marzo, 14 (tel 20 89 44). No sign, but upstairs from the restaurant of the same name. Eight homey rooms. Singles L33,000, with bath L39,000. Doubles with bath L58,000. Am Ex, Visa.

Albergo Leon d'Oro, Viale Fratti, 4 (tel. 77 31 82), off Via Trento. From the station, go 2 blocks left. Functional rooms (no baths), and convenient to the center. Singles L25,000. Doubles L40,000.

Camping: at the Ostello Cittadella (above). The only campground near Parma. Has electrical outlets and a public park nearby. Three-day max. stay. L6000 per person, L6500 per tent. Open April-Oct.

FOOD

The cuisine of Parma is unequalled and wonderfully affordable. Native Parmesan cheese, prosciutto, and an abundance of local sausage varieties fill the windows of the numerous *salumerie* along Via Garibaldi. *Lambrusco* is the wine of choice. When exported, this sparkling red loses its natural fizz so carbon dioxide is added—this is your chance for the real thing. An **open-air market** can be found at P. Ghiaia, off Viale Mariotti, past Palazzo Pilotta (8am-1pm and 3-8pm). Shop for basics at **Supermarket 22,** Via XXII Luglio, 27/C. (Open Mon.-Wed. and Fri.-Sat. 8:30am-1pm and 4-8pm, Thurs. 8:30am-1pm.)

Trattoria Corrieri, Via Conservatorio, 1 (tel. 23 44 26). Whitewashed arches, brick columns, and hanging salami and cheeses. Devour traditional *tortelli di zucca* (ravioli stuffed with sweet squash in a cheese sauce, L6000) or try the *tris,* a mix of *tortelli* with *asparagi* and *erbette* (greens) for L8000. *Lambrusco* L6000 per carafe. *Coperto* L3000. Open Mon.-Sat. noon-2:15pm and 7:30-10:15pm.

Le Sorelle Pachini, Strada Farini, 27. Near P. Garibaldi. Open lunch only, so skip dinner! A delightful traditional *salumeria* which hides one of the best *trattorie* in town in the back. Seems to be a well-kept local secret. Menu changes daily: *primi* L8000, *secondi* L10,000-12,000. Cover L3000. Open Mon.-Sat. noon-2:30pm

Ristorante Nuovo Giardinetto, Borgo Santa Chiara, 10/A (tel. 23 55 51), off Borgo Tommasini, which is off Via della Repubblica. Pasta, a main course, and a *contorno* for L6700—an inspired bargain. Wine L1200 per ½-carafe. Open Sept.-July Mon.-Fri. noon-2pm and 7-9pm.

Pizzeria La Duchessa, P. Garibaldi (tel. 23 59 62). An excellent *trattoria* with a grand variety of *pizze* as well. Large outdoor dining area is great people-watching in the evening. Be prepared to wait for a seat. Pastas average L8000, pizza L600-11,000, and *secondi* L12,000. Open Tues.-Sun. noon-3pm and 7-midnight.

Antica Gelateria Fiore, Strada Petrarca, 1/A. Huge variety of flavors, all delicious. Cones start at L2000.

SIGHTS AND ENTERTAINMENT

Parma's *duomo* and baptistry repose in Piazza Duomo amidst the characteristic calm magnificence of the entire city (though restoration of both buildings currently dispels both calm and majesty). Masterpieces fill the 11th-century Romanesque **duomo** (tel. 23 58 86). The interior houses the *Descent from the Cross* bas-relief by the master Benedetto Antelami in the south transept, and the *Episcopal Throne* supported by piers in the apse. In the cupola Correggio's *Virgin* rises to a gold heaven in a spiral of white robes, pink *putti,* and blue sky. (Some of the art is hidden by restoration work, now nearing completion. Open 9am-noon and 3-7pm.)

The **baptistry** (tel. 23 58 86), in the final stages of exterior renovation, was built over a period of time spanning from Romanesque to Gothic. Through the beautifully sculpted portals by Antelami, the interior showcases stunning 13th-century frescoes. (Open daily 9am-12:30 and 3-8pm. Admission L3000.)

Behind the *duomo* in P. San Giovanni is the **Church of San Giovanni Evangelista** (tel. 23 55 92). Again, restoration efforts currently obscure the Correggio-frescoed cupola. Along the left nave over the first, second, and fourth chapels are frescoes by Parmigianino. (Open daily 6:30am-noon and 3:30-8pm. Free.)

Back toward the river on Strada al Duomo, turn right on Strada Cavour, then take a quick left-right to reach Correggio's **Camera S. Paolo** (tel. 23 33 09) in the small courtyard behind the gate that opens off Via M. Melloni (actually out the back door of the post office). (Open daily 9am-7:30pm. Free.) From the Camera, cross Via Garibaldi and P. Marconi to find the gigantic complex of the **Palazzo della Pilotta.** Constructed in 1602, the palace expresses the authoritarian ambitions of the Farnese dukes. The Farnese built two new clusters, the Pilotta Palace and the **Cittadella** (now a park), in an attempt to unify the city. The never-completed palace was partially destroyed during World War II. Today it houses several museums, the most important being the **Galleria Nazionale** (tel. 23 33 09). Enter the gallery through the **Farnese Theater,** itself built in 1615 in imitation of Palladio's Teatro Olimpico in Vicenza. In the spectacular Farnese style, this much larger version boasts a moveable stage set. This extraordinary collection in the gallery proper includes works of

Correggio and Parmigianino. Leonardo da Vinci's *Testa di una Fanciulla* (Head of a Young Girl), all of Dosso Dossi's work, and the *Pietà* by Cima da Conegliano, are here as well. (Gallery open daily 9am-1:45pm. Admission L10,000. Theater open daily 9am-7:30pm. Admission L4000.) Also in the Palazzo della Pilotta, the sizeable **Museo Archeologico Nazionale** (tel. 23 37 18) displays coins, bronzes, and sculptures of Greek, Etruscan, Roman, and Egyptian origin. Visits to the museum can be made only with advance notice—contact the tourist office. (Open Tues.-Sun. 9am-1:30pm. Admission L4000.)

Outside the *duomo* district a French flavor lingers, the aftertaste of Gallic influences of the 16th to 18th centuries. The **Museo Glauco Lombardi,** in the Palazzo di Riserva at Via Garibaldi, 15 (tel. 23 37 27), has a collection of period pieces devoted to Parma during the reign of Marie-Louise. (Open Tues.-Sat. 9:30am-12:30pm and 4-6pm, Sun. 9:30am-1pm; Oct.-March 9:30am-12:30pm and 3-5pm, Sun. 9:30am-1pm. Free.) Unfortunately, many of the French *palazzi* were blasted to flinders during the war, but enough of the older buildings survive to convey the sophistication depicted by Stendhal.

To remedy cultural overload, retreat to the green flourish of Baroque **Ducal Park,** located west of the Pilotta Palace over the Ponte Verdi bridge. (Open 6am-midnight; Oct.-April dawn-dusk.) South of the park on Borgo Rodolfo Tanzi, the birthplace of **Arturo Toscanini** (1867-1957), conductor *extraordinaire,* now houses a small museum with memorabilia from the maestro's life. (Tel. 28 54 99. Open Tues.-Sun. 10am-1pm. Tues. and Thurs. also 3-6pm . Free.)

Observe the complex production processes of either *Parmigiano* cheese or *prosciutto di Parma* by contacting the **Consortio di Parmigiano** (tel. 29 27 00) at Via Gramsci, 26/A, or the **Consortio di Prosciutto** (tel. 24 39 87) at Via M. Dell'Arpa, 8/B. They'll provide a guided tour of the facilities and free sample at the end.

The city of Parma sponsors fine summer music festival, **Concerti Nei Chiostri,** featuring classical music in the area's churches and cloisters. (Call 28 32 24 for info 5-7pm. Tickets available at the door L23,000; under 18, L18,000.) Contact the tourist office for information and ask them for their brochure which lists the local summer concerts and festivals, including starlit concerts in neighboring castles.

■ Near Parma

Enthusiasts and students of Italian architecture and opera will be pleased by the offerings of the cities and towns around Parma. No composer better embodies the Italian soul than opera giant Giuseppe Verdi, whose native hamlet of **Roncole Verdi** rests on the Parma plain 3.5km outside the city of **Busseto** (from Parma 15 buses daily to Roncole and Busseto, 30min., L4200 and L5200 respectively). To see where this son of a poor innkeeper received his earliest inspiration, visit the house and museum at **Verdi's birth site** (tel. (0524) 924 87) in Roncole. In Busseto proper, within the walls of the ancient **Rocca,** you'll find the famous **Teatro Verdi,** opened in 1868. (Birth site and theater open Tues.-Sun. 9am-12:30pm and 3-7pm; closed Dec.-Mar. except by appointment. Admission to both L4000.) Three kilometers away from Busseto (on the same bus) lies the **Villa Sant'Agata** (tel. (0524) 83 02 10), Verdi's residence during sabbaticals from his work in Milan. Parts of this mansion are open to the public and remain unaltered from the time of his death in 1901. (Open April-Oct. Tues.-Sun. 9-11:40am and 3-6:40pm. Admission L5000.)

■ Piacenza

Tucked into the distant northwest corner of Emilia Romagna, almost bordering on Piemonte, Piacenza eschews a tourist economy to embrace home-grown prosperity. True to its name, this town is pleasantness incarnate. Piacenza is home to several noteworthy monuments of the Renaissance and Middle Ages, and is a convenient stopover on your way through to Parma or Bologna. Piacenza lies on the main rail line between Milan (L5700) and Bologna (L10,500), as well as on a secondary line that connects it to Turin (L13,800) through Alessandria. From the station walk straight across the park on the other side of Via Sant'Ambroglio, take a right on Via Alberoni, another right onto Via Roma, and then a left off Corso Cavour, which leads directly to the **Piazza dei Cavalli.** This central square is named for the two massive 17th-century equestrian statues by Francesco Mochi. Even though the statues were intended as tributes to their riders, Duke Rannucio I and his father Duke Alessandro Farnese, the horses seem to dominate their masters. The true masterpiece of the piazza, however, is the gothic **Palazzo del Comune,** now called **Il Gotico.** The building was built in 1280, when Piacenza was a leading member of the Lombard League (a powerful trading group of city-states in northern Italy). At the opposite end of Via XX Settembre is the **duomo,** constructed between 1122 and 1233, with its reserved, three-aisle nave. The crypt, a maze of thin columns, is one of the most beautiful as well as the spookiest in Italy—grab a friend's hand when you visit. (*Duomo* open Mon.-Sat. 7am-noon and 3:30-7:30pm, Sun. 10-11am and 4-7:30pm.)

The Renaissance **Church of the Madonna di Campagna,** in Piazzale Campagna (take Via Garibaldi from the center), is in the shape of a Greek cross, lacking the typical long nave with aisles. (Open 8am-noon and 4-7pm.)

The **Palazzo Farnese,** in P. Cittadella, was begun in 1588 but, like its counterpart in Parma, was never completed. Walk into the courtyard and note the missing fortifications on its back wall. The *palazzo* houses the **Museo Civico** which houses, among other things, a Botticelli fresco depicting Christ's birth. (Open Tues.-Wed. and Fri. 9am-12:30pm, Thurs. and Sat.-Sun. 9am-12:30pm and 3-6pm. Admission L4000.) The **Galleria Ricci Oddi,** Via Sirio, 13 (tel. 207 42), south of P. Sant'Antonino, exhibits a good collection of contemporary and modern art, including works by Klimt and A. Bocchi.

The **tourist office** in P. Mercatini, 10 (tel. 293 24), tucked in the back of the Municipio near P. dei Cavalli, distributes a map full of useful information on hostels and sights. (Open Mon.-Wed. and Fri.-Sat. 9am-12:30pm and 4-6:30pm.)

As in any Italian town, specialty shops selling meats, cheeses, bread, and fruit are omnipresent. An especially good place to try is **Via Calzolni,** near the center. Local specialties include *tortelli* pasta filled with spinach and ricotta, and **pisarei e fasö,** a hearty bean-and-pea soup. Or head away from the station to **Osteria Del Trentino** (tel. 24 260), Via del Castello, 71, off P. Borgo, a charming restaurant where you can eat indoors or out back in the leafy garden. *Primi* average L7000 and *secondi* L10,000. (Cover L2000. Open Mon.-Sat. noon-3pm and 8-midnight.) The most convenient lodging option is the **Hotel Moderno,** Via Tibini, 31 (tel. 38 50 41 or 292 96; fax 38 44 38). Just walk along the left side of the park in front of you, directly onto Via Tibini. True to its name, it offers modern rooms with new and sturdy furniture and well-scrubbed bathrooms. (Singles L35,000. Doubles L45,000, with bath L56,000.) Piacenza's **post office** is at Via San Antonio, 38-40 (tel. 20 841), the **postal code** is 29100. The **SIP office** is at Via Vittorio Emmanuele, 68 (tel. 28 270) (open 8:30am-1pm and 3-6:30pm). **Telephone code,** 0523. The **train station** information line is 20 637. **Red Cross:** tel. 24 787.

■ Ravenna

Ravenna's moment of geopolitical superstardom came—and went—14 centuries ago, when Justinian and Theodora, rulers of the Byzantine Empire, made Ravenna the headquarters for their attempt to restore order to the anarchic west. In this they were unsuccessful, but Ravenna remained the seat of the Exarchs of Byzantine Italy for two centuries, and the artistic legacy of the period includes the most important examples of Byzantine art outside Istanbul. Ravenna is currently a small city, home also to Dante's bones, and an access to entirely avoidable crowded beaches.

ORIENTATION AND PRACTICAL INFORMATION

Visit Ravenna as a daytrip from Bologna via Castelbolognese (5 trains per day,1 hr. 15 min., L6500) or Ferrara (9 per day, 45min., L5600). There are also frequent trains to Ferrara, where you can change for Venice (3hrs., L13,800). Take a train to Florence via Faenza (3hrs., L13,800) . To go south along the Adriatic coast, take the Rímini line. The train station sits at the east end of town in P. Farini. Viale Farini leads from the station straight into Via Diaz, which runs to P. del Popolo, the center of town.

Tourist Office, Via Salara, 8 (tel. 354 04). From P. del Popolo, take Via Muratori to P. XX Settembre, go right on Via Matteotti, follow it to its end, go left on Via Cavour, then take your 1st right. Useful maps and accommodations information. Open Mon.-Sat. 8am-2pm and 3-6pm, Sun. 9-12:40 and 3-6pm; in winter closed on Sun. Video Info around the corner on San Vitale; a multi-lingual interactive system. **Branch office** at the train station. Open Mon.-Sat. 6:15am-8:20pm.

Budget Travel: CTS, Via Mazzini, 11 (tel. 399 33). Friendly office. English spoken. ISIC cards sold, but no HI cards. Discount airfares. Open Mon.-Fri. 9:30am-12:30pm and 4-7:30pm, Sat. 9am-1pm.

Currency Exchange: Via Diaz is lined with banks. Most open Mon.-Fri. 8:20am-1:20pm and 2:45-3:45pm, Sat. 8:20-11:20am. Also at the Post Office.

Post Office: P. Garibaldi, 1, off Via Diaz before P. del Popolo. Open Mon.-Fri. 8:15am-7pm, Sat. 8:15-12:50. Fermo Posta #1.**Postal Code:** 48100.

Telephones: SIP, Via Rasponi, 22. off P. XX Settembre. Very helpful staff. Open Mon.-Sat. 8:30am-12:30pm and 2:30-5:30pm, Sun. 8:30am-3:30pm (daily 8am-11pm for self-service phone hours). After hours, 10pm-8am, try **Albergo Diana,** Via Rossi, 4. **Telephone Code:** 0544.

Buses: ATR (regional) and **ATM** (municipal) buses depart from outside the train station for the coast and beach towns of Marina di Ravenna, Lido di Classe, etc. Buy tickets at the ATM booth across the piazza from the station (L1600 for most towns)—get a return ticket too, as they're difficult to find in the suburbs. Office hours Mon.-Sat. 6:30am-8:30pm, Sun. 7am-8pm (in winter, slightly less).

Public Toilets: Via Pasolini, off Via Cavour. Super-modern and disinfected after every use. L400. Another at P. Baracca.

Emergencies: tel. 113. **Police:** tel. 112 (emergencies)or 33 333, in P. del Popolo, 26. **Hospital: Santa Maria delle Croci,** Via Missiroli, 10 (tel. 40 91 11). **Medical Assistance:** tel. 33 011.

ACCOMMODATIONS

Most of Ravenna's inexpensive accommodations lie near major transportation lines, and are thus quite noisy. Except during the tanning months of July and August, consider a hotel or campground in one of the quiet beach towns nearby.

Ostello Dante (HI), Via Nicolodi, 12 (tel. 42 04 05). 172 beds. Take bus #1 from Viale. Pallavicini, left of the station (last bus shortly after 9pm, L1000). A no-frills hostel in the eastern suburbs. Hot showers 6-9pm only. 6-bed rooms. Reception open 7-9am and 6-11pm. Curfew 11:30pm. L16,000 per person. Showers, breakfast included. Fine dinner L12,000. Bike rental L10,000 per day (for guests only).

Hotel Ravenna, Viale Marconcelli, 12 (tel. 21 22 04), to the right as you exit the station. Neat, modern (vintage 1960s) rooms with matching furniture. Singles L35,000, with bath L45,000. Doubles L55,000, with bath L65,000. MC, Visa.

Minerva, Viale Marconcelli, 1/A (tel. 21 37 11), across the street from Hotel Ravenna. Clean well-furnished rooms. Singles L35,000. Doubles L50,000, with bath L60,000. Call ahead. Am Ex, MC, Visa.

Albergo Al Giaciglio, Via Rocca Brancaleone, 42 (tel. 394 03). Walk along Viale Farini, then right across P. Mameli. The quietest place in town. All rooms carpeted and clean. Singles L30,000, with bath L35,000. Doubles L45,000, with bath L55,000. Triple L75,000, with bath L85,000. Breakfast in rooms without bath L3500. Excellent meals: ½-pension, L45,000-50,000; full-pension, L70,000-80,000.

Albergo Mokadoro, Via Baiona, 18 (tel. 45 02 72). Take bus #2 northbound and ask the driver to let you off (every 30min. until 11:30pm, about 10min.). 65 modern rooms on an unattractive but quiet road outside town. Singles L25,000, with bath L30,000. Doubles L44,000, with bath L50,000.

FOOD

Those ravennous for sound local fare will find disappointment in Ravenna—you may find yourself saying, "Nevermore!" If you're staying at the hostel, you may wish to avail yourself of the L10,000 dinner or L4000 plate of spaghetti. Hostelers also benefit from the adjacent bargain **supermarket.** (Open Mon.-Wed. and Fri.-Sat.8am-1pm and 3:30-8pm, Thurs. 8am-1pm.) The busy **Mercato Coperto** occupies P. Andrea Costa, up Via IV Novembre from P. del Popolo (open Mon.-Sat. 7am-1:30pm and Fri. 4:30-7:30pm).

Mensa Il Duomo Self-Service, Via Oberdan, 8 (tel. 21 36 88), off P. del Duomo. Well-prepared self-service. Popular; come early. Pasta L2900. Full meals L10,000. Wine L1000 per glass. Cover L1100. Open Sept.-July Mon.-Fri. 11:45am-2:30pm.
Bizantino, in P. Andrea Costa next to the Mercato Coperto. Self service restaurant with stylish, iron detailed interior. *Primi* L4000-6000, *secondi* L3000-7000. Cover L500. Open Mon.-Fri. 11:45am-3pm.
Ristorante/Pizzeria Guidarello, Via Gessi, 7, off P. Arcivescovado, beside the *duomo.* A huge place with surprisingly good food—the only real *trattoria* in town. Try the *Fantasia della Casa,* 3 differently prepared meats with mixed veggies, a complete meal at L15,500. The *Gran Misto Oliver* combines 3 pastas with different sauces (L8500). Cover L2500. Open daily noon-2:30pm and 7-9pm. Around the corner and under the same ownership, on Via Mentana, 31 at **Galleria da Renato** (tel. 23 680), the same fare is available. Wine L6000 per liter. Open Mon.-Sat. noon-2:15pm and 7-10pm. MC, Visa.

SIGHTS AND ENTERTAINMENT

If you are staying in Ravenna, or want to make the full rounds on the church-mosaic-museum circuit, consider buying a cumulative ticket of the city sights, available at any of the monuments listed for L7000. These include the Basilica di San Vitale, the Basilica of Sant'Appolinare, Mausoleum of Galla Placidia, Battistero Neoniano, Museo Arcivescovile, and the Basilica dello Spirito Santo. Inside and out, the 6th-century **Basilica di San Vitale,** Via San Vitale, 17 (take Via Argnetario off Via Cavour) is a sight to behold. Restoration of the imposing ancient structure is nearing completion. An open courtyard overgrown with greenery leads to the awe-inspiring interior, where brilliant mosaics depict familiar scenes from the Bible. The courts of the Emperor Justinian and his wife Theodora stand in formal Byzantine splendor; Christ, seated in the dome, rests on a sphere of blue so vivid it belies its 1400 years. (Open daily 9am-7pm. Admission L3000.)

The oldest and most interesting mosaics in the city clothe the interior of the **Mausoleum of Galla Placidia,** behind the basilica. The coin box for illumination is outside. (Open daily 9am-7pm; entrance included with admission to the Basilica.)

Through the gate between San Vitale and the mausoleum, in the cloisters of a one-time convent attached to the church, lies the sprawling **Museo Nazionale,** Via Fiandrini, (tel. 344 24), with collections from a myriad of periods: Roman, early Christian, Byzantine, and medieval. (Open Tues.-Sun. 8:30am-7:30pm. Admission L6000.)

The **duomo** (tel. 391 96), due south in P. Duomo, is the fusion of everything Baroque. (Open daily 7:30am-noon and 3:30-6:30pm.) In the **Battistero Neoniano** next door on Via Battistero (tel. 336 96), some poorly-restored mosaics in Hellenistic-Roman style reside on the lower level, with three levels of 5th-century mosaics above. (Church open daily 7am-noon and 3:30-6pm. Baptistry open daily 9am-7pm. Admission L3000.)

A small but precious collection of mosaics from the *duomo* is on display in the **Museo Arcivescovile,** nearby in P. Arcivescovado. While you're there, check out the mosaic chapel and the Throne of Maximilian, perhaps the best piece of ivory carving in the Christian world and the zenith of Ravennine sculpture. (Open daily 9am-7pm. Admission L3000.) Compare the mosaics in the orthodox Battistero Neoniano with those in the **Battistero degli Ariani,** on Via degli Ariani off Via Diaz, which was used by the Arians, a sect condemned as heretics for doubting the Trinity. (Open 8:30am-noon and 2:30-sunset.) The **Church of Sant'Apollinare Nuovo,** east on Via di Roma Sud, showcases some huge mosaics along its nave. (Open daily 9am-7pm.) For more mosaics, continue to the **Church of Sant'Apollinare in Classe** (tel. 47 30 04), a 6th-century basilica 5km south of the city (bus #4 or #44, every 30min. from the train station, L1100). The classical style yields to Byzantine depictions of angels and apostles on the heavily decorated triumphal arch. (Open Mon.-Fri. 9am-12:30 and 2-7pm, Sat. and Sun. 2-5pm. L3000 for both.)

For those who (unlike Gustav Klimt) grow weary of Ravenna's mosaics, the **remains of Dante Alighieri** (1265-1321) at the end of Via Dante Alighieri, will satiate that morbid curiosity. There is also a **Dante Museum,** Via Dante Alighieri, 4 (tel. 336 67) whose Dante library is 18,000 volumes strong. (Open Tues.-Sun. 9am-noon and 3-6pm. L3000).

Every Sunday in summer, a **flea market** (books, antiques, etc.) appears in P. Garibaldi, in front of the post office. From the last week in June to the last week in August, the the Church of S. Francesco sponsors **Ravenna in Festival,** featuring operas, concerts, folk music, and drama. The festival culminates in the **concerti d'organo** held in San Vitale, a series of organ recitals. Contact **Teatro Alighieri,** Via Mariani, 2 (tel. 32 577), for programs and information. In winter, opera and ballet animate the Teatro Alighieri. An annual **Dante Festival** during the second week in September brings hell to Ravenna with exhibits, readings, and performances. This festival is also given under the auspices of the Church of S. Francesco (tel. 332 56).

■ Rímini

One face of Rímini, sporting sunglasses and a dark tan, gazes toward the sea: a bohemian Miami Beach with a shortage of bikini tops and an excess of discotheques. Its other face sighs nostalgically toward the inland historic center—an alluring jumble of medieval streets dominated by the Malatesta Temple.

ORIENTATION AND PRACTICAL INFORMATION

Rímini is a major stop on the Bologna-Lecce and Rome-Bologna-Torrino-Lecce train lines, and is served by an airport with service to many European cities (mostly charters). To get to the beach from the station on foot (15min.), walk right from the station along Piazzale C. Battisti, turn right again into the tunnel when you see the yellow arrow indicating *al mare*, then follow Via Principe Amadeo. By bus, take #10 or 11. Tickets (L1200 per hr., L4500 per day) can be bought at the kiosk in front of the station or at *tabacchi*. To reach the historic center of town, take Via Dante Alighieri from the station (5min.).

Tourist Offices: APT, P. Battisti, 1 (tel. 51 331 or 51 480), outside the train station to the left. Be sure to pick up *Book Istantaneo* is an excellent all-purpose guide to Rimini, particularly the beach scene. Open daily 8am-8pm. **Branch office,** P. dell'Indipendenza, 6 (tel. 24 511), at the sea next to the Cassa di Risparmio di Rímini. Open daily 8am-8pm, off-season 8am-2pm. **Promozione Alberghiera:** (tel. 522 69), at the same address as the APT branch office. When you arrive at the train station, they will find you a room for a deposit of L10,000—which is later deducted from your bill. Be insistent about what you can or want to pay for a room—if they're unrealistic, start making noises about going to the hostel. They also run an exchange office. (No commission on cash or traveler's checks.) Open Mon.-Wed. and Fri.-Sat. 8:30am-12:30pm and 3-6:30pm, Tues. and Thurs. 8:30am-12:30pm. Or ask for help at **Hotel Reservations-Adia** in the train station, P. Tripoli (tel. 69 36 28, fax 69 36 04). Phone reservations only. Free. Open summer and at easter 8am-8pm.

Budget Travel: CTS, Beccadelli,16, next to Parco Indipendenza (tel. 55 402). Open Mon.-Fri. 9am-1pm and 3:30-7pm, Sat. 9am-12:30pm. Also **Transalpino** tickets at Via Amerigo Vespucci, 11/C (tel. 265 00). Open 9:30am-1pm and 3:30-7:30pm, Sat. 9am-12pm.

Post Office: Corso Augusto, 8 (tel. 78 16 87), near the Arch of Augustus off P. Tre Mártiri. Open Mon.-Sat. 8:20am-1:20pm and 3-7pm. Also at the beach, Viale Mantegazza at Viale Vespucci. Open Mon.-Fri. 8:15am-1:30pm, Sat. 8:15am-noon, and at Via Roma, 64. Mon.-Fri. 8:30am-7pm. **Postal Code:** 47037.

Telephones: SIP, P. Ferrari, 22, in the mall-like Galleria Fabbri off Via Tempio Matestiano, which intersects with Via IV Novembre; other branches at Viale Carducci, 30 and Viale Trieste, 1. Open daily 8am-10pm. At other times, try any of the many bars along the beach and near the station. **Telephone Code:** 0541.

Trains: Piazzale C. Battisti and Via Dante (tel. 535 12). Trains to Bologna (14 per day, 1hr. 30min.,L8800) and Milan (15 per day, 3hrs., L23,700). Periodic trains to Rome, Paris, Brussels. Trains hourly to Ravenna (1hr., L3900).

Airport: Miramare Civil Airport, Via Flaminia (tel. 37 31 32). Mostly charter flights. Rates vary. Check with CTS (under Budget Travel, above).

Buses: "TRAM." Intercity bus station at Viale Roma at P. Clementini (tel. 39 04 44, fax 39 08 26), a few hundred meters from the station. To many inland towns around Rímini. Bus tickets at train station and P. Tre Mártiri (L1200 intercity, L1600 between cities).

Car Rental: Hertz, Viale Trieste, 16/A (tel. 531 10). Near the beach off Viale Vespucci. L507,000 per week or L111,000 per day with unlimited mileage, including tax. Open Mon.-Sat. 8:30am-1pm and 3-8pm, Sun. 8:30am-1pm. Also an office at the airport (tel. 37 51 08).

Laundry: Lavanderia Self-Service. Via Vespucci, 137, just off Via Tripoli (tel. 39 14 90). Very new, sparkling clean and...instructions in English. L6000 wash, L6000 dry, L1200 detergent. Open daily 7am-11pm, or until 7:30 pm in winter.

Emergencies: tel. 113. **Police:** Corso d'Augusto, 192 (tel. 510 00). **Hospital: Ospedale Infermi,** Via Settembrini, 2 (tel. 705 111). English-speaking doctors. **Medical Assistance:** on the beach at the end of Viale Gounod, beyond Viale Pascoli. Free walk-in clinic for tourists. Open in summer daily 9:30am-noon and 3:30-7pm. **24-hour medic and ambulance:** 38 70 01. **Red Cross:** Via Savonarola, 6 (tel. 26 6 12), near the canal.

ACCOMMODATIONS AND CAMPING

During high season (the last week of June through Aug.), your best chance of finding a room is through the tourist or accommodations offices. Reserve in advance by phone to avoid hassles.

Ostello Urland (HI), Via Flaminia, 300 (tel. 37 32 16), by the airport, 25min. away on bus #9 (L1800). Get off at Via Stokholm (ask bus driver) and follow the signs. Lockout 9am-5pm. Curfew 11pm. L14,000 per person. Non-HI members pay an additional L5000. Breakfast included. Dinners: vegetarian L9000, carnivorous L12,000, pasta only L4000. Call ahead. Open May-Sept. Closed mid-July-mid-Aug.

Albergo Filadelphia, Via Pola, 25 (tel. 236 79). Clean rooms, soft beds and an owner with a soft spot for Americans and *Let's Go* travelers. Singles with bath L20,000. Doubles with bath L40,000, in Aug. L30,000 per person. Reservations help.

Hotel Pigalle, Via Ugo Foscolo, 7 (tel. 39 10 54). Clean and classy hotel on a quiet street. Jazz posters, a peaceful terrace and young and snazzy staff. All rooms with bath. June and Sept., singles L35,000, doubles L70,000. July and Aug. 23-31, singles L42,000, doubles L84,000. Aug. 1-23 singles L55,000, doubles L110,000. Full pension required in Aug.

Pensione Mille Fiori, Via Pola, 42 (tel. 256 17), down the street from currency exchange. Large rooms in lively section of town. Singles with bath: in June L33,000; July L39,500; Aug.1-20 L51,000; Aug. 21-31 L41,500; Sept. L33,000. Doubles with bath, L20,000 per person. Make reservations in July and Aug. Complete pension required in Aug. Open Easter- Sept.

Hotel Cardellini, Via Dante, 50 (tel. 264 12), 100m from the train station, but very respectable. This 2-star offers 63 tidy rooms with big beds, high ceilings, and satellite TV at 1-star prices. Very helpful English-speaking manager. High season (begins at end of July): singles L44,500, with bath L59,000. Doubles L69,000, with bath L94,000. Low season: singles L29,000, with bath L42,000; doubles L44,500, with bath L62,000. MC, Visa.

Camping: Maximum, tel. 37 26 02 or 37 02 71. Take bus #10 or #11 to stop #33 ("Miramare"). July 6-Aug. 24, L5350 per person, L4400 per child, L6600 or L8350 per tent. May 14-July 5 and Aug. 25-Sept., L3900 per person, L3050 per child, L6300 or L8050 per tent. Also try **Italia** (tel. 73 28 82) with campsites and bunga-lows, Via Toscanella, 112 in Viserba di Rímini, 1.5km north of Rímini. From the train station take bus #4 directly to the campsite. L5600 per person, L6000 for a small tent, L9700 for a large tent.

FOOD

Rímini's seaside swarms with sterile cut-purse eateries. Fortunately, you can survive on the resort's delicious snacks. Look in the center of town for affordable full meals. For brown-baggers, Rímini's **covered market,** between Via Castelfidardo and the Tempio, provides an array of comestibles. (Open Mon., Wed. and Fri.-Sat. 7:15am-1pm and 5-7:30pm, Tues. and Thurs. 7:15am-1pm.) The **rosticceria,** in the market, offers cheap seafood and delicious *piadina.* Closer to the beach is the **STANDA Supermarket,** Via Vespucci, 133, (open Mon.-Sat. 8:30am-11pm, Sun. 9am-11pm, MC, Visa) or **Margherita supermarket**, Viale Trieste, 34. (Open 7:30am-1pm and 5-8pm. Closed Thurs. afternoon and Sun.)

Mensa Dopolavoro FerroViario, Viale Roma, 70 (tel. 55 388). Near the train sta-tion, to the left off Via Dante and down a driveway. Food is fresh and service friendly. *Primi* L4500, *secondi* L6000, complete meal L12,000. Menu changes daily. Wine L1600 per ½-liter. Open Mon.-Sat. 11am-3pm and 6-9pm.

Ristorante/Pizzeria Pic Nic, Via Tempio Malatestiano, 30 (tel. 219 16), off Via IV Novembre at the *tempio.* A huge buffet overflowing with gourmet specialties. *Primi* L6000-7000. *Secondi* L9000-17,000. Mozzarella cheese blankets the home-made *lasagne al forno* (L6000). Try the *pizza bianco verde,* a fire-baked cheese and herb delight (L8000). Cover L2000. Open daily noon-3pm and 7pm-1am.

Gelateria Nuovo Fiore, Viale Vespucci, 7 (tel. 23 602), a 2nd location Viale Ves-pucci, 85. Endless flavor selection. Cones L2000-4000. House *aperitivo* L3000. Open March-Oct. daily 8am-3am; Jan.-Feb. Sat.-Sun. 8am-3am.

SIGHTS

Any tour of Rímini's historic center should begin with the Renaissance **Tempio Malatestiano** on Via IV Novembre (tel. 51 130). The church was originally con-structed in Franciscan Gothic style; however, in the 1440s the ruling Sigismondo Malatesta ("Sigmund Headache") modestly transformed the church into a classical monument to himself and his fourth wife, the lovely Isotta.

Sigismondo Malatesta was canonized to hell by the papacy (a privilege unique in history) as a heretic guilty of "murder, violation, adultery, incest, sacrilege, perjury so dissolute that he raped his daughters and sons-in-law and as a boy often acted as the female partner in shameful loves, and later forced men to act as women." But Siggy was also a soldier and patriot who ruled Rímini at its height (1417-1468) and employed such artists as Piero della Francesca and Leon Battista Alberti, who designed the exterior of the new church.

Alberti modeled the front of the temple after the Roman Arch of Augustus, which still stands at the gates of Rímini. The two front arches, originally intended to hold the sarcophagi of Sigismondo and Isotta, are now filled with limestone. The spa-cious, single-aisled interior and its wooden-trussed roof recall the temple's original Franciscan design. In the chapel to the left of the card shop hangs a looming Giotto crucifix. The sprightly sculptures and reliefs found in almost every chapel are the creations of Agostino di Duccio. (Open daily 7am-noon and 3-7pm.)

A short distance from the temple, **Piazza Tre Mártiri,** named after three partisans hanged by the Fascists in 1944, forms the ramshackle, noisy city center on the site of the Roman forum. The most striking vestige of Rímini's former glory is the **Arch of**

Augustus, at the end of Corso d'Augusto. The oldest Roman triumphal arch (27 BC), it blends together arch, column, and medallion.

Rímini's medieval center and favorite hangout, **Piazza Cavour,** off Corso d'Augusto, contains one of the oddest ensembles of buildings in Italy. The tall Renaissance arcade of the **Palazzo Garampi** contrasts dramatically with the adjoining fortress-like **Palazzo dell'Arengo** (1207) and the smaller **Palazzo del Podestà** (1334). Between the first two buildings is an Italian version of Brussels's famous *le pisseur,* elaborated in a full Baroque setting. Perpendicular to the Municipal building, the pink brick **Teatro Comunale** (1857), auditorium (destroyed by a bomb in WWII) completes a second side of the square. On the third side, a motley collection of shops, bars and offices surround the Renaissance entrance to the **fish market.** Four stone dolphins in the corners of the market once filled the small canals (still visible under the benches) with water used to clean the fish. In addition, two curious sculptures pose in the center of the piazza: an eccentric, moss-encrusted fountain (1543), engraved with an inscription recalling the presence of Leonardo da Vinci, and a seated, sumptuously garbed Pope Paul V (1614) brandishing ferocious eagles.

Also worth seeing: the old fortress, **Rocca Malatestiana,** built by Sigismondo between 1437 and 1446 (behind the Communal Theater). Inside the *rocca* is the new **Museo Dinz Rialto** (tel. 239 22), a museum of ethnology with educational exhibits on aboriginal cultures, focusing on Africa and Polynesia. (Open Mon.-Sat. 8am-1pm;Fri.-Sat.also 4-6pm Admission L4000.) Rímini's last two noteworthy churches are the **Church of Sant'Agostino** with its great cycle of Riminese Gothic frescoes in its choir; and the **Church of the Servi,** with its lush, almost theatrical Baroque interior. The **Museo Civico,** Via Gambalunga, 27 (tel. 70 43 25), houses a collection of Roman mosaics and early Italian paintings, highlighted by Giovanni Bellini's *Dead Christ with Four Angels.* (Museum open Tues.-Sun. 8:30am-1pm and 3:30-8:30pm; Sept.-June Mon.-Sat. 8am-1pm. Admission L4000, children L2000.)

ENTERTAINMENT

Rímini is notorious throughout Europe for its sleazy pickup scene. *Passeggiata* is a euphemism for the wild cruising you can witness nightly along the *lungomare* spanning **Viale Amerigo Vespucci** and **Viale Regina Elena.** The discotheques in Rímini are among the largest and most dazzling on the continent—and there are literally hundreds to choose from. Rímini has instituted a **Blue Line and a Red Line—** a bus service (L2000 per night, L10,000 per week) that runs in July and August—for carless disco-goers. The blue line originates at the station and travels between the beach towns nearby (2-5:30am, every 40 min.) and the red line originates in P. Kennedy (10pm-5am, every hr.) and runs to all the clubs within Rimini. Also in P. Kennedy is the "Night Office," an information service located in a double-decker bus open nightly in the summer from 9pm to 3am.

THE MARCHES (LE MARCHE)

The mountain peaks and undulating hills of the Marches taper into the Adriatic Sea and picturesque central Italian hill towns are replaced by endless seaside resorts and tourist traps the farther east you go. Away from the water, however, are numerous valleys and coastal plains, colored by patches of wheat, maize, and olives. Originally inhabited by the Gauls and Picenes, the area later fell under Roman control. It received its present name in the 10th century, when it was a border province of the Byzantine Empire; in the 12th and 13th centuries the powerful Montefeltro family of Urbino and the Malatesta clan of Rímini ruled, significantly altering the faces of many towns with a number of extraordinary churches and palaces.

Since World War II, summer tourism has emerged as the mainstay of the region's economy. A crowded strip of international beach resorts has sprung up beside the ancient cities that dot the Marches' serene shoreline. Each summer sees a migration of Germans to the area, making the coast appear more like the North Sea than the Adriatic. Senigallia and Fano have retained scraps of charm, but a secluded beach is essentially impossible to find in the summer months.

The region's two gems are actually not on the sea but 90 minutes inland; Renaissance Urbino and medieval Áscoli Piceno are easily accessible and should not be missed. Direct trains roll from Rome to Ancona (4hr. 30min.), and vacation buses cross to Urbino, Áscoli Piceno, and the coast from Tuscany and Umbria. The Milan-Lecce coastal line also serves the region.

■ Pésaro

Though Pésaro is on the beach, it is not an entirely beach-oriented town. Rather the beach and the city coexist, allowing tourism to flourish alongside a vital historic center, where buildings record 1000 years of change in casual proximity to each other. Even in modernity Pésaro provides hospitable urban spaces—such as the Piazza Lazzarini at the entrance to the old town and the Piazza della Libertà on the sea at the far end of the main street. The beach itself is standard "Riviera Adriatica" fare. And not the least of the city's attractions is its proximity to magnificent Urbino, less than an hour away.

ORIENTATION AND PRACTICAL INFORMATION

Pésaro lies on the main Bologna-Lecce route along the Adriatic coast. From Rome, take a train toward Ancona (6 or 7 per day), then change at Falconara to one of the frequent *locali* to Pésaro (4hr. 30min., L19,000). The center of the old city is **Piazza del Popolo.** Walk across the small piazza in front of the train station onto Viale del Risorgimento and then continue on Via Branca (5min.). To reach P. della Libertà and the beach, take bus #1, 2, 6, 7, or 11 to Viale Trento (in summer only; L1000). Buses will drop you either at the train station or P. Matteotti. From the latter, take Via San Francesco to P. del Popolo; from there take Via Rossini, which becomes Viale della Repubblica, directly to the beach.

> **Tourist Office: Azienda di Promozione Turistica (APT),** 3 offices. At the train station (tel. 68 78). Open summers only, daily 9:30am-1pm and 4-6:30pm. Via Rossini, 41 (tel. 69 341). Open daily 9am-1pm and 4-6pm. Piazzale della Libertà (tel. 63 690). Open summer only, daily 9am-12:30pm and 4-7pm. Both Via Rossini and the Piazzale offices have friendly and helpful English-speaking staff.
> **Post Office:** P. del Popolo (tel. 69 155), at the beginning of Via Rossini. Open Mon.-Sat. 8:15am-7:40pm. **Postal code:** 61100.
> **Telephones: SIP,** P. Matteotti, 23/24, behind the AGIP station. Open daily 8am-8:30pm. **Telephone code:** 0721.
> **Buses:** P. Matteotti, down Via S. Francesco from P. del Popolo. Buses #1, 2, 4, 5, 6, 7, 9, and 11 stop at P. Matteotti. To: Fano (frequent buses, 15min.), Ancona and Senigallia (5 per day except Sun., 1hr. 30min.), and Urbino (8 per day, 1hr., L3500). Also an express bus to Rome (2 per day, 4hr. 30min.).
> **Bookstore: Pésaro Libri,** Via Abbati, 23. Political, religious and philosophical works in Italian. Student atmosphere. Open Tues.-Sun. 9am-1pm and 4-8pm.
> **Emergencies:** tel 113. **Police:** Main station and foreigners' office (tel. 69 241). **Hospital:** P. Cinelli (tel. 36 11). **Medical Assistance:** tel. 31 444. **Night and holiday Medical Service:** Via Nitti, 36 (tel. 45 53 79). **Emergency: Pronto Soccorso,** tel. 32 957.

ACCOMMODATIONS

Except in July and August, you should have no trouble finding a bed.

> **Ostello Ardizio (HI)** (tel. 55 798), at Fosso Sejore 6km from town. Take the **AMANUP** bus toward Fano from P. Matteotti (6:30am-10pm every 30min., L1000). Get off when you see the "Camping Norina" sign on the beach to your

left. To your right you should have just passed the first junction. Take this road away from the beach, ½ block. Quality hostel with 88 beds, in a serene area close to the beach. Fastidiously kept. Free tennis courts. L14,000 per person. Breakfast included. Meals L12,000. Reservations essential in July and Aug. Open May-Oct.

Pensione Ristorante Arianna, Via Mascagni, 84 (tel. 31 927), 100m from the beach. Spotless, basic rooms, excellent food. Singles L46,000; doubles L70,000. Off-season singles L38,000. Doubles L50,000. Shower included. Reservations essential. Full pension is a good deal (L65,000, low season L48,000) and the food is good.

Hotel Riviera, Via Ninchi, 4 (tel. 30 228). Old but well kept hotel. Freshly painted and thoroughly scrubbed. Prime location on the beach downtown. Singles L29,000, with bath L35,000. Doubles L43,000, with bath L55,000. Compulsory full pension in August, L40,000-50,000 per person for room with bath and meals.

Camping Panorama (tel. 20 81 45), 7km north of Pésaro on the *strada panoramica* to Gabicce Mare. Take bus #1 to the end; from there it's a 20-min. uphill walk. A path leads to a quiet beach. L6000 per person, L1050 per tent. Off-season, L5000 and L8050. Hot showers included. Open May-Sept.

Campo Norina (tel. 55 792), 5km south of the city center on the beach at Fossoseiore. Take the bus for Fano from P. Matteotti (L1000). L7000 per person, L8600 per tent. Off-season, L5000 and L6500. 4-person bungalows L54,000, off-season L50,000. Open April-Oct.

FOOD

Pésaro's **public market** is at Via Branca, 5, off P. del Popolo behind the post office (open Mon.-Sat. 7:30am-1:30pm). **Pizzerie** line the beach, while **alimentari** crowd the sidewalk *bars* on Corso XI Settembre. Best of all is the **STANDA supermarket** upstairs at Via Branca, 52, off P. del Popolo. (Open Tues.-Sat. 8:30am-12:30pm and 4-8pm, Mon. 4-8pm.)

Mensa Arco della Ginevra, Via della Ginevra, 3, near Musei Civici. A self-service cafeteria and bargain-hunter's delight with elephantine portions. Never mind that the vegetables are slightly overcooked: this place has both selection and price. Hearty complete meal with wine or water L8900. Open Mon.-Fri. noon-2:30pm.

Harnold's, P. Lazzarini (tel. 68 786), close to Teatro Rossini. Spanking new look: outdoor seating in the piazza. Fresh, cheap and delicious with a wide range of eccentrically-named, satisfying *panini* (L3000). Open Thurs.-Tues. 11:30am-2am.

Trattoria Pinocchio, Via Venturini on P. Antaldi, 12 (tel. 34 771). Hip trattoria, reasonably priced. Open daily lunch and dinner; closed Sun.

Trattoria da Maria, Via Mazzini, 73 (tel. 687 64). The place to go for a home-cooked meal. Never mind the gruff owner. *Primi* from L5000. *Secondi* from L8000. Try the fresh *zuppa di pesce* (fish soup). Open Fri.-Wed. noon-3pm and 7-11pm.

SIGHTS AND ENTERTAINMENT

The robust arcade and *putti*-weighted window frames of the 15th-century **Ducal Palace,** home of Pésaro's ruling della Rovere clan, preside over the **Piazza del Popolo,** Pésaro's main square. **Corso XI Settembre** and its side streets where narrow passages under blossoming balconies pass open arcades and sculptured doorways. Off the *Corso* on Via Toschi Mosca, the **Musei Civici** (tel. 31 213) house a superb collection of Italian ceramics and primitives. (Open Tues.-Sat. 9am-8pm, Sun. 9am-1pm; Oct.-March Tues.-Sat. 8:30am-1:30pm, Sun. 9:30am-12:30pm. Admission L5000.) An extensive collection of photographs, portraits, theatrical memorabilia, letters, and scores pertinent to the composer's life awaits at the **Rossini Birthplace and Museum,** Via Rossini, 34 (Casa Rossini). (Open Tues.-Sat. 10am-10pm, Sun. 10am-7pm. Admission L2000.)

Most of Pésaro's modest Gothic churches exist behind their more lavish Baroque portals. Among them are the **Chiesa di San Domenico** on Via Branca and the **Chiesa di Sant'Agostino** on Corso XI Settembre. Enter to see its beautiful late 15th-

and early 16th-century wooden choir stalls inlaid with still-lifes, landscapes, and city scenes. (Open 9am-12:30pm and 3:30-8pm.) For a fine example of art nouveau folly, head toward the beach; just before P. della Libertà on the left, early 20th-century **Villino Raggeri** drips with icing-like stucco work. Outside of town is **Villa Imperiale** (4th-15th c.), a mansion currently owned by a duke. The lavish villa and gardens can be visited June 15-Sept. 21 on Tues. at 4pm by making arrangements with the APT (tel. 636 90). Tours depart from Piazzale della Libertà (L5000).

The evening *passeggiata* (high style and *gelato* are *de rigueur*) cruises along Viale Trieste and P. della Libertà. Older folk meander through P. del Popolo, window-shopping in ritzy stores. Popular nightspots for the youthful are **The Bistro,** Viale Trieste, 281, under Hotel Cruiser, and **Big Ben,** Via Sabbatini, 14, between the Palazzo Ducale and the Conservatorio Rossini.

Pésaro hosts the **Mostra Internazionale del Nuovo Cinema** (International Festival of New Films) the second and third weeks of June. Movies are shown in the buildings along Via Rossini, and at the Teatro Comunale Sperimentale off P. del Popolo. 1994 will be the 30th annual festival. New and old films are shown, independent and commercially produced. Organizers make an effort to bring interesting and rarely screened films; last year's line up focused on middle eastern filmmakers as well as a famous Italian director from the '50s, Dino Risi. The fortune of opera composer Rossini (born here) endowed a music school, the Conservatorio di Musica G. Rossini, which sponsors events throughout the year. Contact the conservatory at P. Olivieri for a schedule. The annual **Rossini Opera Festival** begins in early August. Opera performances and orchestral concerts continue until September. Contact the Azienda for exact dates and prices, or reserve tickets through the information office, Via Rossini, 37 (tel. 301 61). For a great view of the **sunset,** head up to **Parco Ortigiuli,** Via Belvedere, near the River Foglia (8am-7pm; free).

■ Urbino

If you only visit one town in Italy, make it Urbino. A perfectly harmonious ensemble, under the aegis of philosopher/warrior Federico da Montefeltro (1444-1482) the city exemplified the finest in Renaissance style and tradition. It is no wonder that Baldassare Castiglione described Federico as the "light of Italy" and set the elegant dialogues of his book *The Courtier* in Urbino's Palazzo Ducale. Urbino's fairy tale skyline has changed little in the last 500 years. And while tourists shape the character of many cities, Urbino owes its flair to its university students, still imbued with the creative spirit of native sons Raphael and Bramante.

ORIENTATION AND PRACTICAL INFORMATION

The **SAPUM bus** from Pésaro's P. Matteotti or train station is cheap, frequent, and direct (10 per day, 1hr., L3500). After winding up steep hills, the bus will deposit you at Borgo Mercatale, above which lies the beautiful city center. A short uphill walk, or a ride in the elevator (in the wall of the city to the right when you face the gateway in; open daily in summer 7am-9pm; L300), takes you to **Piazza della Repubblica,** the city's hub.

Tourist Office: P. Duca Federico, 35 (tel. 24 41 or 26 13; fax 24 41). Distributes a list of hotels and a small map. Open Mon.-Sat. 9am-1pm and 3-7:30pm; off-season Mon.-Sat. 8:30am-2pm.

Buses: Information (tel. 97 05 02). Departures from Borgo Mercatale. Timetable posted at the beginning of Corso Garibaldi, under the portico at the corner bar on P. della Repubblica.

Post Office: Via Bramante, 22 (tel. 25 75), right off Via Raffaello. Open Mon.-Fri. 8:30am-7:40pm, Sat. 8:30am-1pm. **Postal code:** 61029.

Telephones: SIP, P. Rinascimento, 4, off P. Duca Federico. Open daily 8am-10pm. **Telephone code:** 0722.

Public Toilets: Albergo Diurno, Via Battisti, 2, off P. della Repubblica. Toilets L300. Showers L2500. Open daily 7am-noon and 2-7:30pm. Also on Via San Domenico, off P. Duca Federico next to the APT office.

Emergencies: tel. 113. **Police:** P. della Repubblica, 1 (tel. 26 45 or 32 04 91). **Hospital:** Via B. da Montefeltro (tel. 32 93 51, 32 81 21, or 32 81 22), to the north of the city out of P. Roma.

ACCOMMODATIONS AND CAMPING

Cheap lodging is rare in Urbino, and reservations are essential. You might want to consider staying in the youth hostel in Pésaro and taking a day trip to Urbino. For longer stays, write to the Università degli Studi, Calle dei Cappuccini.

Albergo Italia, Corso Garibaldi, 52 (tel. 27 01), off P. della Repubblica, near the Palazzo Ducale. A charming 2-star hotel with affable management. Patio, great view, and elevator. 48 elegant rooms. Singles L35,000, with bath L45,000. Doubles L48,000, with bath L64,000.

Pensione Fosca, Via Raffaello, 61 (tel. 32 96 22). Top floor. Signora Rosina takes good care of her guests. Small, charming rooms. No baths in rooms. Singles L35,000. Doubles L49,000. (Off season L30,000 and L42,000 respectively.)

Hotel San Giovanni, Via Barocci, 13 (tel. 28 27 or 320 55). A relatively modern hotel with a helpful manager. Restaurant downstairs. Singles L35,000, with bath L48,000. Doubles L50,000, with bath L65,000. Triples with bath L75,000.

Camping Pineta, Via San Donato (tel. 47 10), in the *località* of Cesana, 2km from the city walls. L7000 per person (L3500 per child), L14,000 per tent. Open June 1-Sept. 15.

FOOD

Many *paninoteche, gelaterie,* and burger joints are located around P. della Repubblica. Execute comprehensive shopping at **Supermarket Margherita,** Via Raffaello, 37. (Open Mon.-Sat. 7:45am-12:45pm and 5-7:45pm. Closed Thurs. afternoon.)

Ristorante Rustica, Via Nuova, 5 (tel. 25 28), across from Club 83. Traditional atmosphere, excellent food. Pizza from L4000. *Secondi* from L9000. Open Thurs.-Tues. noon-3pm and 7pm-1am; closed July 5-25.

Pizza Evoé, P. S. Franceso, 3 (tel. 48 94). A very popular *pizzeria* with a young crowd. Outdoor seating in a secluded piazza, around the corner from P. della Repubblica. Pizzas from L5000. Cover L500; ½ liter wine L3000.

Pizzeria Le Tre Piante, Via Foro Posterula, 1 (tel. 48 63), off Via Budassi. Spectacular view from the outside tables, in addition to the delicious food. Pizza dinners L4000-6000, others from L15,000. Open Tues.-Sun. noon-3pm and 7pm-2am.

Bar del Teatro, Corso Garibaldi, 88 (tel. (0541) 62 92 84) at the base of the Palazzo Ducale. It's not exactly cheap but it's got the best view in town (P. Ducale on one side, a vista overlooking the valley on the other). A cool, shady place to spend the afternoon. Open daily 7am-2am; closed Sun.

SIGHTS

Urbino's most remarkable monument is the Renaissance **Palazzo Ducale** (Ducal Palace). The façade, which overlooks the edge of town, boasts a unique design attributed to Ambrogio Barocchi: two tall, slender towers enclose three stacked balconies. Most of the rest of the palace, celebrated in Italy as "the most beautiful in the world," was designed by Luciano Laurana. Enter the palace from P. Duca Federico. The interior **courtyard** is the quintessence of Renaissance harmony and proportion. To the left, a monumental staircase takes you to the private apartments of the Duke, which now house the **National Gallery of the Marches.** Federico was one of the great patrons of the early-middle Renaissance period (the Quattrocento— 1400s). Works here reflect the transition into the age of Humanism; perspective in painting is struggled with in Piero della Francesca's *Flagellation of Christ.* Perfection, balance and harmony are witness in the *Ideal City,* artist unknown. The animation and three-dimensionality is tempered by a restraint in passion, later undone by the melodrama of the Baroque period which followed. Also amongst the works are Berruguete's famous portrait of Duke Federico (who sports the world's most famous broken-nosed profile), Raphael's *Portrait of a Lady,* Paolo Uccello's tiny, strange *Profanation of the Host.* The most intriguing room of the palace is the Duke's study on the second floor, where stunning inlaid wooden panels give the illusion of real books and shelves covered with astronomical and musical instruments. Nearby, a circular stairway descends to the Cappella del Perdono and the Tempietto delle Muse, where the Christian and pagan components of the Renaissance commingle. The chapel once served as a repository for holy relics accumulated by the Duke. Eleven wooden panels representing Apollo, Minerva, and the nine muses at one time covered the walls of the temple, but all have been removed (eight of them are currently in Florence's Galleria Corsini). Don't leave the palace without heading underground to see the well-documented "works" of the Palazzo. Here the meandering maze included the Duke's bath, both hot and cold tubs, plus the kitchen, wash room, freezer and lavatory for the staff, an ingenious underground cistern provides water to these rooms, the heating and cooling of which is wisely crafted. It is here where you really get a feeling about how life in Urbino 500 years ago must have been.

At the end of Via Barocci lies the 14th-century **Oratorio di San Giovanni Battista,** decorated with brightly colored Gothic fresco-work of Lorenzo and Giacomo Salimbeni, representing events from the life of St. John. If you speak Italian, the *custode* can give you a wonderful explanation of how fresco painters used lamb's blood as ink for their sketches. (Open daily 10am-noon and 3-5pm. Admission L2000, but you will be obliged to see S. Giuseppe next door for another L2000.) **Raphael's house,** Via Raffaello, 57, is now a vast and delightful museum with period furnishings. His earliest work, a fresco entitled *Madonna e Bambino,* hangs in the *sala.* (Open Mon.-Sat. 9am-1pm and 3-7pm, Sun. 9am-1pm. Admission L5000.) The hike up to the **Fortezza Albornoz** (turn left at the end of Via Raffaello) ends with an awe-inspiring view of the Ducal Palace and the rest of the city; the perfect spot for a picnic. (Open daily 8am-6pm. Free.) For information about English-speaking tours, try contacting Marguerite Laciura at 32 89 40.

ENTERTAINMENT

Urbino's P. della Repubblica serves as a modeling runway for local youth in their boho threads. Take a walk down this fashion ramp and then stroll (or climb) the serpentine streets at dusk. If you seek more active entertainment, dance the night away at **Club 83** on Via Nuova (opens late, best try around midnight). Throughout July you can attend the **Antique Music Festival** in Church of S. Domenico. A cheaper alternative, and more popular with students, is the **University ACLI,** on Via Santa Chiona, a bar with music and small crowds. All this begins in August, when the Italian university summer session convenes. August also brings the ceremony of the **Revocation of the Duke's Court,** replete with Renaissance costumes. Check at the tourist office for the exact date in 1994.

■ Ancona

Named by the Greeks for the elbow (*ankon*) shape of the harbor, Ancona is the archetype of a port city. Its value as a center of trade was first recognized by the emperor Trajan, who developed the city in the first century AD; in the Middle Ages, Ancona reached the height of its importance in trade with the East. Today, the cargo is ferry-borne tourists, not spices and silks. But Ancona retains a certain appeal. The old town is tough and gritty, projecting a muscular and hardened quality. Buildings are high, streets dark and sooty. Unlike most historical centers, commerce exists only around the periphery, and the core is quiet and dilapidated. The cathedral rests on the highest point, from which you can see the sunset over the port and the Adriatic beyond.

FERRIES

Get complete and accurate schedules at the **Stazione Marittima** on the waterfront just off P. Kennedy; bus #1 runs to and from the station (L1000). All the ferry lines operate ticket and information booths. The helpful **information office** at the entrance of the station gives free guided tours of Ancona twice a day in summer, as well as free museum tickets and a coupon good for L4000 worth of snacks in a local bar. (English spoken. Open daily 8am-2pm and 3:20-9:30pm.)

Most travel agents have up-to-date schedules, but ferry service can be fickle, so call and check on dates and prices. An **arrivals/departures board** for the upcoming week hangs inside the main entrance of the station. Most lines give discounts (up to 50%) for round-trip tickets, and student and senior reductions are usually available, too. Make reservations if you're traveling during July or August. **Be at the stazione at least two hours before departure.**

The main lines are: **Karageorgis** (tel. 27 45 54 or 27 72 04), **Marlines** (tel. 20 25 66, fax 411 77 80), **Minoan Lines** (tel. 567 89, fax 20 19 33), **Strintzis** (tel. 286 43 31, fax 20 66 75), **G.A. Ferries** (tel. 20 10 80 or 20 36 37, fax 20 63 31), **Topas** (tel. in Çesme, Turkey (549) 26 916, fax (549) 26 508, 27 932 or 27 933), **Hellenic Mediterranean Lines** (tel. 55 218, fax 29 26 18, or 20 40 41), **Jadrolinija** (tel. in Rijeka, Croatia, (38) (51) 30 899 or 35 418, fax (38) (51) 21 31 16 or 37 110).

ORIENTATION AND PRACTICAL INFORMATION

Ancona is an important junction on the Bologna-Lecce train line and is also served by trains from Rome. The center of town, **Piazza Cavour,** is a 10-minute ride on bus #1 from the train station (L800). Buy the ticket at the station or at the *tabacchi* across the piazza. **Corso Garibaldi** and **Corso Mazzini** connect Piazza Cavour to the port.

Tourist Office: in the train station (tel. 41 703). Open daily 8am-6:30pm. Lightly staffed branch office (seasonal) at Stazione Marittima (20 11 83). Open daily 8am-2pm and 3:20-9:30pm.

Post Office: Viale della Vittoria (tel. 20 13 20 or 51 728). Open Mon.-Fri. 8:15am-7:40pm, Sat. 8:15am-1pm. **Postal code:** 60100.

Telephones: SIP, Corso Stamira, 50, off P. Roma. Also at P. Cavour. Both open daily 8am-9:30pm. **ASST,** P. Rosselli, in front of the station. Open daily 7am-midnight. **Telephone code:** 071.

Buses: departures from P. Cavour and the train station (tel. 20 27 66). Timetables posted at P. Cavour. To: Pescara (3hr.), San Benedetto (2hr.), Urbino Via Fano (2hr. 30min.), Pésaro (1hr. 30min.), and Senigallia (35min.).

Trains: P. Rosselli (tel. 43 933). To: San Benedetto (1hr., L5600); Áscoli Piceno (1hr. 45min., L8800); Pescara (2hr., L10,500); Pésaro (1hr. 30min., L4800); Rome (4hr., L20,000); and Milan (5hr., L33,000).

Car Rental: Avis, Via Marconi, 17 (tel. 50 369). From L600,000 per week with unlimited mileage. Free drop-off anywhere in mainland Italy. They speak English.

Public Toilets: at P. Stamira, Stazione Marittima, and Scalone Nappi.

Emergencies: tel. 113. **Police:** tel. 28 888. **Hospital:** at Via XXV Aprile, 15 (tel. 59 61).

ACCOMMODATIONS AND FOOD

In summer, people waiting for ferries often spend the night at the Stazione Marittima, but you'll find lots of reasonably priced hotels in the lively town center. Avoid the overpriced lodgings in the area by the train station. Make reservations or arrive early—rooms fill quickly in the summer.

Pensione Centrale, Via Marsala, 10 (tel. 54 388), on the 4th floor. Fine rooms with high ceilings. Singles L30,000. Doubles L40,000, with bath L60,000.

Hotel Cavour, Viale della Vittoria, 7 (tel. 20 03 74), 1 block from P. Cavour. Take bus #1 to the beginning of Viale della Vittoria. The fragile-looking elevator will take you to large rooms on the 3rd floor. Doubles with bath L50,000.

Pensione Milano, Via Montebello, 1/A (tel. 20 11 47), at the corner of Via Vecchini, half-way up along flight of stairs. Modern boarding-house design. Avoid rooms overlooking the *autostrada* feeder road below. Singles L30,000. Doubles L40,000. Closed during part of the summer.

The port harbors a good number of inexpensive restaurants. Regional specialties include *brodetto* (fish stew), *pizza al formaggio* (cheese bread), and *vinsgrassi* (lasagna with chicken livers and white sauce). Pack a meal for your ferry ride at the old-fashioned **Mercato Pubblico** (across from Corso Mazzini, 130), where you'll find the four food groups well-represented. (Open Mon.-Sat. 7:30am-12:45pm and 5:15-7:30pm; off-season Mon.-Sat. 7:30am-12:45pm and 4:30-7pm.) **Supermarket SIDIS,** at Via Matteotti, 115, offers the best grocery deals around. (Open Mon.-Sat. 8:15am-12:45pm and 5-7:30pm; closed Thurs. evening.) A word to the wise: the buildings in Ancona are large and occasionally deserted and the town does not go overboard on the street lights, so exercise **caution** when walking at night.

Trattoria 13 Cannelle, Corso Mazzini, 108 (tel. 20 60 12), at P. Roma opposite the fountain. Packed with locals, this place really satisfies. *Primi* L8000. *Secondi* L12,000-20,000. Open Mon.-Sat. noon-2:30pm and 8-10pm.

Osteria del Pozzo, Via Bonda, 2 (tel. 207 39 96), a tiny passage off P. Plebiscito. Look for kelly green. Popular, cheery, and cheap. Specialties include fried fish and *spaghetti al frutti di mare* (with seafood). Full meals around L19,000. Open Mon.-Sat. noon-2:30pm and 7:30-10pm.

SIGHTS

Survey the Anconan sea and sky from **Piazzale del Duomo,** atop **Monte Guasco.** Climb up Via Papa Giovanni XXIII, or take bus #11 from P. Cavour. If you decide to walk, you'll enjoy the beautiful **Scalone Nappi,** a verdant stairway street. (Follow the left-hand steps at the point where the street forks; there are only 244 steps, and the vista is magnificent.) In P. del Duomo you'll find the **Cathedral of San Ciriaco,** erected in the 11th century on the site of a Roman temple to Venus. Its stolid Romanesque design is the outcome of the confluence of Apulian Romanesque from the south and the remnants of Byzantine from the north. (Cathedral open daily 9-10:30am and noon-6pm.)

Via Pizzecolli, the main street of the old quarter, reaches from Via Papa Giovanni XXIII to the fine Venetian-Gothic doorway of the **Church of San Francesco delle Scale** (St. Francis of the Steps) before entering the courtyard of the **Government Palace** and **Piazza Plebiscito.** Up the street, across from the **Loggia dei Mercanti** (Merchants' Gallery), stands the Romanesque **Church of Santa Maria della Piazza,** its façade overcharged with blind arches and bestial sculptures.

After decades of restoration (World War II bombings and a 1972 earthquake were among its trials), the **Museo Archeologico Nazionale delle Marche** is open for business on Via Ferretti above Via Pizzecolli. The impressive collection's best pieces include the Ionian *Dinos of Amandola,* some wonderful Greek vases, and two life-size equestrian bronzes of Roman emperors. (Open Mon.-Sat. 9am-1:30pm, Sun. 2:30-7:30pm.) Ancona's painting gallery, the **Galleria Comunale Francesco Podesti,** is housed in the 16th-century **Palazzo Bosdari** at Via Pizzecolli, 17. Carlo Crivelli's tiny, flawless *Madonna col Bambino* completely shows up Titian's *Apparition of the Virgin,* recently restored to the full glory of its original colors. (Open Tues.-Sat. 10am-7pm, Sun. 9am-1pm. Admission L3000; handicapped, over 60 and students free; Sun. free for all.) Evenings in Ancona demand a stroll on the tree-lined esplanade from Corso Garibaldi past P. Cavour to Viale della Vittoria. The tourist office's booklet *Estate 93* fills you in on events of interest; also pick up a summer cinema schedule. In mid-July, the **Festa della Birra e del Rock** (Rock'n'Beer Fest) features religious hymns and weak tea with milk.

■ Áscoli Piceno

Áscoli Piceno is the hill town secret of Italy. A medieval city like Urbino, it offers the architecture, museums and history without the blight of tourism. As a result, prices are downright reasonable and the near-empty hostel, housed in a 13th-century Palazzo, completes the budget traveler's dream ticket into medieval Italy.

According to legend, Áscoli was settled by Greeks who were guided westward by a woodpecker—a *picchio*—which gave the city its surname and provided a symbol for the Marches. Áscoli was the metropolis of the Piceni people, a quiet Latin tribe that controlled much of the coastal Marches and had the woodpecker as their clan totem. Whatever its origins, Áscoli has always been fiercely independent, from its role as a center of anti-Roman power during the Social Wars to its successful resistance to Nazi occupation. In the late 13th century, this independence produced a splendid architecture that remains unspoiled. Known as the "town of travertine" for the white limestone of which it is built, Áscoli rests on a plain at the confluence of the Castellano and Tronto Rivers, enclosed by the nearby mountains, which form a natural amphitheater. Stick to the historic center; avoid the ungainly new town.

ORIENTATION AND PRACTICAL INFORMATION

Áscoli is about one hour by bus or train from San Benedetto del Tronto, which is itself one hour from Ancona on the Bologna-Lecce train line. **Cotravat** buses, cheaper, less crowded, and more frequent than the trains, leave San Benedetto del Tronto for Áscoli about every 45 minutes (L3200). If you do take the train, you'll still need to hop a city bus (L1000) once you arrive. Walk straight out of the station, one block to Viale Indipendenza, take a right and then walk half a block to the stop. Catch bus #2 or #3 to arrive at the historical center. Get off at the bus station behind the *duomo,* where the Cotravat buses stop as well. Take Via XX Settembre to your left off P. Arringo in front of the *duomo* to Via del Trivio, which connects to Corso Mazzini and P. del Popolo.

Tourist Office: Ufficio Informazioni, P. del Popolo, 17 (tel. 25 52 50). Very helpful. Open April 15-Sept. 30 8:30am-1pm and 3-7:30pm; holidays 9am-1pm.

Post Office: Via Crispi, off Corso Mazzini. Open Mon.-Sat. 8:15am-7:40pm. Fermo Posta open Mon.-Sat. 8:30am-1pm and 4-7:40pm. **Postal code:** 63100. **Telephone code:** 0736.

Buses: all leave from Viale de' Gasperi (behind the cathedral) except Amadio, which runs from Viale Indipendenza. Timetable outside on the wall at **Agenzia Viaggi Brunozzi,** Corso Trento e Trieste, 54/56 (tel. 25 94 60). Buy train and bus tickets here. Open Mon.-Fri. 9am-1pm and 4-7pm. **ARPA** to: Pescara (tel. (0861) 24 83 43; 5 per day, 2hr., L5600) and Rome (daily at 2:20pm, 8hr.). If the Agenzia is closed, you can get tickets to S. Benedetto in a *tabacchi.*

Emergencies: tel. 113.

ACCOMMODATIONS

There are a few quiet and well-kept hotels in Áscoli Piceno, but clearly the best choice for the budget traveler is the city's relaxed youth hostel. If you're looking for a way to make a lot of money in a beautiful city, open a hotel in Áscoli.

Ostello de Longobardi, Via Soderini, 26, Palazzetto Longobardo (tel. 25 90 07). Getting there is tricky, but it is 1 block away from the Ponte Romano, one of the few bridges across the Tronto River. From P. del Popolo take Via del Trivio 3 blocks past S. Francesco until it forks into 2 streets. Take Via Cairoli going left to P. San Pietro Martire until you reach Via Soderini. Continue on for 3 short blocks until Via del Longobardi, and the hostel, on your left. Friendly warden occasionally plays violin for his guests as well as takes them on free tours of the city. No curfew; you get the keys. L12,000 per person.

Albergo Piceno, Via Minucia, 10 (tel. 25 25 53), near the cathedral and the bus stop. Close to the center of things, and so clean you could eat off the floor. If you get a room without bath, you will not have access to a shower. Singles L40,000, with bath L50,000. Doubles with bath L70,000. Triples with bath L90,000.

Cantina Dell'Arte, Via della Lupa, 8 (tel. 25 57 44 or 25 56 20), behind the post office. Take the street to the left of the ugly concrete building (there are no street signs or hotel/restaurant signs). In the medieval heart of town, modern rooms with fine furniture, TVs, and private baths. Singles L45,000. Doubles L65,000. Triples L80,000. Quads L100,000.

Hotel Pavoni, Via Navilella, 135/B (tel. 34 25 75 or 34 25 87), 3km ahead on the road to San Benedetto. Quiet and affordable, partly because it's in outer exurbia. Take bus #3 from P. Arringo (L1000). Singles L20,000, with bath L35,000. Doubles L30,000, with bath L60,000.

FOOD

You can fill your tummy without emptying your pockets here—an excellent meal should run L10,000. There's also an **open-air market** in P. San Francesco, behind P. del Popolo (Mon.-Sat. mornings). In P. Santa Maria Inter Vineas, the small **Supermarket Gierre** sells local *porchetta*. (Open Mon.-Fri. 9am-1pm and 3:30-8pm, Sat. 9am-1:30pm.)

Trattoria Lino Cavucci, P. della Viola, 13 (tel. 503 58). An excellent choice. *Primi* L4500-L5000. Wine L1500 per ½ liter. Open Sat.-Thurs. noon-3pm and 7-11pm.

Cantina dell'Arte, Via della Lupa, 5 (tel. 25 11 35), across from the hotel (no sign). A family-run restaurant with long communal tables. Delicious daily specials. Complete meal L15,000. Open daily noon-3:30pm and 7-10pm.

L'Assaggino, Via Minucia, 24, at the end of Via Civo del Duca (2 blocks from P. del Popolo). A self-service *pizzeria* with indoor and outdoor seating. Inexpensive. Open Mon.-Sat. 11am-2pm and 4-9pm.

Pizzeria Italia, Corso Mazzini, 205. Near the post office. Standing only.

SIGHTS

Piazza del Popolo, the historic center of town, is a calm oasis in this busy city. The 16th-century *portici* which line two sides of the square recall the Piazza San Marco in Venice. The third side houses the 13th-century **Palazzo dei Capitani del Popolo,** whose massive portal and statue of Pope Paul III date from 1548. The history of the edifice is full of Renaissance (and later) intrigue. Originally erected as the palace of the city's hierarch, or captain, the building was burned on Christmas Day 1535 in an inter-familial squabble; the piazza smoldered for two full days. A decade later the palace was refurbished and dedicated to the pope, who brought peace to Áscoli. In 1938 the palace was the seat of the principal Fascist party, only to be wrested for partisan use in early 1945. Through the entrance to the left of the main portal, an excavated area beneath the presumed foundation of the *palazzo* is exposed. Here, remains from the Roman era were revealed in 1982. This discovery legitimated the view that the piazza was originally the "Forum" in "Asculum." Built works from both the Republican and Augustan eras can be viewed here, via a serpentine wooden pathway weaving down and under the structure of the *palazzo*. A museum *in situ* is very handsome and worth a visit, especially since it's free. (Open June 15-Sept. 14 daily 9am-7pm.) The piazza is the forecourt for the elegant eastern end of the **Church of St. Francis** (13th-16th centuries). Its spacious three-aisled interior houses a 14th-century wooden crucifix, the only art object saved from the 1535 fire. At dusk Áscoli's youth gather here for a lively *passeggiata*. (Open 8am-noon and 3-7pm.)

Abutting the church to the south, the gracious **Loggia dei Mercanti** (Merchant's Gallery, 1509-1513), now a favorite meeting place for the town elders, leads to

Corso Mazzini and the austere 14th-century **Church of St. Augustine** (open 9am-noon and 3-7pm).

Via delle Torri, off P. Sant'Agostino, runs past the stone houses of the old quarter to the 13th-century **Church of St. Peter the Martyr** and tiny **Via di Solestà.** This street, one of the oldest in the city, leads to the single-arched **Ponte di Solestà,** one of Europe's tallest Roman bridges. Cross the bridge, or the Ponte Nuovo and walk to the edge of town (turning on Viale Marcello, right or left respectively), to find the church of St. Emidio alle Grotte, a baroque façade grafted onto the natural rock wall. Inside, the walls are formed by a series of catacombs. The first Ascoli Christians are buried here. Back at S. Pietro Martire, and around the corner in P. Venidio Basso stands the diminutive 11th-century Romanesque **Church of SS. Vincenzo e Anastasio** (take Via Trebbiani). The low campanile, divided by two arched windows and topped by a conical spire, is characteristic of the city's medieval churches. Legend has it that water from the crypt's miraculous well has healed the lame and brought sight to the blind.

On the other side of town, **Piazza Arringo** derives its name from the harangues delivered there by local leaders. The massive, travertine **duomo** is a pastiche of art and architecture from the 5th through the 20th centuries. A Roman basilica forms the transept, topped by an irregular octagonal dome from the 8th century. The two towers were built in the 11th and 12th centuries, respectively, while the lateral naves and central apse were constructed in the 1400s, giving the cathedral an overall late-medieval tone that is tempered with a modern twinge. Further embellishments included two interior stairways, the 16th-century façade and mosaics depicting Áscoli's role in World War II (1954). The *duomo's* **Cappella del Sacramento** (Chapel of the Sacrament), an intricately framed polyptych of the *Virgin and Saints* (Carlo Crivelli, 1473) surmounts a 14th-century silver altar. (Open daily 9am-noon and 4-7pm.) Next to the cathedral stands the compact 12th-century **baptistry,** decorated with a *loggia* of blind arches. Works by Crivelli, Titian, van Dyck, and Ribera hang amid red velvet curtains and pink walls in **Pinacoteca Civica,** inside the **Palazzo Comunale** (southern flank of the piazza). (Open Mon.-Sat. 9am-1pm, Sun. 9am-12:30pm. Admission L2500, seniors free.) Visit the **Museo Archeologico,** also on the piazza, for its hall of mosaics. (Open Tues.-Fri. and Sun. 9:30am-1:30pm. Free.)

On the first Sunday in August, Áscoli holds the **Tournament of Quintana,** a medieval pageant in which over 1000 people deck themselves out in traditional costume. The tournament, which features armed jousting and a torchlight procession to P. del Popolo, culminates the four-day festival of Sant'Emidio, the city's patron.

The **carnival** in February is one of the best in Italy. Insanity reigns on the Tuesday, Thursday, and especially the Sunday preceding Ash Wednesday. Residents don costumes, and folk dancers perform in P. del Popolo. Happily, the event is not mobbed by tourists, but you should still make hotel reservations a week ahead.

Abruzzo and Molise

Only a short distance from Rome (about 3 hours by train), but a long stretch from the frenzy of tourism, the highlands of Abruzzo offer the traveler a tranquil reprieve in the well-preserved medieval towns of L'Áquila and Sulmona. Surrounding both cities are easily accessible natural areas: to the south of Sulmona is the **Abruzzo National Park** which offers a glimpse of an Italy before all the civilization: wild animals, mountainous vistas, and pure air. To the north of L'Aquila looms the *Gran Sasso* (big rock), the highest peak of the Apennines. In summer its sheer wall attracts climbers and hikers, while in winter it hosts 3 ski resorts. The coastal region, however, has been reduced to shapeless cultural shambles by "progress." Pescara and the surrounding coast are a vapid tumble of *pizzerie*, discos and beach blankets, completely alien to the rugged and unspoiled interior highland.

The nation's second smallest region, **Molise** is deservedly the least known Italian corner, lacking any cities of distinction. Nevertheless, its mountain areas abutting the Abruzzo National Park offer more unspoiled wilderness, where bears, wolves, and boars roam, trying to avoid assimilation into the local cuisine, which includes *sopprfessate* (smoked boar sausage). Also scattered through the region are several ancient towns, and some ruins dating back to the Golden Age of Greece.

In both regions, train lines are painfully circuitous, so make use of the **ARPA** bus service. For bus information call the Arpa office in Avezzano (tel. (0863) 26 561). Avoid traveling on Sundays, when bus traffic is sharply reduced. If you want to explore Molise, plan on using a car, since the best wilderness and villages lie beyond the scope of public transportation.

■ Térmoli

Overrun by German and Italian tourists in July and August, the resort town of **Térmoli** retains enough authenticity to be interesting, and it's also the cheapest and most convenient Apulian point of departure to the Trémiti Islands.

Orientation and Practical Information Térmoli serves as the end point of the Napoli-Campobasso-Térmoli train line (2hrs., L6500), and is a 90-minute train ride on the Bologna-Lecce line from Pescara to the north and from Fóggia to the south (both L5700). Trains arrive at the station in **Piazza Garibaldi,** while the buses arrive in **Piazza Melchiorre Bega** next door. A **tourist information booth** is located in P. Bega (tel. 70 67 54), or the **principal tourist office** is located through the bus arcade, off Corso Umberto I and around the corner to your right, on the second floor (tel. 70 39 13). Here, find information on boat service to the Trémiti Islands (from Termoli only), bus and train schedules, and on hotels, restaurants. (Open Mon.-Sat. 8am-2pm.) The best information on boats to the Trémiti Islands is found at the offices at the port. **Adriatica Navigazione** (tel. 70 53 41) is the largest company but the **Santa Lucia Lines** (tel. 48 59) might prove a better deal.

The **post office** (tel. 24 05) is located on Corso Milano, 18. (Open Mon.-Sat. 8:15am-5:30pm. **Fermo Posta** Mon.-Sat. 8:15am-1pm., July-Aug. Mon.-Fri. 8:15am-1pm, Sat. 8:15am-noon.) The **postal code** is 86039, and the **telephone code** 0875. Térmoli's responsive **tourist office** at P. Bega (tel. 27 54), through the arcades off Corso Umbergui, has the best information on the Trémiti Islands, and posts bus and train schedules; buses leave from the same piazza. (Open Mon.-Sat. 8am-7pm.)

Accommodations and Food The only affordable place to stay is the **Pensione Villa Ida,** Via Milano, 27 (tel. 70 66 66; open April-November), to the left of the train station toward the beach. Modern, well kept, and located one block from the beach and 2 blocks from the "strip," Corso Nazionale, where the nightly promenade of tourists and locals takes place. (Singles with bath L45,000. Doubles with bath L60,000. Obligatory half-pension in July, L50,000 per person, single, L55,000 per person, obligatory full pension in Aug., L75,000.) Off Via Duomo (on the Borgo Vecchio) at **Osteria Dentro le Mura,** Via Salvatore, 36, yield to the temptation of *crostini* (pieces of grilled bread with sundry toppings), L2500-L3000; open Mon., Tues., and Thurs.-Sun., 8pm-2am.) **Rosticceria Pizzeria Bar Morelli,** on Via Roma, 27, across the street from the entrance to the old quarter (tel. 70 32 86), hustles full meals for around L12,000 and pizza for L1500 a slice. (Open daily 8am-11pm.) If you're up for an adventure and have a little money to burn, stop by **Z'Bass** (tel. 70 67 03), a *trattoria tipica* just off the Corso Nazionale past Via Sannitica, almost at the beach wall. Order their live shellfish antipasto. For the tamer palate, the fish entrees are excellent. Quiet and relaxed during the day but active at night, the **Microbar** (tel. 70 62 38) in P. Vittorio Veneto (on Corso Umberto I, right across from the bus station), is a local, family-run business with the best hours around, open 24 hrs. during July and August, and 7am-3am daily the rest of the year.

Sights The city flaunts the standard Italian beach scene and a small but fairly enchanting old quarter. Walk down Corso Umberto I from the train station and take the first left onto Corso Nazionale to reach the **Borgo Vecchio,** the historic center. Early risers will be treated to a spectacular meeting of sea and sky, framed by medieval streets. The most prominent feature of the Borgo Vecchio is the **Castello Svevo,** built in 1247. It was abandoned for 500 years, until 1799, when the Bourbons used it as a prison to hold 300 revolting *termolesi* (closed to the public). The **cathedral,** behind the castle, offers a unique, 13th-century interpenetration of Byzantine, Moorish, Abruzzese, and Umbrian forms. (Open daily 7:30am-6:30pm.)

Térmoli thrives on summer festivals. For three days around the last weekend in July, the **International Festival of Folklore** lures innocent young dancers, singers, and storytellers from around the world. Every August 4 Térmoli celebrates the **Festa di San Basso** with a bawdy parade of fishing boats and fireworks in honor of the city's patron saint. The **Sagra del Pesce** occurs the last Saturday in August, when fresh fish are cooked in outdoor cauldrons. Every August 15 the **Festivo del Mare** commemorates a Saracen attack by "burning down" the Borgo Vecchio with fireworks. From the last week of July through September Térmoli hosts an exhibition of international contemporary art.

■ ■ ■ L'ÁQUILA

L'Áquila (The Eagle) seems a fitting name for this busy commercial city, perched on a lofty plateau in the heart of the Gran Sasso massif, the highest segment of the Apennines. An earthquake in 1703 partially demolished the medieval city; resulting in its half-modern, half-medieval character.

The oldest and most characteristic monument of L'Aquila is the **Fountain of the 99 Spouts,** each spout representing a different lord of a castle who contributed to the founding of the city. The source of the water remains unknown, although the water has been flowing steadily since its construction in 1292. In fact the number 99 resonates throughout the town in a curious way: there are exactly 99 churches, 99 piazze, and 99 fountains gracing its streets. And every night the bell in the civic tower rings 99 times.

ORIENTATION AND PRACTICAL INFORMATION

The city's historic district centers on **Piazza del Duomo,** joined to the commercial district near the bus station by **Corso Vittorio Emanuele II.** On the other side of the piazza, **Corso Federico II** runs to **Via XX Settembre,** which circumscribes the southern half of the city. At the intersection of Corso Federico II and Via XX Settembre you will find the Villa Comunale. At the northern tip of the city, just to the right of the Corso Vittorio Emanuele is the **Castello** and surrounding park. These patches of greenery mark the north and south perimeter of the city. It is approximately a 30 minute walk between the two. Make sure to pick up a map; navigating the small streets tends to be difficult as street names change every few blocks. An extended portico on Vittorio Emanuele, to the right of the duomo, offers numerous bars and cafés with outdoor seating; a pleasant, sheltered place to spend a few hours, watching the activity of the *città centro.*

> **Tourist Office: EPT,** P. Santa Maria Paganica, 5 (tel. 41 08 08 or 41 03 40). Take Corso Vittorio Emanuele to Via Leosino; hang a right and the office will be on your right. Ask for their map of the Gran Sasso mountain area if you're planning on hiking. Open Mon.-Fri. 8am-2pm and 4-6pm, Sat. 8am-1pm. **Azienda di Turismo:** Located conveniently on Corso Vittorio Emanuele, 49. (tel. 41 08 59). Open daily, 9am-1pm and 4-6:30pm. Helpful staff speaks some English.

L'AQUILA

Post Office: on P. del Duomo (tel. 61 641). Open Mon.-Sat. 8:15am-7:40pm. **Postal Code:** 67100.

Telephones: SIP, Via XX Settembre, 75. Open Mon.-Sat. 9am-12:30pm and 2:30-6pm, Sun. 9am-12:30pm and 3:30-6:30pm. **Telephone Code:** 0862.

Trains: at P. della Stazione (tel. 20 497), in the outskirts. Take bus #1, 3, or 3/5 (L700) from outside the station to the center of town, or follow the signs to the Fontana Delle 99 Cannelle and then hike up the hill to Corso XX Settembre (about 1km total). Trains run on the Sulmona -Terni line, 1 hour from Sulmona (L4300). Connections to Rome, Napoli, and Pescara.

Buses: ARPA (tel. 69 464). To: Rome (16 per day, 9 on Sun., 1hr. 30min., L11,300); Pescara (9 per day, 5 on Sun.; in winter 2 per day, none on Sun., 2hr., L8700); Sulmona (Mon.-Sat. 9 per day, 1hr., L6100); Avezzano (30 per day, 2 on Sun., 1hr. 30min., L5300). Bus tickets in the information booth at Porta Paganica, near the castello whence the buses leave.

Hiking Information: Club Alpino Italiano, Via XX Settembre, 15 (tel. 24 342), on the 3rd floor. The best maps, books, and information on local trails and refuges, though you'll be lucky if you find an English speaker. Open Mon.-Sat. 9am-1pm and 4-8pm. If the club is closed, two bookstores on Via Andrea Bafile offer a good selection of maps and guidebooks on Gran Sasso, Abruzzi National Park, and nearby areas: **Libreria Colacchi,** Via Andrea Bafile, 17 (tel. 25 310). Open Mon.-Fri. 8:45am-1pm and 4-7:45pm, Sat. 8:45am-1pm. **Libri Scalastici,** Via Andrea Bafile, 27 (tel. 22 323). Open Mon.-Fri. 8am-1pm, and 5-8pm, Sat. 8am-12pm.

Public Restrooms for men and women, underground at P. Palazzo, off Corso Principe Umberto.

Emergencies: tel. 113. **Police: Questura,** Via Strinella, 2 (tel. 113). **Red Cross:** tel. 22 333.

ACCOMMODATIONS AND FOOD

L'Aquila is an upscale tourist town dominated by 3-star hotels, and budget accommodations are scarce; arrive early and check with the tourist office.

Albergo Aurora, Via Cimino 21, off P. del Duomo (tel. 22 053). Walk through the courtyard and take stairs up to 2nd floor. Large, quiet rooms. Singles L30,000. Doubles L42,000, with bath L45,000.

Lo Shay, located in Bazzano (tel. 44 15 21), a 10 min. ASM bus ride from town, on the road to the Funivia. Catch the #6 bus in front of the Castello on Via Castello: runs approximately every 30 minutes. Singles L30,000. Doubles L40,000, with bath L50,000. Restaurant on the premises.

Torrone is to L'Aquila what chocolate is Perugia. Torrone, a nougat made of honey and almonds, plain or chocolate, is manufactured in L'Aquila and sold in many establishments along the main streets, Corso Federico II and Corso Vittorio Emanuele. Among other places, look for this local sweet in **Tappirullan,** Via Vittorio Emanuele. There is an **outdoor market** held every morning except Sunday in P. del Duomo, extending to Via Sallustio, or stock up at **Supermercato STANDA,** Via Sant' Agostino, 6, off P. del Duomo under the STANDA department store. (Open Mon. 4-8pm, Tue.-Sat. 9am-1pm and 4-8pm.

Trattoria Stella Alpina, Via Crispomonti, 15 (tel. 41 31 90), off P. del Duomo. Serves hearty regional dishes like *agnello ai ferri* (grilled lamb, L9000) and *spaghetti alla chitarra* (thick spaghetti, L6000). Ask for the *crostini,* a delicious concoction of toasted bread, melted mozzarella, and prosciutto drenched in extra virgin olive oil (L8000)—it's not on the menu. Request the *schiaffoni* and, instead of getting whacked repeatedly across the face, you'll get delicious rigatoni-like pasta in a sauce of cream, peas, and mushrooms (L6000). Cover L2500. Open Sat.-Thurs. 11:30am-3:30pm and 6:30-10pm.

Trattoria Da Lincosta, P. S. Pietro, 19 (tel. 28 662). A short walk from the duomo on a small, sunny piazza. Try one of the specialties: *Chitarra Boscaiola* (pasta with mushrooms, red peppers and tomatoes), L7500; *Agnello ai Ferri* (grilled lamb), L11,000. Staff speaks some English. Cover L3500. Open Mon.-Thu., Sat.-Sun. noon-3pm and 6pm-midnight.

Ghiottonera (tel. 24 049), at the intersection of Corso Vittorio Emanuele and Via Castello. This bar/café, situated in P. Regina Marghenta against the backdrop of Neptune's fountain, offers a tranquil atmosphere and affordable eats. Pizza and calzones for L1200. Ask the proprietor for a hot dog if you miss home—he spent 4 years in the U.S. Open daily 6am-2am.

SIGHTS AND ENTERTAINMENT

L'Áquila's **castello** dominates the pleasant park at the end of Corso Vittorio Emanuele, across and up the hill from the bus station. The Spanish built this hilltop fortress in the 16th century as a defense against rebellious townspeople. Its thick walls now house the outstanding **National Museum of Abruzzo,** which showcases the region's early art. The museum's extensive collection of sacred medieval art includes delicate wooden doors carved with New Testament scenes from a 12th-century church. The paleontological section contains a fossilized mammoth found near the town in 1954. (Open Tues.-Sat. 9am-2pm, Sun. 9am-1pm. Admission L4000.) In the evenings, the path around the fortress's moat is the site of the *passeggiata,* which continues up and down Corso Vittorio Emanuele.

From Via XX Settembre, take Viale Crispi to Viale di Collemaggio to reach the **Basilica of Santa Maria di Collemaggio,** begun in 1287 at the urging of local hermit Pietro da Morrone (who later became Pope Celestine V). The façade, with its elaborate checkered pink and white marble, rose windows and rounded doorways, is in sharp contrast to the interior. The stripping away of baroque embellishments in 1972 and the earlier loss of medieval frescoes have left the church noticably bare, with only the striking white limestone Renaissance **Tomb of San Celestino** left. If you're feeling guilty about anything, make sure to visit on August 29: According to tradition, all sins will be forgiven merely by attending church. Each year on this day, important political figures from all parts of Italy march in procession through the door in hopes of attaining absolution. (Open 8:30am-12:30pm and 4-7pm.)

Closer to the heart of town, walk down Via Sassa (off P. Duomo) for a short tour of L'Áquila's minor architectural prizes. Stop at Palazzetto Franchi, #56, which encloses a graceful Renaissance courtyard made unique by its double *loggia* (now partially sealed). The courtyard of #29A hides the **Church and Convent of Beata Antonia,** run by cloistered nuns. Ring the bell and ask to see the *affresco* (fresco) and you will be escorted to a magnificent 15th-century crucifixion scene covering an entire wall. (Ring between the hours of 9am-noon or 4-6:30pm.)

Down Via San Bernadino lies the **Church of San Bernadino,** built in honor of Bernadino of Siena, who spent the last years of his life here hoping to revive the pure Franciscan faith. Behind the Renaissance façade you'll find two mausoleums (for San Bernadino and Maria Pereira) by Silvestro dell'Aquila, a student of Donatello. The exquisite Baroque wooden ceiling was built after the 1703 earthquake ravaged the original interior.

From November to May, the **Società Aquilana dei Concerti** holds classical concerts in the *castello* (admission L8000-18,000). Also of interest are the recitals at the **Festival of Classical Guitar** in August. For ticket and schedule information, check the Azienda di Turismo, or with the **Ufficio Organizzativo dell'Ente Castello Cinquecentesco,** 67100, L'Aquila (tel. 24 262 or 41 41 61, fax. 61 666). L'Áquila claims one of central Italy's best snow sport resorts, **Campo Felice.** (Weekly lift tickets L100,000, children L80,000.) *Settimana bianca* packages, covering room, board, and lift tickets, begin at L350,000. Write to the Azienda di Turismo or call Campo Felice (tel. 91 78 03; in Rome, (06) 684 11 54), for information.

■ Near L'Áquila

The craggy terrain around L'Áquila conceals isolated medieval towns, ancient churches and monasteries, and abandoned fortresses. East of the city lie the extraordinary ruins of the 15th-century **Rocca Calascio**, one of the world's most sophisticated works of military architecture. It's surrounded by the medieval towns of **Santo Stefano di Sessanio** and **Castel del Monte**, as well as the 9th-century **Oratorio di San Pellegrino** in the town of Bominaco. To the west of L'Áquila lie extensive Roman ruins at **Amiternum**, and the enormous **Lago di Campotosto**, the largest man-made lake in Italy, which supplies electricity to the Abruzzo and surrounding regions. ARPA buses service these sights from both L'Áquila and Sulmona (2-3 departures per day, 1hr. 30min.-2hr. 30min., L3000-4000). North of L'Áquila, the town of **Assergi** contains a beautiful 12th-century abbey, **Santa Maria Assunta**, with well-preserved frescoes reminiscent of Byzantine art. To get there, take one of the hourly #6 municipal buses (1hr., L1200) from Porta Paganico.

12km above L'Áquila rises the snowcapped **Gran Sasso d'Italia** (Big Rock of Italy), the highest peak entirely within Italy and a mountaineer's delight. First procure a map marked *carta topografica per escursionisti* or *Wanderkarte*. Make sure it includes *sentieri* (trails marked by difficulty) and *rifugi* (hikers' huts charging L8000-14,000 per night). Always call these refuges before setting out, and bring food, as prices rise with the altitude. **Club Alpino Italiano** in L'Áquila (tel. 24 342) has the most up-to-date Apennine advice. The accommodations booklet available at L'Áquila's **EPT** contains a list of Abruzzo refuges. From L'Áquila, take bus #6 from Porta Paganico, on Via Castello; make sure it is going all the way to the *funivia*. (about 5 per day, 1hr., L1200; buy an *extraurbano* ticket in a *tabacchi*). Get off at the base of the cableway. If you don't feel like hiking to the top, you can take the *funivia* halfway up (L10,000, Sat.-Sun. L12,000; descent L8000, Sat.-Sun. L12,000; round-trip L15,000, Sat.-Sun. L18,000). The *funivia* runs every half-hour from 8:30am-5pm, except at 1:30pm. Camp and munch at **Camping Funivia del Gran Sasso** (tel. 60 61 63), an immaculate, grassy area down the hill from the eponymous cableway. (L6000 per person, L6000 per small tent, L8000 per large tent; off-season L5000 per person, L5000 per small tent, L7000 per large tent. Electricity L2000. Showers L1000.) The campground restaurant prepares massive *panini* for L3000 and eggplant parmesan L3000. (Open daily 9am-1pm and 3-9pm.) Campground open Nov.-April and June-Sept. 15.

The area around the *funivia* offers several pristine hikes. Trail #10 (about 500m down the road) will take you up to **Monte Della Scindarella**, with a stupendous view of the Gran Sasso and L'Áquila. The upper *funivia* station provides access to several trails; to tackle the mountain itself, take trail #3 to trail #4. In the winter, the Gran Sasso teems with skiers. Skiing at **Camp Imperatore**, the upper end of the *funivia*, starts at L100,000 for a weekly lift pass (valid throughout the season except Dec. 26-Jan. 6 and the Tuesday after Easter). If you're a novice, take a lesson from the Gran Sasso ski school (L35,000 for individuals, less for groups of 2 or more). For useful information on Alpine guides, inquire at the tourist office or write **Collegio Regionale Guide Alpine**, Via Serafino 2, 66100 Chieti (tel. (0871) 69 338).

■ Sulmona

Sulmona's most famous son, the poet Ovid (43 BC-17 AD) stands immortalized in **Piazza XX Settembre**, the city's main meeting space. Despite its preoccupation with the ancient poet, Sulmona owes its beauty to the late middle ages, when prosperity spurred the construction of innumerable churches and palaces. Sulmona's intimate size and noteworthy architecture make it the perfect town to relax for a day or a weekend. Sulmona maintains a distinct sweetness, thanks not only to the residents' friendliness but also to the proliferation of candy stores. Sulmona has been the home of *confetti* candy since the 15th century. These flower-shaped, sugar-coated almonds, now most often supplanted by paper imitations, are thrown at weddings worldwide.

Orientation and Practical Information Sulmona is easily reached by ARPA bus from L'Áquila (9 per day, 1hr. 30min., L4800), and Pescara (5 per day,

1hr. 30min., L5900). For more bus information call 21 04 69. Buy tickets on the bus. The city is more conveniently reached on the Rome-Pescara train line, with 15 daily trains in each direction (Rome, 3hr., L12,100; Pescara, 1hr. 15min., L4400). To get to the town center from the station, take bus A (every 30min., buy tickets from the driver, L1000) or walk the 2km uphill. The **telephone code** is 0864; use the **SIP** phones behind the **Church of the SS. Annunziata** on Largo San Tommasi. (Open daily 8am-10pm.) The **tourist office,** is at Via Roma, 21 (tel. 53 276), off Corso Ovidio. (Open Mon.-Sat. 8am-2pm.)

Accommodations and Food The friendly and helpful proprietors of **Albergo Italia,** P. Tommasi, 3 (tel. 52 308), off P. XX Settembre, offer what is clearly the best budget hotel in Sulmona. Elegant rooms overlook the dome of the church of the SS. Annunziata and the mountains. (Singles L30,000; doubles L50,000-55,000, with bath L60,000-65,000.) **Albergo Stella,** Via Panfila Mazara, 16 (tel. 52 653), is conveniently located off Corso Ovidio. (Singles with bath L35,000. Doubles L42,000, with bath L50,000.) **Ristorante Stella,** downstairs, serves a "Menu Turistica" for L16,000. Open daily noon-2pm and 7-10pm. **Ristorante Cesidio,** P. Solimo (tel. 52 724) is a family-run escape from busy Corso Ovidio and the main *piazze*. A full meal goes for as little as L20,000. (Open Sat.-Thurs. noon-3pm and 7:30-midnight.) For a taste of the local flavor, look for **Ristorante Italia** (tel. 33 070), located in P. XX Settembre. Open Tue.-Sun. 12:30-3pm and 7-10pm. Corso Ovidio is lined with inexpensive pizzerias, cafés and bars if a snack or light meal is what you crave. **Pizzeria Ernano,** Corso Ovidio 263, offers calzones and beer; a good alternative to gelato in the afternoon. Those with a sweet tooth will not want to miss **G. Di Carlo e Figlio,** Corso Ovidio, 185, for his famous *confetti*. (Open daily 8:30am-1pm and 2:30-7pm.) Pick up picnic staples at **Supermercato STANDA,** Corso Ovidio, 15. (Open Mon.-Sat. 9am-1pm and 4-8pm.)

Sights At one end of Corso Ovidio, the **gardens** of Sulmona offer shade to the weary. One of the Abruzzo's most magnificent structures is the nearby **Church and Palace of SS. Annunziata,** an extravagant Baroque church façade which abuts a delicate Gothic-Renaissance *palazzo*. The *palazzo* now houses a small museum focusing on Renaissance Sulmonese goldwork (may be closed for restoration). Throughout the summer months, free classical music concerts fill the *palazzo's* courtyard (check the billboards or with the tourist office).

The colossal **Piazza Garibaldi,** just beyond the church, is dominated by the Renaissance-era **Fontana del Vecchio,** which gushes clear mountain water from a rare medieval aqueduct (1256). A daily **market** takes place here, which is expanded on Tuesdays and Saturdays. Farther down Corso Ovidio, on P. del Carmine, stood the **Church of San Francesco della Scarpa** (St. Francis of the Shoe), but all that remains is a 12th-century portal. Off Corso Ovidio near the gardens, peek into the **Palazzo Tabassi,** built in 1449 by Matro Petro Da Como.

Prohibitively expensive accommodations mean that the mountain resort town **Scanno** is better visited as a daytrip from Sulmona. Its lake is one of the few remaining in Italy that has not been reduced to an enormous pee-puddle. Incredible vistas accompany the twisting, stomach-punishing bus ride (14 per day, 1hr., L2500).

◾ National Park of Abruzzo (Parco Nazionale D'Abruzzo)

The National Park of Abruzzo, a huge wildlife preserve, occupies a vast, mountainous tract in the southwest corner of the region. It contains perhaps the only genuine wilderness in Italy, with vast glaciers and forests, and extensive fauna. Furthermore, the park's villages, with their *pensioni* and restaurants, offer more than just the usual trappings of civilization.

Pescassèroli, the park's administrative center, provides the ideal base for explo ration. According to creative legend, the town was founded by a nasty old coun who had taken advantage of Pesca, the beautiful wife of the knight Serolo. After th young lovers died (Pesca of shame, Serolo of grief) the penitent count joined thei names and built the town around their (the dead people's) tomb.

ORIENTATION AND PRACTICAL INFORMATION

Pescassèroli, like most towns in the preserve, is served by ARPA's **Avezzano-Caste di Sangro** bus line (Mon.-Sat.: 6 per day, Sun.: 1 per day). **Avezzano** (on the Rome Pescara train line) lies 1½hrs. by bus from Pescassèroli (L3400), 1½hrs. from Rom (L5400), 2½hrs. from Pescara (L6900), and 2hrs. from L'Áquila (L6000). An ARP bus links L'Áquila with Avezzano hourly (50min., L3400). **Castel di Sangro** (on th Sulmona-Carpinone train line) is 1hr. from Pescassèroli (L2500). In July and Augus an ARPA bus leaves P. Esedra in Rome for Pescassèroli daily (7am) and returns t Rome in the evening (7:30pm, L8000). For more information, call ARPA at (0863 26 561 or 22 921.

In Pescassèroli, the helpful **tourist office** (tel. 91 04 61) waits on Via Piave acros from the police station. Get accommodations and transportation information here (Open daily 9am-1pm and 4:30-6:30pm.) For an overpriced but essential park ma and similarly expensive books on its plants and critters, try the **Ufficio di Zona** (te 919 55), off P. Sant'Antonio. (Open daily 9am-noon and 3-7pm.) At least it's for good cause; profits go toward maintaining the park.

The dreary town of **Avezzano** is notable only for its location on both the Rome Pescara train line and the main bus route though the National Park. The **touris office,** Via Garibaldi, 35/39 (tel. 352 67), lies directly across the piazza from the trai station and ARPA bus stop. (Open Mon.-Sat. 9am-1pm and 4-6pm.)

The town of **Alfedena,** 1km from its train station and 33km from Pescassèroli showcases picturesque archeological sites. Its tourist office (tel. 873 94), in the mai square, stocks information on the ever-open Roman **acropolis** and **necropolis**.

The **telephone code** for Pescassèroli, Opi, and Avezzano is 0863; for Civitell Alfedena, Alfedena, Castel di Sangro, and Pescocostanzo, 0864.

ACCOMMODATIONS, CAMPING, AND FOOD

Avezzano

If you must stay overnight here, opt for **Creati,** Via XX Settembre, 208 (tel. 41 3 47), with singles for L25,000 and doubles for L40,000 (private bath included). Mos restaurants in Avezzano charge exorbitant prices.

Pescassèroli

Most reasonably priced accommodations in Pescassèroli do not offer single rooms but solo travelers can often finagle a double or quad room to themselves for th price of a single. **Locanda Al Castello** (tel. 91 07 57), across from the park office, i comfortable, charming, and convenient to the bus stop and trails. Full pension is good deal, as the meals are plentiful and delicious. (L25,000 per person, L30,00 Aug. and last week of Dec.; ½-pension L45,000 per person, L55,000 Aug. and year' end; full pension L65,000, L70,000 Aug. and the 6 days of Christmas.) 2km uphil from town, but with mountain views, the **Albergo Valle del Lupo,** Via Collach (tel. 91 05 34), rents fresh new rooms. Walk down Viale S. Lucia off P. S. Antoni and turn right along Viale Colle dell'Oro. Follow the signs from there. (Double L50,000, with bath L57,000. Single and off-season prices are negotiable.) There ar four campgrounds within 21km of town; the best is **Campeggio dell'Orso** (tel. 91 55), by the river on the Opi road (L5000 per person, L5000 per tent).

The best restaurant in town is **Pizzeria Ristorante Picchio** on Via Lungo Sangr (tel. 91 23 33). Enjoy delicious *funghi sott'olio* (L3000) and broccoli-stuffed *torte loni* (L7000) in the shadow of two huge wooden mills that once ground flour fo pasta. Cover is L2000. A full meal, including drinks, will cost around L20,000. (Ope

daily noon-3pm and 7-11:30pm; Sept.-June Thurs.-Tues. noon-3pm and 7-11:30pm.)
Get a pre-hike carbo-boost from **Pizzamama,** Via Colli dell'Oro, 18 (tel. 91 27 69);
don't confuse this street, off P. S. Antonio, with the road out of town. Pizza is L1000
per slice, including *pizza al jurapi,* made with a spinach-like plant that only grows
at altitudes above 1600m. (Open daily 11am-3pm and 5-10pm.) The **A&O supermarket** is on Via S. Lucia, the main highway (open daily 8:30am-1pm and 4-8pm).

Opi

ARPA buses follow the winding road through the park to the village of **Opi** (5km).
Two km past the village on the bus route lies the campground **Vecchio Mulino** (tel.
91 22 32; L6000 per person, L5000 per small tent, L10,000 per large tent). At the
turn-off to Camosciara there's an **information center** (tel. 891 70) for foreign visitors. (Open July 10-Aug. Mon.-Sat. 9am-1pm and 2-5pm.)

Civitella Alfedena

10km past Opi, the bus reaches the village of **Villetta Barrea;** 200m down, the
turn-off to Civitella Alfedena leads to the **Pinas Nigra Campground** (L5000 per person, L5000 per tent. Aug. L1000 extra). The site is large and pleasant, bordered by
the River Sangro. In Civitella Alfedena, make yourself at home at the **Alberghetto
La Torre,** Via La Torre (tel. 89 01 21; doubles L40,000; extra bed L15,000). The ice-
cold **Barrea Lake** cuts majestically into the mountains, stretching 7km between Villetta Barrea and the next village of **Barrea.** The **Colle Ciglio** campground, on the
banks of the lake, is 500m above town on the way to Alfedena, 10km from Barrea.

Alfedena

Stay at **Leon D'Oro** (tel. 87 121; singles L20,000, with bath L22,000; doubles
L34,000, with bath L40,000). **Alimentari Crispi,** off the main square, makes *panini*
(sandwiches) from L2000. A track leads from Alfedena to **Lago Montagna Spac-
cata** (3km away), where the intrepid and insulated can brave the freezing mountain
waters.

FOOD FESTIVALS

During August, eat your way through the park by stopping at a food festival free-for-
all. On the 24th day of the eighth month, Opi hosts the **Sagra degli Gnocchi** (gnoc-
chifest), a nationally renowned eat-along that causes an accommodations squeeze as
thousands converge to consume *gnocchi,* sausages, and cheese while watching
exploding *gnocchi* fireworks. (*Gnocchi,* in case you've been wondering, are potato-
flour dumplings whose consistency ranges from delicate puffs that melt in the
mouth to chewy lumps that land with a thud at the bottom of the stomach.)

EXCURSIONS

You don't really enter the park until you begin the scenic ascent on the bus ride
from Avezzano to Pescasséroli. Fields of poppies, rock outcrops, dazzling valleys,
and dizzying vistas will delight you. To avoid gastronomic *déjà vu,* don't eat too
much before this twisting climb. If you don't see any wildlife in the park, compensate in Pescasséroli by checking out the **zoo** on Via S. Lucia, which includes animals
indigenous to the park and information on natural history. (Open daily 10am-noon
and 3-6pm. Admission L3000.)

Once you get off the bus, you'll find the region undeveloped and its trails poorly
marked. Begin by purchasing a trail map (L8000) from the Ufficio di Zona in Pescasséroli. The clear, detailed map points out where the different animals protected
in the preserve—brown bears, chamois, deer, wolves, and eagles—are most likely
to be found. Some of the best trails are within walking distance of Pescasséroli.
From the town center, turn right at the intersection of Viale S. Lucia with the state
road to reach trail B2, a 2½-hour climb skirting Monte Di Valle Carrara; you might
see a bear (hope it's at zoom-lens distance). Make the beautiful 2½-hour hike to **Valico (Pass) di Monte Tranquillo** (1673m). Take trail C3, which starts at the south-

ern end of town, up through the green Valle Mancina past the Rifugio Della Difesa. Keep climbing and you'll eventually reach the pass, with its impressive view of the mountain peaks to the north. For a more extended excursion, take trail D6, across the stream from town, up to trail E3, which leads to the town of Opi (total time 3hr. 30min.). Or take trail D1, at the same starting point, to trails A9 and A1 (3hr. 30min.). To increase your chances of seeing wildlife, continue on trail A2 (1hr.) to A3 (1hr. 30min.).

If you can tune your hiking timetable to that of the ARPA bus line, venture further afield. A scenic hike snakes its way to the **Valle Fondillo,** 9km from Pescasséroli. To reach it, take a bus to the south-bound road just after Opi (it's at km 51; ask the driver). At the end of this road, trail F2 guides you on a pleasant stroll up to the *Valico Passaggio dell'Orso* (1672m, 2hr. 30min. to the top). If you prefer lumpier terrain, **La Camosciara** is the place for you. To get there, hop the bus to Casone Antonucci, just west of Villetta Barrea (at km 55-56). A paved road leads south for about 3km to P. Camosciara. The strenuous one-hour hike takes you to the **Rifugio Della Liscia** (1650m), at the foot of the rocky peaks.

In winter, this area has excellent skiing, with challenging slopes and copious snowfall. Package deals on **settimane bianche** (white weeks) can run as low as L380,000 for room, lift tickets, and half-pension (full pension L425,000). For more information, contact the tourist office in Pescasséroli. For a regional snow bulletin, call (0862) 665 10.

SOUTHERN ITALY

CAMPANIA

In the shadow of Mount Vesuvius, the fertile crescent of Campania cradles the Bay of Naples and the larger Gulf of Salerno. Italy's most spectacular natural setting welcomes scores of tourists with its famous hospitality and a wealth of historic sights. The world-famous pleasure-island of Cápri is still the main attraction of the region and is in yearly danger of sinking under the combined tonnage of invading tourists. Other candidates for the summerly festival of humanity are the stunning Amalfi coast, the ruins of Pompeii and Herculaneum, and the steaming baths on the isle of Íschia. The oft-ignored inland towns, the ruins of Paestum, and the fiery fields west of Naples offer excellent alternatives to crowds and prices of the better-known areas.

Campania's commercial and cultural history has long been bound up with that of Naples, its capital and major port. Naples' strategic location has been coveted ever since it was established as a Greek colony, Neapolis (New City), around 600 BC. Conquered by the Romans in 327 BC, it became a favorite residence of emperors (Nero made his theatrical debut here) and literary personages, including Virgil. Naples reached the zenith of its prosperity when Charles I of Anjou made it his capital in 1266. The city was subsequently enlarged and embellished with elegant palaces and churches. The subsequent years brought a succession of rulers to the region: Spanish Habsburgs were followed by Bourbons, Bonapartes, and finally the Savoys. Campania became part of the unified Italian nation in 1860.

■■■ NAPLES (NAPOLI)

For too many years, Naples has been synonymous with organized crime, corruption, and poverty. At its core, though, Naples is true to the melodrama of the mandolins. It is home to unwavering fatalists, united by family and tradition, not to mention an ever-sacred soccer team. Rich museums, grand palaces, and a proudly extroverted populace define this city far better than the powerful criminals of the invisible Neapolitan Camorra, and the spate of glistening new buildings are evidence of the faith people have in this city's future. Petty thievery does abound, however, so empty your car and leave anything you value in a safe place at the hotel. Still, as long as you follow simple precautions (see the crime section, below), Naples will reward you greatly with its unending supply of sights, shops, and the world's best pizza.

GETTING IN AND OUT OF NAPLES

Hitching in and around Naples is extremely risky.

Naples is southern Italy's transportation hub: frequent **trains** from Stazione Centrale connect the city to Italy's other major cities, including the port of Bríndisi on the Rome-Lecce line (where the ferries to Greece accept Eurail passes). (See Trains for more information.)

Ferries and hydrofoils run from Naples's Molo Beverello to the islands of Cápri, Íschia, and Prócida. The tourist office brochure *Qui Napoli* and the newspaper *Il Mattino* both carry up-to-date ferry schedules. There are also connections to Sardinia and Sicily. Hyrdofoils only (Alilauro and SNAV) leave the port of Mergellina for the islands and Sorrento. Ferry schedules and prices change constantly, so it's best to check ahead. At both ports, large sings clearly show the departures of the several

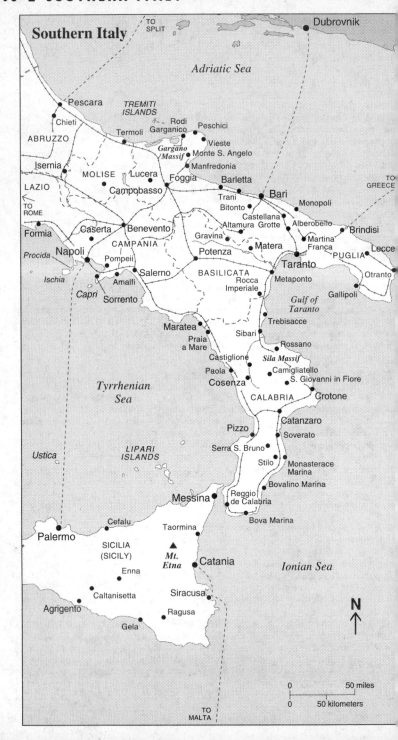

Southern Italy

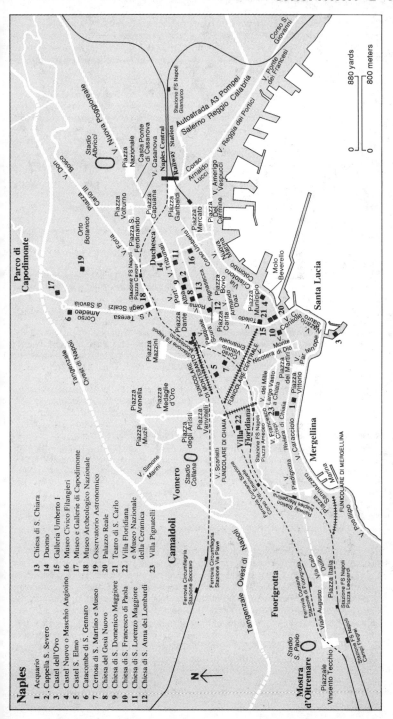

lines. The prices differ minimally between companies. **Caremar** hydrofoils and fer-ries serve all three islands. (To Cápri, 5 per day, 70min., L14,000; to Íschia, 9 per day—5 of these by way of Prócida—70min., L14,000; to Prócida, 6 per day, 60min., L11,000. Less frequent in off-season. Ticket office on Molo Beverello open daily 6am-11pm.) Other key ferries:

Naples-Lípari Islands: Siremar Lines, Agenzia Carlo Genovese, Via Depretis, 78 (tel. 551 21 12, for reservations 761 36 88; open daily 9am-1pm and 3-7:30pm). Ferries leave at 9pm from the Molo Angioino at the Stazione Marittima Thurs.-Tues.; June 1-15 Mon., Thurs., and Sat.; Sept. 27-May 31 Tues. and Fri. To: Strómboli (8hr., L55,000), Lípari (12hr., L60,000), and Vulcano (13hr., L65,000). Fares quoted are June-Sept.; at other times they will be somewhat lower.

Naples-Palermo: Tirrenia Lines, Molo Angioino, Stazione Marittima (tel. 551 21 81). Ticket office open Mon.-Sat. 8:30am-1:30pm and 2:30-7pm, Sun. 3:30-7:30pm. To: Palermo daily at 8pm (11hr., L61,900; Oct.-May L47,900). There is a L2000 port tax upon leaving Palermo.

Naples-Cagliari: Tirrenia. Thurs. and Sat. at 5:30pm; Oct.-May Thurs. at 7:15pm (16hr., L48,400; Oct.-May L37,800).

Naples-Règgio di Calabria-Catania-Syracuse-Malta: Tirrenia. Departs Naples Thurs. at 8:30pm. To: Règgio (10hr. 30min.), Catania (15hr.), and Syracuse (19hr.). All fares L61,900; Oct.-May L47,900. To Malta (25hr., L137,600; Oct.-May L114,000). There is a L15,000 port-tax upon leaving Malta.

Trains: Information, (tel. 554 31 88), lines usually busy. Ticket prices and sched-ules in English and Italian. Also **information booths** and *Digiplan* machines at the Stazione Centrale. Telephone service and information booths open daily 7am-9pm. To: Milan (7hr., L56,700), Rome (1-2 per hr., 2hr. 30min., L15,400), and Syr-acuse (10hr., L43,500). To Bríndisi (for Greece), 6hr. 30min., L27,000.

Flights: Aeroporto Capodichino, Viale Umberto Maddalena (tel. 780 57 63, departures 780 32 35, arrivals 780 30 49), nw of the city. Take bus #14 from P. Garibaldi in the city center. A taxi from P. Dante should be L20,000. Connections to all major Italian and European cities. **Alitalia,** Via Medina, 41/42 (tel. 542 53 33), off P. Municipio. Open Mon.-Fri. 8:45am-5:30pm. **TWA,** Via Partenope, 23 (tel. 764 58 28). They don't handle flights from Naples, but cover Rome and other airports. Open Mon.-Fri. 9am-5:30pm. **British Airways,** Via Partenope, 31 (tel. 764 55 50). Daily flights to London. Open Mon.-Fri. 9am-1pm and 2-5:30pm.

TRANSPORTATION WITHIN NAPLES

Taxis: (tel. 556 44 44). Take only taxis with meters. L2800 plus L100 per 100m or 25sec. (L500 per min.). Sun. and holidays L1200 supplement; 10pm-7am L2000 supplement. L400 per piece of luggage. To the airport should be about L20,000.

Car Rental: Avis, at Stazione Centrale (tel. 28 40 41). Open Mon.-Fri. 8am-1pm and 3-7:30pm, Sat. 8:30am-1pm and 4-6pm. **Hertz,** P. Garibaldi, 69 (tel. 20 62 28). Open Mon.-Fri. 8am-7pm, Sat. 8am-1pm, Sun. 8am-12:30pm. **Europcar,** P. Garibaldi, 69 (tel. 20 65 96), open daily 8am-7:30pm. A small car should be L450,000-550,000 per week at any of these locations.

The city presents numerous public transportation options: bus, tram, subway, funic-ular, and a high-speed suburban train line (*Ferrovia Circumvesuviana*). The fare for all inner-city transport is L1000 per ride. Half-day non-subway passes (6am-2pm or 2-11pm) are valid on buses (ATAN, ACTP, and SEPSA only), trams, and funiculars (L1500, whole-day passes L2500; available in convenience stores throughout the city). Subway passes are the same price but must be purchased separately, and they cannot be used on the other modes of transport. Bus service, especially in the morn-ing and late afternoon, can be a nightmare. People have been known to fall out of or be crushed inside overcrowded buses. To cover long distances (especially from Mergellina to the station), use the efficient and cool subway or tram #4. City buses congregate in P. Garibaldi outside the train station, and have signs clearly indicating their routes and destinations.

Buses #150 and 104: From P. Garibaldi to the center of the city, P. Municipio, and onward to the bay (Riviera di Chiaia) and Mergellina (for the youth hostel and Pozzuoli).

Trams #1 and 4: A picturesque and practical way to get from the station to Mergellina. Stops at the Molo Beverello port. Hop on in front of the Garibaldi statue near Stazione Centrale.

Metropolitana: The subway system is convenient from the train station to points west: P. Cavour (Museo Nazionale), P. Amedeo (funicular to Vómero), Mergellina, and Pozzuoli. Go to platform #4, 1 floor underground, at Stazione Centrale.

Ferrovia Circumvesuviana: (tel. 779 24 44) The fastest way to get to Herculaneum (15min.), Pompeii (45min.), and Sorrento (80min.). One floor underground at the train station.

Funicolare Centrale: The most frequently used of the 3 cable railways to Vómero, connecting the lower city to the hills and S. Martino. Leaves from P. Duca d'Aosta, next to the Galleria Umberto on Via Roma/Toledo.

CRIME

Accompanied by tinkling mandolins, Neapolitans love to glorify their city with a "canzone napolitana," a felicitous and flighty ballad of sun, sea, and *amore*. The Naples of song, however, is only an operatic respite from the modern, urban Naples, a promiscuous and anarchical landscape of haggling market crowds, hell-bent motor vehicles, and packs of volatile youngsters known as *scugnizzi*. Like its *scugnizzi*, Naples possesses an unkempt and dangerous charm that is often difficult to appreciate, especially for the many visitors who fall prey to *lo scippo*, the local term for petty kleptomania.

Women travelers and solo travelers of either sex should be especially on guard, as you will stand out to attackers as potential victims. Follow those common sense safety rules warranted by large cities, and review the Safety and Security and Women Travelers sections in the first part of this book.

ORIENTATION AND PRACTICAL INFORMATION

Naples consists of many *piazze* and quarters. Immense **Piazza Garibaldi,** on the eastern side of Naples, contains the central train station and the major city bus terminal. Broad, tree-lined **Corso Umberto I** leads southwest from P. Garibaldi, ending at P. Bovio. From here Via Depretis branches to the south, leading to P. Municipio and nearby P. del Plebiscito, an area of stately buildings and statues. On the water at the foot of P. Municipio lie **Molo Beverello** and the Stazione Marittima, the point of departure for ferries. Turn north from P. del Plebiscito and go up Via Toledo (also called Via Roma) to reach **Piazza Dante, the university district,** and **Spaccanapoli** (literally "splitting Naples"), a straight, narrow street that changes names every few blocks. Lined with palaces and churches, Spaccanapoli runs through the middle of historic Naples with Roman rectitude. But be careful you don't get yourself *spaccato* by the hordes of youngsters on mopeds who use this alley (only 3 or 4m wide) as a racecourse. To the west, at the foot of the hills, you'll find the **Santa Lucia** and **Mergellina** districts, with their celebrated bayside walks of Via Partenope and Via Caracciolo. Farther west are the most scenic areas of Naples: hillside **Via Posillipo, Via Petrarca** winding up above Mergellina, and **Via Manzoni** running along the crest of the ridge, with stunning vistas from its western end. A park crowns the cliffs of panoramic **Capo di Posillipo.** The hilltop **Vómero** district above Santa Lucia commands a view of Mount Vesuvius to the east, historic Naples below, and the Campi Flegrei (Phlegraean Fields) to the west. The Vómero can be reached by funicular from Via Roma/Toledo or the Montesanto station (northwest of P. Dante).

Tourist Offices: EPT, at the central train station (tel. 26 87 79). Helpful, almost to a fault—you'll have to wait as they exhaustively help the people in front of you. They will also call hotels and ferries for you. Pick up a map and the indispensable guide *Qui Napoli* featuring everything from train schedules to entertainment listings (in English and Italian). English spoken. Open Mon.-Sat. 9am-8pm, Sun. 9am-1pm. **Main office,** P. Martiri, 58, Scala B, second floor (inside Ferragamo's *palazzo*) (tel. 40 53 11). Take bus #150. Open Mon.-Fri. 8:30am-2:30pm. Also at Stazione Mergellina (tel. 761 21 02) and the airport (tel. 780 57 61). In theory open Mon.-Fri. 8:30am-2pm and 5-7:30pm. **AAST information office,** P. Gesù Nuovo (tel. 552 33 28). Take bus #185 up Via Roma toward P. Dante, get off at Via Capitelli, and follow it to the piazza—right in front of the Chiesa del Gesù Nuovo. The most helpful and professional office in the city. Open Mon.-Sat. 9am-7pm, Sun. 9am-2pm. Other offices at Castel dell'Ovo (tel. 764 56 88) and at the hydrofoil port in Mergellina (tel. 761 45 85). **Note:** Plans are in the works to streamline procedures by combining the two main tourist agencies into a single APT office; consequently some of this information may change. For specific information on arts and entertainment, check out the *Posto Unico,* a poster/calendar covering theaters, restaurants, and clubs. **Qui Napoli Computer Information,** terminals located throughout the city in public buildings and sights, offers tourist information and more. Yes, the computers speak English.

Budget Travel: CTS, Via de Gasperi, 35 (tel. 552 00 74). Student travel information, ISIC/FIYTO cards, and booking service. Open Mon.-Fri. 9:30am-1pm and 3-6pm, Sat. 9:30am-12:30pm. **Eurostudy Travel,** Via Mezzocannone, 87 and 119 (119 is the main office) (tel. 552 06 92/09 47 and fax 551 16 42). Open Mon.-Fri. 9:30am-1:30pm and 3-6pm. **CIT,** P. Municipio, 70-72 (tel. 554 54 26). The city's most complete travel agency. Open Mon.-Fri. 9am-1pm and 2:30-6pm. For ferry reservations to Greece, go to **Travel and Holidays,** Via Santa Lucia, 141 (tel. 764 01 29). Take bus #150 from P. Garibaldi. Open Mon.-Fri. 9am-1:30pm and 3-6:30pm, Sat. 9am-1:30pm. **Italian Youth Hostel Organization (Associazione Alberghi Italiani per la Gioventù),** Salita della Grotta, 23 (tel. 761 23 46). An excellent resource for information on youth hostels and special HI and Transalpino plane, train, and ferry discounts. HI cards L30,000. Open Mon.-Fri. 9am-1pm and 4:30-7pm, Sat. 9am-1pm; Oct.-June 9am-1pm and 4-7pm, Sat. 9am-1pm.

Consulates: U.S. (tel. 761 43 03 or 583 81 11; phone lines open 24hr.), on P. della Repubblica (sometimes called "P. Principedi Napoli" on maps) at the western end of the Villa Comunale. Passport and consular services. Mon.-Fri. 8am-1:30pm, mid-Sept.- June Mon.-Fri. 9am-12:30pm and 3-5:30pm.

Currency Exchange: The few banks willing to change money charge commissions of L3000. Try one of the banks' main offices for the most efficient transactions. Closest to the train station is **Banca Nazionale del Lavoro,** P. Garibaldi (tel. 799 71 13), at the corner of Corso Umberto. Open for exchange Mon.-Fri. 8:30am-1:30pm and 2:45-4pm. You can also exchange in the Stazione Centrale, which has the longest hours but bad rates. Open daily 8am-1:30pm and 2:30-8pm.

American Express: contrary to the information printed in the 1993 *American Express Traveler's Companion,* the office in Naples has closed.

Post Office: P. Matteotti (tel. 551 14 56), off Via Diaz, which runs off Corso Umberto at its western end. Fermo Posta L250 per letter retrieved. Offers special *CAI post* service (Posta Celere), which delivers packages anywhere in the world in 3 days (in Europe, starting from L28,900, to USA, starting from L49,500 for packages up to 1kg). Open Mon.-Fri. 8:15am-1:30pm, Sat. 8:15am-12:10pm. Also at Galleria Umberto and Stazione Centrale (both open same hours). **Postal code:** 80100 (for Fermo Posta at P. Matteotti).

Telephones: ASST, at Stazione Centrale. Also at Via Depretis, 40, on the street off P. Bovio at the end of Corso Umberto, heading south towards P. Municipio. Both open 24 hrs. **SIP,** at Galleria Umberto. Open daily 9am-5pm. Also at Via Petronio, 8-18, off Via N. Sauro along the water in Santa Lucia. *Gettoni* and *scheida* cards only. Open daily 8:30am-10pm. The Via Depretis office has the shortest lines. **Telephone Code:** 081.

English Bookstore: Feltrinelli, Via S. T. d'Aquino, 70/76 (tel. 552 14 36). Turn off Via Roma/Toledo onto Via Ponte di Tappia at the Motta restaurant. The store is 20m ahead on the left. An extensive selection, including yours truly. Open Mon.-Fri. 9am-8pm, Sat. 9am-1:30pm. **Universal Books,** Rione Sirignano, 1 (tel. 66 32 17), upstairs on the 1st floor, near Villa Comunale, 1 block east of Via Santa Maria in Portico. Multilingual. Open Mon.-Fri. 9am-1pm and 4-7pm, Sat. 9am-1pm.

So, you're getting away from it all.

Just make sure you can get back.

AT&T Access Numbers
Dial the number of the country you're in to reach AT&T.

*ANDORRA	19◇-0011	GERMANY**	0130-0010	*NETHERLANDS	06◇-022-9111
*AUSTRIA	022-903-011	*GREECE	00-800-1311	*NORWAY	050-12011
*BELGIUM	078-11-0010	*HUNGARY	00◇-800-01111	POLAND¹◆²	0◇010-480-0111
BULGARIA	00-1800-0010	*ICELAND	999-001	PORTUGAL¹	05017-1-288
CROATIA¹◆	99-38-0011	IRELAND	1-800-550-000	ROMANIA	01-800-4288
*CYPRUS	080-90010	ISRAEL	177-100-2727	*RUSSIA¹ (MOSCOW)	155-5042
CZECH REPUBLIC	00-420-00101	*ITALY	172-1011	SLOVAKIA	00-420-00101
*DENMARK	8001-0010	KENYA¹	0800-10	SPAIN	900-99-00-11
*EGYPT¹ (CAIRO)	510-0200	*LIECHTENSTEIN	155-00-11	*SWEDEN	020-795-611
*FINLAND	9800-100-10	LITHUANIA◆	8◇196	*SWITZERLAND	155-00-11
FRANCE	19◇-0011	LUXEMBOURG	0-800-0111	*TURKEY	9◇9-8001-2277
*GAMBIA	00111	*MALTA	0800-890-110	UK	0800-89-0011

Countries in bold face permit country-to-country calling in addition to calls to the U.S. *Public phones require deposit of coin or phone card. **Western portion. Includes Berlin and Leipzig. ◇Await second dial tone. ¹May not be available from every phone. ◆ Not available from public phones. ²Dial "02" first, outside Cairo. ¹Dial 010-480-0111 from major Warsaw hotels. ©1993 AT&T.

Here's a travel tip that will make it easy to call back to the States. Dial the access number for the country you're visiting and connect right to AT&T **USADirect®** Service. It's the quick way to get English-speaking operators and can minimize hotel surcharges.

If all the countries you're visiting aren't listed above, call **1 800 241-5555** before you leave for a free wallet card with all AT&T access numbers. International calling made easy—it's all part of **The _i_ Plan.**℠

Let's Go wishes you safe and happy travels

These people are only a third of the 150 students who bring you the *Let's Go* guides. Most of us were still out on the road when this photo was taken, roaming the world in search of the best travel bargains.

Of course, *Let's Go* wouldn't be the same without the help of our readers. We count on you for advice we need to make *Let's Go* better every year. That's why we read each and every piece of mail we get from readers around the globe — and that's why we look forward to your response. Drop us a line, send us a postcard, tell us your stories. We're at 1 Story Street, Cambridge, Massachusetts 02138, USA. Enjoy your trip!

NAPLES

Luggage Storage: around the corner from the pharmacy in the train station. L1500 per piece per day. Open 24 hrs.

Late-Night Pharmacy: tel. 26 88 81, at Stazione Centrale (leaving the tracks, head to the left by the fountain). Open Mon.-Sat. 8am-8pm. Call 192 for the 24-hr. recording of nighttime pharmacies (in Italian).

Emergencies: tel. 113. **Police:** tel. 794 11 11. English speakers always available. **Ufficio stranieri:** at the Questura, Via Medina, 75, at Via Diaz. **Medical Assistance: Ambulance,** tel. 752 06 96. **Guardia Medica Permanente** (tel. 751 31 77), in the Municipio building, for medical assistance at night or during holidays. **Psychiatric First Aid:** tel. 743 43 43.

ACCOMMODATIONS

When you arrive at the central train station, hotel-hawkers will invariably approach you. If you do need to stay near the train station, and all you want is a cheap bed for the night, this may be the easiest route. Check *Let's Go* first, though, and seek out a good-quality, safe place. However, unless you're only staying over in Naples to catch an early train or ferry the next day, you really should avoid the area around Piazza Garibaldi. Filth, noise, and vice are pervasive—many hotels rent rooms by the hour—and it's particularly unsafe at night, and will leave you with a drastically skewed impression of Naples. There are better alternatives in the area around the **university,** between P. Dante and the *duomo*. Hotels here cater primarily to students and offer well-furnished, immaculate rooms at low prices, though vacancies decrease when school is in session. The **Mergellina** area at the far end of the waterfront (served by subway and trolley) commands outstanding views of Vesuvius and Cápri, but hotels and restaurants range in price from expensive to exorbitant.

Seriously consider paying more for added comfort, security, and respectability in Naples. Always agree on the price *before* you unpack your bags, never give up your passport before seeing your room, and be alert for shower charges, obligatory breakfasts, and the like. When selecting a place to stay, check for double-locked doors and door buzzers. The **ACISJF,** at the Stazione Centrale (tel. 28 19 93) near the EPT, helps women find safe and inexpensive rooms. (Open Mon.-Fri. 3-7pm, Tues., Fri., Sat. 9:30am-1pm and 3-7pm.) Phone numbers are posted at the booth in case nobody's home (or try tel. 40 41 28). For additional information on women-only accommodations contact the **American Women's Club** (tel. 575 00 40). If you have a serious complaint, call the EPT's special number: 40 62 89. (English spoken.) For information on **camping,** see Near Naples below.

Ostello Mergellina (HI), Salita della Grotta, 23 (tel. and fax 761 23 46). Take the Metropolitana to Mergellina and make 2 sharp rights onto Via Piedigrotta. Follow the street underneath the overpass and follow the signs up to your right (*before* you get to the tunnel). A 15-min. walk from the subway and not far from the waterfront. Overpriced, but one of the safest places to stay on a budget in Naples. Well-maintained 2-, 4-, and 6-person rooms, all with bath. Although there are 200 beds, it's best to reserve in July-Aug. Someone is always there, so you can leave luggage. Lockout 9:30am-4:30pm. Check-out 9am. Curfew 11:30pm. L18,000 per person. If you are not a member, you must pay L5000 extra per night. Each such payment earns you a stamp, and with 6 stamps you receive a hostel membership that's good for one year. Breakfast, sheets, and shower included. The self-service cafeteria downstairs offers à la carte items and full meals for L12,000.

Near Piazza Dante and Vómero

Take bus #185, CS, or CD from the train station to the bargain rooms around P. Dante. Although we wouldn't advise walking around here late at night, it makes an acceptable central base for cautious tourists. To reach the more serene Vómero, get off any of the buses running up Via Roma/Toledo toward P. Dante near Galleria Umberto, and take the funicular up.

Albergo Imperia, P. Miraglia, 386 (tel. 45 93 47). From P. Dante, walk east through the arch to the left of the clock tower. Continue on Via San Pietro a

Maiella, to the right of Pizzeria Bellini. Continue walking through a small piazza. At the end, look for two large grey doors on the right side of the narrow street. A 4-floor climb to bright, clean, and recently renovated rooms. Young management accustomed to working with students. Convivial TV room makes a great meeting place. English spoken. Pay telephone. Singles L21,000. Doubles L34,000. Showers included. Call 1 or 2 days in advance July-Aug. and at Easter.

Albergo Duomo, Via Duomo, 228 (tel. 26 59 88). Capacious white-and-baby-blue-trimmed rooms, all with bath. Immaculate. Doubles L70,000. Triples L90,000. Quads L110,000. *Matrimoniale* L50,000. Curfew 1-2am.

Pensione Margherita, Via Cimarosa, 29 (tel. 556 70 44 and 578 28 52), on the 5th floor, in the Vómero outside the central funicular station. A fancy hotel that charges the lowest prices in this posh district. Pleasant breakfast room with paintings, color TV, and oriental rugs. Often full. English spoken. Curfew midnight. Singles L40,000. Doubles L72,000. Triples L99,000. Breakfast and showers included (L1000 for a towel).

Near Piazza Bovio

Albergo Orchidea, Corso Umberto, 7 (tel. 552 40 07), scala B, on the 5th floor. On this noisy but relatively safe piazza you'll find dazzling, high-ceilinged rooms with small balconies and great views (some with views of the sea). All rooms with private shower. Doubles L80,000. Triples L100,000. Quads L120,000.

Near Mergellina and Santa Lucia

More scenic and serene than P. Garibaldi or P. Dante, Mergellina and Santa Lucia harbor a few choice accommodations. Keep on the main streets along the waterfront at night, though, as the small, sinewy alleys can be dangerous.

Pensione Teresita, Via Santa Lucia, 90 (tel. 764 01 05). Cozy and feels secure inside. Singles L30,000. Doubles L40,000. Some rooms have refrigerators.

Near Piazza Garibaldi

Casanova Hotel, Via Venezia, 2 (tel. 26 82 87). Take Via Milano off P. Garibaldi and go left at its end. A good (though noisy) option in a ramshackle region. Airy, clean rooms, knowledgeable management, and a rooftop terrace with bar service. Doubles L40,000, with bath L52,000. Quad with bath L90,000. Breakfast L4500.

Hotel Ginevra, Via Genova, 116 (tel. 28 32 10). Turn right immediately as you exit the station. Walk 2 blocks up Corso Novara, and take the second right onto Via Genova. Pleasant, bright rooms, some with TV. Singles L25,000. Doubles L45,000, with bath L50,000. Breakfast L3500. Laundry service (L4000 per load). Show them your *Let's Go* guide to obtain these rates.

Hotel Prati, Via Rosaroll, 4 (tel. 554 18 02, fax. 26 88 98). Take Corso Garibaldi to the right from the far end of P. Garibaldi to P. Principe Umberto. Well-decorated rooms complete with mini-balconies, phones, wooden dressers, and tiled bathrooms. Very professional, but at the expense of charm. Color TV and fridge in room. English spoken. Special prices for *Let's Go* users: doubles with bath L120,000. L30,000 per additional person. Breakfast L6000. Lunch and dinner L20,000 each. Major credit cards and traveler's checks accepted.

Albergo Zara, Via Firenze, 81 (tel. 28 71 25). From the train station, turn right onto Corso Novara, then take the 1st left. Clean rooms with peeling neoclassical ceilings. Cozy TV room. Singles, doubles, and triples, with or without bath. L25,000 per person.

Hotel de la Ville, Vico S. Alessio al Lavinaio, 16 (tel. 554 03 97). Take a left onto Corso Garibaldi from P. Garibaldi and hang a right on "Il Traverso Garibaldi," which becomes Via Alessio. Less grandiose than its name would imply, the Hotel de la Ville nonetheless offers fine rooms at good rates. Singles L25,000. Doubles L40,000, with bath L50,000. Flash your *Let's Go* for best prices. Traveler's checks.

FOOD

Pizza, that world-famous concoction of crust, tomatoes, and cheese, was an invention of Neapolitans. The unique combination of the skill of the *pizzaiolo* (pizza chef), the sweet local tomatoes, fresh mozzarella cheese, extra-light dough, and a wood-burning oven makes for an exquisite pie. Stands throughout the city sell slices of pizza fresh out of the oven for L1000 each—they're popular late-morning snacks. (Try the stands around P. Capuana and P. Mercato, to the north and south of the train station.) Naples's most venerable (though not oldest) *pizzeria* is **Antica Pizzeria Da Michele,** Via Cesare Sersale, 1/3 (tel. 553 92 04), to the right off Corso Umberto not far from the train station. They only make the two original types of pizza, *Marinara* (tomato, garlic, oregano, and oil, L3000) and *Margherita* (tomato, mozzarella cheese, and basil, L3500). (Open Sept.-mid-Aug. Mon.-Sat. 8am-10pm.)

Seafood in all of its glorious incarnations is the pearl of Neapolitan cuisine. Enjoy the mussels of the gulf in *zuppa di cozze* or *cozze al limone,* or savor *vongole* of all varieties, including razor clams and their more expensive cousin, the oyster. *Aragosta* (crayfish) are sweeter than lobster, and *polipi* (octopus) is one of the cheapest sources of protein around. The city's most notable wines are *lacrima christi* (Christ's tears) which accompanies the seafood, and the red *gragnano.*

Spaghetti, now an Italian staple, was first boiled in the pots of Neapolitan kitchens—and don't mumble any nonsense about Marco Polo and China to the Neapolitans if you want to stay on their good side. Today, Naples's most famous pasta dishes are the savory *spaghetti alle vongole* (with clams) and *alle cozze* (with mussels); both are served in their shells atop the pasta.

Naples's most beloved pastry is *sfogliatella,* filled with sweetened ricotta cheese, orange rind, and candied fruit. It comes in two forms, *riccia,* flaky-crusted variety, and *frolla,* a softer, crumbly counterpart. The city's foremost *sfogliatella* producer is **Pintauro,** Via Roma/Toledo, 275 (tel. 41 73 39), a tiny, worn-marble bakery that has been around since 1785. It sells both varieties, piping hot, for L1300 each. (Open May-July Mon.-Sat. 8:30am-7:30pm, Sept.-April Mon. 8:30am-7:30pm.)

Have fun at Neapolitan **markets.** On **Via Soprammuro,** off P. Garibaldi, you can create your own repast from the street market's edible grab bag. (Open Mon.-Sat. 8am-1:30pm). Find food downstairs at the **STANDA supermarket** at Via Roma/ Toledo, 128. (Open Mon.-Fri. 9am-1pm and 4-7:45pm, Sat. 9:10am-1pm.)

Near Piazza Dante

The historic center around P. Dante, served by buses #185 and CD, shelters some of the city's most delightful *trattorie* and *pizzerie.* Amidst its narrow, winding streets, you'll find some of the cheapest eats on Via dei Tribunali.

Pizzeria Sorbillo, Via Tribunali, 35. A testimony to Neapolitan pizza-making culture. The cheapest pizza in the area (from L2500). In summer, try your pizza with *filetto* (fresh tomato chunks) for L1000 extra. Beer L2000. Service 10%. Open Mon-Sat. 11:30am-3pm and 7-11pm.

Pizzeria Port'Alba, Via Port'Alba, 18 (tel. 45 97 13), inside the Port'Alba arch on the left side of the P. Dante clock tower. Established in 1830, this is the oldest *pizzeria* in Italy. The *vecchia pizza Port'Alba* is the chef's chef d'oeuvre, split into quarters, one with shrimp and calamari, one with tomato and mozzarella, one with capers and olives, one with mushrooms, and in the center a little surprise (L8000). The *pescatore* is loaded with seafood (L8000). The restaurant's non-pizza offerings are also good. Cover for *pizzeria* L1000, for restaurant L2000. Service 15%. Open Thurs.-Tues. 9am-2am.

Le Bistrot dell'Università, Via Sedile di Porto, 51 (off Via Mezzocannone near Corso Umberto). Picnic tables draw an informal college crowd. You'll be hard pressed to beat their L11,000 lunch including cover and service (but not drinks). *Primi* from L3500. Open for lunch Sept. to mid-Aug. Mon.-Fri. noon-4pm. From-Sept.-June the menu goes South American at night (open Wed.-Mon.).

Trattoria Fratelli Prigiobbo, Via Portacarrese, 96 (tel. 40 76 92). Turn off Via Roma at the Motta restaurant and walk 2 blocks. Dirt-cheap seafood *secondi* like roasted *calamari* (L6000). *Primi,* including *gnocchi alla mozzarella,* around L3000. They also have pizza (L3000-5000). Wine L2000 for a ½ bottle. Cover L500. Open Sept. to early Aug. Mon.-Sat. 9am-11pm.

Ristorante-Pizzeria Bellini, (tel. 45 97 74) at corner of Strada Sta. Maria Costanti-nopolo and Via San Pietro, by Port'Alba. Service is slow, but scrumptious entrees make up for it. Fresh fish. Try the *bucatini alla Bellini,* thick spaghetti-like pasta with eggplant, peppers, peas, mushrooms, basil, and mozzarella (L7000). Cover L1500. Service 13%. Open Mon.-Sat. noon-2:30pm and 7:30-10:30pm.

Gelateria Della Scimmia, P. della Carità, 4 (tel. 552 02 72). The bronze monkey that hangs in the storefront has come to symbolize superior ice cream and des-serts. Try the *formetta,* an ice cream sandwich with thin crispy wafers—you pick the flavors (L2000). Cones L1500-3000. Open Thurs.-Tues. 10am-midnight.

Piazza Amedeo and Santa Lucia

Piazza Amedeo, with its own *metropolitana* stop, is a favorite hangout of Naples's chic youth. Along its scenic avenues, just north of the Villa Comunale park, you'll find several trendy *caffè* and pubs. Restaurant prices are high, but you can explore the streets for great snack-bars.

Osteria Canterbury, Via Ascensione, 6 (tel. 41 35 84). Take Via Vittoria Colonna off P. Amedeo, make the 1st right down a flight of stairs, then turn right and immediately left. The best affordable meals in the area. The elegant interior, with lots of wood and fresh flowers, prepares your senses for a delicious meal. Devour the pilgrims' favorite *penne di casa Canterbury* (pasta with eggplant, cheese, and tomato sauce, L9000). Cover L2000. Open Sept.-July Mon.-Sat. 1-3pm and 8:30pm-midnight.

Pizzeria Trianon da Ciro, Via Parco Margherita, 27 (tel. 41 46 78), off P. Amedeo. Same old name, but it's on the cutting edge of Neapolitan *pizzerie.* This stylish and modern place caters to a snobby crowd, but has gained a popular following for its gigantic pizzas (L6000-10,000). *Pizza Trianon* is their hallmark, with 4 dif-ferent sections (L12,000). Cover L2000. Open daily noon-4pm and 6pm-1am. All credit cards accepted. Reservations may be necessary Saturday nights.

Mergellina

Take tram #1 or the subway to **Mergellina,** (4th stop from P. Garibaldi, the first after the tunnel) southwest of P. Amedeo on the waterfront. It's an excellent area for informal but hearty Neapolitan dining. **Piazza Sannazzaro,** in the center of Mergel-lina, is famous for its many *trattorie,* which serve the beloved local *zuppa di cozze.* Via Piedigrotta and the surrounding streets also present affordable alternatives.

Antica Trattoria al Vicoletto, Via Camillo Cucca, 52 (tel. 66 92 90). From the subway exit, walk across the street onto Via Piedigrotta. Follow it about 150m until you see the sign, then turn left into the narrow alley. The food here is *puro, genuino,* and *economico.* An incredible full meal 15,000 (served during the day only; cover and service—but not drinks—included). Try the *tagliatelle al vico-letto,* with eggplant, peppers, tomato, and pesto (L7000). Cover L2000. Service 15%. Open Sept.-July Mon.-Sat. noon-3pm and 7pm-1am.

Pizzeria Da Pasqualino, P. Sannazzaro, 79 (tel. 68 15 24). Outdoor tables and amazing pizza (L4000-8000). Terrific seafood and fried snacks. The *cozze impe-pata* (mussels in pepper broth, L7000) really spices things up. Wine L5000 per bottle. Cover and service included. Open Nov.-Sept. Wed.-Mon. noon-midnight.

Vómero

A cable car up to Vómero brings you to the city's favorite culinary enclave. Restau-rants are generally more expensive, but **Via Bernini** and **Via Kerbaker,** both off Via Scarlatti near the funicular stations, offer some traditional *trattorie.*

Trattoria La Pentolaccia, Via Kerbaker, 124 (tel. 556 71 34). Enter around the corner at P. Durante, 1. A sweet place with lots of locals. Excellent house wines L3000 per liter. Go for the house fish specialty, *farfelle salmone* (L6000). *Pasta e fagioli* L4000. For a savory *secondo* try stuffed squid (L6000). Cover L1000. Open Sept.-July Mon.-Sat. 12:30-3pm and 8-11:30pm.

Trattoria da Sica, Via Bernini, 17 (tel. 556 75 20). Family-run with traditional Neapolitan fare like *vermicelli alla puttanesca* (pasta with tomatoes, olives, and capers, L76000) and *pasta e fagioli* (pasta and bean soup, L5000). Excellent wines from L4000 per bottle. Frequented almost solely by natives. Cover L1000. Service 12%. Open Oct.-Aug. Fri.-Wed. noon-3:30pm and 8pm-midnight.

Osteria Donna Teresa, Via Kerbaker, 58 (tel. 556 70 70). Wonderful, homey place. Most dishes less than L5500. Try the excellent *pasta al forno* (baked pasta, L6000). Their specialty is *spaghetti alle vongole* (L8000). They offer a complete meal (*primi* and *secondi*, plus a glass of wine) for L15,000. Wines L2000 per bottle. Bread L500. Open Sept.-July Mon.-Sat. noon-3pm and 8pm-midnight.

Near Piazza Garibaldi

Tourist-ridden, expensive, and mediocre restaurants dominate P. Garibaldi. Fortunately, high-quality low-cost meals can be found on the side streets just off the piazza. These areas become seedy at night, so eat early.

Trattoria Da Maria, Via Genova, 115, the 2nd right off Corso Novara. No sign. In a city where tradition, simplicity, and hospitality come first, Papà Riccio and his family have kept their small, unrefined *trattoria* true to the Neapolitan style. All pasta L4000. The popular favorite is *bucatini alla puttanesca* (pasta with tomatoes, olives, and capers). *Secondi* from L5000. Local wines L3500-5000. No cover, no service. Open Mon.-Sat. noon-3:30pm and 6:30-10pm. Closed Aug. 15-30.

Pizzeria Trianon da Ciro, Via Pietro Colletta, 44/46 (tel. 553 94 26), near Antica Pizzeria da Michele. From P. Garibaldi, follow Corso Umberto, take a right 200m down on Via Egizaca a Forcella, then a left at the 1st piazza. With marble tables and wood-burning ovens, this ancient *pizzeria* is just as famous as Da Michele down the street, and many prefer its larger and more innovative selections (such as *8-gusti,* a pizza divided into 8 differently flavored sections, L12,000). Beer or soda L2000. Service 15%. Open Mon.-Sat. 10am-4pm and 6-11:30pm, Sun. 6-11:30pm.

Avellinese da Peppino, Via Silvio Spaventa, 31/35 (tel. 28 38 97). From the train station, take the 3rd left on P. Garibaldi. In a well-lit area. Locals and tourists dine in at the outdoor tables, lured by the tasty seafood dishes. Unparalleled *spaghetti alle vongole* (L6500). *Gragnano* wine L4500 per bottle. *Menù* L16,000. Cover L1000. Service 10%. Open daily 11am-midnight.

Trattoria Spina, Piazza Portanova, 1 (tel. 553 99 53). From P. Garibaldi, walk down Corso Umberto, through P. Nicola Amore, and take your 1st right onto Via Starace. On the left in the little piazza just ahead. *Primi* from L4000; try their specialty, *pasta e ceci* (pasta with chick peas, L4500). Or cool off with their splendid *insalata caprese* (buffalo mozzarella, tomato, and basil, L6000). Cover and service included. Open Tues.-Sun., noon-4pm.

SIGHTS

Don't be deceived or disheartened by the unpleasant scene that greets you as you exit the train station—not all of Naples is like this. **Piazza Garibaldi,** locally known as the "Zona Vasta," is a confusing conglomeration of hotels, small bars, parked cars, buses, vendors, and black-market dealers. Naples's main artery, **Corso Umberto,** leading away from the piazza, is an impressive boulevard lined with beautiful cast-iron street lamps and 19th-century buildings that metamorphoses into a transvestite strip at night. A couple of detours lead off the *corso* into the interesting alleys of old Naples. To the north, **Via Sant'Agostino alla Zecca** leads to the dilapidated 18th-century church of the same name. The dramatic interior shows a mighty Christ sharing a cloud with St. Augustine. (Church open daily 8am-12:30pm and 4:30-7pm.)

Corso Umberto ends in **Piazza Bovio** at the 17th-century **Fountain of Neptune,** with a view over P. Municipio to the massive **Castel Nuovo.** Charles of Anjou built it in the 13th century to replace the waterfront Castel dell'Ovo, which was too susceptible to attack. The finely modeled central panel of the remarkable double-tiered **Laurana Arch** (1467) adorning the entrance portrays King Alfonso I in his chariot, surrounded by his court. It is one of the earliest examples of Renaissance sculpture in the city, built to commemorate Alfonso's 1443 arrival in Naples. In the courtyard, the elegant Renaissance portal at the entrance to the 14th-century Chapel of Santa Barbara is surmounted by a Madonna and a flamboyant Gothic rose window. The castle proper houses the offices of the city government and is closed to the public, but you can enter the **museo civico,** containing sculptures and frescoes from the 14th and 15th centuries, along with 15th- to 20th-century bronze and silver works. (Open Mon.-Sat. 9am-1pm. Chapel open same hours as museum. Both free.) Continue away from the station past P. Municipio to **Piazza del Plebiscito,** the most decorative square in the city, dominated by the neoclassical **Church of San Francesco di Paola** (1816-1831). The dome, based on Rome's Pantheon and raised high on a drum, dominates the square. The impressive interior, meanwhile, feels more like a Supreme Court chamber than a church. (Open daily 7am-noon and 4-7:30pm.)

In front of the church stand two equestrian statues, one of Charles III (Don Carlos) and the other of Ferdinando I. The 18th-century Palazzo Salerno and the 1815 Palazzo della Prefettura flank them. The plain, three-story façade of the **Palazzo Reale** (1600-1602) balances the curving mass of the San Francesco church. In the series of niches below the façade, fierce late 19th-century statues represent the eight dynasties that ruled Naples. From the courtyard, enter the huge Staircase of Honor. Its 15th-century bas-reliefs depict the battle between Ferdinand of Aragón and René of Anjou. Above, on the second floor, the former royal apartments now house the **Palazzo Reale Museum** and the plush 18th-century **Court Theater.** Many of the rooms are decorated with Gobelins tapestries, and the palace houses an impressive collection of Romantic paintings. (Palace and museum open Tues.-Sun. 9am-2pm. Admission L6000.) Next to the palace presides the **Teatro San Carlo,** the most distinguished opera theater in Italy after Milan's La Scala. Its gray and white neoclassical façade dates from an 1816 rebuilding. The ticket office is open Tues.-Sun. 10am-1pm and 4:30-6pm when there is a performance. Season runs Oct.-June. (Ticket office tel. 797 23 31 or 32, theater tel. 797 21 11.) Also neighboring the palazzo is the **Galleria Umberto,** a four-story arcade of shops and offices constructed between 1887 and 1890 in imitation of Milan's Galleria Emanuele. Its blending of glass and iron exemplifies a late-Victorian wedding of technology and art.

Spaccanapoli (Historic Naples)

Via Roma, also called Via Toledo, begins to the side of P. del Plebiscito at small and busy P. Trieste e Trento and runs through the heart of the city's historic district. Spanish built the street and gave it its original name, Via Toledo. At the corner of the piazza, the Jesuit **Church of San Ferdinando** (1622) contains a lectern, fonts, and chairs bearing the emblem of the king of Spain. A Ribera painting of Sant'Antonio is tucked away in the sacristy. (Church open daily 8am-12:30pm and 4:30-7pm.)

From here, walk up the street, angling to your right through P. Carità to reach P. Monteoliveto, where you'll encounter the unassuming **Church of Sant'Anna dei Lombardi,** a venerable museum of Renaissance sculpture. Its most noted work, Guido Mazzoni's *Pietà* (1492), sits in the chapel at the end of the right transept. In the Piccolomini Chapel, to the left of the entrance, note the beautiful monument to Maria d'Aragona by Antonio Rossellino and Benedetto da Maiano. Walking up Calata Trinità Maggiore from the church, you'll reach **Piazza Gesù Nuovo.** On one side of the *piazza* stands the **Church of Il Gesù Nuovo.** Erected between 1584 and 1601, its dark pyramid-grid façade taken from a 15th-century Renaissance palace. Colored marble and typically florid Neapolitan frescoes adorn the light interior. (Gesù open daily 7:15am-1pm and 4-7:15pm. Sant'Anna open daily 7:15am-1pm.)

On the other side of the square rises the **Church of Santa Chiara,** one of the principal monuments of Medieval Naples. Constructed in 1310, it was rebuilt in a spare Gothic style after being destroyed during World War II. The large, single-aisled apseless interior is littered with medieval sarcophagi and tombs, many decorated with beautiful Gothic canopies. Exit the left side of the church and walk to the right down the side alley to the entrance of the **Convent of the Clarisse.** Straying from the customary intimacy and delicacy of a medieval cloister, two alleys of trellises—decorated with majolica tiles depicting rural and town scenes, carnivals, and myths—crisscross the overgrown courtyard. This lovely, peaceful spot is a welcome rest. (Church open daily 8am-12:30 and 4:30-7:30pm. Cloister open Mon.-Sat. 8:30am-12:30pm and 4-6:30pm, Sun. 8:30am-12:30pm.)

Return to Via Roma/Toledo and walk right past P. Dante onto Via Pessina to the **Museo Archeologico Nazionale** (tel. 44 01 66), Europe's most important archaeological museum. The collection includes the astonishing treasures of Pompeii and Herculaneum. Pick up an English guidebook at the museum's souvenir shop (L8000), since few pieces are adequately labeled. To get to the museum, take the subway to P. Cavour, or take bus CS, CD, or any other going up Via Roma/Toledo, and get off at P. Museo.

Dominating the Great Masters Gallery on the ground floor are the *Farnese Hercules* and the *Farnese Bull,* the largest surviving sculpture from antiquity, carved from a single block of marble. The back hall exhibits portrait busts including the bald, pug-nosed Socrates, and Seneca, with his protruding tongue and loose folds of skin. Subtle, intricate mosaics from Pompeii rest on the mezzanine upstairs—including the *Mosaic of Alexander,* which portrays a young and fearless Alexander routing a terrified army of Persians. The *Medea* captures the anguish of the mythical sorceress as she contemplates killing her children. (Museum open Tues.-Sat. 9am-2pm, Sun. and holidays 9am-1pm. Admission L8000; under 18 or over 60, free.)

The **Church of San Domenico Maggiore** forms one side of a small piazza of the same name off Via Roma/Toledo between P. Carità and P. Dante. A 14th-century church with a 19th-century Gothic interior, San Domenico combines two styles: the pointed arches, windows and the vaulted side aisles are Gothic, but the color and texture of the decor are strictly Neapolitan Baroque. The 13th-century painting that spoke to St. Thomas Aquinas, a resident of the church's adjoining monastery, hangs in the Chapel of the Crucifix (on the right side of the altar in the nave). To the painting's question, "Well hast thou written me, Thomas. What wouldst thou have as a reward?" St. Thomas replied, "None other than thee." The small **Church of Sant'Angelo a Nilo,** across from San Domenico, takes its name from the ancient statue erected here by the Alexandrian colony. The church sports beautiful 15th-century carved wooden doors and the sepulchre of Cardinal Rinaldo Brancaccio, the product of a collaborative effort by the Florentine artists Donatello, Michelozzo, and Portigiana. (San Domenico open daily 8am-12:30pm and 4:30-7pm, Sant'Angelo a Nilo open daily 8am-12:30pm.)

Hidden on Via De Sanctis, a small side street north of P. San Domenico Maggiore is the **Cappella di San Severo.** The chapel, now a private museum, features the *Cristo Velato (Veiled Christ)* by Giuseppe Sammartino, consummated in 1753. Sammartino's remarkable marble veil over the statue of the wounded, prostrate body of Christ continues to confound experts. Many believe he poured a molten substance over the body to create the incredibly lifelike veil. Downstairs through a door to the right, two truly grisly 18th-century corpses, one of them an obviously pregnant woman, stare from glass showcases. One legend claims that the alchemist Prince Raimondo of the San Severos, who built the chapel, killed his wife and her lover by injecting them with a poisonous elixir that happened to preserve their veins, arteries, and vital organs. (Open Mon. and Wed.-Sat. 10am-1pm and 5-7pm, Tues. 10am-1pm, Sun. 9am-1:30pm. Admission L3000.)

Via Benedetto Croce, Via San Biagio dei Librai, and Via Vicaria Vecchia are just three of the names Spaccanapoli takes as it follows the course of the old Roman

Decumanus Maximus. This is the heart of the old city, a narrow way enclosed by tall tenements and decaying *palazzi*. On Via San Biagio dei Librai alone lie the Renaissance **Palazzo Sant'Angelo** (#121), **Monte di Pietà** (Banco di Napoli, #114), and **Palazzo Marigliano** (#37). The street continues, widening at intervals to accommodate churches and monuments. Via San Biagio ends at Via del Duomo, where you'll find the 18th-century **Church of San Giorgio Maggiore.** In the vestibule of its warm yellow interior stand the antique columns and walls of a primitive paleochristian structure. Diagonally across from the church rises the beautiful Renaissance **Palazzo Cuomo** (1464-90). You can enter the foyers of most of these private palaces Monday through Friday roughly 9am-2pm.

The venerable shops of Naples's traditional artisans line Spaccanapoli and the surrounding alleys. Off the piazza of the church of San Domenico Maggiore at **Calace Strumenti Musicali,** Vico San Domenico Maggiore, 9 (up the stairs on the left of the courtyard to the first floor), mandolins, guitars, and other intstruments are still crafted by hand with techniques passed from master to apprentice over generations. (Open Mon.-Sat. 8:30am-6:30pm.) **Scultura Sacra Lebro,** Via San Gregorio Armeno, 41, a family operation, is one of the last to produce hand-carved and painted religious statues. (Open Mon.-Fri. 9am-1:30pm and 4-7:30pm, Sat. 9am-1:30pm.) The most endearing shop in Old Naples may be the tiny **Ospedale delle Bambole** (doll hospital) (tel. 20 30 67), Via San Biagio dei Librai, 81, near Via Duomo, founded in 1899. The mirthful shopkeeper is perfectly suited to his merciful calling. (Open Mon.-Fri. 10:30am-1:30pm and 4:30-8pm, Sat. 10:30am-1pm. Closed three weeks in August.)

Unlike the cathedrals of other Italian cities, Naples's **duomo** loiters on an obscure side street. The church began as a 5th-century paleochristian basilica. The façade, late 19th-century neo-Gothic, retains its original doors. A Baroque veneer covers the Gothic outlines of all the pointed arches in the interior, except in the two chapels on either side of the high altar. The latter are decorated with 14th-century frescoes, which retain their original form. Halfway down the left side enter the **Church of Santa Restituta,** the first Christian basilica of Naples. Built in the 4th century, it preserves its ancient forms in the nave's columns and in a 5th-century baptistry, whose primitive font was hacked out of the floor (the entrance to the baptistry lies at the end of the right aisle). A beautiful 17th-century bronze grille protects the Baroque **Chapel of San Gennaro.** Relics of St. Januarius are said to have stopped lava from Mount Vesuvius at the gates of the city. A silver reliquary is secreted behind the high altar, bearing the head of the saint and two vials of his coagulated blood. According to legend, disaster will strike the city if the blood fails to liquify at appointed times (the first Saturday of May, Sept. 19, and Dec. 16), when boisterous and confident crowds jam the *duomo*. (Cathedral open daily 8:30am-1pm and 5-7:30pm.) Beneath the *duomo*, excavations have exposed remarkable vestiges of Naples's past. Here you can wander the remarkably intact Greek and Roman roads which run under the modern city. (Excavations open for special tours Sat.-Sun. at 10:30am and 11:30am. Tickets must be reserved in advance from the Azienda di Turismo at P. del Gesù.)

Piazza Capuana, between the *duomo* and P. Garibaldi, forms the center of a vibrant quarter of old Naples. Two ponderous towers frame one of the most beautiful Renaissance archways in Italy, the **Porta Capuana.** On one side of the piazza stands the elegant Renaissance **Church of Santa Caterina a Formiello,** built in 1519 to match the gate. (Open daily 9am-12:30pm and 5-7:30pm.) Via Carbonara serves as the quarter's main street. Its neighborhood church, officially **San Giovanni a Carbonara** (closed in 1993), is known by locals as **Santa Sofia.** Its piazza doubles as a soccer field for neighborhood kids.

Santa Lucia and Mergellina

Walk along the bay in the late afternoon or early evening to see the Villa Comunale fill with locals taking their *passeggiata*. Via Sauro in the Santa Lucia section is the traditional place to watch the sunset. The 12th-century **Castel dell'Ovo** (Egg Castle;

open for exhibits only), a massive Norman structure of yellow brick and incongruously converging angles, stands on the promontory of the port of Santa Lucia, dividing the bay into two parts. To the west lies the **Villa Comunale,** a waterfront park dotted with sycamores and palms and graced by sculptures, fountains, and an **aquarium.** The oldest in Europe, it features a collection of 200 species of fish and marine fauna native to the Bay of Naples. (Tel. 583 31 11. Open during the summer Tues.-Sat. 9am-5pm, Sun. 9am-6pm. Admission L3000.) Off the rocks near the Castel dell'Ovo Neapolitans come to sunbathe and swim. A streetcar runs along the Riviera di Chiaia, where at #200 you'll find the **Villa Pignatelli,** one of the few verdant villa grounds left in the city.

At the foot of the hills of Posillipo, **Mergellina** affords the most celebrated view in Naples: climb Via Petrarca to see the panorama to which no postcard can do justice.

Vómero and the Hills

The breezy calm of the hillside residential district of Vómero is an antidote to the frantic pace of the rest of Naples. A full morning, or perhaps two, should be reserved for visiting Vómero's important historical sights, the Villa Floridiana and the Monastery of St. Martin. Funiculars to this area leave from Via Roma/Toledo across from the Galleria, from P. Amedeo, and from P. Montesanto.

The **Villa Floridiana** (entrance at Via Cimarosa, 77) crowns a knoll notable for its camellias, pine trees, and terrace overlooking the bay. The villa itself, a graceful white neoclassical mansion (1817-19), houses the **Duca di Martina Museum,** which contains porcelain, ivory, china, pottery, and a small group of 17th-century Neapolitan paintings (tel. 578 84 18). Surrounding the villa is a tranquil park. (Museum open Tues.-Sat. 9am-2pm, Sun. 9am-1pm. Admission L4000; free for children under 18 and adults over 65. Park open 9am-one hour before sunset—generally 7pm in summer and 4pm in winter.)

The huge Carthusian **Certosa di San Martino** (Monastery of St. Martin) rises from a spur of the Vómero hill near Castel Sant'Elmo. Erected in the 14th century, it was remodeled during the Renaissance and Baroque periods. It now houses the **Museo Nazionale di San Martino** (tel. 578 17 69), documenting the art, history, and life of Naples from the 16th century to the present. (Open Tues.-Sat. 9am-2pm, Sun. 9am-1pm. Admission L6000; free for those over 65 or under 18). The **Castel Sant'Elmo,** begun in 1349 under the Anjou reign, affords a remarkable view from its ramparts. (Open Tues.-Sat. 9am-2pm, Sun. 9am-1pm. Free.)

The **Museo e Gallerie di Capodimonte** occupy a restored 18th-century royal palace set in the sylvan hills north of the National Museum. Masterpieces and kitsch compete for attention along the walls; the former are usually on the second floor, the latter on the first. Among the many works are Massacio's *Crucifixion,* Filippino Lippi's *Annunciation and Saints,* with Florence in the background, Raphael's portrait of Pope Leo X and two cardinals, Michelangelo's stunning drawing of *Three Soldiers,* and two superb Breughels—*The Allegory of the Blind* and *The Misanthrope.* A haunting *Flagellation* by Caravaggio and a copy of Michelangelo's *Last Judgment* (with the figures unclothed as they were originally painted) by Marcello Venusti also hang here. (Open Tues.-Sat. 9am-2pm, Sun. 9am-1pm. Admission L8000; under 18 or over 60, free.) Take bus #110 or 127 from Stazione Centrale, #22 or 23 from P. del Plebiscito, or #160 or 161 from P. Dante. (The gardens surrounding the museum are open daily 7:30am-8pm; off-season 7:30am-5pm or 6:30pm.)

Down Via Capodimonte from the museum, head into the **Chiesa della Madonna del Buon Consiglio,** which Neapolitans refer to as "Little St. Peter's." Inside, in the third chapel on the left (the Chapel to the Duchesses of Aosta), resides a smaller (but still sizeable) copy of Michelangelo's *Pietà.* Outside under the portico sits a copy of his *Moses.* Outside the church, enter the 2nd-century **Catacombe di San Gennaro,** noted for their frescoed early Christian chapels. (Tours given Fri.-Sun. at 9:30, 10:15, 11, and 11:45am. Admission L4000.)

ENTERTAINMENT

The monthly *Qui Napoli* and the weekly poster *Posto Unico,* both available at the tourist office, provide excellent information on happenings in Naples. Most of the information in *Qui Napoli* is translated into English, including brief descriptions of the city's major sites and tour listings. *Posto Unico* publishes lists of films, discos, and clubs (in Italian).

Luglio Musicale a Capodimonte, a series of free classical music concerts, brings top-notch performers to the Museo di Capodimonte grounds on July nights. The tourist office sponsors free folk concerts with typical Neapolitan and Italian songs throughout the year. The concerts are given Tuesday through Sunday from 9:30-11:15pm in the Partenope Hall of the Royal Hotel, Via Partenope, 38. Get a free pass from your hotel or the tourist office.

Naples is liveliest during its many religious festivals. The **Festa di Piedigrotta** on September 7 and of **San Gennaro,** the patron saint of Naples, on September 19, explode with a communal ardor that is unique to Naples. The festival of **Madonna del Carmine,** held on July 16 at P. del Carmine at the southern end of Corso Garibaldi, culminates in fireworks at the Fra' Nuvolo tower. During Christmas, hundreds of crèches (*presepi*) decorate the city. The sepulchre decorations during Easter and the grand Easter parade in the center of town are also noteworthy.

If you want to enjoy the sun but not stray too far from the city, head to the huge rocks off Castel dell'Ovo. Neapolitans gather here in the heat, and many intimate *caffè* lurk on the promontory below the castle proper.

Naples slumbers at night, except for the Sunday evening *passeggiata,* when the Villa Comunale along the bay fills with folks taking in the cool air. The young elite strut their new threads around **Piazza Amedeo.** Via Posillipo beckons those who savor the smell of the sea (take bus #140 from P. del Gesù) and Via Petrarca is ideal for a romantic stroll (take bus #C21 at P. Plebiscito). Or join legions of amorous couples at the scenic park at Capo di Posillipo (take bus #140 to the end). While strolling Via Posillipo, sample an ice cream from **Bilancione,** Via Posillipo, 398/B, near P. San Luigi. It's a Naples tradition. (Open Sept.-July Thurs.-Tues. 10am-11pm.)

Naples's nighttime hotspots include **Casablanca,** Via Petrarca, 101 (tel. 76 948 82); **Chez Moi,** Parco Margherita, 13 (tel. 40 75 26; take the Metropolitana to P. Amedeo); and the larger **KissKiss,** Via Sgambati, 47 (tel. 46 65 66) in Vómero. A respectable crowd frequents all three. They feature dancing Friday through Sunday from 10pm and charge a L15,000-20,000 cover. (KissKiss puckers up during the week as well. All open Sept.-July.) Ask around to get the latest on the club scene. **The Shaker Club,** Via N. Sauro, 24 (tel. 41 67 75; take bus #150 to Via Partenope—it's in the Albergo Miramare), caters to an older crowd with its more refined nightclub atmosphere. Gay men and women hang out at **Bagatto,** Via Partenope (close to the Hotel Royal) and **Jimmy Club,** Via Manzoni, 28 (take bus C21 from P. del Plebiscito). In the Villa Comunale, another hot spot is **Bar Marotta,** on P. Vittoria. None of these bars is exclusively gay.

If the discos are too pricey for you, on summer evenings **P. Bellini** closes to traffic. *Caffés* and bars set their tables out, and young people fill the piazza. You don't even need to order a costly drink (beer L5000 and up) to sit down.

Shopping

Throughout the city, and particularly in the **Duchesca** region off Via Mancini near P. Garibaldi and the **Pignasecca** region off P. Carità, street markets peddle belts, radios, shoes, and other inexpensive items. Never buy electronic products here—even brand-name packages are known to have contained only bricks. As in all crowded areas in Naples, hold tight to your valuables on Pignasecca's streets. (Markets are generally open Mon.-Sat. 9am-sunset; many close Tues. at 2pm.)

If you feel more comfortable window-shopping at fancy stores, the main shopping districts center around **Corso Umberto, Via Roma/Toledo, Via Chiaia** near P. Trieste e Trento, and **Via dei Mille** in the Santa Lucia region. The most modern and expensive shopping district is in the hills of Vómero along perpendicular **Via Scarlatti** and **Via Luca Giordano.** Two affordable clothes chains that sell contemporary Italian casual wear are **Wiscky & Coca** and **Omonimo.**

THE BAY OF NAPLES

■ West of Naples: Campi Flegrei (Phlegraean Fields)

The Bay of Naples originally served as a strategic trading port for the Greeks, who associated its westerly peninsula with the underworld. The volcanic lakes and bubbling mud baths of the Phlegraean (Burning) Fields did not, however, intimidate either the Greeks or Romans: both built major cities here, and scattered the area with imposing monuments.

Pozzuoli

Although somewhat shabby and neglected ever since a 1980 earthquake, **Pozzuoli** has several worthwhile ancient ruins and makes the best base for exploring the Campi Flegrei. It is also the most convenient jumping-off point for the islands of Prócida and Íschia. The town is serviced by subway from Naples's Stazione Centrale and by the Ferrovia Cumana train from Montesanto in Naples (southwest of P. Dante, L1200). Allow a full day to see the sights of the fields, since they are far apart.

Numerous signs point the way, but if you prefer to have a map visit Pozzuoli's **tourist office,** Via Campi Flegrei, 3 (tel. (081) 526 14 81 or 526 24 19), off P. Capo Mazza. (English spoken. Open Mon.-Fri. 9am-2pm.) **Caremar** ferries (tel. (081) 526 13 35) run three times a day to Íschia (1hr. 30min., round-trip L9000) and Prócida (30min., round-trip L5800). Buy tickets at the **biglieterria marittima** on Via Roma.

Accommodations There are only two semi-budget hotels in Pozzuoli, and unfortunately both have garnered reputations as "pay-by-the-hour" spots for errant couples. They are, however, fine for the night if you have no other options. **Hotel Flegreo,** Via Domiziana, 30 (tel. 526 15 23), about 1km down the road from the tourist office, lets small rooms. (Doubles with bath L60,000. Triples with bath L75,000.) **Albergo Paradiso,** Via Campi Flegrei, 52 (tel. 866 54 69), offers fairly roomy, clean doubles (with or without bath for L55,000). (Sept.-July try to knock off at least L5000.) You can reach it either by walking 3km past the tourist office and following the left-curving road when you reach the Arco Felice locality, or by taking the #1 CTP or the SEPSA bus. The **AVERNO** Campsite, SS. Domiziana, 21 (tel. 804 26 66), offers three-star camping for L8000 per person, L8000 per tent.

Food For cheap picnicking, grab your supplies at the **supermarket** across the street from the tourist office. A full meal in Pozzuoli could cost as much as L35,000, but if you limit your dinner to the main course, you could come out on top at **Trattoria Cagi,** Via N. Fasano, 6 (tel. (081) 526 82 55). Their specialties are the vegetarian *ravioli zucca e salmone* and *spigola al sale.* For dessert *panna cotta* is the choice. (Open Tues.-Sat. noon-4pm and 7pm-1am.) Less expensive is **La Lampara,** Via dell'Emperio, 9 (tel. 526 37 62), serves its well-prepared fish dishes and pizza at outdoor tables overlooking the bay. *Farfelle al salmone* is L8000 and pizza ranges L4500-L8000. (Open Thurs.-Tues. 12:30-2pm and 7-11:30pm. Major credit cards accepted.) **Trattoria Da Don Antonio,** Via Magazzino, 20 (tel. 526 79 41), off the port in shabby but ebullient surroundings, caters to the voracious, serving a full meal of fresh seafood with drink for under L25,000. (Open Sept.-July Mon.-Sat. 12:30-3:30pm and 7-9pm.)

Don't leave Pozzuli without trying *zeppole e panzarotti* (fried dough and potato croquettes) from Orsolina right on the port. For a perfect lunch or even afternoon snack, buy some *friselle* at any market or bakery (large, dark, flat, half-donut breads without yeast). Soak them in water, then squish fresh tomatoes on top of them, and (of course) add olive oil and salt.

Sights From the Ferrovia Cumana, take the pedestrian bridge over the tracks, turn left and then right at the big intersection. From there, follow the curving road to P. Capo Mazza. Pozzuoli's **Anfiteatro Flavio,** built under Vespasian between 69-79 AD, boasts unusually well-preserved underground galleries and arenas which show the complicated mechanics necessary for raising and lowering the animal cages. (Open daily 9am-2hr. before sunset. Admission L4000.) From the Metropolitana station, turn right onto Via Solfatara, turn right again on Via Anfiteatro, and follow it to the entrance. The **Tempio di Serapide** was not a temple at all, but an ancient city market that just happened to enclose a statue of the god Serapis. A strange form of volcanic activity, bradyseism, which causes slow earthquakes that can raise or lower the entire region by several feet over the course of a few months, has intermittently submerged, shaken, and lifted this site. With its puddles of water and eerie, half-submerged pillars, the marketplace looks like a miniature Atlantis just risen from the sea. On Via Solfatara, to the right of the Metropolitana station, snag any of the city buses going uphill to get to the still-active **Solfatara Crater.** Alternately, you can easily walk (20min.) from the train station to see the steaming fissures and bubbling mud. (Open 9am-1hr. before sunset. Admission L4000.)

Baia

Many fascinating sights are within easy bus or car ride from Pozzuoli. You might want to pack a lunch before setting out, though, as the areas offer only small over-priced snackbars to appease grumbling bellies. From any of the SEPSA bus stops located throughout Pozzuoli or by way of the Ferrovia Cumana, take the 20-minute ride to **Baia** (L1000), notable for the Roman baths that have recently been excavated there and for its history as an hotbed of ancient hedonism. (Baths open daily 9am-2hr. before sunset. Admission L4000.) A bit to the north is **Lake Averno,** a spooky haunt that Homer and Virgil described as the entrance to Hades.

Cumae

From the Baia area, you can take a bus (L1200 on the Napoli-Torregaveta line) or the Ferrovia Cumana train line to **Cumae,** the most impressive site in the Campi Flegrei. Cumae was the earliest Greek colony on the Italian mainland (founded in the 8th century BC), and the mother of Pozzuoli, Naples, and many cities of the Magna Graecia. Its highlight is the **Antro della Sibilla,** a long gallery built for the Cumaean Sibyl, the most famous oracle west of Greece. In this great hallway, used as a pizza oven prior to its rediscovery in 1932, devotees awaited the Sibyl's prophecies. Ascend the acropolis to the ruined Temple of Jove (take the steep stairs that tunnel up through the rock) which rewards the climb with a vantage to the curving coast. You may be able to sneak into the huge gallery underneath the promontory; it leads past subterranean cisterns to other ruins farther inland. The whole sprawling site requires at least an hour's visit. Bring a flashlight. (Open daily 9am-2 hr. before sunset. L4000.)

Bácoli and Miseno

If you are intrigued by the Campi Flegrei's combination of volcanic coastline, ancient ruins, and provincial modernity, continue out to **Bácoli** and **Miseno,** at the tip of the peninsula. Hike Bácoli's steep streets, then visit its cisterns: the **Centro Camerelle,** on the via of the same name, whose two subterranean levels supplied a Roman villa and the **Piscina Mirabile,** a huge, pillared underground reservoir that supplied the Roman fleet at Miseno. Under Augustus, the port of **Miseno** was joined to the nearby lake to provide a secure anchorage; various remnants of the Roman camp survive above and below water. Explore the village or climb the towering cape; some also hitch through the tunnel to reach the lighthouse.

Further out on the cape, delve into fabulous beaches and countryside. Many visitors camp unofficially near the sea or by one of the many volcanic lakes. There are several sites with facilities in the area—opt for these safer spots if there are less than three in your group. **Vulcano Solfatara,** Via Solfatara, 47 (tel. 526 74 93), offers sites next to the crater for L9000 per person, L7000 per tent (open April-Oct. 15); Pozzuoli's tourist office provides further information on camping.

■ East of Naples: Pompeii, Herculaneum (Ercolano), and Vesuvius

Mount Vesuvius's fit of towering flames, suffocating black clouds, and seething lava meant sudden death for the prosperous Roman city of **Pompeii** in 79 AD. The eruption buried the city—tall temples, patrician villas, massive theaters, and all—under 10 meters of volcanic ash. Successive layers of ash, dust, pebbles, lava, and rock from the sudden eruption preserved not only the buildings but also the remains of a few of its inhabitants, asphyxiated by the heavy cloud of poisonous gas which preceded the lava. On the other side of the mountain, Herculaneum was discovered when 18th-century farmers sank shafts for wells. The analysis of ancient texts soon revealed another, larger city nearby—Pompeii. Covered with soft material (in contrast to the hard tufa stone over Herculaneum), parts of Pompeii were quickly unearthed beginning in 1748, and the remains have provided us with a basic understanding of daily life in the Roman era.

Archaeological findings indicate that Pompeii was inhabited as early as the 8th century BC and that during the 7th century BC, it fell under the influence of Greeks and Etruscans, who developed it as a commercial center. By the 2nd century BC, Pompeii was a mature city with a Hellenic culture typical throughout southern Italy. Falling under Roman influence around 180 BC, the city developed further both as a trading port and as an aristocratic enclave, until its dramatic and untimely death.

Practical Information The quickest route to Pompeii (25km south of Naples) is the **circumvesuviana train** line from Naples's Stazione Centrale (L2500, Eurail passes valid). A less frequent state train leaves from the main track at the station, stopping at Pompeii en route to Salerno (7 per day 7:10am-1:15pm, L2500). Most travelers take the *circumvesuviana's* Naples-Sorrento line, which lets you off at the Pompeii-Villa dei Misteri stop just outside the west entry. An alternative is to take the *circumvesuviana* from Naples toward Poggiomarino and hop off at the Pompeii Santuario (*not* the Pompeii Valle) stop.

To get to the **site** of Pompeii walk straight from the station, take a right across the P. Immacolata and head about 300m down Via Roma until you see the east entrance. (Entrances open 9am-1hr. before sunset (off season around 3pm). Admission L10,000.) The **tourist office,** Via Sacra, 1 (tel. 850 72 55), across from P. Barto Longo on the way to the east entrance, provides free maps and the informative pamphlet *Notizario Turistico Regionale.* (Open Mon.-Sat. 8:30am-1:30pm.) Another tourist office sits near the west entrance on Via Villa dei Misteri (tel. 861 09 13), to the right of the *circumvesuviana* stop.

Accommodations Unless you wish to tour Pompeii extensively, there is no reason to stay overnight in the dull, modern city. **Soggiorno Pace,** Via Sacra, 29 (tel. 863 60 25), charges L20,000 per person, whatever room you ask for. **Hotel Minerva,** Via Roma, 137 (tel. 863 25 87), near the entrance to the site, rents doubles for L45,000 and triples for L65,000. The cheapest alternative is to stay at one of the local campgrounds, which are all near the ruins. Unfortunately, they tend to be somewhat ruined themselves. **Camping Zeus** (tel. 861 53 20), outside the Villa dei Misteri *circumvesuviana* stop, boasts a swimming pool and restaurant (L6000 per person, L5000 per large tent, L4000 per small tent). Not far away, on Via Plinio, the main road that runs from the ruins, **Camping Pompeii** (tel. 862 78 82), with the same ownership and prices as Zeus, has attractive bungalows for L50,000 for two people and L80,000 for four. If you're desperate you can sack out on the floor of its indoor lobby for L6000 per night. These places are eager for customers, so you can usually bargain them down at least 25%.

Food **La Vinicola,** Via Roma, 29, tempts with a pleasant outdoor courtyard and abundant *gnocchi con mozzarella* (potato dumplings with tomato and cheese, L5000). Also try the *zuppa di cozze* for L4000. (Wine L3000 per ½ liter. Cover L1500. Service 15%. Open daily 10am-midnight Sept.-mid-July Sat.-Thurs. 10am-11pm.) More expensive meals are found at the **Trattoria Pizzeria dei Platani,** Via Colle San Bartolomeo, 8 (tel. 863 39 73), down the street from the Museo Vesuviano, where L6000 buys you a plate of *cannelloni.* The *menù* is L16,500 without drinks. (Cover L2000. Service 15%. Open daily 9:30am-7:30pm.)

Sights The east side entrance to the site admits you by the amphitheater, the west side entrance by the Antiquarium. A comprehensive walk-through will probably take four or five hours; pack a lunch and a water bottle as the two snackbars, although fine in a pinch, are rather expensive.

As you enter from the east, the **Grande Palestra** sprawls to your left. The large structure, enclosed on three sides by a colonnade and pine trees, was used by Pompeiian youths for gymnastic exercises and competitions.

The **amphitheater** across from the gymnasium, built in 80 BC, is the oldest extant, and best-preserved in Italy. With seating for 15,000, it looms over a vista of Pompeii and the mountain beyond but is never used for modern events. Next to the gymnasium, the **House of Loreius Tiburtinus** preserves the essentials of a Roman garden—long rectangular pools surrounded by trellises and formal paintings. Walking toward the Forum, which is near the west or "sea" entrance, you'll pass the **teatro grande,** constructed in the Hellenistic Age (200-150 BC) in the hollow of a hill. Parallel to the stage to the left is the much smaller **teatro piccolo,** built later for concerts and ballet. North of the theater stands the **Temple of Isis,** Pompeii's monument to the cult of the Egyptian fertility goddess. Going north from the temple, you will reach **Via dell'Abbondanza,** the main street (1km long), lined with small shops, taverns, and electoral campaign propaganda.

From Via dell'Abbondanza, backtrack toward the east entrance and turn off to the **Casa di Menandro.** Named after Menander, the Greek poet whose fresco was found in the courtyard, the house is one of the largest and most intact in the city. The pool in the atrium, was used to catch rain water from the ceiling opening.

Head west on Via dell'Abbondanza toward the Forum to reach the **Terme Stabiane** (Stabian Baths), and enter through another *palestra.* The separate men's and women's sides each included a dressing room, cold baths (*frigidaria*), warm baths (*tepidaria*), and hot or steam baths (*caldaria*). The world's oldest profession claimed its own territory one street over in the red-light district of **Vico del Lupanare.** At the top of this street is a small brothel consisting of several bed-stalls. Above each of the stalls a pornographic painting depicts with unabashed precision the specialty of the women who inhabited it.

Via dell'Abbondanza ends at the **Forum,** the commercial, civic, and religious center of the city, framing a wonderful view of Vesuvius. The **basilica** (law courts building), which encloses the south side of the Forum, was the largest building in Pompeii and retains parts of its impressive dais in the southeast corner. Three temples also graced the Forum. On the northern side rises the **Temple of Jupiter.** The **Temple of Apollo** sits across the side street from the basilica, almost hidden from the rest of the city (unlike a Greek temple, which usually reigns from atop a hill). The stone in the middle was used as a sacrificial altar. In the **Temple of Vespasian,** on the western side across the forum from the Temple of Apollo, a delicate frieze on the center altar illustrates the preparation for a sacrifice.

Showcases along the western side of the Forum display gruesome plaster casts of some of the volcano's victims, including a crouching pregnant woman and a running boy. The contorted positions of the humans and even a dog are sufficient to convince that the inhabitants were suffocated by the gases of the eruption rather than crushed by its ashen discharge.

North of the Forum, rest in the cafeteria (go up to its roof for the only aerial view of Pompeii) before starting on a walk to the northwest corner of the site and out to the Villa dei Misteri. Walk up to the massive **Casa del Fauno**, in front of the **Casa dei Vetii.** The Casa dei Vetii contains Pompeii's most remarkable frescoes, all crafted in the latest of Pompeii's styles, involving fantastic architectural designs perspective. The tiny room through the halls on the right contains a two-and-a-half-foot marble statue of Priapus proudly displaying his colossal member. This legendary child of Venus and Adonis is pictured elsewhere in town and phallic images are ubiquitous, but your smirks prove you more dirty-minded than the Romans—*phalli* were believed by the ancients to ward off the evil eye. Next to the room a smaller *triclinium* contains some of the most intact examples of the late style of Roman painting.

Two companies offer **tours of the sites.** Call to find out times for the English tours. **COOP Touring** (tel. 536 96 01) and **G.A.T.A.** (tel. 861 56 61). Otherwise a short search is bound to land you in an English tour to savor the gory details of life and death in the ancient Pompeiian culture.

A short walk from the Casa dei Vetii brings you to **Villa dei Misteri.** A renowned cycle of paintings (in the room directly to the right of the entrance) depicts a ritual of initiation into the forbidden cult of Dionysius.

Ercolano (Herculaneum)

Closer to Naples (12km), **Ercolano (Herculaneum)** would have a sublime seaside view if it weren't 10m underground. Take any *circumvesuviana* train toward Pompeii from Naples's central train station to the Ercolano stop (15min., L1600). Walk 500m down the hill from the station to the **ticket office.** (Open daily 9am-1hr. before sunset. Visitors may remain until 30min. before sunset. Admission L8000.) Before entering, consider purchasing the *Amadeo-Maiuri* guide to Herculaneum, the most comprehensive guidebook, available in the bar across the street (L9000). Neatly excavated and impressively intact, Herculaneum contradicts the term "ruins." Once a wealthy residential enclave on the Roman coast road, Herculaneum does not evoke the same sense of tragedy that Pompeii does—all but a handful of its inhabitants escaped the ravages of Vesuvius. In a much less disorienting (and less crowded) tour than those offered in Pompeii, you can wind your way through the 15 or so houses and baths that are now open to the public. There are no colossal buildings, temples, or off-color frescoes to grab your imagination here, but the houses, with their fresh interior decoration, attest to the cultural development of this affluent community. Two-thousand-year-old frescoes, furniture, mosaics, small sculptures, and even wood paneling seem as vital as the day they were made, preserved by a mud avalanche that tumbled off the volcano on a cushion of gas. The **House of Deer,** so named for a statue of a deer being savagely attacked by greyhounds, is one of the more alluring villas. Probably big partiers, the owners had a statue of a *Satyr with a Wineskin* and an all-too-recognizable statue of the town's patron "saint" Hercules in a drunken stupor trying to relieve himself. The **baths** are quite interesting and largely intact. **The House of the Mosaic of Neptune and Amphitrite** belonging to a rich shop owner is famous for its mosaic depicting—well, take a guess.

Near Ercolano: Mt. Vesuvius

Bad luck. The cheap buses that used to run to **Mount Vesuvius,** the only active volcano on the European continent, from Ercolano are no longer running. The only option for those without their own wheels are taxis—be sure to bargain your price. You can ramble to the top of the volcano (½hr.) for a look inside the astounding crater, but you must be accompanied by a guide (L4000). Expert sources say the trip is safe—there has been no eruption since March 31, 1944.

■ Inland From Naples

Caserta

The main reason to visit Caserta, 45 min. from Naples by train (the first leaves from Stazione Centrale at 7:15am; L2800), is the magnificent **Palazzo Reale** (Royal Palace), locally referred to as the "Reggia." Commissioned by Bourbon Charles III in 1752 to imitate Versailles, the enormous palace contains 1200 rooms, 1790 windows, 34 staircases, and an immense garden. The Royal Apartments are decorated with frescoes on the vaults and intricate marble floors. The three libraries with original manuscripts lead to the *Presepe,* an immense Nativity scene enclosed in a glass structure. Carved by Neapolitan sculptors, the scene shows the Holy Family in the middle of an Italian market. (Tel. 32 14 00. Open Mon.-Sat. 9am-1:30pm, Sun. 9am-12:30pm. Admission L6000.) Bring a picnic lunch and enjoy the fountains and waterfall, 11am-3pm, in the gardens behind the palace. (Gardens open daily 9am-1hr. before sunset. L4000.)

The other attraction in Caserta is the haunting medieval town of **Caserta Vecchia.** The Apulian-Romanesque cathedral dates from 1153 and reveals distinct Middle Eastern influence. (6 buses per day (#11) run to and from Caserta Vecchia from Caserta's train station and from P. Vanvitelli, 30min., L1500. You can purchase the ticket at the ACTC booth near the train station.)

Caserta doesn't abound with cheap places to stay, but if you decide to sleep over, the **Albergo Eden,** Via Verdi, 26 (tel. 32 64 95), to the right of the train station as you exit, should have room. (Singles with bath L30,000. Doubles L55,000, with bath L60,000.) Or try **Albergo Limone,** Via Verdi, 52 (tel. 35 42 68), on the same side as Albergo Eden. (Single with bath L40,000. Doubles with bath L65,000.)

Clean, elegant, and economical, **Farina R&V,** Via S. Giovanni, 7-9 (tel. 32 61 38), off Corso Trieste, offers *primi* for L3000-4000 and *secondi* for L8000-10,000. (Open Mon.-Sat. 8am-8pm.) **Tavola Calda Il Corso,** Corso Trieste, 217-219 (tel. 35 58 59). Serves full meals with drink L15,000. (Open Mon.-Sat. 12:30-3:30pm and 5pm-midnight.) **Royal Food,** Via Verdi 16, right next to the train station (tel. 35 42 68), offers *primi* for L4800, *secondi* for L6000. Cover L1000. (Open Mon.-Fri. 7am-8pm, Sun 8am-10pm.)

Caserta's **EPT** is located at Corso Trieste, 37 (tel. 32 11 37), at the corner of P. Dante. Pick up their brochure on the Palazzo Reale. (Open Mon.-Fri. 8:30am-1:30pm, Sat. 8:30am-noon.) Caserta's **postal code** is 81100; its **telephone code** is 0823. The **Post Office** is in P. Vescoriato off P. Vanvitelli. **Telephones:** SIP in Via Roma 53. **Avis Rent-a-Car** in train station (tel. 44 37 56). (Open Mon.-Fri. 9am-1pm, 2-6pm; Saturday 9am-2pm.)

If you happen to be in town around July 26, you may catch the **Festa Sant'Anna,** when music and fireworks light up the town. The beginning of September brings concerts to Caserta Vecchia, in a festival known as **Settembre al Borgo,** with performances given every night for about 20 days including theater, comedy, music and dancing.

Capua

Capua, founded 47 years before Rome on the banks of the Volturno river as Casilinum, gradually transformed into the Roman outpost Santa Maria Capua Vetere, 5km from today's present city. The Anfiteatro Campano (older and bigger than Rome's) was built here; however, most of its blocks were later used to build parts of the other churches and buildings in Capua Nova, once the pillaging and burning of Santa Maria by Saracens forced the inhabitants to escape to the new town.

Capua is just 15 min. by **train** from Caserta (L1600), or ½ hour by **bus** (#6, L1500, bus terminal on the left of the train station.) Locals pride themselves on having had one of the first three senates (along with Rome and Benevento), as well as city walls that are still intact.

To get into the center of the old city from the station, head straight down Viale Ferrovia and across what used to be the town moat; go through the 16th-century Porta Napoli arch, make a right as you face the Teatro Ricciardi, and then your first left, which heads straight into P. dei Giudici.

The **Museo Provinciale Campano,** through the arch at the end of Via Duomo (tel. 96 14 02), has an extensive, important collection of Etruscan, Egyptian, and Roman artifacts as proof of its former greatness. (Open Tues.-Sat. 9am-2pm, Sun. 9am-1pm. Free.) Capua's **duomo,** first built in 856, with its campanile (861) was renovated and enlarged several times, and should not be missed.

Capua's **Pro Loco** keeps its own hours at P. dei Giudici, 12, the town center. Here you can pick up a map and a guide to the sights. (Theoretically open Mon.-Sat. 8:30am-noon and 4-8:30pm.) Those interested in Capua's history need not even spend the night here if they plan it right. If you do, however, try the **Hotel Mediterraneo** Via Nazionale Appia, km 202, 150 (tel. 96 15 75 or 62 26 11). There is a small, winding road on the right outside the train station, ending on Via Appia, and on the right is the Hotel. Or else follow Viale Ferrovia and take a right on Via Appia. Singles L36,000, with bath L46,000. Doubles L60,000, Triples L80,000 and Quads L100,000, all with baths and telephones. (Fax also in the lobby.) And for excellent edibles, try **Da Nino/La Taverna Fieramosca,** with two entrances, one on Via Amalfitano and one on P. Ethiopia. (Pizza in the evenings from L4500, delicious pasta with the sauce of the day L5000. Open Tues.-Sun. noon-midnight. Tel. 62 24 57.) Even cheaper food can be found at the **mercato** in P. Ethiopia (Mon.-Sat. 8am-1pm). The generous proprietor at **Ristorante Romano,** Corso Appio, 34-36 (tel. 96 17 26), serves full meals for about L17,000. Pizza L3000 and up. (Open Wed.-Sun. 6pm-1am. AmEx and Visa.)

Benevento

The countryside around Benevento is enchanting. The town was first called *Maleventum* (Ill Wind); after the Romans finally defeated Pyrrhus here in 275 BC, however, they decided it might be a "good wind" (*Benevento*) after all. Traces of the Roman Empire include **Trajan's Arch,** constructed in 114 AD and decorated with fine bas-reliefs, and the huge **Roman theater** from the 2nd century BC—one of the largest in Italy. The Church of S. Sofia (762), with an attached monastery, has been transformed into the **Museo del Sannio.** Displays include a large collection of archaeological remains from the area dating as far back as the Iron Age. (Open Tues.-Sun. 9am-1pm. Free.)

Visit the village of **Montesarchio**, with its 15th-century castle, or Sant'Agata dei Goti, with its Romanesque cathedral. (The bus terminal is on the Viale dei Rettori.) In the city's old section is **Albergo della Corte,** P. Piano di Corte, 11 (tel. 548 19). Off Corso Garibaldi, follow the tiny Via Bartolomeo Camerario (across from Banca di Roma), and watch out for cars. It's tiny but luxurious and newly renovated with singles at L35,000 and doubles at L65,000, all with bath. Prices are negotiable depending on number of people and length of stay. Near Trajan's Arch, **Ristorante e Pizzeria Traiano,** Via Manicotti, 48 (tel. 250 13), has meals for about L22,000. (Open Wed.-Mon. noon-3pm and 7:30pm-midnight.)

Benevento can be reached by train from either Caserta or Naples. **EPT** is on Via Giustiniani, 34 (tel 25 424), off Via Mellusi (from Villa Comunale, take any left to reach Via Mellusi). (Open Mon.-Sat. 9am-1pm.) They should have maps, brochures, and guides to the monuments. The **postal code** is 82100; the **phone code** is 0824. To get into the old section, take bus #1 from the train station (every 15min., L800). Before returning to Naples, be sure to sample Benevento's *Strega* (witch) liqueur.

CÁPRI

ISLANDS

Lingering off either shore of the Bay of Naples, the pleasure islands of **Cápri, Íschia,** and **Prócida** beckon the culture-weary traveler with the promise of beautiful natural sights and a variety of first-rate accommodations.

Large ferries (*traghetti*) and hydrofoils (*aliscafi*) leave daily from Naples's **Molo Beverello** at the end of P. Municipio in Naples. (Take bus #150 or tram #1 or #4 from Naples's *stazione centrale.*) **Hydrofoils** also leave from the Mergellina port. **Caremar,** Molo Beverello (tel. 551 38 82, in Cápri 837 07 00) runs the main line to the islands. **Navigazione Libera del Golfo (NLG),** Molo Beverello (tel. 552 55 89, in Cápri 837 08 19), has slightly lower prices and less comfortable boats. Avoid purchasing a round-trip ticket which will subject you to the whims of a single company for the duration. The islands are also accessible Via Sorrento. Ferries run throughout the day from both ports. Check schedules and prices at *biglietterie* located at all ports.

Transport is very affordable: Naples to Íschia, for example, is only L8000. Eight ferries leave for Cápri between 6:40am and 7:40pm (L8000, first departure Sun. 7am). The last boat returning to Naples leaves at 7:20pm. Ferries to Íschia charge the same prices and follow similar schedules, leaving Naples from 6:30am (Sun. 7:05am) to 7:30pm, with a late ferry (via Prócida) at 11pm. Direct ferries to Prócida run between the same hours (5 per day, L5500). There is also service between Íschia and Prócida (L2700), Cápri and Sorrento (L4250), Íschia and Sorrento (L10,000), Amalfi and Cápri (L9000), Íschia and Pozzuoli (L9800), and Prócida and Pozzuoli (L7000). Hydrofoils for all islands leave from the Mergellina marina more frequently, but cost about twice as much as the ferries. From late September to June, ferries run at half their high-season frequency.

■ Cápri

The Roman emperor Augustus became enamored of the fantasy island beauty of Cápri in 29 BC and swapped more fertile Íschia for it. His successor Tiberius passed his last decade here in wild imperial debauchery, leaving several villas dispersed around the island. Today's visitors may seek a certain debauchery too, but in Cápri they are generally content to pay through the nose for en masse ferry excursions to the renowned Blue Grotto, or to gawk at the rich and famous in Cápri town's *piazzeta.* **Ánacapri,** clinging to the side of nearby **Monte Solaro** (589m), is less frequented by daytrippers, and qualifies as a budget version of paradise, with two *affita camere,* (privately rented rooms at affordable rates). Carry your *Let's Go* with you (it may land you discounts). You might consider renting a moped in Sorrento (see below) and bringing it over on the ferry, as the distances between sights, ports, and hotels are long (be advised however, that the rules of the road in Cápri are strictly enforced). Otherwise the bus system will efficiently get you to the most important sights.

ORIENTATION AND PRACTICAL INFORMATION

Most ferries dock at **Marina Grande** on the north side of the island, from which you can take the **funicular** to the town of Cápri (every 15min. 6:35am-9:15pm, L1500). Buses leave from town to **Marina Píccola** (on the south shore) and **Ánacapri** (every 15min. 6:30am-1:40am, L1500). Less frequent buses run directly from Marina Grande to Ánacapri (L1500). The funicular ejects you into **P. Umberto. Via Roma,** Cápri's ritzy strip, leads off to the left. The bus to Ánacapri takes you to **P. Vittoria. Via Giuseppe Orlandi,** running in both directions from the piazza, leads to the cheapest and best establishments.

Tourist Office: in Cápri, at the end of the dock at Marina Grande (tel. 837 06 34). Open Mon.-Sat. 8am-8pm. Also in P. Umberto, (tel. 837 06 86). Open Mon.-Sat.

8am-8pm, Sun. 8:30am-2:30pm; Oct.-May Mon.-Sat. 9am-1pm and 3:30-6:45pm. In Ánacapri, an information office is at Via Orlandi, 19/A (tel. 837 15 24), off the main piazza, to the right as you get off the bus. Open Mon.-Sat. 9am-1pm and 3:30-6:40pm; Sept.-May 9am-1pm. These offices provide a vague map, an updated list of hotels, and ferry and bus schedules. English spoken.

Currency Exchange: Cambio, Via Roma, 33 (tel. 837 07 85), across from the main bus stop in Cápri. Open March 15-Nov. 15 daily 9am-9pm. Also at P. Vittoria, 2 (tel. 837 31 46), in the center of Ánacapri. Open March 15-Nov. 20 daily 8:30am-7:30pm. No commission at either location.

Post Office: central office in Cápri on Via Roma (tel. 837 72 40), a couple of blocks downhill from P. Umberto. Open Mon.-Fri. 8:15am-6:30pm, Sat. 8:15am-12:10pm. In Ánacapri at Viale de Tommaso, 4 (tel. 837 10 15). Open Mon.-Fri. 8:15am-1:30pm, Sat. 8:15am-12:10pm. **Postal code:** 80073.

Telephones: SIP (tel. 837 55 50), behind the funicular stop in Cápri. Open daily 9am-1pm and 3-10:45pm, Oct.-June 9am-1pm and 3-8pm. Public phones in Ánacapri at P. Vittoria, 4 (tel. 837 33 77). Open daily 8am-10pm; Oct.-May 9am-1pm and 3-8pm. **Telephone code:** 081.

Buses: tel. 837 04 20. In Cápri, buses depart from Via Roma for Ánacapri, Marina Píccola, and points in between. In Ánacapri, buses depart from P. Barile off Via Orlandi for the Grotta Azzurra (Blue Grotto), the *faro* (lighthouse), and other points nearby. There's also a direct bus line between Marina Grande and P. Vittoria in Ánacapri. Buses cost L1500 per ride.

Luggage Storage: Caremar ticket office (tel. 837 07 00), across from the Marina Grande dock. L2000 per bag. Open daily 7am-7pm.

Swimming Pool: Bagni Nettuno, Via Grotta Azzurra, 46 (tel. 837 13 62), above the Blue Grotto in Ánacapri. Take the bus from Ánacapri center. Full use of outdoor pool, private beach, reclining chair, shower, and changing room in scenic cliffside surroundings for a special *Let's Go* price of L8000 per day (regular price is L12,000). Open mid-March to mid-Nov. daily 9am-7pm.

Emergencies: tel. 113. **Police,** Via Roma (tel. 837 72 45). They'll connect you with an English speaker. **Hospital: Ospedale Capilupi,** Via Provinciale Ánacapri (tel. 837 00 14 or 837 87 62), between Cápri and Ánacapri. **Hospital Emergency First Aid:** tel. 837 81 49). For minor medical assistance in summer, call the **Guardia Medica Turistica** in Cápri (tel. 837 20 91).

ACCOMMODATIONS

Call in advance and confirm reservations—Ánacapri is your best bet. It's possible to find vacancies impromptu in July, but not in August. Makeshift camping is frowned upon and heavy fines are strictly imposed. But don't be put off by the inconvenience of finding a place to stay: the natural splendor of this legendary island should not be missed.

Ánacapri

Villa Eva, Via La Fabbrica, 8 (tel. 837 20 40). Set high among the gardens and trees and only a 10min. walk to the Grotta Azzurra this is the perfect vacation setting. From the port at Marina Grande take the bus to Anácapri and get off at P. Vittoria. From here call Villa Eva and the warm-hearted Mamma Eva or her husband Vicenzo will actually come pick you up. The tidy, tasteful rooms (with bath and some with terraces) were built by Vicenzo himself. *Let's Go* prices: L18,000-L25,000 per person depending on the room you ask for. Private doubles L50,000. Group discounts. Call a few days in advance to confirm your reservations especially in August. English spoken.

Hotel Il Girasole, Via Linciano, 43 (tel. 837 23 51). Take the Ánacapri bus to the P. Caprile stop and walk down the hill to your left. Take the tiny alleyway with the "Girasole" sign for about a 7-min. walk straight ahead. A real treat for *Let's Go* users—management loves the book and anglophones in general. By next year they may also offer shuttle service from Marina Grande—and serve dinner for L15,000 which also includes a light breakfast in the morning. All rooms have private baths. Bed in double L25,000; in triple L23,000, in quad L20,000. English spoken.

CÁPRI

Hotel Loreley, Via G. Orlandi, 16 (tel. 837 14 40), head down from Piazza Vittoria. In the center of Anacapri, offers a large bright rooms at L30,000 for singles, L50,000 for doubles. All with baths. Larger rooms even cheaper. *Let's Go* and a smile may also lower the price.

Hotel Caesar Augustus, Via Orlandi, 4 (tel. 837 14 21), on main bus route (from port, L2500) before the town center. It's difficult to dispute their claim to "most beautiful view in the world." Once the most expensive luxury hotel on the island, today a comfortable, weathered monument with a gorgeous garden entrance. English spoken. L30,000 per person upon mention of *Let's Go*. Open Easter-Oct.

Cápri Town

Albergo La Tosca, Via Birago, 5 (tel. 837 09 89). Walk up the stairs at P. Umberto at the exit of the funicular and through the 2nd alley on the left, Via Padre S. Cimino. Follow the twisting path, bearing right on Via Valentino, and take a left where the street ends. Spacious rooms, some with ecstatically scenic views and terraces. Singles L30,000. Doubles L70,000, with bath L90,000. Breakast L10,000. Discounts in off-season for stays of 3 or more days.

Pensione Quattro Stagioni, Via Marina Piccola, 1 (tel. 837 00 41). From P. Umberto at the top of the funicular walk downhill on Via Roma. Turn left at the 3-pronged fork in the road and look for the 1st house on the left. Though hot in summer the cozy, flower-filled rooms are clean and have sensational views. Outgoing owner speaks English. Doubles L80,000, with bath L90,000. Breakfast L20,000. Less of a deal in July and Aug. when ½-pension of 1 meal or the costly breakfast is required (L25,000 added to room price). Open March 15-Oct.

FOOD

Caprese food is as glorious as the panoramas from the island's cliffs. Savor their local *mozzarella* alone, or with tomatoes, oil, and basil in a dish known as *insalata caprese,* respectfully considered the best summer meal in the world by many. The *ravioli alla caprese* is hand-stuffed with the tastiest of local cheeses. Don't miss the *torta di mandorla* (chocolate almond cake). Accompany meals with the local red and white wines, which bear the *Tiberio* label.

Restaurant and bar prices in the town of Cápri will make you gasp—buy food from one of the groceries instead. Take the right prong of the fork at the end of Via Roma to reach **Supermercato STANDA** (open daily 8am-1:30pm and 4:30-9pm; in winter Mon.-Sat. 8am-1pm and 3:30-8pm). Ask at Girasole and Villa Eva for local low-cost restaurants.

Ánacapri

Ristorante Il Cucciolo, Via della Fabbrica, 52 (tel. 837 19 17), near the bus stop for the Damecuta ruins on road to Blue Grotto; a 5-min. walk from Villa Eva. Follow the path from the sign. An outdoor restaurant with expansive views of the bay. Homemade *agnolotti* (stuffed pasta) and their fresh fish are the friendly owner's pride and joy. Wine L7000 per bottle. Open daily 12:10-2:30pm and 7:30-10:45pm.

Trattoria Il Solitario, Via Orlandi, 96 (though the tile says #54; tel. 837 13 82), off P. Vittoria. An amazing, ivy-covered hideaway. *Cannelloni alla caprese* L8000, homemade pasta L7000-8000, salads L3500. Wine L5000 per bottle. Cover L1500. Open daily 12:15-3pm and 7pm-midnight; Sept. 21-June 19 Tues.-Sun. 12:15-3pm and 7pm-midnight.

La Quercia, Via della Migliari, 46 (tel. 837 88 20). Only a 5-min. walk from Girasole. Supreme view and divine seafood at discount prices.

Pizzeria Aumm Aumm, Via Caprile, 18 (tel. 837 20 61). Nice, modern place with a lively crowd and excellent service. Wood-burning brick-oven pizza L5000-8000. *Primi* L8000. Open daily noon-1am.

Cápri Town

Buca di Bacco, Via Longano (tel. 837 07 23), off P. Umberto I. Elegant yet affordable. *Primi* L6000-8000, *secondi* L8000-9000. Also pizza at night L5800-10,000. Cover, L2000. Service 12%. Open Thurs.-Tues., noon-3pm and 7pm-midnight.

Moscardino, Via Roma, 28 (tel. 837 06 87). New management. Limited but excellent selection. *Menù* is L25,000. Open daily noon-3pm and 7pm-midnight.

SIGHTS

To appreciate Cápri's Mediterranean beauty from on high, take Via Longano from P. Umberto in Cápri center and then make the trek up to the left on Via Tiberio to **Villa Jovis** (1hr.). This is Emperor Tiberius's ruined, but still magnificent, pleasure dome. Legend has it that Tiberius tossed those who displeased him over the precipice. *Let's Go* advises walking down. (Open daily 9am-1hr. before sunset. Admission L4000.) On the descent along the path, a short detour takes you to the **Arco Naturale,** a majestic stone arch, off Via Matermania on the eastern cliffs. On a clear day you can see as far as Paestum through the weathered arch.

Toward the southern edge of the town of Cápri lies the **Certosa,** a 14th-century Carthusian monastery. (Open Mon.-Sat. 9am-2pm, Sun. 9am-1pm. Free.) The nearby **Giardini di Augusto** (Gardens of Augustus) aren't noted for their horticultural beauty, but a superb series of belvederes makes the visit worthwhile. In one corner of the gardens a small statue is dedicated to Lenin, who fled to Cápri after the failed revolution of 1905. (Garden open daily 8am-1hr. before sunset.) Descend the coiled trail below the gardens if it's open, or take any of the frequent buses to **Marina Píccola** on the southern coast (every 15min., L1500), one of Cápri's most beautiful seaside stretches. Though the beach is a glorified pile of rocks, you can cavort in the clear water among immense lava stones or rent a boat and paddle to even better spots to the west. You can also swim at Marina Grande, near the port.

Take any of the boats near the port or descend north between vineyards from P. Umberto to **Bagni di Tiberio,** a bathing area amidst the ruins of an imperial villa (also accessible by boat from Marina Grande, L7000).

Until the completion of the cliffhanging roadway a few decades ago, only a narrow Phoenician staircase joined **Ánacapri** (literally "over Cápri") to the lower town. From P. Vittoria in Ánacapri, take a 5-min. chairlift (round-trip L7000) to the top of **Monte Solaro.** (Open 9:30am-1hr. before sunset.) The view from the top is terrific: on a clear day, you can see the Apennines to the east and the mountains of Calabria to the south. Another attraction is the **Villa San Michele.** Built earlier this century on the site of another of Emperor Tiberius's villas, it was the lifelong work of the Swedish author and physician Axel Munthe. Classical sculptures throng the villa, retrieved from Cápri's sea bottom where they were hurled after Tiberius's death, allegedly by the ghosts of his victims. (Open daily 9am-1hr. before sunset. Admission L5000.) Below the villa is a nice walk from which one can see all of Cápri; it is especially beautiful at night. From Ánacapri center, take a bus to the **faro,** Italy's second-tallest lighthouse, where you can snorkle, tan, or leap from volcanic rocks along with countless Italians.

Cápri's most famous attraction, the **Grotta Azzurra** (Blue Grotto), has become the area's most fearsome tourist trap. A motorboat from Marina Grande, barely 2km away, costs L8000 round-trip and leaves regularly from 9am until two hours before sunset. From the motorboat you are transferred unceremoniously to rowboats for a tour of the grotto (L10,500, tip expected). The "captains" take you through at such a speed that your eyes scarcely have time to adjust to the remarkable blue glow, best seen in the early evening. You can skip the motorboat ride by taking a bus from Ánacapri to the cliff above the grotto (every 20min., L1500). Many visitors dive into the clear water of the grotto, but swimming is permitted only before 9am and after 6pm when the rowboats are not running. Don't go alone or if the surf is heavy. There is a tiny public "beach" (really a rock and concrete ledge) at Gràdola, just west of the Grotta, poised for diving board action. Also the well-equipped Bani Nettuno is here.

Night-time action is expensive in Cápri. In Anácapri the largest club is the **Zeus** on Via Orlandi, 21 (tel. 837 11 69). Admission is L25,000 but passes from the hotels, including the ones we list, slash off L10,000. If you're looking for live music try the nearby **Underground,** Via Orlandi, 259 (tel. 837 25 23).

■ Íschia

Across the bay from overrun Cápri, larger, less glamorous Íschia has managed to cram many of the characteristics of Campania onto its small surface. Íschia has beautiful beaches, natural hot springs, ruins, forests, vineyards, lemon groves, and a once-active volcano. Unfortunately, the island hasn't escaped the hideous overpricing of a resort island and is perhaps best as a day trip from Cápri or Naples. Íschia's main towns are: **Íschia Porto,** which surrounds a perfectly circular port formed by the crater of an extinct volcano, **Cassamícciola Terme,** an expensive spa with an overcrowded beach, **Lacco Ameno,** another spa town (but one with a lofty pedigree—it's the oldest Greek settlement in the western Mediterranean), and **Fório** on the western coast, sheltering many *pensioni* and the popular **San Francesco beach.**

Ischia's scattered sights offer a break from sun and surf of the beaches. Near Íschia Porto, the **Castello d'Íschia** (1441), built by the King of Spain on the site of a 5th-century BC Greek fortress, is situated on a little island of its own connected to Íschia by a 15th-century footbridge. When Íschia's volcano **Mt. Epomeo** erupted for the last time in 1301, the island's inhabitants fled to the tiny island for safety. After the castle was completed, it sheltered Íschia's entire population, forced to flee the mainland this time due to eruptions of pirates along the shore. When you visit, be sure to see the **nun's cemetery** where the Poor Clares resided in the 18th century. When nuns died, the order built stone thrones to prop the decomposing bodies as a constant (and redolent) reminder to the other nuns of death's presence. The castle also features an exposition room with changing modern art exhibits. (Open daily 9am-8pm. Admission L5000, elevator to top L1000.)

The ruins in Lacco Aveno testify to its antiquity, but the town's most distinctive characteristics are the **Il Fungo** finger-shaped promontory off the coast, and an expensive thermal spa featuring radioactive waters. If you're staying in Fório, stop by its 14th-century sanctuary, **Santa Maria di Loreto,** and the 15th-century tower **Torrione.** Just south is **Citara,** a large beach with giant diving rocks. **Barano d'Íschia,** the southern region of Íschia, contains the **Spaggia dei Maronti,** the most tranquil and scenic swimming area (serviced by boat-taxi from Sant'Angelo) and a convenient base for hikes up the volcano, Mt. Epomeo.

PRACTICAL INFORMATION

Tourist Office: Scalo Porto Salvo (tel. 99 11 46 or 98 30 05), in Íschia Porto. Open Mon.-Sat. 9am-2pm and 3-8pm. A 2nd Azienda Turismo operates on Corso Vittorio Colonna, 104 (tel. 98 30 66). Open Mon.-Fri. 9am-1pm.

Buses: SEPSA, on P. Trieste. To destinations all over the island. Main office and depature point on Íschia Porto. Bus #1 covers Cassamícciola Terme, Lacco Ameno, Fório, and Sant'Angelo. (Every 30min., L1200.) **Tours** of the island by boat (L15,000) and by minibus (L20,000) are available and can be booked through agents along the waterfront. (Bargaining is suggested for these last.)

Ferries: Two major lines, **Casemar** and **Linee Laura,** have the same prices and schedules—they only vary by 30min. To Íschia from: Naples (every 2hr. 6:10am-11pm, Sun. 7:05am-11pm, L7300); Pozzuoli (5 per day, L4900); Amalfi (L13,000); Sorrento (L10,000); Positano (L12,000); and Prócida (L2700).

ACCOMMODATIONS

Hotels in Íschia run the gamut from reasonable to exorbitant. By late July and August rooms are hard to come by without reservations made at least three months in advance. Few hotels offer singles, and since rooms are in such high demand, some hotel owners may not rent rooms for less than a week. Prices plummet from October to May. Get the hotel list from the tourist office for the most detailed maps of the island, or try the most economical way to overnight in Íschia: camping. Íschia is an easy daytrip from both Sorrento and Naples, so you might consider avoiding the search for affordable accommodations altogether.

Íschia Porto

Albergo A. Macri, Via Jasolino, 96 (tel. 99 26 03), near the port off the street that runs along the water. Respectable rooms far from the beaches. Singles L34,000, with bath L40,000. Doubles L64,000, with bath L75,000. Oct.-June singles L29,000, with bath L38,000. Doubles L58,000, with bath L68,000. Flash your *Let's Go* book to get these prices.

Il Crostolo, Via Cossa, 32 (tel. 99 10 94). From the tourist office take Via Jasolino right, but don't follow it to the port. Take the ascending road to the hotel at the top of the curve to the right. Terrace and several of the rooms have super views of the port. Singles with bath L35,000. Doubles with bath L62,500. Sept.-June singles L26,000; doubles with bath L60,000. Breakfast included. Half-pension (L60,000) required in July and Aug.

Cassamícciola Terme

Pensione Quisisana, P. Bagni, 34 (tel. 99 45 20). Take bus #3 from the port to the piazza. Tiny, family-run establishment with plenty of comfort. A 10-min. walk from the beach. Curfew midnight. July-Aug. obligatory full pension L65,000 per person. Open May-Oct.

Fório

Pensione Di Lustra, Via Filippo Di Lustro, 9 (tel. 99 71 63). A 2-second walk from the beach. At first you might think you've mistakenly stumbled into botanical gardens. Gorgeous views inside and out. Doubles with bath L60,000-70,000 including breakfast. Half-pension required in July and Aug. (L50,000). **Pensione Villa Franca,** Strada statale Lacco, 155 (tel. 98 74 20). Take bus #1 from Íschia Porto and get off at the stop for the San Francesco beach. On the street traversed by the bus. Well-kept rooms, a pretty patio, and a swimming pool. A 15-min. walk from the beach. English spoken. Singles L30,000, with bath L35,000. Doubles with bath L60,000.

Camping: The most economical source of accommodations. 2 delightful campgrounds lie near Íschia Porto. The better is **Eurocamping dei Pini,** Via delle Ginestre, 28 (tel. 98 20 69), a 10-min. walk from the port. Take Via del Porto onto Via Alfredo de Luca, walk uphill and take a right on Via delle Terme, where you will see the arrow indicating *Camping.* L9500 per person, L9000 per large tent, L5000 per small tent; Sept.-June L8000, L7000, and L5000. Bungalows with bath and kitchen facilities for 2, 3, 4, or more run L80,000 (reserve ahead). The tent site is more scenic than the bungalow site. Open June-Oct. **Camping Internazionale,** Via M. Mazella (tel. 99 14 49), a 15-min. walk from the port. Take Via Alfredo de Luca from Via del Porto and bear right onto Via M. Mazzella at P. degli Eroe. (Note that there are 2 Via Mazzellas—Michele and Leonardo—running parallel.) Luxuriant foliage and tranquil surroundings. L12,000 per person (L8000-10,000 off-season), L6000 per tent. Immaculate 2-person bungalows with bath L65,000, L15,000 per additional person; off-season L40,000 and L14,000. Bathless bungalows slightly cheaper. Open May-Oct. 20.

FOOD

Íschia has ubiquitous outdoor eateries, numerous *alimentari,* and a plethora of fruit vendors.

Íschia Porto

Da Mastu Peppe o Fraulese (tel. 98 19 12), located behind the tourist office on the waterfront. Lovely outdoor restaurant with a view of the port. Spaghetti

L5000. *Risotto alla pescatore* (with fresh seafood, L11,000). Open Tues.-Sun. 12:30-2pm and 8pm-midnight.

Emiddio, Via Porto, 30, right by the docks. Here the *ravioli alla panna* (L5000) are supreme. Other *primi* L4000-7000. *Menú* is clearly displayed outside with all the prices. Open daily noon-3pm and 7pm-midnight. Cover L1500.

Casamicciola

Ristorante Zelluso, Via Parodi, 41 (tel. 99 46 27). *Primi* L5500. *Menú* L25,000. Open daily noon-2:30pm and 8pm-midnight. Oct.-May closed Mondays.

■ Prócida

A small island of fisherfolk and farmers, Prócida prefers to remain a spectator to its neighbors' summertime transformation into country clubs. Though crowds also swarm to Prócida, they don't stay on long enough to taint its beaches. Take a ferry from Naples (5 per day, L6400), Pozzuoli (L5800 round-trip), or Íschia (L2700). The 14km volcanic coast offers three principal beaches: *Spiaggia Chiaia, Spiaggia Ciraccio,* and *Chiaiolella*. From the main port, the interior sights of the island can be covered in one beautiful trek. From the town center, take Via Principe Umberto out and up the long steep haul (no buses) to the **Abbazia Arcangelo San Michele** (St. Michael's Abbey) on the easternmost and highest hilltop in Prócida. On the way up you'll see the Medieval walls of the **Terra Murata** (citadel) on Via San Michele just below the monastery. The abbey's pastel yellow façade, redone in 1890, belies the interior, where you'll find ornate 15th-century gold-lead frescoes and bleeding Christ figures. (Open daily 9am-6:30pm.) On the way down, revel in the view of the island's second port on the southern side and stop to admire the ochre Pantheon-domed **Santuario Mariano** with an 1810 façade at P. Vittorio Scialoia. Buses don't serve much of the island, but it's only 4km wide and taxi service is available from Marina Grande (tel. 896 87 85). From the center, Via Vittorio Emanuele, buses do wheel you to **Chiaiolella,** a little port where you can cross the footbridge to the islet of **Vivara,** preserved as a wildlife sanctuary and breeding ground for the rabbits Procidano cook up in their famous stew. **Angolo di Paradiso,** Via Salette, 14 (tel. 896 76 57), on the Ciraccio beach, serves excellent, inexpensive dishes. *Spaghetti alla scarpara* is a fried spaghetti dish with myriad spices (L6000). Their *coniglio alla procidana* (local rabbit) will make you hop for joy (L11,000). (Cover L1500. Service 10%. Open May-Sept. daily 1-4pm and 7-10:30pm.)

Of the island's four hotels, only two are affordable. The **Riviera,** at Via G. Da Procida, 36 (tel. 896 71 97), is in the Chiaiolella beach area. (Singles with bath L35,000; doubles with bath L66,000; full pension L85,000. Open April-Sept.) The **Savoia,** on Via Lavadera, 32 (tel. 896 76 16), also has decent rooms. (Doubles L50,000; full pension L60,000.) You can reach the campground **Graziella,** at Via Salette (tel. 896 77 47) on the beach, by taking the island bus from the port to P. Urno and walking one-half km to Spiaggia Ciraccio. Facilities are few but tranquility abounds. (L8000 per person, L7000 per tent. Open May-Sept.) The **ETP Residences office,** Via Principe Umberto, 1, lets apartments from one night to a month depending on availability. In August reservations and a minimum stay of 2 weeks are required. Depending on the month, prices range from L30,000-50,000 per person, per night. The **AAST tourist office** is on Via Marina (tel. 896 96 24). Open Mon.-Fri. 9am-1pm. Stock up on groceries before you get here as food on the island is very expensive.

■ Sorrento

Odysseus's crew shielded their ears from the spellbinding song of the Sirens, who inhabited Sorrento's peninsula. If the Sirens still exist, chances are they chant in English and German to camera-laden foreigners. Nevertheless, there are fates far orse than being shipwrecked on Sorrento's rocky beaches where rooms with ews are still affordable and access to Cápri and the Amalfi coast is convenient.

RIENTATION AND PRACTICAL INFORMATION

orrento is very well organized for tourists of all budgets, and just about everyone peaks at least one foreign language, especially English.

On the tip of the peninsula that leaps for Cápri's throat, 48km south of Naples, orrento is served by frequent *circumvesuviana* trains. Buses run regularly from orrento to the towns of the Amalfi coast.

There's a short throughway which leads you from the stairs outside the station y the phone booths) to **Corso Italia,** Sorrento's main street. To the left lies **Piazza** asso, the center of town. Several smaller *piazze* surround it, as do most of the wn's restaurants, bars, and shops.

Tourist Office: Via L. De Maio, 35 (tel. 878 11 15). Cross P. Sant'Antonino (behind P. Tasso toward the water) to Via L. De Maio; the office is to the right within the Circolo del Forestiere complex, in the room on the left as you enter the building. A large, helpful, English-speaking office with maps, accommodations service, and information on cultural events. Grab a free copy of *Surrentum*, the monthly tourist magazine. Open Mon.-Sat. 8:30am-2:30pm and 4:30-8pm, Oct.-June Mon.-Sat. 8:30am-2:30pm and 4-7pm.

American Express: Acampara Travel, P. Angelina Lauro, 13 (tel. (081) 878 48 00).

Post Office: Corso Italia, 210T-U (tel. 878 16 36), near P. Lauro. Open Mon.-Sat. 8:15am-7:30pm. **Postal code:** 80067.

Telephones: SIP, P. Tasso (tel. 878 24 00), at Via Correale under the church on the far side. Open daily 9am-1pm and 4-9:30pm. **Telephone code:** 081.

Buses: SITA (tel. 878 27 08). All buses to towns on the Amalfi coast leave only from the *circumvesuviana* station. Frequent buses to Positano (L1500), Praiano (L2100), and Amalfi (L2800). From Amalfi, change buses and pay an additional L2100 to go to Salerno or an additional L1100 to go to Atransi, Ravella, Scala, Minori, or Maiori.

Ferries: the cheapest route to Cápri. Descend the stairs at P. Tasso. **Caremar** (tel. 878 12 82) is the most reliable. Boats leave daily at 8am, 10am, 2:45pm, 5:45pm, and 7:40pm (less frequently in winter). Tickets L4800 (45min.). Or **Alilauro** Hydrofoile (tel. 807 30 24) take 15min. for the crossing (L7000). Ferries also to: Íschia (L19,000), and in summer, Ponza (L40,000), and Ventotene (L30,000).

Car and Moped Rental: Sorrento Rent A Car, Corso Italia, 210/A (tel. 878 13 86). Mopeds, day rate about L40,000. They also rent Vespa 125s for L61,880 (inquire about licensing requirements for these).

Laundromat: Terlizzi, Corso Italia, 30 (tel. 878 11 85). Coin-op and drycleaning.

Emergencies: tel. 113. **Police:** Vico 3° Rota, (tel. 878 11 10), a left off Corso Italia 1 block after Viale Nizza, past the hostel. Ask for the English-speaking foreigners' office (*Ufficio Stranieri*). **Hospital: Ospedale Santa Maria Misericordia,** Corso Italia (tel. 878 34 96). English speakers on hand.

ACCOMMODATIONS

ome Sorrento hotels allegedly charge more than their official prices but escape iunicipal reprimand. If you feel you've been overcharged you can write a letter to ie EPT and perhaps eventually get a refund. Still, many bargains exist. It's sensible o call ahead for reservations in July and August.

Ostello Surriento (HI), Via Capasso, 5 (tel. 878 17 83). From train station, go down the stairs by phone booths and follow the through street to Corso Italia. Make a right then look for the old church on your left; Via Capasso runs along its side. Savvy young management, wild decorations, and waterfront location redeem primitive and many-bedded rooms. Free shower. Lockout 9:30am-5pm. Curfew 11:30pm. L12,000 per person. Breakfast L2000. Open March-Oct.

Hotel Linda, Via degli Aranci, 125 (tel. 878 29 16), behind the train station. Despite the barren area, the rooms are clean and cozy. Singles with bath L40,000. Doubles with bath L60,000. Oct.-April prices decrease by L10,000.

Pensione Mara, Via Rota, 5 (tel. 878 36 65). Turn right on Corso Italia from train station, take Via Capasso past youth hostel, and then make your 1st right. Immaculate rooms (some with terraces) in beautiful, quiet area. English spoken. Doubles L70,000. Triples L88,000. Quads L110,000. (Make reservations for summer stays.

Hotel Elios, Via Capo, 33 (tel. 878 18 12). Clean rooms with bay views. Doubles with bath L70,000. Bringing *Let's Go* gets you a discount if you ask politely.

Hotel Nice, Corso Italia, 257 (tel. 878 16 50). Not the most picturesque hotel in this beautiful city but reasonably clean rooms. Nice proprietors. Nice singles L45,000. Nice doubles L66,000. Discounts for doubles during the winter.

Hotel City, Corso Italia, 221 (tel. 877 22 10), on the main street that heads toward P. Tasso from the train station. A colorful, art-filled place. A bit noisy at night. English spoken. Comfortable doubles with bath (some with garden patios) L60,000. Singles available Oct.-June L45,000. Breakfast L7000. Reserve at least months in advance for Aug.

Hotel Savoia, Via Fuorimura, 48 (tel. 878 25 11), on the street off the right hand of the statue in P. Tasso. The best bet if you're arriving in the summer without reservations. Friendly English-speaking management. A few small singles with bath L40,000. Doubles L70,000. Breakfast L7000.

Hotel Loreley et Londres, Via Califano, 2 (tel. 807 31 87). Take Via Capasso past the youth hostel all the way to the waterfront. The Sorrento hotel you've dreamed of, with views of cliffs and sea. Worth the higher price. Doubles with bath and breakfast L85,000. July-Sept. obligatory half-pension L70,000.

Hotel Villa Gerardo, Via Capo 82/84 (tel. 807 30 63). All rooms with bath. Doubles L75,000, 10-15% for extra person. Half pension L65,000. TV and telephone. In winter, singles L40,000. Just opened, so get it while it's good.

Camping: Nube d'Argento, Via del Capo, 21 (tel. 878 13 44). Both of these camp sites have small markets inside. From the train station, follow Corso Italia past P. Tasso until it becomes Via del Capo. L13,000 per person and per tent, L6000 per small tent. 2-person bungalows L80,000. Prices decrease in the off-season (Oct.-March). **Villaggio Verde,** Via Cesarano, 12 (tel. 807 30 28), a 10-min. walk from the town center off Via degli Aranci. L9000 per person and L8000 per tent. 2-person bungalows with kitchen and bath L60,000.

FOOD

Sorrento is famous for its *gnocchi,* plump potato dumplings smothered in a zesty tomato sauce and mozzarella cheese. Also popular are the *cannelloni. Nocillo* is a dark liqueur made from the hefty local walnuts. Unfortunately, few of the affordable restaurants in Sorrento offer local fare, opting instead to cater to the Germans with *Würstel* and to the English with fish and chips. Otherwise, flee the city center and explore the local hangouts in the surrounding area. **Supermercato STANDA,** Corso Italia, 221, sells the cheap stuff (open Mon.-Wed. and Fri.-Sat. 8:30am-12:55pm and 5-9:25pm, Thurs. 8:30am-12:55pm). Follow San Cesareo out until it turns into San Puoro for fresh fruit, fish, or bargain shoes sold at a variety of market stands. (Go in the morning for the best deals.)

In the City

Ristorante e Pizzeria Giardiniello, Via Accademia, 7 (tel. 878 46 16). Take the 2nd left off Via Giuliani (way to the right of Via Dinkins), which runs off Corso Italia at the cathedral. Mamma Luisa does all the cooking in this large family-run establishment. Her *gnocchi* transcend poetry (L6000). Don't miss the *bocconcini al Giardiniello,* tiny oven-baked pizzas with prosciutto and mushrooms (L6000 for about 10). *Vino di Sorrento* L6000 per bottle. Cover L1500. Open daily 11:30am-midnight, Oct.-May Fri.-Wed. 11:30am-midnight.

Ristorante Sant'Antonino, Via Santa Maria delle Grazie, 6 (tel. 877 12 00), off P. Sant'Antonino. Popular with locals as well as tourists for its flora-filled patio and low prices. *Farfalle con zucchine* (butterfly-shaped pasta mixed with zucchini

L6500) and yummy-and-a-half *gnocchi alla sorrentina* (L6000). Also, full menus starting at L14,000. Long wine list. Open July-Sept. daily noon-midnight, Feb. 16-June and Oct.-Dec. Tues.-Sun. noon-midnight.

Outside the City

Taverna del Curato, Via Casarlano, 10b (tel. 877 16 28). 30min. uphill walk from town center in the locality of Casarlano, or take infrequent bus #1 from P. Tasso. From P. Tasso, take Via Fuorimura to Via Atigliana and follow it uphill. Food just like mamma's. They make their own *fettucine del Curato* (hand-cut pasta with cream, ham, mushrooms, and bacon, L7000) and bottle their own wine (L5000 per). Cover L1500. Open daily noon-1am; Oct.-May Thurs.-Tues. noon-1am.

Gigino Pizza a Metro, Via Nicotera, 11, at Vico Equense (tel. 879 84 24), a 10-min. train ride from Sorrento. Take the *circumvesuviana* to the Vico Equense stop, go left as you exit the station, and follow the winding road uphill to its end at P. Umberto. Finally, take a left on Via Roma and another left on Via Nicotera. This is unofficially the world's largest *pizzeria,* a massive 2-story facility with monstrous wood-burning ovens that cook *pizza a metro* (1m-long pizza), supposedly famous throughout Italy. A meter will feed at least 5 starving tourists; starving Italians, however, are likely to eat elsewhere. Overeat *pizza margherita* with fresh tomato and mozzarella (L22,000) or *quattro stagioni* with cheese, prosciutto, mushroom, and tomato (L24,000). ½ liter of beer L2500. Cover L1000. Service 13%. Open daily noon-1am.

Snack Bar 2000, largo Sedil Dominova, off Via San Cesareo. The "2000" dominates a tiny piazza with outdoor tables, a liquor store, and a small *alimentari.* The *menù* is surprisingly good with lasagne and veal cutlet at L13,000.

SIGHTS

The westerly orientation of the beaches makes sunset swims truly memorable. To get to the lovely **Punta di Sorrento,** walk down the Ruderia Romana off Via Capo; after 400m, it turns into a footpath that leads to the water, passing the ruins of a medieval fortress. A bit farther, southwest of the city, the **Villa di Pollio,** a public park, harbors ruins and a fantastic swimming hole. To get there, take a bus to Capo di Sorrento and then walk 12 minutes past the stop.

Nearby **Sant'Agata** (12km by SITA bus from P. Tasso), a tiny city perched high in the hills, is known as the "city on the two gulfs" because from its majestic height you can see both the Bay of Naples and the Gulf of Salerno. The city's church, the **Chiesa di Sant'Agata,** boasts a 13th-century mother-of-pearl altar by the Florentine school. From the church, take an uphill path to the locality of **Deserto,** a tranquil, deserted plain from which you can survey the Campanian coastline far below.

Sorrento hosts several interesting spectacles throughout the year, including an elaborate procession on Good Friday and an international film festival in October. One of the most notable events of the year is the February 15 **Festa di Sant'Antonino,** when the town's fishermen let loose with a market to beat all markets, processions from the church, and a parade of Sant'Antonino's statue through town. Several miracles are attributed to the saint, among them his success in convincing a nasty whale to return a swallowed child to its mother at the *marina grande.* Classical music is performed roughly every other night throughout July and August at the outdoor atrium of the **Chiostro di San Francesco,** near the Villa Comunale on the water. (Showtime 9pm. Admission L20,000, students under 26 L12,000, some shows half-price.) Free events from July through September take place in the Villa Comunale, the Chiostro di San Francesco, and the town's two ports. Get a list at the tourist office. From November to March, the Sorrento Tourist Board organizes **Sorrento Inverno,** a free entertainment program that includes movies, concerts, local folklore exhibits, and guided tours of town. The area around P. Tasso heats up and gets down after dark. People swarm the streets, look out over the bay, and careen around on mopeds. **La Boutique della Birre,** in Ville Pompeiana, Via Marina Grande, 6 (tel. 877 24 28), has gorgeous frescoed rooms, pool tables, over a hundred kinds of beers, and music saturating the air. Food is also available (sandwiches

and pasta). (Open nightly 7:30pm-1am.) For more international flavor go to **South
Compass,** P. Antiche Mura (tel. 878 42 90). Large screen playing MTV, plus sand
wiches, beer, and nightly contests with prizes. Open 8pm-close. You can get bottle
of wine, T-shirts and more. Food is a bit pricey but the place is lively so one can g
just without ordering anything.

AMALFI COAST

The Amalfi Coast is worth every superlative a tourist brochure could heap upon it
Stretches of bold, arresting bluffs typify the region's alluring scenery. A limeston
range marked by deep gorges and fantastically sculpted rocks, the harsh souther
shore of the mountainous peninsula separating the Bay of Naples from the Gulf o
Salerno is tempered by prolific lemon groves, from which comes the newly discov
ered **limoncello,** an aftermeal drink (around L17,000 for the bottle; the fancier th
bottle, the more it costs). On these steep mountain sides you'll also find terraces o
grape vines, olive trees, almonds, camelias, and oleander.

The coast is accessible by frequent SITA buses leaving Sorrento and Salerno ever
two hours, and *circumvesuviana* service from Naples on a less regular basis (th
Meta stop). Some find the route Via Salerno more convenient as Eurail passes are no
honored by the *circumvesuviana* to Sorrento and Meta. You will revere the bu
drivers after this voyage; they manage the dizzying, semi-aerial roads with aplomb
Rent a motorbike for an exhilarating, if treacherous, coastal experience. This i
probably the best bike ride in Italy; distances between towns are short, and on bik
you'll be able to stop anywhere along the way and enjoy the sea vistas or go swim
ming. Due to the character of the road, hitchhiking is inadvisable for hitchers an
drivers alike. You can also reach the Amalfi coast by sea, with the **Metró della Cost**
(Salerno-Amalfi L3000). The fare changes depending on which city you land on.

■ Positano

Ten miles from Sorrento, Positano looks as if it might slip off its tenuous rock perc
right into the sea. As Steinbeck wrote of his old vertical haunt, "You do not walk t
visit a friend, you either climb or slide." Other *artistes,* Tennessee Wiliams amon
them, hit this quiet fishing village. In recent years, Positano has perhaps traded som
authenticity for tourist appeal, but it remains one of a kind, especially when see
from the direction of Sorrento.

Positano is located one hour from Sorrento by SITA bus. From the bus stop a
Chiesa Nuova, either walk down the winding stairway to the village (affectionate
referred to as the "Thousand Steps") or take the bus, which runs every half-hour u
and down the main street (L1200). When leaving, buy tickets in advance from th
Bar Internazionale. The terse but well-informed **tourist office** is at Via del Saracino
4 (tel. 87 50 67). Stop by to pick up a map and a neat, glossy booklet on the tow
(Open Mon.-Sat. 8:30am-2pm.) A row of 10 **SIP telephones** is located directl
behind the tourist office in the alley. The **telephone code** for Positano is 089. /
pharmacy is located at Via dei Mulini (tel. 87 58 63). The **emergency number** is, a
always, 113; the **police** are at Chiesa Nuova (tel. 87 50 50).

Ferries provide extensive service; buy tickets at the *biglietteria marittima* o
the port. Boats run to Cápri (departures 9am and 3:20pm, L12,500), Amalfi (11am
5:20pm, and 6pm, L7000), Íschia (9am, L14,000), Salerno (5:20pm and 6pm
L12,500), Naples (3:20pm, L13,000), and Sorrento (3:20pm and 4:10pm Via Cápr
L13,000).

Homer's Sirens allegedly inhabited the three rocks off Positano's beach. If you to
feel the pull of the Sirens' call, try one of the many *pensioni* in the area. (Reserv
early in the busy summer season.) **Villa Maria Luisa,** Via Fornillo, 40 (tel. 87 50 23
10 minutes from the top of Positano near Fornillo beach, leases splendid views

relaxing terraces and doubles with baths (L60,000-65,000; L25,000 per extra person). Literally next door is the **Casa Guadagno,** Via Fornillo (tel. 87 50 42) with spotless, well-lit rooms. Call ahead as the 10 rooms with bath are a quick sell. (Singles L35,000, doubles L65,000; Oct.-May singles L30,000, doubles L55,000.)

As you descend on the right of Via dei Mulini, the aroma emanating from **Trattoria Giardino degli Aranci** will entice you to their outdoor and indoor tables. Their specialties are spaghetti with mussels (*cozze*) for L9000 and grilled fish for L15,000. Open daily noon-1am; in winter Tues.-Sun. 1-3pm and 8-11pm.) **O'Capurale,** Marina di Positano (tel. 87 53 74), dishes up heaping plates of *bucatini alla caporalessa* (baked pasta with eggplant and cheese) for L7000 (other pasta specialties L7000-11,000), and serves them at outdoor tables facing the beach. Main dishes run L9000-11,000. Wine is L6000 per bottle. (Cover L2000. Service 10%. Open March-Oct. daily 12:30-4pm and 7:30-11pm.)

Spiraling upwards from **Marina Grande,** Positano's grey but attractive beach, **Via dei Mulini,** with its many boutiques and well-clad foreigners, is a study in the well-heeled tourist. For more traditional sight-seeing, however, the 17th-century church of **Santa Maria Assunta,** located in P. Flavio Gioia, crowns the memorable Positano landscape with a beautiful tiled dome. Boats from **Marina Grande** will take you on minicruises to the islets of **Li Galli,** and **La Porta** beach with its 15,000-year-old grotto, the legendary Sirens-ville. Hop the bus from the top of Positano or hike the 45-minute trail to **Monte Pertuso.** On the way, stop at the locals' favorite freshwater spring at the foot of a small Madonna. Monte Pertuso, a high cliff pierced by a large *pertuso* (hole), towers over the beautiful and hamlet of **Praiano,** which basks in newfound popularity.

■ Amalfi

> God created Amalfi one day when he was in a great mood.
>
> —A. Cutole

The first Sea Republic of Italy, Amalfi has been a bustling seaside town since its foundation by the Romans. After a downfall caused by Norman conquest and the 1343 earthquake, Amalfi became the first city to reestablish commercial ties with both the East and West, and created its own coin. Home of Flavio Gioia (inventor of the compass), Amalfi was also the point of origin of the famous *"Tabula de Amalpha,"* an important development in the governing of sea navigation. Today, however, tourism has replaced exotic sea trading. Fortunately, the crunch isn't as intense as in Sorrento, and the milieu is far more enchanting. Amalfi attracts passive lingerers who stroll the beautiful bayside promenades, sip coffee in the intimate piazza in front of the cathedral, or step off on forays into the high hills and winding roads of the surrounding coast.

ORIENTATION AND PRACTICAL INFORMATION

Buses stop in P. Flavio Gioia, named after the developer of the European magnetic compass. Head away from the water and pass through the white, arched portal or the street to the right of P. del Duomo.

Tourist Office: Corso delle Repubbliche Marinare, 27/29 (tel. 87 11 07; fax 87 26 19). On the water in the direction of Salerno from the bus stop. Friendly staff has limited information; ask for the city pamphlet, hotel list, and street map if they're in stock. Open Mon.-Fri. 8am-2pm and 4:30-7pm; Oct.-May Mon.-Sat. 8am-2pm.

Post Office: Corso delle Repubbliche Marinare, 29 (tel. 87 13 30), on the road running along the waterfront. Open Mon.-Fri. 8:15am-6pm, Sat. 8:15am-12:15pm. **Postal code:** 84011.

Telephones: Bar Della Valle, Via Marino del Giudice, 8 (tel. 87 12 65). Take the road that leads uphill from P. del Duomo. Open daily 8am-2pm and 3:30-10pm; Oct.-May closed Sun. **Telephone code:** 089.

Buses: terminal at P. Flavio Gioia, 1 (tel. 87 10 09), at the waterfront. Buses leave regularly for: Sorrento (L3200), Positano (L1600), Salerno (L2400), Ravello (L1500), and other coastal destinations.

Boats: several companies sail from the port near P. Flavio Gioia. Among them, **Gabbiano** propels thrice daily to Cápri June-Sept. (L9000), and to Íschia (L12,500); April 9-May to all locations once daily. To Salerno June-Sept. 4 times daily (L5000). Private boats sail regularly for the Grotta Smeraldo from the docks next to the bus terminal (about L10,000 per person).

Boat Rental: Raffaele Florio (tel. 87 21 47). L10,000 per hr. for a rowboat, L25,000 per hr. with engine and full tank of gas. (The boats are near *Lo Smeraldino* on the waterfront.) Further down the street, **Lido Delle Sirene,** Piazzale dei Protontini (tel. 87 14 89) also rents boats for L60,000 per 2hr. without sailor. A mini-cruise to the **Grotta dello Smeraldo** is L35,000 for 2 people. Groups may receive discounts.

Emergencies: tel. 112. **Police:** Via Casamare, 19 (tel. 87 10 22).

ACCOMMODATIONS

Staying in Amalfi is a pricey treat. Accommodations fill in August, so reserve at least one month in advance. The best bargain is a stone's throw away in the less crowded village of **Atrani.**

Hotel Amalfi, Via dei Pastai, 3 (tel. 87 24 40), to the left off Via Genova as you go uphill. A 3-star establishment with immaculate rooms, attentive management, terraces, and citrus gardens—simply Amalfi's best. All rooms with bath. English spoken. June-Sept. doubles with breakfast L85,000. Oct-May doubles L70,000. Triples L120,000 high season, L100,000 low season. These are the special *Let's Go* prices, so be sure to mention the book. Even greater discounts in low season.

Pensione Proto, Salita dei Curiali, 4 (tel. 87 10 03). Take Via Lorenzo d'Amalfi from P. Duomo and go right into the tiny alley where you see a sign for the Church of Maria Addolorata. Comfy but run-down rooms. Proto-English spoken. Half-pension required July-Aug. L35,000-40,000 depending on room. June and Sept. singles with bath L20,000, doubles with bath L30,000. Cheaper in off-season.

Hotel Lidomare, Via Piccolomini, 9 (tel. 87 13 32), through the passageway off Via Genova across from the *duomo.* Take a left up the flight of stairs, and then go up the steps through the arch on the far right side of the piazza. Posh, pristine, and small. Antique lounge sports color TV and piano. Run by a delightful duo. 1 single with bath and breakfast L55,000, Oct.-May L45,000. Doubles with bath and breakfast L85,000-90,000, Oct.-May L80,000. A/C L7000.

FOOD

Countering the low-quality, high-priced outlets that feed the charter busloads, grocer **N. Anastasio** (tel. 87 10 07) at Via Lorenzo d'Amalfi, 32 (the street that runs by the *duomo),* provides cold cuts (about L1500-3800 per *etto)* and *passolini,* a regional specialty of plump raisins wrapped in inedible lemon leaves (L2000). Also consider a bottle of *Ravello* wine for L4000-7000. (Open Mon.-Sat. 8am-1:30pm and 4:30-9:30pm, Sun. 8am-1pm; off-season closed Sun.) Another local wine is the *Gran Furore* which goes for similar prices.

Bar Il Tarì, Via P. Capuano, near #9 (tel. 87 18 32), on the street that Via Genova runs into. Don't let the name or location throw you; the restaurant Il Tarì is a few doors down, but the snack bar is unmarked. Delectable hot and cold food at delectable prices. *Gnocchi* L5000, sandwiches L3500-4000. Wine L5000 per bottle. Open daily 10am-3pm and 7-11:30pm; Nov.-May closed Tues.

Ristorante La Piazzetta, in Atrani on P. Umberto I (tel. 871 930), well-marked and easy to find on the town's only piazza. Special student and *Let's Go* prices of L16,000 for full *menù* including beverage and service. Fish is their specialty.

Trattoria La Perla, Salita Truglio, 3 (tel. 87 14 40), around the corner from the Hotel Amalfi. Elegant but moderately priced. Terrific seafood. Bounteous *spa-*

ghetti al profumo di mare (with seafood, L9000) and terrific homemade *cannelloni amalfitana* (pasta stuffed with veal and spices, L5000). *Sammarco vino* from Ravello L6000 per bottle. Try mentioning *Let's Go.* Open daily noon-3:30pm and 7pm-midnight; Oct.-May closed Tues.

Bar-Gelateria Royal, Via Corenzo d'Amalfi, 10 (tel. 87 19 82), near the *duomo.* The excellent hand-churned ice cream here is Amalfi's best. Their specialty is the *pastiera napoletana,* with bits of Neapolitan Easter fruitcake. Cones L2000-3000. Open daily 11am-2am; Oct.-May closed Mon.

SIGHTS

The town's principal monument is the **duomo,** off Via Mansone I, at the top of a long flight of stairs overlooking P. del Duomo. Rebuilt in the 19th century according to the original medieval plan, the cathedral (originally 9th-12th century) boasts a startling façade of varied geometric designs typical of Arab-Norman style, but very unusual in Italy. The exceptional bronze doors, crafted in Constantinople in 1066 lead inside to unusually narrow bays which augment its taut elegance. Downstairs, the crypt houses the remains of St. Andrew (all except his head, which the Pope kindly donated to St. Andrew's church in Patras, Greece) and a bronze statue of the apostle sculpted by a pupil of Michelangelo. (Cathedral open daily 7am-1:30pm and 3-8pm. Appropriate dress required.) To the left of the church the **Chiostro Paradiso** (Cloister of Paradise), a 13th-century cemetery, has become a graveyard for miscellaneous column fragments, broken statues, and sarcophagi. Its Arabic arches create a romantic setting for piano and vocal concerts on Friday and Saturday nights July through September. Tickets cost L5000. (Cloister open daily 9am-1:30pm and 3-8pm. Admission L1000.)

The old 9th-century **arsenal** located on the waterfront by the entrance to the city contains relics of and information on Amalfi's erstwhile maritime glory. Continue up the street to the ceramic laboratory **Ceramiche Giovanna Fusco,** Via delle Cartiere, 22, where some of the pottery that saturates P. del Duomo's shops is made before your very eyes. (Open Jan. 7-Aug. 17 and Aug. 26-Dec. 22 Mon.-Sat. 9am-1pm and 3-6pm.) Just before the ceramic lab, several yellow signs point to a path that leads up into one of the treasures of Amalfi, the **Valle dei Mulini** (Valley of the Mills). A short hike up and away from the sea along a stream bed by the old paper mills affords a pastoral view of hillside lemon groves and narrow, rocky mountains.

Near Amalfi: Atrani

Your first excursion from Amalfi should be to **Atrani,** (if you haven't escaped there already), a shimmering beachside town of 1200 inhabitants, a mere 10-minute walk from Amalfi (or 1 bus stop, L1500). At the entrance to a ravine, the **Valley of the Dragons,** Atrani has beachfront with no stairs screened by stunning mountains in the background. The investiture of Amalfi's vacationing doges took place in the town's **Church of San Salvatore dei Birento,** facing you as you enter the town's main archway to the central piazza. The church has been remodeled but the 11th-century Byzantine bronze doors are still intact. Thirteenth-century **Santa Maria Maddalena** is also beautiful, with its tiled cupola and gorgeous view of the coast.

If you can't find a place to stay in Amalfi, consider the **A'Scalinatella,** in Atrani, P. Umberto, 12 (tel. 87 19 30). From Amalfi walk 5min. along the waterfront. Just before you arrive at the tunnel descend the stairs that pass through the Ristorante Zaccaria to the water and take a left. Cross the parking lot and go under the arch into the town's only piazza. Follow signs from there. The congenial family that manages this quasi-hostel caters to students and budget travelers. Special *Let's Go* price of L10,000 (L15,000 in Aug.) for bed and bath. Sheets, use of kitchen facilities and washing machines, and towel are extra.

As you climb up the main street (Via dei Dogi) from the port, **public toilets** are on the left, **phones** are on the right, and the town's best restaurant, **A'Paranza,** crowns the top of the hill on the right, at Via Dragone 1-2 (tel. 87 18 40). Only fresh fish is served at L15,000 for *primi* and around L20,000 for *secondi*. Open daily 12:30-2:30pm and 7:30-11:30pm. Oct.-May closed Tues.

■ Ravello

Ravello's origins are shrouded in mystery; it probably began as a Roman refugee camp in the 6th century AD. By the end of the 11th century the town had blossomed to 36,000 inhabitants, whose numbers dwindled progressively as a result of Pisan raids. Today, with a population of 2500, the town has retained the medieval beauty and landscaping prized by Boccaccio, who dedicated part of the *Decameron* to it, and by Wagner, who made it the setting for the second act of *Parsifal*. Whether or not you sense yourself on the brink of a *magnum opus,* it's worth the journey up the mountain. Hike the 7km up from Amalfi for the most spectacular views.

Orientation and Practical Information Ravello is a short bus ride from Amalfi (every hr., 7am-10pm, L1500). **Piazza Vescovado** hosts most municipal services, while the hotels and restaurants are generally to the left of the piazza when you face the *duomo.* The **tourist office,** at P. Vescovado, 13 (tel. 85 70 96, fax 85 79 77), to the left of the cathedral, is very helpful, offering pretty brochures, maps, and up-to-date accommodations information. English spoken. (Open Mon.-Sat. 8am-8pm.) To the left of the tourist office is the **post office** (open Mon.-Sat. 8:15am-1:30pm). The **postal code** is 84010. Next along the street is the **pharmacy,** while **public toilets** are to the right of the *duomo* by the corner bar. **Exchange currency** at the **Banca Populare,** Via Roma, on the left walking away from the *duomo.* (Open Mon.-Fri. 8:20am-1:15pm.)

Accommodations and Food Two options are available if you're planning to spend the night. The dramatically situated **Hotel Villa Amore** (tel. 85 71 35), en route to Villa Cimbrone, has column-filled niches in the hallways and a garden overlooking cliffs and sea. (Half-pension required at L75,000. June and Sept. singles with bath L53,000, doubles L93,000; Oct.-May singles with bath L45,000, doubles L83,000.) Up the street to the left of the tourist office **Albergo Toro,** Via Emanuele Filiberto (tel. 85 72 11), lets clean, comfortable rooms on an oleander-filled side street. Pretty covered terrace, restaurant downstairs. (Half-pension July-Aug. L75,000; Oct.-June singles L38,000, with bath L43,000. Doubles with bath L76,000. Prices vary in the off-season. AmEx.)

Several *alimentari* and assorted specialty food shops line Via Roma off P. Vescovado. For a sit-down meal try **La Colonna,** at Via Roma, 20 (tel. 85 78 76). The affable young owner Alfonso speaks English and is well-known throughout the town for his delectable fish and homemade pasta. Try his cheese crêpes (L10,000) or ask for his specialty, *tagliatelle con melanzane* (pasta with eggplant, L9000). He's also proud of his tasty *torta caprese,* an almond chocolate cake (L4000). (Open Tues.-Sun. noon-2pm and 7-11pm.) If you're taken by the pottery on the tables and walls, visit brother Pasquale's gallery next door.

Ravello decants some of southern Italy's best **wines.** Three famous types, *Sammarco, Gran Caruso,* and *Episcopio,* are savored around the globe. Pick up a few bottles of *Sammarco* (L4000-5000) at the vineyard's warehouse, **Casa Vinicola Ettore Sammarco,** Via Civita, 9 (tel. 87 23 89), at the SITA bus stop 3.5km from Amalfi on the road to Ravello, where you can also buy some *limoncello.* (Open Mon.-Sat. 8am-1pm and 3-7pm, Sun. 8am-1pm.)

Sights Trees and flowers, small churches, and winding byways enhance the already spectacular setting of Ravello's **Villa Rufolo,** perched 360m above the sea. This 11th-century country estate, built by a wealthy Ravellian family, later housed several popes, Charles of Anjou, and the embittered expatriate Wagner, who exclaimed upon seeing it, "The garden of Klingsor is found." A medieval tower with beautiful Norman-Saracen vault and statues representing the four seasons serves as the entry to the famous Moorish cloister. (Enter from the bus stop at P. Vescovado. Open daily 9:30am-1pm and 3-7pm, Oct.-May 9:30am-1pm and 2-5pm. Admission L3000.)

Outside Ravello's **duomo** you can see the Amalfi coast's third set of spectacular bronze doors (these 12th-century ones were modeled on Amalfi's). Inside, a simple nave arcade of antique columns sets off two fantastic Cosmatesque pulpits, one large enough to be a separate building. To the left of the altar stands the chapel of San Pantaleone, patron of the town, whose "unleakable" blood is preserved in a cracked vessel. (San Pantaleone was beheaded at Nicomedia on July 27, 290. On this day every year the city holds a **festival** and the saint's blood reputedly liquifies. Open daily 9am-1pm and 3-7pm, Oct.-May 9am-1pm.)

Follow the signposts for **Villa Cimbrone** on the small road passing to the right of Villa Rufolo. Floral walkways and gardens are the prelude to some of the most magnificent views in all the Amalfi coast. (Admission L3000.)

Ravello's **classical music festival,** held June 20-30, hosts internationally renowned musicians. Concerts draw crowds to the cathedral and the gardens of Villa Rufolo. Tickets run L12,000-15,000, and may be purchased at the tourist office.

Scala

Established in 400 BC by a group of Roman shipwreck victims, Scala lies 1½km up the hill from Ravello. The tiny little burg spawned both Ravello and Amalfi; unfortunately, those greedy Pisans got to it between 1135 and 1137, and the town has never fully recovered.

Scala faces Ravello from the northwest, dominating the coast from its 400m elevation. Take any of the buses from Amalfi (7am-9pm, L1500) or Ravello (10:30am-9:30pm, L1500). The still air, ebbing mist, and glimmer of the sea behind the cliffs of Ravello below make Scala's inspiring landscape the consummate Amalfi coast image.

Don't be daunted by the unappealing façade of the **cathedral;** the immense structure has three exceptional frescoed plates on its vaulted ceilings. The **Pro Loco** (tel. (089) 85 73 25), in P. Municipio around the corner from the pharmacy, hands out pamphlets (open daily 9am-noon and 5:30-9:30pm). They can also direct you to the **Torre dello Ziro,** the remaining tower in the castle ruins with a lofty panorama of the coast.

After your hike to the tower, savor the views from a table at **Ristorante-Pizzeria Belvedere,** Via d'Amata (tel. 85 73 76), in the Campidoglio area of Scala, 1km uphill from the bus stop. The huge plates of *pasta al sugo di pesce* (with fresh seafood, L12,000) confirm your arrival in heaven. (Cover L1500. Service 10%. Open daily noon-3pm and 7pm-midnight, Oct.-March Sat.-Sun. noon-3pm and 7pm-midnight, April-June Thurs.-Tues. noon-3pm and 7pm-midnight.)

Minori

Minori was once Amalfi's arsenal and as such suffered attacks from all of the bigger port's enemies. In these more settled times, however, the city is better known for its lemons, exported all over the world, and for its beaches and family atmosphere. Accommodations are reasonable, so Minori is a sensible stopover point on your way along the coast.

The coastal SITA bus (L1500) stops right at the center of town, which opens right onto a pebble beach. The **Pro Loco** at P. Umberto I, 18 (tel. (089) 87 70 87 or 87 76 07), is often out of pamphlets, but willing to help as much as possible. (Open Mon.-Sat. 9am-noon and 4-8pm.)

Though far from luxurious, **Albergo Cápri,** Via Dietro la Chiesa, 19 (tel. 87 74 17), on the second floor, is a good bet. Take the road through Church San Trofimena's bell tower. (Doubles L48,000, with bath L48,000, including breakfast.) The **Caporal Hotel,** Via Nazionale (tel. 87 74 08), is a prettier but more crowded hotel with more professional services and English-speaking owner. June-Sept. Singles with bath L60,000. Doubles with bath L80,000. Full board L90,000. L10,000-20,000 off during the other months. AmEx.

For a satisfying meal, try **La Botte,** Via S. Maria Vetrano, 15 (tel. 87 78 93). The management is accommodating, there are wooden outdoor tables, and the *scialetelli con Frutti* is splendid (L8500). Pizza L5000-8000. Cover L2000.

Praiano

Three and a half miles down the coast, Praiano is a rocky city built in the image of Positano, but less touristed than its neighbor and rival in the fish trade. This tiny town has a lovely beach but no tourist office and no real center. A spread of a few shops meets the needs of its 1500 inhabitants.

Enjoy the rapturous panorama from the excellent campground-hotel **La Tranquillità,** Via Roma, 10 (tel. (089) 87 40 84), on the road to Amalfi (ask the bus driver to stop at the Ristorante Continental/La Tranquillità). The rooms here hold a monopoly on the coast's most awe-inspiring views of the surrounding caves, castles, gorges, and sea, while the spotless campsite (the only one on the coast) clings miraculously to precipitous cliffs that hang over the coast. (L12,000 per person; off-season L10,000. Tent included. Clean, new bungalows with bath and often a terrace L25,000-30,000 per person including breakfast.) Don't leave the coast without savoring a meal at the open-air **Ristorante Continental,** above La Tranquillità. The place to go for fresh mountain air, endless views, and exquisite food. *Primi* cost L6000, *secondi* are L9000-15,000, and the local wine runs L6000 per bottle. *Let's Go* bearers receive a 15% discount. (Cover L2000. Open daily noon-3pm and 8pm-midnight. Hotel and restaurant both open March-Nov.) The hotel has a direct staircase to the beach. There's another marvelous beach up the road toward Positano but you must be willing to descend 400 steps (keep the return trip in mind). Alternate accommodations may be found at **Open Gate** (tel. 87 41 48), just up the street from the campground, which offers views and steps to the beach (doubles are about L50,000).

Turn the bend as you leave Praiano and you'll immediately encounter both the sign for the **Grotto dello Smeraldo** and the steps leading to the miniscule fishing village of **Conca dei Marini,** which boasts a Norman tower. The SITA bus from Sorrento to Salerno will drop you off at the elevator entrance to the grotto, to the left of a bar/restaurant/ceramics shop. The grotto is sensitive about its rivalry with Cápri's azure equivalent. The water—of a pleasant green hue due to the light entering through an underground tunnel—isn't as stunning, but the cave is large, and the tour long as multilingual guides show you stalagmites and stalactites in different forms above and below the water level. An Italian television station ruined the natural beauty of the site by sinking a nativity scene in the middle of the cave. The guides tend to dwell on this feature. The elevator down from the road is free; entrance to the cave and boat tour is L4000. (Open daily 9am-5pm.)

■ Salerno

Home to Europe's first medical school, Salerno was where medieval patients received the latest drugs and submitted to the newest surgical techniques; even today it maintains the intellectual snobbery of a university town. After the picturesque and mountainous coastal villages, the big-city atmosphere and dearth of sights are a shock to the system. Nevertheless, inexpensive accommodations and extensive bus and train connections (Eurail passes are good here) facilitate transit to the Amalfi coast and the archaeological sites of Pompeii and Paestum.

ORIENTATION AND PRACTICAL INFORMATION

Salerno is a major stop for trains headed toward Calabria from Rome and Naples. The train station is on Piazza Veneto, from which the expansive and remarkably clean Corso Vittorio Emanuele strikes off to the right (closed to traffic), leading to

Via dei Mercanti. Parallel to Corso Vittorio Emanuele but closer to the sea, Corso Garibaldi runs northwest into Via Roma, and southeast into Corso Torrione. Closer, to the water Piazza della Concordia separates Lungomare Trieste from Lungomare Marconi to the southeast.

Tourist Office: APT (tel. 23 14 32), on P. Ferrovia to the right as you leave the train station. Maps and pamphlets on the Amalfi Coast. *Memo* is an excellent guide to Salerno's *alberghi,* with map, bus schedule, and entertainment listings. English spoken. Open Mon.-Fri. 9am-2pm and 3-8pm, Sat. 9:30am-12:30pm and 3:30-7:30pm. **APT,** Via Roma, 248 (in P. Amendola, tel. 22 47 44). Open Mon.-Fri. 9am-1pm and 4-7pm, Sat. 9am-noon. English spoken.

Budget Travel: CTS, P. St'Elmo (tel. 75 32 72). Open Mon.-Fri. 9am-1pm and 4:30-7:30pm.

Post Office: Corso Garibaldi, 203 (tel. 22 41 54), at Via dei Principati. Open Mon.-Sat. 8:30am-7:30pm. **Postal Code:** 84100.

Telephones: SIP, Corso Garibaldi, 31/2, set in from the street to the left as you leave the train station. Open daily 9:15am-12:45pm and 2:15-5:45pm. **Telephone Code:** 089.

Trains: in P. Ferrovia (tel. 23 14 15), behind P. Veneto. Trains depart regularly 5am-11pm to Pompeii (40min., L2400) and Naples (1hr., L4300). Also several trains to Paestum on the Salerno-Règgio di Calabria line (45min., L3900). Information office outside and to the right of the station open daily 7am-9pm.

Luggage Storage: Follow the signs in the station, to the huge warehouse. Bags L1500, bikes and the like L2000.

Buses: SITA, Via Irno, 2-4 (tel. 79 50 21). Information office open Mon.-Sat. 8am-1pm and 4:30-8pm. Buses to Naples (every 10-15min. 6am-9pm, L4300) leave from Corso Garibaldi outside SITA office. Buses for the Amalfi coast depart from P. della Concordia to: Amalfi (frequent buses 6am-10:30pm, L2400); Sorrento (9 per day 6am-7pm, L5000) with stops at the coastal towns of Praiano (L3200) and Positano (L3900). Buses run less frequently Sun. **ATAC** (tel. 22 58 99) city bus #41 leaves regularly from outside the train station to Pompeii (every 20min. 5:55am-9:55pm, 30min., L2800). Several bus lines run from P. Concordia to Paestum (direction "Sapri," L4000).

Swimming Pool: Piscina Comunale Torrione, Lungomare Marconi (tel. 23 90 41), across the street from the fort-like structure. Admission L5500, under 14 L4000; Sunday L6500 and L5000. Open June-Sept. daily 10am-4pm.

Emergencies: tel. 113. **Police:** tel. 23 18 19. **Hospital: S. Lenardo** (tel. 67 11 11). **Medical Assistance:** tel. 30 19 99.

ACCOMMODATIONS

The hotel supply is just adequate—nothing more, nothing less. Prices have risen dramatically, without a similar rise in quality. Salerno is in no way a budget vacation destination, and a night spent here should be as a stopover. Establishments fill rapidly in late July and August, so arrive early in the morning to secure a place.

Ostello della Gioventù "Irno" (HI), Via Luigi Guercia, 112 (tel. 79 02 51). Exit the train station and make a left. Via Torrione runs along the tracks. After about 300m you'll come to Via Mobilio, which will take you left under the tracks. Approximately 300m ahead you'll see a staircase on your right leading up to Via Luigi Guercia. Clean rooms, kitchen facilities, TV room and gentle management—who could ask for more? Curfew midnight. Lock-out 10:30am-5:00pm. L15,000 per person, L2000 for sheets. Ask at desk for directions to eateries which offer discounts to hostel clientele.

Albergo Cinzia, Corso Vittorio Emanuele, 74 (tel. 23 27 73), down the street from Santa Rosa. Chintz galore. One single L25,000. Doubles L75,000. Make reservations for July and Aug.

Albergo Santa Rosa, Corso Vittorio Emanuele, 14 (tel. 22 53 46), off the piazza in front of the train station. Clean, bright, and a bargain. English spoken. Curfew 12:30am. Singles L35,000. Doubles L50,000.

Hotel Salerno, Via Vicinanza, 42 (tel. 22 42 11). The sign is across the street from Albergo Santa Rose. Furniture was new in the 50s and hasn't died yet. Singles L35,000, with bath L40,000. Doubles L45,000, with bath L60,000.

FOOD

Salerno lays claim to no dish in particular but partakes of the general Campanian culinary genius, serving delightful specialties like *pasta e fagioli* (pasta and bean soup) and all sorts of seafood-based treats. Nearby Battipaglia produces the famous *mozzarella alla buffala,* fresh cheese made from water buffalo's milk. Shop cheap at **Supermercato STANDA,** Corso Vittorio Emanuele, 228 (open Mon.-Tues. and Thurs.-Sat. 9am-1pm and 4-8pm, Wed. 9am-1pm).

Pizzeria Ristorante Fonzie, Via S. Mobilio, 22 (tel. 239 208). Richie, Potsie and the gang cook up excellent, very inexpensive food on the way to the hostel. Delicious mini-pizzas L2000. Open 12:30-2:30pm and 4:30pm-midnight.

Pizzeria Del Vicolo della Neve, Vicolo della Neve, 24 (tel. 22 57 05). Take the side street that intersects with Via Roma before #160; go right and then right again. In the old city, this piece of Salernitan history hasn't changed since its opening 500 years ago. Try traditional dishes like *baccalà in cassuola* (salt cod with tomatoes, oregano, and oil, L7000) or *giambotta* (a mix of potatoes, eggplant, and peppers, L5000). Full meal runs between L20,000 and L30,000. Cover L2000. Service 12%. Open Thurs.-Tues. 8pm-3am.

Trattoria-Pizzeria Da "Sasà" La Casereccia, Via Diaz, 42 (tel. 22 03 30), off Corso Vittorio Emanuele. Black chairs and pink tablecloths demonstrate that this popular restaurant can accessorize. Full meals of delicous fish L15,000-25,000. Cover L2000. Open Sat.-Thurs. 12:30-3pm, and 8-11:30pm, Sun. noon-3pm.

Ristorante Il Caminetto, Via Roma, 232 (tel. 22 96 14). Across the street from the tourist office. A family-run restaurant that keeps its prices low. Savor *risotto alla pescatore,* a delicious mix of rice and seafood, for only L7000. Pizzas bake in the wood-burning oven at night (L4500-7000). *Gragnano wine* L5000 per bottle. Cover L2000. Service 12%. Open Thurs.-Tues. noon-3:30pm and 7pm-midnight.

SIGHTS AND ENTERTAINMENT

Taking Via Molo Manfredi off of the Villa Comunale at the western end of Via Roma, you can stroll onto the seawall that juts into the bay. Once there, revel in the divine Amalfi coastline and in the sights and sounds of the nearby fishing harbor. Although locals claim the water is fine, and there are no signs posted that prohibit swimming, Salerno's sea appears at least to be less than clean. To swim in the area either wear a wetsuit, or hop over to another town on the Amalfi coast—the hamlet of **Vietri sul Mare** is closest (take the SITA bus toward Sorrento, 15min., L1500).

For a spectacular view of Salerno's majestic surroundings, take bus #19 from Teatro Verdi (L1000), west of the Villa Comunale, to the medieval **Castello di Arechi,** which dates from the 8th century. (Open daily 9am-6pm. Free.) Back at city level, visit Salerno's medieval quarter. It was once the capital of the Norman empire (1077-1127) and home of Europe's oldest medical school. (Ninth-century codices were already calling it ancient.) Watched over by a 12th-century Norman tower, the **cathedral,** built between 1076 and 1085 by decree of the Norman leader Robert Guiscard, honors Salerno's patron saint, San Matteo. An ancient pool lies in the center of its colorful atrium. The revered tooth, the holy tooth, and nothing but the tooth of San Matteo awaits worship in the crypt. (Cathedral open daily 9:30am-12:30pm and 4-7pm.)

Don't miss the Sunday evening *passeggiata* when the *lungomare* overflows with people strolling and enjoying ice cream. In June, July, and August, an **arts festival** features free concerts and drama in the atrium of the cathedral and at the city's stadium. Salerno also hosts an **international film festival** in October at Cinema Capitol in the center of the city (admission L6000; ask at the tourist office for details on this and related cinematic events throughout the year). During the month of July, Salerno also hosts an **international blues festival.**

The area around Salerno rocks with discos. June through September, the night-time hotspot is the renowned **Fuenti** (tel. 21 09 33), in the locality of Cetara, 4km west of Salerno. Uniquely situated on the coastal cliffs, it features three full floors of open-air dancing. (Cover L15,000, 1st drink included. Open Sat.-Sun. 10pm-4am.) In the winter, Salerno lives it up at **Living,** Via Gelsi Rossi (tel. 39 92 01), northeast of the train station in the city center. (Open Oct.-May Thurs.-Fri. 8:30pm-2am, Sat. 9:30pm-3am, and Sun. 6:30pm-3am. Free; Sat.-Sun. cover L15,000, first drink included.) The cheapest way to get into these clubs is to look for free passes which are randomly handed out. Also check *MEMO* for special events and more club listings, including those outside of Salerno.

■ Paestum

Paestum's ruins rise up in an open field amid flowers and wild grasses. Founded in the 7th century BC as Poseidonia by a group of Greek colonists from Síbari (near Crotone in the Ionian Sea), Paestum quickly grew into a flourishing commercial center, enjoying an expansive trade with the Etruscans and the lands to the north. Conquered in the 4th century BC by native Italians, it revived under Roman rule with the addition of baths, forums, and amphitheaters. Decline set in when the extension of the Appian Way to the Adriatic allowed Rome to bypass Tyrrhenian trade routes. Recurrent malaria epidemics and Saracen raids during the 9th century hastened the city's demise.

Hotels and restaurants lie north and south of the site. It's most convenient to stay in Salerno, only an hour away and connected by frequent buses and trains. Buses on the Salerno-Sapri line leave from P. Concordia, near the Salerno train station, about every half-hour (first bus at 5:45am); trains run about every two hours. The last bus back to Salerno leaves at 8:10pm, the last train at 9:30pm. Both cost about L3800. Nunzio Daniele's *Paestum: Hypothesis and Reality* is an excellent source of historical information on the area.

The three major temples lie along the Via Sacra. The **basilica** (6th century BC) dedicated to Hera is thought to be the oldest, based on its archaic form. The **temple** is extremely wide (9 columns across—even the Parthenon is only 6), and the tapering of its columns so extreme that it makes the temple's outer colonnade seem to lean outward on both sides. The neighboring **Temple of Neptune** (450 BC) is the largest, most intact Doric structure in the city. The six-by-fourteen column plan gives the temple its long, graceful form. In contrast to the basilica, a slight upward curving of the temple floor corrects the optical illusion that the columns sag outward. Sit facing Neptune on the far wall of the basilica for a remarkable view of this petrified forest of columns. In front of the temples lie the remains of large altars, an imposing block of limestone in front of the basilica, and two basins (the small one Roman and the other Greek). At the opposite end of the grounds, past the forum and ampitheater, stands the small **Temple of Ceres** (circa 500 BC), whose Ionic capitals now grace the museum. Sacrificial altars wallow in front of the temple, and to the right towers a lone votive column.

The **museum** (tel. (0828) 81 10 23), outside the temple grounds on the other side of Via Aquila, displays a fascinating collection of sculpture, architectural fragments, terracottas, and unusual tomb paintings from Paestum and excavations in the nearby plain of Sele. The museum's hours of operation change by season, though in general it is open 9am-7pm. Buy here the ticket which also admits to the Temple grounds. Open 9am-2hrs. before sunset; L8000.

If you decide to spend the night here, try the tranquil **Villa Rita** near the *zona archeologica* (tel. (0828) 81 10 81). A double with breakfast during the summer months is L65,000 (L10,000 less in the low season). Off the main street (**Magna Grecia**) at the end of the temple grounds, to the left of the station is **Pizzeria La Nonne,** for a quick pizza outdoors.

In July and August, Paestum hosts its own international festival of music, drama, and dance. For a program and information, contact the **tourist office** on P. Basilica 151-153 (tel. (0828) 81 10 16; open Mon.-Sat. 8am-2pm). You can also pick up *Paestum Magazine* for info on Paestum as well as other sites in the **Cilento.** It is produced and distributed by **Cointur,** Via Magna Grecia, 69 (tel. (0828) 72 25 20). It also has a limited list of hotels in the area and you can make reservations here (open 9am-1pm and 4-7:30pm).

A popular beach lies about 2km east of the temples, sprinkled with several campgrounds. **FLIC** (tel. (0828) 81 12 91) rents spots with electricity and running water for L9000 (July-Aug. L15,000) plus L4000 per person (July-Aug. L5400). Nearby **Villaggio Desiderio** (tel. 85 11 35 or 72 50 24) has a pool and markets (L8000 per person; Sept.-June L4000 per person. Use of pool L7500).

▓ Apulia (Puglia)

The heel of Italy's boot, Apulia has paid the price for its strategic location relative to the East. Apulia's fertile, flat territory is especially valuable for its position on the dry, rocky Mediterranean coast. The ancient Greeks left few traces of their stay here, but made Apulia one of the flourishing regions of Magna Graecia. For the Romans, the area was an outlet to half the Empire; the Appian Way led to now-dismal Bríndisi. The Middle Ages brought an onslaught of invaders whose combined influences created a fantastic conglomerate culture. Modern Apulia, having served its time on skid row, is regaining its prominence as the richest and most educated region in the *mezzogiorno.* In Apulia's interior, whitewashed, cone-roofed *trulli* houses and remote medieval villages dot a cave-ridden plain; along the shore, ports have a distinctly Middle-eastern air. The region's landscape is remarkably diverse, from the forested Gargàno Massif and the fertile chessboard plain to the Grecian Salentine Peninsula. Unfortunately, a legacy of *machismo* has remained which women may find threatening, especially in the large cities. In public, pointed obliviousness or a withering insult is usually sufficient to dissuade continued obnoxious behavior.

Apulia is as accessible to contemporary tourists as it was to ancient invaders. Direct train lines run from Naples to Bari and from Bologna to Lecce. **Rail service** is supplemented within the region by the private Ferrovie Bari-Nord, Ferrovie Del Sud-Est, Ferrovie del Gargàno, and Ferrovie Calabro-Lucane lines. If you hold a Eurailpass or *cartaverde,* remember that neither one is valid on these lines. The transportation hubs of Fóggia, Bríndisi, and Táranto are perhaps best viewed from the station as you make your connections; base yourself in Bari and Lecce instead.

THE GARGÀNO MASSIF

The Gargàno Massif once ranked among the most popular pilgrimage destinations in Europe: the Archangel Michael was said to have appeared here in a cave here in the 5th century, and in ancient times the same cavern was occupied by a respected dream oracle. In these more secular times, the peninsula is renowned for the 65km of beaches on the northern and eastern coasts, some of the best in continental Italy. The inland is covered by the **Foresta Umbra,** which shelters some of Italy's rare old-growth stands. The forest abruptly gives way to classic Mediterranean terrain on the southern half. The Gargàno is succumbing to the twin blights of southern coastal areas—smokestacks and beach umbrellas—so visit the region soon, before it becomes an industrial tract interrupted by the occasional *villagio turistico.*

Siponto

Three km southwest of Manfredónia, the ancient city of Siponto was abandoned after a 12th-century earthquake and plague. The sole survivor is the remarkable **Church of Santa Maria di Siponto,** which stands in a grove of pines amidst modest pre-Roman ruins. Built during the 11th century in Puglian-Romanesque style, the church's blind arcade shows strong Pisan influence, while the square plan and cupola also point to Byzantine roots. Siponto is the next-to-last stop on the Fóggia-Manfredónia train line.

■ Vieste

Vieste, located on the "spur" of the Italy's boot, is the quintessential Italian beach resort town. In every coastal cove North and South of the city lies a *villagio turistico*, a pastiche of hotels, restaurants, bungalows and campsites, offering boats, bicycles and a variety of other toys and services. The new town offers little but suntan-oil shops, photo outlets and tourist-oriented restaurants (all of which have bilingual menus written in Italian and German). The old town, built on a rocky peninsula jutting out into the sea is in contrast exceptionally scenic; its narrow, pedestrian-only streets, opening to periodic views of the sea eventually lead to a weather-worn *duomo*. According to legend, the site was originally home to an anonymous fishing village inhabited by the handsome fisherman Pizzomunno and the beautiful maiden Vieste. The nearby Sirens (of Odyssey fame), jealous of Pizzomunno's love for Vieste, threw her in the abyss to drown. Pizzomunno turned into white stone, petrified by sorrow. The rocky promontory of Pizzomunno ("tip of the world") lies opposite of Vieste and forms a natural harbor. Every hundred years the lovers come together for one night (tickets L50,000). While Vieste's graceful authenticity abides in spite of the suntanned masses, a certain frivolity undermines the legend.

ORIENTATION AND PRACTICAL INFORMATION

There are two ways of getting to Vieste, both picturesque. If you're coming from the north on the Bologna-Lecce line, get off at San Severo and catch the Ferrovie del Gargàno train to Peschici; a bus continues to Vieste (San Servo-Vieste, 3hr.). A direct Ferrovie del Gargàno **bus** from San Severo to Vieste leaves daily at noon (3hr. 30min.). **SITA** buses run from the south to Vieste from Fóggia Via Manfredónia (6 per day, 3hr., L6900). The **centro** lies a 10-minute walk down Viale XXIV Maggio from the bus stop at P. Manzoni.

Tourist Office: P. Kennedy, 1 (tel. 70 88 06). From the bus stop, walk up Viale XXIV Maggio, which becomes Corso Mazzini. Bear left at the end onto Viale Italia. Tables piled with tourist guides, maps, and practical information on Vieste. English spoken. Open Mon.-Sat. 8am-2pm and 4-10pm, Sun. 8:30am-1pm; Sept. 21-June 21 Mon.-Fri. 8am-1:30pm and 3:30-9:30pm, Sun. 8:30am-1pm.

Post Office: Via Veneto (tel. 70 80 00), next to the public gardens. Open Mon.-Fri. 8:15am-6:30pm, Sat. 8:15am-noon. **Postal code:** 71019.

Telephone code: 0884.

Buses: schedules are posted in the kiosk at the bus stop. **Ferrovia del Gargàno,** tel. (0882) 32 14 14. Buy tickets at one of the *agenzie* in P. Vittorio Emanuele. **SITA,** tel. (0881) 731 17. Buy tickets on the bus.

Ferries: to the Trémiti Islands daily (see Trémiti Islands below).

Emergencies: tel. 113. **Police:** tel. 70 62 22.

ACCOMMODATIONS AND FOOD

Vieste is a summer resort without budget provisions. If you plan to visit between mid-July and August, make reservations or be prepared to dance 'til dawn. Prices change monthly in summer, peaking in August. For information on the **Agriturismo** program, which places tourists at local farms, call 762 04. Rates vary according to season and participants.

Pensione Al Centro Storico, Via Mafrolla, 32 (tel. 70 70 30), at the end of Via Pola. From the bus stop take Viale XXIV Maggio to P. Vittorio Emanuele, which leads to Via Pola. The friendliest proprietor in town keeps the splendid old *palazzo* spotless. She'll give you keys to come and go as you please. Singles L30,000, doubles L45,000. Prices go up by L15,000 per person in July and even more in August. Delicious breakfast included.

Albergo Riviera, Via IV Novembre, 2 (tel. 70 50 00), off Via Veneto. Fastidiously kept. Airy, spartan lodgings. Singles L35,000, doubles with bath L40,000; off-season, singles L25,000, doubles L30,000.

Camping: More than 80 campsites line the beaches north and south of the city. Call ahead to check for vacancies. **Apeneste** (tel. 70 51 91), off Lungomare Mattei. L7000 per person, L8000 per small tent, L18,000 per large tent; July-Aug. 20 L7500 per person, L8500 per small tent, L20,000 per large tent. Open June-Sept.

Around the old town, restaurants occupy basements and stuccoed corners, while a daily produce **market** on Viale XXIV Maggio near the bus station supplies the less table-inclined. At night, wooden carts selling nuts and candies line the streets of **La Villa,** specializing in *torrone* (nougat with hazelnuts). Stock up at the **supermarket** on Via XXIV Maggio near the bus station. (Open Mon.-Wed. and Fri. 8am-1pm and 5-8pm, Thurs. 8am-1pm, Sat. 8am-1pm and 5-9pm.)

Locanda La Macina, Via Alessandro III, 49, at the foot of the *duomo.* One of Vieste's best dining experiences can be had at outdoor wooden tables between 2000-year-old walls. Entrees start at L7000. Open daily 12:30-2pm and 6-11pm.

La Ripa, near the *duomo.* Pricey tourist-trap appearance is just a guise; 3 generations of women serve *troccoli al sugo di seppia* (long, canoe-shaped noodles in cuttlefish ink, L7000) and *cozze piriene* (stuffed mussels, L9000). Other *secondi* L7000-L11,000. Cover L2000. Open May-Oct. 1-2:30pm and 7:30pm-midnight.

Ristorante Box 19, Via Santa Maria di Merino, 19 (tel. 70 52 29), off Corso Mazzini, near Lungomare Europa. The town favorite. Pasta dishes L4500-6000. Try the *melanzane ripiene* (stuffed eggplant) L7000. Wine L5000 per liter. Cover L1500. Service 10%. Open daily noon-3pm and 7pm-midnight.

Il Fornaio, Corso Mazzini, 12, at the end of the street. For Vieste's cheapest and most satisfying meal, partake of the *panzerotti* (deep-fried dough filled with cheese and tomatoes, made fresh every 10min., L1500). Open daily 8am-midnight.

SIGHTS AND ENTERTAINMENT

In southern Vieste, at the end of Via Battisti, the buildings of the well-preserved old town crowd up against the *duomo* in seeming adoration. The weathered **duomo** is the embodiment of architectural understatement. Near the entrance is a wooden statue of Santa Maria; legend has it that the statue sweats, but one can't be sure. From the *duomo,* head southeast on Via Cimaglia to the **Chianca Amara,** a rock where in 1554 the lives and bodies of thousands of *Viestini* were cut short by Turks. A **castle** rising from the town's summit offers a tremendous view of the Gargàno coast. Join the massive swarm of people in Vieste's popular *passeggiata,* which passes around the **Giardini Pubblici Vittorio Veneto** and **Corso Lorenzo Fazzini.** Of Vieste's three **beaches,** the southern beach, **Pizzomunno,** (a.k.a. Spiaggia della Scialara or del Castello) parallel to Lungomare Mattei, is the cleanest. To get to the beaches of postcard fame, however, you must travel farther up or down the coast. Throughout this area, the water is so clear that you can see to the sandy bottom for hundreds of feet out from the shore.

The best way to see the famed Gargàno coastline is to take a two-hour and 30-minute motorboat excursion from Vieste to the local **grottos.** Boats depart from the port daily in summer at 8:30am and at 2:30pm if enough people show (L15,000, under 12 L7000). Buy tickets at hotels or at any of the ubiquitous kiosks.

Worthwhile Vieste festivals include that in honor of **San Giorgio** in late April, featuring a procession, fireworks, and a horse race on the beach; the **Festival of Santa Maria** in early May; and the mid-June **Festival of Sant'Antonio.**

■ Trémiti Islands (Isole Trémiti)

The Homeric king Diomedes, it is said, came here with his army on the way home from the Trojan War. The defeated Trojans, seeking revenge, transformed the army into albatrosses, which are only seen at sunset and sunrise and are said to emit the cry of a newborn baby. The birds' mythical origin is still the only plausible explanation to the evolutionary puzzle of why the species exist in three isolated pockets: here, in Japan, and in Calais, France. Now called *Trémiti* after the small tremors which continually rattle them, the islands provide a woody, sandy escape from the competitive summer tanning of the Adriatic resorts. In July and August, the islands do not escape the sun-seekers, but happily they cluster on just one beach. If you're planning a daytrip, bring your own provisions, since all food bears the price tags of imports. The islands make easy daytrips from Vieste, Térmoli, and several other points. The **tourist office** in Térmoli has the most comprehensive information on the Trémiti (see Térmoli listings under Molise).

Trémiti is a laid-back, easy destination to play in for a week or weekend. It's somewhat rustic—there are no street names for the few (and mostly unpaved) roads. Walking, the prevalent form of transportation, is pleasant with an almost constant view of the sea, and the sound of the wind in the trees.

GETTING THERE

Ferries and hydrofoils ply the islands from a number of Adriatic ports, though Térmoli is now the most convenient departure point. For all departures, be at the port about 45min. before departure.

Adriatica Navigazione runs **ferries** and **hydrofoils** from the largest number of ports, and can be contacted in Vieste at Gargàno Viaggi, P. Roma, 7 (tel. (0884) 70 85 01), and in Térmoli at Intercontinental, Corso Umberto I, 93 (tel. (0875) 70 53 41). **Motonave Vieste,** Via S. Maria di Merino, 8 (tel. (0884) 70 74 89), runs service from Vieste, and **Navigazione Libero del Golfo,** Bar Del Porto, 2707 (tel. 48 59), runs the cheapest boats from Térmoli (in Térmoli call (0875) 70 39 39). Depending on whence you come and which ship you take, you will arrive at either **San Nicola** or **San Domino.**

> **Térmoli-Trémiti: Adriatica Navigazione,** May 1-Sept. 30 daily at 9:20am, 1hr. 45min., L11,200; call for departure times in other seasons. (Also offers expensive—L19,700—hydrofoil service.) **Santa Lucia Lines,** daily at 9:15am, 2hr., L11,200.
> **Vieste-Trémiti: Motonave Vieste,** daily at 8:40am, 2hr., round-trip L28,000.
> **Adriatica Navigazione** also has service May 26-Sept. 30 daily at 9:20am, additional departure Fri. at 7:30pm, 1hr. 45min., round-trip L28,000.

Adriatica hydrofoils also link these and other cities with the islands, but are more expensive (from Vieste L18,100 plus port tax, from Térmoli L19,700). Hydrofoils run daily between the islands and Peschici, Rodi Gargánico, Manfredónia, and Vasto in Abruzzo. Call them for further information.

Whether you've landed on San Nicola or San Domino, you will immediately be assailed by announcements for boat tours of San Domino and its grottos (about L10,000), but be forewarned—the excursion is nothing spectacular. **Luggage storage** at each port is L2000.

Ferries between the two islands run frequently (L1500; don't buy round-trip or you may be stuck without a return boat). Make sure your boat is just going across, and not on a tour; you may be asked to shell out L10,000 once on the high seas.

ONCE THERE

Your choice of island will be guided by the parable of Mary and Martha. If you prefer the contemplative life, head to **San Nicola,** dominated by a massive Benedictine abbey predating the millenium. Access to the sea, the town of San Nicola itself, and the **Church of Santa Maria** all lie within the abbey's boundaries. The church houses a Byzantine crucifix brought to the islands in the year 747, an 11th-century black Madonna, and the fully visible mummified remains of the blessed Tobias, in surprisingly good shape for his 434 years. Also note the Venetian altar and the remnants of Byzantine mosaics on the floor. To the left of the church lies a **courtyard,** lined by Roman and Gothic cloisters, which opens to a remarkable view of the entire archipelago. The abbey is impossible to miss coming from the ferry dock, as it is the only opening in a vast sheet of rock.

If you prefer the pleasures of the active life, hit the beaches of **San Domino,** the largest of the Trémiti, and the only ones with sand. All affordable accommodations are here, as well as a nightly discotheque. An alternative to this beach is **Cala Matana.** To find it, head to the main piazza of San Domino and look for the "Panifico" sign, next to two benches pointing off to a panoramic view of San Nicola. On the left, take the staircase to the sea, then follow the path until you find the flat(ish) rock outcropping of your choice. A more secluded bathing paradise can be found the island's eastern coast, follow the signs off the main road to town to "Villaggio Internazionale," veering right just before the "Villaggio" itself. This will lead you to the northern tip of the island, where you can search out a *cala* (cove) you like.

Mountain bike rental at **Ibiscicli** to the left of the church in the *piazzetta* (tel. 66 30 58; L10,000 for one hour). There is a *medico* (**doctor**) in the small brown hut in the port. He holds court daily 10:30am-noon (Dr. Dauno Morlino, tel. (0330) 82 30 74). The **telephone code** on the islands is 0882.

The cheapest, most scenic, and most lively place to stay on the island is the **Villagio Internazionale,** located at Punta del Diamante (tel. 66 34 05, in winter (0733) 22 61 07). It offers bungalows or prefab aluminum huts for rent. From May 1 to June 27 and then again from Sep. 7 through Sep. 30, you can rent either hut or bungalow by the night (breakfast included. Throughout July and Aug. ½-pension is required, full pension is optional). Prices, per-person, per-day for: hut, L26,000 (no pension), L52,000-70,000 (½-pension), L60,000-78,000 (full pension); bungalow, L47,500 (no pension), L70,000-86,000 (½-pension), L78,000-94,000 (full pension). The restaurant is self-serve, and you can rent canoes or hire a motorboat to explore marine coves.

Most places require full pension in summer, but it's not a bad deal as the food beats restaurant offerings. **Pensione Giovanna** (tel. 66 32 13, Oct.-March, (0875) 70 10 69) has doubles with bath and balcony (full pension L80,000; less in off-season). **Pensione Rossana** (tel. 66 32 49), up the steep hill to the left of the port, requires full pension in July and August. (All double rooms. Half-pension L70,000, L75,000 in July, L80,000-90,000 in Aug. Singles June and Sept. only no pension, L35,000, full pension, L70,000). **Albergo Villa Olimpia** (tel. 66 30 46), to the left off the main road on the way to the island's center, is home to over 40 felines. For humans, the hospitable owner offers rooms without pension. (L40,000 per person. Off season only: March-June, Sept.) Full pension is L70,000-95,000 in June-August per person; off-season L60,000.) Ask for a room with a view if staying more than one night; you get an incredible sweeping vista down to the sea and across to San Nicola.

All supplies must be brought in by ship, so restaurants are expensive. Bring your own provisions and save, or shop at the two *alimentari* in the center, the better one located on the road to the left. Open daily in summer 7:30-11:45am and 5-8pm, and if closed, just ring the bell. The pharmacy next door is permanently closed, so bring any supplies you might need. **Ristorante Belvedere** does indeed have a good view. Across from the *Panifico* sign in the *piazzetta* (tel. 66 33 09), it serves bread, pizza and beer, along with other offerings. (Open all day.) For a bar, discoteca, gelateria, paninoteca, risorante, and fast-food place all rolled into one, try **Diomede,** open all day and most of the night. No cover for the disco, which booms until midnight, and later on weekends.

■■■ BARI

Baresi have good reason to boast. A center of Byzantine power in southern Italy, their city went on to become a major embarkation point for the Crusades, and later the keystone of Frederick II's Mediterranean empire. The new city, a model of 19th-century urban planning, serves as the region's cultural and economic hub. Not the least of Bari's accomplishments is a concerted effort to make the city enjoyable for backpackers, an enterprise conducted in the spirit of the city's most famous resident: Santa Claus.

Bari's old city, reminiscent of an Arab *medina,* is a nucleus of old-style poverty coupled with modern twists: pitiless maniacs on wheels, racism against Albanians and other minorities who have been seeking asylum in record numbers, street crime, and a widespread drug problem. Nevertheless, Bari can be safe as long as you exercise the precautions you would in any large city, and the "Stop-Over in Bari" program makes it an excellent base for daytrips to the surrounding countryside.

The "Stop-over In Bari" Program

Eight years ago, local government and grass roots organizations came up with a unique idea (and if it doesn't stay unique, budget travel guides might very well become obsolete)—to make Bari a mecca for backpackers from all over. The agent would be the *Stop-Over in Bari* program, and the original philosophy would be emblazoned on a flyer distributed across Europe: "Free vacations!" Well, almost free. Between **mid-June** and **mid-September,** *Stop-Over* can be of immeasurable assistance to travelers **under 30** who are not residents of the region.

Outside the train station is the newly inaugurated double-decker bus with a large "Stop-Over in Bari" sign above. Relax while the bilingual (and sometimes trilingual) staff kindly provide you with every possible piece of information you need about Bari and its province, ferries and more. Another **info booth** is inside the stazione marittima. Pick up a daily *Stop-Over* **newsletter** for information on discounted restaurants, supermarket, shops, museums, and cultural events. For additional daily information, tune in to *Stop-Over* **radio** in English at 102 FM. If you have a sleeping bag or tent, take bus #5 (last one leaves at 11pm, but be there no later than 10:45pm) or #3 to **Pineta San Francesco,** a free **campground** with bar, free showers, and free luggage storage. All city buses are free as long as you are under 30 and a non-resident of Bari. Be aware, though, that Bari's bus system leaves a lot to be desired—strikes occur frequently and service is slow.

If you are bereft of sleeping bag or simply want a more luxurious sojourn, take advantage of *Stop-Over's* **Package,** which puts you up in a private home for two nights for a mere L30,000 (L15,000 per additional night). You'll be put up with college students and their ilk, most likely in neighborhoods safer than those in which Bari's squalid *pensioni* cluster. (Call (080) 521 45 38 or fax 521 18 22 to reserve; reservations appreciated but not essential.)

Stop-Over also offers various events and seminars (such as pizza-making) throughout the summer at the Pineta S. Francesco, where the campground is. (All events free.) Tour Bari for free using their **bicycles** and **skateboards** but don't leave them unattended; Stop-Over also offers two free weekly **concerts** and occasional events throughout the summer, as well as free copies of an English edition of Luca Conti's *Inter-Rail Man,* a funny and detailed guide to railpass travel from a personal perspective.

Stop-Over's **main office** at Via Dante Alighieri, 111, has more detailed information on sights and events (tel. 521 45 38; open daily 8:30am-8:30pm). The 24-hr. **summer hotline** is 44 11 86 (at the Pineta).

FERRIES

Getting to Greece from Bari is cheaper and more appealing than going by way of Bríndisi (unless you have a Eurorail or Interrail pass). Ferries ply to **Corfu** (11hr.), **Igoumenitsa** (12hr. 30min.), and **Patras** (15-20hr.). There are no discounts for Eurail passes or *cartaverde,* but most lines offer special student rates. The following are ferry companies with their destinations; the lowest prices (deck class) for each are shown. The **high season** varies slightly from company to company, year to year, and place to place, but is generally from the first week of July to the last week of August. The **port tax** for Greece is L10,000. Tickets and information can be obtained directly at the **stazione marittima** or at the offices listed below. **You must check in at the stazione marittima two hours before departure.** After buying your ticket and paying the tax, you will be given a boarding card to be stamped at the **police station,** conveniently located in the *stazione marittima.* Tickets may also be purchased at **OTE**, the travel agency connected with Stop-Over (open year-round, even after *Stop-Over* is over. See "Budget Travel" in Orientation and Practical Information).

> **Morfimare,** Corso de Tullio, 36/40 (tel. 521 00 22). Boxes #11 and 12 at the port. To: **Patras** (L75,000, high season L90,000; students pay L5000 less; departs odd-number days June-July, evens in Aug., at 9pm); **Igoumenitsa-Corfu** (L50,000, high season L65,000; students L45,000, high season L50,000; departs even days June-July, odds in Aug., at 8pm).
> **Ventouris Ferries,** c/o Pan Travel, Via S. Francesco d'Assisi, 95 (tel. 524 43 64). To: **Patras** (L70,000, high season L90,000; students pay L5000 less; departs daily at 8:30pm); **Corfu** and **Igoumenitsa** (L50,000, high season L70,000; students L45,000, high season L50,000; daily departures July-Aug.).

ORIENTATION AND PRACTICAL INFORMATION

Via Sparano leads north from the train station two blocks to **Piazza Umberto,** the main square in town. Two blocks east of the *piazza* and parallel to Via Sparano runs **Corso Cavour,** Bari's main street. About nine blocks north is **Corso Vittorio Emanuele,** separating the old city to the north and the new city to the south. The main square in the old city is **Piazza Mercantile.**

> **Tourist Office:** Stop-Over should satisfy your every need, but just in case, there's **EPT,** P. Aldo Moro, 33A (tel. 524 22 44), to the right as you leave the station. Regional and local maps of Apulia. English spoken, sort of. Open Mon.-Sat. 9am-1pm, in summer Mon.-Sat. 9am-1pm and 4-8pm.
> **Budget Travel: OTE,** Via Dante, 111 (tel. 521 45 38). From the station, walk 1 block past P. Umberto to the left. Information on student discount travel from the people who run Stop-Over. Open Mon.-Sat. 8:30am-8:30pm.
> **Currency Exchange:** at the information desk in the F.S. train station when banks are closed (open 7:30am-8pm). Also at the **Automobile Club Italiano** at the ferry terminal, but only when boats are arriving or departing.
> **American Express: Morfimare,** Corso de Tullio, 36/40 (tel. 521 00 22), near the port. Open Mon.-Fri. 9am-12:30pm and 3:30-6:30pm.
> **Post Office:** P. Battisti (tel. 39 61 11), behind the university. From P. Umberto, take a left on Via Crisanzio, then the 1st right on Via Cairoli. Open Mon.-Fri. 8:20am-7pm, Sat. 8:20am-1pm. **Postal code:** 70100.
> **Telephones: SIP,** Via Oriani, near the castle. Open daily 8am-9pm. **ASST,** outside the station to the right. Better for international calls. Open daily 7am-10pm. **Telephone code:** 080.
> **Trains:** Bari lies on train lines from Rome (6 per day, last at 10:50pm, 7-8hr., L33,000) and Milan (15 per day, last at 11:42pm, 8-10hr., L60,000). Frequent **trains** connect Bari with Apulia's larger towns: Fóggia (1hr. 30min., L8800), Táranto (2hr., L8800), Bríndisi (2hr., L8800), and Lecce (2hr. 30min., L10,500). The station is also home to several private lines, including the **Ferrovie del Sud-Est** (tel. 558 32 22; to Castellana Grotte, Alberobello, and Martina Franca), on the

last track of the central station, and the **Bari-Nord** (tel. 521 47 14; to Bitonto and Barletta), and the **Ferrovie Calabro-Lucane** (tel. 572 52 22; to Matera in Basilicata), both on the western side of the square.

English Bookstore: Feltrinelli Bookstore, Via Dante, 91/95, one-half-block from Stop-Over's main office. A decent collection of classics and moderns. Open Mon.-Sat. 9am-1pm and 4-8pm.

Emergencies: tel. 113. **Police:** tel. 113. **Carabinieri:** tel. 112. **Ambulance:** tel. 522 15 14. **Fire Department:** tel. 115.

ACCOMMODATIONS AND FOOD

If you are over 30 or it is not summer, the following are the only options. The two-day Stop-Over Package is a better deal than most of these, even if you don't use the second day. Exercise caution in the following locations.

Pensione Giulia, Via Crisanzio, 12 (tel. 523 50 30). From the station, turn left just before P. Umberto. Clean and spacious, the rooms have semi-vaulted ceilings painted with idyllic scenes. Singles L45,000, with bath L65,000. Doubles L60,000, with bath L80,000.

Pensione Romeo, Via Crisanzio, 12 (tel. 521 63 80), in the same *palazzo* as the Pensione Giulia. Recently remodeled. The ground floor is clean and modern, but avoid the upstairs rooms. Sepulchral singles with bath L40,000. Lovelorn doubles with bath L65,000.

Ostello del Levante (HI), Palese Marina, Lungomare Massaro, 33 (tel. 552 02 82). Take the train to the Bari-Palese stop (L800) or bus #1 from Corso Cavour to Palese and walk to the beach. The hostel resides in safer territory outside the city. It doubles as a home for the mentally handicapped, so watch which column you check when you register. 6 beds per room. Lockout 9am-5pm. Curfew 11pm. L12,000 per day. Breakfast included.

Sandwiched between bountiful sea and rich pastures, Bari specializes in seafood, horse, and lamb dishes. Zesty seafood sauces like *ciambotto* (made of fish, olive oil, onions, and tomatoes) accompany pasta. Ricotta cheese made with sheep's milk is Bari's splendid modification on cottage cheese. Many *macellerie* sell whole roasted chickens to go for about L8000. Among the many **markets** in Bari is the daily vegetable frenzy that takes place at P. del Ferrarese. **Supermercato Vito Caldarulo,** Via de Giosa, 97 (tel. 54 43 26), one street east of Corso Cavour, vends at reasonable prices (open daily 8:30am-1pm and 5-8pm). Bari also abounds in places to get *focaccie* for L2500-L3000.

Osteria delle Travi, Largo Chiurlia, 12, at the end of Via Sparano. Turn left through the arches at the entrance to the old city. Support the *Mezzogiorno* in this charming stone cellar by ordering local specialties: pasta with arugula and ricotta, and *braciola* (horsemeat wrapped around stuffing). Full meals L14,000 without drinks. Other prices vary. Open Tues.-Sun. 12:30-2:30pm and 7:30-10:30pm.

Taverna Verde, Largo Adua, 18/19 (tel. 54 03 09), on the *Lungomare* between Molo San Nicola and La Rotunda, at the end of Corso Cavour. Black-tie service at ripped-jeans prices. *Orecchiette alla barese* (the regional pasta speciality) L5000. Local wine L3000 per bottle. Cover L2000. Service 15%. Open Mon.-Sat. noon-3pm and 8pm-midnight.

Vini e Cucina, Strada Vallisa, 23, in the old city. Follow Corso Cavour to P. Mercantile; it's to the left. Pleasant cantina atmosphere. Full meals with house wine L12,000. Open Mon.-Sat. noon-3pm and 6-10pm.

El Pedro Self-Service, Via Piccinni, 152 (tel. 521 12 94). Not a Mexican restaurant but a great cafeteria serving authentic Pugliese specialties, different every day. Complete meal with drink L14,000. Open for lunch only.

SIGHTS

Enjoy Bari, but don't make yourself a target for crime. **Do not venture alone into the old city, especially at night.** As in other southern cities, avoid flashy watches and jewelry, keep valuables in front inside pockets, and hold purses and bags where drive-by thieves can't grab them.

Enter the **old city** at P. Mercantile, the site of a colorful morning **market.** The piazza lies under the open porch and clock tower of the **Sedile,** the medieval meeting place of local councils. Debtors were once tied to the Column of Justice (far right of square).

Yes, Virginia, there is a Santa Claus, and he's dead. His remains were brought to Bari from Asia Minor by 60 sailors in 1087, after the clever Baresi outran some Venetians who had planned to nab the remains of this patron saint of sailors and pawnbrokers. The victorious sailors refused to hand over the saint to the local clergy, saying they had vowed to construct a special temple for the remains, thought to possess miraculous properties. From P. Mercantile, follow Via Palazzo di Città to the **Church of San Nicola,** completed in the 12th century to shelter the remains of St. Nicholas (Santa Claus), who is renowned not only for Christmas loot but also for resurrecting three children who were sliced to bits and plunged into a barrel of brine by a nasty butcher. The church's spartan appearance is better suited for a fortress; in fact, the tower on the right survives from a Byzantine castle that originally occupied the site. The central door exemplifies the motley sources of the Puglian-Romanesque style: Saracen in the arabesques and symbolic figures around the door, classical in the rosettes of the cornice, Byzantine in the solemn angels surrounding the arches, and Lombard in the crude animal carvings of the bases. An 11th-century episcopal throne hides behind the high altar. The crypt, with its windows of translucent marble, houses the remains of St. Nicola beside a beautiful silver reliquary. (Open daily 8am-noon and 4-7pm.)

Bari's Puglian-Romanesque **cathedral** is a short walk from the church. Passing down **strada del Carmine,** you'll be greeted by the vibrant old streets: narrow alleys lined with small whitewashed houses and thronged with children, vendors, and black-swathed women. Begun at the end of the 12th century during the peaceful years of Norman rule, the **cathedral** displays a typically austere Romanesque façade, somewhat modified by Baroque decorations around the doors. Its interior is a fine example of Romanesque architecture, with a choir and chapel protruding gently from the nave. (Open daily 8am-noon and 4-7pm.)

On the outskirts of the old city, not far from the cathedral, the **Castello Svevo** (Swabian Castle) evokes the grandeur and power of three different periods. Ruggiero II the Norman began the structure with the castles proper and four keeps. It was then rearranged by Frederick II (1230-1240) into a trapezoid with two of the towers still standing in the interior. In the north, toward the sea, a pointed door and beautiful mullioned windows also hearken to the 13th century. Finally, Isabel of Aragon and Sona Sforza added the bulwarks and angular keeps, and reorganized the internal court (16th-century). During this time it served as a cultural center headed by Isabella. Much of the castle is closed for the excavation of a recently discovered Roman city on the site. You can, however, admire plasters of Pugliese sculpture of the 11th-16th centuries in the **Gypsoteca** (open daily 9am-1pm; admission L4000, 60 and over and 18 and under free).

Beyond the castle lies a seawalk that trails past the ferry port to a small fishing harbor then on to **Molo San Nicola** (San Nicola's Wharf). The gray-and-white towered building in the distance, the **Palazzo della Provincia** on lungomare N. Sauro (tel. 39 24 23), houses the **Pinacoteca Provinciale** on its top floor. The museum displays paintings by Veronese, Tintoretto, and Bellini, including the latter's *Martyrdom of St. Peter.* Ask to see the works of Francesco Netti, Bari's greatest artist and Italy's only impressive Impressionist painter and the modern sculptor Pino Pascali. (Open Thurs.-Tues. 9am-1pm and 4-7pm, Sun. 9am-1pm. Free.)

ENTERTAINMENT

Bari rivals Naples as the south's cultural nucleus. *Stop-Over* has the latest news on events and hotspots, and sponsors everything from recycling workshops and kite festivals to comic-strip shows. Unfortunately, one of the most renowned theaters in Italy and a glorious landmark for Bari will not be in use for an unspecified time. The **Teatro Petruzzelli** was almost completely destroyed in a fire in October of 1991. You can still admire the imposing red façade (what remains of the teatro). **Teatro Piccinni** (tel. 521 37 17) offers a concert season in the spring. In summer, occasional concerts are held in the *castello*. Entertainment listings crowd *Ecco Bari*, the tourist office's entertainment guide, and the *Bari Sera* section of *La Gazzetta del Mezzogiorno* (the local newspaper). *Stop-Over* also has the scoop on the latest in the nightlife scene.

The great commercial event of the year, the **Levante Fair,** runs for 10 days in mid-September. The largest fair in southern Italy, it displays goods from all over the world in the huge fairgrounds by the municipal stadium, off Lungomare Starita.

For night-life in Bari check out **La Baraonda,** Largo Eroi del Mare, an American-style bar with an Italian crowd. Or try **Caffè Sotto il Mare,** Via Venezia, on the Great Wall in the old town (closed Wed.).

If you feel like traveling out of the area, **Villa Renoir** (Strada S. Caterina) offers some excitement especially on Saturday and Sunday nights. (Take bus #20 from P. Massari and stop on Via Bellomo.) Don't forget that bus service does not go on all night. It would be best to go with a car and with someone who knows the area.

■ Near Bari

Bitonto

For a potent dose of Puglian-Romanesque architecture, take the half-hour train ride from the Bari-Nord station to Bitonto (every hr., L3000 round-trip). When you arrive, a 1km walk down Via Matteotti and a right turn deposits you in the medieval quarter. Once there, many signs with detailed maps will help direct you. Bitonto's glorious **cathedral** stands in the medieval quarter; it was constructed between the 12th and 13th centuries from mellow golden stone in loose emulation of San Nicola in Bari. Majestic side arches enhance the church's compact form, while sculptured lions, griffins, and bas-relief New Testament scenes enliven the main portal. Inside, windows illuminate a finely carved wooden ceiling (a late 19th-century reproduction of the original design), while a splendid pulpit crowns the nave (1229). The **crypt** rests on 30 columns salvaged from a Roman temple. Their capitals were the gifts of 30 members of the city's medieval nobility. Recent excavations of the floor have revealed a mosaic with the design of a griffin.

The rest of medieval Bitonto boasts several interesting buildings, including the Gothic **Church of San Francesco d'Assisi** (1286) and the 16th-century **Palazzo Sylos Calo,** whose Catalan-Gothic doorway opens to an elaborate Renaissance courtyard. In addition to these, almost all of the buildings in Bitonto's *centro storico* can claim provenance in the Middle Ages.

For more information try the local **Biblioteca,** on Via dei Mercanti, 52. (Open Mon.-Fri. 9am-1pm, Tues. and Thurs. 4:30-7pm.) The **Centro Ricerche Storia e Arte Bitontine,** Via Ferrante Aporti (tel. 874 52 94), can also provide maps and historical documents on Bitonto. Open in the afternoons, unless they have something better to do. Finally, the local **police** offer tours of the city and they also have keys to some of the buildings. It is better to call ahead (tel. 951 10 14; no English spoken).

For food shopping there are numerous **supermarkets** in town, including several on Via Matteotti as you come from the train station.

Ruvo di Puglia

Midway between Bari and Barletta on the Bari-Nord line (from Bari 30min., L2800), Ruvo di Puglia began as a Greek colony in about the 8th century BC and reached the pinnacle of its influence four to five centuries later. Ruvo later passed into Roman hands; in 463 AD those fun-loving Goths destroyed the town in a fit of good-humored mayhem. Patient Ruvo whiled away the dog days of the Middle Ages in gradual rebuilding; one of the best products of this epoch is the three-nave Apulian Romanesque **cathedral** begun in the 13th century and restored several times from the 16th to the 19th centuries. Note the exterior ornamentation and the church's large, ornate rose window; other highlights include a 14th-century wooden crucifix and M. Pino da Siena's 1576 *L'Adorazione dei Pastori*. On the façade, note the statue of a man on a throne, reading the Book of the Seven Seals; this is believed to be a portait of our dear friend, Frederick II. To the right of the cathedral stands the resolute **campanile,** antedating the millennium. The newly reopened **Jatta Museum,** on the right of the cathedral, contains a collection of over 2000 classical vases. (Open daily 9am-1pm., Fri. and Sat. 4-7:30pm also. Free.)

To get to the *centro storico* from the station, turn right and then onto Corso Duca della Vittoria; follow the signs that lead to the wooded *piazza.*

Castel del Monte

Situated halfway between the Murge and the sea, **Castel del Monte** is the subject of much speculation. It was originally built for the pleasure of Frederick II around 1240; lacking defensive structures, it probably served no strategic purpose. The edifice is straight out of a *Dungeons and Dragons* module: a perfect octagon, with eight octagonal towers, containing sixteen trapezoidal rooms, connected by three differently structured stairways embellished with twenty-sided dice. It is surmised that charismatic Frederick designed it himself as a pleasure dome, meeting place, and astronomical observatory. In fact, rays of sunlight converge on certain points at each semi-annual equinox, à la Indiana Jones.

The grounds are always open, but you can only visit the inside on Sunday mornings. To get there, take the Bari-Nord train to Andria (35min., L7400 round-trip) and then board one of six daily buses on the Andria-Spinazzola route (45min.; call 30 09 48 for information on departure times).

Bargain eating does not exist in Castel del Monte: best bring a picnic.

Egnazia

Mid-way between Bari and Brindisi on the coast lie the ruins of Egnazia. This former Messapian city was famed for its pottery, characteristically superimposing yellow, purple, and white designs on a glossy black background. You can view examples of these wares at the **archeological museum.** (Tel. (080) 72 90 56. Museum open daily 8:30am-1:30pm; archeological zone also 2:30-7pm. Free.) Egnazia eventually became a Greek port, taking the name Gnathia, and then a Roman stronghold. The ruins of the port are the most extensive Roman remains in Apulia; unfortunately, they're mostly underwater, and are currently being studied by scuba archaeologists. Above ground, see the three-aisled **basilica,** the **forum,** a road leading to Bríndisi, and the **acropolis** atop the hill. Several **tombs** and sections of the ancient **fortifications** survive from the Messapian period.

Travel to Egnazia Via Monópoli, which is 45 min. from Bari by train (almost every hr., L3900) and one hour from Bríndisi (about every 2hr., L5000). From the Villa Comunale in Monópoli, take the bus towards Torre Canne and get off at Egnazia (you will not pass Go; you will not collect $200). There is an Egnazia train station but it's a bit removed from town and the ruins.

If you're lucky enough to have four wheels of your own, don't miss the cave village near the ruins, **San Giovanni.**

Ostuni

Rising out of a landscape of sea, red earth, and olive trees, the *città bianca* (white city) of Ostuni appears completely ethereal. The walls and even the pavement of the *centro storico* are kept pure as the driven snow by local ordinance; walking through the old town, you'll feel surrounded by icebergs. Nevertheless, the most important monuments in Ostuni are polychromatic. The **Convento Delle Monacelle** (Convent of the Little Nuns) on Via Cattedrale sports a Baroque façade and is topped by a blue-, yellow-, and white-tiled dome of evident Moorish inspiration. Further along Via Cattedrale, surprisingly, is the **cathedral.** Built in 1437, it was the last Byzantine building erected in southern Italy. On Via Cavallo, the more modest **Chiesa di San Giacomo di Compostella** (1423) served as a chapel to a noble family.

By far the most breathtaking sight on Ostuni, however, is the panoramic view of the fields rolling out to the sea, from a foreground of white houses. From Via Cattedrale, turn left and head downwards until you reach the edge of the old town. Keep going left, and you'll hit the **Porta Nuova,** a gate commissioned by Robert D'Anson to boost commerce in Ostuni.

From the **train station,** take the shuttle bus (every 30min., every hr. on Sun. L700) to P. Libertà, which abuts on Via Cattedrale at the edge of the old town. (Return buses same times.) The **AAST Tourist Office** (tel. (0831) 30 12 68 or main office 30 37 75; open Mon.-Sat. 9am-12:30pm and 4-7:30pm) is at P. Libertà, 63.

For replenishing and a change of color, go to the kitschy **Osteria del Tempo Perso,** Via G. Tanzarella, 47 (tel. 30 33 20). Good food for easy-to-stomach prices. (Open daily 8:30pm-midnight.)

Frequent **trains** run to Ostuni from Bríndisi (40min., L3200) and Bari (1hr., L5700).

■ Barletta

Barletta is a compact city with a few bursts of fun to offer. Its star attraction is an amusing pageant on the first or second Sunday in September. The city reenacts the 1503 **Disfida** (Challenge), a battle in which 13 Italian knights handily defeated 13 Frenchmen. The victory was somewhat hollow, as the Spanish would later use the pretext that the knights had received Spanish aid to occupy the entire southern half of Italy. Other attractions include some interesting Romanesque churches, a massive bronze statue from antiquity, and an outstanding collection of paintings by Giuseppe de Nittis, one of Italy's great 19th-century artists.

Orientation and Practical Information To reach all of Barletta's sights, walk from the station and turn right on Via Garibaldi. Barletta is 15 min. north of Trani on either the Bologna-Lecce or Bari-Nord train lines (from Bari 40min., L4400). Corso Vittorio Emanuele is closed off to cars around 6pm until 11pm and on Sunday mornings throughout the year.

For more information, the **Azienda Autonoma Soggiorno e Turismo,** Via D'Aragona, 95 (tel. 331 331), can be of help. (Open Mon.-Sat. 8am-2pm.)

Accommodations and Food The only budget accommodations are at **Pensione Prezioso** Via Teatini, 11 (tel. 52 00 46), on P. del Plebiscito. Follow Viale Giannone right in front of the train station, which leads to P. Aldo Moro, keep going straight and eventually you'll end up in P. del Plebiscito. Singles L30,000, doubles with bath L60,000. Also in P. del Plebescito, **Pizzeria Dai Saraceni,** P. del Plebiscito, 65 (tel. 51 71 00), offers complete meals for L20,000. Try their tasty *pizza ai Saraceni* (with ham, artichokes, olives, capers, etc.) for L6500. (Cover L2000, service 20% or less, depending on the waiter's mood. Open daily 12:30-3pm and 7:30pm-1am.) Off Corso Garibaldi, **Supermarket DOK** is on Via G. de Nittis. (Open Mon.-Sat. 8:30am-1:30pm and 4:30-7:30pm.) In an old-fashioned setting lies **Bella Napoli** (tel. 32 231), across from the museum at Corso Garibaldi, 129. The food and service are superb, full meals are L15,000, cover L2000, service 15%. (Open daily noon-3pm and 7pm-midnight.)

Sights The 12th-century **Church of San Sepolcro** graces the center of town on Corso Vittorio Emanuele at Corso Garibaldi. The façade preserves remnants of an original porch, a pointed doorway, and two blind arches. The only decoration remaining in the recently restored church interior is the large 13th-century baptismal font to the left of the entrance, and the tender 16th-century Byzantine-style Madonna at the end of the right aisle. (Open Mon.-Sat. 9:30am-noon and 5:30pm-8:30pm winter, 6:30pm-9pm summer.) On a low podium next to the church towers the 5m **Colosso.** This 4th-century bronze statue from Constantinople represents a Byzantine emperor, possibly Valentinian I, holding the cross and globe, symbols of the two realms of his power. As the Venetians were hauling home the loot from the sack of Constantinople (the Fourth Crusade), shipwreck sent the Colosso to Barletta's shore. It was then dismembered by a group of friars who melted its bronze limbs for use as church bells. The limbs you see were fashioned by a 15th-century sculptor commissioned to restore it.

Continue on Corso Garibaldi and venture into the old town to reach the **Cantina Della Disfios,** where the fabled confrontation of the knights took place. The "cantina" itself is simply the basement of a Gothic palace; note the huge stone cistern in the back. After years of renovations the **Castello** (castle) has finally re-opened to the public. This is actually a fortress first built by the Saracens; subsequently enlarged by the Normans and Frederick II. The final and most substantial change was done by Carl V (from 1532 to 1600).

This place has so much room that it is now used for conventions, in which case it may be closed for tourists. The **Museo** and Pinacoteca have also been moved here and on display are over 10,000 paintings dating from 1200 to 1600 including many by the local Giuseppe de Nittis. (Open Tues.-Sun. 9am-1pm and 4-7pm, Oct.-April 3-4pm. Admission L3000, L1000 for those under age 14. Half-hour guided tour, possibly in English.)

During the summer, it is worth going to **Margherita di Savoia** (go to the bus terminal on Via Manfredi, off of P. del Plebiscito, L1000 one way) for kilometers of beautiful beaches and clear blue water. Unfortunately most of the beach is private but for about L15,000 you can rent a whole package (umbrella, chair, and bed) and the fresh water showers. It is better to shop at a supermarket beforehand. Many of the Stabilimenti turn into piano bars and mini-discos at night.

■ Trulli District

Hundreds of unusual, cone-shaped dwellings, known as *trulli,* cluster in the **Valley of Itria,** between Bari and Táranto. Originally built in the 16th and 17th centuries by pioneers in the great Italian pastime of tax evasion, the mortarless buildings follow a cylindrical design made of stones carved from the rocks below; and are topped by a limestone conical cap. The Spanish levied a harsh tax for each dwelling; however, unfinished houses were exempted. The *trulli* were designed so that the roof could be knocked down in minutes, as soon as the tax man was spotted. The tax codes were changed when the Spanish caught on, but the style persisted. The *trulli* have been incorporated into modern life as residences, restaurants, and even boutiques.

Alberobello

The greatest concentration of *trulli* is in Alberobello, 90 minutes south of Bari on the Ferrovie del Sud-Est line to Táranto (15 trains per day, fewer on Sundays, more on school days, L8600 round-trip).

From the train station, bear left and take Via Mazzini which becomes Via Garibaldi until you reach P. del Popolo. Any left turn will bring you into the thick of the *trulli* zone. Unhappily, the *trulli* are crawling with tourists, and most have become curio shops. Beware the limpid-eyed souls who beg you to "visit" the interior of their *trullo:* you will be expected to buy at least a postcard.

Turn right from P. del Popolo to find the **Pro Loco Tourist Office,** at Corso Vittorio Emanuele, 15 (open Mon.-Sat. 9am-12:30pm and 5-7pm). Continue on Corso Vittorio Emanuele and bear left past the nondescript church at the end. Straight ahead is the **Trullo Sovrano,** or Sovereign Trullo. This mammoth two-story structure, the *only* two-story trullo, was built in the 19th century as headquarters for a religious confraternity and *carbonari* sect. Alberobello's eateries and sleeperies are overtouristed and expensive; it's easier as a Bari-based daytrip. Don't be fooled by the gift boxes of wines—although they might be good wines, they are not from Alberobello. Be sure to bring sunglasses if the day is bright as the white *trulli* are blinding in the sun.

Alberobello offers several options if you plan to spend some time here. At **Hotel Lazillotta,** P. Ferdinando IV, 31 (tel. 72 15 11) for L15,000 per person you get a bed and breakfast in a double. Add L10,000 for a single. The best deal is L55,000 per person for full pension in a double (AmEx, Diners, MC and Visa accepted). If you have a group of four or more, another option is to rent a *trullo* through **Agenzia Immobiliare Fittatrulli,** Via M.S. Gabriela, 66 (tel. 932 27 17). A *trullo* for four people will run between L90,000-L100,000.

To eat in the heart of the *trulli*, **Palomino,** Monte Pasupio, 3 (tel. 932 26 24), has a *menú turistico* for L18,000 (no alcohol and no credit cards).

Alberobello's **phone code** is 080. The **postal code** is 70011.

Martina Franca

You can see other *trulli* sprinkled among fields of flowers in the surrounding Itria Valley by taking the train to Martina Franca, 6km away and the next stop on the train line. Founded in the 14th century as a free (*franca*) city by Philip D'Anson, Martina Franca doesn't have that many *trulli*, but instead it has a beautiful baroque *centro storico*. From the train station, follow Via della Stazione to Viale dei Lecci, then turn left on Corso Taranto, which becomes Corso Italia. Turn left and go through the arch at P. XX Settembre to reach P. Roma, where you can (possibly) pick up a map at the **tourist office,** #35 (tel. 70 57 02; open Mon.-Sat. 9am-12:30pm and 4:30-7:30pm, Nov.-March Mon.-Sat. 8:30-2pm). Next door towers the grandiose **Ducal Palace** (1669) with more than 300 rooms, most of which are now offices. To tour the few accessible rooms, climb the left-hand stairs to the third floor. The walls are draped with multicolored Baroque frescoes depicting contemporary and ancient scenes of leisure and pleasure. Ironically, the rooms host the meetings of the Martina Franca city council. (Open Mon.-Sat. 8am-8pm. Free.) The fanciful Baroque façade of the 18th-century **Church of San Martino** presides over P. Plebiscito (open daily 8am-noon and 4-7:30pm). From Viale de Gasperi, enjoy the vista of the Itria Valley and its *trulli*. Don't miss the true centro on three *vie*: Conte Ugolino, Principe Umberto, and Cavour.

There are no cheap hotels here. One option is the **Albergo La Cremaillere,** 7km away in Locando San Paolo at Via Orimini, 1 (tel. (080) 70 02 65). (Singles L35,000. Doubles with bath, L60,000.) To get there, take a Ferrovie del Sud-Est bus, which leaves from P. Crispi off Via Taranto for Locando San Paolo. Another option is the aforementioned *Agriturismo* deal in Locorotondo. For a good meal, stop by **La Tavernetta,** Corso Vittorio Emanuele, 31 (tel. 70 63 23), off P. Roma. Homemade *orechiette al sugo* go for L6000, main dishes for L8000-12,000; local wine is L5000 per bottle. (Cover L2500. Open daily noon-3pm and 7:30pm-midnight.) Shop at **Supermercato Fontana,** on Via Taranto to the left after turning off Via dei Lecci. (Open Mon.-Sat. 8am-1pm and 5-8pm.)

Martina Franca's **Festival della Valle d'Itria** brings concerts and opera to the city in late July-early August. Tickets for the events range from L5000 to L30,000. During the first weekend in July, the **Festa di San Martino** rouses the town with the outdoor concerts and parades.

Martina Franca is about 45 min. by **train** from Táranto (9 per day, round-trip L5400) and 90 min. from Bari. (Trains leave at 7:15am, hourly from 8:30am-12:30pm and 2:30-6:30pm, and less frequently until 9pm; L9800 round-trip.) **Bus** service from Ferrovie del Sud-Est connects Martina Franca with Táranto's P. del Castello (11 per day, L2400; for information call 40 44 63 in Táranto).

Castellana Grotte

Take a Sud-Est train from Bari toward Alberobello to reach Castellana Grotte, home to Italy's finest caverns (30min.). They are a 2km hike away from the station, though many hitch successfully. Those folk follow the Grotte signs from the train station. You enter from an enormous pit called *La Grave,* which, despite its beauty, was used as a garbage dump until the rest of the caverns were discovered in 1938. The real highlight waits at the end of the tunnel—the *Caverna Bianca* (White Cavern), a landscape of stalactites. Tours (1hr. 45min., L20,000) run from 9am-noon and 3-7pm. Partial tours (40min., L10,000) do not include the *Caverna Bianca,* and leave hourly 8:30am-12:30pm and 2:30-6:30pm. For information, call (080) 896 55 11.

The High Murge

Trains on the **FerroVia Calabro-Lucane** line from Bari to Matera (frequent departures, 1hr., L5800) cross gently rolling paths to the quiet town of **Altamura.** Although one of the largest cities in the Murge region, the old town has managed to retain its tranquil quality. From the FCL train station, go right, through the underpass, and straight on Via Regina Margherita to the gate; feel free to peek through the gates of the villas that line the approach. A portal through the old city wall leads to Via Frederico II di Svevia. On the left down Via Federico you can see the petite **Church of San Nicolò of the Greeks,** a simple church serving the Greek Orthodox community. A bit further down towers the campanile of the **cathedral,** built in Frederick's time. The façade's two towers reveal northern European influences. Inside, look for the treasury and women's gallery. The **Pro Loco** (Tourist Office) is in P. della Repubblica.

The only reasonable place to stay in town is the **Albergo Mercadante,** Via Frederico, 74 (tel. (080) 84 24 92), offering rooms almost as musical as the hotel's namesake—composer Francesco Saverio Mercadante (1795-1870), born across the street. (Singles L20,000. Doubles L30,000.) Il Rè della Griglia grants you tasty calzones (L4500), pizzas, and other regal fare at Via La Maggiore, 2, off Via Federico. (Tel. 84 10 53. Open Tues.-Sun. 9am-1pm and 6pm-midnight.) A **supermarket** is at Via Fillippo 58. (Open Tues.-Sun. 9am-2pm and 5-8pm.)

Gravina in Puglia seems even more rustically tranquil than Altamura until you discover the oddities on the far side of town most natives avoid. To get there, take a Gravina train on one of the FS or FCL lines from Altamura (10 per day, 6am-10pm, 10min., L1600). To the right of the station as you exit stands the church of the **Madonna delle Grazie,** with an apparently annoyed eagle sprawled across its façade. The big bird symbolizes the Orsini clan, a powerful Roman family that, among other things, spawned a number of popes. Though the bird has pals all over town, flee this particularly horrid avian to the far side of the tracks and follow the sign to the *centro* until you hit the big intersection. Go straight onto Corso Aldo Moro, continuing on Via Vittorio Veneto past the **Palazzo di Città.** About 300m up Via Veneto, at the intersection with Via del Museo, a faded blue sign points toward the **Museo Ettore Pomarci Santomasi,** Via del Museo, 20 (tel. 85 10 21), which exhibits archeological finds from the area. (Open Tues.-Sat. 9am-noon.)

Several eerie sights await at the end of Via Matteotti (coming from P. della Repubblica). In P. Domenico, pray that your sins aren't too mediocre because **Purgatory Church** on the right would be a very creepy place to spend eternity. The two skeletons on the portal are supported by bears, which were also Orsini mascots. To the left of the church and right of the **Biblioteca** (built in 1743) lies a street leading to the **Basilica,** an immense four-aisled edifice. Back and towards the left of the Biblioteca, a narrow path runs through a particularly decrepit section of town. At the bottom lies the entrance to the district avoided by all locals. Ravines and the teeming vestiges of antedeluvian cave dwellings bring home the meaning of the name *gravina.* Some of the vestiges take the form of bones, which now rattle around in the **Grotto-Church of San Michele,** their deceased possessors minced by Saracen scimitars. The gate to the grotto area and church stays locked, but pay a few hundred lire to one of the kids nearby to summon the caretaker. Do this as well for the **Church of San Vito Vecchio** on the right towards the top of the hill. It's not hard to see why the whole area is riddled with superstition.

On a lighter note, finish the tour of Bari and surroundings with **Polignano** (about 35km). Several FS trains pass by here daily (L3200 one-way). The town fills with tourists late in the summer, but you can still enjoy the crystal-clear water and beautiful grottos. Before returning to Bari, grab an ice cream from **Il Mago del Gelato,** in P. Garibaldi, and walk through the old town right across from it, where you may land on one of the little squares which are excellent view points of the whole coast.

■ ■ ■ BRÍNDISI

Want to *really* look forward to going home? A visit to Bríndisi will undoubtedly do the trick. Most people linger here just long enough to catch a ferry to Greece, but even rational folk sometimes get stuck overnight.

A look at the architecture indicates that Bríndisi must once have been quite pleasant. The narrow medieval alleys and flowered 19th-century streets remain, sadly obscured and overshadowed by the by-products of a busy port: cheap postwar buildings, piles of garbage, and prostrate transients. The latter are usually young backpackers, but recently they have come to include thousands of Albanian refugees.

Bríndisini react to their city's dreariness in two ways. Some people accept their fate with a wry sense of humor; others bitterly resent anyone who comes from more tolerable climes, though they try to get the most they can out of the run-by tourist.

FERRIES

Bríndisi is Italy's major departure point for ferries to Greece. There is regular service to **Corfu** (8hr. 30min.-9hr. 30min.), **Igoumenitsa** (10hr. 30min.-11hr. 30min.), **Patras** (15-20hr.), and **Cefalonia** (Adriatica lines, 16hr. 30min.). From Patras, there is bus service (4hr., L14,000; buy tickets at the *stazione marittima*) and train service (railpasses valid) to Athens. All ferries leave in the evening.

Bríndisi is served by **Adriatica,** Via Regina Margherita, 13 (tel. 52 38 25) near the *stazione marittima;* **Marlines** c/o **Pattimare,** Corso Garibaldi, 97 (tel. 52 65 48 or 52 65 49); **Hellenic Mediterranean Lines,** Corso Garibaldi, 8 (tel. 52 85 31); and **Fragline,** Corso Garibaldi, 88 (tel. 56 82 32).

Fares to all destinations in Greece are: L60,000 for the deck and L48,000 for the return trip on a round-trip ticket. High season, which is usually from the third week of July to mid-August, the rate jumps to L90,000 and L72,000 for the return. If you plan ahead carefully, you may be able to leave on certain days and get a 50% discount. Deck class is fine in summer—sleeping horizontally outside is more comfortable than spending the night in an airline-type seat in a smoke-filled room. Be sure to bring warm clothes and a sleeping bag if you're on the deck. Bicycles travel free; motorcycles are L30,000, high season L35,000.

Most lines offer discounts to those under 27 and to ISIC-holders. **Eurailpass** holders get free deck passage on Adriatica Lines and Hellenic Mediterranean Lines (space-available basis—you could get bumped by a paying passenger), but must pay a L18,000 supplement from June 10 through September (this includes the port tax); at other times the only charge is the L10,000 **port tax. Cartaverde** holders get a 50% reduction on the same two lines. Buying a round-trip ticket in the off-season saves 20%. Finally, there are group reductions of approximately 10% on one-way and 20% on round-trip tickets (usually 10 people minimum).

Eurail holders should go directly to the main offices listed above to get their tickets, because many travel agencies will advertise either Adriatica or Hellenic Mediterranean tickets and then try to double-talk their way to your money with commission-based services. Those without railpasses should seriously consider leaving from the much more palatable port of **Bari,** where departures can be cheaper (see Bari listing above).

When you buy your ticket, you must pay the obligatory port tax (L10,000), and the office will give you a boarding card, which you must have stamped at the police station on the first floor of the maritime station.

You lose your reservation on most lines if you don't **check in at least two hours before departure.** Allow plenty of time for late trains and the 1km walk from the train station to the ferry station. From mid-July to mid-August, it may be worth the effort to purchase ferry reservations at line offices or travel agents in other cities before you get to Bríndisi.

PRACTICAL INFORMATION

All that ferrygoers need to know about Bríndisi is that **Corso Umberto** runs straight out from the train station, punctuated by fountainous **P. Cairoli. Corso Garibaldi** meets Corso Umberto at **P. del Popolo,** then veers left, leading to the *stazione marittima.* Bríndisi is generally unsafe and crime-ridden; women should beware in the evenings. Lone backpackers are considered particularly easy targets. If your ferry connection is late at night, be aware that theives often stalk tourists along Corso Umberto. Try to walk with a group of people (the more the better; wait until you can collect at least a quartet, preferably of mixed gender).

Tourist Office: Don't follow the bright signs to "tourist information"; they'll lead you to a bare room in the *stazione marittima.* Instead try **EPT,** Lungomare Regina Margherita, 5 (tel. 52 19 44), at the dock to the left of the *stazione marittima,* 1 block to the side of P. Vittorio Emanuele. Helpful official speaks English flawlessly. Open daily 9am-1pm and 4:30-7:30pm.

Currency Exchange: Go to **Banca Nazionale del Lavoro** at Via Santi, 11, off P. Vittoria. Avoid the ripoff rates at the *stazione marittima;* change money at one of the many outfits lining Corso Umberto and Corso Garibaldi, all of which offer direct U.S.-Greek conversions.

Trains: P. Crispi. Both **FS** and **Ferrovie del Sud-Est.** From: Naples (8:52pm, 8hr. L27,000); Rome (via Fóggia, 3 per day, 8hr., L46,800); Milan (via Ancona and Bologna, 6 per day, 10hr., L66,600). To: Bari (frequent departures, 1hr. 30min. L7800); Táranto (every hr., 1hr.,15min., L4400); Lecce (frequent departures 30min., L3200). **Luggage storage:** open daily 7am-11pm; L1500 per bag.

Buses: Ferrovie del Sud-Est, at the train station (tel. 52 59 91). Handles buses throughout Apulia. **Marozzi** c/o Pattimare, Corso Garibaldi, 97 (tel. 52 65 48), or the *Lungomare,* wheels twice daily to Rome (10:10pm, 8hr. 30min., L46,000 *super rapido,* 11am, 7hr. 30min., L53,000).

Post Office: Via San Francesco, off the *Lungomare* (tel. 239 56). Open Mon.-Sat 8:15am-8pm. **Postal code:** 72100.

Telephones: SIP, Via XX Settembre, 6, to the left on your way from the station to the port, near Albergo Venezia. Full service on international calls. Open daily 9am-1pm and 3:30-6:30pm. **Telephone code:** 0831.

Public Showers: Via del Mare, behind the Stazione Marittima. Not the cleanest facilities. Showers L3000. Toilets L300 when they're not on strike. Open daily 9am-1pm and 4-8pm.

Emergencies: tel. 113. **Police:** tel. 113. **Hospital: Ospedale di Summa,** P. Antonio (tel. 20 42). **Ambulance:** tel. 52 14 10.

ACCOMMODATIONS AND FOOD

Not many people choose to stay the night in Bríndisi. If they do, it's often on top of a backpack in one of the piazze along Corso Garibaldi—a miserable and dangerous experience.

Ostello della Gioventù "Bríndisi," is 3km away in Casale (tel. 41 31 23). Take the ferry across the port (every 10min., L200) then follow the signs for 1500m, or

take bus #3 or 4 from the center (L700). Clean place, soft mattresses. Open 7am-midnight. L11,000 per person. Breakfast L3000. 3 meals L10,000.
Hotel/Pensione Altair, Via Tunisi, 4 (tel. 52 49 11), off Via Garibaldi, near the *Stazione Maritima.* Clean, quiet and comparatively safe—even so, venturing out after 9 or 10pm is not recommended. Singles L25,000. Doubles L40,000, with bath L60,000.

A wonderful **open-air market,** off Corso Umberto on Via Battisti, sells fresh fruit by the metric ton. (Open Mon.-Sat. 7am-1pm.) Pizza and *focaccia* are made in huge sheets and sold by weight. **Supermarket Eurospar,** at the end of Corso Garibaldi, near the port, is modern and well stocked but crowded with Greece-bound backpackers. (Open Fri.-Wed. 8:30am-1pm and 4:30-8pm, Thurs. 8:30am-1pm.)

Trattoria da Emilia Spaghetti House, Vico dei Raimondo, 11, off Via San Lorenzo. A selection of fresh pastas (L7000), includes salad, beverages, bread and cover if you bring your *Let's Go.* Open daily 9am-10pm. Ring bell next door if the owner isn't there.
Spaghetti House Osteria Cucina Casalinga, Via Mazzini, 57, parallel to Corso Umberto, not far from the station. Delicious fare and a proprietor who loves *Let's Go* readers. *Lasagne* (L4000). Full meal of pasta, beverage, and bread, (about L7000). Cover L500. Open Mon.-Sat. 11am-2:30pm and 4-8:30pm.
Trattoria L'Angoletto, Via Pergola, 3 (tel. 52 50 29), near the port, off Corso Garibaldi. Pleasant, elegant outdoor eating. Pizza (L5500-8000). Open Sat.-Thurs. 9am-11pm.

SIGHTS AND ENTERTAINMENT

Stand with your back to the port and turn right; on the stairs facing the water you will find the only remaining terminal **column** of the Appian way. If you look closely, you'll see a marble capital graced by the sculpted figures of Jove, Neptune, Mars, and eight tritons. On the other side of the port rises another pillar. This modern counterpart to the Roman relic is a monument to Italian sailors. Surrounded by a vast seaside park, the **Marinaio d'Italia** takes the shape of an oversized rudder 55m high. You can easily hop over on one of the **Casale** ferries that leave every 15 min. from Banchina Montenegro, opposite Via Montenegro (L200).

Back in Bríndisi, wander through the nooks and crannies of the old town. Just above the Appian Way column, you'll stumble across the ruins of the Roman house in which Virgil died on his way home from Greece. P. Duomo introduces the *duomo* itself (12th c. rebuilt in the 18th c.), where Frederick II wed Jerusalem's Yolande.

If you follow the water for 2km or take the Casale ferry, you'll end up at the **Santa Maria del Casale.** The pride of Bríndisi, this multicolored, elaborately adorned building is reminiscent of Byzantine design but also incorporates Gothic ornamentation. It was built by Prince Phillip of neighboring Táranto, who enlisted his countryman Rinaldo da Taranto to paint an impressive Last Judgement fresco. If you're stuck overnight between June 27 and July 14, you can party at the **Festa de L'Unità.** The **P.C.I.** (Italian Communist Party) subverts the minds of capitalism-weary Bríndisini with nightly dancing, movies, music, and even a fashion show. Most events are free and take place in Via Grandi.)

■■■ LECCE

Variously dubbed the "Florence of the Baroque" and the "Athens of Apulia," Lecce is both a happily untouristed cornucopia of 17th-century architecture and one of southern Italy's most important intellectual centers.

A cosmopolitan succession of conquerors—Cretans, Romans, Saracens, Swabians, and more—passed through here, but the city's modern form was defined under the dominance of Habsburg Spain in the 16th and 17th centuries. Competitive merchants, aristocrats, and the religous orders of the Counter-Reformation spawned a plethora of palaces, churches, and arches in the distinctive *barocco Leccese.* Carved from soft, golden sandstone, the exuberant architecture resembles a sumptuous theatrical set. Cornices curl around columns, draperies drip with fatuous *putti,* balconies resemble fruitbowls, and windowsills become flower stalls.

Lecce remains an important center of agricultural trade, which around here means an abundance of olives. The University of Lecce is responsible for restoration projects and archeological studies around the area, as well as a vivacious student scene. The city provides a good starting point for a trip down the Salento Peninsula, Italy's high heel. Small Turkish- and Greek-looking towns dot the peninsula, and in some places you'll hear a dialect similar to Greek.

ORIENTATION AND PRACTICAL INFORMATION

The southeastern terminus of the state railway system, Lecce lies some 35km south and inland of Bríndisi. Twenty-five daily trains connect the Athens of Apulia with the Newark of Apulia (30min., L3200). To get to the center from the train station, walk down Viale Quarta and turn right onto the broad Via Gallipoli. Turn left at Viale Otranto and continue to the end. Past the castle on your left is **P. Sant'Oronzo,** the center of town. The immense Portale Napoli can be reached by following Via Umberto from P. Sant'Oronzo to Via Principi di Savoia, then turning left. Many intersections are bereft of street signs, so trace your path along a map or pleasantly lose yourself.

> **Tourist Office: EPT and AAST,** (tel. main office 30 41 17; branch offices 464 58, 24 64 43 or 30 44 43), in the "Il Sedile" monument in P. Sant'Oronzo. Maps, pamphlets, hotel listings. Helpful, informed, and occasionally English-speaking. Open Mon.-Sat. 8:30am-1:30pm and 4:30-7:30pm. Scheduled to close sometime before 1994—if this is so, call the main office for information.
>
> **Budget Travel: CTS,** Via Palmieri, 89 (tel. 30 18 62). A student travel service. Air and train information, tickets, and discounts. Open Mon.-Fri. 8:30am-1pm and 4:30-8pm, Sat. 8:30am-1pm.
>
> **Post Office:** in Piazzetta Libertini (tel. 30 30 00), at the end of Viale Otranto next to a large indoor market. Open Mon.-Sat. 8:15am-7:30pm. **Postal Code:** 73100.
>
> **Telephones: SIP,** Via Oberdan, 13 (tel. 68 64 22), near P. Mazzini. Open daily 9:15am-12:45pm and 3:30-6:30pm. **Telephone Code:** 0832.
>
> **Trains:** in P. Stazione (tel. 30 10 16), about 1km from the town center. **F.S.** travels north to Táranto (change at Bríndisi, 8 per day, 2hr., L8800). The provincial **Ferrovie del Sud-Est** (tel. 24 19 31) runs down the Salento Peninsula to Gallipoli (8 per day, 1hr., L7600 round-trip) and Otranto (change at Maglie, 4 or 5 per day, 1hr. 30min., L6800 round-trip).
>
> **Buses: STP,** Via Adua (tel. 228 73), parallel to Via Taranto. Connections to the Salento Peninsula. **Sud-Est,** Via Boito, easily accessible by urban bus #7 (L700) from the train station (tel. 64 76 34). To: Otranto (2 per day, 1hr. 30min., L5500); Gallipoli (5 per day, 50min., L4000); Táranto (2 per day, 80min., L7000); and other Apulian destinations.
>
> **Emergencies:** tel. 113. **Police:** Viale Otranto (tel. 47 16). **Hospital: Ospedale Vito Fazzi,** P. Bottazzi (tel. 68 51). **Ambulance:** tel. 68 54 03 or 63 54 11.

ACCOMMODATIONS AND CAMPING

An affordable, decent bed is a rare find indeed.

> **Hotel Cappello,** Via Montegrappa, 4 (tel. 30 88 81). From the station, take the 1st left off Viale Quarta onto Via Don Bosco and follow the signs. Nice and modern but be prepared for a rude awakening by the morning trains next door. Bathless singles with toilet, bidet, and sink, but no access to a shower; however, the affable owner will probably let you shower in an empty room. Singles L30,000, with bath L40,000. Doubles with bath L60,000. Triples L80,000. Quads L100,000.

Camping: Camping Torre Rinalda (tel. 65 21 61), 3km from the beach in the zone of Litoranea. Take bus #18 to Litoranea. July 7-Aug. 26 L7400 per person, L10,600 per tent. Off-season L5400 per person, L6700 per tent.

OOD

egional specialties include *ciceri e tria* (pasta cooked in chick pea broth), *cappello i gendarme* (a pastry shell stuffed with eggplant, zucchini, and veal), and *mercia,* sheep's-milk mozzarella. Buy picnic supplies at **Salumeria Loiacono,** Via Fazzi, l, in P. Sant'Oronzo, a 150-year-old cheese store. The **indoor market** next to the ost office provides a chance to haggle. (Open Mon.-Fri. 5am-1pm, Sat. 5am-1pm id 4-8pm.)

La Capannina, Via Cairoli, 13 (tel. 30 41 59), 700m from the station. Delicious food outdoors, in the middle of an imposing neoclassical piazza. A fun atmo-sphere—don't miss the *antipasti self-serve* (L6000). Meat dishes L8000-12,000. Wine L2000 per half-liter. Cover L1500. Service 15%. Open Tues.-Sun. noon-3pm and 7-11:30pm.

Ristorante Cinese Chinatown, Via della Saponea, 15 (tel. 30 85 58), past the Church of Santa Croce on the right. Complete *menùs* L15,000, L20,000, and L25,000. Open Mon.-Sat. noon-3pm and 7-11pm.

Ristorante-Pizzeria Da Claudio, Via Cavour, 11 (tel. 24 95 29), 1 block down from Alloggio Faggiano. Complete dinner L15,000 (including cover). Pasta from L5000. Meat dishes L5000-7000. Pizza L3500-5000. The excellent house red wine is L3000 per liter. Cover L1200. Open Thurs.-Tues. 7-11pm.

Paninoteca Tipica Leccese, P. Mazzini. This is the place to try *puccia,* a local bread heavily stuffed with your choice of ingredients (L5000). Open Sept.-May Thurs.-Tues. 9:30am-1am.

Ristorante Gambero Rosso, Via Bragacci, 16 (tel. 24 15 69). Full meal includes fruit and beverages L20,000. Coperto L1000, service 10%. Open Sat.-Thurs. noon-3pm and 7-11pm.

IGHTS AND ENTERTAINMENT

he best way to see Lecce is to wander around the old quarter, bumping into iroque monuments at every turn. Start with the **Church of St. Irene** (1591-1639) f P. Sant'Oronzo, a fine example of both Roman Baroque and the more florid :cce style. Unfortunately, like many of the city's architectural treasures, the church closed for restoration. The church in the marvelous complex of **Piazza del uomo,** a short distance away on Via Vittorio Emanuele. In front looms the **cathe- al,** rebuilt between 1659 and 1670 by Giuseppe Zimbalo, the architect of many of :cce's most celebrated buildings. The interior dates mostly from the 18th century, ith the exception of two Leccese altars. (Open daily 8-11am and 4:30-7:30pm.)

To the right of the cathedral (the first building as you enter the square), you'll ncounter the **seminary** (1709) by Cino, a pupil of Zimbalo. Cino was also well- ersed in flamboyant architectural idiom here, stopping just short of debauchery ith the help of a little bilateral symmetry.

Attached to the right of the cathedral, the **Palazzo Vescovile** (Bishop's Palace), stinguished by its open portico, has been remodeled several times since its origi- il construction in 1632. The porticoes held shops in the days when an annual fair ok place in the piazza. The final component of the piazza, the **campanile** (1682), khibits a more restrained elegance. A stroll down Via Libertini takes you to the **orta Rudiae** (1703), past the unfinished Baroque façade of the **Church of Santa eresa** to the simple Renaissance façade of the **Church of Sant'Anna.** At the end the street awaits the phantasmagorically complicated **Church of the Rosary,** mbalo's last work.

Return to P. Sant'Oronzo and walk north across P. Castro Mediano to Lecce's ost uninhibited monument. No amount of extravagant architecture quite prepares ou for the **Church of Santa Croce** (1548-1646), the supreme expression of Leccese Baroque and the city's most vaunted possession. Fantastic monsters and caryatids adorn the façade; the great rose window resembles an upside-down wedding cake. Instead of the surfaces lavished with sculpture and painting favored by many Baroque buildings, two simple rows of Corinthian columns support plain white walls within the church. A wonderfully animated altar (1614) by F. A. Zimbalo, Giuseppe's papa, adorns the chapel to the left of the apse. (Open daily 9am-1pm and 5:30-7:30pm.)

To the left of Santa Croce rises the **Palazzo del Governo.** Zimbalo designed the lower half of the façade while Cino worked on the upper portion. Diagonally across the street sprawls the Florentine-style **Palazzo Adorni,** with a secret enclosed garden in back. (Both open daily 8am-1pm.) From here Via Umberto and Via Principe di Savoia take you to the **Arco di Trionfo,** erected in 1548 in honor of Charles V, whose coat of arms adorns the front. Located in an ancient cemetery beyond the arch, the **Church of SS. Nicolò e Cataldo** was founded in 1180 by the Normans and modified in 1716 by Cino (closed for restoration). Note the Arabic influence especially in the portal. Small mausoleums of every conceivable style cluster around the narrow paths of the cemetery next door.

Little remains of Lecce's Roman city except the 2nd-century AD **amphitheater,** which is camouflaged by the scenery at **Piazza Sant'Oronzo** (and by the restoration equipment and by the plants growing on it). The **Column of Sant'Oronzo** next to the amphitheater is one of the two that once marked the termination of the Appian Way in Bríndisi.

Still more Baroque churches await the as-yet-unsatisfied visitor. The **Church of Santa Chiara** (1694; closed for restoration), at the end of P. Vittorio Emanuele, houses fine Leccese Baroque altars. **Via Arte della Cartapesta,** so named for its manufacture of papier-mâché figures of saints, runs to the left of the church. The **Church of Carmine,** whose whimsical façade (1717) was Cino's last work, contrasts perfectly with the plain façade of the **Church of the Gesù** (1579), providing a definitive expression of Leccese Baroque.

On Viale Gallipoli toward the station, you'll find the urbane **Museo Provinciale.** It houses a collection of bronze statuettes, inscriptions, vases, and rare 4th-century commemorative fish plates. Hours and admission prices change with the politician in charge. (Now open Mon.-Fri. 9:30am-1:30pm and 2:30-7:30pm, Sun. and holidays 9am-1:30pm. Free.) The *pinacoteca* on Via Imperatore Adriano, 79 (Convento Antonio) has a collection of 17th and 18th-century religious paintings. (Open Mon.-Fri. 9am-noon and 4:30-7pm. Free.)

This quiet city comes alive in July and August. **Estate Musicale Leccese** (July-Aug. 15) is a festival of music and dance. Ask at the EPT for *Calendario Manifestazioni 1993,* which details seasonal goings on in the whole province. You can create your own party before then, however, by hanging out at **P. Mazzini** by the beautiful fountain, especially with the help of a good *puccia* and a beer.

SALENTO PENINSULA

While in Lecce, take the time to visit the many medieval fortresses and castles scattered along the **Salento Peninsula.** The castle closest to Lecce (11km away on the road to Struda) is **Acaia,** now a forgotten ruin overgrown with weeds. Huge vaults, remnants of mosaics, narrow staircases, and a desolate courtyard stir medieval fantasies. (3 buses per day leave for Acaia from the Via Adua station in Lecce.)

Other spots in the Salento Peninsula are hard to reach by public transport. The **Ferrovie del Sud-Est,** a private railway, serves most of the larger communities (Gallipoli, Otranto, Gagliano), but is slow and infrequent.

▌Otranto

Otranto is the best starting point for a tour of the Adriatic Coast (9 per day, 1hr. 30min., round-trip L6800; change at Maglie). An ancient city of Greek origin and the easternmost point of habitation in Italy, Otranto was once the capital of Byzantine territory in Apulia and remained a key strategic site throughout the Middle Ages as a Norman outpost and embarkation point for the Crusades. In 1480, the Ottoman Turks attempted to conquer the Italian Peninsula and started the project in Otranto. The invasion was turned back early on, but Otranto's 800 citizens were slaughtered and the town ravaged. The remains of the "martyrs of Otranto" (those who refused Islam) are still found in the phenomenal **cathedral,** which also preserves an 11th-century mosaic pavement of the Tree of Life that extends the entire length of the nave. The crypt houses 42 columns pilfered from Greek, Roman, and Arab structures, all of varying marbles. Alterations over the centuries have left the once-austere exterior with an elaborate Baroque portal from the 18th century and a fine Gothic rose window. The Byzantine **Church of San Pietro** poses covertly in an enclosed square. Built between the 10th and 11th centuries in the shape of a Greek cross, its richly articulated interior contrasts with its staid exterior. The city is also making effort to restore the Aragonese castle and the old city walls to their former grandeur, though even in their present state they are more attractive than the concrete boxes which were built in the modern section of the city.

Practical Information Otranto's **tourist office,** at Via Basilica, 8 (tel. 80 14 56), rests at the foot of the *duomo.* (Open Mon.-Sat. 8am-2pm.) The independent **Cooperativa Turismo Iniziativa Otranto,** on largo Cavour near the *duomo,* is staffed by a jolly bunch who'll help you find a room. They also participate in the national **Agriturismo** program, if you desire to stay at local farms. The cost is usually around L31,000 per person. You can join their tours to local sites. (Open Mon.-Sat. 9am-noon and 5-8pm.) Otranto's **postal code** is 73028. The **phone code** is 0836. A dilapidated **ferry** runs from Otranto to Corfu and Igoumenitsa (Greece), operated by **Roana Lines.** Fares average L49,000 (students L40,000), but they jump to L69,000 (students L60,000) July 29-Aug. 10. Check the byzantine schedule and make inquiries and reservations at the **Stazione Marittima** (tel. 80 10 05). **LINNE Lauro** (tel. 80 15 78, at the port), has similar prices but a different schedule.

Food and Accommodations For a dominating view of the beach and the brightest, whitest rooms around, pick **Hotel Bellavista,** Via Vittorio Emanuele, 19 (tel. 80 10 58). (Singles L35,000, mid-June to mid-July L41,000. Doubles L55,000-64,000. Mid-July to the end of August full pension required L78,500. All rooms with bath.) If you plan to stay, try **Albergo Ester,** Via Papa Giovanni XXIII, 29 (tel. 80 12 96), near the Aragonese castle, rents doubles with bath for L65,000. (Reserve in Aug.) **Pensione de Plancia,** Via Porto Claudio (tel. 80 12 17). Good location right across the northern beach of Otranto. (Nice singles with bath for L45,000, doubles with bath L66,000.) All of Otranto's hotels have obligatory full pension on the order of L80,000 per person in August. You'll find fast food and pizza by the slice at **Pro-fumo di Mare,** Lungomare Terra d'Otranto, 3. The other dishes are a bit expensive. Or sate your hunger with a roast chicken (*pollo arrosto,* L8000), from one of the many *rosticcerie.*

Sights and Entertainment The last weekend of June, Otranto welcomes the summer and tourists with a feast for three days; in August there is another one in honor of the martyrs. Venture a few miles north of Otranto to **Torre dell' Orso,** a *lido* cradled in pine woods at the end of a beautiful inlet. A bemused Madonna sits at the **Grotta della Poesia,** a small pool of clear water enclosed by low cliffs and a natural bridge.

The coast south of Otranto is more rugged, bordered by limestone cliffs and dotted with flat-roofed homes. **Santa Cesárea Terme** is an important resort in the

area, famous for its thermal springs and spectacular location. The **tourist offic**
gathers dust at Via Roma, 209 (tel. 94 40 43). A mere 6km south of here is th
marine cave **Zinzulusa Grotto** (L3000), filled with stalactites and stalagmites (*zi*
zuli in the local dialect). Two Ferrovie del Sud-Est buses per day run to San
Cesárea Terme from Via Adua in Lecce.

■ Gallipoli

To explore the peninsula's Ionian Coast, start at **Gallipoli** (*not* the Gallipoli of Worl
War I fame, which is located in Turkey). (From Lecce by train every 30min., 1h
L3200, or by bus 1hr., L3200.) Named "beautiful city" by the Greeks, the port ha
traditionally traded in olive oil and wine. Its insular old city possesses a distinct
Greek air. Pastel houses enclose narrow winding streets that lead to the seasi
promenade that has replaced the city's ancient walls. Stretching along Gallipoli
northern coast are two picturesque beaches, **Santa Maria al Bagno** and **Sant**
Caterina. Several secluded beaches lie close to town and south of Gallipoli (admi
sion around L500). **Lido San Giovanni**, on the beach road, harbors pebbly sand an
clear water. Gallipoli's extremely modest **Pro Loco tourist office,** Corso Roma, 22
(tel. 47 62 02), can be found next to P. Fontana Greca. (Open July-Aug. Mon.-Fr
10am-noon and 5-7pm.) To see the remains of the true Hellenic Fountain (3rd cer
tury BC) just go around it. The little tower you see in the old part of town is the **Ri**
ellino from which Gallipoli's women used to drop hot oil on the Venetians wh
were attacking the city. Continue up Corso Roma over the bridge and into the ol
town. Fresh fruit is available at an **indoor market**, on the left at Corso Roma,
(Open daily 7am-1:30pm and 5-8pm.) Across the street on P. Imbriani is the **po**
office. (Open Mon.-Fri. 8:30am-1pm.) The **phone code** is 0883.

Unfortunately, Gallipoli has no bargain lodgings. The only semi-reasonable plac
is **Pensione Al Pescatore,** Riviera C. Colombo (tel. 47 36 56), up Corso Roma an
take a right. The large rooms and beautiful courtyard add up to L45,000 for a sing
and L75,000 for a double (all rooms with bath; July-Aug. full pension require
L85,000). **Camping Vecchia Torre** (tel. 20 90 83), about 3km from town, lets bu
galows for two people at L50,000 (off season L25,000). Or pay L7500 per perso
off season L4500. (Open May 15-Sept.) **Baia di Gallipoli** (tel. 26 69 06), about th
same distance from town, rents two-bed bungalows for L85,000, and charges L690
per tent, L9500 per person, off season L4900 per tent, L6800 per person. (Ope
June- Sept.) Both have tennis courts (although no rental equipment) and are close t
the beach. **Agenzia de Luca,** Corso Roma 217 (tel. 26 42 43), offers glass-botto
boat tours for L15,000 per person. Or a true sail-boat experience for L30,000 (up t
8 people). (Open Mon.-Sat. 9am-12:30pm and 4:30-8:30pm. English spoken.)

■■■ TÁRANTO

Legends say Taras, son of Neptune, founded Táranto 1200 years before Rome's cr
ation. As a metropolis of Magna Graecia, Táranto was an important trading port an
center of philosophical thought. Spartans, Normans, and their kin periodical
reduced Táranto to smithereens; only a few premodern traces remain.

Contemporary Táranto is a fascinating microcosm of the ups and downs of th
20th-century *mezzogiornio*. The old city, with its noisy markets and tiny fishin
boats, retains the trappings of the preindustrial South. Flanking this area is a nav
base, the result of Táranto's military build-up during Fascist times; to the north, pos
war smokestacks churn out steel.

ORIENTATION AND PRACTICAL INFORMATION

Táranto is divided into three parts: the **port area** to the north, with the train statio
the **old city,** a small island across Ponte di Porta Napoli from the station; and th
new city, to the southeast across the *canale navigabile*, which houses the majorit

of hotels, restaurants, and offices. Pick up a city map at the information window at the station and then take any bus (L800) to the new city. You may also buy a day pass for L2000 which gives you unlimited travel on city buses, although tickets are not checked very often. **Be careful walking in the old city during the day and definitely avoid it at night.** Don't walk through the old city with a pack on unless you're eager to part with it. At night, stick to the brightly lit, well-populated seaside boulevards.

Tourist Office: Corso Umberto, 113 (tel. 43 23 92), in the new city. Take bus #8 from the station; get off 3 stops after the bridge into the new city. Make a left on Via Acclavio and follow it to Corso Umberto; the office is across Corso Umberto on the corner. Well-equipped, genial. Provides a good map and help with accommodations. English spoken. Open Mon.-Fri. 9am-1pm and 5-7pm, Sat. 9:30am-11:30pm.

Budget Travel: CTS, Via Matteotti, 1 (tel. 43 33 50, fax 452 62 38), just across the bridge in the new city. ID cards and student discounts. Open Mon.-Fri. 10am-1pm and 5-8pm, Sat. 10am-1pm.

Post Office: Lungomare Vittorio Emanuele II (tel. 43 59 51), a few blocks up from the *canale navigabile*. Open Mon.-Sat. 8:15am-6pm. **Postal code:** 74100.

Telephones: SIP, Lungomare Vittorio Emanuele, 20 (tel. 43 90 91), near the post office. Open Mon-Sat. 8am-9:30pm. **Telephone code:** 099.

Trains: in P. Duca d'Aosta for both **F.S.** and **Ferrovie del Sud-Est.** Trains to: Bríndisi (frequent departures, 1hr. 30min., L5000), Bari (also frequent, 1hr. 30min., L8800), Martina Franca (9 per day, 45min., L3200), and Alberobello via Martina Franca (14 per day, 1hr., L3900). There is 1 direct train for Alberobello, daily at 4:30pm. Naples and Rome are possible by train, but most people find the bus to be faster and cheaper.

Buses: AMAT city bus tickets cost L800 or L2000 per day for unlimited travel; buy them at *tabacchi* or at the small office outside the station. **Ferrovie Autobus del Sud-Est** (tel. 35 35 85) buses to Martina Franca (11 per day, 7am-9pm, 1hr., L2500) and Bari (4 per day, 2hr., L8000), leave from P. Castello (in the old city, just across from the *canale navigabile*). Buses to Lecce (4 per day, 2 hr., L7000), leave from Via Magnaghi in the northeastern outskirts of the new city. **SITA** buses depart from P. del Castello for Matera (5 per day, 1hr. 45min., L7000; some require a change at Laterza). Also inquire at Agenzia Ausiello for buses to Naples (7am and 4pm, 4hrs., L25,900); to Rome (8am and 3:30pm, 6hrs., L55,000).

Emergencies: tel. 113. **Police:** tel. 112 or 113. **Hospital: SS. Annunziata,** Via Bruno (tel. 98 51).

ACCOMMODATIONS AND CAMPING

Unlike other Apulian cities, Táranto is not lacking in cheap, comfortable lodgings. Fortunately, most hotels congregate in the brightly lit *Viali* of the new city, and at the end of the well-traveled *Lungomare* in the old city. Nevertheless, exercise caution all throughout Táranto at night. The campgrounds here boast four stars and correspondingly astronomical prices.

Albergo Pisani, Via Cavour, 43 (tel. 24 087), across bridge in the new city off P. Garibaldi. The brightest, newest place in town. Singles L33,000, with bath L40,000. Doubles L63,000, with bath L77,000. Triples with bath L90,000.

Albergo Sorrentino, P. Fontana, 7 (tel. 471 83 90), next to Hotel Ariston. Family-run. Large but run-down rooms. Singles L25,000. Doubles L35,000, with bath L45,000.

Pensione Rivera, Via Campania, 203 (tel. 33 88 90), on the outskirts of town. Take the "Circolare Rossa" bus (L800) from Via Regina Margherita and get off at Via Campania (15min.). Contemporary, comfortable rooms in a residential area. Singles L29,000. Doubles L48,000.

Albergo La Cremaillere, in Locando San Paolo at Via Orimini, 1 (tel. (080) 70 02 65). Quite far out; take the Ferrovie del Sud-Est bus from P. Castello for Martina

TÁRANTO

Franca, and get off at Locando San Paolo (6 per day, 50min.). Right on the *autostrada*. Singles L25,000. Doubles L70,000. All with bath.

FOOD

Táranto swims with seafood. Try *cozze* (mussels) in basil and olive oil. The new city is full of inexpensive restaurants, and the *menù turistico* is a good catch here, often as varied as the regular menu. Grab your daily bread at **Supermercato STANDA** in P. Immacolata (open Mon.-Fri. 9am-1pm and 4:45-8:30pm, Sat. 9am-12:45pm). The daily **market,** in the piazza just across the bridge into the old city, supplies pop music, live snails, stingrays, and yes, fruits and vegetables. (Open daily 7am-1:30pm.)

Trattoria Gatto Rosso da Rino, Via Cavour, 2 (tel. 452 98 75). Specializes in seafood. The *spaghetti mare misto* (literally "mixed sea") is a primo *primo* (L5000), as are the *tubetti alle cozze* (tubular pasta with mussels, L5000). Coperto L1500. Open Tues.-Sun. 11am-3pm and 7-11pm.

Ristorante Basile al Ristoro, Via Pitagora, 76 (tel. 452 62 40), across from the *Giardini Pubblici,* 1 street up from Corso Umberto. An excellent value—pleasant atmosphere, prompt service, and delicious food. Offerings vary according to availability of fresh ingredients. *Primi* around L6000, *secondi* L7000. Pizza and beer, L7000. *Menù* L16,000. Open Sun.-Fri. noon-3pm and 7-11pm.

Birreria Amstel, Via d'Aquino, 27 (tel. 937 58), in the new city, parallel to Corso Umberto off P. Immacolata. Tasty *risotto alla marinara* (rice with seafood, L7000). If you eat in the *tavola calda,* you'll save L1000 per dish and be spared the cover to boot. Splendid pizzas in the evening L4500-6000. Full-choice *menù* L15,000. Wine L2000 per ¼ liter. Cover L1500. Open Aug.-June Thurs.-Tues. 12:30-2:30pm and 7-11:30pm. MC, Visa.

Pan d'Oro, P. Immacolata. American fast food *all'Italiana: tortellini, ravioli, orecchiette* (L2500).

Hong Kong, Eso Umberto, 3 (tel. 284 19). *Menús* L12,000, L15,000 and L18,000. Open Tues.-Sun. noon-3pm and 6:30pm-midnight.

SIGHTS

Other than the cathedral and the superb National Museum, little remains of the city's past glory. Nonetheless, the waterside and main square abide with a certain graciousness. Visit the tree-lined **Lungomare Vittorio Emanuele** in the new city for a far-reaching view over the Mar Grande. On the horizon, between Rondinella Point to the right and lighthoused Capo San Vito to the left, you can see the islands of San Pietro and San Paolo, which enclose the outer harbor. Both are military outposts, however, and can be visited only with permission. The fecund gardens of **Villa Peripato** (or *giardini pubblici*), on the other side of the city, bloom toward a terrace overlooking the Mar Piccolo and the Italian naval base.

Situated across the bridge into the old city, the **Aragonese Castle** was built with a view of both waters and with a hold over the *canale navigabile*. Unfortunately, it still seems to have strategic value; the navy occupies nearly all of it, and only the small **art gallery** (first door on your left crossing into the old town) may be visited. (Gallery open daily 9:30am-1pm and 6-9pm. Free.)

The **old city** invites visitors to wander its dark byways, but exercise appropriate caution. It is home to a remarkable **cathedral,** built in the 10th century and rebuilt in 1713. The church was originally a Greek cross; the Latin arm was added in 1170. The Byzantine exterior walls and cupola are still visible at the sides of the church. Under the chancel, the crypt is doused with 12th-century Byzantine frescoes. Welcome relief from the solemnity of the old town is supplied by the flamboyant decoration of the **San Cataldo Chapel** (end of the right aisle), whose multicolored, intricate marble designs exemplify the Leccese Baroque influence. Compare this structure with Táranto's other prominent cathedral in the eastern part of the new city. Designed by Gio Ponti, this modern Gothic creation takes the shape of a sail. (Both open daily 1-5pm.)

The most telling testimony to Táranto's former importance is found within the excellent **National Museum,** Corso Umberto, 41, at Corso Cavour. This museum's collection of Magna Graecian art now rivals those of Reggio and Naples as the best in Italy; its terra-cotta figure collection is the world's largest. Mostly excavated from the city's necropolis, the collection also includes sculpture and mosaics, imported and local pottery, jewelry, coins, and prehistoric materials. (Open Tues.-Sat. 9am-2pm and 3-7:30pm, Sun. 9am-1pm, Mon. 9am-2pm. Free daily tours in Italian 9:30am and 11am. Admission L6000.)

In summer, an **ACTT** city bus stops along the *lungomare* (10 per day, 8:15am-7:30pm, L800), carrying you to the most beautiful, least crowded **beach** in the area, **Lido Silvana.**

ENTERTAINMENT

Every night from about 6 to 8pm, the entire stretch of **Via d'Aquino** throngs with scoping crowds. The action centers on **Piazza della Vittoria.** Giovanni Filippo Sousa fans sound out a nightly cheer at sundown as the navy band toots to the lowering of the flag where Lungomare Vittorio Emanuele meets the *canale navigabile.*

Táranto's **Holy Week Festival** draws crowds and acclaim from around the country. In a ceremony rooted in medieval Spanish ritual, men don masks and long white robes with pointed hoods and parade a cart through the streets, on a pilgrimage to the Holy Sepulchres housed in Táranto's churches. The festivities begin the Sunday before Easter. Two processions occur Thursday, at 3pm and midnight, and one on Good Friday at 5pm. The Procession of Our Lady of Sorrows leaves at midnight from the Church of San Domenico. A river of people floods the city, walking until noon on Good Friday.

On May 10, the city celebrates the **Festa di San Cataldo** with a procession of boats that escorts the statue of San Cataldo around the harbor. As it passes the Aragonese Castle, the castle lights up beneath a stirring display of fireworks.

BASILICATA

■ Matera

A few decades ago, Matera represented the quintessence of Italian poverty, its destitute inhabitants forced to live in caves (*sassi*) together with pigs and chickens. A river of lire, the source of which is Rome, produced the prosperous, self-satisfied town you see today. Rome's munificence helped build adequate housing, which drew most of the citizens out of their rock caverns. In the 1970s, radicals and visionaries moved to reinhabit the ancient dwellings. Ongoing renovations reflect the effort to provide many Materans with a life in the "interesting" part of town, and the *sassi* are now undergoing rapid gentrification.

ORIENTATION AND PRACTICAL INFORMATION

Ten **SITA** buses depart each day from Metaponto's train station at P. Matteotti (8:25am-9:55pm; 6 per day in winter, 8am-4:50pm; 1hr., L2900) and one departs from Potenza (at 3:45pm, 1hr. 45min., L5100). Seven **Ferrovie Calabro-Lucane** buses leave from Ferrandina's train station on the Potenza-Táranto line (6:30am-9:35pm, 45min., L2900). Calabro-Lucane **trains** also leave every one to two hours from Bari's central train station (6:50am-10:57pm, 1hr. 30 min., L4300). Six SITA buses leave daily from Táranto's bus terminal at P. Castello for Matera (5:50am-7:20pm, 1hr. 45min., L7000). Most service is drastically reduced Sunday and holidays. The heart of the new city is **Piazza V. Veneto**. Via Roma links it to the train and bus stations at P. Matteotti; Via delle Beccherie leads to P. Duomo in the *sassi*.

Tourist Office: EPT, Via de Viti de Marco, 9 (tel. 33 34 52 or 33 19 83). From the station walk down Via Roma and take your 2nd left. Pamphlets in English and a map. Acquire the comprehensive guide to Basilicata. English spoken. Open daily 8am-2pm. **Cooperative Amici del Turista** (tel. 31 01 13), in P. San Pietro Caveoso in the *sassi,* gives out maps and advice on exploring the cave dwellings. Open daily 9:30am-12:30pm; March-May 9:30am-1pm; Oct.-Feb. erratic morning hours. In summer, begin your information odyssey at one of the **information gazebos** near the entrance to the *sassi*. There is one at Via Ribola and another between P. Veneto and Via del Corso. Open daily 9am-1pm and 3-7:30pm.

Post Office: on Via del Corso (tel. 33 18 22), off P. Veneto. Open Mon.-Fri. 8:15am-5:30pm. **Postal code:** 75100.

Telephones: SIP, Via del Corso, 5 (tel. 24 21). Open Mon.-Sat. 9am-1pm and 2-7pm; Sun. 9am-1pm and 3:30-6:30pm. At night, try **Autonoleggio Tommaso,** Vico XX Settembre, 2 blocks from P. Vittorio Veneto. Open 9pm-8am. **Telephone code:** 0835.

Emergencies: tel. 113. **Police:** tel. 33 42 22. **Ambulance:** tel. 33 35 21. **Hospital:** on Via Lanera (tel. 21 14 10).

ACCOMMODATIONS AND FOOD

Insidious rate creep has set in among Matera's former budget hotels as they seek more stars and higher profits. It's possible to find a room if you arrive early in the day, but you'd be best off making reservations a few days in advance.

Albergo Roma, Via Roma, 62 (tel. 33 39 12), downhill from the bus station at P. Matteotti. Friendly, clean, and conveniently located. Fills up fast during festival period (late June-early July). Curfew midnight. Singles L26,000. Doubles L36,000, with bath L40,000.

Hotel President, Via Roma, 13 (tel. 33 57 91, fax 33 58 21). A few affordable rooms without baths. Singles L35,000. Doubles L65,000, with bath L99,000. Breakfast included. Reservations suggested especially during the summer. MC, Visa.

De Nicola, Via Nazionale, 158 (tel. 38 51 11). Follow Viale A. Moro from P. Matteotti to Via Anunzia Tella. To the left, Via Anunzia Tella turns into Via Nazionale. A bit of a hike from the station, but might still have a free room late in the day. Your can also hop on one of the orange city buses (#1, 2, or 6; L800). Singles with bath L52,000. Doubles with bath L84,000.

Matera offers several culinary specialties, including *favetta con cicore* (a soup of beans, celery, chicory, and croutons, all mixed in olive oil) and *frittata di spaghetti* (pasta mixed with anchovies, eggs, bread crumbs, garlic, and oil). Experience true Materan grit by gnawing on *pane di grano duro;* made of extra-hard wheat, this bread stays fresh almost as long as Twinkies. **Panificio Perrone,** Via dei Sariis, 6 (tel. 38 56 56), off Via Lucana, sells large, fluffy loaves (L1800 per kg). They also sell tasty *biscotti al vino,* cookies baked with wine (L7000 per kg). (Open Mon.-Wed. and Fri.-Sat. 8am-2pm and 4-8pm, Thurs. 8am-2pm.) The **market** is between Via Lucana and Via A. Persio, near P. Veneto. (Open Mon.-Sat. 7am-1pm.) Down the block from the tourist office sits **Supermercato Divella,** Via Spine Bianche, 6. (Open Mon.-Wed. and Fri.-Sat. 8:30am-1:30pm and 5-8:30pm, Thurs. 8:30am-1:30pm.)

Ristorante Pizzeria Il Terrazzino, Sui Sussi, Bocconcino due, 7 (tel 33 25 03), off P. Veneto to the left of the Banco di Napoli: follow the path to the sign. Savor local delicacies in a cave dug into the cliffs, or on the outdoor terrace that offers a breathtaking view of the *sassi*. Try hand-made pastas like *cavatelli alla boscaiola,* with a sauce of tomato, mushrooms, and prosciutto (L8000). Pizzas L6000-12,000. Finish with the dazzling *spumoni* (chocolate, coffee, and vanilla ice cream, made *in casa*) L4000. Wine L4000 per bottle. Cover L2000, L1000 for pizza. Service 10%. Open Wed.-Mon. noon-4pm and 7pm-midnight, Tues. noon-4pm (summer only).

Trattoria Lucana, Via Lucana, 48 (tel. 33 61 17), off Via Roma. Matera's best *trattoria.* For *primi*, try the hearty *sfoglia alla lucana*, a lasagna made with local cheeses (L7000). For *secondi*, the *bocconcini alla lucana*, their specialty (diced veal with mushrooms), is a steal at L14,000. Cover L2000. Service 10%. Open Mon.-Sat. 12:30-3pm and 8-10pm. Closed first two weeks of September.

SIGHTS

Before venturing to the *sassi,* take a quick peek in one of the churches on the city's fringes. Walking up Via San Biagio away from P. Veneto, you'll arrive at the 13th-century **Church of San Giovanni Battista**, notable for its decorative portal. The interior is a harmonious Gothic blend of arches, vaults, and columns. Enter the heart of the *sassi* zone by following the *itinerario turistico* leading from Via delle Beccherie away from Via Fiorentilli. You'll ultimately find yourself at Via Duomo, which, as you might guess, leads to the *duomo* in P. del Duomo. Erected between 1268 and 1270, the church is a fine Puglian-Romanesque construction with reaching nave, projecting moldings, rose windows, and richly carved portals. Inside, the 15th-century carved choir stalls compete with the stunning 16th-century **Cappella dell'Annunziata** for your attention. (Churches officially open daily 9am-noon but most remain unlocked until 7 or 8pm.)

From here, you can begin your tour of the *sassi* in the valleys **Sasso Caveoso** and **Sasso Barisano** by following Via Madonna delle Virtù (called the Strada Panoramica dei Sassi) just down the hill from the *duomo.* Of obscure origin, the *sassi* come in four types. The oldest—and crudest—are simply niches in the rock lining Sasso Barisano (across the canyon formed by the Gravina River), in which townsfolk lived over 7000 years ago. The second type includes the carved nooks around Sasso Caveoso dating from around 2000 BC. Third are the homes more elaborately carved from the rock around Via B. Buozzi (stemming from Via Madonna delle Virtù); these are around 1000 years old. Finally come the intentionally constructed dwellings around Via Forentini, no more than 750 years old. Although the *sassi* were almost completely evacuated after the new city was erected, young couples have been renovating and jazzing up nearly all the ancient homes, with the exception of the 6th-century *chiese rupestri* (rock churches). Many still display remnants of Byzantine frescoes dating from the 12th to the 16th centuries. Follow Via Madonna delle Virtù south (to the right) to the **Churches of San Pietro Caveoso** and **Santa Maria d'Idris,** and farther down to the **Church of Santa Lucia alle Malve.** Although the Church of San Pietro Caveoso is currently closed to the public, the two other churches preserve beautiful 11th-century Byzantine frescoes painted on the tufa of the caves. Neither keeps regular hours, but you can try asking for the caretaker who will let you in and provide a brief tour of the place (tip him about L2000). Here, you can also see the inside of a house built in the rocks, furnished as in the old times. (Open during the summer daily 9am-2pm and 3-8pm; fewer hours during the winter; L2000.)

As you roam the Sasso Caveoso, you'll be approached by children who get their spending money by giving "tours." You are better off going with the Amici dei Sassi (tel. 33 10 00) or the Amici del Turista, listed above. Call them first before paying for some kid's *gelato.*

Down Via Buozzi in the direction of P. Veneto, the **Museo Nazionale Domenico Ridola,** Via Ridola, 24 (tel. 31 12 39), off Via Lucana outside the *sassi,* houses an excellent, boldly displayed prehistoric and early classical collection, all in a former 17th-century monastery. (Open Tues.-Sat. 9am-2pm, Sun. 9am-1pm. Free.)

ENTERTAINMENT

Matera lets loose during the **Festival of Santa Maria della Bruna,** held during the last week of June and first week of July. The festival reaches its climax on July 2. At dawn, a procession of shepherds leaves the *duomo,* and at dusk a cart holding a Madonna follows. The ornate cart rumbles along Via XX Settembre, illuminated by thousands of small lights, while warriors in medieval costume and clergy on horse-back march solemnly alongside. At the end of the procession, everyone participates in the *Assalto al Carro,* in which relic-hungry spectators tear apart the cart holding the Madonna after the Madonna itself and other valuables have been removed to safety.

Matera showcases itself in July with **Luglio Materano,** a festival of classical music, dance, and theater. Call ahead to the tourist office to be sure that they're continuing this (new) tradition in 1994. The best evening amusements lie with Matera's 55,000 townspeople: any Friday night you can join them as they strut along P. Veneto and Via del Corso talking up a storm during breaks in *gelato*-snarfing.

■ Metaponto

Like many other towns on Italy's southern coastline, Metaponto is feeling the effects of increased development. A well-known beach resort, its lonely train station and scattered Greek ruins have been joined by a meager (albeit expanding) community development project. A profusion of new clothing stores and food markets are evidence of Metaponto's changing face.

Practical Information The young people who run the **tourist office** on Viale delle Sirene (tel. 74 19 33) may not be able to offer the most complete information, but they're friendly and sport nice tans. Open July-Sept. daily 8am-1pm and 2:30-8pm. There is a **post office** across from Metaponto's Archaeological Museum in the new settlement (open Mon.-Sat. 8:30am-5:30pm) and a **bank,** Cassa di Risparmio di Calabria e di Lucania, located by the beach (tel. 74 19 13; open Mon.-Fri. 8am-1pm). Metaponto's **telephone code** is 0835. Metaponto is an important **train junction** on the Táranto-Règgio line (16 per day to Táranto, 1hr., L3900; 5 per day to Règgio, 6hr., L30,300), with a connection to Naples by way of Potenza (5hr., L18,700). **Bus** service connects the Metaponto station with Matera (8 per day 7am-9pm; in winter 5 per day 7am-5:30pm; L2400).

Food and Accommodations To get to the **Hotel Oasi,** Via Olimpia, 12 (tel. 74 19 30), turn right at the fork in Via Ionio about 100m from the beach. It's at the far end, past the bend in the road and the minimarket in the large, unmarked white building with a red fence. Spacious doubles with bath for L40,000. In July and August the owner usually demands full pension (L65,000 per person). The alternative is the **Hotel Kennedy,** Via Ionio (tel. 74 19 60), on the right side of the fork. Gorgeous doubles with balconies and bath go for L60,000. Full pension is generally required July 15-Aug. 20 (L75,000 per person). **Camping** is probably the best idea if you plan to hang out on the beach for a few days. Attractively situated, **Camping Magna Grecia,** Via Lido, 1 (tel. 74 18 55), lies one-half km off Via Ionio from the strand. (Aug. 1-20, L8000 per person., L8500 per tent; less at other times.) Magna Grecia is really an amusement park in the guise of a campground, complete with shuttle to the beach, tennis courts, swimming pool, game rooms, snack bars, and a disco. (All charge admission—pool, for instance, L2000.) Right on the main Lido with outdoor dining, is **Coop Tur,** Viale delle Sirene, 2, where a complete meal will cost about L18,000 (no drinks included). Open June-mid-Sept. daily noon-2:30pm and 7pm-late for pizza.

Sights and Entertainment To reach the clear water and fine sand of Metaponto's **beach,** catch one of the few buses from the train station (L600, plus L400 for every big bag), or—better yet—walk straight from the station (50m) and take a right onto Via Ionio, being careful not to electrocute yourself on the recently completed pass over the train tracks. From the base of the overpass, it's a 2km walk. Concessions cover only part of the beach; much of it remains untouched and bordered by grassy dunes. Only two reasonable lodging options serve the traveler.

To reach Metaponto's **archaeological sites,** follow the road that leads away from the station. Immediately past the turnoff onto Via Ionio and to the left lies Metaponto's brand new shopping/apartment complex and recently completed **Archaeological Museum.** (Open daily 9am-7pm. Admission L4000.) Further down the road from the station (½ km) lies the turnoff to Metaponto's **Parco Archeologico.** Following the signs, you'll be led to the scanty ruins of the Doric **Temple of Apollo Licius** and the remains of a **Greek Theater** (1.5 km). Continuing on the road from the station for about 3km and turning right on the coastal highway bound for Táranto, it's another 2km to the **Tavole Palatine**—ruins of the Greek temple of Hera. The famous Greek mathematician Pythagoras supposedly taught here until his death in 479 BC.

▨ Calabria

Calabria is Italy's last continental foothold before its lunge for Sicily. Calabria began with the ancient Greeks and the rich towns of **Sibari,** and **Locri;** legions of Byzantines, Saracens, Normans, and Aragonese followed, leaving behind their own marks on the region's population and cities. The coming of the World Wars also marked the formation of organized crime—the *'ndrangheta*—which made thousands of Calabrians leave their homes in search of a better life. Today the effects of the "crime-families" are felt less here than they are in the rest of Italy and, adding to the feeling one gets that somehow everyone, including the mob, has given up on Calabria. The region remains far less organized for tourism than most in Italy, with limited, inconvenient transportation and a dearth of affordable accommodations.

Of the region's four major towns, only two warrant time and energy. Set in the heart of the Sila Massif, a huge granite plateau (1100-1700m), Cosenza appeals to visitors not only for its environs but also for its picturesque old town. Near the southern tip of Calabria is Règgio di Calabria, a dull place whose superb archaeological museum houses the famous Bronze Warriors from Riace. On a venture north along the sandy but often bleak beaches of the Ionian Coast, visit Rossano and Gerace, two little-touristed towns that preserve numerous Byzantine monuments.

■ Cosenza

Cosenza is two-faced: while a flat urban metropolis bursts out of its shell on one side of the Busento River, an old city clings to a hill topped by a citadel—Cosenza's greatest treasures lie between the two. Deep in the Busento River still wallows loot from the first sack of imperial Rome. Besides being *the* site for a spot of speculative fishing, Cosenza's greatest attribute is its location, which makes it the perfect base for hiking in the Sila Massif.

ORIENTATION AND PRACTICAL INFORMATION

Getting around Cosenza isn't difficult, once one realizes there are two train stations *and* two bus terminals. Outside the city, on the Crati River, lies the new train station from which trains service **Paola,** on the Rome-Règgio di Calabria coastal line (several per day, 20min., L2400), and **Metaponto** (11 per day, change at Síbari, 3hr., L8800). Then there's the old train station, from which trains depart for **Camigliatello, San Giovanni,** and other cities in the Sila. Bus #5 connects the stations (every 15min. 6am-12:30am, L1000). The small bus terminal is right outside the old train station at P. Matteotti. One block away stretches **Corso Mazzini,** a main thoroughfare which runs parallel to the tracks extending from the old station and connecting the small bus station with the large one at P. Fera. Once on Corso Mazzini with your back to the old train station and small bus depot, turn left for the old town and right for the central bus station and SIP.

Tourist Office: **APT information office** (tel. 48 26 40), at the new train station. Maps, hotel listings, and information on the Sila. English spoken. Open Mon.-Sat. 8:30am-8pm . There is another one in town (tel. 39 05 95), on Via Rossi. From P. Fera near the central bus station, follow Via Simonetta until you come to Viale della Repubblica. From here, bear up the hill to the right on Via Rossi and cross the rotary at the beginning of the *autostrada*. The office is on the opposite side of the rotary to the left. English spoken. Open Mon.-Fri. 8:30am-2pm. The central **EPT office** advises at Viale Trieste, 50 (tel. 27 821). With your back to the old train station, go right and quickly left if you have any questions the others can't handle. Open Mon.-Fri. 8am-2pm.

Post Office: (tel. 68 41), on Via Vittorio Veneto at the end of Via Piave off Corso Mazzini. Open Mon.-Sat. 8:15am-7:30pm. **Postal code:** 87100.

Telephones: **SIP,** Via dell'Autostazione, above the bus station. Open daily 8:10am-8pm. At other times, try **Croce Bianca,** Via Beato Angelo d'Acri, 29. **Telephone code:** 0984.

Trains: (tel. 48 23 23). The new station (Cosenza) is on Via Popilia at the *super-strada*. Behind the old station is the **Ferrovie Calabro Lucane** station (Cosenza Centrale) off P. Matteotti. Cosenza Monaco, Cosenza Campanella, and Cosenza Casali are three other stations in and near the city.

Buses: off P. Fera, at the opposite end of Corso Mazzini from the train station. Get schedules at the information booths in the new train station. (FCL bus, tel. 36 851, or call 36 853 for all the necessary info on buses and trains.) Gate #5 for Catanzaro, #14 for the Tyrrhenian coast. Snack bar open 24hrs. Buses run erratically Sun. and holidays.

Emergencies: tel. 113. **Police: Questura** tel. 36 001. **Hospital: Ospedale Civile dell'Annunziata** (tel. 68 11), on Via Felice Migliori. On weekends, call 31 831.

ACCOMMODATIONS AND FOOD

The most affordable lodgings cluster around the old station, just a few blocks from the old city, a quarter blessed with good *pensione* and cursed with evil tourist traps. **Albergo Bruno,** Corso Mazzini, 27 (tel. 73 889), just one block from the train station, offers singles for L22,000, with bath L60,000. (Doubles L38,000, with bath L54,000. Triples L50,000, with bath L66,000. Quad with bath L74,000.) Already enhanced by newly renovated bathroom facilities, your stay is topped off with free use of the kitchen and pool-tabled TV room. Under everlasting renovations is the **Hotel Excelsior,** P. Matteotti, 14 (tel. 74 383), facing the old train station. The management equips the large, bright rooms of this once-grand hotel with color TVs and phones. (Singles L50,000. Doubles L80,000. Triples L100,000. Quads L115,000. AmEx, Diners' Club.) The best **camping** in the area is at the Sila Massif (see Near Cosenza) and in the seaside towns of **Scalea** and **Marina di Belvedere** (at least 4 buses per day to each location 6:35am-6pm, 1¼hr., L3000-5000 depending on season). Two sites on Scalea's Tyrrhenian waterfront are **Camping il Gabbiano** (tel. (0985) 20 563). Free hot showers and beach bungalows. (L8000 per person and L9000 per tent during July and August, less during the other months; Open mid-June-mid-Sept.), and **Campeggio Moby Dick** (tel. (0985) 20 278). Well-organized with sporting activites (soccer, beach volleyball, tennis and ping-pong), and a club. Free hot showers and beach bungalows. (L8200 per person and L9000 per tent during the high season; about L5000 in the low season; open June-Sept.). If staying here, pay a visit to another beautiful beach up north, **S. Nicole.**

Consenza's best dishes are prepared *ai funghi,* with fresh mushrooms from the forests of the Sila. Fungus lovers should proceed to **Trattoria Peppino,** P. Crispi, 3 (tel. 73 217), reached by taking a right when you come to the Mario Martire bridge (two blocks from the old train station) leading into the old city. Full meals with drink go for L15,000. (Open Mon.-Sat. noon-10pm.) Crossing over the bridge and going left leads to **Pizzeria Tavola Calda,** Corso Telesio, 214, with its tiny brick oven that churns out the giant *pizza grande* for only L3000. Serves only stand-up or take-out orders. (Open Mon-Fri. 9am-12:30pm and 5-8:30pm, Sat. 9am-12:30pm.) The **Supermercato Standa** vends to do-it-yourselfers at Corso Mazzini, 98 (open Mon.-Fri. 8:45am-12:45pm and 4-8pm, Sat. 8:45am-12:45pm).

SIGHTS AND ENTERTAINMENT

All sights of interest in Cosenza lie in the old city across the small **Busento River** from the old train station. In 410 AD, King Alaric of the Goths headed for Calabria after sacking Rome, but, having forgetten his Cutter's, he died of malaria soon afterward in Cosenza. The despondent tribe buried its leader, clad in his armor and mounted on his horse, beneath the mud of the river bed. Several fruitless digs have been performed in the last few hundred years in hope of unearthing Alaric's hoard.

After crossing the river, turn left onto Corso Telesio, and climb uphill to the **cathedral.** Keep your head up and your mouth closed, for there's no telling what will be tossed from the medieval windows. Despite an excess of garbage, these dark, winding streets are as intriguing as the cathedral itself. Note the mural of the Madonna and Child on the right side of the cathedral, painted in 1863. After the completion of the cathedral in 1222, Frederick II donated what is today the city's most prized possession—the tiny, ornate **Byzantine Cross.** The colorful jewel (204 x 264mm) bears a Christ and mourning Madonna on the left arm, a supplicating St. John the Evangelist on the right, and the archangel Michael above. These days the cross beautifies the Arcivescovato, near the cathedral. Though most bells in the town are rung with the push of a button, you can sound this cathedral's bells the old-fashioned way (Mon.-Fri. 10am-noon). Perched atop the hill, P. XV Marzo guards the **Museo Civico** (tel. 73 387), which houses an impressive collection of prehistoric bronzes. (Open Mon.-Sat. 9am-1pm and Mon. 4-7pm. Free.)

By the spring of 1994, the ninth-century **Teatro Rendano** should reopen its doors for concerts and opera once renovations are completed. You'll also have to wait to see the 12th-century **Norman Castle,** now closed for restoration.

■ The Sila Massif

Located in the heart of Calabria is the **Sila Massif,** 2000 square kilometers of pristine wilderness spread among three main zones: La Greca, the area to the north, La Grande, the central area and La Piccola, a coastal area . These areas together constitute one of Italy's last mountain chains still covered with virgin forest.

To reach **Camigliatello** from Cosenza, you can take either a bus (5 per day, 45min., L3200) or a train (4 per day, 1½hr., L3100 round-trip); San Giovanni is also accessible by both bus (5 per day, 1hr., L4500) and train (8 per day, 2¼hr., L5400 round-trip). Though slower, train travel should not be missed; from the old station in Cosenza (Cosenza Centrale), trains no more than 20m in length inch their way up and through the mountains, accessing incredible views. You'll be awed by the feats of engineering it took to build the route.

Camigliatello

The first major stop you'll come to on the train line from Cosenza is Camigliatello, a lilliputian alpine town with fairytale streets and *castelli*, and the area's best base for exploration. Upon arrival you should immediately confer with the hiking experts at **Pro Loco** (tel. 57 80 91), on Via Roma, 5 to your left as you exit the train station. They give out useful maps of the Sila and offer advice as to where you should and shouldn't go and what's worth seeing. (Generally open daily 9am-12:30pm and 3-7pm.) The office at the **Parco Nazionale** sells maps of hiking trials, but the brave ones can try two interesting hikes from Camigliatello's *castro*. The first involves walking (1½hr.) to **Lago Cecita,** one of five major lakes in the region, sharing a border with the **Parco Nazionale.** Following the signs in front of the station, keep walking until you reach the small pine forest; several dirt roads then branch from the highway, leading ultimately to Cecita's shores. A second, more demanding, and potentially confusing hike from Camigliatello is the three-hour climb to the top of the highest peak in the Sila, **Monte Botte Donato** (1930m). To get there, follow the highway toward Cosenza for about 4km and take the left turn at the *Fago del Soldato* intersection. As you begin climbing, bear left—you'll come to a ski-lift— climb below it until you reach an unmarked road. Turn left onto the road and you'll eventually reach the summit. From the peak of Monte Botte Donato on a clear day, you can see both the Tyrrhenian and Ionian Seas.

Less adventurous souls can visit the nearby pine forest or just savor the fresh mountain air. Pro Loco will help with lodging inquiries, and while their answers are generally expensive, they usually know of a few safe bets. In August and December, **Hotel Mancuso,** Via del Turismo, 55 (tel. 57 80 02), on a street running parallel to Via Roma to your right as you exit the station, requires full pension at L80,000 for pleasant rooms with baths. (Curfew midnight. Off-season singles with bath L35,000, doubles with bath L80,000, triples with bath L105,000, quads with bath L130,000.) **La Baita,** Via Roma, 97 (tel. 57 81 97), to the right as you exit the station, lets singles with bath for L40,000; doubles with bath L78,000; and triples with bath L93,000. In the off-season, Sept.-July 20, doubles with bath are L60,000; triples with bath L75,000. For campers, **La Fattoria** (tel. 57 83 64) lies about 3km from Camigliatello on the road to Lago Cecita. The nicer **Villaggio Lago Arvo** (tel. 99 70 60) awaits on the banks of Lago Arvo in Lórica, 37km from Camigliatello, but is inaccessible by public transportation. Your best bet is to take the bus or train toward San Giovanni in Fiore and get off at Silvana Mansio, which is 15km from Lórica. (Campsite open May-Sept.) For assistance in Lórica, try the **Pro Loco** (tel. (0984) 53 70 69) on Via Nazionale.

While in Camigliatello, picnic on the local specialties—cheeses, cured meats, and marinated mushrooms. The main drag overflows with *salumerie* that can provide you with sandwich supplies. On Via Roma, 44, grab an freshly-baked *cornetto al cioccolat* (chocolate croissant) at **Bar Leonetti** for just L1500 (open Tues.-Sun. 7am-8:30pm). **La Bussola,** Via del Turismo, 75, has full meals without drinks for L22,000 or pizza at night for L3500-6000. Open daily noon-3pm and 7pm-midnight. (Closed Wed. in winter.) To reach some comfortable refuges in the woods, take the path starting at the Cultara Residence Sign ½km along the highway toward Cosenza. Within 10 minutes you'll be surrounded by trees. **Da Sasa Video,** Via Roma, 12, rents two-person car-like bicycles for L5000 per half-hour, and tandems for L5000 per half-hour. Check to see if they have bike trips organized with the tourist office. (Open May-Sept. daily 9am-9pm; rentals only on Sun. in May, June, and Sept.)

Amazing **skiing** conditions draw downhill diehards from Christmas until the Ides of March. Camigliatello's **Tasso Ski Trail** (tel. 57 80 37), on Monte Curcio, is about 3km from town, up Via Roma and left at Hotel Tasso. A lift ticket is L20,000 per day. Hop a ride in summer for memorable views. (Lift runs daily 8:30am-6:30pm; Oct.-June 8:30am-5:30pm. Round-trip L4200.) You can rent skis and boots at **Da Sasa** for L18,000 per day whenever there's snow on the ground.

■ Tyrrhenian Coast

Pizzo

The western coast of Calabria and Basilicata is mountainous with relatively little resort development. Going as far south as **Pizzo** will bring you back to rocky terrain and tourist crowds. The best stretch of territory hugs the northern coast between Praia a Mare and Sangineto; white beaches and the towering rocks of inland mountains meet here to compose a majestic landscape. In Pizzo, there are two accommodations: **Residence Il Giglio,** S.S. 522 Marinella (tel. (0963) 53 48 40). Bungalows that fit 4 people, 40m from the beach. (L88,000 in July. Prices vary in the off-season; open May-Sept.) **Hotel Sonia,** Via Prangi, 112 (tel. 53 13 15). Decent-size rooms with lounge on each floor. (Singles L55,000. Doubles L75,000. Triples L100,000. Aug. full-pension L80,000.)

From Pizzo, any local train headed away from Règgio will take you to the western coast's other seaside villages,**Sangineto, Diamante, Cirella,** and **Scalea;** and in every case you'll travel through Paola (a necessary stopover if you're on your way to Cosenza). If the train workers should suddenly go on strike during your visit, you can also reach Paola's beach by taking a right turn immediately outside the train station and another right under the trestle at the base of the exit camp.

Maratea Marina

Further up the coast lies **Praia a Mare** (train station Praja; from Naples 2½hr., L15,400; from Règgio 3hr., L17,100). Rock formations, caves, and a cozy, pebbled beach await you a few minutes north of Praia in **Maratea Marina.** Officially part of Basilicata, Maratea makes a great daytrip (6 trains per day from Praia, 20min., L600), but don't go on Sundays unless you crave crowds. The closest chow to the beach is **Il Patriarca Pizzeria** (tel. (0973) 87 90 16), 30m up the road to the right as you face away from the train station. (Pizzas from L3500; open daily noon-3pm and 8-11pm.) Or try **White Horse**, S. S. 18 (tel. (0973) 87 90 09). Pizza and beer L10,000 including cover and service.

Lodging is fairly expensive. Two options are **Hotel Calaficara,** Via S. Teresa, 6 (tel. (0973) 87 90 16), near the station. Singles at L55,000 (L65,000 with bath). Doubles for L85,000 (L90,000 with bath). Up to L20,000 less before and after August. The other option is to head for the beach and into the just reopened **Hotel Settebello** (tel. 87 62 77), where you can walk out of your L50,000 single and onto the beach. (Doubles L70,000. All rooms with baths.) Telephones, A/C, and *frigo bar;* reserve July and August.

There are two **tourist offices** here. The main **AAST** office is on Via Santavenere (tel. (0973) 87 69 08). Colorful booklets on the area and surroundings plus helpful listing of hotels and prices. (Open June-Sept. daily (or almost) 9am-1pm and 4-8pm; Sept.-May. morning hours only.) The **post office** can also help (open Mon.-Sat. 8am-2pm and 3-9pm, and Sun. 9am-12:30pm and 5-8pm).

Maratea

Two worthwhile spots to visit around Maratea Marina are the **Grotte di Marina,** a group of stalactite- and stalagmite-coated caverns discovered in 1929 during construction of the *superstrada,* and the town of **Maratea** proper. To reach the caves, simply turn left at Il Patriarca Pizzeria (directions above) and head up to the *superstrada;* the caves are 2km down the road. A free guide service conducts you around their cool interiors. (Open daily 9am-12:30pm and 4-7pm; in winter call the Maratea tourist office for an appointment.) To get to the town of Maratea, simply catch a train from the Marina or travel 3km on the *superstrada* away from the caves. Once in Maratea, orient yourself with your back to Maratea station, then follow the parking lot left, descend along the road to the right, turn right through the tunnel, and continue until the main road with directional signs points right. Once you've walked about 1½km from the station, some more signs point left for **Maratea Porto** and right for **Maratea Santa Vénere** and the historic center. In Santa Vénere, just past the signs, you can pick up a few mildly helpful English booklets from the **AAST tourist office** (tel. (0973) 87 69 08) in the *piazza* (open Mon.-Sat. 9am-8:30pm, Sun. 9am-12:30pm and 5-8pm; reduced hours in winter); you should head downhill, however, for more interesting sights. The best eating option, **Paninoteca Perro Caliente,** opposite the road leading to the port, serves up spicy sandwiches for L5000-7000. (Service 10%; open April-Sept. daily 10:30am-midnight.)

Uphill from Santa Vénere, the **historic center** blankets the side of Monte San Biagio with its of winding, directionless streets. On the top of the mountain lies Maratea's **basilica,** built over the site of a temple where dread pagans once made grisly sacrifices to Minerva. Hovering nearby like an overgrown Christmas ornament, a 22m **Statue of the Redeemer** spreads cheer and redemption throughout the land. Buses run, albeit infrequently, between Maratea Marina, the port, Maratea's central station, Santa Vénere, the historic center, and even up to the basilica (L700; current schedules posted at train stations, tourist offices, and at all ticket sellers). One bus in the morning and two in the late afternoon roll to Maratea Castrocucco, site of **Camping Maratea,** the only accommodation even approaching affordability. (Tel. (0973) 87 90 97. In Aug. L22,500 per person, including parking, light, and hot shower—the works, plus L9000 for extra people.)

■■■ RÈGGIO DI CALABRIA

Completely rebuilt after a 1908 earthquake and currently brimming with designer clothing stores, Règgio just plain lacks mystique. Fortunately, it houses the National Museum, where bronze figures harken to Calabria's ancient glory as part of Magna Graecia, and provides access to the countryside, where olive groves and flower fields cultivated by the perfume industry reflect the sensuous side of Italian life. Less than 35km north is the village of Scilla, within view of Sicily and the Aeolian Islands.

TRAINS AND FERRIES

Règgio has two train stations. All trains stop at **Stazione Centrale,** P. Garibaldi (tel. 98 123), at the southern end of town. The much less frequented (albeit more convenient) **Stazione Lido** sits at the northern end of town off Via Zerbi and near the museum, port, and beaches. As the terminus of the western north-south train line, Règgio is linked to most major cities, including: Milan (3 per day 7:40am-10:50pm, 14hr., L74,700); Rome (several per day 7:35am-1:30am, 7hr., L46,800 plus L16,800 *rapido* supplement, also 2 "express" trains per day; 8:27 and 10pm, 10hr., L46,800); Florence (3 per day 7:40-10:50pm, 11hr., L70,000); Venice (1 per day 6:30pm, 14hr., pre-reserved couchettes only, L72,700 plus L18,500 couchette supplement); Naples (7 per day 1:30am-11:30pm, 5hr., L33,600, also 3 *rapido* trains per day, 7:20am-7:20pm, 4½hr., L12,800 *rapido* supplement.). Though several **ferries** cross the strait to Messina in Sicily, a greater number of ferries and all trains make the crossing from the nearby city of **Villa San Giovanni** (½hr. north by train, L1600). The **Caronte** lines have the most frequent and fastest service (once in Villa S. Giovanni follow the signs to the private ferry services). Nevertheless, three companies do provide service from here to Sicily, Malta, and points throughout Italy. **Ferrovie dello Stato** (tel. (0965) 98 123), at the port five blocks to the left of Stazione Lido facing away from the sea, accepts all InterRail, Eurail, and kilometric tickets for the Sicily crossing. **Tirrenia,** Via B. Bozzi, 31 (tel. 94 003), sits off Via III Settembre three blocks from the Lido station. (Ticket office open Mon.-Fri. 8:30am-1pm and 4-7pm.) **SNAV** (tel. 295 68), next to Ferrovie dello Stato, specializes in hydrofoil service from Règgio to points beyond.

> **Villa San Giovanni-Messina: Ferrovie** ferries 3:20am-4:45pm (14 per day, 20min., L1200).
> **Règgio-Messina: Ferrovie** ferries 6:55am-9:55pm (10 per day, 50min., L1600 one-way, L3000 round-trip). **SNAV** hydrofoils Mon.-Fri. 7:15am-8:40pm (24 per day) and Sat. (18 per day), 20min., L5000 one-way.
> **Règgio-each of the Lípari Islands: SNAV** hydrofoil (June 1-Sept. 30; 4 per day per isle, 2hr.), L29,300 (Vulcano)- L48,100 (Alicudi).
> **Règgio-Catania-Syracuse-Malta: Tirrenia** ferries Tues., Fri., and Sun., stopping in Catania (3hr.) and Syracuse (7hr.); both for L20,000 (Oct.-May L16,000); continuing to Malta (11hr.) for L86,000 (Oct.-May L74,000).

ORIENTATION AND PRACTICAL INFORMATION

Most travel in Règgio is along **Corso Garibaldi,** connecting Stazione Centrale in the south with Stazione Lido in the north. City buses continuously traverse the route (L800), though it is only 1½km from S. Centrale to S. Lido.

Tourist Office: APT booth (tel. 27 120), at the central train station. Useful maps and directions, but irregular hours. "Here is spoken English." Occasionally open Mon.-Sat. 8am-2pm and 2:30-8pm. Two other booths with similar hours at the airport (tel. 64 32 91) and at the main office on Via Roma, 3 (tel. 21 171).

Luggage Storage: at both Centrale and Lido stations (L1500). Open 24 hrs.

Post Office: Via Miraglia, 14 (tel. 24 508), near P. Italia. Open Mon.-Fri. 8am-7pm, Sat. 8am-1pm. **Postal code:** 89100.

Currency exchange: At Corso Garibaldi, 211. Only if you're desperate. Open 9am-noon and 4-7pm. Or at the **FS** info booth inside the station.

Telephones: SIP, Corso Vittorio Emanuele, 110 (tel. 89 75 79). Behind the post office, in the same building. Open 8am-10pm. **Telephone code:** 0965.

Airport: Svincolo Aeroporto, south of town. Catch orange bus #113, 114, or 115 from P. Garibaldi outside S. Centrale (L800). Service to all major cities in Italy.

Emergencies: tel. 113. **Police:** tel. 47 109, on Via Santa Caterina, in the northern end of town near the port. **Medical Assistance:** tel. 34 71 06. **Hospital: Osped-ale Riuniti,** Via Melacrino (tel. 34 71 13).

ACCOMMODATIONS AND FOOD

Staying in Règgio often means depleting your wallet. Hotel quality is notably low and the campgrounds which exist are distant from the city center.

Pensione S. Bernadetta, Corso Garibaldi, 585 (tel. 94 500), right across P. Garibaldi from the central train station all the way up on the 5th floor. Cozy, but acrophobics beware. Singles L26,000. Doubles L35,000.

Albergo Noel, Viale Zerbi, 13 (tel. 33 00 44 or 89 09 65), a few blocks north of Stazione Lido. With the sea behind you, turn left as you exit the station. Great location. TV room and decent restaurant. All rooms with bath. Singles L35,000. Doubles L45,000. Triples L60,000. Breakfast L5000. All credit cards accepted. Reserve in advance in June-Sept.

Albergo Moderno, Via Marconi, 20 (tel. 75 10 02). Singles L30,000, with bath L40,000. Doubles with bath L60,000.

Règgio's chefs feel most at home making *spaghetti alla Calabrese* (noodles dressed in a potent pimento sauce), *capicollo* ham (salami spiced with local hot peppers), and *pescè spada,* swordfish caught off neighboring Bágnara Calabra. A large **market** lies at P. del Popolo, off Via Amendola near the port. (Open Mon.-Sat. 6am-1:30pm.) At Corso Garibaldi, 103, towards the Stazione Lido end also in front of S. Centrale, a **STANDA supermarket** supplies the basics. (Open Mon. and Wed.-Sat. 8:30am-1pm and 5-8:15pm, Tues. 8am-1pm.) There is also an **A&O supermarket** right across from the train station for "the quick shopping" before catching the next train.

Trattoria Del Villeggiante, Via Demetrio Tripepi, 31 (tel. 89 90 01), in the north-ern end of town up the hill from the market. A happy little establishment serving fresh, tasty meals. Hook the *pesce spada,* L10,000. *Primi* L5000; try the *linguine checca,* made with a sauce of tomatoes and *pepperoncini.* Wine L4000 per liter. Cover L1500. Open Mon.-Sat. noon-3pm and 7-11pm.

Cordon Bleu, Via Corso Garibaldi, 203 (tel. 33 24 47), not far from the Museum and STANDA Supermarket. More Italian than it looks. Calamari (L8000) and assorted pastries (from L1000-2000) especially tasty. Wine L4000 per bottle. Cover L1000. Open Thurs.-Tues. 11am-midnight.

La Pignata, Via Demetrio Tripepi, 122 (tel. 27 841), up Via Giutecca from Corso Garibaldi near the SIP. An elegant pizzeria-restaurant with carved wooden ceilings and leather seats. One-eyed giant *pizza polifemo* (with mussels) L6000. *Maccher-oni calabresi* L7000. All meals, including pizzas, come with a tasty appetizer of *bruschette,* pieces of toasted bread rubbed with garlic and topped with a spicy red sauce. Cover L3000. Open Thurs.-Tues. noon-2:45pm and 7:30-11pm.

Don Pepé, Via Roma, 10 (tel. 26 041). Pranzo Turistico, based on meat, L25,000. Or try one of the many fresh-fish-based dishes starting at L12,000. Open Mon.-Sat. noon-3pm and 7-11pm.

SIGHTS AND ENTERTAINMENT

If passing through Règgio, you might as well pass the day by the sea. The **lungomare,** a pleasant park overlooking the water and the rugged Sicilian coast, stretches from one end of Règgio to the other. The main reason visitors stop in Règgio is, however, the world-renowned **Museo Nazionale,** at P. de Nava, on Corso Garibaldi near the Stazione Lido. Documenting Magna Graecia civilization with material from excavations in Calabria and underwater treasure-hunts off the coast, many of the museum's splendid pieces have spent years shuttling about the museums of the world, so expect a few vacant spots along the walls. Especially notable in the non-traveling collection are the works in the upstairs gallery by southern Italian artists such as Antonello da Messina and a set of dramatic Greek tablets from the 5th and 6th centuries BC telling the stories of Persephone, Castor and Pollux, and Achilles and Agamemnon. The two masterpieces of the museum are the extraordinary **Bronzi di Riace** (Bronze Warriors of Riace), two Herculean Greek statues found off the coast of Riace, Calabria, in 1972. These overwhelming figures were miraculously preserved for over 2000 years in the gentle waters of the Ionian. After painstaking restoration, the 2m statues have been identified as Greek originals and dated to the middle of the 5th century BC, the Golden Age of Greek sculpture. (Open Tues.-Sat. 9am-1:30pm and 3:30-7:30pm, Sun. 9am-1pm, and Mon. 9am-1:30pm. Admission L6000, over 60 and under 18 free.)

The tourist office has maps which will also guide you to the **Chiesa degli Ottimati** (ninth century) with its intricate mosaic floor and the **Castello Aragonese.**

■ Near Règgio

Scilla and **Bágnara Calabra,** two picturesque fishing villages, lie about 30km from Règgio along the Tyrrhenian coast. The beach resort of Scilla sits above the famous rock behind which, according to Homer, a female monster with six heads, 12 feet, and a voice like a yelping puppy hid before devouring entire ships that were skirting the harrowing whirlpool of Charybdis. Scilla is accessible from Règgio by train (12 per day, 45min., L4000 round-trip) or by bus (12 per day, last bus 8:30pm, L2200). Avoid Scilla on Sunday, when half of Calabria flocks to its small rocky beach. Scilla may be a better daytrip, but if you do stay, try get one of the tidy rooms in the **Pensione Le Sirene,** Via Nazionale, 57 (tel. (0965) 75 40 19 or 75 41 21). Just one block from the beach (1 block back from the *lungomare*), Le Sirene offers shady communal terraces that overlook the sea and cool rooms with ceiling fans. (Singles with bath L40,000. Doubles with bath L60,000. Triples with bath L75,000. Reservations a good idea June-Aug.) If you forgot to bring a picnic the cheapest meals around are at **Pizzeria San Francesco** on the beach (tel. 75 46 91). Pizza starts at L5500. (Open Thurs.-Tues. 7pm-1am.) Walk 10 minutes from the beach to **Paper Ros** (tel. 75 42 62), an enjoyable locals' *caffè* with a superb view (open daily 10am-midnight). Drinks L200-500. Relax with a nocturnal drink at **Vertigine,** P. San Rocco, 14. Outdoor seats overlook the castle. Drinks from L1500. If you stay out for dinner, try their *Spaghetti alla pescatore* L7000 (seconds vary depending on the fish). Cover L2000, service 10%. Open noon-3pm and 7pm-midnight.

The summer night spot is the open disco created under the arch of a bridge of the *superstrada.* **Il Ponte** offers giant screen video music. Open nightly 9am-close.

Bágnara Calabra, 8km north of Scilla, is tucked among cliffs and grottoes. Painted swordfishing boats with tall lookout towers bob just offshore. The road north of town commands a view of Sicily and the Lípari Islands. Bring a picnic, as local prices are astronomical.

Aspromonte, a protuberance Calabria developed after kicking Sicily one night, presides over the southernmost tip of the Italian peninsula in pine-and-birch covered glory, awaiting those who can't get all the way to the Sila for their nature break. To reach the center of the area, take one of the nine daily blue buses (#127 or 128) from in front of Règgio's central train station to **Gamberie** (L2000). Here visitors enjoy a fabulous view of Sicily and the straits of Messina from the heights of **Puntone di Scirocco** (1660m), accessible by chairlift.

■ The Ionian Coast

The barren beaches which stretch between Règgio di Calabria and Metaponto are sparsely populated with Italian and German tourists and rarely frequented by anyone else. If a strip of sand is all you desire, consider hopping onto the Règgio-Catanzaro line and getting off wherever you feel looks right. **Soverato** (130km from Règgio, L10,500) offers one of the most expansive, scenic, and popular strips; however, the beaches at **Bovalino Marina, Palizzi,** and **Brancaleone** are closer and almost as agreeable. All travelers should be forewarned before planning their itineraries that trains traversing the Ionian coast often have erratic schedules and multiple connections: give yourself ample time to get where you want to go. There are a number of campgrounds in this area. In Bovalino try the **Eurocamping Palazzi di Casignana,** S. S. 106 (tel. (0964) 91 14 07). L7300 per person in August, and L6500 for a large tent. A couple thousand lire less during the other summer months.

Locri and Gerace

Locri (80km from Règgio, L6200) is a sleepy modern town with a seemingly endless, smooth beach and a surfeit of tennis courts. Three km south of Locri lie the remains of the city that Plato called the "Flower of Italy". At **Locri Epizephyrii,** you can find the remains of the only Ionian temple of the Magna Grecia.

Locri is the more organized of the several towns which lie along this coast. An inferno of flavor and spice, the **Trattoria Manglaviti,** Via Roma, 116, cooks up a L15,000 *menù* for elderly card-shuffling locals who have been drinking and dealing for years. (Open daily 3-11pm.) **Public telephones** are found on P. Re Umberto, 25, off of Via Matteotti. (Open Mon.-Fri. 8:30am-12:30pm and 3-9:30pm.) The **post office** is on Via Trento (open 8:30am-5:30pm).

To get to the taciturn town of **Gerace,** 10km inland from Locri and high above the Calabrian countryside, grab a bus from in front of Locri's train station (Mon.-Sat. 6 per day 7am-4:30pm, 20min., L1500, round-trip L2400, return 30min. after each of the Locri departure times). Gerace lives and breathes medieval architecture, and its heart is the **cathedral,** Calabria's largest. As you enter, you'll immediately notice the structure's imperial crypt, supported by 26 ancient Greek columns pilfered from Locri. From the crypt, climb the stairs into a Romanesque interior of the grandest proportions. Outside, to the left of the entrance, note the exquisitely detailed Gothic portal. Another extraordinary portal graces the **Church of San Francesco** (1252), down the street to the right of the cathedral entrance. Its geometric design reveals Byzantine influence. For the best local fare try **Hostaria Lo Sparviero,** Via Luigi Cadorno, 1 (tel. 35 68 26). Full meals L15,000-L25,000. (Open daily noon-midnight June 15 to mid-September.)

Locri may be a good starting point for wilderness lovers. Take the bus from the train station to **Ciminá,** and start your hike up on **Monte Trepitó.** Camp anywhere around here if you don't mind wild pigs and the occasional wolf, or try **Ristorante "Le Quiete Dei Monti"** (tel. (0966) 62 40 00). You can camp for free on their site as long as you spend some money at the restaurant. From up here you can also reach the *belvedere* and see both the Ionian and Tyrrenian Seas. During the summer, all of Locri meets at **La Playa,** Via Lungomare (tel. (0964) 21 431). Well-organized with piano bar nights and disco right off the beach. Close to the water for a midnight swim. For information about Gerace and Locri, consult the **tourist office** in Locri, Via Fiume, 1 (tel. (0964) 296 00). To get there, follow Via G. Matteoti towards the library (#160) and park/maze off Via Umberto; Via Fiume is a small street to your left. (Open Mon.-Sat. 8am-8pm, Sept.-June Mon.-Fri. 8am-2pm.)

SICILY (SICILIA)

Throughout the ages, every great Mediterranean civilization has at one time turned its attention towards Sicily, transforming its landscape and its people but never conquering its independent spirit. The Greeks, Romans, Arabs, Normans, and Aragonese have all held Sicily—usually with the support of an invading army. But while this series of hostile takeovers may have been unwelcome for Sicilians at the time, it's a blessing for the modern traveler: each of the insurgent peoples has left its own imprint upon the island, offering the twentieth-century visitor a fascinating cultural landscape. Today, Sicily is invaded only by tourists eager to take in the legacy of three millennia and more. Nonetheless, the island remains intact, the synthesis of centuries of occupation, creation, and destruction.

In the 5th and 6th centuries BC, the city-states of Sicily were the most powerful and populous in the Magna Graecia, the extension of Greek civilization in the western Mediterranean. In the 9th century, the island became a Muslim outpost second in importance only to Spain. It later served as the seat of the Norman court, and subsequently became the pawn of Renaissance dynasties. The island ultimately fell under harsh Aragonese rule. The Bourbons' shortsighted agricultural policies bled the rich volcanic soil and reduced much of the Sicilian interior to a parched wasteland. In 1860 Garibaldi and his "redshirts" defeated the Bourbon troops and declared the island "liberated," though in fact it became part of the Kingdom of Italy; economic conditions, however, failed to improve.

The bloodshed of Sicilian political life has been matched by the cruelty of Mother Nature. To Giuseppe Lampedusa, Sicily's Prince-turned-writer, it was a "landscape which knows no mean between sensuous sag and hellish drought." The island's position at the edge of the European geologic plate has resulted in a succession of seismic and volcanic catastrophes that have periodically wiped clean the gains of its inhabitants. Those not destroyed seem to have drawn strength from survival; the fruits of Sicily's artistic and intellectual heritage range from Selinunte's stark grandeur to Noto's baroque frivolity, from the irrefutable logic of Pythagoras to the wry irrationalities of Pirandello. Not all have chosen to remain in its harsh territory, however. In the late 19th and early 20th centuries, hundreds of thousands of Sicilians left the island in favor of the promised lands of the United States and Argentina.

Modern Sicily quietly bears the scars of its history. Unlike those of other regions of Italy, the people of Sicily do not revel in their island's traditions. Rather they speed, unabated, toward the future, installing condom vending machines in front of medieval cathedrals and raising petrochemical refineries beside Greek acropolises. For years a point of exodus, Sicily now attracts thousands of immigrants from North Africa. And the Mafia—which until recently seemed to be fading from sight—has renewed its presence, both in Sicily and on the mainland. More and more Sicilians, however, are for the first time expressing their frustration with continued activity of the mob and the perceived stasis exhibited by a government that has had only limited success in stemming the tide of violence. Recent demonstrations against the Mafia have brought thousands to the streets, demanding an end to corruption. Change, unfortunately, is not likely to happen overnight; the number of defendants currently awaiting trial will fill courtrooms until the end of the century.

Because of Sicilian immigration to the United States, and to some extent because of the welcomed American invasion in 1942, *Statunitensi,* (particularly *Sicilo-Americani)* receive an exceptionally warm welcome. Women, however, should be aware that male attention in Sicily is often aggressive, and foreigners, unequipped with the extensive lexicon of Sicilian cut-downs, are particularly susceptible. Though this behavior often extends to verbal harassment, cases of physical harassment and assault are few, if also infrequently reported. But whereas violent crime is

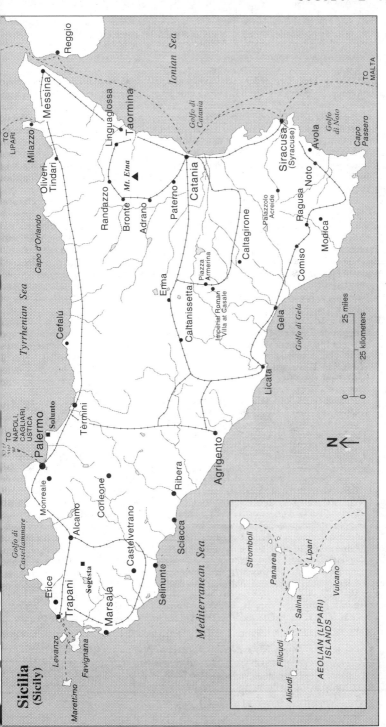

Sicilia
(Sicily)

Tyrrhenian Sea

Ionian Sea

Mediterranean Sea

Reggio

Messina

Milazzo

TO
LIPARI

Oliveri
Tindari

Linguaglossa

Taormina

Randazzo

Mt. Etna

Bronte

Adrano

Paternò

Catania

*Golfo di
Catania*

TO
MALTA

Siracusa
(Syracuse)

Avola

*Golfo
di Noto*

*Capo
Passero*

Noto

Palazzolo
Acreide

Ragusa

Modica

Comiso

Gela

Golfo di Gela

Licata

Enna

Piazza
Armerina

Caltagirone

Caltanissetta

Imperial Roman
Villa at Casale

Capo d'Orlando

Cefalù

Termini

Soluntu

TO
NAPOLI,
CAGLIARI,
USTICA

Palermo

Monreale

Alcamo

Corleone

Ribera

Agrigento

Sciacca

Castelvetrano

Selinunte

Segesta

Marsala

Erice

Trapani

Levanzo

Favignana

Marettimo

*Golfo di
Castellammare*

25 miles

25 kilometers

N

Strómboli

Panarea

Lipari

Salina

Filicudi

Alicudi

Vulcano

AEOLIAN (LIPARI)
ISLANDS

rare (by American standards), petty crime is rampant. The larger cities (Palermo, Catania, Messina, and Trápani) enjoy notoriety for their pickpockets and purse-snatchers, and their downtown districts can be unsafe at night. Travel in groups if you can, or stay close to frequented areas.

In summer, Sicily swelters for weeks at a time (35-45°C). The burning African *scirocco* winds can scorch your vacation in July and August. In addition, haze and random fires often obscure vistas in the summer months. Spring and autumn are ideal times to visit the island. Holy Week in Sicily is noted for its colorful processions: the most celebrated are Good Friday in Enna, where marchers don white, hooded costumes in the Spanish tradition, and Easter Sunday in Prizzi, which features the dance of the devil and of death. For complete details, pick up the booklet "Easter in Sicily," available at most tourist offices. For the traditional tour of Sicily, follow the coast; for a tour of traditional Sicily, venture into the heartland. If you do visit in summer, follow local custom: eat a big lunch, take a two-hour nap, and enjoy the island in the cool early evenings.

TRANSPORTATION

Flights from all major Italian cities service Palermo and Catania. The cheapest way to reach Sicily is a train-ferry combination to Messina (from Rome Via Règgio di Calabria, L46,000). **Tirrenia** (tel. (0923) 218 96), the largest private ferry service in Italy, is the most extensive and reliable, although you should still expect considerable delays; **Grandi-Traghetti** (tel. 091 58 79 39) offers better off-season rates to Palermo from Genoa and Livorno. Prices vary according to specific dates, although approximate prices are given below. Listings are for Tirrenia lines unless otherwise stated.

Règgio di Calabria-Messina: 12 per day on the state railroad ferry 5am-10pm; 1hr.; L1400. To cut this scenic 50-min. crossing to 20min., take the *aliscafo* from the same terminal at the Règgio port (L5000).

Villa San Giovanni-Messina: 22 per day on the state railroad ferry 3:20am-10:05pm (L1000).

Genoa-Palermo (22hr.): **Grandi-Traghetti Lines** Sat.-Mon. at 1pm, Wed. at 4pm. *Poltrona* (L98,000); July 25-Aug. 10 (L118,000); Oct.-June 14 (L78,000). **Tirrenia Lines** year-round Tues., Thurs., and Sat. at 4pm; July 16-Sept. 10 also Sun. noon; July 9-Sept. 30 also Sun. at 4pm. *Poltrona* (L102,200); Oct.-May (L80,300).

Naples-Palermo (10hr. 30min.): 1 per day at 8:00pm. *Poltrona* (L61,900); Oct.-May (L47,900).

Cagliari-Palermo (14hr.): Fri. at 7pm. *Poltrona* (L44,300); Oct.-May (L34,500).

Livorno-Palermo (18hr.): **Grandi-Traghetti** Tues. and Thurs. at 6pm and Sat. at 5pm. *Poltrona* (L91,000); July 23-Aug. 10 (L117,000); Oct.-June 17 (L78,000). Deck seats (L80,000), available only if all other classes are filled.

Naples-Catania-Syracuse (15hr. 30min., 18hr. 45min.): Thurs. at 8:30pm. Deck seats L44,000. *Poltrona* (L61,900) for either destination. Off-season (L47,900).

Règgio di Calabria-Catania-Syracuse (3hr. 15min.): To Syracuse Tues., Fri., and Sun. at 8:30am. A bargain. Deck fare to either port (L14,700). *Poltrona* (L22,000); off-season (L20,400).

Cagliari-Trápani (11hr.): From Cagliari Sun. at 7pm, from Trápani Tues. at 9pm; *Poltrona* (L44,300); Oct.-May (L34,500).

La Goulette (Tunisia)-Trápani (8hr.): Mon. at 8pm. *Poltrona* (L84,700); Oct.-May (L71,000).

Kelibia (Tunisia)-Trápani: SNAV hydrofoils Tues., Thurs., and Sat. at 8:45am (3hr.); Tues.-Wed., Fri., and Sat.-Sun. at 8:45am (3hr. 45min., Via Pantelleria). Fare (L75,000).

Trains in Sicily only partially deserve their reputation for tardiness; the diminutive *Elettromotrici* are reasonably reliable and convenient. Two major bus companies, the private, air-conditioned, and punctual **SAIS,** and the public, often steamy **AST,** serve many of the destinations inaccessible by train. There's no central transportation authority in Sicily, so check in every city and with every driver for the bus schedules to your next destination. Give yourself a few extra hours to get where you're going, especially if you're heading for isolated ruins.

Hitchhiking is difficult on long hauls; hitchers are reputed to have better luck near the turn-offs to roads for short, specific trips. **Hitchhiking is extremely risky—Let's Go does not recommend it. Solo women in particular should not hitchhike in Sicily. Driving** in Sicily is only for the fearless. You'll need an International Driver's Permit (available at AAA; see Documents and Formalities in General Introduction), a rental car, and nerves of steel. Travelers (drivers and pedestrians alike) should be aware that most Italians drive as if they're behind the wheel of a Ferrari F40, even if it's actually a Fiat 500. And Sicilians seem to be particularly fond of using their car horns, which can be annoying but may just save your life. When cruising down a highway, a cryptic Italian highway pictogram may or may not indicate "imminent death." **Pedestrians** should note that simple tasks like crossing the street can become a real challenge here. One strategy is to follow other people across, using them as a buffer between you and the speeding cars. Another alternative is to treat oncoming traffic as if it were a charging rhinoceros: make eye contact and pray to the local saint. Italy is a small country, and the Italians do not waste space—their streets are just wide enough for a car to pass through. Make your mother happy, and look both ways, twice, before crossing the street.

■ Messina

History has handed Messina misfortune after misfortune. Initially colonized in the 8th century BC, the city was first captured (and renamed Messene) by Anaxilas in 493 BC. One hundred years later the Carthaginians came and razed the site. Thereafter, the city began its life as a trading card, falling into the hands of everyone from the Marmertines to the Normans to Richard the Lionheart. The city grew to prosperity under Norman rule and burgeoned as a Crusader port, for 600 years remaining a proud bastion at the periphery of European civilization.

Since the 17th century, though, Messina has been on a downhill slide. After rebelling against Spanish rule in the late 1600s, the city lost its special privileges and declined to one-eighth of its former size. Its slow convalescence was only temporary, for Messina was devastated by plague in 1743, demolished by an earthquake in 1783, bombarded from the sea in 1848, struck by cholera in 1854, slammed by more earthquakes in 1894 and 1908 and flattened by both Allied and Axis bombs during World War II. What is left is a city that has struggled time and again to rebuild itself, and now seems to have taken a few too many body blows to get up off the canvas anymore. Buildings in Messina generally date back no more than several decades, and nearly all appear to have been hastily constructed; even the cathedral, rebuilt twice in this century alone, seems new. A sense of impermanence hangs about, as if Messina's inhabitants know that yet another disaster will soon prove the futility of their efforts.

Unfortunately, Messina is the main point of entry into Sicily from the mainland, so you will probably have to pass through here. Although no city is without its virtues (the fruit stalls in Piazza Carducci near the university sell juicy blood-oranges for less than L200 a piece), you'll probably want to move on as soon as possible, if only because your money is much better spent elsewhere in Sicily. Messina has all of the costs of a place like Taormina, and none of the charm.

ORIENTATION AND PRACTICAL INFORMATION

Major transportation routes and tourist offices cluster around the train station at P. della Repubblica. **Via I° Settembre** connects it with **Piazza del Duomo,** intersecting with **Corso Garibaldi** en route. Corso Garibaldi runs along the harbor to both the hydrofoil dock and Corso Cavour. Take a left from P. della Repubblica on Via G. Farina to arrive at **Via Tommaso Cannizzaro.** This is Messina's main drag; it leads to the center of town, meeting Viale San Martino at **Piazza Cairoli.** Women should

MESSINA

not walk alone in Messina at night—and *no one* should roam streets near the train station or the harbor after 10pm. Stick close to the streets near the *duomo* and the university, where more people are out and about. Be wary of pickpockets and purse-snatchers; keep your money in a secure place.

Tourist Office: Ufficio Informazioni Communali, outside the Central Station to the right in P. della Repubblica (tel. 67 29 44). Affable, English-speaking, and replete with materials and maps. Also has information on Lípari Islands, Taormina, and other areas within the province of Messina. Open Mon.-Sat. 8:30am-1pm. **APT,** Via Calabria, 301 (tel. 67 56 75 or 67 53 56), to the right of the station past the information office. A deluge of maps and information. The English-speaking agents can provide information and help you find a room. Open Tues.-Fri. 8am-2pm and 4-7pm, Mon. and Sat. 8am-2pm. **AAST,** P. Cairoli, 45 (tel. 293 35 41). Open mornings only.

Currency Exchange: Cambio/Ufficio Informazioni (tel. 67 52 34 or 67 52 35), right inside the train station. Good rates plus information on trains and buses.

Post Office: at P. Antonello, off Corso Cavour near the *duomo* (tel. 77 41 90). Italy's only outdoor post office. Fermo Posta at window #12. Open Mon.-Fri. 8:30am-6:15pm, Sat. 8:30-1pm. **Postal Code:** 98122.

Telephones: ASST, on your right from the train station. Open daily 8am-7:45pm. **Telephone Code:** 090.

Trains: at P. della Repubblica (tel. 67 52 34). Tickets purchased at the *biglietteria*. To: Palermo (19 per day, 3hr. 30min., L17,100); Syracuse (13 per day, 3hr., L13,800); Rome (6 per day, 8-10 hr., L46,800); Milazzo, the main port for the Lípari Islands (at least 20 per day, 40min., L3200). **Luggage Storage: Deposito Bagagli** L1500 per bag for every 24 hrs. Always open.

Buses: SAIS, at P. della Repubblica, 46 (tel. 77 19 14), to the left of the train station. To: Taormina (14 per day, 1hr. 30min., L5100) and Catania (20 per day, 2-3hr., L9100); Rome (2 per day, 10hr., L60,000, student fare L45,000). **Giuntabus** (tel. 77 37 82), in the town center, at the corner of Viale San Martino and Via Terranova. To Milazzo (11 per day, 40min., L5500).

Public Transportation: ATM, the orange buses that leave from P. della Repubblica and go into town, L700. Purchase tickets at any *tabacchi* or newsstand. Detailed bus info on the signs with yellow borders outside the station.

Ferries: Stazione Marittima, on the water, 300m to the right of P. della Repubblica. To Règgio (10 per day, 50min., L6100). **Hydrofoils: SNAV** (tel. 36 40 44, 36 77 75 for reservations), a blue, one-story building on Corso Vittorio Emanuele II, 1km north of train station off Corso Garibaldi. To the Lípari Islands (4-5 per day June 1-Sept. 30, 2hr., L28,000-33,000). Save L10,000 by taking the train to Milazzo and catching the ferry there.

Lost Property: at the **Municipio di Messina** (tel. 67 37 52), where Via Vettovaglie hits the harbor (to the right from P. della Repubblica). Open Mon.-Sat. 9am-noon. Ask for **oggetti smarriti.**

Late-Night Pharmacy: (tel. 192) all pharmacies are open during the day 8:30am-1pm and 4:30-8pm. After that, they are on a rotation so that there are always at least two open during the night and on weekends. The pharmacy **LoJacono** (tel. 67 20 18), at Corso Garibaldi 69, is close to the center of town.

Emergencies: Police, (tel. 113). **Hospital: Ospedale R. Margherita** Via Libertà (tel. 36 51); **Policlinico Universitario,** Messina-Gazzi (tel. 22 11, nights and weekends 67 50 48).

ACCOMMODATIONS AND CAMPING

Some smaller establishments are wary of foreign backpackers; check your bags at the station while searching.

Albergo Roma, P. Duomo, 3 (tel. 67 55 66). Ideally situated 100 yds. to the left of the *Duomo* (take bus #8 from the station). The beds sag and there's no hot water, but the high ceilings and balconies off most rooms make up for any shortcomings. Management keeps the front door locked at all times and is reluctant to open up later than midnight. Still, it's Messina's best bargain: singles, L15,000. Doubles, L30,000.

Hotel Touring, Via Scotto, 17 (tel. 293 88 51). As you exit the train station, take a hard left and then bear right under an overpass. Hallways of mirrors and faux-marble give off onto spare, modern rooms. A convenient choice for travelers stranded between trains. Singles, L30,000, with bath, L50,000. Doubles L60,000, with bath, L100,000.

Hotel Monza, Viale San Martino, 63 (tel. 67 37 55), at Via Cannizzaro. Sylvan lobby welcomes you to comfortable, modern rooms. Singles L32,000, with bath L55,000. Doubles L55,000, with bath L90,000.

Camping: Il Peloritano, (tel. 34 84 96). Take bus #28 from the station to the small town of Rodia-Tarantonio. Make sure to stock up on food before you go. Showers available. L3300 per person, per tent. Open mid-May-Oct.

FOOD

Relatively inexpensive restaurants and *trattorie* crowd the area around Via Risorgimento, reached by following Via Cannizzaro (see Orientation above) one block after P. Cairoli. In summer, try the legendary *pescespada* (swordfish) direct from the Straits of Messina, delectable enough to earn Homer's mention in the *Odyssey*. On Via S. Cecilia, eight blocks from P. Maurolico down Via C. Battisti, there is an outdoor **market** (open daily 6am-2pm).

Osteria del Campanile, Via Loggia dei Mercanti, 9 (tel. 71 14 18), behind the *duomo*. Ask for the *menù pizzeria* and choose from two dozen different kinds of pizza (L3500-9000). Cover L2000. Visa, MC, AmEx accepted. Open daily noon-3pm and 8-11pm.

Porta Messina, (tel. 67 38 31), to the right of the train station, where Via Calabria meets Via Valore by the harbor. Budget dining in between trains: snacks, *gelato*, *panini* (under L3000) and simple pasta dishes (all under L5000). Open Sun.-Fri. 7:30am-midnight.

Supermarket: STANDA, P. Cairoli. Go into the main entrance of the department store (also called STANDA), take a right and go down the stairs. Although it's cheaper to buy fruit and vegetables from street vendors, STANDA is your best bet for everything else. Open Mon.-Sat. 9am-1pm and 4-8pm; closed Wed. afternoons.

SIGHTS

The disasters that have befallen Messina have left few of its monuments intact. It is a city undergoing a constant facelift: many sights are currently shrouded in scaffolding and large white tents.

The Piazza del Duomo's wide open spaces and large flagstones provide some Renaissance relief from the asphalt hustle-and-bustle of the rest of Messina. The piazza contains the 12th-century **duomo** (open 8am-12:30pm and 4-7pm, currently under restoration) and the squat **Church of SS. Annunziata dei Catalaní** from the same period. The cathedral's stark exterior features an ornate portal portraying the Archangel Gabriel and the Madonna with saints. In front of the church is the **Fontana di Orione** (circa 1547, also under restoration), the work of Michelangelo's pupil Angelo Montorsoli, where lazy nudes recline on a richly embellished base. The clock tower houses what is supposedly the world's largest astronomical clock. The grim reaper keeps time until the grand spectacle at noon, when a mechanical procession of animals, angels, and legendary figures re-enacts the local legend of the Madonna della Lettera, patron saint of the city. A **festival** in her honor takes over the town every June 3; another festival, the **Ferragosto Messinese,** takes place Aug. 14-15, featuring a procession 150,000 strong.

Just down the road from the port is the **Civic National Museum** (tel. 35 53 33). Founded in 1806 with five private collections, it was adopted by the state in 1904 as a repository for the furnishings, valuables, and works of art recovered from churches and civic buildings after the 1894 earthquake. Today it includes a collection of Renaissance and Baroque masterpieces, among them *The Polyptych of the*

Rosary (1473) by local hero Antonello da Messina, an Andrea della Robbia terracotta of the Virgin and Child, and Caravaggio's *The Adoration of the Shepherds* (1608) and *Resurrection of Lazarus* (1609). Take bus #8 from the station or P. Duomo and get off at P. Museo (20min.); walk part of the way back to view the harbor's scythe-shaped form, which gave Messina its original name Zanclon, from the Greek *zancle* (scythe). (Museum open Mon., Wed., Fri., and Sun. 9am-1pm, Tues. Thurs., Sat. 9am-1pm and 3-5:30pm.)

Messina is not renowned for its beaches. Still, the route traveled by bus #8 (departs from the train station, L700) through the ramshackle fishing villages provides some great waterfront scenery. Get off at whichever stop catches your interest, or wait until the **Lungolago** (20 minutes from the start). This is literally a "long lake," lined with cafés and palm trees, and overlooked by crumbling villas.

AEOLIAN ISLANDS (ISOLE EOLIE)

Seven jewels set in the sparkling Mediterranean, the **Aeolian** (or **Lípari**) **Islands** are all places of diverse and remarkable beauty. They are first mentioned in Homer's *Odyssey* as the domain of Aeolus, King of the Winds. According to this tale, Aeolus gave Odysseus the gift of a bag of winds to help quicken his return trip. His sailors—not the brightest of seafarers—ignored the warning labels and opened the bag blowing themselves right back to the islands.

Still fairly blustery, today's Lípari Islands are renowned for their fiery volcanoes and long and rocky beaches. Long overlooked, the islands have been discovered recently as one of the last areas of unspoiled seashore in Italy. Food and accommodations are more expensive than in the rest of Sicily; prices peak, unsurprisingly, in the August high season, for which you'd better make reservations on the main islands no later than May. Fortunately, there is a youth hostel. Of the seven isles, visit Lípari for a well-equipped tourist center, a castle, and easily navigable vistas; Vulcano for bubbling mud baths and a sulfurous crater; Strómboli for luxuriant vegetation and a restless volcano; Panarea for inlets and a more elite clientele; Salina for grottoes and pilgrims; Filícudí for winding trails and coastal rock formations; and Alicudi for a rare dose of solitude.

Getting There

The seven-island archipelago lies off the Sicilian coast north of **Milazzo,** the principal and least expensive embarkation point (on the Messina-Palermo train line; 1hr from Messina, L3200; 4hr. from Palermo, L13,800). **Giuntabus** also services the town. (Tel. (090) 67 37 82; 19 per day from Messina 5:45am-7pm, 4 on Sun., 45min. L5500; also daily from Catania airport June-Sept., L20,000.) Ferries leave much less frequently from **Naples's** Molo Beverello port. Hydrofoils (about twice the price of ferries) run regularly in late July and August from **Messina, Naples, Cefalù, Palermo,** and **Règgio di Calabria.** Both **SNAV** and **Siremar** have complete hydrofoil schedules available at every port (ask for *un orario generale).* To get to the port in Milazzo, it's easiest to take the blue bus in front of the station. Get your ticket at the bar (L600) and ask to get off at the ferries *(tragbetti).* If you're up for a long walk, cross Piazza Marconi from in front of the train station and bear left on Via XX Luglio. 1km later you'll hit the port as Via XX Luglio becomes Via dei Mille and then, as it curves to the right hugging the port, Via Luigi Rizzo. Ferry offices can be found on Via dei Mille, while *aliscafi* (hydrofoils) and their owners repose on Via Rizzo.

Siremar (tel. (090) 928 32 42 in Milazzo) and **Navigazione Generale Insulare** (tel. 928 34 15) run reliable ferries out of Milazzo. Siremar also services several smaller islands and Naples (tel. (081) 551 21 12 in Naples). Frequencies listed are for June through September. Prices are the same for both lines. Connections can be made between any stops in a line.

Milazzo-Vulcano-Lípari-Salina: To Vulcano 1hr. 30min., Siremar L9100, NGI L8300; Lípari 2hr., Siremar L9800, NGI L8900; Salina 3hr., Siremar L12,500, NGI L11,300. **Siremar:** 4-5 per day 7am-6:30pm. **NGI:** 2-3 per day 6:30am-10pm.

Milazzo-Panarea-Strómboli Via Vulcano and Lípari: To Panarea 3hr. 15min., Siremar L11,700, NGI L10,700; Strómboli 5hr., Siremar L15,800, NGI L11,300. **Siremar**: 1 per day 8-9am. **NGI:** Friday only, 6:30am and 10pm.

Milazzo-Filícudí-Alicudi Via Vulcano, Salina, and Lípari: To Filícudí 4hr. 30min., Siremar L17,100, NGI L15,400; Alicudi 5hr. 30min., Siremar L21,000, NGI L19,000. **Siremar:** 1 per day 6:45-7am. **NGI:** Fri. only 6:30am and 10pm.

Naples-Strómboli-Panarea-Salina-Lípari-Vulcano: To Strómboli 8hr., L47,900; Panarea 10hr. 30min., L51,100; Salina 11hr. 30min., L51,100; Lípari 12hr. 30min., L53,800; Vulcano 13hr. 45min., L54,300. **Siremar:** Daily (except Wed.) 9pm from the Molo Beverello port.

The increasingly popular **hydrofoils (aliscafi)**, running twice as often as ferries, for twice the price, and in half the time, are operated by **Siremar** and **SNAV** (tel. 928 45 09 in Milazzo, 36 40 44 in Messina). From May 15 to October 15, SNAV runs to Lípari from Messina (5 per day 7am-6:20pm, L28,200), Règgio di Calabria (5 per day, L29,600), Cefalù (3 per week, L36,000), Palermo (2 per day, L55,100), and Naples (1 per day, L116,000). Cabins are air-conditioned, although its never quite as strong as one might hope. Frequencies listed above are for June through September; off season schedules are more erratic—with as few as a third the number of trips. Connections can be made between any two points in a route.

Milazzo-Vulcano-Lípari-Salina: To Vulcano 35min., Siremar L16,700, SNAV L15,200; Lípari 50min., Siremar L17,900, SNAV L16,300; Salina 1hr. 15min., Siremar L22,600, SNAV L20,500. **Siremar:** 10-12 per day 6:30am-7:15pm. **SNAV:** 6 per day 7:30am-7:30pm.

Milazzo-Panarea-Strómboli Via Vulcano and Lípari: To Panarea 1hr. 40min., Siremar L21,500, SNAV L19,500; Strómboli 2hr. 30min., Siremar L28,900, SNAV L25,900. **Siremar:** at least 3 per day 7:05am-3:05pm. **SNAV:** 2 per day at 10:30am and 4pm.

Milazzo-Filicudi-Alicudi Via Vulcano and Lípari: To Filicudi 2hr., Siremar L30,800, SNAV L28,000; Alicudi 2hr. 30min., Siremar L38,000, SNAV L34,500. **Siremar:** 2 per day at 7am and 2:15pm. **SNAV:** 1 per day 7:45am, plus a second Mon.-Wed. and Sat. at 1:40pm.

The **telephone code** for the islands is **090.** (You must pay extra for inter-island calls.)

■ Lípari

...a floating island, a wall of bronze and splendid smooth sheer cliffs.
—Homer

Lípari is the largest and most beautiful of the islands off the coast of Sicily. In the town of the same name, pastel-colored houses dot a small promontory crowned by the walls of a medieval *castello,* the site of an ancient Greek acropolis. Although placid in appearance, Lípari belies an effusion of summer activity, from folk festivals to discos. The town's best beaches, **Spiaggia Bianca** and **Spiaggia Porticello,** are easily reached by bus. Lípari is an ideal base for daytrips to the neighboring six islands and their splendid beaches.

ORIENTATION AND PRACTICAL INFORMATION

The looming *castello* sits at the heart of the town, with the ferry dock to the right and the hydrofoil landing just to the left as you approach by sea. From Piazza Ugo di Sant'Onofrio in front of the hydrofoil dock, **Via Garibaldi** runs around the base of the *castello* to Piazza Mazzini, shadowing the ferry dock. Farther inland the main street **Corso Vittorio Emanuele** runs parallel to the harbor.

Tourist Office: Corso Vittorio Emanuele, 202 (tel. 988 00 95), up the street from the ferry dock. English spoken. Useful free handouts. Open Mon.-Fri. 8am-2pm and 4:30-7:30pm, in Aug. 4:30-10pm; Sat. 8am-2pm.

Currency Exchange: Banca del Sud and **B.A.E.,** both on Corso Vittorio Emanuele. AmEx checks accepted. Open Mon.-Fri. 8:30am-1pm. Unofficial exchanges will change money at rip-off rates, but are always available in an emergency. Compare rates with exchange available at the post office (cash only).

Post Office: Corso Vittorio Emanuele, 207 (tel. 981 13 79), 1 block up from the tourist office, in the building that looks like 2 stacked steam-pipes. Fermo Posta. Open Mon.-Fri. 8:30am-6pm, Sat. 8:30am-1pm. The **postal code** for Lípari is 98055, for Canneto-Lípari 98052, and for the rest of the islands 98050.

Telephones: SIP, (tel. 981 12 63) in the no-name boutique with the yellow awning on Via Maurolico, off Corso Vittorio Emanuele. Open Mon.-Sat. 8:30am-12:45pm and 4:30-8:45pm, Sun. 9am-12:45pm. At other times use the Hotel Augustus, Via Ausonia, the first right off Corso Vittorio Emanuele from the port. Open daily 9am-11pm. **Telephone Code:** 090.

Public Transportation: Autobus Urso Gugliemo, Via Cappuccini (tel. 98 12 62).

Taxis: Corso Vittorio Emanuele (tel. 981 11 10) or Marina Corta (tel. 981 11 95).

Bike/Moped Rental: Foti Roberto, Via F. Crispi, 31 (tel. 981 23 52), on the beach to the right of the ferry port. Bicycles L5000 per hr., L20,000 per day. Mopeds and scooters L12,000 per hr., L30,000 per day. They ask for a L100,000 deposit and your passport number. Open Easter-Oct. 15 daily 9am-6pm.

Public Showers: Salone Doccie, at the barbershop of the Fratelli Acquaro, Corso Vittorio Emanuele, 261, across from Officina Fonti motor service near the ferry dock. Hot showers for men L5000. One of the pleasant Acquaro brothers will give you a pampering chair shave for L4000. Open Mon.-Sat. 9am-noon and 4-8:30pm.

Pharmacy: Farmacia Internazionale, Corso Vittorio Emanuele, 128 (tel. 981 15 83). English-speaking doctor often on duty. Open Mon.-Sat. 9am-1pm and 5-9pm

Emergencies: tel. 113. **Police:** tel. 981 13 33. **Medical Emergency:** tel. 988 52 26. **Night Emergency:** tel. 988 52 67. **Hospital:** tel. 988 51.

ACCOMMODATIONS AND CAMPING

As you ply the port or walk the streets, locals will ask if you are looking for *affitta camere* (private rooms and apartments). These are often the best bargains but prices vary according to demand; proprietors ask for higher prices earlier in the day, then lower the costs later if their rooms haven't filled up. Try bargaining, but expect to pay at least L10,000-15,000 per person from September to June; start at L20,000 in August. Inquiring at local shops (try the bait-and-tackle store on Via Garibaldi near the hydrofoil dock) is often a useful route for finding *affitta camere*.

Lípari is invaded by more and more tourists as the summer progresses, and reaches full capacity in August. Hotels fill almost instantaneously and owners raise their prices by as much as 25%. Make reservations as far in advance as possible.

Locanda Salina, Via Garibaldi, 18 (tel. 981 23 32), near the hydrofoil port. Beautiful rooms overlooking the water. Singles L30,000. Doubles L55,000. Breakfast L5000 (no breakfast in Aug.). Reserve several days in advance for June, months ahead for August.

Ostello Lípari (HI), Via Castello, 17 (tel. 981 15 40, off season 981 25 27), 120 beds, on the hill within the walls of the fortress, next to the cathedral. Strict management sternly enforces midnight curfew. Nevertheless, it's probably the best deal on the islands. Keep an eye on your valuables. Reception open daily 7:30-9am and 6pm-midnight, downstairs only noon-2pm (to check in luggage). L10,000 per person. Cold showers only. Sheets and blankets included on request. Kitchen facilities. Breakfast L3000. Lunch and dinner each L10,000-L14,000 only if enough demand (book them in the morning). HI card only required when near capacity. Reservations recommended in July and Aug. Open March-Oct.

Hotel Europeo, Corso Vittorio Emanuele, 98 (tel. 981 15 89). Awesome location on the bustling corso. Singles L40,000, with bath L45,000. Doubles L70,000, with bath L80,000. Showers L1500. Reserve early for June-Aug.

Camping: Baia Unci (tel. 981 19 09), 2km from Lípari at the entrance to the hamlet of Canneto. This diminutive, shady expanse has an amiable management and a cheap self-service restaurant (roasted swordfish a bargain at L11,000). L8500 per person, tent included. Open April-Oct. 15. Restaurant open daily noon-2pm and 7-11pm.

FOOD

Try any dish with the island's famous *cápperi* (capers), and accompany it with the indigenous *Malvasia* wine. Unfortunately, eating cheaply on Lípari is something of a challenge. The **Upim Supermercato d'Anieri Bartolo** (tel. 981 15 87), Corso Vittorio Emanuele, 212, stocks the basics. (Open Mon.-Tues. and Thurs.-Sat. 8:30am-1pm and 4-8:45pm, Wed. 8:30am-1pm. AmEx, Visa, MC.) The *alimentari* lining Corso Vittorio Emanuele are generally open Sunday.

Self-Service "Dal Napoletano," Via Garibaldi, 12 (tel. 988 03 57), down the block from Locanda Salina, above. As suggested by the name, this is a self-service joint, which means you can avoid the *coperto* and service charge common elsewhere. In fact, they'll bring your order to you at the outdoor tables. *Gnocchi alla Napoletana,* L7000. *Menu* L18,000. Beer on tap. Open Tues.-Sun. 24hrs., Oct.-May Tues.-Sun. 9am-3pm and 6pm-midnight.

Trattoria d'Oro, Via Umberto I, 28 (tel. 981 13 04). Look for the red and white sign pointing off Corso Vittorio Emanuele. The *menù* is an especially good buy (L15,000). Try the *polpo all'insalata* (marinated octopus salad, L10,000). Open daily 11:30am-3:30pm and 6:30pm-midnight. AmEx, Visa, MC.

Trattoria A Sfiziusa, Via Roma, 39 (tel. 981 12 16), 100m from the hydrofoil dock. They make a mean pasta. *Primi* L5000-7000, *secondi* L10,000-15,000. Best bet is the *menù* at L18,000. Open daily noon-2:30pm and 7pm-midnight; closed Fridays in winter. Visa accepted.

Il Galeone, Corso Vittorio Emanuele, 214 (tel. 981 14 63). Good pizzas and a handy location, close to the ferry docking site. Tempts with 32 types of pizza, L6000-12,000 apiece. Open March-Nov. Tues.-Sun. 8am-11pm (pizza in the evenings only, other courses in the daytime).

Pasticceria Subba, Corso Vittorio Emanuele, 92 (tel. 981 13 52). If you still have room after dinner, try anything from this *pasticceria,* recently named one of Italy's best by a popular magazine. Readers of Dante should go for the *paradiso,* a lemon-stuffed dumpling topped with almonds. Open daily 7am-2am.

SIGHTS AND ENTERTAINMENT

Lípari Town

A medieval **castello** crowns the town; within its walls stand four churches and a **duomo.** The latter contains an 18th-century silver statue of San Bartolomeo (above the high altar) and a 16th-century Madonna (in the right transept). The ruins opposite the cathedral in the *parco archeologico* reveal layers of civilization that date back to at least 1700 BC. Many of the artifacts found here decorate the exterior of the superb **Museo Archeologico Eoliano,** which occupies the two buildings flanking the cathedral. (Open Mon.-Fri. 9am-2pm, Sun. 9am-1pm. Free.) Inside the museum is the *serione geologico-vulcanologica,* an exposition of the volcanic history of the islands. The fortress holds a small archeological park and a neoclassical amphitheater hosts events during July's riotous **Festival delle Isole Eolie.** (Open daily 9am-2pm and 3:30-7pm; off season 9am-4:30pm. Free.) But even just a walk around the island or town is itself a treat. The twilight view of the Marina Lunga from near the *municipo* is unbelievably picturesque (right at the base of the *castello* entrance—look for the illuminated cross on the far peak). Even better—for both your eyes and your camera—is a sunset ferry ride to the islands.

As the sun sets and the zephyrs meander in from the sea, squeeze into your spandex and bop over to the **Discoteca Turmalin**, outside the castle walls and to the right as you exit. (Tel. 981 15 88. Cover L12,000. Open daily 10am-2am, Sept.-June Sat. only 10am-2am.) For a dose of American pop culture, visit the **Megaton Bar** at Via XXIV Maggio, 51 (tel. 981 26 19), across from the disco. Enjoy big-screen TV and loud music while sampling a variety of teas, beers, sandwiches, and cocktails. (Open daily 9am-4am, Sept.-May 4pm-2am.) In a blowout party to mark the end of the summer tourist season, Lípari goes crazy with a colorful procession, fireworks, and other festivities on **August 24**—the day of the cathedral's patron saint, St. Bartholomew.

Around the Island

Lípari is known for its beaches and hillside panoramas. Go all out—rent a moped or a bike and take a day to tour the island (but keep your wits about you—the roads are narrow and the cars go fast). Work your way counterclockwise from Lípari's marina, where you'll first stop at **Canneto,** a small town fronted by a rocky beach. To get to the **Spiaggia Bianca** (White Beach) north of Canneto, take the waterfront road to the "No Camping" sign, then walk up the stairs of Via Marina Garibaldi and bear to your right down the narrow cobblestoned path along the water's edge for one-third of a kilometer. There's good swimming all along this area. The beach is the spot for topless (and sometimes bottomless) sunbathing. Protect your delicate flesh, though—those pebbles are sharp and the sun is hot; dive in and stay in. And watch out for occasional public autoeroticism by the shameless locals. From Canneto center, explore the secluded sandy coves flanking Spiaggia Bianca by renting one of the rafts, kayaks, or canoes that line the beach at Via M. Garibaldi. (L6000-8000 per hour, L25,000-35,000 per day.) Buses leave the Esso station at Lípari's ferry port for Canneto nine times per day (16 in July and Sept.; 21 in Aug.; L1500), and for Porticello (Cave di Pumice) 7 times per day (9 in Aug., L2000).

Just a few kilometers north of Canneto lies **Pomiciazzo,** where dozens of pumice mines line the road. On clear days, spectacular views of Salina, Panarea, and Strómboli hang on the horizon. Travel a few kilometers north and you're at **Porticello,** where you can bathe at the foot of the pumice mines while small flecks of the stone float on the sea's surface. As you dive beneath the waves for polished black obsidian, note the red and black veins (pumice and obsidian) which stretch from the beach into the seabed.

After passing through Acquacalda, the island's northernmost city, you'll see signs for the **Duomo de Chisea Barca,** right on the border of **Quattropani.** Head up the slope toward the church and check out some of the homes chopped into the obsidian hills. After a series of twists, turns, and some *very* steep inclines you'll finally reach the church and be granted a vista only those of saintly stature deserve.

Traveling south, across the island from Lípari Town, you'll pass through **Varesana** where the road splits: one route leads to **M.S. Angelo** (dominating the center of the island; follow signs for **Pirrera**) and the other runs to **Pianoconte,** where lava-coated battle gear has been unearthed. Here the road splits again, with one path leading to the **Thermal Baths** at **San Calogero** (on the west side of the island opposite Lípari), notorious during Roman times. The salty sulphate-bicarbonate waters bubble at a steamy 54°C (130°F), but don't be tempted to jump in; a doctor must first certify that you need the jolt. In the opposite direction perches **Quattrocchi** (Four-Eyes), so-called for its view of the four headlands that lie off the island's coast. If you make it to the Quattrocchi Belvedere (4km from Lípari, but a heady climb), you receive in return a noble vista of Lípari's *castello,* Vulcano, and the *Faraglione,* a series of monoliths rising from the sea between Vulcano and Lípari.

South of Quattrocchi sits **Monte Guardia,** home to UNESCO's **Geophysical Observatory** (not open to the public) and, for the rest of us, a close-up view of Vulcano.

Infrequent buses wend their way all the way around the island (3 per day, 1hr. 30min., round-trip L5000; check with tourist office for current times). More often visitors grab boats from the hydrofoil port in Lípari and tour around Lípari and its neighboring islands. Excursions are run by **SEN** (Società Eolie di Navigazione, tel. 981 23 41), which conducts tours of Salina and Lípari (daily at 10am, return 6:15pm, L30,000); Alicudi and Filicudi (Tues. and Fri. at 9am, return 8:30pm, L48,000); Panarea (daily at 10am, return 5:30pm, L30,000); Stromboli (daily at 3pm, return 11pm, L40,000); and Vulcano (daily at 9am, return 1pm, L16,000 for tour around island, L6000 for direct trip). If these prices are too high, try privately contracting a fishing boat for a personalized excursion. Bargain for a decent price—about L12,000 per person per hour is reasonable. Consult the NGI office, Via F. Crispi, 96 (tel. 981 19 55), near the ferry port, for other ways to experience the islands.

■ Vulcano

> *Stretch out and immerse yourself; the hand of the god Vulcan will hold you gently, transforming thoughts into bubbles of music and culture.*
> *—a signpost in Vulcano*

The psychedelic sensations promised by these words may elude you, but if you are seeking an escape from the crowds of Lípari, this island could be worth a visit. Climb up to the sulfurous crater; take a dip in the bubbling sea or sink deeply into the therapeutic mud. But beware: some geologists think the gurgling volcano may explode within the next twenty years. For now, though, the great crater lies dormant at the island's center. Easy access from Lípari (by hydrofoil, L3400; by ferry, L1800) makes Vulcano an excellent daytrip. For those who can stomach the smelly fumes, longer stays are affordable and relaxing. The island's history, not surprisingly, has always been tied to its volcano. The Greeks (among them Aristotle and Thucydides) repeatedly mention eruptions on Vulcano, including the one which created Vulcanello in 183 BC. Ancients believed this was the primary residence of Hephaestus (Vulcan), god of fire and blacksmiths, while medieval lore took the crater to be the entrance to hell. The 19th century introduced industry to the island, which a series of enterprising entrepreneurs purchased with the aim of extracting alum and sulfur. These industrial high hopes, however, were blown to bits by the earthquake of 1890. Vulcano continues to simmer, huffing and puffing but not blowing anything down—yet.

Vulcano is a summer island—if you get here before June or after September, most restaurants will be closed and it will be tough to find a place to stay (some spots do remain open, but a larger island like Lípari is more convenient in the off-season.)

Orientation and Practical Information Ferries and hydrofoils dock at **Porto di Levante,** on the eastern side of the isthmus between **Il Cardo** (the mountain to the left as you approach the port) and the Vulcanello peninsula (to the right). **Porto di Ponente,** along with **Spiaggia Sabbie Nere** (Black Sands Beach—the only smooth one on the Aeolian Islands), lie across the isthmus on the west side of the isle. Vulcano has no street signs, so it will often take more than an address to find what you're looking for. Don't be afraid to ask directions, even if you don't speak Italian (the old men who sit outside the bar at the port are especially happy to oblige.) From the dock at P. di Levante, Via Provinciale curves to the left (toward the volcano) and Via Porto Levante to the right leads into the center of town. After 200m Via Porto Levante bears to the left and turns into Via Lentia; a bit farther on you'll hit Via Porto Ponente, which leads to the right down to the port of the same name. For information about Vulcano, stop by the **tourist office (AAST)** on Via Porto di Levante (tel. 985 20 28 summer only). **Farmacia Bonarrigo,** at Via Faualauoro, 1 (tel. 985 22 44) is open daily 9am-1pm and 5-9pm. For **medical emergencies,** dial 985 22 20; for **police,** call 985 21 10. There are lots of places to rent boats, autos, scooters, or bicycles, including **Porticciolo di Ponente** (tel. 985 24 77) and **Pino Marturano** (tel. 985 24 19). There's a **post office** on the other side of the island in the hamlet of Vulcano Piano, on Via Piano (tel. 985 20 49; open Mon.-Fri. 8am-1:30pm, Sat. 8am-11:20pm). **Scaffidi Tindaro** (tel. 985 20 94) run 7 **buses** per day from the port to Vulcano Piano (9am-6pm, L2000).

Accommodations Keep in mind that all of Vulcano reeks with pervasive sulfur vapors—the island's accommodations are no exception. The run-down but comfortable **Togo Bungalows,** at the far end of Via Lentia (tel. 985 21 28), provides small, four-person bungalows with stoves for L20,000 per person; there are lockers for valuables. **Agostino,** Via Favoloro, 1 (tel. 985 23 42), has comparatively simple doubles at decent prices (Sept.-June L50,000; July-Aug. L60,000). The **Residence Lanterna Blù,** Via Lentia, 58 (tel. 985 21 78), rents cozy apartments for longer stays. Each has a tiny kitchen, a bath, and a private terrace shaded by flowering vines (Two-person apartments May-June L20,000-L25,000; July and Sept. L70,000; August L90,000. Extra bed L20,000; a one-time fee of L18,000 will be charged for cleaning the apartment at the end of your stay. Open Jan. 16-Dec. 14.) Somewhat cheaper is the **Pensione La Giara,** Via Provinciale, 18 (tel. 985 22 29) with twenty rooms at L35,000 (L70,000 in August) per person (breakfast included). The largest and most conveniently located campground is **Campeggio Togo** (tel. 985 23 03), 800m from the port in the Vulcanello area behind the Sabbie Nere beach. Its rather rudimentary facilities cost L7500, L3500 per tent. (Open June-Sept.)

Food The **general store Agostino** is located on Via Favoloro off Via P. Levante (Open daily 8am-1pm and 4-8pm.) **Panificio Alongi,** Via Mercalli, 28, is the island's best bakery. To get there, hook a left on Via P. Levante from Via Provinciale as you're heading away from the port.

The only truly stellar eating experience on the island is the **Ristorante al Cratere** at Via Provinciale, 31 (tel. 985 20 45), just past the entrance to the path to the crater. Its *fettucine fresche al cratere* and aromatic grilled swordfish (L16,000) can be savored with excellent imported beer (from L3000; open daily 12:30-3pm and 7-11pm). If you're seeking a more spartan gastronomical experience, the **Taverna del Marinaio,** just across from Agostino on Via Favoloro, offers pizzas from L7000. (Open noon-2:30pm and 7pm-midnight.) Quality *gelato* can be had at the **Ristorante-Bar Vincenzino,** Via Porto Levante (tel. 985 20 16). Finally, for some fun, check out **Il Diavolo Dei Polli,** in Vulcano Piano (tel. 985 21 97). It's a bit out of the way, but worth it for the view and conversation (Italian only) with the owner Franco. (Grilled specialties; *primi* L5000-6000, *secondi* L10,000-12,000. Open noon-3pm, 6pm-midnight. Franco also drives the island's taxis, so if you try calling and he isn't busy, he may give you a ride up. Show him your *Let's Go* guide for even more attention and possible discounts.)

Sights and Entertainment One way to begin your visit to Vulcano is to tackle the one-hour hike to the **Gran Cratere** (Great Crater) along the snaking foot path beside the crater's fumaroles. Be warned: between 11am and 3pm the sun transforms the side of the volcano into a furnace, so head out in the early morning or late afternoon. The climb is not too difficult, but there are some steep inclines to look out for. On a clear day, having reached the top, you'll be able to see all the other islands. Don't linger long, however: the sulfur smoke spouting from the volcano is saturated with toxins. To get to the path from the port, follow Via Piano for 100m to the bird statues; the path to the crater **(Sentiero per il cratere)** begins on your left on Via Provinciale, just past the **Pizzeria Steak House** and the small yellow sign reading "Marcelleria." Follow the cobblestones there.

Just up Via Provinciale from the port sits the **Laghetto di Fanghi** (mud pool) to our right, a bubbling pit where hundreds of zealots come to spread the allegedly therapeutic glop all over their bodies. If you have no dermatological crises or just think the whole thing is a tad too silly, wade in the nearby waters of the **acquacalda** just behind the *laghetto.* Here, underwater volcanic outlets make the sea percolate like a jacuzzi; don't scald your feet! For cooler pleasures, visit the crowded beach and crystal-clear waters of Sabbie Nere, just down the road from the *acquacalda* (follow the signs off Via Ponente through the black sand).

A **bus** runs from the pier to **Volcano Piano** on the other side of the island (see above). There's little to do except visit the skeleton of the **Church of Saint Angelo,** admire the vistas, and savor the aroma of sun-ripened ginger. In the opposite direction from the pier lies **Vulcanello** with a peninsula all to itself. Like its bigger (and more interesting) sibling across the way, it comes complete with noxious fumes; on the other hand, the colors of the rocks along the way help to compensate for the odor.

■ Strómboli

Viewed from Lípari or Vulcano, the island of Strómboli looks like a giant iceberg jutting out of the water in the distance. Drawing nearer, it becomes clear that the opposite is true: Strómboli is a volcano, and an active one at that. But despite the volcano's year-round activity, Strómboli town (pop. 370) lies dormant until the bustling summer tourist season. Foreigners from all over converge on the island from midJune to early September, making cheap accommodations almost impossible to find—don't plan on staying unless you camp overnight. On the other hand, in the low off season, either *pensioni* are closed or their owners are reluctant to rent rooms for fewer than three nights at a time. If you can manage it, see Strómboli on a day trip out of Lípari. (Ferry times and fares may make it difficult; shoot for the less expensive *nave* if possible.) Otherwise, camp out on the volcano's peak and watch the rocks roll.

Two towns cling to the volcano's slopes. Minuscule **Ginostra** huddles in the southern corner, essentially cut off from the rest of the island. On the opposite side, the adjoining villages of Piscità, Ficogrande, San Vincenzo, and Scari have fused to comprise Strómboli town on the island's northeast corner. The **Church of San Vincenzo** rises above the town and commands a tremendous view from its piazza, complete with Rodinesque sculptures of the Holy Trinity. From the ferry and hydrofoil dock, Via Roma leads up the hill to the church at Piazza Vincenzo. Corso Vittorio Emanuele, dipping and turning from P. Vincenzo to the edge of town, is as close as Strómboli comes to having a main drag. Via Filzi and Via Nunziante branch off of the Corso to the right; both meet up with Via Marina (which originates at the ferry dock) at the black sand beach of **Ficogrande** (big fig). From here 2km in the distance rises **Strómbolicchio,** a gigantic rock with a small lighthouse perched on its rim. The ravages of the sea have eroded the rock (56m high only 100 years ago) to a mere 42m and dropping. **Boats** for hire make their way out to the base of Strómbolicchio (L10,000-15,000), from which one can climb the stairs (reinforced with concrete in the 1920s).

Practical Information Strómboli's **post office** lies on Via Roma (open Mon.-Fri. 8:05am-1:30pm, Sat. 8:05-11:20am), and the island's only bank, **Banco Agricola Etriea,** is next to the Gabbiano (open June-Sept. Mon.-Fri. 8:30am-1:30pm). Change money here or at **Le Isole d'Italia** (also on Via Roma), a travel agency (tel. 98 62 74; open daily in the summer 5pm-8pm). The town **pharmacy** is also on Via Roma (tel. 98 60 79; open 9am-1pm and 5-9pm, Sept.-June 14 9am-noon and 4-8pm). For **medical emergencies** call 98 60 97 or go to the Guardia Medica on the Ficogrande side of the church; for **police** call 98 60 21.

Accommodations Hotels on Strómboli are booked solid in August by the pr
vious winter. In other months. **Pensione la Nassa** (tel. 98 60 33) is a good bet o
Via Marina just 20m before the beach at Ficogrande as you depart from the port.
jovial phys-ed teacher rents rooms from June to September. **Pensione Roma** (te
98 60 88), next to the Bar Roma, is five minutes from the ferry dock up on V
Roma, almost at the top of the hill to the right. The rooms are cool and comfortabl
(July-Aug. doubles L60,000; March-June 14 and Sept.-Oct. singles L20,000, double
L40,000. In winter, singles L15,000.) Farther past the church **Locanda Stella,** Via
Filzi, 14 (tel. 98 60 20) offers warm doubles and triples. (Obligatory half-pensio
L35,000 per person including breakfast. Open June-Aug.) **Villa Petrusa,** Via Solda
Panetrieri, 3 (tel. 98 60 45) has singles and doubles ranging from L40,000-70,000 p
night. **Affitta camere** are available for extended periods of time. Inquire at bars an
stores, or check with the tourist office.

Food The best deals can be had at the **Duval Market** (tel. 98 60 52), to the left o
Via Roma right before the church (open daily 8:30am-1pm and 5:30-8:30pm), an
Supermercato MC7 (tel. 98 60 19) on Via Nunziante (open daily 9am-1pm an
4:30-8:30pm). Just a few meters down on Via Roma is the *rosticceria* **La Trattol**
Pizza runs L9000-12,000 per pie. (Open daily in the summer 8:30am-11pm.) On
breezy terrace overlooking the sea you'll find **La Lampara,** on Via Vittorio Ema
uele between the church and Via Nunziante. Grilled swordfish (L12,000) and my
iad pizzas (L6000-10,000) are unequivocally filling. Try the *tiramisù,* a heaven
conglomeration of coffee-and-rum-soaked cake and sweet mascarpone crea
(L5000). (Cover L1000. Open end of May-Oct. daily noon-2:30pm and 6pm-mi
night.) **Il Gabbiano,** on Via Nunziante above the beach at Ficogrande, moonlights
a free disco (summer only).

Sights An ordinance passed in 1990 has made hiking the volcano officially illega
but it has not seemed to stop people. If such criminality doesn't suit you, look into
trip with the **Guide Alpine Autorizzate** (tel. 98 62 63), the island's authorize
guides. These expeditions leave daily at 5pm from the group's offices in P. Vi
cenzo, returning around 11pm. (April-Oct., L25,000 per person; you may be able
negotiate for less.) Despite large warning signs, it is possible to hike the volcar
unguided. (The guide office seems to be concerned about the fact that backpacke
ignore local ordinances and because they're missing out on L25,000 at the sam
time.) Travelers are likely to have trouble stashing their bags anywhere in tow
they try asking politely further down the road at the Villa Petrusa (see below). In
pinch, they hike up to where the terrain starts getting difficult, and hidetheir heav
non-valuables somewhere until they can pick them up on your way back down. Hi
ers take sturdy shoes, a flashlight, snacks, warm clothes for the exposed summ
(sleeping bag is a real bonus), and *at least* 2 liters of water. The hike takes abo
three hours up and two down. Ideally, reaching the summit around dusk—it
almost impossible to see anything but smoke during the day—allows adventurers
camp out and see the brilliant lava flows by night. High-speed film increases th
chances of good nighttime photos.

To get to the volcano, hikers follow Corso Vittorio Emanuele (from P. Vincenz
a good kilometer or so until they come to a large warning sign and a fork in the roa
they then bear to the left. When a secluded stretch of beach comes into view, th
path turns upward and (after 400m) cuts between two white houses, the last stru
tures hikers see except for the bar/ristorante L'Osservatorio a little farther on. If tra
elers see any shortcuts, they take only those that are well-trodden—anything els
will land them in a maze of thick brambles and reeds. Halfway up the slope is th
island's best view of the tremendous **Sciara del Fuoco** ("Trail of Fire") streamin
down the mountain into the sea, and a glimpse of the crater. Finally, the trail dege
erates into a scramble up volcanic rock and ash, where it pays to follow the red-an
white striped rock markings. The warning signs at the top ridge are sincere: sever

ears ago a photographer fell to her death in search of a closer shot. A red triangle with a black vertical bar means "danger," not "no parking." Hikers think very seriously about climbing with heavy loads or in the dark, since the last part does get steep. Europe's most active volcano belches forth a thundering shower of molten boulders every 15 minutes or so to the cheers of onlookers. For an overnight trip, hikers bring a sturdy food bag, plastic to place between themselves and the wet sand, warm clothing, and foul weather gear for the frigid fogs that envelop the peak. **Società Navigazione Stromboli** runs an evening **boat trip** from Strómboli to see the molten crimson trail of the *Sciara del Fuoco.* Boats leave Ficogrande port at 9pm and return at 10pm (L20,000).

Other Islands

The remaining four *Eolie* provide an uncrowded detour from the ordinary, whether you're in the mood for a rural fishing village or an overindulgent resort.

Salina

A verdant paradise and the second-largest isle, **Salina** is renowned for rock formations at Semaforo di Pollara and Punta Lingua, and for some of the best *Malvasia* wine. Salina is relatively uncorrupted by tourism; its beaches are uncrowded, its sleepy character intact. Even so, there's talk going around that it is going to be the next Capri, as the island gets more and more popular every year with Romans and other mainlanders. Salina's main port, where both the ferries and hydrofoils dock, is the Porto Santa Marina. Unless otherwise noted, the listings for food and accommodations that follow are all located in the small settlement that rises above S. Marina's docks. From the port, Via Lunga Mare heads to the right toward Malfa and Pollara, site of the last eruption on the island some 12,000 years ago. From Malfa a road cuts through the center of the island through Valdichiesa and down the slopes of Rinella, where some of the hydrofoils dock. The town of Lingua, famed for its lucid water, lies just south of **Santa Marina,** 3km to the left on Via L. Marel. From Lingua and Valdichiesa, paths extend to the peak of **M. Fossa delle Felci,** towering an impressive 962m above the island. If you show up on August 15 for the Feast of the Assumption of the Virgin you'll be surrounded by pilgrims en route to the **Sanctuary of the Madonna del Terzito,** nestled in Valdichiesa and dating back to the early 1600s. **Buses** run frequently (10 per day) to any of these towns from the port; consult the schedule posted outside the SNAV ticket office next to the docks.

Pensione Mamma Santina, Via Sanità, 40 (tel. 984 30 54), has doubles with bath for L55,000 March to June (July-Sept. obligatory half-pension L70,000). Mamma Santina's is a long steep walk through narrow streets. To get there from the port, walk up into town and take a right on the first cross street you see, Via Risorgimento; after about 250m, a sign for Mamma Santina's will point out the way. Traipse along Via Lunga Mare about 25m to the right of the port; Via Sanità is a narrow staircase woven into the hill. **Villa Orchidea,** on Via Roma in Malfa (tel. 984 40 79), is run by a friendly Australian woman. (Doubles with bath L72,000-95,000 in low season. July-Aug. obligatory half-pension L100,000.) Take the bus or *aliscafo* to Rinella for Salina's only true budget accommodations. **Camping Tre Pini** (tel. 980 91 55) charges L10,000 per person, L8000 per tent and is open April to October. A market, bar, and restaurant are on the premises. **Ristorante da Franco** (tel. 984 32 87) is a long haul but there's no better view on all of Salina. Follow signs from the top of Via Risorgimento. Homegrown anitipasti and primi are L10,000. If you've got some cash to throw around, order one of the celebrated (but expensive) seafood specialties; which run as much as L40,000 a plate. (Open year-round noon-3pm and 8pm-midnight; July-Aug. evenings only.) **Mamma Santina** also runs a small eatery, especially convenient if you're staying there for the night. The *menù* goes for L28,000, wine included. (Dinner only 8-11pm.) The cheapest way to eat, as usual, is the cold lunch route; try any *alimentare* or market you find on Via Risorgimento. **Posta Telegrafo** is at Via Risorgimento, 130 and is open Mon.-Sat. 8am-1:20pm. **Police** in Salina are at

984 30 19. There is a cluster of **SIP telephones** down by the port, and a **bank** ne
door where you can change your money (open summer only). The only year-rou
bank is down the road 7km in Malfa. The **Farmcaica Comunale** (tel. 984 30 98) s
at the bottom of Via Risorgimento, ready to help Tues.-Fri. 9am-1pm and 5:3
8:30pm, Mon. 5-8pm.

Panarea

If *La Dolce Vita* were being filmed today, it would be set in **Panarea.** In the la
three or four years, this tiny island (3.5 sq. km) midway between Salina and Stró
boli has become the favorite spot for wealthy northerners, who come to private v
las or to hotels that run a steep L150,000 or more per person. The island
renowned for its immaculate waters and striking natural rock sculptures. **Pun**
Milazzese, on the southern tip of the island was the site of a Bronze Age prehisto
village, while the opposite end is marked by a sulfurous fumarole.

Filicudi

West of Lípari, **Filicudi** presents an array of volcanic rock formations and t
enchanting **Grotta del Bue Marino** (Grotto of the Monk Seal) on the side oppos
the port (accessible only by boat). Heading to the right up the hill of **Montepal**
ieri as you arrive at the port brings you rapidly to the rocky terraces of **Fossa Fe**
(774m) and the island's **post office,** adjacent to (and located in the same buildi
as) the **Pensione La Canna.** (Tel. 988 99 56; July-Aug. doubles L75,000, full pensi
L90,000; off season doubles with bath L65,000; full pension L80,000.) As you he
further up to the town of **Valdichiesa** with its rapidly deteriorating church (note
precariously balanced bell tower), paths run around to the western edge of t
Fossa and down to **Pecorini,** home to a set of ancient Greek inscriptions. T
island's one paved road carries you back to the port from here, as the peninsu
Capo Graziano reaches effortlessly into the sea from the right. **La Canna,**
impressive rock phallus (71m high, 9m wide), skyrockets from the sea a kilome
from Filicudi's west coast. It's easily visible if you make it on the footpath around t
Fossa; otherwise rent a boat (L15,000-20,000) or grab a ferry to **Alicudi** (Sirem
L7200) which will pass right by the suggestive rock.

Alicudi

On the westernmost fringes of the Aeolian islands sits **Alicudi,** at five square km,
tle more than a speck in the sea. With one telephone, a hotel, 120 inhabitants,
paved roads, and recently installed electricity (Feb. '91), Alicudi is just the place
go if you're headed nowhere in particular. Heading up Via Regina Elena leads y
rapidly to the island's **church,** as well as, farther on, the **castle.** It's rumored th
women used to hide from pirates in the nooks and crannies of the **Serra della Fa**
cona; if you reach **M. Filo d'Arpa's crater** (675m) you'll see why—just getting
there is a task. Left of the port, make your way over the stones to untourist
Tonna. The **Albergo Ericusa** (tel. 988 99 02, it's *the* phone) caters to the few vi
tors who aren't visiting family; half-pension runs at L80,000 and full pension
L90,000. (Open June-Sept., but call before you come—it's a long way back to civ
zation.) Full pension is advisable; with their isolation, vendors sell food at inor
nately high prices, so be prepared.

■ Cefalù

Ostensibly named for the head-shaped promontory (now called the Rocca) th
stares down upon what once was a sleepy fishing village, Cefalù remains a cache
Arab, Norman, and medieval architecture. The fishermen have opened shops a
restaurants to serve the streams of visitors drawn to its pleasant streets and san
beaches in the summer. Hotels fill up during the summer, and the prospects of fir
ing an inexpensive *pensione* are fairly dismal even in the off-season. Visit Cefalù a
stopover or daytrip from Palermo, only an hour away by train (14 each weekd

L5000; 6 trains per day to Milazzo, 5 hr., L10,500—if you're en route to the Lípari islands). You can easily tour the town in half a day and still have time for a swim—in the crowded but still unspoiled waters right below town or at the beaches a short bus ride away.

PRACTICAL INFORMATION

Via A. Moro leads to the right from the station into town. At the first big intersection, **Via Roma** runs off to the left and into Cefalù's modern quarter. To get to the **old city,** continue on Via Moro as it turns into Via Matteotti and then (at P. Garibaldi) into Corso Ruggero. **Via Lungomare** runs the length of Cefalù's main beach before it passes into the old city as **Corso Vittorio Emanuele.**

Tourist Office: Corso Ruggero, 77 (tel. 210 50), in the old city. English-speaking staff helps with accommodations and stocks a map of the city. If you don't see anyone, check in back. Open Mon.-Fri. 8am-2pm and 4:30-7:30pm, Sat. 8am-2pm.

Exchange: Banca S. Angelo, near the station at the corner of V. Giglio and V. Roma. Open weekdays 9am-1pm. For 24-hr. access, try the change machine by the **Banca di Sicilia,** in P. Garibaldi.

Post Office: Via Vazzana (tel. 215 28), off Via Roma. Open Mon.-Fri. 8am-5:30pm, Sat. 8-1:30pm. **Postal Code:** 90015.

Telephones: Agenzia San Mauro, Via Vazzana, 7 (tel. 234 43). In front of the *lungomare.* Open Mon.-Sat. 9am-1pm and 4-7:30pm. **Telephone Code:** 0921.

Buses: SAIS, to Castelbuono and Geraci. **SPISA,** Via Umberto I, 28 (tel. 243 01), up the right from P. Garibaldi. Inquire at the Bar Musotto (SPISA leaves from here and from the station); their buses serve all local towns for under L2000.

Emergencies: tel. 113. **Police:** tel. 113. **Hospital:** Via A. Moro (tel. 211 21). **Nighttime Medical Emergency:** tel. 236 23.

ACCOMMODATIONS, CAMPING, AND FOOD

Cefalù's hotels cater primarily to deep-pocketed northern Europeans; cheap lodgings are an endangered species. Consider camping and spend your money on a nice meal overlooking the water instead.

Pensione delle Rose, Via Gibilmanna (tel. 21 885). Turn right on Via A. Moro from the station. At the first stoplight, turn right onto Via Mazzini and continue up the hill until it turns right again on Via Umberto which soon turns into Via Gibilmanna. Make a final right at the *pensione* sign, and left up the tree-lined stairs. Rooms with spectacular views of the town. Singles L30,000. Doubles L45,000, with bath L55,000. Oct.-May singles L25,000, doubles L40,000, with bath L50,000.

Locanda Cangelosi, Via Umberto I, 28 (tel. 21 591), off P. Garibaldi. *The* budget shack. Only 4 rooms, so call in advance for the cheapest bed in the old city. Singles L34,000. Doubles L50,000. Showers included. Oct.-May singles L20,000, doubles L30,000.

Pensione La Giara, Via Veterani, 40 (tel. 21 562), off Corso Ruggero, a block from the beach. Comfortable rooms with balconies opening onto a picturesque street with a sea view. July-Aug. half pension required, L72,000 per person. Sept.-June singles L24,000-L33,000, doubles L44,000-55,000.

Camping: Costa Ponente (tel. 20 085), 3km west at Contrada Ogliastrillo (a 45-min. walk or a short ride on the Cefalù-Lascari bus, L2000). Swimming pool and tennis court. L6500 per person, L5500 per small tent, L8000 per large tent; Sept.-June L6000 per person, L4800 per small tent, L6900 per large tent. Nearby **Camping Sanfilippo** (tel. 201 84) charges L5000 per person, L4500 per small tent, L6500 per large tent. Both campgrounds run markets in the summer, but you're probably better off stocking up at the STANDA in the center of Cefalù (see below).

Affordable restaurants cluster around Corso Ruggero and Via Vittorio Emanuele, and many fine *pizzerie* converge on Via C.O. di Bordonaro and the *lungomare*, some with balcony dining. Shop for basics at **STANDA,** Via Vazzana (tel. 24 500) near the post office. (Open Mon.-Tues. and Thurs.-Sat. 8:30am-1pm and 4:30-8pm, Wed. 8:30-1pm.)

Al Bastione, Cortele Pepe (tel. 23 228), off Corso Ruggero to the left past the *duomo* as you head toward the sea. Eat outdoors in a tiny courtyard under a grapevine, or indoors in the air-conditioned basement. Fabulous seafood (from L10,000), cheap *primi* (from L6500) and pizza (from L6000). Open daily noon-3:30pm and 6:30pm until they decide to close. AmEx, MC, Visa.

Pizzeria "da NINO," (tel. 22 582) to the right down the *lungomare*. Low prices, outdoor dining and a seaside view make it worth the tourist crowd. Simple entrees like *pizza margherita* (L4000) or *spaghetti al pomodoro* (L5000) make the best deals.

SIGHTS AND ENTERTAINMENT

In P. Duomo off Corso Ruggero you'll find Cefalù's austere 11th-century Norman **cathedral,** supposedly erected by Roger II in gratitude for divine protection from a shipwreck. The golden stone and square-towered solidity echo the monumentality of the Rocca behind it. Inside, 16 Byzantine and Roman columns support superb capitals as well as elegant horseshoe arches that exemplify the Saracen influence on Norman architecture in Sicily. The bright Byzantine mosaics depict angels, a compassionate Christ, the Madonna, and the Apostles. (Open daily 9am-noon and 3:30-7pm. Proper dress required—shoulders and knees should be covered.)

Opposite the cathedral, down Via Mandralisca, the private **Museo Mandralisca** houses a fine collection of paintings, Greek ceramics, Arab pottery, antique money, and Antonello da Messina's *Ritratto di Ignoto* ("Portrait of an Unknown Man," 1470-1472), the face featured on most Sicilian tourist brochures. (Open daily 9am-12:30pm and 3:30-7pm. Admission L4000.)

At the end of Via XXV Novembre on Via Vittorio Emanuele (hugging the beach) is the curious semi-subterranean 16th-century **lavatoio medievale** (medieval laundromat). Don't drink the water coming from its fountains and try your best not to inhale the noxious fumes spewed from the ancient tubs.

For a bird's-eye view of the city, make the half-hour haul up the **Rocca** by way of the Salita Saraceni, which begins near P. Garibaldi off Corso Ruggero. On the mountain, walkways lined with ancient stone walls lead to the **Tempio di Diana** (Temple of Diana). Dating back to the 4th century BC, it was first used for sea-cult worship and later as a defensive outpost.

At night the beach party moves to **Le Sabbie d'Oro,** one town over in S. Lucia (tel. 213 40). From July to September, Cefalù hosts the **Incontri d'Estate,** which features classical, contemporary, and Sicilian folk music, as well as opera, in outdoor concerts. The Sicilian Symphony Orchestra is a featured performer at these concerts. Shows are moved to the *duomo* August 4-6 to accommodate the **Fiesta di San Salvatore** in honor of Cefalù's patron saint, celebrated with a rousing display of fireworks and marching bands.

Cefalù's best beaches, **Spiaggia Mazzaforno** and **Spiaggia Settefrati,** are located west of town on SPISA's Cefalù-Lascari bus line (L1500-L2000).

Near Cefalù: The Ruins of Tyndaris

Seventy-five kilometers east of Cefalù and just 15km west of Milazzo (whence ferries depart to the Aeolian Isles) lies **Tíndari,** site of the ruins of **Tyndaris.** Dating from the 4th century BC, the Greek settlement was founded high on a hill as a fortification against enemy attacks. Tindaris chose wisely, siding with Rome in the Punic Wars and supplying ships for the expedition that destroyed Carthage in 146 BC. However, an earthquake in 365 AD destroyed the city, and the Arabs mopped up the remains in 836. Unearthed only in the mid-1900s, the ruins are now home to a museum, several archeological curiosities, olive groves, and spectacular views of the Aeolian Isles.

The first sight you'll see upon climbing the hill to the ancient site is the **Santuario di Tíndari,** erected less than 30 years ago for the **Madonna Nera** (Black Madonna). Local legend has it that a statue of this eastern madonna washed up on the shores of Tíndari hundreds of years ago. The current sanctuary stands on the site where the first church in her name once stood. Across from the entrance to the sanctuary, a path leads to the heart of the ruins, including the **basilica** and **agora**. The **theater** perches 125m further down, characteristically cut into the hill with an impressive panorama of the surrounding seascape. The **museum,** adjacent to the theater, has a series of knick-knacks uncovered from the site as well as some drawings illustrating what life was like in the ancient town. (Museum open daily 9am-2pm. Site open daily 9am-1 hr. before sunset. Both free.) Just in front of the museum proceeds the main street of the town, the **decumanus.** Follow it to the right as you exit the museum; it will curve past the base of the basilica and lead you to the **Casa Romana,** an old Roman house replete with intricate mosaics. All around the site stand bits and pieces of the city's walls, as well as the original city gate on the main road en route to the *santuario*. If you have the chance, drop by Tíndari to see **Greek drama** in the theater; the tourist office in Cefalù has listings of current plays and performance times.

The best way to get to the ruins at Tíndari is to take a train to **Patti.** Buses run from the station to the center of town (L1000); switch there to one of the 4-5 buses a day that run directly to the site (L2000). Be sure to double-check when buses are returning; Tíndari is no mecca and you can readily find yourself stranded there late in the day. The ruins are also accessible by taking the train to Oliveri-Tíndari and making the hike up the hill. Follow your first right out of the station until the street ends; bear left here under the highway and then to the right past a grove of lemon trees. When you come to a green gate, go left (following the white arrows). Finally, bear right when the path forks. Tíndari is at the top, 40 steep minutes away.

■■■ PALERMO

The people and palaces of Palermo, capital of Sicily, proclaim it as a crossroads of Mediterranean cultures. First in the Phoenecian orbit, then under Roman and Byzantine sway, Palermo blossomed under Saracen (831-1071) and Norman rule (1072-1194), emerging as one of Europe's most prominent cities. Hohenstaufen, Angevin, Aragonese, and Bourbon overlords followed. Enjoying unusual goodwill and tolerance, the city became the intellectual bastion of southern Italy and a junction for trade between East and West (thus its original name, "Palominos," meaning "all harbor"). In modern times, Palermo has earned notoriety of a less lofty sort: it is considered to be the cradle of Italian organized crime. Having risen to prominence in the late 19th century, the loose affiliation of *uomini d'onore* (men of honor) known as the Mafia saw its power diminished by Fascist-era purges, then augmented by cooperation with invading Allied forces during World War II. Since the mid-80s the government has once again tried to curtail Mafia influence, with inconclusive results. Among the palermitani, though, one thing is certain: they've had enough and won't stand for the Mafia's domination any longer. Banners and advertisements hang from balconies all over the city, commemorating the judges and public officials who have died fighting the mob, and calling for an end to cosa nostra. Although the ongoing battle of intimidation and assassination continues to make headlines and coffee-shop conversation, petty thievery and drive-by snatchings are far more likely to trouble the traveler. Women should be especially alert in Palermo. Be cautious, especially as you stray further from the center of this fascinating, patchwork city.

ORIENTATION AND PRACTICAL INFORMATION

Palermo and its crescent-shaped harbor lie at the end of a fertile basin called the **Conca d'Oro** (Golden Conch). To the north, 610m of Monte Pellegrino's limestone mass separate the city from **Mondello,** its beautiful beach. As you exit the front of the station onto P. Giulio Césare, **Via Roma** runs straight into Palermo, cutting through the city. Ten blocks from the station it is intersected by **Corso Vittorio Emanuele,** racing from the sea toward the mountains and, 10 blocks after that, by **Via Cavour,** running parallel to Corso Vittorio Emanuele. One block to the left of Via Roma as you exit the station lies **Via Maqueda,** paralleling Via Roma through its intersection with Corso Vittorio Emanuele at P. Verdi all the way to the Teatro Mássimo at Via Cavour. At this point it transforms into **Via Ruggero Séttimo,** and at Via E. Amari (in **Piazza Castelnuovo**) into **Viale della Libertà.**

Behind the once-grand *palazzi* lining the main avenues you'll find a maze of alleys and courtyards. These innards of historic Palermo are a sharp contrast to the sterile grid of the modern quarter west of P. Castelnuovo. Shop for food at markets off Via Roma on Via Divisi, and between the Palazzo dei Normani and the station at P. Ballaro; for clothing, try Via Bandiera near the Church of San Domenico. Ritzier shops plume themselves along Via Roma, Via Maqueda, and viale della Libertà. With the exception of restaurants, everything in Palermo closes from noon to 3pm and then again around 8pm.

CRIME

Don't let crime ruin your stay in Palermo. Pickpockets and moped-mounted bag-snatchers will get you if you fail to take precautions. Keep wallets in moneybelts or neck pouches, *not* in front pockets or handbags. Leave all bags, valuables, expensive watches and other jewelry at your hotel; if your room is not secure, however, you may have to choose between two evils. Avoid the dark, deserted back streets of old Palermo at night, sticking instead to the fancier, more modern sections of the city, which are comparatively safer than the side streets. The Via P. di Belmonte (between Via Roma and Via Maqueda, one block before P. Castelnuovo) is a good choice; so is the popular beach at Mondello (see below). The area between Via Roma, Corso Vittorio Emanuele, and the water (to the right as you're leaving the station), known as "La Cala," is notorious for being unsafe. Women—simply do not carry purses.

Tourist Office: P. Castelnuovo, 34 (tel. 58 38 47), 2km north of the train station. Take bus #7 or 46 going toward Teatro Politeama; the tourist office is in the building with the huge SICILCASSA sign. Open Mon.-Fri. 8am-8pm; Sat. 8am-2pm. Another office is in the **train station.** Open Mon.-Fri. 8am-2pm. Both offer detailed info on Palermo (maps, brochures) and other places of interest such as Cefalù, Monreale, and Ústica. English spoken. The booth at the airport (tel. 59 16 98) is open daily 8am-8pm.

Budget Travel: CTS, Via Garzilli, 28/G (tel. 32 57 52). Take Via Maqueda to P. Castelnuovo; go 1 block past P. Castelnuovo on Via Libertà and turn left on Via Carducci. Two blocks farther you'll hit Via Garzilli. The office is then to your right. Harried but efficient. Open Mon.-Fri. 9am-1pm and 4-7:30pm, Sat. 9am-1pm.

Consulate: U.S., Via G.B. Vaccarini, 1 (tel. 30 25 90), off viale della Libertà. Take bus #28 from V. della Libertà. Open Mon.-Fri. 8am-12:30pm and 3-5pm. Emergencies only. **U.K.** citizens should contact their consulate in Naples (tel. (081) 66 35 11); **Australian** citizens should contact their embassy in Rome (tel. (06) 83 27 21) as should **Canadians** (tel. (06) 440 30 28) and **New Zealanders** (tel. (06) 440 29 28). **Germany** (V. E. Amari, 124; tel. 58 33 77) and **Tunisia** (P. I. Florio, 24; tel. 32 89 96) both have embassies in Palermo.

American Express: G. Ruggieri, Via E. Amari, 40 (tel. 58 71 44). Follow Via E. Amari from P. Castelnuovo toward the water. Very busy. Open Mon.-Fri. 9am-1pm and 4-7pm, Sat. 9am-1pm.

Post Office: Via Roma, 322 (tel. 160), by the Museo Archeologico, 2 blocks from Via Cavour. Open Mon.-Sat. 8:15am-7:30pm for letters, 8:15am-1:20pm for packages. Fermo Posta at windows #15-16. Open Mon.-Fri. 8:15am-7:30pm, Sat. 8:10am-1:30pm. **Postal Code:** 90100.

Telephones: ASST, Via Lincoln, across from the train station. Open 24 hrs. **SIP,** in P. Ungheria,, to the left off V. R. Settimo past Teatro Massimo. Open Mon.-Sat. 8am-8pm, Sun. 8am-noon and 4-5:30pm. **Telephone Code:** 091.

Flights: Cinisi-Punta Raisi (tel. 59 16 90), 31km west of Palermo. Public buses connect the airport to P. R. Settimo in front of the Politeama (15 per day 5:30am-10:30pm, L4500). Taxis charge at least L50,000-60,000 for the same route.

Trains: P. G. Césare (tel. 616 18 06), on the eastern side of town. To Milan (2 per day, 22hr., L78,700); Rome (3-4 per day, 15hr., L63,200); Naples (3-4 per day, 13hr., L50,100).

Luggage: Deposito Bagagli, L1500 per bag for 24 hrs. Open 6am-10pm.

Public Transportation: City buses (AMAT), (tel. 35 01 11). Fare L1000 for a 1hr. ticket, L3000 for a 1-day pass. Buy tickets from coin-operated machines inside buses (exact change only), from *tabacchi,* or at the bus depot. The main terminal is in front of the train station.

Buses: Filli Camilleri-Argento, (tel. (0922) 390 84). To Agrigento (2-3 per day, 2hr., L10,200) from Via Balsamo around to the right of the train station as you face P. G. Césare and Via Roma. **Autoservizi Segesta,** Via Balsamo, 26 (tel. 616 79 19) has over 20 departures per day direct to Trápani (1hr. 45min., L11,000). **SAIS,** Via Balsamo, 16 (tel. 616 60 28). To Catania (16 per day, 2hr. 30min., L16,000) continuing on to Syracuse (L5200 extra).

Ferries: Tirrenia (tel. 33 33 00) in Palazzina Stella Maris within the port. Entry to port off Via Francesco Crispi. Open 8:30am-1pm. **Grandi Traghetti,** Via M. Stabile, 53 (tel. 58 78 32). Open Sun.-Fri. 8:30am-5pm. **Siremar,** Via Francesco Crispi, 120 (tel. 58 24 03). Open 8am-1pm and 3-5pm. Siremar has daily ferries to Ústica (Mon.-Sat. at 9am, Sun. at 7:30am, 2hr. 20min., L15,800) as well as hydrofoils 3 times daily in July and Aug. (at 7am, 2:45pm and 6pm, 1hr. 15min., L28,300). Tirrenia and Grandi Traghetti serve more distant ports: Tunisia, South America, Northern Europe.

Gay Men's Resource Center: Arci-Gay, Via Trápani, 3 (tel. 32 49 17 or 32 49 18). Information on events. Open Mon.-Fri. 9:30-11:30pm.

Lost and Found, in the Palazzo del Municipio, P. Pretoria (tel. 33 93 30), off Via Maqueda near Via Vittorio Emanuele. Open daily 8:30am-1:30pm.

Public Toilets and Showers: Albergo Diurno, at the train station. Clean and convenient. Showers L7500. Shampoo L6000. Open daily 8am-8pm.

Late-Night Pharmacy: Lo Cascio, Via Roma, 1 (tel. 616 21 17), near the train station. Open Mon.-Fri. 24 hrs, Sat.-Sun. 8pm-9am. Consult tourist office for seasonal openings.

Emergencies: tel. 113. **Police:** tel. 112. **Hospital: Civico Regional e Generale,** Via Lazzaro (tel. 606 11 11). **Medical Emergency:** tel. 606 11 11.

ACCOMMODATIONS AND CAMPING

Finding a decent and inexpensive place to stay here is a breeze. A surfeit of *alberghi* blesses **Via Roma** and **Via Maqueda,** but women should avoid the eastern part of town by the train station after dark.

Hotel Cortese, Via Scarparelli, 16, (tel. 33 17 22). From the train station, walk 10min. down Via Maqueda to Via dell'Universita; look for the sign to the left. Turn left and go another 200m. Probably the nicest hotel in its price range. Impeccable, modern rooms with new furniture. A perk: June 15-Sept. 15 you get free tickets to the beach—sun umbrellas and cabanas included. Huge market right next door. Singles L22,000, with shower L28,000. Doubles L36,000, with shower L45,000. Hall showers free. Half or full pension available. Visa, MC.

Pensione di Fiore, V. Roma, 391 (tel. 58 80 36). Smack in the middle of town. The gloomy spiral staircase leads up to bright rooms at the lowest prices around. Singles L22,000. Doubles L34,000. Free showers in the hall.

Albergo Orientale, Via Maqueda, 26 (tel. 616 57 27), just a few blocks from the station. Don't come for the stark rooms; come for the surreal experience of meandering through the halls of this gloriously run-down 17th-century *palazzo*. Singles L30,000. Doubles L45,000, with bath L50,000. The only triple (with bath) has a balcony Mussolini would have died for (L60,000).

Albergo Cavour, Via Manzoni, 11 (tel. 616 27 59), on the 5th floor. From P. G. Césare in front of the station hang a right on Via Lincoln; Via Manzoni is the first street on your left. Well-sized rooms, classic wood-panelled elevator. Singles L24,500. Doubles L34,000. Showers L4000.

Albergo Letizia, Via Bottai, 30 (tel. 58 91 10). From Via Roma head on Corso Vittorio Emanuele toward the water. Via Bottai is the 8th street on your right, just before the entrance to P. Marina. A little out-of-the-way, but the rooms are as fresh as the bottles of rainwater the owner collects in his spare time. Singles L27,000, with bath L33,000. Doubles L40,000, with bath L50,000. Extra bed L17,500. Expect prices here to rise by as much as L10,000 in the summer.

Albergo Bristol, Via Maqueda, 437 (tel. 58 92 47). Peek through your lace curtains to see Teatro Massimo and P. Verdi, Palermo's most fashionable square. The young staff welcomes students with open arms. Singles L30,000. Doubles L40,000, with bath L50,000.

Albergo Alessandra, Via Divisi, 99 (tel. 616 70 09), off Via Maqueda. Recently renovated, with beautifully decorated ceilings. Singles with bath L35,000. Doubles L50,000, with bath L60,000.

Hotel Odeon, Via E. Amari, 140 (tel. 33 27 78). Directly to the right of the Teatro Politeama as one faces it from P. Castelnuovo. Clean but depressing rooms in a super-convenient location. Lots of old-timers so don't make too much noise. Singles L18,000. Doubles L45,000.

Hotel Capri, Via Maqueda, 129 (tel. 616 82 49). Clean though charmless rooms; brand-new bathrooms in the hall. Singles L25,000. Doubles L45,000.

Hotel Ariston, Via M. Stabile, 139 (tel. 33 24 34), in the busy part of town far from the station. Head up Via Roma 3 blocks past Via Cavour or take bus #7 or 46 and jump off before Via E. Amari. Modern rooms overlooking a quaint courtyard. Singles L30,000, with bath L40,000. Doubles L45,000, with bath L55,000.

Petit Hotel, Via Principe di Belmonte, 84 (tel. 32 36 16), to the left off Via Roma 2 blocks before Via E. Amari as you head from the station. Quiet, clean, and in a relatively safe neighborhood crowded with posh *caffè*. Drop by Frankie's place downstairs (Bar Fiore) for a late-night snack. Doubles with bath L48,000-60,000.

Camping: Trinacria, Via Barcarello (tel. 53 05 90), at Sferracavallo by the sea. Take bus #28 from Teatro Mássimo. L5000 per person and per tent. Also at Sferracavallo is **Campeggio dell'Ulivo,** Via Pegaso (tel. 53 30 21). It's cheaper, but lower quality. L6000 per person, tent included.

FOOD

Palermo is famous for its *pasta con le sarde* (with sardines and fennel) and *rigatoni alla palermitana* (with a sauce of meat and peas). The best seafood platter is swordfish, either plain (*pesce spada*) or rolled and stuffed (*involtini di pesce spada*). Eggplant comes in every shade of purple, in forms ranging from slender to stout. Have it cold in a tasty sauce, deep-fried in sandwiches, or in a dish called *caponata di melanzana*, stewed with onions, celery, green olives, and capers. At certain stands in the markets you can get octopus simmered to order (snack portion about L1500). Also try *panelle,* tasty fried balls of chick-pea flour sliced and sandwiched. For the apotheosis of local cuisine, have *spaghetti al broccoli affogati alla palermitana,* spaghetti combined with spicy fried broccoli. And, of course, partake of the heady local wines.

The **STANDA supermarket** has outlets at Viale della Libertà, 30 (tel. 33 16 21), in the northern end of town past Piazza Castelnuovo, at Via R. Séttimo, 16/22 (tel. 58 60 19), and at the corner of Via Roma and Via Divisi, near the station (tel. 616 40 93). (All three open daily 9am-1pm and 4-8pm.)

Trattoria Shanghai, Vicolo de Mezzani, 34 (tel. 58 97 02), overlooking P. Caracciolo. Hook a right on Corso Vittorio Emanuele off Via Roma as you journey from the station and then a left on Via Vucciría just 1 block farther. As you enter P. Caracciolo, bear right onto Vicolo de Mezzani. Despite this *trattoria's* name, the food here is pure Palermo. Arrive for lunch and watch the marketeers do their stuff. Great *gamberi* (shrimp) L8000. Cover L1000. Service 10%. Open daily noon-3:30pm and 6:30-midnight.

Il Cotto e il Crudo, P. Marina, 45 (tel. 58 97 02). From Via Roma, head toward the water on Corso Vittorio Emanuele, then right on Via Bottai into P. Marina. So diminutive and peaceful you'd never know it was there. Look for the *trattoria* sign in front. Don't miss the *farfalle verdissime* (butterfly-shaped pasta in a spinach, rughetta and parmesan sauce, L6000). Well-presented self-serve antipasto table L5500. Cover L1500. Service 10%. Open Fri.-Wed. 12:30-3pm and 7:30-11pm.

Trattoria-Pizzeria Enzo, Via Maurslico 17, to the left as you exit the station onto P. G. Césare. Filling and fabulous for the fantastically frugal. Full meals (*primi, secondi,* and beverage) L13,000. Open Sun.-Fri. 9:30-11pm.

Hostaria al Duar 2, Via E. Amari, 92 (tel. 32 16 78), off Via Roma as you angle towards the port. Award-winning Italian and North African cuisine. Experience Tunisia's finest with the *Completo Tunisio* (L14,000, food, drink, and cover included) or else the more traditionally Italian *penne all'arrabiata*, pasta so hot it's "mad." Cover L1500. Open Thurs.-Tues. noon-3pm and 7-11:30pm. AmEx, MC, Visa.

Hotel Patria, Via Alloro, 104 (tel. 616 11 36). Take Via Paternostro off Corso Vittorio Emanuele until you see the fading red Hotel Patria coat of arms to your left past P. San Francisco. Palermitans line up to eat delicious food al fresco in one of the city's most romantic courtyards. Try the *tagliatelle alla norman* (L6000), noodles in a sauce of eggplant and tomato. *Secondi* L6000-12,000. Cover L500. Service 10%. Open Mon.-Sat. 1-3pm and 8-11pm.

Bar Fiore, Via Principe di Belmonte, 84 (tel. 33 25 39), left off Via Roma near the Teatro Politeama. A cheap and decent eatery in this otherwise expensive pedestrian mall. If you have a whole meal, jovial owner Frank, Palermo's greatest extrovert, will treat you to a glass of *zibbibbo,* an Olympian ambrosia that Bacchus brought to Palermo. Pasta of the day L3000; large and light *insalata mista* L5000. Try his superb *frullata,* the Italian milkshake (L4000). Top it off with some amazing pizza, your choice of artichoke, spinach, or mushroom (L2500). Draft beer on tap. Possible discounts for groups carrying *Let's Go.* (Frank's a big fan.) Open daily 6am-midnight.

Il Mirto e la Rosa, V. P. Granatelli, 30 (tel. 32 43 53). A vegetarian restaurant (will wonders never cease?) that features a fine lunch-time *menù convenienza* (*primo,* salad and drinks L10,000). If you're not in such a hurry, try their *crepes con funghi* (L8000). Coperto L2500. Open daily 12:30-3pm and 8-11pm; their tea room is open 4:30-7:30pm. MC, Visa.

Antica Foccacceria S. Francesco, Via Paternostro, 58, off Corso Vittorio Emanuele across from the Church of S. Francesco on the piazza. A 150-year-old *pizzeria:* dark wood, cast iron, and aged cacophony. Supposedly Garibaldi took his first meal here after liberating Palermo. Pizza about L2000 per slice. A tribe of locals lines up for *pane ca' meusa,* small sandwiches of ricotta and marinated tripe for L2200. *Arancina,* a fried-rice-and-meat ball, costs L1700. Beer L2500-3000. Eat outside (you bring it out yourself) on the steps of S. Francesco. Open Tues.-Fri. 9:30am-10:30pm, Sat.-Sun. 9:30am-midnight.

Trattoria Trápani, P. Giulio Césare, 16 (tel. 61 61 642). On the right side of the square as you exit the train station. A real handy cheap-eat. *Primi* L3200-L4000, *secondi* L5000-L7000. *Coperto* L500. Service 10%. Minimum of L8000 per person. Open Mon.-Sat. noon-3pm and 6-10:30pm.

Trattoria dei Vespri, P. Sta. Croce dei Vespri, 6/A (tel. 617 20 19), 2 blocks south of Corso Vittorio Emanuele. Turn left off Via Roma onto Via Discesa dei Giudici at the large Tarantino sign heading away from the station, then bear left and walk 1 piazza past the church of Santa Anna. A gourmet oasis in the midst of the dark old city. Enjoy the food at an outdoor table in an otherwise deserted piazza. The

pescespada arrosto (roasted swordfish) is unbeatable (L10,000). Service 10%
Open Mon.-Sat. 1-3pm and 6:30pm-midnight.

Osteria Lo Bianco, Via E. Amari, 104 (tel. 58 58 16), off Via Roma as you're
headed towards the port. Local crowds wipe the sweat from their brows between
each delectable bite. They have a printed *menù,* but, in truth, it changes daily. If
you're lucky they'll have some *pesce spada* (swordfish, L9000), but everything's a
treat. Sample local wines from the stainless steel barrels perched safely overhead
(L3000 per liter). Open Mon.-Sat. noon-3pm and 7-11pm.

SIGHTS

After ancient glory and then seven centuries of neglect, Palermo is an incongruous
mix of the splendid and the shabby. The bizarre sight of Palermo's half-crumbled
soot-blackened 16th-century *palazzi* startles visitors accustomed to the cleaner historic districts of northern Italy. In the past several years, however, efforts have
slowly begun to clean, rebuild, and reopen structures like the magnificent Teatro
Mássimo, closed due to water damage for, unbelievably, over 20 years. Peek into
random courtyards on your path to find the *cortili* for which the city is famous. The
courtyards themselves often seem to be held together only by the ivy laced across
their facades. For a glimpse of Palermo's ravaged splendor, climb the red marble
staircase at Via Maqueda, 26, across from the Orfeo cinema, to the tremendous balustrade on the top floor.

From Quattro Canti to San Giovanni degli Eremiti

The intersection of Corso Vittorio Emanuele and Via Maqueda forms the **Quattro
Canti,** where each corner celebrates a season, a king of Spain, and one of the city's
patron saints. The Canti date from the early 17th century when Sicily was under
Spanish rule. Just a few steps away to your left as you proceed down Via Maqueda
toward the station sits **Piazza Pretoria** with a fountain (1555-1575) originally
intended for a Florentine villa, but currently more likely to be found in the pages of
Penthouse: the fountain features, among other things, a circle of nude men and
women trying (but failing) to cover their privates and eyeing one another sugges-
tively. Palermitans were so shocked when it was unveiled that they nicknamed the
sculpture "the fountain of shame." Flanking the piazza are the 16th-century **Palazzo
del Municipio** and the splendid baroque **Church of Santa Caterina** (1566-1596).

Next to the statue of Philip III in the Quattro Canti, the dismal gray façade of the
Church of San Giuseppe dei Teatini (1612) belies its "as much as you can put on
the walls without tearing them down" Baroque interior. Don't miss such details as
the upside-down angels supporting the fonts at the entrance, or the frieze of children playing musical instruments on the wall of the south transept. (Open daily
7:30am-noon and 6:30-8:15pm.)

Farther down Via Maqueda and to the left as you approach the station, **Piazza
Bellini** embraces the **Church of San Cataldo** (1154), a Norman building whose red
domes and arches give it the air of a mosque. **La Martorana,** or, more properly
Santa Maria dell'Ammiraglio (built for an admiral of the Norman king Roger II)
shares San Cataldo's leafy platform. Mediocre Baroque additions partially conceal its
12th-century structure. The Byzantine mosaics inside are the 12th-century equivalent of celebrity photos: here's Roger I and Jesus, there's George the Admiral with
the Mother of God. (Both open Mon.-Sat. 8:30am-1pm and 3:30-7pm, Sun. 8:30am-
1pm.)

Across Via Maqueda from P. Bellini and to the right as you close in on the station,
Via Ponticello winds through a crowded neighborhood to the **Chiesa del Gesù**
(or Casa Professa, built 1363-1564). Look for its green mosaic dome. The ochre
stucco conceals a dazzling, multicolored marble interior and an almost Dalí-like
depiction of the Last Judgment. Standing in Il Gesù's courtyard, you can see traces of
American bombing during World War II; the **Quartiere dell'Albergheria,** the
inner core of the city, never quite recovered from the war's destruction—as evinced

by the numerous shattered buildings, including the one next to the Chiesa. (Church open daily 7am-noon and 5-6:30pm.)

Farther along Via Ponticello, one of Palermo's two main open-air **markets** extends from **Piazza Ballarò** to the **Church of the Carmine.** This 17th-century *chiesa* has a mosaic dome that it is all emerald fans and gold swirls—it looks like a cross between a Ming vase and a parlor room tea-cup. This area, replete with narrow streets and hidden gardens, warrants further exploration.

Venturing from the Quattro Canti onto **Corso Vittorio Emanuele,** heading away from the harbor, you will pass the dilapidated *palazzi* of the **Piazza Bologni** to the left and a spindly statue of Charles V (1630) before confronting the striking exuberance of Palermo's **cattedrale** up on the right. Begun by the Normans in 1185, it absorbed elements of every architectural style from the 13th through 18th centuries, though the best exterior elements are the original Norman towers and the three-apsed grandeur of the eastern side. Inside, the chapels on the left contain six royal tombs (four canopied and two set in the wall) of Norman kings and Hohenstaufen emperors dating from the 12th to 14th centuries. The *tesoro* (treasury, L1000), to the right of the apse, contains a dazzling array of sacerdotal vestments from the 16th and 17th centuries as well as episcopal rings, chalices, and croziers. (Open daily 7am-noon and 4-7pm.) The cattedrale is connected by the flying buttresses to the former Archbishop's palace (1460).

Set behind a tropical garden across from the church, the **Palazzo dei Normanni** (entrance around the back) contains the **Cappella Palatina** (1132-40). Built by Roger II, it too exhibits a fantastic fusion of styles—a carved wooden stalactite ceiling, a cycle of golden Byzantine mosaics rivaled only by those of Ravenna and Istanbul, and marble walls with geometric designs. In the apse, an enormous Christ looms above a 19th-century mosaic of the Virgin. Before leaving, visit the **Sala di Ruggero** (King Roger's Hall, one floor above the Palatina), a room adorned with mosaics in flora and fauna motifs. Because the *palazzo* is now the seat of the Sicilian Parliament, you must wait at the desk for an escort. (Palace open Mon. and Fri.-Sat. 9am-noon unless Parliament is in session. Chapel open Mon.-Fri. 9am-noon and 3-5pm, Sat.-Sun. 9-10am and noon-1pm. Chapel closed Sunday and holiday afternoons.)

Perhaps the most romantic spot in Palermo is the garden and cloister of the **Church of San Giovanni degli Eremiti** (St. John of the Hermits), Via dei Benedettini, 3. Built in 1132 by fanciful Arab architects, it is topped by winsome pink domes. Beside the church a tropical garden shades 13th-century cloisters. (Open Mon., Thurs., and Sat. 9am-2pm; Tues., Wed., and Fri. 9am-1pm and 3-5pm; Sun. 9am-1pm. From April to September 30, closes at 6pm.) Exiting the Cappella Palatina, follow the castle walls around to the right until Piazza della Pinta; V. dei Benedettini is to the right. To get there from the station, take bus #9.

Walk back to Corso Vittorio Emanuele to see the **Porta Nuova,** a huge gate topped by a pyramidal roof. The gate was erected to commemorate Charles V's triumphal entrance in 1535, but modified in 1668 with the rugged figures which now embellish the entrance arch.

From the Church of San Francesco to the Villa Giulia

The churches and palaces east of Via Roma toward the old port (La Cala) lie in a maze of tiny, serpentine streets. The 13th-century **Church of San Francesco d'Assisi,** Via Paternostro, off Corso Vittorio Emanuele about five blocks from Via Roma and to the right as you head toward the harbor, features an intricate rose window and a zigzag design on the outside common to many other churches in the area. The church's restored Gothic interior was augmented by side chapels in the 14th and 15th centuries and adorned with Renaissance and Baroque accessories. (Open daily 7-11am and 4-6pm.)

The **Oratory of San Lorenzo,** just a few doors down Via Imacolatella (to the left as you face the church of San Francesco), was decorated by the master of stucco,

PALERMO

Giacomo Serpotta (1656-1732). This monochrome stucco has a hard finish tha
seems to be carved stone when looked at from afar. Caravaggio's last known work
The Nativity (1609), was stolen from the altar in 1969—hence the seven locks or
the oratory door. The inlaid mother-of-pearl benches are too impressive to sit or
(Open erratically; the oratory is curated by an elderly neighbor in her spare time. T
enter, ring at #5, prepared to make a L3000 *offerta*.)

The **Giardino Garibaldi,** a park several blocks further toward the sea on Cors
Vittorio Emanuele, is replete with royal palms, fig trees, and giant banyans. The tw
fig trees are oldest and most distinctive: they grow wildly, each with over 100 sep?
rate trunks sprouting from the ground that fuse into three or four main arteries. ?
crumbling mish-mash of churches, palaces and modern apartments surround th
square (P. Marina). From the nearby **Church of Santa Maria della Catena** you ca
see the small inlet of **La Cala,** once the harbor and now a fishing port. Corso Vi
torio Emanuele ends at the war-scarred remains of the **Porta Felice** (begun i
1582). Once a fashionable seaside drive, the **Foro Italico** is now a tacky boardwal
strip. Follow signs from P. Marina to the **Museo delle Marionette,** which show
cases Sicily's proud tradition of puppetry, as well as collections of puppets fror
India, England and the Congo. (Open Mon., Wed. and Fri. 9am-1pm and 4-7pn
Tues., Thurs. and Sat. 9am-1pm. Puppet shows on request. Admission L5000 ge
eral, L2000 student.) Signs in Piazza Marina also point towards the part-Gothic, pa
Renaissance Palazzo Abatellis (1495), which houses one of Sicily's superb region?
galleries. Upstairs, an entire room is devoted to painter Antonello da Messina (143(
1479), Sicily's number-one son. Works by Leandro Bassano (1557-1622), Vincenz
da Pavia, and Leonard Macaluss round out the Sicilian gang. (Open Mon., Wed., an
Sat. 9am-1:30pm, Tues., Thurs., and Fri. 9am-1:30pm and 3-7:30pm, Sun. and hol
days 9am-12:30pm. Admission L2000.)

Heading down Foro Italico to the east, there is a **small amusement park,** whic
opens everyday in the late afternoon when the Sicilian sun has gotten cool enougl
Farther down, on Foro Umberto I along the harbor, **Villa Giulia** has a weary garder
which harbors a little something for everyone: band shells, playgrounds, menage
ies, sculpture, floral gardens, and cenotaphs.

From the Church of San Matteo to the Museo Archeologico

Most of Palermo's other noteworthy sights lie along **Via Roma** north of Corso Vi
torio Emanuele as you amble away from the station. The Baroque **Church of Sa
Matteo** (on Corso Vittorio Emanuele) conceals an ornate marble interior and fou
statues by Serpotta in the pilasters of the dome. (Open daily 8am-noon and 4-7pm
On Via Roma to the right just a block from its intersection with Corso Vittorio Ema
uele, again as you move away from the station, is the 12th-century **Church ?
Sant'Antonio,** revamped in the 14th and 19th centuries. You can still see the orig
nal structure in the square frame and the columns of the chancel. (Open Mon.-Sa
8am-noon and 6:30-8:15pm, Sun. 7:30am-1pm. Closed for restoration in 1992.) Ju
past the intersection, on Via Vucciría off Corso Vittorio Emanuele, is another **ma
ket.** Dozens of varieties of fish, seafood, fruits and vegetables, including six-foot zu?
chini, tantalize the palate and the eye. (Open 8am-8pm; closed Wed.)

The **Church of San Domenico** fronts the piazza of the same name on Via Rom?
to the right with the station behind you. Rebuilt in 1640, the church is Sicily's Pa?
theon, containing tombs and cenotaphs of distinguished citizens. The **Oratorio d?
Rosario,** behind San Domenico on Via dei Bambinai (ring at #16), houses a famou
altarpiece by Van Dyck, *Madonna of the Rosary with St. Dominique and th
Patroness of Palermo* (1628). (Both open 7:30am-noon.)

Via Meli extends from Piazza San Domenico and leads, appropriately enough, ?
Piazza Meli. By bearing left on Via dei Bambinai, through Piazza Valverde, and on?
Via Squarcialupo, you'll find the **Church of Santa Cita** to your left on V. Valverd?
The exterior was damaged during the war, but a rose window remains, showerir
the interior with baroque color and texture. The marble arches on the east wall ?

the choir and the sarcophagus in the second chapel on the left remain from the original Renaissance structure. The **Oratorio di Santa Cita,** behind the church (ring at Via Valverde, 3), is decorated with Serpotta's *Virtues,* reliefs of New Testament scenes, and, on the short wall near the entrance, a depiction of the Battle of Lepanto, where Cervantes lost a hand. (Both open 8-11am and 4-5:30pm.)

The **Museo Archeologico Regionale** is found at P. Olivella, 4 (tel. 58 78 25) and is accessible by hanging a left on Via Bara two blocks before Via Roma hits Via Cavour as you head away from the station. This museum occupies a 17th-century convent and displays a relatively unremarkable collection in two beautiful courtyards. The museum's been under restoration, and though all the rooms are now open, the occasional workman may get in your way. See the building for its *cortile.* In the bronze collection is the *Ram of Syracuse* (Greek, 3rd century BC), renowned for its realism. (Open Mon., Wed.-Thurs., and Sat. 9am-2pm., Tues. and Fri. 9am-1:30pm and 3-6pm, Sun. and holidays 9am-1pm. Admission L2000.)

Other Sights

Across Via Maqueda from the Archeological Museum, the **Teatro Mássimo,** constructed between 1875 and 1897 in a robust neoclassical style, is the largest indoor stage in Europe after the Paris Opera House. The Mássimo unfortunately has been undergoing reconstruction since 1985; the projected completion date is in 2010 (or maybe 3010, given the pace of progress in Sicily). The exiled opera and symphony perform in the **Politeama Garibaldi** (farther up Via Maqueda, which becomes Via Ruggero Settima), a huge circular theater built in 1874. The entrance is a triumphal arch crowned by a bronze chariot and four horses. The theater also houses the **Galleria d'Arte Moderna.** (Theater performances Jan. to late May and mid-July to Aug. Admission from L30,000. Gallery open daily 4-10pm. Sept.-June Tues., Wed. and Sat. 9am-1pm and 3-6pm; Thurs., Fri.-Sun. 9am-1am. Admission L5000.)

The **Convento dei Cappuccini** welcomes amateur paleontologists into its catacombs; 8000 bodies, some mummified and intact, inhabit lengthy subterranean corridors. (Open daily 9am-noon and 3-5pm; tours offered by friars intermittently. Admission free, but *offerta* expected.) Take bus #27 from P. Castelnuovo or bus #5 from Stazione Centrale.

Monte Pellegrino, an isolated mass of limestone rising from the sea, is Palermo's principal natural landmark, separating the city from the beach at Mondello. Near its summit, the **Santuario di Santa Rosalia** marks the site where Rosalia, a young Norman princess, sought ascetic seclusion. Her bones were discovered in 1624 and brought to Palermo, where they vanquished a raging plague. The present sanctuary is built over the cave where she performed her ablutions; its trickling waters are said to have thaumaturgic powers. The summit of Monte Pellegrino (a half-hour climb from the sanctuary) offers a gorgeous view of Palermo, Conca d'Oro, and on a clear day, the Lípari Islands and Mount Etna. Take bus #12 from P. XIII Víttime to the sanctuary.

ENTERTAINMENT

Palermo shuts down entirely at night. After about 9 or 10pm, there is virtually nothing to do—which is just as well, since walking any later is not a particularly wise idea. Summer nights belong to the *lido* of **Mondello,** on the cape beyond Monte Pellegrino. To join the crowds of young Palermitans in their *passeggiata,* take bus #14, 15, or 77 from P. Sturzo behind the Teatro Politeama and get off at the last stop (L1000). In summer, express bus #6 ("Beallo") also runs to Mondello, beginning at the train station and stopping along Via della Libertà. The bar and disco at **Villa Boscogrande,** the gorgeous *palazzo* where director Lucino Visconti filmed *The Leopard,* attract a posh crowd. Take bus #28 from Via della Libertà.

The major summer event in Palermo takes place at the **Teatro di Verdura Villa Castelnuovo.** From the first week of July through the first week of August, an international festival of ballet, jazz, and classical music jams in this open-air seaside theater. For tickets and information, contact the **Politeama Garibaldi, P.** Ruggero Séttimo (tel. 605 33 15; open Tues.-Sat. 10am-1pm and 5-7pm, Sun. 10am-1pm), across from the tourist office. The **Festa di Santa Rosalia,** held July 10-15, gives the city an excuse to shed its usual sobriety and go on a binge of music and merriment.

Palermo resorts to two other beaches aside from the Lido at Mondello. **Sferracavallo** is a roomier but rockier beach (take bus #28 from Via della Libertà), while **Addaura** entertains the young Palermitan jet-set crowd in summer (bus #3 from the train station or Via della Libertà).

For more in-depth information on cultural events and nightlife, pick up a copy of *Un Mese a Palermo,* a monthly brochure in Italian, available at any APT office.

Ardent mafia buffs may want to see the **Carcere Giustiziario,** an imposing structure looming where Via Francesco Crispi becomes Via Monte Pellegrino. The prison, reputedly Italy's most secure, houses *cosa nostra* kingpins and terrorists.

■ Near Palermo

Términi Imerese

About 30km east of Palermo at the base of Monte Calógero sits **Términi Imerese,** a rapidly developing resort first frequented by Greeks and Romans, who began taking advantage of the town's supposedly therapeutic springs in 600 BC. Home to an impressive Baroque *duomo* and a wonderful view of the northern coast. Términi makes a reasonable choice as a stopover on the way to Cefalù. All trains from Palermo (30min. away) stop at the base of the hill on which the city stands. As you exit the station onto Via Aurora, orange AST buses head to the top of the town (L600); hopping off at Via Garibaldi will land you just a block away from P. Duomo, with its 16th-century statues. Inside the **Duomo** check out Marabitti's *Madonna del Ponte* and a crucifix painted by Ruzzolene in the late 1400s. Near P. Duomo you'll find the **Museo Civico** (thoughtfully located on Via Museo Civico) which contains some archaeological goods from the ruins of ancient Greek Himera and a few simple paintings. The museum (tel. 814 49 11) is only open in the morning from 9am-2pm, but you can hang out with the young people in the afternoon shade just in front of the *duomo*. Bars and caffès are sprinkled around the piazza. Try **Uscateria Bazzone** just behind the *duomo*. This kiosk sells *gelato* (L1500) and *uscata* (L3000), a type of *calzone* peculiar to Términi Imerese.

If you're hungry, there's **Magros Supermarket** at Piazza Francesco Crispi, 14, off Via Aurora two blocks to the left as you exit the station en route to the *duomo*. Farther up, there's a **STANDA** in P. Duomo. If you have to spend the night, the only option is **Il Gabbiano (Dipendenza)** at Via Libertà 221 (tel. 811 32 62), over 1km to the left as you exit the station. It serves mainly travelers who get off from the nearby *autostrada*. (L40,000 per person; reservations recommended. Make sure you ask for the rooms in the *Dipendenza*, otherwise you'll pay a lot more.)

Between six and 12 buses per day leave from Términi Imerese's train station to **Cáccamo,** home to 8600 vivacious Sicilians and a gargantuan 12th-century **castle.** A Duke of Cáccamo lived here until the early 1900s, at which time it was handed over for public use. If the front door is closed, turn around and head toward the war memorial; buzz Signor La Rosa at Corso Umberto, 6. He'll take you to all the spots worth seeing—down deserted alleys and secret passageways (his services are free, but he's not too proud to accept a tip, if you're so inclined). After seeing the castle, float around the town and check out the **duomo** dedicated to St. George; note the fiery reliefs about the door by Gaspare Guercio. Unfortunately, Cáccamo doesn't offer travelers any places to stay; head down the hill to Términi Imerese instead.

Monreale

About 10km southwest of Palermo lies the golden city of **Monreale** and its magnificent Norman-Saracen **duomo** (circa 1174). The church's incredible medieval mosaics supposedly inspired Jacques Cartier to name his Canadian city Montreal. Against a brilliant gold background, the Old and New Testaments are depicted in 130 panels, over which a massive Christ Pantocrator (Ruler of All) presides. To read this brilliant Bible, start at the upper right-hand corner of the inner nave with the creation and work your way back to the present under Christ Pantocrator where Virgin and Child sit with attendant angels, among whom you can find Thomas à Becket, canonized just as work on the mosaics began (L500 to light up mosaics). The net overhead testifies to Monreale's nemesis—termites have been making a meal of the carved and gilded timber ceiling since the early 19th century. The *tesoro,* off the transept, is housed in one of the most raucously rococo chapels in Italy (L2000). Outside, circle around to see the Arab-style inlay behind the apse, and a spectacular view of the *conca d'Oro* below. Then step in to see the intricate arches and multicolored inlays of the cloister (partially under restoration), renowned for the capitals of its colonnade, each one unique. Considered to be the richest collection of Sicilian sculpture anywhere, the capitals run the gamut of styles: Greco-Roman, Saracen, Norman, Romanesque, Gothic, and various combinations. In the corner by the lesser colonnade and its fountain, look for the capital depicting William II offering the Cathedral of Monreale to the Virgin. Be sure to climb up to the roof and look down on the central apse. Two doors down from the cloister is the entrance to a series of quiet gardens which look out over Palermo and its sprawling expanse. (Cathedral open daily 8am-12:30pm and 3:30-6:30pm. Cloister open daily 9am-7pm; Nov.-March Mon.-Sat. 9am-1:30pm, Sun. 9am-12:30pm. Admission to cloister L2000; to roof L2000.) Get off at the end of the line and walk uphill (toward the Rocca) until you come to a fork in the road. Here, pay another L1000 for the ride in a mini-bus up to Piazza V. Emanuele in Monreale. When you hop off the bus, the *duomo* is to the right; Via Roma runs uphill to the right. **Tourist information** (tel. 65 64 270) resides in the building to the left of the church.

Sate your hunger at **Trattoria-Pizzeria da Peppino,** Via B. Civiletti, 12 (tel. 640 77 70), off Via Roma to the left as you're headed away from the *duomo. Primi* start at L8000, *secondi* at L5000-10,000. The *pizza bastardo* sports the local cheese *caciocavallo* (L7000). (Open Sat.-Thurs. 10am-3pm and 5pm-midnight.) For picnics, plunder the produce stores that line Via Roma. The **Salumeria Fratelli Madonia,** Via Roma, 22 (tel. 640 44 97), will provide not only a quick nutrition fix, but a lesson in pasta nomenclature. (Open Mon.-Sat. 7am-1:30pm and 4-8pm; Sun. 7am-1pm.) For cookies, cakes, pizza, and other delights, the bloodhound consumer heads for **Panificio Conca D'Oro,** Via P. Novelli, 25 (tel. 640 45 13, open until 8pm), whose enticing aromas you can smell over a block away.

Soluntum and Ústica

If windswept ruins make you swoon, you might consider paying a visit to the Phoenician and Roman site at **Soluntum** (Solunto), perched on a precipitous promontory about 15km east of Palermo on Cape Zafferano. Come to poke around the remains of dwellings, sewers, cisterns, a forum, and a theater, or just to take in the panorama of Palermo and environs. Take strada statale 113 to Porticello, then turn left and continue past Aspra to the site.

The volcanic island of **Ústica** also lies within reach of Palermo, 36 miles off the coast. Settled first by our friends the Phoenicians, then by pirates and exiled convicts, this marine reserve features prime snorkeling and waterborne grotto-hopping opportunities. Inquire at the Palermo tourist office for further details. **Siremar** runs ferries and hydrofoils out to the island (see Orientation and Practical Information: Ferries).

■■■ TRÁPANI

Unlike much of urban Sicily, Trápani is a remarkably livable and energetic city. You'll find the center surprisingly clean and traffic-free; the major arteries are closed to automobiles for much of the day. Surrounded by the ocean on three sides, Trápani stays cool under even the hottest Mediterranean sun. Its residents display a combination of Sicilian candor and North African effusiveness that has earned Trápani its designation as "Sicily's friendliest city." While its sights are not at the top of most tourists' itineraries, it makes a perfect base for expeditions to the beaches of the western coast, the luckless ruins of Greek temples, and the breathtaking mountain-town of Érice. If you're in Trápani for more than a few hours, the Baroque churches peppered throughout the town, fashioned at the crossroads of European and African influences, merit more than just the harried glance of a traveler in transit.

FERRIES

Ferries and hydrofoils leave Trápani for the Égadi Islands (Lévanzo, Favignana, and Maréttimo). Both leave from the docks off Via Ammiraglio Staiti, which runs the length of the port just south of Corso Italia. Tickets for ferries are available from **Siremar,** Via Ammiraglio Saiti, 61 (tel. 54 05 15; open Mon.-Fri. 6am-2pm, 4-6pm and 9pm-midnight; Sat. 6am-2pm, 4-5pm and 9pm-midnight; Sun. 6am-2pm). Ferry tickets are also available from **Traghetti delle Isole,** Via Ammiraglio Staiti, 13 (tel. 217 54; open Mon.-Fri. 9am-1pm and 4-7pm, Sat. 9am-noon.) Siremar has its hydrofoil ticket office (tel. 277 80) right on the docks, along with that of the other hydrofoil line, **Alilauro** (tel 240 73). These open up at least a half-hour before each hydrofoil departs. The following departure times are for mid-June through mid-September only. The prices are the same on all lines.

> **Trápani-Favignana:** 6 per day (7am-2pm, 1hr.-1hr. 30min., L4600). 11 hydrofoils per day (7am-7:15pm, 20min., L8400).
> **Trápani-Lévanzo:** 4 per day (7am-2pm, 1hr.-1hr. 30min., L4600). 11 hydrofoils per day (7am-7:15pm, 20min., L8400).
> **Trápani-Maréttimo:** 1 per day at 9am (2hr. 30min., L10,400). 3 hydrofoils per day (8:15am-6:15pm, 1hr., L19,100).
> **Trápani-Pantelleria:** Ferries depart daily at 9am and midnight (4hr. 30min., L33,400).
> **Trápani-Tunis (Tunisia): Tirrenia** runs a ferry every Mon. at 9am (9hr., L85,000); **Alimar** has one on Wednesdays at 11am (L78,000). Tickets for both lines are available at **Sudovest Viaggi** (tel. 271 01), located 50m back from the port.

ORIENTATION AND PRACTICAL INFORMATION

Trápani sits on a peninsula, three hours west of Palermo by train (L13,800). An express bus makes the trip in two hours, rolling from Via Paolo Balsamo, 26, near the train station in Palermo, to P. Garibaldi in Trápani (L10,500). Trains run from Marsala (13 per day, 45min., L3700). From Agrigento, **S. Lumia** (tel. 204 14) runs 4 buses per day from P. Garibaldi (behind the movie theater, near the post office; 6:20am-2:10pm, L14,500). Trápani's station sits in a mixed-up area midway between the old part of the city and the new town. **Via Osorio** starts a little to the left of the station, ending near **Corso Italia.** At the end of Corso Italia sits **Piazza S. Agostino,** and beyond the piazza, Trápani's main thoroughfare **Corso Vittorio Emanuele** cuts through the old city to the tip of the peninsula. The **bus depot** is just around the corner to the left as you exit the station. **Corso Vittorio Emanuele II** runs through the old town, intersecting **Via Roma,** which spans the peninsula. The old town lies directly in front of the train station; the new town is behind it. The **bus depot** is just around the corner to the left as you exit the station.

> **Tourist Office:** P. Saturno (tel. 29 000). Take Via Osorio from the Mobil sign, turn left at the end, and then go right onto Corso Italia all the way to the *piazzetta.* Armfuls of handouts. English spoken. Open Mon.-Sat. 8am-8pm, Sun. 9am-1pm. **Information booth** at airport. Open for incoming flights. **APT main office,** Via Vito Sorba, 15 (tel. 27 077), 4 blocks behind the station to the right. Open Mon.-Sat. 8am-2pm, Wed. and Thurs. 3-7pm.

Post Office: P. Veneto (tel. 28 087), up Via Osorio and then right on Via XXX Gennaio. Open Mon.-Fri. 8am-5:30pm, Sat. 8am-2pm. **Postal Code:** 91100.

Telephones: SIP, Via Scontrino, near the station. Open daily 9am-12:30pm and 4:30-8pm. **Telephone Code:** 0923.

Flights: V. Florio Airport (tel. 84 11 30), 16km outside the city in Birgi en route to Marsala. Buses leave 1hr. before flight time from outside **Salvo Viaggi,** Corso Italia, 52/56 (tel. 87 36 36, fax. 28 436). To Rome (L179,000), Pantelleria (L80,500), and special chartered flights on Saturday from Milan (price varies).

Trains: at P. Stazione (tel. 28 071 or 28 081).

Buses: AST (tel. 25 875) buses to Érice leave from P. Malta (Montalto), around to the left of the train station (Mon.-Sat. 13 per day 6:30am-7pm, Sun. 5 per day 9am-6:15pm; L2500, round-trip L4300). Catch the return bus in Érice on Via Pepoli (7:30am-7:55pm). To Segesta: **Tarantola,** (tel. 31 020 or 32 598) runs 3 per day. To Palermo: **Segesta** leaves from P. Malta (Montalto).

Luggage Storage: at the train station, L1500 per piece. Open 7am-9:20pm.

Emergencies: tel. 113. **Police:** Via Orlandini, 19 (tel. 27 122). **Hospital: Ospedale Sant'Antonio Abate,** Via Cosenza very far from town (tel. 80 94 50).

ACCOMMODATIONS AND CAMPING

Hotels are much better and only slightly more expensive in the beach resort **Capo San Vito**; take a bus from P. Malta (Montalto) (8 per day, 1hr., round-trip L7300).

Pensione Messina, Corso Vittorio Emanuele, 71 (tel. 21 198), on a Renaissance courtyard just a few blocks from P. S. Agostino. Spacious rooms, firm beds, and a rather loud pink bathroom. Run by a friendly, if slightly rambunctious family. Singles L18,000. Doubles L35,000. Showers L2500.

Albergo Moderno, Via Genovese, 20 (tel. 21 247). Turn right off Corso Vittorio Emanuele (heading away from P. S. Agostino) onto Via Roma, then take a left on Via Genovese. Trápani's oldest hotel, this once-proud *palazzo* hosted the Princess of Spain. Quiet, clean rooms all with a nautical theme. Singles L25,000, with bath L40,000. Doubles L40,000, with bath L52,000.

Sabbia d'Oro, Via Santuario, 49 (tel. 97 25 08), on the beachfront in San Vito Lo Capo. Impeccable, great location, and a bargain for the area. Singles L30,000. Doubles L50,000. Sept.-June singles with breakfast L26,000. The same management runs **Pensione Ocean View** (tel. 97 26 13) in the same building. Less opulent rooms. L19,500 per person, L22,500 with bath.

Albergo Nuovo Russo, Via Tintori, 4 (tel. 22 166), off Corso V. Emanuele to the left. 6 floors of wooden furniture, long carpets and soft armchairs. You can live it up at a low price, but only if you're alone and you don't mind not having your own bathroom (singles without bath L34,000). Singles with bath L53,000. Doubles L63,000 with bath L81,000.

Albergo Maccotta, Via degli Argentieri, 4 (tel. 28 418), behind the tourist office on P. Saturno. Quiet location, airy rooms. Singles L30,000-40,000. Doubles L70,000.

Camping: Capo San Vito and Castellamare del Golfo, on the opposite side of the cape, harbor most of the nearby campgrounds (buses daily to Castellamare at 12:30pm and 2:30pm, 1hr. 30min., round-trip L6400). **Near Capo San Vito: Camping La Fata,** Via Mattarella (tel. 97 21 33) charges L7000 per person, L6500 per small tent, L11,500 per large tent. **Camping Soleado,** Via della Secca (tel. 97 21 66) charges L7500 per person, L7000 per small tent and L10,000 per large tent. Both open year-round. **Near Castellamare del Golfo: Baia di Guidaloca** (tel. 59 60 22); **Lu Baruni** (tel. 39 133); **Nausicaa** (tel. 31 518); and the cheapest, **Ciauli** (tel. 318 33), which charges L5500 per person, L5500 per small tent, L7500 per large tent. The other places charge about L1500 more. All open June-Sept., except Lu Baruni, which is open year-round.

FOOD

Take your money to the **open-air market** in P. Mercato di Pesce (at the end of Via Torrearsa), and let it loose. (Open Mon.-Sat. 8am-1pm.) This market is such an institution that the piazza was named after it. Pick up essentials at the supermarket **Margherita,** Via San Domenico, 32, between the port and the train station. (Open Mon.-Sat. 8am-1:30pm and 5-8pm.) Trápani is known for its sardines and its *couscous con pesce,* in which said sardines often lurk. Also try a *biscotto coi fichi,* the Italian fig-newton; all of the bakeries along Corso V. Emanuele stock them for about L400 each.

Pizzeria Calvino, Via Nasi, 75 (tel. 214 64), 1 block off Corso Vittorio Emanuele as you're headed toward the port. All of Trápani comes here for take-out pizza (small L5000) before soccer games. Sit-down or take-out. Savor *lasagne al forno* (L5000). Open daily noon-2pm and 5pm-1am.

Pizzeria Mediterranea, Corso Vittorio Emanuele, 195 (tel. 54 71 76). Only 2 choices: *pizza origanata,* with whole tomatoes, garlic, oregano, anchovies, and *pecorino* cheese; or *pizza quattro gusti* with ham, basil, anchovies, and mozzarella. Small L5000-6000, large L15,000-16,000. Both pies are drool-worthy. Beer L4000 per mug. Open Fri.-Wed. 9am-1pm and 5pm-1am.

Trattoria la Botte, Corso Vittorio Emanuele, 191 (tel. 8711 50). Full of merry locals. The hearty food is good but the atmosphere is the prime (and primal) draw. *Primi* L6000, *secondi* L6000-8000. Try the local wine from one of the wooden casks above the bar (L4000 per liter). Cover L1500. Open Mon.-Sat. 10:30am-3pm and 7-11pm.

Casablanca, Via San Francesco d'Assisi, 69 (tel. 200 50), near the port at Via Serisso. More soothing than Bogart's voice. Bubbling fountain, a large ceiling fan, and soft classical music. Pricey, but worth it. Try the local specialty *couscous con pesce* (L9000). Wine L500 per liter. Cover L2000. Open Tues.-Sun. noon-4pm and 7pm-1am.

Mensa Ferrovieri, at the train station. This employees' cafeteria is also open to tourists. All dishes made to order. Full meals (bread, pasta, meat, salad and beer or wine) L10,000. Open daily 11am-3:30pm and 6-10:30pm.

SIGHTS AND ENTERTAINMENT

You can tour Trápani's major sights in a pleasant afternoon. Begin one block off Corso Italia on Via S. Elisabetta, where the Gothic-Renaissance **Church of Santa Maria** displays a beautiful marble baldachin (1521) sheltering a Della Robbia terracotta. Farther up Corso Italia you'll hit Piazza S. Agostino which runs right into Piazzetta Saturno by way of Via S. Agostino, where the buildings begin to get older and more ornate and the cars aren't allowed to go. Here you'll find the façade of the former **Church of Sant'Agostino** (14th century), which preserves a Gothic portal and rose window. The **Fountain of Saturn,** a triple-tiered basin supported by sirens, dates from the late 16th century.

The main street of the old city, **Corso Vittorio Emanuele II,** around the corner, is lined with elaborate façades. At one end, the 17th-century **Palazzo Seratorio** houses temporary art exhibits on its main floor; the **Collegio dei Gesuiti** (1636) contains an 18th-century carved walnut cupboard; and the **cattedrale** displays a striking green-tiled dome and pink stucco walls. Down a small street to the left on Via Giglio, the tiny Baroque **Chiesa del Purgatorio** sports a free-standing sculpture and a small emerald dome outside, and a group of 20 incomprehensible wooden statues inside. This collection, called *I Misteri* (The Mysteries), is carried in a procession around the town on Good Friday. At this time, their bearers call out, asking if anyone knows whose they are or what they're used for. No one ever does, so they are returned to the church for another year. Their identification has been a mystery for over 600 years.

Viale Regina Elena runs along the port to **Viale Duca l'Acosta,** where fishermen dry and mend their nets. For a treat, get up at the crack of dawn, head down to see the fishermen do their stuff, and continue up to the tip of the city to see the sunrise at the **Torre di Ligny.** From the Torre you can take Via Libertà past the fish market at piazza Mercato de Pesce to **Via Garibaldi,** whose cream-colored *palazzi* are rivalled only by those of Corso V. Emanuele. Past the pink, twisted columns of the Chiesa del Carminello, a broad flight of steps to the right brings you to the **Church of San Domenico.**

Farther out in the new section of town visit the **Museo Nazionale Pepoli.** (It's a grueling walk; buses to the museum are run by **SAU** and they leave from Via G. Fardella, 2 blocks to the right of the station—take bus #1 or 10, L700.) The museum's magnificent Baroque interior staircase leads to a collection of local sculpture, painting, coral carvings, and folk-art figurines. (Open Wed. and Sat. 9am-1pm; Tues.-Fri. 9am-1pm and 3-6pm; Sun. 9am-12:30pm. Admission L2000, Sun. free.)

Trápani sponsors a festival of opera, ballet, and drama, **Luglio Musicale Trapanese** (tel. 229 34), which attracts troupes from abroad. It takes place in an open-air theater in the city park, the Villa Margherita, during the last three weeks of July. (Shows begin at 9pm. Admission from L12,000.) **Settimana dell'Egadi,** in late May, greets the new crop of tourists with music, food, and archeological tours, and of course there's the **Processione dei Misteri,** where you can moan and groan to the beat of the bemasked and becolored townsfolk as they march through the city on Good Friday, quizzing their clueless comrades about the statues they carry.

At night the young and the restless populate the beer gardens in P. XVIII Novembre or the *gelaterie* along Via Turetta, but only until 8:30pm, when the entire town passes out.

■ Near Trápani

San Vito lo Capo

The gentle shores of San Vito Lo Capo present an immense, sandy beach and a vast selection of *gelaterie.* Although it's a major resort for northerners, the town remains inexpensive, genuine, clean, and an ideal place to relax for a day. For more seclusion, drive 12km, or make the bus connection through Castellamare to Guida Loca, to the **Riserva dello Zingaro,** a nature preserve whose pastoral, cow-studded trails lead to crystalline coves and a grotto that could serve as the entrance to Dante's *Inferno.* Buses to San Vito leave from the Trápani *autostazione* at P. Malta (8 per day 7am-6:30pm, 1hr. 15min., L4400 one way, L7300 round-trip). The last bus back to Trápani on weekdays leaves at 8:15pm (Sun. return trips from 10am-8:15pm). For more on the Zingaro nature reserve, ask for information (in English) at the Trápani tourist office.

In recent years, more and more visitors have been flocking to the concrete-city **Gibellina Nuova.** Razed to the ground by a 1968 earthquake, the city has been rebuilt over the last 25 years with ultra-modern buildings and monuments which (the brochure says) "are themselves works of modern art." (From Trápani 6 buses per day 6am-5pm, returning 6:25am-5:50pm, 1hr.)

Érice

Only a short distance from the coast, Érice soars 750m above sea level. In ancient times, Érice was one of Sicily's most revered sites. As such, the city has been the mythical home to successive goddesses of fertility: first the Elymnian Astarte, then the Greek Aphrodite and the Roman Venus. Both the city itself and the vistas it affords are a visual delicacy. The outer walls date back to the 16th century BC, and the town is virtually unchanged from medieval times. The city has a number of worthwhile sights to visit, particularly the **Norman castle,** with its medieval towers (in typical Sicilian fashion, adorned with TV broadcast aerials), and the lush adjoining gardens. There is also a 14th-century **duomo** with a 13th-century bell tower. But the greatest pleasure is in strolling Érice's cobblestone streets, savoring the well-preserved buildings and the overwhelming views. The panoramas out over Trápani (occasionally reaching all the way to Tunisia) are tremendous.

The **Tourist Office (AAST)** is at Via C.A. Pepoli, 11, on the hill near the bus stop (tel. 869 388 or 869 173; open Mon.-Sat. 8am-2pm and 4-7pm; Sun 8am-2pm). The bus from Trápani leaves from P. Malta (Montalto) (Mon.-Sat. 12 per day, 6:30am-6:15pm., Sun. 5 per day 9am-6:15pm. Last bus back weekdays at 8:30pm, Sun. at 7:15pm, 45min., L4300 round-trip). As hotel prices tend to be as lofty as the altitude, Érice is best as a daytrip from Trápani. If you're stuck, the cheapest place is the **Edelweiss,** Cortile P. Vincenzo (tel. 86 91 58); singles with bath L80,000, doubles L120,000. Good cheap food is also hard to come by, and **La Pentolaccia,** Via Guarnotti, 17, is as close as you'll come (tel. 86 90 99). *Primi* run L7000 and *secondi* L8000; try the *farfalle dello chef* for a real treat. (Cover L2500. Open March-Nov. Sat.-Thurs. 12:30-3pm and 7:30-10pm. Closed Dec.-Feb.) Just down the block, the **Antica Pasticceria del Convento,** Via Guarnotti, 1 (tel. 869 005), makes sinfully good sweets for the nuns and the public alike. L16,000 buys a kilo, enough to earn four people an afternoon in purgatory. (Open daily 8:30am-1pm and 3pm-midnight.)

Égadi Islands (Isole Égadi)

The mid-afternoon summer sun is far kinder to the Égadi Islands than to their scorched neighbor, Sicily. Cats and local elders lounge on the terraces of the white-washed tufa houses nestled above the harbors, soothed by the warm massage of the scirocco. Pass by Favignana, tourist trap and home to the remnants of the archipelago's tuna trade, and head straight for the outlying islands of Maréttimo and Lévanzo. Connected by frequent ferry and hydrofoil service (both between islands and between the islands and Trápani; see Trápani, Ferries), these rough and barren islands—strewn with bushes, wildflowers, and lost sheep—offer archeological wonders, cool sea grottos, and hiking trails with incredible views.

Favignana

Site of a large military camp, industrial, gritty Favignana sports a traditional beach, the Lido Burrone, 3km across the island from the main harbor. Rent a bike (L5000 per day) and pedal to one of Italy's hidden treasures, an old quarry by the sea called the **Bue Marino** (Elephant Seal). A small number of overpriced *pensioni* and distant campgrounds await on Favignana; hop the hydrofoil to Maréttimo or Lévanzo. For food, raid the *alimentari* and pizzerias on Corso V. Emanuele.

Lévanzo

The prehistoric cave art in the **Cava del Genovese,** about an hour on foot from the port, is only viewable on a guided tour (in decipherable Italian only). Signor Castiglione, who will lead you to the caves on his burro, generally meets all hydrofoil arrivals and can be found at the Siremar office above the dock. (Fee: L15,000-20,000. You can also call him at 92 40 32.) The Paleolithic incisions are the most fascinating for their veracity and curvilinear form; one shows a horse with its head turned in a style of representational depth that predates the Renaissance by centuries. The Neolithic paintings of animals (such as pigs and cows) no longer inhabiting the islands illuminate the geological history of the archipelago. The island also offers a number of secluded beaches and grottos for swimming. Though no accommodations on the Egadi Islands are cheap, Levanzo is your best be if you refuse to stay on the mainland. Levanzo has only two *pensioni,* and though the prices are high, they are not outrageous. The first it **Pensione Paradiso** (tel. 92 40 70), which offers newly renovated rooms overlooking the sea. (Singles L40,000; Doubles L60,000. In July-Aug., full pension is obligatory, L100,000 per person. If it's in the off season, don't be afraid to bargain with them—they're as desperate as you are.) 15m up the hill is the **Pensione dei Fenici** (tel. 92 40 83), which has a large terrace and an even better view. (Singles L40,000; doubles L67,000.) Pick up groceries or bring food from Favignana or Trápani.

Sundown draws locals, travelers, and resident expats to the seaside café, where an evening of cards and a warm North African sirocco can easily stretch one cappuccino (L1500) into four. (Open until everyone decides to go to bed.)

Maréttimo

Maréttimo, the most remote of the Égadi Islands, offers the most remote atmosphere as well. Newly established hiking trails take you up and down the rocky cliffs of the island, and on clear days, the view stretches as far as Tunisia. A handful of cafés, *gelaterie,* and the **Torrente Trattoria,** on P. Umberto across from the Siremar office, vend sandwiches and *gelato.* If you like Maréttimo enough to stay overnight, ask at the Tratorria about renting a room in a private house for L20,000-25,000 per night. (There are no official accommodations on the island.)

■ Pantelleria

The appeal of this sun-baked volcanic island is rooted in its North African feel, tranquil countryside, and characteristic dome-roofed *dammuso* dwellings. You can climb the extinct volcano or meander through the terraced vineyards which yield raisins and Tanit, a famous raisin wine. The *sesi,* resembling the *nuraghi* of Sardinia and the *trulli* of Apulia, are the neolithic remnants of the island's earliest inhabitants. Ferries (**Siremar** and **Traghette delle Isole**, both L33,400) connect the island daily with Trápani. **Alitalia** flights leave from Trápani daily (call 87 36 36 for information) and from Pantelleria for the return trip; the airplane's a lot faster, but also more expensive (30min., L80,500). The cheapest place to stay is at the **Miryam,** Corso Umberto, 1 (tel. (0923) 91 13 74). Singles with bath L45,000-55,000, doubles with bath L80,000-96,000. The **Agadir,** Via Catania, 1 (tel. 91 11 00), offers half-pension for L60,000. In low season, singles with bath run L35,000 and doubles L60,000. Ask around on the docks about lodging in private homes, which can save you a lot.

The **Pro Loco,** Via San Nicola, 1 (tel. 91 18 38), can help you find a place if you're desperate. (Open Mon.-Sat. 9am-12:30pm and 5-8pm.) A **post office** and **bank** sit in the center of Piazza Cavour. Nearby is the home of Gianni Gabriele, who rents mopeds for only L30,000 a day (tel. 91 17 41); call to find out if anybody's home and to get directions to his unmarked house.

■ Segesta

One of the best-kept secrets of the archaeological world is the unfinished 5th-century Greek temple at Segesta. As you make the 1km hike from the train station, you'll catch glimpses of the **temple** ahead; note the ancient **theater** crowning the hill on the left. The ruins constitute the sole remains of the once-flourishing city of the native Sicilian people (Sikels). From mid-July until the first week of August during odd-numbered years, classical plays are performed in the ancient theater. Special buses leave P. Politeama in Palermo (1hr. 45min. before showtime) and P. Marina in Trápani (1hr. before showtime). Buy the L15,000-25,000 tickets from a travel agent in Palermo or Trápani. To reach the theater, walk up the road from the *bar* (20min.). Trains from Palermo and Trápani make daily stops at Segesta's station, but only in the summer (Palermo-Segesta L10,200; Trápani-Segesta L3200). **Buses** to Segesta are run by **Autoservizi Tarantola** (tel. 31 020), leaving Trápani at 8am, 10am, and 2pm Mon.-Sat., returning at 11am, 1pm, and 6pm (L4000 one-way, L6700 round-trip).

■ Marsala and Mozia

The island-city of **Mozia** began as an outpost of nearby Carthage, and passed an uneventful four centuries producing textiles until its destruction at the hands of the Syracusans in 397 BC. The survivors fled to the mainland of Cape Lilybeo and founded what is now **Marsala**. (The Arabs renamed *Lilybaeum* "Mars-Alí," port of Alí.) In 1575, Emperor Charles V successfully averted pirate attacks by hastily blocking off the port. An unfortunate side effect of this action, however, was a steady decline of the city which lasted several centuries. In 1860 Giuseppe Garibaldi and his army landed here to begin his infamous campaign of unification. These days, most Italians know the city as home to the famous Marsalan wine. Although Marsala is best visited just passing through on your way to the enigmatic Mozia, the city's museums and archaeological sites do have something to offer.

From the train station, Via Roma is a straight shot into Marsala's historic center, changing into Via XI Maggio at P. Matteotti. Following Via XI Maggio will land you in front of the 18th-century **Palazzo Comunale,** and the Baroque **duomo,** which stand in **Piazza della Repubblica.** A variety of sculpture from the 16th-century school of Gagini decorates the church's vast interior. Behind the *duomo* at Via Garraffa, 57, the **Museo degli Arazzi** contains Philip II's eight elaborate 16th-century tapestries illustrating Titus's war against the Jews. A polite request will get you a guided tour from the enthusiastic custodian. (Open daily 9am-1pm and 4-6pm. Admission L1000.) At the end of Via XI Maggio lies P. della Vittoria, separating the city from the sea. To the right is the entrance to Marsala's *zona archeologica*; to the left is the **Museo Baglio Anselmi,** which houses a 35m Carthaginian warship believed to have sunk during the Battle of the Égadi Islands, which ended the First Punic War in 241 BC. (Open Mon.-Tues. and Thurs.-Fri. 9am-1pm, Wed. and Sat.-Sun. 9am-1pm and 3-6pm. Free.) The nearby **Villa Romana** (Roman Tenement), one of the few buildings excavated in the vast archaeological zone, further documents Marsala's ancient past. (Open upon request at the Museo Lilybeo.) The small **Church of San Giovanni,** next to the museum, covers Grotta della Sibilla, a cave where a mythical Sibyl proclaimed her oracles.

To witness the production of Marsala wine, take a free tour of the **Cantina Florio** facilities, located on Lungomare Mediterraneo just past Via S. Lipari, to the left behind the train station. (Open to the public Mon.-Fri. 9am-noon and 3-6pm.) Marsala's **Pro Loco,** at Via Garibaldi, 45 (tel. 71 40 97), off Via XI Maggio, will direct you to other Marsala distillers and help find accommodations. (Open Mon.-Sat. 8am-2pm and 4-7pm.) **Trattoria da Pino,** Via San Lorenzo, 25 (tel. 71 56 52), offers a decent L18,000 *menù.* To get there from P. Repubblica, head away from the station on Via XI Maggio and bear left on Via Curatolo, which eventually becomes Via San Lorenzo. Nearby at Via San Lorenzo, 8, an unmarked **bakery** sells fresh, warm bread at L1100 a loaf (get there before noon). The cheapest hotel in town is the **Garden,** Via Gambini, 36 (tel. 98 23 20), follow signs from the right of the train station. (Singles L30,000, with bath L45,000. Doubles L55,000, with bath L70,000.)

Mozia (now known as San Pantaleo) was the scene of a monumental naval battle in which Dionysius of Syracuse annihilated the Carthaginian Himilco in 397 BC with the aid of that new super-weapon, the catapult. The near-deserted islet lies 8km north of Marsala, across a thin strait traversed hourly by a rickety little boat (Mon.-Sat. 9am-1pm and 3-6pm). Remains of the original, child-sacrificing Phoenician inhabitants are plentiful, from the ritual altar to the dry dock on the other side of the tiny island. Many of the island's archaeological finds are displayed in the tiny museum at the port.

To get to Marsala from Trápani, take a bus from P. Malta (5 per day, departs 6:50am-2pm, returns 7am-2:15pm, L3600 each way). The bus company in Marsala (**Municipilizatta,** tel. 95 11 05) runs six buses a day to and from Mozia, leaving from P. del Popolo. (Bus #4, L800, departs 6:45am-2:50pm, returns 7:15am-3:35pm.) The boat to Mozia leaves from a pier at the end of the road where this bus will let you off.

■ Selinunte

A magnificent jumble of ruins atop a plateau overlooking the Mediterranean, Selinunte (from the Greek *Selinus,* the wild celery that once grew in the valley) awes with its immensity and desolation. Composed primarily of three temples to the east (the only one standing was reconstructed in 1958) and an acropolis across the valley to the west (restructured 1925-1927), these piles of rubble recall Selinunte's glory as an ally of Syracuse in the 6th century BC. The city fortunes took a decided downturn after 409 BC, when the place was sacked by Segesta and Carthage; it was finally destroyed by its own people in 241 BC in anticipation of a Roman attack. Selinunte remains shrouded by an air of mystical isolation that justifies the sobriquet given it by the Arabs: "the place of the idols." (Open 8am-sunset. Admission L1000.) About a kilometer inland, the enormous half-quarried drums for unbuilt columns lie abandoned in a stone outcropping. In the field below is the one that got away.

Getting to Selinunte is a hassle. From Palermo, Trápani, or Marsala, take the bus or train to Castelvetrano. Blue buses leave for Selinunte from Castelvetrano's train station (at 2 and 5:50pm, not returning until the next day, 30min. L1500). To get there, follow Via Minghetti up the hill from the left of the train station. Make a left at the top onto Via Vittorio Emanuele; when this street comes to an end, go to the right through P. Garibaldi. P. San Giovanni is just beyond. If you miss the bus to Selinunte, Hotel Zeus, Castelvetrano's one hotel, is up the hill from the station at Via Veneto, 6 (tel. (0924) 90 55 65; singles L40,000, doubles L70,000). Cheaper stays (and more pleasing countryside) can be found in Selinunte. Costa d'Avorio, Via Stazione, 5 (tel. 46 207) has singles for L25,000 (with bath L30,000) and doubles for L40,000 (with bath L50,000). If you're desperate, see if the staff at Pro Loco in P. Garibaldi (see directions above) can help. (Open Mon.-Sat. 8am-1pm and 4-8 pm; no phone.)

■■■ AGRIGENTO

The Greek poet Pindar once lauded Agrigento as "Man's Finest City." The centuries since Pindar have introduced some tough competition for the title, but who's to say that Agrigento doesn't deserve it still? Agrigento's *centro storico* is a cobblestoned web of welcoming streets where butcher shops and Gucci boutiques sit comfortably side by side. The city has tree-lined Parisian-style avenues and squares, plus 4km of golden beach thrown in for good measure. Luigi Pirandello, winner of the 1934 Nobel Prize in Literature, was born here—something no Agrigentan will let you forget. Add to all this the fact that the city also boasts some of the world's best preserved classical Greek architecture, there's no contest. Pindar's been right all along.

ORIENTATION AND PRACTICAL INFORMATION

Agrigento marks the midpoint of Sicily's southern coast. The transportation terminals, along with a park in P. Moro, divide the Medieval from modern cities. Trains arrive at the station in **Piazza Marconi. Viale della Vittoria** is the arrow-straight, tree-lined boulevard that leads to the train station, then veers uphill to the right, coming to an end in **Piazza Vittorio Emanuele.** The staircase which leads up from P. Marconi brings you to one edge of **Piazzale Moro.** The cobblestoned **Via Atenea,** the old city's main drag, begins nearby. Along it you'll find most of the town's shops and restaurants.

Trains run from the station to Palermo (11 per day, 1hr. 30 min., L10,700), and Catania via Caltanissetta and Enna (4 per day, 3hrs., L12,800 to Catania, 2hr., L8800 to Enna). **Buses** gather up the hill past P. Vittorio Emanuele, in P. Roselli, an otherwise empty lot. From Trapani, **Autoservizi Lumia** (tel. (0922) 20 414) runs **4 buses** daily to Agrigento (departures from Trapani's P. Garibaldi; 4hr., L14,500). From Marsala, take the train to Castelvetrano (15 per day, 1hr., L3700), and then one of four daily buses to Agrigento (L9600) via Selinunte and Ribera. From Ragusa, take an **AST** bus (tel. (0932) 62 1249) to Gela (3 per day, L5400), where you can switch to a **Licata** bus to Agrigento (tel. (0922) 40 1360; 5 per day, L6800). **Autoservizi Cuffaro** (tel. (0922) 91 63 49) makes 6 trips a day to and from Palermo's P. Balsamo (2hr. 15min., L10,200).

Finally, **SAIS** buses (tel. (0922) 59 52 60) ticket and info office down the hill from P. Roselli serve Catania (8 per day, 2hr. 30min., L16,000).

Tourist Office: AAST, Via Atenea, 123 (tel. 20 454). Convenient and unusually enthusiastic with good map and helpful information and handouts. Open Mon.- Sat. 8 am-2 pm and 4:30-6:30 pm.

Post Office: P. Vittorio Emanuele, with the great Fascist "worker style" mosaics out front. Full services (including telegraphs and **currency exchange**) open Mon.-Fri. 8:10am-noon. Basic services (letters, stamps, packages) Mon.-Sat. 8:10am-7:30pm.

Postal Code: 92100.

Telephones: SIP, Via Atenea, 96. Open daily 9am-noon and 4:30-7:45pm. **Telephone Code:** 0922.

Buses: Most city buses depart from the train station. #8, 9, 10 and 11 run to the Valley of Temples, #10 to San Leone. Fare L600. Buy tickets at any newsstand or tabacchi.

Ferries: Siremar, Porto Empedocle (tel. 63 66 83). Take a bus from the train station (at least 1 per hr., L2000). To the **Pelagie Islands,** Linosa (L40,000) and Lampedusa (L 50,000). 1 departure per day at midnight, arriving Linosa at 5:45am, Lampedusa at 10:15am, and Linosa at noon. Tickets at the Siremar office in the port. Get there at least an hour before departure.

Emergencies: tel. 113. **Police:** P. Moro (tel. 59 63 22). **Hospital: Ospedale Civile San Giovanni di Dio** (tel. 40 13 44), off P. S. Giuseppe on Via Atenea.

ACCOMMODATIONS AND CAMPING

Hotel Bella Napoli, P. Lena, 6 (tel. 20 435), off Via Bic Bac, which leads uphill from the high end of Via Atenea. Simple, clean rooms are adequately furnished; rooftop terrace overlooks the valley. Singles L25,000, with bath L35,000. Doubles L40,000, with bath L55,000.

Hotel Concordia, Via San Francesco, 11 (tel. 59 62 66). Close to the train station. Take Via Pirandello from the top of the steps that lead into P. Moro. The rooms are tiny, but spotless. Sits on an active market square. Singles L25,000, with bath L30,000. Doubles L40,000, with bath L60,000.

Hotel Villa Belvedere, Via San Vito, 20 (tel. 20 051), at the top of the stairs which begin by the Restaurant Kalos, opposite P. Moro. The modern rooms are dark, clean, and quiet. A two-star establishment, for whatever that's worth. Singles L30,000, with bath L50,000. Doubles L50,000, with bath L70,000.

Camping in Agrigento is fairly expensive and removed from the city. The two campgrounds do, however, have beautiful beach fronts, so if you want to bum around California-style, this is the place.

Internazionale San Leone (tel. 41 612). L7000 per person, L5000 per small tent, L8000 for large ones. Open April-Oct.

Internazionale Nettuno (tel. 41 62 68) L6500 per person, L5000 for small tents. Open year-round. Check with tourist office before heading out as bus service is sporadic. The sites are popular and have similar facilities (showers, restaurants, markets), though Int'l San Leone has a bit more shade. It's best to bring your own food in from town, as the campground "markets" are expensive. Occasional #10 buses to San Leone come out this far (a zone called "Le Dune," the Dunes), otherwise you'll have to hike the 3 km from the center of S. Leone (face the beach and walk to the left).

FOOD

There are a couple of small fruit and vegetable stands in front of the Hotel Concordia (Open Mon.-Sat. mornings). Agrigento's **STANDA** doesn't stock food, so your best bet is one of the small *alimentari* lining Via Pirandello or Via Atenea. Indulge a sweet tooth at the candy stalls along Via della Vittoria (open all day and well into the evening). The specialty is *torrone,* a heavy, creamy, nut-filled toffee. The "market" by the soccer field consists of a bunch of stalls selling cheap clothes.

Trattoria Atenea, Via Ficani, 12 (tel. 20 247), the 4th right off Via Atenea from P. Moro. 2-course lunch L15,000; dinner *menù* L12,000. Extensive sea-food offerings. *Calamari* (squid) or *gamberi* (shrimp), both L9000. Wine L4000 per liter. Open Mon.-Sat. noon-3:30pm and 7-midnight.

Ristorante Pizzeria, La Corte degli Sfilzi, 4 (tel. 59 55 20), in the *cortile* (garden) Contarini off Via Atenea. Fancy floral-print tablecloths bear witness the fine food.

Go for the *pizza menù,* your choice of pizza, *insalata mista,* and wine or beer, including cover and service (L12,000). Regular *menù* L14,000. Open Thurs.-Tues. noon-3pm and 6:30pm-midnight. Summer weekdays, open for dinner only.

Trattoria Black Horse, Via Celauro, 8 (tel. 23 223), off Via Atenea. An interesting family-run establishment. Ask the cook to sing as you wait and you'll be treated to some Verdi. *Tronchetto dello chef* (L6500) is the specialty: a thick lasagna packed with peas, ham, and meat sauce. Veal Scallopine "Black Horse" is a worthy *secondo.* Wine L5000. Cover L2000. Open Mon.-Sat. noon-3pm and 7-11pm. AmEx, MC, Visa.

Paninoteca Manhattan, Salita M. Angeli, 9, (tel. 59 66 95), up the steps to the right off Via Atenea near P. Moro. Creative Italian sandwiches with creative American names. The "Rokhfeller" combines tuna, pepper, lettuce, *insalata russa,* tabasco, and a healthy dose of whiskey (L4000), while the "Brooklin" sports 'shrooms, cheese, lettuce, and *pancetta* (L4000). Innumerable brands of beer L3500. Open Mon.-Sat. 8:30am-3pm and 5:30pm-midnight.

Trattoria La Forchetta, P. San Francesco, off Via Atenea. Authentic Agrigentan cuisine in a restful setting. *Primi* from L6000. *Secondi* from L8000. Excellent *calamari fritto* (fried squid) L9500. Cover L1000. Service 10%. Open Mon.-Sat. 12:30-3pm and 6:30-11pm.

▌IGHTS AND ENTERTAINMENT

▪lle dei Templi

▪grigento's star attraction is the **Valle dei Templi** (Valley of the Temples), a couple
▪ kilometers down the hill from the modern city. Take bus #8, #9, #10, or #11 from
▪e train station (last bus back at 9:45pm; L600) and ask to be dropped off at the
▪uartiere *Ellenistico-Romano* (Hellenistic-Roman Quarter). With its four roads ter-
▪ed building complex, it provides an excellent idea of the old city's organization.
▪escend the hill to the **Museo Nazionale Archeologico di San Nicola** to orient
▪urself. The museum contains a notable collection of artifacts, especially vases
▪m Agrigento and the rest of central Sicily. (As of 1993, the museum's hours have
▪en cut down for lack of personnel; open Mon.-Fri. 9am-1pm, Sat. 9am-5pm. Free.)
▪e adjacent **Church of San Nicola,** a small 13th-century Romanesque-Gothic
▪urch on the site of a Greek sanctuary, preserves Roman sarcophagi with reliefs
▪picting the death of Phaedra (2nd chapel on the right). Unfortunately, the church
▪only opened for weddings (if you're lucky and one is in progress, it's no problem
▪ sneak in and have a look around). Walking 1km down the busy road in front of
▪e museum will bring you to a dirt lot, a snack bar, and lots of tour buses: the cen-
▪r of the Valley of the Temples.

▪With the exception of the temples of Concord and Juno, the structures here were
▪stroyed by a combination of earthquakes and early Christian anti-paganism. In the
▪e adjacent to the parking lot are the ruins of the **Tempio di Giove Olimpico.** Had
▪ construction not been halted by the Carthaginian sack of the city in 406-405 BC,
▪would have been one of the largest Greek temples ever built. Now little is left;
▪ost of the temple's stone was carted away in the 18th century to build a jetty at
▪arby Porto Empedocle. The temple's 38 18m columns were supported by 8m
▪*lemones*—figures standing in as supporting columns. A reconstructed *telemon*
▪s alongside the ruins. Further along in the same area, the four columns supporting
▪ entablature represent the piecemeal effort to rebuild the 5th-century BC **Tempio**
▪ **Castore e Polluce** (Castor and Pollux). Across from the parking lot are the few
▪maining columns of the **Tempio di Ercole** (Heracles), the oldest temple (6th cen-
▪ry BC) here.

▪Uphill from the Temple of Hercules looms the **Tempio della Concordia,** the most
▪tact (34 columns!) Greek temple in the world after the Temple of Theseus in Ath-
▪s. The temple was erected in the mid-5th century out of limestone, now faded
▪lden. It owes its remarkable preservation to early sanctification as a Christian
▪urch by the then-Bishop of Agrigento San Gregorio delle Rape (St. Gregory of the

Turnips). The niches in the interior walls originally created for Christian worship a still visible.

In Agrigento

The **Tempio di Giunone** (Juno) dates from the same period as the Temple of th Concord and though nowhere near as well-preserved, it commands the greate view from the top of the hill. On your way down, you'll pass the **Paleochristia Necropolis,** those holes in the ground that look more like a beehive.

The most interesting building in Medieval Agrigento is the small, 11th-centu Norman **Church of Santa Maria dei Greci,** which occupies the site of a 5th-centu BC Doric temple. (Follow the signs up the hill from the top of Via Bac off Via A nea.) Part of the wooden Norman ceiling remains, as well as a portion of the 14t century Byzantine frescoes. Look for the astonishing secret tunnel, which you ca enter from the courtyard. It preserves the stylobate (the platform beneath the c umns) and the six stumps of the ancient temple. (If closed, call 59 54 79.)

The **Chiesa del Purgatorio** (Church of Purgatory) in P. Purgatorio houses eig statues representing the Virtues and a few stuccos by Serpotta. The left of th church, underneath a sleeping lion, is the entrance to a network of undergroun channels and reservoirs built by the Greeks in the 5th century BC. Wanderin behind the church on Via Fodera will lead you to **Santo Spirito,** a complex contai ing a chapel, charterhouse, and refectory (now used as a library), founded by Ciste cian nuns at the end of the 13th century. The church displays more beautif stuccos (1693-1695) by Serpotta, illustrating scenes from Christ's life; ring the be on the church door to enter.

For a change of pace you can visit the birthplace of playwright **Luigi Pirandello** P. Kaos (named for Pirandello's most famous work). Take bus #11 to this sma museum of books and notes, honored by his gravestone in the backyard. (Op weekdays 9am-1hr. before sunset; Sat.-Sun. 9am-1pm. Free.) The **Settmana Pira delliana,** a week-long festival of plays, operas, and ballets performed out-of-doors P. Kaos takes place in late July and early August (tickets L10,000-20,000; cancelled 1993 for lack of funds—check with the tourist office or call (0922) 26 333 for inf mation on the status of the '94 festival).

The first Sunday of February brings the **Almond Blossom Festival,** an intern tional folk event in the Valley of the Temples. In early July, townsfolk throw bre to the effigy of St. Calogero in gratitude for curing the city of a deadly yeast e demic. **San Leone,** 4km from Agrigento (easily accessible by bus #10), is laden wi splendid stretches of beach. Beginning in the early evening, *ragazzi* gather in fro of the beach-side **Aster** game room/pizzeria to strut their stuff and sing along to th music pouring out of all the cafés. Last bus to Agrigento at 9:45 pm.

Near Agrigento: Pelágie Islands

The islands of **Lampedusa** and **Linosa,** though geologically part of the African con nent, belong politically to the province of Agrigento. They're an easy, budget-bu ing ferry ride from Porto Empedocle (one-way to Lampedusa L50,000 to Lino L40,000). The island is noted for its peculiar Arabic architecture, peregrine falcor seals, and virile sea turtles; revel in fauna at the Isola dei Conigli nature reserve. Lin sa's greatest riches lie underwater: the island is famous for unbeatable snorkelin and diving. Unfortunately, the port areas have become infested with bacteria and balls from the islands' sewage facilities.

Accommodations aren't cheap on the islands. **Albergo Oasi** (tel. 97 06 30) le singles for L40,000 and doubles with bath for L80,000; **Albergo Belvedere** (tel. 01 88), offers half-pension at L75,000 per person. On Linosa try **Hotel Algusa.** (T 97 20 52. Singles with bath L40,000. Doubles with bath L75,000.)

Lampedusa has the most to choose from. **Albergo Oasi** (tel. 97 06 30) lets singl for L13,500 and doubles for L22,500, or try **Albergo Belvedere** (tel. 97 01 8 where singles with bath are L18,000 and doubles with bath L31,500. You won't I

ssing the night on Linosa without a fat wallet; a 3-star **Hotel Algusa** is cheapest.
el. 97 20 52. Singles with bath L65,000-90,0000. Doubles L100,000-150,000.)

Enna

his is Sicily's best-kept secret. Soaring above the poorest and only landlocked prov-
ce in Sicily, inviolate Enna invites you to view the life of the island's interior.
nans are prone to modesty and self-deprecation, and coastal Sicilians view them
th a condescending eye, a combination which has made Enna Sicily's best-kept
cret: a cool, animated city with numerous piazze offering panoramas of the sur-
unding countryside. Ennans are quick to point out that theirs is a city of true tran-
ility, and the only capital without a mafia presence. They take their time and
rely fret: perched atop a mountain 948m above sea level, watching over the entire
nd, there is no need to worry.

Throughout its history, the town has been a popular military base, passing from
e hands of its original inhabitants to Greek, Roman, Arab, Norman, Lombard, and
urbon rule. The only vestiges of this past are a huge medieval castle, a Lombard
wer, and a curiously remodeled 13th-century cathedral.

RIENTATION AND PRACTICAL INFORMATION

nna, located at the center of the island, is known as the "navel of Sicily." It is easily
ccessible by bus from Palermo or Catania; voyaging from the south requires trans-
rs at either Caltanissetta (Mon.-Sat., 4 per day, 1hr., L4000) or Gela (2 daily, 1hr.,
600). Buses leave Catania from the train station (7 per day, 3 on Sun., 1hr. 15min.,
000) and Palermo from Via P. Balsamo, 16 (3 per day, 2 on Sun., 2 hr., L11,000).
here is also train service from Catania (11 per day, 1hr. 30min., L6500) and Pal-
mo (6 per day, 2hr., L13,200), but Enna's train station is 5km downhill from the
nter of town. Fortunately there are hourly buses connecting the station and the
ty center (schedule posted in the train station, L1500). To get to the center of Enna
m the bus depot, turn right onto Viale Diaz in front of the station and then take
other right onto Corso Sicilia; walk until Via Sant'Agata branches off to the right.
his runs directly into **Via Roma,** Enna's main strip, at P. Matteoti. This *via* then
ads past **Piazza Vittorio Emanuele** and up to the **Castello di Lombardia** on the
ft, to the right it winds through a residential and shopping district, eventually com-
g to an end in the vicinity of the **Torre di Federico.**

Tourist Office: AAPIT, Via Roma, 413 (tel. 50 05 44 or 50 05 48). One of Sicily's
best. Extremely informative and well-organized. Pick up the fine map of Enna
with a very detailed map of the whole island on the obverse. Open Mon.-Fri.
8:30am-1:30pm and 3:30-6:30pm, Sat. 8:30am-1:30pm. **ASST,** P. Colajanni, 6 (tel.
26 119), 100m up from the AAPIT and to the right. Smaller, but also well-organized. Open Tues.-Fri. 8am-2pm and 4:30-7:30pm (winter 4-7pm), Mon. and Sat.
8am-2pm.

Currency Exchange: Banks along Via Roma, between P. Vittorio Emanuele and P.
Umberto I.

Post Office: Via Volta, 1 (tel. 21 729). Take a left off Via Roma just before the
AAPIT, and walk to the right behind the building labeled "Provincia." Open Mon.-
Fri. 8am-7:30pm, Sat. 8am-2pm. **Postal code:** 94100.

Telephones: SIP, P. Scelfo (tel. 24 034), below P. Vittorio Emmanuele. Open daily
8am-8pm. At other times, try **Albergo Sicilia,** P. Colajanni. **Telephone code:**
0935.

Buses: SAIS, Viale Diaz (tel. 50 09 02), outside the city center. Open daily 6am-
2pm and 3:15-8:30pm.

Emergencies: tel. 113. **Police:** tel. 112. **Hospital: Ospedale Umberto I,** tel. 452
45. **Guardia Medica:** tel. 45 489.

ACCOMMODATIONS AND FOOD

The town's only hotel is the **Hotel Sicilia,** P. Colajanni, 5 (tel. 50 08 50), on V
Roma past the AAPIT office. This modern building is posh and clean, with a gr
view and there's a TV in every room. (Singles L77,000. Doubles L134,000. Tripl
L167,000. All-you-can-eat breakfast included. All rooms with shower.) If there are
vacancies at the hotel, or too many vacancies in your wallet, head down the mor
tain to the smaller (and cheaper) lakeside town of **Pèrgusa.** Buses #4 make the 7k
trip hourly from the bus station and from Via Roma just below P. Vittorio Emma
uele (L600). In Pèrgusa, the **Miralogo** (tel. 54 12 72), right before the entrance
town, charges L30,000 for singles and L50,000 for doubles (both with bath). I
past the center of town, **Hotel La Pergola** (tel. 54 17 33) offers singles for L24,0
and doubles for L37,000 (both with bath), overlooking Pèrgusa's totally-out-of-c
text **Formula One racetrack.** There is a **campsite** on the lake, but in 1993 it w
occupied by the Italian Army, because of worries over increased Mafia activity in S
ily. Check at the AAPIT in Enna for current status.

Enna's most famous comestible is its *piacentino* cheese, sharp, spicy, and it
be sampled at the **market** on Via Mercato Sant'Antonio, off Via Roma at P. Umbe
I. (Open Mon.-Sat. 7:30am-2pm and 4-8:30pm.) **Centro Formaggi** at Via Merc
Sant'Antonio, 33, has a much larger selection. **TOPS Discount Alimentare,** up
steps behind the bus station, is a warehouse-style supermarket. (Open Mon.-S
8am-2pm and 4:30-9pm, Sun. 8am-1pm.) For a quick fix and a hip mix, try **Knu**
Via Restivo, 14, off Via Roma to the left just past P. Umberto and the Municip
What is Sicily's coolest bar-eatery (named after a Herman Hesse novel) doing in p
vincial Enna? Don't ask, just groove to the James Brown or jam on your own w
the guitar and bongos in the corner. The **Panino Funny Bread** has strong g
gonzola cheese, prosciutto, and chicory (L4000). The menu also features a w
array of vegetarian *panini* (L3000) and Guinness on tap (L6000 for a large be
(Open daily 11am-2pm and 6pm-2am. Closed Mon. in winter.)

SIGHTS AND ENTERTAINMENT

Via Roma ascends through the old city, leading to the **cathedral.** Founded in 1
and renovated in the 16th century, it has a slender Baroque façade. The polygo
transepts, the apses, and the south door remain from the original medieval str
ture. Behind the church, the small **Museo Alessi** displays the *duomo's* treasury a
some Greco-Roman artifacts and medieval paintings. (Open Tues.-Sun. 9am-1
and 4-7pm. Free.) There is the nearby **Museo Varisano,** which exhibits pott
shards and figurines. (Open Mon.-Sat. 9am-1:30pm and 3:30-6:30pm, Sun. 9:30
1pm and 3:30-6:30pm. Free.)

The **Castello di Lombardia,** constructed on a 5000-year-old foundation at
eastern end of town, was built by Frederick II to maintain control of the center
the island. Six of the original 20 towers remain. One of its three courtyards is n
used as an open-air theater. The castle offers a thrilling view of the mete
impressed Lago Pèrgusa; myth has it that Hades abducted Demeter's daughter Pe
phone from its shores. The small town you see clinging to the next mountain ove
Calascibetta. Behind the castle, at the summit of the mountain, is Demeter's sac
ground, the **Rocca di Cerere,** imparting a view of the fertile fields below. (Ca
open daily 9am-7pm. Free.)

The **Torre di Federico II,** an octagonal lookout with excellently preserved Got
vaulting, rises 24m at the opposite edge of the city, surrounded by the city's pu
garden. (Garden open daily 9am-8pm. Free.) A secret tunnel, still visible from
tower's third level, once connected the tower with the Castello di Lombardia.
get to the tower, walk along Via Roma past the Upim department store (away fr
P. Vittorio Emmanuele). Via Roma eventually turns into Via della Libertà. Turn
onto Viale 4 Novembre to reach the foot of the public gardens. (Access to the tov
only by permission from the gatekeeper, whose house is on the grounds of the p
lic gardens. Tower under restoration in 1993.)

One of Enna's largest festivals is the **Festa della Madonna,** held on July 2, marked by the incessant popping of firecrackers and the interminable eating of renowned *mastazzoli* (apple cookies). Parties also accompany the feasts of **Saint Anna** on the last Sunday in July and **Saint Valverde** on the last Sunday in August. Enna's most renowned festival, however, is its **Holy Week.** Different groups and religious orders don unique costumes, revealing the Spanish influence once quite strong in Sicily.

Down the hill at the **Autodromo di Pèrgusa,** processions are of another (faster) sort. Pèrgusa's lakeside racetrack hosts international Gran Prix car races year-round. The most important ones take place in June, July, September, and October (tel. 25 660 for info).

Near Enna: Piazza Armerina

The golden Baroque buildings of **P. Armerina** rise gracefully on three knolls over-looking the Ennese countryside. Nearby is the **Villa Romana del Casale,** a Roman country house that preserves some of the ancient world's finest mosaics.

The villa lies 5.5km southwest of town. Officially known as the Villa Romana del Casale, it was probably a hunting lodge of Maximanius Heraclius, co-emperor with Diocletian under the Principate. The villa was built around 300 AD and was occupied until the Arab period. Sacked in 1160 and buried by a landslide soon after, it remained undiscovered until 1916. The villa houses no less than 40 rooms of vivid **mosaics,** the largest and most intact of their kind in the world. In the Corridor of the Big Game Hunt, a varied landscape of hills, trees, rocks, and villas surrounds hunters pursuing their game while the hunted animals themselves chase smaller prey. The *sala ragazze in bikini* ("bikini-girl room") is just what its name suggests: women in skimpy swimsuits play beach ball and lift weights. More soft porn comes your way in the *cubicolo scena erotica,* near the exit to the villa. Be sure to pick up a guide to the villa (along with a map) at the tourist office in Enna or Piazza Armerina—it helps immeasurably to find your way around and discover what's what. (From May 1-Sept. 30 buses (L500) shuttle back and forth between the villa and Piazza Armerina. Departures on the hour, 9-11am and 4-6pm.) Flag the bus down as it rolls past the Hotel Villa Romana (see below). (The villa is open daily 9am-7pm. Admission L2000, under 18 and over 60, free.) If you're really taken by it, ask for information about some of the other nearby villas, such **Morgantina, Ardone,** and **Nicosia.**

Piazze filled with pine, eucalyptus, poplar, and cedar trees punctuate P. Armerina's narrow medieval streets. In the center is **P. Garibaldi,** with several 18th-century buildings. The **duomo** (1627) at the summit of the town peers down with its impos-ing Baroque façade (17th-18th c.) and a 15th-century Gothic-Sicilian belfry. Inside, the painted crucifix and the Madonna in the chapel to the left both date from the 15th century. Above the high altar, a baroque tabernacle contains a Byzantine icon of the *Madonna della Vittoria,* a gift of Pope Nicholas II. It is carried in procession during the **Feast of the Assumption** (August 15). The Feast of the Assumption is preceded on August 13-14 by the **Palio dei Normanni,** a costumed horse race com-memorating the presentation of the key to the city to the Norman Count Roger III.

P. Armerina is a 45-minute **bus** ride from Enna (7 per day, 3 on Sundays and holi-days; L3700). Buses also run directly to Palermo, Catania, and Syracuse via Catania. To reach Ragusa on the way east or south, take a bus to the petrochemical waste-land of Gela (several per day, 1hr., L4600; ask at least 3 bus drivers hanging out in P. Gen. Cascino to triangulate the correct times). From Gela, the best option is the train (7 per day, 1hr. 30min., L5700). Be sure to allow time to catch the last bus out (around 4pm), or you'll find yourself stranded.

In general, buses in Piazza Armerina gather in Piazza Generale Cascino, which sits on the new city's principal street, Via Generale Muscarà. The streets to follow to get to the old city (an easy walk) are well-indicated by a yellow sign at the edge of P. Cascino. City tourist information, Via Cavour, 15 (tel. 68 02 01) is signposted from Piazza Garibaldi, once you've arrived in *centro.* (Open Mon.-Sat. 8am-2pm and 4:30-7:30pm.) Piazza Armerina has no inexpensive accommodations, but if you're stuck, try the **Hotel Selene** (tel. 68 22 54). Walk up Via Muscarà several blocks away from the old city and make a diagonal right across the first large piazza you come to. (Spacious singles with bath L55,000. Doubles L85,000. AmEx, MC, Visa.) Another option is the **Hotel Villa Romana,** Piazza Alcide de Gasperi (tel. 68 29 11), at the bottom of Via Roma, which begins in P. Garibaldi. (Singles with bath L60,000. Doubles with bath L90,000.) They also offer some budget rooms with communal bathrooms and showers. (Singles L25,000; doubles L40,000.) The problem is that these go fast and there are very few to begin with. Out by the turn-off for the mosaics (4km. outside of the city), the **Trattoria La Ruota** (tel. 68 05 42) also runs an informal **campground.** The owners are helpful, the food is yummy, and the price is negotiable (L2000-4000 per person; bring your own tent.) **Picnics** are the best eating option in Piazza Armerina. **Supermercato CRAI** on Via Muscarà a few blocks from the buses has good deals and friendly service. (Open Mon.-Sat. 8am-1pm and 4:30-8pm, Sun. 8:30am-12:30pm.)

■ Ragusa

The provincial capital of Ragusa has quietly avoided the frenetic pace of other Sicilian cities, simultaneously managing to escape inclusion on most tourist itineraries. The city has grown uphill from its beginnings at **Ragusa Ibla,** so that walking the streets is tantamount to following an architectural timeline. The old city begins with a well-preserved Baroque center, constructed 300 years ago after the town was completely destroyed by an earthquake, then winds up and down the hills toward a frenzy of construction in the new city, near the station. Along the way, the city displays all of the intervening stylistic periods. The streets here evolve from an orderly grid into a chaotic weave of terraced alleys. The citizens seem to acknowledge the taxonomy of new and old town: the young hang out in the former, while their elders congregate in the latter. Though the Ragusan pace of life is somewhere between comatose and dead, the old city will reward the dedicated street-wanderer with architectural treasures and near-perfect solitude.

ORIENTATION AND PRACTICAL INFORMATION

The train and bus stations are in P. del Popolo and nearby P. Gramsci, respectively. To reach the city center from these adjacent *piazze,* hang a left as you exit either station onto **Viale Emanuele Lena,** go through P. Libertà, and walk up to the Ponte Senatore F. Pennavaria, the northernmost of three bridges crossing the Vallata Santa. The *ponte* runs directly into **Via Roma,** which continues across town to its abrupt end at the edge of a moonscape. **Corso Italia,** off Via Roma, leads downhill several blocks, changes into Via 24 Maggio, and ends at the **Chiega di Santa Maria delle Scale.** From here, stairs zig-zag the rest of the way down the hill to **Ragusa Ibla.**

The only big city that's well-connected to Ragusa by **train** is Syracuse (5 per day, 2hr. 15min., L8800). There are also 5 per day from Gela (1 hr. 30 min., L5700). One or two trains per day make the trip from Agrigento (4hr., L13,800) or Palermo (L22,000). AST **buses** run regularly from Syracuse's Piazzale Marconi (Mon.-Sat. 8 per day, Sun. at 9am and 2:30pm; 3hr., L7500). There are three buses per day to Palermo (L17,900), and three to Gela (1hr. 30min., L4500), where a connection can be made to Agrigento (4 per day, 1hr. 30min., L9600). From Enna, take the bus to Gela (1hr. 30min., L8600) and then the train (1hr. 30min., L5700).

Tourist office: AAPIT Via Capitano Bocchieri, 33 (tel. 62 14 21), in Ragusa Ibla, signposted in P. del Duomo. (For directions to Ragusa Ibla and P. del Duomo, see *Sights and Entertainment* below.) You'll be welcomed royally (red carpet included) to this former *palazzo* by a flood of thick guides and brochures on the city and the province. Open Mon.-Sat. 8am-2pm.

Currency exchange: banks on Via Lena and Via Roma. Outside of banking hours, try **Viaggi Turismo** (tel. 65 43 31) on Via Lena near the bus station. Open Mon.-Fri. 9am-1pm and 4-7:30pm, Sat. 9am-1pm.

Post Office: P. Matteotti, (tel. 62 23 21), 2 blocks down Corso Italia from Via Roma. Open Mon.-Sat. 8am-7:30pm. **Postal code:** 97100.
Telephones: SIP, Via Maiorana, on the city side of Ponte Vecchio (the middle bridge). Open Mon.-Sat. 9am-12:30pm and 4:30-8pm. **Telephone Code:** 0932.
Buses: AST (tel. 62 12 49), in P. Gramsci. Schedules posted on side of building bordering the depot. Buy tickets on bus. **ETNA** to Catania (10 per day, 6 on Sun.; 3hr., L8900). A ticket office and schedule is located in the GranBar, across from P. Gramsci.
Emergencies: tel. 113. **Police:** tel. 62 34 00 or tel. 112. **Hospital: Ospedale Civile,** right across from the train station on Via Leonardo da Vinci (tel. 62 14 10 during the day; tel. 62 39 46 for nighttime and holiday emergencies).

ACCOMMODATIONS AND FOOD

Hotel San Giovanni, Via Transpontino, 3 (tel. 62 10 13), off the center bridge on the station side. A quiet, clean hotel with great beds and marble bathrooms. TV in every room. Singles L39,000, with bath L55,500. Doubles L50,000, with bath L85,000. AmEx, MC, Visa.
Hotel Jonio: Via Risorgimento, 4a (tel. 62 43 22). Closest to the train station; walk down Viale Sicilia from P. del Popolo. Darker than the San Giovanni, but the showers are strong and hot. TV in every room. Singles L26,000, with bath L55,000. Doubles (with bath only) L75,000. MC, Visa.
Camping: Ragusa's campgrounds are at Marina, 20 km to the south. Tumino buses (tel. 62 31 84) run regularly from P. Gramsci in Ragusa to P. Duca degli Abruzzi in Marina (30min.; L2900, round-trip L4900). **Baja del Sole,** (tel. 39 844). L6000 per person, L6000 per small tent, L9000 per large tent, L7000 per person with sleeping bag. **Villa Nifosì** (tel. 39 118) runs L7000 per person, L7000 per tent, L10,000 per large tent, L7000 per person with sleeping bag. Oct-May, prices drop by L500-1000. Buy supplies at SMA in Ragusa before heading out *(see below)*.

While in Ragusa, make a point to try some *panatigghie,* thin pastries filled with cocoa, cinnamon, and ground meat. Unfortunately, they aren't cheap, and neither are the *trattorie* where they're sold. If you're tapped for cash, visit the immense **SMA Supermarket** on Viale Sicilia, down hill to the right from the train station (open Mon.-Sat. 8:30am-1:30pm and 4:30-8pm, Wed. 8:30am-1:30pm only).

Pizzeria La Grotta, Via G. Cartia (tel. 55 795), the 2nd right off Via Roma at the red sign. Melt-in-your-mouth pizzas (L2000 per slice) and *calzoni* (L2000); draft beer L2500 and up. Open Wed.-Mon. 6am-2pm and 5pm-midnight.
La Valle, Via Risorgimento, 66 (tel. 293 41). From the station take a right onto Viale Sicilia, then walk downhill past the gas station. *The* place young Ragusans recommend, though on the pricey side. Pasta L5500-8000. A wide variety of pizzas L6000-8000. Open Sat.-Thurs. noon-3pm and 8pm-midnight. AmEx, MC, Visa.
Latalena Self-Service, Via Risorgimento, 30 (tel. 65 25 88), just a few blocks from the station, to the left off Viale Sicilia. Savor the L12,000 *menù* or pizza and explore the delicacies under the glass next to the register. Green tablecloths (tasteful light green) and a view. Upscale. Open Tues.-Sun. noon-3pm and 7pm-midnight.
Caffè Trieste, Corso Italia, 76 (tel. 62 21 10), across from the post office. Superior Sicilian pastries (L1500-2000) and perfect iced espresso (L1500). No seats, just pit-stop consumption. Open Mon.-Sat. 6:30am-10pm.

SIGHTS AND ENTERTAINMENT

Judge Ragusa and Ibla by their exteriors—church interiors rarely match their elaborate Baroque façades. The many side streets delight with their ornamented doorways. The upper town boasts an **Archaeology Museum** (tel. 62 29 63) that lies one door down and in back of the STANDA off Via Roma, with artifacts from the nearby Syracusan colony of Camarina. (Open Mon.-Sat. 9am-2pm, daily 3-6:30pm, Sun. 9am-1pm. Free.) Via Santa Anna, your first right off Via Roma, is crossed by Via della

Frecce and Via dei Vespri, two small streets lined with some of Ragusa's mo charming homes.

To get to **Ragusa Ibla,** take the #3 city bus (L600, tickets in *tabacchi*), leavi every hour on the half-hour from in front of the train station at P. del Popolo, a every hour on the hour from Via Roma. The bus ride is long and indirect; you'd better to make the steep 10-minute walk from the **Chiesa di Santa Maria de Scale,** at the very bottom of Corso Italia (Via 24 Maggio).

The stairs at Santa Maria offer a stellar view of Ragusa Ibla, crowned by a mon tery and the 18th-century dome of **San Giorgio.** Descend under the roadway to Repubblica, at the bottom of 200m of tricky staircases. The road to the right he circumscribes the town, passing abandoned monasteries and a lush valley of far land. You will eventually come to the beautifully arranged **P. del Duomo di S Giorgio,** at the top of the city. **Corso 25 Aprile** runs downhill from the bottom this piazza, finishing at the **Giardino Ibleo,** home to two churches and walks shad by palm trees. Below the entrance to the gardens is the **Portale di San Giorgio,** o of the few 14th-century structures to survive the 1693 earthquake. An **Antique Ma ket** takes place the last Sunday of each month at Giardino Ibleo.

In summer, any citizen who can fit into a swimsuit spends the weekend at **Mari di Ragusa,** a drab resort strip. Autolinee Tumino (tel. 62 31 84) runs 14 buses p day to Marina (last bus leaves 8:30pm; last bus returns 10pm; L2900, round-tr L4900). A complete schedule is posted in the Polleria Giarrosto in Marina's P. Du degli Abruzzi. In the same piazza savor Marina's best ice cream at **Delle Rose,** whe the scoops are so enormous they give you *two* cones.

The resort's most animated eatery, **Pub Shaker,** is located at the beginning of Lu gomare Mediterraneo, and serves a variety of *panini,* including the oddly stuff *tropicale,* with prosciutto, pineapple, lettuce, and mustard. Bottled beers are L22 and up. (Open daily 7pm-4am.)

■ Syracuse (Siracusa)

Sicily's dignified Grecian city, Syracuse radiates the classical romance of Rome a harbors the climate of a vacation island. The city did, in fact, begin on an islar **Ortigia.** The town grew quickly, swelling over the 50-yd. strait that separated from *terra firma,* and extending into a much larger and even more prospero development (Neapolis) on the mainland. That was in the 7th century BC—toda *Siracusani* can only lament their city's millennia-long decline. Some say the c began to slide in 668 AD, when the bathing Byzantine emperor Constans was blu geoned to death with a soap dish. Others set the fatal date at 211 BC: Syracuse ju hasn't been the same since being sacked by the Romans. Certainly the glory-da were long ago; from the 6th to 3rd centuries BC, Syracuse was arguably the great city in the world, cultivating such luminaries as Pindar, Theocritus, and Archimed and claiming among its diverse feats the creation of both the world's largest thea and the first known cookbook. The young metropolis wielded a military might un valed in the Mediterranean. Syracuse can no longer claim to be the center of the c ilized world, but the decline of this ancient New York has been gradual, as the bu *caffè* and businesses of ancient Ortigia and the latter-day *palazzi* of Neapolis atte

ORIENTATION AND PRACTICAL INFORMATION

Syracuse rests on and off the southeastern coast of Sicily. Most of the historic city on the island of Ortigia, which is connected by two bridges to the mainland. T principal bridge leads to **Corso Umberto** on the mainland, which runs throu **Piazzale Marconi,** the main bus terminal. The first right off this Piazzale (Via Ca nia) leads to Corso Gelone, cutting through the modern city and out towards t **archaeological park.** The other important street off P. Marconi is **Via Frances Crispi,** which leads to the train station.

Tourist Office: APT, Via San Sebastiano, 45 (tel. 67 710). Take a right onto Viale Teocrito at the end of Corso Gelone; the office is down a street to the left (near the Catacombs). It's a good 15-min. walk from the bus and train stations, but they have maps, brochures, and speak a little English. Open 8am-2pm and 4-7pm. Also try **AAT** (tel. 66 932) at Via Maestranza, 33, near P. Archimede in Ortigia.

Currency Exchange: The city has plenty of **banks,** especially in Ortigia. Also at the ticket office in the train station, where the rates are just as good as a bank's. Open 9-11:30am and 4-6pm. The post office also offers exchange services.

Post Office: P. delle Poste, 15 (tel. 68 416), left after you cross the bridge into Ortigia. Fermo Posta (tel. 66 995). Open Mon.-Sat. 8am-7:45pm. **Postal code:** 96100.

Telephones: SIP is now located on Via Teracati (near the Motel Agip), a hell of a long walk past the end of Corso Gelone. Open daily 8am-8pm. Better to try the Bar Belcaffè Tamanaco, P. Marconi, 19, or else make do with street-phones. **Telephone Code:** 0931.

Trains: Via Francesco Crispi, midway between the old city and the archaeological park. To: Catania (15 per day, 1hr. 30min., L6500); Taormina (14 per day, 2hr., L10,500); Messina (14 per day, 3hr., L13,800); Ragusa (6 per day, 3hr., L8800).

Buses: From Piazzale Marconi on Corso Umberto. **SAIS** ticket office (tel. 667 10), at the intersection off Corso Umberto and Via Francesco Crispi. To Catania (8 per day, 3 on Sun., 1hr. 15min., L6100), Palermo (4 per day, 1 on Sun., 4hr., L22,100), and Noto (11 per day, 3 on Sun., 1hr., L3700). **AST** ticket office (tel. 65 689), next door to the post office in Ortigia; **city buses** leave from here. To: Catania (14 per day, 7 on Sun., L6100); Noto (15 per day, 4 on Sun., L3700); and P. Armerina (at 7am, 3hr., L11,600). All inter-city buses leave from P. Marconi; you can buy tickets on the bus.

Ferries: Tirrenia, Via Mazzini, 5 (tel. 66 956).

Emergencies: tel. 113. **Police:** Via S. Sebastiano (tel. 65 424). **Hospital:** Via Testaferrata (tel. 68 555). **Late-night Emergencies: Guardia Medica,** on Via Reno just a block from the station (tel. 22 555).

ACCOMMODATIONS AND CAMPING

Syracuse offers copious cheap accommodations in the new city and by the train station, but, if you'd prefer seashells and cobblestones, a room in charismatic Ortigia is well worth the expense. Women should be wary of the area around the station.

Hotel Milano, Corso Umberto, 10 (tel. 66 981). Rooms vary from spacious to bunk-bedded, but its low price and convenient location at the entrance to the bridge to Ortigia make it a good choice. Singles L25,000, with bath L35,000. Doubles L40,000, with bath L55,000.

Pensione Pantheon (tel. 22 985), at #22 in the Foro Siracusano, off Corso Umberto. Close to the bus station, yellow, modern, and extremely basic. Singles L30,000, with bath L35,000. Doubles L40,000, with bath L50,000. The **Pensione Bel Sit,** Via Oglio, 5 (tel. 60 245; signposted off Corso Gelone), has a similar set-up and the same prices, only the rooms are white and the proprietors more personable. Both hotels are *way* up high, on the 5th floors of their respective buildings.

Gran Bretagna, Via Savoia, 21 (tel. 68 765). Take your 3rd right past the bridge in Ortigia (at Temple of Apollo). This weathered hotel-house is proudly kept by its manager-owner, Dr. Pulvino, who also writes poetry and is head-chef in the hotel's restaurant. Each room has some distinctive decoration; one preserves 19th-century frescoes, another has a spiral staircase and private terrace. Curfew midnight. Singles L38,000, with bath L42,000. Doubles L62,000, with bath L75,000. Extra bed L19,000. Breakfast (8-9:30am) included. Open Dec.-Oct. Am Ex, MC, Visa.

Hotel Centrale, Corso Umberto, 141 (tel. 60 528), follow signs from train station. If your train from Rome gets in at 1am, this is just the thing to tide you over until the daylight hours. Modern, clean. Singles L20,000. Double L38,000. Showers included.

Camping: Fontane Bianche (tel. 79 03 33), near the beach. Take bus #21 or 22 from the post office (L600); 20km from Syracuse. L6500 per person, L6500 per small tent, L10,000 per large tent, L5000 per sleeping bag. Open May-Oct. Buy your basics at a Syracuse supermarket before heading out.

FOOD

Pizza is about the only budget option in Syracuse other than the **market** on Via Trento, near the Temple of Apollo. (Open Mon.-Sat. 7am-early afternoon.) For staples, try the **Supermercato Linguanti,** Corso Umberto, 186, across from the Hotel Centrale just a block from the station. (Open Mon.-Tues. and Thurs.-Sat. 7am-1pm and 3-8pm, Wed. 7am-1pm.)

Spaghetteria do Scugghiu, Via D. Sciná, 11, off P. Archimede. An ancient Syracusan institution. 22 delicious types of spaghetti, all L6000. *Secondi* L8000-10,000. Cover L1500. Open Tues.-Sun. noon-3pm and 7pm-midnight.

Stella del Porto, Via Tripoli, 40 (tel. 60 582), just a few doors down from P. Marconi. Mostly locals; the cooks will drag you into the kitchen to choose your fare. Menu changes daily, depending on the day's catch. Full meals L20,000-25,000. Open Mon.-Sat. noon-3pm and 7pm-midnight.

Trattoria Paolina, Via F. Crispi, 14, up from P. Marconi. No tourist in sight; just you and the old men who sit outside. *Primi* L400-5000. Good protein selection: *ceci* (chickpeas) or *lenticchie* (lentils) (L3000). Open Mon.-Sat. noon-3pm and 7-10pm.

Trattoria la Foglia, Via Capodieci, 29 (tel. 46 15 69), at the far end of Ortigia, near the Fontana Aretusa. Sicily's chic-est (and only?) vegetarian restaurant has been favorably reviewed by, among others, the *New York Times*. The woman who owns the place cooks the food, and her husband the sculptor fills the room with quirky artwork. Expensive. Pasta L8000 and up; 4-person vegetable plates L30,000. Cover L3000. Open Wed.-Mon. 11:30am-3pm and 7-11pm. AmEx.

Tuttopizza, Lungomare Alfeo, 12, below the Fontana Aretusa. Investigate the wonderful results of trysts between dough and tomato sauce, all served outside at candlelit tables (L4000-10,000). Try the *Alfeo,* their finest match, topped with eggplant, prosciutto, olives, mushrooms, tomato, and mozzarella (L7000). Beer L3500. *Servizio* 30%. Open Thurs.-Tues. 7pm-late. After your dinner of *tuttopizza,* you can have **Tuttogelato** in the same place.

SIGHTS

The historic sights are concentrated in two areas a few km apart: the enclosed archaeological park in the north part of town, and the island of Ortigia.

Ortigia

From the main approach to the island, Corso Umberto, cross over the bridge into Ortigia and you feel the breezy relief of an island refuge, of having left the sweltering mainland behind.

The ruins of two Greek temples and several Gothic and Renaissance churches and palaces are sprinkled along the winding streets of the island. Cross the bridge to Ortigia to find the ruins of the **Temple of Apollo**: the oldest Doric temple in Sicily (565 BC). All that remain are two columns supporting a piece of entablature and parts of the *cella* wall, which manifests traces of the subsequent Byzantine church.

Up Corso Matteotti to the right **Piazza Archimede,** the principal square of the old city. The 15th-century Palazzo Lanzo (#6), is graced by original Gothic fenestration and a beautiful Catalan 14th-century staircase in the courtyard. Down Via dei Montalto, a small passageway leads to a fantastic external view of the **Palazzo Montalto** (1397), the fanciest of the Gothic palaces in town, with triple windows set in Arab-decorated pointed arches.

The **duomo** (P. del Duomo) is one of the most extraordinary buildings in all of Italy. More than 2300 years separate the 18th-century baroque façade from the attached 5th-century BC **Temple of Athena,** and the intervening centuries each made their own additions. The cumulative effect is the representation of every period of Italian architecture. Once admired by Cicero, the temple was converted to a three-aisled Christian basilica in the 7th century. The columns were embedded in a solid wall, and arches were carved out of the interior (as at Agrigento's Temple of Concord). 26 of its original 34 columns remain, not only on the sides but also in the entrance and in the Byzantine chapel at the end of the north aisle. The 16th-century wooden ceiling is inscribed with an excerpt from a papal bull issued by Leo X in 1517 asserting the importance of the church.

P. del Duomo, in front of the cathedral, is lined with fragrant oleander trees and elegant *palazzi*. At #24, the graceful façade of the **Palazzo Benevantano,** reconstructed in 1788, conceals a serpentine balcony (all but invisible in 1993 because of scaffolding). At the far end of the square, wiggly columns frame the entrance to the church of **Santa Lucia alla Badia** (1695-1703; open only during church services and closed for restoration in 1993). Santa Lucia, martyred at the hands of Christian-hating emperor Diocletian in the third century AD, is Syracuse's patron saint.

From the piazza, a trip down Via Picherale will bring you to the ancient **Fonte Aretusa,** a "miraculous" freshwater spring by the sea. Legend has it that the nymph Arethusa escaped through a tunnel from her admirer Alpheus and was transformed into this fountain by the goddess Diana. Alpheus in turn was transformed into the eponymous river in Greece, which supposedly feeds the spring to this day through a getaway tunnel. Steps lead to the **Foro Vittorio Emanuele,** a tree-lined walk along the harbor.

Walk back up into the city from the fountain along Via del Capodieci to get to the opulent **Galleria di Palazzo Bellomo** (#16; tel. 69 511). This 14th-15th-century *palazzo* is a treasure trove of all kinds of artwork: from ornate Sicilian carriages to Byzantine Bible scenes to colorful wax crèches depicting the birth of Christ. Paintings of note are *The Annunciation* by Antonello da Messina, and the enormous *Burial of Santa Lucia* by Caravaggio. (Museum open Mon.-Sat. 8am-2pm, Sun. 8am-1pm. Admission L2000, free for those under 18 or over 60.)

Archaeological Park

Syracuse's larger monuments are in or near the Archaeological Park on the north side of town; follow Corso Gelone until it is intersected by Via le Teocrito; the entrance to the park is down Via Augusto to the left. (Open daily 9am-6pm, winter 9am-3pm. Admission L2000.) The **Greek theater,** scooped out of solid rock at the beginning of the 5th century BC, is the largest of its kind in existence. The *cavea,* or auditorium, originally had 59 rows of seats (now 42) in nine wedges, seating up to 15,000 people. You can still distinguish the three divisions of the theater—the *cavea,* the semi-circular orchestra pit, and the rectangular stage, which had a two-story permanent set with niches and colonnades.

The **Paradise Quarry,** outside the entrance to the Greek theater, is a flowered area in front of the chalk cliffs, with two large grottos: the **Orecchio di Dionigi** (Ear of Dionysius) and the **Grotta dei Cordari** (Cordmakers' Cave). The former is an artificial grotto of cathedral proportions (65m long, 5-11m wide, 23m high). Its name is derived from its resemblance to a giant earlobe and its exceptional acoustics.

Exiting the theater/quarry area, you come up against a fence through which you can see the **Altar of Hieron II** (241-215 BC), which was used for public sacrifices. At 198m by 23m, it is the largest altar known. To take a closer look, walk up the hill and enter through the same gate that leads to the **Roman amphitheater,** constructed in the 2nd century AD. A stage is occasionally set up in the amphitheater for dance and dramatic performances. Contact the tourist office for precise information.

At the very end of Corso Gelone, where it turns into Viale Teracati, the **tomb of Archimedes** sits behind a fence on a busy street corner. The tomb is dug entirely out of rock, even down to the triangular portico and crude columns at its entrance.

The **Catacombe di San Giovanni,** a few blocks away down Viale Teocrito, are extensive, sporadically frescoed catacombs dug between 315 to 360 AD. Outside the catacombs lie the ruins of a building said to be the first Christian church in Sicily. Below the ruins hide frescoed the 4th-century crypt of San Marziano, also home to some hauntingly faded frescoes, complete with Latin inscriptions. (Open Thurs.-Tues. 10am-noon and 4-6pm; mid-Nov.-mid-March 10am-noon. Admission L2000, under 18 or over 60 free.) The entire city is rumored to rest on a labyrinth of similar underground galleries, some running all the way to Catania, dug to provide refuge from invaders. Located down Viale Teocrito from the park, the three-year-old **Museo Archeologico Regionale Paolo Orsi,** on the grounds of the Villa Landolina, is credited with one of the world's best collections of Greek artifacts. (Open Tues.-Sat. and 1st and 3rd Sun. of each month 9am-1pm. Admission L2000, under 18 or over 60 free.) Across from the museum is Syracuse's newest monument, the space-age **Santuario della Madonna delle Lacrime.** The sanctuary is being built to commemorate the four-day period in 1953 when a statue of the Madonna cried for four days on end. The statue's tears were accompanied by several vaguely described events referred to as "miracles," and the spot has been a favorite with pilgrims ever since.

ENTERTAINMENT

Every even-numbered year, **Greek classical drama** is performed in the spectacular setting of the Greek Theater during May and June. The cheapest seats cost L15,000-20,000; ask for details at the APT office. July and August bring all kinds of music and theater to the Roman amphitheater. (Admission L7000-25,000.)

Beachcombers can bus the 18km from Syracuse to **Fontane Bianche** (bus #21 or 22, L600), an endless, silken beach frequented by a jet-set crowd. A smaller, less spectacular beach, more popular with the locals, is **Arenella,** 8km from the city (bus #23, L600). To play in waters of a different sort, take a daytrip to the **Fiume** and **Fonte Ciane,** home of the world's only major papyrus groves outside of Egypt. Take AST bus #21 or 22 from the post office to the Fiume Ciane bridge (15min., L600; let the driver know where you want to go); then walk along the path up to the source.

Natives rate Ortigia nightlife a *"niente"* (nothin'), but don't give up so easily. Much tax money has been spent on lighting the monuments, and the tiny island becomes a stage for the *passeggiata.* The prime place to promenade is along the port in the **Foro Vittorio Emanuele.** From about 8pm onwards, a sea of *Siracusani* mills around by the water, taking breaks in the cafés, admiring the trinkets for sale, or gawking at the foreign luxury yachts docked nearby. For a roof over your socializing head, **Flirt,** Via Cavour, 4, off P. Duomo, is home to the artsy and demure. During the winter, boogie at **Il Trabochetto,** Via delle Vecchie Carceri, 30, near the *duomo* (L12,000).

Near Syracuse: Noto

After suffering complete destruction in a 1693 earthquake, Noto, 32km southwest of Syracuse, was rebuilt in Baroque opulence by the wealthy Landolino family. A cascade of palaces and churches, some set atop monumental staircases and others behind tropical gardens, glitters along **Corso Vittorio Emanuele**, which begins right above Noto's **Giardini Pubblici** (Public Gardens) at the **Porto Reale.** The **APT tourist office,** P. XVI Maggio (tel. 83 67 44), on Corso Vittorio Emanuele, provides a free map of the most beautiful buildings. (English spoken. Open daily 8am-2pm and 4-7pm; winter 8am-2pm and 3-6pm.) You'll note that while proud Noto lavishes care on its 18th-century edifices, its Romanesque, Gothic, and modern structures languish in acute disrepair. Evidently the architectural rule of thumb is, "If it ain't Baroque, don't fix it." Apart from the general atmosphere, the town's most noteworthy sight is the **duomo,** a few blocks before the tourist office. The construction of the cathedral was begun immediately following the earthquake of 1693. You'll note it bears the mark "S.P.Q.N." above the door, Noto's twist on *senatus populusque romanus*.

Noto is best seen as an easy daytrip from Syracuse. If you choose to stay over, the one hotel is the clean and pleasant Albergo Stella, Via F. Maiore, 44 (tel. 83 56 95). (Singles L23,000. Doubles L42,000, with bath L47,000. Showers L2000.) **Trattoria del Carmine,** Via Ducezio, 9 (tel. 83 87 05), the first right off Via S. La Rosa downhill from P. XVI Maggio, serves home-cooked *ravioli di ricotta* (L5000). Full meals are L12,000-15,000. (Open Tues.-Sun. noon-3pm and 7-midnight.) Eggplant is a specialty at **Trattoria al Buco,** Via Zamardelli (tel. 83 81 42), the first left off Corso Vittorio Emanuele after the Porto Reale. Try the *tagliatelle alla melanzane* (egg noodles with eggplant) for L5000. (Open daily noon-3:30pm and 7:30-10:30pm; winter noon-3:30pm and 6-10pm.)

SAIS and AST **buses** leave from Syracuse in a steady stream from 5:45am to 7:50pm (28 per day, 7 on Sun., 1hr., L6100 round-trip), and the last bus back heads out at 9:15pm (7:15pm Sundays). Noto can also be reached by any local train on the Syracuse-Ragusa line (12 per day, 30min., L4300 round-trip), but it's a 20-min. walk uphill to town from the station. Fine beaches are only 7km away at **Marina di Noto;** buses leave from the Giardini Pubblici (4 per day, L2000, none on Sundays).

In a river gorge about 30km northwest of Syracuse near Sortino, the remote, eerie neolithic necropolis at **Pantalica** merits a visit. The gouged-out sockets of hundreds of tombs stare out from looming cliffs. Bring a flashlight. Pantalica is most easily accessible by car, but you can take a bus from Syracuse to Sortino and walk the remaining 6km or else call up **Zuccalà** (tel. 46 42 98), who run ½-day tours from Syracuse for L30,000 per person.

■ Catania

Catanians claim their city prepares them for every surprise the rest of the world has to offer. Certainly the metropolis is intimidating, with its chaotic traffic, immense, collapsing housing projects, and unfortunate status as Italy's most crime-ridden city. Especially give heightened Mafia activity in the last two years, it's hard to step off the bus in Catania without fearing that you'll be caught in the crossfire as the Marlon Brando look-alike strutting along the sidewalk is gunned down at your feet. That's what movies (and some newspapers) would have us believe, but beneath the squalid veneer of its sooty *palazzi* and its black reputation, Catania reveals an intriguing urban mosaic. Perpetual prey to the nearby volcano, this ancient city has been leveled and rebuilt many times; the present appearance dates from reconstruction following the monstrous 1692 earthquake, after which G. B. Vaccarini embellished the city with sumptuous Baroque buildings. Walls of dark volcanic stone lend a characteristic pall to the historic quarters, matched by gray concrete elsewhere.

So in spite of what you've been told, the city is not merely a den of thieves: people *live* here, and go about their lives with an appealing mixture of composure and flair.

ORIENTATION AND PRACTICAL INFORMATION

Catania lies between Messina and Syracuse on Sicily's eastern coast. The main street, **Via Etnea,** runs north from P. del Duomo to P. Gioeni, but there is little of interest beyond P. Cavour. From the train station walk inland along Corso Mártiri della Libertà to bank-laden **Corso Sicilia,** which intersects with Via Etnea. From here thrifty accommodations and boutiques await to your right all the way to P. Cavour; to the left is the **duomo** and **Via Vittorio Emanuele II** running to the water and P. dei Mártiri.

By European standards, Catania (like Palermo) is quite crime-ridden, but anyone who's ever spent a night in New York, London, or Paris, etc. will have a level of street-smart sophistication sufficient to be safe. Visitors should, however, be particularly wary of anything which might be intended as a distraction—a (staged) fight, someone pointing out a stain on your clothes, even an intentional fender-bender to get you out of your car. Be cautious walking around the city, especially at night; sin-

CATANIA

gle women should be particularly watchful. Leave expensive watches or clunky jewelry somewhere safe (in your hotel, *if secure*), and don't be afraid to make a scene if you feel threatened. Check the General Introduction sections on Safety and Security and Women Travelers for further important information.

Tourist Offices: AAPIT, Largo Paisiello, 5 (tel. 31 21 24 or 31 77 20), up the hill on Via Pacini, off Via Etnea near the post office. Maps, guides, cultural information. Open Mon.-Fri. 9am-1pm and 4:30-6pm, Sat. 9am-1pm. **Train station branch office,** right on the tracks (tel. 53 18 02). Open Mon.-Sat. 8am-8pm. **Airport branch office,** (tel. 34 19 00). Open Mon.-Fri. 8:30am-1:30pm and 2:30-7:45pm.

Budget Travel: CTS, Via Garofalo, 3 (tel. 715 04 34), up the hill from the intersection of Via Etnea and C. Sicilia. Student travel information. Open Mon.-Fri. 9:30am-1pm and 4:30-7pm, Sat. 9:30am-12:30pm. In winter it opens ½hr. earlier.

American Express: La Duca Viaggi, Via Etnea, 65 (tel. 31 61 55). Cardholders can get emergency cash and pay monthly AmEx bills here. Also a good place to inquire about **ferries** to Malta (from L60,000). Open Mon.-Fri. 9am-1pm and 4-7:30pm, Sat. 9am-noon.

Currency Exchange: Banks near intersection of Via Etnea and Corso Sicilia, or else the **Ufficio Informazioni** near the ticket office in the train station. Open 8am-8pm; English spoken.

Post Office: Via Etnea, 215 (tel. 31 15 06), in the big building next to the Villa Bellini Gardens. Open Mon.-Sat. 8:15am-7:40pm. **Postal code:** 95100.

Telephones: SIP, Corso Sicilia, 67. Open daily 9am-12:30pm and 4:30-7:30pm. **IRITEL,** P. Papa Giovanni XXIII, 12, across from the train station. Open 8am-10pm. **Telephone code:** 095.

Flights: Fontanarossa, (tel. 34 53 67). Bus #24 from the train station. Daily flights to Malta (round-trip L238,000; under 25, L194,000) with **Air Malta,** Via Ventimiglia, 117 (tel. 53 99 83), where Corso Sicilia turns into Corso Mártiri della Libertà.

Trains: (tel. 53 16 25), in P. Papa Giovanni XXIII. To: Syracuse (18 per day, 1hr. 45min., L6500); Messina (every hr., 2hr. L7200); Enna (11 per day, 1hr. 30min., L6500); Palermo (5 per day, 4hr., L17,100).

Buses: Interurban buses arrive in front of the train station. **SAIS,** Via D'Amico, 181 (tel. 53 61 68), in the right corner of the piazza as you exit the train station. Open 6am-9pm. To: Messina (8 per day, 1hr. 30min., L9500); Taormina (15 per day, 1hr. 30min., L5100); Syracuse (8 per day, 1hr. 30min., L6100); Enna (7 per day, 1hr. 15min., L8000); Palermo (22 per day, 3hr., L16,600); Agrigento (7 per day, 3hr., L16,000). In the same offices, **ETNA** (tel. 53 27 16) takes you from the train station to P. Armerina (7 per day, 2hr., L8600) and Ragusa (10 per day, L8900). **AST,** Via Luigi Sturzo, 220 (tel. 28 12 80), in the left corner of the same piazza. Open 6am-7pm. In addition to local routes, service to Syracuse (13 per day, 1hr. 30min., L6100). All bus services are reduced considerably Sun. **City Buses: AMT,** From Via Etnea, headed towards the *duomo*, buses #29 and 36 to the central train station; bus D (June-Sept. only) to the beach. From the train station, bus #24 to the airport; bus #27 to the beach. Buy tickets (L1000, L1700 for 3hr.) at *tabacchi* or newsstands. If you're caught without one, you'll suffer a fine of a mere 60 times the ticket price.

Ferries: Gozo Channel, office at Fratelli Bananno, Via Anzalone, 7 (tel. 32 66 08). Nearly all ferry service to Malta and Gozo Channel (except for expensive ones at La Duca Viaggi) has been suspended indefinitely.

Late-Night Pharmacy: Crocerossa, Via Etnea, 274 (tel. 31 70 53).

Emergencies: tel. 113. **Hospital:** Via Vittorio Emanuele, off Via Plebiscito (tel. 32 65 33). **Guardia Media:** tel. 726 26 00 (night-time and holidays). **Police:** tel. 112 or 31 77 33.

ACCOMMODATIONS AND FOOD

Pensione Gresi, Via Pacini, 28 (tel. 32 27 09), off Via Etnea near Villa Bellini and the post office. Don't let the charred doors on the 1st floor discourage you; the *pensione* on the 3rd floor is spotless. Every room has at least one Baroque angel fluttering on the ceiling to watch you while you sleep. Singles L37,000. Doubles L58,000, with bath L72,000.

Pensione Ferrara, Via Umberto, 66 (tel. 31 60 00), off Via Etnea just a few blocks from Via Pacini. Randomly furnished rooms with high ceilings. Balconies and 3rd floor breezes keep things cool. Singles L31,000, with bath L38,000. Doubles L52,000, with bath L65,000.

Pensione Südland, Via Etnea, 270 (tel. 31 24 94), across from the post office. Immense and elegant, though somewhat noisy and often full. Singles L35,000, with bath L46,000. Doubles L48,000, with bath L61,000. Breakfast L5000.

Pensione Rubens, Via Etnea, 196 (tel. 31 70 73). Rooms of Rubensesque proportions. Singles L30,000. Doubles L47,000. Showers L3000.

Don't leave Catania without trying their famous eggplant and ricotta spaghetti, named after Catanese composer Vincenzo Bellini's well-known opera, *Norma*. A sprawling **market** extends from the end of Via Pacini (off Via Etnea) all the way to Corso Sicilia (open Mon.-Sat. early morning-2pm). Another, almost as big, can be found off P. del Duomo; the main attraction is fish, but there are foods of all kinds. There is an **SMA Supermarket** at Corso Sicilia, 50 (open Mon.-Fri. 8:30am-1pm and 5-8pm, Sat. 8:30am-1pm; closed Wed. afternoon. MC, Visa).

Trattoria la Paglia, Via Pardo, 23 (tel. 34 68 38), across from the *duomo* behind the fountain near the fish market. Catch of the day, *spaghetti marinara,* vegetable, fruit, and wine L18,000. Try *insalata di polipo* (octopus salad) L6000. Area not recommended for single women at night. Open Mon.-Sat. noon-11pm.

Pizzeria Mungibeddu, Via Corridoni, 37, off Via Umberto I east of Via Etnea. Delicious pizza L4000-8000. *Coperto* L1500. Three-course *menù* L10,000. Open Sat.-Thurs. 11am-3pm and 6pm-midnight.

Trattoria Casalinga, Via Biondi, 19 (tel. 31 13 19), 3rd left off Via Antonio di Sangiuliano, which is to the right of Via Etnea as you walk from the *duomo*. The menu changes daily, but they're always happy to do the classic *norma*. Full meals only: L18,000-25,000. Open for lunch only and for as long as the clientele stays.

Gastronomy G. Conte, Via Etnea, 158 (tel. 31 10 89). An excellent eatery. *Pizzette* and other *tavola calda* snacks L1800-2000. Counters only, so come early. Also take-out service. Open Mon.-Sat. 7am-9pm.

Spinella, Via Etnea, 300 (tel. 32 72 47). Super pastries and coffee right across from the Bellini gardens. Open Thurs.-Tues. 7am-10:30pm. Next door, the **Pasticceria SaVia** (tel. 32 23 35) is slightly cheaper and has a bigger selection.

SIGHTS

At the center of Catania's **P. del Duomo,** Vaccarini's lava-built **Fontana dell'Elefante** (Elephant Fountain, 1736) boasts a unique anatomical feature. Vaccarini, true to reality, carved his elephant without visible testicles. When the statue was unveiled, horrified Catanian men concluded that this was a slur on their virility and demanded corrective measures; Vaccarini's acquiescence was monumental. Residents pledge that visitors may attain citizenship by smooching the elephant's massive tush, but the altitude of the pachyderm's posterior precludes any such aspirations. Stand behind the cool-flowing fountain on the far end of the square for a good view of the **cathedral,** introduced by an open space at its side, allowing the full play of Baroque regalia. The other buildings on the square (the 18th-century Palazzo del Municipio on the left, the former Seminario dei Chierici on the right) are striped black and white to mirror the side of the *duomo*.

The church interior, now with a Baroque barrel-vaulted nave and domed side aisles, once looked quite different, as 1950s restoration work revealed. Stumps of the old columns were found, as well as the tall pointed arches of the original three apses. The two transept chapels have exquisitely paneled Renaissance frames (1545). One of them, the Norman **Cappella della Madonna** (right), also preserves a beautiful Roman sarcophagus and a 15th-century statue of the Virgin. 1994 is the

100th anniversary of Catania's beloved priest, the Beato Cardinale Dusmet. You can see his body lit up by fluorescent lights 25 ft. from the chapel, his bony (quite literally) fingers sticking out of the vestments. Near the main entrance (to the right as you come in) is **Bellini's tomb.** The words and music inscribed above are from *sonnambula,* one of the composer's four principal works. He died at the young age of 33.

Via Crocíferi, which runs parallel (three streets away) to Via Etnea from P. di San Francesco to Villa Bellini, is packed with Baroque churches. Via Gesuiti, which branches off from Via Crocíferi at the church with an octagonal tower, climbs a hill to the **Church of San Nicolò,** the largest and most frightening in Sicily. A giant unfinished façade with amputated columns and black protuberances encloses a cavernous interior. Up the hill from the P. del Duomo at Via Vittorio Emanuele 266 is the entrance to the **Greco-Roman Theater.** Behind the amphitheater (entrance around back) is the similar but smaller **Odeon.** Mt. Etna's 1669 eruption coated the marble of both theaters in lava. (Open daily 9am-1hr. before sunset. Free.) In mid-July, **Catanio Musica Estate** takes place on a stage set up in the Odeon; inquire at AAPIT.

Up Via Etnea **Bellini Gardens** offer a lush refuge against Mt. Etna's backdrop. A few blocks before the gardens, at the intersection of Via Etnea and Corso Sicilia, are the ruins of a second-century **Roman amphitheater** just below street level. The more recent inscription reads: "For me, Christ made the city of Catania sublime."

ENTERTAINMENT

The **Teatro Bellini** (tel. 31 20 20) is the city's principal theater for opera and concerts. The opera and symphonic seasons begin in October. Symphonies run until January (tickets from L6000); operas until June (from L13,000). From July to September, the city and province host performances (mostly in the Odeon) of music, theater, and dance. All events are free and schedules are plastered about town. The AAPIT is very active culturally and puts out a free monthly bulletin ("Lapis") on **nightlife** in Catania: movies, concerts, festivals. Catania has a dynamic **punk rock/ heavy metal** scene; check the area around the university (P. della Università) for hand-scrawled posters announcing concerts (usually free).

La Plaja is a pleasant but crowded beach within view of a nearby power-plant (take bus #27 or D, June-Sept. only). Farther away from Catania's port, **La Scogliera** is a better choice with a clear bathing area spread out beside igneous cliffs (bus #34 from P. Duomo, 30min.).

Near Catania: Mount Etna

Mt. Etna is one of the world's largest active volcanoes and (at 3350m) the largest and highest in Europe. The Greek poet Hesiod envisioned Etna as the home of Typhon, the last monster conceived by the Earth to fight the gods before the dawn of the human race. If so, Typhon remains restless; a 1985 eruption destroyed much of the tourist station near the summit. Etna blew its top again in 1992, unsettling residents of some of the towns along its slopes.

The trains of **Ferrovia Circumetnea** circumnavigate the volcano's base, stopping at local villages. From Catania, use **Stazione Borgo,** Via Caronda, 350 (tel. 54 124); Via Caronda is the street that forks off Via Etnea to the right just after the Bellini Gardens. At this station, you can hop on a train that runs around Etna's entire inland perimeter, finishing near the coast at Giarre-Riposto (5 per day, last one leaves Catania at 4:10pm, 3 hr. 30min., L7500). From Giarre-Riposto you can make connections onto the national railway and get back to Catania (or go on to Taormina) in less than an hour. If you'd like to do some real hands-on exploring, an AST **bus** leaves from Catania's central train station at 8:15am for **Rifugio Sapienza,** making a 10 min. rest stop at Nicolosi (where you can fill up your picnic basket), and returns at 4:15pm (round-trip L6700). From Sapienza (1900m), you can hike up to **Torre del Filosofo** ("The Philosopher's Tower," 2920m; as high as you're allowed to go) and back in about 5hrs. The hike is difficult, because the ashy pebbly terrain slips underfoot; it's

TAORMINA

like climbing up a beach at a 35° angle. The other option is the (expensive) cable-car service that runs to 2500m and is then supplemented by 4x4s up to 2920m (9am-4pm, last down 4:30pm; one-way to 2500m L14,200, round-trip L25,700; one-way to 2920m L25,700, round-trip L45,000; children under 10 ½-price; closed if winds are high).

However you choose to get up the volcano, you're in for a thrill: the hardened lava, and huge boulders and craters are unearthly. Bring sweaters and windbreakers; winds are ferocious, and even in mid-July pockets of snow sometimes remain.

Stock up on food before you leave; as a last resort the self-service cafeteria at the tourist station serves decent L2000 pizzas and pasta dishes for L7000. Based in Taormina, **CIT,** Corso Umberto, 101 (tel. (0942) 23 301), runs pricey package tours to Etna. **SAT,** Corso Umberto, 73 (tel. 24 653), offers similar deals. Trips to 1900m are L30,000 per person; to the Philosopher's Tower L65,000.

■ Taormina

The story goes that Neptune shipwrecked a boat full of Greeks off the eastern coast of Sicily in the 8th century BC, and only one sailor, Teocle, survived to crawl ashore. He was so inspired by the beautiful scenery that he decided to found a city, and Taormina was born.

2500 years later, Otto Geleng, a Prussian painter, stopped in Taormina, painted a few idyllic scenes, and rushed back to Northern Europe (canvases in hand) to show the rest of Europe. Fascinated by Geleng's landscapes, hundreds of aristocrats and art critics converged upon the town, and Taormina the resort came into being.

These days it's a precious combination of both: a cliff-top city of mansions, pine trees and purple flowers, with a hazy-blue coastline stretching out below. In the past 30 years some high-rise hotels have sprung up along the beaches, but if you stay up high in the old city, there's not a steel beam or a plexiglass window to be seen.

ORIENTATION AND PRACTICAL INFORMATION

The easiest way to get to Taormina is by **bus** from Messina (13 per day, L5100) or Catania (16 per day, L5100). Although **trains** are more frequent—from Messina (30 per day, 50min., L3100) and Catania (29 per day, 45min., L3900)—the train station is located far below Taormina, and access to the city depends on buses which make the run uphill every 15 to 75 minutes until 10:25pm (L1500).

From the bus depot, take a left up Via Pirandello until **Corso Umberto I,** the main drag, which runs the length of the town. Innumerable stepped side streets branch from the *corso.* Via Naumachia leads downhill to **Via Bagnoli Croci,** which continues on to the public gardens. The 4 principal *piazze* are along Corso Umberto.

Tourist Office: P. Santa Caterina (tel. 23 243), off Corso Umberto at P. Vittorio Emanuele in Palazzo Corvaia. Helpful and well-organized, if they slow down enough to notice you. Will help with your accommodations search (difficult in Aug.). English spoken. Excellent city map. Open Mon.-Sat. 8am-2pm and 4-7pm.

Currency Exchange: Cambio Valuta, Corso Umberto, 224, right before P. S. Antonio. Open Mon.-Sat. 9am-1pm and 4-8pm. Also, hordes of other places on the *corso.* The ticket office in the bus depot (open early morning until 7pm), will exchange cash only.

American Express: La Duca Viaggi, Via Don Bosco, 39 (tel. 62 52 55), right on P. IX Aprile. Cash advances, traveler's check refunds; will hold mail for 1 month. Open Mon.-Fri. 9am-1pm and 4-7:30pm, Sat. 9am-noon.

Post Office: P. S. Antonio (tel. 21 242), at the top of Corso Umberto near the hospital. Open Mon.-Sat. 8:10am-7:10pm. **Postal code:** 98039.

Telephones: SIP, Via San Pancrazio, 6 (tel. 246 69), at the top of Via Pirandello in the Avis office. Open Mon.-Sat. 9am-12:30pm and 4-7:30pm. **Telephone Code:** 0942.

Buses: SAIS (tel. 62 53 01). To Catania, Messina, and local destinations. Also, tours to Etna like ones offered by CIT (see Mt. Etna above). Both offer "Etna Tramonto," a sunset trip up the volcano (June-Oct., Mon. and Wed., L65,000 per person).

Car Rental: Avis, Via San Pancrazio, 6 (tel. 23 041). Open Mon.-Sat. 9am-12:30pm and 4-7:30pm, Sun. drop-off only 9am-noon.

Moped Rental: Sicily on Wheels, Via Bagnoli Croci, 90 (tel. 62 56 57). Scooters L18,000 per day, L110,000 per week. Vespa 2-seaters L26,000 per day, L180,000 per week. Must be over 15. Open daily 7am-12:30 and 4-8pm. **California,** nearby at #86 (tel. 23 769), rents the same at considerably higher prices.

English Bookstore: Libreria Interpress, Corso Umberto, 37 (tel. 24 989). Look for the awning that says "Book Shop." Also, books in French and German. Open daily 8:30am-1pm and 4-8:30pm.

Emergencies: tel. 113. **Police:** tel. 112. **Late-Night Medical Emergency: Guardia Medica,** tel. 62 54 19. **Hospital: Ospedale San Vincenzo** (tel. 23 149), in P. San Vincenzo.

ACCOMMODATIONS AND CAMPING

Reservations are a must in August. The following *pensioni* usually have vacancies in the off-season, but most will not accept phone reservations from late June through September. If you are determined to stay overnight in summer, have the tourist office book a room for you. Cheaper accommodations are available in the nearby towns of Mazzarò, Spisone, and Giardini-Naxos, but bus service to these areas stops about 9pm; the only alternative for the first two is a long hike down steep trails.

Pensione Svizzera, Via Pirandello, 26 (tel. 23 790; fax. 62 59 06), between the bus station and the town center. A little expensive, but well worth every *lire*. The rose-colored building looks out over the magnificent coastline. Kept so neat, even the Swiss would be impressed. All rooms with bath. Singles L32,000. Doubles L52,000. Triples L60,000. Breakfast L7000. Open March-Nov.

Villa Pompei, Via Bagnoli Croci, 88 (tel. 23 812), across from the public gardens. You can smell the flowers from the rooms. Run by sweet, caring sisters. Singles L30,000. Doubles L48,000, with bath L54,000. Extra bed L15,000. Showers L2000. Reservations for June-Sept. required a month in advance with deposit.

Inn Piero, Via Pirandello, 20 (tel. 23 139), near the base of Corso Umberto. Tidy, recently renovated rooms. All with shower. Singles L37,000. Doubles L58,000.

Pensione Minerva, Via Paternò, 6 (tel. 23 496). From P. S. Antonio, head straight up the hill on Via Apollo Arcageta. After about 200m, Via Paternò branches off to the left. The rooms are a little dusty, the carpet is a little shabby, but this *pensione* sits at one of the highest points in the city, and all the doubles have great views. Singles L30,000. Doubles L45,000, with bath L55,000. Breakfast L8000.

Camping: Campeggio San Leo (tel. 24 658), on the cape 200m up the hill from the train station, and can be reached by any bus from Taormina that passes the station on its route (L1500). L7000 per person, L8000 per small tent, L10,000 per large tent. **Eurocamping Marmaruca** (tel. 36 676), 5km from Taormina in the Letojanni area. Marmaruca is accessible by buses from Taormina headed in the direction of Messina (L1500). L5600 per person, L4500 per small tent, L7700 per large tent. Both places have foodstores within ½km.

FOOD

Cheap eateries are few and far between; avoid everything off Corso Umberto I. Even buying bread, cheese, and fruit can be expensive unless you try the **Supermercato STANDA** on Via Apollo Arcageta, at the end of Corso Umberto, one block up from the post office. (Open Mon.-Sat. 8:30am-1pm and 5-9pm.)

U Lantirnaru, Via Apollo Arcageta, 14 (tel. 24 565), at the end of Corso Umberto. Watch the chickens spinning in their huge wood-burning oven. ¼ of a big bird, a large plate of french fries, bread, and a beverage for L13,000 (*menù turistico*). Open Mon. and Wed.-Sat. noon-2pm and 5-11pm, Sun. 10:30am-2pm.

Pace, P. San Pancrazio, 3 (tel. 23 184), at the end of Via Pirandello. Outdoor tables, plenty of company, and a great location. Pizza (L5000-9000). *Cannelloni alla Siciliana* L7000. *Coperto* L1500. Open Wed.-Mon. noon-2:30pm and 7-11pm.

Trattoria da Nino, Via Pirandello, 37 (tel. 21 265), between the buses and the town center. The owner rolls all his pasta fresh in the kitchen (*primi* from L5500). He's also proud of his *minestrone* (L6500); "You haven't tasted *minestrone* until you've tried ours." Open Sat.-Thurs. 11:30am-3pm and 6:30pm-late.

Café L'Arco, Via C. Patricio, 28 (tel. 21 121), uphill from the start of Corso Umberto. The young clientele doesn't wait for the savory pastries to cool; a burned tongue is a small price to pay for such *buon gusto.* The *cipolline* is stuffed with mozzarella, prosciutto, tomatoes, and onions (L2500). Take-out available. Open Tues.-Sun. 9am-2pm and 5:30-11pm.

SIGHTS AND ENTERTAINMENT

Goethe thought the 3rd-century **Greek Theater** in Taormina commanded one of the most beautiful views in the world; see if you would sell your soul for the vista. (Open daily 9am-1hr. before sunset. L2000, under 18 or over 60 free.) To get there, walk up Via Teatro Greco, off Corso Umberto at P. Vittorio Emanuele. As you exit the theater, check out the grand Timeo Hotel to your left: this was Taormina's first hotel, started by painter Otto Geleng for his friends, who were arriving in droves.

On the other side of P. Vittorio Emanuele, behind the tourist office, is the **Roman Odeon,** a small theater now partly covered by the Church of Santa Caterina next door. A ways up Corso Umberto, P. del Duomo showcases Taormina's 13th-century **duomo,** rebuilt during the Renaissance. ("It's open when the Monsignor wants it to be open," but try the morning or early evening hours.) The Gothic interior shelters paintings by Messinese artists and a fine alabaster statue of the Virgin.

Walk along Via Circonvallazione, running parallel to and above Corso Umberto. A small set of steep stairs snake up the mountainside to the **castello,** hands-down Taormina's finest view.

In the summer, the city hosts **Taormina Arte,** an international festival of theater, music, and film (late July-Sept.). Most performances are in the Greek Theater or in the public gardens. (Admission L7000-50,000. For information call 21 142, visit the outdoor offices in P. Vittorio Emanuele, or inquire at the tourist office.) Taormina is home to a number of overpriced, uneventful discotheques. This sort of nightlife mostly concentrates in nearby Giardini-Naxos (see below). One worthwhile nightspot in Taormina is **Tout Va,** Via Pirandello, 70 (tel. 238 24), an open-air club with great views, although it's a tiring half-hour trek from town. (Cover, depending on the night, begins at L15,000. Open in summer daily 10pm-3:30am.) **Le Perroquet** (tel. 24 462), on Via Roma and P. S. Domenico de Guzman (walk downhill from P. IX Aprile), is a popular **gay club.** (Cover L15,000. Open daily July 15-Sept. 15.)

Near Taormina

Taormina's closest and most popular beach is the Lido Mazzarò below town. Down the road to the right and 100m off the coast is the tiny **Isola Bella,** a national nature preserve. The *lido* is accessible by the funicular from Via Pirandello in Taormina (every 15min.; L2000; last car up at 8:30pm, in Aug. 1am). Huge lines form for the return trip at "rush hour" from 5 to 7pm. Some of the nearby towns—**Castelmola** in particular—are also scenic, and a short bus ride out of town.

Nearby **Giardini-Naxos** was the site of the first Greek colony in Sicily (725 BC). Recent excavations in the **archaeological park** have revealed the outlines of the city walls, built with monstrous irregular blocks of solidified lava. This sounds promising, but the remains are so scanty that they're unlikely to interest anyone who isn't a Ph.D. candidate in archaeology. (Open daily 9am-6pm. Free.) On the way into Giardini-Naxos from Taormina, along Via Roma, you'll find affordable **accommodations;** many of the places here and in the center of Giardini-Naxos are cheaper than the options available in Taormina. SAIS buses leave from Taormina's bus terminal every 15 to 45 minutes (L 1500, round-trip L2500).

SARDINIA (SARDEGNA)

"Not a bit like the rest of Italy..." declared D.H. Lawrence, inspired by Sardinia's harsh, mountainous terrain and rustic, undeveloped villages. Though the interior persists in its untamed state, 20th-century concrete beehive condominiums and tourist amenities have long since cluttered several destinations along the coast. Elsewhere, however, long stretches of untouched beaches, coves, and cliffs remain to tempt the traveler weary of Riviera-style tourist traps. In the major cities, people dress as elegantly, drive as recklessly, and profess the same passion for gelato as the "continentals." The Sardinians, however, retain their keen sense of honor and hospitality. Most proudly speak the native Sardo dialect, an orphan Romance language bearing little resemblance to Italian.

Nonetheless, an old Sardinian legend reveals a sense of inferiority: when God finished making the world, he had a handful of dirt left over, which he threw into the Mediterranean and stepped on, thus creating Sardinia. Other curious landscaping phenomena took place over 3500 years ago; the island is dotted with *nuraghi*, monuments to ancient civilizations constructed around the 2nd millenium BC. The cone-shaped fortified tower-houses were built of huge blocks of stone without the aid of mortar. Over 7000 survive. The same civilization erected the 500 **Giants' Tombs** to house *en masse* the remains of its rich and famous.

The first historically recorded invaders of Sardinia were the seafaring Phoenicians and the Carthaginians. It was the methodical and business-minded Romans, however, who turned the island into an agricultural colony. Sardinia's history has been one of violent and almost constant struggle against foreign invaders, including the Pisans, the Aragonese (who took over Alghero and kicked out its inhabitants), and the cruel and oppressive Spanish who were finally overpowered in the 18th century. Even Napoleon tried (and failed) to take Sardinia in 1793 in an offensive launched from Corsica. Vittorio Emanuele, who became king of Italy in 1861, began his campaign to unify Italy from Sardinia (helped by its favorite son Giuseppe Garibaldi) and made it part of the unified whole. Mussolini did much for the island and its transport networks, and is still fondly remembered by many. These days, the island is home to twenty-four NATO bases, as well as the foreign tourists who reside in coastal towns during the summer months. Throughout the centuries of foreign influence, however, Sardinians have clung firmly to their traditions with a characteristic hauteur forged through centuries of confrontations with foreign invaders.

Well into this century, the economy of Sardinia still depended exclusively on agriculture. Only decades ago, *padroni* (landlords) still held the land and poor farmers toiled under a system akin to serfdom. Owing to the growing influence of the Italian Communist Party (both its founder, Antonio Gramsci, and its late Secretary General, Enrico Berlinguer, were Sardinians), much of the land is now owned by those who work it, although large sections of Sardinia's scenic coastline have fallen into the hands of foreign speculators. Industrialization and modernization have polarized Sardinian society, sidelining many who cling to traditional ways of life; recently, tourism and industry have emerged as significant forces in Sardinia. Still, despite a massive campaign launched on the continent to promote Sardinia as a vacation destination, many of the island's attractions remain virtually inaccessible without a car, and despite (or perhaps because of) the American military base on La Maddalena, few Sardinians care for Anglophones.

■ Getting There

The cheapest way to go is *posta ponte* (deck class) from Civitavécchia to Olbia (L17,000). Beware the summer tourist rush (late July and August) and the omnipresent possibility of strikes when planning your trip to Sardinia. If you plan on traveling

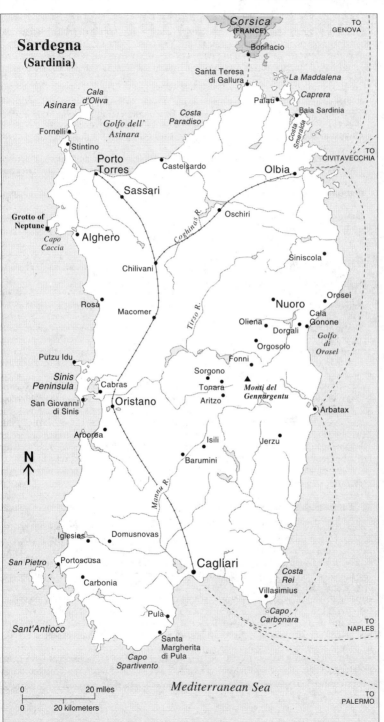

Sardegna
(Sardinia)

at the height of the season, reserve two weeks prior to departure. Prices listed below are for *poltrone* (reserved reclining chairs). *Posto ponte* fares are often available only when all the *poltrone* are taken. **Tirrenia** operates the most ferries and offers the cheapest fares, but long delays occasionally mar the service. Tickets can be purchased at many travel agencies in Italy and the U.S. In Italy, look for Terrenia signs outside travel agencies.

Civitavécchia-Olbia: daily both ways at 11pm, July-Aug. also at 11am (7hr., L31,000). There is also a **Ferrovie dello Stato** connection to Golfo Aranci, near Olbia (4 per day, 8hr. 30min., L16,700), a better choice if you've got a car.

Civitavécchia-Cagliari: daily at 6:30pm from Civitavécchia and Cagliari (13hr., L50,700).

Civitavécchia-Arbatax: Tues. and Fri. from Civitavécchia at 6:30pm. Departs Arbatax for Civitavécchia Sun. and Thurs. 10pm and midnight; in winter midnight only (8hr. 30min., L39,400.)

Genoa-Olbia: daily at 6pm from Genoa, Aug. at 5 and 11:45pm. Daily at 8:30pm from Olbia, Aug. 8:15am and 8:30pm (13hr., L57,400).

Genoa-Cagliari: Tues., Thurs., and Sun. at 4:45pm from Genoa. Mon., Wed., and Sat. at 3pm from Cagliari (20hr. 30min., L80,200).

Genoa-Porto Torres: daily at 8pm from both cities, in Aug. at 8:15am, 10am, 5pm, 7pm, and midnight (12hr. 30min., L56,500).

Genoa-Arbatax: Mon. and Fri. at 6pm from Genoa, in Aug. at 7pm. Tues. and Sat. at 2pm from Arbatax, in Aug. at 4pm (19hr. 30min., L59,100).

Naples-Cagliari: Thurs. at 5:30pm from Naples. Tues. at 6:30pm from Cagliari. (16hr., L51,400.)

Palermo-Cagliari: Sat. at 7pm from Palermo. Fri. at 7pm from Cagliari (13hr., L47,300).

Trápani-Cagliari: Tues. at 8pm from Trápani. Sun. at 7pm from Cagliari (11hr., L37,500).

Tunis-Cagliari: Mon. at 8pm from Tunis. Sun. at 7pm from Cagliari (21hr., L103,400).

Tirrenia offices can be found in **Civitavécchia,** Stazione Marittima (tel. (0766) 288 01 23); **Genoa,** Stazione Marittima, Ponte Colombo (tel. (010) 25 80 41); **Palermo,** Via Roma, 385 (tel. (091) 33 33 00); **Livorno,** Agenzia Marittima Carlo Laviosa, Via Scali d'Azeglio, 6 (tel. (0586) 89 06 32); and **Rome,** Via Bissolati, 41 (tel. (06) 474 20 41).

Flights also link Olbia, Alghero, and Cagliari to most major Italian cities, as well as to Paris, Geneva, Zurich, Munich, and Frankfurt. A Rome-Olbia flight runs L131,500, but night flights are cheaper (L106,000). Check with local tourist offices for schedules, fares, and discounts.

■ Transportation

Public transportation in Sardinia is an inexpensive but somewhat inefficient way to see the island. Buses tend to miss many of Sardinia's treasures such as campgrounds next to Roman ruins or hidden coves with private bathing in spectacular natural settings. Instead they go to its cities and more crowded campgrounds, which are not the reasons to come to Sardinia. It is possible, however, to plan a decent itinerary around the bus schedule. If you get stuck in the middle or (worse) the end of the day in a town you're ready to escape you may end up spending the night there. The two main bus companies are ARST and PANI. **ARST** links almost every village on the island to the nearest big town. Its service is oriented toward local residents; the bus stops on request at any cluster of houses as well as at the planned stops. **PANI,** by contrast, connects only the major cities—Cagliari, Sássari, Oristano, and Núoro— and although some buses stop at one or two intervening towns, many stop only at their final destination.

Train service has improved in recent years and remains significantly less expensive than buses. If you aren't in a hurry, they can provide vistas of the unique beauty of the countryside that highway travel sacrifices.

The most prized destinations simply cannot be reached without a car. **Car rental** rates have recently come within the range of many budget travelers. The ideal Sardinian holiday combines a rented car with stays at the many campgrounds set in magnificent natural settings. The best car rental deals will be found in larger cities. **Mopeds** are another option, running about L50,000 per day; finding rental outlets, however, is a challenge. **Bikes** seem an enticing option, but unless you have the leg muscles of an Olympian, Sardinia's mountainous terrain will reduce you to a hiker with a two-wheeled backpack. Anyone traveling alone should think twice about bicycling in some of the less populated inland areas south of Nuòro, and women are especially cautioned. Also, women should never go on hikes alone in the countryside. **Hitchhiking in Sardinia can be very dangerous, especially for women—even when traveling in pairs.** *Let's Go* does not recommend hitchhiking.

■ Accommodations and Food

Virtually all growth in Sardinia's rapidly expanding vacation industry has been in the luxury sector. Most cities lack an adequate selection of moderately priced accommodations. Consult the local tourist office, and ask for the semi-reliable and comprehensive *Annuario Alberghi,* which lists prices for all hotels, *pensioni,* and official campsites on the island. You can usually find a decent single in town for about L30,000, but during peak season single travelers will probably have to scrounge for roommates. Rooms are scarce in August. The two **youth hostels** (in Alghero and Porto Torres) provide an inexpensive but unreliable alternative, as they often fill up or shut down unexpectedly. Both lie near the beach and have crowded but airy rooms. **Camping** outside official campsites is illegal, but discreetly practiced nonetheless. **Agriturismo** is an excellent alternative to *pensioni;* tourists live on farms in the countryside and eat dinners with their host families but a car is almost always necessary to reach these rural destinations (bed and breakfast approximately L25,000, half-pension L37,000, full pension L50,000). Ask the tourist office for a list of participating farms in the area, or contact one of the two agencies that run *agriturismo* centers in Sardinia. They will make reservations without the usual booking fee generally required for the summer months. If you write early enough they will send you a complete directory of their *agriturismo* locations in Sardegna, complete with photos: **Agriturismo di Sardegna,** (tel. (0783) 41 80 66) Cooperativa Allevatrici Sarde 09170, Oristano, Caselle Postale 107; **Terra Nostra,** Associazione Sarda per l'Agriturismo, Via Sassari, 3, 09123 Cagliari (tel. (070) 66 83 67).

For those interested in an alternative vacation with forays into pristine natural settings, Sardegna has much to offer. Over 50% of Italy's endangered species are found here: a battle is currently engaged between various wildlife federations and the Italian government to establish more wildlife sanctuaries here to protect these species from the constant encroachment of the tourist industry into the natural landscape. **Hiking and trekking** have become increasingly popular as guides from various cooperatives lead groups along shepherds' paths in the golden hills of the interior. Most local tourist agencies have information on local trekking adventures, or contact Ignazio Porcedda, an English speaker who arranges excursions in Sardegna with **Guide GAE Ambientali Escursionistiche,** Cooperative Turistica "Sinis" Campeggio Nurapolis 09070 Narbolia (Oristano), (tel. (0783) 522 83 or 575 03). Sardinians have raised beautiful horses for centuries. Horse lovers can design their own trekking adventures by contacting one of the local centers (ask at the tourist office) or by contacting **Ante Sardo,** the association of Sardinian riding centers, Via Ravenna, 24, 09100 Cagliari, (tel. (070) 30 46 10).

Sardinia's **cuisine,** like its terrain, is rustic and rugged. A menu often includes hearty dishes like *sa fregula* (pasta in broth with saffron—a spice rarely used on the mainland), *malloreddus* (dumplings with saffron), or *culurgiones* (ravioli stuffed with cheese and beetroots, covered with tomato sauce, lamb, and sausage). The most celebrated dishes are a vegetarian's nightmare: grilled pigs or goats, *cordulu* (lamb entrails), and pork cooked in lamb's stomach. Fish and shellfish abound on the island and are often served in novel ways (even on pizza). Unfortunately, it's hard to find these typically Sardinian dishes except in expensive restaurants. Still don't leave the island without sampling such distinctive local specialties as *pane frattau*, a thin bread covered with eggs, cheese, and tomato sauce, and *sebada*, a delicious dough stuffed with cheese, sugar, and honey. Vegetarians will find it tough going in Sardinia. Check our listing of markets, vegetarian products, and in any small town, a *panino alle melanzane* (roll with eggplant in olive oil) can be found at a local bar. Look for daily outdoor markets in older neighborhoods, where you can get fresh bread and fruit, goat and sheep cheese, and then go tend your own flock for the completely authentic experience. In the summer months local fuits such as apricots, peaches, and nectarines provide succulent picnic makings. The local honey spread on bread makes an excellent breakfast. Sardinian bee pollen is an unusual and inexpensive delicacy you wouldn't want to miss. The local wines, often sweet and strong, reward a taste or two. Try *vernaccia d'Oristano* (with a heady, almond aftertaste) with fish, or the robust *cannonau di Sardegna* with meat.

■■■ CAGLIARI

Cagliari earns the superlatives among Sardinian cities; it is the island's capital, its largest metropolis, the chief and most agreeable port, and one of the best destinations on the island. The city yields such improbable and delightful surprises as Roman ruins, Spanish churches, medieval citadels, exquisite beaches, and a large pink flamingo population. Founded and raised to prosperity under the Carthaginians, Cagliari passed through the hands of numerous conquerors, Romans, Spaniards, and Pisans among them. The city's present disposition, however, seems more influenced by the sun and pleasant climate than by its sanguinary history. From Cagliari, you can make daytrips to the *nuraghic* ruins near Barumini, the Phoenician-Roman city of Nora, and the Costa del Sud beaches.

ORIENTATION AND PRACTICAL INFORMATION

Via Roma (where the PANI bus drops you) hugs the harbor, framed on one side by **Piazza Matteotti,** which houses the tourist office and town hall with the train and ARST stations nearby. Facing the train station, to the left one finds **Piazza Deffenu**, the PANI station, and the Tirrenia docks. To the right, the city sweeps upwards onto a steep and unforgiving hill crowned by the **castello,** which commands a fantastic view of the city and sea from the historic center of town.

Azienda di Turismo, P. Matteotti (tel. 66 92 55 or 66 49 23). Look for a weirdly shaped cubicle in the park/garden. Wonderfully helpful and pleasant if somewhat harried. English spoken. Free maps, detailed picture pamphlets, etc. Open Mon.-Sat. 8am-8pm.

Budget Travel: CTS, Via Cesare Balbo, 4 (tel. 48 82 60). Information on discounts and travel packages for students. Sells HI cards. Open Mon.-Fri. 9am-1:30pm and 4-7:30pm, Sat. 9am-1:30pm. **Associazione Italiana Studenti Sardi: Memo Travel,** Via Pitzolo, 1/A (tel. 40 09 07). General travel information, English-speaking staff. Open Mon.-Fri. 9am-1pm and 4:30-8pm, Sat. 9am-1pm.

Currency Exchange: in the train station at the information desk (tel. 65 62 93). Excellent rates. Open Mon.-Sat. 7am-10pm.

Post Office: P. del Carmine near P. Matteotti (tel. 66 83 56). **Fermo Posta** L250 per letter. Open Mon.-Sat. 8am-4:40pm, but some services close at 1pm. **Postal code:** 09100.

Telephones: ASST, Via Angioy, off P. Matteotti. An efficient but expensive office. Open 24 hrs. for international calls. **SIP,** Via Cima, 9, off Via Manno. Open daily 8am-9:30pm. **Telephone code:** 070.

Airport: in the village of **Elmas** (tel. 24 01 11, 24 00 46, or 24 01 69). Free ARST buses for ticketholders run between the airport and the city terminal at P. Matteotti (20min.) before each flight.

Trains: Ferrovie dello Stato (tel. 65 62 93), P. Matteotti. In summer, 9 trains per day to: Olbia (L18,200), Porto Torres (L19,500), Sássari (L18,700), and Oristano (L6300). **Ferrovie Complimentarie della Sardegna** (tel. 49 13 04), P. della Repubblica. A private railroad.

Buses: PANI, P. Darsena, 4 (tel. 65 23 26). Nonstop service to Sássari at 7am and 2:15pm (L28,000). Open Mon.-Sat. 9am-2pm and 5-7pm, Sun. 1-2pm and 5:15-6:15pm. **ARST,** P. Matteotti, 6 (tel. 65 72 36), serves local towns (see above for more info). Office open 5am-10pm.

Ferries: Tirrenia, Via Campidano, 1 (tel. 66 60 65), at the end of the Via Roma arcade. Service to Genoa (L77,200), Civitavécchia (L47,700), Palermo (L44,300), and Tunis (via Trápani, L100,400). Open Mon.-Fri. 9am-1pm and 4-7pm. The new office in Stazione Marittima in the port opens 1hr. before ships depart.

Car Rental: Ruvioli, Via dei Mille, 11 (tel. 65 89 55). Minimum age 18. Major credit card recommended or L500,000 deposit. Rates are L96,000 per day, L142,000 per weekend, L486,000 per week. Reserve one week in advance. Another branch location at the airport (tel. 697 33). Open Mon.-Sat. 8:30am-1pm and 3:30-8pm.

Laundry: Lavanderia a Gettone, Via Concezione, 3/A. Self-service. Open Mon.-Fri. L3000 per kg. Open 8:30am-1pm and 4-8pm.

English Bookstore: La Bancarella, Via Roma, 169. Classics and a complete selection of romance novels. Open Mon.-Fri. 9am-1pm and 4:30-8pm, Sat. 9am-1pm.

Pharmacy: Farmacia Dr. Spano, Via Roma, 99 (tel. 65 56 83). Gives out a free booklet with helpful phrases concerning illness (in 4 languages). Open Mon.-Sat. 9am-1pm, and 4:30-10:10pm.

Emergencies: tel. 113. **Police: Questura,** Via Amat, 9 (tel. 602 71). **Hospital:** military hospital on Via Ospedale, 46 (tel. 66 57 55), by the Chiesa di San Michele. Near the beach Il Poetto, try **Ospedale Marino,** Viale Poetto, 12 (tel. 37 36 73). **First Aid:** tel. 267.

ACCOMMODATIONS

Cagliari has an ample stock of inexpensive pads, but there is fierce competition year-round: university students from September until mid-July, tourists from July to mid-September. Ask the tourist office in P. Matteotti for help.

Albergo Firenze, Corso Vittorio Emanuele, 50 (tel. 65 36 78), on the 5th floor. Current proprietress is sweet as can be, renting clean, airy rooms in a manner that makes you feel welcomed into an Italian home. The walls are covered in paintings and sketches by her mother, her guests, and other notable persons. Singles L25,000. Doubles L30,000.

Allogio Londra, Viale Regina Margherita, 16 (tel. 66 90 83), right next to the PANI station. The huge, chipped wooden doors, high ceilings, and lace curtains house comfortable rooms. British proprietess very helpful on directions for local beaches and sights. Lock-out times from 9:30am-1pm while they clean the rooms. Singles L28,000, with bath L32,000. Doubles L40,000, with bath L48,000.

Locanda Las Palmas, Via Sardegna, 14 (tel. 65 16 79), next to La Perla. Good location, adequate rooms, unusual bedspreads. Singles L28,000. Doubles L41,000.

Pensione Vittoria, Via Roma, 75 (tel. 65 79 70) on the 3rd floor, next to the movie theater. A small, elegant *pensione* with cavernous, majestic rooms, inlaid mosaic floors, beautiful furnishings, and views of the sea. Singles L38,000, with bath L44,000. Doubles L56,000, with bath L70,000.

FOOD

For basic picnic fare, try the far end of Via Sardegna where one finds several small shops that provide fruit and bread.

Panetteria Mura, Via Sardegna, 40 (open 7:30am-1pm and 5-8:30pm). Vegetarians will be pleased to find soy milk and other hard-to-find protein products.

Trattoria Barrilicu, Via Sardegna, 78 (tel. 65 29 70). Established 80 years ago and run by the same family, this trattoria resides in a single, ancient room with wooden beams on the ceiling, shaped with tapestries. A wild boar's head greets you as you enter. Try their *spaghetti ai gambini* (L8,000). (Open Mon.-Sat. noon-3pm and 8-11pm.)

Da Bruno, Via Cavour, 17 (tel. 653 54). True Sardinian cuisine in a warm, hospitable atmosphere. Try the *malloreddus alla Campidanese* (traditional cornflour dumplings with saffron and *peccorino* cheese, L7000) and the *porchetto sardo* (roast pork with Sardinian seasoning, L12,000). Open Tues.-Sun. 12:30-2:30pm and 7:30-11pm. MC, Visa.

La Cantina, Via dei Mille, 3 (tel. 66 64 30). A cavernous interior with fast-food offerings and prices. Fantastic salads with fresh, crisp, vegetables for malnourished travelers for L2000-L3000. Stuff yourself for less than L4000. Open Mon.-Sat. 9am-3pm and 5-10:30pm.

SIGHTS

The conspicuous pink towers of the **Bastione di San Remy** mark the division between the modern port and the cramped medieval quarter on the hill above. A steep climb up the stairway to the terrace offers a spectacular view of the Golfo degli Angeli, the marshes to the west, and the "Devil's Saddle," a rock formation set amidst the mountains surrounding Cagliari. The slender steps behind the *bastione* lead to medieval Cagliari, where wrought-iron balconies overflow with flowers. Narrow streets lead uphill to the **duomo,** a charming exemplar of Pisan geometry refinished in 1933 by Giarrizzo in the Romanesque style of the Pisa cathedral. The pulpits at the entrance, depicting scenes from the New Testament, are the work of Guglielmo Pisano, as are the four wrestling lions at the base of the 12th-century altar. Before leaving, glance below at the sanctuary carved into the island rock in 1618. The colorful marble inlays with animated miniatures of Sardinian saints cover the 292 niches containing the relics of early Christian martyrs.

The age-blackened **Torre di San Pancrazio** (1305) is up the hill on P. Indipendenza, and its mate, **Torre dell'Elefante** (1307), lies below on Via Università. These towers shade the **Museo Nazionale Archeologico,** a repository of grave artifacts from the earliest period of Sardinian history. Prehistoric figurines stand beside elegant Greek statues, and the curves of Roman vases reflect sparkling Phoenician jewelery. Most impressive are the broad-shouldered warriors and pot-bellied gods crafted in bronzed stone by the people of the mysterious nuraghic civilization. Unfortunately the museum has been closed since February 1992 to move to a new location. Check with the tourist office to see if it has reopened.

Pass under the Torre di San Pancrazio to the **Arsenale,** from whose lofty towers you can admire the model-like cityscape. There you will find the **Cittadella dei Musei,** a modern complex of research museums that houses Oriental art. A short stroll down a curving lane leads to the public gardens at the end of Viale R. Elena. To the left of the **museo civico** is a gallery of contemporary Sardinian painting and sculpture. (Open Tues.-Sat. 9am-1pm and 4-7pm. Free.) To the left of Viale Buon Cammino is the **Roman amphitheater,** the most significant Roman ruin in Sardinia. It was constructed in the 2nd century from a natural depression in the rock. Continue down Via San Ignazio da Laconi to the university **botanical gardens** with over 500 species of plants. (Open Tues.-Sun. 8:30am-8pm; admission L1000, children L500.)

A small pagan temple from the Roman era was incorporated into the **Church of San Saturno** in 470 AD. The oldest church on the island, it was built in the shape of a Greek cross with a dome to designate the site where Saturnus was martyred during the reign of Diocletian. The church now stands closed and forlorn in an empty lot in P. San Cosimo off Via Dante near the cemetery.

ENTERTAINMENT

A **flea market** fires up on Sunday mornings at the **Bastione di San Remy** (Terrazza Umberto). Comb through used clothes, toys, and assorted junk to the thumping beat of reggae and rap. Also on Sundays, explore the **food market** on the far side of the stadium in Borgo Sant'Elia. Fresh fruit and seafood are yours if you're willing to bargain in this huge local gathering.

During the first four days of May, Sardinians flock to Cagliari for the stupendous **Festival of Sant'Efisio,** faithfully honoring a vow made 300 years ago to a deserter from Diocletian's army who saved the island from the plague. A costumed procession escorts his effigy from the capital down the coast to the small church that bears his name.

From July to September, the city hosts an **arts festival.** The amphitheater rejuvenates with classic plays, and outdoor movies are shown at the Marina Piccola, off Spiaggia del Poetto (see below).

■ Near Cagliari

Beaches

C.S. Elia and **Il Poetto** (4km and 6km southeast of the city, respectively) are grand sandy beaches. The latter stretches 10km from the mountainous Sella del Diavolo (Devil's Saddle) to the Margine Rosso (Red Bluff); behind it are the salt-water **Stagno di Molentargius** (Ponds of Molentargius), a popular flamingo hangout. City bus P leaves every 20 min. from Via Roma going away from the train station (20min., 1100, ticket must be bought beforehand at newsstand). After arriving at the beach stay on the bus to reach areas not packed with locals. Better yet, head for **Cala Mosca,** a smaller, less crowded beach surrounded by dirt paths that lead to isolated coves for more private sunning and swimming. To get here, take city bus 5/12 to Stadio Amsicora (ask the driver or look out the window to your left) and then city bus 11 to the beach. It takes a bit longer to reach than Il Poetto but is well worth it.

Uta, Barúmini, and Nora

The tiny village of **Uta** (20km west of Cagliari) shelters the **Church of Santa Maria,** one of the island's most notable Romanesque buildings. Built around 1140, the church is a deft fusion of French and Pisan architectural styles. Eleven ARST buses per day depart for Uta (40min., L2800).

Barúmini, an agricultural bastion in the rolling countryside 60km north of Cagliari, lies 1km west of the **Nuraghi of Su Nuraxi.** (Open daily 8am-dusk.) These ruins are the best-preserved complex of *nuraghi* in Sardinia. Set atop a hill, the village is constructed of huge, rough-hewn blocks in an intricate layout, vividly illustrating the defensive nature of this civilization. The only direct service from Cagliari to Barúmini is the daily ARST run at 2:10pm (1hr. 30min., L7000). To return, take the FCS bus at 6:30pm (L3200) to San Luri. Once in San Luri, go to the FS train station to catch the commuter train to Cagliari at 7:10pm (L4200).

Partially submerged, **Nora,** said to be the oldest city in Sardinia, was settled by the Phoenicians (circa 850 BC), who coveted its strategic position at the end of a high, narrow peninsula surrounded by the Mediterranean. The town prospered, becoming in time a Roman stronghold. Its luck faltered, however, with the onslaught of pirate raids, and by the 8th century, Nora was abandoned completely. From its rugged location, strong winds whipping across the ancient wall, one gains a clear understanding of how the various sea-based empires of antichita might have appeared; the ancient central square of the town is enclosed by a temple with only one column left standing, but the theater remains in excellent condition. What was once a busy marketplace two centuries ago has now been worn away by the erosion of the sea. Several former dwellings of merchants display the intricate mosaics of their flowers preserved almost intact. Those with an interest in archeology and a basic knowledge of Italian should pick up the archeological guide by Carlo

Tronchetti at the entrance (L8000). It deepens the experience of Nora, describing intriguing details in the excavated ruins. (Open daily 9am-8pm; off-season 9am-12:30pm and 2-5pm. Admission L3000, children over 10, L1500, 10 and under, free.) Nearby is a pleasant beach. ARST buses make a run to Pula every hour (30min., L3300). From Pula, it's a 4km walk to Nora; follow Corso Emanuele, turn left when it ends, and follow the signs.

NÚORO AND ITS PROVINCE

Invasions and foreign domination have defined the political history of coastal Sardinia; older Sardinian culture was forced to retreat inland. If true *Sardi* exist today, they must live in Núoro, where the jagged terrain of Sardinia's interior has sculpted a diffident *campagnola* (rural) mentality in its inhabitants. Proud peasant women, dressed in magpie black, drape Spanish *fazzolletti* (shawls) over their shoulders and murmur in a dialect studied by academics worldwide for its similarity to Latin, while their children sport Levi's and cruise the streets on mopeds. A car is ideal for visits to the Núoro province's smaller villages, as much of the region is inaccessible by public transport and is less well-adapted to tourism than Sardinia's larger cities but is perfect for the traveler who wants to take on the rugged natural landscape through trekking and other adventures.

■■■ NÚORO

PRACTICAL INFORMATION

From the station, follow Via Lamarmora to **Piazza della Grazie.** From there Corso Garibaldi leads to Piazza Vittorio Emanuele II, the ARST station, the *duomo,* and the main shopping area on Via Manzoni. Behind you and up the hill along Via IV Novembre you'll find the Piazza d'Italia, the tourist office, and the PANI station. To the right of the **Chiesa della Grazie** lie the privately-run train station and a residential area.

Tourist Office: P. Italia, 9 (tel. 300 83). Armed with an array of booklets and brochures, the staff is eager to evoke Núoro's past. English spoken. Usually open Mon.-Fri. 9am-1pm and 4-7pm.

Post Office: P. Crispi, 8 (tel. 302 78), off Via Dante. Open Mon.-Sat. 8am-7:40pm. **Postal Code:** 08100.

Telephones: SIP, Via Brigata Sassari, 6, at P. d'Italia 1 block from the tourist office. Open Mon.-Sat. 8:30am-12:30pm and 3-7pm, Sun. 8am-1pm. **Telephone code:** 0784.

Fax: Eliografa Legatoria, Via Lamarmora, 54. Open Mon.-Fri. 8am-1pm and 4-7pm, Sat. 8am-1pm.

Trains and Buses (PANI): Station located at the corner of Via Lamarmora and (appropriately) Via Stazione. At Piazza Emanuele (2 blocks from the *duomo*), is a center of youth activity and also the local **ARST** station where you can catch a bus to the train/PANI station. Daily service to: Cala Gonzone (L4500); Dorgali (L3500); Oliena (L1500); Orgósolo (L2500); Cagliari (L18,500); and Monte Ortobene (L1200). Trains fairly reliable. Tickets for PANI available at Tobacco/Bar attached to the Lamarmora station.

Car Rental: Autonoleggio Maggiore, Via Convento, 32 (tel. 304 61). Open Mon.-Sat. 8am-1pm and 4-7pm.

Emergencies: tel. 113. **Ambulance/Medical Emergency:** tel. 363 02. Volunteer ambulance service only.

ACCOMMODATIONS AND FOOD

Inexpensive establishments are few and far between in Núoro, and the camp-grounds are miles away. If you are unable to find accommodations here, consider staying in Orgósolo or Oliena where rooms tend to be available.

Il Portico, Via Mons. Bua (tel. 375 35), near the end of P. Vittorio Emanuele. Pleas-ant, clean rooms with private showers and baths and a rustic decor. Management runs great restaurant below. Singles L40,000. Doubles L50,000. Reserve ahead.
Mini Hotel, Via Brofferio, 13 (tel. 331 59), off Via Roma. Overlooks an enormous construction site. Homey, clean, and noisy, with an effusive staff. Ask for a one of the back rooms which face a small courtyard. All rooms with baths. Singles L50,000. Doubles L65,000.
Hotel Grillo, Via Mons. Melas, 14 (tel. 386 78), off Via Manzoni. Residential neigh-borhood away from center, across from the judo school. Baths in every room, and full of fine touches. Singles L65,000. Doubles L87,000.

Cheap restaurants are scarce. Try the well-hidden but very friendly **supermarket** on Via Manzoni, next to the Alitalia office. (Open Mon.-Fri. 8am-1pm and 4-7:30pm, Sat. 8am-1pm.) Closer to the ARST station is the **Supermarket Vina** (Via Veneto, 5), with low prices and local products. (Open Mon.-Fri. 8am-1pm and 4-8pm, Sat. 8am-1pm.) For fresh fruit, cheese, and meat, explore the enclosed **market** at P. Mameli, 20, also off Via Manzoni. (Open Mon.-Tues. and Thurs.-Sat. 8am-1pm and 4:30-7pm, Wed. 8am-1pm.)

Pizzeria Del Diavolo, Via Dante, 10, near the post office. A variety of sinfully good pizzas (cheese L2000, mushroom L2500) and *panini*. This is where black-garbed locals come for take-out. Open Mon.-Sat. 8:30am-2pm and 5-10pm.
Il Portico, Via M. Bua (tel. 331 59), off the north end of P. Vittorio Emanuele. Con-nected to the hotel, this restaurant serves delicious, elegant meals to locals. Pizzas L5500-7000. Cover L2000. Open Tues.-Sun. noon-2:30pm and 8:15-10:30pm.

SIGHTS AND SEASONAL EVENTS

Despite Núoro's provincial appearance, there are a few small treasures to be found. As you walk in the streets above P. Mazzini, keep your eyes open for stark leftist **murals,** similar to those at Orgósolo. The surreal **Piazza Sebastiano Satta,** named for the local poet, lies off Via Roma. Alcoves cut into twisted pillars of rock cradle statuettes that tell his story. The recently renovated *duomo* in P. Santa Maria della Neve merits a visit. The major attraction in town is the **Museo della Vita e delle Tradizioni Popolari Sarde** (Museum of Sardinian Life and Popular Traditions), Via Mereu, 56. Follow the signs up from the cathedral. The museum has masks, tradi-tional costumes, and various artifacts recalling the pastoral past of Núoro's inhabit-ants. One of the better known masks is the farmer's mask and costume replete with sheep fur, cowbells, and a grimace worn during primitive Sardinian festivals. (Open Tues.-Sat. 9am-1pm and 3-7pm, Sun. 9am-1pm. Free.) Núoro celebrates one such festival—the **Sagra del Rendetore,** on the last two Sundays of August. Núoro's natives claim that while in other parts of Sardinia such rites exist to placate tourists, here they are "proprio sentiti" (truly felt).

Núoro also provides housing to the **Museo Regionale del Costume,** Viale San Francesco, with exhibits of more traditional clothing, and the **Museo Civico Speleo,** an archeological museum of items found in the Nuraghic province. The latter is a great way to learn about the region's geography. (Both open Tues. and Thurs. 9am-1pm and 3-7pm, Wed., Fri., and Sun. 9am-1pm. Free.) The **Casa di Grazia Deledda** has been preserved as a museum exhibiting the personal effects of the 1926 Nobel Prize winner in literature. (Open daily 9am-1pm. Free.) Sardinians are very proud of their writer; myriad *vie* and *piazze* are named in her honor. For more information about her life ask for the English language pamphlet at the tourist office.

■ The Province

For a picnic, take the orange APT bus from P. Vittorio Emanuele up to **Monte Orto-bene** (3 per day, 10min., L1200). At the peak lies a shady park from which a large bronze statue of Christ the Redeemer overlooks the neighboring hamlets. From the bus stop on top of Monte Ortobene, walk 20m down the road to get a good view of colossal **Monte Corrasi,** dwarfing the town of **Oliena** below.

If the view intrigues you, hop on a bus and check out Oliena up close (30min., L1500). In this undeveloped heartland village the black-clad women attend mass daily while old men cluster in the piazze and discuss the weather and their wives' cooking. There are several churches in Oliena; **Santa Croce** on Via Grazia Deledda, begun in 1580, is still largely intact and well worth a visit. The stone exterior is surrounded by flowers, and the interior contains an ancient wooden tabernacle with an eerily life-like wooden sculpture of Christ's body in a coffin (used during the rites of Saints' Week). Ask the **Pro Loco** (tourist office; tel. (0784) 28 87 77) for the keys to visit; to reach the office continue straight on Via Vittorio Emanuele II (after the bus drops you off at the little white chapel) and take the large stairway to your left. The office is in the middle of a flight of stairs on your right. No maps of the city exist, but they can give you directions. (Open daily 9am-1pm and 3:30-7:30pm.)

Ci Kappa, on Via Martin Luther King (tel. (0784) 28 87 33) is a famous bar, restaurant, and hotel, with a view onto Corso Vittorio Emanuele II and the mountain. The rooms are modern and comfortable, and all have private baths. (Singles L53,000; doubles L72,000.) Another acclaimed hotel/restaurant in the area is **Su Gologone** (tel. (0784) 28 75 12), advertised throughout Sardinia for its "traditional" cuisine and snazzy accommodations with horseback riding, pool, bars, and disco. The only hitches are the price (of course) and the fact that it rests 8km outside of Oliena toward Dorgali. Singles are L79,000 and doubles are L110,000; while a complete meal will run you upwards of L45,000. **Carrus,** Via N. Bixio, 11 (tel. (0784) 28 90 66) is an *agriturismo* farm. Bed and breakfast are L25,000 if you stay one night, and drop to L20,000 per night for extended stays. (Check with the Terranostra agency.)

Venturing past Oliena is problematic since the scarcity of public transportation limits exploration of the hill towns south of Núoro. **ARST** buses run round-trip at inconvenient hours. One remote town easily accessible from Núoro is **Orgósolo,** a pleasant 40-minute ride (L2400) through rolling, ochre-colored countryside punctuated by vineyards. The area's bloody history of *banditismo* (banditry) was made famous throughout Italy by the 1963 film *The Bandits of Orgósolo.* Even today the town still has an air of living beyond the reach of justice. Check out Orgósolo's colorful 1960s **murals,** a series of leftist and nationalist paintings covering walls on **Corso Repubblica,** the town's main street. A local teacher initiated the paintings after studying art in Latin America. A mural decrying American imperialism lies on Via John Kennedy. In **Piazza Caduti in Guerra,** a spring trickles from a water-gouged rock, a memorial to the town's war dead. Across the street, a mural depicts an old man resting, decorated with a war medal. A Brechtian inscription reads, "Happy are the people who have no need of heroes."

If you desire repose and an evening in town, stay at **Hotel Sa'e Jana,** Via Lusu (tel. (0784) 40 24 37), a family-run hotel with large rooms, balconies, private baths, and a rustic atmosphere rarely found in Italian hotels. Anyone with a smidgen of Italian should not lose the chance to question the grandmother about her personal experiences with Orgosolo's banditismo in the 1950's. Good, simple, food at low prices in the restaurant downstairs. Ask the proprietor about his tri-weekly "peasant" feasts accompanied by traditional Sardinian folksongs. (Singles L35,000, doubles L70,000.) Closer to the center of town lies the **Petit Hotel,** Via Mannu, 9 (tel (0784) 40 20 09), off Corso Repubblica, in a small cluster of dirty buildings. It offers comfortable rooms and prices (singles L25,000, with bath L30,000; doubles L36,000, with bath L40,000). If you miss the last bus back to Núoro and are tempted to hitch after dark, reconsider—**hitchhiking is not safe here.** *Bandito* activity occasionally resurfaces in the countryside, though it is usually not directed at tourists, but reserved instead for the locals. **Women should not walk alone in the countryside here.**

Just over one hour east of Núoro by ARST bus (5 per day Via Dorgali, L4400) lies **Cala Gonone,** the gateway to a number of spectacular beaches and caves. Take the steps through the wooded area when you get off the bus.

The beaches at Cala Gonone are pebbly and crowded. A walk or ride down the dirt road along the coast rewards the effort with sandier, less-populated beaches. Boats leave four times per day, more often in July and August (L14,000), for the stunning **Grotta del Bue Marino** (Cave of the Monk Seal), one of the last haunts of this elusive creature. The seals rarely appear during the day, however, and the cave itself is the main attraction. Nearly 1km of its more than 5km expanse of caverns, stalactites, and lakes is illuminated. However, stampeding crowds and the locked gate isolating the glowing grotto mar the experience. Just down the coast is the vast beach of **Cala Luna.** Encircled by marshes and caverns, the beach is accessible only by boat (L13,000, combined grotto/Cala Luna ticket L19,000). Boats also run to the more remote and equally breathtaking beaches of **Cala Sistre** (L22,000), **Biriola d'Aguglia** (L29,000, reservation required), and **Cala Mariolu** (L27,500), all accessible only by boat. **Consortto Marittimo Transport** has monopolized the boat transport market to beaches. Call for reservations (tel. (0786) 93 305). **Cala Osal** is accessible only by car.

Cala Gonone has wholeheartedly embraced the creed of tourism, making budget accommodations a sacrilege. Try the convenient (if noisy) **Albergo Gabbiano** at P. Porto, in the port (tel. 93 130). Rooms overlook the water. (Singles L35,000, doubles L45,000.) One step up is the newly renovated **Piccolo Hotel,** Via Colomba, 32 (tel. 93 232). The gracious proprietor lets elegant, immaculate rooms with balconies overlooking a quiet garden. (Singles with bath L50,000; doubles with bath L80,000, with mandatory summer pension L90,000 per person.) A large, well-equipped, and expensive **campground** on Via Collodi (tel. 931 65), across from the city park, charges L14,900 per person (L18,600 in July and August), and L2000 for a lamp. (Open April-Sept.)

ORISTANO AND ITS PROVINCE

Oristano sustains a quiet life, keeping the beauty of the Sinis peninsula beaches and ruins to itself. During the prehistoric times, the mineral wealth of the region attracted settlers from the Nuraghic civilization who left stone monuments as evidence of their presence here. The town of Oristano, capital of the province, saw the height of its independent splendor in the 14th century when the princess Eleanora d'Arborea led the last stages of native resistance to mainland invaders. Part of her legacy was a massive legal code in ancient Sardinian that was adopted throughout the island. Oristano's provincial, agricultural feel sets it apart from the more touristed towns in Sardegna. It is a good base for visiting nearby beaches and archeological sites.

■ Oristano

ORIENTATION AND PRACTICAL INFORMATION

Piazza Roma is the center of town. From the station, follow **Via Vittorio Veneto,** the street furthest to the right as you exit the station, straight to **Piazza Mariana,** then take **Via Mazzini** to Piazza Roma. The **ARST** station and **tourist office** are located on the south end of Via Cagliari. There is a large map outside of the ARST station. To get to P. Roma form there, follow **Via Emanuele** from nearby **Piazza Mannu.** From the PANI station (located on Via Lombarda on the other side of town—north of P. Roma) head toward Via Tirso. Make a right and then a quick left

ORISTANO

onto Via Cagliari. When you come to Via Tharros, turn left and this will take you directly into the square.

Tourist Office: Via Cagliari, 278 (tel. 73 191 or 74 191), 6th floor, near P. Mannu across from the ARST station. Extremely helpful, well-informed staff with information on the town and region. Open Mon. and Thurs.-Fri. 8am-2pm, Tues.-Wed. 8am-2pm and 4-8pm. **Pro Loco,** Vico Umberto, 1 (tel. 70 621), off Via de Castro, between P. Roma and P. Eleonora d'Arborea. Independent tourist office with information on Oristano only. Open Mon.-Fri. 9am-noon and 5-8pm, Sat. 9am-noon. A Pro Loco **trailer** summers on P. Roma. Open daily 9:30am-9pm. A new Pro Loco office is in the works on Via Vittorio Emanuele.

Post Office: Via Mariano IV, 10 (tel. 30 27 34). Open Mon.-Sat. 8:15am-7:40pm. **Postal code:** 09170.

Telephones: SIP, P. Eleonora d'Arborea, 40, opposite the Church of San Francesco. Open Mon.-Fri. 8:30am-12:30pm and 3-7pm, Sat. 8:30am-12:30pm. **Telephone code:** 0783.

Trains: P. Ungheria (tel. 72 270), about 1km from the town center. Trains to: Sássari (4 per day, 3hr., L12,400), Olbia (4 per day, 4hr., L14,200), and Cagliari (15 per day, 1hr., L7400).

Buses: PANI, Via Lombardia, 30 (tel. 21 268), at a bar. Three buses leave daily to: Cagliari (8:55am, 4:19pm, and 9:35pm, 1hr. 30min., L11,000); Núoro (7am, 3:30pm, and 7:50pm, 2hr., L11,000); Sássari (7am, 3:30pm, and 7:50 pm, 2hr. 15min., L13,000). **ARST,** Via Cagliari (tel. 780 01), connects local routes and runs 2 slower buses to Cagliari (7:10am and 2:10pm, 2hr. 15min., L11,000).

Laundry: Lavanderia Espresso, Via Sardegna, 137, across from the Bonsai restaurant. L3000 per kg. Open Mon.-Fri. 8:30am-1pm and 4-7pm.

Emergencies: tel. 113. **Ambulance/Medical Emergency:** tel. 78 222. **Main hospital,** Via Fondazione Rockefeller (tel. 74 261). **First Aid:** tel. 74 333.

ACCOMMODATIONS AND CAMPING

Prices and quality here are consistent with those of northern cities. Oristano caters more to traveling Sardinian businessmen than to tourists and competition is low, keeping prices bloated.

Piccolo Hotel, Via Martignano, 19 (tel. 71 500), off Via Crispi. From P. Eleonora d'Arborea, walk in the direction of the statue's stare. Take a right, an immediate left, the 3rd right, and then a left. Tidy, tiny rooms, all with baths, several with massive balconies overlooking the Medieval city. Helpful, philosophically-inclined management. Singles L55,000. Doubles L80,000.

I.S.A., P. Mariano, 50 (tel. 36 01 01). If the Piccolo is full the only other option is this medium-range hotel with a lobby carpeted in purple velours, elevators, gleaming glass panes, and silver surfaces everywhere. Well-furnished, pleasant rooms are appropriate for the price. Singles L65,000. Doubles L100,000. Off-season: singles L35,000, doubles L60,000.

Camping: Marinadi Torre Grande, Via Stella Maris (tel. 22 228), 100m out of Torre Grande on the road to Oristano (7km). Facilities galore, but packed in summer. L6000 per person, L10,000 per tent. Open July-Sept. There are also bungalows available for rent. They house up to 4 and are a bargain at around L80,000 (off season L50,000).

Agriturismo: ask at the tourist office for information. Spots generally run L35,000 per person including half-pension.

FOOD

You can buy the basics for rock-bottom prices at the **Euro-Drink market,** P. Roma, 22. (Open Mon.-Sat. 8am-1pm and 5-8pm.) The **STANDA supermarket** is at the corner of Via Diaz and Via Cavour. (Open Mon.-Fri. 8:30am-1pm and 4:30-8pm, Sat. 8:30am-1pm.)

Bonsai, Via Sardegna, 140 (tel. 73 546). Sit down in the back or take out from the bar to take advantage of their fantastic sandwich menu (L3500-4500) or try a full sit-down meal with wine (L16,000). Very friendly service, popular with the locals and worth the walk. Open Wed.-Mon. 7:30am-11pm.

Arborea, P. Roma, 15 (tel. 70 363). Boisterous locals dine under huge murals that portray the astounding and rapid succession of Sardinian civilizations, invasions, and governments. Try the outstanding *spaghetti alle arselle* (scallops, L9000). *Menù* L25,000. Open daily noon-3pm and 7-11pm.

SIGHTS AND ENTERTAINMENT

The center of town is **Piazza Roma,** dominated by the 13th-century **Tower of St. Christopher.** On summer evenings, young *oristanesi* rock and ramble through the piazza and the adjoining **Corso Umberto.** The pastel **Church of San Francesco** (1838) stands at the end of Via de Castro, at P. Eleonora d'Arborea. In the sacristy of this Pantheon-inspired building, the 16th-century polyptych of *St. Francis Receiving the Stigmata* and the 14th-century statue of San Basilio by Nino Pisano evince deep reverence. The main sanctuary displays a wooden crucifix, a simple, straight cross on which the emaciated and tortured body of Christ is draped (typical of 14th-century German art, left altar), and a balustrade formed from fragments of an 11th-century pulpit (right transept).

A statue in P. Eleonora d'Arborea by the *municipio* commemorates **Eleonora d'Arborea,** Sardinia's Joan of Arc. This local heroine was a 14th-century princess who successfully defended independent Sardinia against the encroaching Aragonese. She is remembered for drafting the *Carta de Logu* (Code of Laws) in 1395, setting down the Sardinian legal system for almost 500 years and preserving the ancient Sardinian language in which it was written. The matriarchal tradition continues in Oristano to this day—many provincial officials, including the most recent governor and mayor, have been women.

Down Via E. d'Arborea from P. E. d'Arborea is the **duomo,** a delightful amalgam of a 13th-century skeleton and 18th-century embellishment. Outside, a rainbow-colored cupola sits on top of the octagonal bell tower. Inside are chandeliers, tapestries, paintings, and even some stained glass. Patterns of yellow, blue, and lavender create halos around the icons and altars. Three kilometers out of town on the road to Cagliari is the equally remarkable 12th-century **Basilica of Santa Giusta,** typically Sardinian in its synthesis of Lombard and Pisan influences. The sculpted façade depicts two lions dismembering and devouring a deer. Set against this macabre backdrop is a tremendous square cross of dark blocks. The interior is simple and severe, so as not to distract the pious during uninspiring sermons.

On the last Sunday of **Carnevale** (in March) and the following Tuesday (inquire at the tourist office), Oristano celebrates the **Sartiglia,** a traditional race first run in the 16th century in which masked horsemen try to pierce six-inch metal stars with their swords as they gallop down the street. Those who pierce a lot of stars bring *Fortuna* upon the next harvest. In nearby **Cabras** (on the road to Tharros), **La Corsa degli Scalzi** is performed the first Sunday in September. This procession of white-clad, barefoot runners, bearing a statue of San Saivatore, reenacts the brave feat of Oristanese women at the time of the Moorish invasion. While the men remained to defend the town of San Salvatore, the women carried the statue of the town's saint away to safety in neighboring Cabras. On July 6 and 7, the town of **Ardia** sponsors a frenzied and occasionally fatal horse race in which zealous riders circle a church seven times to commemorate Emperor Constantine's victory at the Milvian Bridge in 312 AD. Go early to get a good standing place; the horse cavalcade begins between 6 and 7pm. There is no public transportation to the event.

■ Sinis Peninsula and the Costa Verde

The coastal areas surrounding Oristano offer everything that the better-known resorts do—except the concrete and crowds.

20km west of Oristano, in the southernmost tip of the peninsula, lie the ruins of the ancient Phoenician port of **Tharros.** Much of the city remains submerged, but excavations have revealed Punic fortifications, a Roman temple dedicated to Demeter, a paleochristian baptistry, and a Punic shrine. Additionally, the impeccable beaches here are beautiful and serene. To reach Tharros, take an ARST bus (40min., one way L2500, round-trip L5000) directly to the site. Student guides paid by the Council of Cabras lead informative free tours of the ruins in Italian. On the way to Tharros you'll pass two interesting churches: **San Salvatore,** built above a pagan temple whose Roman deities (Venus, Cupid, and Hercules) are still visible on an underground wall, and **San Giovanni in Sinis,** a part-pagan, part-Christian structure dating from the 5th century that seems, in structure and spirit, to be a distant ancestor of Oristano's Santa Giusta. During the 1960s San Salvadore was converted into a Mexican-American "Old West" village for several spaghetti westerns.

On the other side of the isthmus from Tharros are the beaches and village of **San Giovanni di Sinis.** To go directly there, take the ARST bus (4 per day at 8am, noon, 2pm, and 6:50pm; L2500, round-trip L5000). The two sites, Tharros and San Giovanni, are close enough that you might buy a ticket for the ruins and then cross over to San Giovanni on foot.

15km north of San Giovanni on the peninsula are the beaches of **Putzu Idu** and **Cala Saline.** Beautiful, white-sanded, and largely empty, they're worth a swim or even a few quiet days of lolling. Three villages lie in close proximity on this remote corner of the peninsula. The only affordable accommodation is at **Hotel "Su Pallosu,"** Via Sa Margosa, 2, in Marina di S. Vero Milis (tel. (0783) 580 21). (Singles L40,000. Doubles L70,000.) The local fishing community frequents the bar. You can find cheap food, live music and a friendly gathering every night at **Club Tomoka;** just ask at the hotel for directions. To get to Putzu Idu from Oristano, take the ARST bus (direction Barátili or San Pietro) and get off at Riola (25min.). Walk down Via Roma, which dead-ends onto Via Umberto, and turn right. Wait for the connecting bus a few meters down the street, across from the motocycle repair shop. The connecting bus (use the same ticket) will be marked "Cala Saline"; take it for another 8km (10-15min.) right to the beach. (Bus leaves Oristano 9:50am; returns at 1pm and 7pm; L3000.) Walk a few kilometers south along the coast to see the stunning cliffs at **Capo sa Starraggia.** Approximately 7km south, the lovely cliffs and white beach of **Is Arustas** await the hardy hiker; the less ambitious can take an ARST bus directly to Is Arutas (same line as San Giovanni, L3500).

About 35km south of Oristano, the **Costa Verde** stretches nearly 40km, a happy mingling of sandy coves and scintillating ocean. Yet apart from the two coastal towns of Porto Palma and Marina di Arbus (where there is a rudimentary campsite), there are few denizens to speak of, and even fewer travelers. ARST buses take you part of the way to Arbus (*not* Marina di Arbus or Diane) at 8:10am, 2pm, and 5:45pm (1hr. 30min., L5500) but you'll have to fend for yourself from there.

■■■ ALGHERO

For a place originally labeled "L'Aleguerium" because of the abundance of seaweed cluttering its shores, Alghero has come a long way. Its serpentine cobblestone streets, stately eucalyptus trees, and parasol pines overlook a magnificent expanse of ocean. In the 11th century, the Genovese transformed Alghero from an insignificant fishing village into a major trading post; in 1350 a wave of Catalonian immigrants repopulated the city. Natives still speak the melodious Catalan language, a number of restaurants serve *paella,* and many of the piazze are called *plaças.* In fact, the town's Spanish air has earned it the nickname of the "Barcelonetta of Sardinia."

ORIENTATION AND PRACTICAL INFORMATION

From **Piazza Porta Terra,** with one's back to the tourist office, the **ARST** and city buses stop to one's left, on **Via Garibaldi** and in the park, the medieval quarter lies downhill to one's right, and straight ahead along **Via Simon** and **Via Kennedy** lies the hotel district, a more modern quarter where one can find lodgings for the night.

Getting to and from Alghero by public transportation usually requires going through Sássari. Alghero is one hour from Sássari by ARST **bus** (5 per day, L4500), SFS bus (10 per day, L4500), and by **train** (10 per day, L3200). ARST buses also run directly to Porto Torres (4 per day, 50min., L4800).

Tourist Office: P. Porta Terra, 9 (tel. 97 90 54), near the bus stop. On your right as you walk toward the old city from the park. Pleasant staff provides a street-indexed map, list of accommodations, and bus and train schedules. Ask about lodgings at one of the **Agriturismo** farms in nearby villages: there are many local possibilities. English spoken. Open daily Mon.-Sat. 8am-8pm; Oct.-June Mon.-Sat. 8am-2pm and 5-8pm.

Currency Exchange: Largo San Francesco, 21. 24-hr. automatic machine. Also **Banca Commerciale Italiano**, Viale Giovanni XXIII. Open Mon.-Fri. 8:20am-1pm.

Post Office: Via XX Settembre, 108 (tel. 97 93 09). Open Mon.-Sat. 10am-7:30pm, Fermo Posta 10am-1:20pm. **Branch Office,** Via Colombano, 44, near the tourist office (tel. 97 92 45). Open Mon.-Fri. 8:10am-1:15pm, Sat. 8am-12:45pm. **Postal code:** 07041.

Telephones: booths at P. Sulis. Phone cards available in bars on the piazza. **Telephone code:** 079.

Trains: at Via Don Minzoni and Via Castelsardo (tel. 95 07 85), in the northern part of the city. Take the AP or AF city bus from the *fermata* 1 block north of the tourist office (every 20min.) or stroll 1km along the port. Open daily 5:30am-9:30pm. There is also a tiny and more convenient terminal beyond the main station on Via Garibaldi, adjacent to the port, with Sássari service only (10 per day, 40min., L3200, more scenic and cheaper than the bus).

Buses: ARST (information tel. 26 00 48) and **SFS** buses depart from Via Catalogna, by the park. Purchase ARST tickets on board, SFS tickets at *caffè* or kiosks in the park. To Sássari (L4500) and Porto Torres (L4800).

Taxis: P. Porta Terra (tel. 97 53 96), across from the tourist office.

Bike/Moped Rental: Noleggio di Tilocca Tomaso, Via Garibaldi, 39, at the harbor (tel. 97 65 92). Bikes L12,000 per day, mountain bikes L18,000 per day, tandem bikes L20,000 per day. Mopeds L25,000 per day. Scooters L50,000 per day. Insurance included. If you don't speak Italian, ask for their English-language brochure with a complete listing of prices and restrictions. Another location on Via La Marmora, 29. Open Mon.-Sat. 8:30am-1pm and 4-8:30pm, Sun. 8:30am-noon.

Car Rental: Budget, Via Sassari, 7 (tel. 93 51 67). L90,000 per day. Must be 21 years old.

Horse Rental: Club Ippico Capuano (tel. 97 81 98). 3km from Alghero. L25,000 per hour to rent a horse. Special guided excursions for an afternoon with reservations recommended 2-3 days in advance. They will come to get you in Alghero for a charge of L5000 per person.

Emergencies: tel 113. **Police:** P. della Mercede, 4, tel. 113. **Hospital: Ospedale Civile** (tel. 95 10 96), Regione la Pietraia, a few blocks north of the main train station on Via Don Minzoni.

ACCOMMODATIONS AND CAMPING

Prices escalate and rooms vanish in July and August unless one has made a reservation far in advance or is willing to pay *meta pensioni* prices which don't come cheap here. If all else fails, friendly **Masia Margherita** at Via Angelo Roth, 12 (tel. 97 53 93), may have a room in a private house for about L25,000 per single and L50,000 per double with shower.

Ostello dei Giuliani (HI), Via Zara, 3 (tel. 93 03 53), 7km from Alghero in Fertilia—great for getting to beach. Take the yellow AF city bus from (from Via La Marmora next to the train station, every hr., 15min., L1100). ARST buses around the corner also go there. Curfew 10pm. L14,000 per person. Showers L2500. Break-

ALGHERO

fast L3000. Scrumptious lunches and dinners L12,000. (Meals served July and Aug. only.) *Always* reserved to capacity in July and August, but call and ask about cancellations. Open April 15-Oct. 15.

Pensione Normandie, Via Mattei, 6 (tel. 97 53 02), a 10-min. walk from the port. From Via Cagliari (which turns into Via Papa Giovanni XXIII), turn right on Via Mattei. Adequate rooms in friendly, family-run place. Doubles L40,000.

Hotel San Francesco, Via Machin, 2 (tel. 97 92 58). From the tourist office, follow Via Simon along the old city boundary and take the 2nd right. Tranquil, comfortable rooms in the church cloister, each with private bath. Breakfast included. Occasional concerts. Reserve ahead in summer. Singles L40,000. Doubles L85,000. Off season singles L37,000. Doubles L65,000.

Hotel Miramare, Via G. Leopardi, 9 (tel. 97 93 50). A step up in price and quality, perfect for those who desire the leisure-lifestyle hotel-by-the-sea. Carefully furnished rooms, clean modern bathrooms and balconies with views of the sea. Half pension required during the summer L65,000 per person, full pension only a bit more at L70,000 per person (regardless of room). Off season singles with bath L40,000. Doubles with bath, L66,000. Am Ex, Visa accepted.

Camping: Calik (tel. 93 01 11), 6km away, before the bridge into Fertilia. Large and crowded, 50m from the beach. L12,500 per person. Open June-Nov. La **Mariposa** (tel. 95 03 60), Via Lido, 3km away on the Alghero-Fertilia road and near the beach. Packed in summer. L15,000 per person, L7000 per auto. Open June-Oct.

Agriturismo: available at **Dulcamara** (tel. 99 91 97) and **Carboni Margherita** (tel. 99 90 93) and **Sa Giorba** (tel. 99 90 01) in S. Maria la Palma. Minumum stay 3 days. Bed and breakfast L25,000 per person; half pension L45,000; L10,000 booking tax per person. Rent an "agricultural house" for a minimum of 7 days for L23,000 per person with a deposit of L100,000 required against possible damages. Sa Giorba has horses that can be rented for L25,000 per hour, L70,000 for hours. Also by **Corredu Francesca,** Birio Aeroporto Militare (tel. 99 90 24) and **Baia Santos,** Via Guttierrez, Pod 3 (tel. 99 90 53) both in Fertilia, 3km from the beach Riviera del Corallo. Corredu Francesca costs L48,000 for half pension but allows tents to be pitched for only L13,500 per night. Baia Santos costs L2800 per person including breakfast, L48,000 for half pension, and L30,000 per person to rent an "agricultural house." Inquire for pamphlets at tourist office.

FOOD

Investigate the **market** by the park at the bus stop—enter from Via Cagliari (open Tues.-Sun. 7am-1pm). Every Wednesday, crowds engulf the **open-air market** on Via de' Gasperi (open 8am-1pm). The **Supermercato STANDA** near the station on Via Don Minzoni, 98, provides the basics. (Open Mon.-Sat. 9am-1pm and 4:30-8:30pm.

Ristorante La Muraglia, Bastioni Marco Polo (tel. 98 08 43). Outdoor tables framed by medieval buildings on one side and the raging sea on the other. A potentially ecstatic dining experience on the ancient walls overlooking the sea not to be missed. Homemade pasta. *Spaghetti al pomodoro* L8000, fresh fish L7000. *Coperto* L2000. Am Ex accepted.

Ristorante da Marco, Via Roma, 23 (tel. 97 95 79). Stretch out in wooden booths covered by checkered table cloths. The bargain find of Alghero. Pizza, pasta, and vino in tourist menus of L13,500, L23,000 or L26,000. Open Mon.-Sat. noon-3pm and 7pm-midnight. Am Ex, Visa accepted.

Paninoteca al Duomo, P. Civica, 2. Don't be frightened off by the English-language sign beckoning you to enter or the greasy look, this place *is* a bargain and it *is* good. Basic Italian fare: pizzas, panini, pastas, for fairly low prices. *Margherita pizza,* L3000, *quatro stagioni,* L5800. *Coperto* L1500 for hot dishes such as pasta or hamburgers. Open Mon.-Sat. 10am-3pm and 6pm-midnight.

Ristorante El Pultal, Via Colombano, 40 (tel. 97 80 51), in the old city near the post office branch. Expensive main dishes (L8000-12,000), but reasonable prices on large pizzas (L4500-8500; served only at dinner). Interior designed as a canvas of Catalonian motifs: dine under brown arches that cut through a dining room with dolls, masks, and flowers nestled in corners and wine bottles displayed in wooden shelves extending to the ceiling—all of which contrast with the idyllic Hallmarkish sunset scene painted in pastels over the fireplace. Open daily noon-3:30pm and 8pm-midnight.

SIGHTS AND ENTERTAINMENT

A leisurely walk through the **Città Vecchia** (Old City) reveals tiny alleyways, half-hidden churches, and the ancient town walls. Don't miss the fantastic vistas of the sea along Bastioni Marco Polo. From P. Sulis, Via Carlo Alberto takes you to the 14th-century **Church of San Francesco,** whose heavy neoclassical façade conceals a gracious Gothic presbytery. In July and August, the classical music of the **Estate Musicale Internazionale** (Summer Music Festival), sponsored by the tourist office, fills the cloisters. Schedules and tickets are available from the tourist office. Brown and green shutters complement the beige walls along nearby Medieval **Via Principe Umberto.** At #7 you'll find the **Casa Doria,** with its beautiful 16th-century façade, built by the powerful Doria clan of Genoa who fortified the fishing village of Alghero in the 11th century. Down the street you can get the most interesting view of the cathedral—the backside. Begun in 1552, the cathedral took 178 years to build, resulting in a motley Gothic-Catalan-Renaissance façade. Rebuilt in the 19th century, the church retains its striking Gothic choirs and campanile.

There are three strategically located Medieval **towers** in Alghero. **Torre del Portal,** on Piazza Porta Terra, was one of two access routes to the fortified Catalan city, complete with a drawbridge and (at the time) an artificial moat. **Torre de l'Espero Reial,** in Piazza Sulis, is a circular fortification with a grand view of the ocean. The **Torre de Sant Jaume** is commonly known as the **Torre dels Cutxos** (Dog's Tower) since it served as a 15th-century dog pound.

For a look at what's underneath the waves, visit the **Mare Nostrum Aquarium,** Via XX Settembre, 1 (tel. 97 83 33), across from the old city. The aquarium displays representatives of the local fish and reptile populations, along with piranhas and sharks. (Open daily 10am-1pm and 5-11pm; Oct.-June Mon.-Fri. 10am-noon and 4-8:30pm, Sat.-Sun. 4-9pm. Admission L8000.)

After a day in the sun, head for **Birdlands,** Via Roma, 50 (tel. 97 79 03) in the historic center. Live music blares nightly in the lounge upstairs (open 9:30pm-1am) and a bar and *gelateria* occupy the downstairs (open 11am-1am). Ask at the *azienda* about seasonal events, which include Catalan music and folk performances.

■ Near Alghero

The **Grotte di Nettuno** (tel. 94 65 40) is a vast natural wonder, an eerie cavern complex of dagger-like stalactites and mushrooming stalagmites. The caves delve into Capo Caccia, a steep promontory which projects from Porto Conte (25km by land from Alghero, 15km by sea). (Groups are admitted hourly 9am-6pm; Oct.-April 9am-2pm. Admission L10,000; children L6000.) Boats leave Alghero's Bastione della Maddalena every hour on the hour at **Compagnie Navisanda** (round-trip 3hr., L13,000). The SFS bus combs the beautiful coast (leaving at 9:15am, 2:50pm, and 5:15pm, returning at noon, 3:45pm, and 6pm, 50min., round-trip L5700, one way L3000). Mopeds can reach the *grotte* in 30 minutes. Once there, descend the memorable 654 steps that plunge between massive white cliffs all the way to the sea. If you're on moped, stop at the beaches of Porto Conte and exquisite Capo Caccia, as well as the **Nuraghe of Palmavera** (10km out of Alghero), where an intriguing central tower dates from 1500 BC. (Mandatory tour L3500. Open daily April-Oct. 9am-1pm and 4-8pm.) If you've rented a moped for the whole day, ride 10km toward Porto Torres to the **Necropolis of Anghelu Ruju,** the largest in Sardinia, a group of 38 tombs built by the local fishing tribes around 3000 BC. You can also take the ARST bus from Alghero (departures at 7:05am, 1:45pm, and 4:35pm, L1500).

At **Bosa,** 45km south of Alghero, make a short climb down the hillside away from town to several outstanding beaches. A bus departs from Alghero at 9:55am and 6:50pm, and returns via an interior route at 5:30pm. Follow the sea away from Alghero to the magnificent beaches of **Spiaggia di San Giovanni** and **Spiaggia di Marta Pia,** north of town, where you'll find lots of clear water and few tourists. The **Spiaggia Le Bombarde,** close to Fertilia and the hostel, is even less crowded but is receding rapidly into the sea. A determined walk to **Torre del Lazzaretto** farther along the shore will be more rewarding. The ASP city buses serve Porte Corte and the beaches.

■■■ SÁSSARI

Sardinia's second-largest city sits atop a limestone plateau, where its founders sought refuge from the foreign invaders and malaria epidemics common to coastal territory. Today Sássari is an important petrochemical center, with modern suburbs ringing its compact Medieval core. In the capital of Italy's largest province, Sassarians enjoy the highest standard of living in Sardinia, as well as the continental pretensions of its grandiose 18th-century Piazza d'Italia and sole boulevard, Via Roma. The pleasant, old-fashioned character of Sassari manifests itself in the evening gathering of Sassarians, young and old, in Piazza d'Italia, in an ancient form of society reenacted for centuries.

ORIENTATION AND PRACTICAL INFORMATION

All roads radiate from the newly restored **Piazza d'Italia.** As you stand facing the Banco di Napoli in the *piazza,* **Via Roma** and the **PANI station** are on your left. **Emiciclo Garibaldi** and the **ARST station** are straight ahead, with the leafy **Piazza Castello** behind it. The main shopping street, **Corso Vittorio Emanuele,** and the **train station** are on your right. The towns of Alghero and Porto Torres are conveniently located 37km southwest and 18.5km northwest, respectively.

Tourist Office: (tel. 23 35 34) Viale Umberto, 72. In an unobtrusive, grey office building on the left, coming from the Piazza d'Italia and at the northwest corner of Piazza d'Italia. Very helpful staff, willing to spend time to answer your personal questions and give advice on itineraries for local destinations. Open Mon.-Fri. 8am-2pm and 4-6pm, Sat. 8am-noon.

Currency Exchange: Banca Commerciale Italia, Piazza d'Italia, 23. Open Mon.-Fri. 8:20am-1:35pm and 3:15-4:45pm.

Budget Travel: CTS, Via Costa, 48 (tel. 23 45 85), off Viale Italia. Open Mon.-Fri. 10:30am-7pm.

Post Office: Via Brigata Sassari, 13 (tel. 23 21 78), off P. Castello. Open Mon.-Fri. 8:15am-7:40pm. Many services not available after 1pm. **Postal code:** 07100.

Telephones: SIP, Viale Italia, 7/A. Open Mon.-Fri. 9am-12:30pm and 4:30-7:30pm. **Telephone Code:** 079.

Flights: 28km south, near Alghera Fertilia. Free ARST buses leave for airport from station 75min. before departures. Both domestic and international flights. **Airport Information:** tel. 93 50 33.

Trains: P. Stazione (tel. 26 03 62), 1 block from P. Sant'Antonio. To: Olbia (9 per day, 2hr., L8800); Oristano (7 per day, 2hr. 45min., L10,800); Cagliari (6 per day, 3hr. 30min., L19,300); Porto Torres (9 per day, 20min., L1600); Palau (2 per day, 4hr., L10,500); Alghero (10 per day, 40min., L3400). Ask for a complete schedule of local trains at the tourist office. Take the #8 bus from the station to avoid the long uphill trek to Piazza d'Italia. Buy tickets in the newstand at the station (L1100).

Buses: PANI, Via Bellini, 25 (tel. 23 69 83 or 23 47 82), off Via Roma, 1 block from P. d'Italia. To: Cagliari (at 6:35am and 9:30am, 2pm, and 7:15pm, 4hr., L26,000 direct at 6am and 2:15pm and 6pm, 3hr. 15min.); Núoro (3 per day, 2hr. 30min. L13,000); Oristano (5 per day, 2hr. 15min., L12,500). Open Mon.-Sat. 5:30am 6:30am, 9:15am-2:15pm, and 5:30-7:15pm. Ask at the desk for a complete sched

ule of local buses. **ARST,** Emiciclo Garibaldi, 23 (tel. 26 00 06). Serves most local
routes. **SFS,** tickets in the bar next door at #26 (tel. 24 13 01). Runs buses to
Alghero (10 per day, 90min., L4500), Porto Torres (L2000), Castelsardo (L3500),
and Torrelba (L4000). Open Mon.-Sat. 7am-1:30pm and 2-8pm. **Luggage Storage
ARST:** L2000. Open Mon.-Sat. 10am-4:30pm.
Car Rental: Avis, Via Mazzi, 2/A (tel. 20 30 55 46). 1 day L94,000. 1 week
L450,000. Must be 21 years old.
All-Night Pharmacy: Simon, Via Brigata Sassari, 2 (tel. 23 32 38). Posts a weekly
list of other all-night pharmacies.
Emergencies: tel. 113. **Police:** Via Copino (tel. 23 23 43). **Medical Emergency:
Ospedale Civile,** Via de Nicola, off Via Costa (tel. 22 05 00). **First Aid:** tel. 22 06
21.

ACCOMMODATIONS

Cheap rooms in Sássari are tough to find in July and August.

Pensione Famiglia, Viale Umberto, 65 (tel. 23 95 43). A large establishment run by
8 women whose communal proprietary interest in clients evokes Fellini's house
of women as depicted in the film 8½. They let large rooms with cathedral-high
ceilings. However, the beds are cots, and hot water is scarce. Don't let the flies in
the lobby deter you. Curfew midnight. Singles L20,000. Doubles L28,000.
Hotel Giusy, P. Sant'Antonio, 21 (tel. 23 33 27). Very clean, modern, and professional. All rooms with private bath. Singles L40,000. Doubles L54,000.

FOOD

A wide selection of *pizzerie* lines **Corso Emanuele.** Any student ID allows you to
eat at the **University Mensa,** Via Padre Manzella, 2 (tel. 21 91 11), off P. Gramsci. A
basic, filling meal is yours for L6500 but better yet, see if you can get a student out-
ie to sell you a ticket for about L1000. (Open Mon.-Sat. 12:30-2:20pm and 7:30-
9pm.) The large, enclosed **market** occupies P. Mercato, down Via Rosello from Via
Vittorio Emanuele. (Open Mon.-Fri. 8am-1pm and 5-8pm, Sat. 8am-1pm.) The
STANDA supermarket is on Viale Italia at Via Sardegna. (Open Mon.-Fri. 8:45am-
1pm and 4:30-8:15pm, Sat. 9am-1pm.) Or try the well-stocked minimarket (tel. 26
? 13), to the left as you exit the station (open Mon.-Fri. 8am-1pm and 5-8pm, Sat.
8am-1pm). Vegetarians will find soy products, raw nuts, and other protein products
at the *alimentari* at 34 Via Brigita Sassari. Many Japanese products found here as
well. (Open Mon.-Fri. 8am-1pm and 5-7:30pm, Sat. 8am-1pm.)

Trattoria Da Peppina, Vicolo Pigozzi, 1 (tel. 23 61 46), off Via Emanuele. A small,
simple place filled with locals. Reservations recommended. Vegetarians beware:
all the sauces here have meat in them. *Primi* L4000-7000, *secondi* L6500-10,000.
Open Mon.-Sat. noon-3pm and 7-10pm.
Pizzeria Al Corso, Corso Emanuele, 148 (tel. 23 42 10). Perhaps the island's best
pizza, loaded with cheese and toasted to perfection in a wood-burning oven
(L4500-9000). Even the plain mozzarella *margherita* will send your tastebuds
into orbit. Vegans can ask for a special pizza not on the menu with different local
vegetables but without cheese. Open Tues.-Sun. 7pm-1am.

SIGHTS AND SEASONAL EVENTS

The **Museo Giovanni Antonio Sanna,** Via Roma, 64 (tel. 27 22 03), houses reconstructed *nuraghi*, Sardinian paintings, traditional costumes, and a pleasant garden.
The graceful Roman statues and mosaics are a treat, but best of all is the droning
rythm of Sardinian pipe music played in the ethnographic section. (Open Mon.-Sat.
9am-2pm, Sun. 9am-1pm, 2nd Wed. of each month 4:30-7:30pm. Admission L4000.)
The **Cathedral of San Niccolò,** originally a 13th-century Romanesque structure,
gained a Spanish Colonial Baroque façade in the 17th century, dubbed "an immense
flower of stone," by Elio Vittorini. Entry is not allowed, however. The **Church of
Santa Maria di Betlem,** near the train station, is another hybrid: its 14th-century

Gothic vaults shelter elegant Baroque altars, and the adjacent cloister preserve
bronze-spigoted medieval fountain. (Open 10am-6pm.)

The lavish **Sardinian Cavalcade,** held on the second-to-last Sunday in May, is S
dinia's most notable folk festival. The festivities include a morning procession of c
tumed emissaries from dozens of villages all over Sardinia, an afternoon *Pa*
(horserace), and an evening song-and-dance show.

I Candelieri, the festival of the candlesticks (great wooden columns in the sha
of enormous tapers), takes place on Assumption Day (August 14), when the *Gre*
or farmers' guilds, parade giant replicas of candles and matches through the stree
The festival dates back to the 16th century, when people reasoned that it was a la
of candle offerings to the Virgin that caused the latest plague.

■ Near Sássari

Castelsardo's striking location on a lofty promontory and its proximity to san
beaches make it a popular junction along Sardinia's Costa Paradiso. Only 34
northwest of Sássari, it is also a convenient daytrip (10 ARST buses per day, L350
The hilltop town offers few cultural sights other than a late-Gothic **cathedr**
shamelessly replastered in drab stucco, which shelters an impressive 15th-centu
painting of the *Madonna with Angels.* The **castle** at the top of the hill affords a
mendous view of the northern coast (open daily 8am-8pm).

There are no rooms in the old town. Try **Pensione Pinna,** Lungomare Anglona
(tel. (079) 47 01 68), across the street from the harbor. Ask for one of the rooms
the second floor with views of the sea. (Singles L27,000-45,000. Doubles L65,0
80,000.)

Some easily accessible *nuraghi* await you 30km south of Sássari—most notal
Nuraghi Santu Antine at **Torralba.** Some of the most interesting prehistoric arc
tecture in the western Mediterranean can be found just off the road. The cent
tower dates from the 9th century BC and the fortifications surrounding it from t
7th. (Site open daily 8:30am-8:15pm.) The must-see **Museum of the Valley of t**
Nuraghi at Via Carlo Felice, 97 (tel. 84 72 98), in Torralba, provides information
the *nuraghi,* next to excavated relics. (Open Tues.-Sun. 9am-1pm and 3-8p
Admission L4000, under 18 free.) The Torralba **train station** (on the Cagliari-Sáss
line) lies 1km from the monument, and PANI and ARST buses also run to the tov
(4km from the site, L4000).

The most convenient **beach** from Sassari is found in **Platamona,** a long wh
expanse of sand, where the locals go on weekends. Take the orange city b
labelled Via Budi Budi from Via Torse Tonda in the middle of the public garde
(every 40min., 30min., L3600 round trip). Buy tickets at the **SFS office,** 26 Emci
Garibaldi. This bus also goes to the best place to stay near Sássari, if you have can
ing gear: the **International Cristina Camping Village,** Platamona (tel. 31 02 30). C
off the bus when you see the large sign on your right. A decent campground, a
crowded with many trailers nestled away in the trees, but featuring its own beauti
beach that makes it a worthy stopover for several days. Prices L70,000 per bun
low (houses 5 persons).

NORTHERN COAST

The crowded northern shore of Sardinia includes the Emerald Coast (Costa Sm
elda), arguably the area of Italy most victimized by the Eurotourist deluge, Santa T
esa di Gallura, a coastal retreat rapidly succumbing to the same tourist-glutted fa
and the Costa Paradiso, which developers are trying to push as the "next Co
Smeralda." To round things off, there's the justly untouristed petrochemical cen
of Porto Torres, and the once-charming town of Stintino. Unless you're longing

ind a hotel that literally charges a million lire a night, or you miss the crush of Rimini and Piazza San Marco, the north coast should be avoided.

■ Porto Torres

There is little to rave about in a town whose most scenic spot is a three-bench park next to the main bus stop. Founded by Caesar, it once enjoyed considerable importance as an ancient Roman harbor. Today it is a terminal for petrochemicals and ferries to and from Civitavécchia, Genoa, and Toulon (France). Do as Caesar would have done: come, see, and leave quickly.

Orientation and Practical Information Trains, buses, and ferries come and go from the port. As you stand with your back to the water, straight ahead is **Corso Vittorio Emanuele II,** the main street, which leads from the port to the church of San Gavino.

Tourist Office: Pro Loco, Via Roma, 30 (tel. 51 50 00). The office is hidden down a back street. From the port take Via Emanuele II into town. Turn left on Via Roma, the 1st cross street. English-speaking attendants will present you with maps, brochures, and information. Open July-Sept. 8am-7pm with 1hr. off for lunch.

Post Office: Via Pacinotti, 4 (tel. 50 21 90). Open Mon.-Fri. 8:10am-1pm, Sat. 8am-12:45pm. **Postal code:** 07046. **Telephone code:** 079.

Trains: Via Ponte Romano, 89 (tel. 51 46 36), next to the port. To: Sássari (L1800). Trains stop in the middle of the street. Open daily 5:30am-8:30pm.

Buses: ARST buses run to and from **Sássari** incessantly (L2000) and **Alghero** (5 per day, L4500). For service to **Stintino,** walk 2 blocks from the port to P. Umberto, where you can also catch the bus to Sássari. It's best to purchase tickets in advance at the **Bar Acciazo** on Corso Vittorio Emanuele, halfway between the port and P. Umberto (look for the big pink sign).

Ferries: Tirrenia, Stazione Marittima in the port (tel. 51 41 07). Service to Genoa, Livorno, and Toulon. Ticket office open Mon.-Sat. 8:30am-noon and 3-8pm, Sun. 3-6pm.

Car Rental: Mureddo, Via Mare, 8 (tel. 51 01 81, after hours 27 46 29), across from the port. Must be 21. Also **bike rental.** *Let's Go* gets you a 20% discount. Open daily 8:30am-1pm and 3:30-7:30pm.

Emergencies: tel. 113. **Medical Emergency: Pronto Soccorso,** Via delle Terme, 5 (tel. 51 03 92), off Via Ponte Romano. Some English spoken.

Accommodations and Food There's no need to stay or eat in Porto Torres, since Sássari is only 30 minutes away by bus. Prices for rooms (when available) are high, and the windows of restaurants on the main street are plastered with outrageous "tourist menus." The tiny **Ostello per la Gioventù Balai (HI)** (youth hostel) is an option at Via Balai (tel. 51 30 01). Walk 2km from the port along the coastal road to Castelsardo until you reach the intersection of Via Balai and Strada Litoranea, or take the local bus which leaves every half-hour from the *fermata* in front of the port. It's often full, so call ahead. (Reception open 6-11pm. L16,000 per person. Dinner L12,000. Open July-Oct.) Stock up on munchies at the immense **Turrismarket,** Via Pacinotti, 1, at Via Sacchi beyond San Gavino. (Open Tues.-Sat. 8:15am-12:45pm and 5:30-8pm, Mon. 8:15am-12:45pm.) Choose from a variety of *panini* (L4500-7000) at **Pizzeria Il Drago,** Via Ponte Romano, 54 (open Tues.-Sun. 6-11:30pm), or settle down for a superb seaside meal at **Ristorante Scaglio Lungo,** Via Lungo Mare, 12 (tel. 50 13 00). Meals start at L16,000. (Open daily 7pm-4am.)

Sights To the untrained eye, the ruins of a Roman bath (*Terme Centrale*) next to the train station look like marble rubble. Medieval townspeople, themselves uncertain, named them "Il Palazzo del Re Barbaro" (Palace of the Barbarian King). In the museum, you can see headless statues, cornucopias, and ancient gamblers' dice, all

excavated from the bath. A guide is usually free to take you through the ruins an
recount tales of their once-licentious use. (Open daily 9am-1pm and 3-7pm.) You
need no assistance to identify the seven marble arches that span the narrow Tu
tano River nearby as part of a **Roman bridge.**

Porto Torres's finest sight is the **Church of San Gavino,** a masterpiece of Sardinia
architecture. An 11th-century variation on a Pisan Romanesque theme, it has a se
ond apse in front replacing the formal façade. The somber interior, lit only by tall sl
windows, shelters a double row of 28 ancient columns and a wooden truss ceilin
Outside, tiny, dilapidated houses with external staircases enclose antique cour
yards.

Near Porto Torres: Stintino

Stintino, 24km northwest of Porto Torres on the Capo del Falcone, was unt
recently a legitimate fishing village. It is now a prototypical victim of developmen
The winter population of 746 increases to almost 20,000 in summer. Much of Stin
no's transformation can be attributed to the stunning beauty of **Spiaggia di Pelosa,**
beach 4km outside town, whose sparkling turquoise waters glisten against th
bone-dry **Isola Asinara,** an island penal colony. An easy 500m wade through thig
deep water takes you to a tiny islet and its marooned 18th-century Aragonese towe
It's a great day trip to the best beach near Sássari. One bus per day in summer (
2:20pm, 30min., L3500) serves Stintino from Porto Torres, and doesn't return unt
the next morning. Instead, return through Sássari (4 per day, 1hr., L4500), or bett
yet, leave from Sássari in the morning. Don't miss the last bus, as impromptu cam
ing is nearly impossible. If you're desperate, try **Albergho Silvestrino** at Via Sássar
12 (tel. 52 30 07), where singles run L35,000, with bath L40,000, and doubles a
L65,000, with bath L70,000.

■ Santa Teresa di Gallura

Perched on Sardinia's northwest tip, Santa Teresa di Gallura is a pastel beach tow
It's very *pleasing,* in a banal, soporific kind of way—the only scene here is the fan
ily vacation. From the small, immaculate beach **Rena Bianca,** though, you can act
ally see Corsica across the turquoise waters. This is the perfect beach for those wh
desire breaking waves to ride to shore.

Orientation A dirt path leads away from the beach up the hill. At the fork, th
lower path leads to **Isola Municca,** a stadium-like islet with high rocks that ring
field of grass. The higher trail twists between magnificent granite formations an
offers an excellent view of Corsica and Capo Testa, especially in the morning. Fo
low the hill to reach the isthmus connecting **Capo Testa** with the mainland. Othe
wise, go back into town and take Via Capo Testa (3km) or the ARST bus from th
post office mornings and afternoons. There are beaches on both sides of the ist
mus—check the direction of the wind and choose the leeward side. From Capo Te
ta's lighthouse, you can walk down to a secluded series of scenic coves. Paths lea
south through the spectacular granite quarries of the *Valle della Luna.*

Practical Information Santa Teresa's **Azienda,** P. Vittorio Emanuele, 24 (te
(0789) 75 41 27), can assist you with accommodations and has dozens of pamphle
advertising local services, such as boat, moped, and horse rentals. (Open dai
8:30am-1pm and 4:30-7pm; Oct.-May Mon.-Sat. 8:30am-1pm and 4:30-7pm.) Fro
Santa Teresa, daily **ferries** sail to Bonifacio in Corsica (1hr., L13,000, French vi
required). Both **Tirrenia** (tel. 75 41 56) and **Navarma** (tel. 75 52 70) staff offices
the tiny port. If you wish to cross into French waters yourself, rent a sailboat o
motorboat from **Circolo Nautico Capo Testa** (tel. 75 54 56) on the isthmus, whic
also runs a scuba-diving school (Open May 15-Oct.15 daily 8am-8pm). Alternativel
explore *terra firma* by renting a horse at **Centro Ippico Ruoni** (tel. 75 15 90), 5kr
out of town in Ruoni. Bike and moped rentals are available from **GULP,** Via Nazio

ıle, 58 (tel. (0789) 75 56 89). Mountain bikes go for L22,500 per day, Piaggios for ₋30,000; Vespa 125's are L60,000 per day, and scooters are L45,000 per day. (Open Mon.-Fri. 9am-1pm and 4-7:30pm, Sat. 9am-1pm.) All-day (9:30am-5pm) boat excur-sions to the archipelago islands are available, complete with lunch and horse ride ̇or L70,000. Reserve two days ahead from **ONDA**, Via Carlo Alberto, 9 (tel. 75 41 ₄9). **ARST buses** travel to Olbia (5 per day, 1hr. 30min., L6500), Sássari (2 per day, ̇hr., L14,500), and Palau (40min., L3000) from Via Eleonora d'Arborea, adjacent to ̇he post office off Via Nazionale. Tickets can be purchased at the Black and White ̇ar across from the station on Via Nazionale.

Accommodations Cheap hotels are often full in July, *always* in August. Most ̇emand at least half-pension. Prices are listed for low and high seasons respectively ̇where possible.

Hotel Bellavista, Via Sonnino, 8 (tel. 75 41 62), at the edge of town overlooking Rena Bianca. Huge rooms, private baths, and balconies. Singles L55,000-65,000. Doubles L60,000-65,000.

Riva Hotel, Via Galliano, 26 (tel. 75 42 83). Funky tropical motifs in pleasant rooms. Nice management, no pension. Singles L50,000. Doubles L60,000.

Hotel del Porto, Via del Porto, 20 (tel. 75 41 54). From Via Nazionale turn onto Via del Porto and follow it to the port. Worth the walk: large, almost elegant rooms with peaceful views of the water, and the Sardinian countryside. Singles L25,000-30,000. Doubles L50,000-60,000. Am Ex, Visa, MC accepted.

Camping: Arco Balleno, 10km from Porto Pozzo (tel. 75 20 40). L13,500 per per-son, including tent and car. Open June-Sept.

Food Most local restaurants are astronomically expensive. For hearty low-cost ̇asics, an *alimentare*, fruit and vegetable markets, and delis are easy to find on Via Aniscara off P. Vittorio Emanuele (open during regular business hours).

Papa Satan, Via La Marmora, 20/22. No phone. Look for the sign off Via Nazionale. Futuristic flaming patio in back. Wood-burning ovens. Try the devilishly good *spa-ghetti alla Papa Satan* (L11,000-13,000). Open daily noon-2:30pm and 7pm-mid-night.

Panino's Shop, Via XX Settembre, off P. Emanuele. Ultracool owner plays rap while making chewy pizza (L3500). Open daily 7am-3am.

■ Costa Smeralda

Once upon a time, the windy, craggy coastline above Olbia was nothing but a series ̇f poor fishing villages. Then, in 1962, a consortium of foreign investors led by the Aga Khan developed the area into a posh resort and renamed it the Emerald Coast. Today, the fine sand beaches and clean waters are blocked off by a swarm of luxury ̇hotels, restaurants, and shops. Accommodations and food run to outrageous sums, ̇nd the alert police force actively discourages unofficial camping. Crowds are size-̇ble year-round, and downright unbearable in July and August. It is impossible to ̇ind a room anywhere on the coast in August. The less crowded, less expensive, ̇more appealing southern coasts provide a better destination than the over-priced ̇tourist culture of the north.

A bland town of pastel stucco and reinforced concrete, **Arzachena** is notable ̇mainly for its nearby gulf. The town is a central depot on the northern coast, half-̇way between Olbia and Santa Teresa di Gallura on the ARST bus route, one hour ̇from each (10 per day from Olbia, L3000). If you must pause here, the **Azienda di Turismo** has an office on Via Risorgimento (tel. 82 624. Open Mon.-Fri. 8am-1:30pm and 3-7:15pm, Sat. 8am-1:30pm). Catch all buses two blocks down the hill ̇behind the *azienda*.

■■■ OLBIA

While not particularly seedy, Olbia is hardly the stuff of which poetry is made—it's just another dot on Italy's map of lackluster, well-trafficked ports. One exception is the pleasant, if tourist-oriented **Corso Umberto**, a good place to find a refreshment before moving on. Celebrate your arrival in Sardinia by stocking up on essentials and escaping to further destinations as quickly as possible.

PRACTICAL INFORMATION

Ferries arriving at the port are greeted by blue ARST buses and a train timed to meet incoming passengers. The cluster of buildings to the right as you disembark houses a bar, newsstand, and televisions to entertain stranded travelers. To reach Olbia's *centro,* take the waiting train to the first stop: tickets can be purchased on board. (The train continues on to Sássari, a much better choice if you can handle a bit more travel.) To get to the tourist ofice, walk directly from the station up Via Pala until it intersects with **Corso Umberto,** with the ARST station about 200m to your right. Turn left and continue past **Piazza Margherita** on your right (Olbia's youth hang-out) until you reach Via Catello Piro (also on your right), where you will find the tourist office. It's likely, however, that your boat will arrive long before business hours. If this is the case, revive youself at one of several *caffè* along Corso Umberto where you can sip espresso and enjoy cream-filled pastries with other weary travelers while waiting for the tourist office to open.

- **Tourist Office:** Via Catello Piro, 1 (tel. 214 53), off Corso Umberto. The best thing in Olbia: excellent map of the town supplied by very friendly English-speaking staff. Ask for the *Annuario Alberghi,* an invaluable list of prices for almost every hotel in Sardinia and a beautiful guide in English that presents itineraries to explore Sardegna's coasts, archeological sites, and "trekking adventures." Open Mon.-Sat. 8am-1pm and 4-7pm, Sun. 8am-noon; Oct.-May Mon.-Sat. 8:30am-1pm and 4-7pm, Sun. 8:30am-noon.
- **American Express: Avitur,** Corso Umberto, 139 (tel. 243 27). Check-cashing for cardholders on weekday mornings. Friendly staff. Open Mon.-Fri. 9am-1pm and 4-7pm, Sat. 9am-1pm.
- **Post Office:** on Via Acquedotto (tel. 222 51), 2 blocks off P. Matteotti. Open Mon.-Sat. 8:30am-7pm. **Postal code:** 07026.
- **Telephones: SIP,** Via dei Filippi, 14, near P. Matteotti. Closed in 1993 for recon-struction. Currently a gaping, empty pit in the middle of the street. Scheduled to reopen by the summer of 1994. The three bars on Piazza Margherita sell phone cards and public phones are there as well. **Telephone code:** 0789.
- **Trains:** Via Pala, off Corso Umberto by the bus station (tel. 224 77). Before the ferry departure, trains run directly from the station, originating in Sássari, to the port. Trains depart regularly for Sássari (L8800) and Golfo Aranci (L2400).
- **Buses: ARST,** at the far end of Corso Umberto, 168 (tel. 211 97). Buy tickets in the bar to the right of the station. To: Núoro (4 per day, about L12,000); Arzachena (10 per day, L3000); Santa Teresa di Gallura (5 per day, L6500); Palau (L4000). Schedule posted in station. Open 4am-1am. Local buses (orange) traverse the town and trek from Olbia's center to the airport (#2). Local rides cost L1200-1300; buy tickets on board from coin-only machines.
- **Ferries: Tirrenia,** Corso Umberto, 17 (tel. 226 88). Service to Civitavécchia and Genoa. Open Mon.-Sat. 8:30am-1:30pm and 4:30-6pm. **Port office** (tel. 224 82) open when ferries are running—check 1hr. 30min. in advance for schedule changes. **Linea dei Golfi** (tel. 221 26), in the port office, runs lines to Piombino (the port for Elba) and Livorno in Tuscany.
- **Bike and Moped Rental: Smerelda Express** (tel. 691 92), at the Olbia airport. A Vespone PX moped runs L50,000 per day, a Piaggio Bravo bike L30,000 per day (plus 19% tax). Unlimited mileage. Liscense required to rent a moped. Open 6am-midnight.

Pharmacy: Farmacia Lupacciolu, Via Porto Romano, 2 (tel. 213 10). Open Mon.-Sat. 9am-1pm and 4:40-10pm, Sun. 8-10am.

Emergencies: tel. 113. **Hospital: Ospedale Civile** Via Aldo Moro (tel. 522 00 or 522 01). Some English spoken. **Guardia Medica,** Via Fern, 4 (tel. 224 91), near the Church of San Simplicio. For medical assistance evenings and weekends. Open Sat. 2pm-Mon. 8am, Tues.-Fri. 8pm-8am.

ACCOMMODATIONS AND FOOD

Albergo Terranova, Via Garibaldi, 3 (tel. 223 95). A cheaper stopover place with small, clean rooms with balconies that open to the bustle of Piazza Margherita. Singles L35,000. Doubles L55,000. Sinks in rooms.

Albergo Minerva, Via Mazzini, 6 (tel. 211 90). Clean, well-lit rooms and friendly young management, 50m from Terranova but slightly quieter location. Singles L32,000, with bath L40,000. Doubles L50,000, with bath L60,000.

Dining in Olbia can either be inexpensive and bland or very expensive and delicious. For self-service bargains, shop at the **Mercato Civico** on Via Acquedotto (open Mon.-Sat. 7:30am-1pm and 4:30-8pm), or at the **STANDA Supermarket** at Corso Umberto, 156 (open Mon.-Sat. 9am-8:30pm). Vegetarians should stock up on soy milk and other supplies here: there will be few other chances to do so on this island.

Pizzeria Al Ciclope, Via Acquedotto, 24. No telephone number, no drinks, no one-eyed clientele, nothing but fine pizza. Cheese slice L1800. Open daily 11am-1pm and 5:30-10pm.

A Tavole di Leone o Anna, Via Barcelona, 90 (tel. 263 33). A hike northwest of the train station, or take bus #1. Via Sassani turns into Via Barcelona. Floral booths, a handsome wooden bar, and superb Sardinian cuisine. *Spaghetti alla pescatora* (spaghetti with a fresh fish sauce) L15,000. Homemade ravioli L15,000. *Aragosta alla Catalana,* their lobster specialty, L18,000. Open Wed.-Mon. noon-3pm and 8-11:30pm.

SIGHTS AND NEAR OLBIA

Nearly all traces of Olbia's Greek, Roman, and medieval past have disappeared. The one exception is the 12th-century **Church of San Simplicio** behind the train station. Built in the Pisan Romanesque style, the structure features an attractive asymmetrical façade of off-white granite. Inside, half-formed faces leer out from stone pillars. (No set hours.)

Excursions from Olbia include trips to **S'Abe** (6km away) on the road to **Castello Pedrese,** and the "Giants' Tombs" of **Su Monte.** If you're taking the bus to Núoro, not far out of Olbia you'll pass the surrealistic **Isola Tavolara,** an immense prism of rock protruding 450m out of the sea. Five buses per day run to **San Teodoro,** 30km from Olbia (L3000), where a long, luxurious beach eases into the ultramarine water. Especially in July and August, you'll be marching straight into the ranks of the tourist phalanxes, but go ahead—it's worth it. Stay at the **Albergho L'Esagono** (tel. (0784) 86 57 83), a complex of red clay buildings right on the beach, off Via Cala d'Ambra (doubles with obligatory half-pension L80,000; full pension required in August for L95,000). Up the road is the **Cala d'Ambra campground** (tel. (0784) 86 56 50) with satisfactory facilities (L8500 per person in July; L9500 in August; L7500 during the year; tent included; reservations strongly recommended for the summer).

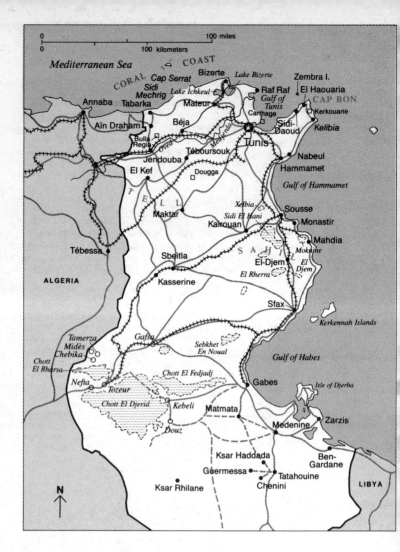

TUNISIA

Queen Dido of Phoenicia sailed to Carthage in the 9th century BC to found a nation "rich in wealth and harsh in the pursuit of war." The ensuing centuries have drawn western myths upon the Tunisian landscape: from the Odyssey's land of the lotus-eaters to Hannibal at Carthage to modern-day exoticism (Berber villages of the Sahara served as the location of Luke Skywalker's home planet, Tatooine, in Star Wars). These western assumptions are not helped by tourist brochures which often exploit them in order to further sell the country to European mass tourism of the package-holiday variety.

A trip into Tunisia's varied geography will quickly dispel these simple cultural stereotypes. As the government increasingly puts effort into expanding the tourist industry, many areas, along with Tunisia's cultural intricacies, are becoming increasingly possible to reach. At the same time, most European travelers haven't caught on to this wave, leaving the inland and south delightfully in peace. The beautifully diverse landscape ranges from the surprisingly green, mountainous north with miles of palm-treed beaches (some even without Germans) to the semi-islamicized Berber villages which dot the Saharan border in the south.

PLANNING YOUR TRIP

Most of the information contained in the Italy Essentials Section also applies to Tunisia. The following addenda should complement what you already know.

The **Tunisian National Tourist Office (ONTT)** is a good source of information and brochures about the country and its regions. The country's central tourist office is at 1, av. Mohammed V, 1002 Tunis (tel. 34 10 77, fax 35 09 97). In the U.S., write or call the **Embassy of Tunisia,** Cultural Section in Charge of Tourism, 1515 Mass. Ave. NW, Washington, DC 20005 (tel. (202) 862-1850, fax 862-1858). The ONTT in the U.K. is at 77a, Wigmore St., London W1H 9IJ (tel. 071 224 5561, fax 071 224 4053). In Italy, contact the **Centro Turistico della Tunisia,** Via Baracchini, 10, 20123 Milan (tel. 87 11 26). For the U.S. State Department's *Background Notes* on Tunisia, write to the Superintendent of Documents, U.S. Government Printing Office, Washington, DC 20402. Major Tunisian cities also operate a local tourist office called the **Syndicat d'Initiative,** referred to in listings as the "Syndicat."

No visa is required of U.S. citizens to enter Tunisia for up to four months, or of Canadians and U.K. citizens for up to three months. Australians, New Zealanders and South Africans must obtain a visa before departure from the nearest Tunisian consulate (do this at least 1-3 weeks before you leave).

■ Money

US $1 = .94 dinar (D)	1D = US $1.06
CDN $1 = .81D	1D = CDN $1.24
UK £1 = 1.61D	1D = UK £0.62
AUS $1 = 0.72D	1D = AUS $1.39
NZ $1 = 0.59D	1D = NZ $1.70
SA R = .32D	1D = SA R3.16

The dinar (D) consists of 1000 millimes (ml). Sums are written with periods: 14.300 means 14 dinars, 300 millimes. Amounts under 5D are frequently expressed in thousands of millimes. Change is often scarce, so hang on to it, especially the precious 100ml pieces used in pay phones. Save your exchange receipts: with them, only 30% of what you originally change can be reconverted, up to a maximum of 100D (without them, you can't reconvert any currency at all). It is illegal to import or export Tunisian currency.

Banks are generally open for exchange in summer Monday through Friday 8-11am and in winter Monday through Thursday 8-11am and 2-4pm, Friday 8-11am and 1:30-3pm. During **Ramadan** (see Festivals and Holidays), banks are open Monday through Friday 8-11:30am and 1-2:30pm. A few large hotels and all airports provide exchange services outside regular hours.

HEALTH

■ Health

Two of the health concerns outlined in the Italy Essentials section should be emphasized for the Tunisian tourist: diarrhea and overexposure to the sun.

To avoid diarrhea while in Tunisia select produce that can be peeled, or wash it thoroughly with *bottled* water. Don't eat creamy pastries or any food that has been standing out. Although sandwiches and salads in restaurants are for the most part fine, if you want to play it safe, stick to cooked vegetables. Don't drink the local water in any form, and resist the tempting but treacherous, ice-cold glasses of *citronade*. Beware as well of ice cubes, and be careful even when brushing your teeth. If you have diarrhea that persists beyond a couple of days, don't hesitate to seek out a Tunisian doctor. If the diarrhea is a sign of something more serious, waiting until you get home could be dangerous.

Always wear a sun hat in the interior to prevent heatstroke and carry plenty of bottled water, especially in the desert (for some additional advice on desert survival see Southern Tunisia). Finally, be sure that, along with sunscreen, your medical kit includes chewable Pepto Bismol or Kaopectate tablets.

The only vaccination recommended for travelers to Tunisia is a gamma globulin—consult your doctor for specifics.

■ Safety and Security

Tunisia's nationwide **emergency phone number** is 197.

Despite perceptions that North African countries are crime-ridden and dangerous, tourists to Tunisia will rarely encounter problems if they take care to understand their surroundings. For general information on safety while traveling, see the Italy Essentials: Safety and Security section of this book.

Urban areas in which extra caution is in order are the *souks* (market streets) and the *medinas* (old cities). The maze-like *medinas* vary in size and intricacy, but in general, don't rely solely on the tourist office maps to guide you through them. As in any labyrinth, extreme caution should be used at night in many *medinas*. When in doubt, ask your hotel proprietor or hostel manager for advice and directions before venturing out. Carry sums of over 10D or 15D in a moneybelt or necklace pouch. When purchasing anything, keep your money securely in hand or belt until you have agreed on a price. Always pay with small bills and request them when you exchange money.

Some tourists have had problems with con artists who claim to be guides. If someone offers to show you around a city or give you directions, they may later turn around and demand compensation for being your "guide." In general, if there's something you don't want and won't pay for, make this absolutely clear right up front and always negotiate a price for a service *beforehand*.

In contrast to much of North Africa, Tunisia has very harsh laws regarding the possession or use of drugs. **Do not attempt to bring drugs in, take them out, buy them, or use them.** Don't even talk to dealers, who are likely to approach you with hashish in the more heavily touristed areas. Some drug dealers might be narcs, and even if they're not, you would not want to be caught in a compromising position—Tunisian law allows for guilt by association.

Note that the U.S. is not universally popular in the Arab world, particularly given recent intervention in the Persian Gulf and U.S. support for Israel. Although Tunisia does not have as powerful Muslim extremists as its neighbors (due to an aggressive crackdown by the present government), do not assume that your American flag-Budweiser t-shirt will earn you instant respect.

Most of Tunisia's **electric current** runs at 220v AC.

■ Women Travelers

Jnlike more fundamentalist Muslim countries, women in Tunisia experience a good leal of freedom. Still, some precautions do apply: dress conservatively outside of the European-dominated tourist areas (*Let's Go* should help you avoid these areas anyway). Women traveling alone in the touristed cities of the north will encounter only ninor hassles, but in the interior or the south might want to go accompanied by nother woman or (unless it really cramps your style) a man you know well.

■ Language

The official language is Arabic, but all Tunisian secondary school students study French, and most people who commonly deal with tourists speak a smattering of English and German as well. French is common among educated Tunisians even in the interior. If you don't speak French, try to brush up on your sign language.

GETTING THERE

■ By Plane

There are no direct flights between North America and Tunisia. North Americans should fly to London or Rome, and then make their way to Tunis by plane, train, or boat. **Tunis Air** flies from most major European and North African cities and offers a confusing array of round-trip deals. Flights to London cost 142D, but a charter company will reduce that by about 50%. Tunis Air flights to and from France are about the same price. Flights between Tunis and Marseille cost around 155D.

■ By Boat

As far back as 204 BC, boatloads of visitors were coming from Italy to present-day Tunisia. It still is, without a doubt, the best manner to get there. Try calling **Tirrenia** tel. (0923) 23 819 in Trápani) for ferry information:

Trápani-Tunis (7hr. 30min.): chair L85,000; Jan.-May L74,000. Departures from Trápani Mon. at 9am; from Tunis Mon. at 8pm; arrives Tues. at 6:30am.
Alimar (tel. (0923) 27101): departures from Trapani Wed. at 11am; from Tunis (May-June only) Sat. at 1pm. (L78,000).
Calgiari-Tunis (20hr.): chair L103,400; Jan.-May L87,700. Departures from Cagliari Sun. at 7pm; from Tunis Mon. at 8pm.

Report for all ferries leaving the port of La Goulette (a 15-min. ride on the TGM commuter train from downtown Tunis, get off at Vieille Goulette) **two hours in advance,** or you'll miss the boat. During the last two weeks of August, book tickets well in advance—all boats from Tunisia are packed with Europe-bound migrant workers. To buy a ferry ticket, you must show your bank receipt for the purchase of dinar and obtain a *Bons de Passage* from the bank itself—a minor but requisite bureaucratic hassle. You can buy tickets from all major travel agents. In the late summer crunch, fight it out at the crowded **Tirrenia Ticket Office,** 122, rue de Yougoslavie, 1000 RP, Tunis (tel. (01) 24 28 01).

All boat lines are supervised by the **Compagnie Tunisienne de Navigation (CTN),** which provides information and runs ticket offices at 5, Rue Dag Hammarskjold in Tunis (tel. 24 28 01), at La Goulette (tel. (01) 73 51 11), at Ponte Colombo (Gare Maritime) in Genoa (tel. (010) 26 981), at Rione Sirignano, 2, in Naples (tel. (081) 761 36 88), and at 12, rue Godot de Mauroy in Paris (tel. (331) 52 66 60 19).

On arrival, you will have to fill out a detailed **customs** declaration, although it is unlikely that you will have any of the items asked about (refrigerators, firearms).

ONCE THERE

■ Getting Around

Trains

A major **train** line runs south from Tunis to Sousse, and then splits into an eastern line through Sfax, which ends in Gabès, and a western line to Tozeur and Gafsa. Another line runs west through Jendouba to the Algerian border and splits into northwest branches ending in Bizerte and Tabarka. Although service is infrequent, the trains are comfortable and air-conditioned. Second-class prices compete with the cost of other modes of transportation. For information, contact **Société Nationale de Chemins de Fer Tunisienne (SNCFT)** at the train station (Gare Tunis-Ville in pl. de Barcelone (1000 RP, Tunis), between rue de Hollande and av. de Carthage, at av. Farhat Hached (tel. 24 44 40). Pick up a train schedule for the entire country at the information booth in the Tunis train station. Student discounts are available.

Buses

Buses are the most common form of intercity transit. They are inexpensive and convenient, but crowded. Try to board at the terminal (*gare routière*)—this increases your chance of finding a seat and may get you onto an express coach. Schedules change frequently and service can be painfully slow, especially in rural areas. The **Société National des Transports (SNT),** 74, av. de Carthage, Tunis (tel. 24 64 13) operates buses between Tunis and its suburbs. The **Société du Métro-Léger de Tunis (SMLT),** av. Muhammad V, Tunis (tel. 78 44 33), operates the light rail system, and the **Société de Transports Rural et Interurbain (SNTRI),** passage Mazaguan, Tunis, operates rural, intercity, and international routes.

Louages

Tunisia has a well-developed network of inter-city taxis, or **louages.** These are without a doubt the most convenient form of transportation as they are faster and more comfortable than buses and much more frequent than trains. Most towns have at least one, if not two louage "stations," usually vacant lots near the bus station.

Louages are usually white Peugot station wagons with a red or blue stripe around the side. The small placard displayed on the roof does not necessarily indicate where the louage is headed, just where it's been registered. There is room inside for five passengers, and the car will take off like mad for its destination only after all the seats have been filled. For most routes this will only require a 5-10 minute wait. If your destination is more obscure (a small town or a ruin), the driver may charge you extra for the unfilled seats; don't fall for this unless you're sure that there is indeed no one else headed that way.

Most drivers have regular routes with fairly fixed prices (although these are only displayed in Arabic). Use the rate of 2.500D per hour per person as a general yardstick to determine the correct fare. If you feel you're being overcharged, though, use your fellow passengers as a reference. Tunisian *louage* riders know the going rate; don't ever pay more than what another rider has paid for the same trip.

Private Cars

A **private car** is indispensable for touring the Sahara, where public transportation is scarce. You must be at least 21 and have a valid international driver's license. Get four people together and rent a cozy two-door four-seater with unlimited mileage, and you can cover transportation costs with 20D per day per person. Ask to inspect the car *before* you sign. If you're planning to travel through the desert, be sure to bring ample water, since breakdowns can occur.

Hitchhiking

Let's Go does not recommend hitchhiking.

Hitchhiking is illegal in Tunisia, but many foreigners find it fairly easy. **Women should never hitch alone in Tunisia.** Keep in mind that many Tunisians consider hitching tantamount to freeloading, and may request a contribution. Hitching doesn't save money, since public transportation is so cheap, but it does save time and if you get stranded, it might be your only hope.

Accommodations

Tunisia supports nearly 30 Youth Centers and HI **youth hostels,** all designed to house soccer teams. They tend to be large, functional, and clean. Some are as charming as locker rooms, and while convenient to the local stadium, they are often far from the center of town. Not all are safe for women. The HI affiliate in Tunisia is the Association Tunisienne des Auberges de Jeunesse, 10, Rue Ali Bach Hamba, BP 320-1015 Tunis, RP (tel. 24 60 00).

The ONTT classifies **hotels** on a zero- to four-star scale, and provides listings of all official hotels. Budget travelers should stick with the unrated (1-4D per person), one-star (5-8D per person), and two-star (9-12D per person) establishments.

Organized **camping** hasn't yet come of age in Tunisia, except in the south, where it may be your only alternative. Nevertheless, a handful of campgrounds do exist. As for unofficial camping, the ONTT guide states, "You can pitch your tent where you wish on beaches and in parks after having first obtained permission from the property owner or from the nearest Police or National Guard station." In practice, it can be hard to get such permission, or even to find the right people to ask. In a pinch, most youth hostels will allow camping on their grounds for 300ml-1D per person, including use of the facilities. Public beaches are the most popular places for setting up camp. Freelance camping could be dangerous, though—think twice before pitching your tent (especially given the low cost of regular accommodations). **Don't ever camp alone.** Keep in mind that in Tunisia, toilet seats and hot showers are a rare luxury. Bring your own toilet paper.

Food

Tunisian cooking reflects the competing foreign influences in the country. A single bakery may sell French pastry, Berber date cake, and Near Eastern *halvah.* The staple starch is potatoes, usually cooked in a spicy tomato sauce. All restaurants serve *couscous,* a steamed semolina wheat preparation, topped with almost any kind of sauce. *Couscous* can be a life saver for vegetarians; when all else fails, ask for *cous cous aux legumes* (with veggies) or *sans viande* (without meat). Beef and chicken are Tunisia's principal meats, typically served roasted, either plain or skewered (*en brochette*). *Merguez,* one of the country's most common meat dishes, is spicy sausage, often served with tomatoes and other vegetables. *Odja* consists of eggs and tomato sauce with a bit of sausage, and *koucha* is a meat and potatoes mixture in a spicy red sauce. Fresh seafood is available on the coast, squid being particularly popular. *Tajine* resembles quiche. Vegetables, mostly tomatoes, cucumbers, and onions, are finely chopped in *mechouia,* Tunisia's national salad. Fast-food stands serve *brik à l'oeuf* (eggs, potatoes, and a green vegetable in a puff-pastry shell). When in the south, fresh almonds (*looz*) are a readily available, satisfying snack.

In cafés, try the sharp-tasting but soothing *thé vert,* tea richly steeped with mint and heavily sugared. Although Islam frowns on drinking, beer and wine are widely served. *Celtia,* the most common brand of beer, costs 1200D per bottle. Tunisian red wines are heavy, but *gris de Tunisia* and *Koudiat,* both rosés, are quite good. The local liqueurs *bookha* (distilled from figs) and *thibarine* (distilled from dates) ought to at least be sampled.

Be advised that Tunisian cooking involves a great deal of preparation, restauran often run out of certain entries towards the end of the day, so arriving on the la end of lunch or dinner hours could affect your food selection.

■ Keeping in Touch

Tunisian **telephones** take 100ml coins—one is enough for local calls and about s are needed to call anywhere in the country briefly. The unused balance will k returned. Dial direct using the **regional area codes:** Tunis and suburbs 01, Bizert Cap Bon region 02, Sousse-Mahdia-Monastir region 03, Sfax region 04, Gabes-Jerl region 05, Gafsa region 06, Kairouan region 07, and El Kef and the North 08. Certa rural areas can be reached only with the operator's assistance (tel. 15). Internation calls may be placed from telephone offices and from major hotels. The quickes cheapest way to call abroad is to find a phone that accepts 1D and 500ml coins, an dial direct (00—country code—area/city code—phone number). Direct calls to th U.S. cost 2400D per minute. Expect a 20-minute wait if you call collect *(en P.C.V.)*

Letters to the U.S. and Canada weighing up to 20g cost 500ml; postcards ai 400ml. Letters to Europe are 450ml; postcards are 350ml. Post offices (called th P.T.T., for *Poste, Téléphone, & Télégraphe)* are generally open from 8am-noon an from 3-6pm Monday through Friday and Saturday mornings; in winter from 7:30a -1:30pm Monday through Saturday. Ramadan hours are usually 8am-3pm. Allow least three weeks for mail sent from Tunis to the U.S., two weeks for Europea addresses. Send **telegrams** and telexes from telephone offices or post office (Stamps are also sold at newsstands and tobacconists.)

■ Bargaining

The name of the game is hard bargaining. Asking prices are about ten times th actual value. If you really intend to buy, avoid mingling with tour groups, and sh(late in the day when salespeople are anxious to unload their wares. Refusing, tui ing your back, and walking away will decrease the price substantially. It is often p(sible to barter in Tunisia; pens, T-shirts, and sport caps are especially coveted item

LIFE AND TIMES

■ History and Politics

Tunisia has long treasured its physical and ideological openness. Centuries of imn gration and empire-building as well as various foreign influences have left their ma on this tiny nation, which today belongs as much to the Mediterranean as to th Maghreb.

The earliest evidence of settlement in Tunisia dates from about 750 BC, but le end attributes the founding of **Carthage** to the Phoenecian Queen Dido in 814 B(By the 6th century BC, already prosperous from coastal and North African trade, th city had become a major power in the Mediterranean. When both Carthage ar Rome intervened in Sicily, the two empires went to war with one another in a serii of conflicts known as the **Punic Wars,** comparable in size and scope to the Wor Wars of our century. Of the three wars, the second was the most spectacular ar devastating. **Hannibal,** the Carthaginian general, led an army that included 370 el phants over the Alps to surprise the Romans from the north, and trounced th Romans at Lake Trasimeno and Cannae. Nevertheless, the clever Roman leade Fabius Cunctator ("the delayer") prevailed over Hannibal in the end, with his stra egy of "delaying," or avoiding combat. Subsequent Italian governments appear t have hung onto this delaying concept, though without the same fortuitous ou comes. The Second Punic War ended with a Roman victory in 201 BC, but the infl ential Roman Senator Cato the Elder made *Cartago delenda est* ("Carthage must be destroyed") his cry, and eventually people listened. Perhaps to quiet Cato, the Romans declared the Third Punic War, which permanently settled the conflict in their favor (146 BC).

Despite the Romans' attempt to prevent Carthaginian resurgence by sowing the city site with salt, Carthage soon flourished as a provincial capital. Tunisia was Rome's primary African granary; the richness of its archaeological remains attests to the colony's wealth. Like much of the Empire, it was sacked by the Vandals and reconquered by the **Byzantine Empire.** As the Arabs began to dismember Byzantium, the region was overrun in 698 and incorporated into the Abassid Empire centered in Baghdad. The four dynasties that ruled Tunisia established the Islamic faith locally and built the *medinas* (old cities) at the center of present-day Tunisian cities.

In the late 16th century, the **Ottoman Turks** seized the area, but within a century relinquished control to the **Beys,** a dynasty of Turkish origin. Under these rulers, Tunisia acquired its present-day name and borders. When they weren't cavorting within their Bardo Palace, the Beys supervised the adoption of the 1861 constitution—the first in any Arab country—and pushed Tunisia toward Westernization. The latter efforts led to economic dislocation and allowed European nations to "manage" Tunisia's economy.

After invading Tunisia in 1881, the **French** did a great deal to organize and develop the country; they also seized all the best land for their own settlers. Their lasting legacy is the Tunisian civil service, one of the best in the developing world. Although French rule remained relatively liberal in Tunisia, a nationalist consciousness developed among the intelligentsia, who formed the reformist **Destour Party** shortly after WWI. They were soon superseded by a new generation of young agitators led by a lawyer named Habib Bourguiba, who split and formed the more radical Neo-Destour party. Bourguiba, whom the French jailed before he escaped into exile, returned triumphantly in 1955 to negotiate Tunisia's relatively painless transition to independence, which came on March 20, 1956. A year later he deposed the last Bey, then the titular head of state, and became President-for-Life.

A pragmatist, Bourguiba encouraged the French to stay, to the benefit of Tunisia's economy. Social reforms were introduced, including equal rights for women, liability reform, and greater and more equitable educational opportunities. By the last decade of Bourguiba's reign, however, Tunisia was in financial turmoil and a state of civil unrest. After 31 years in office, the elderly Bourgiba was deposed in a bloodless coup on November 7, 1987. His influence, though, is still strongly felt and his face continues to adorn the currency. He was replaced by President Aine el Abidine ben Madj Hamita Ben Ali. General Ben Ali has attempted to reverse the economic decline with new economic programs and active pursuit of Middle Eastern unity. While Tunisia today faces high unemployment and a tradition of autocracy, it also remains one of the more open and stable of the Arab states.

■ Festivals and Holidays

Islam is the primary cultural force molding Tunisian life; the major celebration each year is **Ramadan,** the Muslim month of fasting that comes at different times of the Gregorian year, depending on the lunar calendar. Ramadan affects all aspects of daily life. Shops and services close down for the afternoon. Muslims are forbidden to eat, drink, or smoke between sunrise and sunset. After sunset, streets swell with people, shops and businesses reopen, and the festivities last until well past midnight. The end of Ramadan is marked by Id al-Fitr, a three-day celebration during which all commercial activity comes to a standstill. In rural areas and smaller towns, restaurants and cafés close throughout the day. Concerned about how little work gets done during the month-long holiday, President Bourguiba once moved to cancel Ramadan—an action akin to outlawing Lent in the Vatican. A nationwide revolt quickly compelled Bourguiba to abandon his ill-advised position.

Southern Tunisia regularly hosts national festivals, which invariably include camel fights as well as such less-raucous forms of traditional culture as folkloric presentations and parades.

■■■ TUNIS

Tunis is a Maghreb city that tries very hard to be Paris. Modern and prosperous by North African standards, its million-and-a-half inhabitants cloak themselves in a swirling mixture of Western fashion and traditional garb. The ancient heart of the city, the *medina,* where tumultuous *souks* (bazaars) unfurl around immense mosques, possesses a specious Arab authenticity belied by the clutter of a tourist trap. The stately structures and tree-lined boulevards of colonial Tunis vacillate between a bizarre imitation of European culture and a pleasant Islamic variation on the City of Light. On the outskirts sprawls a typical third-world urban margin: innumerable, identical blocks of ugly high-rise apartments and miles of muddy shantytowns.

Originally an appendage of Carthaginian Thynes, Tunis survived the destruction of its mother city to become a prominent outpost in Roman and Byzantine times. By the 13th century it had matured into a bastion of Islam. Under the Hafsid Dynasty, the city acquired a reputation for liberal ideas and progressive ways that it continues to cultivate. By the 1800s, when the Turks had come and gone, the French occupation set Tunisia's capital flying on a course toward Westernization, and it hasn't looked back since. While the *medina* and the old city still pulse with silk and arabian nights, no one would deny that the center of attention has been transferred. *La ville nouvelle* is where today's action is—in the pizza places, near the record stores, behind the wheel of a Peugeot.

ORIENTATION AND PRACTICAL INFORMATION

The new center of Tunis was laid out by the French with their colonial penchant for wide, tree-lined streets and ornate façades. Major boulevards often change names after large intersections. The primary east-west axis is **avenue Habib Bourguiba,** which becomes **avenue de France** several blocks before the *medina.* The avenue is intersected by the major north-south artery, **avenue de Carthage,** which becomes **avenue de Paris** and then **avenue de la Liberté** as it proceeds north. The former stretches from the water's edge to the *medina;* the latter extends from the southbound bus station to the verdant **Belvedere Park.** Av. Habib Bourguiba is *the* thoroughfare, home to most of the city's major banks and travel agencies. The body of water at the end of the avenue is not the Mediterranean, but **Lac de Tunis,** an enclosed expanse of salt water. A causeway carries the electric TGM commuter train across the lake to the harbor at **La Goulette,** where the ferries dock. To get to the TGM station from the port road on the left, take a right at the castle, a left at the statue, and walk straight (10min.). The TGM train will take you to Tunis for 230ml. The *Métro,* a newly opened above-ground trolley, connects the TGM station with the train station. The TGM line continues north to the archaeological sites of Carthage, the village of Sidi Bou Said, and the beaches at La Marsa.

Tourist Office: ONTT Reception Office (tel. 34 10 77), pl. d'Afrique at av. Bourguiba and av. Mohammed V. Not too informed and not too helpful. Many brochures, little information, even less English. Ask for a map of the city and hope it isn't in Arabic. Open Mon.-Sat. 8am-6pm; Sun 8am-noon. For advice and intelligible maps, try the ONTT branch offices at the **train station** (same hours), or on the 2nd floor of the Tunis-Carthage **airport.**

Budget Travel: Sotutour-Stav, 2, rue de Sparte (tel. 24 70 48), off av. de Paris. Standard agency; sells ISICs too. Open Mon.-Sat. 8:30am-12:30pm and 2:30-8pm.

Embassies: U.S., 144, av. de la Liberté (tel. 78 25 66). **Canada,** rue du Senegal (tel. 79 80 04). **U.K.,** 5, pl. de la Victoire (tel. 34 14 44), at the entrance to the *medina.* Also the only service for citizens of **Australia** and **New Zealand.** For a visa—required of U.S. and Canadian citizens staying longer than 3 mo., and of Australian

TUNIS

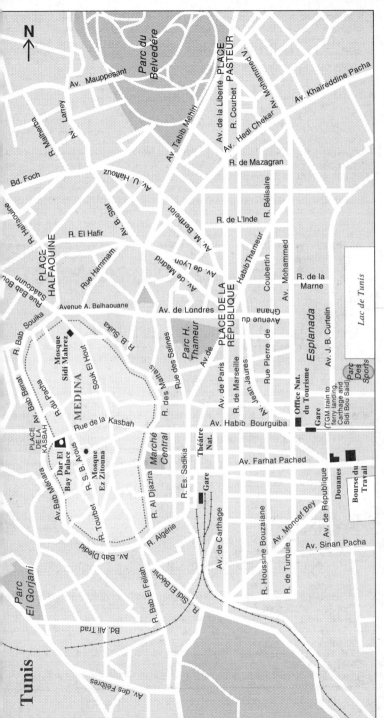

Tunis

citizens visiting for any length of time—bring 7.500D to the consulate at 136, av
de la Liberté (tel. 28 00 55). **Algeria,** 18, rue du Niger (tel. 28 31 66). Minimum
sum for **money exchange** about 1000 Algerian Dinars. **Italy**, 37, rue G. Abder
nasser (tel. 34 18 11). **Germany**, 1 rue El Hamra Mutuelle ville (tel. 78 64 55).

American Express: Carthage Tours, 59, av. Habib Bourguiba (tel. 34 70 15). No
banking services. Emergency check cashing for cardholders only; others can only
report lost or stolen traveler's checks here. Don't expect a warm reception. Open
Mon.-Fri. 8am-noon and 2:30-7pm, Sat. 8am-noon.

Post Office: 30, av. Charles de Gaulle, (tel. 65 01 21), off av. de France. Limited ser
vices only in the afternoon. **Poste Restante** at window #8 (150ml per letter
received). Open Mon.-Fri. 7:30am-1pm and 5-7pm, Sat. 7:30am-1pm, Sun. 9-11am
Sept.-June open Mon.-Sat. 8am-6pm.

Currency Exchange: any of the **banks** along av. H. Bourguiba. They're all open
8am-noon (Mon.-Fri.). Some then close and re-open later (from 4:30-6pm) while
others remain open throughout the afternoon until 4pm.

Telephones and Telex: 29, rue Gamal Abdel Nasser, entrance around the corner
from the post office. Inefficient. Some phones here take 1D and 500ml pieces, so
you can make direct international calls. Send **telegrams** from here or the post
office. Open 24 hrs. 24-hr. payphones also in the underpass at av. de Paris-av. de
Ghana intersection. **Telephone Code:** 01.

Flights: Tunis-Carthage International Airport (tel. 23 60 00). 24-hr. **currency
exchange.** Take bus #35 from av. Bourguiba to the airport (*aérodrome*) and back
(about 320ml). Note: the TGM Aéroport stop is actually a beach named
Aéroport—not the airport. **Tunis Air** has temporary offices at 47, av. Farhat
Hached (tel. 33 01 00), while its main offices are being renovated.

Trains: SNCFT Tunis Ville Station, pl. de Barcelone (tel. 24 44 40), between rue
de Hollande and av. de Carthage. The new *Métro* connects this station to the
TGM station. To: Hammamet and Nabeul (2.250D); Sousse (4D); Sfax (6.650D)
Gabes (9.700D); Bizerte (2.100D). **Commuter Trains: TGM,** at the foot of av
Bourguiba. Carthage-La Marsa via La Goulette and Sidi Bou Said. Speedy, frequent
tram service 5am-midnight. 350ml to Carthage and La Marsa, 200ml between mid
dle stops.

Buses: City buses at av. Dr. Habib Thameur at **Jardin Thameur** before av. de
Paris; also next to the **TGM Tunis-Marine Station.** Buses also stop at pl. de Bar
celone, in front of the Tunis-Ville train station and along av. Bourguiba. Fare
140ml and up, depending on distance traveled. **Southbound** and **Hammamet**
Nabeul Buses: SNT (tel. 57 11 11). The SNT station is at the end of av. de
Carthage across from the cemetery to the right. Walk or take municipal bus #8
from av. Bourguiba or #50 from Gamal Abdel Nasser (200ml).

Ferries: La Goulette (tel. 27 50 00). Take the TGM train to Vieille Goulette, 1km
from the port. Ferry tickets at any of the travel agencies along av. Bourguiba
Arrive at least 2hr. before departure.

Taxis: tel. 78 33 11. Always metered. Three passengers is the usual maximum. 50%
surcharge after 9pm. To airport about 2D.

Car Rental: Europcar, 17, av. Habib Bourguiba (tel. 34 03 03). The cheapest
Renault Super 5s cost 180D for 3 days, 400D for a week. Open daily 8am-12:30pm
and 2-7pm. **Hertz,** 29, av. Bourguiba (tel. 24 85 59), or at the airport (tel. 23 60
00). **Avis,** in the lobby of the Hotel Africa (tel. 78 05 93). It is illegal for a rental
car to carry more than 5 people including the driver. Always have passports ready
for security checks. You must be 21 to rent and drive, and have had a license for
more than 1 yr.

Swimming Pool: in the **Parc du Belvédère,** at the end of av. de la Liberté. Open
July-Sept. 10am-5pm. 500ml. Take bus #5, 28, or 38 from av. Bourguiba.

Laundromat: There are no coin-operated laundromats in Tunisia, but some dry
cleaners take laundry by the kilo. Try **Laverie**, 15, rue d'Allemagne, across from
the produce market. Open Mon.-Sat. 7am-6:30pm.

Late-Night Pharmacy: 43, av. Bourguiba (tel. 25 25 07), or 20, av. de la Liberté
(tel. 24 35 20).

Hospital: Hôpital Charles Nicolle (tel. 66 30 10), bd. du IX Avril 1938 at rue Paul
Bourde.

Emergencies: Police, tel. 197. Less than helpful. **Ambulance:** tel. 190 or 34 12 50. **Medical Emergency:** tel. 34 12 50.

ACCOMMODATIONS

Finding a budget hotel in Tunis is no problem except in the height of summer; the problem is finding one that seems safe. Think twice before staying in the cheapest hotels (anything under 4D) or in the *medina*. If you exercise the same precautions you would in any major city, however, you should not have a problem.

Hotel Bristol, 30, rue Mohamed el Aziz Taj, (tel. 24 48 36), off av. de Carthage behind the Café de Paris. Clean, cheap cubbyholes. Singles 4D. Doubles 6D. Triples 9D. Quads 11D.

Hotel Agriculture, 25, rue Charles de Gaulle (tel. 24 63 94), near the post office. Decent and well-kept. Singles 4.500D. Doubles 8D, with bath 10D. Triples 12D, with bath 14D. Showers (cold in summer) 1D.

Hotel Cirta, 42, rue Charles de Gaulle (tel. 24 15 82), across from the Agriculture. Tiny but unsullied rooms, many with balconies overlooking the bustling street. Singles 6D. Doubles10D. Triples 13D. Quads 15D. Showers 1D.

Victoria Hotel, 79, av. Farhat Hached (tel. 34 28 63), across from the bus stops in front of the train station. Colorful sheets and floors; some rooms have bathrooms that look like mini-mosques. Singles 7.500D. Doubles 11D. Triples 11D, with shower 12D. Quad with large bathroom 15D.

Hotel Commodor, 17, rue d'Allemagne (tel. 24 49 41), 2nd right off av. Charles de Gaulle from av. de France. A cut above, and not much more expensive. Polished wood lobby and spotless rooms. Singles 8D, with bath 11D. Doubles 15.750D, with bath 17.900D. Triples 22.250D, with bath 24.400D.

Hotel de France, 8, rue Mustapha M'Barek (tel. 24 58 76), off pl. de la Victoire. Hands down, nicest of the bunch: grand lobby, cafe, amiable management. Hallways are gloomy, but rooms are simple and comfortable. Singles 10.250D, with shower 11.650D. Doubles 12.500D, with shower 15.300D. Breakfast 1.850D.

Hotel de Suisse, 5, rue de Suisse (tel. 24 38 21), in a narrow alley between rue de Hollande and rue Gamal Abdel Nasser, by the train station. Tidy and affordable. Singles 7D. Doubles 10D, with bath 11D. Showers 1D.

Hotel Central (tel. 24 04 33) across the street from the Suisse, offers sardine-can rooms which are real bargains if you're in a group of two or more. Doubles 7.500D. Triples 11D. Quads 14D. Mat on roof 2D. Shower 1.500D.

Hotel Rex, 65, rue de Yougoslavie (tel. 25 73 97), at rue Ibn Khaldoun. Breezy rooms with imitation parquet floors. The bathrooms (in every room) are an architectural landmark. Singles 12D. Doubles 12D. Triples 14D.

Hotel de la Paix, 8, rue de Annibal (tel. 25 44 95), around the corner from the Hotel de France. This place beats even the Central for economy. Singles and Doubles 6D; 3D for each additional person. No showers.

FOOD

Tunis is most cosmopolitan when it comes to cuisine. You can feast on *spaghetti alla bolognese* cooked to an *al dente* perfection that would be the envy of any Italian chef, continue with a savory platter of spiced roast lamb, and finish with a delicate *éclair au chocolat* worthy of the finest french *pâtisseries*—all for under 4D. Unfortunately, this gastronomic ideal is surrounded by pitfalls: many places are dirty, and often the clean places are overpriced. The stand-up *rôtisseries* and sandwich shops off av. Bourguiba and av. de la Liberté are usually rip-offs. The farther away from av. Bourguiba you go, the less you'll have to pay. Those on a budget can survive on the hot snacks sold at most *pâtisseries:* mini pizzas, hot anchovy rolls, tuna rolls, and meat pies (about 350ml). Peruse the stalls of the comprehensive **central market,** on rue Charles de Gaulle between rue d'Allemagne and av. d'Espagne (open daily 6am-2pm). **Monoprix,** a large supermarket with stores off av. Bourguiba on rue Charles de Gaulle and on rue de la Liberté at rue du Koweit, also stocks a selection of inexpensive edibles. (Open daily 8:30am-7:30pm.)

Restaurant Carcassonne, 8, av. de Carthage (tel. 25 67 68). Clean, quiet, friendly, and efficient. Try the *tajine* (a bit like quiche, 1.600D). Four-course Ménu du Jour a super-bargain at 2.900D. Open daily 8am-10pm.

Restaurant Abid (tel. 25 70 52), 98, Rue de Yugoslavie. Similar to the Carcassone, and right around the corner. Most entrees 1500D; few vegetarian options. Open daily 10:30am-10:30pm.

M'Rabet (tel. 26 17 29), at the center of the *medina* in Souk Et-Trouk. The 300-year old building contains the *sarcophagi* of an Ottoman sheik, his servant, and his daughter, for whom the restaurant is named. Smoke a *sheeshah* (water pipe, 1.500D) or sip Turkish coffee (300ml). Upstairs is a tea salon, decorated with old curved mirrors and paintings, and a copper furnace reminiscent of Aladdin. Main courses are served (dinner 11-12D) as a belly dancer gyrates to the plinking of a *sitar* (6D for the show). Open Mon.-Sat. noon-3 pm and 8pm-midnight. Shows in the evening only.

Mic Mac (tel. 34 28 67), at rue de Yougoslavie and Ibn Khaldoun. One of the few stand-up sandwich shops that's not a rip-off. Reasonably clean. Massive, greasy *chaourma* sandwich and fries 1.100D. Open Mon.-Sat. 7am-10:30pm.

Restaurant Neptune, 3, rue du Caire (tel. 24 48 20), across from Hotel Africa. Prompt service, large portions and decent fare. Nothing on the menu over 3D. Open daily 11am-3pm and 6-10pm.

Restaurant Des Palmiers, 11, rue d'Egypte (tel. 28 54 07), off av. de la Liberté. Well worth the 15-min. walk from av. Bourguiba. Dishes are fresh, Tunisian, and served quickly. Try the *meloukya,* a delicious meat dish which looks extremely unappetizing (1.450D). Open Mon.-Sat. noon-10:30pm. Closed mornings during Ramadan.

Restaurant Ennil, 9, rue du Caire (tel. 34 93 80). Mediocre food at reasonable prices. Open daily 10am-10pm.

Restaurante du Caire (tel. 25 77 01), across the street from Ennil at #6, serves similarly uninspired but affordable fare. Open 11am-10pm.

SIGHTS

The New City

French-built modern Tunis is best seen as you stroll up **av. Habib Bourguiba,** known as the city's Champs Elysées. Including its tree-filled park median, the boulevard spreads nearly 70m. The Tunisian passion for flowers is evident—florist stalls and young boys vending jasmine blossoms line its entire length. Along the way, you can also stock up on such Tunisian souvenirs as Levis 501 T-shirts and Michael Jackson bootlegs. The **place d'Afrique,** at the intersection of av. Muhammed V, was once occupied by an equestrian statue of Bourguiba. That statue now resides in front of La Goulette, and in its place rises a four-legged clock tower. The site has been officially renamed **place du 7 Novembre 1987,** commemorating the recent *coup d'état.*

Nowhere is the stamp of the French colonial period clearer than at the juncture of av. Bourguiba and pl. d'Afrique, in the heart of the city. After you cross av. de Carthage on the boulevard, you will reach the **Artisanat** (a bastion of overpriced local crafts) on the left, and after it, the wedding-cake white **National Theater.** At **place de l'Indépendance,** where av. Bourguiba comes to an abrupt halt, you may suddenly feel you are in Paris: on the left is the oversized French Embassy, a miniature Elysées palace hiding behind its elegant black iron fence. Then the street narrows suddenly and av. Bourguiba becomes av. de France. The next block on the same side forms a continuous arcade in the manner of a 19th-century Parisian boulevard. Across the street the massive Roman Catholic **cathedral** incorporates keyhole-shaped Islamic arches into its Gothic form (1882). The blend is only slightly more successful than the efforts the French made within the edifice to convert Tunisians to Christianity. (Cathedral open for Mass: weekdays 8:15am and 6:30pm., Sun. 9am and 11:00am.) If you are in search of a little leafy peace, head to the **Jardin Thameur,** av. Habib Thameur, a large park that's a popular place to sit and talk, play soccer, and steal kisses on the sly.

Medina

In most Arab cities, the fortified medieval city, or *medina,* seems worlds apart from its 19th- and 20th-century surroundings. This is true only of the fringes of Tunis's *medina,* however, since the central areas have become so filled with vulgar souvenir shops that they seem a continuation of av. Bourguiba, which leads directly toward them. The Medieval *souks*—itinerant weekly markets specializing in handmade wares—have become so commercialized that there is now a Souk Burger, next to Mustang Jeans by the mosque. Stuffed toy camels decorate every curb, and for your convenience, the street vendors do take VISA and American Express.

Nevertheless, the *medina* is certainly worth a few hours; and despite the heavy commercialization, you'll be surprised to find real Arab life only a few steps away from the main drags. Take a left or a right down some small alley and you'll find yourself on a side street full of laughing children where the signs are only in Arabic. Be careful however: exploring the *medina* by day is less risky than at night, when it's unsafe for anyone. (The police will be unsympathetic if you're mugged.) On av. Bourguiba and by the mosque, young men claiming to be students may offer either to guide you around the sights (they will expect payment) or to accompany you to the grossly over-priced artisan shops (they will receive a commission). Also beware of merchants who drag you upstairs to see their "terraces," and then request an outrageous fee for the exalted privilege of having entered their shop.

To escape the tourist traps, take **rue de la Kasbah** (on the right) rather than **rue Djamaa ez Zitouna** (on the left) from pl. de la Victoire. Both are lined with shops, though Tunisians themselves tend to shop on the former. Near the mosque, turn right and wind slowly up the Bab Souika. **Place Bab Souika,** just outside the *medina* walls to the north but at the core of the old city, numbers among the most atmospheric spots in Tunis. Head across the street, up rue Halfouine to the benches and stalls in front of the **mosque Saheb Ettabaa,** stronghold of Arab culture.

Most visitors to the *medina* start at its center, with the **Great Mosque,** on rue Djamaa ez Zitouna. Known formally as Djamaa ez Zitouna (Mosque of the Olives), the Great Mosque—also home to the first university in the Arab world—maintains vague visiting conditions for non-Muslims—especially during the summer. Generally, you are permitted to visit the courtyard between 8:30am and noon (except on Fri.) if your arms and legs are fully covered. Alternatively, visit the terrace of one of the surrounding shops and look down into the courtyard—prayer times are quite a sight. As you enter the courtyard of the mosque, a long row of carved wooden doors studded with iron stands on your left. These conceal the prayer area and the *mihrab,* which faces east toward Mecca. Opposite, you'll find the gigantic minaret, rising above the entire *medina.* Modified in the 19th century, it is far more decorative than the courtyard or prayer room. The prayer room's 184 columns were salvaged from temples and other abandoned buildings of Roman Carthage.

Be prepared for aggressive salesmen who will sprinkle your hand with fragrance if you stop for a moment in **Souk el-Attarine** (the perfumers' market). At the end of Souk el-Attarine, take a right and a few steps on Sidi Ben Arous to come to the stylish 17th-century **Hamouda Pacha Mosque** with its elegant minaret and adjoining mausoleum. Close to Sidi Ben Arous is the **Souk des Chechias,** a market of tailors whose stacks of red fezzes would turn any Shriner green with envy. Further along Souk el-Attarine is **Souk et-Trouk,** where they sell just about everything, from carpets to t-shirts. If you're in search of a new fez, cheap sandals, or just a piece of dried fruit to snack on, this is the place to come. Following Souk et-Trouk to rue Sidi Ben Zaid, you'll see on the left side the 17th-century **Sidi Youssef Mosque,** with its octagonal minaret, opposite the 18th-century **Dar el Bey** palace on your right, now housing the Ministry of Foreign Affairs. Walk back toward the minaret of the Grand Mosque and along its back wall through the **Souk el-Koumach** (also called Souk des Etoffes). Multicolored scarves, light dresses, and other women's garments hang in high rows in this 15th-century alleyway. Don't miss the narrow turn-off onto **Souk el-Leffa,** where you'll find luxurious handmade carpets.

Many of the larger emporiums have intricately tiled terraces from which you can see the rooftops of the *souks* and the surrounding *medina*. The most famous is that of the **Palais d'Orient,** the large bazaar at #58 Souk el-Leffa. Their enameled tile terrace dates from the 15th century; its view is featured on hundreds of postcards.

Souk el-Leffa turns into **Souk es-Sekkajine,** the saddlemakers' *souk,* still proffering reins and halters. Retrace your steps, turn right onto Souk el-Kouafi, and on your right will be the miniature maze of **Souk des Orfèvres**—the jewelers' neighborhood. In this beehive of shops, hunched artisans cut stones, engrave silver, and fashion pendants out of ancient coins.

Walk back in front of the main porch of the Grand Mosque and cut uphill along Souk el-Attarine for a quick turn-off right onto **Souk el-Blag-Djia**, a market with all sorts of shoes, some fresh from the factory, and some made on the premises. Souk el-Blag-Djia becomes tiny rue el-Jelloud. Where you see the sign "el-Jelloud," take a left into a cul-de-sac (Impasse Echemmahra). At the far end, you can ring the doorbell at #9 and ask to visit the small, elegant 17th-century **Tomb of Princess Aziza,** now a private residence. Other sights of interest in the *medina* lie farther from the central market area. The stately **Mosque of Sidi Mahrez** at the far northern tip of the *medina,* can be reached by passing through completely untouristed *souks* where local residents do their shopping. From the area of the Grand Mosque, walk back toward the new city along rue de la Kasbah, and take the left fork onto the narrow **Souk du Cuivre** (copper souk), which rings with a chorus of metalworkers' hammers. You can buy teapots, lamps, pipes, and hammered metal plates here directly from the artisans (5.000-25.000D). At the end, turn left onto Souk el-Grana, which eventually turns into Souk el-Out. If you follow the covered market route, the *souks* will eventually give way to **Sidi Mahrez,** a large white mosque on the street of the same name. The 17th-century edifice is noted for its strong Turkish influence, with four small domes grouped around a single large central dome. (The domes are not visible from the street and entrance is off limits, but you can catch a glimpse from the rooftop bar of the Hotel International.) Across the street, through two bronze doors, lies the fascinating **Zaouïa Sidi Mahrez.** Walk straight in and turn left to find a well where women come to bathe in holy fertility water.

Make the stroll over to the southern corner of the *medina*. From the Grand Mosque, follow rue Djamaa ez-Zitouna, and take the first right onto Souk el-Balat, which leads to rue des Teinturiers. Here, at #31, you'll find the **Mosquée des Teinturiers**—dyers' mosque, built in 1716. Although closed to non-believers, the mosque is worth seeing for its fancifully colored eaves in red, green, and yellow. A few steps farther, signs point the way to **Dar Ben Abdallah,** an ornate 18th-century palace that houses the **Museum of Traditional Arts.** (Open Tues.-Sun. 9:30am-4:30pm. Admission 1D.) If you retrace your steps from the courtyard of the palace and continue along rue des Teinturiers, you'll eventually reach the **Souk des Teinturiers,** the dyers' colorful *souk,* where looms rattle and dye trickles into a gutter in the middle of the street.

The Bardo Museum

While a trip to North Africa generally means escape from the endless "must-see" museums of Europe, Tunis offers no better diversion than the **Bardo Museum,** home to one of the world's finest collections of ancient art. The Bardo is most renowned for its Roman mosaics; the finest works have been transported here from various archaeological sites throughout the country and more than compensate for the uninspiring ruins at Carthage and other sites.

Initiate yourself on the ground floor at the cross-shaped baptistery in the **Paleochristian Room,** which also features brightly colored mosaic tombstones with dyspeptic icons and Latin admonitions. Around the corner to the right in the **Room of Baal Hammon,** ritual slabs illustrate the Carthaginian procedure for sacrificing children to their dark goddess, Tophet (read the explanation to find out how). If you don't intend to try this out, move on to Room VI, which exhibits artifacts from **Bulla**

Regia, highlighted by twice-life-size statues of Roman gods, as well as a mosaic of Perseus and Andromeda. The ornate geometric mosaics uncovered at **Thuburbo Majus** are in Room VIII. Take refuge from the dead by ascending the staircase into the land of the immortal: Room IX, (**Carthage**) the central exhibition hall, is a court-yard with a Turkish twist, used by the bey's harem. Now it houses sculpture and mosaics excavated at Carthage. The **Hadrumetum Room** is decorated below by an immense mosaic from Sousse, the *Triumph of Neptune,* while the walls above are a backdrop for three semi-circular works depicting rural houses and a 4th-century piece entitled *Mosaïque du Seigneur Julius.* The adjacent Room XI mounts a superbly preserved *Neptune in his Chariot.* Across from this the **Virgilius Room** devotes almost all its space to the exhibition of a single, small mosaic of the poet himself with a Muse standing on either side of him. High-school Latin scholars can have some fun (finally) by trying to guess exactly which verse of *The Aeneid* Virgil is holding in his lap. Room XXVII houses the finds from **Dougga,** including a cele-brated mosaic that depicts *Ulysses and the Sirens,* the latter quite homely and the former frightened nonetheless. Complete your odyssey at the **Uthina Room,** where a wall-mounted mosaic depicts the love-lorn and face-less Orpheus enchanting the beasts with his inspired strumming.

The Bardo is open Tues.-Sun., 9:30am-4:30pm; during Ramadan until 4pm. (Admission 2D; 1D extra for permission to take photos.) Take bus #3 from av. Bour-guiba or metro #4 from av. Habib Thameur (both cost 320 ml). Either one will let you off within 500m of the museum; it's further down the road on the right. Or take a cab (2D) to avoid the sweat and grind of public transportation.

■ Near Tunis: Carthage and Sidi Bou Said

The environs of Tunis were made for daytrips. Efficient TGM commuter trains make **Carthage** (30min., 450ml) and **Sidi Bou Said** (35min., 450ml), easy, quick rides. Trains come every 15 minutes or so. The spectacular 30km beach of **Raouad** begins just past **Gammarth;** but both these towns (and La Marsa as well) are now overrun tourist nightmares.

Carthage

> There was an ancient city (Tyrian settlers inhabited it), Carthage,
> opposite Italy and the far-off mouths of the Tiber, a city rich in wealth
> and terribly harsh in the pursuit of war. Juno is said to have loved this one
> city more than all lands...
>
> —Virgil, The Aeneid I 12-16

> Carthage must be destroyed.
>
> —Cato

If you come to see the ruins of this great city you will understand Juno's sentiment; if you visit the modern suburb which has taken its place, you will probably side with the Senator. Contemporary Carthage is a bland, pretentious collection of mansions and tourist traps—even a bottle of soda costs 600ml here. The ruins are scattered over a wide area that coincides with the stops of the TGM train line. Successive stops are close together and can be traversed easily on foot. If you're short on stam-ina or time, get off at the **Carthage-Hannibal** station, visit the Roman baths, then get back on the TGM to **Carthage-Byrsa** and visit the Tophet and the Punic Ports. The nearby beaches of the Bay of Tunis offer a refreshing alternative to yet another ruin. Buy a ticket for all Carthage sites at either the Carthage Museum or the Roman baths. (2D, free with ISIC. Be ready to fend off guides or use up some loose change.)

Carthage-Byrsa: Though most of the uncovered ruins of Carthage date to the Roman era, evidence of the original Punic settlement has been discovered here in the form of a cemetery. At the site of the **Tophet** (also called the **Sanctuary of Tanit**) quiet bushes conceal stones shaped like the planks of picket fences, engraved with a simple design: a circle atop a rectangle that balances on a triangle. The pictogram represents the figure of the bloodthirsty goddess Tanit, who demanded the sacrifice of first-born 12- and 14-year-olds in time of hardship. Each stone mourns one of the 1200 children who were sacrificed here. (Open daily 7am-7pm.) To reach the Tophet, cross the tracks and head towards the sea, then take a right onto rue Hannibal.

Almost nothing remains of what was the world's greatest harbor in its time, but determined archeologists have reconstructed the contours of the original **Punic Ports.** Inside the "Antiquarium" (the custodian will unlock it for you) are detailed models of the military port from the Punic and Roman periods. (Site open daily 7am-7pm.) To reach either site, walk toward the large palm tree you can see from the Carthage-Byrsa station. Beyond this palm, there's a small lake. From here, the Tophet is your first right (rue Hannibal) and the Punic Ports are further on, around the lake to your left.

Carthage-Hannibal: the **National Museum of Carthage** occupies the site where an immense Roman temple once stood. The remains are scattered throughout the surrounding gardens. Inside you'll find only a few Punic funerary steles and two expressive 4th-century sarcophagi made from Italian Carrara marble—an indication of the city's former wealth. (Open daily 8am-7pm.) To reach the museum from the station, follow the palm-lined avenue up to its crest, and just as it's about to slope down again, make a left up a narrow dirt path. The most substantial rubble of Carthage lies in the village named after the general who struck fear into the hearts of thousands of Romans. From the station, walk toward the water and turn left on rue Septime Severe to find the 2nd-century Roman **Baths of Antoninus**—the single most impressive ruin in Carthage. Once rivaling Rome's Baths of Caracalla in size, the baths were gradually destroyed by villagers who used the site as a quarry. You can't enter this forest of humpbacked pediments and fallen pillars; the sea breeze is your only solace as you wander around them. Further away from the water, back near the entrance, you'll discover a tiny underground Christian chapel, whose floor is patterned with an ornithological mosaic. (Open daily 8:30am-7pm; off-season 8:30am-5pm.)

Head farther up the road, cross beneath the railway tracks, and follow the signs to the **Roman Villas** and **Archeological Gardens,** where you'll find two Byzantine churches and a Punic necropolis. The guides will tell you that the elegant villa was Hannibal's Palace; they refuse to admit that Hannibal wasn't Roman and died 400 years before the villa was built. Over the hill lies the well-preserved 3rd-century **Odeon.** (Open daily 8am-7pm.) From the station, cross the tracks and go uphill to reach the remnants of the Roman **amphitheater.** Another 2km ahead, the scrupulously restored **Theater of Carthage,** provides the backdrop for the **Festival of Carthage** (July to mid-Aug.). For information, contact the tourist office in Tunis or see the schedule in *La Presse*.

Sidi Bou Said

After spending the day getting sweaty and sandy in Carthage, the village of Sidi Bou Said (10 min. further down the TGM line) is the perfect spot to repair to. The streets are all smooth cobblestone, the houses all a fresh-painted blue and white, and purple flowers and century plants spill out of wall-top gardens everywhere. Though popular with European visitors, Sidi Bou Said is where you'll see your first Arab tourist. Indeed, the TGM is packed with city-dwellers who make the trip in the late afternoon for the sea-breezes and the café culture. Decorative detail is the secret the town's charm: doors studded with patterns of giant black nails, metal knockers in the shape of the Hand of Fatima, brightly painted metal window grills, and wooden window boxes thick with flowers.

From the TGM station, proceed to the right and turn left at the police station. Walk up the hill along av. Docteur Habib Thameur to the tiny **town square.** The TGM whisks you back to Tunis until midnight. Follow rue Sidi Bou-Fares from the main square, turn left, and hike up the hill. A small tip will persuade the guardian to let you climb the **minaret.** Or continue from the town square until you see the steep flight of 254 stairs to the right; these descend to the small beach. Before 10am or after 9pm, ask around the port about lending a hand on one of the fishing boats that ply the sea all night and return at dawn. You'll have a great time, and if you can spare several days, you may even get paid. The **Hotel Sidi Bou-Fares,** up the hill from the main square at #15 (tel. 74 00 91), maintains eight simple, spotless rooms with stone floors around a garden courtyard in the shade of an immense fig tree. The ambiance here suggests something between a luxurious Mediterranean villa and a 1960s commune. The genial owner occasionally cooks lunch, and trades insults with the guests. Call ahead; a room here is the most pleasant base for exploration in Tunis. (Singles 10.500D. Doubles 17D. Triples with bath 24D. Breakfast included.)

Restaurant Chergui, off the main square (tel. 74 09 87), is the cheapest and one of the most appealing restaurants in town. Try the excellent *couscous poulet* for 2.500D, the *brik à l'oeuf* for 700ml, or the *tajine de fromage* (a meatless quiche) for 2.500D, all served in a large courtyard at low, Arab-style tables. (Open daily noon-10pm.) For dessert, pick up some *bambolini,* a fried dough concoction swamped in sugar (200ml) from the stands that line the beach.

Sidi Bou Said exists only for the evening. As the sun sets, the city's unrivaled cafés jolt awake from mid-day slumber. The expensive and trendy restaurants are at the bottom of the cliff. A better view and more authentic experience can be had atop the cliff at **Café Sidi Chabaane,** with its irregular tiers and delicate teas.

CAP BON PENINSULA

Stretching northeast toward Sicily, Cap Bon defines the Bay of Tunis on one side and the Gulf of Hammamet on the other. The cape's hillsides, rich with olive and orange groves, and its shimmering sea provide welcome relief from both the scorching heat of the south and the wearying bustle of Tunis. Vacationing Europeans crowd the peninsula's fine beaches and fill its azure waters in the beach towns of Kelibia, Hammamet and Nabeul. Frequent and packed buses link the villages of the peninsula with Tunis and each other. Unfortunately, inexpensive hotels are rare, though staying at hostels will help salvage your budget.

■ Nabeul

Nabeul is both a pleasant, inexpensive place to spend a few days and an excellent anchor for excursions throughout the rest of the Cap Bon Peninsula. Its beaches may be less spectacular than the more famous ones at nearby Hammamet (12km south), but Nabeul's lower prices and less artificial atmosphere make up for it. Locals and foreigners alike come here to relax and swim in what is perhaps Tunisia's only authentic beach town. Nabeul's other claim to fame as tile and ceramics capital of Tunisia makes it a nexus for tourists who equate travel with shopping. The place becomes a madhouse on Friday mornings, when tourists are bused in for a contrived, so-called **camel market.** Flee to the beach when you hear them coming.

Orientation and Practical Information If you arrive by train (from Tunis, 7 per day, 2.250D, 1 hr. 30 min.), exit the **train station,** in front of you will be **place du 7 Novembre,** with a tree growing out of a massive ceramic vase. Across the street and slightly to the right is a small **museum** of Carthaginian and Roman artifacts (open Tues.-Sun. 8am-1pm, 4-7pm, 600ml). To get to the **tourist office,** av. Taïeb Mehiri (tel. 86 800), head straight one block, and take a right on av. Taïeb Mehiri. Proceed almost to the beach; it's on your right. They're extremely helpful by Tunisian standards: they speak English *and* they have a map. (Open 7:30am-1:30pm and 4-7pm, Sept.-June 8:30am-1pm and 3-5:45pm.) If you come by bus, you will arrive somewhere on the main street in town, which changes name (from west to east) from av. Thameur to **av. Farhat Hached** (the major shopping street) to rue Zarrouk. **Av. Bourguiba** is a perpendicular cross street; the train station and pl. 7 Novembre are two blocks south of the intersection. The **post office** (tel. 85 297) and **police station** (tel. 85 474) both reside on av. Bourguiba, at numbers 170 and 73, respectively. (Post office open July-Sept. Mon.-Fri. 8am-1:30pm and 5-7pm, Sat. 8am-1:30pm, Sun. 9-11am; Oct.-June Mon.-Fri. 8am-6pm, Sat. 8am-1:30pm.) Nabeul has several public **telephone** spots, or "taxiphones." The most centrally located is near the police station on av. Bourguiba (open daily 8am-11pm).

Louages for the south and for Tunis (2.500D) leave from av. Thameur about two blocks before the intersection with av. Bourguiba. (Negotiate a price *before* you get in.) Every half-hour, **buses** leave for Tunis (1hr. 30min., 2.250D) and Hammamet (12km away, 420ml). Buses and *louages* to Kelibia and other northern Cap Bon destinations cities in northern Cap Bon depart from the El-Mahfar station (tel. 85 407) towards the end of av. Farhat Hached, a block beyond the town square. (To Kelibia: 12 per day from 9am-6pm, 1.800D.) Behind the buses you can find Nabeul's **central market,** where you can pick up anything from onions to can-openers.

Accommodations and Food   Nabeul is blessed with a magnificently located and painstakingly managed **HI Youth Hostel** (tel. 85 547), lodged between two luxury beachside hotels. Walk several blocks away from the train station (in the direction of the tourist office) and turn right on rue Mongi Slim, where you can wait for the local bus or walk the mile to the beach. Groups fill the crowded bunks in summer, but getting a mattress and camping out in the courtyard is never a problem. Half (5D) or full (7.500D) pension is now required, but the simple, delicious food is well worth it, and you don't have to stray from the beach. Membership is required. Lockout's at midnight, but if there aren't many lodgers the manager will give you keys. Back in town, you'll find the **Pension Les Roses** on rue Sidi Abdel Kader (tel. 85 570), off av. Farhat Hached. Rooms are clean and fresh as the pension's mint-green interior (though that could change, last year everything was pink!) (5D per person, July-Aug. 6D; cold shower 500ml). The **Hotel Les Jasmins** (tel. 853 43), 2km from the bus station down the Hammamet road, allows **camping** on its grounds for 1.900D per person, 1.300D per tent (cold showers included).

Restaurant de la Jeunesse, 76, av. Farhat Hached, attracts a healthy mix of tourists and locals. Dishes run 1-2.500D; the *merguez grillé* is excellent at 2D. (Open daily 9am-9pm.) Try **Ideal Restaurant,** up rue Mongi Slim from the youth hostel, a friendly, family-run place where most dishes run 1D and a tasty steak 2D. If you're not interested in what they proudly refer to as their "english food," ask about their *couscous* (available every other day or so)—you can have a meal which includes a main course, salad, and beverage for 5D. (Open daily 8am-11pm.) Also on rue Mongi Slim, 500m up from the Ideal at #50, you can get basic goods at a small **supermarket** (open daily 9am-2:45pm and 4-9pm).

Near Nabeul: Hammamet

Whatever beauty Hammamet once had is now lost in the slick, commercial, money-sucking vortex that is its 20th-century incarnation. (Not even the Garden of Eden could maintain its charm if invaded by sixty-odd hotels.) Admittedly, the beaches are impressive, but there is little to do in Hammamet except stare disapprovingly at the relentless tides of tourists. The most entertaining sights in Hammamet are the signs advertising various establishments, which range from "Ismail's Deutsches Restaurant" to "Sinbad's Bazar-Snackbar-Cafe-Boutique-Frisör." Moving from the ridiculous to the sublime, Hammamet's one impressive sight is its 15th-century **fort,** which presides over the rows of hotels and restaurants (open 8:30am-9pm, Oct.-April 8:30am-6pm, 1D). However, the adjacent **medina** is, predictably, an artificial, latter-ay cave of thieves. As always, hang onto your dinars, or they're apt to leave your pocket by means both fair and foul.

To get to the beach from the **train station** head left as you exit the station and go downhill along av. Bourguiba. **Tourist Information** (tel. 80 423) is at the foot of the avenue, within sight of the beach and the fort. **Trains** leave Tunis for Hammamet (8 per day, 1hr. 30min., 2.250D, change at Bir Bou Rekba). **Buses** leave from Tunis' Gare Routière Sud (10 per day, 2.450D) and arrive at av. Bourguiba, near the fort in Hammamet. A comparably-priced *louage* (2.500D) is probably the best bet.

Kelibia

If Hammamet gets to you and even Nabeul seems too much of a circus, Kelibia, just an hour north, may provide you with an escape. It's a ramshackle fishing village, the sort in which you might expect to run into Ishmael and Ahab, taking a breather before resuming their hunt. A magnificent 6th-century fortress rises above the port, but otherwise there's not much to see in Kelibia proper. The main attraction is the white sands of **El-Mansourah** (2km north), without a doubt the Cap Bon's finest beach. Further north at **Kerkouane** are the best-preserved Punic ruins in all of Tunisia. Since Kelibia doesn't concern itself much with tourism there's a real scarcity of affordable lodging and food; the town and its surroundings are best seen as an easy daytrip from Nabeul.

Orientation and Practical Information Arriving by either bus or *louage*, you will be deposited in Kelibia town, a dusty, modern place noteworthy only for its 10 mosques, all with varied minarets. To get to the more attractive seaside section (2.5km away), head right, with the arches of the bus station behind you. Walk a short distance until you come to a large street with a flower-laden divide, where you should turn right; you'll pass the **supermarket** on your left. At the end of this street, you should see a sign for the **Hotel Florida** and **Kelibia Plage.** Catch a cab (250-350ml), walk a couple of blocks further to the **bus stop** (every 30min, only in July and August), or hike from there.

14 buses per day leave Tunis leave for Kelibia from the SNT station at the end of av. de Carthage (2hr., 3.500D). 12 buses per day run to and from Nabeul (1hr. 30min., 1.800D); a *louage* is about the same.

Accommodations The best value for accommodations is the signposted **Hotel Florida** (tel. 96 248), which has singles for 14.500D and doubles for 22D. Although a bit pricey, it's right on the sand and has a view of the fortress. The Florida also has a reasonably good **restaurant,** with a 5D menu. **Club Nautique,** a windsurfing school next door, rents sailboards in high season for about 5D an hour. Across the street, the **Restaurant de la Jeunesse** (tel. 96 171) serves grilled fare at 6-8D for a full menu. A little further down the road, around to the right as the road to El-Mansourah splits off to the left, is the **Cafe Sidi El-Bahri.** Stop in, sit on a terrace overlooking the sea, and sample some of the most marvelous *café au chocolat* you'll ever taste (500ml). 200m farther, at the beginning of the road to El-Mansourah, the **HI youth hostel** (tel. 96 105) rents bunks in barracks (4D) to members and non-members alike. Look sharp: there are no signs, and though the words "youth hostel" are prominently displayed on the building itself, they're written in Arabic and so won't be much help. It's a large blue and white building with the Tunisian flag flying out front. The only other accommodation is the **Pensione Anis** (tel. 95 777), signposted about 500m outside of Kelibia town on the road to the port. Spotless rooms vary in price according to the tourist season. (Singles 10.500-13D. Doubles 15-17D. Breakfast and hot showers included.) Free-lance **camping** is often tolerated along Mansourah beach and the long stretches of deserted beach further north. Again, try to check with any possible owner of the site or the police, and be sure to consider safety.

Sights The remarkably intact **Borj,** or fortress, sits between Kelibia and Mar
sourah. Along with the fort at Hammamet, it controlled the eastern portion of the
Cap Bon peninsula. Little remains of the original 4th-century BC walls; most of the
present battlements were added by the Romans and Byzantines in the subsequen
centuries. In the 16th and 17th centuries, the Spanish wrested control of the for
from its Fatimid occupants and built the crenellations atop the walls. It was late
occupied by the Turks and then the French. The anti-aircraft gun emplacements are
adornments from our own century; the fort's Axis occupants came under attack b
Allied aircraft. The fort is generally open all day during the summer, but accessibilit
depends on whether the local occupant and guardian is there to greet you.

The road that winds around the base of the fort lead to El-Mansourah and its ivor
beaches 2km away. There's no public transportation, but it's a quick, breezy wall
with beach cottages on one side of the road and farmland on the other. Nor sign
point you towards the beach; just follow one of the sandy paths that lead to the blu
water.

■ El Haouaria

Tiny El Haouaria, right at the tip of the Cap Bon peninsula, is about the size of Kelib
ia's pinky. With one real road, five stores and three cafés, this town is on the ma
only because it is home to one of the most unusual and unexpected sites in all c
Tunisia: the **Grottes Romaines** (Roman Caves), a labyrinth of underground pyr
mids carved out of the limestone rock along the shore. You can explore the grotto
yourself; though there are quite a few, the path between them is simple and a loca
guide (no matter what he tells you) just won't be necessary. The first you'll come t
is the Ghar el Kebir, or "Big Cave." In the center sits a massive piece of rock with
vaguely discernible hump and head. Everyone swears that the crude sculpture is
camel. A whole series of other man-made grottos is linked to this first one, most c
which are pyramidal, with holes at the top to admit sunlight. The shafts of ligh
streak down at angles, illuminating only part of the smooth, packed-sand cave floor
When you tire of the solitude, join the packs of El Haouarian boys who take advan
tage of the caves and rock formations below the caves to plunge into the Mediterra
nean. (Grottos open daily 8am-7pm; 600ml to enter.)

El Haouaria can be reached by bus from either Tunis or Kelibia. Buses depart dail
from Tunis's Gare Routière du Nord (near the Bab Saadoun), itself a bus trip on th
#3 from the center of town (5 per day, 2hr. 15min., 3.390D; check return time
with the driver). Service is much more frequent to and from nearby Kelibia, runnin
every hour or so. To reach the caves themselves, walk straight through town alon
av. Bourguiba and then head 1.5km past the end of town and towards the shore
You'll come to a café patio with a thatched roof; the rocks slope down to the se
from here. The entrance to the "camel" cave is a short distance off to the right.

Between Kelibia and El Haouaria lies **Kerkouane,** an abandoned site which wa
buried under the sand; you can clearly see the layout of the town in the Punic ruin
(12km north of Kelibia, open 9am-noon and 2-5pm). Take a *louage* between Kelibi
and El Haouaria and the driver can let you off 1km from the site.

■ Sousse

In spite of its popularity as one of Tunisia's major tourist locations, Sousse remain
clean, inexpensive, and basically agreeable. The city was first founded by the Phoe
nicians, possibly as early as the 9th century BC. Between the 3rd century BC and th
8th century AD, two tourist activities were consistently in vogue here: capturing th
city and changing its name. The place became, in sequence, Hadrumetum under th
Romans, Hunsericopolis under the Vandals, Justinopolis under the Byzantines, an
finally Sousse under the Aghlabid Arabs. Its glory days came in the 9th century AD
when the Aghlabids built the existing city walls and most of the major monuments
In recent years the city has enjoyed rapid growth and prosperity. (Tunisia's Pres

nt Ben Ali hails from Sousse—a little pork barrel politics never hurt any city.) Take
Sousse itself, and then branch out to see the other cities of the Sahil.

rientation and Practical Information If you come in by train, you will
rive at the **central station** (9 trains per day from Tunis, 2hr. 30min., 4.050D; 8 per
y from Nabeul, 2-3hr., 3.050D; change at Bir Bou Rekba). Turn right as you exit
d walk about 100m until you see **place Farhat Hached,** where pedestrians, buses,
rs and even the occasional train all compete for the same space. Just as you arrive,
e **tourist office** (tel. 25 157) will be on your left at 1, av. Bourguiba. (Open Mon.-
t. 7:30am-7:30pm, Sun. 8:30am-noon in July-Aug.; 8:30am-1pm and 3-5:45pm,
lf-day Fri.-Sat., closed Sun. rest of year.) The entrance to the *medina* will be visible
ross the square to your right. Most buses and *louages* end their routes at the **bus
ation,** alongside the walls of the *medina*, to the right of the *medina* entrance.
uages to Monastir and Mahdia, however, congregate to the left of the entrance to
e medina. Also note: trains to and from Monastir and Mahdia use the **Sousse Bab
did** station (not the central *gare*), located near the port 200m past place Farhat
ached. (To Monastir: 16 per day, 30 min., 630ml. To Mahdia: 8 per day, 1 hr.,
630D. Fewer trains to both cities on Sun.) The **post office** is on av. de la Répub-
que, which also branches off pl. Farhat Hached; most everything else is on av.
urguiba, which runs away from pl. Farhat Hached and the port down towards the
en sea. This includes the Monoprix **supermarket** (open daily 8:30am-12:30pm
d 3:30-7:30pm), the **police station** (tel. 25 566), and numerous **banks.** (Most open
r changing money Mon.-Fri. 8-11:30am and 2-5pm, Sat.-Sun 9am-noon.) A **phar-
acy** is located at #5, av. Bourguiba (tel. 24 414; open Mon.-Sat. 8:30am-1:30pm
d 4:30-8pm). Around the corner from the Monoprix, on rue du Caire, is a **tele-
one** office, where you can pay in cash at the dek for international calls (to the U.S.
out 2.800D per min.; open daily 7am-11pm).

ccommodations and Food A good choice is the (perhaps wistfully
med) **Hotel de Paris,** 15, rue du Rampart Nord (tel. 20 564). Angle to the right as
u enter the *medina*; it's just inside. Rooms can be minuscule (i.e. exactly as long
a bed) but they're neat, the showers are hot, and there's even a rooftop terrace.
ingles 7D. Doubles 12D.) Near the mosque and the Ribat, in place de la Grande
osquée, the rooms at the **Hotel Ahla** are not as immaculately kept as those at the
aris, but with blue doors, wooden furniture and thick blankets on the beds, they've
t a little more character. (Singles 6D, doubles 12D, triples 16D; Oct.-April singles
D, doubles 10D, triples 13D. Hot showers.) More upscale is the **Hotel Medina** (tel.
722), which rises above the Grand Mosque. It's got plenty of rooms, so it's a
od fallback. The luxurious entry room and lounge is something right out of Ali
ba. (Prices vary according to tourist season: singles 9-12D, none in high season;
ubles 14D-20D. Showers and breakfast included.)
Eating out in Sousse is generally expensive. As a rule, avoid any place right on av.
urguiba or pl. Farhat Hached. An exception to this rule is the **Restaurant Sidi-
ahia,** right at the entrance to the *Medina* (look for the black and red awning). It's
t a touristy location, but the clientele is strictly Tunisian. Most entrees here are hot
hell and under 1D. Otherwise, for decent, fairly cheap food try the three alleys
pposite the two big movie theatres on av. Bourguiba. (If you're lucky, you can stop
and see a Hindu-original action-romance subtitled in French and Arabic; you'll
ver again think an American movie atrocious.) The inauspiciously titled **Big Mac
rves** food more or less worthy of the name; **Restaurant de la Jeunesse,** (tel. 23
49), one block over on rue Ali Bach Hamra is in essentially the same league. A plate
either place runs about 1.500-2.500D.

ights The **medina** itself is the heart and soul of Sousse, even more so than in
ost Tunisian cities. It is also distinctive, if only by its size—almost everything of
terest lies within the old city. The streets are noticeably wider, the merchants

somewhat more civilized. But most striking are the remarkably preserved ou
walls. One look at the extensive fortifications serves as an unforgettable reminder
what the *medinas* really were before the introduction of fast-multiplying T-sh
vendors; entire fortified cities once could and did resist sieges. Enclosed within t
walls is the **Ribat,** a fortress-within-a-fortress constructed in the 8th century. T
coastal *ribats* served as "fighting sanctuaries," wherein a special class of warri
monks (sort of the Islamic counterpart to the Christian Knights Templars) divid
their time between prayer and practice smiting their fellow man. Climb the tow
for an excellent view of the *medina*. (Open April 1-Sept. 30 Tues.-Sun. 8am-7p
admission 1D, photo permit 1D.) Close by is the **Grand Mosque,** constructed und
the Aghlabites in 850 AD. While (as elsewhere) the prayer hall is closed to non-M
lims, the simple, elegant courtyard is open to all visitors. (Open 8am-1pm; admissi
300ml.) Outside the *medina* walls is a small but worthwhile **Museum of Antiq
ties,** with one of the best collections of mosaics outside of the Bardo Museum
Tunis. To get there, head uphill from the main entrance to the *medina* (created
an Allied bomb during Word War II) and walk about a kilometer along blv
Maréchal Tito. The museum is just beyond the point where the Army and Police b
racks guard each other across the street. (Open Tues.-Sun., April-Sept. 9am-no
and 3-6:30pm; Oct.-March 9am-noon and 2-5:30pm.)

■ Monastir

Monastir's rich historical legacy is now barely tangible. Its origins go back to t
Phoenicians and the Romans; the city enjoyed a stint in the limelight when near
Kairouan slipped into decline in the 11th century. More recently, Monastir was t
birthplace of ex-President Bourguiba, and his association with the city is still qu
salient. However, unless you happen to be an ardent personal fan of the man, do
bother spending more than a half-day here (though if you do, you might enjoy t
huge **Bourguiba Mosque,** the twin-towered **Bourguiba Family Tombs,** and t
gold-leafed **Statue of Bourguiba,** all on or near **Avenue Bourguiba.**)

Although the government (believe it or not, under Bourguiba) poured money ir
"improving" the old quarters of Monastir, the end result is a sterile, artificial tou
locale. Cut straight through the *medina* to the sea and Monastir's one item of int
est: the **Ribat** (a monastery-like that of Sousse), founded in 796 AD and expanded
the 9th and 11th centuries, remains both genuine and unharmed. (Open 8am-7p
admission 1D.) Climb the tower for a splendid view of the sea in one direction, a
Bourguiba-land in the other. Then catch the next train at the Gare du Metro, r
Salem B'chir, for the equally historic and much more charismatic city of Mahdía o
hour south (8 per day, 1.190D). Buses (#52) to or from Sousse run hourly (750m
Louages to Sousse cost about 800ml.

■■■ MAHDÍA

A bit removed from the well-worn tourist track, Mahdía remains a peaceful locati
almost entirely free of the milling crowds so common elsewhere. The city's fortur
have waxed and waned since the Fatimid leader, Obeid Allah, first realized the t
mendous strategic importance of the long, thin peninsula upon which the c
resides. Obeid Allah, reverently known as *el-Mahdi* ("the Deliverer") proceeded
occupy the peninsula of Cape Africa between 916-921, establishing a fortress an
city. The wisdom of these defenses, which included a 30-foot wall across the pen
sula, was proven in 945, when Mahdía resisted an 8-month siege led by Muslim pu
tan Abu Yazid. After his failed siege attempt, Mr. Yazid was stuffed and used as a t
for the Caliph's monkeys, ending his career as a puritan.

Shortly thereafter, Mahdía began to flourish as the capital of the (Shiite) Fatin
Dynasty, and for a time it even eclipsed Kairouan in importance. Obeid Allah h
constructed the main fortress facing east toward Cairo in the hope that his r

would soon extend that far. In 968, the Fatimids did gain control of Cairo, fulfilling Obeid Allah's dream. However, their capital's glory proved short-lived—within a century, Mahdía was sacked by the first of a succession of Christian and Muslim occupiers. The city was left with a handful of impressive monuments and the memory of a heroic past. Present-day Mahdía is a fishing village with a lively port and a *medina* unencumbered by aggressive merchants hawking souvenirs. Someday, this may change: sooner or later, resort hotels will exploit the 17km of beautiful beaches nearby. At least for now, though, Mahdía remains untouristed, quiet, and endearing.

ORIENTATION AND PRACTICAL INFORMATION

Upon arrival by bus or train, walk with the water to your right until you see a large square with the Banque de Tunisie on the far side. Up the street to your left is the massive stone entryway, or **Skifa Bub Zaouïa,** to the **medina.** Further along the water is the squat Obeidite **Mosque;** the easily recognizable **Borj** (fortress) is 200m past the mosque, on the tip of the peninsula. The *medina's* charming, narrow main street, rue Oubad Allah el-Mahdi (street signs in Arabic) originates at the Skifa and passes through place du Caire and then place Kadi Noamene, thus hitting all three of the old city's focal points. Just inside the Skifa, the **Syndicat d'Initiative** occupies the first building on the street (tel. 81 098). The office doubles as a paint shop and distributes hand-sketched maps, but the knowledgeable official speaks several languages and may invite you for coffee. **Buses** depart from the port area for Monastir (10 per day, 1hr., 1.580D), and Sousse (14 per day, 1hr. 45min., 2D). The last buses leave around 8:30pm. **Louages** are a more convenient option to and from Mahdía, as service is frequent and competitively priced to Sousse (2.150D), and El Jem (1.500D). *Louages* leave from the Esso station next to the port, two blocks from the Skifa across from the **train station.** Eight metro trains per day leave for Monastir (1hr., 1.090D), and continue on to Sousse's Bab Jedid station (1hr. 30min., 1.630D), along the port a few blocks from pl. Hached.

Near the Banque de Tunisie you'll find a **late-night pharmacy** ("pharmacie de nuit"; tel. 81 490), which is open all night, and public **telephones** (open daily 7:30am-1:30pm and 3:30-10:30pm). **Avenue Itabib Bourguiba** begins from outside the Skifa and is the new city's main artery; along it you'll find most **banks** and travel agents. A **police station** sits at #71 (tel. 81 673). Next door is the Magasin General, a **supermarket** (open Tues.-Sat. 8am-12:30pm and 2:45-7pm; Sun. 8am-12:30pm. MC, VISA). Down the road there's a **post office** on the left (open Mon.-Sat. 8am-6pm, Sun. 9-11am; Jul.-Aug. 7:30am-2pm; Sun. 9-11am).

ACCOMMODATIONS

The paucity of visitors to Mahdía means few budget accommodations, but what does exist is clean and affordable. Avoid arriving late in the day in summer without reservations. Mahdía's handful of restaurants clusters in the port area. Evenings in the *medina* revolve around cozy **place du Caire,** where outdoor café tables brim with locals.

Hotel Al Jazira, 36, rue Ibn Fourat (tel. 81 629). Walk from the Skifa to pl. du Caire, turn left onto rue du Corrique, and walk to the water. Jazira is on your left. An incredible bargain. Clean, cozy rooms, some overlooking the sea. Genial family management, attractive rooftop terrace. Vacancies hard to come by in summer. (Singles 5.500-8.500D, doubles 13.000D; in winter singles 4.500D, doubles 9.000D. Showers and kitchen privileges included. Women should exercise caution crossing the *medina* at night.)

Hotel Rand, 20, av. Taïeb Mehiri (tel. 80 448), several blocks from an excellent beach. From the Skifa, walk up av. Bourguiba, bear left at the fork, and turn left at the first big intersection (the beach is to the right). Spacious, spic-and-span rooms and gracious management. 6D per person. July-Aug. supplement 1.000D. Free baths. Breakfast 1D.

Hostel: Maison des Teunes (tel. 81 559). Large and impersonal, but super-clean and well-kept. Everyone is welcome but priority is given to **HI** members. Curfew midnight. 3D per bed in a double, triple or quadruple. To get there follow the road that begins at the ESSO station uphill, away from the water.

Camping: El Asfour, on the public beach along the Sousse road, between the El-Mehdi and Sables d'Or hotels. This is actually just a down-and-out beachside café, but they've got a lot of property and will let you camp for 2D per person. Bring your own tent.

FOOD

Restaurant El Madina (tel. 80 607), in the market building behind the large Banque de Tunisie. Don't look for the sign (it's in Arabic), look for the Maitre d' with the Salvador Dalí moustache. Somewhat spicy fare at mild prices. Amazing *brik à l'oeuf* (700ml) and *couscous au poisson* (2D). Open daily 7am-11pm.

Restaurant El Moez, 2nd alleyway after turning to the right inside the Skifa. The owner is a Tunisian St. Nick and serves up spicy spaghetti (900ml) and various fish dishes (from 2D). Open daily 8am-9pm.

SIGHTS

The **Skifa Bab Zouila** (Dark Entrance) is, as the name suggests, the gateway to the *medina,* and a logical place to start a tour of Mahdía. It originally served as the only land gate to the heavily fortified Fatimid capital. Keep in mind that the Skifa was just the gateway of the fortifications—it's clear that the architects of Mahdía's defenses really meant business. The Skifa's walls are over 10m thick, while its dark namesake passageway stretches over 44m. From the Skifa, walk down rue Oubad Allah el-Mehdi to **place du Caire** and the glazed tile façade of the **Moustapha Hamza Mosque.** Mahdía's most venerable monument lies a little farther toward the water at place Kadi Noamene. The **Obeidite Mosque** is Islam's oldest Fatimid mosque, and after the Great Mosque in Kairouan, Tunisia's holiest. Obeid Allah first erected the structure in 921, but a cycle of gradual deterioration and restoration has continued, with the most recent restoration occurring in 1961-65. Despite major reconstructions, the simple linearity of the original Fatimid design has been preserved. The arcaded courtyard conducts you to a colonnaded sanctuary. Unadorned pillars separate modest rush mats that cover the floor of the prayer room. At all times, visitors are restricted to the main courtyard, and extremely modest attire is required. (Inquire at the *syndicat* for the entrance hours. If they're closed, check the mosque Sat.-Thurs. in late afternoon.) Continue from the Great Mosque along the *medina's* waterfront, where you're likely to see young locals diving for octopus. The **fishing port,** Tunisia's busiest, is the scene for intriguing arrivals (human and ichthyoid) in the early morning and at dusk. Ahead looms the immense **Borj el-Kebir** (literally "big fort") which is also fittingly named. Built by the Turks in 1595, the Borj, with its strategic location, commands a view of all approaches to the city. (Open Tues.-Sun. 9am-1pm and 2-6pm. Admission 600ml, photo permit 1D.) From mid-July to August, the Borj hosts **The Nights of Mahdía,** the equivalent of the International Festival of Sousse, featuring the same shows. Tickets are sold at the gate (2-5D, students half-price).

Farther along the peninsula, hewn out of the rocky shoreline, the 1000-year-old **Fatimid Port** continues to harbor fishing boats. At the tip of windblown Cape Africa, a solitary lighthouse presides over Mahdía's sprawling cemetery. The famous treasures from a sunken Roman ship discovered off the cape in 1907 are currently on display at the Bardo Museum in Tunis. After the circuit of the peninsula, continue down the coast toward Monastir and you'll come upon the **municipal beach.** Farther along the route to Sousse, the beaches remain unmarred by the debris of resort hotels that have littered the coastline to the north.

Near Mahdía: El Jem

uth of Mahdía, off the road to Ksour Essaf, lies **Salakta.** Turn off at the sign and
llow the road to the coast; then veer left and you'll reach **Sullecthum,** an ancient
oman seaport that once engaged in lucrative trade. Though small, the **archaeolog-
al museum** houses interesting relics, including a remarkable mosaic of a lion. (A
) to the caretaker will open the museum anytime.) South along the white, sandy
:ach and all around the museum are found the ruins of the port.

In the tiny town of El Jem, monkeys compete with Peugeots, and wherever you
) you can hear the sheep bleat. El Jem has one hotel, one market, and one café.
id a Roman coliseum. The sixth largest coliseum in the world, in fact. A collection
' ramshackle buildings huddles at its feet, and it seems as if the coliseum is all that's
ving modern-day El Jem from being swallowed up by the hot Tunisian sands.

During his brief 3rd-century reign, the rebel emperor Gordian constructed the
nphitheater by an old Roman road, exactly halfway between Sousse and Sfax.
owever, he neglected to buy the support of the Third Augustan Legion, which
romptly beat up on both Gordian and the rest of the province. In its day, the
nphitheater held 30,000 spectators and hosted games of all sorts—you can still
:er into the pits in its sandy floor to see the cellars where the beasts and gladiators
armed up.

Every bit as impressive as its distant cousin in Rome, the amazingly intact arena
flects the skill of the Roman engineers responsible for its construction. The dam-
;e you see is no fault of theirs, but rather of an overzealous government official,
ho in 1695 ordered artillery fired at the coliseum in an attempt to flush out a band
' tax evaders who had fortified themselves within. (Arena open 7am-7pm. Admis-
:n 2D; photo permit 1D). For the first three weeks of July, the colosseum is the
:ectacular setting of the **Festival International de Musique Symphonique** (with
e catchy slogan, "El Jem que j'aime"). For information call 90 224. On the road
uth to Sfax (a 10-min. walk from the amphitheater) lies the **Archeological
useum** and another, smaller amphitheater. Mosaics in the museum once adorned
oman villas at Thydrus, the predecessor of the modern village. (Open daily 7am-
m. Admission 2D. Ticket is the same as for the amphitheater.)

The drab main avenue of El Jem still bears the once-obligatory name of Bourguiba
id is home to some auto mechanics and a couple of goats. At the end opposite the
ena and next to the **train station,** you will find El Jem's only hotel: **Hotel Julius**
:l. 90 044 or 90 419), with plush singles for 7.500D, doubles for 13D. (Breakfast
id private bathrooms included.) There are a few hole-in-the-wall eateries in El Jem,
it the only good bargain is **Restaurant de Bonheur** (tel. 90 421), one block from
e hotel down the road to Sfax. Go with the *poulet rôti* (2.500D) and salads
.200D) or request an excellent omelette (1D, not on the menu; open daily 8am-
)pm).

Facing the coliseum from the train station, there's a **police station** (tel. 90 700)
id a **late-night pharmacy** up the road to the right. Down the same road but to the
ft, you'll find (all near Restaurant de Bonheur) a **post office** (tel. 90 139; open
on.-Sat. 8am-1:30pm, Sept.-June 8am-noon and 3-6pm), **telephones** (open daily
im-10pm), and a couple of **banks.** El Jem is served by 5 trains a day to Sousse and 4
 Sfax (both 2.250D). Bus service is infrequent, but there are at least 2 each after-
)on to both Sousse and Sfax (2.150D). *Louages* to Sousse, Sfax and Mahdía. Both
ises and *louages* depart from the square in front of the Hotel Julius, across from
e train station.

Sfax

ax may be Tunisia's second city in terms of size (a quarter of a million residents),
it it has not yet assumed corresponding importance as a cultural or tourist center.
ie massive wall surrounding the *medina* is all that's left to remind you that Sfax is
er one thousand years old, in spite of the banks and the business and the tall build-

ings. Inside the walls, the interior of the old city is relatively devoid of tourists, and (whether by cause or effect) also somewhat lacking in items of interest. Even the **Great Mosque,** almost exactly in the center of the *medina* leaves something to be desired; you could easily walk past it mistaking it for a carpet factory or a fish warehouse. Really the best thing to do while you're in Sfax is to walk a few blocks from the train station and sit for while in the pretty gardens to the left of the *medina* entryway, shaded by the huge walls of the old city.

If you didn't get your fill of mosaics at the Bardo in Tunis, the **Archaeological Museum** (tel. 29 744) has a few more. It's on the ground floor of the stately, dome-roofed town hall, a few blocks down from the trains station on **avenue Habib Bourguiba,** Sfax's main thoroughfare, which runs across town from the train station to the port.

Staying overnight in Sfax will likely cause loneliness and depression. If you do get stuck here, however, there's a proliferation of hotels just inside the entrance to the *medina,* all more or less within the same (cheap: 4-7D per person) price range. None come too highly recommended, but the cleanest of the bunch are the **Hotel Medina** (tel. 20 354) and the **Hotel Jerid** (tel. 23 890), both on rue Mongi Slim; and the **Hotel Maghreb** (tel. 20 051) on the right as soon as you enter the old city. For good food, try the *couscous aux legumes* (1D) at the **restaurant** with no name (#14) next to the Hotel Maghreb. There's also a vendor at the entry to the *Medina* who sells delicious peanut muffins for 120ml each.

The **Syndicat d'Initiative** (tel. 24 606), located in a glass pavilion on ave. Bourguiba several blocks up from the train station, can give you a map and info on the Kerkennah Islands. A **police station** (tel. 29 700) sits about 100 meters back from the *syndicat,* and a **late-night pharmacy** (tel. 21 626; open 8pm-8am) can be found at #24, rue Leopold Senghor (branching off the square by the town hall). The **post and telephone office** (open Mon.-Sat. 7:30am-1pm; Sept.-June Mon.-Sat. 8am-6pm, Sun. 9-11am) is across from the train station to the right, as is the S.N.T.R.I. **bus station** (to the left). Occasional buses run to the mostly nearby cities, including eight daily to Gabès (4.780D).

Five trains run daily to and from Sousse via El Jem (2hr., 3.700D), two per day to and from Gabès (3hr., 4.050D). *Louages* leave from outside the *medina* walls and hit all the above destinations much more frequently. The ferry dock is the point of departure for **SONOTRAK** ferries to the Kerkennah Isles. To get to the ferry terminal, walk 12 long blocks (about 900m) straight from the train station, and turn left (about 400m more).

Near Sfax: Kerkennah Islands

Only 21km off the coast and due east of Sfax, the Kerkennah Isles are the consummate antithesis of that busy, metropolitan city. In fact, these isles are almost completely undeveloped. While lacking amenities, they also lack the typical mobs of tourists found at Hammamet and Jerba. It's one of the rare places in Tunisia where you stand a reasonable chance of finding a beach all to yourself. Kerkennah is excellent place for getting your feet wet (the water is too shallow for real swimming), watching the sunset or counting palm trees—and not much else. And dreamy and as romantic as that may sound, be warned—these islands are no nirvana. The terrain is rough and dusty and there's no one to pick up after the island's few residents, who care a lot more about fishing than about preserving Kerkennah's natural beauty or impressing you. Given its isolation and solitude, Kerkennah's great advantage (or problem) is that there is absolutely nothing to do.

To get to the Isles, catch a ferry from the terminal at Sfax (tel. 22 216) for the unbelievably small fee of 500ml. (Sept.-mid-June, ferries leave 4 times daily in each direction, 1hr. 30min. From Sfax at 7:30 and 11:30, 3 and 6pm. From the islands 5:30am and 9am, 1pm and 4:30pm. Mid-June until the end of August, the number of ferries is doubled: from Sfax every 2hr. 6am-8pm, from the islands every 2hr. 5am-7pm.) On arrival, you will be at the westernmost point in the archipelago,

Gharbi, which is connected to **Chergui** (the other major island) by a causeway. Four hotels cluster together in **Sidi Frej,** on Chergui. Take the municipal bus (with a red placard that reads 'Hotel' in the window) and ask to be let off at the *Zone touristique.* It's about a 15-minute ride; be sure to get off at your stop, or you'll end up someplace disturbingly nowhere with about a two-hour wait to catch the bus heading the other way. Along the way, you'll marvel at the flat appearance of the Kerkennah islands: no point on the islands is more than 35 feet above sea level.

When you get off the bus, you'll be at a crossroads where signs point the way to the hotels. Because the Kerkennah Islands have so little to keep you busy, one thing to do might be to treat yourself to a night or two at one of Chergui's two-star resort hotels. The **Farhet** (tel. 81 236) and **Grand Hotels** (tel. 81 266) are comparably priced and have well-kept grounds and swimmable beaches; both have pool tables and airy lounges; the Farhat boasts a swimming pool and tennis courts. (Prices vary according to season 14-24D per person, based on double occupancy. By yourself, expect to pay about 7D more. MC, VISA. Breakfast and private bathroom included.) If your budget won't afford such indulgence, the **Hotel Cercina** (tel. 81 228) decent singles and doubles (14.500D and 22.000D, less in winter; breakfast and private bathroom included) and rock-bottom bungalows (5D per person) with shared bathrooms. The restaurant at the Cercina is moderately priced (dinner 4-5D) and has fresh seafood. (Full pension at the Farhat or the Grand will run you about 8D extra per day.) If the idea of a resort hotel doesn't suit you, the final option is to stay on the bus for another 7km until you hit the island's biggest "town," **Renla.** Here, in addition to the very basic **Hotel el Jazira** (tel. 81 058; 6D per person with breakfast), you'll find a **supermarket** and a couple of **pâtisseries.** A **pharmacy** (tel. 81 074), a **police station** (tel. 81 053), and a **bank** (tel. 81 024) are all nearby.

SOUTHERN TUNISIA

The vast emptiness of the Sahara stands as a reminder of humanity's insignificance. Villages cling to hilltops or huddle in oases; the immense desert scarcely deigns to acknowledge them except with continual gusts of sand. Berbers still dwell in caves, Bedouins still herd camels and harvest dates, and 20th-century civilization is still a rare mirage in the vast ocean of sand. But the diversity of the desertscape is surprising. The Great Eastern Erg undulates with endless sand dunes. But the Sahara of southern Tunisia has many other faces: the marshy salt flats of Chott el Jerid, the jagged Ksour Mountains, the lunar landscape of Matmata, and the bursts of green foliage in the oases.

Desert Survival

Summer temperatures soar in the Sahara. The body loses a gallon or more of liquid per day—*drink a liter of water every hour and a half or so,* and keep drinking at regular intervals, even if you're not thirsty. Thirst is the first sign of dehydration, which comes on rapidly. Drinking enormous quantities of water *after the fact* is not effective—in fact, it's dangerous to do so in high temperatures. If you're using sweet beverages, dilute them with water to avoid over-reacting to high sugar content—even orange juice should be diluted at least by 50%. Alcohol and coffee cause dehydration; better not to indulge, but if you do, compensate with a lot of water. For long-term stays, a high-quality beverage with potassium compounds and glucose, such as ERG (an industrial-strength Gatorade), will help keep your strength up.

Light-colored, breathable long sleeves and trousers actually keep you cooler and protect you from the sun. Keep clothing on (light colors reflect heat), not off. Wearing a sweaty shirt, though uncomfortable, will prevent dehydration more effectively than removing it. Thick-soled shoes and two pairs of socks can help to keep feet comfortable on a hike during the summer as the sand can register a scorching 150-

200°F. Make sure to carry sunglasses with 100% UV protection, sunscreen of sufficient strength (even if you don't usually burn), and a hat. *Always keep your head covered*—you can buy a wide-brimmed straw hat on the street for about 4D. A bandana or towel dipped in water and wrapped around the head might add protection and relief. Temperatures fluctuate unpredictably, so consider bringing a sweater or jacket. In winter temperatures in the Sahara approach the freezing point, and it occasionally snows.

■ Gabès

Gabès is first and foremost a Saharan frontier town. Its atmosphere is reminiscent of the old American West, when Billy the Kid was king: hot sun, low buildings, bursts of wind that scatter sand across the streets, and equally sudden moments of calm when everything is perfectly still. The city gives the impression of everything and nothing going on simultaneously: it's a frontier town, as well as a big industrial center. The reason for Gabès's existence since the 7th century, and the reason to visit is for its beautiful oasis, a thick belt of palms several kilometers long that surrounds the city

The *oasis* is not meant for passive viewing—a glance from the exterior and all you see are a bunch of scraggly, old, withered palms. It becomes both cooler and more interesting as you hike inside on the paths. According to legend, Muhammed's barber Sidi Boulbaba founded Gabès on an old Roman site because of the forest of palms and cool water there. The more pragmatic reasons are its strategic coastal position and location on the edge of the great Sahara. Over the past 50 years appreciating the palm trees has become increasingly difficult in the face of the smokestacks and warehouses that have sprung up. Even so, because it's a transportation hub and because it's always been the gateway to the Sahara, gritty Gabès is a good place to re-group, water your horse, and rest a while before moving on into the desert.

Practical Information Gabès has two major streets, **avenue Farhat Hached** and **avenue Habib Bourguiba,** which intersect to become **avenue Habib Thameur,** which continues on another 500m to the beach. The other important street is **avenue Monji Slim;** this avenue runs parallel to av. Farhat Hached before merging into it at a small triangular park with a dome-topped clock in the middle. Streets are long and the city is spread out, stretching over 2km from one end of av. Farhat Hached to the other. The **tourist office** is on av. H. Thameur, 300m down from the intersection of avenues Bourguiba and Hached (tel. 70 254; open loosely Mon.-Sat. 9am-noon and 3-6pm). Unless you're going to the beach anyway, it's not worth the walk, as the staffers are apt to close up shop and take off for a few days without any advance notice. There's also a **Syndicat d'Initiative** (tel. 70 344) right at the intersection, but opening times here are even more mysterious and prone to change. Rumor has it that if you catch them with the door open, you can sneak a peek at their up-to-date and informative list of phone numbers: "Gabès 1974." The **train station** is on av. Monji Slim; you'll arrive at av. Farhat Hached by heading straight one block. Two air-conditioned trains per day zoom to Tunis (3:40 and 10:30pm, 9.700D, *direct-climatisé*). After the merge with av. Monji Slim, and in the opposite direction of the intersection with av. Bourguiba, the **louage** station is in a dusty lot on av. Farhat Hached. Further along still, at the tip of av. Farhat Hached (just before it turns into the large road to Sfax), you'll come upon the **bus station** or *gare routière* (it looks abandoned—it's only when you go around through the side entrance that you find any signs of life). **SNTRI** and **SORTREGAMES** run to Jerba (6 per day, 7am-3pm, 4hr., 5.600D), Matmata (11 per day, 5am-6:30pm, 1hr., 1.510D), Kebili (5 per day, 9am-3:30pm, 2hr., 3.600D), Douz (1 per day at noon, 3hr. 4.650D), and Gafsa (7 per day, 5:30am-1:30pm, 4.600D). The **post office** near the *louage* lot doubles as a **currency exchange,** but they accept cash only. (Open Mon.-Sat. 8am-1pm and 3-6pm, July-Aug. Mon.-Sat. 7:30am-2pm.) For traveler's checks, try one of the **banks** on av. Bourguiba. One block to the right of the train station, on av. Monji Slim, a **late-night pharmacy** stays open 8pm-8am. Past this a block and a half, **Magasin General** (the Tunisian STANDA), sells all the pasta, canned goods, and yogurt you'll ever need (open daily 8am-12:30pm and 3-7pm; MC, Visa). Gabès has plenty of **telephones,** and you'll find **taxiphones** (the Tunisian national telephone company) nearly every block on av. Bourguiba or av. Farhat Hached (open daily 8am-9:30pm). Back at the intersection of avenues Bourguiba and Farchat Hached, **Hertz** (tel. 70 525) and **Europcar** (tel. 74 720) compete to send you thundering out into the Sahara in one of their rentals. A **police station** (tel. 70 390) is six blocks up av. Bourguiba.

Accommodations and Food Most of the hotels are either near the bus and *louage* stations, or by the Hached-Bourguiba intersection, closer to the beach. The former are more convenient if you're only going to be in Gabès overnight, but if you're considering staying longer, look around on ave. Bourguiba (a kilometer or so away), where there are fewer cars and more of a small-town atmosphere. **Hotel Ben Nejima,** rue Ali Jemel, 66 (tel. 21 062) at ave. Farhat Hached between the louage and bus stations, maintains immaculate rooms, and a lounge with life-sized oasis pictures on the wall (5.500D per person, showers included). **Hotel de la Poste** (tel. 20 218) is two blocks from the famous Bourguiba-Hached intersection, on ave. Bourguiba. High-ceilinged and airy, this hotel is on the nice side of town and is very kind to your wallet (4D per person, showers included). In Gabès the **youth hostel** is **Centre de Stages et de Vacances (HI)** (tel. 71 270). From ave. Farhat Hached, between the train and louage stations, turn at Hotel Salama onto rue Sadok Lassoued. Continue to the end of the street, then turn right (ave. Bourguiba) and take an immediate left. The hostel is 200m ahead on the left. (10pm curfew; clean doubles and triples for 4D per person; well-shaded camping 2D per person, 500ml per tent; HI members only when the hostel is near capacity, usually late July-Aug.) **Hotel Medina** (tel. 74 271) on rue Ali Jemel up the road from Hotel Ben Nejima. Well-furnished rooms, some with balconies, and all with cute little throw rugs (5D per person, cold showers included).

　A la Bonne Boufe, av. Bourguiba, 62 (tel. 20 992) near the Bourguiba-Hached intersection. Try the immense, delicious *couscous d'agneau* for 1.600D. (Open daily noon-3pm and 6-10pm.) **Restaurant Bouka Chouka** (tel. 20 387) on rue Ali Jemel, next to Hotel Ben Nejima. Delicious food served lightning fast for about 3D a meal. *Pommes de terre à la Viande* is 1.500D. (Open daily 7am-11pm). Next door, the **Restaurant Ben Nejima** (below the hotel of the same name) serves similar fare at similar prices.

Sights and Entertainment What you see is what you get—there are no great mosques (except the one under construction) or museums here (except the souk that tries to attract customers by calling itself one). So when it comes to things to do in Gabès, use your imagination. Hike through the oasis on the shady trails that begin behind the bus station, or hire a horse-and-buggy. Across the street from the Hotel Ben Nejima, there's a **boulangerie** where the affable bakers will show you around their ceiling-high ovens before sending you off with a hot 3-foot loaf for only 130ml. And finally, there's the inevitable **souk-stroll.** In Gabès, the best souks are towards the end of av. Bourguiba, far from the Hached-Bourguiba intersection. Straw hats (a great Sahara accessory) seem to be the biggest item here; they range in price from 1.500D-4D.

■ ■ ■ ISLE OF JERBA

The island of Jerba was supposedly the residence of the mythical "Lotus Eaters" from Homer's *Odyssey*. According to the narration, Odysseus's crew, while on shore leave, stumbled upon a couple barrels of the local lotus wine and decided that going home wasn't such a pressing concern after all. Roughly three millennia later, Jerba still bills itself as a haven of R&R, but the rise of Islam has made the famous local product a lot harder to come by. Despite the best efforts of the tourist industry, Jerba does manage to retain some of its natural beauty.

While Homer and the local tourist office paint a picture of Jerba as a merry island where bottoms are always up, the reality of the island's history has been much less relaxed. The Phoenicians first arrived in the 6th century BC and the Carthaginians later built the 7km El Kantara causeway connecting the island to the mainland (still in use today). Thereafter, the island passed into the hands of the Romans, the Ibadite Muslims, the Hilalian Arabs, the Kings of Sicily, and the Hafsids. In 1560, French, Spanish and Neapolitan troops attacked the island, then a pirate haven in an effort to wrest it from the control of the infamous Dragut. An excessively bloodthirsty fellow, Dragut massacred the invading forces with the help of the Turkish fleet and constructed a tower out of their more than 5000 skulls. The tower was given an annual whitewash and remained until 1848, when some concerted pleading led to the bones' removal and burial.

Despite this nasty lesson, Europeans still invade Jerba; daily direct flights from most continental capitals keep Jerba's 27 luxury hotels and beaches full. However, though the island is no longer the mythical paradise it once was, you'd be missing out if you came to Southern Tunisia and didn't stop off for a day or two. If you've spent any time washing dust out of your mouth in Gabès or Sfax, breezy leafy Jerba will be a great relief. It's wisest to avoid the string of expensive shoreline hotels and instead stay in **Houmt Souk,** the island's largest city and transportation hub. From Houmt Souk, at the center of the northern shore, a short bus trip or about a 2.500D taxi ride takes you to the start of the beaches, about 12km east. A bus trip (#10 or 11) around the island costs about 1.500D. About the only item of interest is the **El Ghriba Synagogue** in Er Ridah. The synagogue is modern but the site is supposedly one of the oldest in the world. Jerba's small but enduring Jewish community claims to be descended from a group that fled Jerusalem in 584 BC.

■ Houmt Souk

Arriving at the bus station and following the downhill road to the right, you will be on **avenue Bourguiba,** a broad, leafy boulevard reminiscent of Tunis' own av. Bourguiba. The cafés that set up tables in the shade are good spots to wile away the hot mid-afternoon hours, and there are enough tourists around Houmt Souk so that you feel secure, but not enough to make you ashamed of being one.

Practical Information 200m down the avenue on your left will be the **Syndicat d'Initiative** (tel. 50 915), in a nice pavilion; on your right will be the confusing tangle of streets and souks where most of the hotels are found. The Syndicat can give you a handout with a map and answer (in English) any questions. (Open Mon.-Sat. 9am-12:30pm and 3-6pm.) There is a **Tourist Office** (tel. 50 544) in town, but it's not worth the 1km walk since the Syndicat should be able to tell you all you need to know (open Mon.-Sat. 8am-1pm and 3-5:45pm). Back on av. Bourguiba, a **post office** (open Mon.-Sat. 8am-2:30pm; also **exchanges money**) and **telephones** (open daily 7am-7pm) are near the Syndicat. Most hotels rent **bikes and mopeds** (both great ways to see the island), but at rip-off rates (1D per hour, 6D per half day, 10D per day). Better deals can be found on the other side of the souks, in a small garage on av. Abdelhamid el Cadhi. The blue hand-painted sign reads "Location Cycles" (tel. 50 303; bikes 4D, mopeds 24D for a full day.) Wherever you rent, bargain hard and be picky about which bike or moped you get; once you've paid, it's tough to get a refund even if the bike falls to pieces beneath you. There is a **late-night pharmacy** (open 8pm-8am) behind the bus station 100m past the ESSO station. The **police** (tel. 50 528) are on call at the top of av. Bourguiba, 50m down from the bus station.

Accommodations Jerba has a wealth of classy accommodations that fall about mid-range on the affordability scale. To get to most of them, either cut through the souks (short cut), or follow the signs from in front of the Syndicat that read "Hotel el Arischa." Either way you'll end up in the aforementioned sandy lot. From here, the **Hotel el Arischa** (tel. 50 384) is down an alley to the right where you can see the twin spires of a Catholic church rising. The Arischa used to be a *fondouk*, where camel merchants would stay whenever they came to town. Its beautiful courtyard even includes a (murky) swimming pool. (6D per person, breakfast and showers included.) Without question the best deal in town is the **Auberge de la Jeunesse (HI)** (tel. 50 619) where a bed with breakfast, showers, and use of the kitchen comes to 4D. This is no ordinary hostel: the rooms are mainly doubles, they have a sitting room with polished wood furniture—real hotel quality. Recently painted a fresh blue and white, with a young and friendly staff. Manager speaks English. (HI members only. Meals 3D each. Curfew midnight, but if you want to go out dancing, they will understand.) The hostel is next to the entrance to the "Hotel Touring Club Marhala," which is signposted in the sandy lot. The **Hotel Essalem** (tel. 51 029), near the bus station, is also a fair deal. Head one block down av. Bourguiba and turn right at the police station. Rooms are basic and clean, some with balconies. (Prices vary 4-5D per person according to the season; breakfast and showers included.) The **Hotel Sables d'Or** (tel. 50 423), close to the Arischa, has shiny checkerboard floors and ornate walls and bannisters. (Singles 8D; doubles 15D; triples 21D. Shower stalls in every room. No breakfast.)

Food One can eat relatively cheaply at either the **Restaurant du Palmiers,** 45, rue de Bizerte (open 11am-4pm and 6pm-midnight), or the **Restaurant du Sportif** on av. Bourguiba (open noon-9:30pm). A rich and filling meal at either place comes to about 3D. **Buses** run from Gabès (5 per day, 4hr., 5.600D) and depart via Gabès once daily each for Sfax (8D), Sousse (11.700D) and Tunis (15.200D). **Louages** generally run slightly more often and congregate in front of the bus station. **Tunis Air** also flies once daily to Jerba from Tunis.

Sights Near the Tourist Office, the **Borj Ghazi Mustapha** *is* worth the walk. Houmt Souk's fortress and another Dragut memento, it sits on the coast looking out to sea. To get there, plunge fearlessly into the *souk*, until you reach a sandy lot on the other side; the large tree-lined street opposite is rue Taieb Mehiri, leading straight to the Borj. (Open 8am-noon and 3-6pm. Admission 600ml, photo permit 1D. Known to be inexplicably closed at times; if you can't get in, even just walking around the perimeter is worth it.)

■ Matmata

When the makers of *Star Wars* were searching for a setting for a desert planet, they came upon the otherworldly scenery surrounding Matmata. A scorched landscape of twisted mountains and sprawling craters stretches to the horizon. (Don't miss the incongruous sight of "Welcome to Matmata" appearing suddenly in large letters in 3 languages on a mountainside in the middle of the desert.) Although the film crews and jawas packed up long ago, nature adds its own special effects at sunset, when the ominous landscape assumes an eerie red glow. With moonrise, all becomes peaceful. Walk just a kilometer or so along either the Tamezret or Gabès roads and savor some memorable images. Brief but repetitive rains have carved gutters and valleys in the rock; Berbers now build dams to reroute the water to their olive trees.

At first glance, the desert surrounding Matmata appears entirely uninhabited. The Berber population has developed a remarkable mode of habitation in which a large central pit is carved in the ground (usually about 10m deep and 10m wide), while tunnel passageways connect a constellation of adjoining chambers. The present-day Berbers of Matmata have made some 20th-century concessions—many of their "primitive" dwellings sprout television antennas at ground level. Local children will be more than delighted to show you their homes for a few hundred millimes. On the whole, however, Matmata's residents may come off as somewhat jaded, showing none of the interest in foreigners that inhabitants of larger cities like Gabès do.

Orientation and Practical Information Matmata is easily seen as a day-trip from Gabès, but you might consider an overnight stay: the daylight hours are an endless parade of tour buses deploying battalions of tourists and the town becomes vastly more pleasant in the evenings, when the buses depart and sunset introduces a cool, serene nightfall. And finally, there's the added novelty of staying in Matmata's unique hotels ("Luke Skywalker slept here"): if you've always wanted to go underground, here's your chance.

Matmata's **Syndicat d'Initiative** (up the hill from the main bus stop) celebrated its grand opening in May 1993. They don't have a lot to offer in the way of literature, but the English-speaking official evidently likes his new job and is forthcoming and enthusiastic. They're open daily 8am-7pm and after hours they leave a bus schedule posted on the door (no matter what they tell you, show up a good 45 minutes before the bus's scheduled departure time, as the drivers tend to be loose about their comings and goings). Next door to the Syndicat, Matmata's small **post office, telephones,** and **currency exchange** are all in the same building. The telephones are direct-dial, pay-after. Currency exchange will change hard cash only and, at last check, were refusing U.S. dollars because, "the dollar is too easy to counterfeit." Try anyway. (All three open Mon.-Fri. 7:30am-1:30pm; Sept.-June Mon.-Thurs. 8am-noon and 3-6pm, Fri. 8am-12:30pm.)

11 buses per day run between Matmata and Gabès (1.510D), supplemented by *louage* service. They depart from the dirt lot near the Hotel Ben Nejima, close to the regular stations. Confirm that your ride is going all the way to "Matmata *ancien*," and not "Matmata *nouvelle*," 15km short of the village. If you do wind up in the new town, however, don't despair; *camionettes* make the trip to "Matmata *ancien*" frequently (600ml).

Accommodations and Food Three of Matmata's hotels are, like the Berber homes, holes in the ground. All are signposted and within easy reach of the bus stop and the center of town. The famous cantina scene in Star Wars was filmed at **Sidi Driss** (tel. 30 005). Unfortunately, nearly all of the decor from that period has since been removed, so you'll have to use the Force of your imagination. The one-bulbed, polybed rooms are cool and reasonably clean (4.900D per person, including breakfast; showers 1D). **Les Berberes** (tel. 30 024) is almost a rerun of Sidi Driss: same prices and facilities, though you're also less likely to get stomped on by tourists. It's never been toasted by aliens, but down-to-earth three-course meals (2.200D) are tasty nonetheless. (5.500D per person, including breakfast and showers.) The **Marhala Touring Club Hotel** (tel. 30 015) puts fewer beds into cleaner rooms. It's also more expensive and more touristed. If you arrive in high season early in the day, they may insist on full pension (11D), but the meals of soup, egg pastry, and couscous are well worth it. (Singles 6.700D. Doubles 10D. Showers 1.200D. Breakfast included.) Matmata does have one or two restaurant-cafés, but the hotel pension-plans are probably the best bargains. At Sidi Driss and Les Berberes, full pension runs about 10D per person. If you prefer a picnic, there are also several small grocery shops that sell bread, yogurt, canned goods, and juice.

Near Matmata

The sleepy subterranean village of **Haddej** remains untainted by mass tourism and George Lucas. Chances are you'll be greeted by a band of local children shouting whatever French they know: "Bonjour! Bonjour! Un Stylo!" A small gift (Bic pens are preferred) will earn you a tour around to the Troglodytes (more Berber-style homes), the inexplicably named **Marriage Cave,** and to an **olive press** where fresh oil is squeezed every day. The easiest way to get to Haddej is to take one of the

Gabès-Matmata buses and get off at Tijma, 5km outside of Matmata; a sign points out the paved road leading east to Haddej, a peaceful, 3-km walk away. There is a small path connecting the village to Matmata, though it's much easier to hire a **donkey** in Matmata (20D per day). **Tamezret,** 13km to the west of Matmata, is a well-preserved Berber village carved into the cliffs along the side of a mountain, commanding a dramatic view of the bleak landscape. Its stone houses huddle tightly together in defensive Berber style, and are best seen from above. At the top of the town by the steepled building, enjoy a cup of mint tea with almonds at the café (400ml) or clamber onto the roof for a look at the village below. One bus per day runs at noon from Matmata to Tamezret (500ml), supplemented very sporadically by *camionettes* (1D). Even if you don't make it to the village, a hike on the road is worthwhile for the dramatic landscape above. 23km east along the bumpy road lies **Toujane,** scenically perched on the edge of a cliff, and split in two by a deep gorge. There are no restaurants or cafés here, but children tote small buckets with bottles of lukewarm soft drinks for 300ml. No public transportation is available to Toujane. If you don't have your own car, see what kind of a deal you can arrange to hire a *camionette* and driver for the day (a fair price would be around 20-25D).

■ Tataouine and Chenini

Venturing out south from Gabès, one comes to the **Berber towns,** on the fringes of inhabited Tunisia. The Berber villages, or *ksour*, have noticeably different names and styles from the Arab cities to the north. As often as not, these settlements are located in astoundingly inhospitable settings, unforgettable evidence of the Berbers' ability to adapt themselves to their harsh desert surroundings.

Tataouine

The most convenient base from which to explore the Berber homelands is **Tataouine,** sometimes also called Foum Tataouine. The 125-km journey from Gabès south to Tataouine proceeds by way of **Medenine,** itself a Berber city of some interest until the 1960s, when the government, in its proven wisdom, decided to bulldoze the entire place as part of a plan to improve it. Don't stay in the new, improved Medenine longer than it takes to change buses (Gabès to Medenine, more or less hourly from 7am, 1hr. 30min., 2.400D). From Medenine take a connecting bus to Tataouine (1hr., 1.600D). On arrival, the bus station is on rue 1 Juin 1955, about a block from the two main streets, av. Bourguiba and av. Farhat Hached. **Louages** depart from a plaza with a clock tower on av. Farhat Hached, one block to the right as you exit the bus station (Gabès, 2hr. and 4.250D, Medenine, 40min., 1.900D). Tataouine's **post office** sits right under a mountain at the end of av. Bourguiba (open Mon.-Sat. 7am-1:30pm, Sept.-June Mon.-Sat. 8am-6pm). Across the street is a **late-night pharmacy,** open 8pm-8am. One block back towards the center of town and to the right, the **police** are on call (tel. 197). The **telephone office** across from the Hotel Ennour is open 7am-midnight. Accommodations and eating in Tataouine are generally affordable, and both are options at the inelegant but inexpensive **Hotel Ennour** (tel. 60 131) at one end of av. Bourguiba, unmistakable as you enter town. (Dusty rooms 3D per person, showers upon request.) Plates in the restaurant below run 1.500-2.500D. Worthy of extra-special attention is the **Restaurant El Kaïma,** which serves heaping delicious bowls of the best *couscous aux legumes* in all Tunisia (1.500D). To get there, make a right off either av. Bourguiba or av. Farhat Hached onto rue 2 Mars, one block before the post office.

Chenini

Apart form the **movie theater** on av. Bourguiba which shows such classics as *Fist Fighter: There's Only One Vanquisher* (500ml), Tataouine does not have much to see or do. The best daytrip in the area is to **Chenini,** and if you've come this far south, it would be a shame to skip this treasure of a Berber village. The cheapest way to make the 8km trip to Chenini is to grab a seat in one of the *camionettes* that leave from in front of the Café du Sud on rue 2 Mars, near the post office. They charge only 1D each way, but departure times are very irregular. If you don't have any luck, the only other alternative is to specially charter a *louage*. They'll try to hit you up for 25D, but be stubborn and never pay anything more than 15D for the round-trip. The ride out to Chenini features some spectacular desert landscape; and for once there's not a telephone wire, souvenir stand, or TV antenna to be seen. You'll be dropped off at the **Relais Chenini,** which serves a standard, fixed-price meal for 3D. Below are the **post office (PTT)** and the town's lone **telephone.** Above, the stone path snakes upwards towards the village itself, cut and built into the side of the mountain. Follow the path around the mountain to the other side for a fantastic view of the desert's vast expanse.

Keep in mind that while Chenini is the most impressive of the Berber villages in the vicinity of Tataouine, it is also the most touristed. In this rough country, the tour-bus hordes have become the land-rover hordes. Most tourists groups schedule their visits for Mondays and Thursdays (market days in Tataouine) but don't let the crowds daunt you—the steep, rocky hills and the endless views make Chenini worth it. Less-frequented villages include **Guermessa, Ghomrassen,** and **Ksar Hadada.** Much farther south (78km) lies the town of **Remada.**

■ Douz

After visiting **Douz,** you'll have a lasting impression of what the word "oasis" means. It may not be what you expect, though; it isn't the archetypal pool of water accompanied by Bugs Bunny or Lawrence of Arabia. Rather, it is a sizeable expanse of cultivated palm trees and irrigation channels that ripple like small streams, surrounded by desert in all directions. The palm trees here give dates, so an *oasis* is little more than a date farm. Situated between the Great Eastern Erg and the vast *Chott,* Douz makes an ideal base for desert adventures and is perhaps the best of the Tunisian oases to visit. The town began as a rallying point for the M'Razig, a nomad tribe. Legend has it that Douz got its name when the French army's 12th battalion bivouacked here in the 19th century—*douze* means "twelve" in French. Modern Douz still has an army barracks (don't try to take photos—it's *not* appreciated), but the town is also becoming increasingly touristy. Between 10am and 7pm, the streets here are a sizzling frying-pan of heat and humidity. Twilight among the cultivated plots brings the only respite. Wandering boys may pour you a cup of palm sap for 100ml; try it in the morning when it's sweetest. The town swells with migrant farm-workers in late fall for date-harvesting season.

Public transportation puts Douz within easy reach. Direct **buses** to larger cities are infrequent—there's only one per day to Tozeur (8am, 3.600D) and Gabès (6:45am, 4.500D), but buses run to nearby Kebili (900ml), where you can make the necessary connections. **Louages** speed off to Kebili (1.150D) even more often than the buses.

Orientation Arriving in Douz, the first thing you see is a statue of a camel, his rider a Bedouin with a particularly pained expression on his face. This is the **place du 7 Novembre,** which turns into an avenue of the same name that runs along one side of Douz's **market square.** 25m past the statue is the small SNTRI **bus station;** another 25m around the corner **louages** line up under a 50s style drive-thru canopy. **Avenue Taieb Mehri** leads diagonally to Douz's main street, **av. Habib Bour. Avenue des Martyrs** begins at another entrance to the market square and extends straight out of town towards the desert.

Practical Information From a café on av. des Martyrs, the well-informed **ONTT tourist office** (tel. 95 351) arranges **camel rides** and **buggy rides** (3.500D and 1.800D per hr., respectively). (Open Mon.-Sat. 8:30am-noon and 4-6pm; Sept.-June Mon.-Thurs. 8:30am-1pm and 3-6pm, Fri. and Sat. closed afternoons.) The **post office, telephone office,** and **currency exchange** (tel. 95 300) are grouped together in the PTT building on av. Taieb Mehri. (Open Mon.-Thurs. 7:30am-1pm; Sept.-June Mon.-Thurs. 8am-noon and 3-6pm, Fri.-Sat. 8am-12:30pm.) Douz has three **pharmacies,** which trade off late-night responsibilities; there's one near the post office, and another on av. Rue 7 Novembre. (Open 8am-1pm and 4-8pm.) A **bank** is located next to the police station (tel. 95 333) a block up the Kebili road.

Accommodations The fact that you're in the desert never escapes you, even in your sleep. Regardless of price or location, all hotels in Douz have a thin film of sand that extends everywhere. The **Hotel Bel Habib** (tel. 95 309), on av. 7 Novembre, rents out the cleanest rooms with elegantly decorated showers for 4D per person. Some rooms have balconies overlooking the market square. Take your mattress out on the terrace for a snooze *en plein air*. The **Hotel 20 (Vingt) Mars** (tel. 95 495), on the market square, lets rooms with more dust and fewer frills for 3D per person. The **Hotel Splendide** (tel. 95 173; to the left behind the lounge station) doesn't quite live up to its name, but comes pretty close with a set-up like the Bel Habib's. The owner is exceedingly proud of the camel rides he arranges for guests. (Rooms 3.500D per person, showers included.) All three of these places offer breakfast for an additional 1D. Down the av. des Martyrs into and past the oasis, convoys of tour buses disgorge hapless tourists at expensive hotels with swimming pools and air conditioning. **Hotel Roses des Sables** (tel. 95 484) parts with singles for 11D, doubles for 16D. (Breakfast included.) **Hotel Saharien** (tel. 95 337) provides comfortable rooms with polished wooden desks in the heart of the oasis. (Singles 15-18D; doubles 24-30D, depending on the season. Breakfast included.)

Camping is an option in Douz only if you have your own tent and your own trees for shade. **Desert Club Camping** on rue des Affections, off av. des Martyrs, isn't much more than an empty lot with an overpriced Italian restaurant attached. The 3D (5D per person in a big tent) they charge is as much as the hotels.

Food The **Restaurant Bel Habib** (tel. 95 309), below the hotel, serves meat-filled *tajine* for 2D. The friendly people at the **Restaurant El-Kods** (tel. 95 495), besides conversing in about five languages, prepare tasty, sizeable meals for 2D. The **Restaurant Ali Baba,** one block up the Kebili road, is only slightly bigger than its two tables, but cannot be accused of being pretentious. (*Couscous* 1.500D.)

Sights For local adventures try the **mountain bike rental** "Location de Velo" (tel 95 554) in pl. 7 Novembre. For longer journeys into the Sahara by car and camel, drop by **Abdelmoula Voyages** (tel. 95 282) on av. des Martyrs or **Douz Voyages** (tel. 95 179) on pl. 7 Novembre. (Both offer package deals for 30D per person, per day; meals and camping included.) You can also explore the rippling, powdery sands of the **Great Dune** (truly out of a Bugs Bunny desert scene) by the fort-like **Hotel Mehari,** 2 km past the tourist office. Standing amidst the palm trees on this big sandy bump, the oasis sits behind you, and desert stretches out in front: no trees, no bushes, just sand. An excellent **oasis hike** begins near the entrance to the market on av. des Martyrs. Following the signs for "Desert Club Camping" will bring you to the edge of the oasis. Take a right down the sandy road and into the thick of the palms. This track continues (bear right at the fork) through a kilometer of quiet green before hitting a small paved road. A left here will take you through more oasis, past the Hotel Saharien and the abandoned Hotel Marhala, through a small village, and, finally, out of the oasis. The hike is about 3km long ending with a fantastic desert view at the stadium in the Place du Festival. Vacant 51 weeks of the year, the stadium on the town's outskirts comes to life in late December for **Douz's Festival International du Sahara,** when you can watch Berber tribes playing sand hockey with a bran-filled ball or cheer on fighting, racing camels. Hundreds of tourists saturate the town during that week, and most hotels tack extra dinars onto their prices.

TOZEUR

Near Douz You can take buses to smaller, less-touristed towns deeper in the desert. Four buses a day (6:45am-2:30pm, 420ml) run to **Zaafrane,** 10km away along a predominantly paved road. The **Zaafrane Hotel** offers singles for 13.500D, doubles for 21D (tel. 95 074; half-pension 3D extra). The buses continue through fantastic scenery to **Es-Sabria** and finally **El-Faouar** (1.300D), 41km away, where beautiful palms shade squat, modern buildings. The only hotel in El-Faouar, the creatively named **Faouar Hotel** (tel. 95 085), is a three-star and prices its rooms accordingly. (Singles 28.500D, doubles 42D. Prices drop by 15-20D in the off season. Half-pension 3D extra.) Four **buses** per day (6:30am-3:30pm) return from El-Faouar via Zaafrane. **Camionettes** serve both towns for the same price as the buses, but with a lot more frequency. They are the only way to get to **Nouil** (550ml), another nearby desert village with a small *oasis*. **Novil Campement** has offices on av. Taieb Mehri in Douz, and offers hotel-style accommodation in large Bedouin tents. (7D per person. Half-pension 2.500D extra.)

■ Tozeur

Situated over 120km across the Chott el Jerid (salt flats) from Douz, Tozeur is the largest (and almost the only) city in southwest Tunisia. Like Douz, it's an oasis and makes an excellent base for desert excursions. Tozeur's distinctive characteristic is its 8th-century Mesopotamian-style brickwork, which incorporates geometric designs into the walls themselves. The designs are particularly visible in the walls of mosques and the *medina*.

Orientation and Practical Information Two major avenues (remarkably enough, named **avenue Farhat Hached** and **avenue Habib Bourguiba**) cross to form a T. Arriving by bus or *louage*, you will find yourself on av. Farhat Hached to the east of av. Bourguiba, which runs north-south. The **Syndicat d'Initiative** (tel. 50 034), located at the intersection, isn't much help unless you want to book a tour somewhere. The regional **tourist office** (tel. 50 503) is much more helpful, but they're 2km away—all the way to the end of av. Bourguiba and then down av. Abou el-Kacem ech Chabbi, which heads off to the west. (Open Mon.-Sat. 8:30am-1pm and 3-5:45pm.) **Telephones** are near the Syndicat, **currency exchanges** are found on the two main avenues (if you have traveler's checks, the best bank to go to is the STB at the end of av. Habib Bourguiba), and the **post office** (tel. 500 00) is just off av. Bourguiba (open Mon.-Sat. 7:30am-1pm; Sept.-June Mon.-Fri. 8am-noon and 3-6pm, Sat. 8am-12:30pm). The **police** (tel. 50 016) are 1km away on the Gafsa road; the **hospital** (tel. 50 400) is located in town. (In medical emergencies you can always call 198 for help.) The regional **bus** company (on av. Farhat Hached; sign in Arabic) runs 6 times a day to Nefta (30min., 750ml). Across the street, SNTRI provides bus service to Douz via Kebili (1 per day, 2hr., 4.680D) and Tunis via Kairouan (5 per day, 4hr., 9.650D to Kairouan; 7hr., 14,180D to Tunis). **Louages,** leaving from an alley 100m from the SNTRI office, have routes to all these cities as well.

Accommodations Tozeur's **youth hostel,** the **Auberge de Jeunes (HI)** (tel. 52 335—walk east on av. Farhat Hached and follow the sign at the clock tower 100m) is less depressing than most Tunisian hostels, with a shower in every 4-6 person room (HI members only; curfew midnight; 3D per person). The **Residence Essalem** (tel. 50 981) is more upbeat and is located in the same area. The young guys behind the receptionist's desk are into Bob Marley and Joe Cocker, so if you need a music fix... The cool and breezy rooms go for 6D per person, including free showers and breakfast whenever you want. Across from two on the way to the tourist office on av. Abou el-Kacem Chebbi, the **Residence Warda** (tel. 52 597) has a similar set-up. The terrace here has a great view of town and some rooms even have air conditioning for an extra 3D. (6.300D per person, breakfast and showers included.) A step up is the **Hotel Splendid** (tel. 50 053), off av. Bourguiba. All the rooms have fans, and although the swimming pool wasn't working in 1993, it may be fixed by 1994. (Singles 11.500D; doubles 17D; breakfast included; showers 1.300D.) The **Hotel Essaada** (tel. 50 097), also off av. Bourguiba, is the place to go if you're counting pennies. Beds sag, but at 2.500D, there's not much room to complain (showers 500ml). For once camping is also a viable option. One kilometer past the tourist office, **Campement Beaux Rêves** (tel. 51 242) is a veritable garden of Eden: flowers, grapes, even grass, all amidst palms at the edge of the oasis. Pitch your own tent or take a bed in one of their palm-frond bungalows for the same price (3.500D per person, showers included).

Food   Tasty cheap eats aren't tough to find either. Among the options are **Restaurant le Paradis** (tel. 51 432) off av. Bourguiba, **Restaurant le Soleil** (tel. 50 220) on av. Abou el-Kacem Chebbi, and the **Restaurant du Sud** (tel. 50 826) on av. Farhat Hached. A good plate of *couscous Tunisien* at any of these places costs 1.500-2D. The Restaurant du Sud specializes in cuisine from Sfax, which is a sight better than the city itself. An *omelette sfaxienne*, stuffed with tuna and tomatoes, goes for 1.200D.

Sights   Tozeur's *medina* extends off to the left as you walk down av. Bourguiba past the Syndicat. The **Museum of Archeology and Traditional Arts** (tel. 50 034) inside isn't worth the time; three small rooms present more dust than exhibits. (Open 8am-noon and 3:30-6:30pm; off season 8am-1pm and 3-5pm; admission 1D.) Tozeur's park, **Le Paradis,** is filled with flowers and a profusion of palm trees. From the end of av. Bourguiba, veer right and walk about half a kilometer; there will be a sign to the left. (If the walking is getting to you, another anonymous "Location de Velo" is on the same road as Le Paradis. They rent rickety **bikes** (for 1D per hour or 5D for 24 hours) as well as peculiar two-wheeled vehicles common in Southern Tunisia, called *byscles*. Still farther along, past the tourist office, is the **cultural center;** it's unclear which culture this is the center of, but it's certainly not Tunisian. This four-bus rest stop boasts an impressive new building, lots of places to spend money, and another tourist-oriented, overpriced museum, the private **Musée Dar Cherait** (tel. 51 000; admission 2.500D; open daily 7am-midnight). A sandy path leads from the left of the cultural center, past a mosque under construction, and into the oasis. The track winds its way along a small stream for another kilometer before it finishes at the **Belvedere,** an awesome collection of rocks and gorges from which you can look back on all 2500 acres of palm trees, plus part of the Chott.

West of Tozeur: Nefta and Vicinity

Nefta is another of the Tunisian oases, lying 23km due west of Tozeur. It is known for its numerous non-volcanic hot springs, which are scattered about the area. It is also to a lesser extent a religious center as evidenced by the many mosques in town. But Nefta is most noteworthy for the **Corbeille de Nefta,** a natural bowl-shaped depression filled with palms. The site is eye-catching, but the view is marred by an architectural eyesore—the Sahara Palace Hotel. More worthy structures occupying the bowl's edge are the several mosques that comprise the **Ridge of Domes.** While the Corbeille is attractive, it's not quite as fabulous as the tourist offices might claim—especially if you've already seen the oases at Douz and Tozeur.

To get to Nefta and the Corbeille, take the bus from Tozeur (750ml); you'll pass the **Syndicat d'Initiative** (tel. 57 184) on your way in. Personable, English-speaking staff will answer specific questions, but their services may not be necessary. To reach the rim take av. Bourguiba until it splits just past the post office, then the unpaved right fork to the first street to the right, and keep heading in that direction for about 250m. On reaching the rim, take the dirt track down and enter the Corbeille itself. It's important to remember that while this is Nefta's big tourist attraction, it is (like most oases) just farmland, and as such, private property. Don't be surprised or frightened at the scrappy guard puppies that patrol the area—their bark is a lot worse than their bite.

10km down the road past Nefta, the Sahara begins in earnest. Except for a small shack or two and the scraggly bushes that grow by the side of the road, there are no signs of life for miles around. Though desolate, the terrain offers an authentic Tunisian desert experience, with the Chott on one side of the road and rolling dunes on the other. One of the shacks is actually the **Marché des Roses des Sables,** an outdoor market for "sand roses": those curious rock formations (crystallized gypsum) that are found in *souks* all over Tunisia. Moving past the market, you can walk out onto the *Chott* (salt flats). The location is also a particularly good one for seeing mirages (or, at least, things which *look* like mirages).

If you return to the road and walk a kilometer past it into the desert, the vegetation will gradually decrease until there's nothing but fine sand and large dunes. Here you can explore the trackless desert in complete solitude, though you'll probably feel too hot to do anything more than return to the road. (As always, **be sure to bring at least one liter of water per person per hour.)**

Buses, louages, and **camionettes** all pass the Marché on their way to the Algerian border and will be more than happy to leave you stranded for around 1.200D. Since traffic back to Nefta is extremely light, hitchhiking is very difficult; the few cars that do pass are either reluctant to stop or stuffed to the brim with immigrating Algerians. The safest way to see the Marché is to charter a *louage* in Nefta to take you there and back (10D round-trip). Another 24km along the same road is the Algerian frontier, along which one of the few points of entry is found at **Hazoua.** You can reach Hazoua by bus directly from Tozeur twice daily from Nefta at 8am and 5pm (1hr., 1.200D); *louages* and *camionettes* also make the trip. Once there, be prepared for a long wait at the Tunisian border and a 3km walk to the Algerian frontier post unless you can catch a *louage*. At present—especially in the aftermath of the assassination of the Algerian President in July 1992—the Algerians are likely to give you a cool reception. You'll need an entry visa and will probably be required to change 1000 non-convertible Algerian Dinars (US $250-300) which you cannot take back out with you. Good luck.

East of Tozeur: Chebika, Tamerza, and Mides

The mountains, deserts, and oases surrounding Tozeur constitute some extremely difficult terrain, but they also offer what is without question some of the most spectacular scenery in all of Tunisia. The three towns of Chebika, Tamerza, and Mides reward the intrepid traveler with something unique and marvelous to behold. Ideally, see them all as a full-day trip from Tozeur; otherwise at least try to reach Tamerza, the most worthwhile and accessible of the three.

By and large, the roads in the region are impassable in anything less than a Range Rover. Your best option is to hire a 4x4 vehicle and a guide for the day. Get a group together and pile as many people as you can into the car—they can seat up to eight passengers. Bargain for the total price of the trip: typical rates will be 100-120D for the day. You can try asking at the Syndicat for information, but a good source of vehicles and guides is **Tunisie Voyages** (tel. 52 439) in Tozeur, 1km down av. Farhat Hached in the direction of Nefta. They offer a whirlwind half-day tour for 75D; the more leisurely full-day package goes for 100D (unless you want them to provide lunch, which they're glad to do for an extra 50D; brown-bag it instead). **Mehari Voyages** (tel. 50 387) is generally more expensive, but they have offices right next door so you can shop and compare (120D for a full day; no ½-day option).

The road to Chebika is especially tough, but if you're content just to see Tamerza and Mides, a cheaper option is to take a louage to **Metlaoui** (1.900D) and then to **Redeyef** (1,800D). In Redeyef, ask to be let off near the camionettes. From in front of the park, small pick-up trucks and the occasional bus make the trip to Tamerza and sometimes to Mides (1D; no buses to Mides). You're taking a chance, though; even if you're lucky enough to get out there, it's hell trying to find a way back. It is possible to persuade a *camionette* driver to take you on a quick tour of both towns for around 5D. If you do end up getting stranded, Tamerza has two hotels. One's a four-star (70D per person, in case you're wondering), but the other, the **Hotel Les Cascades,** offers rooms at 11D per person (breakfast included).

After traversing roads which challenge even the best shock-absorbers, you first encounter the *oasis* of Chebika. Although the inhabitants have recently relocated to newer buildings alongside the old village, Chebika itself is an ancient village community perched on a mountainside, with a cluster of palms between mountains to one side and desert to the other. For a handful of change, a local will take you along the path that climbs through the hills to the source of the spring, which flows downhill as a small stream. Striking though it is, the stream is dwarfed by the one at Tamerza, which is famous throughout Tunisia for its two waterfalls—cool, lush and beautiful sanctuaries in the midst of the parched desert. The last location, only 3km from the Algerian border, is Mides, where you can visit a gorge which cuts into the rock.

If you're lucky enough to have your own vehicle (not necessarily a Land Cruiser), the best route to take is the road to Metlaoui and then to Redeyef. Beyond Redeyef, 25km of paved road leads straight to Tamerza; the turn-off for Mides 5km before Tamerza is bumpy but easily negotiable. You'll have to skip Chebika; the roads from Tamerza are steep and rocky. Somethings to keep in mind before undertaking any **desert expeditions** with your own vehicle: above all make sure that your car has been recently serviced and is in good running condition. Carry water for drinking and for the radiator, and make sure your car is equipped with a spare tire and necessary tools. Five gallons of water is recommended for each vehicle. For any trips off major roads, a board and shovel are useful in case your car gets stuck in sand; the board can be shoved under a tire to gain traction and the shovel can take care of minor quagmires. **Stay with your vehicle if it breaks down:** it is easier to spot than a person. In the most nightmarish scenario—being stranded in extreme heat with little or no water—find whatever shade you can, drench yourself with (but don't drink) cooled radiator water to ward off dehydration, burn motor oil in a hubcap to send smoke signals, and if you must move, do so only at night. If you see the temperature gauge climbing while driving, turn off the air conditioning. If an overheating warning light comes on, stop immediately and wait about a half hour before trying again. Never pour water over the engine to cool it; you can crack the engine block.

Throughout your trip you can take in breathtaking desert vistas and remarkable mountain panoramas. (Don't be put off if you round a deserted mountain bend and suddenly encounter a traffic jam of 10 or 20 Range Rovers lined up at a photo spot.) And on the way home, don't miss out on that desert sunset. Try to leave in the early morning or after midday to avoid the most oppressive heat, and tote loads of water (buying it later will cost you plenty).

THE NORTHERN (CORAL) COAST

The Tunisian National Tourist Office advertises the country's northern, or coral, coast as "Green Tunisia," and for once, their description is not too far from the truth. The forests are lush and the fields thick with grass, and the only sands are the white beaches that make up the stunning coastline which runs from Tunis all the way to the Algerian border. In fact, the coral coast (so-named for the large reefs found offshore) has a lot more in common with neighboring Sicily (about 200 miles away) that it does with the rest of Tunisia; the principal cities, Bizerte and Tabarka, with their tree-lined streets and red-tile-roofed dwellings, only serve to reinforce this impression. Add to this the fact that the north coast is virtually undiscovered by tour groups and hotel complexes; this is where you can come to escape the crowds of Hammamet and Jerba. Northern Tunisia is perhaps the country's most visitor friendly area (less hot, better beaches) and it also has the fewest tourists. This may change in the near future, however, as the tourist offices is promoting Tabarka very actively.

■■■ BIZERTE

Situated at Africa's northernmost point, Bizerte has long been seen as an important strategic port. The Carthaginians were the first to settle here, and dug the canal linking the Mediterranean Sea to the inland Lake Bizerte. The Romans built atop the Greek and Carthaginian contributions, and were followed in their turn by the Byzantines and Arabs. The city changed hands repeatedly during the 16th-century Hapsburg-Ottoman wars. In the 17th century, the city gained notoriety as a pirates' nest, serving as a base for raids on European ships. World War II again demonstrated the city's importance, as it was a key objective during the see-saw North African battles. The French were so attached to the site that they ceded control of the city when Tunisia was granted independence in 1956, but refused to abandon the port and naval base. Five years of mounting tensions led to a major confrontation and over 1000 Tunisian military casualties. The Bizerte Crisis of 1961 led to the opening of diplomatic discussions, and two years later the French withdrew entirely. Only bitter memories and the solemn cemetery remain from that time; the white beaches and old quarters of the town remain timeless.

ORIENTATION AND PRACTICAL INFORMATION

The compact town center can be perplexing because many roads run diagonally. A good landmark is **avenue de l'Algérie,** which begins at the main **bus station** by the canal, cuts through the main square (**place 7 Novembre 1987**), crosses **avenue Habib Bourguiba,** and finishes in place Slah-Edine Bouchoucha, near the **Old Port.** The resemblance to Venice is uncanny, and the effect is beautiful. Bizerte's *medina* sits on the Old Port. A long stretch of beaches (called "The Corniche") begins here.

Blue-and-orange **buses** depart from the main station for nearby beach towns Ras Jebel (8 per day, 1.230D) and Ghar-el-Melh (3 per day, 1.230D), both about an hour's ride. Buses leave for Tunis's Bab Saadoun station every half-hour (1½hr., 1st class 2.450D, 2nd class 2.130D). "Confort" means 1st class, with air conditioning in a Greyhound-style bus. One bus per day goes to Le Kef (6.200D), but leaves from in front of the **train station,** 500m further along the canal (away from the drawbridge). Four slow trains crawl daily to Tunis (3 on Sun., 2.350D). For the same price, *louages* make the same trip in two-thirds of the time; they congregate in the shadow of the drawbridge just up from the bus station.

Tourist Office: O.N.T.T., 1, rue de Constantinople (tel. 32 703). From the bus station, walk along the water past the bridge and the *louages* and make a left at the sign. Friendly and English-speaking, but so poorly informed and supplied that they can't even give you a map to help you on your way. Open daily 8:30am-1pm and 3-5:45pm, July-Aug. 7:30am-1:30pm and 4-7pm.

Post Office: (tel. 31 585) ½-block up from pl. 7 Novembre on av. de l'Algérie. Open Mon.-Sat. 8am-6pm, Sun. 9-11am; July-Aug. Mon.-Sat. 7:30am-1:30pm and 5-6pm, Sun. 9-11am. The **telephone office** is across the street and around the corner on rue du 1er mai. Open daily 8am-5pm, July-Aug. 7:30am-1:30pm.

Currency Exchange: There's one in the post office, but you'll get better service in the **banks** on pl. 7 Novembre.

Bicycle/Moped Rental: Any of the small bike shops along av. Bourguiba. Bicycles 1.500D per hour, 7D per day. Mopeds 5D per hour.

Late-night Pharmacy: rue Ali Belhaouane, off av. Bourguiba, facing the Old Port. Open nightly 7:30pm-7:30am.

Hospital: rue du 3 Août (tel. 31 422).

Police: (tel. 197) on the square with the fountain between av. Bourguiba and av. 2 Mars 1934.

ACCOMMODATIONS AND FOOD

The expensive resort hotels along the beach are packed with tour bus groups, and most cheap hotels in town fill in July and August, so arrive early.

Hotel Continental, 9, rue du 2 Mars 1934 (tel. 31 436). Walking from the main square on av. de l'Algérie, it's the second right after the post office; the sign is broken, so look sharp. Big rooms with firm, wooden beds and large curtains. Clean bathrooms with some of the wildest tile-patterns ever. (Singles 5.500D. Doubles 9D. Showers included.)

Remel Youth Hostel (HI), (tel. 40 804), 4km south of town on the road to Tunis. Take "Menzel Jemil" bus #8A or a "Ras Jebel" bus (both 210ml) and ask to get off at Remel Plage. The hostel is a funk-o-matic ramshackle place in the woods behind the Ecole des Pêches. The white sands and teen hangout of Remel Beach are just 100m through the trees. HI Members only. 3D per person. Shower included. Breakfast 1D. Lunch or dinner 2.500D. Cooking facilities available.

Hotel Zitouna, 11, place Slah-Edine Bouchoucha (tel. 38 760), at the end of av. de l'Algérie, 1 block from the Old Port. Tiny, dingy rooms with sagging beds. Singles 4D. Doubles 6D. Showers 500ml.

Fruit vendors sprout in great numbers in **place Slah-Edine,** and a lively covered market flourishes near the base of the old port. There's a **Monoprix Supermarket** on rue 2 mars 1934 (open daily 8:30am-12:30pm and 3:30-7:30pm; opens on Sun. at 9am). From pl. 7 Novembre, walk diagonally on av. Taleb Mahri past the Office National des Pêches in the upper left-hand corner of the square.

Rôtisserie du 1er Mai (tel. 38 087), near the post office, on the corner of rue du 1er Mai and av. de l'Algérie. Steaming, scrumptious spaghetti or *couscous* 1D. Sample the *couscous* with rice and *haricots* (long, thin string beans). Jolly owner, quick service. Try flashing *Let's Go* for some extra friendliness and attention. Open daily 6:30am-10pm.

Pizzeria du Vieux Port, Chez Belahouel, on av. Bourguiba, facing the Old Port. A restaurant name that runs through 3 languages and the place to stop if you've had *couscous* once too often. Pizza 550ml per 100 grams. Open daily noon-10pm.

SIGHTS

In the celebrated **Old Port,** the combined smells of coffee and rotten fish waft through the air. Facing the Old Port, **place Slah-Edine Bouchoucha** is ringed with fruit and vegetable stalls, above which rise the twin minarets of the Debaa and Grand Mosques. The entrance to the sturdy 18th-century **kasbah** is at the end of the Old Port, 100m from the sea (open daily 9am-noon and 3-7pm; adults 400ml, children 200ml). There's a cozy café on the top level; from here, the *kasbah's* crenellated battlements command a broad view of the port, the coast, and (peeking inside) the *medina.* The **Andalusian Quarter,** with its ancient archways, winding alleys, and nail-studded doors, lies just to the north. Sheep wander the streets and chew hay, and in every other shop, a caged parakeet or two twitters merrily. On the neighboring hilltop, the 16th-century **Spanish Fort** is now an open-air theater. Confusingly, the fort was actually built by the Turks, and received its name when the Arabs captured it from Don Juan of Austria.

Cap Blanc, which forms Africa's northernmost point, is perhaps the most spectacular sight near Bizerte. To get there, follow av. de la Corniche along the beach and up the coast to the *Radiophare du Cap Blanc* sign, where you turn right. The rough road struggles to the top of **Jebel Nador** (288m), the perfect perch for a glorious sunset vista. Below, chalky Cap Blanc protrudes into the sea. To reach its tip, descend the mountain and follow the trail leading off the road. The bike ride is scenic and challenging; count on three hours round-trip.

Two "luxury" beach hotels (4km out along the Corniche), the **Jalta** and the **Nadhour,** monopolize sports and entertainment. Both rent **horses,** though the Nadhour is cheaper (7D per hour, with guide), and **bikes** (2D per hour). The Nadhour also offers **windsurfing** and **tennis** (each 5D per hour). If you like **waterskiing,** ask at the Jalta's reception desk. Both complexes are too far to walk: the quickest way to get to either one is with the "La Corniche" #1 **bus**, which departs regularly from av. Bourguiba near the Old Port. The trip also makes a nice bike ride.

■ Near Bizerte: Raf Raf and Utica (Utique)

Raf Raf

Along the coast of Bizerte, the mountains at **Raf Raf** plunge into the sea, forming a crescent-shaped beach by the water. During the summer, much of the beach suffocates under the weight of vacationing Tunisians, beach umbrellas, and plastic bottles. Just a 1km walk past all this, however, the contrast is striking: secluded stretches of white sand, the rocky island of Pilav jutting out of the crystal clear waters in front of you, and mountains of dark pine forests at your back, within 50m of the beach (without a doubt the finest in the vicinity of Bizerte). Shallow water and strong surf make for good bodysurfing and boogieboarding.

In July and August, there are four **buses** per day direct from Bizerte to "Raf Raf Plage" (1hr., 1.750D); otherwise, take one of the year-round "Ras Jebel" buses to Ras Jebel (8 per day, 1hr., 1.230D), and hop on a connecting bus for the remaining 6km to Raf Raf (every 1½hrs., 15min., 450ml). The last bus returns from Raf Raf at 6:30pm. If you get caught overnight, there's one hotel in town, the **Hotel Dalia** (tel. 41 530), which is down the street towards the water from the main bus stop. (Prices vary according to season. Singles 11.500-14.500D. Doubles 16-20D. Breakfast/showers included.)

Utica

Utica is North Africa's oldest port and was once its greatest, but the passage of three millennia has seen the city fall into decline and abandonment. What remains today dates from a late period in the city's history and consists mostly of first to 4th century aristocratic Roman residences. To get to Utica, take any non-direct **bus** along the Bizerte-Tunis line in either direction (more or less hourly, 40min., 980ml) and get off at Utique. From the rather lonely bus stop in town, cross over the highway and follow the signposted road 2km to "Utique ruines"; you'll come to a small **museum** with two rooms of Punic and Roman exhibits, and some of the mosaics not taken to the Bardo Museum. Get your ticket to enter 800m farther along at the site marked by a yellow sign so rusted it looks like an antique itself. The only remnant of Utica's Carthaginian period is the ancient (8th century BC) **Punic necropolis.** Most of the rest of the site consists of Roman houses, the most noteworthy of which is the **Maison de la Cascade** (House of the Fountain). Herein, you'll find tattered mosaics, intricate marble work, and of course, a fountain. (Site open daily 8am-6pm; museum open Tues.-Sun., same hours. Admission 1D, students with ISIC cards free; photo permit 1D.)

■ Tabarka

The mellow beach town of Tabarka is the great prize of the North Coast, remaining almost entirely untouched by tourism. Welcome breezes blow through the streets of Tabarka town, which is flanked on one side by a beach, the other by rocky cliffs, and overlooked by a fortress dramatically perched above it. Tabarka is as laid back as Nabeul, but more beautiful and upscale. This year 3-4 luxury hotels have opened up and an international airport was built.

Orientation and Practical Information Tabarka's biggest street, av. **Habib Bourguiba,** runs from the beginning of town straight to the sea. Halfway there, it opens up into a lush, well-monitored park, whose centerpiece is an immense statue of you-know-who with his pet dog. On av. Bourguiba just beyond the park is Tabarka's **tourist office** (tel. 44 491; open Mon.-Thurs. 8:30am-1pm and 3-5:45pm, Fri.-Sat. 8:30am-1:30pm; July-Aug. Mon.-Fat. 7:30am-1:30pm). They can give you a map and some brochures, but the town's small enough that you can do without their grouchy services. There's a **post office** and **currency exchange** at the end of av. Bourguiba, near the beach (open Mon.-Fri. 8am-noon and 3-6pm, Sat. 8am-12:30pm; July-Aug. Mon.-Sat. 7:30am-1:30pm). **Taxiphones** and the two **banks** are found on the main drag, but back towards the center of town. The **late-night pharmacy** on rue Alzouaoui (off av. Bourguiba near the entrance to town; across from the Hotel Novelly) is on call from 8pm-7:30am. **Police** (tel. 197) are at the end of the park closest to the mountains.

The town has two **bus** companies. The first, situated at the beginning of av. Bourguiba, is **regional** and runs one morning bus per day to Bizerte, Le Kef, and Jendouba; service is more frequent to nearby Ain Draham. **SNTRI**, the national company, has seven buses per day to and from Tunis (last bus leaves Tabarka at 3:45pm; 1st class 6.150D, 2nd class 5.400D). Tunis buses depart from rue du Peuple, parallel to av. Bourguiba and close to the Hotel Corail. There are few *louages* (serving Ain Draham, Jendouba only), originating near the regional bus station.

Accommodations There are only a few hotels in Tabarka, and most of these are pricey and geared towards people in multiples of two. If you arrive by yourself in high season (July-Aug.), expect to have to pay the cost of a double room. The cheapest place in town is the **Hotel Corail** (tel. 44 544), at 1 rue Tazerka, off av. Bourguiba between the park and the beach. Clean and spacious, with lots of open-air hallways and staircases; its rooftop terrace is one of the highest in the city. (Singles 6D. Doubles 10D. July-Aug. 12D per room, single or double. Showers included.) The **Hotel de la Plage** (tel. 44 039), at 7, rue des Pêcheurs (near the beach), is also reasonably priced by Tabarka's standards. Year-round, singles are 9D and doubles are 14D (showers included). Hospital-like hallways but at least it's near the water.

Food The best part of town for low-priced, filling meals is rue Farhat Hached, off av. Bourguiba one block down from the park in the direction of the water. **Restaurant El Hana,** offers a savory, sizable bowl of *couscous* for 1.200D (open daily 10am-10pm). Also on rue Farhat Hached is the **Restaurant Triki** (tel. 44 170, open 8am-10pm daily), where the main attractions are the meat dishes (2-3D). You can get picnic supplies at the **supermarket** ("Magasin General") across from the statue of Habib.

Sights Tabarka's most captivating sight is its **Genoese Fort,** an integral part of the city's history. It was built by the Lomellini family, who received the Isle of Tabarka as ransom for the release of the Turkish pirate Dragut, who spent four years rowing a Genoese galley after being captured. Dragut proceeded to prove himself worthy of such a price; after his release, he captured Tripoli, destroyed a Spanish fleet, and conquered Jerba. Meanwhile, Tabarka remained in the hands of the Lomellinis for over 200 years. Tabarka's other sight of note is the cluster of rocks at the very end of town known as **Les Aiguilles** ("The Needles"). These huge (20m) natural spires shoot out of the water and are framed against the sky. There is also a museum at **La Basilique,** the site of a French basilica, featuring mostly mosaics. (Admission 1D.)

■ Near Tabarka: Ain Draham

Halfway between Tabarka and Teboursouk lies Ain Draham, a town whose fame rests upon its mountaintop location and the surrounding cork forests. The 8-10km along the way to Ain Draham do provide some winsome vistas, although the effect of seeing a cool mountaintop forest may not be quite the same for people who haven't spent their life living in a desert. If you're traveling between Tabarka and Jendouba, Ain Draham is a good place to stop off for a mid-morning hike. And if fate lands you here on the morning of June 18th, you can watch as villagers dressed in traditional costumes parade through the streets to commemorate the martyrdom of **Fini-el-morg** ("the fair boy"). Legend has it that this light-haired local hero died in 974 defending the village from invaders.

To get to Ain Draham, take a bus or *louage* from either Tabarka or Jendouba (from Tabarka 40min., 760ml; from Jendouba 1hr., 1.370D). Four buses per day also run directly to Tunis (last bus back at 1:30pm, 7.600D).

TELL

The mild climate and fertile fields of this northern interior region have made it a preferred spot throughout history. Wheat, olives, hay...passing through Tell you'll see sweeping countryside and an agriculture industry that's both a surprise and a relief after visiting Tunisia's mostly bone-dry, barren semi-desert. Bulla Regia and Dougga, the finest archaeological sites in Tunisia, testify to Tell's five centuries as Rome's primary granary. The walled city of Le Kef has attracted worshipful Romans, Christians, Muslims, and legions of plundering mercenaries.

■■■ LE KEF

Le Kef (also "El Kef") means "The Rock," an appropriate name for a fortress town built atop a craggy mount. Le Kef's commanding position was important as late as 1956, when it proved an invaluable post for the French, who wished to observe Algerian rebel stations during the Franco-Algerian war. Even after Tunisian independence was granted, the French troops abandoned the vital position only after the Tunisians stopped asking politely and started shooting.

The city's reputation dates far back, to when the rulers of Carthage shipped their rowdy Sicilian mercenaries here. Arab refugees from the Christian *Reconquista* of Spain later settled the town, reminded of the rocky hills and sweeping plains of Andalusia. However, the city's association with gentler things also dates back to ancient times. The Romans built a libidinous temple to Venus at Le Kef, and perpetuated the belief that every year Venus flew between Rome and Le Kef, accompanied by a flock of doves (the ruins of the Temple of Venus are 5km away up a road negotiable only in a 4x4). Islamic pilgrimages to Kairouan and to Mecca traditionally pass through Le Kef to solicit the doves' blessing.

ORIENTATION AND PRACTICAL INFORMATION

With hills reminiscent of San Francisco, and views that stretch forever, the *medina*, lurking under the towering *kasbah*, feels like the *centro storico* of an Italian hilltown. The bus and *louage* station lies in the new city, five minutes downhill from the *medina*—take a right out of the bus lot and up to the top of the hill, turn right again, then take the second left on rue Ali Belhaouane. This street ends at **place de l'Indépendence;** the *medina* is up high; **av. Habib Bourguiba** (the main road to Tunis) begins in pl. de l'Indépendence, and heads uphill and to the right out of town. Frequent *louages* supplement bus service to Jendouba (4 per day, 1hr., 1.700D), Tunis (16 per day, 4hr., 5.930D), Bizerte (1 per day at 7am, 4hr. 30min., 6.200D), Sfax (2 per day at 4am and 12:30pm, 5hr., 8.100D), and Gafsa (1 per day at 5:30am, 5hr., 6.200D).

Tourist Office: (tel. 21 148), next to Café du Dinar in pl. de l'Indépendence. Comfortable couches and wooden tables make this unusual office a good place to unwind; Mohamed Tlilli, the friendly and knowledgable volunteer director of the bureau, also heads the *kasbah* restoration effort. Open loosely 9am-8pm; known to close for long lunch breaks or when it gets too hot.

Post Office, Telephone Office, Currency Exchange: P.T.T., on the corner of rue Hedi Chaker and rue d'Algerie. Bear left at the fork downhill from the tourist office and walk 2 blocks. Open Mon.-Sat. 8am-6pm, Sun. 9-11am, July-Aug. Mon.-Sat. 7:30am-2pm. For exchanging traveler's checks, try the **bank** in pl. de l'Independance. More telephones at Taxiphone (open 6am-midnight). Bear right at the fork downhill from the tourist office.

Late-night Pharmacy: On the small street that winds upward from pl. de l'Indep022 pendance, 50m from Café du Dinar. Open daily 8pm-8am.

Police: tel. 197, in a large building up the hill from the bus station.

ACCOMMODATIONS AND FOOD

Hotel de l'Auberge, (tel. 20 036), at the foot of the *medina,* up from pl. de l'Independance. The hotel has deteriorated considerably since Eisenhower passed the night here during WWII, but 3D will get you a big room with a balcony and a great view of Tell. Showers included.

Hotel de la Source (tel. 21 397), up to the left of the Auberge; you can't miss their "billboard." Basic rooms and yellow walls for 5D per person. In the winter, heated rooms are 6D; 4D with no heat. Showers in every room.

Hotel Medina, 18, rue Farhat Hached (tel. 23 214). Walk up av. Bourguiba past the "Tunis" sign and then bear left (uphill). Horribly bland, but the rooms are clean and there's a rooftop terrace. Singles 6.500D. Doubles or triples 5D per person. (Strong showers 500ml.)

Le Kef has few sit-down restaurants. You can eat cheaply at any of the five or six places on **rue Hedi Chaker,** just below pl. de l'Independance. Be warned: these are small operations and many run out of food (or else have severely limited menus) by about 7pm. There is also an air-conditioned **Monoprix Supermarket** halfway up the hill from the bus station (open daily 8am-noon and 4-8pm).

Restaurant de l'Afrique (tel. 22 079), rue Hedi Chaker. All the Tunisian classics, from *couscous* to *mermez* to *mloukia* (1.500D each). Open Mon.-Sat. 9:30am-10pm.

Restaurant El Andelous, also on rue Hedi Chaker. Similar to the l'Afrique, but a little cheaper and more popular with insects. Open daily 8am-8pm.

SIGHTS

Sightseeing in Le Kef is a pleasure because it's so informal, slow-paced, the way tourism *should* be. None of the sights charge admission, have a regular staff, or keep strict opening hours (though most try to stick to an 8am-noon and 3-6pm schedule). Most places of interest have an old guardian or caretaker; if he's around, you're in luck: they are invariably friendly, and enthusiastic, and will likely give you a history lesson along with your tour.

Climb up through the *medina* from the steps starting to the right of the Hôtel de la Source. These will lead you to the foot of the **kasbah** (1601), crowning the peak of Le Kef's once impregnable rock and affording a fine vista of irrigated plains and the bustling new town. The *kasbah* is currently under restoration, but during the day, the wooden entrance door is almost always left open. Beneath the *kasbah,* the well-preserved 4th-century **Christian Basilica** surrounds an open-air court with massive, oblong columns. During the 8th century, the basilica was converted into a mosque, making it one of the oldest in the country; villagers call it Djamaa el-Kebir, or Grand Mosque. The fluted domes and slender minaret of the **Mosque of Sidi Bov Makhlouf** clash with the rocky mass of its imposing neighbors, the *kasbah* and the basilica. Inside are the brightly ornamented coffins of several saints. If the caretaker is around, ask him to let you climb the minaret. The view is worth the uncomfortably compact stairway and the pigeons that get in your way. The main street that runs alongside the *kasbah* winds around to the right and ends in a large square. Across the square rue Jendouba leads to the **Bab Ghedive,** one of the few gateways in Le Kef's extensive set of walls and fortifications. Le Kefians call it **Bab-Ghdar,** or the Gate of Treachery, because of the popular belief that Governor Ghedive opened the gates for the French in 1881. The tourist office historians don't believe a word of it; they point out that the French attacked from Algeria, which is in the opposite direction. Whatever the case, it makes this gate a lot more interesting. Beyond the *bab,* you abruptly step from the city out into a deserted meadow below a steep cliff face. Beyond the stone walls is a series of holes in the ground (they look like wells) which you can peer into for a glimpse of the **Roman cisterns,** an ancient sewage and water-processing network that runs under all of Le Kef. If you want to go inside, ask at the tourist office. They'll take you down into another set of cisterns right next to the Hotel de la Source. Across from these cisterns are the ruins of some fourth-century **Roman baths.** On the street behind Hotel Medina, the **Église de Saint Pierre** predates both the French and the Arabs, who call it Dar el-Kous. This 4th-century Roman basilica stands empty now, save for a few columns left standing. For an unusual outdoor excursion you can take a hike up the **Jugurtha's Table,** a huge slab of stone with an exhaustive vista. To get there, take a *louage* from Le Kef to the village of **Kalaat Senan** (2.200D). A 4km path leads to a 1,500-year-old staircase cut into the living rock. From the top, you can look out over Algeria and the fields of the Tell.

■ Bulla Regia

With your first glance around the site, the trip to remote Bulla Regia will hardly seem worth the trouble. But look a bit deeper (literally) and you'll see that your efforts have paid rich dividends. Bulla Regia's treasures remain buried beneath the ground, in a series of underground mansions and sites. The city was the capital of the Numidian kingdom until the last of the Numidian heirs, Jugurtha, was defeated by the Romans 25km away. Affluent Romans of the 2nd and 3rd centuries AD gentrified the location, rebuilding the city and then duplicating their villas below ground to escape the summer heat. A 7th-century earthquake destroyed most of the above-ground sections, but left numerous subterranean rooms and mosaics (of Bardo Museum quality) intact.

Orientation and Practical Information To reach Bulla Regia, catch one of the four morning buses from Le Kef to **Jendouba** (2hr., 1.700D); a *louage* (2.050D) will cut your travel time in half. In Jendouba, all buses and *louages* stop in or near the pl. 7 Novembre 1987. Blue-and-white **buses** run hourly to the museum (8km away); they leave from in front of the FINA gas station, 100m past pl. 7 Novembre in the direction of Ain Draham (fare 300ml). If you miss the bus, flag down one of the yellow **taxis** that shuttle back and forth *louage*-style between Jendouba and Bulla Regia (400ml per person); a regular taxi costs about 1.500-2D, and can accommodate 3 passengers). There are three bus companies in town, which provide service to a variety of destinations between them. Buses also run north to Ain Draham (1hr., 1.370D) and on to Tabarka. The last bus back to Le Kef is at 3pm; *louages* (2.050D) make the run until mid-afternoon. *Don't* get caught in Jendouba after about 4pm, or you'll find yourself stranded in a no-horse town with absolutely no way to get out.

Sights Purchase your entrance ticket at the **museum** across the road from the site. (Open daily 7am-7pm, Sept.-March 8:30am-5:30pm. Admission 1D. Photo permit 1D.) Here, you can wise up on your Bulla Regia history (assuming you read French or Arabic); relics include a relief of a Numidian horseman and a terrifying mosaic of Medusa. The main entrance to the site stands by the extensive 2nd-century **Baths of Julia Memma,** dominated by a massive arch. Follow the yellow sign that reads "Maison de la Chasse." The first Bulla Regia mosaics are found in the **Maison du Tresor** (House of the Treasure). A few steps past it to the right is the above-ground **Christian Basilica,** which holds badly blotched but surprisingly vivid mosaics. The site's real prizes await further along the path: 50m ahead are steps leading down to the most intact and evocative site, the **Maison de la Chasse** (Hunting Villa). Five entire rooms survive below, surrounding the most beautiful courtyard in Bulla Regia. Graceful Corinthian columns support the underground ceiling, while the blue sky looks down upon the central patio. In the adjacent above-ground rooms to the north, mosaics vividly display gazelles, birds, and other animals, as well as a scene of porters bearing the prey. The cavernous **Maison de la Pêche** (Fishing Villa), to the right, shelters a clam-shaped fountain and a large mosaic of two fishermen and assorted undersea life: squids, octopi, eels, and catfish. The house served as a tribunal and prison: the judge sat by the underground fountain and sent miscreants into cells behind him. Another yellow sign points out the way to the **Maison d'Amphitrite** (House of Venus); Inside is an exquisite mosaic of Venus flanked by Poseidon and other mer-creatures. Cupids hold a crown over her head, and fish, garlands, and mirrors float by her feet. It's Botticelli's *Birth of Venus* minus the big clam. Across from the Venus is a beautiful portrait-mosaic of a woman. Both of these are so superb it's a wonder they haven't been moved to the Bardo Museum in Tunis. Above-ground and facing the baths, paths to the right lead to a small **Byzantine fort;** the bumpy track through the grass to the left leads to what remains of the **Temple of Apollo.** From here, cross the market and you'll end up behind the substantial remains of Bulla Regia's **theater,** which easily rivals that of Dougga.

■ Sbeïtla

Most visitors to Tunisia would at least recognize **Sbeïtla**—it's one of the sites most often photographed by the Tunisian Tourist Office. The Capitoline temple that graces so many "Tunisie" posters, is the best-preserved building in a complex of ruins which were once the Roman town of Sufetula. Step through history as you walk through Roman, early Christian, and Byzantine ruins dating from the first through 6th centuries AD.

The origins of Sufetula remain uncertain, but the Romans appear to have built the town from scratch at the end of the first century AD. The place never attained real prominence, except possibly for a short time in the 7th century. In the year 646, the Patriarch Gregory elected to challenge the Byzantine authorities in Constantinople, proclaiming himself Emperor and making Sbeïtla his capital. He chose poorly—the following year 20,000 Arabs under Abdullah ibn Saad came by and beat the daylights out of Sbeïtla, a blow from which neither Gregory nor Sbeïtla ever really recovered.

On arrival at the one-room bus station, turn right with the train tracks behind you. Walk two blocks to av. Belhaouane, and turn left. Walk straight along av. Belhaouane 1km until you come to the ruins, nicely heralded by the **Triumphal Arch,** which formerly marked the entrance to the city. A little further along is the small but well-kept **museum** and the entrance to the site. (Ruins open daily 6am-8pm, off-season 8am-6pm; museum open daily 8am-1pm and 3-6pm, off-season 8am-noon and 1-5:30pm; 1D ticket gets you into both; photo permit 1D.) Entering opposite the museum and disregarding anyone attempting to sell you real, authentic Roman coins and statues, turn left and pass the 7th-century **Byzantine Forts.** You can head through the still-discernible town grid to the three-bayed Arch of **Antoninus Pius.** Step right through it into the **Forum** and view the high point of your tour—the **Temples to the Capitoline Trinity.** Although they are characteristically combined into one temple, Sbeïtla for some reason constructed separate, adjacent temples to the trio of Jupiter, Juno, and Minerva. Exiting between the temples, you can head off to the right to find some early (3rd- to 6th-century) **Christian basilicas.** There is a superbly preserved mosaic baptistry in the **Basilica of Vitalis.**

Three buses per day make the trip from the Kairouan bus station to Sbeïtla (1:30-4:30pm, 2hr., 3.800D). Sbeïtla is also connected to the Roman ruins at Maktar (4 buses daily, 8am-2:30pm, 1hr. 30min., 3D) from which connections can be made to Tunis and Le Kef. If you find you've missed the last bus back to Kairouan (not at all hard to do) take a *louage* to Sousse or Kasserine and then another to Kairouan. It will cost upwards of 5D, but it's the only alternative, since there's no direct Sbeïtla-Kairouan *louage* service.

■ Dougga

The Roman metropolis of Dougga, the largest and best-preserved ancient site in Tunisia, is everything you expected from Carthage but failed to find. From its temple to its toilets, the ancient city remains almost completely intact; indeed, it was inhabited up to a century ago, when a new town was built down the hill for its denizens who, it was felt, were distracting the tourists. Framed by pastures, olive trees, and grain fields, perched on a high bluff, Dougga is also the most scenically situated of Tunisia's ruined Roman cities. Dougga extends over a large area, requiring the better part of a day for a complete tour. Fortunately, the major ruins are concentrated in a small area around the ancient forum.

Orientation and Practical Information You can get to the ruins at Dougga by going to the town of the same name, on the Le Kef-Tunis **bus** line. Just take any of the 16 daily buses from Le Kef to Tunis and ask to be let off at Dougga (1hr., 2.220D). If you're coming from Tunis, there are nearly as many from that direction (2hr., 3.800D). In Dougga town, the road to the ruins is marked and begins at the Mobil station. It's a 3km hike to the site; the road is paved but steep in places. Just before you hit the ruins, the pavement stops. Either plunge into the thick of things here, or continue along the dirt road 250m up to the main entrance. At the entrance, a guide will tell you that your visit will be immeasurably poorer without his services. Unless you can agree in advance on a reasonable price (1-2D), shrug him off. To get home, you can easily flag down a bus on the main road headed for Tunis (every hour) or Le Kef (every 1½-2 hrs.). The buses are green and white and run late into the evening. Note that the ruins at Dougga can also be reached by way of **Teboursouk,** a neighboring village also on the Le Kef-Tunis line. The roads are better on this side of the hill, but the walk is twice as long (6km).

Sights The main entrance to the site leads directly to Dougga's second-century **theater.** The entire structure is intact, even down to the columns of the *skene*. The Tunisian National Tourist Office now schedules performances of classical drama here during the annual **Dougga Festival,** in July early August. Tickets for shows (in French and Arabic) cost 2-5D. Ask at the tourist office in Tunis. A short walk uphill from the theater brings you to the remains of the **Temple of Saturn.** Only four columns are still standing, silhouetted against the skyline and staring out over miles of grain fields.

Continuing down the road from the theater, you will come to the former center of town and the **Capitol of Dougga.** This 2nd-century building deserves its reputation as one of the finest examples of Roman construction in Tunisia. Six slender, fluted columns, 10m high and crowned with a full triangular portico, recall the grandeur that was Rome. Inside there's half a marble head of Jupiter, surrounded by a crossword puzzle of fragmented Latin inscriptions (the cellar of this temple has become a storehouse for the extra inscriptions found at the sight). Adjacent to the capitol are the **Forum** and the **Plaza of the Twelve Winds,** where the careful eye will discern a circular compass rose carved into the marble pavement. All around the compass' border, the names of the winds are also carved. Turning your back to the Capitol, the path leading to the left ends at a set of stairs which descend into the large **Lycinian baths.** The baths are well-preserved, with many of the massive walls and interior colonnades still standing; below, you can step down to the service tunnels. Exiting from the service tunnels drops you in the residential part of town, more or less in front of the remarkably intact **House of Ulysses.** The place takes its name from a particularly well-preserved mosaic, since moved to the Bardo Museum. Across the street, stairs lead down to the **House of Trifolium.** Dougga's largest building was not a temple or government structure—it was a brothel. Numerous small rooms, about whose functions archaeologists can only speculate, branch off the central courtyard. In its day, the Trifolium would have been heralded by a stone *stele* depicting a huge phallus. At some point over the centuries, this was removed, aving behind two elegant but much more subdued Corinthian columns atop the aircase. Next door are the **Cyclops Baths,** where clients probably dropped by to vash up.

The pagoda-like tower visible down the hill is the **Lybido-Punic Mausoleum,** built n the second century BC in honor of a Numidian prince. It is about the only signifi-ant example of Punic architecture in Tunisia. Once they had taken over Carthagin-an territory, the Romans didn't leave much standing. 250m to the left are the feet of he now-broken **Arch of Septimus Severus.** Walking back past the Capitol and nto the olive groves, you'll pass through the 3rd-century **Arch of Severus Alex-nder.** A few strides further west on the path through the olive trees is the stately **Temple of Juno Caelestis.** A dozen freestanding columns and a semicircular wall orm a courtyard surrounding a central platform. (Site open 8am-7pm. Admission D. Photo permit 1D.)

AHIL

ulging from Tunisia's central eastern shore is a wide stretch of land called the Sahil, r "coastal plain." The hot, arid landscape sustains endless groves of olive trees. Myr-d sheep forage aimlessly in unlikely places—courtyards, public squares, and even upermarkets. Diversity reigns in this region: while the northern city of Sousse wells its massive *medina* with package-tour visitors, the southern city of Sfax has ndustrialized with nary a tourist in mind. Monastir, the coastal birthplace of former resident Bourguiba, offers only the inflated trappings of a personality cult. Down he coast, the ancient port of Mahdía enchants with its forthrightness. Inland, Tuni-a's most sacred mosque reposes in Kairouan, while at sleepy El Jem, a Roman coli-eum bears witness to a great and cruel civilization.

■■■ KAIROUAN

or centuries the faithful have made their way across the desert to pay their respects t the most sacred mosque in the Maghreb region—the **Mosque of Sidi Oqba** at ,airouan, dedicated to the saint who spread Islam across North Africa. Kairouan is he fourth holiest city in Islam, eclipsed only by the sacred triad of Mecca, Medina, nd Jerusalem. Religious fervor and a strategic location have accounted for the forti-ed city's growth in the inhospitable steppe of central Tunisia. Popular convention olds that seven pilgrimages to Kairouan equal one to Mecca—sufficient to absolve our sins entirely. Kairouan, also home to some of the most interesting architecture nd decorative work in all of Tunisia, is fortunately one of only two Islamic holy cit-es that admit non-Muslims (Jerusalem is the other). According to legend, Sidi Oqba on Nafi, a companion of Muhammed, founded the city in 670 when a spring sud-enly sprouted at his feet, revealing a precious gold chalice that had mysteriously isappeared from Mecca. For good measure, Oqba banished all the scorpions, nakes, and reptiles from the region. After all this, the sanctity of the spot was imme-iately acknowledged, and the city became known as "Kairawan"—camping place or camels. Kairouan's first century or so was a bit rocky—the city was captured and illaged, then captured and pillaged again. During the golden age of the Aghlabid ynasty (800-1057), most of Kairouan's major buildings were constructed, and the ity attained a religious and cultural preeminence which it retains to this day.

ORIENTATION AND PRACTICAL INFORMATION

,airouan is sprawling. Most historical sights are spread around the large *medina,* nd services are not conveniently clustered together, but are instead scattered about ll over the place outside the walls of the old city. To make matters worse, Kair-ouan's residents rarely use street names. In spite of all this, don't get discouraged;

once you've gotten lost a couple of times, you'll have a feel for the city and thing will improve immeasurably.

Arriving by *louage,* you'll find yourself in a dirt lot 400m from the *medina's* pr mary northern entrance, the **Bab et Tounes.** The bus station (Gare Routière) is clea on the other side of the old city. Take a right out of the bus lot and then a left alon the *medina* walls and you'll end up (after 2 blocks) in a large square in front of th **Bab ech Chouhada,** the old city's main southern entrance. The two *babs* ("gates' are connected by **av. 7 Novembre,** which begins at Bab et Tounes, cuts through th center of the *medina,* and then continues through Bab ech Chouhada and beyon The city limits are loosely defined by **av. de la République,** which runs around Kai ouan's entire perimeter, except for the eastern side. A final spot to keep in mind **place de la Victoire,** marked by a giant pedestal that once supported a statue Habib Bourguiba. This square lies several blocks off av. 7 Novembre by way of av. la République.

Note: old (pre-1987) maps and pamphlets show av. 7 Novembre as av. Bourguib (or rue Ali Bel Hovane); they also show the section of av. de la République betwee pl. de la Victoire and av. 7 Novembre as av. Farhat Hached. Since Bourguiba wa deposed in 1987, Kairouan seems to be one of the few cities to have taken steps t erase his memory, along with av. Farhat Hached for good measure.

Tourist Office: Syndicat d'Initiative (tel. 20 452) and **Tourist information** (te 21 797), in the same building near the intersection of av. de la République and ru des Aghlabites. From Bab et Tounes, walk to the right, then past the *louage* st tion, and then straight down the wide rue des Aghlabites; the offices are 1k down, at the end of the road to the right. The Syndicat speaks English and sells special combined admission ticket to all Kairouan's sites (2D). You can pick up free but inaccurate map at Tourist Information, in general the less helpful offic of the two. Both open daily from 8am-5:30pm. You may have to fill out and sign bureaucratic "Petition to the Mayor of Kairouan to see the sites of the city almost more amusing than it is annoying.

Currency Exchange: Banks can be found all over, but in particular on the stree that lead from Bab ech Chouhada to av. de la République.

Post Office: pl. de la Victoire (tel. 22 555). Open Mon.-Sat. 7:30am-1pm and 7pm, Sun. 9-11am; winter Mon.-Sat. 8am-6pm, Sun. 9-11am.

Telephone Office: up 2 blocks from the post office on the road to Tunis ("Ta phone," on your right). Open daily 6:30am-1am. Another office in the pedestria mall outside Bab ech Chouhada also offers **fax** services. Open daily 8am-10pm.

Louages: in a dirt lot 200m to the right outside Bab et Tounes. Continuous servic to and from Sousse (2.550D), Tunis (5.550D), and smaller neighboring towr until around 8pm.

Buses: Gare Routière. From Bab ech Chouhada, take a left and then a right at th sign. Avoid this place if possible, because it can be very difficult to get on th right bus. The employees are friendly and (seemingly) knowledgeable and wi impress you by reciting from memory all the departure times for a given destina tion on a given day—but departure times vary with employees. Get a second third, and even fourth opinion. When the buses *do* finally arrive, there is som times (but not always) a man who stands by the door and shouts out their destina tions. **SNTRI** runs to and from Tunis (13 per day, 3hr., 5.600D). A **regional** bu company serves Sbeïtla (4 per day, 2hr., 3.800D) and Le Kef by way of Makthar (4 per day, 2hr., 3.800D to Makthar; 2hr, 2.500D more to Le Kef).

Taxis: Leave from in front of the post office, Bab ech Chouhada, and Bab I Tounes.

Swimming Pool: at the **Hotel Continental,** across from the tourist office. Admi sion 2D.

Late-night Pharmacy: Pharmacie de Nuit, outside the *medina* walls. With Ba ech Chouhada behind you, take a right along the walls and then another right the first 4-way. Open daily 7:30pm-8:30am.

Police: (tel. 20 477 or 197) offices in the middle of the *medina* or else off av. de la République near Hotel Splendid.

Hospital: (tel. 20 036 or 198) across from the tourist office.

ACCOMMODATIONS AND FOOD

Hotel Sabra (tel. 20 260), just outside the *medina* at Bab ech Chouhada. Not the dirt-cheapest, but certainly the best value in town. 30 clean rooms plus 2 lounges and a panoramic rooftop terrace (a good place to do laundry). Rooms have good light, spotless bathrooms, and showers. Singles 5D. Doubles 9D. Includes breakfast.

Hotel Barrouta, av. 7 Novembre. A neatly kept (if small) place in the heart of the *medina,* near restaurant of same name. Colorful tiles line the hallways and stairs, and most of the floors are marble. 2.500D per person, grimy shower included.

Hotel Sidi Belhassen (tel. 20 676), boulevard Sadikia. Follow the large sign from Bab et Tounes. Clean beds squeezed into shoebox rooms, some with no windows. (3D per person. Showers included.)

There are few bargains for hungry visitors. Many of the cheaper restaurants in Kairouan inflict fixed-price menus upon unsuspecting stomachs. Due to the high heat levels and the greedy vendors, beverages go for a whopping 500ml. (Café Sabra next to the tourist office sells soda for 300ml.) Always inquire about prices before you chow or chug. Your cheapest eating options are the roast chicken places along av. de la République. The **Magasin General** (1 block past the pedestrian mall opposite Bab ech Chouhada) is bigger than most Tunisian supermarkets and is an excellent option (open Mon.-Sat. 8am-12:30pm and 3:30-7:45pm, Sun. 8am-12:15pm). If all else fails, make a pilgrimage to Kairouan's sweet shops for the divine *makroudh* (Tunisian Fig Newtons), small biscuits stuffed with dates and smothered in honey (800ml per kilo).

Restaurant Barrouta, behind the Barrouta and under the Hotel. Small change will buy an ample dinner. Walk through the kitchen to get to the tables or eat outside. Most entrees 1.200-1.500D. The *macaroni-agneau* satiates nicely, and a wonderful spicy sauce blankets omelettes. Open daily noon-3pm and 6:30-9:30pm.

Restaurant Fairouz (tel. 21 862), marked by large signs off av. 7 Novembre in the *medina* near Bab et Tounes. Gracious hosts serve excellent Tunisian fare accompanied by French folksongs blaring from the radio. *Couscous d'agneau* 3D. Open daily 10am-10pm.

Restaurant Sabra (tel. 25 095), av. de la République, 2 blocks from pl. de la Victoire. Neat and prompt. 3-course *menu* of *couscous,* meat, and salad for 3.500D. Open daily noon-3pm and 6-10pm. (Not to be confused with hotel and café of the same name.)

SIGHTS

Plan your walking tour of Kairouan around the comprehensive ticket available at the tourist office. The sights included are the most interesting and the only ones open to non-Muslims. As usual, you can enter the courtyard of the **Great Mosque** (Sidi Oqba) but not the main prayer room. (Zebra-striped robes provided for those not in proper attire, i.e. knees and shoulders covered.) Peer through the tall carved door of banana wood on the right to catch a glimpse of the *mihrab* (prayer niche) and *minbar* (pulpit) brought from Baghdad in 862, two of the oldest examples of luster tile decoration in the world. The 296 columns throughout the prayer hall are topped with Roman, Greek, and Punic capitals collected from all over Tunisia. The oldest Islamic monument in the Western world, the mosque was erected in 688 and rebuilt in 695. Most of what you see today is 9th-century Aghlabite work that has been renovated and altered over the centuries. Opposite the sanctuary stands the oldest **minaret** in the world, built in 836. Its ponderous appearance hints at a secondary, defensive purpose—note those decorative arrow-slits in the crenellations near the top.

Follow av. de la République 1km past the giant **Aghlabite Pools** to the **Mauso leum of Abou Zama,** also known as the **Zaouia de Sidi Sahab,** in reference to Abou Zama's role as a companion to the Prophet. The Zaouia is home to a religious broth erhood and its founder's tomb. From the baseboards to eye-level, flowery blue tile cover the walls, and then from eye-level up, minutely filigreed gypsum. A colon naded corridor and a second, domed foyer are paneled similarly. The final court yard, surrounded by cells and vessels containing saints' remains, is clad in tile patterned with buildings and trees.

Heading back into the old city, Kairouan's carpet-walled **souks** are clustered along av. 7 Novembre. On some afternoons in the covered **Souk des Tapis,** you can watch women auction the rugs they've knotted and woven to eager merchants. Across from the Souk des Tapis, up the stairs in a brown building is the **Bir Bar routa.** Within its narrow confines a blindfolded camel circles endlessly, powering a 14th-century contraption that lifts water from a sacred spring far below the cham ber. For a small donation you can sample this refreshing water that, according to leg end, flows directly from Mecca. Up the side street, the 9th-century **Mosquée de Trois Portes** glorifies its namesake three portals with a delicate façade.

Close by the Bab Ech Chouhada is the **Zaouia Sidi Abid El Ghariani.** It is hard to imagine a more serene final resting place than the tiny courtyard of striped black and-white Moorish arches. In a side room, the saint rests in peace under an ornate wooden ceiling. In **Rakkada,** 7km away on the road to Sfax, the **Museum of Islamic Art** houses parchments, paintings, and other artistic treasures from the city of Kair ouan. Those who are serious about studying Tunisian antiquities can take one of the hourly buses (420ml) to Rakkada from the Kairouan bus station. (Museum open Tues.-Sun. 9am-4pm, admission included on tourist office ticket. Great Mosque open Sat.-Thurs. 8am-2pm, Fri. 8am-noon. All other monuments open Sat.-Thurs. 8am-5:30pm, Fri. 8am-noon.)

Kairouan draws crowds of pilgrims from across Tunisia (and even other coun tries) for the festive religious celebration of **Mouled,** the prophet Muhammed's birthday. Streets are covered in garlands and lit up at night, as streams of partiers promenade through the old city. (Since Muslim holidays are celebrated according to the lunar calendar, precise dates vary from year to year.)

■ Near Kairouan: Makthar

Although one of the least-visited archaeological sites in the country, Makthar fea tures a surprisingly extensive spread of ruins. Located 110km west of Kairouan, the site is that of the former Carthaginian and later Roman city of **Mactaris.** The site wouldn't be worth a special trip, but if you're traveling in between Makthar and Kairouan, it's an excellent stop. The Roman-built **Bab el Ain arch** serves as the divider between modern Makthar, a small and unremarkable little town, and ancient Mactaris. Just beyond, a three-room **museum** serves as the entrance to the site; inside are a few well-crafted funerary steles and a rare example of Latin carved in its elegant, cursive script. (Open April-Sept. 8am-6pm; Oct.-March 9am-noon and 2 5:30pm. Admission 1D, photo permit 1D.)

Presiding over the entire site from its center is the second-century **Arch of Trajan.** From a distance the arch appears to stand alone; as you approach you'll catch glimpses of the forum that lies behind it, strewn with fallen columns and broken rock. The **Roman baths,** 200m down from the arch, are Makthar's largest ruins. Even now, the walls tower 18m above the ground, an indication of the Roman rev erence for that which comes next to godliness: cleanliness. Traces of the mosaic remain upon the floor. The remnants (mostly foundations) of a number of other buildings and temples are scattered about the site, which you can inspect virtually undisturbed.

A few buses run daily from Kairouan; inquire about details and be certain about the last return time. One bus leaves daily from Le Kef at 3pm (1½hr., 2.300D). Buses depart opposite the Hotel Restaurant Mactaris.

APPENDIX

Language

Modern Italian, a descendant of medieval Latin, was standardized in the late Middle Ages, thanks to the literary triumvirate of Dante, Petrarch, and Boccaccio, who all wrote in the Tuscan dialect. Today, although most Italians still converse at home in local dialects, they can also communicate in "standard" Italian, which is taught and spoken at school, and which reigns though the universal medium of television. If you don't speak Italian, you'll probably be able to manage with English. More Italians are likely to know a smattering of French than English, and cognates often help Spanish speakers.

Knowing a few basic terms, however, will make your trip much easier, and you'll find that even mangled Italian can evoke enthusiastic appreciation. Take a phrase book (the *Barron's* book is fairly useful; and *Berlitz* has some useful phrases, though the vocabulary is geared toward business travelers) and practice with it before you leave. If you can learn only one complete sentence, learn *Parla inglese?* (PAHR-lah een-GLAY-say: Do you speak English?). Remember that when writing numbers, Italians often cross their sevens and use a comma instead of a decimal point (and vice versa). Even more often, what they write is completely illegible to the American-trained eye—once you've learned the numbers, ask the train information people to speak rather than write the time and track you want.

■ Pronunciation

Pronunciation is easy: it's almost entirely phonetic, but remember that no letter (except H) is ever silent.

There are only 7 vowel sounds in Italian. **A, I,** and **U** are always pronounced the same way, whereas **E** and **O** each have two possible pronunciations, depending on whether the sound is stressed or unstressed.

a	(father)	*casa*	*papa*
e	(bed)	*è*	*bello* (stressed)
e	(ate)	*sete*	*e* (unstressed)
i	(marine)	*bigoli*	*misti*
o	(rosy)	*dove*	*nome* (stressed)
o	(lost)	*cosa*	*posta* (unstressed)
u	(ruse)	*lusso*	*virtù*

Italian consonants will give you few problems, except the few quirks noted here.

C and G: before **a, o,** or **u** c and g are hard, as in *cat* and *goose* or as in the Italian *colore* (koLORay) or *gatto* (GAT-to). They soften into "ch" and "j" sounds when suceeded **i** or **e,** as in the English *cheese* and *jeep* or the Italian *ciao* (chow) and *geLAto* (jehlahtoh).

CH and GH: ch and gh are always followed by an **i** or **e** and return c and g to their hard counterparts, thus *chiave,* (KYAvay) and *laghi* (LAgee).

GN and GL: pronounce **GN** like the **NI** in *onion,* thus *bagno* is "BAHNyo." **GL** is said like the **LI** in *million,* so *sbagliato* is said "sbalYAHto."

S and Z: An intervocalic **s** is pronounced as the English z, thus *casa* sounds like "kahza." A double **s** or an initial **s** has the same sound as English s, so *sacco* i "SAHK-co." **Z** always has a ts sound; *stazione* is thus "statSYOHnay."

SC and SCH: When followed by **a, o,** or **u, sc** is pronounced as "sk," so *scus* yields "SKOOzee." When followed by an **e** or *i*, however, the combination is pro nounced *sh* as in *sciopero* (SHOpehroh). The combination **sch** only precedes an or **e** and is always hard (sk) as in *pesche* (PEHskay).

Doubled consonants: Most likely to cause the English speaker difficulties and blank stares is the difference between double and single consonants in Italian When a doubled consonant appears, a good approximation of proper pronuncia tion is to tack the consonant to both the end of one syllable and the beginning o the next, thus *sette* should be "SEHT-te" while *sete* is said "SEH-te." This may seem minor, but if you mean "I'm thirsty" ("Ho sete"), you don't want to end up saying "I'm seven years old" ("Ho sette").

Stress

For most Italian words, stress falls on the next-to-last syllable. When a word's stres falls on the last syllable, it is written with a grave accent: *città, unità.* In general, th endings **-ia, -ie,** and **-io** act as a single syllable for stress purposes, with the stress fall ing on the preceding syllable, which you'd otherwise consider the third-to-last. The main exception to this last rule is the group of words ending in the **-ria** suffix tha indicates a shop; their stress falls on the last **i**: *trattoRIa, rosticceRIa, paneficeRIa salumeRIa, lavandeRIa,* etc. Because place names so often deviate from thes rules, *Let's Go* indicates stress in the names of cities throughout the book by the us of acute accents, which Italians are phasing out of their language: Pésaro, Táranto and so on (some of the accents are standard to written Italian, thus Règgio di Cala bria is written, as in Italian, with a grave accent—and when referring to the islan Cápri (CAHpri), remember only the car is named cuhPREE.

Italians do not pluralize by adding an **s,** but change the last vowel of a word. A word that ends in an **a** in the singular (mela—MEH-lah) ends with an **e** in the plura (mele—MEH-lay). A word that ends with an **o** in the singular takes an **i** (*conto t conti* the plural, as does a word that ends in an **e** in the singular (*cane/canie* A wor whose last letter is accented, such as **caffè,** stays the same in the plural. A word tha doesn't end with a vowel is also stable (one *autobus,* two *autobuse*

■ Phrases

Reservations by phone

Mastery of the following phrases should allow you to get through the process o reserving a room on the telephone. Remember, many proprietors are using to dea ing with the minimal Italian of callers; even without any real knowledge of Italian, i is quite possible to get a room.

Pronto! (prohn-toh): phone greeting.

Parla inglese? (PAHR-lah een-GLEH-say): Hopefully, the answer is "Sì," or better yet, "Yes. If not, struggle gamely on ...

Potrei prenotare una camera singola (doppia) senza/con bagno per il due agosto (POH-tray preh-noh-TAH-ray OO-nah cah-MEH-rah seen-GO-lah (DOHP-pyah) SEHN sa/kon BAHN-yoh pehr eel doo-ay ah-GOS-to): Could I reserve a single (double) roor without/with bath for the second of August?

Mi chiamo (mee KYAH-moh): My name is ...

Arriverò alle quattordici e mezzo (ahr-ree-veh-ROH ahl-lay kwaht-TOR-dee-chee ay MET tsoh): I will arrive at 14:30 (remember, Italian use the 24-hour clock, so add twelve to afternoon/evening arrival times).Return phrases to watch out for: *Mi dispiace* (mee dis PYAH-chay, I'm sorry); *No, siamo completo* (noh, syah-moh com-PLEH-toh, Nope we're full); *Non si fa prenotazioni per telefono* (nohn see fah preh-no-tat-SYO-ne pehr te-LEH-fo-no, We don't take telephone reservations); *Deve arrivare primo dell quattordici* (DEH-vay ahr-ree-VAH-ray PREE-moh dehl-lay kwaht-TOR-dee-cee, Yo must arrive before 2pm).

Numbers

	uno		19	dicianove
	due		20	venti
	tre		21	ventuno
	quattro		22	ventidue
	cinque		30	trenta
	sei		40	quaranta
	sette		50	cinquanta
	otto		60	sessanta
	nove		70	settanta
0	dieci		80	ottanta
1	undici		90	novanta
2	dodici		100	cento
3	tredici		101	centuno
4	quattordici		102	centodue
5	quindici		1000	mille
6	seidici		2000	duemila
7	diciasette		10,000	diecimila
8	diciotto			

Time

che ora...?	ah chay orah	At what time...?
che ore sono?	chay oray sono	What time is it?
sono le due e mezzo	SO-no lay doo-ay ay MEHT-tsoh	It's 2:30.
mezzogiorno	eh meht-tsoh-jor-noh	It's noon.
mezzanotte	eh meht-tsah-noht-tay	It's midnight.
adesso	ah-DEHS-so	now
domani	doh-MAH-nee	tomorrow
oggi	OJ-jee	today
eri	ee-EH-ree	yesterday
presto	PREH-sto	soon, quickly

Months (i mesi) are not capitalized in Italian: *gennaio* (jen-NAHY-oh), *febbraio* (feb-BRAHY-oh), *marzo* (MART-soh), *aprile* (ah-PREE-lay), *maggio* (MAHJ-jo), *giugno* (JOON-yo), *luglio* (LOOL-yo), *agosto* (ah-GOS-to), *settembre* (sayt-TEHM-bray), *ottobre* (ot-TOH-bray), *novembre* (no-VEHM-bray), *dicembre* (dee-CHEHM-bray). Days of the week (la settimana) are not capitalized either: *lunedì* (Monday, loo-neh-DEE), *martedì* (mahr-teh-DEE), *mercoledì* (mayr-coh-leh-DEE), *giovedì* (jo-veh-DEE), *venerdì* (veh-nayr-DEE), *sabato* (sah-BAH-to), *domenica* (doh-mehn-EE-cah).

General phrases

Ciao	chow	Hi/So long (informal)
Buon giorno	bon JOR-noh	Good day/Hello
Buona sera	BWO-nah SEH-rah	Good evening
Buona notte	BWO-nah NOHT-tay	Good night
Arrivederci	ahr-ree-vay-DEHR-chee	Goodbye
Per favore	pehr fah-VO-ray	Please
Grazie	GRAHT-zee	Thank you
Prego	PRAY-go	You're welcome/May I help you
Va bene	vah-BEH-nay	Fine, OK
Scusi	SKOO-zee	Pardon
Sì/No/Forse	see/noh/fohr-say	Yes/No/Maybe
Non lo so	non lo so	I don't know
Non parlo italiano.	non PAHR-lo ee-tahl-YAH-no	I don't speak Italian.
Non capisco	non cah-PEE-sko	I don't understand
C'è qualcuno	chay kwahl-KOO-noh	Is there someone
qui chi	qwee kee	here who
parla inglese?	PAHR-lah een GLAY-say	speaks English?
Potrebbe mi aiutare?	poh-TREHB mee iy-oo-TAH-ray	Could you help me?

Parla lentamente	PAR-la lehn-tah-MEN-tay	Speak slowly.
questo	KWEH-sto	this
quello	KWEHL-lo	that
quale	KWAH-lay	which
dove	DOH-vay	where
quando	KWAN-doe	when
perchè	payr-CHAY	why/because
più	pyoo	more
meno	MEH-noh	less
Come si dice...?	CO-may see DEE-chay	How do you say...?
Come si chiama	CO-may see KYAH-mah	What do you call
questo in italiano?	KWEH-sto een ee-tahl-YAH-no	this in Italian?

Basic Necessities

Vorrei...	VOHR-ray	I would like...
Quanta costa?	KWAN-tah CO-stah	How much does it cost?
Dov'è... ?	doh-VEH	What is...?
un biglietto	oon beel-YEHT-toh	a ticket
solo andato	SO-lo ahn-DAH-to	one way
andato e ritorno	ahn-DA-to e ree-TOR-no	round trip
il gabinetto	eel gah-bee-NEHT-to	the bathroom
il consolato	eel con-so-LAH-to	the consulate
la stazione	la staht-SYO-nay	the station
l'alimentari	la-lee-men-TAH-ree	the grocery store
l'ostello	lo-STEHL-lo	the hostel
il ponte	eel POHN-teh	ridge
la chiesa	lah KYAY-zah	church
il duomo		the cathedral
il museo		the museum
il teatro		the theater
il telefono	eel tay-LEH-fo-no	the telephone
il mare	eel MAH-ray	the sea
la spiaggia	la spyahj-jah	the beach
l'ospedale	los-peh-DAH-lay	the hospital
aperto	ah-PEHR-to	open
chiuso	CYOO-zo	closed
l'ufficio postale	loof-FEE po-STAH-lay	the post office
l'ingresso	leen-GREHS-so	the entrance
l'uscita	loo-SHEE-tah	the exit
il treno	eel TREH-no	the train
l'aeroplano	lay-ro-PLAH-no	the plane
l'autobus	LAOW-toh-boos	the (city) bus
il pullman	eel POOL-mahn	the (intercity) bus
il traghetto	eel tra-GEHT-to	the ferry
l'aliscafo	lah-lee-SCAH-fo	the hydrofoil
l'arrivo	lahr-REE-vo	the arrival
la partenza	la par-TEHN-zah	the departure
il binario	eel bee-NAH-reeoh	the track
il volo	eel VO-lo	the flight
la prenotazione	preh-no-taht-SYOH-nay	the reservation
l'affitta camera	lahf-feet CA-meh-ra	the private room for rent
una camera singola (doppia)		a single (double) room
con bagno/doccia	con BAN-yo/DOCH-CHA	with bath/shower

Directions

Dov'è...?	Doh-veh	Where is...?
Ferma a...?	Fehr-mah ah	Do you stop at...?
A che ora parte...?	a kay o-rah PAHR-tay	What time does the...leave?
vicino	vee-CHEE-noh	near
lontano	lohn-TAH-noh	far
Gira a sinistra.	GEE-rah see-NEE-strah	Turn left.
Gira a destra.	GEE-rah ah DEH-strah	Turn right.

mpre diritto	SEHM-pray dee-REET-toh	straight ahead
etro l'angolo	dee-AY-troh lan-GO-lo	around the corner
petta!	ah-SPEHT-tah	Wait!
rma!	FEHR-mah	Stop!
uto!	iy-OO-toh	Help!

estaurant Basics

meriere	waiter
meriera	waitress
ltello	knife
cchaio	spoon
rchetta	fork
atto	plate
ntipasto	the appetizer
primo piatto	the first course
secondo piatto	the second course
contorno	the side dish
dolce	the dessert
formaggio	the cheese, cheese course
rima) colazione	breakfast/lunch
anzo	lunch
na	dinner
coperto	the cover charge
servizio	the service charge/tip
conto	bill

Glossary

ne following is a glossary of art, architecture, and historical terms used in the book,
oth Italian and English. Scattered among these terms are a number of Italian words
at have appeared in the preceding pages, interesting and mundane.

bbazia: also *Badia,* an abbey.

griturismo: a program which allows tourists to stay in farmhouses throughout
ly. Depending on the region, the cost of the stay may be off-set by laboring on the
rm.

isle: sides of a church flanking the nave, separated from it by a series of columns.

mphora: large antique vase, usually used to hold oil or wine.

pse: a semicircular, domed projection at the east (altar) end of a church.

trium: entrance court, usually to an ancient Roman house or a Byzantine church.

aldacchino: baldachin. A stone or bronze canopy over the altar of a church sup-
orted by columns.

alze: a region of crags, cliffs, or ravines

asilica: In ancient Rome, a building used for public administration. Christians
dopted the architectural style, a rectangular building with aisle and apse but no
ansepts, for their churches.

attistero: a baptistry, (almost always) a separate building near the town's *duomo*
here all city baptisms were performed.

orgo: A suburb or street leading into a suburb from the center of town (these sub-
bs are now often just another section of town).

alvary chapels: a series of outdoor free-standing chapels commemorating the
ages of Christ's Passion.

ampanile: a bell tower, usually free-standing.

amposanto: a cemetery.

antoria: choir gallery of a church.

artoon: a large preparatory drawing for a penile fresco or painting.

aryatid: a column in the shape of a female figure.

assone: a painted chest.

Castrum: the base structure from which many Italian cities grew, a rectilinear c with straight streets, the chief of which would be the decumanus.

Celle: cells of a monastery.

Cenacolo: the Last Supper (often to be found in the refectory of an abbey or co vent).

Chancel: the enclosed space around the altar in a medieval church reserved clergy and choir; in most Italian churches the space has been opened.

Ciborium: A box or tabernacle that holds the host.

Cipollino: onion marble, marble with veins of green or white.

Cloister: a quadrangle with covered walkways along its edges, usually with a gard in the center.

Comune: the government of a free city of the Middle Ages.

Condottiere: the captain of a mercenary band hired by Italian cities to fight th medieval and Renaissance wars.

Corso: principal street.

Crenellations: battlements, the shape of which often reflects medieval politi Guleph (see below) crenellations are swallow-tailed, while **Ghibelline** crenellatic are square.

Cupola: dome.

Diptych: a panel painting in two sections.

Duomo: cathedral, the official seat of a diocesan bishop, and usually the cent church of an Italian town.

Façade: the front of a building, or any other wall given special architectural tre ment.

Fiume: a river.

Forum: in an ancient Roman town, the central square containing most of t municipal buildings.

Fresco: *affresco,* a water-color painting made on wet plaster. When it dries, t painting becomes part of the wall.

Funicolare: funicular, a cable railway ascending a mountain.

Ghibellines: one of the two great medieval factions, originally this party support the Holy Roman Emperor (Frederick II when the troubles began) in his strugg against the papacy. Later distinctions became completely blurred and being a G belline merely meant that the rival town down the road or the rival family up t street were Guelph.

Giardino: garden.

Graffiti: *sgraffito* white design scratched on a prepared wall.

Greek Cross: a cross whose arms are of equal length.

Grotesque: painted, carved, or stucco decorations (often heads) on a Roman or I uscan homes, named for the work found in Nero's buried (grotto) Golden House Rome.

Intarsia: inlay work, usually made of marble, metal, or wood.

Latin Cross: a cross whose vertical arm is longer than its horizontal arm.

Loggia: The covered gallery or balcony of a building.

Lungo, Lung: literally "along," so that a *lungomare* is a boardwalk or promena alongside the ocean, and a *lungarno* in Florence is a street running alongside t river Arno. Except, naturally, in Venice, where a steet bordering a canal is a *fonc menta.*

Lunette: A circular frame in the ceiling or vault of a building that holds a painting sculpture.

Maestà: The Madonna and Child enthroned in majesty, always accompanied angels and in later medieval and Renaissance art, accompanied also by saints.

Narthex: the entrance hall before the nave of a church; in a Byzantine church, t portico.

Nave: the central body of a church.

era: the office charged with building a public structure, most often a city's omo.

la: A large altarpiece.

lazzo: an important building of any type, not just a palace.

lio: a banner. Now also means a horserace in which the neighborhoods of a city mpete for a banner.

nsione and pension: *Pensione* originally meant a boarding house, but is now ed interchangeably with *albergo* (hotel). Many *pensioni* relive their roots by fering their guests "pension" or a set price per person which includes board and lging (half-pension includes two rather than three meals a day).

azza: a city square. In Venice, the term *campo* (literally field) is usually used stead.

età: a scene of the Virgin, sometimes accompanied, mourning the dead Christ.

etra Serena: a soft grey sandstone, easily carved, often used for interior decora-n in Tuscany.

scina: a swimming pool.

lyptych: a painting made in many panels or sections (more than three, at any te).

edella: a step, in medieval beds, the low boxes surrounding a bed, the meaning is ken over in painting of altarpieces to signify the small paintings, usually in several ctions, beneath the main painting or altarwork.

esepio: a crib or manger, or a group of statuary figures arranged around the nativ- scene (a *crêche*).

tto: (*pl. putti*) the little nude babies that flit around Renaissance art occasionally, d Baroque art incessantly.

uatrefoil: a four-lobed design typical of Gothic framing.

figio: (*pl. rifugi* refuges (alpine huts) scattered all over the Alps and Dolomites hich offer beds and meals for hikers.

uola: the Venetian name for a confraternity.

ettimana Bianca: literally "white weeks," special packages for weeks of skiing, hich offer a set price for room and board (sometimes the rate includes ski passes, metimes it doesn't—check before you make reservations).

nopia: the red pigment sketch made on a wall as a preliminary study for the fresco hich will cover it.

igmata: miraculous body pains or bleeding the resemble the wounds of the cruci- d Christ.

rada: street.

elamones: (also *telamons*) supporting columns sculpted as male figures (the unterparts to caryatids).

ondo: a round painting.

ransept: either one of the arms of a cruciform church.

ravertine: the chief building material of Rome, ancient and modern, when they eren't using marble. Always light-colored, but sometimes with black speckles.

riptych: a painting in three panels or parts.

rompe l'oeil: "to deceive the eye," a painting or other piece or art whose purpose to trick the viewer with perspectival wit, as in a flat ceiling painted so as to appear med.

ia: street.

illa: a country house, usually a large estate with a formal garden.

ittorio Emanuele II, *et al.* The main street of just about every town in Italy is amed for one of four figures crucial to the *risorgimento:* Vittorio Emanuele II, the st King of Italy; his crafty minister, **Camillo de Cavour;** the idealistic, popular ero **Giuseppe Garibaldi,** whose group of volunteers *I mille* (The thousand) liber- ed much of Southern Italy from the Bourbons; and **Giuseppe Mazzini,** the "father the Italian nation" who provided a vision of unified Italy that help spur the *risorg- nento* into being.

Index